THE INTERNATIONAL FEDERATION

World of Tennis
1986

The year 1985 will be remembered as a particularly exciting one for tennis, in which the long-established supremacy of the Americans was challenged by European players, and in particular by the explosive new West German teenager, Boris Becker. As usual, all these events are fully reported in *World of Tennis 1986*, which provides a comprehensive review of all that is happening in the game.

Published in association with the International Tennis Federation and now in its eighteenth edition, *World of Tennis* has long been recognised as the sport's foremost reference book. Its 480 pages are packed with photographs, accounts and results of all the world's major tournaments including: the four Grand Slam events; the women's International Series; the men's Grand Prix; international team competitions such as the *Davis Cup*, *Federation Cup* and Wightman Cup; as well as the satellite circuits. The detailed reference section contains biographies of more than 200 of the top world-ranking men and women players and portraits of the all-time greats, plus the Championship Rolls.

Special feature articles by top tennis journalists around the world include reports on the current controversy about a proposed minimum age limit for girl players, and the growth of satellite circuits for those trying to break into the game. Ted Tinling assesses the unique contribution to tennis of Kitty Godfree, the Wimbledon champion in 1924 and 1926, who captured the hearts of millions at the centenary celebrations of the women's championship in 1984; and Paul Haedens pays tribute to the remarkable career of the French 'Musketeer', Jean Borotra.

World of Tennis 1986 is not just an ideal work of reference for all tennis enthusiasts, but contains superb accounts of great performances in the recent and distant past and looks ahead to future developments in the game.

THE INTERNATIONAL TENNIS FEDERATION

World of Tennis

1986

Edited by John Barrett
Compiled by Lance Tingay
Biographies by Steve Flink

Willow Books
Collins
8 Grafton Street, London
1986

Assistant Editor (USA): **Dewey Blanton**

Editorial and design preparation for Willow Books by Christine Forrest

Abbreviations used in this book

ARG	Argentina	**HK**	Hong Kong	**POR**	Portugal
AUS	Australia	**HU**	Hungary	**RU**	Rumania
AU	Austria	**IND**	India	**SA**	South Africa
B	Belgium	**INDO**	Indonesia	**SING**	Singapore
BERM	Bermuda	**IRE**	Ireland	**SP**	Spain
BOL	Bolivia	**IS**	Israel	**SW**	Sweden
BR	Brazil	**IT**	Italy	**SWZ**	Switzerland
BUL	Bulgaria	**J**	Japan	**TAI**	Taiwan
C	Canada	**JAM**	Jamaica	**THAI**	Thailand
CH	Chile	**K**	Korea	**TU**	Turkey
CHI	China	**MAL**	Malaysia	**UAR**	United Arab
COL	Colombia	**MEX**	Mexico		Republic
CR	Costa Rica	**MON**	Monaco	**UG**	Uganda
CU	Cuba	**MOR**	Morocco	**UR**	Uruguay
CZ	Czechoslovakia	**NIG**	Nigeria	**USA**	United States of
D	Denmark	**NOR**	Norway		America
EC	Ecuador	**NTH**	Netherlands	**USSR**	Union of
EG	Egypt	**NZ**	New Zealand		Soviet Socialist
F	France	**PAK**	Pakistan		Republics
FIN	Finland	**PARA**	Paraguay	**VEN**	Venezuela
G	Germany	**PER**	Peru	**YU**	Yugoslavia
GB	Great Britain	**PH**	Philippines	**Z**	Zimbabwe
GR	Greece	**POL**	Poland		

Cover photograph: Boris Becker, Wimbledon 1985 (Michael Cole Camerawork)

Willow Books, William Collins plc
London · Glasgow · Sydney · Auckland · Toronto · Johannesburg
Published in Great Britain 1986

British Library Cataloguing in Publication Data

World of tennis. – 1986
1. Tennis—Periodicals
I. International Tennis Federation
796.342'05   GV991

ISBN: *Cased edition* 0 00 218208 4   *Limp edition* 0 00 218209 2

Typeset, printed and bound in Great Britain by
Hazell Watson & Viney Limited,
Member of the BPCC Group,
Aylesbury, Bucks

CONTENTS

On 27 December, 1985, Harry Hopman, the game's most successful *Davis Cup* captain, who led his Australian teams to 16 successes in 21 finals between 1938 and 1968, died suddenly at his home in Florida, at the age of 79.

Harry, a small, sharp-eyed, energetic man, had been a leading world-class player in the 1930s, with three Australian men's doubles titles, plus four Australian and one US mixed titles with his first wife, Nell, to his credit, as well as three appearances in the Australian singles final. He became a journalist, and in 1950 started to travel regularly overseas with young Australian teams. By insisting on strict discipline and a high work-rate, he helped to develop the talents of several generations of world champions from Frank Sedgman to John Newcombe. No fewer than 14 of his charges won at least one Grand Slam singles title.

In 1970, after Nell had died, Harry moved to the USA and began a new coaching career. With his new American wife, Lucy, he went first to the Port Washington Tennis Academy, and then for a short time to Treasure Island in St Petersburg, Florida. Finally he went to the nearby Bardmoor Country Club in Largo. There Harry Hopman's International Tennis became the home of many leading circuit players and the regular stopping-off place for many more, who sought the advice and help of the greatest motivator the tennis world has ever seen. Harry Hopman's death closes an era. He will be sorely missed. – J.B.

PREFACE

Our sport, it seems, is incapable of adapting peacefully to the problem of growth. After 18 years of open tennis we are still fighting wasteful internecine battles in the men's game that will certainly be more costly and probably more damaging to the whole fragile edifice of professional tennis than any of the squabbles that have gone before. Having survived the corporation fees crisis of 1969, the appearance of a WCT circuit in 1971 as a direct rival to the Grand Prix, and the banning of contract professionals in 1972; having seen proved at Wimbledon 1973 (the year of the boycott by 79 members of ATP, the newly formed players' union) the fundamental truth that the game is bigger than any of its performers; having watched the contortions of WCT as they hopped into and out of the Grand Prix and then sued the management of the game as a prelude to returning on vastly better terms; having survived all these traumatic events, we are now faced with a battle between the Men's International Professional Tennis Council and the management companies who represent some of the star players for control of the game itself.

Or that is what the MIPTC would have us think. Personally I do not believe that the management companies have ever wanted to control tennis. They recognise, as any knowledgeable observer does, that the game must have an independent governing body. Perhaps the time has come to appoint a Commissioner on the American model. Unfortunately the MIPTC is far from independent. Its representatives from the International Tennis Federation, the Association of Tennis Professionals and the Tournament Directors all have vested interests which they seek vigorously to protect.

Nevertheless many Grand Prix tournaments have freely sought the professional help of the management companies to revive their sagging fortunes and have been delighted with the results. Indeed the major Championships themselves have sensibly sought their help in areas where they are more proficient than their own employees. If certain tournaments have abdicated their responsibilities to the game by handing over management roles which they should properly have controlled themselves, then that is their shortcoming. Never, for instance, should any company which represents players have control of the allocation of wild cards, the scheduling of matches or the appointment of a referee or linesmen. A voice perhaps, control never. Surely, though, these safeguards could be written into the rules of the Grand Prix. It is also undoubtedly true that certain tournaments have experienced occasional acts of coercion, which at best have been questionable and at worst criminal. This calls for stronger and better organised tournament committees. It also argues strongly for close discussions between the parties in dispute to remove these practices.

While the game insists on growing (and the Beckermania phenomenon alone is proof of that) there will be problems in accommodating new events with popular appeal. Yet it is surely the duty of the governing body to recognise the need for change. Tennis is evolving into something that is part sport and part showbiz. Of course the great traditional Championships and team events that have stood the test of time must be protected and nurtured; so must the income that these create for the development of tennis. But, as WCT, the World Team Cup, the European Champions Championship and the World Young Masters have proved, the MIPTC does not have a monopoly on good ideas. A way must be found of embracing sensible new events. By including them in the game's structure and utilising the expertise of the management companies in their development, further income could be produced for building up the game around the world. Otherwise, in a free society with too much money chasing too few weeks, the inevitable result will be a rash of new special events replacing existing tournaments. A peaceful solution must be found to the present problems, and above all personal animosities must not be allowed to cloud the real issue, which is about sensible management of a growing sport. A time-wasting war is not the solution. In a legal war only the lawyer benefits.

This year *World Of Tennis* has been forced to take the painful decision to end the women's year on 31 December, 1985. Thus we cannot include, until our next publication, the last segment of the Virginia Slims Series between January and March this year when the VS Championships conclude the 1985/86 season. Happily in 1986 the women's circuit will coincide with the calendar year. Thus, the problem is solved.

The task of assembling much of the statistical material and writing some of the key pieces has once more fallen to that reliable stalwart, Lance Tingay, who, with the passing years, seems to increase rather than diminish his output. Long may it be so. Again I suspect that his self-effacing wife, Daphne, is partly responsible. Without the continuing support of my media colleagues from around the world, masters of the written word and the telephoto lens, this publication could not survive. To them all I extend my thanks for meeting the new earlier deadlines without fuss and with their customary professionalism. Equally I am indebted once again to Dewey Blanton, our Assistant Editor in the United States, for his contribution to the collection of material. As he departs from the tennis scene to another area of challenge in the communications industry we all wish him well.

Another indispensible colleague is Steve Flink, the Senior Writer of *World Tennis* magazine, whose prodigious output of biographical material on the leading 250 players is a triumph of collation. Our readers are as grateful as I am that he is prepared each year to ruin his Christmas – though I'm not sure that his lovely wife, Frances, shares our enthusiasm. At the ITF headquarters, the capacity of Shirley Woodhead to carry in her head the minutiae of the multifarious topics with which she deals in the course her overcrowded year continually amazes me. There has been admirable support from Helen Demetriou, Jane Byrne and Jackie Nesbitt; they make an impressively efficient team. It is pleasing to hear that the ITF office is about to go electronic; a computer information service will be a significant advance.

The two players' organisations, the ATP and the WTA, have once again been unfailingly helpful in searching out obscure facts and in producing their year-end statistics. Ron Bookman, George Pharr and Temple Pouncey at the former and Peggy Gossett, Joe Page and Peachy Kellmeyer at the latter are all, by now, used to my impossible telephone requests which they take in their stride. I want them all to know that they are much appreciated.

Similarly the ladies of the impressively well-organised Virginia Slims organisation, Diane Desfor, Annalee Thurston and Marcia Robbins (another to whom we send our best wishes as she moves on to pastures new) are a tower of strength on the road. No less important is their tireless computer SlimStat whose friendly welcome as I plug into its mammoth memory banks always brings a fresh glow of gratitude for modern technology. We were talking a year ago of a similar database for men's tennis. I am told Hewlett-Packard will soon be offering a service from the ATP headquarters.

The first year of media information service from the MIPTC, under the direction of John Hewig, has been an unqualified success. There were never any doubts about the earnestness to provide what was necessary and if there were some early hiccups, the irritations were magically smoothed away by the charming ladies who worked round the clock to make the system work. Sandy Genelius, Jennifer Proud and Marieke Van Der Drift can look back on a year of signal service, which was much appreciated.

For four years now I have been coaxed and cushioned, prodded and protected by the remarkable Christine Forrest, our freelance production editor. Her ability to get the best from everyone – publisher, printer and Editor – speaks volumes for her patience and her genuine love of the detail of her work. It is no exaggeration to say that the final appearance of this volume is entirely due to her. We both hope that it serves its purpose of informing, amusing and enlightening its ever wider circle of readers.

JOHN BARRETT
London, 1986

FOREWORD

Welcome, once more, to *World of Tennis*, the official publication of the International Tennis Federation, which provides the most comprehensive records of events, results and trends in our ever-expanding game.

Throughout these pages you will, I hope, find much which will entertain as well as inform you. Despite the inevitable commercialism which dominates so many aspects of top tennis and indeed all sports at the highest level these days, we should try wherever possible to keep the fun in the game. In its 18th year of publication, *World of Tennis* has much history to record, not least of course the stunning exploits of West Germany's Boris Becker, who became Wimbledon's youngest and first unseeded champion. It was a year of growth in all areas of ITF responsibility, from juniors to those ever-enthusiastic veterans, and a particularly successful time for European tennis, which provided the men's singles winner of all four Grand Slam tournaments for the first time since 1934.

Disappointingly, it was a year, too, in which the official game had to resort to litigation in response to action being taken against it, which so many of us feel could destroy the basic structure on which the game's healthy future depends. Certainly we know we had to fight to try and make sure tennis remains under the control of those who are answerable to it, rather than those whose first priority must be the benefit to themselves and their clients.

World of Tennis 1986 will, I hope, provide you with an ideal anthology and reference book of what tennis is really all about – the personalities past and present and the important matches which have been played.

PHILIPPE CHATRIER
President, International Tennis Federation

THE YEAR IN REVIEW

Ronald Atkin

The thunderstorm which ripped off a chunk of Wimbledon's masonry and flooded the All England Club's elegant premises, and the so-called 'small tornado' which devastated Flushing Meadow during the US Open were nature's special, spectacular contributions to a tennis year of administrative upheaval and significant changes on court.

The Men's International Professional Tennis Council declared war on agents Mark McCormack, Donald Dell and Ray Benton in a flurry of law-suits and swingeing adjectives in early November, only a day after unanimously approving a rule requiring mandatory drug testing of players. Long and expensive (indeed, potentially financially crippling) litigation seems likely as a result of MIPTC's action, which was a counterclaim to a suit originally filed against the Pro Council in April by Volvo – the former sponsor of the men's Grand Prix circuit – and Dell's company, ProServ, later joined by McCormack's IMG. If the costs will be high, so are the stakes: nothing less, in fact, than the destination of the game's long-term future.

The Pro Council's suit, filed in the US Federal District Court in New York, accused the agents of 'holding the game hostage and seeking to strangle it in an illegal web of pervasive conflicts, intimidation, fraud and corruption'. The full details of the Pro Council's case ran to 99 pages, in which the agents were charged with 'exerting extensive power over players from the cradle to the grave – that is, over junior, world class and senior men's professionals'. The indictment went on: 'Through the coercive use of their power over players and the abuse of their power, ProServ and IMG have been able to seize control or have a substantial financial interest in at least 24 of the 37 major tournaments, plus many other tournaments in the 1985 Nabisco Grand Prix'.

Philippe Chatrier, president of the International Tennis Federation and former chairman of the Pro Council, stressed that no one in the ITF, the Association of Tennis Professionals or the tournament directors, the three factions which compose the nine-member, non-profit Pro Council, had gone out looking for a fight. 'There comes a time, however, when if you are under almost constant, insidious attack, especially from outside influences whose chief, if not sole consideration is exploitation of the game for their own and their clients' commercial gain, then you have to say "enough is enough" ', said Chatrier.

This dramatic, if belated, bid to limit the mushrooming influence of agents in the game was by far the most portentous off-court happening of the year and quite overshadowed the long debate about the advisability of 12- and 14-year-olds competing intensively in international competitions – a topic covered in depth elsewhere in these pages. It also dwarfed the drug-testing decision, in itself one of the most important ever taken in the history of open tennis. As Chatrier said, 'Our concern has not been so much the belief that there is a drug problem in tennis but to try to allay the suspicion of others that there may be a problem and we are afraid to do something about it'. The Pro Council was also anxious to take a responsible line on drugs in good time for the Olympic Games of 1988, when tennis will return as a fully competitive event.

So tennis marched into 1986 with its administrators enjoying a high public image. The game, too, ended the year on an uplifting note with that marvellously exciting *Davis Cup* final between Sweden and West Germany in Munich, where the holders just resisted the one-man assault mounted by the exciting figure of Boris Becker. The burly, blond

With a first US Open title, Ivan Lendl stamped his authority on the year as the world's No. 1, despite disappointments in Paris, where he lost his title, and at Wimbledon. (M. Cole)

teenager was indisputably the arrival of the year. His storming conquest of Wimbledon was the summit of a wonderful year for Europe and a miserable one for the United States in the men's game, with all four Grand Slam titles falling into European hands. Jimmy Connors, sliding from the peak as he moved past his 33rd birthday, and John McEnroe were eclipsed at the biggest events. McEnroe, it is true, won eight Grand Prix tournaments in 1985 and also captured the heart of Tatum O'Neal, but he surrendered the Wimbledon and US Open titles.

McEnroe also lost his position as the world's No. 1 to Ivan Lendl. The tall, lugubrious Czech, a resident of the United States if not yet one of its citizens, enjoyed the sort of year which forced even him to break into a smile. He won 11 tournaments in 1985, including three in a row on different surfaces (Fort Myers, Monte Carlo and the WCT Championships in Dallas), and after achieving his lifetime's ambition of lifting the US Open title, following three years as runner-up, he embarked on another impressive victory streak, winning events in Stuttgart, Sydney, Tokyo and Wembley. On top of that, Lendl stepped outside the confines of Grand Prix competition to earn himself a staggering £650,000 in a day at Antwerp, where he won the competition's first prize of £150,000 and then set off for the nearest bank vault, bearing the gold-and-diamond-encrusted tennis racket worth half a million pounds. Little wonder that even this cautious man felt able to increase the number of the German shepherd dogs which act as companions and security guards at his mansion home in Greenwich, Connecticut.

Lendl's ambitions of clinging onto the French crown he had won in 1984 were torpedoed by the self-effacing Mats Wilander, who thus ended what had until then been a barren year for him. In the Monte Carlo final in the spring Wilander's baseline style had been shredded by Lendl's combination of fire-power and patience. The Swede took the lesson to heart, switched to a more adventurous pattern, slaughtered McEnroe in straight sets in tne French semi-finals and then overturned the confident Lendl, who had not dropped a set on his way to the final. It was Wilander's fourth Grand Slam title – two French and two Australian – all achieved well before his 21st birthday. Not even Bjorn Borg did that. In the second round Wilander demolished Becker for the loss of six games and although the young German had defeated Vitas Gerulaitis in the first round at Roland Garros, there was little indication of the record-breaking impact he was about to make when he crossed the Channel to play on the grass of England.

Having won the Young Masters title indoors at Birmingham at the beginning of the year, Becker had the media reaching for their superlatives as he tore through the field at Queen's Club. After losing to him in the final, Johan Kriek made the prophetic comment that Becker could go on to win Wimbledon. The way was undoubtedly smoothed for him as the top seeds toppled: Wilander was blasted out in Wimbledon's first round by Slobodan Zivojinovic, the massive Yugoslav known more simply as Bobo, who was to wreak further damage by eliminating McEnroe from the Australian Open in December, and securing the singles victories which ensured France's shock relegation from the World Group of the *Davis Cup*. Kevin Curren, the laconic South African who now flies an American flag of convenience, removed the holder, McEnroe, in Wimbledon's quarter-finals at a cost of only eight games, then put out Jimmy Connors, the third seed, with even more impressive ease. Ivan Lendl who, like McEnroe, had gone back to the United States after the French Open to prepare for Wimbledon away from pressures and prying eyes, was ambushed in the fourth round by the cheerful Frenchman, Henri Leconte, giving Fleet Street's headline writers the gift of 'Hooray Henri'.

Becker, who had needed five sets to get past Joakim Nystrom and Tim Mayotte, saw off Leconte in four sets, then beat Anders Jarryd by a similar margin to reach the final. His family hurried over from Germany to watch, and the rest is history. Herr Becker's son became the youngest-ever champion in a Grand Slam tournament, the youngest-ever Wimbledon finalist, the first unseeded Wimbledon champion and the first German to win the title. The legend was launched.

Becker's manager, Ion Tiriac, who had been saying at the German Open less than two months previously that his protégé was promising enough to win Wimbledon in three years' time, sat staring at the Centre Court scene from the VIP's box. He failed to rise to join in the ecstatic applause for Becker and had to be pulled to his feet by the player's coach, Gunther Bosch. Already Tiriac was preoccupied with the forthcoming marketing job on the bright new star in the tennis firmament. 'Beckermania' swept Germany as its new *wunderkind* spearheaded the assault on the *Davis Cup*. In August a United States team lacking McEnroe and Connors (following their refusal to sign good-conduct pledges) was beaten 3–2 amid such scenes of hysteria that one of the American team, Eliot Teltscher, said: 'I felt like we were extras.'

The bad fdeling and appalling behaviour which had so embarrassed the US Tennis Association officials at the 1984 *Davis Cup* final against Sweden, and which led to the ill-received demand for good-conduct pledges from the 1985 competitors, eventually led to the resignation of Arthur Ashe as team captain after five years in the job, during which the USA had twice won the Cup. Meanwhile, Becker's Germany and the multi-talented Swedes marched towards a meeting in the final. Both nations marked up crushing 5–0 wins in their semi-finals – Sweden over an injury-crippled Australia and the Germans over a Czech team lacking Lendl in the singles because of arm trouble. By then, however, Lendl was the champion of the US Open and apparently so little interested in helping his native country in the *Davis Cup* that he subsequently went on record as saying he would not be playing in the event any more.

Stefan Edberg's brilliant victories over Lendl in the semi-finals and Wilander in the final of the Australian Open secured a clean sweep of the men's Grand Slam titles for Europe.

At long last there was a change, too, even if it was not so sweeping as in men's tennis, among the women. Martina Navratilova and Chris Lloyd battled it out, as ever, in the French (where Mrs Lloyd won a three-set thriller) and at Wimbledon, where Miss Navratilova had her revenge. Then in the US Open the elegant Hana Mandlikova finally fulfilled her wonderful promise and overturned the two leading ladies of the sport in successive matches to win the crown and snap the Navratilova-Lloyd domination of Grand Slam championships at 15. Miss Mandlikova could not maintain the impetus at the Australian Open, where the big two again contested the final (Navratilova winning 6–4 4–6 6–2). For the statistically-minded, that win upped Martina's winnings by the end of 1985 to the brink of ten million dollars. Mrs Lloyd's appearance in the Australian final was her 32nd in a Grand Slam, of which she was won 17. Miss Navratilova's was her 19th, of which she has now won 13, ten of them over Mrs Lloyd.

By December both McEnroe and, perhaps less expectedly, Lendl, were under suspension and Connors had already served a spell out of action for misbehaviour in the autumn. All the more significant, then, that after Sweden had completed their successful defence of the *Davis Cup* in the face of a fanatically partisan crowd in Munich, their coach, Hans Olsson, said of his perfectly behaved players: 'They don't even really need an umpire out there.'

That final brought the year to an even-tempered conclusion, though Becker caused a ripple or two after the tie by calling for the resignation of his team captain, Wilhelm Bungert, and the installation of his own coach, Gunther Bosch. It would be tragic if Becker, so admirably talented, powerful and determined and such a glorious breath of fresh air in tennis, started to gain a reputation for the wrong sort of aggressiveness.

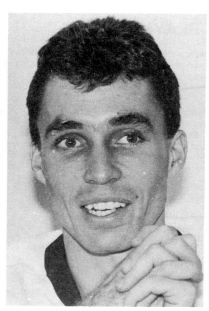

Above left: Stefan Edberg won a first Grand Slam title in Melbourne. *Above right:* Ivan Lendl — undisputed No. 1. (T. Hindley) *Below left:* Boris Becker, who broke records at Wimbledon. *Below right:* Mats Wilander collected a second French title. (M. Cole)

PLAYERS OF THE YEAR

Lance Tingay

BORIS BECKER

One might say that this remarkable young man from Germany was more even than *the* player of the year. In terms of Wimbledon he was the player of the century. In winning he compiled a list of superlatives which have become almost trite by repetition. He was the first unseeded winner, which perhaps reflects the weakness of the seeding method by computer, and was the first German male singles victor, although Gottfried Von Cramm, finalist three years running in the 1930s, was not all that far away.

What belongs to him alone, to his nature as a player, is the fact that he was 17 years 227 days old on the last Sunday when he became the youngest by nearly two years to win Wimbledon. Yet he not only had the physique of a champion – was he not Lew Hoad all over again? – but he had the mental equipment as well. He pulled off a strong-armed victory, losing eight sets in the course of winning. Ted Schroeder was the only other champion to do that.

When early in the year this prodigious young man carried off the Young Masters Under-21 event in Birmingham, he seemed young even for that. Yet when he was back in Britain and winning at Queen's Club, it was obvious that not only were the young players of the world going to be challenged, but the big champions also. Then, at the year's end, he underlined his rich quality by beating both Stefan Edberg and Mats Wilander in the *Davis Cup* final in Munich, as Germany went down 2–3 to Sweden. They were the victories of a born champion, who went on to reach the final of his first Masters.

Perhaps events at Wimbledon fell out in a way that favoured Becker. Kevin Curren did much damage on his behalf. But when it came to the crunch – and what bigger crunch is there than the final? – the flair, the maturity and finishing power belonged to one who, did he but know his place in the game, should have been among the juniors.

IVAN LENDL

It could be said that this splendid Bohemian, who is in the succession of such notable players as Jan Kodes, Jaroslav Drobny and, going back into the mists, Roderick Menzel and Karol Kozeluh, came of age in 1985. He did so at the age of 26 when he made himself US Open Champion. He was, of course, already among the great ones of the game. His French success in 1984 was proof enough of that. But the question remained whether Lendl had won, or whether McEnroe had lost? Certainly the American cast away a two-sets-to-nil lead in abject fashion.

Although McEnroe was certainly not at his pristine best late that Sunday afternoon at Flushing Meadow, the Czech victory belonged very definitely to the positive merits of a sparkling game. Once Lendl had rid himself of his poor start, his tremendous pace-making from the ground, his glorious passing shots, and his venomous volleys built the victory of a major champion. Behind him was the memory of three defeats at the same stage in as many years. But Lendl was a player transformed, maybe by his new coach Tony Roche, maybe by his rigorous diet, maybe merely by the passing of time, into a man of more than usual might among a mighty field.

What was important was not the dollar value of the prize, which was enormous, but the spirit by which his efforts gave him the most honoured and prestigious tennis crown after that bestowed by Wimbledon. He finished the year in triumph with a third Masters crown, leaving the world in no doubt regarding his supremacy. Clearly, now, there is nothing beyond his powers.

MATS WILANDER

During the season Jimmy Connors made the point, seemingly in a spirit of criticism, that Mats Wilander did not give his full effort all the time. In the big events, yes; in lesser tournaments, he relaxed. Whether the assessment be accurate is known only to Wilander. But if he tries his hardest on the most vital occasions, what is that but sound sense – and good strategy?

The bloom of his precocious 1982 triumph in France now belongs to the past. Wilander, a player of maturity cast in the same superb mould as the creator of modern Swedish success, Bjorn Borg, waxed his brightest once again in 1985 on the demanding shale courts at the Stade Roland Garros. Obviously he tried his hardest there and a fine Swedish name was imprinted again on the roll of Grand Slam champions. It was for him the second leg of a possible Grand Slam, for he had won the Australian title (on grass, so utterly different from shale) in Melbourne at the end of 1984 – a title he was to lose to compatriot Stefan Edberg only at the last hurdle. Wimbledon put a quick end to the possibility but Wilander did far better at Flushing Meadow, where he inspired McEnroe to his best and a sparkling match. Yet it was back in Paris that this pleasing player, lithe, handsome and clean cut, made himself a player of the year.

STEFAN EDBERG

In 1983 the 17-year-old Stefan Edberg from Vastervik in Sweden became outstanding, even for a Swede, in winning the Grand Slam of junior championships. It was therefore no surprise that by the end of 1985 he had taken himself to the forefront of the international game.

Throughout the season he was always edging towards the front of the pack. In the Young Masters event at Birmingham he looked like being a winner until falling to the even more insistent Boris Becker in the title match. In Paris he surpassed his seeding status when as 14th seed he beat the sixth, his compatriot Anders Jarryd, and yielded only to the third seed, Jimmy Connors, in the quarter-final. At Wimbledon he followed the book. Again seeded 14 he reached the fourth round before bowing to Kevin Curren, the number eight. For Flushing Meadow he had earned promotion to the 11th spot, and once more he fell in the fourth round to the more highly rated Connors, at number four.

In Melbourne, in the Australian championships, he threw away the form guide. Now seeded five, he made his leap upwards in a dramatic semi-final where Ivan Lendl, the best in the world, was worsted 9–7 in the fifth set. He then took his Swedish senior, Mats Wilander, almost as a matter of course in the final. Thus emerged a new Grand Slam champion. Few players did better in 1985 than this 19-year-old.

MARTINA NAVRATILOVA

When you have become as good as this wonderful Czech-born player was in 1984, when she won the Grand Slam and when, in doubles as well as singles, she was as near invincible as any woman in modern times, there is no room to move upwards. You either stay where you are, on a plateau of perfection, or you move downwards, making room for someone else on the step of the ladder. So with Martina Navratilova in 1985. Chris Lloyd beat her in the French final; Hana Mandlikova beat her in the final at Flushing Meadow. The two victors played superbly, and the US affair was a toss-up anyway. When you win two tie-break sets, as did Miss Mandlikova, there has to be an element of luck.

You make your own luck to some extent and Miss Navratilova did not on that occasion do so. Yet at Wimbledon she was her old supreme self. As she continued her reign as queen, all pretenders to the throne were thrust back. Indeed she was still very much *the*

Above left: *Hana Mandlikova had reason to smile in 1985. (T. Hindley)* ***Above right:*** *Chris Evert Lloyd.* ***Below:*** *Martina Navratilova, still the world's No. 1.* *(A. Evans)*

player of the year in 1985. It became a stupendous happening for anyone to beat her, although she was beaten more than had been her wont.

Yes, she diminished in stature. But the general standard of her play, her astonishing capacity to treat the ball and order her tactics as though she had the muscle and reactions of a man, made her the prize target of all who competed against her. She was the Mount Everest to be conquered. And when conquered, the majestic difficulties of the peak still remained. Players like Miss Navratilova do not arise in every generation.

HANA MANDLIKOVA

There must have been many who reacted to the spectacular triumph of Hana Mandlikova in the final of the US Open (7–6 1–6 7–6 against the redoubtable Martina Navratilova) on the lines of: 'And it's about time, too.' In 1980 the enigmatic Miss Mandlikova won the Australian title after losing the US Open in the final to Chris Lloyd. In 1981 she won the French singles. A little later she was in at the death at Wimbledon, yielding in the final to Chris Lloyd. In 1982 she was again in the US final, losing . . . to Chris Lloyd, need I say? Her brilliance, her apparent couldn't-care-less air, reminded one of Evonne Cawley, albeit with Australian *joie de vivre* tempered by the rigours of mid-Europe and Kafka's cynicism. How beautifully she hit the ball. How wonderful were her shots. How killing. How punishing – when she was paying attention.

There had been many disappointments, but in the autumn of 1985 a Czech sun shone brightly. There at Flushing Meadow she faced her old enemy, Chris Lloyd, in the semi-final, where she won after a fine match. Then it was Czech against Czech. Miss Mandlikova, who had ball-girled for her opponent in Prague, was the stronger-armed in the crises. So she became US champion. What a splendid comeback!

CHRIS EVERT LLOYD

As an impressive 16-year-old, Chris Evert came on to the international scene in 1971, a paragon of classic tennis virtues from Fort Lauderdale. She won her first Grand Slam title in 1974. Since then no season has passed without her winning at least one such title, and her triumph in 1985 was the title with which she made her début as one of the great all-time players – the French Championship.

In the last year or two there have been hints that Mrs John Lloyd, as she now is, might be going 'over the hill', which would not be surprising, with her 31st birthday falling at the end of 1985. Whether or no the French Championship was her swan-song, time alone will tell. But what reward this fine player has given us over the years, with beautiful play, impeccable sportsmanship and grace in every inch of her! The 1985 season would not have been the same without her.

THE INTERNATIONAL TENNIS FEDERATION

THE ITF YEAR
DAVIS CUP, FEDERATION CUP
MEMBERS' ADDRESSES
NATIONAL RANKINGS
1985 RESULTS

Helena Sukova, with her compatriot Hana Mandlikova, shouldered the singles responsibility for Czechoslovakia as they won the Federation Cup by NEC for the third successive year in Nagoya, Japan.

(M. Cole)

THE ITF YEAR

John Parsons

In a year when the International Tennis Federation inevitably became embroiled in the political warfare and legislation which too often distracts attention from its more necessary role of development, it is heartening to record the considerable progress which nevertheless was made. More than 50 countries, the vast majority falling into the category most in need of guidance and encouragement, benefited either directly or indirectly from the various schemes which the ITF has been able either to introduce or expand since Doug MacCurdy became Director of Development towards the end of 1984. This aid has taken the form of workshops for coaches or officials in several parts of the world; help with the organisation and sponsorship of tournaments, especially for juniors; the provision of equipment and the setting up of the Competitive Development Fund.

A donation of £100,000 by Wimbledon, later supplemented by an equally generous boost from the French Open, provided both the inspiration and the feasibility to introduce this scheme which will allow young boys and girls to develop their skills internationally in a way which might not otherwise have been possible. For instance, when a nation has a particularly promising young player who needs to test his or her abilities against sterner opposition in overseas tournaments and that association lacks the funds to finance such a trip, then they can seek help from this fund. Applications are reviewed once a quarter, and the ITF has made it clear that these will be looked upon much more favourably when they come from nations who are also doing all they reasonably can to help themselves.

Despite the continued dominance in women's tennis of Martina Navratilova, now in her 30th year, and Chris Evert Lloyd, who was 31 in December 1985, there is no doubt that in the main the stars of the game are getting younger. Two teenagers — Boris Becker, then 17, and Stefan Edberg, 19 — won men's Grand Slam singles titles in 1985. The need for the ITF to expand its development work still further, and over as broad a field as possible, cannot therefore be stressed too highly.

Clearly it is likely to be some time before standards of opportunity and play in black Africa and parts of Asia and the Middle East reach those in countries where tennis has a long history of tradition and success. Yet in a year when Europe most definitely wrested the continental supremacy from the United States, after a decade or more in which they had taken over from Australia, the progress in South America was particularly impressive. Juniors from that part of the world, some of them like Gabriela Sabatini already totally absorbed in senior events, made a considerable mark during 1985. Indeed, two Mexicans made it to the final of the junior boys' singles at Wimbledon, and Jaime Yzaga from Peru reached the last 16 of the US Open, where he took a set from the eventual champion, Ivan Lendl — the only set he lost.

The wide spread of the Grand Slam tournament titles in 1985 is exactly in keeping with the ITF's aims and desires, for tennis can only benefit when many different competitors from different countries are striving for the top honours. Just as four men shared the senior Grand Slam titles, so four boys shared the honours in the junior singles at those most prestigious events on the ITF's junior ranking circuit, on which there were 99 tournaments during 1985, compared with 88 in 1984.

Another innovation by the ITF in 1985, with youth and development in mind, was the staging for the first time of the World Youth Cup, a team competition for boys and girls aged 16 and under. It was held in Kobe, Japan, where the 16 qualifiers from regional competitions held earlier in the year, gathered to compete. Australia beat the United States 2–1 in the final of the boys' event and Czechoslovakia, in keeping with their status as three-times winners of the *Federation Cup*, demonstrated their strength in depth by winning the girls' trophy.

This event enabled the ITF to complete its band of international competitions for juniors in all the recognised age groups, although some adjustments will be necessary in future for the Sport Goofy events which have been catering for the under-14 and under-12 groups. They will need to take account of the age qualifications for major international competition introduced at the start of 1986 on the recommendation of the ITF's Eligibility Commission. This was established to investigate the growing fears that too many young players were playing too much senior tennis too soon, putting undue mental and physical strain on themselves.

The Commission heard a wide cross-section of opinion and expert advice, open forums being held both at Delray, during the Lipton International Players Tournament, and then in Paris at the French Open. The Commission finally produced a set of regulations which were accepted by the MIPTC but were regarded as excessive by WIPTC, and a compromise was reached over the number of events in which girls aged 14 and under could play in women's competitions. It was agreed unanimously, however, that international events for the 12-and-under group should be dropped.

At the other end of the age scale, the ITF continued to play its full role in the activities of the international tournament game's two governing councils, the MIPTC and the WIPTC, helping in particular to push for those changes in the fundamental international calendar which will give both the men's and women's circuits a much more orderly appearance. In 1986 there will be two Nabisco Masters and two Virginia Slims Championships, so that they can in future relate directly to the same year in which all the qualifying points are obtained. Although hopes that the Italian Championships would once again be a tournament for both men and women in 1986 were not to be fulfilled, this is still something the ITF would like to see happen in the not too distant future.

Membership of the ITF continues to expand, the total number of affiliated nations at the end of 1985 being 124, of which 82 were full members and 42 associate members. New full members since 1984 are Bangladesh, Ivory Coast and Malta, while the new associate members are Butan, Cook Islands, Fiji, Guinea Conakry, Mali, Montserrat, Nepal, Qatar and Togo. With the popularity of tennis growing in so many different parts of the world, so too the interest and support for such major international events as the *Davis Cup* by NEC, also broadens. Full details of last year's eventful competition, with its thrilling climax in Munich, are given elsewhere, but for 1986 there has been a record entry of 71 nations. For the first time, there will be an African Zone, the winners of which will then progress to two European Zones.

No less than three of the four individual Grand Slam champions took part in the *Davis Cup* final, in which Sweden successfully retained the trophy. Czechoslovakia were equally successful in the *Federation Cup*, winning for a third successive year, although once more it was disappointing that a number of prominent nations, including the United States and West Germany, were unable to field their strongest teams in this competition.

ITF WORLD CHAMPIONS

The ITF men's World Champion is decided annually by the ITF's panel of former champions: Don Budge, Fred Perry, Frank Sedgman and Tony Trabert. The Women's Champion for 1985 was taken from the Virginia Slims points table.

	MEN	WOMEN
1978	Bjorn Borg	Chris Evert
1979	Bjorn Borg	Martina Navratilova
1980	Bjorn Borg	Chris Evert Lloyd
1981	John McEnroe	Chris Evert Lloyd
1982	Jimmy Connors	Martina Navratilova
1983	John McEnroe	Martina Navratilova
1984	John McEnroe	Martina Navratilova
1985	Ivan Lendl	Martina Navratilova

THE *DAVIS CUP* by NEC

Richard Evans

For the first time since Fred Perry led Britain to four successive victories in the 1930s, a European nation retained the *Davis Cup* when Sweden defeated West Germany 3–2 at the Olympiahalle in Munich. The dramatic fifth rubber which saw Michael Westphal twice edge ahead of Stefan Edberg before bowing to the Swede's superior talent, 3–6 7–5 6–4 6–3, provided the perfect final act to one of the most pleasing and closely contested *Davis Cup* finals since the abolition of the challenge round in 1972. Amazingly it was the first final for 21 years to be decided in the fifth rubber, Roy Emerson being the last player to be called upon to win the Cup at the very last hurdle, when he defeated Chuck McKinley in Cleveland in 1964.

If crowds of just under 14,000 at the Olympiahalle were brought to the very edge of well-behaved hysteria by the heroic exploits of Boris Becker and his team-mates, the thrilling climax was no more than the 1985 *Davis Cup* campaign as a whole deserved. Seldom in its 85-year history has this uniquely fascinating competition created more global interest or excitement. Apart from the two finalists, nations with as disparate tennis histories as Australia, Paraguay, India, Yugoslavia, the USSR and Britain were affected by *Davis Cup* fever, not merely as a result of success in the main stages of the world group but also through the nerve-jangling drama created in the relegation and promotion battles.

To this observer at least, it seems that the late ITF secretary, David Gray, got it absolutely right when he devised the world group and zonal group system which came into force in 1981. Although the idea of compressing the whole thing into a two-week *Davis Cup* festival at one venue still has its supporters, it is hard to see how the advantages of such an idea would outweigh the interest generated by nations staging successful home ties.

Paraguay and Yugoslavia were prime examples of this in 1985, but no country benefited more from the present home and away system spread over four weeks than West Germany. Quite apart from broadening the already happy smile of the loyal Japanese sponsors, NEC, home ties against the United States in Hamburg and against Sweden in Munich helped fan the flames of Becker's Wimbledon triumph, creating still greater interest in tennis in one of the most affluent high-tech markets in the world.

In stricter tennis terms, the year was immensely satisfying because it saw the consolidation of the finest and most powerful all-round *Davis Cup* team since Neale Fraser was able to call upon the likes of Rod Laver, Ken Rosewall and John Newcombe in the early 1970s. Hans Olsson's men are a true credit to tennis, not merely for their abundant and varied skills but for the refreshing spirit of camaraderie and sportsmanship that they bring to a game badly in need of it. In marked contrast to Gothenburg 12 months before, when the referee, Alan Mills, had to consider defaulting Jimmy Connors, Patrick Flodrops, the French referee in Munich, found himself pleasantly under-employed. Olsson was not so very far from the mark when, in a reply to a flippant question about the need for code of conduct agreements, he replied, 'My boys are so good they don't even need umpires'.

Quite naturally Olsson was most delighted by his team's ability to prove that they could win away from home. The draw had favoured them in 1984, but the new champions found themselves a very long way from Gothenburg or quaint little Bastad when they travelled to Santiago for their first-round tie against Chile. Within hours of arrival an earthquake sent the team running for their lives ('I was scared', said Mats Wilander, who

Above: Stefan Edberg thrown jubilantly aloft by his Swedish team-mates. ***Below left to right:*** Nystrom, Wilander, Edberg, Jarryd and Hans Olsson (non-playing captain) after beating West Germany 3–2 in Munich. *(T. Hindley)*

caught the first plane out), and a few weeks later it was left to Stefan Edberg and Jan Gunnarsson to make the trip back down to South America to finish the job. Next on the list for the Swedes was a passage to India; all the way to Bangalore, where David Lean shot most of his epic film. The tie was less than an epic, with the Swedes calling the grass unplayable, but still winning on it despite some brave resistance from the veteran Amritraj brothers, Vijay and Anand.

In the semi-final, Sweden were allowed to play at home again and, rather than risk the early October weather in Bastad, as they had done the previous year, they took Australia indoors in Malmö and beat Neal Fraser's depleted squad 5–0. Anders Jarryd set the Swedes on their way with a brilliant display of serving against Peter McNamara on the specially laid clay court, but McNamara, playing his first *Davis Cup* tie for almost three years after knee surgery, showed much of his old flair before going down 13–11 in the third set. Ironically McNamara had been pressed into service because his old doubles partner Paul McNamee was unfit.

West Germany's path to the final had been just as impressive. After disposing of Spain at home, a McEnroe-less America were led onto the slow, damp clay of Hamburg's famous Rothenbaum Club where they were beaten 3–2 with Becker, the recently baptised idol of German sport, shrugging off the pressure most 17-year-olds would have felt at having to win the tie in the fifth rubber by battering Aaron Krickstein into submission 6–2 6–2 6–1. And it was supposed to have been Krickstein's sort of court! Becker, deservedly, got most of the plaudits, but with Ken Flach and Robert Seguso keeping the US alive in the doubles, even after Becker had served for the match at 5–4 in the fifth set, it was Hans Schwaier's five-set victory over Krickstein that provided the crucial point for the Germans and proved, as Westphal was to emphasise in the semi-final against Czechoslovakia, that the Germans are not entirely a one-man band.

Westphal, in fact, beat his drum for six hours and one minute against that tireless trouper, Tomas Smid, on a very fast carpet at Frankfurt's Festhalle before clinching a famous victory 6–8 1–6 7–5 11–9 17–15. In terms of games played (85) it was the longest live rubber in *Davis Cup* history, because the 86-game marathon between Arthur Ashe and Christian Kuhnke in Cleveland in 1970 was played with the US already 4–0 up. But the McEnroe-Wilander duel in St Louis in 1982 lasted 31 minutes longer. For Westphal, however, it was quite long enough. 'I could only have managed another two or three more games', he admitted, after giving the Germans a commanding 2–0 lead over a Czech team that had Ivan Lendl playing doubles only, because of an arm injury. With the new US Open champion rarely able to offer his best, Lendl and Smid crashed to Becker and Andres Maurer in straight sets.

We have been saying for years that anything can happen in *Davis Cup* and in 1985 France proved it. One of the most talented teams in the competition not only lost to Paraguay in Asuncion in the first round but compounded the error by crashing to the mighty Slobodan Zivojinovic and his Yugoslav colleagues in the relegation battle in Belgrade later in the year. For a team containing Yannick Noah and Henri Leconte to suffer such a fate seemed almost unthinkable, but the French will have a whole year to ponder the consequences of not preparing properly for *Davis Cup* ties, while they try to restore the cockerel's pride. Almost as surprising was the Soviet Union's 3–2 victory in Buenos Aires, with Andrei Chesnokov beating the highly experienced José-Luis Clerc 6–2 in the fifth set of the fifth rubber, after trailing by two sets to love. So Argentina, finalists in 1981, and France, finalists in 1982, both discovered how quickly the wheel of fortune turns.

For Boris Becker, of course, it had become a whirl of triumph which remained quite untarnished by West Germany's defeat in Munich. He could, it is true, have done better in the doubles, with or without the unnecessary excuse of an injured hip, but his performances in both singles, first in beating Edberg on the Friday and then in keeping the tie alive for the Germans by outplaying as solid a competitor as Wilander on the Sunday, were performances that required an extraordinary level of determination and self-belief. Like any true champion, he seems to revel in pressurised situations, and the record he turned in after his first year of *Davis Cup* play was staggering. Still 17 until one

Advice for Becker from Wilhelm Bungert, who Becker suggested after the tie should be replaced as captain by his own coach, Gunther Bosch − a statement later retracted. (T. Hindley)

month before the final, he remained unbeaten in live singles matches and lost two sets in four ties. No wonder the West Germans are crazy about him.

But not even Becker could beat the Swedes on his own. Proving their amazing versatility and depth of talent, Olsson's team were able to shrug off the loss through illness of Anders Jarryd, their No. 2 singles player and doubles expert, and still win on a German-made carpet that was really too fast for good quality tennis. It was a tribute to the skills of all the players that we saw anything other than one-shot rallies.

Olsson's remark after beating Australia in Malmö − 'Germany can choose whatever court they want; I have the players for it' − was not the statement of an over-confident captain. It was merely the truth. With Wilander beating Westphal in the first rubber despite the young German's 19 aces; Wilander and the brilliant Joakim Nystrom taking advantage of Maurer's service weakness to win the doubles; and Edberg overcoming his nerves (and another 22 aces from Westphal) to prove that he now has the character to match his talent, Sweden's right to retain the Cup was never questioned either by impartial observers or even by the Bavarian crowd who devised a new form of noisy support for their players by clapping rhythmically between every point. The best team won and, to their credit, the Germans were the first to recognise it. Now they have beaten such stalwart opposition on an alien court, with a new No. 2 singles player and a reserve doubles team, it is difficult to see how anyone is going to take the Cup away from the Swedes in the forseeable future. But in *Davis Cup* who knows?

DAVIS CUP **PRIZE MONEY 1985** (provided by NEC)

NON-ZONAL COMPETITION: Champion nation: $200,000. Runners-up: $100,000. Semi-finalists: $75,000. Quarter-finalists: $45,000. Play-off winners: $35,000. Play-off losers: $25,000.
ZONAL COMPETITION: $2,800 per tie. *Bonuses* − Winners: $3,200. Semi-finalists: $1,600. Quarter-finalists: $800. First round winners: $400.
Overall total: $1,153,200.

Non-Zonal Competition

FIRST ROUND	QUARTER-FINALS	SEMI-FINALS	FINAL	CHAMPION
USA				
Japan	USA 5–0			
Spain		West Germany 3–2		
West Germany	West Germany 3–2			
CZECHOSLOVAKIA			West Germany 5–0	
USSR	CZECHOSLOVAKIA 3–2	CZECHOSLOVAKIA 5–0		
Argentina				
Ecuador	Ecuador 4–1			SWEDEN 3–2
Paraguay	Paraguay 3–2			
France		AUSTRALIA 3–2		
Yugoslavia			SWEDEN 5–0	
AUSTRALIA	AUSTRALIA 3–2			
India	India 3–2			
Italy		SWEDEN 3–0		
Chile				
SWEDEN	SWEDEN 4–1			

With the exception of USSR, capital letters denote seeded countries.

RELEGATION ROUND

FIRST ROUND	QUARTER-FINALS
Japan / Spain	Spain 3–2
USSR / Argentina	USSR 3–2
France / Yugoslavia	Yugoslavia 4–1
Italy / Chile	Italy 3–1

Zonal Competition

EUROPEAN ZONE A

FIRST ROUND	QUARTER-FINALS	SEMI-FINALS	FINAL	PROMOTED
Turkey / Iran	RUMANIA			
	Turkey w.o.	RUMANIA 5–0		
HUNGARY / Morocco	HUNGARY 4–1		RUMANIA 4–1	
Egypt / Algeria	Egypt 4–1	Egypt 3–2		
Senegal / Monaco	Monaco 4–1			DENMARK 3–2
Cyprus / IRELAND	IRELAND 4–1	Monaco 3–2		
Bulgaria / Belgium	Belgium 3–1		DENMARK 5–0	
DENMARK	DENMARK	DENMARK 5–0		

EUROPEAN ZONE B

FIRST ROUND	QUARTER-FINALS	SEMI-FINALS	FINAL	PROMOTED
	ISRAEL			
Finland / Netherlands	Netherlands 4–1	ISRAEL 4–1		
	AUSTRIA		ISRAEL 3–2	
Norway / Greece	Greece 4–1	AUSTRIA 3–2		
Poland / Zimbabwe	Zimbabwe 3–2			GREAT BRITAIN 4–1
Tunisia / SWITZERLAND	SWITZERLAND 5–0	SWITZERLAND 5–0		
Portugal / Luxembourg	Portugal 5–0		GREAT BRITAIN 3–0	
GREAT BRITAIN	GREAT BRITAIN	GREAT BRITAIN 5–0		

EASTERN ZONE

FIRST ROUND	QUARTER-FINALS	SEMI-FINALS	FINAL	PROMOTED
	NEW ZEALAND			
Chinese Taipei / Sri Lanka	Chinese Taipei 5–0	NEW ZEALAND 4–1		
	CHINA		NEW ZEALAND 5–0	
Hong Kong / Singapore	Hong Kong 4–1	CHINA 3–2		
Philippines / Malaysia	Philippines 5–0			NEW ZEALAND 4–0
	THAILAND	Philippines 4–1		
South Korea / Indonesia	South Korea 5–0		South Korea 5–0	
	PAKISTAN	South Korea 4–1		

AMERICAN ZONE

FIRST ROUND	QUARTER-FINALS	SEMI-FINALS	FINAL	PROMOTED
BRAZIL / Venezuela		BRAZIL 5–0		
			BRAZIL 4–1	
URUGUAY / Colombia		Colombia 3–2		MEXICO 4–1
C. Caribbean / CANADA		CANADA 4–1		
			MEXICO 3–2	
Peru / MEXICO		MEXICO 3–2		

THE *DAVIS CUP* by NEC, 1985

NON-ZONAL COMPETITION

FIRST ROUND – USA d. Japan 5–0, Kyoto City (E. Teltscher d. K. Maruyama 6–1 6–1 6–1; A. Krickstein d. S. Shiraishi 6–4 6–1 3–6 6–4; K. Flach/R. Seguso d. S. Nishio/S. Sakamoto 6–2 6–3 6–1; Krickstein d. Maruyama 6–1 6–1; Teltscher d. Shiraishi 6–3 6–2); *West Germany d. Spain 3–2, Sindelfingen* (M.Westphal d. S. Casal 10–8 6–3 2–6 2–6 6–4; B. Becker d. J. Aguilera 6–3 6–4 6–4; Becker/A. Maurer d. Casal/E. Sanchez 4–6 6–3 1–6 6–3 6–4; Becker lost to Casal 4–6 6–1 5–7; Westphal lost to Aguilera 4–6 6–3 3–6); *Czechoslovakia d. USSR 3–2, Tbilisi* (M. Mecir d. K. Pugaev 6–4 6–3 9–7; T. Smid d. A. Zverev 6–3 6–4 6–3; Smid/L. Pimek lost to Zverev/S. Leoniuk 6–3 6–4 9–11 6–8 5–7; Mecir d. Zverev 6–3 8–6 0–6 8–6; Pimek lost to Pugaev 6–8 2–6); *Ecuador d. Argentina 4–1, Buenos Aires* (A. Gomez d. J. L. Clerc 4–6 6–4 13–11 6–3; R. Viver lost to M. Jaite 4–6 7–5 7–5 2–6 3–6; Gomez/R. Ycaza d. Clerc/Jaite 13–11 6–3 3–6 6–4; Gomez d. Jaite 6–1 6–4 6–4; Viver d. R. Arguello 6–1 4–6 6–3); *Paraguay d. France 3–2, Asuncion* (V. Pecci d. Y. Noah 6–8 15–13 2–6 8–6 10–8; F. Gonzalez d. H. Leconte 4–6 6–3 3–6 6–3 6–4; Gonzalez/Pecci lost to Leconte/Noah 2–6 6–3 8–6 5–7 3–6; Gonzalez lost to Noah 6–3 3–6 15–17 4–6; Pecci d. Leconte 6–3 6–4 3–6 7–5); *Australia d. Yugoslavia 3–2, Split* (P. McNamee d. M. Ostoja 3–6 3–6 10–8 6–0 6–4; P. Cash lost to S. Zivojinovic 5–7 7–5 8–10 4–6; Cash/J. Fitzgerald d. G. Prpic/Zivojinovic 7–5 10–12 6–8 6–4 6–4; Cash d. Ostoja 6–2 6–0 6–2; McNamee lost to Zivojinovic 6–3 3–6 3–6); *India d. Italy 3–2, Calcutta* (R. Krishnan d. F. Cancellotti 6–3 11–9 4–6 3–6 6–4; V. Amritraj d. C. Panatta 6–1 6–4 5–7 3–6 6–3; An. Amritraj/S. Menon lost to C. Panatta/G. Ocleppo 3–6 3–6 7–9; V. Amritraj d. Cancellotti 5–7 4–6 6–4 6–3 8–6; Krishnan lost to C. Panatta 8–6 4–6 1–6); *Sweden d. Chile 4–1, Santiago* (S. Edberg lost to H. Gildemeister 3–6 6–2 4–6 5–7; H. Sundstrom d. P. Rebolledo 7–9 6–2 6–0 9–7; Edberg/J. Gunnarsson d. R. Acuna/Gildemeister 6–1 1–6 6–3 6–3; Sundstrom d. Gildemeister 6–1 3–6 7–5 6–2; Edberg d. Rebolledo 6–4 4–6 6–2).

QUARTER-FINALS – West Germany d. USA 3–2, Hamburg (B. Becker d. E. Teltscher 6–2 6–2 6–3; H. Schwaier d. A. Krickstein 2–6 6–1 2–6 6–1 8–6; Becker/A. Maurer lost to K. Flach/R. Seguso 2–6 8–6 1–6 6–4 5–7; Schwaier lost to Teltscher 4–6 6–2 7–5 4–6 2–6; Becker d. Krickstein 6–2 6–2 6–1); *Czechoslovakia d. Ecuador 5–0, Guayaquil* (I. Lendl d. A. Gomez 5–3 ret'd; M. Mecir d. R. Viver 6–0 6–1 6–3; Lendl/T. Smid d. M. Aguirre/R. Ycaza 7–5 6–4 6–4; Mecir d. Ycaza 6–4 6–3; Smid d. Aguirre 6–0 6–1); *Australia d. Paraguay 3–2, Sydney* (P. McNamee d. F. Gonzalez 3–6 6–0 6–3 6–1; J. Fitzgerald lost to V. Pecci 2–6 3–6 6–1 4–6; McNamee/M. R. Edmondson lost to Gonzalez/Pecci 3–6 10–8 3–6 6–1 3–6; McNamee d. Pecci 6–8 7–5 6–2 9–7; Fitzgerald d. Gonzalez 6–3 9–7 7–5); *Sweden d. India 4–1, Bangalore* (A. Jarryd d. V. Amritraj 3–6 7–5 2–6 6–3 6–4; M. Wilander d. R. Krishnan 6–3 6–3 6–2; S. Edberg/Jarryd d. V./An. Amritraj 21–19 2–6 6–3 6–4; Wilander lost to V. Amritraj 6–8 7–9; Jarryd d. Krishnan 6–3 4–6 6–1).

SEMI-FINALS – West Germany d. Czechoslovakia 5–0, Frankfurt (B. Becker d. M. Mecir 6–3 7–5 6–4; M. Westphal d. T. Smid 6–8 1–6 7–5 11–9 17–15; Becker/A. Maurer d. I. Lendl/Smid 6–1 7–5 6–4; Becker d. L. Pimek 6–1 6–4; Westphal d. Mecir 6–3 6–4); *Sweden d. Australia 5–0, Malmo* (A. Jarryd d. P. McNamara 6–4 6–4 13–11; M. Wilander d. W. Masur 6–1 6–1 6–0; S. Edberg/Jarryd d. M. R. Edmondson/J. Fitzgerald 6–4 6–3 6–4; Wilander d. McNamara 6–4 6–3; Jarryd d. Masur 6–1 6–2).

FINAL – Sweden d. West Germany 3–2, Munich (M. Wilander d. M. Westphal 6–3 6–4 10–8; S. Edberg lost to B. Becker 3–6 6–3 5–7 6–8; Wilander/J. Nystrom d. Becker/A. Maurer 6–4 6–2 6–1; Wilander lost to Becker 3–6 6–2 3–6 3–6; Edberg d. Westphal 3–6 7–5 6–4 6–3).

RELEGATION ROUND – Spain d. Japan 3–2, Tokyo (S. Casal d. S. Shiraishi 4–6 7–5 6–3 6–3; E. Sanchez d. T. Fukui 7–5 6–1 6–1; Casal/Sanchez d. T. Yonezawa/E. Takeuchi 6–3 6–3 6–4; Spain conceded reverse singles matches); *USSR d. Argentina 3–2, Buenos Aires* (A. Chesnokov d. M. Jaite 6–0 6–4 6–2; A. Zverev lost to J. L. Clerc 4–6 6–2 3–6 6–3 5–7; S. Leoniuk/Zverev d. Clerc/Jaite 6–4 1–6 9–7 6–2; Zverev lost to Jaite 4–6 6–3 2–6; Chesnokov d. Clerc 2–6 1–6 6–4 6–2); *Yugoslavia d. France 4–1, Belgrade* (G. Prpic d. Y. Noah 3–6 4–6 6–1 6–4; S. Zivojinovic d. H. Leconte 4–6 7–5 6–1 6–2; Prpic/Zivojinovic lost to Leconte/Noah 4–6 4–6 1–6; Zivojinovic d. Noah 6–4 6–4 6–4; Prpic d. Leconte 8–6 6–8 6–3); *Italy d. Chile 3–1, Cagliari* (C. Panatta d. J. A. Fernandez 6–2 7–5 6–1; F. Cancellotti lost to R. Acuna 3–6 2–6 6–4 6–2 5–7; G. Ocleppo/Panatta d. Acuna/J. P. Queirolo 6–4 6–2 6–4; Cancellotti d. Fernandez 6–1 7–5 6–2).

ZONAL COMPETITION

AMERICAN ZONE

FIRST ROUND – Brazil d. Venezuela 5–0, Caracas (M. Hocevar d. C. Claverie 6–3 14–16 6–4 6–4;

C. Motta d. A. Mora 6–1 6–1 7–5; C. Kirmayr /Motta d. R. Scheller /I. Calvo 6–4 6–2 6–2; Kirmayr d.
Mora 6–3 6–3; D. Campos d. Claverie 6–3 6–3); *Colombia d. Uruguay 3-2, Montevideo* (A. Jordan
d. M. Filippini 6–3 6–2 6–3; L. A. Gonzalez lost to D. Perez 1–6 0–6 0–6; Jordan /R. Gomez d. Perez /H.
Roverano 8–6 6–4 3–6 6–4; Jordan lost to Perez 0–6 1–6 1–6; Gonzalez d. Filippini 6–2 3–6 6–4 6–1);
Canada d. Commonwealth Caribbean 4–1, Chicoutimi, Quebec (M. Wostenholme d. R. Smith
6–4 9–7 6–3; S. Bonneau d. R. Hale 7–9 7–5 6–3 6–4; J. Brabenec Jun. /D. Segal lost to Hale /Smith
6–3 7–5 6–4; Wostenholme d. Hale 6–2 6–2 7–5; Bonneau d. Smith 4–6 17–15 6–3); *Mexico d. Peru
3–2, Mexico City* (J. Lozano lost to C. Di Laura 9–7 3–6 6–8 5–7; F. Maciel d. P. Arraya 6–3 2–6 7–5
7–5; L. Lavalle /F. Perez d. F. Maynetto /J. Izaga 8–6 3–6 6–1 3–6 6–3; Lozano lost to Arraya 6–3 5–7
3–6 6–4 2–6; Maciel d. Di Laura 6–4 6–4 6–2).
SEMI-FINALS – Brazil d. Colombia 4–1, Porto Alegre (D. Campos d. C. Gomez 6–2 6–4 6–1; C.
Motta lost to A. Jordan 7–5 6–3 5–7 2–6 2–6; C. Kirmayr /Campos d. Jordan /Gomez 6–4 6–4 6–1; M.
Hocevar d. L. Gonzalez 6–0 6–1); *Mexico d. Canada 3–2, Chicoutimi, Quebec* (F. Maciel d. S.
Bonneau 8–6 4–6 7–5 6–2; L. Lavalle lost to M. Wostenholme 5–7 3–6 8–6 6–8 2–6; Maciel /A.
Moreno lost to G. Michibata /M. Greenan 7–9 7–9 4–6; Maciel d. Wostenholme 6–2 6–3 6–0; Lavalle
d. Bonneau 12–10 6–1 6–2).
FINAL – Mexico d. Brazil 4–1, Porto Alegre (L. Lavalle d. D. Campos 6–1 6–3 6–2; F. Maciel d. J.
Goes 6–3 7–5 6–4; J. Lozano /R. Ramirez lost to C. Kirmayr /C. Motta 6–1 3–6 7–9 6–3 0–6; Lavalle d.
Goes 5–7 6–1 6–1 6–1; Maciel d. Campos 3–6 7–5 6–3).

EASTERN ZONE

FIRST ROUND – Chinese Taipei d. Sri Lanka 5–0, Taipei (Huang-Jung Hsu d. N. Casiechitty 6–1 6–1
6–0; Chang-Rung Wu d. A. Fernando 6–3 9–7 6–4; Huang-Jung Hsu /Chang-Rung Wu d.
Casiechitty /Fernando 6–1 6–4 7–5; Huang-Jung Hsu d. Fernando 6–4 6–2; Chang-Rung Wu d.
Casiechitty 6–1 6–1); *Hong Kong d. Singapore 4–1, Singapore* (Kelvin Ng d. A. Teo 9–7 7–5 6–1; M.
Bailey lost to M. Hassan 6–4 3–6 4–6 6–3 4–6; Ng /R. King d. Hassan /V. Pereira 9–7 3–6 8–6 6–3; Ng d.
Hassan 6–1 6–2 9–7; Bailey d. Teo 6–4 6–4 6–2); *Philippines d. Malaysia 5–0, Kuala Lumpur* (F.
Barrientos d. S. Selvarajoo 6–1 6–2 6–3; R. Rafael d. A. Malik 4–6 6–4 6–4 6–0; Barrientos /R. Suarez d.
Malik /Selvarajoo 6–3 6–4 6–3; Barrientos d. Malik 9–7 7–5; M. Tolino d. Y. K. Wah 6–4 6–2); *Korea d.
Indonesia 5–0, Seoul* (Tap-Taik Ro d. T. A. Wibowo 6–4 6–2 6–2; Yeong-Dae Jeon d. Suharyadi 8–6
6–2 2–6 0; Bong-Soo Kim /Jin Sun d. Ludiwiyono /D. Wailan 6–4 10–8 6–2; Jeon d. Wibowo 6–3 ret'd; Ro
d. Suharyadi 6–1 6–3).
QUARTER-FINALS – New Zealand d. Chinese Taipei 4–1, Auckland (D. Mustard d. Huang-Jung
Hsu 6–1 6–1 6–1; R. Simpson d. Chang-Rung Wu 6–4 6–2 6–3; D. Lewis /Mustard d. Huang-Jung
Hsu /Chuang-Hsing Liu 6–3 6–1 6–4; Lewis d. Chang-Rung Wu 6–1 6–3; Simpson lost to Chuang-Hsing
Liu 3–4 ret'd); *China d. Hong Kong 3–2, Shanghai* (Wei You d. M. Bailey 9–7 6–1 6–3; Zhao Xie d. C.
Grant 3–6 6–0 6–0 6–2; Fan Zhang /Shuchen Li lost to Bailey /Grant 12–14 2–6 8–10; Wei You d. Grant
3–6 2–6 6–1 6–8 6–3; Zhao Xie lost to Bailey 3–6 5–7); *Philippines d. Thailand 4–1, Bangkok* (R.
Rafael d. C. Tritilanant 6–4 6–1 6–3; F. Barrientos d. N. Srijaroen 7–5 12–10 4–6 6–1; Barrientos /R.
Suarez d. V. Samret /S. Phukaeow 6–2 1–6 6–4 6–2; M. Tolentino lost to Srijaroen 6–4 0–6 0–2 ret'd;
Suarez d. Tritilanant 6–2 6–0); *Korea d. Pakistan 4–1, Islamabad* (Yeong-Dae Jeon d. Hamidul Haq
6–2 6–2 6–4; Bong-Soo Kim d. Islamul Haq 6–4 6–2 6–3; Kim /Jon-Seon You d. Islamul Haq /M. Zia 6–3
6–4 3–6 6–4; Kap-Taik Ro d. Rashid Malik 7–5 6–2; You lost to Zia 6–1 3–6 4–6).
SEMI-FINALS – New Zealand d. China 5–0, Wellington (C. J. Lewis d. Wei You 6–1 6–2 6–4; R.
Simpson d. Zhao Xie 4–6 1–6 6–2; Lewis /K. Evernden d. Wei You /Zhao Xie 6–4 3–6 3; Lewis d. Fan
Zhang 7–5 7–5; S. Guy d. Wei You 6–1 6–1); *Korea d. Philippines 5–0, Manila* (Yeong-Dae Jeon d.
M. Tolentino 6–3 3–6 6–0 6–3; Jon-Seon You d. R. Rafael 8–6 10–8 6–0; You /Bong-Soo Kim d. Rafael /R.
Suarez-Yoo 4–6 6–1 1–6 8–6 6–3; Jeon d. Rafael 6–3 6–2; Kim d. Tolentino 6–0 6–2).
FINAL – New Zealand d. Korea 4–0, Christchurch (K. Evernden d. Kap-Taik Ro 6–3 6–2 6–4; C. J.
Lewis d. Bong-Soo Kim 6–4 6–4 6–2; Evernden /R. Simpson d. Yeong-Dae Jeon /Jon-Seon You 5–7 6–3
6–2 6–4; Evernden d. Kim 9–7 6–4).

EUROPEAN ZONE A

FIRST ROUND – Turkey w.o. Iran; Hungary d. Morocco 4–1, Casablanca (F. Zentai lost to A.
Chekrouni 4–6 9–7 4–6 6–2 1–6; B. Taroczy d. H. Saber 3–6 6–3 4–6 6–4 6–2; R. Machan /Taroczy d.
Chekrouni /Saber 6–2 6–2 6–4; Zentai d. Saber 4–6 9–7 6–4 6–0; Taroczy d. Chekrouni 14–12 6–1);
Egypt d. Algeria 4–1, Cairo (A. El Mehelmy d. A. Azzi 6–0 6–0 3–6 2–6 6–3; T. El Sakka d. D.
Boudjemline 6–1 6–4 6–3; El Mehelmy /El Sakka d. Azzi /R. Joueurgalou 7–5 3–6 3–6 6–2; El
Mehelmy lost to Boudjemline 2–6 7–5 3–6; El Sakka d. K. Harrad 6–3 6–2); *Monaco d. Senegal 4–1,
Dakar* (R. Balleret d. N. Kabaz 6–2 6–2 6–1; G. Ganancia lost to Y. Doumbia 2–6 3–6 1–6; Balleret /J.

Vincileoni d. Doumbia /Kabaz 4–6 9–11 6–4 11–9 6–3; Ganancia d. Kabaz 6–2 6–3 6–2; A. Viviani d. M. Doumbia 6–4 5–7 6–4); *Ireland d. Cyprus 4–1, Nicosia* (M. Doyle d. Y. Hadjigeorgiou 6–0 6–1 6–3; S. Sorensen d. A. Papamichael 6–1 6–4 8–6; Doyle /Sorensen d. H. Asdjian /P. Zachariades 6–1 6–2 6–4; Doyle lost to Papamichael 6–3 5–7 4–6; Sorensen d. Hadjigeorgiou 6–2 6–1); *Belgium d. Bulgaria 3–1, Brussels* (J. van Langendonck d. K. Lazarov 6–2 2–6 6–4 7–5; K. Demuynck lost to Y. Stamatov 5–7 6–3 1–6 9–7 4–6; van Langendonck /A. Brichant d. K. /M. Lazarov 6–2 6–1 6–0; Demuynck d. K. Lazarov 6–3 4–6 6–4 2–6 6–4).

QUARTER-FINALS – Rumania d. Turkey 5–0, Istanbul (F. Segarceanu d. Y. Erkangil 6–3 6–0 6–1; A. Marcu d. N. Demir 6–2 6–2 6–1; A. Dirru /Segarceanu d. A. Karagoz /Erkangil 6–4 6–3 6–2; Segarceanu d. Karagoz 6–0 6–1; Marcu d. Erkangil 6–3 6–2); *Egypt d. Hungary 3–2, Cairo* (A. El Mehelmy d. F. Zentai 6–1 6–2 6–4; T. El Sakka lost to B. Taroczy 5–7 4–6 0–6; El Mehelmy /Sakka d. Taroczy /R. Machan 5–7 7–5 11–9 3–6 10–8; El Sakka d. Zentai 6–4 6–4 7–5; El Mehelmy lost to Taroczy 5–7 4–6); *Monaco d. Ireland 3–2, Monte Carlo* (G. Ganancia lost to M. Doyle 7–5 6–4 4–6 0–6 4–6; B. Balleret lost to S. Sorensen 7–5 2–6 5–7 2–6; Balleret /J. Vincileoni d. Doyle /Sorensen 6–3 2–6 4–6 6–4 6–4; Balleret d. Doyle 6–3 6–3 6–3; Ganancia d. Sorensen 8–6 3–6 3–6 6–4 9–7); *Denmark d. Belgium 5–0, Holte* (P. Bastiansen d. B. Boileau 6–3 5–7 6–4 6–3; M. Mortensen d. J. van Langendonck 5–7 1–6 6–1 6–1 6–3; Bastiansen /Mortensen d. A. Brichant /van Langendonck 6–4 3–6 6–2 6–3; Mortensen d. Boileau 6–2 6–2; Bastiansen d. van Langendonck 6–3 6–1).

SEMI-FINALS – Rumania d. Egypt 4–1, Bucharest (F. Segarceanu d. T. El Sakka 7–5 3–6 6–0 6–2; A. Dirzu d. A. El Mehelmy 6–6 3 6–1; Segarceanu /Dirzu d. El Sakka /El Mehelmy 6–3 3–6 6–3; Segarceanu d. El Mehelmy 6–4 6–2; Dirzu lost to El Sakka 4–6 2–6); *Denmark d. Monaco 5–0, Monte Carlo* (M. Mortensen d. G. Ganancia 6–3 6–3 6–1; P. Bastiansen d. B. Balleret 6–4 8–6 4–6 3–6 6–4; Bastiansen /Mortensen d. Balleret /J. Vincileoni /Balleret 6–0 2–6 6–0 11–9; Bastiansen d. Ganancia 6–1 6–1; M. Tauson d. A. Viviani 6–4 6–4).

FINAL – Denmark d. Rumania 3–2, Bucharest (P. Bastiansen d. A. Marcu 1–6 6–4 6–1 6–2; M. Tauson lost to F. Segarceanu 3–6 1–6 3–6; Bastiansen /M. Mortensen d. I. Nastase /Segarceanu 6–3 6–4 9–7; Bastiansen lost to Segarceanu 6–8 6–2 4–6 2–6; Tauson d. Marcu 6–4 3–6 6–1 7–5).

EUROPEAN ZONE B

FIRST ROUND – Netherlands d. Finland 4–1, Hilversum (M. Oosting d. L. Palin 6–2 6–1 6–2; M. Schapers d. O. Rahnasto 6–4 0–6 1–6 6–4 6–2; H. van Boekel /Oosting d. Palin /Rahnasto 6–3 6–4 6–8 6–3; Schapers d. Palin 4–6 7–5 6–1; Oosting lost to Rahnasto 6–8 3–6); *Greece d. Norway 4–1, Athens* (T. Bavelas lost to T. Jonsson 3–6 4–6 6–2 6–0 4–6; G. Kalovelonis d. M. Ronneberg 10–12 6–4 6–2 6–3; Kalovelonis /C. Efremoglou d. Ronneberg /J. E. Rustad 6–2 6–4 6–4; Bavelas d. Ronneberg 10–8 6–4 6–2; Kalovelonis d. Jonsson 2–6 6–2 6–2); *Zimbabwe d. Poland 3–2, Warsaw* (P. Tuckniss lost to W. Kowalski 1–6 2–6 4–6; H. Ismail lost to W. Rogowski 6–1 3–6 3–6 3–6; Ismail /Tuckniss d. Kowalski /L. Bienowski 8–6 6–2 6–3; Tuckniss d. Rogowski 6–1 4–6 4–6 6–1 6–3; Ismail d. Kowalski 6–8 3–6 6–3 6–4 6–2); *Switzerland d. Tunisia 5–0, Tunis* (R. Stadler d. H. Soudani 6–1 6–0 6–0; D. Utzinger d. A. Soudani 6–4 6–4 6–1; Utzinger /M. Gunthardt d. A. /M. Soudani 6–2 6–3 6–1; Stadler d. M. Soudani 6–0 6–2; Utzinger d. E. Bramly 6–2 6–2); *Portugal d. Luxembourg 5–0, Lisbon* (J. Silva d. J. Goudenbour 6–2 6–1 6–4; P. Cordeiro d. M. van Kauvenbergh 6–1 6–0 6–1; Silva /Cordeiro d. G. Faber /Goudenbour 6–3 6–2 6–4; Cordeiro d. Goudenbour 4–6 6–3 6–3; Silva d. van Kauvenbergh 6–1 6–3).

QUARTER-FINALS – Israel d. Netherlands 4–1, Ramat Hasharon (S. Glickstein d. H. van Boeckel 6–2 6–4 11–9; A. Mansdorf lost to M. Schapers 2–6 9–11 3–6; Glickstein /S. Perkis d. van Boeckel /Schapers 2–6 7–5 6–4 6–3; Glickstein d. Schapers 4–6 6–1 3–6 6–0 6–0; Mansdorf d. van Boeckel 10–8 7–5); *Austria d. Greece 3–2, Athens* (T. Muster d. G. Kalovelonis 6–4 6–1 6–1; B. Pils d. T. Bavelas 4–6 8–6 5–7 6–2 6–2; P. Feigl /A. Antonitsch d. Kalovelonis /C. Efremoglou 8–6 6–3 7–5; Antonitsch lost to F. Bazeos 6–3 3–6 4–6; Pils lost to Kalovelonis 4–6 4–6 4–6); *Switzerland d. Zimbabwe 5–0, Weggis* (H. Gunthardt d. H. Ismail 6–0 6–1 6–1; J. Hlasek d. P. Tuckniss 6–2 6–2 6–4; Gunthardt /Hlasek d. Ismail /Tuckniss 6–1 6–1 6–1; Hlasek d. Ismail 6–1 6–3 6–4; R. Stadler d. Tuckniss 6–2 6–0 6–1); *Great Britain d. Portugal 5–0, Nottingham* (S. Shaw d. J. Silva 6–3 6–1 6–1; M. J. Bates d. P. Cordeiro 6–4 6–2 6–0; Bates /Shaw d. Silva /Cordeiro 6–3 6–4 6–2; Shaw d. Cordeiro 6–4 8–6; Bates d. Silva 6–4 6–4).

SEMI-FINALS – Israel d. Austria 3–2, Hartberg (A. Mansdorf lost to T. Muster 5–7 6–1 3–6 0–6; S. Glickstein d. B. Pils 6–8 6–4 4–6 6–4 6–1; Glickstein /S. Perkis d. A. Antonitsch /P. Feigl 7–5 7–5 8–6; Mansdorf d. Pils 2–6 7–5 6–1 6–2; Glickstein lost to Muster 6–3 8–10 2–6); *Great Britain d. Switzerland 3–0, Eastbourne* (J. M. Lloyd d. J. Hlasek 5–7 2–6 6–4 7–5 6–4; M. J. Bates d. H. Gunthardt 6–0 6–3 2–6 6–1; C. Dowdeswell /Lloyd d. Hlasek /Gunthardt 7–5 3–6 4–6 6–3 6–2).

FINAL – Great Britain d. Israel 4–1, Eastbourne (M. J. Bates lost to S. Glickstein 7–9 6–3 5–7 6–3 3–6; J. M. Lloyd d. A. Mansdorf 14–12 6–3 4–6 6–3; Lloyd /C. Dowdeswell d. Glickstein /S. Perkis 6–4 3–6 7–5 2–6 6–3; Lloyd d. Glickstein 6–1 6–1 3–6 6–3*; Bates d. Mansdorf 6–2 1–6 6–3*).

*Played indoors at Herstmonceux.

DAVIS CUP by NEC 1986

Non-Zonal Competition

FIRST ROUND 7–9 March	QUARTER-FINALS 18–20 July	SEMI-FINALS 3–5 August	FINAL 19–21 December
WEST GERMANY*			
Mexico†			
USA			
Ecuador†			
AUSTRALIA			
New Zealand†			
SPAIN			
Great Britain†			
USSR			
Yugoslavia†			
India			
CZECHOSLOVAKIA			
Italy†			
PARAGUAY			
Denmark†			
SWEDEN			

Seeded nations in capital letters.
Play-off ties 3–5 October, 1986.

† Choice of ground.
* Choice of ground if decided by lot.
Choice of ground if decided by lot.

Zonal Competition

AMERICAN ZONE

FIRST ROUND 17–19 January	SECOND ROUND 7–9 March	SEMI-FINALS 18–20 July	FINAL 3–5 October	
	CHILE†			Winner promoted to Non-Zonal Group 1987
	Canada			
	Brazil			
	Commonwealth Caribbean‡			
	Peru			
	COLOMBIA†			
	ARGENTINA*			
Uruguay				
Venezuela†				

AFRICAN ZONE

FIRST ROUND 17–19 January	SECOND ROUND 7–9 March	SEMI-FINALS 4–6 April	
	ZIMBABWE†		Winner to European Zone A
	Libya		
	MOROCCO†		
	Kenya		
	SENEGAL*		Winner to European Zone B
Nigeria			
Tunisia†			
	Ivory Coast		
	ALGERIA†		

EUROPEAN ZONE A

FIRST ROUND 9–11 May	SECOND ROUND 11–15 June	SEMI-FINALS 18–20 July	FINAL 3–5 October	
Luxemburg	FRANCE			Winner promoted to Non-Zonal Group 1987
Turkey†	†			
EGYPT†				
Malta				
Cyprus				
Bulgaria†				
Winner of African Zone – top half				
Portugal†	AUSTRIA†			
Finland	†			
Poland†				
	RUMANIA			

EUROPEAN ZONE B

FIRST ROUND 9–11 May	SECOND ROUND 13–15 June	SEMI-FINALS 18–20 July	FINAL 3–5 October	
Iran	MONACO†			Winner promoted to Non-Zonal Group 1987
Hungary†				
Greece†	SWITZERLAND*			
Syria				
Winner of African Zone – bottom half†				
Norway				
Saudi Arabia†	NETHERLANDS			
Belgium				
Ireland†	ISRAEL			

EASTERN ZONE

FIRST ROUND 7–9 March	SECOND ROUND 9–11 May	SEMI-FINALS 18–20 July	FINAL 3–5 October	
Singapore†	JAPAN†			Winner promoted to Non-Zonal Group 1987
Taiwan				
Hong Kong	CHINA*			
Malaysia†				
Bangladesh				
Thailand†				
PHILIPPINES				
Indonesia†				
Pakistan				
Sri Lanka	KOREA†			

Hana Mandlikova led the Czech team to a fourth victory in the Federation Cup by NEC *over a depleted US team.* *(T. Hindley)*

THE *FEDERATION CUP* by NEC

John Parsons

Inspired by her success a month earlier at the US Open, a confident and impressive Hana Mandlikova led Czechoslovakia to victory for the third successive year in a splendidly staged *Federation Cup* in Nagoya, Japan. During a week which drew enthusiastic crowds totalling 37,953 Miss Mandlikova was very much the dominant personality, winning all five of her singles and the two deciding doubles, as Czechoslovakia defeated Greece 2–1, Switzerland 2–1, Hungary 3–0, Bulgaria 2–1 and finally the US 2–1.

In the final, which had to be spread over two days, Czechoslovakia defeated a United States team which was not only without Martina Navratilova and Chris Evert Lloyd but also Zina Garrison, their deputed number one, who had been taken ill with a kidney infection on the eve of the semi-final against Australia. One can only speculate whether a full-strength United States team would have prevented Czechoslovakia joining them as the only nation to have won this event three times in a row. Tom Gorman, the United States captain, thought they could have done. Miss Mandlikova, who had beaten both the world's top two at Flushing Meadow, thought otherwise.

Czechoslovakia were already well in sight of renewed success when rain, which ended several days of mainly humid and hot weather, halted the final. Helena Sukova, after playing herself both into and out of trouble, had won the opening singles from Elise Burgin, the fiercely competitive replacement in the American team, 6–3 6–7 6–4. In a patchy contest, Miss Burgin recovered from 1–4 to take the second set and Miss Sukova did the same from 1–3 in the third to take the match, her serve and volley power and control returning just in time. Miss Mandlikova had reached 7–5 3–0 15–30 on Kathy Jordan's serve when the rain came, and she needed only a further ten minutes on the Monday to complete what in fact was little more than a formality.

Miss Sukova, however, often found herself under pressure. Against Switzerland she had been beaten by Lilian Drescher and against Bulgaria by Katerina, the younger of those remarkable Maleeva sisters who, together with their mother, Yulia, as team captain, make such a formidable combination. Even against Hungary, before Miss Mandlikova won a lively contest with Andrea Temesvari, Miss Sukova had surprisingly dropped a set against the tall, big-serving Csilla Bartus. For her part, however, Miss Mandlikova wavered only once, conceding the opening set to Manuela Maleeva before striking back superbly to take the next two, 6–2 6–1. Certainly the crowd appreciated her play, and the way she led her team, during the closing ceremonies, in Japanese-style bows to each of the stands.

Even if it was only on the Thursday, a public holiday, that the 8,500-seater stands were almost full, NEC, the generous sponsors, must have been delighted by the considerable television and newspaper exposure they received in their home country. The Western influence in Japan is now notable in most things, although some Japanese customs were being absorbed by the visitors, rows of tennis shoes outside the dressing rooms demonstrating how one Japanese tradition was being honoured. It was disappointing for Thursday's crowd that, after watching a close struggle between the United States and Argentina, kept alive by Gabriela Sabatini defeating Miss Garrison, they then saw the host nation beaten by Britain.

One deficiency in Nagoya, where the light tended to fade rapidly soon after 4 p.m., was the absence of floodlights. After two lengthy three-setters, in which Anne Hobbs lost to Masako Yanagi 5–7 6–3 6–2 and Annabel Croft beat Etsuko Inoue 7–6 6–7 6–3, the deciding doubles had reached the point where Miss Inoue and Miss Yanagi had taken the first set 7–6 against Miss Hobbs and Jo Durie and it was 2–2 in the second when they were forced to stop. The following day, although Miss Durie opened the proceedings with a double-fault, she and Miss Hobbs quickly demonstrated their strength as a pair and took just 45 minutes to transform their deficit into a 6–7 6–3 6–2 victory.

Britain had earlier beaten West Germany, who had originally been named as second seeds. That, however, was before the withdrawal for various reasons of their top four players – Steffi Graf, Claudia Kohde-Kilsch, Bettina Bunge and Sylvia Hanika – all of whom had originally indicated their availability and willingness to play. In the quarter-finals, Britain went out to Bulgaria, who also gave Czechoslovakia their toughest fight. The Bulgarian win over Britain was virtually assured once Katerina Maleeva, at 16 already ranked 25 in the world, hit back from 3–5 in the final set, with a succession of astute winners, to beat Jo Durie.

Meanwhile, in the other half of the draw, as Australia and the United States moved towards their expected semi-final clash, there was an early surprise when France lost to New Zealand after Belinda Cordwell upset Pascale Paradis. Only 48 hours earlier France had also lost their place in the World Group of the *Davis Cup* by failing in Yugoslavia. In reaching the last four, the United States defeated Korea, the Republic of China and then Argentina. Australia, with Anne Minter, Wendy Turnbull and Liz Smylie, came through convincingly against Denmark, Spain and Italy.

Following the withdrawal of Miss Garrison, the Australians had looked likely to repeat the semi-final success they had scored over the Americans a year earlier. Then Miss Minter had beaten Kathy Horvath, Miss Turnbull had lost to Miss Jordan and the Australians had won the doubles. This time everything went the other way. First a splendid effort by Miss Burgin against Miss Minter put the Americans ahead; next Miss Turnbull avenged her defeat by Miss Jordan over three long, tense and exciting sets and then the same two Americans beat Miss Turnbull and Miss Smylie, 0–6 6–1 6–4, in a doubles delayed at 2–2 overnight and finished on the morning of the final.

The last act of a fine event was the handing over of the *Federation Cup* flag to Helena Sukova's father, Cyril Suk, the president of the Czech Tennis Federation; it will be in his safe keeping until the 1986 *Federation Cup* in Prague. Czechoslovakia will not easily be dislodged as champions.

THE *FEDERATION CUP* by NEC

NAGOYA, JAPAN, 7–13 OCTOBER
PRELIMINARY ROUND – **Belgium d. Uruguay 3–0** (S. Wasserman d. C. Van der Weck 6–3 6–0; K. Schuurmans d. L. Rodriguez 6–0 6–1; I. de Ruysscher /A. Devries d. M. Clavijc /Van der Weck 6–0 6–2); **Ireland d. Thailand 3–0** (S. Nicholson d. V. Vichienchair 6–1 6–1; J. Thornton d. C. Wattana 6–7 7–5 7–5; D. Craig /Nicholson d. Wattana /P. Samawanthana 6–2 6–4); **Chinese Taipei d. Finland 2–1** (Chui-Mei Ho lost to A. Aallonen 6–2 2–6 5–7; Su-Ling Lai d. A. Happonen 2–6 7–5 6–3; Su-Ling Lai /Sui-Tsuan Wen d. Allonen /Happonen 6–3 6–7 9–7); **Norway d. Chile 2–1** (A. Sunde lost to P. Sepulveda 6–3 4–6 6–2; A. Jonsson d. N. Rodriguez 4–6 6–4 6–3; Jonsson /Sunde d. Rodriguez /Sepulveda 6–3 3–6 6–1); **China d. Indonesia 2–1** (Li Xinyi d. S. Aggarkusuma 0–6 6–4 6–2; Ni Zhong d. Y. Basuki 1–6 6–1 6–2; Xiufen Pu / Qindi Weng lost to Aggarkusuma /Basuki 1–6 5–7); **Republic of Korea d. Philippines 2–1** (Min-Kyeong Seol lost to D. Castellajo 4–6 4–6; Jeong-Soon Lee d. J. Saberon 6–3 6–2; Soo-Ok Kim /Eun-Ok Cho d. Castellajo /Saberson 6–2 6–2).

FIRST ROUND – **Czechoslovakia d. Greece 2–1** (H. Mandlikova d. A. Kanellopoulou 6–2 6–0; H. Sukova d. O. Tsarbopoulou 6–1 6–4; R. Marsikova /A. Holikova lost to Kanellopoulou /Tsarbopoulou 3–6 2–6); **Hungary d. Belgium 3–0** (A. Temesvari d. I. de Ruysscher 7–5 6–3; C. Bartos d. S. Wasserman 6–3 7–6; Temesvari /Bartos d. de Ruysscher /K. Schuurmans 6–2 6–2); **Canada d. Sweden 2–1** (C. Bassett d. C. Lindqvist 6–4 6–3; J. Young d. C. Karlsson 7–5 6–1; Bassett /H. Pelletier lost to Lindqvist /M. Lindstrom 6–4 3–6 4–6); **Bulgaria d. USSR 3–0** (M. Maleeva d. L. Savchenko 6–7 6–4 6–1; K. Maleeva d. E. Eliseenko 6–4 6–2; K. /M. Maleeva d. S. Cherneva /N. Bykova 6–3 7–5); **Yugoslavia d. Ireland 3–0** (S. Goles d. S. Nicholson 4–6 6–4 6–3; M. Jausovec d. J. Thornton 6–3 6–0; Goles /A. Winkler d. D. Craig /Thornton 6–2 6–2); **Switzerland d. Netherlands 2–1** (C. Jolissaint lost to

M. Mesker 3–6 6–4 4–6; L. Drescher d. N. Schutte 6–2 7–6; Jolissaint /Drescher d. Mesker /Schutte 6–3 6–2); *Japan d. Austria 3–0* (E. Inoue d. P. Huber 7–5 6–7 6–2; M. Yanagi d. B. Pollet 6–4 6–3; Inoue /Yanagi d. Huber /Pollet 7–5 6–2); *Great Britain d. West Germany 3–0* (A. Croft d. M. Schropp 6–3 6–1; J. M. Durie d. P. Keppeler 6–4 6–0; Durie /A. E. Hobbs d. Keppeler /A. Betzner 6–4 3–6 6–1); *Italy d. Chinese Taipei 3–0* (R. Reggi d. Chiu-Mei Ho 6–1 6–1; S. Cecchini d. Su-Ling Lai 6–1 6–0; Reggi /Cecchini d. Su-Ling Lai /Sui-Tsuan Wen 6–1 6–0); *Mexico d. Norway 3–0* (H. Steden d. A. Sunde 6–3 6–4; C. Hernandez d. A. Jonsson 7–6 6–1; Staden /M. E. Llamas d. Jonsson /J. Jensen 7–5 6–3); *Spain d. Hong Kong 2–1* (A. Almansa d. P. Hy 6–0 6–0; E. Guerra lost to P. Moreno 3–6 2–6; Almansa /R. Bielsa d. Hy /Moreno 3–6 7–6 6–3); *Australia d. Denmark 3–0* (W. M. Turnbull d. T. Scheuer-Larsen 6–2 7–6; A. Minter d. A. Moeller 6–2 6–2; Turnbull /Mrs E. Smylie d. Scheuer-Larsen/Moeller 6–3 6–3); *Argentina d. Peru 3–0* (G. Sabatini d. Mrs L. Gildemeister 6–3 6–3; A. Villagran d. P. Vasquez 7–6 6–7 8–6; Sabatini/M. Paz d. Gildemeister/Vasquez 6–0 7–6); *New Zealand d. France 2–1* (B. Cordwell d. P. Paradis 6–3 6–2; J. Richardson lost to N. Tauziat 6–3 3–6 2–6; Cordwell/Richardson d. I. Demongeot/Tauziat 6–0 7–5); *China d. Brazil 3–0* (Li Xinyi d. N. Dias 6–4 7–6; Ni Zhong d. C. Monteiro 6–3 6–4; Xiufen Pu/Qindi Weng lost to C. Faillace/Monteiro 4–6 2–6); *USA d. Republic of Korea 3–0* (Z. Garrison d. Min-Kyeong Seol 6–0 6–0; K. Jordan d. Soo-Ok Kim 6–3 6–4; Jordan/S. A. Walsh d. Jeong-Soon Lee/Eun-Ok Cho 6–0 6–0).

SECOND ROUND – Czechoslovakia d. Switzerland 2–1 (H. Mandlikova d. C. Jolissaint 7–6 6–1; H. Sukova lost to L. Drescher 6–7 3–6; Mandlikova /Sukova d. Jolissaint /Drescher 6–1 6–2); *Hungary d. Canada 2–1* (A. Temesvari lost to C. Bassett 3–6 1–6; C. Bartos d. J. Young 7–6 6–2; Temesvari /Bartos d. J. Hetherington /H. Pelletier 7–5 6–3); *Bulgaria d. Yugoslavia 3–0* (M. Maleeva d. S. Goles 6–1 6–3; K. Maleeva d. M. Jausovec 6–4 6–2; K. /M. Maleeva d. Goles /A. Winkler 6–4 7–6); *Great Britain d. Japan 2–1* (A. Croft d. E. Inoue 7–6 6–7 6–3; A. E. Hobbs lost to M. Yanagi 7–5 3–6 2–6; J. M. Durie /Hobbs d. Inoue /Yanagi 6–7 6–3 6–2); *Italy d. Mexico 3–0* (R. Reggi d. H. Steden 6–4 3–6 7–5; S. Cecchini d. C. Hernandez 6–2 6–4; Cecchini /L. Garrone d. Hernandez /M. E. Llamas 6–3 6–3); *Australia d. Spain 3–0* (W. M. Turnbull d. A. Almansa 6–1 6–1; A. Minter d. E. Guerra 6–4 6–0; Minter /J. Byrne d. Almansa /R. Bielsa 6–1 7–5); *Argentina d. New Zealand 2–1* (G. Sabatini d. B. Cordwell 6–1 6–0; M. Paz d. J. Richardson 6–3 6–4; Sabatini /A. Villagran lost to Cordwell /Richardson 2–6 2–6); *USA d. China 3–0* (Z. Garrison d. Li Xinyi 6–0 6–2; K. Jordan d. Ni Zhong 6–1 6–0; Jordan /S. A. Walsh d. Li Xinyi /Ni Zhong 6–2 6–2).

QUARTER-FINALS – Czechoslovakia d. Hungary 3–0 (H. Mandlikova d. A. Temesvari 6–3 6–4; H. Sukova d. C. Bartos 6–7 6–2; R. Marsikova /A. Holikova d. Temesvari /Bartos 6–4 6–3); *Bulgaria d. Great Britain 2–1* (M. Maleeva d. A. Croft 6–2 6–2; K. Maleeva d. J. M. Durie 6–2 4–6 8–6; K. /M. Maleeva lost to Durie /A. E. Hobbs 4–5 ret'd); *Australia d. Italy 3–0* (W. M. Turnbull d. R. Reggi 6–2 6–1; A. Minter d. S. Cecchini 6–3 6–2; Turnbull /J. Byrne d. Reggi /L. Garrone 6–1 6–3); *USA d. Argentina 2–1* (Z. Garrison lost to G. Sabatini 7–5 1–6 1–6; K. Jordan d. A. Villagran 6–1 6–1; Jordan /S. A. Walsh d. Sabatini /Villagran 5–7 6–3 6–4).

SEMI-FINALS – Czechoslovakia d. Bulgaria 2–1 (H. Mandlikova d. M. Maleeva 3–6 6–2 6–1; H. Sukova lost to K. Maleeva 6–6 6–7; Mandlikova /Sukova d. K. /M. Maleeva 6–3 7–6); *USA d. Australia 2–1* (K. Jordan lost to W. M. Turnbull 4–6 7–6 5–7; E. Burgin d. A. Minter 6–3 6–4; Jordan /Burgin d. Turnbull /Mrs E. Smylie 0–6 6–1 6–4).

FINAL – Czechoslovakia d. USA 2–1 (H. Mandlikova d. K. Jordan 7–5 6–1; H. Sukova d. E. Burgin 6–3 6–7 6–4; R. Marsikova /A. Holikova lost to Burgin /S. A. Walsh 2–6 3–6).

CONSOLATION PLATE

FIRST ROUND – Belgium d. Thailand 3–0; Brazil d. Indonesia 3–0; Netherlands d. Denmark 3–0; Hong Kong d. Norway 2–1; Greece d. Chile 2–1; USSR d. Austria 2–1.
SECOND ROUND – Korea d. Sweden 2–1; Philippines d. Belgium 2–1; Brazil d. Peru 2–1; Netherlands d. Ireland 2–1; Hong Kong d. Finland 2–1; West Germany d. Greece 3–0; USSR d. Taiwan 3–0; France d. Uruguay 3–0.
QUARTER-FINALS – Korea d. Philippines 3–0; Brazil d. Netherlands 2–1; West Germany d. Hong Kong 2–1; USSR d. France 2–1.
SEMI-FINALS – Korea d. Brazil 2–1; USSR d. West Germany 3–0.
FINAL – USSR d. Korea 3–0.

Saab – Official car for the ITF

An exclusive car for exclusive people

In many ways, the qualities that characterize a truly great ambassador may be used to describe a truly great car.

Case in point, the Saab 9000 Turbo 16.

Bold, sophisticated, confident, daring, stylish and powerful – it's a car fitting the noblest courtier. A perfect mix of strength and grace.

The heart of the 9000 Turbo 16 is the 16-valve turbocharged engine. This powerful muscle has double overhead camshafts, a microprocessor controlled fuel injection system, APC and an intercooler, which allows the 9000 Turbo 16 to dominate the road. But it does so in impeccable taste. Its streamline aerodynamic design is a feast for the eyes and its spacious interior makes the 9000 Turbo 16 one of the most comfortable cars on the market.

A car such as the 9000 Turbo 16 isn't designed for everyone. It's for the discriminating connoisseur who demands the most from himself and the things around him. It's for somebody such as yourself.

Write or call us and we'll send you more information about the exciting Saab 9000 Turbo 16.

Saab-Scania, Saab Car Division
S-611 81 Nyköping, Sweden.
Telephone: (+46)155 44 000

FEDERATION CUP by NEC 1985

PRELIMINARY ROUND	FIRST ROUND	SECOND ROUND	QUARTER-FINALS	SEMI-FINALS	FINAL
	CZECHOSLOVAKIA	CZECHOSLOVAKIA 2–1	CZECHOSLOVAKIA 2–1	CZECHOSLOVAKIA 3–0	CZECHOSLOVAKIA 2–1
	Greece				
	Netherlands	Switzerland 2–1			
Uruguay / Belgium	Switzerland				
	Belgium 3–0	Hungary 3–0	Hungary 2–1		
	Hungary				
	Canada	Canada 2–1			
	SWEDEN				
	BULGARIA	BULGARIA 3–0	BULGARIA 3–0	BULGARIA 2–1	
	USSR				
Thailand / Ireland	Ireland 3–0	Yugoslavia 3–0			
	Yugoslavia				
	Austria	Japan 3–0	GREAT BRITAIN 2–1		
	Japan				
	West Germany	GREAT BRITAIN 3–0			
	GREAT BRITAIN				
	ITALY	ITALY 3–0	ITALY 3–0	AUSTRALIA 3–0	USA 2–1
Finland / Taiwan	Taiwan				
	Mexico	Mexico 3–0			
Norway / Chile	Norway 2–1				
	Spain	Spain 2–1	AUSTRALIA 3–0		
	Hong Kong				
	Denmark	AUSTRALIA 3–0			
	AUSTRALIA				
	ARGENTINA	ARGENTINA 3–0	ARGENTINA 2–1	USA 2–1	
	Peru				
	France	New Zealand 2–1			
	New Zealand				
Indonesia / China	Brazil	China 2–1	USA 3–0		
Philippines / Republic of Korea	China				
	Republic of Korea 2–1	USA 3–0			
	USA				

Capital letters denote seeded countries.

The ITF Committee of Management (left to right): A. Metreveli, R. Nikolic, H. Grimm, E. Kawatei, D. N. Hardwick, P. Llorens, P. Chatrier, H. L. Delatour, B. R. Tobin, A. Pena, G. D. Jorgensen, D. Jude.

THE INTERNATIONAL TENNIS FEDERATION

The International Tennis Federation
Church Road, Wimbledon, London SW19 5TF
Telephone: 01 946 5587. Cables: Intennis, London SW19. Telex: 919253 ITF G and 943119 ITF G.
Telecopier: 01 946 3659.

President 1985–87: Mr P. Chatrier.
Honorary Life Vice-Presidents: Mr J. Borotra, Dr G. de Stefani, Mr A. Heyman.
Honorary Life Counsellors: Mr L. E. Ashenheim, Mr J. E. Carrico, Mr L. Gorodi, Mr J. S. Harrison,
Padma Bhushan R. K. Khanna, Mr S. Malless, Mr S. B. Reay, Mr W. H. Woods.
Committee of Management 1985–87: Mr P. Chatrier, Mr H. L. Delatour, Dr H. Grimm, Mr D. N.
Hardwick, Mr G. D. Jorgensen, Mr E. Kawatei, Mr P. Llorens, Mr A. Metreveli, Mr R. Nikolic, Mr A.
Pena, Mr B. R. Tobin.
Vice-Presidents 1985–87: Mr H. L. Delatour Jr, Mr P. Llorens, Mr B. R. Tobin.
Honorary Treasurer 1985–87: Mr D. Jude.
Auditors 1985–87: Messrs Ernst & Whinney, Becket House, 1 Lambeth Palace Road, London SE1 7EU.
Legal Counsel: Mr J. W. Lillie.
Sub-Committees 1985–87: *Davis Cup*; *Federation Cup*; Finance; Junior Competitions; Olympic;
Rules; Technical; Veterans.
Commissions: Media; Medical.
Secretariat: Miss S. Woodhead – General Secretary; Mr T. Hallberg – Director of Men's Tennis; Mr
D. MacCurdy – Director of Development; Miss B. Wancke – Director of Women's Tennis.
Sponsorship and Business Consultant: Dr P. Angeli.

MEN'S INTERNATIONAL PROFESSIONAL TENNIS COUNCIL

ITF representatives: Mr P. Chatrier, Mr F. Hainline Jr, Mr D. N. Hardwick. *Player representatives:*
Mr M. G. Davies (Chairman), Mr R. Moore, Mr H. Solomon. *North American tournaments:* Mr C.
Pasarell. *European tournaments:* Mr F. Bartoni. *Rest of World:* Mr B. R. Tobin. *Administrator:* Mr
M. Marshall Happer III. *Assistant Administrators:* Mr D. Cooper, Mr T. Eugenio (New York) and Mr
P. Svehlik (Paris).

WOMEN'S INTERNATIONAL PROFESSIONAL TENNIS COUNCIL

ITF representatives: Mr P. Chatrier, Ms J. Cella, Mrs A. Jones. *WTA representatives:* Mr J.
Diamond, Ms P. Kellmeyer, Ms C. Reynolds. *North America:* Ms E. McGoldrick. *European
tournaments:* Mr R. Stammbach. *Rest of World:* Mr B. R. Tobin. *Managing Director:* Ms M.
Oliveau.

THE AFRICAN YEAR

The year 1985 was an exciting one for African tennis. It began on a most positive note with the eighth
ITF West African Junior Championships /Air Afrique Trophy, which attracted competitors from 23
countries and is now believed to be the largest junior sporting event in Africa. On the final day, a
crowd of more than 1,000 watched Ivory Coast narrowly retain the team championship, with Senegal,
Morocco, Algeria and Togo filling the other places in the top five. An all-West African team was then
selected on the basis of their performances and sent, under ITF colours, to train for one month in
Blois, France, and during the summer they also competed in six junior tournaments in France.
    Later in the year came the much-welcomed formation of an African Zone of the *Davis Cup*. Since
the number of African nations participating in the competition had increased and the quality of the
players improved, it was felt that the time was right to take this important step in the development of
the worldwide game. In October the African Tennis Confederation staged the African Senior
Championships for adults. This tournament, now in its sixth year, is held annually in Tripoli, Libya.
Zimbabwe provided both the boys' and the girls' teams for the ITF World Youth Cup, an international

16-and-under competition held in Kobe, Japan in November, as a result of the African qualifying tournament in Zeralda, Algeria.

ASIAN TENNIS FEDERATION

President: General Jonosewojo (Indonesia); *Deputy President:* Goro Fujikura (Japan); *Secretary:* Eiichi Kawatei (Japan); *Treasurer:* Ed Hardisty (Hong Kong).

It was another year of improvement for Asian tennis, both in the number of tournaments staged and in the standard of play achieved. New junior tournaments in Korea, Indonesia, Sri Lanka and the Philippines brought the number of Asian events on the ITF junior ranking calendar to 15, and many of the leading juniors expressed an intent to move into senior tennis. Doug McCurdy, the ITF Director of Development, organised teachers' workshops in the Middle East and Asia with a three-day course in Bahrain and a five-day course in Japan. Many Asian coaches took part and were enthusiastic about the value of courses like these. Accordingly they will become a regular part of the annual programme so that coaching standards throughout the area can be improved. Facilities, too, were being improved throughout Asia. In Korea, for instance, the Olympic tennis complex, with its 18 separate courts and a 10,000-seat stadium, was already well advanced. China was hoping to build a large facility in the centre of Bejing, while in Japan the new Tokyo Tennis Centre already has 48 courts, and there are plans to build a 10,000-seat stadium. These three centres, together with the Jubilee Centre in Hong Kong, with its unique facilities ideal for residential coaching seminars, will become the heart of Asian tennis development. There were three important international events held in Japan during 1985. The *Federation Cup* by NEC was another success for the Czech girls. The University Games and the World Youth Cup, both staged in Kobe, were the first major contests played on sand-filled synthetic grass, and most of the players liked the performance of the product. Already the Asian tennis world is looking towards the 1988 Olympic Games, hoping to produce better players at all levels to compete there.

EUROPEAN TENNIS ASSOCIATION

President: Heinz Grimm; *Vice Presidents:* J. Chargelegue and R. Nikolic. *Members:* K. Hehenkamp, H. Klosterkemper, G. Paish, F. Ricci-Bitti, J. M. Tintore, B. Victor.

For the European Tennis Association 1985 was a memorable year. In March, for instance, the Association celebrated its tenth anniversary, and no less than 25 member nations were represented at the Annual Meeting which took place in Geneva. By the end of the year the developing strength of European tennis was plain for all to see, not only in the *Davis Cup* and *Federation Cup*, but in Grand Slam tournaments in which European men, for the first time since 1934, won all the titles and European-born women won three of the four.

Heinz Grimm, the ETA President, during his address in Geneva, could point with justifiable satisfaction to the progress already made and the principal objectives for the future, which included the creation of new tournaments for women, the improvement of officiating, and the continuing search for general sponsorships. In this respect, the arrival of Badische Adilin & Soda Fabrik (BASF) as sponsors of the BASF European Cup (formerly the King's Cup) in January was a great step forward. Another long-term goal was also achieved with the launching of a European women's team championship along similar lines to the men's event, and a major sponsorship of this competition in time for 1987 is expected.

Meanwhile, the two important European stops on the Virginia Slims Series, the Indoors — played for the second time in Zurich — and the Outdoor event — staged for the first time in Lugano — were both a considerable success. The ETA, with its huge commitment to junior activities, of course, especially through the European Junior Championships and the increasingly popular range of Summer cups, will continue to do its best to serve all aspects of European tennis to the highest possible level.

THE PANAMERICAN TENNIS CONFEDERATION

President: A. Plaza (Venezuela); *Vice-Presidents:* D. Nelthropp (Virgin Island); A. Marin (Colombia); H. Pistelli (Argentina); *Secretary:* G. Mejia (Dominican Republic); *Treasurer:* R. Velez (Puerto Rico); *Vocal:* Ms S. Hagey (USA), A. Lucas (Venezuela), J. Marquez (Brazil).

The main objective of the Panamerican Tennis Confederation is to regulate tennis tournaments of the Olympic circle in the American continent — the Bolivarian Games, Central American and Caribbean Games and the Panamerican Games. During 1985 the first Panamerican Veteran Championships were also organised and staged in the Romana 'Club de Campo' in the Dominican Republic. The 1986 Championships in September will be held in Caracas, Venezuela.

THE SOUTH AMERICAN YEAR

COSAT – President: A. Plaza (Venezuela); *Committee:* C. Rymer (Uruguay), W. Jones (Peru), J. Villadeamigo (Argentina) and W. Chechia (Brazil); *Secretary:* R. Gomez.

The objects of the South American Tennis Confederation, which embraces Argentina, Brazil, Bolivia, Colombia, Chile, Ecuador, Paraguay, Peru, Uruguay and Venezuela, are to promote tennis throughout the Region and to co-ordinate the activities of member nations. In particular this involves many important junior events, especially the South American Junior Championships and the Nations Cup for men and women. In addition, every March an international South American Senior Championship is organised by Otto Hausser in the three age groups for men (45, 55 and 60) and two for women (40 and 50). There is also an annual club championship, the winner of which competes against the European Champion club. Success by many South American junior players in international tournaments for all age groups is a heartening indication of the progress being made throughout the Region.

Leonardo Lavalle of Mexico, son of the President of the Mexican LTA, delighted the family by winning the Wimbledon junior singles title and earning a world ranking in the top 100.　　　　　　　　　　　　　　　　　　　　　　　　　　　　　　　　*(T. Hindley)*

The youngest player ever to win a Grand Prix tournament, Aaron Krickstein found it difficult to maintain the impetus of his remarkable young career. He started the year ranked 12 and ended it at 30. (T. Hindley)

THE ITF FOUNDATION

The ITF Foundation was created in 1980 to establish liaison and co-operation between the International Tennis Federation and manufacturers of tennis related products, and to ensure a constant exchange of views and comments mutually beneficial to the sport.

Membership of the Foundation, for an annual subscription of £1,000, enables each company to be officially recognised at various ITF activities during the year and also to be offered a direct line of communication with any of the 124 nations affiliated to the ITF. In return, the finance generated enables the ITF Development Programme to give help, ranging from coaching, the training of coaches and officials, tennis leadership workshops and the provision of equipment in countries and regions where it is most needed. To date, for instance, members have provided the ITF with more than 10,000 obsolete rackets, which have been passed on, in turn, to National Tennis Associations for use in specified national programmes.

The following are currently working with the ITF:

ASICS, Japan; **Adidas**, France; **AMF Head**, USA; **Bolltex**, Sweden; **DHL**, Great Britain; **Diadora**, Italy; **Dunlop**, Italy; **Dunlop**, Great Britain; **Fischer**, Austria; **Gosen**, Japan; **Kim Top Line**, Italy; **Lacoste**, France; **Marlboro Leisure Wear**, Italy; **Mizuno**, Japan; **Nassau**, Republic of Korea; **Penn**, USA; **Pirelli**, Italy; **Prince**, USA; **Rossignol**, France; **Slazengers**, Great Britain; **Supreme (Allwetter)**, West Germany; **Tacchini (Sandys)**, Italy; **Tennis Australia**; **Tennis De France**; **Tennis World**, Great Britain; **Tretorn**, Sweden; **Wilson**, USA; **Yamaha**, Japan.

NATIONAL ASSOCIATIONS, RANKINGS AND CHAMPIONSHIPS

MEMBERS WITH VOTING RIGHTS (82)

Abbreviations: C.=Cable address, T.=Telephone number, TX.=Telex number.

ALGERIA

Federation Algerienne de Tennis, Centre des Federations Sportives, Cite Olympique, BP 88 El Biar, Algiers.
T. (213) 79 /39 /39 or 78 /63 /63; TX. 52691 CFS DZ; *Pres.* Mr L. Benazzi; *Sec.* Mr R. Bouakkaz.

ARGENTINA

Asociacion Argentina de Tenis, Av. San Juan 1315 /1317, (1148) Capital Federal, Buenos Aires.
C. Argtennis, Buenos Aires; T. (1) 26 1569 /27 0101 /26 4696; TX. 17336 ARGEN AR; *Pres.* Mr J. J. Vasquez; *Secs* Mr F. Turno, Mr L. J. Rival.

AUSTRALIA

LTA of Australia Ltd, Box 343, South Yarra, Victoria 3141.
C. Tencourt, Melbourne; T. (3) 267 4277; TX. 36893 TENCRT; *Pres.* Mr B. R. Tobin; *Sec.* Mr C. McDonald.
MEN: **1** Paul McNamee; **2** Pat Cash; **3** Simon Youl; **4** John Fitzgerald; **5** Wally Masur; **6** Peter Doohan; **7** Mark Edmondson; **8** Broderick Dyke; **9** Darren Cahill; **10** Mark Woodforde.

AUSTRIA

Osterreichischer Tennisverband, Hainburgerstrasse 36, A 1030 Vienna.
C. Austriatennis, Vienna; T. (222) 753345 /733352; TX. 131652 OETEN A; *Pres.* Dr T. Zeh; *Sec.* Mr P. Nader.
MEN: **1** Thomas Muster; **2** Hans Peter Kandler; **3** Bernhard Pils; **4** Al. Antonitsch; **5** Reininger; **6** Peter Feigl; **7** Horst Skoff; **8** K. Oberparleiter; **9** Gerald Mild; **10** Michael Bauer.
WOMEN: **1** Petra Huber; **2** Barbara Pollet; **3** Judith Poelzl; **4** Ingrid Sommerauer; **5** Ingrid Vlach; **6** Heidi Sprung; **7** Karin Hinterwirth; **8** Claudia Tranker; **9** Susanne Kotzmaier; **10** Karin Oberleitner.

National Closed Championships
MEN'S SINGLES – Semi-finals: P. Feigl d. T. Muster 4–6 7–6 0–6; G. Mild d. H. P. Kandler 3–6 7–6 7–6. ***Final:*** Muster d. Mild 6–0 6–2 6–1.
WOMEN'S SINGLES – Semi-finals: P. Huber d. B. Pollet 6–4 6–4; J. Polzl d. A. Pesak 6–4 6–1. ***Final:*** Huber d. Polzl 6–2 6–0.

BAHRAIN

Bahrain Lawn Tennis Federation, PO 26985, Bahrain.
C. Tennis, Bahrain; T. (973) 687236; TX. 8292 GPIC BN; *Pres.* Dr Tawfecq Al-Moayed; *Sec.* Mr Adnan Fakhro.

National Closed Championships
MEN'S SINGLES – Semi-finals: V. C. Jacob d. P. Panton 6–0 6–0; K. E. Mammen d. D. Fisher 6–1 6–2. ***Final:*** Jacob d. Mammen 6–0 6–0.

BANGLADESH

Bangladesh Tennis Federation, Tennis Complex, Ramna Green, Dacca 2.
C. Tennisfed, Dacca; T. (2) 506650; TX. 642401 SHER BJ (mark: for tennis); *Pres.* Lt Gen. H. M. Ershad; *Hon. Sec.* Mr Wahedul Karim.
MEN: 1 Iftekhar Sardar; 2 Maroof Rahman; 3 Haroonur Rashid; 4 Khaled Salahuddin.

National Closed Championships
MEN'S SINGLES – Semi-finals: I. Sardar d. K. Salahuddin 6–3 6–2; M. Rahman d. H. Rashi 6–4 6–3. *Final:* Sardar d. Rahman 6–2 6–4.

BELGIUM

Royal Belgian Tennis Federation, Passage International Rogier 6, BTE 522, 1210 Brussels.
C. Tennisfeder, Brussels; T. (2) 217 2365; TX. 24023 TENFED B; *Pres.* Mr P. P. de Keghel; *Secs.* Mr W. Goethals and Mr F. Lemaire.
MEN: 1 Bernard Boileau; 2 Jan Van Langendonck; 3 Alain Brichant; 4 Karel Demuynck; 5 Jean Fisette; 6 Denis Langaskens; 7 Jacques Grandjean; 8 Pierre Godfroid; 9 Johan Depreter; 10 Eric Brawerman.
WOMEN: 1 Kathleen Schuurmans; 2 Ann Devries; 3 Sandra Wasserman; 4 Ilse De Ruysscher; 5 Isabelle Dumont; 6 Annick Claes; 7 Anne Gabriel; 8 Greet Vervloet; 9 Klaartje Van Baarle; 10 Nicole Mabille.

National Closed Championships
MEN'S SINGLES – Semi-finals: J. De Preter d. J. Van Langendonck 6–4 6–1 6–4; B. Boileau d. A. Brichant 6–3 6–4 6–0. *Final:* Boileau d. De Preter 6–4 6–3 6–2.
WOMEN'S SINGLES – Semi-finals: I. De Ruysscher d. K. Schuurmans 6–2 6–1; S. Wasserman d. A. Devries 7–6 1–6 6–2. *Final:* De Ruysscher d. Wasserman 6–3 6–0.

BOLIVIA

Federacion Boliviana de Tennis, Calle Mexico 1638, Casilla 20887, La Paz.
C. Fedboltenis, La Paz; T. 378769; *Pres.* Sr T. Sagarnaga P.; *Sec.* Sr M. Adriazola.

BRAZIL

Confederacao Brasileira de Tenis, Rua Anfilofio de Carvalho No. 29, Grupo 407 /8-ZC-20.030 Centro, Rio de Janeiro.
C. Cebetenis, Rio de Janeiro; T. (21) 220 5444, 251 3920; *Pres.* Mr Eugenio Saller; *Sec.* Mr C. A. Martelotti.
MEN: 1 Julio Goes; 2 Cassio Motta; 3 Marcos Hocevar; 4 Nelson Aerts; 5 Givaldo Barbosa.
WOMEN: 1 Niege Dias; 2 Patricia Medrado; 3 Luciana Corsato; 4 Claudia Monteiro; 5 Silvana Campos.

National Closed Championships
MEN'S SINGLES – Final: C. Motta d. L. Mattar 6–3 6–0.
WOMEN'S SINGLES – Final: N. Dias d. P. Medrado.

BULGARIA

Bulgarian Tennis Federation, 18 Tolbuchin Blvd., 1040 Sofia.
C. Besefese Tennis, Sofia; T. 80-3710 or 8651; TX. 22723 or 22724 BSFS BG; *Pres.* Mr S. Ganev; *Sec.* Mr T. Tzvetkov.
MEN: 1 Liuben Petrov; 2 Iulian Stamatov; 3 Ruslan Raynov; 4 Krasimir Lazarov; 5 Egveni Jeliazkov; 6 Edmond Derderian; 7 Asen Dishkov; 8 Teodor Bachev; 9 Stefan Chamurliisky; 10 Rumen Mihov.
WOMEN: 1 Manuela Maleeva; 2 Katerina Maleeva; 3 Dora Rangelova; 4 Adriana Velcheva; 5 Bogdana Marinova; 6 Diana Moskova; 7 Marina Mondova; 8 Elizabeth Nikolova; 9 Mirela Kraycheva; 10 Milena Arsova.

National Closed Championships
MEN'S SINGLES – Semi-finals: I. Stamatov d. K. Lazarov 7–6 7–6 5–7 6–3; L. Petrov d. R. Raynov 7–6 6–4 7–5. *Final:* Petrov d. Stamatov 7–6 6–4 4–6 6–3 6–1.

WOMEN'S SINGLES – Semi-finals: A. Velcheva d. M. Kondova 6–2 6–0; D. Rangelova d. B. Marinova 1–6 7–5 6–3. *Final:* Rangelova d. Velcheva 6–3 6–2.

CAMEROON

Federation Camerounaise de Lawn Tennis, BP 1121, Yaounde.
C. Fecatennis-MJS. Yaounde; T. 233860 /1310 or 224329; TX. 8568 KN or MNFA 8261 KN; *Pres.* Brig. Gen. J. J. Tataw; *Sec.* Dr N. Mboulet.
MEN: **1** Zacharie Mougnol; **2** Jean Ngoue; **3** Joseph Onguene; **4** Michel Fondjeu; **5** Nkoueleu; **6** Harari; **7** Michel Atana; **8** Eyap; **9** Ateba; **10** Ribouem.
WOMEN: **1** Razac Vilanova; **2** Languin; **3** Imhof; **4** Faury; **5** Bon; **6** Soulier; **7** Billet; **8** Esclafit; **9** Mametz; **10** Gacha.

National Closed Championships
MEN'S SINGLES – Semi-finals: Z. Mougnol d. J. Onguene 6–3 ret'd; J. Ngoue d. M. Fondjeu 6–4 6–3. *Final:* Mougnol d. Ngoue 6–4 6–3 7–6.
WOMEN'S SINGLES – Semi-finals: R. Vilanova d. Faury 6–2 6–2; Languin d. Imhof 6–2 2–6 6–2. *Final:* Vilanova d. Languin 6–3 7–5.

CANADA

Canadian Tennis Association, 3111 Steeles Avenue West, Downsview, Ontario, Canada M3J 3H2.
C. Sportrec, Ottawa; T. (416) 665-9777; TX. 053 3660 SPORTREC OTT; *Pres.* Mr F. Godbout; *Exec. Dir.* Mr D. Steele; *Dir. High Performance:* Ms D. Wilson.
MEN: **1** Glenn Michibata; **2** Stephane Bonneau; **3** Chris Pridham; **4** Martin Wostenholme; **5** Hatem McDadi; **6** Andrew Sznajder; **7** Martin Laurendeau; **8** Doug Burke; **9** Grant Connell; **10** Derek Segal.
WOMEN: **1** Carling Bassett; **2** Jane Young; **3** Helen Kelesi; **4** Karen Dewis; **5** Marjorie Blackwood; **6** Jill Hetherington; **7** Rene Simpson; **8** Helene Pelletier; **9** Marianne Groat; **10** Wendy Pattenden.

National Closed Championships
MEN'S SINGLES – Semi-finals: S. Bonneau d. D. Segal 6–2 7–6; M. Laurendeau d. G. Michibata 6–1 6–4. *Final:* Bonneau d. Laurendeau 7–6 3–6 6–3.
WOMEN'S SINGLES – Semi-finals: J. Young d. M. Blackwood 6–4 7–5; K. Dewis d. J. Hetherington 6–7 7–5 6–0. *Final:* Young d. Dewis 7–6 6–3.

CHILE

Federacion de Tenis de Chile, Almirante Simpson No. 36, Casilla 1149, Santiago.
T. (2) 2227279; TX. 241328 COCH CL; *Pres.* Mr A. Peric; *Sec.* Mr A. Alvarez.
MEN: **1** Ricardo Acuna; **2** Pedro Rebolledo; **3** Hans Gildemeister; **4** José Antonio Fernandez; **5** Alvaro Fillol; **6** Belus Prajoux; **7** Gerardo Vacarezza; **8** Juan Pablo Queirolo; **9** Kerman Urresti; **10** Ivan Camus.
WOMEN: **1** Paulina Sepulveda; **2** Patricia Hermida; **3** Isabel Ubilla; **4** Carolina Garcia Huidobro; **5** Natacha Marcucci; **6** Monica Fuentealba; **7** Carolina Espinoza; **8** Jakeline Rivas; **9** Eugenia Fernandez; **10** Pamela Gonzalez.

CHINA, PEOPLE'S REPUBLIC OF

Tennis Association of the People's Republic of China, 9 Tiyuguan Road, Beijing.
C. Sportchine, Beijing; T. 751313; TX. 22323 CHOC CN; *Pres.* Mr L. Zhengcao; *Sec.* Mr Liu Huaitang.
MEN: **1** Zhao Xie; **2** Keqin Ma; **3** Fan Zhang; **4** Shuhua Liu; **5** Zhiqiang Zhao; **6** Shuchen Li; **7** Shiquin Li; **8** Qianghua Meng; **9** Depeng Li; **10** Jianguo Wang.
WOMEN: **1** Xiufen Pu; **2** Ping Wang; **3** Lilan Duan; **4** Ni Zhong; **5** Ping Guo; **6** Qindi Weng; **7** Qingqing Gong; **8** Xiaoyun Zhu; **9** Ruichun Yang; **10** Yan Sun.

National Closed Championships
MEN'S SINGLES – Semi-finals: Shuchen Li d. Shuhua Liu 6–1 6–4 7–6; Keqin Ma d. Zhao Xie 6–4 6–3 7–5. *Final:* Keqin Ma d. Shuchen Li 6–2 7–5 6–4.
WOMEN'S SINGLES – Semi-finals: Xinyi Li d. Ni Zhong 7–5 2–6 6–4; Lilan Duan d. Xiaoyun Zhu 6–4 6–3. *Final:* Xinyi Li d. Lilan Duan 6–2 6–0.

CHINESE TAIPEI

Chinese Taipei Tennis Association, 10th Floor, 53 Ren-Aird, Section 3, Taipei, Taiwan.
C. Sinovision, Taipei; T. (02) 7716190; TX. 25080 CHINA TV; *Pres.* Mr H. P. Chung; *Sec.* Mr E. S. C. Wang.

MEN: 1 Chang-Rung Wu; 2 Huang-Jung Hsu; 3 Chung-Hsing Liu; 4 Fei-Shyong Gong; 5 Yu-Tien Lin; 6 Chun-Mo Lin; 7 Hong-Long Wu; 8 Kuo-Long Ho; 9 Chi-Hwa Kuo; 10 Chun-Nan Lin.
WOMEN: 1 Chiu-Mei Ho; 2 Su-Lin Lai; 3 Fang-Ling Lin; 4 Hsiu-Tsuan Wen; 5 Mei-Chu Hsu; 6 Dai-Hwa Wang; 7 Su-More Lin; 8 Li-Chuan Shieh; 9 Su-Ying Lai; 10 Su-Sing Lin.

National Closed Championships
MEN'S SINGLES – Semi-finals: Chang-Rung Wu d. Fei-Shyong Gong 6–4 6–0; Huang-Jung Hsu d. Chung-Hsing Liu 4–6 6–4 6–3. *Final:* Chang-Rung Wu d. Huang-Jung Hsu 6–2 6–2.
WOMEN'S SINGLES – Semi-finals: Shi-Ting Wang d. Dai-Hwa Wang 6–4 6–2; Su-Ling Lai d. Fang-Ling Lin 6–3 6–0. *Final:* Su-Ling Lai d. Shi-Ting Wang 6–2 6–0.

COLOMBIA

Federacion Colombiana de Tenis, Apartado No. 10.917, Bogota 1.
C. Fedetenis, Bogota; T. (2) 81 8330; TX. 41275 ICJD CO; *Pres.* Mr G. Obando; *Sec.* Mr K. Wodak Jr.
MEN: 1 Carlos Gomez; 2 Alvaro Jordan; 3 Javier Restrepo; 4 Orlando Agudelo; 5 Rene Gomez; 6 Mario Rincon; 7 Ivan Molina; 8 John Restrepo; 9 Jorge Falla; 10 Raul Ordonez.
WOMEN: 1 Elsa Rodriguez; 2 Liliana Fernandez; 3 Luz Gonzalez; 4 Gloria Escobar; 5 Adriana Isaza; 6 Jeanette Torres; 7 Maria Moggio.

National Closed Championships
MEN'S SINGLES – Semi-finals: C. Gomez d. A. Jordan 5–5 ret'd; H. Sy Corvo d. O. Agudelo 6–3 6–4. *Final:* Gomez d. Sy Corvo 4–6 6–2 9–7.
WOMEN'S SINGLES – Semi-finals: L. Fernandez d. L. Gonzalez 7–5 1–6 7–5; E. Rodriguez d. G. Escobar 4–6 6–2 6–3. *Final:* Rodriguez d. Fernandez 6–3 6–3.

CUBA

Federacion Cubana de Tenis de Campo, Calle 13 NR 601 ESQ AC, Vedado Habana 4.
C. Olimpicuba, Habana; T. (7) 418883 /402921 /415394; TX. 0511332 INDER CU; *Pres.* Mr R. Martinez; *Sec.* Mr M. Osorio.
MEN: 1 Mario Ivan Perez; 2 Wilfredo Henrry Torriente; 3 Juan Antonio Pino Perez; 4 Nelson Cruz Noguera; 5 Tomas Rodriguez Sanchez; 6 Joel Gonzalez; 7 Jesus Borrego Valdes; 8 Eloy Cuevas Gil; 9 Pedro Pablo Del Valle Aguila; 10 Oscar Ortega Modrono.
WOMEN: 1 Belkis Rodriguez Abreu; 2 Odalis Moreno Gonzalez; 3 Maria Esther Rodriguez Luis; 4 Paula Hernandez Alvarez; 5 Celia Artze Gourriel; 6 Lesvia Arteaga Menses; 7 Maria Del Garcia Mayedo; 8 Karelia Echevarria Acosta; 9 Rita Pichardo Pavon; 10 Yoanny Montesino Rodriguez.

National Closed Championships
MEN'S SINGLES – Semi-finals: W. Henrry d. J. Pino 6–3 4–6 6–2; M. Tabares d. J. Borrego 6–1 7–5. *Final:* Tabares d. Henrry 6–4 6–1.
WOMEN'S SINGLES – Semi-finals: B. Rodriguez d. C. Artze 6–1 6–4; O. Moreno d. M. Rodriguez 6–1 6–4. *Final:* Rodriguez d. Moreno 6–2 6–4.

CYPRUS

Cyprus Tennis Federation, Nikitara Str. 19, PO Box 3931, Nicosia.
C. Tennis, Nicosia; T. (02) 450 875; TX. 5300 OLYMPIC CY; *Sec.* Mr D. Solomonides.
MEN: 1 Yannos Hadjigeorgiou; 2 Phivos Zachariades; 3 Alexis Photiades; 4 Haik Ashdzian; 5 Yannakis Constantinides; 6 Rodger Lee; 7 Christos Karamallakis; 8 Loucas Christofides; 9 Simon Aynedjian; 10 Christos Christofides.
WOMEN: 1 Eleni Pilava; 2 Natia Iacovou; 3 Sylvia Loizidou; 4 Tereza Apostolidou; 5 Angela Georgiou; 6 Roulla Mina; 7 Christina Panatoniou; 8 Chryso Loucaidou; 9 Stalo Tritti; 10 Marina Potoudi.

National Closed Championships
MEN'S SINGLES – Semi-finals: Y. Hadjigeorgiou d. Y. Constantinides 6–1 6–1; P. Zachariades d. H. Ashdjian 6–3 4–6 6–4. *Final:* Hadjigeorgiou d. Zachariades 7–5 6–3.
WOMEN'S SINGLES – Semi-finals: E. Pilava d. A. Georgiou 6–2 6–4; T. Apostolidou d. S. Loizidou 6–4 6–0. *Final:* Pilava d. Apostolidou 3–6 6–0 7–5.

CZECHOSLOVAKIA

Ceskoslovenska Tenisova Asociace, Na Porici 12, 115 30 Prague 1.
C. Sportsvaz, Prague; T. (2) 249451-5 /245167; TX. 122650 CSTVC; *Pres.* Mr C. Suk; *Sec.* Mr M. Polak.
MEN: **1** Ivan Lendl; **2** Miloslav Mecir; **3** Tomas Smid; **4** Libor Pimek; **5** Pavel Slozil; **6** Marian Vajda; **7** Jaroslav Navratil; **8** Karel Novacek; **9** Stanislav Birner; **10** Milan Srejber.
WOMEN: **1** Hana Mandlikova; **2** Helena Sukova; **3** Regina Marsikova; **4** Iva Budarova; **5** Andrea Holikova; **6** Katerina Skronska; **7** Lea Plchova; **8** Marcela Skuherska; **9** Olga Votavova; **10** Hana Fukarkova.

National Closed Championships
MEN'S SINGLES – Semi-finals: M. Mecir d. T. Smid 6–4 3–6 6–4; L. Pimek d. P. Slozil 6–4 6–3. *Final:* Mecir d. Pimek 7–5 6–4 6–3.
WOMEN'S SINGLES – Semi-finals: J. Novotna d. H. Fukarkova 7–6 6–4; H. Sukova d. A. Holikova 6–1 6–4. *Final:* Sukova d. Novotna 6–4 6–3.

DENMARK

Dansk Tennis Forbund, Idraettens Hus, Brondby Stadion 20, DK 2605 Brondby.
C. Tennisforbund, Copenhagen; T. (2) 455555 Ext. 276 or 242; TX. 33111 I DRAET DK (mark: Attn Tennis); *Pres.* Mr J. Bertelsen; *Sec.* Mr J. Ahlstrand.

National Closed Championships
MEN'S SINGLES – Semi-finals: P. Bastiansen d. L. Elvstroem 7–6 6–2; M. Tauson d. M. Christensen 6–3 6–2. *Final:* Bastiansen d. Tauson 3–6 6–2 6–1.
WOMEN'S SINGLES – Semi-finals: L. Vandborg d. L. Holm Larsen 6–1 6–0; T. Arildsen d. A. Moeller 6–3 6–0. *Final:* Vandborg d. Moeller 3–6 6–4 6–0.

ECUADOR

Federacion Ecuatoriana de Tenis, PO Box 4587, Guayaquil.
C. Fedetennis, Quito; T. 512123 or 524060; TX. 3862 EMPRES ED; *Pres.* Mr N. Macchiavello; *Sec.* Mr C. Carbo.
MEN: **1** Andres Gomez; **2** Raul Viver; **3** Ricardo Ycaza; **4** Martin Aguirre; **5** Hugo Molina; **6** Axel Reich; **7** Donny Lovo; **8** Hernan Luque; **9** Eduardo Medina; **10** Erich Reich.
WOMEN: **1** Montserrat Martinez; **2** Martha Camizares; **3** Maria Gallegos; **4** Mercedes Ramos; **5** Maria Olvera.

EGYPT

Egyptian Lawn Tennis Federation, 13 Kasr el Nil Street, Cairo.
C. Gyplawnten, Cairo; T. (2) 753235; TX. 93697 SAFLM UN (mark: Att. Tennis) or 21554 STC MN; *Pres.* Mr G. El Nazer; *Sec.* Dr A. Tewfik.

FINLAND

Suomen Tennisliitto, Radiokatu 12, Box 27, 00250 Helsinki 25.
C. Tennisliitto, Helsinki; T. (0) 4737255; TX. 121797 SVUL SF; *Pres.* Mr A. Narakka; *Sec.* Mr E. Kiuttu.
MEN: **1** Leo Palin; **2** Pasi Virtanen; **3** Olli Rahnasto; **4** Kimmo Alkio; **5** Mika Hedman; **6** Jari Koho; **7** Joakim Berner; **8** Matti Timonen; **9** Veli Paloheimo; **10** Pasi Montonen.
WOMEN: **1** Tarja Koho; **2** Anne Aallonen; **3** Marianna Ansio; **4** Mervi Mannisto; **5** Hanna Thoren; **6** Sarianna Ansio; **7** Anne Happonen; **8** Laura Sarkilahti; **9** Petra Thoren; **10** Nanne Dahlman.

National Closed Championships
MEN'S SINGLES – Semi-finals: P. Virtanen d. A. Eranne 7–6 6–3; K. Alkio d. P. Montonen 6–7 6–2 6–1. *Final:* Virtanen d. Alkio 3–6 7–6 6–2.
WOMEN'S SINGLES – Semi-finals: A. Aallonen d. H. Thoren 6–4 6–4; T. Koho d. L. Sarkilahti 6–4 0–6 6–2. *Final:* Koho d. Aallonen 6–2 6–4.

Here at Wimbledon, Henri Leconte showed us the brilliance of his shot-making as he swept past Lendl to the quarter-finals, where he produced a magnificent but unavailing performance against Becker, who beat him in four sets. *(A. Evans)*

FRANCE

Federation Française de Tennis, Stade Roland Garros, 2 Avenue Gordon Bennett, 75016 Paris.
C. Tennisfedet, Paris; T. (1) 47 43 96 81; TX. TENFED 611871F; *Pres.* Mr P. Chatrier; *Sec.* Mr J. C. Collinot.
MEN: **1** Yannick Noah; **2** Henri Leconte; **3** Thierry Tulasne; **4** Guy Forget; **5** Tarik Benhabiles; **6** Jerome Potier; **7** Pascal Portes; **8** Bruno Dadillon; **9** Philippe Fleurian; **10** Loic Courteau.
WOMEN: **1** Pascale Paradis; **2** Catherine Tanvier; **3** Nathalie Tauziat; **4** Isabelle Demongeot; **5** Catherine Suire; **6** Sophie Amiach; **7** Christine Calleja; **8** Corinne Vanier; **9** Nathalie Herreman; **10** Nathalie Phan Than.

National Closed Championships
MEN'S SINGLES – Semi-finals: B. Dadillon d. T. Benhabiles 7–6 2–6 7–5; G. Forget d. O. Delaire 6–2 6–3. *Final:* Forget d. Dadillon 3–6 6–3 6–1 6–1.
WOMEN'S SINGLES – Semi-finals: N. Tauziat d. M. Calleja 6–2 6–0; P. Paradis d. I. Demongeot 6–2 5–7 9–7. *Final:* Tauziat d. Paradis 6–4 7–5.

GERMAN DEMOCRATIC REPUBLIC

Deutscher Tennis-Verband der DDR, Storkower Strasse 118, 1055 Berlin.
T. (2) 54 98 533; TX. 114919 DTSB DD; *Pres.* Mr K. H. Sturm; *Sec.* Mr W. Joch.

GERMANY, FEDERAL REPUBLIC OF

Deutscher Tennis Bund e.V., Leisewitzstr. 26, 3000 Hannover 1.
C. Tennisbund, Hannover; T. (511) 281067; TX. 921378 DTB D; *Pres.* Dr C. Stauder; *Exec. Dir.* Mr G. Sanders.
MEN: **1** Boris Becker; **2** Hansjoerg Schwaier; **3** Andreas Maurer; **4** Michael Westphal; **5** Ricki Osterthun; **6** Damir Keretic; **7** Wolfgang Popp; **8** Tore Meinecke; **9** Hans-Dieter Beutel; **10** Peter Elter.
WOMEN: **1** Claudia Kohde-Kilsch; **2** Steffi Graf; **3** **eq** Bettina Bunge, Sylvia Hanika; **5** Eva Pfaff; **6** Myriam Schropp; **7** Petra Keppeler; **8** Sabine Hack; **9** Gabriela Dinu; **10** Isabel Cueto.

National Closed Championships
MEN'S SINGLES – Semi-finals: H. Beutel d. Gau 7–5 6–3 6–1; R. Gehring d. K. Eberhard 6–4 6–1 6–4. *Final:* Beutel d. Gehring 4–6 6–4 6–4 7–5.
WOMEN'S SINGLES – Semi-finals: P. Keppeler d. Ms Gartner 7–6 6–4; S. Hack d. Ms Wieser 6–4 6–2. *Final:* Hack d. Keppeler 6–0 2–6 8–6.

GREAT BRITAIN

The Lawn Tennis Association, Barons Court, West Kensington, London W14 9EG.
C. Lawntenna, London W14; T. 01-385 2366; TX. 8956036 THELTA G; *Pres.* Mr G. B. Brown; *Sec.* Mr J. C. U. James.
MEN: **1** John Lloyd; **2** Jeremy Bates; **3** Stephen Shaw; **4** Stuart Bale; **5** Colin Dowdeswell; **6** Nick Fulwood; **7** Jonathan Smith; **8** Leighton Alfred; **9** Jason Goodall; **10** Robin Drysdale.
WOMEN: **1** Annabel Croft; **2** Jo Durie; **3** Anne Hobbs; **4** Sara Gomer; **5** Virginia Wade; **6** Amanda Brown; **7** Sally Reeves; **8** Rina Einy; **9** Jo Louis; **10** Julie Salmon.

National Closed Championships
MEN'S SINGLES – Semi-finals: N. A. Fulwood d. C. Dowdeswell 6–4 6–4; M. J. Bates d. J. R. Smith 2–6 6–4 6–4. *Final:* Bates d. Fulwood 6–3 6–2.
WOMEN'S SINGLES – Semi-finals: A. E. Hobbs d. A. N. Croft 6–4 6–3; V. Wade d. J. V. Wood 6–2 6–2. *Final:* Hobbs d. Wade 7–6 6–7 9–7.

GREECE

Hellenic Tennis Federation, 89 Patission Str., 104 34 Athens.
C. Efotennis, Athens; T. (1) 8210478 or 8815804; TX. 222415 EFOA GR; *Pres.* Mr D. Stefanides; *Sec.* Mr D. Gangas.
MEN: **1** George Kalovelonis; **2** Fotis Vazeos; **3** Konstantinos Egremoglou; **4** John Rigas; **5** Anastasis Bavelas; **6** Panayiotis Kambadelis; **7** John Kambakoglou; **8** Fotis Ekonomou; **9** Efstathios Haritonides; **10** Dionissis Kipriotis.

WOMEN: 1 Angeliki Kanellopoulou; 2 Olga Tsarmbopoulou; 3 Xenia Anastasiadou; 4 Barbara Mihalopoulou; 5 Fotini Priovoulou; 6 Amanda Mitropoulou; 7 Eleftheria Kavadia; 8 Anna Lagou; 9 Christina Papadaki; 10 **eq** Elpida Koll, Amalia Vafiadou.

National Closed Championships
MEN'S SINGLES – Semi-finals: F. Vazeos d. J. Kambakoglou 0–6 6–2 6–2; G. Kalovelonis d. E. Haritonides 6–0 6–0. *Final:* Kalovelonis d. Vazeos 2–6 6–1 6–4 7–6.
WOMEN'S SINGLES – Semi-finals: O. Tsarbopoulou d. X. Anastasiadou 6–0 6–0; A. Kanellopoulou d. B. Mihalopoulou 6–3 6–1. *Final:* Kanellopoulou d. Tsarbopoulou 6–2 6–0.

HONG KONG

Hong Kong Tennis Association Ltd, Room 911, Queen Elizabeth Stadium, Oi Kwan Road, Hong Kong. C. Tennis, Hong Kong; T. (5) 741546; TX. 73411 RYODEN HX; *Pres.* Dr P. Kwok; *Sec.* Dr E. W. Hardisty.
MEN: 1 Kelvin Ng; 2 Colin Grant; 3 Randall King; 4 Mark Bailey; 5 Kester Ng; 6 Robin Fok; 7 Shum Yat Wai; 8 Pang Lui; 9 Christopher Lai; 10 Paul Bailey.
WOMEN: 1 Patricia Hy; 2 Paulette Moreno; 3 Lisa Kwok; 4 Christine Kwok.

National Closed Championships
MEN'S SINGLES – Semi-finals: C. Grant d. R. King 0–6 6–4 7–5; A. Brothers d. M. Bailey 6–3 7–5. *Final:* Grant d. Brothers 7–5 6–0 7–6.
WOMEN'S SINGLES – Semi-finals: E. Lightbody d. D. Hung 6–0 6–0; G. Tijou d. N. Omori 7–5 6–2. *Final:* Lightbody d. Tijou 6–1 6–1.

HUNGARY

Magyar Tenisz Szovetség, Dozsa Gyorgy ut 1-3, H-1143 Budapest.
C. Comsport Tennis, Budapest; T. (1) 630-852; TX. 225105 OTSH HV; *Pres.* Mr I. Gulyas; *Sec.* Mr F. Zentai.
MEN: 1 Sandor Kiss; 2 Ferenc Zentai; 3 Laszlo Zsiga; 4 Janos Guti; 5 Vilmos Lazar; 6 Ferenc Csepai; 7 Karoly Banhidi; 8 Gabor Lukacs; 9 Otto Puski; 10 Istvan Gulyas Jr.
WOMEN: 1 Eva Rozsavolgyi; 2 Rita Kowaczics; 3 Lilla Buza; 4 Anna Nemeth; 5 Katalin Fagyas; 6 Reka Szikszay; 7 Judit Budai; 8 Antonia Homolya; 9 Bea Hanak; 10 Ildiko Guba.

National Closed Championships
MEN'S SINGLES – Final: F. Zentai d. S. Kiss.
WOMEN'S SINGLES – Final: C. Bartos d. E. Rozsavolgyi 6–4 6–2.

INDIA

All India Lawn Tennis Association, Power Centre Private Ltd, 755 Mount Road, Madras 600 002.
C. Powerpack, Madras; T. (44) 812725; TX. 41 7869 GSET IN; *Pres.* Mr R. Masturlal; *Hon. Sec.* Mr L. Reddy.
MEN: 1 Nandan Bal; 2 Enrico Piperno; 3 Mayur Vasant; 4 H. P. Raghuveer; 5 K. G. Ramesh; 6 Dinesh Rajagopal; 7 Tej Bhandari; 8 Sheil Kumar; 9 Vijay Venkatesh; 10 K. Somnath.
WOMEN: 1 Radhika Krishnan; 2 Bela Pandit; 3 Gowri Krishnan; 4 Nasreen Sujatali; 5 Monisha Muthanna; 6 Malini Mukherjea.

National Closed Championships
MEN'S SINGLES – Semi-finals: N. Bal d. S. Narendra 6–1 6–4; E. Piperno d. M. Vasant 6–2 6–1. *Final:* Bal d. Piperno 6–3 7–5.
WOMEN'S SINGLES – Semi-finals: N. Rangarajan d. R. Krishnan 3–6 6–2 6–2; B. Pandit d. N. Sujatali 7–6 4–6 6–3. *Final:* Rangarajan d. Pandit 6–4 6–3.

INDONESIA

Indonesian Tennis Association, Jln. Olahraga V /3 Kemanggisan, Slipi, Jakarta 11.480.
C. Tennis Indonesia, Jakarta; T. (0646) 5482488; TX. 45214 KONI IA; *Pres.* Major Gen. H. Jonosewojo; *Sec.* Mr S. Nartomo.
MEN: 1 Tintus Wibowo; 2 Justedjo Tarik; 3 Suharyadi; 4 Donald Wailan; 5 Sulistyono; 6 Hawin Sutopo; 7 Deddy Tedjomukti; 8 Ludywijono; 9 Josafat Sihombing; 10 Yanuar Mangitung.
WOMEN: 1 Suzana Anggarkusuma; 2 Yayuk Basuki; 3 Utaminingsih; 4 Lucky Tedjomukti; 5 Conny Maramis; 6 Luciana Lolong; 7 Tutut Nugroho; 8 Yusti.

National Closed Championships
MEN'S SINGLES – Semi-finals: J. Tarik d. Suharyadi 6–2 6–2; T. Wibowo d. D. Wailan 6–2 6–2. *Final:* Tarik d. Wibowo 4–6 6–4 6–4.
WOMEN'S SINGLES – Semi-finals: S. Anggarkusuma d. T. Nugroho 6–3 6–1; Y. Basuki d. T. Sumarno 6–3 6–3. *Final:* Anggarkusuma d. Basuki 6–1 6–4.

IRAN

Tennis Federation of Islamic Republic of Iran, Department of International Affairs, PO Box 11 1642, Tehran.
C. Olympic Tehran; T. (21) 826999; TX. 212691 VARZ IR; *Pres.* Mr G. H. Noorian; *Sec.* Mr M. Sefatti.
MEN: **1** Mohharam Ali Khodaee; **2** Kambiz Derafshi Javan; **3** Jehanbakhsh Soori; **4** Abbas Kheyltaash; **5** Hossein Akbari; **6** Seifullah Behzadpoor; **7** Mohammad Atshani; **8** Abbas Dehghani; **9** Ahmad Reza Jamalian.

National Closed Championships
MEN'S SINGLES – Final: M. A. Khodaee d. J. Soori.

IRAQ

Iraqi Tennis Federation, c/o Iraqi National Olympic Committee, PO Box No. 441, Baghdad.
C. Iroq, Baghdad; T. (1) 97390 (am) 98879 (pm) or 98874 (pm); TX. 2824; *Pres.* Mr N. Shaker; *Sec.* Mr G. Bakose.

IRELAND

Irish Lawn Tennis Association, 22 Upper Fitzwilliam Street, Dublin 2.
C. Irishtennis, Dublin; T. (01) 606332; TX. 31295 ILTAEI; *Pres.* Mr C. J. Brennan; *Sec.* Mrs M. Hogg.
MEN: **1** Matt Doyle; **2** Sean Sorensen; **3** Michael Nugent; **4** Sean Molloy; **5** Conor McCullough; **6** Peter Lowther; **7** Michael Cowhie; **8** Owen Casey; **9** Peter Minnis; **10** Glenn Beirne.
WOMEN: **1** Siobhan Nicholson; **2** Rhona Howett; **3** Jennifer Thornton; **4** Diane Craig; **5** Louise Edgar; **6** Lesley O'Halloran; **7** Bernadette Griffith; **8** Gillian Chandler; **9** Rosemary Langford; **10** Carmel O'Sullivan.

National Closed Championships
MEN'S SINGLES – Semi-finals: M. Nugent d. D. Miley 5–7 6–4 6–3; S. Molloy d. C. McCullough 4–6 6–1 6–1. *Final:* Nugent d. Molloy 6–4 2–6 6–4.
WOMEN'S SINGLES – Final: S. Nicholson d. B. Griffith 6–1 6–4.

ISRAEL

Israel Tennis Association, PO Box 20073, Tel Aviv 61 200.
C. ILTA, Tel Aviv; T. (3) 613911 /625864; TX. 341118 BXTVIL Ext. 5348; *Chmn* Mr D. Harnik; *Sec.* Mr Z. Meyer.
MEN: **1** Shlomo Glickstein; **2** Shachar Perkis; **3** Amos Mansdorf; **4** Gilad Bloom; **5** Amit Naor; **6** Eylon Sinai; **7** Oded Ya'acov; **8** Raviv Weidenfeld; **9** Boaz Merenstein; **10** Haim Zion.
WOMEN: **1** Ilana Berger; **2** Dalia Koriat; **3** Sagit Doron; **4** Sarit Shalev; **5** Zahavit Gal-On; **6** Soffi Rafael.

National Closed Championships
MEN'S SINGLES – Semi-finals: S. Glickstein d. G. Bloom 6–4 6–2; S. Perkis d. A. Mansdorf 4–6 7–5 6–2. *Final:* Glickstein d. Perkis 6–2 6–2.
WOMEN'S SINGLES – Semi-finals: D. Koriat d. S. Doron 4–6 6–3 7–5; I. Berger d. S. Shalev 6–4 6–3. *Final:* Berger d. Koriat 6–2 6–3.

ITALY

Federazione Italian Tennis, Viale Tiziano 70, 00196 Rome.
C. Italtennis, Rome; T. (6) 36858 213 /210 or 3960092; TX. 613330 FIT I; *Pres.* Avv. P. Galgani; *Sec.* Dott. G. Annibali.
MEN: **1** Francesco Cancellotti; **2** Claudio Panatta; **3** Alessandro De Minicis; **4** Claudio Mezzadri; **5**

Gianni Ocleppo; **6** Simone Colombo; **7** Massimo Cierro; **8** Paolo Cane; **9** Claudio Pistolesi; **10** Luca Bottazzi.
WOMEN: **1** Raffaella Reggi; **2** Anna Maria Cecchini; **3** Laura Garrone; **4** Federica Bonsignori; **5** Caterina Nozzoli; **6** Laura Golarsa; **7** Barbara Romano; **8** Silvia La Fratta; **9** Sabina Simmonds; **10** Patrizia Murgo.
National Closed Championships
MEN'S SINGLES — Semi-finals: S. Colombo d. A. De Minicis 6–2 6–0; C. Panatta d. M. Fioroni 6–1 6–4. **Final:** Panatta d. Colombo 6–1 6–4.
WOMEN'S SINGLES — Semi-finals: B. Romano d. S. La Fratta 6–3 7–5; L. Garrone d. F. Bonsignori 3–6 7–5 6–1. **Final:** Garrone d. Romano 6–3 3–6 6–3.

IVORY COAST

Federation Ivoirienne de Tennis, 08 BP 300 08, Abidjan 01.
T. 41 40 57; TX. 3484; *Pres.* Mr J. C. Delafosse; *Sec. Gen.* Mr K. Kouadjo.

JAMAICA

Jamaica Lawn Tennis Association, 2A Piccadilly Road, PO Box 175, Kingston 5.
C. Lawntenna, Kingston; T. New Kingston 2441 /2442; TX. 2442; *Pres.* Mr W. A. Scholefield; *Sec.* Mrs Y. K. Walsh.

JAPAN

Japan Tennis Association, c /o Kishi Memorial Hall, 1-1-1 Jinnan Shibuya-ku, Tokyo 150.
C. Niplotenis, Tokyo; T. (3) 481 2321; TX. JAAA J 27697 (mark attn: Japan Tennis); Telecopier: 03 467 5192; *Pres.* Mr T. Kosaka; *Sec.* Mr S. Shimizu.
MEN: **1** Tsuyoshi Fukui; **2** Shozo Shiraishi; **3** Toru Yonezawa; **4** Joel Bailey; **5** Shin-Ichi Sakamoto; **6** Jun Kamiwazumi; **7** Ken-Tchi Hirai; **8** Tetsu Kuramitsu; **9** Takayoshi Shibuya; **10** Hitoshi Shirato.
WOMEN: **1** Etsuko Inoue; **2** Masako Yanagi; **3** Akiko Kojimua; **4** Yukte Koizumi; **5** Emiko Kagawa; **6** Miki Mizokughi; **7** Kumiko Okamoto; **8** Maya Kodowaki; **9** Fumiko Furuhashi; **10** Masako Morikawa.
National Closed Championships
MEN'S SINGLES — Semi-finals: T. Fukui d. T. Kuramitsu 6–2 6–2; T. Yonezawa d. S. Shiraishi 6–1 6–4. **Final:** Fukui d. Shiraishi 6–2 6–3 7–6.
WOMEN'S SINGLES — Semi-finals: E. Inoue d. Y. Koizumi 6–2 6–4; M. Yanagi d. M. Mizokuchi 6–3 6–3. **Final:** Inoue d. Yanagi 6–0 6–0.

KENYA

Kenya Lawn Tennis Association, PO Box 43184, Nairobi.
C. Tennis, Nairobi; T. 567256; TX. 22575 KATE NBO; *Chmn* Mr J. Carneiro; *Hon. Sec.* Mrs. M. E. Walker.
MEN: **1** Saleem Rana; **2** James Ilako; **3** David Lowe; **4** Sammy Kipkoech; **5** Peter Mithamo; **6** Charles Ilako.
WOMEN: **1** Jane Ndunda; **2** Carol Hughes; **3** M. Bommelauer; **4** Wanjiku Murigu; **5** Rosemary Strachan; **6** Camilla Wekesa.
National Closed Championships
MEN'S SINGLES — Semi-finals: S. Rana d. D. Lowe 6–1 6–4; P. Wekesa d. N. Odour 6–2 6–0. **Final:** Wekesa d. Rana 6–3 6–3.
WOMEN'S SINGLES — Semi-finals: J. Ndunda d. L. Wekesa 6–4 6–1; C. Hughes d. C. Wekesa 6–2 6–2. **Final:** Hughes d. Ndunda 4–6 6–4 6–2.

KOREA, REPUBLIC OF

Korea Tennis Association, Room 505, Sports Building, 19 Mukyo-Dong, Chung-Ku, Seoul.
C. Kortennis, Seoul; T. 777 4028 or 777 6081-9 Ext. 52; TX. KOCSEL K24989; *Pres.* Mr C. K. Cho; *Sec.* Mr Y. M. Huh.
MEN: **1** Dong-Wook Song; **2** Young-Dae Jeon; **3** Woo-Yong Lee; **4** Choon-Ho Kim; **5** Ja-Yeol Gu; **6** Seong-Hoon Choi; **7** Chang-Dae Jeon; **8 eq** Jin-Sun Yoo, Gap-Taik Ro; **10 eq** Deok-Mo Hwang, Jong-Hyun Choi.

America's 20-year-old Lisa Bonder suffered some unlucky draws in 1985, but was encouraged to beat Rinaldi in New Orleans, where she bowed to Evert Lloyd in the semi-finals. *(M. Cole)*

WOMEN: **1** Jeong-Soon Lee; **2** Min-Kyeong Seol; **3** Soo-Ok Kim; **4** Yang-Ja Park; **5** Jeong-Ok Choi; **6** Eul-Sun Choi; **7 eq** Eun-Ok Cho, Eun-Sook Han; **9** Jeong-Myeong Lee; **10** Eun-Hee Choi.

National Closed Championships
MEN'S SINGLES — Final: Dong-Wook Song d. Choon-Ho Kim.
WOMEN'S SINGLES — Final: Jeong-Soon Lee d. Soo-Ok Kim.

KUWAIT

Kuwait Tennis Federation, PO Box 1462, Hawalli.
C. Tennis, Kuwait; T. 424948; TX. COMITE 23192 KT (mark: Attn. Tennis Assn); *Pres.* Mr K. A. Al-Bannai; *Sec.* Mr A. Alrifae.
MEN: **1** Khalid Ashkanani; **2** Mohammad Ali; **3** Bassam Al Hajeri.

LEBANON

Federation Libanaise de Tennis, PO Box 113-5591, Hamra, Beyrouth.
C. Tennispong, Beyrouth; T. (961) 34 22 82; TX. 20653 GESPA LE (mark for E. A. Yazbeck); *Pres.* Mr A. K. Matar; *Hon. Gen. Sec.* Mr E. A. Yazbeck.

LIBYA

Jamahiriya Tennis Federation, PO Box 879, Tripoli.
C. Almadrab, Tripoli; T. (21) 39156; TX. 20710 RIADAH LY or 20420 LY LIBOLYMPIC; *Pres.* Mr A. N. Oweiti; *Sec.* Mr M. Krewi.
MEN: **1** Said Karam; **2 eq** Sabah Baz, Ali Tawbeh; **4** Raymond Kattoura; **5 eq** Rabih Baz, Salah Skaff; **7 eq** Michel Philippdes, Tony Rizk, Roger Saliba; **10** Adoni Abounaoum.
WOMEN: **1** Maya Hajjar; **2** Nahya Aboukhalil; **3** Tania Zeitouni; **4** Nazek Yared; **5** Raja Siblini; **6 eq** Lena Zeitouni, Nadia Zeitouni, Sherine Rebeiz.

National Closed Championships
MEN'S SINGLES — Final: S. Karam d. S. Baz 6–4 6–4 6–4.
WOMEN'S SINGLES — Final: M. Hajjar d. T. Zeitouni 6–3 6–1.

LUXEMBURG

Federation Luxembourgeoise de Tennis, 7 Avenue Victor Hugo, Luxemburg 1750.
C. Federation Luxembourgeoise de Tennis, Luxemburg; T. 47 31 57; TX. 3556 COSL LU; *Pres.* Mr G. Logelin; *Gen. Sec.* Mrs A. Berger.
MEN: **1** Johny Goudenbour; **2** Mike Van Kauvenbergh; **3** Paul Hoffmann; **4** Dariusz Wieczorek; **5** Jacques Radoux; **6** Fernand Claude; **7** Stephan Kinsch; **8** Serge Bruck; **9** Joa Neuman.
WOMEN: **1** Karin Kschwendt; **2** Simone Grandjean; **3** Ginette Huberty; **4** Nadia Faber; **5** Vera Stejskalova; **6** Pascale Welter; **7** Anne Toussaint.

National Closed Championships
MEN'S SINGLES — Semi-finals: J. Goudenbour d. J. Radoux 6–1 6–2; M. Van Kauvenbergh d. P. Hoffmann 6–1 7–6. *Final:* Goudenbour d. Van Kauvenbergh 6–1 6–3.
WOMEN'S SINGLES — Semi-finals: K. Kschwendt d. N. Faber 6–0 6–1; S. Grandjean d. G. Huberty 7–5 6–0. *Final:* Kschwendt d. Grandjean 6–1 6–0.

MALAYSIA

Lawn Tennis Association of Malaysia, Dept of Educational Studies, Faculty of Education Studies, UPM Serdang, Selangor.
C. Tennis Kuala Lumpur; T. (03) 586101 Ext. 471; TX. UNIPER MA37454; *Pres.* Hon. Mr A. G. Baba; *Sec.* Mr A. A. Zakaria.

MALTA

Malta Lawn Tennis Association, PO Box 50, Sliema Post Office, Sliema.
T. 512368; *Pres.* Mr. J. P. Galea; *Sec.* Mr G. J. Bonello.
MEN: **1** Gordon Asciak; **2** Christopher Gatt; **3** Steven Schranz; **4** Denis Galea; **5** Daryl Delicata.

WOMEN: 1 Helen Degiorgio Asciak; 2 Carol Curmi; 3 Alexia Gera; 4 Katherine Camilleri; 5 Karen Pace.

MEXICO

Federacion Mexicana de Tenis AC, Durango No. 225-301, 06700 Mexico DF.
C. Mextenis, Mexico City; T. (5) 514-37-59; TX. 1761056 FMDTME; *Pres.* Mr L. Lavalle; *Sec.* Mr L. Riefkohl.
MEN: 1 Leonardo Lavalle; 2 Francisco Maciel; 3 Hector Ortiz; 4 Javier Ordaz; 5 Enrique Haro; 6 Guillermo Stevens; 7 Alfonso Gonzalez; 8 Yves Lemaire; 9 Fernando Perez; 10 Alejandro Flores.
WOMEN: 1 Heleane Steden; 2 Claudia Hernandez; 3 Maria Elena Llamas; 4 Monica Munoz; 5 Susana Rojas; 6 Terevsa Lisci; 7 Claudia Salsamendi; 8 Maricarmen Casta; 9 Alejandra Vallejo; 10 Lucila Becerra.

National Closed Championships
MEN'S SINGLES – Semi-finals: L. Lavalle d. H. Ortiz 6–1 6–3 7–6; F. Perez d. E. Haro 6–1 7–6 6–3.
Final: Lavalle d. Perez 6–3 6–4 6–3.
WOMEN'S SINGLES – Semi-finals: C. Hernandez d. M. Casta 6–0 7–5; M. Munoz d. C. Ortega 4–6 6–3 6–1. **Final:** Hernandez d. Munoz 6–1 6–1.

MONACO

Federation Monegasque de Tennis, 46 Rue Grimaldi, 98000 Monaco.
C. Federation-Tennis-Monaco; T. (93) 30-01-02; TX. CONG 469760 MC (mark: for LTA); *Pres.* Mr L. Caravel; *Sec.* Mr J. C. Riey.
MEN: 1 Gilles Ganacia; 2 Bernard Balleret; 3 Jacques Vincileoni; 4 Albert Viviani; 5 Michel Borfiga; 6 Christophe Bogetti; 7 Jacques Guglielmi; 8 Olivier Perret.
WOMEN: 1 Agnes Barthelemy; 2 Nadine Balleret; 3 Lara Viviani; 4 Sandrine Moreno; 5 Sylvene Seneca.

MOROCCO

Federation Royale Marocaine de Tennis, Maison des Sports, Parc de la Ligue Arabe, Casablanca.
C. Tenisfede, Maroc; T. 27-87-31 or 26-75-53; TX. FRTENNIS 23745 M; *Pres.* Mr M. M'Jid; *Sec.* Mr M. Moufid.
MEN: 1 Saber Houcine; 2 Chekrouni Arafa; 3 Nadini Abdelkhalek; 4 Dlimi Mohamed; 5 Assouadi Bouchaib; 6 Bennis Abdelilah; 7 Amechrak Mustapha; 8 Alami Mokhtar; 9 Sebti Rachid; 10 Dislam Mustapha.

National Closed Championships
MEN'S SINGLES – Final: S. Houcine d. D. Mohamed.

NETHERLANDS

Koninklijke Nederlandse Lawn Tennis Bond, PO Box 107, 1200 AC Hilversum.
C. Tennisbond, Hilversum; T. (35) 46941; TX. 73250 LINE NL; *Pres.* Mr K. T. M. Hehenkamp; *Vice Pres.* Mr J. F. Steensma; *Sec.* Mr Y. Buruma.
MEN: 1 Michiel Schapers; 2 Huub van Boeckel; 3 Menno Oosting; 4 Tom Nijssen; 5 Johan Vekemans; 6 Chris Vermeeren; 7 Mark Koevermans; 8 eq Vincent van Gelderen, Robert Jan Bierens, Rene Moos.
WOMEN: 1 Marcella Mesker; 2 Marianne Van Der Torre; 3 Nanette Schutte; 4 Karin Moos; 5 Hellas ter Riet; 6 Hester Witvoet; 7 Digna Ketelaar; 8 Manon Bollegraf; 9 Carin Bakkum; 10 eq Nicole Jagerman, Simone Schilder, Marielle Rooimans.

National Closed Championships
MEN'S SINGLES – Semi-finals: M. Schapers d. J. Vekemans 7–5 6–2 1–6 6–4; M. Oosting d. M. Koevermans 6–2 6–2 4–6 6–2. **Final:** Schapers d. Oosting 6–7 4–6 6–0 6–3 6–3.
WOMEN'S SINGLES – Semi-finals: M. Van Der Torre d. N. Schutte 6–2 7–5; M. Bollegraf d. Y. der Kinderen 6–1 6–4. **Final:** Van Der Torre d. Bollegraf 3–6 6–4 6–3.

NEW ZEALAND

New Zealand Lawn Tennis Association, PO Box 11541, Manners Street, Wellington.
C. Tennis, Wellington; T. (41) 731 115; *Exec. Pres.* Mr I. D. Wells; *Exec. Sec.* Mrs S. A. Reeve.
MEN: **1** Chris Lewis; **2** Russell Simpson; **3** Bruce Derlin; **4** David Mustard; **5** Kelly Evernden; **6** Steve Guy; **7** David Lewis; **8** James Dunphy; **9** Stephen Harley; **10** Paul Smith.
WOMEN: **1** Belinda Cordwell; **2** Brenda Perry; **3** Michelle Parun; **4** Julie Richardson; **5** Sally Moorfield; **6** Edith Tatana; **7** Ruth Seeman; **8** Linda Stewart; **9** Angelique Lodewyks; **10** Lyn Meachen.

National Closed Championships
MEN'S SINGLES – Semi-finals: K. Evernden d. J. Dunphy 6–4 4–6 6–0; D. Lewis d. S. Guy 6–4 6–0. *Final:* Evernden d. Lewis 7–6 6–4.
WOMEN'S SINGLES – Semi-finals: B. Perry d. J. Richardson; B. Cordwell d. L. Stewart. *Final:* Perry d. Cordwell 7–5 5–7 7–6.

NIGERIA

Nigeria Lawn Tennis Association, National Stadium, Syrulere, PO Box 145, Lagos.
C. Tennis Natsports, Lagos; T. (1) 83 0649; TX. 26559; *Pres.* A. R. A. Adejumo; *Sec.* L. A. Ayorinde.

NORWAY

Norges Tennisforbund, Hauger Skolevei 1, 1351 Rud.
C. Norsktennis, Oslo; T. (2) 134290; TX. 78586 NIF N; *Pres.* Mr A. Melander; *Sec.* Mr T. Kverneland.
MEN: **1** Morten Roenneberg; **2** Tony Joensson; **4** Truls Midtboe; **5** Anders Haaseth; **6** Jan Svensen; **7** John Erik Rustad; **8** Baard Gundersen; **9** Terje Persson; **10** Morten Unneberg.
WOMEN: **1** Astrid Sunde; **2** Amy Joensson; **3** Ellen Grindvold; **4** Froeidis Forberg; **5** Kjersti Jensen; **6** Hanne Helgoe; **7** Bente Baemark; **8** Ingrid Gjerdene; **9** Stine Vogt Andersen; **10** Monica Wiese.

National Closed Championships
MEN'S SINGLES – Semi-finals: M. Roenneberg d. A. Jensen 6–2 6–1 6–3; T. Joensson d. T. Midtbo 4–6 6–0 4–6 6–3 6–2. *Final:* Roenneberg d. Joensson 1–6 7–6 6–2 7–6.
WOMEN'S SINGLES – Semi-finals: A. Sunde d. F. Forberg 7–6 6–3; A. Joensson d. E. Grindvold 6–4 7–5. *Final:* Sunde d. Joensson 6–1 6–1.

PAKISTAN

Pakistan Tennis Federation, Rawalpindi Club, PO Box 16, The Mall, Rawalpindi.
C. Paktennis, Rawalpindi Cantt; T. (51) 64026; TX. 5830 SAEED PK; *Pres.* Gen. Rahim Uddin Khan; *Sec.* Mr Muneer Pirzada.
MEN: **1** Islam Ul Haq; **2** Hamid Ul Haq; **3** Haseeb Aslam; **4** Mushaf Zia; **5** Inam Ul Haq; **6** Rasheed Malik; **7** Meer Mohammed; **8** Jaleel Riaz.
WOMEN: **1** Alya Nasir; **2** Farah Khursheed; **3** Nausheen.

PARAGUAY

Asociacion Paraguaya de Tenis, Colon 1054, Casilla de Correo 26, Asuncion.
T. 43350; TX. 362 PY HORIZONTE; *Pres.* Dr A. V. Ugarte; *Sec.* Dr M. A. Salcedo; *Gen. Man.* Mr D. L. Llamosas.
MEN: **1** Victor Caballero; **2** Roberto Stogni; **3** Alberto Grossbrown; **4** Hugo Chapacu; **5** Francisco Arrellaga; **6** Juan A. Dominguez; **7** Oscar E. Napout; **8** Edgardo Aranda; **9** Luis Perez; **10** Carlos D. Carvallo.
WOMEN: **1** Patricia Perez; **2** Gloria Benitez; **3** Laura Ugarriza; **4** Marta Laterza; **5** Sita De Lindgren; **6** Giselle Cases.

National Closed Championships
MEN'S SINGLES – Semi-finals: R. Stogni d. C. Carvallo 6–3 6–2 6–1; A. Grossbrown d. L. Perez 6–1 6–2 6–0. *Final:* Stogni d. Grossbrown 6–2 4–6 6–1 6–4.
WOMEN'S SINGLES – Semi-finals: P. Perez d. L. Ugarriza 6–3 6–2; G. Benitez d. M. Laterza 6–4 7–5. *Final:* Benitez d. Perez 6–2 6–0.

PERU

Federacion Peruana de Tenis, Casilla 2243, Lima.
C. Fepetennis, Lima; T. 24 99 79; TX. 25740 PE MORALES; *Pres.* Mr L. Morales Costa; *Sec.* Mr A. Pereda Pareja.

PHILIPPINES

Philippine Tennis Association, Rizal Memorial Sports Complex, Vito Cruz Street, Manila.
C. Philta, Manila; T. (2) 58 35 35 or 86 46 81; TX. 45967 FPTC PM or 64619 FPTC PN; *Pres.* Col M. B. Barba; *Sec.* Mr N. R. Reyes.

POLAND

Polski Zwiazek Tenisowy, Ul. Marszalkowska 2, IIIrd Floor, 00-581 Warsaw.
C. Poltenis, Warsaw; T. (22) 21 80 01 or 29 26 21; TX. 816494 PAISP PL or 812466 COS PL; *Pres.* Mr R. Garbaczewski; *Hon. Sec.* Mr K. Tarasiewiez; *Gen. Sec.* Mr P. Dudzinski.

National Closed Championships
MEN'S SINGLES – Semi-finals: W. Rogowski d. T. Maliszewski 7–6 6–3 4–6 7–6; W. Kowalski d. W. Jamroz 6–4 6–1. *Final:* Rogowski d. Kowalski 7–5 6–7 2–6 3–6.
WOMEN'S SINGLES – Semi-finals: D. Dziekonska d. D. Szwaj 6–3 6–4; M. Waniek d. E. Zerdecka 6–1 6–3. *Final:* Waniek d. Dziekonska 6–1 6–3.

PORTUGAL

Federacao Portuguesa de Tenis, Instalacoes Municipais de Tenis, Parque Florestal de Monstano, 1300 Lisbon.
C. Portugaltenis, Lisbon; T. (1) 648067; TX. 13109 TENLIS P; *Pres.* Mr A. Vaz Pinto; *Gen. Sec.* Mr J. F. Dias.

National Closed Championships
MEN'S SINGLES – Semi-finals: P. Cordeiro d. J. Silva 6–4 6–7 6–4 1–6 7–5; P. Silva d. J. Maio 6–4 7–6 6–3. *Final:* Cordeiro d. Silva 3–6 7–5 6–0 7–5.
WOMEN'S SINGLES – Semi-finals: I. Costa d. P. Valadas 7–5 6–1; S. Marques d. Sandra Marques 6–1 6–4. *Final:* Marques d. Costa 6–4 6–2.

RUMANIA

Federatia Romana de Tenis de CIMP, Str. Vasile Conta 16, 70139 Bucharest.
C. Sportrom, Bucharest; T. (0) 11 97 87; TX. 11180 SPORT R; *Pres.* Mr I. Gheorghe; *Gen. Sec.* Mrs. F. Mihai.
MEN: **1** Florin Segarceanu; **2** Adrian Marcu; **3** Andrei Dirzu; **4** Laurentiu Bucur; **5** Dumitru Haradau; **6** Razvan Constantinescu; **7** Emil Hnat; **8** Marius Comanescu; **9** Mihai Sovar; **10** Radu Harnut.
WOMEN: **1** Daniela Moise; **2** Teodora Tache; **3** Luminita Salajan; **4** Aurelia Gheorghe; **5** Maria Romanov; **6** Monica Radu; **7** Otilia Pop; **8** Liliana Pop; **9** Diane Samungi; **10** Florentina Curpene.

National Closed Championships
MEN'S SINGLES – Semi-finals: F. Segarceanu d. L. Bucur 6–1 6–1 6–1; A. Marcu d. A. Dirzu 6–2 7–6 6–1. *Final:* Marcu d. Segarceanu 4–6 7–6 6–1 4–6 6–2.
WOMEN'S SINGLES – Semi-finals: D. Moise d. M. Voinea 6–3 6–3; F. Curpene d. T. Tache 2–6 7–5 7–5. *Final:* Moise d. Curpene 2–6 6–3 6–2.

SAUDI ARABIA

Saudi Arabian Tennis & Table Tennis Federation, PO Box 4674, Riyadh 11412.
C. Koratawia, Riyadh; T. (1) 4788145 /7966; TX. 204130 TENNIS SJ; *Pres.* Mr S. Al-Jabhan; *Sec.* Mr Saud Ali Abdulaziz.
MEN: **1** Khalid Hussein Fitiani; **2** Fahmy Mohamed Saleh; **3** Dr Ali Alaa El Din; **4** Rushdi Hisham Malhas; **5** Khalid Hussein El Siah; **6** Gamal Mohamed El Oshban; **7** Mazen Hussan Giniedy; **8** Abdel Aziz El Kridies; **9** Adnan Hassan Hawary; **10** Salah El Din Al Homoud.

National Closed Championships
MEN'S SINGLES – Final: K. H. Fitiani d. F. M. Salah.

With a stunning victory over Pam Shriver in the Australian Open, Catarina Lindqvist reached the quarter-finals and lifted her world ranking to 13 — her best finish yet, and the highest a Swedish girl has ever achieved. *(A. Evans)*

SENEGAL

Federation Senegalaise de Lawn Tennis, BP 510, Dakar.
T. 22 44 67; TX 3159 SG CTDSENE; *Pres.* Mr Y. Ndiaye; *Sec.* Mr A. Ndiaye.
MEN: **1** Thierno Ly; **2** Lamine Sonko; **3** Abou Berthe; **4** Nagy Kabaz; **5** Alioune Toure; **6** Miloud Doumbia; **7** Moustapha Diop; **8** Lamine Diedhiou; **9** Cheikh Berthe; **10** Madicke Samb.
WOMEN: **1** Saida Berthe; **2** Sadia Berthe; **3** Myriam Berthe; **4** Neissa Doumbia; **5** Khady Lacote; **6** Nafissa Diop; **7** Ida Diop; **8** Ami Berthe; **9** Salimata Sow; **10** Diama Seck.

National Closed Championships
MEN'S SINGLES – Semi-finals: T. Ly d. M. Doumbia 6–3 7–5; L. Sonko d. A. Berthe 6–4 6–4. *Final:* Ly d. Sonko 6–4 6–3.
WOMEN'S SINGLES – Semi-finals: Saida Berthe d. M. Berthe 6–2 6–4; Sadia Berthe d. N. Doumbia 7–5 6–4. *Final:* Saida Berthe d. Sadia Berthe 6–2 3–6 6–4.

SINGAPORE

Singapore Lawn Tennis Association, Apartment 13, Dover Close East No 15 – 212, Singapore 0513.
T. 4733533; TX. MAPAL RS 37679 or MBL RS 23527; *Pres.* Dr. O. L. Boon; *Sec.* Mr T. Teo.

SOUTH AFRICA

The South African Tennis Union, PO Box 2211, Johannesburg 2000.
C. Tennis, Johannesburg; T. (011) 402 3580; TX. 425976 SA; *Pres.* Mr A. de W. Horak; *Sec. /Treasurer* Mr G. L. Talbot.
MEN: **1** Kevin Curren; **2** Eddie Edwards; **3** Danie Visser; **4** Christo Van Rensburg; **5** Barry Moir; **6** Christo Steyn; **7** Kevin Moir; **8** Gary Muller; **9** Denys Maasdorp; **10** Robbie Venter.
WOMEN: **1** Rosalind Fairbank; **2** Yvonne Vermaak; **3** Beverly Mould; **4** René Uys; **5** Elna Reinach; **6** René Mentz; **7** Jennifer Mundel; **8** Monica Reinach; **9** Dinky Van Rensburg; **10** Brigette Ferreira.

National Closed Championships
MEN'S SINGLES – Semi-finals: B. Pirow d. E. Edwards 6–3 6–1; C. Steyn d. D. Maasdorp 3–6 6–4 6–3. *Final:* Steyn d. Pirow 6–7 7–5 6–3.
WOMEN'S SINGLES – Semi-finals: E. Reinach d. G. Boon 6–3 6–1; D. Van Rensburg d. R. Mentz 6–2 6–0. *Final:* Reinach d. Van Rensburg 7–6 6–4.

SPAIN

Real Federation Espanola de Tenis, Avda. Diagonal 618 3 D, 08021 Barcelona.
C. Fedetenis, Barcelona; T. (3) 2005355 or 2010844; *Pres.* Mr A. P. Niubo; *Sec.* Mr T. G. Balmaseda.
MEN: **1** José Higueras; **2** Juan Aguilera; **3** Sergio Casal; **4** Fernando Luna; **5** Emilio Sanchez; **6** José Lopez; **7** Jorge Arrese; **8** Gabriel Urpi; **9** Alberto Tous; **10** José M. Clavet.
WOMEN: **1** Ana Almansa; **2** Inmaculada Varas; **3** Michelle Garth; **4** Rosa Bielsa; **5** Ninoska Souto; **6** Margarita Vaquero; **7** Beatriz Pellon; **8** Georgina Maresma; **9** Begona Erana; **10** Elena Guerra.

National Closed Championships
MEN'S SINGLES – Semi-finals: E. Sanchez d. F. Luna 6–3 6–1 6–0; S. Casal d. J. Arrese 7–6 5–7 6–4 6–3. *Final:* Sanchez d. Casal 6–1 6–3 7–5.
WOMEN'S SINGLES – Semi-finals: A. Sanchez d. J. Souto 6–2 7–5; N. Souto d. I. Varas 6–7 6–4 6–4. *Final:* Sanchez d. Souto 7–6 6–2.

SRI LANKA

Sri Lanka Tennis Association, 45 Sir Marcus Fernando Mawatha, Colombo 7.
C. Tennis, Colombo; T. (1) 91425; TX. 22082 XPOINT CE or 22291 XPOINT CE; *Pres.* Mr E. Perera; *Sec.* Mr J. Madugalle.

National Closed Championships
MEN'S SINGLES – Semi-finals: F. Sebaratnam d. N. Casiechetty 4–6 7–6 6–2 6–2; A. Fernando d. A. Perera 6–2 6–1 6–1. *Final:* Fernando d. Sebaratnam 6–0 6–0 6–0.
WOMEN'S SINGLES – Semi-finals: P. Sebaratnam d. S. De Silva 6–3 2–6 8–6; L. Weerasuriya d. M. Karunaratna 7–5 6–1. *Final:* Weerasuriya d. Sebaratnam 6–0 5–7 6–2.

SUDAN

Sudan Lawn Tennis Association, PO Box 1553, Khartoum.
T. 70081; *Pres.* Mr A. E. Bakr; *Sec.* Mr M. A. Amer.

SWEDEN

Svenska Tennisforbundet, Lidingovagen 75, S 115 37 Stockholm.
C. Svensktennis, Stockholm; T. (8) 679770; TX. 12234 TENNIS S; *Pres.* Mr L. Olander; *Sec. Gen.* Mr R. Levin.
MEN: 1 Mats Wilander; 2 Anders Jarryd; 3 Henrik Sundstrom; 4 Joakim Nystrom; 5 Stefan Edberg; 6 Jan Gunnarsson; 7 Thomas Hogstedt; 8 Stefan Simonsson; 9 Kent Carlsson; 10 Magnus Tideman.
WOMEN: 1 Caterina Lindqvist; 2 Carina Karlsson; 3 Catrin Jexell; 4 Carin Anderholm; 5 Elisabeth Ekblom; 6 Anneli Bjork; 7 Stina Almgren; 8 Asa Flodin; 9 Karin Schultz; 10 Helena Olsson.

National Closed Championships
MEN'S SINGLES – Semi-finals: U. Stenlund d. J. Gunnarsson 4–6 6–3 6–1; J. Karlen d. J. Kjellsten 7–6 7–6. *Final:* Srenlund d. Karlen 6–2 6–0.
WOMEN'S SINGLES – Semi-finals: M. Lindstrom d. K. Karlsson 6–2 2–6 6–3; C. Lindqvist d. E. Ekblom w.o. *Final:* Lindstrom d. Lindqvist 6–4 7–6.

SWITZERLAND

Schweizerischer Tennisverband, Talgut-Zentrum 5, PO Box 3063 Ittigen /Berne.
C. Suissetennis, Bern; T. (031) 58 74 44; TX. 911391 STV CH; *Pres.* Mr B. Frischknecht; *Dir.* Mr R. Julita.
MEN: 1 Heinz Gunthardt; 2 Jakob Hlasek; 3 Roland Stadler; 4 Dominik Utzinger; 5 Marc Krippendorf; 6 Stephan Bienz; 7 Jarek Srnensky; 8 Christoph Meyer; 9 Stephan Medam; 10 Thierry Grin.
WOMEN: 1 Petra Delhees Jauch; 2 Christiane Jolissaint; 3 Lilian Drescher; 4 Karin Stampfli; 5 Csilla Cserepy; 6 Eva Krapl; 7 Susanne Schmid; 8 Celine Cohen; 9 Monika Weber; 10 Claudia Pasquale.

National Closed Championships
MEN'S SINGLES – Semi-finals: H. Gunthardt d. S. Bienz 6–4 7–6; R. Stadler d. Z. Kuharszky 6–2 6–1. *Final:* Gunthardt d. Stadler 6–1 6–3 1–6 2–6 6–3.
WOMEN'S SINGLES – Semi-finals: C. Jolissaint d. L. Drescher 2–6 6–3 6–3; P. Delhees Jauch d. K. Stampfli 6–4 6–2. *Final:* Delhees Jauch d. Jolissaint 6–4 6–4.

SYRIA ARAB REPUBLIC

Syrian Arab Tennis Federation, PO Box 421, Damascus.
T. 225026 /34 /52; TX. HOTECH SY 411935; *Pres.* Dr. S. Al Jabi; *Sec.* Mr M. Hendi.

THAILAND

The Lawn Tennis Association of Thailand, c /o Sports Promotion Organisation of Thailand, Hua Mark, Bangkok 10240.
C. Thai Tennis, Bangkok; T. (2) 314 0808 or 314 6142; TX. 20843 MIDASIA TH; *Pres.* Col S. Amornwichet; *Sec.* Capt. B. Phantawong.

TRINIDAD & TOBAGO

The Lawn Tennis Association of Trinidad & Tobago, c /o Trintoc, PO Box 601, Port-of-Spain, Trinidad.
C. Lawntenna, Port-of-Spain; T. 62 32911; *Pres.* Mr V. E. Bruce; *Sec.* Mr G. A. Matthew.

TUNISIA

Federation Tunisienne de Tennis, Cite Sportive Bourguiba, El Menzah, 1004 Tunis.
T. (1) 238 144; TX. 14637 TOPMED TN; *Pres.* Mr F. Farah; *Sec.* Mr M. Azzouz.
MEN: 1 Abdelmajid Soudani; 2 Aziz Zouhir; 3 Raouf Ben Farhat; 4 Lies Bramly; 5 Jalel Becheur; 6 Jilani Bouhafa; 7 Mongi Khadraoui; 8 Hassen Soudani; 9 Hichem Riani; 10 Karim Hamida.
WOMEN: 1 Lilia Maaref; 2 Mounira Bey; 3 Bassima Mahersi; 4 Amina Razgallah; 5 Samia Benismail; 6 Zohra Bouhafa; 7 Nejha Ayari; 8 Mejda Bey; 9 Dora Kannou; 10 Nadia Sebai.

National Closed Championships
MEN'S SINGLES – Semi-finals: A. Soudani d. C. Dahhel 3–6 7–5 6–4; J. Bouhafa d. H. Debbeche 6–4 1–6 6–2. **Final:** Soudani d. Bouhafa 6–2 7–5 6–3.
WOMEN'S SINGLES – Semi-finals: Mounira Bey d. A. Hachani 6–1 6–1; Mejda Bey d. O. Ayadi 3–6 6–2 6–4. **Final:** Mounira Bey d. Mejda Bey 6–2 6–2.

TURKEY

Turkiye Tenis Federasyonu, Ulus Is Hani, Ankara.
C. Tennis Sport, Ankara. T. (41) 12 41 50 /261; TX. 42251 TFF TR; *Pres.* Mr Y. Das; *Sec.* Mr Y. T. Kurat.
MEN: 1 **eq** Yavuz Erkangil, Alaaddin Karagoz; 3 **eq** Necvet Demir, Husnu Guzel; 5 Kaya Saydas; 6 **eq** Huseyin Karasu, Mert Ertunga; 8 Atlihan Binoz; 9 Muzaffer Arpacioglu; 10 **eq** Ali Colak, Oguz Azkara, Ural Ates, Temel Soysal, Metin Curel, Mehmet Tinaz.
WOMEN: 1 Elif Oguz; 2 Sevtap Akdere; 3 Gul Guzelbey; 4 **eq** Gigdem Kayagan, Duygil Aksit, Emel Erden, Muge Ozgenel; 8 **eq** Yesim Oguz, Ayse Coknaz; 10 **eq** Nuray Derman, Lale Kaya.

National Closed Championships
MEN'S SINGLES – Semi-finals: Y. Erkangil d. A. Karagoz 6–3 6–3 1–6 1–6 6–4; N. Demir d. H. Karasu 6–1 6–3 6–0. **Final:** Erkangil d. Demir 6–2 4–6 4–6 6–2 8–6.
WOMEN'S SINGLES – Semi-finals: S. Akdere d. G. Kayagan 7–5 6–1; G. Guzelbey d. E. Oguz 7–5 6–1. **Final:** Guzelbey d. Akdere 6–0 2–6 6–2.

USA

United States Tennis Association Incorporated, 51 East 42nd Street, New York, NY 10017.
C. Ustennis, New York; T. (212) 949-9112; TX. 42449 ULTA UI; *Pres.* Mr H. L. Delatour Jr; *Exec. Dir.* Mr D. F. Conway; *Exec. Sec.* Mr M. J. Burns.
MEN'S SINGLES: 1 John McEnroe; 2 Jimmy Connors; 3 Kevin Curren; 4 Tim Mayotte; 5 Johan Kriek; 6 Paul Annacone; 7 Brad Gilbert; 8 Eliot Teltscher; 9 Scott Davis; 10 Greg Holmes; 11 Jimmy Arias; 12 Aaron Krickstein; 13 David Pate; 14 Mike Leach; 15 Tim Wilkison; 16 John Sadri; 17 Sammy Giammalva; 18 Robert Seguso; 19 Tom Gullikson; 20 Bud Schultz; 21 Matt Anger; 22 Hank Pfister; 23 Brian Teacher; 24 Mark Dickson; 25 Ken Flach; 26 Lawson Duncan; 27 Jimmy Brown; 28 Jonathan Canter; 29 Larry Stefanki; 30 Marty Davis; 31 Ben Testerman; 32 Vitas Gerulaitis; 33 Peter Fleming; 34 Vince Van Patten; 35 Leif Shiras; 36 Mike DePalmer; 37 Francisco Gonzalez; 38 Mel Purcell; 39 Terry Moor; 40 Robert Green; 41 Todd Nelson; 42 Tim Gullikson; 43 Harold Solomon; 44 Roger Knapp; 45 Glenn Layendecker; 46 Steve Denton; 47 Chip Hooper; 48 Andy Kohlberg; 49 Jay Lapidus; 50 Matt Michell; 51 Tom Cain; 52 Jim Grabb; 53 Dan Goldie; 54 Robert Van't Hof; 55 Bill Scanlon; 56 Lloyd Bourne; 57 Mike Bauer; 58 Norman Schellberger; 59 Blaine Willenborg; 60 Marcel Freeman.
MEN'S DOUBLES: 1 Ken Flach /Robert Seguso; 2 Mike DePalmer /Gary Donnelly; 3 Scott Davis /David Pate; 4 Mark Dickson /Tim Wilkison; 5 Francisco Gonzalez /Matt Michel; 6 Tim /Tom Gullikson; 7 Hank Pfister /Ben Testerman.
WOMEN'S SINGLES: 1 Martina Navratilova; 2 Chris Evert Lloyd; 3 Pam Shriver; 4 Bonnie Gadusek; 5 Zina Garrison; 6 Kathy Rinaldi; 7 Kathy Jordan; 8 Barbara Potter; 9 Stephanie Rehe; 10 Peanut Louie; 11 Kathleen Horvath; 12 Elise Burgin; 13 Pam Casale; 14 Robin White; 15 Terry Phelps; 16 Debbie Spence; 17 Alycia Moulton; 18 Anne White; 19 Kate Gompert; 20 Lisa Bonder; 21 Susan Mascarin; 22 Molly Van Nostrand; 23 Betsy Nagelsen; 24 Melissa Gurney; 25 Ann Henricksson; 26 Camille Benjamin; 27 Caroline Kuhlman; 28 Kim Shaefer; 29 Grace Kim; 30 Patty Fendick; 31 Mary Lou Piatek; 32 Michelle Torres; 33 Barbara Gerken; 34 Kristen Kinney; 35 Linda Gates; 36 Gigi Fernandez; 37 Leigh Thompson; 38 Lea Antonoplis; 39 Beth Herr; 40 Marianne Werdel; 41 Candy Reynolds; 42 Vicki Nelson; 43 Terry Holladay; 44 Shawn Foltz; 45 Lori McNeil; 46 Amy Holton; 47 Jenny Klitch; 48 Cecilia Fernandez; 49 Beverly Bowes; 50 Ginny Purdy; 51 Wendy White; 52 Tina Mochizuki; 53 Sharon Walsh Pete; 54 Penny Barg; 55 Kim Sands; 56 Heather Ludloff; 57 Linda Howell; 58 Eileen Tell; 59 Lisa Spain; 60 Barbara Bramblett.
WOMEN'S DOUBLES: 1 Martina Navratilova /Pam Shriver; 2 Barbara Potter /Sharon Walsh Pete; 3 Betsy Nagelsen /Anne White; 4 Gigi Fernandez /Robin White; 5 Zina Garrison /Kathy Rinaldi; 6 Beth Herr /Terry Phelps; 7 Elise Burgin /Alycia Moulton; 8 Zina Garrison /Lori McNeil.

URUGUAY

Asociacion Uruguaya de Lawn Tennis, Calle Pablo De Maria 1065, Montevideo.
C. Urutennis, Montevideo; T. (2) 4 63 63; TX. CADE UY 22333; *Pres.* Mr C. R. Estrada; *Sec.* Dr G. Inda.
MEN: 1 D. Perez; 2 H. Roverano; 3 V. Valdarelli; 4 M. Filippini; 5 N. Zurmendi.

WOMEN: 1 S. Casaretto; 2 N. Clavijo; 3 L. Rodriguez; 4 P. Miller.
National Closed Championships
MEN'S SINGLES – Final: H. Roverano d. M. Filippini 6–3 4–6 7–5.
WOMEN'S SINGLES – Final: S. Casaretto d. M. Clavijo 6–2 6–1.

USSR

Lawn Tennis Federation of the USSR, Luzhnetskaya Naberezhnaya 8, 119270 Moscow.
C. Sportkomitet, Moscow; T. (095) 201 08 64; TX. 411287 PRIZ SU; *Pres.* Mr B. Volynov; *Sec. Gen.* Mr V. Yanchuk.
MEN: 1 Andrei Chesnokov; 2 Aleksandr Zverev; 3 Konstantin Pugaev; 4 Aleksandr Volkov; 5 Sergei Leoniuk; 6 Gennady Avdeev; 7 Girtas Dzelde; 8 Andrei Olkhovsky; 9 Andris Vysand; 10 Iosif Krochko.
WOMEN: 1 Larisa Savchenko; 2 Elena Eliseenko; 3 Yulia Salnikova; 4 Natalia Bykova; 5 Liudmila Esmanova; 6 Nina Avdeeva; 7 Elena Gishjants; 8 Svetlana Parkhomenko; 9 Viktoria Milvidskaya; 10 Natalia Reva.

VENEZUELA

Federacion Venezolana de Tenis, Apartado 70539, Los Ruices, Caracas 1070-A.
C. Fevetenis, Caracas; T. (2) 9792421 /1487 /0697; TX. 28465 FVT VC; *Pres.* Mr A. P. Rivas; *Sec.* Mr G. Barrera.

YUGOSLAVIA

Tenis Savez Yugoslavije, Terazije 35, Belgrade.
C. Tesaj, Belgrade; T. (11) 33 33 36; TX. 12 595 SFKJ YU; *Pres.* Mr R. Nikolic; *Sec.* Mr Z. Peric.

ZIMBABWE

Tennis Association of Zimbabwe, PO Box 2346, Harare.
T. (10) 32901; TX. 2501 ZW LIQUOR; *Pres.* Mr I. D. F. Godden; *Sec.* Mrs C. Greener.
MEN: 1 Haroon Ismail; 2 Orlando Loourenco; 3 Philip Tuckniss; 4 Mark Gurr; 5 Clive Wilson; 6 Graham Cohen; 7 Greg Rodger; 8 Larry Katz; 9 Byron Black; 10 Graham Martin.
WOMEN: 1 Angela Longo; 2 **eq** Sally Ann Birch, Charmaine Olivier; 4 Lyndsay Standen; 5 Sally Stephens; 6 Sue Roux; 7 **eq** Julia Muir, Paula Iverson; 9 Nicki Hagstaff; 10 Fiona Martin.

Associate Members Without Voting Rights (42)

AFGHANISTAN Afghan Lawn Tennis Association, c /o National Olympic Committee of Afghanistan, National Stadium, Kabul.
C. Olympic Kabul; TX. 20579; *Pres.* Mr O. Saraj; *Sec.* Mr H. Osman.
BAHAMAS The Bahamas Lawn Tennis Association, PO Box N-10169, Nassau.
T. (809) 326 1625 or 322 2694; TX. BRAMLINCOL 20318; *Pres.* Mr P. Phillips; *Sec.* Mrs S. Ryan.
BARBADOS Barbados Lawn Tennis Association, PO Box 615c, Bridgetown.
T. 427 5298; *Pres.* Mr N. F. Symmonds; *Sec.* Mr B. Hackett.
BENIN Federation Beninoise de Lawn Tennis, Club du Benin, BP 63, Akpakpa Cotonous II.
C. Lawn Tennis Box 516; T. 31 34 94; *Pres.* Mr G. Ligan; *Sec.* Mr C. Martins.
BERMUDA Bermuda Lawn Tennis Association, PO Box 341, Hamilton 5.
C. Ernsaudit, Bermuda; T. (29) 57272; TX. 3680 ERNST BA; *Pres.* Mr W. F. Way.
BHUTAN Bhutan Tennis Federation, PO Box 103, Thimphu.
Pres. Mr T. Dorji; *Sec.* Mr L. Tsering.
BOTSWANA Botswana National LTA, PO Box 1174, Gaborone.
T. 53029 or 51743; TX. 2538 AUTOG BD; *Pres.* Dr J. Letsunyane; *Sec.* Mrs L. Ranasinghe.
BRITISH VIRGIN ISLANDS British Virgin Islands Lawn Tennis Association, PO Box 201, Road Town, Tortola.
C. Veritatem, Tortola; T. (809) 49 42616; TX. 7918; *Pres.* Dr K. Adamson; *Sec.* Mr N. Barton.
BRUNEI DARUSSALEM Brunei Darussalam Lawn Tennis Association, PO Box 1300, Bandar Seri Begawan.
TX. DCABWN BU 2267; *Pres.* Mr T. R. Butcher; *Sec.* Mr A. Ajmain.

BURMA   Burma Tennis Federation, Aung San Memorial Stadium, Kandawgalay Post Office, Rangoon.
C. Ubsped, Rangoon; T. 01 71731; *Pres.* Mr K. K. Gyi; *Sec.* Mr A. Thein.

CAYMAN ISLANDS   Tennis Federation of the Cayman Islands, PO Box 1352, Grand Cayman Island, British West Indies.
T. (1809 94) 92077; TX. 4310 CORPSER CP; *Pres.* Mr D. Price; *Sec.* Mr. G. Barlow.

CONGO   Federation Congolaise de Lawn Tennis, BP 2092, Brazzaville.

COOK ISLANDS   Cook Islands Tennis Association, PO Box 610, Rarotonga.
T. 22327; TX. 62026 SSIRARO; *Pres.* Mr B. R. Baudinet; *Sec.* Mr W. Jon.

COSTA RICA   Federacion Costarricense de Tenis, PO Box 326-1005, B Mexico, San José.
C. Hopec, San José; T. 236133; TX. 2101 HOPEC; *Pres.* Mr F. Holtermann; *Sec.* Mr R. Mendieta;

DJIBOUTI   Federation Djiboutienne de Tennis, Rue Pierre-Pascal, BP 728, Djibouti.
C. PO Box 728, Djibouti; T. 35 22 86; *Pres.* Mr H. Houmed; *Sec. Gen.* Mme M. A. Farah.

DOMINICAN REPUBLIC   Federacion Dominicana de Tenis, Club Deportivo Naco, Calle Central, Ens. Naco, Santo Domingo, Rep. Dominicana.
T. 565 4836 or 685 8059; TX. 3460418 BONELLY; *Pres.* Mr G. Mejia; *Sec.* Mr J. Ravello.

EL SALVADOR   Federacion Salvadorena de Tenis, Apartado Postal (01) 110, San Salvador.
C. Molino, San Salvador; T. (503) 23 38 92; TX. 20542 MOLINO; *Pres.* Ing. R. Sanchez; *Sec.* Ms P. Rodriguez.

ETHIOPIA   Ethiopia Lawn Tennis Federation, PO Box 3241, Addis Ababa.
C. Addis Ababa (c /o Sports Commission); T. (01) 156205; TX. 21377 NESCO ET; *Pres.* Mr H. Balcha; *Sec.* Mr H. Afework.

FIJI   Fiji Lawn Tennis Association, PO Box 313 BA, Fiji Islands.
T. 60870; *Pres.* Mr B. K. Reddy; *Sec.* Mr P. R. Singh.

GHANA   Ghana Tennis Association, National Sports Council, PO Box 1272, Accra.
C. Ghansport; T. 63924 or 63927; *Pres.* Mr E. Annan; *Sec.* Mr A. K. Ocloo.

When he beat Wilander in the first round of Wimbledon, Zivojinovic confirmed the promise he had shown as the National Yugoslav Champion in every age group from 12 to 21, and his victory over McEnroe in the Australian Open proved the point.   (A. Evans)

GUATEMALA Federacion Nacionale de Tenis, Palacio de Los Deportes Zona 4, Guatemala.
T. (2) 310261; *Pres.* Mr J. Mansilla; *Sec.* Mr R. Rivera.

GUINEE CONAKRY Federation Guineene de Tennis, Ministere e la Jeunesse et Sports, BP 262, Guinee Conakry.
T. 44 19 62; TX. 2102 MJ GUI; *Pres.* Mr M. L. Damba.

GUYANA Guyana Lawn Tennis Association, PO Box 10205, Georgetown.
C. Lawntenna, Georgetown; T. 02 71195 (President), 02 67826 (Secretary); TX. 2281 CALA GY; *Pres.* Mr T. B. E. Richmond; *Sec.* Dr G. Muller.

HAITI Federation Haitienne de Tennis, c/o Mr J. Etienne, Box 1728, 1377 Rue Carlstroem, Port-au-Prince.
C. Joetienne, Port-au-Prince; T. 5-0703 or 5-1377; *Pres.* Mr J. Etienne; *Sec.* Mr O. Nadal.

JORDAN Jordan Tennis Federation, PO Box 35121, Amman.
C. Tenfed, Amman; T. 962-6 662707; TX. 22500 HILAL JO; *Chmn* Dr M. Al-Fawwaz; *Sec.* Mr I. Jarallah.

KOREA, PEOPLE'S DEMOCRATIC REPUBLIC OF Tennis Association of the Democratic People's Republic of Korea, Munsin-Dong, Dongdaewon Dist., Pyongyang.
C. Tennis, DPR Korea; T. 6-2386 or 6-3998; TX. 5-472; *Pres.* Mr P. Jung Yang; *Sec.* Mr Li Won-Gun.

MALAWI Lawn Tennis Association of Malawi, PO Box 1417, Blantyre.
Sec. Mrs S. Windsor.

MALI Federation Malienne de Tennis, Ministere des Affairs Etrangeres Koulouba.
T. 225489 /225633 /225092; *Pres.* Mr A. Nafo; *Sec.* Mr A. Traore.

MAURITIUS Mauritius Lawn Tennis Association, Rose-Hill Club, Bruce Street, Rose-Hill.
C. Tennis, Mauritius; T. 4-1666; *Pres.* Mr C. Cure; *Sec.* Mlle C. de Maroussem.

MONTSERRAT Montserrat Tennis Association, PO Box 386, Plymouth, Montserrat, British West Indies.
T. 491 5363 /5368; *Pres.* Mr L. Arnold; *Sec.* Miss E. Fenton.

MOZAMBIQUE Federacao Mocambicana de Tenis, Caixa Postal 4351, Maputo.
T. 27027; TX. 6-597 SATCC MO; *Pres.* Mr P. M. Figueiredo; *Sec.* Mr J. Nhabangue.

NEPAL All Nepal Tennis Association, PO Box 2090, Dasarath Stadium, Kathmandu.
T. 211732 or 215712; TX. 2390 NSCNP; *Pres.* Mr S. Singh; *Sec.* Mr P. K. Shrestha.

NETHERLANDS ANTILLES Netherlands Antilles Tennis Association, PO Box 3360, Emmastad Curacao.
T. 44192; *Pres.* Mr Ing. M. R. Paula; *Sec.* Mr H. Thomas.

PANAMA, REPUBLIC OF Comision Nacionale de Tennis de Panama, Apartado 6-6717, El Dorado, Panama.
T. 600019 or 262785 /60; TX. 2534 INDE PG; *Pres.* Mr H. Spalding; *Sec.* Mr E. Palomo.

PUERTO RICO Puerto Rico Tennis Association, Box 40456 – Minillas Station, Santurce, Puerto Rico 00940.
T. 721-9112 or 721-1655; TX. 3454212; *Pres.* Mr J. Baldrich; *Sec.* Mrs L. de la Rosa.

QATAR Qatar Tennis Federation, PO Box 4959, Doha.
T. 831788 or 831786; TX. 4059 QTSF DH; *Pres.* I. G. Al Kawari; *Sec.* Mr K. Al Dafa.

SAN MARINO Federazione Sammarinese Tennis, Republic of San Marino 47031.
C. Piazza M. Tini n. 15-47031, DOGANA; T. 905303; TX. 550885 SP RSMI; *Pres.* Mr A. S. Belluzzi; *Sec.* Mr E. Belluzzi.

TANZANIA Tanzania Lawn Tennis Association, PO Box 965, Dar es Salaam.
T. (51) 23351; TX. 41009; *Pres.* Mr A. Fernandes; *Sec.* Mr R. Rugimbana.

TOGO Federation Togolaise de Lawn Tennis, BP 4632, Lome.
T. 21456; TX. 5015 CNOT TO; *Pres.* Mr A. Kokou; *Sec.* Mr G. Tohonou.

UNITED ARAB EMIRATES United Arab Emirates Tennis Association, PO Box 87, Dubai.
T. (04) 434 989; TX. 46347 FAGEN EM; *Pres.* Lt Col S. Khalfan; *Sec.* Mr N. Madani.

YEMEN P.D.R. Yemen Tennis & Table Tennis Federation, PO Box 157, Aden.
C. Madhrab, Aden; T. 53244 or 53639; *Pres.* Mr A. H. Salem; *Sec.* Mr I. Mohammed.

ZAMBIA Zambia Lawn Tennis Association, PO Box 31299, Lusaka.
C. Parliament, Lusaka; T. (01) 218991; TX. PARLY ZA 44390; *Pres.* Mr M. Chibesakunda; *Sec.* Miss E. Mabo.

100% SUPPORT IS ASSURED EVEN FOR HUNDREDS TIMES OF DASH AND STOP.

ASICS TIGER's tennis shoes, designed on biomechanical principles, satisfy the world top players' requirements.

TLL504 TOP SEED SL

Ideal for reasonable play on hard court. The upper is made of R-9100 special synthetic leather.
The outersole is made of polyurethane compounded with rubber, which is constructed to keep softness and lightness of urethane material and strength of rubber material alive for smooth play.
Size : 5-10 $\frac{1}{2}$.
Color : White/Silver navy.
 White/Ice blue.

ANDERS JARRYD

ASICS Corporation Overseas Operations Division
1-1, Minatojima-Nakamachi 7chome, Chuo-ku, KOBE, 650 JAPAN Phone : 078-303-3333 Telex : 5622-916 ASICSA J
Cable : ASICSPI KOBE Tele-facsimile : 078-303-2244
ASICS TIGER CORP.
3030 South Susan Street Santa Ana, California 92704 U.S.A. Phone : 714-754-0451 Telex : 685533
Tele-facsimile : 714-754-0507
ASICS TIGER GmbH
Welser Strasse 1, D-4040 Neuss, F. R. Germany Phone : 02101-38020 Telex : 8517431 ASI D Tele-facsimile : 00149-2101-37341

THE JUNIOR GAME

European success, already forcefully reflected in other areas of world tennis, was equally apparent on the junior scene, especially in the ITF's Junior World Ranking Series of international tournaments. Two of the top three boys and girls in the rankings at the end of 1985 were Europeans and it was a particularly triumphant year for the Italians, who saw Claudio Pistolesi win the Orange Bowl to finish on top of the boys' list and Laura Garrone win both the French and US Open junior events, to head the girls' rankings.

As always in this 18-and-under age range, the overlap of senior and junior competition means that the talents of some players are not reflected to the full. This was especially so in the case of Leonardo Lavalle from Mexico, who won the junior title at Wimbledon but was not in the top three in the ITF rankings. Lavalle was one among many South American boys and girls who made great headway during 1985. In fact Argentina's Patricia Tarabini and Mariana Perez Roldan, high in the girls' singles list, also finished joint number one in the girls' doubles. There were also joint leaders in the boys' doubles – Czechoslovakia's Petr Korda and Cyril Suk, younger brother of Helena Sukova.

Another outstanding highlight of the junior year was that three Swedish boys finished champions at the Port Washington Rolex International – Ulf Stenlund (18s) Per Henricksson (16s) and Nicklas Kulti (14s). The Bjorn Borg heritage shows no sign of losing its thrust.

JUNIOR WORLD RANKING LEADERS

Singles
1978   Ivan Lendl (CZ) and Hana Mandlikova (CZ)
1979   Raul Viver (EC) and Mary Lou Piatek (USA)
1980   Thierry Tulasne (F) and Susan Mascarin (USA)
1981   Pat Cash (AUS) and Zina Garrison (USA)
1982   Guy Forget (F) and Gretchen Rush (USA)
1983   Stefan Edberg (SW) and Pascale Paradis (F)
1984   Mark Kratzman (AUS) and Gabriela Sabatini (ARG)
1985   Claudio Pistolesi (IT) and Laura Garrone (IT)

Doubles
1982   Fernando Perez (MEX) and Beth Herr (USA)
1983   Mark Kratzman (AUS) and Larisa Savchenko (USSR)
1984   Augustin Moreno (MEX) and Mercedes Paz (ARG)
1985   Petr Korda (CZ), Cyril Suk (CZ) and Patricia Tarabini (ARG) and Mariana Perez
       Roldan (ARG)

A dejected Pat Cash suffered a frustrating, injury-plagued year, for after reaching the Wimbledon doubles final with Fitzgerald, he missed the rest of the season and slipped from eight to 67 in the rankings. (T. Hindley)

ITF JUNIOR WORLD RANKING CIRCUIT 1985

DATE	TOURNAMENT	BOYS' SINGLES FINAL	GIRLS' SINGLES FINAL
27 Dec–1 Jan	ITF West African	G. Cohen d. P. Koffi 6-0 6-2	M. Berthe d. O. Bouchanou 6-4 6-2
31 Dec–6 Jan	Copa Ford	H. Skoff d. K. Steeb 6-1 6-2	M. Perez Roldan d. P. Tarabini 1-6 7-6 6-3
31 Dec–6 Jan	Coqui Bowl	C. Bergstrom d. S. Enochs 6-1 6-1	K. Skulj d. S. Stafford 6-3 6-3
31 Dec–6 Jan	Western Australian	B. Hamburg d. K. McCreery 6-0 6-3	N. Crutchley d. J. Bottrill 6-4 6-3
7–13 Jan	Coffee Bowl	M. Merez d. J. Sanchez 6-4 6-4	K. Skulj d. L. Stern 6-4 6-1
8–13 Jan	Copa Pony	H. Skoff d. J. Silva 6-2 4-6 7-5	P. Tarabini d. M. Perez Roldan 6-4 6-3
15–20 Jan	Guayaquil Bowl	J. Silva d. S. Mora 6-1 7-6	H. Ter-Riet d. I. Driehuis 6-2 2-6 7-5
22–27 Jan	Inka Bowl	J. Silva d. J. Izaga 6-2 6-1	K. Strohmeier d. M. Moran 6-1 7-6
29 Jan–3 Feb	Start, Sofia	I. Saric d. M. Nicolae 6-4 6-3	O. Pop d. D. Rangelova 1-6 6-3 6-3
29 Jan–3 Feb	Condor De Plata	J. Silva d. M. Filipini 6-4 7-6	E. Moran d. M. Morel 2-6 6-3 6-4
5–10 Feb	Santiago	J. Silva d. M. Yoma 6-2 6-4	P. Sepulveda d. K. Strohmeier 2-6 6-2 6-2
11–17 Feb	Carrasco Bowl	J. Silva d. F. Davin 6-1 6-4	M. Perez Roldan d. P. Tarabini 7-6 6-0
15–19 Feb	Winkler Indoor	P. Korda d. M. Nastase 6-4 6-2	C. Singer d. W. Probst 7-5 5-7 6-2
19–24 Feb	Argentina Bowl	F. Davin d. D. Pons 7-5 6-4	P. Tarabini d. K. Sipos 6-2 0-6 6-4
25 Feb–3 March	Asian Junior	S. Matsuoka d. W. Tongkumchoo 6-2 6-4	L. S. Kim d. P. Moreno 6-4 6-3
25 Feb–3 March	Sun Cup	I. Saric d. D. Goodfroid 6-3 6-2	R. Zrubakova d. A. Devries 2-6 6-4 6-2
26 Feb–2 March	Asuncion Bowl	T. Srichaphan d. D. Pons 6-1 4-6 12-10	E. Hirose d. K. Codiani 7-5 7-5
4–10 March	Bangkok	T. Srichaphan d. Z. Ali 6-1 6-2	A. Kijimuta d. J. M. Lee 7-5 6-2
4–10 March	Banana Bowl	F. Davin d. J. Silva 7-5 6-4	P. Tarabini d. M. Perez Roldan 6-1 6-3
11–16 March	Siam Motors	T. Thongkhamchu d. T. Srichaphan 3-6 6-4 7-6	Y. Zhu d. Y. Busuki 6-3 3-6 6-4
18–24 March	SAA	B. Farrow d. J. Blake 6-3 6-7 7-5	E. Reinach d. D. Van Rensburg 7-6 6-1
19–24 March	Indonesia Junior	T. Indrawan d. A. Zeeshan 7-5 6-3	B. Yayuk d. T. Lucky 6-1 7-6
26–31 March	Marcos Open	F. Barrientos d. R. Harrison 6-4 6-2	J. Saberon d. J. Basuki 6-2 5-7 6-4
1–7 April	Governor Rodriguez	F. Barrientos d. S. Matsuoka 6-3 3-6 6-1	E. Olivarez d. P. Moreno 7-5 6-0
1–7 April	Grasse	P. Lacombrade d. A. Schott 6-4 6-4	F. Martin d. S. Niox-Chateau 6-3 6-4
3–8 April	Trofeo Ellesse	S. Mezzadri d. C. Pistolesi 5-7 7-5 6-0	L. Golarsa d. A. De Vries 6-1 4-6 6-0
7–12 April	Tel Aviv	A. Naor d. S. Zysk 6-2 6-4	Z. Gal-On d. D. Koriat 6-1 7-6
8–14 April	Nice	C. Bergstrom d. S. Mora 6-1 6-1	H. Dahlstrom d. S. Niox-Chateau 6-3 6-1
9–14 April	Hong Kong	F. Barrientos d. Z. Ali 6-1 6-2	J. Saberon d. R. Basuki 6-2 2-6 6-1
13–17 April	Jerusalem	A. Naor d. T. Nydahl 6-4 1-6 9-7	D. Koriat d. Z. Gal-On 6-3 4-6 6-3
14–20 April	Katoro Cup	H. Holm d. O. Bakaric 4-6 6-2 6-2	K. Skulj d. S. Pfitzner w.o.
15–21 April	Taipei	F. Barrientos d. S. Matsuoka 7-6 7-5	J. M. Lee d. I. S. Kim 6-1 6-1
22–28 April	Jal Cup	J. Boytim d. C. Garner 7-6 6-1	J. Young d. A. Kijimuta 6-0 6-2
22–28 April	Spring Bowl	D. Engel d. F. Davin 2-6 7-6 6-2	R. Zrubakova d. S. Wasserman 6-2 7-5
29 April–5 May	Acropolis Cup	A. Padovani d. C. Pistolesi 6-1 6-2	A. Dechaume d. S. Niox-Chateau 6-4 6-2
5–11 May	Italian Junior	G. Perez Roldan d. F. Davin 6-2 2-6 7-5	P. Tarabini d. L. Golarsa 6-1 6-0
13–18 May	Trofeo Cassa	J. Saric d. C. Suk 6-2 6-3	P. Tarabini d. M. Perez Roldan 6-2 6-1
16–19 May	Berlin	G. Perez Roldan d. F. Davin 6-3 6-2	M. Gartner d. W. Probst 6-2 3-6 6-2
20–25 May	Trofeo Banca	P. Korda d. C. Bergstrom 6-0 6-1	M. Perez Roldan d. B. Fulco 6-2 3-6 6-1
27 May–1 June	Astrid Bowl	J. Izaga d. T. Muster 2-6 6-3 6-0	M. Perez Roldan d. H. Witvoet 6-2 4-6 6-1
3–9 June	French Junior	G. Tesorone d. U. Pigato 6-2 6-1	L. Garrone d. D. Van Rensburg 6-1 6-2
10–15 June	Trofeo Cremona	W. Kowalski d. G. Vanderveeren 6-3 7-6	A. Kalatian d. A. Winkler 6-4 6-1
10–16 June	White Devils Junior	F. Davin d. G. Perez Roldan 6-3 7-5	A. Devries d. I. Driehuis 6-3 6-2
10–16 June	Apple Bowl	T. Theine d. C. Araya 6-2 6-3	M. Ghezzi d. J. Alexander 7-6 6-2
17–23 June	Golden Shoes	Abandoned owing to bad weather	J. Pospisilova d. M. Jaggard 6-2 7-5
18–23 June	LTA Grass Thames Ditton		L. Field d. V. Lake 6-2 1-6 6-2

Dates	Event	Boys' Singles	Girls' Singles
22-30 June	Open Danish	F. Fetterlein d. K. Brendstrup 6-3 6-4	E. Broers d. A. Aalonen 4-6 6-3 6-4
25-30 June	LTA Int Surbiton	J. Izaga d. P. Trigieuro 6-1 6-4	M. Turk d. T. Price 7-6 6-4
1-7 July	Wimbledon	L. Lavalle d. E. Velez 6-4 6-1	A. Holikova d. J. Byrne 7-5 6-1
8-13 July	Friendship Cup	L. Nemecek d. Z. Ali 6-1 6-1	H. Adamkova d. P. Langrova 6-2 6-2
8-13 July	Netherlands Junior	F. Vermeer d. J. Dwyer 7-5 6-4	T. Wilmink d. J. Schreuks 7-6 6-1
8-14 July	Hannen-Alt Cup	M. Strelba d. T. Theine 6-0 1-6 6-4	S. Meier d. R. Wieser 6-3 4-6 6-2
15-21 July	Klosters	U. Pigato d. P. Wekesa 6-2 1-6 6-3	B. Paulus d. K. Oberleitner 4-6 6-3 6-2
15-21 July	Tunisia	P. Chinelatto d. S. Sorisini 6-2 6-1	S. Ballat d. M. Martinez 7-6 6-2
18-23 July	Crystal Cup	M. Strelba d. C. Suk 6-3 7-6	D. Samungi d. P. Sedlackova 6-3 7-5
23-27 July	Slovakia Cup	M. Strelba d. L. Nemecek 6-1 6-4	T. Tache d. D. Samungi 6-4 6-3
27 July-4 Aug	South American Junior	S. Cortes d. M. Filipini 4-6 6-4 6-3	G. Miro d. P. Sepulveda 6-1 6-2
27 July-4 Aug	Kenya	P. Wekesa d. E. Polo 6-1 7-5	S. Seeber d. C. Wekesa 6-3 6-2
28 July-4 Aug	European Junior	C. Bergstrom d. C. Pistolesi 6-2 5-7 7-5	A. Holikova d. L. Meskhi 6-3 6-1
29 July-3 Aug	Winchester	D. Ison d. N. Jones 6-2 6-1	K. Rickett d. V. Lake 6-2 3-2 ret'd
3-11 Aug	USTA Nationals	J. Berger d. F. Hunt 6-0 3-6 6-3 5-7 6-4	S. Rehe d. C. MacGregor 7-5 6-2
5-10 Aug	All Nigeria Junior	S. Akinloye d. A. Nweje 7-5 6-1	B. Paulus d. K. Kschwendt 7-6 6-7 7-6
12-18 Aug	S-Sparkassen Cup		
12-18 Aug	USTA Grass	J. Blake d. K. Kuperstein 6-4 6-2	N. Arendt d. L. Haldas 6-2 6-1
13-17 Aug	BMC Botswana	B. Black d. G. Jeftha 6-1 6-2	N. Wagstaff d. C. Rosenburg 6-4 6-0
16-20 Aug	Sri Lanka	N. Rajapakee d. S. Soysa 6-1 6-1	L. Weerasuriya d. T. Viragh 6-0 6-1
19-24 Aug	Indianapolis	A. Moreno d. A. Naor 6-3 7-6 6-3	C. Schuschel d. L. Novello 4-6 6-2 6-2
26-30 Aug	Coupe De Zeralda	M. Benyebka d. V. Wadle 6-2 6-2	K. Czoske d. W. Bouchabou 6-1 6-4
26 Aug-1 Sept	Rumania	A. Popovici d. E. Dascalu 7-5 6-4	T. Tache d. D. Samungi 6-4 6-7 6-2
27-31 Aug	Bata Zimbabwe	B. Black d. P. Dalleau 6-0 6-2	J. Muir d. E. Seeber 6-2 6-2
31 Aug-8 Sept	Canadian Junior	C. Bergstroem d. J. Blake 6-1 6-1	N. Arendt d. A. Kiimuta 6-4 6-3
2-8 Sept	Caracas	M. Merz d. N. Pereira 6-7 6-4 21-19	M. Sanchez d. E. Gibson 6-0 6-3
2-8 Sept	Sofia	Z. Cica d. A. Radev 6-4 6-4	E. Nikolova d. E. Pampoulova 6-3 6-2
9-15 Sept	US Open	T. Trigueiro d. J. Blake 6-2 6-3	J. Garrone d. A. Holikova 6-2 7-6
9-15 Sept	Aphrodite Cup	M. Tuma d. T. Kabakoglou 6-3 6-0	Cancelled
9-15 Sept	Agua De Luso Portugal	C. Silva d. P. Flintsoe 7-6 7-6	A. Allonen d. C. Curmi 6-3 6-3
16-22 Sept	Tbilisi	V. Gabrichidze d. I. Krochko 6-3 6-2	I. Meskhi d. I. Fishkina 7-5 6-3
20-24 Sept	Tashkent	V. Gabrichidze d. A. Chernetsky	N. Zvereva d. I. Fishkina
23-28 Sept	Manolo Orantes Cup	N. Bendtsen d. P. Flintsoe 6-4 6-4	T. Elver-Jorgensen d. M. Vinas 6-2 6-3
25-29 Sept	Seoul	S. S. Lee d. T. S. Kim 4-6 6-3 6-2	J. M. Lee d. I. S. Kim 2-6 6-2 6-1
25-29 Sept	Belgrade	P. Flintso d. G. Ivanisevic 6-3 4-6 6-3	T. Elver-Jorgensen d. A. Fetehagic 6-7 7-5 6-2
1-6 Oct	East Asian	S. S. Lee d. M. S. Lee 6-3 6-3	J. M. Lee d. I. S. Kim 6-1 6-3
7-13 Oct	China	S. Zhiwei d. H. Bo 6-0 5-7 6-0	Y. Lihua d. Z. Yu Yu 6-1 6-4
14-20 Oct	Japan Open	S. Matsuoka d. R. Tsujino 5-7 6-4 7-6	A. Kijimuta d. M. Yokota 6-3 7-5
9-20 Nov	Queensland	N. Bonwick d. J. Stead 6-3 7-6	J. Lundquist d. S. Faulkner 6-3 6-3
15-19 Nov	Stockholm	U. Stenlund d. P. Wennberg 7-6 6-2	J. Jonerup d. M. Ekstrand 6-3 3-6 6-4
16 Nov-14 Dec	New South Wales	P. Korda d. B. Custer 6-4 7-6	L. Field d. K. Deed 6-1 2-6 6-3
21-24 Nov	Helsinki	U. Stenlund d. T. Nydahl 7-5 6-2	A. Jonsson d. M. Ekstrand 7-5 4-6 7-5
25-29 Nov	Victorian Junior	S. Barr d. P. Flynn 6-4 6-2	M. Turk d. K. Deed 6-1 7-6
30 Nov-8 Dec	Australian Junior	S. Barr d. S. Furlong 7-6 6-7 6-3	J. Byrne d. L. Field 6-1 6-3
16-20 Dec	South Australian Junior	P. Korda d. M. Jeffrey 6-4 7-5	J. Dwyer d. T. Morton 6-4 6-3
16-23 Dec	Orange Bowl	C. Pistolesi d. B. Oresar 6-2 6-0	M. J. Fernandez d. P. Tarabini 7-6 6-1
26-30 Dec	Western Australian	C. Turich d. B. Hamburg 6-1 6-2	J. Crutchley d. J. Ledder 7-5 6-2
26 Dec-1 Jan	Rolex	U. Stenlund d. S. Ohta 6-2 6-1	P. O'Reilly d. J. Pospisilova 7-6 6-3
26 Dec-1 Jan	Copa Casablanca	J. Sanchez d. W. Kowalski	C. Moss d. M. Kemper

WORLD YOUTH CUP

Australia and Czechoslovakia shared the honours when the leading 32 teams for boys and girls from all parts of the world came together in Kobe, Japan, in November, 1985, for the first staging of the ITF's World Team Cup for players aged 16 and under. The finals were organised by the ITF in conjunction with the Japan Tennis Association after the majority of teams had earlier fought their way through regional qualifying events in South America, Africa, Asia and Europe.

The televised finals featured a particularly exciting finish to the boys' event when Australia, who had defeated the USSR in the semi-final, beat the United States 2–1. After the singles matches had been shared, the Australian doubles team of Shane Barr and Jason Holtenberg beat John Falbo and Francisco Montana 7–5 in the third set after saving four match-points in the second. In the girls' event, Czechoslovakia beat France 2–1 to reach the final, where they defeated Australia, 3–0 winners over Britain in the semi-finals, also by 3–0.

Placement ties also took place and the final listing was:

BOYS: Champion nation – Australia; runners-up – USA; 3rd – USSR; 4th – Venezuela; 5th – Italy; 6th – Argentina; 7th – Czechoslovakia; 8th – Brazil; 9th – Netherlands; 10th – India; 11th – West Germany; 12th – Korea; 13th – Spain; 14th – Zimbabwe; 15th – Japan; 16th – Jamaica.

GIRLS: Champion nation – Czechoslovakia; runner-up – Australia; 3rd – France; 4th – Great Britain; 5th – USA; 6th – Hong Kong; 7th – Japan; 8th – Peru; 9th – West Germany; 10th – Belgium; 11th – Brazil; 12th – Zimbabwe; 13th – Korea; 14th – Bulgaria; 15th – Venezuela; 16th – Jamaica.

KOBE, JAPAN, 13–17 NOVEMBER
BOYS' EVENT – Semi-finals: Australia d. USSR 2–1 (R. Fromberg lost to A. Cherkassov 3–6 2–6; S. Barr d. D. Kacharava 6–7 6–3 6–3; Barr /J. Stoltenberg d. Kacharava /Cherkassov 6–0 7–5); **USA d. Venezuela 3–0** (F. Montana d. J. C. Bianci 6–0 6–1; J. A. Falbo d. N. Pereira 6–3 3–6 6–3; Montana /Falbo d. Bianci /F. Sydow 6–4 6–4). **Final: Australia d. USA 2–1** (Fromberg lost to Montana 2–6 2–6; Barr d. Falbo 6–4 6–4; Barr/Stoltenberg d. Montana/Falbo 4–6 7–6 7–5).
GIRLS' EVENT – Semi-finals: Czechoslovakia d. France 2–1 (J. Pospisilova lost to A. Dechaume 4–6 4–6; R. Zrubakova d. S. Niox-Chateau 6–1 6–3; Pospisilova /Zrubakova d. Dechaume /Niox-Chateau 6–2 6–2); **Australia d. Great Britain 3–0** (S. McCann d. T. Catlin 6–3 6–0; N. Provis d. A. Simpkin 6–2 6–3; Provis /W. Frazer d. Simpkin /S. McCarthy 6–0 6–1). **Final: Czechoslovakia d. Australia 3–0** (Pospisilova d. McCann 6–4 6–4; Zrubakova d. Provis 7–6 7–5; Pospisilova /Zrubakova d. Provis /Frazer 7–5 6–4).

ITF WORLD CHAMPIONSHIPS FOR PLAYERS AGED 14, 12 AND UNDER 'THE SPORT GOOFY TROPHY'

The third Sport Goofy Trophy was held at Walt Disney World in Florida from 18–22 September at the Lake Buena Vista Club, with 128 players from some 40 countries competing for honours. Eligibility for the Sport Goofy Trophy is via regional competitions of Asia, Europe, East Africa and South America and by a selection of wild cards by the ITF Junior Competitions Committee to cover other geographical regions with no means of qualification. Under the sponsorship of Walt Disney Productions, the Sport Goofy Programme enables children to enjoy tennis in an atmosphere of good sportsmanship and international fellowship. Winners of the 1985 World Championships for players aged 14, 12 and under were as follows:

BOYS' 14 SINGLES – Final: M. Chang (USA) d. N. Kulti (SW) 7–6 6–2.
BOYS' 12 SINGLES – Final: T. Ho (USA) d. A. Ito (J) 6–1 6–1.
GIRLS' 14 SINGLES – Final: N. Zvereva (USSR) d. M. Kriebel (G) 4–6 6–2 6–1.
GIRLS' 12 SINGLES – Final: M. Seles (YU) d. K. Kessaris (USA) 6–1 6–1.

GALEA CUP

Men's 20 and under team championship
Zone A: Norway d. Hungary 3–2. **Zone B:** Poland d. Great Britain 3–2. **Zone C:** Monaco d. Portugal 3–2. **Zone semi-finals:** Italy d. Denmark 5–0; USA d. Yugoslavia 4–1; Spain d. USSR 4–1; Czechoslovakia d. Austria 4–1. **Semi-finals:** USA d. Spain 3–2; Italy d. Czechoslovakia 3–2. **Final:** Italy d. USA 3–2 (P. Cane d. L. Jensen 6–2 6–1 8–6; C. Pistolesi lost to R. Reneberg 3–6 3–6 3–6; Cane/M. Fioroni lost to Jensen/B. Pearce 1–6 6–3 1–6 2–6; Pistolesi d. Pearce 10–8 4–6 4–6 6–1 6–1; Cane d. Reneberg 6–3 6–0 6–4).

The Australian team, who won the ITF's inaugural World Youth Cup in Kobe, Japan —
(l-r) Jason Stoltenberg, Shane Barr, Richard Fromberg, Max Bates (captain). (R. Adams)

ANNIE SOISBAULT CUP

Women's 20 and under international team championship
Quarter-finals: USA d. Switzerland 2–1; Argentina d. West Germany 2–1; Czechoslovakia d. Holland
2–1; USSR d. Great Britain 3–0. **Semi-finals:** Argentina d. USA 2–1; Czechoslovakia d. USSR 2–1.
Final: Czechoslovakia d. Argentina 3–0 (A. Holikova d. P. Tarabini 3–6 7–5 6–4; O. Votavova d. M.
Perez Roldan 0–6 6–3 6–2; Holikova /J. Novotna d. Tarabini /Perez Roldan 7–5 7–5).

VALERIO CUP

Boys' 18 and under international team championship
Zone A: Italy d. USSR 4–1. **Zone B:** West Germany d. France 3–2. **Zone C:** Sweden won round robin
between 3 teams. **Zone D:** Czechoslovakia d. Great Britain 3–0. **Semi-finals:** Sweden d. West
Germany 4–1; Italy d. Czechoslovakia 4–1. **Final:** Italy d. Sweden 3–2 (A. Baldoni lost to D. Engel 2–6
1–6; C. Pistolesi/S. Mezzadri d. C. Allgaardh/T. Nydahll 6–4 6–4; Pistolesi d. Allgaardh 6–3 6–4; U.
Colombini d. C. Bergstrom 7–6 6–2; O. Camporese lost to U. Stenlund 0–6 3–6).

COPA SM LA REINA

Girls' 18 and under international team championship
Zone A: Sweden d. USSR 3–2. **Zone B:** Italy d. Yugoslavia 3–2. **Zone C:** Czechoslovakia d. Rumania
5–0. **Semi-finals:** Italy d. Czechoslovakia 4–1; Sweden d. Yugoslavia 5–0. **Final:** Italy d. Sweden 4–1
(L. Lapi lost to C. Dahlman 0–6 1–6; L. Garrone/L. Golarsa d. A. K. Ollson/M. Lundquist 6–1 6–3;
Garrone d. H. Dahlstrom 6–2 6–7 6–2; C. Nozzoli d. Ollson 6–4 6–4; Golarsa d. Lundquist 6–2 6–0).

SUNSHINE CUP

Boys' 18 and under international team championship
Quarter-finals: Argentina d. France 3–0; Italy d. USA 2–0; Sweden d. Spain 2–1; Mexico d. Brazil 2–1.

Semi-finals: Argentina d. Italy 2–0; Sweden d. Mexico 3–0. **Final:** Argentina d. Sweden 2–0 (F. Davin d. U. Stenlund 5–7 7–5 6–3; G. Perez Roldan d. C. Bergstroem 6–4 6–1).

MAUREEN CONNOLLY BRINKER CONTINENTAL PLAYERS CUP

Girls' 18 and under international team championship
Quarter-finals: USA d. Rumania 3–0; Italy d. USSR 3–0; Sweden d. France 2–1; Argentina d. Czechoslovakia 2–1. **Semi-finals:** Italy d. USA 2–0; Argentina d. Sweden 2–0. **Final:** Argentina d. Italy 2–0 (M. Perez Roldan d. C. Nozoli 7–5 6–0; P. Tarabini d. L. Garrone 6–4 1–6 6–1).

JEAN BOROTRA CUP

Boys' 16 and under international team championship
Zone A: Sweden d. Hungary 5–0. **Zone B:** France d. Belgium 4–1. **Zone C:** Italy d. Austria 4–1. **Zone D:** West Germany d. Spain 4–1. **Semi-finals:** France d. West Germany 3–2; Sweden d. Italy 4–1. **Final:** Sweden d. France 3–2 (P. Henricsson lost to A. Boetsch 3–6 2–6; P. Wennberg d. P. Ventura 6–2 6–2; N. Utgren d. S. Blanquie 6–1 6–2; M. Zeile d. C. Sebastiani 6–1 6–3; Henricsson/Utgren lost to Boetsch/R. Pedros 2–6 6–3 4–6).

HELVETIA CUP

Girls' 16 and under international team championship
Zone A: Czechoslovakia d. Italy 5–0. **Zone B:** France d. Switzerland 5–0. **Zone C:** Sweden d. Great Britain 5–0. **Zone D:** West Germany d. Poland 4–1. **Semi-finals:** West Germany d. Czechoslovakia 3–2; Sweden d. France 4–1. **Final:** West Germany d. Sweden 4–1 (M. Schurhoff d. M. Ekstrand 6–2 4–6 6–4; M. Gartner/S. Hack lost to M. Strandlund/M. Nilsson 3–6 3–6; Gartner d. J. Jonerup 7–6 6–2; Hack d. Strandlund 6–1 6–1; W. Probst d. Nilsson 6–1 6–1).

COPA DEL SOL

Boys' 14 and under team championship
Zone A: Austria d. Spain 5–0. **Zone B:** France d. West Germany 5–0. **Zone C:** Italy d. USSR 5–0. **Zone D:** Czechoslovakia d. Holland 3–1. **Semi-finals:** Austria d. France 4–1; Italy d. Czechoslovakia 3–2. **Final:** Austria d. Italy 5–0 (G. Bohm d. F. Casa 6–4 6–2; T. Buchmayer /O. Fuchs d. S. Pescosolido /F. Pisilli 6–2 6–3; Buchmayer d. Pescosolido 6–3 4–6 6–4; Fuchs d. Pisilli 6–3 7–6; H. Prilled d. M. Ardinghi 6–2 6–1).

EUROPA CUP

Girls' 14 and under international team championship
Zone A: USSR won round robin between 3 teams. **Zone B:** Belgium d. Sweden 4–1. **Zone C:** Italy d. cCzechoslovakia 5–0. **Zone D:** West Germany d. Holland 3–2. **Semi-finals:** Italy d. Belgium 4–1; USSR d. West Germany 4–1. **Final:** USSR d. Italy 3–2 (N. Zvereva d. A. Dell'Orso 6–2 4–6 6–4; T. Tchernysova lost to F. Romano 3–6 2–6; E. Brihovec lost to S. Favini w.o.; A. Blumberga d. G. Boschiero 6–3 4–6 6–4; Zvereva/Tchernysova d. Boschiero/Dell'Orso 6–4 6–3).

ITF VETERANS COMPETITIONS

The continuing enthusiasm for veterans' tennis round the world seems almost insatiable. Entries for the major traditional events and demands for new ones continue to snowball, with an increase of almost 25 per cent over the 1984 total of 356 competitors on the VIP Circuit. At a meeting of the Veterans Committee, its chairman, Radmilo Nikolic from Yugoslavia, submitted a paper proposing various ways in which they should harness and develop this extraordinary upsurge of interest. Among the most important points were to maintain the team events as the most important competitions each year; to develop veteran tennis through regional and national veteran organisations, particularly in parts of the world where it is not yet organised on a sound and on-going basis; and to organise the veteran game purely on an amateur basis, following the spirit of the Olympic Games, no prize money being awarded to players in veteran tournaments and team events.

One of the great highlights of the veterans' year was the staging of the ITF Veterans Championships in Melbourne in March. For the first time a 35-and-over section, which helps to bridge the gap between what might be termed the natural tournament circuit and the veteran stage, was introduced. West Germany's Jurgen Fassbender enjoyed singles and doubles success in that category. Hugh Stewart, a prolific activist for the veterans' game, won the men's over-55 singles and doubles in a year when he also retained his place at the top of the VIP points circuit.

ITALIA CUP

Men's 35 and over
REGGIO CALABRIA, ITALY, 2–5 MAY
Quarter-finals: West Germany d. Argentina 3–0; Italy d. Great Britain 2–1; USA d. Spain 3–0; France d. Austria 3–0. ***Semi-finals:*** Italy d. West Germany 3–0; USA d. France 3–0. ***Final:*** USA d. Italy 2–0 (G. Malin d. G. Pozzi 7–5 2–6 6–3; B. Seewagen d. S. Rohrich 6–3 6–4).

DUBLER CUP

Men's 45 and over
PERTH, WESTERN AUSTRALIA, 18–24 MARCH
Quarter-finals: West Germany d. Italy 3–0; Great Britain d. Belgium 3–0; Australia d. Switzerland 3–0; USA d. Canada 3–0. ***Semi-finals:*** West Germany d. Great Britain 2–1; Australia d. USA 2–1. ***Final:*** West Germany d. Australia 2–1 (B. Nitsche d. B. Casey 3–6 6–2 6–4; K. Fuhrmann lost to I. Barclay 3–6 5–7; B. Nitsche /K. Fuhrmann d. B. Casey /I. Barclay 6–3 2–6 6–4).

AUSTRIA CUP

Men's 55 and over
PERTH, WESTERN AUSTRALIA, 18–24 MARCH
Quarter-finals: France d. Great Britain 2–1; Australia d. Sweden 3–0; USA d. West Germany 3–0; New Zealand d. Ireland 3–0. ***Semi-finals:*** USA d. New Zealand 2–1; Australia d. France 3–0. ***Final:*** Australia d. USA 3–0 (F. Sedgman d. H. Stewart 6–1 6–3; R. Howe d. J. Morton 4–6 6–3 6–2; B. McCarthy /M. Lord d. E. Kauder /K. Lambert 6–3 7–6).

BRITANNIA CUP

Men's 65 and over
POERTSCHACH, AUSTRIA, 10–17 JUNE
Quarter-finals: USA d. Yugoslavia 3–0; Norway d. Brazil 2–1; Great Britain d. West Germany 2–1; Australia d. Mexico 3–0. *Semi-finals:* USA d. Norway 3–0; Australia d. Great Britain 2–1. *Final:* USA d. Australia 3–0 (G. Mulloy d. G. Henley 6–3 6–2; A. Swetka d. H. Paine 6–2 6–2; R. Hippensteil /A. Ritzenberg d. G. Henley /H. Paine 6–4 6–2).

CRAWFORD CUP

Men's 70 and over
BRAND, AUSTRIA, 29 MAY–1 JUNE
Quarter-finals: USA d. West Germany 3–0; Australia d. Denmark 2–1; Austria d. Sweden 2–1; Finland d. Great Britain 2–1. *Semi-finals:* USA d. Australia 3–0; Austria d. Finland 2–1. *Final:* USA d. Austria 3–0 (C. Steele d. Hannemann 6–1 6–1; G. Mulloy d. M. Rossler 6–1 6–1; F. Klein /M. Rossler d. G. Hughes /Hanneman 6–3 6–0.

YOUNG CUP

Women's 40 and over
POERTSCHACH, AUSTRIA, 10–17 JUNE
Quarter-finals: USA d. Netherlands 2–1; West Germany d. Canada 3–0; Italy d. Spain 2–1; France d. Australia 2–1. *Semi-finals:* West Germany d. USA 2–1; France d. Italy 3–0. *Final:* West Germany d. France 3–0 (Masthoff d. Bouteleux 7–5 6–1; H. Orth d. Darmon 7–5 6–2; Masthoff /Orth d. Bouteleux /Sanchez 6–4 6–2).

MARIA ESTHER BUENO CUP

Women's 50 and over
BREMEN, WEST GERMANY, 25–28 JUNE
Quarter-finals: USA d. New Zealand 3–0; Canada d. Norway 3–0; France d. Sweden 2–1; Great Britain d. Italy 3–0. *Semi-finals:* Great Britain d. France 3–0; USA d. Canada 3–0. *Final:* USA d. Great Britain 3–0 (J. Crofford d. L. Cawthorne 6–0 6–3; N. Reed d. R. Lauder 7–6 6–7 7–5; Crofford /Hayward d. Cawthorne /Illingworth 6–2 7–5).

ITF VETERAN CHAMPIONSHIPS

MELBOURNE, AUSTRALIA, 25–31 MARCH
MEN'S OVER 35 SINGLES – FINAL: J. Fassbender (G) d. M. Broom (AUS) 6–3 6–1.
MEN'S OVER 35 DOUBLES – FINAL: J. Fassbender (G) /F. Gadoni (IT) d. B. Burns /M. Pettman (AUS) 6–3 6–3.
MEN'S OVER 45 SINGLES – Final: I. Barclay (AUS) d. K. Fuhrmann (G) 6–2 4–6 7–6.
MEN'S OVER 45 DOUBLES – Final: R. Duesler /J. Nelson (USA) d. K. Gyorgi /B. Nitsche (G) 7–6 6–2.
MEN'S OVER 55 SINGLES – Final: H. Stewart (USA) d. E. Kauder (USA) 6–4 6–4.
MEN'S OVER 55 DOUBLES – Final: J. Morton /H. Stewart (USA) d. A. Bailey /M. Lord (AUS) 6–0 6–2.
MEN'S OVER 60 SINGLES – Final: R. Sorlein (USA) d. V. Zabrodsky (SW) 6–4 7–6.
MEN'S OVER 60 DOUBLES – Final: T. Johansson /V. Zabrodsky (SW) d. O. Jierkowsky /J. Karlhofer (AU) 6–1 7–5.
MEN'S OVER 65 SINGLES – Final: J. Gilchrist (AUS) d. A. Ritzenberg (USA) 6–3 6–4.
MEN'S OVER 65 DOUBLES – Final: F. Klein /A. Ritzenberg (USA) d. H. /G. Butler (AUS) 3–6 7–6 6–0.
MEN'S OVER 70 SINGLES – Final: F. Klein (USA) d. J. Haanes (N) 6–1 6–4.
MEN'S OVER 70 DOUBLES – Final: G. Mulloy (USA) /J. Dreyfus (USA) d. A. Kay /A. Matthews (AUS) 6–3 3–6 6–4.
OPEN MIXED DOUBLES – Final: A. Basford /A. Tulloh d. A. /J. Mills 6–2 3–6 7–5.
WOMEN'S OVER 40 SINGLES – Final: H. Orth (G) d. K. Seelbach (G) 6–1 6–3.
WOMEN'S OVER 40 DOUBLES – Final: J. Dalton /H. Orth (G) d. J. Emmerson /A. Tulloh (AUS) 4–6 6–3 6–2.
WOMEN'S OVER 50 SINGLES – Final: I. Michael (G) d. L. Cawthorne (GB) 3–6 6–3 7–6.
WOMEN'S OVER 50 DOUBLES – Final: A. Fotheringham /H. Polkinghorne (AUS) d. L. Stock /L. Forbes (AUS) 6–2 6–3.

The 1952 Wimbledon champion, Frank Sedgman, still competes vigorously on the 45-and-over circuit with the same racket skill but slightly less mobility.   (A. Cole)

Elna Reinach of South Africa, ranked five in her country and 205 in the world, strove to improve those positions on the Satellite circuit, winning both singles and doubles at Cumberland and Lee-on-Solent. *(A. Evans)*

BUILDING THE SUPERSTRUCTURE

Ron Atkin

The fact that Doug MacCurdy, the International Tennis Federation's Director of Development, spent Christmas Day in 1985 working on an ITF project in the Ivory Coast was perhaps the supreme example of the Federation's fundamental object in tennis – to assist the world-wide development of the game. In his first year as Director of Development, MacCurdy advised at coaching courses, workshops and other missionary visits in more than 50 countries. The impression that MacCurdy brought back from his world travels was of a strong theme of progress, assisted significantly by the return of tennis to the Olympic Games. There is now a greater awareness of the sport and, more important, a greater willingness on the part of Sports Ministries and National Olympic Committees to put effort and cash into the promotion of the game.

The chief beneficiaries of this boom are the youngsters. As Philippe Chatrier, the ITF President, said in his end-of-year newsletter, among the most important facilities being offered by the Federation are scholarships and the raw materials of tennis, while the growth of the junior game has been one of the real success stories since the inauguration of official youth competition in 1978. The junior champions in that year were Ivan Lendl and Hana Mandlikova, so very little else needs to be said about the importance of junior development programmes. Since then the junior world champions have included Pat Cash, Stefan Edberg and Gabriela Sabatini.

At the end of 1985 nine different countries had representatives in the top 12 boys' singles rankings, while the girls went one better with ten nations represented in the best dozen. In 1981 the international junior circuit was offering some 60 tournaments in 30 countries, involving about 3,000 youngsters. In 1985 this had mushroomed to 103 tournaments in 59 countries – both records. There could be no finer statistics to show what the ITF calls its 'determination to ensure that the grass-roots of tennis have the healthiest base and the broadest opportunity to develop'.

The ITF was entitled to sound pleased with itself when it reported: 'Juniors from almost every country in the world now have an opportunity to take part in at least one international ranking tournament'. Lendl, who ended 1985 as the world's number one player, and Edberg, winner of the Australian Open and the victor for Sweden in the deciding rubber of the 1985 *Davis Cup* final against West Germany in Munich, are the supreme examples of the benefits of supervised development of the junior game, but perhaps the most heartening sight, and not only from the ITF's point of view, was the sheer variety of countries producing promising talent.

The top three boys were Claudio Pistolesi (Italy), Christian Bergstrom (Sweden) and Franco Devin (Argentina), and while none of these nations is exactly a stranger to success in world tennis there were some new nations (in tennis terms, anyway) with candidates vying for fame. Jaime Yzaga of Peru, Leonardo Lavalle of Mexico, Joao Silva of Portugal and Shuzo Matsuoka of Japan were all numbered in the leading 20, with youngsters from Chile, Finland, Mexico and Israel in strong contention. Italy possessed the top girl, too, in Laura Garrone, but Japan, Chile, Brazil, Holland and Belgium were also well represented. No longer do players from the United States, Czechoslovakia, Sweden and Australia monopolise the rankings. Never has tennis, in every sense of the word, been more open.

Not that these 'big names' are in immediate danger of being superseded. When the first-ever World Youth Cup was held in Kobe, Japan, in November, 1985, Australia won the boys' title and the Czechs were the girls' champions. But, more important, 32 leading teams competed in this 16-and-under event's final stages after qualifying tournaments held in Africa, Asia, Europe and South America.

To assist the smooth development from junior to intermediate and senior levels, the ITF has inaugurated a Competitive Development Fund. Wimbledon contributed £100,000 from its takings, the French Open put in a similarly generous amount and among the first to benefit from the fund were young players from Pakistan, Senegal and Israel who were awarded grants to enable them to play tournaments in Europe, something they would otherwise have been unable to do.

The Competitive Development Fund could prove vital in helping to bridge the gap in the grooming of promising youngsters from poorer or underdeveloped nations. Yannick Noah is a prime example of the benefits of assistance at a vital period in his life. He showed great promise as a child in the Cameroons but benefited mainly from the experience and greater facilities available to him when he made the move to France as a teenager. 'It is largely from the age of about 13 that the gap starts to widen very quickly, and a lot of it is the difference in the amount of competitive tennis available', said MacCurdy.

However, despite the heartening progress, there remains the major handicap that in many countries the tennis infra-structure is not well enough developed for that progress, at the moment, to be on anything other than a short-term basis. So while the ITF can help, and is helping, with junior progress, it cannot provide more courts and other necessary facilities to take the development a stage further. It is therefore heartening to be able to report the continued healthy advance in the growth of satellite events. These satellite circuits, consisting of a four-week series of tournaments plus a 'Masters' week, have proved invaluable in providing up-and-coming players with not only a modest amount of prize money but also with the points which are so vital in order to establish themselves on the ranking computer.

Satellites got under way in 1978, the same year as official world junior competition, and they have grown steadily since that first year in which a total of $427,000 was offered in prize money in Europe. This cash was on offer at the traditional places where tennis has flourished in the past – France, Italy, Spain, Sweden, Holland, Austria and Britain. By 1985 the nations involved included Bulgaria, Finland and Yugoslavia, a total of 21 satellite events offering $710,000 in prize money, with a further $400,000 available in the 'Challenger' events, which paid out between $25,000 and $75,000. These 13 'Challenger' competitions, held in such out-of-the-way spots as Parioli, Tampere and Thessaloniki, helped boost the total on offer to the lower-grade professionals to just over a million dollars.

In 1986 the Association of Tennis Professionals' satellite circuit will embrace 38 five-week events. The United States will organise seven of these, while Britain has two and other countries involved are India, Brazil, West Germany, France, Italy, Spain, Yugoslavia, Mexico, Bulgaria, Finland, Holland, Canada, Hungary, Switzerland, Austria, Belgium, Australia, Argentina and South Africa.

The progress in setting up a women's satellite circuit has been slower, but Barbara Wancke of the International Tennis Federation was able to reveal that the pace of development is speeding up at last. 'In 1985 we were working hard on a comprehensive set of regulations and organisational guidelines for a world-wide circuit', she said. 'The main intention is to persuade the national associations which can afford it to fund them because sponsorship is not easily obtained.'

As with the men, Europe is the best-organised continent for women's satellites, but the ITF, which took over the setting up of these circuits from the Women's Tennis Association in 1984, reports steady and heartening advances from Latin America and Asia. This year more than $600,000 will be on offer at women's satellites in Europe and Barbara Wancke was able to state: 'The major development of the women's game is now happening at the lower end. . . . Our ultimate ambition is to have a well-established series of satellite circuits feeding into $25,000 tournaments, which in turn will feed into the $50,000 and $75,000 events and then the competitors would eventually move up, if they are good enough, into the main Virginia Slims women's competitions. That in turn will help foster the development of promising juniors into top-flight professionals.

GRAND SLAM TOURNAMENTS

**FRENCH CHAMPIONSHIPS
WIMBLEDON CHAMPIONSHIPS
US OPEN CHAMPIONSHIPS
AUSTRALIAN OPEN CHAMPIONSHIPS**

Chris Evert Lloyd (left) and Martina Navratilova, who have dominated the Grand Slam championships for the past decade. Since 1974 they have won between them 29 of the world's major singles titles.   *(M. Cole)*

FRENCH CHAMPIONSHIPS
David Irvine

Thanks to the world-wide coverage given by the media, most enthusiasts denied the chance of attending the French championships have been able to create for themselves a mental picture of what tennis at the Roland Garros Stadium in Paris is like. Clay-court matches, as they have been taught, are won from the baseline, not the net. Usually long, they tend to be cat-and-mouse contests, decided more often than not on errors rather than winners; often predictable and rather dull for those accustomed to faster surfaces.

Imagine the surprise, then, when the 1985 tournament – and in particular the men's event – turned out to be nothing like that. What occurred may have fallen short of outright revolution but the whiff of change was unmistakable. Overnight the French Open had become an adventure.

Why? Some attributed it to the sun which blazed down from the start; others to an unusually interesting draw, and a few – reluctantly – to the fact that, though denied the ultimate prize 12 months earlier, John McEnroe had nevertheless demonstrated that attacking tennis could be a viable alternative to the percentage approach. Whatever the reason, the mood was very different, with nearly everyone on the offensive. It was fun.

It could be argued that in the final analysis there was no significant change. Mats Wilander won the men's title for the second time in four years and Chris Lloyd the women's for the sixth time in 12. Yet both adopted a far more positive approach than in previous years. Wilander, at 17 the youngest player to become a French singles champion in 1982, confessed a conscious willingness to present himself to the public as 'more interesting' than he had been hitherto. In that aim he undoubtedly succeeded. The Swede, who had not won a tournament of any sort since lifting the Australian crown in Melbourne six months previously, delighted a sell-out crowd in prising the championship from Ivan Lendl's grasp by a margin – 3–6 6–4 6–2 6–2 – which accurately reflected the pattern of play. Mrs Lloyd's 6–3 6–7 7–5 victory over Martina Navratilova, which earned her a 17th Grand Slam singles title, was flavoured with even greater drama providing a timely face-saver after the overall mediocrity of the women's event.

Neither champion began the Paris fortnight as a favourite. Wilander's failures in Hamburg and Rome, where he was mesmerised by Miloslav Mecir, had suggested that his career might be in decline. And though no-one expressed surprise at finding Mrs Lloyd in the women's final, her recent record against the world No. 1 – only one win in their 16 previous encounters – scarcely provided the basis for a persuasive case to be made for her regaining the crown.

Though few were prepared to look beyond Miss Navratilova for a probable women's winner, McEnroe, Lendl and Yannick Noah, who had shown touches of his 1983 form in winning the Italian championship, all appeared better bets than Wilander for the men's title. Only the Swedish press corps had absolute faith in their man, because 'this is the one he really wants'. All the same Wilander must have been mightily relieved to find himself in the opposite half of the draw to Mecir, his *bête noire*, and among non-Swedish journalists there was still no discernible shift in the odds on Wilander until he routed Germany's golden boy, Boris Becker, 6–3 6–2 6–1 in the second round with a display which cast an entirely different light on the 20-year-old's attitude.

A triumphant conclusion to one of the season's best matches left Chris Evert Lloyd once more queen of clay, following her thrilling win over Martina Navratilova in the French Open final. *(T. Hindley)*

If Wilander's positive play delighted, his frank dealings with the press proved more intriguing still. 'There have been times recently when I've been very bored with tennis', he admitted, 'but I've been looking forward to the French for some months. I agree I play well in big events – I don't know why. Maybe deep inside I'm not concentrating 100 per cent at some other tournaments.' He acknowledged that the French public had disliked the way he had played in winning the title in 1982. 'And so did I', he added. 'Unfortunately that was the only way I knew how to play then. Now I'm trying to change. I want to be more interesting.'

During the World Team Cup in Düsseldorf the week before the French, McEnroe had questioned Wilander's motivation and speculated whether the Sweede really wanted to be the best. 'I'm trying as hard as I can to be No. 1', was Wilander's assurance, 'but if it means practising eight hours a day I'm not prepared to do that. It's not worth it.' Wilander had a more direct answer to McEnroe in the semi-finals, where he beat him 6–1 7–5 7–5, matching the American for touch at the net and then destroying him with the accuracy of his passing shots. It was a lesson which must have left the world champion regretting, still more, his failure to lift the title in 1984, when he had led Lendl by two sets in the final. An opportunity like that may not come his way again.

Lendl's progress to his sixth defeat in seven Grand Slam finals was even more convincing than Wilander's, for at no time did he drop a set. When the crunch came, though, the Czech's serve let him down, and once again his inflexibility left him without an alternative strategy to fall back on. His appearance – gaunt, hollow-eyed and nervous – revealed the enormous strain he felt. Wilander, though, played with almost carefree abandon, his subtle command of the conditions (seen best in the confident way he spiralled so many lobs into the wind) underlining his absolute belief in himself.

For the second successive year all four top men's seeds made the semi-finals. Two other seeds, Jimmy Arias (16) and Eliot Teltscher (8), both lost to qualifiers; the former to Robert Saad from Argentina in the first round, the latter in the second round to Andrei Chesnokov, the first Russian in the men's event since Alex Metreveli a decade earlier. Other notable upsets were the defeat of Andres Gomez (15) by France's Henri Leconte, and that of an exhausted-looking Mecir (11) (who in one match was reduced to serving under-arm) by Martin Jaite, the Argentine most likely to take over the mantle of Guillermo Vilas and José-Luis Clerc.

It was the overall quality of many men's matches that attracted and thrilled the record crowds. Wilander v Becker, Noah v Clerc, McEnroe v Joakim Nystrom, Stefan Edberg v Anders Jarryd – all provided marvellous contests. Yet none compared with the fourth-round match which brought together the Frenchmen Noah and Leconte. By any standards that was a classic, and Leconte's fifth-set recovery, after losing a two-sets lead, marked the lefthander as a player of exceptional talent.

In contrast the women's matches were almost uniformly drab. There was obvious interest in the progress to the semi-finals of Gabriela Sabatini, the 15-year-old Argentinian who many believe will ultimately challenge for the highest honours, but at no time did any player perform well enough to suggest she might threaten the Lloyd–Navratilova empire. Yet when the two great champions finally shared centre stage, they produced an epic; all Mrs Lloyd early on, as she built a 6–3 5–2 lead, and then a shift to Miss Navratilova as she recovered to win the second set and then, at 5–5 in the third, led 40–0 on her opponent's serve. 'On paper I had pretty much lost it at that moment', said Mrs Lloyd. But paper scores have never impressed her that much. Sheer determination saw her extricate herself from that seemingly impossible situation as victory somersaulted back into her sights. Two glorious backhand passes settled it. 'What satisfied me most was that I never gave up', she said. 'I was really proud of myself the way I hung in.'

Defeat cost Miss Navratilova the chance of becoming the first player since Margaret Court in 1964 to win three French titles in one year for, with Pam Shriver, she won the women's doubles (their eighth consecutive Grand Slam championship) and, with Switzerland's Heinz Gunthardt, the mixed. Veterans Mark Edmondson and Kim Warwick won the men's doubles – the first Australians to do so since John Newcombe and Tony Roche in 1969.

After a miserable start to 1985, Mats Wilander captured the French title with a brilliant win over the holder, Ivan Lendl. *(T. Hindley)*

JUNIOR EVENTS

BOYS' SINGLES – Final: J. Yzaga (PER) d. T. Muster (AU) 2–6 6–3 6–0.
GIRLS' SINGLES – Final: L. Garrone (IT) d. D. Van Rensburg (SA) 6–1 6–3.
BOYS' DOUBLES – Final: P. Korda (CZ) /C. Suk (CZ) d. V. Gadrichidze (USSR) N. Volkov (USSR) 4–6 6–0 7–5.
GIRLS' DOUBLES – Final: M. Perez Roldan (ARG)/P. Tarabini (ARG) d. A. Holikova (CZ)/R. Szrubakova (CZ) 6–3 6–7 6–4.

FRENCH CHAMPIONSHIPS PRIZE MONEY

MENS' SINGLES –Winner 1,338,200fr. Runner-up 669,060fr. Semi-finalists 334,580fr. Quarter-finalists 169,530fr. Fourth round losers 98,140fr. Third round losers 53,530fr. Second round losers 31,230fr. First round losers 15,060fr.
Total: 6,959,340fr.
WOMEN'S SINGLES – Winner 1,262,700fr. Runner-up 640,500fr. Semi-finalists 315,675fr. Quarter-finalists 160,125fr. Fourth round losers 78,690fr. Third round losers 41,175fr. Second round losers 21,046fr. First round losers 11,437fr.
Total: 5,868,810fr.
MEN'S DOUBLES (per team) – Winner 535,400fr. Runners-up 267,680fr. Semi-finalists 133,900fr. Quarter-finalists 53,540fr. Third round losers 26,770fr. Second round losers 13,380fr. First round losers 7,800fr.
Total 1,962,880fr.
WOMEN'S DOUBLES (per team) – Winners 384,300fr. Runners-up 301,300fr. Semi-finalists 104,770fr. Quarter-finalists 56,730fr. Third round losers 30,200fr. Second round losers 15,500fr. First round losers 8,690fr.
Total 1,789,740fr.
MIXED DOUBLES (per team) –Winners 46,000fr. Runners-up 28,000fr. Semi-finalists 16,400fr. Quarter-finalists 10,000fr. Second round losers 5,600fr. First round losers 2,400fr.
Total 230,000fr.
Overall total 19,895,600fr.

MEN'S SINGLES

Holder: I. Lendl (CZ)

Final result: 3–6 6–4 6–2

Columns: FIRST ROUND · SECOND ROUND · THIRD ROUND · FOURTH ROUND · QUARTER-FINALS · SEMI-FINALS · FINAL

First Round
- J. P. McENROE (USA) (1)
- R. Agenor (HA)
- F. Segarceanu (RU)
- P. Annacone (USA)
- M. Bauer (USA)
- T. Warneke (USA)
- P. Arraya (PER)
- B. Taroczy (HU)
- T. Muster (AU)
- M. Vajda (CZ)
- V. Van Patten (USA)
- M. Flur (USA)
- M. R. Edmondson (AUS)
- G. Urpi (SP)
- H. SUNDSTROM (SW) (12)
- B. GILBERT (USA) (15)
- H. Gildemeister (CH)
- S. Zivojinovic (YU)
- S. Shaw (GB)
- M. Ostoja (YU)
- L. Botazzi
- J. Arrese (SP)
- G. Barbosa (BR)
- S. Youl (AUS)
- M. Leach (USA)
- E. Bengoechea (ARG)
- M. Ingaramo (ARG)
- M. DePalmer (USA)
- J. Brown (USA)
- H. D. Beutel (G)
- J. NYSTROM (SW) (7)
- M. WILANDER (SW) (4)
- T. Tulasne
- V. Gerulaitis (USA)
- B. Becker (G)
- E. Sanchez (SP)
- G. Prpic (YU)
- H. van Boeckel (NTH)
- E. Winogradsky (USA)
- D. Cahill (AUS)
- M. Dickson (USA)
- D. Cassidy (USA)
- K. Eberhard (G)
- R. Arguello (ARG)
- A. Tous (SP)
- J. SMID (CZ) (13)
- Y. NOAH (9)
- L. Pimek (CZ)
- M. Schapers (NTH)
- B. Derlin (NZ)
- A. Ganzabal (ARG)
- R. Simpson (NZ)
- J. Clerc (ARG)
- J. Lapidus (USA)
- H. Leconte
- T. Wilkison (USA)
- P. Portes
- I. Kley (BR)
- K. Carlsson (SW)
- P. Westphal (G)
- P. Slozil (CZ)
- A. GOMEZ (EC) (5)

Second Round
- McENROE (1) — 6–0 6–2 7–5
- Segarceanu — 6–5 7–7 6–2
- Hocevar — 6–3 6–2 4–6 6–4
- Warneke — 3–6 6–1 6–4 7–6
- Taroczy — 7–5 3–6 7–5
- Vajda — 6–4 3–6 4–6 6–3 6–3
- Flur — 6–2 7–6 6–4
- SUNDSTROM (12) — 6–3 6–3 6–1
- Gildemeister — 7–5 6–4
- Zivojinovic — 6–4
- Ostoja — 4–6 6–2 2–6 6–3 8–6
- Arrese — 2–6 7–6 7–5 6–3
- Youl — 6–4 3–6 7–6 6–3
- Bengoechea — 7–5 2–6 6–4 6–7 6–3
- DePalmer — 5–7 6–3 6–7 7–6 6–3
- NYSTROM (7) — 6–2 4–6 6–1 6–0
- WILANDER (4) — 6–1 6–4 6–2
- Becker — 6–3 6–7 6–1 6–1
- Sanchez — 6–3 5–7 2–6 6–1 6–0
- van Boeckel — 1–6 6–3 2–6 6–4 9–7
- Cahill — 3–6 6–2 6–1 2–6 14–12
- Cassidy — 6–3 6–3 5–7 6–4 6–2
- Arguello — 6–4 6–4 7–6
- SMID (13) — 7–6 6–3 6–3
- NOAH (9) — 6–7 6–1 7–5 6–4
- Schapers — 6–4 6–0 6–4
- Ganzabal — 6–3 6–2 6–2
- Clerc — 6–4 6–3 6–1
- Leconte — 7–5 6–2 6–1
- Portes — 7–5 6–4 7–6
- Carlsson — 6–2 6–1 6–3
- GOMEZ (5) — 6–1 3–6 6–3 6–3

Third Round
- McENROE (1) — 6–2 6–4 6–4
- Hocevar — 6–1 4–6 7–5 6–4
- Taroczy — 4–6 6–3 6–7 6–4 6–4
- SUNDSTROM (12) — 6–1 2–6 6–4 6–2
- Gildemeister — 5–7 7–6 6–3 7–5
- Arrese — 7–5 6–4 6–2
- Youl — 2–6 7–5 7–6 6–1 7–5
- NYSTROM (7) — 3–6 1–6 7–6 6–3 6–4
- WILANDER (4) — 6–3 6–2 6–1
- Sanchez — 6–1 6–2 6–4
- Cahill — 6–0 6–1 6–2
- SMID (13) — 6–4 3–6 6–1 6–4
- NOAH (9) — 6–1 6–1 6–4
- Clerc — 6–3 6–3 6–3
- Leconte — 6–2 6–1 6–3
- GOMEZ (5) — 6–2 6–4 6–1

Fourth Round
- McENROE (1) — 6–2 6–1 6–2
- SUNDSTROM (12) — 6–3 6–4 6–7 6–3
- Gildemeister — 7–5 6–1 6–2
- NYSTROM (7) — 6–2 6–0 6–2
- WILANDER (4) — 3–6 6–4 6–3 6–3
- SMID (13) — 6–2 6–2 6–2
- NOAH (9) — 6–1 6–7 6–4 4–6 8–6
- Leconte — 6–3 6–4 6–4

Quarter-Finals
- McENROE (1) — 6–3 7–5 6–2
- NYSTROM (7) — 7–6 6–1 6–1
- WILANDER (4) — 6–3 6–4 6–4
- Leconte — 6–3 6–3 6–7 4–6 6–1

Semi-Finals
- McENROE (1) — 6–7 6–2 6–2 3–6 7–5
- WILANDER (4) — 6–4 7–6 6–7 7–5

Final
- WILANDER (4) — 6–1 7–5 7–5

M. WILANDER (SW) (4)

First round

A. JARRYD (SW) (6)
S. McCain (USA)
J. Higueras (SP)
J. McNamara (AUS)
V. Pecci (PARA)
C. J. Lewis (NZ)
S. Glickstein (IS)
D. Perez (UR)
J. Frawley (AUS)
S. Simonsson (SW)
J. Hlasek (SWZ)
P. Elter (G)
C. Panatta (IT)
S. EDBERG (SW) (14)
J. ARIAS (USA) (16)
R. Saad (ARG)
H. Schwaier (G)
F. Cancellotti (IT)
C. Motta (BR)
K. Novacek (CZ)
H. de la Pena (ARG)
G. Forget
T. Benhabiles
T. Nelson (USA)
J. M. Lloyd (GB)
G. Ocleppo (IT)
B. Willenborg (USA)
C. Roger-Vasselin
W. Popp (G)
J. S. CONNORS (USA) (3)
E. TELTSCHER (USA) (8)
D. Campos (BR)
A. Chesnokov (USSR)
E. Adams (USA)
R. Viver (EC)
J. Fitzgerald (AUS)
H. Gunthardt (SWZ)
D. Kerenic (G)
M. Jaite (ARG)
P. Cane (IT)
T. Allan (AUS)
M. Mitchell (USA)
D. Visser (SA)
S. Meister (USA)
M. Navratil (CZ)
M. MECIR (CZ) (11)
A. KRICKSTEIN (USA) (10)
F. Luna (SP)
G. Vilas (ARG)
W. Masur (AUS)
J. Lopez-Maeso (SP)
W. Fibak (POL)
P. McNamee (AUS)
J. Lumberger (AUS)
J. Potier
Z. Kuharszky (SWZ)
L. Duncan (USA)
J. P. Fleurian
J. Gunnarsson (SW)
P. Kutchka (CZ)
E. Edwards (SA)
I. LENDL (CZ) (2)

Second round

JARRYD (6) 6-0 6-3 7-5
Higueras 7-5 6-1 6-3
Aguilera 6-2 8-3 7-5
Lewis 6-1 3-6 6-2 7-5
Holmes 6-3 7-5 4-6 6-4
Frawley 6-3 6-1 6-3
Hlasek 6-3 6-2 6-2
EDBERG (14) 7-6 6-3 6-3
Saad 6-1 6-4 7-5
Cancellotti 6-3 6-2 6-7-3-6 6-0
Motta 7-5 6-4 5-7 1-6 7-5
de la Pena 7-6 5-7 6-1 6-3
Benhabiles 6-7 5-7 7-6 6-3 6-3
Lloyd 6-3 6-3 6-1
Willenborg 6-4 1-6 2-6 6-3 6-4
CONNORS (3) 6-4 6-1 7-5
TELTSCHER (8) 6-4 6-2 6-1
Chesnokov 6-2 6-3 6-1
Viver 5-7 6-4 6-2 6-1
Gunthardt 6-0 6-3 6-4
Jate 7-5 7-5 6-2
Allan 6-0 6-2 6-3
Visser 6-2 6-3 6-3
MECIR (11) 6-1 4-6 6-1 6-3
KRICKSTEIN (10) 6-3 6-2 6-2
Vilas 6-3 6-2 6-1
Lopez-Maeso 6-0 6-2 6-1
McNamee 6-0 6-2 6-1
Potier 6-1 1-6 4 6-1
Duncan 6-2 6-4 6-4
Gunnarsson 7-5 7-6 7-5
LENDL (2) 6-1 6-3 6-1

Third round

JARRYD (6) 6-3 6-4 6-1
Aguilera 4-6 6-4 6-3 7-5
Frawley 1-6 6-3 3-6 6-3 6-2
EDBERG (14) 6-2 6-3 6-4
Cancellotti 6-4 6-4 6-3
Motta 6-4 6-2 6-4
Benhabiles 6-3 6-2 7-6
CONNORS (3) 6-1 6-3 6-0
Chesnokov 5-7 7-5 6-3 6-4
Gunthardt 7-6 4-6 6-1 6-1
Jate 6-4 6-4 6-3
MECIR (11) 6-2 6-4 6-3
KRICKSTEIN (10) 6-4 3-6 6-1 6-3
McNamee 6-0 6-0 6-4
Potier 6-7 6-1 6-0 6-0
LENDL (2) 7-6 6-3 6-2

Fourth round

JARRYD (6) 6-4 6-2 6-2
EDBERG (14) 7-6 6-3 6-0
Cancellotti 6-3 6-3 3-6 7-6
Motta 6-4 6-2 6-4
CONNORS (3) 6-3 4-6 7-5 7-5
Gunthardt 7-6 4-6 6-4 4-6 8-6
Jate 6-2 6-4 6-3
KRICKSTEIN (10) 7-5 5-7 1-6 6-2 6-1
LENDL (2) 6-1 6-2 6-2

Quarter-finals

EDBERG (14) 6-3 6-7 6-4 6-2
CONNORS (3) 3-6 6-0 6-2 6-2
Jate 6-1 6-2 6-3
LENDL (2) 6-2 6-2 6-0

Semi-finals

CONNORS (3) 6-4 6-3 7-6
LENDL (2) 6-4 6-2 6-4

Final

LENDL (2) 6-2 6-3 6-1

Capital letters denote seeded players. Number following player's name gives seeding order.

WOMEN'S SINGLES

Holder: M. Navratilova (USA)

Winner: M. NAVRATILOVA (USA) 6–3 6–7 7–5

FIRST ROUND	SECOND ROUND	THIRD ROUND	FOURTH ROUND	QUARTER-FINALS	SEMI-FINALS	FINAL
M. NAVRATILOVA (USA) (1)	NAVRATILOVA (1) 6–1 6–0	NAVRATILOVA (1) 6–3 6–0	NAVRATILOVA (1) 6–0 6–0	NAVRATILOVA (1) 6–4 6–1	NAVRATILOVA (1) 6–2 6–2	NAVRATILOVA (1) 6–4 6–4
P. Teeguarden (USA)						
S. V. Wade (GB)	Wade 7–5 6–4					
S. Gomer (GB)						
M. Skuherska (CZ)	Tanvier 6–2 6–3	Tanvier 6–4 6–4				
C. Tanvier						
K. Sasak (YU)	Sands 7–6 1–6 6–3					
K. Sands (USA)						
R. Reggi (IT)	Reggi 6–0 4–6 6–0	Reggi 6–2 7–5	Reggi 6–2 6–0			
S. Amiach						
M. Jausovec (YU)	Jausovec 6–2 6–0					
A. Croft (GB)						
H. Kelesi (C)	Skronska 6–4 2–6 6–1	RINALDI (13) 6–4 6–0				
K. Skronska (CZ)						
T. Mochizuki (USA)	RINALDI (13) 6–4 6–0					
K. RINALDI (USA) (13)						
B. POTTER (USA) (12)	Scheuer-Larsen 6–3 6–2	Scheuer-Larsen 6–3 6–1	Scheuer-Larsen 6–1 4–6 6–1	Cecchini 6–3 6–2		
T. Scheuer-Larsen (D)						
B. Herr (USA)	Herr 6–1 6–0					
M. Mesker (NTH)						
V. Ruzici (RU)	Horvath 6–4 2–6 6–3	Horvath 7–6 6–1				
K. Horvath (USA)						
M. Yanagi (J)	Keppeler 6–4 1–6 6–2					
P. Keppeler (G)						
A. Holton (USA)	Cecchini 6–0 6–1	Cecchini 6–0 6–1	Cecchini 7–5 5–7 6–4			
T. Holladay (USA)						
C. Cecchini (IT)	Karlsson 4–6 6–3 6–1					
C. Jolissaint (SWZ)						
E. Inoue (J)	Jolissaint 7–6 6–2	Jolissaint 2–6 6–3 6–0				
E. Pfaff (G)						
H. SUKOVA (CZ) (5)	SUKOVA (5) 6–1 6–2					
H. MANDLIKOVA (CZ) (3)	MANDLIKOVA (3) 6–1 7–5	MANDLIKOVA (3) 2–6 6–4 7–5	MANDLIKOVA (3) 6–3 6–0	MANDLIKOVA (3) 7–6 6–2	KOHDE-KILSCH (7) 6–4 6–4	
E. Burgin (USA)						
R. Fernandez (USA)	Burgin 7–5 4–0 ret'd					
J. Klitch (USA)						
M. Washington (USA)	Longo 6–4 6–2	Garrone 7–5 6–2				
E. Longo (ARG)						
K. Steinmetz (USA)	Garrone 6–1 6–1					
L. Garrone (IT)						
A. Henricksson (USA)	Henricksson 3–6 6–3 6–3	Villagran 3–6 6–1 6–4	Spence 6–0 6–1			
I. Budarova (CZ)						
A. Villagran (ARG)	Villagran 6–2 6–0					
R. Einy (GB)						
Mrs D. Balestrat (AUS)	Spence 6–3 2–6 6–3	Spence 7–5 6–2				
D. Spence (AUS)						
L. Savchenko (USSR)	LINDQVIST (9) 6–4 6–3					
C. LINDQVIST (SW) (9)						
A. TEMESVARI (HU) (15)	Paradis 7–6 3–6 6–3	Mascarin 6–0 6–2	Hanika 6–2 0–6 6–3	KOHDE-KILSCH (7) 5–7 6–0 6–3		
P. Paradis						
A. Brown (GB)	Mascarin 6–3 7–5					
S. Mascarin (USA)						
S. Hanika (G)	Hanika 7–5 6–4	Hanika 6–0 6–1				
A. E. Smith (USA)						
C. Benjamin (USA)	Benjamin 4–6 6–3 6–0					
C. Jexell (SW)						
K. Maleeva (BUL)	K. Maleeva 6–3 7–5	K. Maleeva 6–1 6–1	KOHDE-KILSCH (7) 6–4 6–3			
E. Tail (USA)						
M. Brown (USA)	Spain Short 6–1 5–7 6–3					
L. Spain Short (USA)						
M. Torres (USA)	Medrado 6–2 6–2	KOHDE-KILSCH (7) 6–4 6–4				
S. Solomon (USA)						
C. KOHDE-KILSCH (G) (7)	KOHDE-KILSCH (7) 6–2 6–2					

MRS J. M. LLOYD (USA) (2)

Round 1

Player	Result
Z. GARRISON (USA) (6)	GARRISON (6) 6–3 6–0
J. Golder (USA)	
R. Fairbank (USA)	Fairbank 7–5 6–2
A. E Hobbs (GB)	
F. Bonsignon (IT)	Herreman 7–5 6–4
N. Herreman (USA)	
I. Cueto (G)	Cueto 7–6 5–7 6–3
E. Minter (AUS)	Suire 7–6 6–2
J. Russell (USA)	
C. Suire	
S. Schmid (SWZ)	A. White 6–2 4–6 9–7
A. White (USA)	
S. Goles (YU)	Barg 3–6 6–2 6–4
P. Barg (USA)	
L. Drescher (SWZ)	SABATINI (14) 6–2 6–2
G. SABATINI (ARG) (14)	
B. GADUSEK (USA) (10)	GADUSEK (10) 6–3 6–2
N. Dias (BR)	
J. Foltz (USA)	Jaeger 6–4 7–5
A. Jaeger (USA)	
M. Schropp (G)	A. Minter 6–2 6–2
A. Minter (AUS)	
C. Calmette	Calmette 6–2 6–1
M. Paz (ARG)	
B. Mould (SA)	Holikova 6–2 6–1
A. Holikova (CZ)	
L. Bernstein (USA)	Calleja 4–6 6–3 6–4
M. Calleja	
P. Delhees Jauch (SWZ)	Delhees Jauch 7–5 6–3
S. Collins (USA)	
M. MALEEVA (BUL) (4)	M. MALEEVA (4) 6–3 6–3
C. BASSETT (C) (8)	BASSETT (8) 7–6 7–6
A. Betzner (G)	
J. Mundel (SA)	Mundel 6–1 6–3
G. Rush (USA)	
I. Demongeot	Nelson 6–2 6–2
V. Nelson (USA)	
G. Dinu (G)	Dinu 7–5 7–5
M. Quinlan (USA)	
T. Phelps (USA)	Phelps 6–4 6–4
R. Uys (SA)	
J. M. Durie (GB)	Derly 7–5 0–6 6–4
E. Derly	
W. White (USA)	Tauziat 6–0 6–7 7–6–2
N. Tauziat	
J. Cummings (USA)	CASALE (16) 6–3 6–1
P. CASALE (USA) (16)	
S. GRAF (G) (11)	GRAF (11) 7–5 6–4
E. Okanawa (J)	
E. Eliseenko (USSR)	Kim 6–1 6–2
G. Kim (USA)	
B. Bunge (G)	Bunge 6–1 6–1
P. Vasquez (PER)	
L. McNeil (USA)	McNeil 6–1 6–0
G. Purdy (USA)	
A. Leand (USA)	Gildemeister 6–3 6–2
L. Gildemeister (PER)	
A. Kanellopoulou (GR)	Kanellopoulou 7–5 3–6 6–4
B. Nagelsen (USA)	
C. Vanier	Bonder 7–6 2–6 6–0
J. Thompson (AUS)	
MRS J. M. LLOYD (USA) (2)	LLOYD (2) 6–2 6–1

Round 2

- Fairbank 7–6 2–6 13–11
- Cueto 6–4 6–0
- A. White 6–0 7–6
- SABATINI (14) 6–1 7–6
- GADUSEK (10) 6–1 6–1
- Calmette 6–1 6–4
- Calleja 6–3 4–6 6–3
- M. MALEEVA (4) 6–0 6–1
- BASSETT (8) 6–3 6–2
- Dinu 4–6 7–5 6–2
- Phelps 6–3 6–2
- Tauziat 6–7 7–6 6–2
- GRAF (11) 6–0 6–4
- Bunge 6–1 6–1
- Kanellopoulou 6–3 6–4
- LLOYD (2) 6–3 7–5

Round 3

- Fairbank 4–6 7–6 6–3
- SABATINI (14) 6–1 7–6
- GADUSEK (10) 6–2 6–0
- M. MALEEVA (4) 6–0 6–1
- BASSETT (8) 7–5 6–4
- Phelps 6–3 1–6 6–2
- GRAF (11) 6–1 7–6
- LLOYD (2) 6–3 7–5

Quarter-finals

- SABATINI (14) 6–0 1–6 7–5
- M. MALEEVA (4) 7–5 6–3
- Phelps 4–6 6–0 6–3
- LLOYD (2) 6–2 6–3

Semi-finals

- SABATINI (14) 6–3 1–6 6–1
- LLOYD (2) 6–4 6–0

Final

LLOYD (2) 6–4 6–1

Capital letters denote seeded players. Number following player's name gives seeding order.

MEN'S DOUBLES

Holders: H. Leconte (F)/Y. Noah (F)

Winner: M. R. EDMONDSON (AUS)/K. WARWICK (AUS) (8) 6–3 6–4 6–7 6–3

FIRST ROUND

SLOZ/LUSMID (1)
Davis/Dunk
Hermann/Meinecke
Cahill/Carter
Pham/Varner
Strode/Wittus
Canel/Colombo
GONZALEZ/MITCHELL (10)
DePALMER/DONNELLY (15)
A.M. Hocevar
Cassidy/Tarr
Hlasek/Panatta
Honey/Steyn
C. Fancutt/J. Frawley
De Miguel/Tous
EDMONDSON/WARWICK (8)
LECONTE/FITZGERALD (3)
Jate/Minussi
S. Simonsson/Simpson
Gottfried/Holmes
Campos/Roese
Katzman/Youl
Soares/Smensky
GIAMMALVA/WILLENBORG (12)
GERULAITIS/LEWIS (14)
Gunnarsson/Mortensen
Fibak/Leach
Edwards/Visser
Benhabiles/Portes
Gitlin/Lloyd
NYSTROM/WILANDER (6)
ANNACONE/VAN RENSBURG (7)
Gildemeister/Prajoux
Graham/Warder
Maurer/Pop
Acuna/Fillol
Arias/Korita
Dickson/Wilkison
DYKE/MASUR (9)
MEISTER/TELTSCHER (11)
Bauer/Motta
Gildemeister/Van Patten
McNamara/McNamee
Courteau/Forget
Pimek/Zivojinovic
Schapers/Segarceanu
EDBERG/JARRYD (4)
H. GUNTHARDT/TAROCZY (5)
Casal/Sanchez
Evernden/Robertson
Flur/McCain
M. Gunthardt/Kuharszky
Clerc/Nastase
Fleuran/Winogradsky
GLICKSTEIN/H. SIMONSSON (16)
BARBOSA/KLEY (13)
Poter/Lusse
Arraya/Ostoja
Mustard/J. Smith
Dowdeswell/Levine
Bengoechea/Johnson
Adams/Birner
FLACH/SEGUSO (2)

SECOND ROUND

Davis/Dunk 6–3 5–7 6–2
Hermann/Meinecke 6–3 6–7 6–4
Strode/Wittus 6–2 7–6
GONZALEZ/MITCHELL (10) 7–6 6–4
DePALMER/DONNELLY (15) 6–3 6–2
Hlasek/Panatta 6–3 7–6
C. Fancutt/J. Frawley 6–4 6–2
EDMONDSON/WARWICK (8) 6–4 4–6 11–9
LECONTE/FITZGERALD (3) 6–4 6–3
S. Simonsson/Simpson 6–1 5–7 6–2
Katzman/Youl 6–4 6–2
GIAMMALVA/WILLENBORG (12) 6–4 6–2
Gunnarsson/Mortensen 6–2 6–4
Edwards/Visser 7–5 7–6
Bathman/Tideman 6–4 6–4
NYSTROM/WILANDER (6) 4–6 6–3 6–4
ANNACONE/VAN RENSBURG (7) 7–6 1–6 18–16
Graham/Warder 6–3 7–6
Acuna/Fillol 7–6 6–4
Dickson/Wilkison 3–6 6–4 6–2
MEISTER/TELTSCHER (11) 7–5 6–3
McNamara/McNamee 6–4 6–4
Courteau/Forget 6–3 6–4
EDBERG/JARRYD (4) 6–3 6–4
H. GUNTHARDT/TAROCZY (5) 6–3 6–3
Flur/McCain 6–0 6–2
Clerc/Nastase 3–6 6–3 6–2
GLICKSTEIN/H. SIMONSSON (16) 7–6 6–4
BARBOSA/KLEY (13) 6–3 6–3
Mustard/J. Smith 6–1 6–3
Dowdeswell/Levine 7–5 6–3
FLACH/SEGUSO (2) 6–2 6–7 6–0

THIRD ROUND

Davis/Dunk 4–6 6–4 6–3
GONZALEZ/MITCHELL (10) 7–5 6–3
DePALMER/DONNELLY (15) 7–6 1–6 6–4
EDMONDSON/WARWICK (8) 7–6 6–2
LECONTE/FITZGERALD (3) 6–3 7–5
GIAMMALVA/WILLENBORG (12) 7–6 6–3
Gunnarsson/Mortensen 7–5 6–4
NYSTROM/WILANDER (6) 6–1 6–3
ANNACONE/VAN RENSBURG (7) 7–5 6–4
Dickson/Wilkison 6–7 6–4 6–2
Meister/Teltscher 6–2 1–6 6–3
EDBERG/JARRYD (4) 6–1 6–3
H. GUNTHARDT/TAROCZY (5) 6–4 6–1
GLICKSTEIN/H. SIMONSSON (16) 6–1 6–4
Mustard/J. Smith 7–6 6–3
FLACH/SEGUSO (2) 6–3 6–2

QUARTER-FINALS

GONZALEZ/MITCHELL (10) 7–6 5–7 6–3
EDMONDSON/WARWICK (8) 5–7 6–3 8–6
GIAMMALVA/WILLENBORG (12) 6–4 6–4
NYSTROM/WILANDER (6) 6–3 6–4
ANNACONE/VAN RENSBURG (7) 7–6 7–7–5
EDBERG/JARRYD (4) 7–6 6–3
GLICKSTEIN/H. SIMONSSON (16) 6–7 6–4 6–4
FLACH/SEGUSO (2) 6–3 6–3

SEMI-FINALS

EDMONDSON/WARWICK (8) 5–7 6–3 6–4
NYSTROM/WILANDER (6) 7–6 6–3
EDBERG/JARRYD (4) 6–3 6–2
GLICKSTEIN/H. SIMONSSON (16) 6–2 6–2

FINAL

EDMONDSON/WARWICK (8) 6–4 6–1 7–5
GLICKSTEIN/H. SIMONSSON (16) 6–3 6–4 6–1

Capital letters denote seeded pairings. Number following players' names gives seeding order.

WOMEN'S DOUBLES

Holders: M. Navratilova (USA)/P. H. Shriver (USA)

Winner: M. NAVRATILOVA (USA)/P. H. SHRIVER (USA) (1) 4–6 6–2 6–2

FIRST ROUND

- NAVRATILOVA/SHRIVER (1)
- McDaniel/W. White
- Campos/Corsato
- Crowe/Steinmetz
- Croft/Purdy
- Drescher/Inoue
- Mochizuki/Rimes
- COLLINS/LEAND (13)
- MRS. J. LLOYD/PARADIS (11)
- Demongeot/Tauziat
- A. Brown/Uys
- Murgo/Romano
- Gomer/Pelletier
- Elissenko/Savchenko
- Gulley/Sasak
- HORVATH/RUZICI (7)
- BUNGE/PFAFF (4)
- Kinney/Whytcross
- Remilton/Sato
- Hetherington/Rush
- Bonder/Mascarin
- Cecchini/Gildemeister
- Delhees-Jauch/Schropp
- HOLLADAY/JAUSOVEC (16)
- MANDLIKOVA/A. SMITH (9)
- Dias/Kannellopoulou
- Gadusek/Lindqvist
- Benjamin/Kaplan
- McNeil/Sands
- Longo/Reggi
- Garrison/Rinaldi
- NAGELSEN/A. WHITE (6)
- BASSETT/TANVIER (5)
- Herr/Phelps
- Sure/Wade
- Calmette/Derly
- Romanov/Spence
- Holikova/Skronska
- Amiach/Vanier
- A./E. MINTER (15)
- BURGIN/TEMESVARI (12)
- Etchemendy/Herreman
- K./M. Maleeva
- Manset/Vasquez
- Casale/Goles
- Medrado/Monteiro
- Golder/Nelson
- FAIRBANK/HOBBS (3)
- JOLISSAINT/MESKER (8)
- Hy/Jexell
- Po/Sabatini
- Murundel/Teeguarden
- Holton /Ounlian
- Barg/Villagran
- Budarova /Skuherska
- HENRICKSSON/B. JORDAN (10)
- MOULD/P. SMITH (14)
- Kuczynska/Parry
- Fairlie/Reis
- Okagawa/Schenk
- Karlsson /Scheuer-Larsen
- Blount/Farrel
- Graf /Russell
- KOHDE-KILSCH/SUKOVA (2)

SECOND ROUND

- NAVRATILOVA/SHRIVER (1) 6–1 6–1
- Campos/Corsato 1–6 6–4 8–6
- Drescher/Inoue 6–2 7–5
- COLLINS/LEAND (13) 6–4 6–4
- LLOYD/PARADIS (11) 6–4 6–2
- Murgo/Romano 6–1 6–2
- Elissenko/Savchenko 6–2 6–1
- HORVATH/RUZICI (7) 7–5 6–1
- BUNGE/PFAFF (4) 6–3 6–2
- Hetherington/Rush 6–3 7–5
- Cecchini/Gildemeister 6–7 6–2
- HOLLADAY/JAUSOVEC (16) 6–7 6–2 6–4
- MANDLIKOVA/A. SMITH (9) 6–3 6–1
- Gadusek/Lindqvist 6–3 6–3
- McNeil/Sands 4–6 6–3 6–4
- NAGELSEN/A. WHITE (6) 2–6 6–3 6–4
- Herr/Phelps 7–6 6–0
- Sure/Wade 6–4 6–1
- Holikova/Skronska 6–3 6–1
- A./E. MINTER (15) 6–3 6–3
- BURGIN/TEMESVARI (12) 7–6 6–3
- K./M. Maleeva 6–1 6–0
- Casale/Goles 7–5 6–0
- FAIRBANK/HOBBS (3) 6–0 6–3
- Hy/Jexell 6–4 7–6
- Mundel/Teeguarden 6–6–3
- Barg/Villagran 6–2 6–2
- Budarova /Skuherska 6–3 6–3
- MOULD/P. SMITH (14) 7–6 6–3
- Fairlie/Reis 6–2 6–3
- Blount/Farrel 6–4 6–2
- KOHDE-KILSCH/SUKOVA (2) 7–5 7–5

THIRD ROUND

- NAVRATILOVA/SHRIVER (1) 6–3 6–1
- COLLINS/LEAND (13) 6–3 6–8 6–6
- LLOYD/PARADIS (11) 6–4 6–3
- HORVATH/RUZICI (7) 7–5 4–6 6–4
- BUNGE/PFAFF (4) 6–1 6–3
- Cecchini/Gildemeister 6–4 6–3
- MANDLIKOVA/A. SMITH (9) 7–5 6–4
- NAGELSEN/A. WHITE (6) 6–3 5–7 6–3
- Sure/Wade 6–4 6–2
- Holikova/Skronska 6–4 7–6
- BURGIN/TEMESVARI (12) 6–4 6–2
- FAIRBANK/HOBBS (3) 7–6 6–4
- Mundel/Teeguarden 6–2 6–3
- Barg/Villagran 6–2 6–1
- MOULD/P. SMITH (14) 2–6 6–3 6–2
- KOHDE-KILSCH/SUKOVA (2) 6–1 6–0

QUARTER-FINALS

- NAVRATILOVA/SHRIVER (1) 6–1 6–0
- LLOYD/PARADIS (11) 4–6 6–1 6–3
- BUNGE/PFAFF (4) 4–6 6–0 6–4
- NAGELSEN/A. WHITE (6) 6–2 6–4
- Holikova/Skronska 3–6 6–3 11–9
- BURGIN/TEMESVARI (12) 4–6 7–5 6–3
- Barg/Villagran 6–2 6–7 6–3
- KOHDE-KILSCH/SUKOVA (2) 7–6 6–3

SEMI-FINALS

- NAVRATILOVA/SHRIVER (1) 6–3 6–3
- NAGELSEN/A. WHITE (6) 6–1 6–2
- BURGIN/TEMESVARI (12) 6–4 6–4
- KOHDE-KILSCH/SUKOVA (2) 6–2 6–1

FINAL

- NAVRATILOVA/SHRIVER (1) 6–3 6–4
- KOHDE-KILSCH/SUKOVA (2) 6–4 7–5

Capital letters denote seeded pairings. Number following players' names gives seeding order.

MIXED DOUBLES

Holders: R. L. Stockton (USA)/Miss A. E. Smith (USA)

Winner: H. GUNTHARDT (SWZ)/M. NAVRATILOVA (USA) (1) 2-6 6-3 6-3

FIRST ROUND	SECOND ROUND	THIRD ROUND	QUARTER-FINALS	SEMI-FINALS	FINAL
Bye					
H. Gildemeister/Bunge	H. Gunthardt/Navratilova (1)				
M. Gunthardt/Kuczynska	H. Gildemeister/Bunge 6-3 7-6	H. Gunthardt/Navratilova (1) 6-3 6-1			
Kley/Teeguarden	Kley/Teeguarden 7-6 4-6 6-3	Kley/Teeguarden 6-1 7-6	H. Gunthardt/Navratilova (1) 6-3 6-1		
Dowdeswell/Inoue	Herman/Pfaff				
Bye				H. Gunthardt/Navratilova (1) 6-4 7-6	
Bye	Feaver/Wade				
Forget/Paradis	Suk/Sukova 6-4 6-4	Suk/Sukova 6-4 4-6 6-2			
Suk/Sukova	Donnelly/Herr 6-4 5-7 7-5	Donnelly/Herr 6-7 6-3 6-4	Suk/Sukova w.o.		
Donnelly/Herr	Dunk/B. Jordan (8)				
J./C. C. Vanier					
Bye					
Bye	Van Patten/Garrison (4)	Van Patten/Garrison (4) 6-4 6-4			
B. Strode/Benjamin	B. Strode/Benjamin 6-2 6-7 6-4				
Benhabiles/Calleja	Bengoechea/Longo	Prpic/Goles 6-4 6-1	Prpic/Goles 7-5 6-3		
Bye					
Prpic/Goles	Prpic/Goles 7-6 6-2			Prpic/Goles 6-4 6-4	
Ostoja/Jausovec	Tideman/Lindqvist 6-3 6-7 6-4	Chesnokov/Reva 6-4 6-1			
Tideman/Lindqvist	Chesnokov/Reva				
Van Rensburg/Reinach			Warder/Minter (6) 6-1 6-0		
Bye					
Hocevar/Dias	Hocevar/Dias 6-2 3-6 7-5	Warder/Minter (6) 7-6 6-4			
Fleurian/Calmette	Warder/Minter (6)				
Bye					H. Gunthardt/Navratilova (1) 6-4 6-1
Bye					
Barbosa/Medrado	Bauer/Tanvier (5)	Bauer/Tanvier (5) 6-2 1-6 9-7			
Champion/Etchemendy	Barbosa/Medrado 6-1 6-4				
Motta/Villagran	Motta/Villagran 6-3 6-4	Motta/Villagran 6-3 4-6 6-2	Bauer/Tanvier (5) 3-6 6-3 6-1		
Davis/Dollins	Bahrami/Suire				
Bye				Bauer/Tanvier (5) 7-6 7-5	
Bye					
Meister/Barg	Meister/Barg	Meister/Barg 7-5 6-4			
Vinogradsky/Demongeot	Meister/Barg 6-2 6-3		Meister/Barg 6-7 6-3 6-3		
Graham/Whytcross	Kuharszky/Jolissaint 6-3 7-5	Kuharszky/Jolissaint 6-2 6-4			
Kuharszky/Jolissaint	Fibak/Bassett (3)				
Bye					
Bye					
Giammalva/A. Smith (7)	Giammalva/A. Smith (7)	Giammalva/A. Smith (7) 1-6 6-3 13-11			
Vajda/Holikova	Vajda/Holikova 6-4 7-6				
Sanchez/K. Maleeva	Sanchez/K. Maleeva 6-7 6-4 6-3	Sanchez/K. Maleeva 6-0 3-6 6-3	Sanchez/K. Maleeva 7-5 7-5		
Portes/Herreman	Warwick/Burgin				
Bye				Gonzalez/P. Smith 4-6 6-1 6-4	
Mitchell/Leand	Mitchell/Leand 6-1 7-5	Mitchell/Leand 7-5 3-6 6-3			
Haillet/Phan Thanh	H. Simonsson/Karlsson				
Bye			Gonzalez/P. Smith 6-3 6-1		
Gonzalez/P. Smith	Gonzalez/P. Smith 6-4 7-5	Gonzalez/P. Smith 4-6 6-4 9-7			
Ismail/Sands	Flach/Shriver (2)				
Bye					Gonzalez/P. Smith 6-7 6-4 6-4

Capital letters denote seeded pairings. Number following players' names gives seeding order.

LACOSTE

LA CHEMISE LACOSTE
8, RUE DE CASTIGLIONE · 75001 PARIS · TÉLÉPHONE (1) 2603264 · TÉLEX : 211183 F

WIMBLEDON CHAMPIONSHIPS
Lance Tingay

The Lawn Tennis Championships extended to new frontiers in 1985. It was a tournament of superlatives, the most eventful, the most exciting and the most crowded. It brought a new champion, Boris Becker, who, at 17 years 227 days, was the youngest and the first unseeded winner of the singles since seeding was introduced in 1927. He was the first German men's singles victor, and his was the most hard-earned victory.*

What failure there was, too! John McEnroe, the favourite, vanished from the singles almost tamely and, having yielded in the doubles also, was not to be seen on court on finals day. It was not like that since 1977.

Form was generally followed among the women. Martina Navratilova won the singles for the fourth successive year and for the sixth time in all. The last to do four in a row was Mrs Helen Moody in 1927–30. Yet even Miss Navratilova astonished in failure, for she and Pam Shriver, winners of eight previous women's doubles Grand Slam titles, fell in the final. The incomparable Miss Navratilova compensated by taking a second title none the less – the mixed doubles with Paul McNamee. She did so adventurously, playing not only the longest mixed in Wimbledon's history (her semi-final was 69 games and included a record set at 23–21) but a total of 117 games on the last day; her stint comprised the mixed quarter-final, semi-final and final. Louise Brough, in 1949, played as many, including the singles final. The sum of Miss Navratilova's Wimbledon titles was boosted to 13.

British players were sparsely represented in the later stages, although Virginia Wade, just short of 40 years old, added to the records by winning two rounds in the singles, pushing her total of Wimbledon matches to 207 in 24 successive years; only Bunny Ryan (218), Jean Borotra (221) and Billie Jean King (265) have done more.

The cauldron of Wimbledon records bubbled continuously. The men's No. 4 seed, and French champion, Mats Wilander, lost in the first round, the No. 2, Ivan Lendl, in the fourth, while the overwhelming favourite, John McEnroe, did not survive his quarter-final and third seed Jimmy Connors failed in the semis. The South African-born, newly naturalised American, Kevin Curren, beat both McEnroe and Connors as if the two former champions were county-class men playing a major tournament by mistake – yet he threatened only fleetingly in the final against the incredible Becker.

A first-round men's doubles match re-wrote the records. When the Swede Jan Gunnarsson and the Dane Michel Mortensen beat the Australian John Frawley and Victor Pecci of Paraguay by 6–3 6–4 3–6 7–6, the fourth set tie-break reached 26–24, its 50 fluctuating points marking the longest in any recorded event.

All this came after a miserable start, abysmal weather allowing only one match to be completed on the first day and but a handful on the second. The sole opening-day victor was Lendl against the American Mel Purcell. Yet Lendl grumbled mightily at being so lucky, perhaps foreseeing the sad standard of his performance three rounds later against the happy dash of France's Henri Leconte. By the end of the first Saturday (which produced a record attendance for that day of 35,234) the schedule was well behind. Only four men were in the last 16 of the singles, only five in the women's. The seeding list was already sorely damaged, with only nine men and ten women surviving in the singles. Wilander (4) had lost to the tall Yugoslav Slobodan Zivojinovic; Pat Cash (6) fell to qualifier

It was a record-breaking occasion as West Germany's Boris Becker became the youngest Wimbledon men's champion, the first German and the first unseeded player to win that title. (A. Evans)

Ricardo Acuna of Chile; Johan Kriek (9) had gone and so had Aaron Krickstein (10), Miloslav Mecir (12), Eliot Teltscher (13 and with the British John Lloyd as his conqueror) and Tomas Smid (15).

The week's casualties among the women featured Claudia Kohde-Kilsch (6), whose defeat by Jo Durie fleetingly fuelled British hopes. Bonnie Gadusek (9) was out, with Kathy Jordan (10), Caterina Lindqvist (12), Carling Bassett (13) and Gabriela Sabatini (15).

All, or nearly all, was sunshine in the second week. McEnroe, Curren, Connors and the Swede, Anders Jarryd, reached their appointed places in the last eight, while Acuna, the Swiss Heinz Gunthardt, Leconte and Becker were the unseeded intruders. Becker already had two seeds to his credit — Joakim Nystrom (7) in round three and Tim Mayotte (16) in the fourth. Against Nystrom, Becker won only by 9–7 in the fifth set, and Mayotte pushed him even harder, leading two sets to one and being within two points of victory in the fourth-set tie-break. The incredible young German, powerful, tireless, apparently with every shot in the book and without nerves, thereafter never played a fifth set.

In the other half of the draw the mercurial hitting of Curren, who popped down service aces with intimidating frequency, laid waste the surviving aristocrats, winning in three sets in successive matches against Stefan Edberg, McEnroe and Connors. McEnroe won but eight games, Connors only five. One wondered why two such champions could be so frail.

Curren's status as favourite did not endure beyond the opening set of the final. The climax of the meeting proved stimulating and spectacular, the rallies short and sharp, the lightning winners, whether in attack or defence, breathtaking. It was a machine-gun duel, Becker with the heavier ammunition. Curren came back with a fine recovery in the tie-break of the second set. Behind at 2–4, he won the next five points. But Becker remained utterly remorseless in his power, his burly frame belying the speed of his footwork as he frequently dived headlong for his winners. He emerged a very, very impressive champion. And the Mexican who won the junior event was four months his senior!

That he was unseeded made Becker's victory even more spectacular. He had, though, the week before the draw, demonstrated his prowess on grass by winning at Queen's Club from a strong field. Had the old seeding system been in operation, with the referee and committee exerting personal judgment, Becker would surely have been seeded. But on the computer list, he was only number 20.

The right of Wimbledon to make their own assessment was exerted in the women's singles. Although the computer said that Chris Lloyd should be the top seed, no-one who knew a racket from a cricket bat would have disputed the right of Miss Navratilova to stand as the favourite on Wimbledon's grass. So rather than make a preposterous order the committee exercised their right of choice by giving both equal status as number one seeds.

The women's singles turned out to be the two-horse race all took for granted, Miss Navratilova having the more onerous journey to the final in that she lost more games than Mrs Lloyd, although there was not the remotest danger to either. The final was good, but by no means great and nothing like the wavering conflict in France where Mrs Lloyd had won so valiantly. The virtues of a superbly strong baseline game were evident in the early stages as Mrs Lloyd won the first set. The strain of thwarting so able a server and so deft a volleyer as Miss Navratilova eventually sapped the power of Mrs Lloyd. She was in the hunt at all times, but inevitably fell behind more and more as the majestic, overpowering attack of the champion had its reward. Many a time one would have thought that a man, not a woman, was in action bringing Mrs Lloyd to a weary submission.

There were 126 other matches in the event and none had any significance in the final result. Kathy Rinaldi and Zina Garrison had the kudos of being semi-finalists, while three other Americans, Barbara Potter, Pam Shriver and the qualifier, Molly Van Nostrand, were in the last eight and the only non-American quarter-finalist was the Czech Helena Sukova. The third seed, Hana Mandlikova, failed in the third round to the Australian Elizabeth Sayers Smylie who became very prominent in the closing stages of the tournament. Fourth-seeded Manuela Maleeva from Bulgaria fell two rounds short of where she should have been when Miss Van Nostrand achieved her downfall. It was

Miss Wade who did as well as anyone for Great Britain and in her last singles at Wimbledon, her 87th in all, she fell honourably in three sets to the fifth-seeded Miss Shriver.

The distinction of Mrs Smylie was to take the women's doubles, where she and Kathy Jordan were the third seeds. For Miss Jordan it was not a first for she and the Texan Anne Smith had won in 1980. The final victory over Miss Navratilova and Miss Shriver was against all odds, save only that Miss Navratilova had won her singles title only a couple of hours before.

The subsequent success of Miss Navratilova in the mixed I have already mentioned. The title holders, of 1984 and 1983, the British John Lloyd and the Australian Wendy Turnbull, were not able to whip up the patriotic fervour of those years, falling on the last day in the quarter-final against Mark Edmondson and Miss Jordan who were in turn beaten by the ubiquitous Mrs Smylie and Fitzgerald.

The men's doubles produced popular champions in the Swiss Heinz Gunthardt and the Hungarian Balazs Taroczy, formerly known for their hard-court expertise. Seeded eight, they had their severest test in the quarter-final against the American-South African pairing of Paul Annacone and Christo Van Rensburg, where the fifth-set tie-break reached 24–22 after five hours and five minutes on court. Thereafter the champions glided downhill, with a four-set win over the former champions, Paul McNamee and Peter McNamara, and another in the final against the Australian Davis Cup pair, Cash and John Fitzgerald.

The weather also set records. A lightning flash on the first day sent crashing to the ground a piece of masonry from the new complex of building on the east of the Centre Court. On the second Friday came the mother and father of all thunderstorms at about two o'clock. One and one half inches cascaded down in 20 minutes, a tree by the hard courts was split in two by lightning and traffic in the road disrupted. Yet, with the courts covered, the delay was only an hour and a half.

The tournament finished on time but noon became the starting time on all courts after the early rain which diminished the opening week's attendance by 10,000 compared to the year before. Subsequently the turnstiles never ceased to turn; the second Tuesday's 38,577 was a record for any day at any time and the total for the 13 days was 397,983, the highest ever.

In 1986 Wimbledon stages its 100th Championship. Will McEnroe reassert his genius? For the first time since 1978 he played no final. Does the lawn tennis world now belong to Becker?

* Only Becker and Ted Schroeder, in 1949, have lost as many as eight sets on their way to the title. Schroeder's figures were: sets 21–8, games 172–119, a losing percentage of games of 40.89. Becker's figures were: sets 21–8, games 166–126, a losing percentage of 43.15. Four champions lost a total of seven sets, of whom Ashley Cooper in 1958 won 21–7 sets, 172–140 games, with a losing games percentage of 44.87. In 1927 Henri Cochet won 21–7 sets, 146–114 games, with a losing percentage of 43.85; Rene Lacoste in 1928 won 21–7 sets, 154–107 games, with a losing percentage of 40.99; and Jimmy Connors had a losing percentage of 39.48 when, in 1974, he won 21–7 sets and 164–107 games.

MEN'S SINGLES

Holder: J. P. McEnroe (USA)

FINAL

CURREN (8)
6–2 6–2 6–1

6–3 6–7 7–6 6–4

FIRST ROUND

- J. P. McENROE (USA) (1)
- P. McNamara (AUS)
- N. Odizor (NIG)
- G. Muller (SA)
- S. M. Shaw
- C. J. Lewis (NZ)
- C. Steyn (SA)
- G. Barbosa (BR)
- A. Maurer (G)
- J. Frawley (AUS)
- H. Schwaier (G)
- R. Van't Hof (USA)
- J. B. Fitzgerald (AUS)
- A. Giammalva (USA)
- V. Pecci (PARA)
- J. C. KRIEK (USA) (9)
- S. EDBERG (SW) (14)
- P. Doohan (AUS)
- M. Ostoja (YU)
- T. Wilkison (USA)
- J. Hlasek (SWZ)
- T. Moor (USA)
- C. Hooper (USA)
- B. Taroczy (HU)
- D. G. C. Mustard (NZ)
- S. M. Bale
- M. J. Bates
- R. Viver (EC)
- M. DePalmer (USA)
- L. Stefanki (USA)
- K. CURREN (USA) (8)
- J. S. CONNORS (USA) (3)
- S. Simonsson (SW)
- K. Evernden (NZ)
- T. Navratil (CZ)
- B. P. Derlin (NZ)
- R. Krishnan (IND)
- G. Forget (F)
- L. R. Bourne (USA)
- L. Shiras (USA)
- L. Alfred
- B. Testerman (USA)
- C. A. Miller (AUS)
- C. H. Cox (USA)
- R. Simpson (NZ)
- T. SMID (CZ) (15)
- M. MECIR (CZ) (12)
- T. R. Gullikson
- J. Arias (USA)
- J. Lapidus (USA)
- M. Vajda (CZ)
- M. Bauer (USA)
- R. Harmon (USA)
- R. Seguso (USA)
- T. E. Gullikson (USA)
- S. B. Denton (USA)
- D. Pate (USA)
- N. A. Fulwood
- M. Benhabiles (F)
- R. Acuna (CH)
- T. Nelson (USA)
- P. CASH (AUS) (6)

SECOND ROUND

- McENROE (1) 6–4 6–3 6–4
- Odizor 6–7 6–7 6–6 3–6 3
- Lewis 6–4 6–2 6–3
- Steyn 6–4 6–4 6–2
- Maurer 7–5 6–3 7–5
- Schwaier 6–3 6–2 6–4
- Fitzgerald 6–4 7–5 6–1
- KRIEK 6–4 6–0 4–6 7–5
- EDBERG (14)
- Wilkison 6–4 6–0 2–6 7–6
- Moor 6–3 3–6 6–7 7–6 7–5
- Hooper 7–5 7–6 6–3
- Mustard 7–6 6–2 4–6 6–4
- Flur 6–4 6–3 6–4
- DePalmer 6–3 3–6 6–3
- CURREN (8) 7–6 6–3 6–4
- CONNORS (3)
- Evernden 6–4 6–4 6–4
- Krishnan 6–2 7–5 4–6 7–6
- Bourne 3–6 6–3 6–4
- Shiras 6–3 7–6 6–3
- Testerman 3–6 6–3 6–4 6–2
- Giammalva 6–0 6–4 5–7 6–4
- SMID (15) 6–4 6–7 7–5 6–3
- T. R. Gullikson 4–6 6–3 6–4 6–7 6–3
- Lapidus 6–4 4–3 3–6 6–7 7–5
- Bauer 5–7 7–6 7–5 6–2
- Seguso 6–4 6–3 6–0
- Denton 6–4 6–3 3–6 6–3
- Pate 6–3 6–4 6–4
- Acuna 6–3 6–4 6–4
- CASH (6) 2–6 6–2 7–5 6–7 6–3

THIRD ROUND

- McENROE (1) 7–6 6–1 7–6
- Steyn 3–6 7–6 6–4 6–4
- Maurer 6–3 7–5 7–5
- KRIEK (9) 3–6 7–6 7–5 6–1
- EDBERG (14) 6–1 7–5 3–6 6–7 9–7
- Hooper 6–4 6–4 7–5
- Mustard 7–6 6–4 2–6 6–4
- CURREN (8) 7–5 5–7 6–4 6–4
- CONNORS (3) 6–3 6–2 6–1
- Krishnan 6–4 7–5 6–2
- Testerman 6–4 6–7 4–6 6–1 7–5
- Giammalva 6–3 6–1 6–2
- T. R. Gullikson 6–7 6–7 6–4 6–2 6–3
- Seguso 6–3 6–4 6–4
- Pate 7–6 6–4 6–4
- Acuna 7–6 6–3 3–6 6–7 7–6 4

FOURTH ROUND

- McENROE (1) 6–3 7–5 6–4
- Maurer 6–1 6–4 3–6 6–3
- EDBERG (14) 6–3 6–4 6–4
- CURREN (8) 6–3 6–3 7–5
- CONNORS (3) 7–5 5–7 7–5 6–2
- Giammalva 4–6 6–3 7–5 7–6
- Seguso 4–6 6–3 7–5 6–2
- Acuna 7–5 6–4 6–2

QUARTER-FINALS

- McENROE (1) 6–0 6–4 6–2
- CURREN (8) 7–6 6–3 7–6
- CONNORS (3) 6–3 6–4 6–3
- Acuna 6–4 7–6 6–2

SEMI-FINALS

- CURREN (8) 6–2 6–2 6–4
- CONNORS (3) 6–1 7–6 6–2

B. BECKER (G)

Champion: Becker 2-6 7-6 6-3 6-3

First round (entrants)

- A. JARRYD (SWI) (5)
- C. Panatta (IT)
- E. Davis (USA)
- B. Moir (SA)
- T. Champion (F)
- M. Mitchell (USA)
- P. Elter (G)
- V. Van Patten (USA)
- D. T. Visser (SA)
- M. Davis (USA)
- J. Gunnarsson (SW)
- H. Sundstrom (SW)
- G. Holmes (USA)
- B. Schultz (USA)
- A. KRICKSTEIN (USA) (10)
- Y. NOAH (F) (11)
- R. Gilbert (USA)
- E. Edwards (SA)
- C. Dowdeswell
- V. Amritraj (IND)
- J. Canter (USA)
- B. D. Drewett (AUS)
- S. McCain (USA)
- V. Gerulaitis (USA)
- M. Fleming (USA)
- C. Motta (BR)
- J. Sadri (USA)
- B. Teacher (USA)
- H. P. Gunthardt (SWZ)
- S. Zivojinovic (YU)
- M. WILANDER (SW) (4)
- J. NYSTROM (SW) (7)
- J. M. Goodall
- D. Goldie (USA)
- P. Annacone (USA)
- M. W. Anger (USA)
- Z. Kuharszky (SWZ)
- B. Becker (G)
- H. Pfister (USA)
- P. McNamee (AUS)
- S. Meister (USA)
- R. B. Green (USA)
- R. Saad (ARG)
- P. Slozil (CZ)
- K. Flach (USA)
- T. Allan (AUS)
- T. S. MAYOTTE (USA) (16)
- E. TELTSCHER (USA) (13)
- G. Ocleppo (IT)
- J.M. Lloyd
- W. Popp (G)
- H. Leconte (F)
- C. M. Dunk (USA)
- W. Masur (AUS)
- D. Cassidy (USA)
- J. Lopez-Maeso (SP)
- S. Glickstein (IS)
- M. R. Edmondson (AUS)
- W. Fibak (POL)
- M. Leach (USA)
- M. Purcell (USA)
- I. LENDL (CZ) (2)

First round results

- JARRYD (5) 4-6 3-6 6-4 6-4 6-3
- Davis 6-2 6-2 6-3
- Mitchell
- Van Patten 6-3 6-7 7-5 6-4
- Visser 7-6 6-4 6-7 6-3
- Gunnarsson 6-3 6-2 3-6 6-3
- Holmes 6-3 4-6 6-7 6-4 6-2
- Schultz 6-4 3-6 7-6 6-4
- NOAH (11) 6-4 3-6 7-6 6-7 6-3
- Edwards 6-3 6-3 6-3
- Amritraj
- Drewett 7-6 7-5 6-4
- Gerulaitis 6-2 5-7 6-4 3-6 6-3
- Sadri 6-3 6-2 6-3
- Gunthardt 6-4 7-5 6-7 6-2
- Zvojinovic 6-2 5-7 7-5 6-0
- NYSTROM (7)
- Annacone 5-7 7-5 6-1 1-6 9-7
- Anger 5-7 6-2 6-2 3-6 6-1
- Becker 6-4 3-6 2-6 6-4
- McNamee 6-2 6-4 7-6
- Saad 6-3 6-2 6-4
- Flach 6-3 7-6 6-1 7-6
- MAYOTTE (16) 7-5 6-4 6-2
- TELTSCHER (13) 5-7 7-6 7-6 6-0
- Lloyd 6-2 6-4 7-6
- Leconte 6-3 7-6 7-6
- Masur 7-6 7-6 6-1
- Glickstein 7-6 6-3 6-1
- Gonzalez 6-3 6-2 7-6
- Leach 6-3 6-2 7-6
- LENDL (2) 6-4 7-6 7-6

Second round

- JARRYD (5) 5-7 7-6 7-5 6-4
- Van Patten 7-5 6-3 6-2
- Visser 6-7 6-4 6-4 7-6
- Holmes 6-4 6-7 6-2 6-3
- NOAH (11) 4-6 6-4 7-6 6-2
- Amritraj 7-6 7-6 7-5
- Gerulaitis 5-7 6-4 3-6 7-6 6-4
- Gunthardt 6-4 4-6 6-3 6-4
- NYSTROM (7) 7-5 7-5 6-3
- Becker 6-0 6-1 6-3
- McNamee 6-3 7-6 7-6
- MAYOTTE (16) 6-4 6-4 6-4
- Lloyd 6-3 6-4 4-6 3-6 7-5
- Leconte 4-6 6-4 7-6 6-3
- Glickstein 6-3 6-4 3-6 7-5
- LENDL (2) 6-3 1-6 6-2 6-7 6-4

Third round

- JARRYD (5) 6-3 6-3 6-1
- Visser 6-3 4-6 6-7 6-0 10-8
- Amritraj 4-6 7-6 6-3 7-6
- Gunthardt 6-3 6-7 6-1 3-6 7-5
- Becker 3-6 7-6 6-1 4-6 9-7
- MAYOTTE (16) 3-6 4-6 7-6 6-2 6-0
- Leconte 5-7 6-3 6-4 6-4
- LENDL (2) 7-6 4-6 6-3 6-2

Quarter-finals

- JARRYD (5) 6-1 6-4 6-1
- Gunthardt 6-4 6-4 6-1
- Becker 6-3 4-6 6-7 7-6 6-2
- H. Leconte 3-6 6-4 6-3 6-1

Semi-finals

- JARRYD (5) 6-4 6-3 6-2
- Becker 7-6 3-6 6-3 6-4

Final shown

- Becker 2-6 7-6 6-3 6-3

Capital letters denote seeded players. Number following player's name gives seeding order.

WOMEN'S SINGLES

Holder: M. Navratilova (USA)

4–6 6–3 6–2

FIRST ROUND	SECOND ROUND	THIRD ROUND	FOURTH ROUND	QUARTER-FINALS	SEMI-FINALS	FINAL
MRS J. M. LLOYD (USA) (1)	LLOYD (1)	LLOYD (1) 6–3 6–0	LLOYD (1) 6–2 6–1	LLOYD (1) 6–0 6–4	LLOYD (1) 6–2 6–1	LLOYD (1) 6–2 6–0
M. L. Piatek (USA)						
S. E. Mascarin (USA)	Mascarin 7–6 3–6 6–3					
T. Scheuer Larsen (D)						
J. Byrne (AUS)	Byrne 6–2 6–3	Byrne 6–2 6–3				
S. Amiach (F)						
Y. Vermaak (SA)	Vermaak 6–3 6–4					
M. Jausovec (YU)						
M. Skuherská (CZ)	Drescher 6–1 6–2	Demongeot 6–4 6–3	A. E. Smith 6–2 6–4			
L. E. Drescher (SWZ)						
B. K. Jordan (USA)	Demongeot 6–1 6–4					
I. Demongeot (F)						
V. L. Nelson (USA)	A. E. Smith 6–0 6–2	A. E. Smith 2–6 6–4 6–2				
A. E. Smith (USA)						
H. A. Ludloff (USA)	Gadusek (9) 6–0 6–2					
B. Gadusek (USA) (9)						
C. Lindqvist (SW) (12)	Potter 6–1 6–1	Potter 6–4 7–5	Potter 7–6 6–1	Potter 7–6 7–6–1		
B. C. Potter (USA)						
B. A. Mould (SA)	Gomer 6–7 7–6 6–3					
S. L. Gomer						
P. A. Fendick (USA)	Fendick 6–4 6–1	Fendick 6–1 6–3				
M. L. Brown (USA)						
K. B. Cummings (USA)	Cummings 6–3 6–4					
K. J. Brashe						
E. M. Burgin (USA)	Burgin 7–6 6–2	Burgin 6–0 6–3	Durie 7–5 7–5			
P. S. Medrado (BR)						
A. C. Villagran (ARG)	Villagran 6–7 6–4 6–3					
J. L. Klitch (USA)						
Mrs L. A. Shaefer (USA)	Durie 6–3 6–2	Durie 4–6 6–1 6–2				
J. M. Durie						
B. Nagelsen (USA)	Kohde-Kilsch (6) 7–6 6–1					
C. Kohde-Kilsch (G) (6)						
H. Mandlikova (CZ) (3)	Mandlikova (3) 6–0 6–1	Mandlikova (3) 4–6 6–2 7–5	Smylie 6–1 7–6	Rinaldi (16) 6–2 6–1	Rinaldi (16) 6–1 1–6 6–1	
I. Budarova (CZ)						
N. P. Dias (BR)	Balestrat 6–0 6–2					
Mrs C. M. Balestrat (AUS)						
J. C. Russell (USA)	Russell 5–7 7–6 2–6–1	Smylie 6–4 6–4				
P. Keppeler (G)						
Mrs P. D. Smylie (AUS)	Smylie 6–1 6–2					
A. C. Leand (USA)						
B. A. Herr (USA)	Moulton 6–3 6–4	Moulton 6–2 6–4	Rinaldi (16) 7–6 6–4			
A. A. Moulton (USA)						
R. L. Einy	Reeves 6–3 5–7 6–4					
S. E. Reeves						
M. Schropp (G)	Fairbank 7–5 6–4	Rinaldi (16) 7–5 6–4				
R. D. Fairbank (SA)						
A. Betzner (G)	Rinaldi (16) 6–3 7–5					
K. Rinaldi (USA) (16)						
W. M. Turnbull (AUS) (14)	Turnbull (14) 7–5 6–3	Turnbull (14) 7–5 7–5	Paradis 2–6 7–5 6–1	Sukova (7) 6–4 7–6		
G. A. Rush (USA)						
M. Yanagi (J)	E. A. Minter 6–3 6–3					
E. A. Minter (AUS)						
S. M. Hanika (G)	Hanika 6–4 6–2	Paradis 7–6 6–7 6–3				
S. Suire (F)						
E. Okagawa (J)	Paradis 6–2 6–1					
P. Paradis (F)						
C. J. Wood	Henricksson 6–1 7–5	W. E. White 6–4 2–6 6–4	Sukova (7) 6–1 6–4			
A. B. Henricksson (USA)						
K. Kinney (USA)	W. E. White 6–3 2–6 6–4					
W. E. White (USA)						
E. A. Holton (USA)	Ruzici 4–6 6–4 7–5	Sukova (7) 6–1 6–4				
V. Ruzici (RU)						
C. Jexell (SW)	Sukova (7) 6–3 6–3					
H. Sukova (CZ) (7)						

M. NAVRATILOVA (USA) (1)

First round

- Z. L. GARRISON (USA) (8)
- E. Reinach (SA)
- K. Skronska (CZ)
- T. Phelps (USA)
- P. Casale (USA)
- A. Holikova (CZ)
- K. Gompert (USA)
- M. A. Mesker (NTH)
- M. E. Gurney (USA)
- S. J. Leo (AUS)
- M. M. Groat (C)
- C. Tanvier (F)
- C. Benjamin (USA)
- E. Eliseenko (USSR)
- G. SABATINI (ARG) (15)
- K. JORDAN (USA) (10)
- J. M. Tacon
- L. Savchenko (USSR)
- S. Goles (YU)
- Mrs M. H. Walsh Pete (USA)
- M. Van Nostrand (USA)
- P. Louie (USA)
- E. Kelesi (C)
- S. Pfaff (G)
- S. P. Foltz (USA)
- S. L. Collins (USA)
- R. M. White (USA)
- J. Thompson (AUS)
- T. A. Holliday (USA)
- M. B. Washington (USA)
- M. Maleeva (BUL) (4)
- P. H. Shriver (USA) (5)
- A. H. White (USA)
- A. E. Hobbs
- C. G. M. Kim (USA)
- C. Vanier (F)
- B. Gerken (USA)
- L. Antonoplis (USA)
- S. J. Wade
- E. Inoue (J)
- E. Ekblom (SW)
- C. C. Rehe (USA)
- C. Jolissaint (SWZ)
- K. Temesvari (HU)
- K. Maleeva (BUL)
- Mrs L. Spain Short (USA)
- S. Graf (G) (11)
- C. K. Bassett (C) (13)
- M. Paz (ARG)
- J. Uys (SA)
- J. Louis
- Hu Na (CHI)
- A. N. Croft
- C. Karlsson (SW)
- L. Pichova (CZ)
- A. M. Cecchini (IT)
- J. A. Salmon
- B. Bunge (G)
- L. M. McNeil (USA)
- A. L. Minter (AUS)
- P. Vasquez (PR)
- L. Bonder (USA)
- M. NAVRATILOVA (USA) (1)

Second round

- GARRISON (8) 6-3 6-1
- Phelps 6-2 6-1
- Holikova 6-3 6-3
- Mesker 6-3 4-6 6-4
- Gurney 5-7 6-1 6-3
- Tanvier 7-5 6-4
- Benjamin 6-3 6-2
- SABATINI (15) 6-4 6-0
- JORDAN (10) 3-6 6-3 6-3
- Savchenko 6-0 6-2
- Van Nostrand 6-1 4-6 6-3
- Louie 7-5 6-3
- Pfaff 6-2 6-4
- R. M. White 6-3 6-3
- Holladay 6-2 6-2
- MALEEVA (4) 6-1 6-3
- SHRIVER (5) 6-7 6-1 6-4
- Hobbs 6-3 6-7 6-3
- Gerken 6-4 6-2
- Wade 6-3 6-2
- Inoue 6-4 7-5
- Rehe 6-2 6-1
- Temesvari 6-4 6-3
- GRAF (11) 3-6 7-6 6-4
- BASSETT (13) 6-7 6-4 6-2
- Uys 6-0 3-6 6-3
- Hu Na 7-6 4-6 6-2
- Pichova 6-3 7-5
- Cecchini 2-6 6-4 6-3
- Bunge 7-6 6-1
- A. L. Minter 6-3 6-3
- NAVRATILOVA (1) 6-0 6-2

Third round

- GARRISON (8) 6-3 6-1
- Mesker 6-2 6-7 6-3
- Tanvier 6-3 6-4
- SABATINI (15) 6-3 6-4
- Savchenko 7-5 3-6 6-3
- Van Nostrand 6-2 6-3
- R. M. White 6-3 6-2
- MALEEVA (4) 6-7 6-1 6-4
- SHRIVER (5) 6-3 6-2
- Wade 6-3 6-7 7-5
- Rehe 6-1 6-3
- GRAF (11) 6-3 7-6
- Uys 0-6 7-6 6-3
- Hu Na 7-5 6-4
- Bunge 6-3 6-2
- NAVRATILOVA (1) 6-4 6-1

Fourth round

- GARRISON (8) 6-3 6-1
- Tanvier 6-7 6-4 6-1
- Van Nostrand 7-6 3-6 7-5
- MALEEVA (4) 6-3 6-3
- SHRIVER (5) 6-2 5-7 6-2
- GRAF (11) 6-3 6-2
- Uys 6-2 4-6 6-0
- NAVRATILOVA (1) 7-6 6-3

Quarter-finals

- GARRISON (8) 6-1 6-3
- Van Nostrand 7-5 6-2
- SHRIVER (5) 3-6 6-2 6-4
- NAVRATILOVA (1) 6-2 6-2

Semi-finals

- GARRISON (8) 2-6 6-3 6-0
- NAVRATILOVA (1) 7-6 6-3

Final

- NAVRATILOVA (1) 6-4 7-6

Capital letters denote seeded players. Number following player's name gives seeding order.

First successes at Wimbledon came for Kathy Jordan and Elizabeth Smylie (above l-r), who ended the run of 109 wins by Navratilova and Shriver, and for Heinz Gunthardt and Balazs Taroczy (below r-l), who went on to win these WCT doubles trophies. (T. Hindley)

MEN'S DOUBLES

Holders: P. Fleming (USA)/J. P. McEnroe (USA)

Champion: H. P. GUNTHARDT (SWZ)/B. TAROCZY (HU) (8) 6–4 6–3 4–6 6–3

FIRST ROUND	SECOND ROUND	THIRD ROUND	QUARTER-FINALS	SEMI-FINALS	FINAL

FIRST ROUND

- P. FLEMING/J. P. McENROE (1)
- M. Purcell/V. Van Patten
- T. C. Fancutt/I. Lendl
- J. Hlasek/C. Panatta
- C. H. Cox/A. Kohlberg
- G. Donnelly/B. Teacher
- M. Davis/C. M. Dunk
- B. DYKE/W. MASUR (10)
- H. LECONTE/Y. NOAH (12)
- M. Hocevar/J. Soares
- D. Cassidy/E. Korita
- K. Evernden/M. Robertson
- A. Maurer/W. Popp
- Tim Gullikson/Tom Gullikson
- B. Becker/M. Leach
- J. NYSTROM/M. WILANDER (7)
- S. EDBERG/A. JARRYD (4)
- J. G. Alexander/R. Simpson
- D. Honey/C. Steyn
- T. Delatte/B. Gilbert
- M. J. Bates/J. W. Feaver
- W. Fibak/S. Zivojinovic
- K. CURREN/J. C. KRIEK (14)
- B. MEISTER/E. TELTSCHER (15)
- E. Fernandez/J. D. Pate
- J. B. Dowdeswell/M. Shaw
- S. Herrmann/F. Menecke
- J. Gunnarsson/M. Mortensen
- J. Frawley/V. Pecci
- S. M. Bale/R. A. Lewis
- P. CASH/J. B. FITZGERALD (5)
- H. P. GUNTHARDT/B. TAROCZY (8)
- S. Glickstein/T. Wilkison
- M. Bauer/F. Maciel
- G. Layendecker/G. Michibata
- V. Amritraj/J. M. Lloyd
- M. Gunthardt/Z. Kuharszky
- B. D. Drewett/C. J. Lewis
- F. GONZALEZ/J. M. MITCHELL (11)
- P. ANNACONE/C. J. VAN RENSBURG (9)
- D. Cahill/S. Sanchez
- R. Acuna/D. Gitlin
- D. Graham/L. Warder
- H. Levine/E. Van't Hof
- V. Gerulaitis/D. T. Visser
- N. Brown/D. C. Feigate
- K. FLACH/R. SEGUSO (3)
- M. EDMONDSON/K. WARWICK (6)
- D. Dowlen/N. Odizor
- A. Amritraj/L. R. Bourne
- E. Edwards/C. D. Strode
- M. Stefanki/R. Van't Hof
- G. Barbosa/I. Kley
- S. E. Davis/S. B. Denton
- A. /S. GIAMMALVA (13)
- H. Pfister/M. Testerman
- M. DePalmer/B. D. Manson
- M. Kratzman/S. Youl
- P. McNamara/P. McNamee
- M. Freeman/J. Turpin
- D. Cahill/B. P. Derlin
- P. SLOZIL/T. SMID (2)

SECOND ROUND

- FLEMING/McENROE (1) — 6–3 6–4 3–6 6–4
- Fancutt/Lendl
- Cox/Kohlberg — 7–6 7–6 6–3 6–4
- Davis/Dunk — 6–1 7–6 2–6 7–6
- LECONTE/NOAH (12) — 7–6 7–6 6–4
- Evernden/Robertson
- Tim/Tom Gullikson — 7–6 4–6 5–7 6–4
- EDBERG/JARRYD (4) — 7–5 6–3 7–6
- Honey/Steyn — 6–2 7–6 7–5
- Bates/Feaver — 6–7 7–6 6–1
- CURREN/KRIEK (14) — 6–4 6–2 7–5
- MEISTER/TELTSCHER (15) — 6–4 6–4 6–4
- Dowdeswell/Shaw — 7–6 7–6 6–3
- Gunnarsson/Mortensen — 6–3 6–4 3–6 7–6
- CASH/FITZGERALD (5) — 6–2 6–3 6–4
- H. P. GUNTHARDT/B. TAROCZY (8) — 6–7 6–4 6–3 6–4
- Layendecker/Michibata — 6–7 6–3 6–3 6–3
- V. Amritraj/Lloyd — 6–7 7–6 3–6 6–3 6–2
- Drewett/Lewis
- ANNACONE/VAN RENSBURG (9) — 5–7 6–3 7–6 6–3
- Graham/Warder
- Levine/E. Van't Hof — 6–4 7–6 5–7 7–6
- Brown/Feigate — 7–6 3–2 8–7 6–6
- Dowlen/Odizor — 7–6 7–6 4–6 8–6
- Edwards/Strode
- Stefanki/R. Van't Hof — 6–4 4–6 6–2 6–4
- A. /S. GIAMMALVA (13) — 6–3 2–6 4–4
- Pfister/Testerman — 6–7 6–5 5–7 7–5
- DePalmer/Manson
- McNamara/McNamee — 6–4 4–6 8–6
- SLOZIL/SMID (2) — 6–7 6–2 6–4 6–4

THIRD ROUND

- FLEMING/McENROE (1) — 7–6 3–6 6–3 6–2
- Cox/Kohlberg — 6–3 7–6 6–3
- Evernden/Robertson — 6–7 7–5 ret'd
- Tim/Tom Gullikson — w.o.
- EDBERG/JARRYD (4) — 6–2 6–2 6–7 6–7 6–4
- CURREN/KRIEK (14) — 7–6 6–4 6–3
- MEISTER/TELTSCHER (15) — 6–2 6–4 6–4
- CASH/FITZGERALD (5) — 5–7 4–6 6–3 6–4 6–4
- H. P. GUNTHARDT/TAROCZY (8) — 6–4 6–7 7–6
- V. Amritraj/Lloyd — 7–5 6–1 5–7 6–2
- ANNACONE/VAN RENSBURG (9) — 6–2 6–3 6–3
- Levine/E. Van't Hof — 7–6 6–7 6–3 6–4
- Edwards/Strode — 6–3 6–7 6–4 6–3
- Stefanki/R. Van't Hof — 6–4 6–1 3–6 6–3
- DePalmer/Manson — 6–3 7–6 6–3
- McNamara/McNamee — 6–4 7–5 6–3

QUARTER-FINALS

- FLEMING/McENROE (1) — 6–3 6–4 6–4
- Tim/Tom Gullikson — 6–7 6–3 7–5 7–5
- CURREN/KRIEK (14) — 6–4 3–6 6–4 7–6
- CASH/FITZGERALD (5) — 6–4 6–3 6–4
- H. P. GUNTHARDT/TAROCZY (8) — 6–4 6–0 6–4
- ANNACONE/VAN RENSBURG (9) — 7–6 6–1 7–6
- Edwards/Strode — 7–6 5–7 6–3 7–5
- McNamara/McNamee — 6–3 7–5 6–4

SEMI-FINALS

- FLEMING/McENROE (1) — 6–3 6–4 7–6
- CASH/FITZGERALD (5) — 6–1 7–5 6–4
- H. P. GUNTHARDT/TAROCZY (8) — 6–4 2–6 6–4 6–7 24–22
- McNamara/McNamee — 6–1 6–4 6–2

FINAL

- CASH/FITZGERALD (5) — 7–6 2–6 6–1 6–4
- H. P. GUNTHARDT/TAROCZY (8) — 6–7 6–1 6–2 6–4

Capital letters denote seeded pairings. Number following players' names gives seeding order.

WOMEN'S DOUBLES

Holders: M. Navratilova (USA)/P. H. Shriver (USA)

FINAL: K. JORDAN (USA)/MRS P. D. SMYLIE (AUS) (3) 5–7 6–3 6–4

FIRST ROUND	SECOND ROUND	THIRD ROUND	QUARTER-FINALS	SEMI-FINALS	FINAL
M. NAVRATILOVA/P. H. SHRIVER (1)	NAVRATILOVA/SHRIVER (1) 6–1 6–0	NAVRATILOVA/SHRIVER (1) 6–1 6–2	NAVRATILOVA/SHRIVER (1) 6–0 6–3	NAVRATILOVA/SHRIVER (1) 7–6 6–1	NAVRATILOVA/SHRIVER (1) 6–4 6–2
J. Golder/V. L. Nelson					
B. A. Borneo/J. M. Tacon	Borneo/Tacon 6–4 3–6 6–4				
A. M. Fernandez/Hu Na					
Z. L. Garrison/K. Rinaldi	Garrison/Rinaldi 6–1 6–1	Holladay/Jausovec 6–2 2–6 6–4			
A. J. Brown/R. Uys					
T. A. Holladay/M. Jausovec	Holladay/Jausovec 6–2 6–1				
C. Jolissaint/M. A. Mesker					
J. M. DURIE/Mrs J. M. LLOYD (10)	DURIE/LLOYD (10) 6–2 6–4	DURIE/LLOYD (10) 6–4 6–3	DURIE/LLOYD (10) 5–7 6–4 6–4		
I. Kuczynska/H. Pelletier					
R. Casals/S. Kloss	Amiach/Gerken 4–6 6–4 6–4				
S. Amiach/B. Gerken					
K. Copeland/Mrs H. A. Mochizuki	Dias/Medrado 6–3 6–3	BUNGE/PFAFF (7) 6–7 7–5 6–1			
N. P. Dias/P. S. Medrado					
A. L./E. A. Minter	BUNGE/PFAFF (7) 4–6 7–6 8–6				
B. BUNGE/E. S. PFAFF (7)					
H. MANDLIKOVA/W. M. TURNBULL (4)	MANDLIKOVA/TURNBULL (4) 6–3 6–3	MANDLIKOVA/TURNBULL (4) 6–3 7–6	MANDLIKOVA/TURNBULL (4) 6–1 6–2	MANDLIKOVA/TURNBULL (4) 6–4 6–3	
A. M. Cecchini/M. Schropp					
R. A. Fendick/H. A. Ludloff	Fendick/Ludloff 6–3 6–3				
C. L. C. Gracie					
C. Suire/S. V. Wade	Suire/Wade 6–4 6–2	BURGIN/MOULTON (11) 6–2 6–3			
S. Graf/A. E. Smith					
K. Kinney/P. J. Whytcross	BURGIN/MOULTON (11) 6–1 6–3				
E. M. BURGIN/A. A. MOULTON (11)					
C. K. BASSETT/A. C. LEAND (15)	BASSETT/A. C. LEAND (15) 6–3 3–6 6–3	Demongeot/Tauziat 6–7 6–0 11–9	CHERNEVA/SAVCHENKO (6) 4–6 7–6 6–2		
B. Gomer/J. A. Salmon					
I. Demongeot/M. Schenck	Demongeot/Tauziat 6–4 6–3				
K. McDaniel/M. E. White					
H. A. Crowe/K. A. Steinmetz	McDaniel/White 7–6 6–2	CHERNEVA/SAVCHENKO (6) 6–1 6–2			
S. CHERNEVA/L. SAVCHENKO (6)					
R. D. FAIRBANK/A. E. HOBBS (8)	CHERNEVA/SAVCHENKO (6) 6–0 6–0				
P. Paradis/C. Tanvier					
J. M. Hetherington/G. A. Rush	Paradis/Tanvier 6–3 6–1	Paradis/Tanvier 6–4 6–2	RUZICI/TEMESVARI (14) 0–6 6–4 6–4		
J. L. Klitch/C. Vanier					
I. Budarova/M. Skuherska	Hetherington/Rush 6–4 6–3				
V. RUZICI/A. TEMESVARI (14)					
L. ANTONOPLIS/C. S. REYNOLDS (12)	Budarova/Skuherska 7–5 6–3	RUZICI/TEMESVARI (14) 6–2 6–1			
C. C. Monteiro/Y. Vermaak					
B. A. Jordan/N. S. Seagin	RUZICI/TEMESVARI (14) 6–4 6–3				
J. A. Mundel/M. Van Nostrand					
S. P. Foltz/R. Reis	Monteiro/Vermaak 6–0 6–2	Monteiro/Vermaak 6–4 3–6 6–4	JORDAN/SMYLIE (3) 6–1 6–0	JORDAN/SMYLIE (3) 6–2 7–6	JORDAN/SMYLIE (3) 5–7 6–1 6–4
T. Karlsson/T. Scheuer-Larsen					
R. L. Blount/D. L. Farrell	Mundel/Van Nostrand 6–0 6–1				
K. JORDAN/Mrs P. D. SMYLIE (3)					
B. C. POTTER/Mrs M. H. WALSH PETE (5)	Karlsson/Scheuer-Larsen 6–1 6–2	JORDAN/SMYLIE (3) 6–3 6–1			
B. A. Herr/Mrs L. A. Richardson					
M. L. Piatek/R. M. White	JORDAN/SMYLIE (3) 6–1 6–1				
B. J. Remilton/N. Sato					
M. Paz/G. Sabatini	POTTER/WALSH PETE (5) 6–3 6–7 7–5	POTTER/WALSH PETE (5) 6–2 6–3	POTTER/WALSH PETE (5) 3–6 7–5 6–3		
S. L. Collins/S. Goles					
B. A. MOULD/P. G. SMITH (16)	Piatek/R. M. White 6–2 7–6				
S. NAGELSEN/A. H. WHITE (9)					
A. Henri/Mrs L. A. Shaefer	Paz/Sabatini 5–7 6–2 6–4	MOULD/SMITH (16) 6–3 6–7 6–4			
C. Benjamin/J. C. Kaplan					
P. Casale/P. Louie	MOULD/SMITH (16) 6–2 6–4				
A. N. Croft/L. Howell					
A. E. Holton/M. A. Quinlan	NAGELSEN/A. H. WHITE (9) 7–5 7–5	NAGELSEN/A. H. WHITE (9) 6–1 6–1	KOHDE-KILSCH/SUKOVA (2) 7–6 6–4	KOHDE-KILSCH/SUKOVA (2) 7–6 4–6 6–3	
C. KOHDE-KILSCH/H. SUKOVA (2)					
	Benjamin/Kaplan 0–6 7–5 6–2				
	Henrickson/Leo 6–3 7–5	KOHDE-KILSCH/SUKOVA (2) 6–4 6–0			
	KOHDE-KILSCH/SUKOVA (2) 6–0 6–4				

MIXED DOUBLES

Holders: J. M. Lloyd (GB)/W. M. Turnbull (AUS)

Winner: P. McNAMEE (AUS)/M. NAVRATILOVA (USA) (2) 7–5 4–6 6–2

FIRST ROUND

- J. M. LLOYD/W. M. TURNBULL (1)
- J. D. Newcombe/A. C. Leand
- H. Pfister/C. Benjamin
- I. Kievit/L. Corsato
- M. Bauer/T. Tanvier
- L. Warder/A. L. Minter
- T. Fancutt/E. A. Minter
- B. Buffington/J. C. Kaplan
- J. R. Smith/N. Sato
- S. Hermann/C. Karlsson
- Z. Kuharszky/C. Jolissant
- J. Fillol/P. Casale
- K. Warwick/E. M. Burgin
- D. Fernandez/Mrs B. M. Perry
- D. Graham/P. J. Whytcross
- M. R. EDMONDSON/K. JORDAN (6)
- R. SEGUSO/J. A. E. HOBBS (3)
- F. D. McMillan/B. F. Stove
- C. Honey/G. A. Rush
- O. K. Davidson/J. N. Croft
- B. Teltscher/A. H. White
- E. Teltscher/A. H. White
- C. Cox/W. E. White
- H. Cox/W. E. White
- D. Campos/M. Van Nostrand
- C. Motta/C. C. Montero
- R. Meyer/L. Howell
- R. Hocevar/N. P. Dias
- M. C. Riessen/R. Casals
- N. C. Fulwood/L. Gracie
- A. D. Roche/D. E. Dalton
- D. Gitlin/J. Golder
- J. B. FITZGERALD/Mrs P. D. SMYLIE (7)
- S. E. DAVIS/B. NAGELSEN (8)
- G. S. Dibley/E. Inoue
- G. Michibata/P. Hy
- B. H. Levine/Y. Vermaak
- T. S. Okker/Mrs C. M. Balestrat
- M. T. Fancutt/C. S. Reynolds
- C. Dowdeswell/R. D. Fairbank
- C. J. Van Rensburg/M. Reinach
- C. J. Wittus/B. Gerken
- E. Doohan/R. Remilton
- G. Barnes/C. M. Maleeva
- S. Meister/P. Barg
- P. McNamara/A. Temesvari
- M. Kratzman/J. Byrne
- S. SLOZIL/H. SUKOVA (4)
- S. B. DENTON/J. M. DURIE (5)
- M. J. Bates/S. Gomer
- T. Gullikson/M. Maleeva
- H. P. Van Boeckel/M. A. Mesker
- R. Harmon/Z. L. Garrison
- A. Gonzalez/P. G. Smith
- A. Giammalva/A. E. Smith
- R. Acuna/L. M. Hetherington
- S. Stewart/S. Kloss
- G. Holmes/C. K. Bassett
- J. W. Feaver/S. V. Wade
- C. D. Strode/L. Savchenko
- B. Testerman/Mrs M. H. Walsh Pete
- P. McNAMEE/M. NAVRATILOVA (2)

SECOND ROUND

- LLOYD/TURNBULL (1) 6–1 5–7 12–10
- Pfister/Benjamin 6–2 7–5
- Bauer/Tanvier w.o.
- Fancutt/E. A. Minter 6–1 6–2
- Smith/Sato 7–5 6–2
- Kuharszky/Jolissant w.o.
- Warwick/Burgin 7–5 6–7 6–4
- EDMONDSON/JORDAN (6) 6–2 6–2
- SEGUSO/A. E. HOBBS (3) 6–2 7–6
- Honey/Rush 4–6 7–6 6–4
- Teltscher/A. H. White 6–4 7–6
- Campos/Van Nostrand 6–4 7–6
- Motta/Montero 6–1 6–4
- Riessen/Casals 6–3 1–6 6–1
- Fulwood/Gracie 6–2 7–5
- FITZGERALD/SMYLIE (7) 6–2 6–2
- DAVIS/NAGELSEN (8) 6–3 6–4
- Robertson/Lys 7–5 6–7 7–5
- Levine/Vermaak 6–3 7–6
- Dowdeswell/Fairbank 7–5 7–6
- Van Rensburg/Reinach 6–4 7–5
- Doohan/Remilton 6–3 5–7 6–4
- McNamara/Temesvari 7–5 7–5
- SLOZIL/SUKOVA (4) 6–2 6–2
- DENTON/DURIE (5) 6–4 6–3
- Gullikson/M. Maleeva 6–4 6–3
- Harmon/Garrison 6–4 6–3
- Giammalva/A. E. Smith 6–4 3–6 6–3
- Acuna/Hetherington 6–3 7–5
- Holmes/Bassett 6–2 7–5
- Strode/Savchenko 6–2 6–4
- McNAMEE/NAVRATILOVA (2) 6–4 6–1

THIRD ROUND

- LLOYD/TURNBULL (1) 6–1 7–6
- Bauer/Tanvier 7–6 3–6 6–4
- Kuharszky/Jolissant 6–4 6–4
- EDMONDSON/JORDAN (6) 6–2 6–4
- Honey/Rush w.o.
- Teltscher/A. H. White 6–4 6–4
- Motta/Montero 6–4 7–6 2
- FITZGERALD/SMYLIE (7) 6–1 6–4
- DAVIS/NAGELSEN (8) 6–4 1–6 6–3
- Dowdeswell/Fairbank 6–4 6–2
- Doohan/Remilton 3–6 6–2 6–3
- SLOZIL/SUKOVA (4) 6–2 6–3
- DENTON/DURIE (5) 5–7 6–2 6–4
- Giammalva/A. E. Smith 7–5 4–6 6–4
- Acuna/Hetherington 6–4 3–6 6–3
- McNAMEE/NAVRATILOVA (2) 4–6 6–2 6–0

QUARTER-FINALS

- LLOYD/TURNBULL (1) 6–3 6–7 6–3
- EDMONDSON/JORDAN (6) 6–7 6–4 6–3
- Teltscher/A. H. White 5–7 6–3 6–4
- FITZGERALD/SMYLIE (7) 6–1 6–0
- DAVIS/NAGELSEN (8) 6–7 6–4 6–2
- SLOZIL/SUKOVA (4) 6–4 6–2
- DENTON/DURIE (5) 3–6 6–4 10–8
- McNAMEE/NAVRATILOVA (2) 6–3 3–6 6–2

SEMI-FINALS

- EDMONDSON/JORDAN (6) 7–6 7–6
- FITZGERALD/SMYLIE (7) 7–6 6–4
- DAVIS/NAGELSEN (8) 6–3 6–4
- McNAMEE/NAVRATILOVA (2) 6–4 6–2

FINAL

- FITZGERALD/SMYLIE (7) 7–6 7–5
- McNAMEE/NAVRATILOVA (2) 6–7 7–5 23–21

Capital letters denote seeded pairings. Number following players' names gives seeding order.

WIMBLEDON CHAMPIONSHIPS PRIZE MONEY

MEN'S SINGLES: Winner £130,000. Runner-up £65,000. Semi-finalists £32,500. Quarter-finalists £16,500. Fourth round losers £8,680. Third round losers £4,860. Second round losers £2,865. First round losers £1,750.
Total: £676,880.
WOMEN'S SINGLES: Winner £117,000. Runner-up £58,500. Semi-finalists £28,500. Quarter-finalists £13,950. Fourth round losers £6,950. Third round losers £3,750. Second round losers £2,210. First round losers £1,350.
Total: £561,020.
MEN'S DOUBLES (per team): Winners £47,500. Runners-up £23,750. Semi-finalists £11,880. Quarter-finalists £5,450. Third round losers £2,810. Second round losers £1,490. First round losers £870.
Total: £190,970.
WOMEN'S DOUBLES (per team): Winners £41,100. Runners-up £20,550. Semi-finalists £9,500. Quarter-finalists £4,360. Third round losers £2,100. Second round losers £1,100. First round losers £640.
Total: £152,970.
MIXED DOUBLES (per team): Winners £23,400. Runners-up £11,700. Semi-finalists £5,850. Quarter-finalists £2,730. Third round losers £1,370. Second round losers £680. First round losers £300.
Total £89,160.
WOMEN'S PLATE: Winner £3,315. Runner-up £2,145. Semi-finalists £1,465. Quarter-finalists £730. Third round losers £350. Second round losers £195. First round losers £140.
Total £19,470.
MEN'S 35 AND OVER SINGLES: Winner £10,000. Runner-up £8,000. Semi-finalists £5,000. Quarter-finalists £3,000. First round losers £2,000.
Total: £56,000.
MEN'S 35 AND OVER DOUBLES (per team): Winners £8,000. Runners-up £6,000. Semi-finalists £4,000. First round losers £2,000.
Total: 30,000.
QUALIFYING COMPETITION: Qualifying round losers: Men's singles £875. Women's singles £675.
Total: £19,400.
Overall Total: £1,934,760 (including contributions to Grand Prix Bonus Pool and ATP).

WIMBLEDON PLATE

WOMEN'S SINGLES – Final: E. Reinach (SA) d. T. A. Holladay (USA) 6–4 6–2.

JUNIOR EVENTS

BOYS' SINGLES – Final: L. Lavalle (MEX) d. E. Velez (MEX) 6–4 6–4.
GIRLS' SINGLES – Final: A. Holikova (CZ) d. J. Byrne (AUS) 7–5 6–1.
BOYS' DOUBLES – Final: A. Moreno (MEX) /J. Yzaga (PER) d. P. Korda (CZ) /C. Suk (CZ) 7–6 6–4.
GIRLS' DOUBLES – Final: L. Field (AUS) /J. Thompson (AUS) d. E. Reinach (SA) /J. Richardson (NZ) 6–1 6–2.

35 AND OVER EVENTS

MEN'S INVITATION SINGLES – Final: S. R. Smith (USA) d. J. Fillol (CH) 4–6 7–6 7–6.
MEN'S INVITATION DOUBLES – Final: C. S. Dibley (AUS) /Fillol d. M. C. Riessen (USA) /S. E. Stewart (USA) 4–6 7–6 7–6.

100
WIMBLEDON
CHAMPIONSHIPS
John Barrett

This official celebration of 100 years of the
Wimbledon Championships has been
meticulously researched and captures the magical
atmosphere of this unique annual event.

350 photographs including 32pp colour

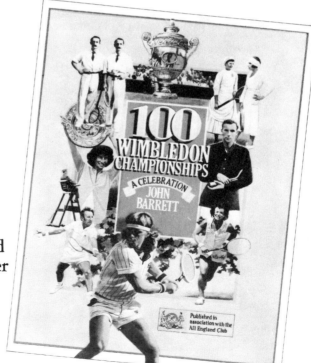

**Published
in October**

£14.95

COLLINS
WILLOW

The glittering talents of Czechoslovakia's Hana Mandlikova were thrillingly revealed at the US Open, where in successive rounds she beat Evert Lloyd and Navratilova to win the title for the first time in her third final. *(M. Cole)*

US OPEN CHAMPIONSHIPS

Bud Collins

Czech-mated as no major tournament had ever been, the US Open was ruled by a couple of Praguematic characters who destroyed the prevalent theory that the champions would repeat. That may be stretching the pun because even though Hana Mandlikova did grow up as a Bohemian girl in Prague, the Ostrava Ghost, Ivan Lendl, is a Moravian. Still, he has done plenty of Prague time.

The forlorn fact for jingoists at Flushing Meadow was that not only did Hana and Ivan take both titles to Europe for the first time in 99 years of the Championships for both women and men, but stockpiled them in the smallest country yet to produce champions of the US Open. Czechoslovakia's 49,000 square miles isn't a lot of room when you're talking acreage to an American. Only a scattering of the 50 states are smaller than the European country, which covers roughly the same amount of ground as New York, but it was room enough to spawn a pair of big hitters who dispossessed the left-handed tenants of the throne room, Martina Navratilova and John McEnroe. Neither was a stranger in the final round. Some felt it was only a matter of time before these two talented sharpshooters came through and others believed that neither Hana nor Ivan could win when it really counted.

Dispelling the latter notion must have been tremendously satisfying to Hana, who had failed before Chris Lloyd in the 1980 and 1982 title bouts, and Ivan, who was on the verge of equalling an ignominious 60-year-old record: four consecutive finals lost. Mandlikova had to beat her two chief tormentors – Evert Lloyd (against whom her match record was 3–18) and Navratilova (5–14) – while Lendl had to overcome his – Jimmy Connors (11–13) and McEnroe (11–13). Mandlikova, against the seemingly invincible Navratilova, was fire-ice-and-steel in their decisive overtime passage to win the closest of all major finals 7–6 (7–3) 1–6 7–6 (7–2). Lendl resisted a set-point in the opening set with a wondrous forehand passer at 2–5 before asserting himself 7–6 (7–1) 6–3 6–4.

Unbearably high heat and humidity, and hard footing, had combined to make Fortress Flushing a formidable sanctuary for US citizens since 1978 when their Open settled there. Hitherto impregnable to outlanders seeking singles booty, the Meadow's ramparts were startlingly overrun by Europeans as never before. A record six men and four women from Europe reached the quarter-finals. The men were Swedes Mats Wilander (3), Anders Jarryd (6), Joakim Nystrom (10); Frenchman Yannick Noah (5); Swiss Heinz Gunthardt and, of course, Lendl. West Germans Claudia Kohde-Kilsch (5) and Steffi Graf (11); Czechs Mandlikova (3) and Helena Sukova (7) were the women. The Swedish triumvirate were the largest European male delegation from a single country in the last eight since three of France's illustrious Four Musketeers – Jean Borotra, Jacques Brugnon, Rene Lacoste – made it in 1927. Added to the fact that Mandlikova is the first European woman to win the US Open (the only other finalist being Poland's Jadwiga Jedrzejowska in 1937) was her rare feat of beating two ex-champs *en route*. That last happened in 1962 when Margaret Smith Court took the first of her five titles by stopping Darlene Hard (winner in 1960 and 1961) and Maria Bueno (1959). Lendl, who clubbed fourth-seeded Connors in a semi, 6–2 6–3 7–5, could say the same, although such had happened among the men much more recently, when McEnroe destroyed Ilie Nastase and Connors during his 1979 dash to the crown.

Navratilova, a prospective wearer of the first triple crown since Billie-Jean King's singles, doubles and mixed triumphs of 1967, had to settle for one – the mixed in the company of Heinz Gunthardt. Their 6–3 6–4 victory over 1983 champs, Aussies Liz Sayers

Smylie and John Fitzgerald, gave Martina a 33rd Grand Slam championship. It also gave the US the astonishingly low sum of two titles in a tournament where Americans were top seeds in every category. Gunthardt, the first Swiss to win a US title, was the sole alien at the top of the seedings.

The other seeding justifiers were Americans Ken Flach and Robert Seguso, who beat France's Henri Leconte and Yannick Noah in a controversial doubles final, 6–7 7–6 7–6 (8–6) 6–0. The French might have won in straight sets, having held five set-points in the second and three in the third. However, at the acrimonious conclusion, each side was accusing the other of malfeasance. On one of the set-points in the third set, with Seguso serving at 4–6 in the tie-break, a Leconte shot skipped off the net cord and appeared to graze Flach before landing beyond the baseline. Leconte and Noah charged that Flach should have called the point against himself, but Flach, uncertain, demurred, he and Seguso leaving it to the umpire, who 'didn't see a touch' and awarded the Americans the point. They in turn accused the sulking French of unprofessionally tanking the fourth set, an accusation that seemed justified.

Having etched a doubles Grand Slam in 1984 and at Paris won a sixth successive Slam title, Navratilova and Pam Shriver stumbled shockingly by their standards. Following their Wimbledon defeat they lost a second straight major doubles final, 6–7 6–2 6–3, to the 'Twin Towers', 6ft 1in Kohde-Kilsch and 6ft 2in Sukova, the latter bringing Czechoslovakia a share in a third title, and Kohde-Kilsch achieving Germany's first title in the US Open.

The keenly anticipated quarter-final, pitting the 17-year-old Wimbledon emperor Boris Becker against McEnroe, didn't happen. Two months after he had twice served for their match in the fifth set at Wimbledon, Nystrom at last pinned Becker 6–3 6–4 4–6 6–4 in the fourth round. Boris, seeded eigth, fell too far behind, his last-hour heroics unavailing. McEnroe almost didn't happen at all. He barely survived Shlomo Glickstein in an opening round horror-show 6–1 6–7 (3–7) 2–6 6–3 7–6 (9–7), during which he was two points from elimination on four occasions in the fifth set. It was the closest call at the starting gate for a first seed since John Newcombe took a spill to Jan Kodes in 1971. But Kodes was reigning French champion while Glickstein, within grasp of an all-time act of *lèse-majesté* – two points away at 4–5 15–30 and 30–all on McEnroe's serve, 6–6 in the tie-break on his own and then 7–7 on McEnroe's – was ranked 175.

Yet the first round wasn't safe from saboteurs, one of whom made it quickly evident that Flushing would stage no Wimbledon championship rematch. Fifth-seeded Kevin Curren, who had ambushed McEnroe and Connors there, got a look at neither, bounced immediately in straight sets by the previously forgettable Guy Forget, a 20-year-old Frenchman ranked 63. Gone, too, was Henrik Sundstrom of Sweden (14), thrashed by the Argentine, Martin Jaite, who, two rounds up the line, bowed to the stylish Gunthardt, usually more useful at doubles. Despite his non-seeded status, Leconte – conqueror of Lendl at Wimbledon – seemed likely to take Curren's reservation in the quarters, but Gunthardt's volleying held up profitably against Henri, placing him opposite Connors.

Ranked 47, Gunthardt was the only unseeded crasher in the quarters, where Connors rationed him to eight games. Nystrom, Jarryd and Noah respectively couldn't take a set from McEnroe, Wilander or Lendl, and the semis fell as expected: seeds one and three (McEnroe–Wilander) and second and fourth seeds, Lendl–Connors. Jimmy Connors, who had set tournament records for matches won (77) and consecutive semi-final appearances (12), twisted his left ankle in practice and never got started against Lendl. Considering Lendl's fitness, strength and resolve (he lost but one set, to Peruvian Jaime Yzaga in the fourth round), and his championship performance against McEnroe, Connors's ankle woes may have been irrelevant.

Only the gumption of a great champion prevented Mats Wilander from providing the climactic opposition to Lendl. McEnroe, reeling 0–2 from service breaks in both the fourth and fifth sets, fought back grimly on the 115-degree griddle, hounding the stubborn Swede through nearly four hours to pull out a 3–6 6–4 4–6 6–3 6–3 triumph and enter his fifth final. McEnroe could justifiably exult, 'It was one of my best performances for hanging in, winning on mental toughness'.

But nothing would save him the following afternoon. Having won all his previous finals

—Vitas Gerulaitis (1979), Bjorn Borg (1980 and 1981), Lendl (1984)—McEnroe commenced as authoritatively, winning the first three games on the loss of a point as Lendl bungled in over-hitting. Ivan looked unconcerned, confident of his course. Refusing to temporize, he was soon in tune, slugging his passing groundies to spike McEnroe's advances. What's more, he seized the net, volleying with unprecedented effect, not merely keeping a point alive but killing it swiftly. Lendlian power was irresistible in every phase as he riddled the groping McEnroe in composing possibly his finest work in a significant event. With each stroke he became more dominant, never allowing McEnroe past 30 on his serve after losing it in the second game. Ivan's handsome topspin lob — duplicating his match-saver against Pat Cash in a 1984 semi — scored the interring break to 5–4 in the third, whereupon he served himself to his richest career dessert: the US Open frosted with $189,500.

In the female sector the other half of the Teutonic Teenies — Steffi Graf, aged 16 years and two months — was the lone serious disturber of the seeded order, taking out Manuela Maleeva (8) and Shriver (4) on the way to the semi-finals. Yet another Czech, lefty Andrea Holikova, registered the other noteworthy upset, dumping Wimbledon semi-finalist, ninth seed Kathy Rinaldi. A couple of lightly regarded young Californians also took notable scalps early, Caroline Kuhlman knocking Andrea Temesvari (16) from the second round, and Robin White chasing Bonnie Gadusek (12) from the third. A worn-out Gabriela Sabatini, seeded tenth, was no problem for Barbara Potter, who should have been seeded.

For Mandlikova-watchers, taken by her shorter, more businesslike manner — in hairstyle and working hours — life was much easier. There were none of those mindless three-set nail-biters against anonymous foes, and when she did drop a set in the fourth round to the dangerous unseeded Kathy Jordan, Hana regrouped with poise for a 6–1 finish. That was the single set lost by any of the top four on their way to the quarters where top seed Evert Lloyd beat Kohde-Kilsch 6–3 6–3; Navratilova (2) brushed aside Zina Garrison (6) 6–2 6–3; and Mandlikova won the championship of Prague over Sukova, 7–6 7–5.

Shriver, however, was caught up with Graf in the tightest match in the history of women's Grand Slam tourneys, gaining a three-point margin over the better part of three hours, playing 39 games in the longest match at the Open since the tie-break was introduced in 1970. Shriver, who may have played the best match of her life with 14 aces and countless brilliant volleys, led 4–1 in the third set, served for it at 5–3 . . . and was beaten, 7–6 (7–4) 6–7 (4–7) 7–6 (7–4), because the flaxen-haired kid just wouldn't let go. Though ahead 4–3 in the tie-break with two serves to come, Pam was too eroded to cope any longer with Steffi's unrelenting and purposeful drives.

That was it for the German, disciplined sharply by Navratilova, 6–2 6–3, and when Evert Lloyd captured the first set of the next match the 67th episode in the Martina–Chrissie show appeared inevitable. But it was cancelled, not for lack of interest but for the abundance of it that Mandlikova summoned for the second and third sets in a 4–6 6–2 6–3 spectacular.

Uncompromising in her desire to attack, Mandlikova began to win the big points and the nerve-clanging games that customarily had gone to the paragon Evert Lloyd, playing in her record 15th straight semi. A run of five games carried Hana 1–0 in the third set, and with diving or flying volleys she came from 0–40 to go ahead 2–1, then 3–1. Though she lost her serve to 3–2, Hana hurdled the stonewaller in the critical sixth game, which after ten deuces and eight match-points for Chrissie, took the score to 4–2.

When it came to vital points, Hana delivered. It will be long speculated whether any one of eight break-points in the 11th game would have assured Navratilova of her third championship. But Hana wasn't about to collapse with one of the greatest finals only warming up — a match of such excruciating twistings and turnings that it was truly in doubt until the last stroke, a gorgeous lunging backhand volley that concluded two and a quarter hours of Sunday punching on a Saturday afternoon.

Curiously it was only the second time in virtually a century that the loser had racked more games than the champ, the prior such disappointment belonging to the same Martina, who outscored Tracy Austin 18–15 in 1981.

In their mutual race to the net, these marauders presented the finest of Flushing finals, the best since Billie Jean King and Evonne Goolagong bombed each other all the way to a 7–5 third set for King in 1974. Within 20 minutes Mandlikova had roared to within tasting distance of a bagel at 5–0, set-point. Abruptly the wide opening began to close as Navratilova battled back to 5–5 and 21,169 witnesses went mad.

Stunned, Mandlikova skidded to 0–40. She was through. Or was she? Eight break-points and nine deuces later she had the game, and would win the set in a tie-break. Martina controlled the second, but stumbled in losing serve to 3–5 in the third. Two points from the abyss at deuce, she counter-punched once more by breaking with a whirling forehand passer.

The shotmaking feast would go to a last roulette spin – another tie-break which went 7–2 to the unintimidated Mandlikova, who clutched the first six points. Hana had done her part in the Czechoslovak double. A day later, Ivan did his, completing a shipment of titles to the land of Kafka, author of *Metamorphosis*. This was the tennis version: final-round losers metamorphosing to champions.

JUNIOR EVENTS

BOYS' SINGLES – Final: T. Trigueiro d. J. Blake 6–2 6–3.
BOYS' DOUBLES – Final: J. Blake /D. Yates d. P. Flynn (AUS) /D. McPherson (AUS) 3–6 6–3 6–4.
GIRLS' SINGLES – Final: L. Garrone (IT) d. A. Holikova (CZ) 6–2 7–6.
GIRLS' DOUBLES – Final: R. Zrubakova (CZ) /A. Holikova (CZ) d. P. Tarabini (ARG) /M. Rocdau (ARG) 6–4 2–6 7–5.

SENIOR EVENTS

MEN'S SINGLES – Final: R. C. Lutz d. S. R. Smith 6–3 7–6.
MEN'S DOUBLES – Final: M. C. Riessen /S. E. Stewart d. J. Fillol (CH) /T. S. Okker (NTH) 6–4 6–4.
WOMEN'S DOUBLES – Final: L. DuPont /V. Ziegenfuss d. B. F. Stove (NTH) /M. Guerrant 7–6 6–1.

US CHAMPIONSHIPS PRIZE MONEY

MEN'S AND WOMEN'S SINGLES – Winner $187,500. Runner-up $93,750. Semi-finalists $46,875. Quarter-finalists $23,750. Fourth round losers $12,500. Third round losers $7,000. Second round losers $4,126. First round losers $2,515.
Total $975,000 each event
MEN'S AND WOMEN'S DOUBLES (per team) – Winners $65,000. Runners-up $32,500. Semi-finalists $16,250. Quarter-finalists $8,250. Third round losers $5,250. Second round losers $2,250. First round losers $1,312.
Total $275,000 each event
MIXED DOUBLES (per team) – Winners $19,000. Runners-up $ 9,000. Semi-finalists $4,000. Quarter-finalists $2,250. Second round losers $1,400. First round losers $550.
Total $65,000
MEN'S QUALIFYING COMPETITION – Third round losers $1,000. Second round losers $700. First round losers $400.
Total $64,000
WOMEN'S QUALIFYING COMPETITION – Third round losers $1,000. Second round losers $700. First round losers $400.
Total $32,000
SENIOR MEN'S SINGLES – Winner $9,000. Runner-up $5,000. Semi-finalists $3,000. Quarter-finalists $2,000. First round losers $1,500.
Total $40,000
SENIOR MEN'S AND WOMEN'S DOUBLES (per team) – Winners $14,000. Runners-up $8,000. Semi-finalists $4,000. Quarter-finalists $2,500.
Total $40,000 each event
Overall total $3,073,500 (including $292,500 for Bonus Pools and Players' Association Fees)

DHL WORLDWIDE EXPRESS

A service no one else can deliver

DHL with more offices in more countries
than any other air express company. DHL delivers
documents and packages world-wide.

· W O R L D W I D E ·

Supersure, Superfast, Super express.

Official freight courier to the International Tennis Federation.

MEN'S SINGLES

Holder: J. P. McEnroe (USA)

FINAL: 7-6 6-3 6-4

FIRST ROUND / SECOND ROUND

First Round	Second Round
J. P. McENROE (1)	McENROE (1) 6-1 6-7 2-6 6-3 7-6
S. Glickstein (IS)	
M. Wostenholme (C)	Wostenholme 4-6 3-3 6-3 6-6-3
H. Gildemeister (CH)	
B. Schultz	Schultz 7-6 6-4 6-2
M. Leach	
R. Matuszewski	Matuszewski 6-7 7-6 6-7 6-4 6-3
S. Denton	
S. Arias	Arias 6-1 6-3 6-1
R. Arguello (ARG)	
A. Mansdorf (IS)	Mansdorf 4-6 7-6 6-1
J. Sadri	
G. Vilas (ARG)	Vilas 7-6 6-7 6-4 3-6 6-1
W. Masur (AUS)	
M. Flur	SMID (16) 6-3 7-5 6-2
T. SMID (CZ) (16)	
J. NYSTROM (SW) (10)	NYSTROM (10) 6-4 7-5 6-1
C. Hooper	
R. Green	Green 7-6 7-6 6-4
R. Agenor (HA)	
D. Goldie	Goldie 6-4 6-3 3-6 3-6 7-5
M. Davis	
M. Vajda (CZ)	Vajda 2-6 2-6 6-3 7-6 7-5
M. DePalmer	
K. Evernden (NZ)	Evernden 6-4 6-2 6-2
L. Duncan	
L. Bourne	Bourne 6-3 7-5 2-6 6-4
T. Brown	
H. Van Boekel (NTH)	Van Boekel 6-1 6-2 3-6 4-6 6-4
J. Fitzgerald (AUS)	
P. Doohan (AUS)	BECKER (8) 6-4 6-1 6-2
B. BECKER (G) (8)	
M. WILANDER (SW) (3)	WILANDER (3) 6-2 6-4 6-4
V. Amritraj (IND)	
S. Foxworth	Foxworth 6-7 6-4 4-6 6-3 6-3
S. Zivojinovic (YU)	
Tom Gullikson	Annacone 6-4 6-4 3-6 6-1
P. Annacone	
P. Fleming	Fleming 6-4 6-2 7-6
R. Acuna (CH)	
M. Ostoja (YU)	Ostoja 6-4 6-7 2-6 7-6
R. Saad (ARG)	
D. Visser (SA)	Visser 6-4 6-1 6-2
R. Viver (EC)	
G. Holmes	Holmes 6-3 2-6 6-4 6-7 7-6
C. Motta (BR)	
P. McNamee (AUS)	KRIEK (12) 6-4 6-2 6-4
J. KRIEK (12)	
T. MAYOTTE (13)	MAYOTTE (13) 6-2 6-4
T. Moor	
J. M. Lloyd (GB)	Lloyd 7-5 7-5 7-5
V. Pecci (PARA)	
N. Odizor (NIG)	Odizor 6-4 6-2 6-0
B. Drewett (AUS)	
J. Canter	Canter 4-6 4-6 6-3 6-4
T. Segura	
T. Wilkison	Wilkison 6-4 6-3 4-6 7-5
V. Van Patten	
P. Slozil (CZ)	Slozil 6-3 6-3 4-6 7-6
F. Gonzalez (PARA)	
M. Bauer	Bauer 6-4 6-4 4-6 6-3
I. Nastase (RU)	
M. Pernfors (SW)	JARRYD (6) 6-3 7-6 6-4
A. JARRYD (SW) (6)	

THIRD ROUND

- McENROE (1) 6-0 7-5 6-1
- Schultz 6-3 6-4 7-6
- Arias 6-4 6-7 0-1 ret'd
- SMID (16) 6-2 6-2 6-1
- NYSTROM (10) 6-3 3-6 6-3 6-0
- Goldie 1-6 6-3 6-2 6-2
- Evernden 6-4 6-3 6-4
- BECKER (8) 6-3 6-0 6-2
- WILANDER (3) 6-3 7-5 6-3
- Annacone 2-6 7-5 7-5 6-1
- Holmes 2-6 6-3 6-4 6-1
- MAYOTTE (13) 4-6 6-1 7-6 7-5
- Odizor 7-6 2-6 6-2 7-6
- Wilkison 6-1 6-3 6-1
- JARRYD (6) 6-4 6-3 6-3

FOURTH ROUND

- McENROE (1) 6-3 6-4 6-4
- SMID (16) 4-6 6-7 6-3 6-3 7-6
- NYSTROM (10) 6-0 6-1 1-1 ret'd
- BECKER (8) 7-6 6-3 7-6
- WILANDER (3) 6-3 7-5 6-3
- Holmes 6-4 6-1 2-6 6-2
- MAYOTTE (13) 7-5 6-4 6-3
- JARRYD (6) 6-0 6-1 6-4

QUARTER-FINALS

- McENROE (1) 6-3 7-5 6-2
- NYSTROM (10) 6-3 6-4 4-6 6-4
- WILANDER (3) 6-3 6-4 4-6 6-4
- JARRYD (6) 7-6 7-6 6-4

SEMI-FINALS

- McENROE (1) 6-1 6-0 7-5
- WILANDER (3) 2-6 6-2 3-0 ret'd

FINAL

- McENROE (1) 3-6 6-4 4-6 6-3 6-3

I. LENDL (CZ) (2)

First round:

K. CURREN (5)
G. Forget (F)
H. Leconte (F)
W. Fibak (POL)
H. Schwaier (G)
B. Taroczy (HU)
T. Mmoh (NIG)
T. Hogstedt (SW)
H. Gunthardt (SWZ)
R. Krishnan (IND)
M. Purcell
L. Pimek (CZ)
B. Perez (SP)
S. Meister
M. Jaite (BR)
H. SUNDSTROM (SW) (14)
S. EDBERG (SW) (11)
J. L. Clerc (ARG)
K. Flach
L. Lavalle (MEX)
B. Gilbert
C. Van Rensburg (SA)
L. Jensen
M. Mitchell
T. Tulasne
J. Navratil (CZ)
P. Lundgren (SW)
S. Perkis (IS)
H. Pfister
S. McCan
G. Muller (SA)
J. S. CONNORS (4)
Y. NOAH (F) (7)
M. J. Bates (GB)
J. Grabb
J. Barbosa (BR)
V. Gerulatis
T. Benhabiles (F)
M. Dickson
J. Berger
D. Rostagno
E. Bengoechea (ARG)
C. Dowdeswell (GB)
B. Teacher
A. Ganzabal (ARG)
M. Cierro (IT)
S. DAVIS (15)
M. MECIR (CZ) (9)
C. Kohlberg
D. Pate
D. Oresar (YU)
D. Cassidy
E. El Mehlenry (EG)
J. Yzaga (PER)
J. Hlasek (SWZ)
H. de la Pena (ARG)
L. Palin (FIN)
C. Panatta (I)
Tim Gullikson
W. Scanlon
B. Testerman
B. Lapidus
I. LENDL (CZ) (2)

Round 2:

Forget 7–7 6–1 6–2
Leconte 3–6 6–3 6–4 4–6 6–4
Schwaier 6–7 6–4 7–5
Mmoh 6–4 8–3 6–6–1
Gunthardt 5–7 6–3 4–6 7–6 6–4
Purcell 6–3 6–4 6–2
Perez 6–3 6–3 6–4
Jaite 2–6 6–2 6–3
EDBERG (11)
Flach 7–5 6–2 2–6 6–1
Gilbert 6–2 6–2 6–2
Jensen 6–2 6–2 6–2
Tulasne 6–7 6–3 6–7 6–3 6–0
Lundgren 6–4 7–6 6–2
Pfister 6–3 6–4 6–4
CONNORS (4) 6–4 6–3 4–6 6–2
NOAH (7) 6–3 7–6 6–2
Grabb 6–2 6–7 7–5 6–3
Gerulatis 6–3 8–7 7–5
Nelson 7–6 4–6 7–6
Berger 6–4 6–7 0–6 7–5 6–4
Bengoechea 4–6 7–6 7–5 6–4
Teacher 6–1 6–4 7–5
S. DAVIS (15) 6–4 6–0 6–4
MECIR (9) 5–7 4–6 7–6 6–3 6–1
Pate 6–2 6–3 2–6 6–0
Cassidy 6–4 6–7 6–0 6–3
Yzaga 5–7 7–5 3–6 6–4 6–3
de la Pena 3–6 6–3 6–2 4–6 6–4
Panatta 7–6 6–3 2–6 6–4
Scanlon 7–6 7–6 0–6 5–7 6–3
LENDL (2) 6–2 6–1 6–3

Round 3:

Leconte 6–4 6–4
Schwaier 5–7 6–7 7–5 7–5 6–3
Gunthardt 5–7 6–2 6–1 6–2
Jaite 6–3 7–6 6–3
EDBERG (11) 7–5 6–3 6–4
Gilbert 6–3 6–2 6–3
Tulasne 7–6 1–6 7–5 6–3
CONNORS (4) 6–3 6–4 6–2
NOAH (7) 7–6 6–3 6–2
Gerulatis 6–2 3–6 6–2 7–6
Berger 6–1 6–3 6–2
Teacher 6–3 7–6 6–3
Pate 6–4 6–0 6–3
Yzaga 6–7 6–3 6–7 6–17–5
de la Pena 6–7 7–5 7–6 6–3
LENDL (2) 6–2 6–0 6–3

Round 4:

Leconte 6–2 6–1
Gunthardt 6–7 3–6 7–6 6–4 6–1
EDBERG (11) 4–6 6–4 6–1 6–4
CONNORS (4) 7–5 6–2 6–4
NOAH (7) 6–3 6–4 6–3
Berger 4–6 7–5 6–4 7–6
Yzaga 6–3 6–3 7–6
LENDL (2) 6–1 6–1 6–3

Quarterfinals:

Leconte 6–2 6–1
Gunthardt 7–6 6–2 3–6 4–6 6–3
CONNORS (4) 7–5 6–2 6–4
NOAH (7) 6–7 6–2 6–3 6–1

Semifinals:

Gunthardt 7–6 6–2 3–6 4–6 6–3
CONNORS (4) 6–4 3–6 6–3 6–4
LENDL (2) 4–6 6–3 6–4 6–0

Final region:

CONNORS (4) 6–2 6–2 6–4
LENDL (2) 6–2 6–2 6–4

LENDL (2) 6–2 6–3 7–5

Capital letters denote seeded players. Number following player's name gives seeding order.

WOMEN'S SINGLES

Holder: M. Navratilova (USA)

7-6 1-6 7-6

FIRST ROUND	SECOND ROUND	THIRD ROUND	FOURTH ROUND	QUARTER-FINALS	SEMI-FINALS	FINAL
MRS J. M. LLOYD (1)	LLOYD (1) 6–1 6–3	LLOYD (1) 6–0 6–3	LLOYD (1) 6–0 6–2	LLOYD (1) 6–2 6–4	LLOYD (1) 6–3 6–3	MANDLIKOVA (3) 4–6 6–2 6–3
J. Thompson (AUS)						
C. Karlsson (SW)	Reggi 4–6 6–3 6–3					
R. Reggi (IT)						
M. L. Piatek	Piatek 6–2 6–4	Kim 7–6 7–6				
C. Joilissant (SWZ)						
B. Bunge (g)	Kim 6–4 6–4					
G. Kim						
C. Tanvier (F)	R. White 0–6 7–6 6–4	R. White 6–2 6–2	R. White 1–6 6–1 6–2			
A. Betzner (G)						
P. Keppeler (G)	Keppeler 6–1 3–6 6–3					
M. Jausovec (YU)	Jausovec 7–5 6–1					
D. Balestrat (AUS)						
G. Fernandez	GADUSEK (14) 6–2 7–5	GADUSEK (14) 6–0 4–6 6–2				
W. M. TURNBULL (AUS) (12)	TURNBULL (12) 6–4 6–1	TURNBULL (12) 7–5 6–2	TURNBULL (12) 7–6 6–1	KOHDE-KILSCH (5) 5–7 7–5 6–2		
V. Ruzici (RU)						
B. Herr	Herr 6–3 6–2					
Mrs S. Walsh Pete						
M. Torres	Torres 7–6 6–7 6–2	Torres 3–6 6–2 6–0				
Mrs K. Shaefer						
S. Amiach (F)	Skronska 6–4 6–7 6–2					
K. Skronska (CZ)						
K. Henricksson	Henricksson 6–1 6–4	Henricksson 6–1 6–4	KOHDE-KILSCH (5) 6–3 6–4			
K. Horvath						
S. Gomer (GB)	M. J. Fernandez 6–1 6–4					
M. J. Fernandez						
A. Villagran (ARG)	Villagran 7–6 3–6 6–4	KOHDE-KILSCH (5) 6–1 6–1				
A. Kanellopoulou (GR)						
N. Dias (BR)	KOHDE-KILSCH (5) 7–6 6–1					
C. KOHDE-KILSCH (G) (5)						
H. MANDLIKOVA (CZ) (3)	MANDLIKOVA (3) 7–6 6–1	MANDLIKOVA (3) 6–3 6–3	MANDLIKOVA (3) 6–3 6–4	MANDLIKOVA (3) 7–5 3–6 6–1	MANDLIKOVA (3) 7–6 7–5	
A. Brown (GB)						
A. Croft (GB)	Croft 6–2 6–1					
M. Skuherska (CZ)						
C. Suire (F)	Allen 6–1 7–5	Hanika 6–0 6–0				
L. Allen						
S. Hanika (G)	Hanika 6–4 6–2					
R. Fairbank (SA)						
K. Jordan	Jordan 7–6 6–3	Jordan 3–6 6–2 6–2	Jordan 7–5 6–1			
K. Mesker (NTH)						
A. Jaeger	Jaeger 2–6 6–1 6–2					
L. Gildemeister (PER)						
S. Rehe	Phelps 7–5 2–6 6–1	Phelps 5–7 7–5 6–3				
T. Phelps						
B. Potter	Potter 6–1 6–4					
C. SABATINI (ARG) (10)						
I. BASSETT (C) (15)	BASSETT (15) 6–1 6–4	BASSETT (15) 6–2 6–1	BASSETT (15) 6–4 6–4	SUKOVA (7) 4–6 7–6 7–5		
I. Budarova (CZ)						
M. Paz (ARG)	Paz 6–0 6–7 7–5					
V. Nelson						
L. Gates	Gates 6–4 6–2	Gates 0–6 6–2 6–3				
L. Antonoplis						
L. Spain Short	Spain Short 6–3 6–4					
A. M. Fernandez						
C. Benjamin	Benjamin 6–4 6–3	Benjamin 6–1 6–2	SUKOVA (7) 6–0 7–5			
I. Demongeot (F)						
B. Jordan	Garrone 6–4 6–3					
C. Garrone (IT)						
B. Bowes	Bowes 6–2 6–4	SUKOVA (7) 6–3 6–1				
J. Mundel (SA)						
H. SUKOVA (CZ) (7)	SUKOVA (7) 6–1 6–0					

H. MANDLIKOVA (CZ) (3)

Women's Singles draw (lower half)

Entry	1st round	2nd round	3rd round	4th round	Quarter-final	Semi-final	Final
M. MALEEVA (BUL) (8)	MALEEVA (8) 6-1 6-1	MALEEVA (8) 6-0 7-6	MALEEVA (8) 6-4 7-5				
S. Mascarin							
J. Klitch	Cueto 6-4 7-5						
I. Cueto (G)							
P. Huber (AU)	Huber 7-6 6-1	Burgin 6-4 6-4		GRAF (11) 6-2 6-2			
D. Spence							
E. Burgin	Burgin 6-0 6-1						
Y. Vermaak (SA)							
H. Kelesi (C)	A. White 6-3 2-6 6-4	A. White 6-4 6-1	GRAF (11) 6-4 6-2				
A. White							
P. Louie	Foltz 6-4 6-4						
S. Foltz							
A. Minter (AUS)	A. Minter 6-3 6-4	GRAF (11) 6-3 7-6			GRAF (11) 6-2 6-2		
E. Minter (AUS)							
P. Fendick	GRAF (11) 4-6 7-5						
S. GRAF (G) (11)							
A. TEMESVARI (HU) (16)	TEMESVARI (16) 6-2 4-6 6-2	Kuhlnan 6-4 6-4				GRAF (11) 7-6 6-7 7-6	
K. Maleeva (BUL)							
C. Kuhlnan	Kuhlnan 6-4 6-4						
L. McNeil							
A. Moulton	Moulton 6-2 7-5	Moulton 7-5 6-4	Moulton 6-4 1-6 7-6				
B. Mould (SA)							
R. Uys (SA)	Goles 6-7 6-1 7-6						
S. Goles (YU)							
R. Casals	Casals 1-0 ret'd	Hobbs 6-2 6-4		SHRIVER (4) 6-2 6-4			
B. Nagelsen							
A. E. Hobbs (GB)	Hobbs 7-5 6-1						
J. M. Durie (GB)							
E. Pfaff (G)	Hu Na 6-4	SHRIVER (4) 6-2 6-3	SHRIVER (4) 6-2 6-3				
Hu Na (CHI)							
T. Scheuer-Larsen (D)	SHRIVER (4) 6-3 6-3						
P. H. SHRIVER (4)							
Z. GARRISON (6)	GARRISON (6) 6-2 6-4	GARRISON (6) 6-2 6-4	GARRISON (6) 6-4 6-4		GARRISON (6) 6-3 6-2		
E. Gerken							
E. Rossides	Casale 6-3 6-2						
P. Casale							
M. Werdel	Werdel 6-2 6-4	Cordwell 6-2 7-6		GARRISON (6) 6-4 6-4			
M. Schropp							
B. Cordwell (NZ)	Cordwell 6-3 6-4						
M. Lindstrom (SW)							
P. Medrado (BR)	Gompert 6-3 6-4	Gompert 6-3 6-1	Gompert 6-4 7-6				
K. Gompert							
J. Russell	Young 7-6 6-3					NAVRATILOVA (2) 6-2 6-3	
J. Young (C)							
T. Holladay	Drescher 6-0 6-2	Holikova 6-3 2-6 6-4		LINDQVIST (13) 7-5 6-0			
L. Drescher (SWZ)							
A. Holikova (CZ)	Holikova 7-6 7-6						
K. RINALDI (9)							
C. LINDQVIST (SW) (13)	LINDQVIST (13) 6-2 6-0	LINDQVIST (13) 6-1 6-2	LINDQVIST (13) 7-5 6-0		NAVRATILOVA (2) 6-4 7-5		
M. Gurney							
Mrs E. Smylie (AUS)	Holton 5-7 6-4 6-1						
L. Hotton							
S. Collins	Thompson 6-1 3-6 6-1	Thompson 6-4 2-5 ret'd		NAVRATILOVA (2) 6-0 6-1			
E. Rapponi-Longo (ARG)							
R. Marsikova (CZ)	Marsikova 6-3 6-2						
W. White							
M. Van Nostrand	Van Nostrand 7-6 6-1	Cecchini 6-4 6-4	NAVRATILOVA (2) 6-0 6-1				
S. Cecchini (IT)	Cecchini 2-6 6-1 6-2						
E. Inoue (J)							
L. Bonder	Bonder 6-2 4-6 6-3						
A. Ivan		NAVRATILOVA (2) 6-1 6-1					
P. Paradis (F)	NAVRATILOVA (2) 6-2 6-1						
M. NAVRATILOVA (2)							NAVRATILOVA (2) 6-2 6-3

Capital letters denote seeded players. Number following player's name gives seeding order.

MEN'S DOUBLES

Holders: J. Fitzgerald (AUS)/T. Smid (CZ)

Winner: K. FLACH (USA)/R. SEGUSO (USA) (1) 7–6 6–7 7–6 6–0

FIRST ROUND	SECOND ROUND	THIRD ROUND	QUARTER-FINALS	SEMI-FINALS	FINAL

FIRST ROUND

- K. FLACH/R. SEGUSO (1)
- C. Garner/B. Papell
- D. Cassidy/D. Graham
- P. Doohan/R. Knapp
- L. Jansen/C. Steyn
- An. Amritraj/M. Fancutt
- P. McNAMARA/P. McNAMEE (11)
- W. FIBAK/L. PIMEK (10)
- S. McCain/S. Perkis
- F. Gonzalez/J. Lapidus
- M. Mortensen/H. Simonsson
- M. Bauer/B. Willenborg
- D. Dowlen/N. Odizor
- R. Baxter/G. Gitlin
- J. FITZGERALD/M. MITCHELL (8)
- H. GUNTHARDT/B. TAROCZY (3)
- M. DePalmer/G. Donnelly
- V. Amritraj/J. Sadri
- E. Edwards/D. Visser
- M. Acuna/E. Fernandez
- R. Doyle/R. Meyer
- H. GILDEMEISTER/V. PECCI (13)
- K. CURREN/J. KRIEK (16)
- B. Gilbert/V. Van Patten
- A. Giammalva/B. Manson
- J.M. Lloyd/R. L. Stockton
- J. G. Alexander/B. Walts
- G.G. Key/ ...
- B. Cox/B. Strode
- M. R. EDMONDSON/K. WARWICK (6)
- P. ANNACONE/C. VAN RENSBURG (7)
- M. Davis/C. Dunk
- K. Evernden/M. Robertson
- T. Delatte/M. Purcell
- S. Meister/E. Wittus
- S. Masur/F. Wittus
- A. Kohlberg/R. Van't Hof
- B. DYKE/W. MASUR (9)
- H. LECONTE/Y. NOAH (12)
- C. Panatta/C. Jones
- B. Becker/S. Zivojinovic
- N. Aerts/J. Soares
- P. Hjertquist/D. Tarr
- C. Hooper/L. Shiras
- P. SLOZIL/T. SMID (4)
- J. NYSTROM/M. WILANDER (5)
- L. Palin/D. Perez
- L. Courteau/G. Forget
- B. Gilde.../C. Kennedy
- D. Dickinson/J. Manset
- L. Bourne/M. Freeman
- E. Adams/M. Wooldridge
- S. DAVIS/D. PATE (14)
- S. DENTON/P. FLEMING (15)
- J. Hlasek/C. Motta
- J. Andrews/G. Layendecker
- B. Levine/E. Van't Hof
- M. Dickson/T. Wilkison
- J. Arias/G. Holmes
- H. Pfister/B. Testerman
- S. EDBERG/A. JARRYD (2)

SECOND ROUND

- FLACH/SEGUSO (1) 6–0 6–1
- Doohan/Knapp 6–4 2–6 6–3
- Jansen/P. McEnroe 6–4 6–1
- McNAMARA/McNAMEE (11)
- FIBAK/PIMEK (10) 7–6 3–6 6–2
- Mortensen/Simonsson 6–2 2–6 6–2
- Dowlen/Odizor 6–4 3–6 6–1
- FITZGERALD/MITCHELL (8) 6–3 6–3
- DePalmer/Donnelly
- Tim/Tom Gullikson 6–3 3–6 6–4
- Acuna/Fernandez
- GILDEMEISTER/PECCI (13) 7–6 6–2
- CURREN/KRIEK (16) 6–3 6–2
- Giammalva/Manson 6–4 7–6
- Alexander/Walts
- EDMONDSON/WARWICK (6) 6–1 6–4
- ANNACONE/VAN RENSBURG (7)
- Evernden/Robertson 6–7 7–5 6–4
- Meister/Wittus
- Kohlberg/R. Van't Hof 6–1 7–6
- LECONTE/NOAH (12)
- Becker/Zivojinovic 6–2 6–2
- Aerts/Soares 6–3 6–2
- Hooper/Shiras 7–5 6–2
- NYSTROM/WILANDER (5) 6–3 6–1
- Courteau/Forget 6–3 6–3
- Dickinson/Manset 6–4 7–6
- S. DAVIS/PATE (14) 6–4 5–7 6–4
- DENTON/FLEMING (15) 5–7 6–3 6–4
- Levine/E. Van't Hof 7–6 7–6
- Dickson/Wilkison 6–2 6–2
- EDBERG/JARRYD (2) 7–5 6–1

THIRD ROUND

- FLACH/SEGUSO (1) 6–4 6–3
- McNAMARA/McNAMEE (11) 6–4 1–6 6–3
- Mortensen/Simonsson 6–4 6–4
- FITZGERALD/MITCHELL (8) 4–6 6–2 6–3
- DePalmer/Donnelly 2–6 7–6 7–6
- Acuna/Fernandez 6–4 6–4
- CURREN/KRIEK (16) 6–4 6–3
- EDMONDSON/WARWICK (6) 7–6 3–6 6–1
- ANNACONE/VAN RENSBURG (7) 6–3 7–6
- Kohlberg/R. Van't Hof 6–4 7–6
- LECONTE/NOAH (12) 6–7 7–6 7–6
- Aerts/Soares 6–4 3–6 6–3
- NYSTROM/WILANDER (5) 6–3 7–6
- S. DAVIS/PATE (14) 3–6 6–3 6–0
- DENTON/FLEMING (15) 6–2 6–7 7–6
- Dickson/Wilkison 4–6 6–4 6–3

QUARTER-FINALS

- FLACH/SEGUSO (1) 6–4 6–7 7–6
- Mortensen/Simonsson 6–7 6–4 6–3
- DePalmer/Donnelly 7–6 6–2
- CURREN/KRIEK (16) 6–0 7–5
- Kohlberg/R. Van't Hof 6–3 2–6 6–4
- LECONTE/NOAH (12) 7–5 7–6
- NYSTROM/WILANDER (5) 6–3 7–6
- DENTON/FLEMING (15) 6–7 7–5 7–6

SEMI-FINALS

- FLACH/SEGUSO (1) 6–4 7–5 6–2
- DePalmer/Donnelly 6–1 7–6 4–6 7–6
- LECONTE/NOAH (12) 7–6 4–6 5–7 7–6 7–6
- NYSTROM/WILANDER (5) 6–3 6–4 6–4

FINAL

- FLACH/SEGUSO (1) 6–1 6–7 5–7 7–6
- LECONTE/NOAH (12) 6–3 7–6 6–4

Capital letters denote seeded pairings. Number following players' names gives seeding order.

WOMEN'S DOUBLES

Holders: M. Navratilova (USA)/P. H. Shriver (USA)

Winner: C. KOHDE-KILSCH (G)/H. SUKOVA (CZ) 6–7 (2) 6–2 6–3

FIRST ROUND

- M. NAVRATILOVA/P. H. SHRIVER (1)
- C. MacGregor/J. Richardson
- C. Benjamin/R. Blount
- J. Kaplan/I. Kuczynska
- S. Goles/E. Rappan-Longo
- M. Jausovec/M. Schropp
- B. Jordan/B. Stove
- G. REYNOLDS/P. SMITH (11)
- S. FERNANDEZ/R. WHITE (9)
- S. Foltz/M. Quinlan
- Y. Vermaak/I. Kloss
- J. M. Durie/S. Graf
- P. Fendick/J. Hetherington
- A. Holikova/K. Skronska
- L. Bonder/S. Mascarin
- E. BURGIN/A. MOULTON (7)
- H. MANDLIKOVA/W. M. TURNBULL (4)
- A. Brown/S. Gomer
- S. Collins/M. L. Piatek
- N. Sodupe/S. London
- M. Paz/G. Sabatini
- P. Barg/R. Reis
- A. E. HOBBS/C. JOLISSAINT (16)
- K. M. MALEEVA (14)
- C. Lindqvist/J. Russell
- C. Cecchini/N. Dias
- K. McDaniel/W. White
- C. Karlsson/T. Scheuer-Larsen
- B. Loue/Mrs K. Shaefer
- K. BUNGE/E. PFAFF (6)
- C. BASSETT/Mrs J. M. LLOYD (8)
- L. Drescher/E. Inoue
- I. Budarova/M. Skuherska
- J. Golder/V. Nelson
- P. Casale/R. Reggi
- L. Antonoplis/A. Henricksson
- K. Allen/K. Copeland
- V. HORVATH/K. RUZICI (13)
- R. FAIRBANK/B. GADUSEK (10)
- B. Mould/P. Whytcross
- Z. Garrison/K. Rinaldi
- A. Jaeger/A. White
- Mrs L. Gildemeister/A. Holton
- J. Amach/B. Gerken
- J. Mundel/M. Van Nostrand
- K. JORDAN/A. E. SMYLIE (3)
- B. POTTER/Mrs S. WALSH PETE (5)
- N. Sato/K. Steinmetz
- T. Mochizuki/E. Okagawa
- H. Crowe/A. M. Fernandez
- A./E. Minter
- T. Holladay/L. Howell
- P. Huber/A. Kanellopoulou
- M. MESKER/P. PARADIS (12)
- A. TEMESVARI/A. VILLAGRAN (15)
- L. McNeil/K. Sands
- P. Demongeot/N. Tauziat
- E. Goolagong/T. Pelletier
- R. Casals/J. E. Smith
- S. Suire/S. V. Wade
- C. KOHDE-KILSCH/H. SUKOVA (2)

SECOND ROUND

- NAVRATILOVA/SHRIVER (1) 6–4 6–2
- Benjamin/Blount 6–3 6–3
- Jausovec/Schropp 6–4 6–4
- REYNOLDS/P. SMITH (11) 3–6 6–1 6–2
- FERNANDEZ/R. WHITE (9) 6–2 6–1
- Durie/Graf 5–7 6–3 6–1
- Fendick/Hetherington 7–5 6–3
- BURGIN/MOULTON (7) 6–4 6–4
- MANDLIKOVA/TURNBULL (4) 6–1 6–1
- Collins/Piatek 6–2 6–4
- Herr/Phelps 6–3 2–6 6–3
- HOBBS/JOLISSAINT (16) 6–4 7–5
- K.M. MALEEVA (14) 6–2 6–3
- Lindqvist/Russell 7–6 6–1
- Karlsson/Scheuer-Larsen 6–4 6–2
- BUNGE/PFAFF (6) 7–6 6–0
- BASSETT/LLOYD (8) 6–2 6–4
- Budarova/Skuherska 6–2 6–3
- Casale/Reggi 6–1 6–1
- HORVATH/RUZICI (13) 6–1 6–1
- Garrison/Rinaldi 6–4 6–3
- Gildemeister/Holton 5–7 7–6 7–6
- JORDAN/SMYLIE (3) 7–6 6–3
- POTTER/WALSH PETE (5) 6–2 7–6
- Crowe/Fernandez 3–6 6–2 6–4
- A./E. Minter 6–2 6–2
- MESKER/PARADIS (12) 2–6 6–2 6–3
- McNeil/Sands 6–2 6–3
- Demongeot/Tauziat 6–3 6–2
- Casals/A. Smith 6–2 6–3
- KOHDE-KILSCH/SUKOVA (2) 6–4 6–4

THIRD ROUND

- NAVRATILOVA/SHRIVER (1) 6–4 6–2
- REYNOLDS/P. SMITH (11) 6–2 6–0
- FERNANDEZ/R. WHITE (9) 6–4 7–6
- MANDLIKOVA/TURNBULL (4) 6–2 6–2
- HOBBS/JOLISSAINT (16) 3–6 6–4 6–3
- Lindqvist/Russell 6–0 6–4
- BUNGE/PFAFF (6) 6–2 6–4
- BASSETT/LLOYD (8) 6–3 6–4
- HORVATH/RUZICI (13) 0–6 7–6 6–3
- Garrison/Rinaldi 6–3 6–2
- Gildemeister/Holton 6–3 6–3
- POTTER/WALSH PETE (5) 6–3 6–3
- MESKER/PARADIS (12) 6–4 3–6 7–5
- McNeil/Sands 7–6 6–1
- KOHDE-KILSCH/SUKOVA (2) 6–2 7–5

QUARTER-FINALS

- NAVRATILOVA/SHRIVER (1) 6–2 6–2
- FERNANDEZ/R. WHITE (9) 6–2 6–2
- MANDLIKOVA/TURNBULL (4) 6–3 6–4
- Lindqvist/Russell 6–7 6–4 6–0
- BASSETT/LLOYD (8) 6–4 6–2
- Garrison/Rinaldi 6–1 6–2
- POTTER/WALSH PETE (5) 3–6 6–1 7–6
- KOHDE-KILSCH/SUKOVA (2) 6–7 6–4 6–4

SEMI-FINALS

- NAVRATILOVA/SHRIVER (1) 6–3 6–0
- MANDLIKOVA/TURNBULL (4) 6–1 3–6 6–1
- Garrison/Rinaldi 6–2 6–3
- KOHDE-KILSCH/SUKOVA (2) 6–7 6–4 6–3

FINAL

- NAVRATILOVA/SHRIVER (1) 6–3 6–4
- KOHDE-KILSCH/SUKOVA (2) 5–7 6–4 6–3

Capital letters denote seeded pairings. Number following players' names gives seeding order.

MIXED DOUBLES

Holders: Tom Gullikson (USA)/Miss M. Maleeva (BUL)

Winner: H. GUNTHARDT (SWZ) / M. NAVRATILOVA (USA) (1) 6–3 6–4

FIRST ROUND

- H. GUNTHARDT/M. NAVRATILOVA (1)
- G. Barbosa/P. Medrado
- B. Dyke/H. Crowe
- S. Perkis/P. Barg
- D. Graham/P. Casale
- K. Warwick/S. V. Wade
- M. Mitchell/P. Louie
- I. NASTASE/H. MANDLIKOVA (7)
- S. DENTON/K. JORDAN (4)
- S. Meister/I. Kloss
- D. Gitlin/J. Russell
- M. Bauer/E. Burgin
- T. Delatte/C. Reynolds
- L. Shiras/K. Horvath
- M. Fancutt/B. Gadusek
- TOM GULLIKSON/M. MALEEVA (6)
- H./L. GILDEMEISTER (8)
- M. Freeman/Z. Garrison
- R. Acuna/J. Hetherington
- H. Gildemeister/B. Bunge
- C. Motta/C. Monteiro
- B. Walts/R. White
- K. Strode/K. Maleeva
- J. M. LLOYD/W. M. TURNBULL (3)
- G. DONNELLY/P. SMITH (5)
- H. Pfister/Mrs K. Shaefer
- M. R. Edmondson/P. Whytcross
- J. G. Alexander/R. Casals
- C. Dunk/M. L. Piatek
- M. Davis/Mrs S. A. Walsh Pete
- J. FITZGERALD/MRS E. SMYLIE (2)

SECOND ROUND

- GUNTHARDT/M. NAVRATILOVA (1) 6–1 6–4
- Perkis/Barg 6–4 7–6
- Warwick/Wade 6–3 6–3
- NASTASE/MANDLIKOVA (7) 6–1 6–4
- Meister/Kloss 6–2 6–4
- Gitlin/Russell 6–2 6–2
- Shiras/Horvath 7–6 3–6 7–6
- TOM GULLIKSON/M. MALEEVA (6) 7–6 6–7 7–6
- Freeman/Garrison w.o.
- H. Gildemeister/Bunge 6–3 6–4
- Walts/R. White 6–4 7–5
- LLOYD/TURNBULL (3) 6–2 6–4
- DONNELLY/P. SMITH (5) 6–4 6–4
- Edmondson/Whytcross 2–6 7–6 6–2
- Dunk/Piatek 6–3 3–6 6–3
- FITZGERALD/SMYLIE (2) 6–4 6–4

QUARTER-FINALS

- GUNTHARDT/NAVRATILOVA (1) 6–2 6–3
- Warwick/Wade 6–7 6–4 7–5
- Gitlin/Russell 3–6 7–5 6–3
- Shiras/Horvath 6–4 6–2
- Freeman/Garrison 7–6 6–4
- LLOYD/TURNBULL (3) 7–5 6–7 6–1
- DONNELLY/SMITH (5) 6–2 6–7 6–4
- FITZGERALD/SMYLIE (2) 7–5 6–3

SEMI-FINALS

- GUNTHARDT/NAVRATILOVA (1) 6–3 3–6 6–3
- Shiras/Horvath 7–6 6–7 6–3
- LLOYD/TURNBULL (3) 6–4 6–4
- FITZGERALD/SMYLIE (2) 6–2 7–5

FINAL

- GUNTHARDT/NAVRATILOVA (1) 6–4 6–2
- FITZGERALD/SMYLIE (2) 6–4 6–3

Capital letters denote seeded pairings. Number following players' names gives seeding order.

After winning a dour first set on a tie-break, Lendl blunted the attack of the holder, John McEnroe, to complete a straight-sets victory that ended a run of three successive final losses in the US Open. *(T. Hindley)*

With a first Grand Slam win in Melbourne, 19-year-old Stefan Edberg gave notice to Wimbledon's young champion, Boris Becker, that the battle for world supremacy would be a stern one.
(R. Gould)

AUSTRALIAN OPEN CHAMPIONSHIPS

Alan Trengove

Any player seeded fifth in a Grand Slam championship ought to be good enough to stand a reasonable chance of winning the title, but nobody seriously considered that Stefan Edberg would win the Australian Open, except possibly the young Swede himself. Although he had proved himself at Kooyong two years before, when he had won the fourth leg of his junior Grand Slam, this was the strongest field yet for the Australian Open, and all four players seeded above Edberg – Ivan Lendl, John McEnroe, Mats Wilander and Boris Becker – appeared to hold far superior credentials.

Yet some of the more fancied stars were clearly either under-prepared for a major grass-court championship, or were simply not in the mood to play their best tennis. Displaying great self-discipline and courage, as well as a fine brand of aggressive serve-and-volley tennis, Edberg – then still not 20 years of age – won his first Grand Slam crown by comfortably beating the holder, Wilander, 6–4 6–3 6–3 in a rain-delayed final. This was the first time (though surely not the last) that two Swedes had fought out a Grand Slam final. The Open was also significant in that, for the first time, all four semi-finalists were Europeans, although the much vaunted Boris Becker, the reigning Wimbledon champion, wasn't one of them. In fact Becker did not survive his first match in the second round. History was made, too, when no Australian reached the quarter-finals. Even allowing for the indisposition of Pat Cash and Paul McNamee, this failure – following the inglorious Australian displays in the men's singles at Wimbledon and the US Open – underlined the decline in Australian tennis.

The Open was marred by very wet weather, which made the courts more slippery than usual, to the irritation of the top two seeds. Both Lendl and McEnroe were highly critical of the state of the courts, their court behaviour and press statements costing them public sympathy, and their negative attitudes probably contributing to their defeats. Having spent the previous few months playing indoor tennis, both found adjustment to wind, rain, spasmodic sunshine, and capricious grass courts extremely difficult.

McEnroe, who did not arrive in Melbourne until the day the event started, looked tired and strained. On the morning after his arrival he became involved in an unseemly scuffle with a news reporter in the lobby of his city hotel and later gave a long, rambling press conference which was likened by some participants to a group therapy session. McEnroe had not taken his girlfriend, Tatum O'Neal, to Wimbledon for fear of press intrusion, and had resented the separation. Here, he was accompanied by Miss O'Neal, but was highly sensitive to any press questions about their relationship. His private life would not normally be relevant to the championships but this time it appeared to have a bearing on what transpired. He frequently denied that he and Miss O'Neal were married or were to become parents. But within a day of the conclusion of the championships he announced that he *was* to become a father. The conflict in his mind perhaps helps to explain his tetchiness and lack of concentration on the court.

McEnroe had been through a relatively poor year, failing at all the other Grand Slam tournaments. He turned up at Kooyong because, after pulling out at the eleventh hour the previous year, he had promised tournament director Colin Stubs that he would do so, and also because he still hoped to win one Grand Slam title, to retain some chance of ousting Lendl from the pinnacle of the game. However, his mind was in too much of a turmoil to permit him to do justice to his extraordinary talent.

He struggled bad-temperedly to beat Danie Visser and Nduka Odizor, and should have been beaten by Henri Leconte in the fourth round. The latter match was played, at

McEnroe's insistence, on one of the field courts, where only 1,500 people could be accommodated. When Leconte led by two sets to one and by five points to one in the fourth-set tie-break, McEnroe looked almost resigned to defeat, but had just enough determination and competitive know-how to hang in and allow the over-excited Frenchman to destroy himself. In his quarter-final against Slobodan Zivojinovic, the American was again erratic, this time paying the full penalty as he lost in five sets to the powerful Yugoslav. He was booed off the centre court by a section of the crowd who thought he had 'tanked' the last few points, and hurriedly left the grounds without attending the mandatory press conference. For this misdemeanour he incurred a $1,000 fine, which brought his total for the tournament to $3,750, exceeding the 12-month limit on fines, so that a 21-day suspension followed.

At times, Lendl seemed as disgruntled as McEnroe. For his on-court excesses he was fined a total of $1,850, necessitating a 21-day suspension for him, too. Despite his misgivings about the courts, he looked to be running into good form when he overwhelmed an in-form John Lloyd in their quarter-final. The power of his service, the severity of his groundstrokes and his new-found volleying dexterity were proving a devastating combination. He had not lost a Grand Prix match since before the US Open and, above all, he had Tony Roche in his corner.

In the semi-finals, however, Lendl had the misfortune to meet young Edberg, who had improved with every match — and needed to, his form having been indifferent at the start of the championships. Unlike most of the other seeds, Edberg had played in the Western Australian Open before heading for Kooyong. He had lost there in the first round to a little-known local player, Roger Grant, and was still trying to find confidence in the opening rounds at Kooyong. In the third round he trailed Matt Anger by 5–7 and by 1–6 in the second-set tie-break. And in the fourth round he lost the first two sets to Wally Masur, saving two match-points in the third before winning in five sets. Had Masur not been suffering from a thigh strain, the Swede almost certainly would have lost.

After this match, Edberg's rhythm and timing rapidly improved. He comfortably disposed of the Dutchman, Michiel Schapers, who had sensationally eliminated Becker, 3–6 6–4 7–6 4–6 6–3, in one of the biggest upsets in the history of the tournament. The fearless hitting which often had saved the young German at Wimbledon looked, on this occasion, merely reckless, and his inexperience was obvious. The rain-protracted match between Lendl and Edberg was the best of the fortnight, yet after the first two sets had been split it seemed that the Czech was close to 'tanking' in the third, in which he won only one game. Lendl was fretting about the slipperiness and unevenness of the court, as well as a sore knee, but then, after a rain-delay at 4–all in the fourth set, he hit some sizzling shots to take the next two games and break Edberg's opening service in the fifth set. It said volumes for Edberg's character that he could weather Lendl's onslaught and immediately break back. The fifth set developed into a thriller, with Edberg's sustained big serving and brilliant backhand finally giving him victory at 9–7.

Meanwhile, Wilander, winner of the title in 1983 and 1984, was waiting confidently for his opponent in the final to emerge. Though wearing a brace to support a strained right arm, he was in even better touch than in 1983, and had beaten Leif Shiras, Tim Wilkison, Johan Kriek and Zivojinovic without dropping a set. Unfortunately, he either peaked a little too soon or lost his momentum because of the long waits caused by rain, and was never really in the final, which was dominated by Edberg's almost flawless serving and volleying. Wilander reached 30 on Edberg's serve only five times, and 40 but once. It was an impressively mature piece of grass-court tennis by the youngster, and the sporting manner in which the final was played was appreciated by a crowd that had found the tantrums of the top seeds more than tiresome.

In contrast to the men's singles, the women's championship was largely uneventful, with only Pam Shriver of the top eight seeds failing to take her place in the quarter-finals. Miss Shriver succumbed to a barrage of accurate groundstrokes from the Swede, Catarina Lindqvist, after leading 6–3 3–1.

Main interest was focused once again on the rivalry between Chris Evert Lloyd, the No. 1 seed, and Martina Navratilova, the No. 2, who both agreed that this championship would determine the world championship for 1985. Each had prepared assiduously for the showdown. Navratilova had played — and won — the two lead-up tournaments in Brisbane and Sydney, while Evert Lloyd had been practising for a week at Kooyong with her husband, John, and coach, Bob Brett. Navratilova also hoped to atone, if possible, for her dramatic defeat by Hana Mandlikova in the US Open final.

As it turned out, Navratilova gained increasing satisfaction in her last three matches, for in her quarter-final she met Helena Sukova, who had beaten her in a semi-final here in 1984, and outclassed her 6–2 6–2; then she recovered from a few shaky moments to overcome Mandlikova 6–7 6–1 6–4, assisted by her opponent's ten double-faults.

If anything, Evert Lloyd had an even more comfortable run to the final, conceding a set to Betsy Nagelsen in the second round, but easily accounting for Manuela Maleeva in the quarters, and then stopping a dangerous Claudia Kohde-Kilsch, 6–1 7–6. Playing their 67th match against each other, the finalists were both tentative at first, but Navratilova settled down more quickly. A double-fault and a badly fluffed volley by Evert Lloyd in the fourth game hurt her confidence to such an extent that she uncharacteristically made a string of errors to lose the first set 6–2. Like the great fighter she is, she came to terms with the swirling wind, tightened her groundstrokes and took the second set 6–4 on her eighth set-point. The reverse prompted Navratilova to become more decisive. In the third set she showed an even greater willingness to force the issue at the net and she made the crucial breakthrough in the fourth game. An umpiring mix-up in the next game dashed one of Evert Lloyd's last remaining hopes, and Navratilova took her rival's service yet again to secure the match and her third Australian crown.

The doubles events were even more affected by the inclement weather than the singles, and only one men's doubles match was staged on the centre court over the entire tournament. In the men's doubles final, which was played on an outside court while the women's doubles final was being held on centre court, Paul Annacone and Christo Van Rensburg won their first Grand Slam title by beating Mark Edmondson and Kim Warwick 3–6 7–6 6–4 6–4. Defending champions Navratilova and Shriver crushed Kohde-Kilsch and Sukova 6–3 6–4 in the women's final.

JUNIOR EVENTS

BOYS' SINGLES – Final: S. Barr d. S. Furlong 7–6 6–7 6–3.
GIRLS' SINGLES – Final: J. Byrne d. L. Field 6–1 6–3.
BOYS' DOUBLES – Final: B. Custer /D. McPherson d. C. Suk (CZ) /P. Korda (CZ) 7–5 6–2.
GIRLS' DOUBLES – Final: J. Thompson /Byrne d. A. Scott /S. McCann 6–0 6–3.

AUSTRALIAN OPEN PRIZE MONEY (US $)

MEN'S SINGLES: Winner 100,000. Runner-up 50,000. Semi-finalists 24,903.21. Quarter-finalists 12,774.19. Fourth round losers 6,903.22. Third round losers 4,064.51. Second round losers 2,506.13. First round losers 1,612.90.
Total: 503,290.06.
WOMEN'S SINGLES: Winner 100,000. Runner-up 50,000. Semi-finalists 24,600. Quarter-finalists 12,450. Third round losers 6,300. Second round losers 3,650. First round losers 2,400.
Total: 434,600. Contribution to WTA 32,258. Contribution to Players' Bonus Pool 12,903.
MEN'S DOUBLES (per team): Winners 34,193.53. Runner-up 17,032.25. Semi-finalists 8,580.64. Quarter-finalists 4,451.61. Third round losers 2,451.61. Second round losers 1,354.84. First round losers 903.23.
Total: 141,935.50.
WOMEN'S DOUBLES (per team): Winners 40,000. Runners-up 20,000. Semi-finalists 10,300. Quarter-finalists 5,000. Second round losers 2,600. First round losers 1,350.
Total: 143,000.

MEN'S SINGLES

Holder: M. Wilander (SW)

6–4 6–3 6–3

FIRST ROUND	SECOND ROUND	THIRD ROUND	FOURTH ROUND	QUARTER-FINALS	SEMI-FINALS	FINAL
Bye	I. LENDL (CZ) (1)	LENDL (1) 6–4 6–0 6–4 6–2	LENDL (1) 6–3 1–6 6–3 6–2	LENDL (1) 6–3 6–2 6–7 6–2	LENDL (1) 7–6 6–2 6–1	EDBERG (5) 6–7 7–5 6–1 4–6 9–7
Bye	L. Lavalle (MEX)					
B. Testerman (USA)	Testerman 7–6 6–3 –6	Testerman 6–1 6–7 7–6 7–6				
T. Cain (USA)	Teacher 7–6 6–2 4–6 3–6 15–13					
K. Teacher (USA)	Steyn 6–4 6–3 6–3	Steyn 6–4 3–6 6–3 6–2	Steyn 2–6 6–4 6–4 7–5			
C. Evernden (NZ)	Warder 6–2 6–0 5–7 6–7 8–6					
C. Steyn (SA)						
B. Derlin (NZ)	S. Perkis (IS)	GILBERT (10) 6–3 6–3 7–6				
L. Warder	B. GILBERT (USA) (10)					
R. Osterthun (G)	T. SMID (CZ) (11)	Lloyd 7–5 6–7 7–6 6–3	Lloyd 6–3 6–4 6–3	Lloyd 5–7 7–6 3–6 7–6 6–4		
Bye	J. M. LLOYD (GB)					
Bye	Denton 6–3 6–4 5–7 3–6 6–3					
S. Denton (USA)	Hlasek 6–4 6–2 6–4	Hlasek 6–4 5–7 7–5 6–4				
G. Layendecker (USA)						
J. Hlasek (SWZ)	Bourne 6–1 6–3 7–5	Frawley 2–6 6–7 6–2 6–1 10–8	NYSTROM (6) 4–6 7–5 6–3 6–4			
C. Limberger	Frawley 6–4 6–4 6–4					
L. Bourne (USA)						
M. R. Edmondson	S. Giammalva (USA)	NYSTROM (6) 6–3 6–2 5–7 6–4				
J. Frawley	J. NYSTROM (SW) (6)					
S. Bonneau (C)	B. BECKER (G) (4)	Schapers 3–6 6–4 7–6 4–6 6–3	Schapers 6–2 6–4 7–6	Schapers 7–6 ret'd	EDBERG (5) 6–0 7–5 6–4	
Bye	Schapers 6–1 6–7 6–3 1–6 6–3					
Bye	van Boeckel 7–5 ret'd	van Boeckel 7–5 6–3 6–3				
M. Schapers (NTH)						
W. Popp (G)	N. Aerts (BR)	Tim Gullikson 4–6 6–2 6–4 6–4	Tim Gullikson 6–4 6–3 3–6 6–4			
H. van Boeckel (NTH)	Tim Gullikson (USA)					
C. Dowdeswell (GB)	Lewis 2–6 6–3 1–6 6–3 6–2					
Bye	Cahill 6–4 6–4 4–6 6–2	Cahill 3–6 7–6 6–3 6–0				
C. J. Lewis (NZ)						
M. Mitchell (USA)	D. PATE (USA) (15)	Dyke 6–2 6–2 6–3	Masur 4–6 6–3 6–2 6–2	EDBERG (5) 6–7 2–6 7–6 4–6 6–2		
T. Cahill	H. SUNDSTROM (SW) (14)					
D. Benhabiles (F)	B. Dyke					
Bye	Masur 6–7 6–3 6–0 6–0	Masur 6–3 6–4 3–6 6–4				
Bye						
W. Masur	Youl 7–6 7–6 6–7 6–3	Anger 6–2 6–1 5–7 6–2	EDBERG (5) 5–7 7–6 6–4 7–5			
M. Oosting (NTH)	M. Anger (USA)					
J. G. Alexander	Glickstein 6–3 7–6 7–6					
S. Glickstein (IS)	Schultz 6–4 7–6 6–2	EDBERG (5) 6–3 6–4 7–6				
S. Bale (GB)	S. EDBERG (SW) (5)					
B. Schultz (USA)						
C. Miller						
Bye						

S. EDBERG (SW) (5)

Round 1

- Bye
- T. Nelson (USA)
- R. Rasheed (NZ)
- P. Doohan
- A. Chesnokov (USSR)
- Bye
- J. Lapidus (USA)
- M. Doyle (USA)
- M. Woodforde
- E. Edwards (SA)
- Bye
- Bye
- M. Leach (USA)
- J. Canter (USA)
- T. Wilkison (USA)
- A. Zverov (USSR)
- M. Flur (USA)
- M. J. Bates (GB)
- L. Shiras (USA)
- G. Forget (F)
- Bye
- Bye
- M. Dickson (USA)
- M. Bauer (USA)
- F. Gonzalez (USA)
- J. B. Svensson (SW)
- M. DePalmer (USA)
- J. Fitzgerald
- D. Keretic (G)
- S. Shaw (GB)
- Bye
- Bye
- A. Mansdorf (IS)
- P. McNamara
- Bye
- B. Drewett
- M. Wooldridge (USA)
- Bye
- N. Odizor (NIG)
- D. McPherson
- D. Visser (SA)
- W. Scanlon (USA)
- Bye

Round 2

- J. KRIEK (USA) (7)
- D. Mustard (NZ)
- Nelson 6-4 6-1 6-3
- Doohan 6-0 6-1 6-2
- D. Thrupp
- Lapidus 6-0 6-4 1-6 6-7 6-3
- Woodforde 7-6 6-4 3-6 6-3
- G. HOLMES (USA) (16)
- P. ANNACONE (USA) (12)
- S. Green (USA)
- Leach 7-5 7-6 5-7 3-6 6-4
- Wilkison 6-2 6-3 6-0
- Flur 7-6 7-7-5 6-4 7-5
- Shiras 4-1-6 6-3 6-2
- M. WILANDER (SW) (3)
- T. MAYOTTE (USA) (8)
- Dickson 7-6 6-2 7-6
- R. Saad (ARG)
- Gonzalez 6-2 6-4 6-2
- DePalmer 6-2 6-2 6-2
- Keretic 6-2-1 ret'd
- S. Zivojinovic (YU)
- S. DAVIS (USA) (9)
- H. LECONTE (F) (13)
- Mansdorf 6-7 6-2 6-4 6-4
- J. Sadri (USA)
- Drewett 7-6 6-3 7-6
- D. Cassidy
- Odizor 7-6 7-6 6-1
- Visser 4-6 7-6 6-2 7-6
- J. P. McENROE (USA) (2)

Round 3

- KRIEK (7) 6-4 4-6 6-3 6-4
- Doohan 6-4 7-6 6-1
- Lapidus 7-6 6-4 7-6
- Woodforde 1-6 6-1 6-4 6-2
- ANNACONE (12) 6-7 7-6 6-4 7-5
- Wilkison 6-4 6-0 6-2
- Shiras 4-6 1-6 6-4 6-0 9-7
- WILANDER (3) 3-6 6-3 7-6 6-4
- MAYOTTE (8) 6-4 6-4 6-4
- Saad 1-6 7-6 6-4 7-5
- DePalmer 6-2 6-2 6-2
- Zivojinovic 7-5 3-6 6-1 6-3
- LECONTE (13) 6-4 6-2 7-5
- Sadri 6-7 7-6 7-6 6-3
- Odizor 6-4 3-3 6-6 4
- McENROE (2) 6-4 6-2 6-4 6-2

Round 4

- KRIEK (7) 7-5 6-4 6-0
- Lapidus 6-7 6-3 6-4 2-6 7-5
- Wilkison 7-5 6-3 6-3
- WILANDER (3) 6-2 6-3 6-2
- MAYOTTE (8) 7-6 6-7 6-4 6-4
- Zivojinovic 6-7 6-3 6-2 6-2
- LECONTE (9) 7-6 6-3 7-6
- McENROE (2) 4-6 6-2 6-4 6-2

Quarter-finals

- KRIEK (7) 6-3 6-4 6-3
- WILANDER (3) 7-6 6-3 6-3
- Zivojinovic 2-6 6-4 6-4 6-4
- McENROE (2) 5-7 7-6 3-6 7-6 6-1

Semi-finals

- WILANDER (3) 6-3 7-5 6-2
- Zivojinovic 2-6 6-3 1-6 6-4 6-0

Final

- WILANDER (3) 7-5 6-1 6-3

Capital letters denote seeded players. Numbers following player's name gives seeding order.

WOMEN'S SINGLES

Holder: Mrs J. M. Lloyd (USA)

Winner: M. NAVRATILOVA (USA) (2) 6–2 4–6 6–2

FIRST ROUND

Player	Second round result
Mrs J. M. LLOYD (USA) (1)	LLOYD (1) 6–1 6–2
R. Fairbank (SA)	
C. Nagelsen (USA)	Nagelsen 4–6 6–3 8–6
A. Brown (GB)	
B. Gerken (USA)	Brown 6–2 1–6 6–0
Mrs D. Balestrat	
B. BUNGE (G) (12)	Balestrat 6–4 6–2
K. MALEEVA (BUL) (16)	
Mrs S. A. Walsh Pete (USA)	K. MALEEVA (16) 7–5 6–4
M. Yanagi (J)	
A. Moulton (USA)	Yanagi 6–3 6–2
M. Schropp (G)	
M. Messker (NTH)	Schropp 6–3 6–4
L. Antonoplis (USA)	
M. MALEEVA (BUL) (7)	M. MALEEVA (7) 6–1 6–1
P. H. SHRIVER (USA) (4)	
A. Holikova (CZ)	SHRIVER (4) 6–1 6–1
R. Bryant	
L. Gates (USA)	Bryant 2–6 6–4 6–2
E. Inoue (J)	
E. Minter	Inoue 6–4 7–5
R. Marsikova (CZ)	
C. LINDQVIST (SW) (10)	LINDQVIST (10) 7–5 6–2
J. M. DURIE (GB) (13)	
A. Minter	DURIE (13) 6–4 6–4
S. Gomer (GB)	
L. Spain-Short (USA)	Gomer 6–2 7–6
G. Fernandez (USA)	
C. Karlsson (SW)	Fernandez 6–1 6–4
C. Croft (GB)	
C. KOHDE-KILSCH (G) (5)	KOHDE-KILSCH (5) 7–5 6–4
Z. GARRISON (USA) (6)	
K. Skronska (CZ)	GARRISON (6) 6–4 4–6 6–4
T. Holladay (USA)	
A. Henricksson (USA)	Skronska 6–3 6–3
J. Byrne	
L. Field (USA)	Henricksson 4–6 7–6 6–4
L. BONDER (USA) (14)	
W. M. TURNBULL (9)	BONDER (14) 6–3 6–3
S. Leo	
Mrs E. Smylie	TURNBULL (9) 6–0 6–0
C. Suire (F)	
S. V. Wade (GB)	Smylie 6–2 4–6 6–3
C. Van Nostrand (USA)	
C. Benjamin (USA)	Wade 6–3 5–7 6–2
H. MANDLIKOVA (CZ) (3)	
H. SUKOVA (CZ) (8)	MANDLIKOVA (3) 6–2 6–2
J. Thompson	
R. White (USA)	SUKOVA (8) 6–4 6–4
L. McNeil (USA)	
E. Jolissaint (SWZ)	White 6–4 5–7 6–1
E. Burgin (USA)	
M. A. Dingwall	Jolissaint 5–7 6–4 6–2
P. PARADIS (F) (15)	
B. POTTER (USA) (11)	Dingwall 6–2 6–2
B. Norton (USA)	
A. E. Hobbs (GB)	POTTER (11) 6–3 6–1
Hu Na (USA)	
N. Provis	Hobbs 6–3 6–2
S. Amiach (F)	
D. A. Hansell (USA)	Provis 6–2 6–3
M. NAVRATILOVA (USA) (2)	NAVRATILOVA (2) 6–2 6–1

THIRD ROUND

- LLOYD (1) 4–6 6–4 6–0
- Balestrat 6–0 7–5
- K. MALEEVA (16) 6–3 7–6
- M. MALEEVA (7) 6–2 6–3
- SHRIVER (4) 6–4 6–1
- LINDQVIST (10) 6–0 7–5
- DURIE (13) 6–2 6–3
- KOHDE-KILSCH (5) 6–1 6–2
- GARRISON (6) 6–1 6–1
- Henricksson 2–6 6–3 9–7
- TURNBULL (9) 6–0 6–0
- MANDLIKOVA (3) 6–2 7–6
- SUKOVA (8) 6–4 6–3
- Dingwall 6–2 7–6
- Hobbs 6–4 7–5
- NAVRATILOVA (2) 6–2 6–1

QUARTER-FINALS

- LLOYD (1) 6–4 6–1
- M. MALEEVA (7) 6–2 6–1
- LINDQVIST (10) 3–6 6–3 6–2
- KOHDE-KILSCH (5) 3–6 6–1 6–2
- GARRISON (6) 4–6 6–1 6–3
- MANDLIKOVA (3) 6–3 6–4
- SUKOVA (8) 6–3 6–1
- NAVRATILOVA (2) 6–3 6–1

SEMI-FINALS

- LLOYD (1) 6–3 6–3
- KOHDE-KILSCH (5) 6–4 6–0
- MANDLIKOVA (3) 2–6 6–3 6–3
- NAVRATILOVA (2) 6–2 6–2

FINAL

- LLOYD (1) 6–1 7–6
- NAVRATILOVA (2) 6–7 6–1 6–4

Capital letters denote seeded players. Number following player's name gives seeding order.

MEN'S DOUBLES

Holders: M. R. Edmondson (AUS)/S. E. Stewart (USA)

Winner: P. ANNACONE (USA)/C. VAN RENSBURG (SA) (2) 3–6 7–6 6–4

FIRST ROUND	SECOND ROUND	THIRD ROUND	QUARTER-FINALS	SEMI-FINALS	FINAL
Bye	WILANDER/NYSTROM (1)	WILANDER/NYSTROM (1) 6–4 6–1	WILANDER/NYSTROM (1) 6–3 6–2	WILANDER/NYSTROM (1) 6–3 6–4 7–6	EDMONDSON/WARWICK (4) 7–5 4–6 7–5 4–6 6–3
Bauer/Bourne	Bauer/Bourne 7–6 6–2				
Alexander/Woodforde	Custer/McPherson 6–7 7–6 6–3	Custer/McPherson 6–7 7–5 6–3			
Custer/McPherson	GLICKSTEIN/PERKIS (10)				
Mmoh/Utzinger	DICKSON/WILKISON (13)	DICKSON/WILKISON (13) 3–6 6–4 7–5	DICKSON/WILKISON (13) 4–6 7–5 6–2		
Bye	Shaw/Steyn 7–5 6–3				
Bye	Canter/Lavalle 1–6 6–1 7–5	Canter/Lavalle 6–3 7–6			
Shaw/Steyn	DAVIS/PATE (6)				
Carlsson/Svensson	EDMONDSON/WARWICK (4)	EDMONDSON/WARWICK (4) 4–6 3–6–2	EDMONDSON/WARWICK (4) 6–4 3–6 6–4	EDMONDSON/WARWICK (4) 3–6 6–3 7–5 6–4	
Arons/Lavendecker	Antonitsch Schapers 6–3 6–4				
Canter/Lavalle	Cassidy/Warneke 7–6 7–6	Cassidy/Warneke 6–3 6–7 6–3			
Bye	LEACH/ODIZOR (15)				
Antonitsch Schapers	DYKE/FANCUTT (11)	Emerson/Tyson 7–5 7–6	Emerson/Tyson 7–6 6–7 6–4		
Doyle/Keretic	Emerson/Tyson 6–4 7–6				
Cassidy/Warneke	McNamara/Shiras 6–4 6–7 6–3	DENTON/STEWART (7) 6–3 3–6 6–2			
Derlin/Mustard	STEWART/DENTON (7)				
Bye	DOOHAN/DePALMER (8)	DOOHAN/DePALMER (8) 7–6 6–3	Miller/Warder 6–4 6–4	Miller/Warder 7–6 7–5 6–2	ANNACONE/VAN RENSBURG (2) 7–6 7–5 6–4
Aerts/Rudeen	Gonzalez/Teacher 6–3 6–4				
Emerson/Tyson	Miller/Warder 6–4 6–7 6–7	Miller/Warder 6–4 6–2			
McNamara/Shiras	EDWARDS/VISSER (14)				
Kratzman/Youl	DREWETT/MITCHELL (16)	DREWETT/MITCHELL (16) 6–3 6–7 6–3	Letts/Robertson 3–6 6–4 10–8		
Bye	Barlow/Limberger 7–6 6–3				
Gonzalez/Teacher	Letts/Robertson 7–6 6–3	Letts/Robertson 2–6 6–2 6–1			
Gilbert/Graham	FITZGERALD/SMID (3)				
Miller/Warder	EDBERG/FORGET (5)	Bates/Mansdorf 4–6 7–6 6–4	BECKER/ZIVOJINOVIC (9) 6–4 6–4	ANNACONE/VAN RENSBURG (2) 5–7 7–6 5–7 7–6 9–7	
Giammalva/Holmes	Bates/Mansdorf 6–3 6–4				
Bye	Evenden/Testerman 7–6 6–3	BECKER/ZIVOJINOVIC (9) 7–6 2–2 ret'd			
Gullikson/McCain	BECKER/ZIVOJINOVIC (9)				
Barlow/Limberger	DOWDESWELL/LLOYD (12)	DOWDESWELL/LLOYD (12) 6–7 6–4 6–4	ANNACONE/VAN RENSBURG (2) 7–5 6–1		
Letts/Robertson	Eyre/Fancutt 6–4 3–6 13–11				
Oosting/Woodbridge	Cahill/Carter 7–6 6–4	ANNACONE/VAN RENSBURG (2) 3–6 6–3 6–4			
Bye	ANNACONE/VAN RENSBURG (2)				
Jeffrey/Furlong					
Bates/Mansdorf					
Evenden/Testerman					
Frawley/Lewis					
Bye					
Eyre/Fancutt					
Popp/van Boeckel					
Cahill/Carter					
Dickinson/Van't Hof					
Bye					

Capital letters denote seeded pairings. Number following players' names gives seeding order.

WOMEN'S DOUBLES

Holders: M. Navratilova (USA)/P. H. Shriver (USA)

FIRST ROUND	SECOND ROUND	QUARTER-FINALS	SEMI-FINALS	FINAL
NAVRATILOVA/SHRIVER (1)	NAVRATILOVA/SHRIVER (1) 6–2 6–1	NAVRATILOVA/SHRIVER (1) 7–6 4–6 6–3	NAVRATILOVA/SHRIVER (1) 6–4 6–2	NAVRATILOVA/SHRIVER (1) 7–6 6–2
Field/Turk				
Lindstrom/Karlsson	Thompson/Byrne 6–4 6–4			
Thompson/Byrne				
Mesker/Paradis	Mesker/Paradis 7–6 6–1	Mesker/Paradis 2–6 6–4 6–3		
Betzner/Schropp				
Amiach/Gerken	BURGIN/SMYLIE (5) 6–1 3–6 6–4			
BURGIN/SMYLIE (5)				
TURNBULL/MANDLIKOVA (3)	TURNBULL/MANDLIKOVA (3) 6–2 7–6	Lloyd/Lindqvist 6–3 7–6	Durie/Hobbs 6–4 6–1	
Suire/McNeil				
Cordwell/Richardson	Lloyd/Lindqvist 6–2 1–6 6–3			
Lloyd/Lindqvist				
Durie/Hobbs	Durie/Hobbs 7–6 6–2	Durie/Hobbs 6–1 6–3		
Brown/Gomer				
Nagelsen/Smith	FAIRBANK/REYNOLDS (7) 7–6 6–3			
FAIRBANK/REYNOLDS (7)				
G. FERNANDEZ/WHITE (6)	G. FERNANDEZ/WHITE (6) 6–1 7–6	Garrison/Wade 7–6 4–6 7–5	POTTER/WALSH PETE (4) 6–3 3–6 6–4	
A./E. Minter				
Garrison/Wade	Garrison/Wade 6–7 6–3 6–3			
Dingwall/Gulley				
Bonder/Croft	Bonder/Croft 7–5 7–6	POTTER/WALSH PETE (4) 6–3 6–4		
Antonoplis/A. Fernandez				
Leo/Whytcross	POTTER/WALSH PETE (4) 3–6 6–2 6–1			
POTTER/WALSH PETE (4)				
K./M. MALEEVA (8)	K./M. MALEEVA (8) 6–3 6–4	Moulton/Gates 4–6 6–2 13–11	KOHDE-KILSCH/SUKOVA (2) 6–4 5–4 ret'd	KOHDE-KILSCH/SUKOVA (2) 3–6 6–4 6–1
Holikova/Skronska				
Moulton/Gates	Moulton/Gates 6–3 6–4			
Jolissaint/Henricksson				
Holladay/Ludloff	Holladay/Ludloff 6–4 4–6 6–3	KOHDE-KILSCH/SUKOVA (2) 6–7 6–2 6–3		
Benjamin/Van Nostrand				
Crowe/Steinmer	KOHDE-KILSCH/SUKOVA (2) 6–4 5–7 6–3			
KOHDE-KILSCH/SUKOVA (2)	KOHDE-KILSCH/SUKOVA (2) 6–2 6–1			

M. NAVRATILOVA (USA)/
P. H. SHRIVER (USA) (1)
6–3 6–4

NABISCO GRAND PRIX

GRAND PRIX REVIEW
POINTS AND PRIZE MONEY
POINTS EXPLANATION
NABISCO GRAND PRIX TOURNAMENTS
NABISCO MASTERS
WCT YEAR

The elegant Czech, Miloslav Mecir, started the year in brilliant fashion by beating Connors to reach the final in Philadelphia, winning Rotterdam and Hamburg and reaching the final in Rome to earn a No. 9 world ranking for 1985. *(A. Evans)*

Despite winning eight Grand Prix titles, John McEnroe failed on all the big occasions — in Paris, at Wimbledon, at Flushing Meadow and at Melbourne — to lose his No. 1 ranking and raise doubts about his future. *(A. Evans)*

GRAND PRIX REVIEW

John Parsons

Whatever doubts there may have been concerning who would be nominated as world champion for 1985 – at least until Stefan Edberg conveniently assisted Ivan Lendl by defeating his one serious rival, Mats Wilander, in the final of the Australian Open – the American-based Czech was an impressive winner of the Nabisco Grand Prix points table. Once his year began to take off at the end of March, it soon became evident that Lendl, rather than last year's undoubted number one, John McEnroe, was most likely to become the front runner for most of the season's honours. In the event, the four Grand Slam titles went to four different players (and for the first time since 1934 entirely to Europeans) but in terms of the overall Grand Prix, Lendl won more titles on more surfaces than anyone else to win the top prize in the bonus pool, which had risen from $300,000 to $800,000 since he last won it in 1981.

For the record Lendl won ten tournaments, the same number as McEnroe in 1984, between Fort Myers at the end of March and Wembley in mid-November – four indoors, four on clay and two on hard courts. In winning the Buick WCT Finals in Dallas in mid-April, even before he had entered his most confidently assured period of the year, he carved a significant new niche for himself in tennis history, for by defeating Tim Mayotte, Lendl achieved the remarkable feat of winning successive Grand Prix titles on three different surfaces in as many weeks. His early-morning Texas triumph, staged more with television in mind than the best interests of the players or the game, followed his victories on clay in Monte Carlo and on hard courts at Fort Myers. In 15 days, therefore, he had collected more than a quarter of his $1,063,074 major tournament prize money for the year.

The success of Lendl, who has never been lower than third in the points table since 1980, certainly mirrored the continuing advance by European tennis in 1985 even if, in his case, it seems as if Americanisation is almost complete. In 1984 there were six Europeans among the 12 who qualified for the Masters in New York, and for the event winding up the 1985 circuit, the proportion was even greater in an expanded event, with Europeans filling ten of the 16 places.

Although failing to win a Grand Slam title for the first time since 1978, McEnroe remained a considerable force in many other Grand Prix tournaments, collecting eight of the 23 titles won by 13 different American players over the year. Just as Lendl had a particularly impressive flourish towards the end of the year, winning 32 successive Grand Prix matches until Edberg upset him in the semi-finals of the Australian Open, so too McEnroe had enjoyed emphatic supremacy at the start of the year which made his later lapses all the more surprising. McEnroe won his first four tournaments, including the Ebel US Pro Indoors at Philadelphia for the fourth successive year, where he won 12 of the last 14 games and looked as awesome as ever against the unseeded Miloslav Mecir in the final. Then suddenly, during the WCT Finals in Dallas, cracks began appearing in the McEnroe armoury which, although he was to win four more titles, were never wholly repaired.

For his part the lanky, often languid Mecir, was the discovery of the year until his serving confidence faded so drastically that he was reduced to serving underarm in Rome and Düsseldorf, at a stage in the year when a certain Boris Becker was beginning to demonstrate a talent and maturity way beyond his tender years. Becker's exploits, well chronicled in other pages, made him both the player and personality of the year. Nevertheless Mecir, despite his problems, still stayed high enough in the points standings to join Wimbledon's youngest champion, Becker, as one of seven first-time qualifiers for the Masters. The others were Edberg, who added the Australian Open title to the

Australian junior title he had won two years earlier, Tim Mayotte, Henri Leconte, Brad Gilbert and Paul Annacone. Mayotte, working as enthusiastically as ever to try to prove that there really is life still in American tennis after McEnroe and Jimmy Connors, won the inaugural Lipton International Players tournament in Delray. Connors, for the first time since 1971, when he was 19, went through the whole year without winning a significant title.

The calendar continued to occupy the attention of the Men's International Professional Tennis Council probably as much as anything else, at least until the Volvo-Pro Serv-IMG lawsuit came along. Although finding sponsorship or other support for Regular Series events, especially outside the main areas of tennis influence, remains a problem, the Super Series list has become more crowded than ever.

The current year, of course, marks the beginning of major changes in the pattern, with the German Open moving from May to September and the Australian Open switching from November to January (which means the next event is not until January 1987). Most important of all, the Grand Prix Masters will be staged in future in December. That means there will be two Masters in 1986 – one in January, related to 1985, and the other in December as the climax to 1986.

Another important development for the Grand Prix in 1985 was the introduction of full-time professional umpires on the circuits, employed and deployed by the MIPTC. Jeremy Shales from Great Britain and Richard Kaufman from the United States were the two officials, out of several who were interested, chosen to take up their permanent duties in mid-summer.

Of the new names to make an impact on the Hewlett-Packard ATP rankings during 1985, New Zealander Kelly Evernden, who swept from nowhere to 89, Mexican junior Leo Lavalle, who finished at 86, and Sweden's Peter Lundgren, who soared from 276 to 27, were among the most prominent. Lundgren was actually a qualifier when he won his first Nabisco Grand Prix title in Cologne in October, and so too was Sergio Casal when he became a first-time winner in Florence, while Larry Stefanki's first Grand Prix win followed his wild-card entry at La Quinta.

If variety in terms of venues and winners is good for tennis, as surely it must be, then 1985 was an excellent year, because the various Grand Prix tournament winners came from eleven different countries, two more than in 1984, and the 71 titles won in 19 different countries were spread among 37 players. In addition to Lundgren, Casal and Stefanki, another 14 won titles for the first time – Martin Jaite, Miloslav Mecir, Claudio Panatta (in Bari after saving four match-points), Horatio de la Pena, Andreas Maurer, Tom Gullikson (in his 11th year on the circuit), Ricky Osterthun, Paul Annacone, Diego Perez, Matt Anger, Jan Gunnarsson, Eddie Edwards, Jonathan Canter and Boris Becker at Queen's Club, eight days before embarking on his historic achievement at Wimbledon.

Tom Gullikson was not alone in being rewarded for persistence. After nearly three years without winning a tournament, Thierry Tulasne claimed three, while Yannick Noah also contributed to eight in total won by French players with a triumph in Rome which was his first since his victory at Roland Garros in 1983. Success for Eddie Edwards right at the end of the year, in Adelaide, was the first for this likeable South African in ten years on the circuit.

Against that it was a year probably best forgotten by three of those who had made so much headway a year earlier. Pat Cash from Australia, Andres Gomez from Ecuador, and Henrik Sundstrom from Sweden were all severely restricted, Cash most of all, by lingering injury complications. It was also a year in which another of the circuit's long-term stalwarts, José Higueras, decided it was time for him to retire after 12 years of international tournament play.

Whatever one's views about exhibitions and special events, it is difficult to see how a sensible, orderly tournament structure, offering employment to an adequate number of players and entertainment to millions, can be sustained without a Grand Prix circuit. It was therefore encouraging that the blue riband events on that circuit, the Grand Slam tournaments, all reported record attendances, despite the terrible weather which struck Wimbledon and the Australian Open in particular.

Sweden's Peter Lundgren, a qualifier when he won his first Grand Prix title in Cologne, leapt from 276 to 27 in the world. (T. Hindley)

Doubles forms an integral, if not always fully reflected part of the Nabisco Grand Prix and although, by necessity, it is not always easy for partnerships to be sustained permanently, because of various individual commitments, some, like Ken Flach and Robert Seguso who took the doubles scene by storm in 1984, had another great year. They finished on top of the team points table by winning five events together, including the US Open where, sadly, there was controversy over a vital point in the final against Yannick Noah and Henri Leconte. It led to much debate about whether a player should acknowledge that he had touched the ball when it was going out, even though the umpire had not noticed the incident.

Flach and Seguso, always an exciting partnership to watch, both also had the satisfaction of registering major gains in their singles world rankings, but the year's individual winner in terms of successes in doubles was surely Anders Jarryd. The Swedish player, robbed of his place in the *Davis Cup* final by illness, took eight Grand Prix titles during 1985 with six different partners. Three were won with Edberg and the others with Peter Fleming, Heinz Gunthardt, Mats Wilander, John Fitzgerald and Guy Forget.

Finally, in a year when, because of Gomez's injury Lendl had to abandon plans to launch a major new partnership with him, but Spain's Sergio Casal and Emilio Sanchez emerged as a new team to be feared, it is worth noting that, as in the singles, the four Grand Slam events produced four different champions. Mark Edmondson and Kim Warwick won in Paris, Heinz Gunthardt and Balazs Taroczy at Wimbledon, Flach and Seguso at Flushing Meadow and Paul Annacone and Christo Van Rensburg in Australia.

It was both an exhausting and stimulating year.

NABISCO GRAND PRIX 1985

DATE	VENUE	SINGLES FINAL	DOUBLES WINNERS
1–6 Jan	London	—	K. Flach/R. Seguso
7–13 Jan	Auckland, NZ	C. J. Lewis d. W. Masur 7–5 6–0 2–6 6–4	J. Fitzgerald/C. J. Lewis
21–26 Jan	Philadelphia	J. P. McEnroe d. M. Mecir 6–3 7–6 6–1	J. Nystrom/M. Wilander
28 Jan–3 Feb	Memphis	S. Edberg d. Y. Noah 6–1 6–0	P. Slozil/T. Smid
4–17 Feb	Delray Beach, Fla	T. Mayotte d. S. Davis 4–6 4–6 6–3 6–2 6–4	P. Annacone/C. Van Rensburg
18–24 Feb	La Quinta, Cal.	L. Stefanki d. D. Pate 6–1 6–4 3–6 6–3	H. Gunthardt/B. Taroczy
18–24 Feb	Toronto	K. Curren d. A. Jarryd 7–6 6–3	P. Fleming/A. Jarryd
25 Feb–2 March	Houston	J. P. McEnroe d. K. Curren 7–5 6–1 7–6	P. Fleming/J. P. McEnroe
25 Feb–2 March	Buenos Aires	M. Jaite d. D. Perez	M. Jaite/C. Miniussi
11–17 March	Brussels	A. Jarryd d. M. Wilander 6–4 3–6 7–5	S. Edberg/A. Jarryd
18–24 March	Rotterdam	M. Mecir d. J. Hlasek 6–1 6–2	P. Slozil/T. Smid
18–24 March	Nancy	T. Wilkison d. S. Zivojinovic 4–6 7–6 9–7	M. Freeman/R. Harmon
25–31 March	Milan	J. P. McEnroe d. A. Jarryd 6–4 6–1	H. Gunthardt/A. Jarryd
25–31 March	Fort Myers, Fla	I. Lendl d. J. S. Connors 6–3 6–2	K. Flach/R. Seguso
1–17 April	Monte Carlo	I. Lendl d. M. Wilander 6–1 6–4 4–6 6–4	P. Slozil/T. Smid
1–17 April	Chicago	J. P. McEnroe w.o. J. S. Connors	J. Kriek/Y. Noah
8–14 April	WCT Dallas	I. Lendl d. T. Mayotte 7–6 6–4 6–1	
8–14 April	Nice	H. Leconte d. V. Pecci 6–4 6–4	C. Panatta/P. Slozil
15–21 April	Bari	C. Panatta d. L. Duncan 6–2 1–6 7–6	C. Panatta/A. Ganzabal
22–28 April	Atlanta	J. P. McEnroe d. P. Annacone 7–6 7–6 6–2	P. Annacone/C. Van Rensburg
22–28 April	Marbella	H. de la Pena d. L. Duncan 6–0 6–3	A. Gomez/C. Motta
29 April–5 May	Las Vegas	J. Kriek d. J. Arias 4–6 6–3 6–4 6–2	P. Cash/J. Fitzgerald
29 April–5 May	Hamburg (German Open)	M. Mecir d. H. Sundstrom 6–4 6–1 6–4	H. Gildemeister/A. Gomez
6–12 May	WCT Forest Hills, NY	I. Lendl d. J. P. McEnroe 6–3 6–3	K. Flach/R. Seguso
6–12 May	Munich	J. Nystrom d. H. Schwaier 6–1 6–0	M. R. Edmondson/K. Warwick
13–19 May	Rome (Italian Open)	Y. Noah d. M. Mecir 6–3 3–6 6–2 7–6	A. Jarryd/M. Wilander
13–19 May	Madrid	A. Maurer d. J. Duncan 7–5 6–2	G. Barbosa/I. Kley
20–26 May	Florence	S. Casal d. J. Arias 3–6 6–3 6–2	D. Graham/L. Warder
27 May–9 June	Paris (French Open)	M. Wilander d. I. Lendl 3–6 6–4 6–2 6–2	M. R. Edmondson/K. Warwick
11–17 June	Queen's Club, London	B. Becker d. J. Kriek 6–2 6–3	K. Flach/R. Seguso
11–17 June	Bologna	T. Tulasne d. C. Panatta 6–2 6–0	P. Cane/S. Colombo
17–23 June	Bristol	M. Davis d. G. Layendecker 4–6 6–3 7–5	E. Edwards/D. Visser
24 June–7 July	Wimbledon	B. Becker d. K. Curren 6–3 6–7 7–6 6–4	L. Pimek/S. Zivojinovic
8–14 July	Boston	M. Wilander d. M. Jaite 6–2 6–4	W. Fibak/T. Smid
8–14 July	Gstaad	J. Nystrom d. A. Maurer 6–4 1–6 7–5 6–3	P. Doohan/S. Giammalva
8–14 July	Newport, RI	Tom Gullikson d. J. Sadri 6–3 7–6	

DATE	VENUE	SINGLES FINAL	DOUBLES WINNERS
15–21 July	Washington, DC	Y. Noah d. M. Jaite 6–4 6–3	H. Gildemeister /V. Pecci
15–21 July	Bastad	M. Wilander d. S. Edberg 6–1 6–0	S. Edberg /A. Jarryd
22–28 July	Indianapolis (US Clay Courts)	I. Lendl d. A. Gomez 6–1 6–3	K. Flach /R. Seguso
22–28 July	Hilversum	R. Oosterhun d. K. Carlsson 4–6 4–6 6–4 6–2 6–3	H. /S. Simonsson
22–28 July	Livingston, NJ	B. Gilbert d. B. Teacher 4–6 7–5 6–0	M. DePalmer /P. Doohan
5–11 Aug	Stratton Mountain	J. P. McEnroe d. I. Lendl 7–6 6–2	S. Davis /D. Pate
5–11 Aug	Kitzbuhel	P. Slozil d. M. Westphal 7–5 6–2	S. Casal /E. Sanchez
12–18 Aug	Montreal	J. P. McEnroe d. I. Lendl 7–5 6–3	K. Flach /R. Seguso
12–18 Aug	Cleveland	B. Gilbert d. B. Drewett 3–6 7–6 7–6	L. Palin /O. Rahnasto
19–25 Aug	Mason, Ohio	B. Becker d. M. Wilander 6–4 6–2	S. Edberg /A. Jarryd
26 Aug–8 Sept	Flushing Meadow (US Open)	I. Lendl d. J. P. McEnroe 7–6 6–3 6–4	K. Flach /R. Seguso
9–15 Sept	Palermo	T. Tulasne d. J. Nystrom 6–3 6–1	C. Dowdeswell /J. Nystrom
9–15 Sept	Stuttgart	I. Lendl d. B. Gilbert 6–4 6–0	I. Lendl /T. Smid
16–24 Sept	Los Angeles	P. Annacone d. S. Edberg 7–6 6–7 7–6	S. Davis /R. Van't Hof
16–24 Sept	Geneva	T. Smid d. M. Wilander 6–4 6–4	S. Casal /E. Sanchez
16–24 Sept	Bordeaux	D. Perez d. J. Brown 6–4 7–5	D. Felgate /S. Shaw
23–29 Sept	San Francisco	S. Edberg d. J. Kriek 6–4 6–2	P. Annacone /C. Van Rensburg
23–29 Sept	Barcelona	T. Tulasne d. M. Wilander 0–6 6–2 3–6 6–4 6–0	S. Casal /E. Sanchez
7–13 Oct	Johannesburg	M. Anger d. B. Gilbert 6–4 3–6 6–3 6–2	C. Dowdeswell /C. Van Rensburg
7–13 Oct	Brisbane	P. Annacone d. K. Evernden 6–3 6–3	B. Drewett /M. Davis
7–13 Oct	Toulouse	Y. Noah d. T. Smid 6–4 6–4	R. Acuna /J. Hlasek
14–20 Oct	Sydney	I. Lendl d. H. Leconte 6–4 6–4 7–6	J. Fitzgerald /A. Jarryd
14–20 Oct	Basle	S. Edberg d. Y. Noah 6–7 7–6 6–1	Tim /Tom Gullikson
14–20 Oct	Tokyo	S. Davis d. J. Arias 6–17–6	S. Davis /D. Pate
21–27 Oct	Tel Aviv	B. Gilbert d. A. Mansdorf 6–3 6–2	B. Gilbert /I. Nastase
21–27 Oct	Tokyo	I. Lendl d. M. Wilander 6–0 6–4	K. Flach /R. Seguso
21–27 Oct	Melbourne	M. Davis d. P. Annacone 6–4 6–4	B. Drewett /M. Mitchell
21–27 Oct	Cologne	P. Lundgren d. R. Krishnan 6–3 6–2	A. Antonisch /M. Schapers
4–10 Nov	Stockholm	J. P. McEnroe d. A. Jarryd 6–1 6–2	G. Forget /A. Gomez
11–17 Nov	Wembley	I. Lendl d. B. Becker 6–7 6–3 4–6 6–4 6–4	A. Jarryd /G. Forget
18–24 Nov	Hong Kong	A. Gomez d. A. Krickstein 6–3 6–3 3–6 6–4	B. Drewett /K. Warwick
18–24 Nov	Vienna	J. Gunnarsson d. L. Pimek 6–7 6–2 6–4 1–6 7–5	B. Donnelly /M. DePalmer
25 Nov–8 Dec	Melbourne (Australian Open)	S. Edberg d. M. Wilander 6–4 6–3 6–3	P. Annacone /C. Van Rensburg
9–15 Dec	Sydney	H. Leconte d. K. Evernden 6–7 6–2 6–3	D. Dowlen /N. Odizor
16–20 Dec	Adelaide	E. Edwards d. P. Doohan 6–2 6–4	M. R. Edmondson /K. Warwick
26–29 Dec	Melbourne	J. Canter d. P. Doohan 5–7 6–3 6–4	D. Cahill /P. Carter
14–19 Jan 1986	New York (Nabisco Masters)	I. Lendl d. B. Becker 6–2 7–6 6–3	S. Edberg /A. Jarryd

NABISCO GRAND PRIX 1985 – POINTS EXPLANATION

The Nabisco Grand Prix is a world-wide points-linked circuit of 71 tournaments, in 23 countries with $23 million prize money under the management of the Men's International Professional Tennis Council. There are 18 separate points categories – from the Grand Slam championships of France, Wimbledon, the US Open and the Australian Open to the Regular Series tournaments with prize money of $88,000. There are five categories – Grand Slam; other 2-week tournaments; Super Series, Doubles Series, Tournament of Champions and London Doubles; Open Week Series; Regular Series. There is no limit to the number of Grand Prix tournaments in which a player may compete each year.

POINTS TABLE

Except for the 128-draw Grand Slam and Two-Week tournaments, the points below are based on 32-draw tournaments. For Super Series tournaments the points shall be increased by one category for each additional 16 places in the draw up to a maximum of two categories. For Regular or Open Week Series the points will be increased one category only for an additional 16 places in the draw. Only points earned shall be awarded (e.g. in a final that could not take place the two finalists would each receive runners-up points). Bonus Points are not awarded until a player has won a round (including advancement by default).

Player Compensation	Grand Slam		Other Two-Week Events		Tournament of Champs.		$495,000 and over		$465,000 to $494,000		$435,000 to $464,000		$405,000 to $434,000		$375,000 to $404,000		$345,500 to $374,000		$315,000 to $344,000		$285,00 to $314,000		$267,000 to $284,000		$231,000 to $266,000		$202,000 to $230,000		$174,000 to $202,000		$145,500 to $173,000		$117,000 to $145,000		$94,200 to $116,000	
	Sgls	Dbls	Sgls	Dbls	Sgls	Dbls	Sgls	Dbls	Sgls	Dbls	Sgls	Dbls	Sgls	Dbls	Sgls	Dbls	Sgls	Dbls	Sgls	Dbls	Sgls	Dbls	Sgls	Dbls	Sgls	Dbls	Sgls	Dbls	Sgls	Dbls	Sgls	Dbls	Sgls	Dbls	Sgls	Dbls
Winner	700	120	550	110	450	90	400	80	375	75	350	70	325	65	300	60	275	55	250	50	225	45	210	42	200	40	175	35	150	30	125	25	100	20	80	15
Runner-up	500	84	350	70	298	63	280	56	263	52	245	49	227	—	210	45	192	38	175	35	157	31	145	29	140	28	122	24	104	20	87	17	70	14	56	10
Losing semi-finalists	350	48	200	40	180	36	160	32	150	30	140	28	130	—	120	26	110	22	100	20	90	18	85	17	80	16	76	14	60	12	50	10	40	8	32	6
Losing quarter-finalists	200	24	100	20	90	18	80	16	75	15	70	14	65	—	60	13	55	11	50	10	45	9	42	8	40	8	35	7	30	6	25	5	20	4	16	3
Losers in round of 16	100	12	50	10	45	9	40	8	37	8	35	7	32	—	20	7	27	6	25	5	22	5	21	4	20	4	17	3	14	3	12	2	10	2	8	—
Losers in round of 32	50	5	25	5	21	—	19	—	18	—	17	—	16	—	15	—	13	—	12	—	11	—	10	—	10	—	9	—	7	—	6	—	5	—	4	—
Losers in round of 64	25	—	12	—	—	—	—	—	—	—	—	—	—	—	—	—	—	—	—	—	—	—	—	—	—	—	—	—	—	—	—	—	—	—	—	—

Singles and doubles points are earned separately at each tournament, and at the year's end the top 64 men on the singles points list and the top 24 doubles players receive bonuses from the $4 million bonus pool. This pool contains a direct contribution by Nabisco and contributions from each tournament ranging from $150,000 from Grand Slam Championships to $11,200 from the smallest Regular Series tournament. To qualify for a bonus, a player must compete in at least 14 tournaments and these 'self designations' may be amended by the Council according to an agreed formula in order to maintain the quality of entry for the entire circuit. The Grand Prix year ends with the Nabisco Masters which in 1985 became a 16-man knock-out tournament in singles. There were eight doubles pairs. Qualification is based on points won in singles and doubles at Grand Prix tournaments.

NABISCO GRAND PRIX 1985 – FINAL STANDINGS

SINGLES

		POINTS	BONUS			POINTS	BONUS
1	I. Lendl (CZ)	4,459	$800,000	33	M. Anger (USA)	549	$14,000
2	J. McEnroe (USA)	4,103	550,000	34	G. Holmes (USA)	546	14,000
3	M. Wilander (SW)	3,308	400,000	35	L. Pimek (CZ)	540	14,000
4	S. Edberg (SW)	2,511	250,000	36	E. Teltscher (USA)	529	14,000
5	B. Becker (G)	2,233	150,000	37	R. Krishnan (IND)	528	14,000
6	J. S. Connors (USA)	2,178	100,000	38	M. Leach (USA)	479	12,000
7	Y. Noah (F)	1,886	75,000	39	J. L. Clerc (ARG)	479	12,000
8	A. Jarryd (SW)	1,860	55,000	40	A. Maurer (G)	462	12,000
9	J. Kriek (USA)	1,497	45,000	41	S. Giammalva (USA)	442	12,000
10	J. Nystrom (SW)	1,482	40,000	42	B. Schultz (USA)	416	12,000
11	T. Mayotte (USA)	1,454	35,000	43	L. Duncan (USA)	413	10,000
12	T. Smid (CZ)	1,348	30,000	44	L. Stefanki (USA)	413	10,000
13	M. Mecir (CZ)	1,311	26,000	45	D. Perez (UR)	408	10,000
14	H. Leconte(F)	1,277	26,000	46	P. Slozil (CZ)	393	10,000
15	B. Gilbert (USA)	1,271	26,000	47	M. Davis (USA)	376	10,000
16	P. Annacone (USA)	1,205	26,000	48	H. Schwaier (G)	375	9,000
17	S. Davis (USA)	1,138	26,000	49	M. Dickson (USA)	371	9,000
18	K. Curren (USA)	1,127	22,000	50	F. Cancellotti (IT)	360	9,000
19	M. Jaite (ARG)	964	22,000	51	G. Vilas (ARG)	360	9,000
20	J. Arias (USA)	959	22,000	52	H. de la Pena (ARG)	352	9,000
21	A. Gomez (EC)	879	22,000	53	W. Masur (AUS)	341	8,000
22	H. Sundstrom (SW)	842	22,000	54	K. Flach (USA)	339	8,000
23	D. Pate (USA)	794	19,000	55	S. Perkis (IS)	318	8,000
24	T. Wilkison (USA)	758	19,000	56	J. Brown (USA)	317	8,000
25	A. Krickstein (USA)	744	19,000	57	J. Fitzgerald (AUS)	314	8,000
26	J. Hlasek (SWZ)	735	19,000	58	B. Testerman (USA)	312	6,000
27	T. Tulasne (F)	704	19,000	59	Tom Gullikson (USA)	312	6,000
28	J. Gunnarsson (SW)	691	16,000	60	G. Forget (F)	303	6,000
29	H. Gunthardt(SWZ)	683	16,000	61	S. Casal (SP)	296	6,000
30	S. Zivojinovic (YU)	666	16,000	62	V. Gerulaitis (USA)	294	6,000
31	J. Lloyd (GB)	596	16,000	63	R. Seguso (USA)	293	5,000
32	J. Sadri (USA)	589	16,000	64	K. Evernden (NZ)	289	5,000

DOUBLES

		POINTS	BONUS			POINTS	BONUS
1	R. Seguso (USA)	769	$165,000	13	M. R. Edmondson (AUS)	412	13,000
2	K. Flach (USA)	765	120,000	14	B. Taroczy (HU)	379	12,000
3	C. Van Rensburg (SA)	671	90,000	15	S. Davis (USA)	302	11,000
4	K. Warwick (AUS)	587	70,000	16	S. Edberg (SW)	296	10,000
5	P. Annacone (USA)	584	50,000	17	M. DePalmer (USA)	290	8,000
6	A. Jarryd (SW)	574	40,000	18	A. Gomez (EC)	271	8,000
7	T. Smid (CZ)	513	30,000	19	Y. Noah (F)	270	7,000
8	M. Wilander (SW)	467	25,000	20	G. Donnelly (USA)	249	7,000
9	P. Slozil (CZ)	452	20,000	21	P. Fleming (USA)	237	5,000
10	J. Fitzgerald (AUS)	437	17,000	22	D. Pate (USA)	234	5,000
11	H. Gunthardt (SWZ)	423	15,000	23	P. Cash (AUS)	225	4,000
12	J. Nystrom (SW)	417	14,000	23	E. Sanchez (SP)	225	4,000

It was a year of significant progress for Heinz Gunthardt, who was a quarter-finalist at Wimbledon, where, with Taroczy, he won the doubles, and at the US Open, where he won the mixed with Navratilova. *(T. Hindley)*

DOUBLES

TEAMS	POINTS	TEAMS	POINTS
1 K. Flach (USA)/R. Seguso (USA)	765	6 H. Gunthardt (SW)/B. Taroczy (HU)	366
2 P. Annacone (USA)/C. Van Rensburg (SA)	575	7 S. Edberg (SW)/A. Jarryd (SW)	283
		8 S. Casal (SP)/E. Sanchez (SP)	218
3 M. Edmondson (AUS)/ K. Warwick (AUS)	384	9 P. Cash (AUS)/J. Fitzgerald (AUS)	217
		10 M. DePalmer (USA)/G. Donnelly (USA)	173
4 P. Slozil (CZ)/T. Smid (CZ)	366		
5 J. Nystrom (SW)/M. Wilander (SW)	365		

SEGMENT 1: 21 JANUARY–3 MARCH

Richard Finn, Malcolm Folley and Bryan Cutress

US PROFESSIONAL INDOOR CHAMPIONSHIPS ($300,000)

In from the sub-zero temperatures that gripped the city walked top-seeded John McEnroe to take the singles title at this traditional Super Series opener of the Nabisco Grand Prix season. McEnroe's passage through the 48-player field without the loss of a set, while beating Marty Davis, Brad Gilbert, Yannick Noah, Scott Davis and Miloslav Mecir, was not surprising. His victory was his fourth in succession on the Supreme court at the Spectrum, which is a surface that caters perfectly for his serve-and-volley tactics.

What was surprising, however, was the appearance of the soft-spoken, bearded Czech, Mecir, in the best-of-five-sets final. Mecir entered the week unseeded, unknown and ranked 61 in the world. He left ranked 29, with his first appearance in a Super Series final to his credit and victories over, among others, Joakim Nystrom and Jimmy Connors. Mecir beat Connors 5–7 6–4 6–3 in the semi-finals, with a patient baseline game built on strong and deep groundstrokes and fleet coverage of the court that wore down the second seed's patience. In the final Mecir scared McEnroe by taking a 5–1 lead in the second set before losing 6–3 7–6 6–1. 'He's really quick around the court', said McEnroe afterwards.

There were other surprises in store for the 82,648 fans. Unseeded Scott Davis reached the semi-finals, upsetting Tomas Smid and Eliot Teltscher before bowing to McEnroe. Qualifier Joao Soares of Brazil beat David Pate and Greg Holmes, two of the top young American stars, to reach the quarter-finals where he lost to Mecir. Holmes had kept alive his reputation of being a giant killer by knocking out the third-seeded Mats Wilander in the second round.

Wilander, a virtual stranger to the indoor American tour, was still able to enjoy his week by taking the doubles title with Nystrom. In a stunning round of upset wins, the Swedish pair knocked off the No. 3 team of Ken Flach and Robert Seguso, the No. 5 team of Fritz Buehning and Ferdi Taygan, the No. 2 team of Heinz Gunthardt and Balazs Taroczy and, in the final, the No. 4 team of Wojtek Fibak and Sandy Mayer. – R.F.

SPECTRUM STADIUM, PHILADELPHIA, 21–27 JANUARY
MEN'S SINGLES – Quarter-finals: J. P. McEnroe d. Y. Noah (F) 6–2 6–4; S. Davis d. E. Teltscher 6–3 6–2; M. Mecir (CZ) d. J. Soares (BR) 7–5 7–5; J. S. Connors d. M. Purcell 6–4 7–6; **Semi-finals:** McEnroe d. Davis 6–2 6–4; Mecir d. Connors 5–7 6–4 6–3. **Final:** McEnroe d. Mecir 6–3 7–6 6–1. **MEN'S DOUBLES – Final:** J. Nystrom (SW) /M. Wilander (SW) d. W. Fibak (POL) /A. A. Mayer 3–6 6–2 6–2.

US INDOOR CHAMPIONSHIPS ($250,000)

A rarely seen snowfall paralysed the city of Memphis on the Thursday of the tournament, but it did little to slow down the Swedish steam-roller, Stefan Edberg, as he ploughed his way to his first title in almost a year. The 19-year-old, who had won in Milan the previous March, returned to the winner's circle in emphatic fashion on the Supreme court at the Racquet Club of Memphis by routing defending champion and top seed Jimmy Connors 6–1 6–4 in the semi-finals and an injured Yannick Noah 6–1 6–0 in the final. In five matches, Edberg did not lose a set.

The third-seeded Noah, in his first final in 50 weeks (La Quinta in 1984 had been the last), played the championship match with a pain in his left ankle and anxiety in his heart.

The pain came from a sprained lateral ligament suffered during a quarter-final victory, 6–3 3–6 6–3 over Shachar Perkis. Heavy strapping and the flow of adrenalin carried him through a thrilling and gutsy 3–6 6–1 7–5 semi-final win over the No. 2 seed, Eliot Teltscher, but his lack of mobility caught up with him in the final and was too much of a handicap against the shot-making skills and serving prowess of Edberg in the 54-minute final. Edberg had two love service games and served three aces to open the final game of the match with a flourish.

Noah's anxiety was triggered by an early-morning phone call from his wife Cecilia, who, eight months pregnant, was calling from a New York hospital. Although she reassured her husband that it was a false alarm: 'It shook me up', said Noah, who endeared himself more to the fans after the final by announcing that he would donate a portion of his $22,500 cheque to CARE for aid to refugees in Ethiopia. Noah asked for donations from the fans and an estimated $6,350 was collected on the spot.

Connors abandoned his prototype graphite mid-size racquet for good at the start of the week, pulling out his trusty, antique T-200 steel frames from his bag. Although he struggled past the thunder of the sixth seed, Kevin Curren, 7–6 6–4 in the quarters, he simply couldn't cope with the powerful serving and crisp net play of Edberg in the semi-finals.

The Czech team of Tomas Smid and Pavel Slozil won their fifth title in 13 months by beating Curren and Steve Denton in the doubles final. – R.F.

MEMPHIS, 28 JANUARY–3 FEBRUARY
MEN'S SINGLES – Quarter-finals: J. S. Connors d. K. Curren (SA) 7–6 6–4; S. Edberg (SW) d. B. Gilbert 6–4 6–2; Y. Noah (F) d. S. Perkis (IS) 6–3 3–6 6–3; E. Teltscher d. G. Holmes 7–6 6–3. **Semi-finals:** Edberg d. Connors 6–1 6–4; Noah d. Teltscher 3–6 6–1 7–5. **Final:** Edberg d. Noah 6–1 6–0. **MEN'S DOUBLES – Final:** P. Slozil (CZ) /T. Smid (CZ) d. Curren /S. Denton 1–6 6–3 6–4.

LIPTON INTERNATIONAL PLAYERS CHAMPIONSHIPS ($300,000)

When Tim Mayotte played his opening match in the inaugural Lipton International Players Championships he could hardly have guessed that he was embarking on the most exciting journey of his tennis career. His first-round encounter with Nigeria's Nduka Odizor went on court late at night, when the temperature at Laver's Resort, Delray Beach, Florida had dipped alarmingly. Less than a fortnight later, Mayotte, No. 45 in the world, was $112,000 richer and the holder of the first Lipton title. At 24, his reputation for sportsmanship had long since been established. All he needed, he felt, was a crown of his own.

With ATP Vice-President John McEnroe declining to enter what was, in effect, the players' championships, Ivan Lendl was the top seed. Lendl survived three rounds – even calling his own score, along with Larry Stefanki, after umpire Luigi Brambilla deserted the chair towards the end of their first-round match – but went out to Sweden's Stefan Edberg. The match started on Monday afternoon, but rain caused it to be postponed until the following morning with Edberg ahead 6–4 5–6. Publicists had christened the new two-week event for men and women 'winter Wimbledon' and here was the weather to illustrate their campaign! Edberg, seeded 13, needed just ten minutes to wrap up his victory over Lendl, 6–4 7–6. Although it boasted a 128–man draw, in common with the Grand Slam tournaments, Lipton did not introduce best-of-five-sets matches until the quarter-final stage.

By then, Edberg was one of only four seeds left in the event, the others being Yannick Noah (9), Tomas Smid (11) and Vitas Gerulaitis (12), of whom only Smid was destined to last a further round. Number two seed, Mats Wilander, was shown the door by American Mike Leach, and Henrik Sundstrom, seeded three, failed to surmount the first hurdle, losing to Yugoslav Marco Ostoja. Scott Davis accounted for Edberg in straight sets in the quarter-finals, having previously beaten Brad Gilbert, Paul Annacone and Marc Flur without a loss of a set. Then just before midnight on the second Friday, Davis clinched his place in the final by outplaying Smid 7–6 6–4 4–6 6–3.

Awaiting him was Mayotte, who earlier in the day had disposed of Sweden's Jan

Gunnarsson. Mayotte had reached the final without meeting a seed and, like Davis, was unseeded. Mayotte hoped the final would show a nationwide TV audience that other members of the cast could entertain and excite on a tennis court, but for one and a half sets it was as flat as yesterday's breakfast pancakes, as Davis capitalised on Mayotte's nervousness. But then Mayotte discovered the confidence to attack his one-time team-mate from Stanford University as he courageously fought back to a 4–6 4–6 6–3 6–2 6–4 victory. Davis's break-point in the first game of the third set could have broken his rival's spirit: Mayotte averted that crisis with a service winner. Davis had another break-point for a 2–1 lead. However, his volley was called 'long' but then corrected, and when the point was replayed Mayotte won it with another service winner. Charged up like never before, Mayotte took the match by the throat and Davis was gradually betrayed by his touch, which at the outset had been lethal.

A day that had dawned with the two young men, rivals yet friends, hitting up with each other came to an end when Mayotte struck away a smash to win the first championship of his professional career. He was just happy that he and Davis had put on an exhibition fit for the occasion. It was also typical of the man that, in his moment of triumph, he cast his mind back to his opening match against Odizor. 'At the beginning of the tournament, I played at midnight and the crowd comprised one drunk', he said. 'I finished playing in the final on national television.'

Paul Annacone from New York and Christo Van Rensburg from South Africa proved unstoppable dark horses in the doubles. Unseeded in a quality field, they walked off with the $45,000 winners' cheque by defeating the experienced duo of Sherwood Stewart and Kim Warwick 7–5 7–5 6–4 in the final. Potential champions such as Slozil and Smid and Edberg and Jarryd fell at the quarter-final hurdle, while Frenchmen Yannick Noah and Henri Leconte, the only seeds, at eight, to survive to the semis, where swept aside by Stewart and Warwick. – M.F.

DELRAY BEACH, FLORIDA, 4–17 FEBRUARY
MEN'S SINGLES – Quarter-finals: S. Davis d. S. Edberg (SW) 6–1 6–4 7–5; T. Smid (CZ) d. Y. Noah (F) 6–3 6–3 7–5; J. Gunnarsson (SW) d. V. Gerulaitis 2–6 6–3 6–4 6–2; T. Mayotte d. M. Leach 6–2 6–3 6–2. **Semi-finals:** Davis d. Smid 7–6 6–4 4–6 6–3; Mayotte d. Gunnarsson 7–6 6–2 4–6 7–5. **Final:** Mayotte d. Davis 4–6 4–6 6–3 6–2 6–4.
MEN'S DOUBLES – Final: P. Annacone /C. Van Rensburg (SA) d. S. Stewart /K. Warwick (AUS) 7–5 7–5 6–4.

PILOT PEN CLASSIC ($300,000)

A dream came true for Larry Stefanki in the $300,000 Pilot Pen Classic at La Quinta in February. As touring professional for the host club, he had invited 55 of his colleagues to compete in the tournament and expected to be one of the many spectators enjoying a week of superb tennis and warm, pleasant weather. Instead he was given a last-minute wild-card spot and went on to win the title above such names as Jimmy Connors, Henrik Sundstrom, Joakim Nystrom, Aaron Krickstein, Johan Kriek, Tomas Smid, Guillermo Vilas and Scott Davis. The last wild-card had been held back by tournament director Charlie Pasarell because there was a possibility that Mats Wilander or Stefan Edberg might want to enter. But a couple of days before the start, Stefanki was told that he had been given the last spot in the draw – and he made the most of his good fortune by beating David Pate 6–1 6–4 3–6 6–3 in the final. 'I was never nervous playing before the home crowd', he said after picking up a $51,000 cheque and 49 computer bonus points which sent him shooting up the ranking list from 143 to 35.

Stefanki's success must rank on the season's list of shocks only slightly lower than Boris Becker's incredible Wimbledon performance. Like Becker later, he had most of his problems solved for him by other competitors, for Greg Holmes put out Smid in the third round and Connors 6–0 6–3 in an amazing quarter-final, while Ben Testerman dismissed second-seeded Henrik Sundstrom 7–5 6–3 in the second round. Pate did his bit by beating Nystrom, Hank Pfister and Krickstein, all in three sets, and Libor Pimek 7–6 6–4 in the

Sweden's intensely competitive Anders Jarryd came close to beating Becker in the Wimbledon semi-finals, but illness kept him from an active role in the Davis Cup final in Munich. *(A. Evans)*

semi-final. Meanwhile, Stefanki was easing his way past Kevin Belcher, Juan Aguilera, Scott Davis, Tarik Benhabiles and Holmes to reach the final.

He made a magnificent start to the title match which attracted 7,500 spectators. His groundstokes were sharp and accurate as he took the first two sets against the obviously nervous Pate, who had already decided to give ten per cent of his winnings to famine relief in Ethiopia. But Stefanki, who later admitted that he felt 'dead tired' after that opening flourish, conceded the third set before he got his second wind and went on to take the biggest pay cheque of his career and his first Grand Prix Super Series title.

The doubles title went to Heinz Gunthardt and Balazs Taroczy who later became Wimbledon champions. After beating Pavel Slozil and Smid in the semi-finals they downed Ken Flach and Robert Seguso, the latter showing no sign of the knee injury he sustained while losing to John Lloyd in the second round of the singles. – B.C.

LA QUINTA, CALIFORNIA, 18–24 FEBRUARY
MEN'S SINGLES – Quarter-finals: G. Holmes d. J. S. Connors 6–0 6–3; L. Stefanki d. T. Benhabiles (F) 7–5 7–6; L. Pimek (CZ) d. J. M. Lloyd (GB) 6–1 1–6 6–4; D. Pate d. A. Krickstein 6–2 2–6 6–1. **Semi-finals:** Stefanki d. Holmes 6–2 4–6 6–3; Pate d. Pimek 7–6 6–4. **Final:** Stefanki d. Pate 6–1 6–4 3–6 6–3.
MEN'S DOUBLES – Final: H. Gunthardt (SWZ) /B. Taroczy (HU) d. K. Flach /R. Seguso 3–6 7–6 6–3.

WCT HOUSTON ($300,000)

A new tournament on the Nabisco Grand Prix tour saw some familiar names in the winner's circle at the Sam Houston Coliseum. The singles winner was the top-seeded John McEnroe, who ran his year's match record to 10–0 by mowing down Wojtek Fibak, Tom Gullikson, Brad Gilbert, Peter Fleming and Kevin Curren. McEnroe then teamed with Fleming to win their 53rd career doubles title, over Hank Pfister and Ben Testerman, which took them to the top of the all-time Open list. They had joined Bob Hewitt and Frew Macmillan on 52 by winning the Masters in January. The clean sweep of the hardware was the 30th in McEnroe's prolific career.

Like all great athletes, McEnroe is at his most vulnerable in the early rounds before he has had time to get into a groove. Here it was the veteran Fibak, fresh from a semi-final showing in Toronto the previous week, who most extended the champion before losing 6–2 6–7 7–5. Playing a very deliberate game, taking all the time allotted between the points to unbalance McEnroe's timing and patience, Fibak was able to fight a long but losing battle. Fibak's time-oriented strategy backfired at 5–5 in the final set, when he was assessed a point penalty for delay of game to give a break-point to McEnroe, who cashed in on it and served out the match. The next four opponents felt the wrath of the McEnroe fury as he brushed them aside without the loss of a set and in the final he beat Curren 7–5 6–1 7–6.

In the land of the shootout and fast draw, it was only fitting that serving was the name of the game in the bang-bang showdown between the top two seeds. McEnroe got the better of the battle, firing in 14 aces to Curren's three. Curren was looking for his second title in as many weeks, following a win in Toronto. He dropped the first set with a lost service at 5–5. In the third set Curren looked to have the upper hand as he grabbed a 3–0 lead, but a double-fault on break-point at 3–1 opened the comeback trail for McEnroe. In the tie-break McEnroe slammed three aces to raise the victory flag. 'I wasn't even in the match. I was on the ropes', said Curren.

Shachar Perkis of Israel continued to enjoy the indoor circuit, reaching the semi-finals for the first time in a Grand Prix tournament. Unseeded he beat the eighth seed, Ramesh Krishnan, as well as Terry Moor and Mark Dickson before bowing to Curren. – R.F.

25 FEBRUARY–3 MARCH
MEN'S SINGLES – Quarter-finals: J. P. McEnroe d. B. Gilbert 6–3 6–3; P. Fleming d. L. Shiras 6–3 6–3; S. Perkis (IS) d. M. Dickson 7–6 6–0; K. Curren (SA) d. T. Mayotte 7–5 7–6. **Semi-finals:** McEnroe d. Fleming 6–4 6–0; Curren d. Perkis 6–2 6–2. **Final:** McEnroe d. Curren 7–5 6–1 7–6.
MEN'S DOUBLES – Final: Fleming /McEnroe d. H. Pfister /B. Testerman 6–3 6–2.

SEGMENT 2: 11–31 MARCH

Richard Evans, Malcolm Folley, Hugh Jamieson

BELGIAN INDOOR CHAMPIONSHIPS ($210,000)

Not for the only time in 1985, a Super Series Grand Prix event turned out to be a Swedish festival when Anders Jarryd defeated his country's No. 1, Mats Wilander, 6–4 3–6 7–5 in the final of the Belgian Indoor Championships. Jarryd had to beat three compatriots in five rounds on the way to the title and only the 19-year-old Australian, Pat Cash, with a 6–4 6–2 defeat of Joakim Nystrom in the quarters, prevented an all-Swedish semi-final round. Twice in 1984 — at Cincinnati (cement) and Barcelona (clay) — this amazing group had three of their number in the semi-finals. Now they had achieved it indoors. Apparently their consistency and versatility know no bounds, for they achieved it again at the Stockholm Open.

Even so there were a few points of interest in Brussels that were not draped in Sweden's blue and yellow flag. The site itself was new, Eric Drossart having secured the use of the Brussels Exhibition complex in a move that gave him an extra 2,000 seats in comparison with the 4,000 capacity of the Forest National Stadium. By the weekend the place was packed, despite live TV coverage, transmitted locally in both French and Flemish.

On court, the opening days were dominated by the sight of a big, copper-headed West German boy of whom big things were expected. Boris Becker out-hit Robert Green in straight sets in the first round before going down in a thriller to the unrelenting Tomas Smid of Czechoslovakia, 5–7 7–6 7–5.

Cash, in his first Grand Prix event of the year, provided most of the other early interest. He had played only one serious match between competing in the Australian Open early the previous December and the *Davis Cup* tie against Yugoslavia just prior to Brussels in March. Such a long lay-off was surely unnecessary and Cash's year became doubly sad when a back injury forced him onto the sidelines immediately after Wimbledon. In retrospect, Brussels proved to be one of the high points of his year. Using his aggressive serve-and-volley game to its best advantage on the medium-paced carpet, he overpowered Mike DePalmer and Matt Mitchell before playing a well-controlled match against the steady Nystrom, gaining in authority and confidence as the match progressed, to win 6–4 6–2.

Wilander, however, provided a sterner test in the semi-final and Cash's lack of match practice over the preceding months caught up with him. After Wilander had earned the first set 6–3 with a barrage of volleys reminiscent of the style he adopts on grass at Kooyong, Cash battled back and actually led 5–1 in the second-set tie-break before coming apart at the seams. Two poor backhand errors allowed Wilander to close out the tie-break and the match 8–6.

Strangely, Wilander looked far more inhibited against Jarryd although that is sometimes the case when one is confronted by a friend and compatriot. But it was Jarryd who proved the more positive, and even during Wilander's period of ascendancy in the second set, Anders never allowed his head to drop. The whoop of joy the 'unsilent Swede' let out after storming the net to force a final error out of his country's No. 1 revealed the intensity of Jarryd's competitive spirit.

The Swedes were also in the ascendancy in the doubles, Jarryd and Stefan Edberg triumphing over Kevin Curren and Wojtek Fibak, 6–3 7–6. – R.E.

BRUSSELS, 11–17 MARCH
MEN'S SINGLES – Quarter-finals: M. Wilander (SW) d. H. Gunthardt (SWZ) 6–1 5–7 7–5; P. Cash

(AUS) d. J. Nystrom (SW) 6–4 6–2; S. Edberg (SW) d. S. Giammalva (USA) 7–6 6–3; A. Jarryd (SW) d. T. Smid (CZ) 6–4 6–4. **Semi-finals:** Wilander d. Cash 6–3 7–6; Jarryd d. Edberg 7–6 6–3. **Final:** Jarryd d. Wilander 6–4 3–6 7–5.
MEN'S DOUBLES – Final: Edberg /Jarryd d. K. Curren (SA) /W. Fibak (POL) 6–3 7–6.

ABN WORLD TENNIS TOURNAMENT ($250,000)

Although the pre-event publicity was built around John McEnroe's entry in the $250,000 ABN World Tennis tournament, the cardboard cut-out of the world champion on the Dunlop promotion stand was all the Dutch public saw of McEnroe. Jakob Hlasek shed no tears about that, for McEnroe's withdrawal through a wrist injury left a gap in the 32-man draw for the Czech-born Swiss, who proceeded to the final, beating two seeds, Ramesh Krishnan (8) and Tomas Smid (6), in the process.

Of the top five seeds, four of whom were Swedish, only Joakim Nystrom (5) reached the semi-finals, where he was despatched in straight sets by eventual winner, Miloslav Mecir from Czechoslovakia. Apart from toppling Nystrom, Mecir defeated the second seed, Anders Jarryd, and Boris Becker. The only set he dropped throughout the tournament was the one he conceded in the first round to Australian Paul McNamee.

Top seed Mats Wilander survived a first-round scare against John Lloyd 7–6 6–2 – the British No. 1 led 5–1 in the opening-set tie-break – only to lose in three sets against the hard-serving American, John Sadri. Stefan Edberg, the other seeded Swede, was a first-round casualty in more ways than one. He pulled a stomach muscle during his defeat there by Francisco Gonzalez and withdrew from the doubles, as well as the following tournament in Milan, where he would have been defending champion. The flamboyant Vitas Gerulaitis, seeded seventh, gained first-hand experience of the havoc Becker was to create later in the summer, when he lost 6–2 4–6 7–6 to the German teenager. Becker was disappointed that he was unable to finish off the New Yorker in straight sets, apparently oblivious to the fact that Gerulaitis served for the match three times in the final set!

Much was expected of the young Australian, Pat Cash, a semi-finalist at both Wimbledon and the US Open in 1984 and now seeded third. He overcame Kim Warwick and Dutchman Huub van Boeckel without too many problems, but Nystrom proved an altogether tougher nut to crack. When Cash served for the match at 5–3 in the final set, the emotionless Swede refused to yield, saving one match-point with a nerveless lob, and a second with a forehand drive that arced over the tramlines before landing in court. The Australian's chance disappeared with that pass, and Nystrom rattled off the tie-break 7–4 to win 2–6 6–3 7–6.

Mecir, though, had the measure of the Swede, just as he had the game to halt Hlasek's ambition in the final, benefiting, no doubt, from his first-ever Grand Prix final – against John McEnroe in Philadelphia two months earlier. On the circuit, the 6ft 3in Czech had already been christened 'Mecir the cat', the nickname being designed to illustrate the deceptive pace with which he disarms rivals. After his 6–1 6–2 defeat Hlasek commented: 'Mecir moves so smoothly, you can't see him move.'

Gerulaitis gained a measure of revenge over Becker in the doubles when, partnering Paul McNamee, he reached the final by beating the German teenager and Vijay Amritraj in two tie-break sets. But the American-Australian combination had to accept the consolation prize, falling 6–4 6–4 to No. 1 seeds Pavel Slozil and Tomas Smid. – M.F.

ROTTERDAM, 18–24 MARCH
MEN'S SINGLES – Quarter-finals: T. Smid (CZ) d. J. Sadri (USA) 6–1 6–3; J. Hlasek (SWZ) d. F. Gonzalez (USA) 6–2 4–6 6–4; J. Nystrom (SW) d. P. Cash (AUS) 2–6 6–3 7–6; M. Mecir (CZ) d. B. Becker (G) 6–4 6–2. **Semi-finals:** Hlasek d. Smid 6–3 6–7 6–3; Mecir d. Nystrom 6–3 6–3. **Final:** Mecir d. Hlasek 6–1 6–2.
MEN'S DOUBLES – Final: P. Slozil (CZ) /Smid d. V. Gerulaitis (USA) /P. McNamee (AUS) 6–4 6–4.

CUORE CUP ($300,000)

When John McEnroe took the Cuore Cup for the fourth time, he extended his winning streak to 15–0 and picked up the $60,000 cheque without dropping a set. Following his routine 6–4 6–1 win over Sweden's Anders Jarryd, he was awarded the Fila Cup from Bjorn Borg, who received a standing ovation from a sell-out crowd.

It still seemed incomprehensible then that 17-year-old West German Boris Becker would emerge from a first-round defeat at the hands of McEnroe to take the tennis world by storm. For although both McEnroe and Borg included Becker in their list of up-and-coming kids for the future no-one could possibly have forecast the impact that the West German boy was soon to make. Becker gave us a clue to his thoughts after making McEnroe, still suffering from the effects of a wrist injury, work hard for his 6–4 6–3 first-round win: 'McEnroe is not my hero any more because I suddenly found that I didn't fear him. But it was a good experience for me to play against the world No. 1 and something that I hope will do me good for the future.' Upset by Becker's insistence on disputing a number of calls, McEnroe channelled all his aggression into the business of winning but admitted: 'He's obviously one for the future.'

Still the most gifted player in the world, McEnroe was king – and the Italian fans loved him for every minute as he packed the Palalido and paraded his girl-friend Tatum O'Neal in public – both seemingly oblivious to the kind of pressures and distractions that were eventually to cost him his Wimbledon and US Open titles. In Milan Jarryd, the man who had beaten McEnroe in Montreal 12 months earlier, found himself out-thought and out-played with his cupboard bare of shots when it came to the crunch.

The world No. 1 was in the mood to win. He did more than brush Czechoslovakia's Jacob Hlasek aside in the semi-finals with a 6–3 6–2 victory: he produced a shot that brought gasps of astonishment from the fans and floored the unfortunate Hlasek. Chasing an almost impossible recovery, McEnroe scampered into a corner of the court before flicking a backhand crosscourt return over his shoulder to leave Hlasek motionless at the net as it turned into a winning drop-shot. Jarryd had more problems getting to the final, defeating on his way the artistic Indian, Vijay Amritraj, big-serving John Sadri and the resilient Tomas Smid in a second-set tie-break, during which the Czech paid the penalty for some schoolboy errors.

But at least Jarryd gained some crumb of comfort with his third doubles title of the year after winning Toronto with Peter Fleming and Brussels in partnership with fellow-Swede Stefan Edberg. This time he partnered Switzerland's Heinz Gunthardt as they cruised to the title with a 6–2 6–1 triumph over the likeable Aussies, Brod Dyke and Wally Masur. – H.J.

MILAN, 25–31 MARCH
MEN'S SINGLES – Quarter-finals: J. P. McEnroe (USA) d. H. Leconte (F) 6–3 6–4; J. Hlasek (SWZ) d. Tim Gullikson (USA) 7–6 4–6 6–4; T. Smid (CZ) d. V. Gerulaitis (USA) 6–3 7–6; A. Jarryd (SW) d. J. Sadri (USA) 6–2 6–4. **Semi-finals:** McEnroe d. Hlasek 6–3 6–2; Jarryd d. Smid 6–3 7–6. **Final:** McEnroe d. Jarryd 6–4 6–1.
MEN'S DOUBLES – Final: Jarryd /H. Gunthardt (SWZ) d. B. Dyke (AUS) /W. Masur (AUS) 6–2 6–1.

SEGMENT 3: 25 MARCH–12 MAY

Bob Greene

PAINE WEBBER CLASSIC ($315,000)

Jimmy Connors appropriately reached the final of the Paine Webber Classic in Fort Myers, Florida, staged in the new Stadium bearing his name. The hard-court surface was the same type on which Jimbo had won the US Open in 1982 and 1983. In both of those title matches, Connors had defeated Ivan Lendl, who was fittingly once again on the other side of the net in Florida, pitting his powerful serve against the man with the best return of serve in the game.

Connors, seeking his first Nabisco Grand Prix title since 1984, had returned to his old Wilson T2000 racket. He had to battle his way to the final, stopping seventh seed Johan Kriek in the quarters and struggling past No. 3 Andres Gomez in a three-set semi-final. Connors was the first seed Lendl faced, as Aaron Krickstein (4) had fallen to Sammy Giammalva in the second round and Yannick Noah (5) had been upset by Brad Gilbert in the first. Connors's half of the draw was intact to the quarters, where Gomez eliminated Eliot Teltscher, the No. 6 seed.

The key to the final, played in bright sunshine and 43°(C) temperatures, came in the third game of the opening set when Lendl, behind 15–40 on his serve, unleashed the first of his eight aces, and pulled back to deuce. Connors gained another break-point, but Lendl drew even with another ace. It was the closest Connors would come as Lendl's game matched the temperature, and in the end it was Lendl who picked up the winner's cheque with an easy 6–3 6–2 victory.

Both finalists had taken time off from the tour, but had different theories on how their holidays had affected them. 'I wish every time I take six weeks off, I could come back and win a tournament', Lendl said. Connors insinuated that his one-month layoff may have hurt his timing. Seven years older than Lendl, he also mentioned that his hard-fought 3–6 6–3 6–4 semi-final victory over Gomez the day before may have taken a lot out of him.

The pairing of Ken Flach and Robert Seguso took the doubles title over Sammy Giammalva and David Pate.

FORT MYERS, FLORIDA, 25–31 MARCH
MEN'S SINGLES – Quarter-finals: I. Lendl (CZ) d. B. Gilbert 6–4 6–2; S. Giammalva d. S. Davis 6–2 6–3; A. Gomez (EC) d. E. Teltscher 7–5 6–0; J. S. Connors d. J. Kriek 6–3 6–2. *Semi-finals:* Lendl d. Giammalva 6–2 6–1; Connors d. Gomez 3–6 6–3 6–4. *Final:* Lendl d. Connors 6–3 6–2.
MEN'S DOUBLES – Final: K. Flach /R. Seguso d. Giammalva /D. Pate 3–6 6–3 6–2.

CHICAGO ($250,000)

After 13 years on the tour, there aren't too many things that Jimmy Connors hasn't done, but at the Volvo Tennis /Chicago tournament, he posted another first. According to Jimbo, winner of more tournaments than any other male player, he had never defaulted a match in his professional career until having to do so before the Chicago final, where he was to have met John McEnroe. (Actually he was forgetting his default to the same player in the Colgate Masters in January, 1979, when he had retired with blistered feet when McEnroe was 7–5 3–0 ahead.) He had injured his back in a 6–4 4–6 7–5 quarter-final defeat of Brad Gilbert and aggravated it in a 6–4 6–3 semi-final victory over Ecuador's Andres Gomez.

The veteran lefthander had easily disposed of Jay Lapidus 6–2 6–3, and David Pate 6–4 7–6.

McEnroe, meanwhile, had comfortably moved through the top half of the draw by crushing Peter Doohan 6–0 6–1 before ousting Mike Leach 6–1 6–2, Paul Annacone 4–6 6–4 6–1, and Scott Davis 6–4 6–1. Annacone pulled off something of a coup in taking only the second set the feisty New Yorker had lost in his first four tournaments of the year, the other being to Wojtek Fibak in Houston.

The week was not without its excitements. In a second-round battle between seventh-seeded Tim Mayotte – who had been extended to a third-set tie-break by qualifier Nduka Odizor – and John Sadri, the latter took a 6–3 lead in the first-set tie-break before Mayotte fought back to save three set-points and eventually win the tie-break 9–7. Throughout the second set, which Mayotte won 7–5, Sadri vented his rage in verbal outbursts, and when the match ended, he refused to shake hands with his conqueror.

Mike Bauer upset No. 5 seed Eliot Teltscher 5–7 6–1 6–2 in the first round, while Terry Moor knocked off Yannick Noah (4) 4–6 7–6 7–6, Bauer then falling to Gilbert in the second round, 6–4 6–1, and Moor being victimised by Scott Davis in the quarters. Johan Kriek, the No. 6 seed, was ambushed 2–6 7–5 6–4 by Annacone in the second round, while Gomez eliminated Mayotte in the quarter-finals.

Noah and Kriek, playing together for the first time in five years, won the doubles title, beating the American *Davis Cup* duo of Ken Flach and Robert Seguso, 3–6 4–6 7–5 6–1 6–4, the title match having been extended to the best of five sets because of Connors's withdrawal.

1–7 APRIL
MEN'S SINGLES – Quarter-finals: J. P. McEnroe d. P. Annacone 4–6 6–4 6–1; S. Davis d. T. Moor 6–4 6–4; A. Gomez (EC) d. T. Mayotte 6–3 3–6 6–1; J. S. Connors d. B. Gilbert 4–6 6–4 7–5. **Semifinals:** McEnroe d. Davis 6–4 6–1; Connors d. Gomez 6–4 6–3. **Final:** McEnroe w.o. Connors.
MEN'S DOUBLES – Final: J. Kriek /Y. Noah (F) d. K. Flach /R. Seguso 3–6 4–6 7–5 6–1 6–4.

WCT ATLANTA ($300,000)

John McEnroe's favourite surface is an indoor carpet where the bounce is true, there are no weather conditions to worry about, and victories come almost automatically. It's no wonder he enjoyed – and won – the WCT Atlanta championships, an indoor event, although the Alexander Memorial Coliseum on the Georgia Tech University campus was not air-conditioned and McEnroe said it was the hottest indoor tournament that he's ever played. His game, a marvellous one of touch and genius, was as hot as the weather both inside and outside the Coliseum.

The field was filled with big servers who made gigantic leaps up the computer rankings in 1985, and the first victim was Sweden's Stefan Edberg, the No. 7 seed, who fell to American Mike Leach in the opening round. The first round also saw fourth-seeded Tomas Smid of Czechoslovakia stumble before the erratic American, John Sadri. India's Ramesh Krishnan was the only player whose game is not set up by a blistering or bewildering serve to gain the second round, where he met McEnroe, who had ousted fellow-American Brian Teacher to begin his successful run.

McEnroe eliminated the smooth-stroking Krishnan 6–1 7–5 before running into American Tim Mayotte, whose confidence had soared after he won the inaugural Lipton International Players Championships earlier in the year. Mayotte had knocked off Hank Pfister and Ken Flach before extending McEnroe to three sets while losing. It was just the warm-up McEnroe needed, as he was to face two more players with power games before the title was his.

After eliminating Edberg, Mike Leach edged qualifier Steve Denton, 7–6 6–7 6–2, then upset the tournament's No. 3 seed, Pat Cash, 6–4 3–6 6–2. After scrambling to the semi-final in his most successful Nabisco Grand Prix tournament this far, Leach found himself facing McEnroe. The top seed needed 77 minutes to end this surprising run as the loser double-faulted three times in the ninth game of the first set.

McEnroe's foe in the championship match, Paul Annacone, made his move through the bottom half of the draw by stopping Sadri, eliminating No. 8 seed Brad Gilbert and enjoying a walkover against second-seeded Kevin Curren, who was stricken with an intestinal illness.

Against McEnroe in the best-of-five-sets final, Annacone served up 13 aces, three of them in the opening game, and finished with 39 service winners. But McEnroe was also on his game, serving 44 service winners, including six aces, in his 7–6 7–6 6–2 victory. A double-fault and a loose error on an approach shot put Annacone behind 1–4 in the opening-set tie-break, and McEnroe made him pay for it, winning 7–2. He also took leads of 5–1 and 6–2 in the second tie-break, which he won 7–5, before breaking Annacone's service in the opening game of the third set, which he took easily.

Paul Annacone and Christo Van Rensburg took the doubles title, defeating Steve Denton and Tomas Smid 6–4 6–3.

22–28 APRIL
MEN'S SINGLES – Quarter-finals: J. P. McEnroe d. T. Mayotte 6–3 3–6 6–2; M. Leach d. P. Cash (AUS) 6–4 3–6 6–2; P. Annacone d. B. Gilbert 7–6 3–6 7–6; K. Curren (SA) d. S. Davis 6–2 7–6. ***Semi-finals:*** McEnroe d. Annacone 7–6 7–6 6–2.
MEN'S DOUBLES – Final: Annacone /C. Van Rensburg (SA) d. S. Denton /T. Smid (CZ) 6–4 6–3.

ALAN KING CAESAR'S PALACE CLASSIC ($400,000)

The $400,000 Alan King Caesar's Palace Tennis Classic had two big surprises: the unseeded Johan Kriek took the title and top-seeded Jimmy Connors was a first-round loser in a Grand Prix tournament for the first time since 1981. The big shocker came from the veteran Vijay Amritraj, whose classic strokes had also handed John McEnroe his only first-round defeat in 1984. The Indian used his fluent all-court game with great intelligence on the hard court, constantly moving Connors from side to side and baseline to net as he won 6–1 7–6, taking the tie-break 7–1.

American Jimmy Arias, more at home on clay, took out fourth-seeded Pat Cash, also in the first round, 1–6 6–3 7–6, and the No. 5 seed, Eliot Teltscher, in the quarter-finals, before reaching the final by way of a hard-earned win over Ken Flach. Kevin Curren, the No. 2 seed, who was trying to shake off a stomach virus, fell 6–1 6–1 to Stefan Edberg in the first round, before the Swede in turn lost in the second round to West Germany's Boris Becker, who was wild-carded into the tournament. But although Becker was able to beat Edberg 6–3 6–7 6–2, he couldn't handle the veteran Tomas Smid of Czechoslovakia, who won their quarter-final battle 6–4 6–7 7–6.

Meanwhile, Kriek was fighting his way through the lower half of the draw. He defeated John Sadri, eliminated Vince Van Patten – a wild-card entry who had disposed of the third seed, Aaron Krickstein – then upset eighth-seeded Tim Mayotte to gain the semi-finals, where he played his best tennis of the tournament, winning eight straight games in one stretch as he beat Smid, 6–4 6–3.

Both players suffered from blistered feet on the hot and sticky court as the temperature reached 32°C when the two unseeded finalists met, Arias playing in his first final since July 1983. Kriek started out slowly, struggling on every service game and putting no pressure on Arias's serve as he stayed back and made errors from the baseline. Arias took the first set 6–4 before Kriek captured his 13th career tournament singles crown by sweeping the next three sets 6–3 6–4 6–2. He began to serve better in the second set and, although falling behind on his serve several times, was broken only once in the match.

There was consolation in the doubles final for Pat Cash who, with fellow-Australian John Fitzgerald, defeated the previous week's winners, Paul Annacone and Christo Van Rensburg.

LAS VEGAS, 29 APRIL–4 MAY
MEN'S SINGLES – Quarter-finals: K. Flach d. J. M. Lloyd (GB) 6–4 4–6 6–4; J. Arias d. E. Teltscher 6–7 6–4 7–6; T. Smid (CZ) d. B. Becker (G) 6–4 6–7 7–6; J. Kriek d. T. Mayotte 4–6 7–6 6–3. ***Semi-finals:*** Arias d. Flach 7–6 7–5; Kriek d. Smid 6–4 6–3. ***Final:*** Kriek d. Arias 4–6 6–3 6–4 6–2.

MEN'S DOUBLES – Final: P. Cash (AUS) /J. Fitzgerald (AUS) d. P. Annacone /C. Van Rensburg (SA) 7–5 6–7 7–6.

WCT TOURNAMENT OF CHAMPIONS ($500,000)

It was the last WCT Tournament of Champions under the old format, whereby only winners of tournaments over the previous 52 weeks made up the field on the Har-Tru clay courts in the shadow of the majestic Tudor-style manor at Forest Hills. And when the day of the championship match came, it was what everybody expected: top-seeded John McEnroe against No. 2 Ivan Lendl, who captured the £500,000 tournament for the second time. Even McEnroe, the defending champion who was playing in front of his hometown fans, was impressed with the Czech's thorough domination in the final. 'It wasn't a case of my playing that badly', he said. 'He played a good match.'

Vitas Gerulaitis, the No. 6 seed and winner of this title in 1980, fell in the first round to the Czech, Marian Vajda, who in turn was no match for Yannick Noah in the second round. Lawson Duncan, an American with a penchant for clay, marched smartly into the quarter-finals by ousting, among others, Israel's Shlomo Glickstein, fifth-seeded Johan Kriek and Argentinian Guillermo Rivas. However, his quick quips weren't enough when facing Lendl in the quarters.

The only other non-seeded player to reach that stage was Italy's Claudio Panatta, who made McEnroe suffer before escaping with a 3–6 6–2 7–6 victory. With his first serve deserting him in the semis, McEnroe also had to struggle against Henrik Sundstrom, who had beaten him on clay in the *Davis Cup* final in 1984. The Swede made only 12 unforced errors in the first two sets, and had two break-points on McEnroe's serve in the opening game of the third set. But the American saved both points, broke Sundstrom for a 3–1 lead with two forcing backhands, and ran out the match, 6–2 3–6 6–2.

Lendl had no problems in the bottom half of the draw until he faced third-seeded Aaron Krickstein in the semis, where Krickstein won the second set, the only set Lendl dropped in the tournament. But after taking a long game early in the third set, Lendl was in full gallop, romping away with the match, 6–1 2–6 6–1.

That set up the title match, and with Lendl on the top of his game, there wasn't much McEnroe could do to stem the tide as the Czech took his fourth consecutive tournament title – a string that saw him win on hard court, red clay, indoors and now Har-Tru. McEnroe won only eight points against serve in the second set as Lendl seemed to anticipate everything. And if his thundering serve and forehand were not enough, Lendl had developed a heavy topspin crosscourt backhand that found all of his opponents pawing the air with their rackets. 'I've been working hard, and it's coming a little early', Lendl said of his game. 'I didn't expect it for another six or nine months.'

In the doubles, Ken Flach and Robert Seguso took their second title of the year by beating Brazilians Givaldo Barbosa and Ivan Kley.

FOREST HILLS, NEW YORK, 6–12 MAY
MEN'S SINGLES – Quarter-finals: J. P. McEnroe d. C. Panatta (IT) 3–6 6–2 7–6; H. Sundstrom (SW) d. T. Moor 6–1 6–2; A. Krickstein d. B. Gilbert 6–3 7–6; I. Lendl (CZ) d. L. Duncan 6–3 6–3. **Semi-finals:** McEnroe d. Sundstrom 6–2 3–6 6–2; Lendl d. Krickstein 6–1 2–6 6–1. **Final:** Lendl d. McEnroe 6–3 6–3.
MEN'S DOUBLES – Final: K. Flach /R. Seguso d. G. Barbosa (BR) /I. Kley (BR) 7–5 6–2.

A finalist in Hamburg and a quarter-finalist in Paris, Henrik Sundstrom spent the rest of the year nursing a stomach injury, which, with a reduced diet of tournaments, pulled his ranking down from 7 to 22.   *(T. Hindley)*

SEGMENT 4: 1 APRIL–19 MAY

Richard Evans, John Barrett and Malcolm Folley

JACOMO MONTE CARLO OPEN ($325,000)

For reasons that would be quite understandable to a modern-day professional tennis player and quite incomprehensible to the rest of mankind, Ivan Lendl did not want to play in the 1985 Jacomo Monte Carlo Open. It was, he said, quite ridiculous of the Pro Council to designate him to a clay-court event in Europe between a cement-court tournament in Florida and the indoor WCT Dallas Finals. However, by the time he had taken this historic and prestigious title by beating Mats Wilander 6–1 6–3 4–6 6–4 in the final, he was looking mildly mollified. So he should have been; anyone should derive considerable satisfaction from seeing his name etched on one of those marble plaques that line the clubhouse walls. History pervades the place and sometimes one can imagine the eye of a Tilden or a Lenglen peering out from behind the shutters of the long-deserted house that sits atop the little hill between the club and the sea. They say the house is haunted.

The way in which Henrik Sundstrom surrendered the title he won so worthily the year before will haunt him for some time to come. The Swede's interrupted semi-final with Lendl was the match of the tournament and one of the great matches of the Grand Prix year. Sundstrom took the first set 6–4, trailed 2–4 in the second and then battled back to 6–6 before losing the tie-break by seven points to three. The duel was absorbing. Long rallies would have sent the crowd to sleep had they not been liberally interspersed with Sundstrom's probing, inventive play that sent Lendl chasing all over the court in pursuit of heavily topspun forehands. Occasionally, the Swede would dart in to punch away a surprisingly assured volley.

Yet such was Lendl's dogged resistance and physical power that Sundstrom could never quite gain the upper hand, not even when he broke serve from 40–0 in a classically played fifth game of the third set. For straight away Henrik found himself 15–40 down. Two cracking serves followed to the net for winning first volleys — brave tactics for a base-line specialist — got him out of trouble, but it was still even at 4–4 when a darkening sky forced play to be abandoned for the night. On the Sunday morning the match sparkled with the same intensity of effort and skill as it had the night before. First Sundstrom and then Lendl had to fight his way out of break-points against serves. So, after more than four hours total playing time, the second tie-break of the match would decide the issue. Sundstrom led 4–2; played two bad points but still found himself serving at 5–4. Then it was Lendl's turn to charge the net and this final act of courage enabled him to wrap it up by seven points to five to win 4–6 7–6 7–6. 'It was a pity someone had to lose a match like that', Lendl said graciously afterwards. Too true.

Wilander, who had disposed of young Aaron Krickstein and Libor Pimek in the previous two rounds, decided that attack was the best approach in the final. But Ivan had his eye in by then and passed with ever-increasing accuracy and confidence.

Lendl, who had not yet dropped a set, shrugged off the loss of the third set and bore down once again on the man who was appearing in his consecutive final in his adopted principality. When it was all over, Lendl permitted himself a smile and decided it wasn't so bad playing in Monte Carlo after all.

Two more Czechs, Tomas Smid and Pavel Slozil took the doubles title over an unlikely pair of finalists, Shlomo Glickstein and Shachar Perkis of Israel, by 6–2 6–3. – R.E.

1–7 APRIL
MEN'S SINGLES – Quarter-finals: I. Lendl (CZ) d. F. Cancellotti (IT) 6–2 6–1; H. Sundstrom (SW) d.

M. Westphal (G) 6–4 6–2; A. Krickstein (USA) d. T. Smid (CZ) 3–6 6–1 6–2; M. Wilander (SW) d. L. Pimek (CZ) 6–3 6–1. *Semi-finals:* Lendl d. Sundstrom 4–6 7–6 7–6; Wilander d. Krickstein 6–2 6–3. *Final:* Lendl d. Wilander 6–1 6–4 4–6 6–4.
MEN'S DOUBLES – *Final:* P. Slozil (CZ) /Smid d. S. Glickstein (IS) /S. Perkis (IS) 6–2 6–3.

EBEL GERMAN OPEN CHAMPIONSHIPS ($250,000)

Miloslav Mecir, the tall curly-haired Czech with the imposing beard of a sea captain, sailed serenely through a powerful field of clay-court experts on the waterlogged courts of Hamburg's Rottenbaum Club to claim his second Nabisco Grand Prix title of the year when he sank fifth-seeded Henrik Sundstrom 6–4 6–1 6–4 in the final of the Ebel German Open, taking the first prize of $45,500 plus a handsome gold Ebel watch worth another $9,000. This win, together with another spectacular display in Rome two weeks later where he reached his fourth final of the year, was to lift his ranking from 25 to 12, securing him a seeding of 11 in the forthcoming French Championships.

The form of Mecir was a revelation. Caressing the heavy, damp balls with sweet touch on the slow, rain-soaked surface he did not lose a set all week. A succession of opponents became ensnared on his tactical web of varied shot-making that mixed safe, deep drives with delicate drops, teasing lobs and intelligent forays to the net to keep them guessing. Sundstrom was the third Swede in succession that Mecir torpedoed; earlier he had sunk the other half of the Swedish *Davis Cup* team, Joakim Nystrom and Mats Wilander, whose flailing top-spin made no impression on him. No doubt Stefan Edberg was glad he had decided to miss Hamburg this year. Neither fourth-seeded Nystrom (who was losing to the Czech for the third time in 1985) nor Wilander, the top seed, could solve the problem of Mecir's disguise and variety of shot that had them both constantly off balance. Wilander admitted: 'I have never felt so helpless on a clay court. He moves the best of anyone on the circuit. He seems slow, but he's deceptive . . . he can reach any ball. Perhaps the only way to beat him is to hit as many aces as possible and come to the net as often as possible.'

Sundstrom started the final as if he would follow Wilander's advice. The world's 11th-ranked player believed he was playing well and certainly his wins over the No. 2 seed, Andres Gomez (6–3 6–0), and José-Luis Clerc (6–3 6–4) suggested he was right. The Swede's 4–2 lead in the opening set further indicated that he, at any rate, would not become mesmerised by Mecir's deceptively innocent game. Nine games later we all knew how wrong that assessment was. Mecir had won them all with frustrating ease. Sundstrom stopped the rot – but only with a single game as the Czech reeled off another five games that left him ahead 4–0 in the third set – and visibly nervous as he neared the moment of victory. With Mecir teetering, the forceful Sundstrom surged back to four games all. However, in the nick of time Mecir steadied his nerves and won the next two games for his second Nabisco Grand Prix title of the year. It had been an impressive performance by someone who is delightfully ignorant of the secret of his success.

The doubles provided some consolation for Andres Gomez. With the Chilean veteran, Hans Gildemeister, he provided a powerful serve and some deft volleying touches as the South American pair beat the experienced Europeans Heinz Gunthardt and Balazs Taroczy 1–6 7–6 6–4 in an exciting final that left the winners $13,500 richer. – J.B.

HAMBURG, 29 APRIL–5 MAY
MEN'S SINGLES – *Quarter-finals:* M. Wilander (SW) d. G. Vilas (ARG) 6–3 6–0; M. Mecir (CZ) d. J. Nystrom (SW) 6–2 6–2; J. L. Clerc (ARG) d. J. Gunnarsson (SW) 6–4 6–2; H. Sundstrom (SW) d. A. Gomez (EC) 6–3 6–0. *Semi-finals:* Mecir d. Wilander 6–1 6–2; Sundstrom d. Clerc 6–3 6–4. *Final:* Mecir d. Sundstrom 6–4 6–1 6–4.
MEN'S DOUBLES – *Final:* H. Gildemeister (CH) /Gomez d. H. Gunthardt (SWZ) /B. Taroczy (HU) 1–6 7–6 6–4.

ITALIAN OPEN CHAMPIONSHIPS ($350,000)

A Roman holiday for Yannick Noah at the Foro Italico: the quiet, sensitive Frenchman could certainly be excused for interpreting his triumph in the $350,000 Italian Open in that fashion, because it brought him his first title for two years, since he was crowned French champion in Paris in 1983. He became the first European since Bjorn Borg in 1978 to capture the Italian championship, as he overcame Czechoslovakia's rising star, Miloslav Mecir, 6–3 3–6 6–2 7–6 in a final that was a duel by sabre, not broadsword.

It was Noah's touch and slice, against Mecir's placement and change of pace. Whenever the Frenchman won a point in this cerebral warfare, his huge grin lit up the afternoon. And when, after three hours, Mecir struck a backhand wide to give Noah the fourth-set tie-break – and the match – by seven points to four, the Frenchman fell to his knees and blew kisses to his wife, Cecilia. In the middle of the second set, light aircraft trailing advertising banners started a bizarre fly-past over the centre court, followed by a police helicopter. It made concentration extremely difficult and one wondered what players of a more volatile nature would have made of it all.

It was at the Foro Italico a year earlier that Noah had injured himself after colliding with a net post. This year, in the quarter-final against José-Luis Clerc, he took an injury time-out, suffering a recurrence of the hamstring injury he had sustained in his right leg during his previous match with Anders Jarryd. Clerc later argued that ninth-seeded Noah was given the benefit of two time-outs, therefore contravening the rules. But during the first stoppage the Frenchman was unable to receive treatment as ATP trainer Bill Norris was elsewhere treating Mats Wilander.

Top-seeded Wilander fell to Mecir in the semi-final, as he had done in Hamburg. At the other end of the draw, defending champion Andres Gomez was beaten in the first round by Sweden's Jan Gunnarsson, who journeyed into the quarters, and Australian Paul McNamee also sprung an upset by beating the No. 4 seed, Aaron Krickstein. But Italian Claudio Mezzadri, ranked 183 in the world, who a year earlier had accounted for Pat Cash, kept up his one-man war on Aussies by beating McNamee in the second round. Mezzadri then defeated the No. 16 seed, Guillermo Vilas, before falling to Mecir.

The Italian Open was a watershed for the 17-year-old German prodigy, Boris Becker. He beat Tarik Benhabiles, Thierry Tulasne, Juan Aguilera (No. 15 seed) and Gunnarsson to arrive at his first Grand Prix tournament semi-final. But Noah's strategy proved too much for him.

Ken Flach and Robert Seguso, defending champions in the doubles, were relieved of their title by the unusual Swedish partnership of Mats Wilander and Anders Jarryd, who overcame the US *Davis Cup* pairing, 4–6 6–3 6–2. – M.F.

ROME, 13–19 MAY

MEN'S SINGLES – Quarter-finals: M. Wilander (SW) d. H. Sundstrom (SW) 7–5 6–2; M. Mecir (CZ) d. C. Mezzadri 6–1 6–2; B. Becker (G) d. J. Gunnarsson (SW) 6–4 6–4; Y. Noah (F) d. J. L. Clerc (ARG) 6–1 7–5. ***Semi-finals:*** Mecir d. Wilander 6–2 6–4; Noah d. Becker 6–3 3–6 6–2 7–6. ***Final:*** Noah d. Mecir 6–3 3–6 6–2 7–6.

MEN'S DOUBLES – Final: A. Jarryd (SW) /Wilander d. K. Flach (USA) /R. Seguso (USA) 4–6 6–3 6–2.

SEGMENT 5: 8–29 JULY

Sandy Genelius and Jennifer Proud

UNION WARREN US PRO TENNIS CHAMPIONSHIPS ($210,000)

Perhaps it was only appropriate that, in what appears to be the 'Year of the Youngsters', three of the final four contestants at the Union Warren US Pro Tennis Championships, America's oldest professional tennis tournament, should have been under the age of 21. The fourth, striking a symbolic blow for the 'senior set', provided record crowds at the Longwood Cricket Club with some of the best tennis he has played in years.

Mats Wilander, the leader of the 'kiddie korps' of professional tennis, had already captured his second French Open singles crown when he arrived in Boston for his first US Pro. The 20-year-old Swede swept through the 56-man field without the loss of a set, climaxed by his 6–2 6–4 triumph over Argentina's Martin Jaite in the Monday evening final, which was played before what is becoming yet another Longwood tradition – a sell-out throng of tennis-hungry spectators. Wilander displayed a rock-steady baseline game, his established forte in over five years on the tour, but, as he had done time and again in 1985, he flavoured his play with many well-timed forays to the net, which kept his 20-year-old opponent off balance. After racing to a 6–2 first-set victory on three breaks of Jaite's serve, the Swede encountered a more determined player in the second set and, in fact, Jaite held a brief advantage at 4–3 when he broke the world's number three player in that seventh game. Wilander, however, returned the favour in the eighth game to level the set score and, after holding serve to push to a 5–4 lead, broke the Argentine in the final game to seal the victory and stake his claim to the winner's purse of $35,700.

Jaite's victim in the semi-finals was a virtual unknown when he arrived in Beantown. The 18-year-old Yugoslav, Bruno Oresar, who has claimed his country's national title in six different age groups, managed to win eight matches in eight days, including qualifying rounds, before falling to Jaite in Sunday's semis, 7–6 6–1. The soft-spoken blond high-schooler, who borrowed funds for the trip from his parents, has also taken the Orange Bowl title in three age categories. By the end of the week, he had won over the Longwood crowds with his impressive quickness on the green clay and his overall gutsy play.

To balance this influx of adolescents, long-time Boston favourite Guillermo Vilas, at the age of 32, played his best week of tennis in over a year. Perhaps drawing inspiration from the Longwood crowds, he straight-setted defending champion and fourth seed Aaron Krickstein in the second round, and eighth seed Libor Pimek of Czechoslovakia in the quarter-finals, before bowing 6–1 6–3 to Wilander in the semis.

The doubles final offered a nail-biting finish to a tremendous week of tennis as Pimek and Slobodan Zivojinovic, the Yugoslav whose name is being pronounced correctly more and more, squeaked past sentimental favourites and two-time Wimbledon doubles champions, Peter McNamara and Paul McNamee, 2–6 6–4 7–6, to claim the first Nabisco Grand Prix doubles title of the year for both players. The Mac attack fell just short in the final as the affable Aussies lost the third-set tie-break, 8–6. They had, however, knocked off the first- and third-seeded teams *en route* to the final and, perhaps more importantly, had served a large dose of confidence to McNamara, who is attempting a comeback from serious knee surgery, which had rendered him virtually inactive on a tennis court for 27 months. – S.G.

BOSTON, 8–15 JULY
MEN'S SINGLES – Quarter-finals: M. Wilander (SW) d. H. Sundstrom (SW) 6–3 6–3; G. Vilas (ARG)

d. L. Pimek (CZ) 6–4 6–2; B. Oresar (YU) d. J. Aguilera (SP) 6–3 7–6; M. Jaite (ARG) d. P. McNamee (AUS) 2–6 6–2 6–0. *Semi-finals:* Wilander d. Vilas 6–1 6–3; Jaite d. Oresar 7–6 6–1. *Final:* Wilander d. Jaite 6–2 6–4.
MEN'S DOUBLES – Final: Pimek /S. Zivojinovic (YU) d. P. McNamara (AUS) /McNamee 2–6 6–4 7–6.

DC NATIONAL BANK CLASSIC ($210,000)

The 1985 DC National Bank Tennis Classic proved that the Washington, DC, area does not lack for tennis fans. Despite the usual heat and humidity, Rock Creek Tennis Stadium was packed with record crowds for seven straight days. It also proved the clay-court talents of Yannick Noah. The athletic Frenchman captured the title on Monday night with a 6–4 6–3 win over Argentina's Martin Jaite before a sellout crowd of 6,100 fans which brought the week's attendance to 88,100.

Noah, perhaps suffering a bit of a letdown from his semi-final victory over Jimmy Connors the previous night, started sluggishly as Jaite raced to a 4–1 lead. The Frenchman was quick to revive, however, employing his aggressive game to smother the net. His offensive arsenal came into play, and he eventually served out the set at love. A service break in the opening game of the second set, and another love game on his serve, made it seven straight games for Noah, giving him a 2–0 advantage in the second set. The match proceeded on serve for the next six games until Jaite, serving at 3–5, netted two backhand volleys to give Noah the match and the championship.

For the second consecutive week the 21-year-old Jaite had found himself in the final of a Grand Prix Super Series event, and he again walked away with the runner-up cheque ($18,445). The likeable Jaite also left with a smile, his ranking raised to 22. Noah had won his second title for the year, a $35,700 cheque and a world ranking of No. 8.

But it had not been a cakewalk for Noah. Semi-final Sunday provided the long-awaited match-up with Connors, which was preceded by a three-set struggle between Jaite and fellow-Argentine Marcelo Ingaramo. Jaite's improving net game kept Ingaramo off balance when it counted, while the press centre was thrown askew by urgent calls from the media in Argentina, thirsting for news of the proceedings on court. By the time Noah and Connors stepped on court, just after 7 p.m., the temperature had 'cooled' to a mere 35°C. Two hours later they were into a third set, with Noah's big serve blunting Connors's returns. The Frenchman served ten aces in the match, three of which came successively in the fifth game of the set to give him a 4–1 lead. Connors, disputing the call on the third ace, thereafter lost his concentration and the match.

In addition to Connors, another revered name performed well. Guillermo Vilas came from Boston with his adrenalin flowing and breezed through the first three rounds with straight-sets victories over Thierry Tulasne, Francesco Cancellotti and José-Luis Clerc. But in the quarter-finals he faced another fellow-Argentine, Marcelo Ingaramo, who had already disposed of Mecir and whose chief claim to fame was being the only Argentine other than Clerc to have beaten Vilas in professional competition. He did it again, easily, 6–1 6–4.

In doubles, Hans Gildemeister and Victor Pecci were winners over David Graham and Balazs Taroczy, 3–6 6–1 6–4. – J.P.

WASHINGTON, DC, 15–21 JULY
MEN'S SINGLES – Quarter-finals: J. S. Connors d. J. Hlasek (SWZ) 6–2 6–4; Y. Noah (F) d. A. Krickstein 6–2 6–4; M. Jaite (BR) d. P. Arraya (PER) 6–2 6–3; M. Ingaramo (ARG) d. G. Vilas (ARG) 6–1 6–4. *Semi-finals:* Noah d. Connors 6–4 3–6 6–2; Jaite d. Ingaramo 6–4 5–7 6–2. *Final:* Noah d. Jaite 6–4 6–3.
MEN'S DOUBLES – Final: H. Gildemeister (CH) /V. Pecci (PARA) d. D. Graham (AUS) /B. Taroczy (HU) 3–6 6–1 6–4.

France's New York resident, Yannick Noah, a proud husband and father, had a more settled year, with wins in Rome and Washington that contributed to a year-end ranking of seven. (T. Hindley)

US OPEN CLAY-COURT CHAMPIONSHIPS ($300,000)

From day one it was no secret that Ivan Lendl was not thrilled to be playing the US Open Clay Court Championships, unwilling to compete on clay five weeks before the US Open, particularly with a sore arm, irritated by playing on the grass courts at Wimbledon. He had been designated to Indy by the Men's International Professional Tennis Council, faced with the unenviable task of balancing the fields among all the Super Series events. After much haggling, Lendl agreed to play, but he had no qualms about letting the world know his displeasure. He came, he ranted, he conquered; pretty much routinely at that, disposing of defending champion Andres Gomez in the final, 6–1 6–3, and dropping a set only to Boris Becker in the semi-finals.

Sunday's final was played under sunny skies with the humidity as comfortable as it had been all week. Gomez's serve, which had been infallible the day before, left him flat. Lendl took the early lead with a break for 2–1, then ran away with the set when Gomez double-faulted twice in the seventh game. Another double-fault – on break-point at 2–3 – gave Lendl the service break he needed. He did not do badly for a man playing with regrets, walking away with a first-place cheque for $51,000. Gomez took home $25,500, which was his biggest pay-cheque to date in 1985.

Now, Becker: that was another story. In his first Nabisco Grand Prix competition since Wimbledon, he was under some pressure to prove it was no fluke. His first match was with Mikael Pernfors, played before a packed stadium Tuesday night, featuring fans in 'Boris Becker Backer' T-shirts. Pernfors, the Americanised Swede, had made a mark by winning consecutive NCAA singles titles in 1984 and 1985 but was an unknown among the tennis élite. It looked easy for Boris. But he faced a match-point in the second set, managing to save it and four more to send the match to a decisive set. The squandered chances broke Pernfors mentally, and Becker reeled off the winner, 6–2.

Becker and Lendl breezed to their much-anticipated semi-final meeting, and it took the Czech the first set – which he lost 5–7 – to figure out how to handle Becker's incredible serve. Retreating a good ten feet behind the baseline, Lendl was able to return effectively again, thereby ending the Wimbledon champ's 16-match winning streak.

Despite his final drubbing, Gomez had a good week. Plagued by injuries, he came to Indianapolis lacking in confidence and match play. He played solidly, setting up a semi-final meeting with Yannick Noah, where, making good on nearly 80 per cent of his first serves, Gomez won the first 11 games, allowed Noah one game, then served out the match, 6–0 6–1. Andres described the 51-minute masterpiece as 'probably the best match I've ever played'.

The top-seeded team of Ken Flach and Robert Seguso defeated Pavel Slozil and Kim Warwick for the doubles title. – J.P.

INDIANAPOLIS, 22–29 JULY
MEN'S SINGLES – Quarter-finals: I. Lendl (CZ) d. M. Jaite (ARG) 6–2 6–3; B. Becker (G) d. M. Mecir (CZ) 6–2 7–5; A. Gomez (EC) d. J. Navratil (CZ) 6–2 6–3; Y. Noah (F) d. H. Schwaier (G) 6–3 6–1. **Semifinals:** Lendl d. Becker 5–7 6–4 6–2; Gomez d. Noah 6–0 6–1. **Final:** Lendl d. Gomez 6–1 6–3.
MEN'S DOUBLES – Final: K. Flach /R. Seguso d. P. Slozil (CZ) /K. Warwick (AUS) 6–4 6–4.

SEGMENT 6: 5–25 AUGUST

Dewey Blanton and Nora McCabe

VOLVO INTERNATIONAL ($250,000)

In order to win the $250,000 Volvo International, his sixth Grand Prix title of the year, John McEnroe had to defeat both his brother, Patrick, and his brother-in-arms. McEnroe handled his younger brother, a wildcard entry, in the first round, 6–1 6–2, in what was an extremely uncomfortable match. Five days later he thumped Ivan Lendl, the other half of the most talented duo in men's tennis right now, to take home the $40,000 first prize.

The tournament was viewed as an especially important one for McEnroe, as it was his first Nabisco Grand Prix competition since his disappointing loss to Kevin Curren in the Wimbledon quarter-finals, after which the 26-year-old had said he felt 'old' and 'overpowered'. No such comments emanated from Stratton, however, where McEnroe did not lose a set and was not seriously threatened anywhere along the way.

Perhaps his biggest hurdle was the mental one imposed by the prospect of playing his younger brother. When they were drawn against one another, John himself was silent on the prospect, whereas his witty father commented that he thought Patrick would be sorry that John was destined to be out of the tournament so early. Joking aside, John was clearly uneasy about the whole affair and following his win, he said bluntly, 'I hope we don't have to do that again for a long time'.

His other five opponents that week would have echoed those very sentiments. McEnroe, his Wimbledon débâcle behind him, seemed a new man, serving and volleying with a vengeance. In the final, however, Lendl did not go gently to defeat. The Czech trailed his arch-rival 0–3 in the first set, only to rally and eventually force a tie-break in which McEnroe prevailed 7–4. In the second set McEnroe raced to a 5–0 advantage, from which point Lendl could stage but a 'semi-rally', getting one break of serve back to 5–2 before the American served out the match.

Other than McEnroe, the big winner in Stratton was Robert Seguso, who had his best tournament ever as a singles player, perhaps under the steadying influence of US *Davis Cup* experience, for he came to Stratton having teamed with partner Ken Flach to win a dramatic Cup doubles in Hamburg. After weeks on clay, no-one, least of all himself, held much hope for him on the DecoTurf courts at Stratton. But the likeable 'Goose' beat fourth seed Johan Kriek and sixth seed Scott Davis *en route* to a semi-final meeting with McEnroe. It was a wonderful week for a man accustomed to doing well only with help on his side of the net.

Seguso proved no contest for McEnroe, although at one point the US No. 1 felt it necessary to point out the anomaly of Seguso excelling in singles. Protesting a Seguso shot which he saw as out but the linesman saw as good, McEnroe pointed to the spot in the doubles alley where (he claimed) the ball landed. 'You are used to calling these kind good for him', McEnroe said, 'but today these are out.'

Seguso excelled in doubles, too, reaching the final, where he and Flach lost to Scott Davis and David Pate. – D.B.

STRATTON MOUNTAIN, VERMONT, 5–11 AUGUST
MEN'S SINGLES – Quarter-finals: J. P. McEnroe d. P. Annacone 6–2 6–3; R. Seguso d. S. Davis 6–2 7–6; J. S. Connors d. T. Mayotte 6–4 6–0; I. Lendl (CZ) d. B. Gilbert 6–3 6–3. **Semi-finals:** McEnroe d. Seguso 6–2 6–3; Lendl d. Connors 6–0 4–6 6–4. **Final:** McEnroe d. Lendl 7–6 6–2.
MEN'S DOUBLES – Final: Davis /D. Pate d. K. Flach /Seguso 3–6 7–6 7–6.

ATP CHAMPIONSHIPS ($300,000)

Wimbledon introduced the tennis world to Boris the Boomer, as the implacable Becker made sporting history. That remarkable fortnight left little doubt as to the vast reserves of courage and talent possessed by the 17-year-old, although some questions remained as to how potent he would be on a harder, less forgiving surface. After all, the lad had won two Grand Prix titles – Wimbledon and Queens Club – where his penchant for throwing his body around the court caused consternation only with his mother; grass stains pose a difficult laundry problem.

Well, the $300,000 ATP Championship introduced the world to Boris the Comic Kamikaze. Not only did he toss his body around the unyielding DecoTurf courts with little regard for life or limb, but he also revealed a certain wit following his 6–4 6–2 thrashing of Mats Wilander in the final. Acknowledging Wilander's triumphs in the tournament the two previous years, Becker said: 'If I had lost this match, they would have had to change the name of this tournament to the Mats Wilander Championship.' Then, in describing his own performance: 'I played my second best [tournament]. I think you know my best one.'

It *was* a stunning showing. Becker moved through the draw in his first Nabisco Grand Prix event since Wimbledon with the greatest of ease, losing sets only to John Sadri and Hank Pfister; the latter observed afterwards that Becker was the best, at his age, that he had ever seen. Certainly his bazooka serve, so much in evidence at Wimbledon, adapted well, for Becker recorded 56 aces for the week. His manhandling of Wilander in the final was merciless; this after Mats had dropped his serve only twice during the entire week. The win was worth $48,000 for Becker, while Wilander earned $24,000 as runner-up.

The ATP Championship proved the optimum forum for tennis daredevils. Tim Wilkison, the affable North Carolinian who has made a career out of scraping his elbows and knees, scratched, battled and drove his way into the semi-finals, chalking up a win over Yannick Noah *en route*. Wilkison, 25, had been serving brilliantly all week, yet against Wilander in the semis he dropped his serve seven consecutive times. Let us not doubt it any longer: Swedes can most definitely play on cement.

In 1984 there were four Swedes in the quarter-finals of the ATP Championship. A year later, the same four were back again, but the (un)luck of the draw meant only two would advance any further. Wilander disposed of Stefan Edberg in three tough sets, while Joakim Nystrom beat Anders Jarryd, 6–2 6–1. In what has become the rule rather than the exception, it was a fine week for Sweden. The doubles final was an all-Swedish affair, with Edberg and Jarryd beating Nystrom and Wilander, 4–6 6–2 6–3. For Jarryd, the top-ranked doubles player on the ATP computer, it was his sixth title of the year. It was also a good week for the ATP Championship, as the tournament drew a record number of 74,865 fans. – D.B.

CINCINNATI, 19–25 AUGUST
MEN'S SINGLES – Quarter-finals: M. Wilander (SW) d. S. Edberg (SW) 6–3 6–7 6–2; T. Wilkison d. J. Brown 6–3 6–4; J. Nystrom (SW) d. A. Jarryd (SW) 6–2 6–1; B. Becker (G) d. H. Pfister 5–7 6–1 6–4. ***Semi-finals:*** Wilander d. Wilkison 6–2 6–1; Becker d. Nystrom 6–4 7–5. ***Final:*** Becker d. Wilander 6–4 6–2.
MEN'S DOUBLES – Final: Edberg /Jarryd d. Nystrom /Wilander 4–6 6–2 6–3.

JOHN PLAYER'S CANADIAN OPEN ($300,000)

As John McEnroe observed after losing the US Open, he has to be at the top of his game to beat Ivan Lendl easily – unless the Czech is having a bad day. Three weeks earlier, in Montreal, Lendl was not having an especially off-Sunday and McEnroe beat him 7–5 6–3, scoring his second straight-sets victory in eight days over his arch-rival. McEnroe, while not in peak form, none the less dominated Lendl, handily thwarting the Czech's attempts

John McEnroe had some harsh words to say about the media's treatment of his private life, but nevertheless he won eight tournaments throughout the year. *(T. Hindley)*

to serve and volley his way to victory by continually jumping on Lendl's second serves to catapult himself to net. Yet the final was not particularly noteworthy. Both contestants looked tense, served less well than earlier in the week, rushed routine shots and hit few outright winners. If the match is remembered at all, it will be as a harbinger of Flushing Meadow where Lendl finally assembled the winning combination of booming serves and screaming forehands, interlaced with crisply executed volleys.

A victim of his own faulty groundstrokes the week before at Stratton Mountain, Lendl scrapped his conservative baseline game and gambled – frequently injudiciously. Rushing the net off both first and second serves, he won 24 of the 38 times he approached but he erased these gains with 34 unforced errors, six on volleys. Not only did he fail to break McEnroe throughout; in striving to bowl McEnroe over with blistering second serves, Lendl committed key double-faults, one in the 12th game contributing to the only break in the first set, and three more in the eighth game of the second causing the other break in the match. As much as anything, it was these Lendl mistakes that gave McEnroe his second consecutive Player's International title.

Severely frustrated, Lendl was goaded into outbursts of rage over two disputed line calls. One prompted him to stop play until the tournament referee could adjudicate, leaving Lendl still fuming later about the competence of umpire Jeremy Shales, one of two full-time officials paid by the Pro Council. The other cost him $500 for unsportsmanlike conduct.

Once again the Canadian Open had a star-studded, but top-heavy, field that robbed many matches of any real drama. Neither McEnroe nor Lendl, who annihilated fifth-seeded Anders Jarryd 6–1 6–0, allowing the Swede just five points against serve in their quarter-final, dropped a set *en route* to the final.

In the semi-finals, McEnroe, blasting 13 aces, five on game points, cruised past a flat-footed Jimmy Connors, who the day before had shellacked the talented but erratic Stefan Edberg, by reeling off the last 12 points of the match. Conceding that his almost-33-year-old legs could no longer muster the effort that made his 1984 US Open slugfest with McEnroe so thrilling, the third-seeded Connors instead substituted boorish behaviour, yelling obscenities and making crude gestures that earned him a $1,500 fine for visible obscenity to compound his 6–2 6–3 loss.

Actually, it was Canadian champion Stephane Bonneau and the struggling Jimmy Arias who grabbed the limelight. To the ecstasy of the Montreal partisans, the Quebec native, ranked 212, knocked off two players in the top 50 – No. 12 seed Tomas Smid and Jakob Hlasek, ranked 45 – before Jarryd ended his glory ride. On the eve of his 21st birthday, Arias revved up his formidable forehand to throttle the fourth-seeded Wimbledon finalist, Kevin Curren, 4–6 6–3 6–2 in the third round. Facing Lendl's own ferocious forehand in the semis, Arias was overpowered, squandering his first and only break-point by netting an easy overhead, after which he folded 6–4 6–2.

After back-to-back wins over Connors and Lendl, McEnroe, with Tatum O'Neal in tow, left town looking the clear favourite for the approaching US Open. Yet Lendl was not dispirited as he flew back to Connecticut for some pre-Open volley tutoring from Tony Roche. 'I need to find the right mix . . . That will help a lot', he said.

The ubiquitous pairing of Ken Flach and Robert Seguso were winners in the doubles, beating Edberg and Jarryd 5–7 7–6 6–3 in a close final. – N.McC.

MONTREAL, 12–18 AUGUST
MEN'S SINGLES – Quarter-finals: J. P. McEnroe (USA) d. R. Krishnan (IND) 6–3 6–2; J. S. Connors (USA) d. S. Edberg (SW) 6–4 6–1; J. Arias (USA) d. E. Teltscher (USA) 6–1 7–6; I. Lendl (CZ) d. A. Jarryd (SW) 6–1 6–0. **Semi-finals:** McEnroe d. Connors 6–2 6–3; Lendl d. Arias 6–4 6–2. **Final:** McEnroe d. Lendl 7–5 6–3.
MEN'S DOUBLES – Final: K. Flach (USA) /R. Seguso (USA) d. Edberg /Jarryd 5–7 7–6 6–3.

SEGMENT 7: 16–29 SEPTEMBER

Richard Evans and Edward Johnson

VOLVO TENNIS ($210,000)

Just when one was beginning to despair of American tennis being able to produce a young player capable of breaking through to take a Nabisco Super Series title on a Grand Prix circuit that, increasingly, was being dominated by youthful European talent, Paul Annacone jumped the queue and won the Volvo Tennis/Los Angeles title with a wonderfully exciting 7–6 6–7 7–6 victory over Sweden's Stefan Edberg. It was the first Grand Prix title of the 22-year-old New Yorker's career and did much to confirm the promise he had shown at Wimbledon the year before when he sprang from nowhere to reach the quarter-finals.

The excellence of the final which, for sheer drama and excitement, ranked amongst the best of the year, did much to alleviate the mood of depression that had hung over the tournament on the Saturday night when poor Jack Kramer had to walk out in front of an expectant 6,000 crowd at the UCLA Tennis Centre to inform them that they were not going to see John McEnroe play that night and, because of the late information they had received concerning McEnroe's fever and severe nausea, all they would get to see was a doubles semi-final.

With Jimmy Connors already missing from the draw as a result of an MIPTC suspension over an accumulation of fines, even some of the more knowledgable Los Angeles tennis fans felt that much of the interest had evaporated from the event. Not for the first time this pessimistic attitude and strange fixation with 'star' names proved groundless. The real tennis connoisseur could not have asked for anything better than the match Annacone and Edberg produced for a large crowd the following day, and pro tennis was well served, not just by the standard of play but also by the demeanour in which it was played.

Edberg, who had saved five match-points before winning the second-set tie-break by ten points to eight, endeared himself to everyone by refusing an 'out' call on a mis-hit Annacone overhead at 40–30 on the American's serve at 5–5 in the final set. The umpire called 'deuce' but before the first words of protest were out of Annacone's mouth, Edberg was walking to his chair, signalling 'good'. Justifiably, the 19-year-old Swede received a rapturous ovation when he returned to the court.

Edberg's contribution to the proceedings had been considerably more substantial than gentlemanly conduct, however. His superb service action and classical backhand volleys had kept the rampant Annacone under some sort of control for long periods of the match, but when a couple of Edberg errors allowed the American to take a six-points-to-two lead in the third and decisive tie-break it seemed all over. Even then the excitement would not subside as Edberg set off in pursuit of a volley and whipped a backhand crosscourt for a stunning winner. That was the sixth match-point the Swede had saved and Annacone was forced to relinquish a seventh before he finally put away a smash to collect his $50,000.

It was somehow fitting that Annacone should have taken a title that had been earmarked for McEnroe. If it is possible to imitate the McEnroe style this quiet, darkly handsome and totally dedicated young player comes nearest to it. Annacone's style is based on relentless, all-out aggression. If there was a point during the entire match against Edberg on which he did not take an early ball and charge the net, then I missed it. Even on high-kicking first serves, Annacone stepped in; sliced a high backhand; raced in and said, in effect, 'Pass me'. It is wearying and worrying to play against someone like that and often Edberg became hypnotised by the image of his opponent standing there, seemingly defenceless at the net, and would hit his return right onto Paul's big-framed racket.

These seemingly suicidal tactics not only won Annacone the match against the world's eighth-ranked player but also had kept him alive throughout the week. He had not, in fact, dropped a set in outmanoeuvring Dan Goldie, Vince Van Patten and the No. 3 seed, Scott Davis, on his way to the semi-finals where he benefited from a walk-over at McEnroe's expense. Edberg's progress had been just as impressive as he brushed aside such heavyweight opposition as Mark Dickson (the only man to take a set off him prior to the final), Brad Pearce, Ramesh Krishnan and Johan Kriek, the No. 4 seed, whom he overwhelmed 6–3 6–3.

There was one major upset in the doubles when the US Open doubles champions, Ken Flach and Robert Seguso, lost to the eventual winners, Scott Davis and Robert Van't Hof. The Californian pair beat Annacone and his regular partner from South Africa, Christo Van Rensberg, 6–3 7–5 in another thoroughly entertaining final. – R.E.

LOS ANGELES, 16–22 SEPTEMBER
MEN'S SINGLES – Quarter-finals: J. P. McEnroe d. B. Gilbert 4–6 6–0 6–3; P. Annacone d. S. Davis 6–4 6–2; J. Kriek d. J. Arias 2–6 7–5 7–6; S. Edberg (SW) d. R. Krishnan (IND) 6–2 6–4. **Semi-finals:** Annacone w.o. McEnroe; Edberg d. Kriek 6–3 6–3. **Final:** Annacone d. Edberg 7–6 6–7 7–6.
MEN'S DOUBLES – Final: S. Davis /R. Van't Hof d. Annacone /C. Van Rensburg (SA) 6–3 7–5.

TRANSAMERICA OPEN ($210,000)

Stefan Edberg followed his hair-breadth defeat in Los Angeles with as emphatic a triumph as could be imagined in San Francisco, where he needed only 53 minutes to overwhelm Johan Kriek 6–4 6–2 in the final of the TransAmerica Open.

As this was one of those rare tournaments that Bjorn Borg had failed to win, one had to go back a long way to find a former Swedish winner of this long-standing event that has been nurtured to its present level of professional expertise over the past couple of decades by the former Kramer touring pro, Barry MacKay. Jan-Erik Lundquist won it in 1962 when it was still being played at the Berkeley Tennis Club across the Bay and Sven Davidson before that in 1957. But neither, I suspect, won it in quite such dashing style as this rapidly maturing 19-year-old from Vastervik. Well as he had played in Los Angeles, Edberg has a preference for Supreme Courts indoors and the additional confidence he derived from the conditions at the Cow Palace were quickly apparent.

He dismissed Larry Stefanki, John Sadri and the dangerous Brad Gilbert in the early rounds without dropping a serve or a set and was given only momentary pause by Paul Annacone in the semi-final. The match never reached the heights of their dramatic duel six days before and only once, in the eighth game of the second set, did Annacone's net-rushing tactics force the kind of errors that had earned him victory at the UCLA Centre. Annacone admitted he had not played nearly as well on this occasion, but the plain truth was that Edberg was not allowing anyone to play particularly well – as Kriek found out the following day.

The new American citizen went into his match with Edberg full of confidence, which was hardly surprising as he had caused the upset of the week in outplaying John McEnroe 7–6 3–6 6–1 in the quarter-finals. There were, of course, some valid explanations for the severity of McEnroe's demise in the third set. He was still a little weak from the virus that had laid him low the previous week, and John Lloyd had done nothing to help his condition by pushing him all the way to a third-set tie-break in their second-round encounter. Having lost the first set 6–1, the British No. 1 took the second 7–5 and came within two points of victory at 6–6 in that third-set tie-break. McEnroe was full of praise for Lloyd's performance and admitted he had been a little lucky in preventing the Englishman from scoring what would have been the best victory of a long and chequered career.

The Lloyd match obviously took a lot out of McEnroe and Kriek ruthlessly exploited his condition the following day. Few people can gauge Johan's moods on a tennis court, least of all, apparently, the man himself. He can be brilliant or simply awful – and the brilliance had been notably lacking in the months preceding San Francisco. It was almost as an act of desperation that he had asked MacKay for a wild card and even Barry was forced to see the funny side of the fact that the man he allowed into his event promptly knocked out his biggest draw card.

With the verve and panache that are the hallmarks of his game when he is playing well very much in evidence, Kriek let rip with a couple of superb service returns in the first-set tie-break, which gave him the set by seven points to three. Then, after a mini-McEnroe revival, he tore into the New Yorker's serve once again in the third set to break that much feared delivery no less than three times in succession. McEnroe was as honest as usual afterwards. 'I didn't have it in me today', he said. 'I'm annoyed at the way I'm playing. I'm simply not hitting the ball as I should be. I'm trying to give it my best but at the moment my best isn't good enough.'

Kriek continued in similar vein in crushing the surprise semi-finalist, Bob Green (a convincing winner over Eliot Teltscher in the quarters), but Edberg was something else altogether. Given the pace at which the modern game is played, it requires a certain level of excellence and consistency to beat anyone in 53 minutes, let alone a player of Kriek's calibre in the final of a Super Series event. But Edberg managed it with the streamlined efficiency of a true champion, never allowing Kriek to look at his high-kicking serve and volleying with such power and precision than even a man of Johan's fleetness of foot was given little opportunity to use his speed. It was, in every aspect, an extremely impressive performance.

The consistent pair of Paul Annacone and Christo Van Rensburg won the doubles title, beating Brad Gilbert and Sandy Mayer in the final, 3–6 6–3 6–4, and afterwards Mayer announced his retirement from regular tournament play. The former Wimbledon semi-finalist and doubles champion has gone into business in the San Francisco area. – R.E.

SAN FRANCISCO, 23–29 SEPTEMBER
MEN'S SINGLES** – **Quarter-finals: J. Kriek d. J. P. McEnroe 7–6 3–6 6–1; R. Green d. E. Teltscher 7–6 6–4; P. Annacone d. T. Mayotte 6–3 6–4; S. Edberg (SW) d. B. Gilbert 6–2 6–2. ***Semi-finals:*** Kriek d. Green 6–2 6–1; Edberg d. Annacone 6–2 3–6 6–1. ***Final:*** Edberg d. Kriek 6–4 6–2.
MEN'S DOUBLES** – **Final: Annacone /C. Van Rensburg (SA) d. Gilbert /A. A. Mayer 3–6 6–3 6–4.

TROFEO GODO MARLBORO SPANISH CHAMPIONSHIPS ($210,000)

When Sweden's top-seeded world No. 3 moved smoothly into his fourth successive final at Barcelona's exclusive Real Club, they were all ready to rename the historic trophy the Mats Wilander Cup. As it was, the question of finding a new name for the $210,000 Trofeo Godo Marlboro was academic, for the three-time champion fell in five torrid sets to the brilliant tennis of the 22-year-old Frenchman, Thierry Tulasne, whose 0–6 6–2 3–6 6–4 6–0 victory was his first Super Series success.

The oppressive heat only partly explains Wilander's humiliation in the closing stages as he persevered with his attacking game on the slow clay, despite the growing confidence of the Frenchman on passing shot and lob. Two harrowing losses to Czech Miloslav Mecir in Hamburg and Rome in May had caused Wilander to adopt a much more positive, attacking attitude in Paris, where he had been spectacularly successful in winning his first tournament of the year.

The same attacking tactics served him well in Barcelona *en route* to the final. Hitting hard from the back of the court, taking the half-court ball on the rise and volleying with skill and discretion, Mats lost only 30 games in five matches as he cut down Cierro, Valda, Perez, Casal and Jaite without conceding a set. The unseeded Tulasne lost one set to Taroczy in the second round, but dropped no others in disposing of Damir Keretic of Germany and three seeds – Germany's Schwaier (13), Jarryd (3) of Sweden and fellow-Frenchman Leconte (8) – with his ungainly but effective whirling, stiff-arm topspin.

If the 7–6 6–0 win over the world's No. 5, Jarryd, in the quarter-finals was unexpectedly one-sided, the 6–3 6–2 win over French and Wimbledon quarter-finalist, Leconte, in the next round was more satisfying personally, for his fellow-countryman, like Tulasne himself, was enjoying the best season of his career. Tulasne's own year had included wins in Bologna and Palermo, victories that provided a large dose of confidence. Clearly Tulasne realised that his performance in Barcelona would be carefully noted by the French *Davis Cup* captain, Jean Paul Loth, and the French national coach, Eric Deblicker, who were among the spectators. Loth noted with pleasure Tulasne's change to a more aggressive style than usual.

The final was a curious match, in which Wilander's attack, all-consuming at first, gradually became more ragged as he tired in the middle-day heat. Tulasne never looked as if he would flag. Trailing one set to two the Frenchman surged to 3–0 in the fourth, but when he lost his break to leave Wilander serving at 4–5, it appeared that the less experienced man had let his chance slip. However, the set-back seemed to rekindle Tulasne's determination as he swept through the next seven games for the match. Wilander commented: 'I never saw Thierry play that well before.' For Loth it was some compensation for seeing Yannick Noah, the No. 2 seed, beaten in his second match, 7–6 2–6 6–4, by Robert Arguello of Argentina.

Not only did Tulasne profit financially from the best win of his career – the $33,600 winner's prize was his biggest tournament pay cheque – but, perhaps more importantly, he also saw his ATP computer ranking improve from 48 to 26.

For the capacity crowd of more than 5,000 at the Real Club there was a happy ending to the afternoon when Sergio Casal and young Emilio Sanchez brought the doubles title home with a 6–3 6–3 victory over Jan Gunnarsson of Sweden and Michael Mortensen of Denmark. Neither pair had been seeded, but the Spaniards in particular had looked every inch the equals of the select pairings as, in succession, they had eliminated Leconte and Noah (4), Tim Gullikson and Wilander (7) and Slozil and Smid (1). When you realise that the last time a Spaniard had won a title in Barcelona was in 1976 when Orantes had beaten Dibbs, and the last time any home player had been in the doubles final had been two years before that when Nastase and Gisbert had beaten Orantes and Vilas, you begin to understand why the cheer that greeted Casal and Sanchez as they went forward to receive their $11,340 prize could have been heard in Madrid. – E.J.

BARCELONA, 23–29 SEPTEMBER
MEN'S SINGLES – Quarter-finals: M. Wilander (SW) d. S. Casal 6–1 6–2; M. Jaite (ARG) d. K. Carlsson (SW) 7–6 6–3; H. Leconte (F) d. E. Sanchez 6–4 6–4; T. Tulasne (F) d. A. Jarryd (SW) 7–6 6–0. **Semi-finals:** Wilander d. Jaite 7–5 6–3; Tulasne d. Leconte 6–3 6–2. **Final:** Tulasne d. Wilander 0–6 6–2 3–6 6–4 6–0.
MEN'S DOUBLES – Final: Casal /Sanchez d. J. Gunnarsson (SW) /M. Mortensen (D) 6–3 6–3.

SEGMENT 8: 7–27 OCTOBER

Edward Johnson, Richard Yallop and John Barrett

ALTECH SOUTH AFRICAN OPEN ($210,000)

At the quarter-final stage of the $210,000 Altech South African Open there was no clue that anything was amiss. True, three of the seeded players – Scott Davis (3), Larry Stefanki (6) and Vitas Gerulaitis (7) had fallen respectively to Matt Anger, Martin Wostenholme and Mike DePalmer, but such upsets are an every-day occurrence on the modern circuit, where the average standard of play is continually rising.

At opposite ends of the draw Kevin Curren and Johan Kriek, former South Africans but now both US citizens, had come safely through, albeit with some difficulty. Kriek had been pushed to a twelve-game second set by the fast-improving Israeli, Shachar Perkis, and Curren had lost the opening set to South African Christo Steyn before surviving 6–7 6–2 11–9. However, there seemed no reason to suppose that the top two seeds would not profit from the match practice and proceed towards their anticipated final-round clash.

But the strong young men had other ideas. Jimmy Arias, having slipped from a No. 6 world ranking at the end of 1983 to 25, was learning the hard facts of tennis life at the ripe old age of 21. Winning was a habit easily lost. Clearly it was time to reassert himself. Unfortunately for Curren the furious aggression of Jimmy's lethal forehand was at its most effective on the fast asphalt courts, and when they met in the last eight the youngster ripped through the Wimbledon finalist's defences 6–4 6–3. In the semi-finals a similar fate awaited Kriek who, after surviving narrowly against DePalmer 4–6 6–3 6–1, was too wild against the consistent Californian Brad Gilbert, a winner already of two tournaments in 1985 on the same hard court surface at Livingstone, New Jersey, and Cleveland.

Meanwhile, Anger, having built upon his victories over Scott Davis and the near-veteran Harold Solomon, proceeded to inflict a 4–6 6–2 6–4 defeat on the No. 8 seed, John Sadri, whose bullet-like serves held no terrors for the man who had beaten Pat Cash to win Wimbledon's prestigious junior event in 1981. Nor did a semi-final meeting with Arias unduly alarm Anger, for the two were great pals and regular practice partners, and although he was ranked a modest 100 on the ATP computer, he knew how to thwart the forehand power of the No. 5 seed. If he could serve well and employ his natural, aggressive volleying game in the rarefied air, he was certain that Arias would find it difficult to pass him with any consistency. Anger held all his service games in the first and last sets (he did lose two in the second, however) and watched gratefully as costly double-faults contributed to Arias's 7–5 4–6 7–5 defeat.

The final revealed how large a part psychology plays in any tennis match. When Gilbert raced to 4–0 40–15 on his own serve in the opening set of the best-of-five-sets final, worth $42,000 to the winner, the result seemed to be a formality. But, unaccountably, Gilbert let his man off the hook as he dropped that game and five more in succession to lose a set that had been his for the taking. Although Anger lost the second set he was now playing with renewed conviction, and a single break of serve in the long fourth game of the third set was enough to give Anger a two-sets-to-one lead. With Gilbert now appearing to feel discomfort in his serving shoulder (which he had fallen on heavily in the doubles semi-final the previous evening), the chances of a major upset became increasingly likely, and an injury time-out requested by Gilbert after he had lost his serve in the opening game of the fourth set signalled his mental state.

Anger, having won the psychological battle, soon completed a physical one 6–4 3–6 6–3 6–2 – a first major success for the likeable young man from Pleasanton, California. Analysing his performance for the eager media representatives he said: 'I guess I played pretty solidly every match. Generally I served well and I didn't give much away . . . I just told myself to buckle down and play some serious tennis.' Spoken like a man who knew that, at the age of 22, his outstanding junior career was at last behind him; he had proved that he could survive among the predators of the professional jungle. But he knew, too, that his new ranking of 33, down from 177 at the start of the year, would be under attack from the hungry young lions who are his contemporaries.

The doubles title was won by Britain's Colin Dowdeswell and his South African partner,

Inspired by his first US Open triumph, Lendl stormed to four autumn wins in Stuttgart, Sydney, Tokyo and London, before losing to Edberg in the Australian Open semi-final. (M. Cole)

Christo Van Rensburg. In a tense final they beat the Israeli pair, Amos Mansdorf and Shachar Perkis, 3–6 7–6 6–4. – E.J.

JOHANNESBURG, 7–13 OCTOBER
MEN'S SINGLES – Quarter-finals: J. Arias (USA) d. K. Curren (USA) 6–4 6–3; M. Anger (USA) d. J. Sadri (USA) 4–6 6–2 6–4; B. Gilbert (USA) d. M. Wostenholme (C) 6–4 6–2; J. Kriek (SA) d. M. DePalmer (USA) 4–6 6–3 6–1. **Semi-finals:** Anger d. Arias 7–5 4–6 7–5; Gilbert d. Kriek 6–4 6–4. **Final:** Anger d. Gilbert 6–4 3–6 6–3 6–2.
MEN'S DOUBLES – Final: C. Dowdeswell (GB) /C. Van Rensburg d. A. Mansdorf (IS) /S. Perkis (IS) 3–6 7–6 6–4.

CUSTOM CREDIT AUSTRALIAN INDOOR CHAMPIONSHIP ($225,000)

Ivan Lendl had come to Australia for seven different singles events prior to the 1985 Indoor Championship, and had not won one of them. Australia always seemed to see the worst of him, apparently going to water when one of the big boys stood up to him. 'I've never played well in Australia, so I'm keen to win this tournament', Lendl said, after his opening 6–0 6–4 victory over the Australian, Craig Miller. He was speaking as the newly-crowned world No. 1, having been a worthy winner over John McEnroe in the US Open final a month earlier. The question was, could he keep it up?

He gave a resounding 'Yes' in Sydney when, for the first time, Australia saw Lendl the champion, who showed his new-found resilience and versatility (baseline and net, power and touch). True, he did not beat one top ten player, McEnroe, the second seed, having pulled out three days before the start, but everything he did supported the theory that we were witnessing the 'new Lendl'. He did not concede a set all week. In the semi-final he asserted himself over Paul Annacone, the fourth seed, 6–4 6–3, and in the final he destroyed Henri Leconte's psychological hold over him, winning 6–4 6–4 7–6. Of their eight meetings before Sydney, Leconte had won five, the last being at Wimbledon in July.

The tournament saw Australian men's tennis at its weakest for years. Both Pat Cash and Paul McNamee were out with prolonged injuries, and there was just one Australian in the top hundred – John Fitzgerald, ranked 47. The 20-year-old Simon Youl was spurred on to beat fellow-Tasmanian David MacPherson in the first round, while in the second he slew the giant-killer, Bud Schultz, who had surprised Jarryd, the defending champion and second seed, 6–4 6–4 the night before. Youl, a gritty, old-style Aussie serve-and-volleyer, lost a close three-setter in the quarters to Fitzgerald, who had shown glimpses of his best form during the week, before bowing to Leconte's greater talent in the semi-final.

Leconte won the hearts of the Sydney public with his on-court gallantry and his bursts of brilliance which overcame Wally Masur, Brian Teacher, third seed Andres Gomez and Fitzgerald, but he needed something more sustained to overcome the turbo-charged Lendl.

Jarryd ensured he did not have a wasted week by teaming up with Fitzgerald to win the doubles, beating the Australian veterans, Mark Edmondson and Kim Warwick, 6–3 6–2 in the final. – R.Y.

SYDNEY, 14–21 OCTOBER
MEN'S SINGLES – Quarter-finals: I. Lendl (CZ) d. B. Testerman (USA) 6–3 6–1; P. Annacone (USA) d. C. Hooper (USA) 4–6 6–3 6–4; H. Leconte (F) d. A. Gomez (EC) 6–4 6–4; J. Fitzgerald d. S. Youl 7–6 6–7 6–3. **Semi-finals:** Lendl d. Annacone 6–4 6–3; Leconte d. Fitzgerald 6–3 6–3. **Final:** Lendl d. Leconte 6–4 6–4 7–6.
MEN'S DOUBLES – Final: Fitzgerald /A. Jarryd (SW) d. M. Edmondson /K. Warwick 6–3 6–2.

SEIKO SUPER TENNIS ($300,000)

In its eighth year, Tokyo's Seiko Super Tennis tournament in the lofty Yoyogi Stadium which had been built for the swimming events of the 1964 Olympic Games, provided a perfect showcase for the talents of the US Open champion, Ivan Lendl. Hitting the ball with intimidating power on the medium-paced supreme court carpet, the world's No. 1

cut down the high-class field without dropping a set in five matches. Try as they would, Scott Davis, David Pate, eighth-seeded Tim Mayotte, the fourth seed, Boris Becker, and the second favourite, Mats Wilander, could not prevent Lendl from pocketing the first prize of $60,000. This was Lendl's 50th Grand Prix victory in seven years as a professional, and the 300 Nabisco Grand Prix bonus points he earned lifted him past John McEnroe on the bonus pool table with its year-end top prize of $800,000.

However, money was the last thing on Ivan's mind as he completed his week of executions with a devastating 6–0 6–4 win in the final against second-seeded Mats Wilander of Sweden. Watching the severity of Lendl's hitting on both wings, it was hard to believe that the last time these two had met, in the final of the French Open, Mats had out-hit and out-volleyed the Czech to score a one-sided victory in four sets. Now the roles were completely reversed. There were five screaming Lendl aces in the first set, as well as a barrage of heavy winners from the back of the court, as a run of twelve consecutive points from 30–30 in the opening game on Wilander's service took him to 3–0. Three games later, Ivan had lost only six more points in clinching the opening set in 21 minutes. One break of serve in the fifth game of the second set was all Lendl required to complete a 56-minute victory as Wilander, playing at least respectably now, prolonged the end until the tenth game.

The semi-finals produced a much-anticipated rematch between the 17-year-old Wimbledon champion, Becker, and the US Open title-holder, Lendl. They had met at the same stage in Indianapolis before the Czech's triumph at Flushing Meadow, and on the fast American clay Becker had won the opening set before being out-hit by Lendl, 5–7 6–2 6–2. On his favourite indoor surface where he can move comfortably and positively, Lendl won again, although the 6–3 7–6 victory produced some marvellous moments of Becker magic, including seven aces, to suggest that these two are likely to have some memorably close encounters in the months ahead. The crucial game was the third of the match when Becker, serving at one-all, failed to consolidate a 40–0 lead. After saving two break-points he carried the game to seven deuces before a flashing Lendl winner finally achieved the break. A further break in the ninth game gave Lendl the opening set. When Lendl was penalised for racket abuse in the seventh game of the second set as he lost his serve, you could sense his pent-up anger. Unfortunately for the German the anger was vented on him, as three more blazing forehand winners and a forced error cost Becker his serve to love as he served for the second set at 5–4. In the tie-break that followed Lendl was rock-like, sweeping six successive points from 1–1 to clinch the match in an hour and 48 minutes.

The other semi-final was literally a non-event for Jimmy Connors, in beating Vince Van Patten, had strained his back. When he tried to practise the next day he could hardly stand straight and was forced to retire. Andres Gomez, the sixth seed, had also suffered a back strain as he lost a magnificent quarter-final against Wilander 6–4 2–6 7–6 and could not take part with Lendl in their doubles semi-final against the top seeds, Ken Flach and Robert Seguso.

Thus there were only two matches instead of the advertised four – a gap that was gratefully filled by Flach and Seguso, who played an exhibition match against Vitas Gerulaitis and Anders Jarryd. The practice obviously did them good because, the following day, they won a thrilling final, 4–6 6–3 7–6 against Scott Davis and David Pate for a first prize of $18,000. – J.B.

TOKYO, 22–27 OCTOBER
MEN'S SINGLES – Quarter-finals: I. Lendl (CZ) d. T. Mayotte (USA) 6–4 7–5; B. Becker (G) d. A. Jarryd (SW) 7–6 6–4; J. S. Connors (USA) d. V. Van Patten (USA) 7–5 6–2; M. Wilander (SW) d. A. Gomez (EC) 6–4 2–6 7–6. **Semi-finals:** Lendl d. Becker 6–3 7–6; Wilander d. Connors w.o. **Final:** Lendl d. Wilander 6–0 6–4.
MEN'S DOUBLES – Final: K. Flach (USA) /R. Seguso (USA) d. S. Davis (USA) /D. Pate (USA) 4–6 6–3 7–6.

SEGMENT 9: 4–17 NOVEMBER

Bjorn Hellberg and Ian Barnes

STOCKHOLM OPEN ($250,000)

What a difference a year can make! In 1984, John McEnroe captured his third Stockholm Open title in singles, but behaved in a way which almost got him disqualified, making it obvious to everyone that the temperamental American was in need of a rest from tennis. Then, 12 months later, McEnroe returned to Royal Hall in the Swedish capital, played brilliant tennis and charmed everyone with his fine sporting manners. Without dropping a set, he won the title once again, defeating Anders Jarryd 6–1 6–2 in the final. It was only in the semis against Edberg that McEnroe faced anything approaching a problem. With the American serving for the match at 5–4 in the second set, the home player fought back with bravery, saving five match-points to level at 5–5. But in the tie-break that followed, it was all McEnroe, who won it 7–4.

McEnroe's record in the tournament is truly remarkable. He has entered five times and won the first prize in 1978, 1979, 1984 and 1985. He also reached the final in 1980, losing to Bjorn Borg on an extremely slow carpet, which was removed immediately after the event. 'I enjoy playing here in Stockholm', McEnroe said after being presented with the winning cheque by Princess Lilian. 'The crowd has a great knowledge of the game, and I really like to perform here.'

For the local organisers, it was a great success in many ways. A capacity crowd followed the play throughout the week, and, for the first time in the 17-year history of the tournament, three Swedes advanced to the semis. Yet the best home player of the lot, Mats Wilander, surprisingly lost in the first round to Thierry Tulasne, the vastly improved Frenchman who had also beaten Wilander in the five-set final in Barcelona a few weeks earlier. This was the first time Wilander had disappointed a Swedish crowd since he earned his fantastic breakthrough as a 17-year-old champion at Roland Garros in 1982. He had won the Swedish Open in Bastad every time he entered (1982, 1983 and 1985), and also reached the final of the Stockholm Open in 1982 (lost to Henri Leconte), 1983 (defeated Tomas Smid) and 1984 (lost to McEnroe). 'I feel a little guilty to all my tennis friends here in Sweden', the deeply disappointed Wilander admitted after his 1–6 6–2 6–2 departure to Tulasne.

For many other Swedes, the week was brighter. Especially for 20-year-old Peter Lundgren, who was ranked 208 in the world before the US Open in August. Since then, the hard-hitting Lundgren, who used to practise a lot with Bjorn Borg, had won a Grand Prix event in Cologne as well as ATP tournaments in Thessaloniki and Bergen. Those achievements brought Peter a wild card in Stockholm. 'Thank you', the young Swede smiled. 'I am going to use this one.' He did too. After beating both Tomas Smid and Scott Davis, he jumped to number 28 on the ATP computer.

Peter Lundgren is only the second top player to emerge from the northern part of Sweden, the first being Joakim Nystrom, who now reached the semis in Stockholm for the first time. Nystrom then faced Anders Jarryd in the most dramatic encounter of the week. 'Jocke' has beaten his *Davis Cup* compatriot only once – in Cincinnati in August 1985 – in 11 meetings, but this time he almost came back from a seemingly impossible position. Jarryd was leading 6–3 5–0 when Nystrom hit back to level at 5–5, and in the tie-break Nystrom was 4–2 up against his shaky opponent before losing 9–7. The previous year, Jarryd had been two points from victory against McEnroe in the semi-final, but this time the Swede, who had played a doubles match until past midnight, was completely outclassed by the inspired McEnroe.

In the doubles, Ecuador's Andres Gomez and Frenchman Guy Forget had too many guns for the Americans, Mike DePalmer and Gary Donnelly, whom they beat 6–3 6–4 in the final. – B.H.

4–10 NOVEMBER
MEN'S SINGLES – Quarter-finals: J. P. McEnroe (USA) d. P. Lundgren 6–1 6–3; S. Edberg d. S. Casal (SP) 6–4 6–1; J. Nystrom d. Y. Noah (F) 6–2 7–5; A. Jarryd d. J. Hlasek (SWZ) 6–2 6–0. **Semi-finals:** McEnroe d. Edberg 6–3 7–6; Jarryd d. Nystrom 6–3 7–6. **Final:** McEnroe d. Jarryd 6–1 6–2.
MEN'S DOUBLES –Final: G. Forget (F) /A. Gomez (EC) d. G. Donnelly (USA) /M. DePalmer (USA) 6–3 6–4.

BENSON AND HEDGES CHAMPIONSHIPS ($300,000)

Ivan Lendl and Boris Becker gave the tenth anniversary Benson and Hedges championships the perfect ending in a final of superb drama and excitement. Lendl, the champion of the United States, successfully defended his Wembley title against Wimbledon winner Becker. The big two of 1985 fought for almost four hours in front of 9,000 enthralled fans, before Lendl edged to the $60,000 winner's cheque with a 6–7 6–3 4–6 6–4 6–4 victory. It was Lendl's fifth successive Grand Prix tournament win, his tenth of the year, and took his winning streak since the triumph of Flushing Meadow to 27 matches, although he had to produce his best to halt 17-year-old Becker's remarkable run of success in England.

Starting with the Young Masters at Birmingham in January, Becker had won all his previous matches in British tournaments, apart from a minor setback on damp grass against Tim Mayotte in the event at Beckenham in June. His all-action tennis at Wembley threatened to provide a repeat of his successes at Queen's Club and at Wimbledon in Britain's longest-running and most important indoor event. Becker admitted: 'I played better tennis and played a better match in the final than I did at Wimbledon.'

But Lendl is a far tougher proposition than any Becker faced at Wimbledon. He generates such power on his groundstrokes, and one of the keys to his successful 1985 has been a dramatic improvement in his back-hand. He also has a new-found confidence at the net as well as the fitness and speed to exploit even the slightest opening. Because of this, he is mentally stronger. Yet Becker frequently had him worried – in the third set, when Lendl lost his momentum at the crucial point with Becker serving at his fiercest, and again in the fourth, when he allowed a 2–0 lead to slip. But this time Lendl stepped up the pace and imposed his will on the match. Becker's sixth double-fault, a tremendous running backhand passing shot, and an inch-accurate lob gave Lendl the vital service break for 5–4, which left him serving for the set instead of serving to save the match. It was the opening he needed. He won 20 of 23 points on the way to levelling the contest and taking a 3–1 grip on the final set.

Lendl had played similar, dominant tennis most of the week after losing his first set of the tournament to American Larry Stefanki. Lendl had arrived in London from New York only late the previous evening and needed time to adjust to the uneven lighting of the end-to-end, two-court Wembley lay-out. Once he had acclimatised, he dropped only two more games to Stefanki, two to Tomas Smid and three to Johan Kriek on the way to a semi-final against the most aggressive outsider of the tournament, David Pate. The refreshing and engaging Pate had proved his durability by battling past Andreas Maurer, 7–6 6–4, third seed Stefan Edberg, 6–7 6–4 7–5, and eighth seed Joakim Nystrom, 6–2 3–6 7–5, before falling 6–4 6–7 6–3 to Lendl in a tremendously combative semi-final.

With Mike Leach removing Scott Davis (seeded seven) and John Sadri upsetting the fourth favourite, Yannick Noah, Becker had a comparatively easy ride to the last four, where he needed two tie-breaks to defeat fifth seed Anders Jarryd. Becker's toughest match, to the delight of the British fans, was against Jeremy Bates, a wild-card entry, who confirmed his improved form in 1985 by taking the Wimbledon champion to 7–5 7–6 in the second round.

In doubles, the star of the week was Frenchman Guy Forget, who partnered Jarryd to a 7–5 4–6 6–4 final victory over Becker and the formidable Slobodan Zivojinovic. Forget, who was the first French player to win a title at Wembley, was partnering Jarryd for the first time. It is a tribute to Jarryd's ability to get the best out of his partners that on the way to the championship they beat such experienced pairings as Steve Denton and Sherwood Stewart, the Wimbledon champions Heinz Gunthardt and Balazs Taroczy, and the title holders, Andres Gomez and Lendl. – I.B.

WEMBLEY, 12–17 NOVEMBER
MEN'S SINGLES – *Quarter-finals:* I. Lendl (CZ) d. J. Kriek (USA) 6–2 6–1; D. Pate (USA) d. J. Nystrom (SW) 6–2 3–6 7–5; A. Jarryd (SW) d. R. Krishnan (IND) 6–1 7–5; B. Becker (G) d. M. Leach (USA) 6–4 5–3 ret'd. ***Semi-finals:*** Lendl d. Pate 6–4 6–7 6–3; Becker d. Jarryd 7–6 7–6. ***Final:*** Lendl d. Becker 6–7 6–3 4–6 6–4 6–4.
MEN'S DOUBLES – *Final:* Jarryd /G. Forget (F) d. Becker /S. Zivojinovic (YU) 7–5 4–6 6–4.

In one of the year's greatest finals, Boris Becker came within a few points of upsetting Lendl at Wembley. *(M. Cole)*

OTHER NABISCO GRAND PRIX RESULTS

BENSON & HEDGES OPEN ($80,000)

AUCKLAND, NEW ZEALAND, 7–13 JANUARY

MEN'S SINGLES – Quarter-finals: J. Fitzgerald (AUS) d. B. Drewett (AUS) 7–6 7–5; W. Masur (AUS) d. K. Evernden 6–4 2–6 9–7; C. J. Lewis d. G. Layendecker (USA) 7–5 6–3; D. Saltz (USA) d. P. Doohan (AUS) 6–4 6–3. *Semi-finals:* Masur d. Fitzgerald 5–7 7–5 7–5; Lewis d. Saltz 7–6 7–6. *Final:* Lewis d. Masur 7–5 6–0 2–6 6–4.

MEN'S DOUBLES – Final: Fitzgerald /Lewis d. Drewett /S. McCain (USA) 6–3 6–4.

MOLSON LIGHT CHALLENGE ($125,000)

TORONTO, 18–24 FEBRUARY

MEN'S SINGLES – Quarter-finals: A. Jarryd (SW) d. P. Fleming (USA) 7–6 6–0; E. Teltscher (USA) d. R. Krishnan (IND) 6–2 6–4; K. Curren (SA) d. D. Schultz 6–2 6–0; W. Fibak (POL) d. G. Mayer (USA) 6–1 1–6 6–4. *Semi-finals:* Jarryd d. Fibak 4–6 6–4 6–3; Curren d. Teltscher 6–3 6–3. *Final:* Curren d. Jarryd 7–6 6–3.

MEN'S DOUBLES – Final: Fleming /Jarryd d. G. Layendecker (USA) /G. Michibata 7–6 6–2.

WCT FUJI FILM WORLD DOUBLES CHAMPIONSHIP ($200,000)

LONDON, 1–6 JANUARY

ROUND ROBIN RED GROUP – First: W. Fibak (POL) /A. A. Mayer (USA) (d. H. Gunthardt (SWZ) /B. Taroczy (HU) 6–3 5–7 6–4 7–6, d. A. Jarryd (SW) /H. Simonsson (SW) 3–6 6–4 6–1 3–6 6–1, d. T. Smid (CZ) /P. Slozil (CZ) 6–3 6–4 6–3). *Second:* Gunthardt /Taroczy (d. Jarryd /Simonsson 3–6 6–3 1–6 7–5 7–6, d. Smid /Slozil 6–3 6–4 7–6). *Third:* Jarryd /Simonsson (d. Smid /Slozil 4–6 6–2 6–4 7–5).

ROUND ROBIN GREEN GROUP – First: K. Curren (SA) /S. Denton (USA) (d. K. Flach (USA) /R. Seguso (USA) 4–6 6–4 7–6 7–5, d. F. Buehning (USA) /P. Fleming (USA) 3–6 6–7 6–3 7–6 6–3, d. M. R. Edmondson (AUS) /S. E. Stewart (USA) 6–4 7–6 6–3). *Second:* Flach /Seguso (d. Buehning /Fleming 3–6 6–7 6–2 7–5 6–3, d. Edmondson /Stewart 6–4 6–2 6–1). *Third:* Buehning /Fleming (d. Edmondson /Stewart 6–1 6–3 7–5).

PLAY-OFFS – Semi-finals: Flach /Seguso d. Fibak /Mayer 4–6 7–6 6–4 6–4; Gunthardt /Taroczy d. Curren /Denton 6–4 3–6 6–3 6–2. *Final:* Flach /Seguso d. Gunthardt /Taroczy 6–3 3–6 6–3 4–6 6–0. *Fifth place:* Jarryd /Simonsson d. Buehning /Fleming 6–3 3–6 7–5. *Seventh place:* Slozil /Smid d. Edmondson /Stewart 6–0 7–6.

BUENOS AIRES ($80,000)

25 FEBRUARY–3 MARCH

MEN'S SINGLES – Quarter-finals: D. Perez (UR) d. R. Arguello (ARG) 6–3 6–3; J. Brown (USA) d. R. Viver (EC) 6–3 6–3; M. Jaite d. F. Maciel 6–3 6–1; H. de la Pena d. M. Ingaramo 6–3 6–4. *Semi-finals:* Perez d. Brown 6–2 6–4; Jaite d. de la Pena 7–5 6–2. *Final:* Jaite d. Perez 6–4 6–3.

MEN'S DOUBLES – Final: Jaite /C. Miniussi d. Perez /E. Bengoechea 6–2 6–4.

LORRAINE OPEN SNVB ($80,000)

NANCY, 18–24 MARCH

MEN'S SINGLES – Quarter-finals: T. Wilkison (USA) d. J. Frawley (AUS) 6–4 4–6 8–6; P. Portes d. H. Leconte 6–4 1–6 6–2; C. Hooper (USA) d. R. Gehring (G) 7–5 6–3; S. Zivojinovic (YU) d. B. Pils (G) 6–2 7–6. *Semi-finals:* Wilkison d. Portes 6–1 6–1; Zivojinovic d. Hooper 7–6 3–6 6–4. *Final:* Wilkison d. Zivojinovic 4–6 7–6 9–7.

MEN'S DOUBLES – Final: M. Freeman (USA) /R. Harmon (USA) d. J. Navratil (CZ) /J. B. Svensson (SW) 6–4 7–6.

BUICK WCT FINALS ($500,000)

DALLAS, 9–14 APRIL
MEN'S SINGLES – First round: J. Nystrom (SW) d. H. Sundstrom (SW) 6–3 6–3 6–4; T. Mayotte d. A. Gomez (EC) 7–6 6–4 6–2; S. Edberg (SW) d. A. Jarryd (SW) 1–6 6–2 6–2 5–7 6–3; A. Krickstein d. E. Teltscher 7–5 2–6 6–3 2–6 7–5. **Quarter-finals:** Nystrom d. J. P. McEnroe 6–4 7–6 6–3; Mayotte d. M. Wilander (SW) 6–3 6–1 7–6; I. Lendl (CZ) d. Edberg 3–6 7–6 3–6 6–1 6–2; J. S. Connors d. Krickstein 7–5 6–2 6–3. **Semi-finals:** Mayotte d. Nystrom 6–4 4–6 6–2 7–5; Lendl d. Connors 6–3 2–1 ret'd. **Final:** Lendl d. Mayotte 7–6 6–4 6–1.

NICE ($80,000)

9–14 APRIL
MEN'S SINGLES – Quarter-finals: H. Leconte d. F. Luna (SP) 7–6 6–4; H. Schwaier (G) d. S. Zivojinovic (YU) 5–7 7–6 6–4; V. Pecci (PARA) d. T. Benhabiles 6–2 4–6 6–1; D. Perez (UR) d. R. Arguello (ARG) 6–2 6–0. **Semi-finals:** Leconte d. Schwaier 7–5 6–4; Pecci d. Perez 6–4 6–2. **Final:** Leconte d. Pecci 6–4 6–4.
MEN'S DOUBLES – Final: C. Panatta (IT) /P. Slozil (CZ) d. L. Courteau /G. Forget 3–6 6–3 8–6.

KIM TROPHY ($80,000)

BARI, 15–21 APRIL
MEN'S SINGLES – Quarter-finals: C. Panatta d. C. Pistolesi 7–6 6–0; J. Lopez-Maeso (SP) d. R. Arguello (ARG) 6–4 6–0; H. Schwaier (G) d. H. de la Pena (ARG) 7–5 6–4; L. Duncan (USA) d. M. Jaite (BR) 3–6 7–5 6–3. **Semi-finals:** Panatta d. Lopez-Maeso 6–0 3–6 6–4; Duncan d. Schwaier 6–3 6–2. **Final:** Panatta d. Duncan 6–2 1–6 7–6.
MEN'S DOUBLES – Final: Panatta /A. Ganzabal (ARG) d. M. Freeman (USA) /L. Warder (AUS) 6–4 6–2.

PUENTO ROMANO OPEN ($100,000)

MARBELLA, 22–28 APRIL
MEN'S SINGLES – Quarter-finals: L. Duncan (USA) d. P. Arraya (PER) 7–5 6–3; E. Bengoechea (ARG) d. R. Agenor 7–5 7–6; H. de la Pena (ARG) d. J. Lopez-Maeso (SP) 6–2 6–4; S. Shaw (GB) d. A. Ganzabal (ARG) 7–6 6–3. **Semi-finals:** Duncan d. Bengoechea 7–6 6–3; de la Pena d. Shaw 6–4 3–2 ret'd. **Final:** de la Pena d. Duncan 6–0 6–3.
MEN'S DOUBLES – Final: A. Gomez (EC) /C. Motta (BR) d. L. Courteau (F) /M. Schapers (NTH) 6–1 6–1.

MUNICH ($100,000)

6–12 MAY
MEN'S SINGLES – Quarter-finals: J. Nystrom (SW) d. C. Motta (BR) 6–2 3–6 6–0; J. L. Clerc (ARG) d. M. Mecir (CZ) 7–5 6–3; H. Schwaier d. K. Eberhard 6–3 6–3; D. Perez (UR) d. E. Sanchez (SP) 6–3 7–5. **Semi-finals:** Nystrom d. Clerc 6–2 6–4; Schwaier d. Perez 6–4 6–4. **Final:** Nystrom d. Schwaier 6–1 6–0.
MEN'S DOUBLES – Final: M. R. Edmondson (AUS) /K. Warwick d. S. Casal (SP) /Sanchez 4–6 7–5 7–5.

MADRID ($80,000)

13–19 MAY
MEN'S SINGLES – Quarter-finals: A. Maurer (G) d. D. de Miguel 6–4 6–2; K. Novacek (CZ) d. R. Agenor (HA) 7–6 4–6 6–3; A. Mansdorf (IS) d. C. Limberger 2–6 6–3 6–4; L. Duncan (USA) d. M. Ingaramo (ARG) 6–2 6–2. **Semi-finals:** Maurer d. Novacek 7–5 6–3; Duncan d. Mansdorf 6–2 6–3. **Final:** Maurer d. Duncan 7–5 6–2.
MEN'S DOUBLES – Final: G. Barbosa (BR) /I. Kley (BR) d. A. Tous /J. Bardoni (IT) 7–6 6–4.

FLORENCE ($80,000)

20–26 MAY
MEN'S SINGLES – Quarter-finals: S. Casal (SP) d. M. Dickson (USA) 6–2 6–4; E. Bengoechea (ARG) d. J. Brown (USA) 6–1 7–6; M. DePalmer (USA) d. L. Duncan (USA) 5–7 6–4 6–4; J. Arias (USA) d. M. Ingaramo (ARG) 6–1 6–4. *Semi-finals:* Casal d. Bengoechea 7–5 6–3; Arias d. DePalmer 6–2 6–3. *Final:* Casal d. Arias 3–6 6–3 6–2.
MEN'S DOUBLES – Final: D. Graham (AUS) /L. Warder (AUS) d. B. Derlin (NZ) /C. Limberger (USA) 6–1 6–1.

BOLOGNA ($80,000)

10–16 JUNE
MEN'S SINGLES – Quarter-finals: A. Tous (SP) d. Z. Kuharszky (SWZ) 6–4 6–1; C. Panatta d. M. Narducci 6–7 6–2 6–3; T. Tulasne (F) d. R. Agenor (HA) 6–2 3–6 6–4; D. Keretic (G) d. G. Prpic (YU) 6–4 3–6 6–4. *Semi-finals:* Panatta d. Tous 7–5 6–3; Tulasne d. Panatta 6–0 6–4. *Final:* Tulasne d. Panatta 6–2 6–0.
MEN'S DOUBLES – Final: P. Cane /S. Colombo d. J. Arrese (SP) /Tous 7–5 6–4.

STELLA ARTOIS CHAMPIONSHIPS ($200,000)

QUEEN'S CLUB, LONDON, 10–16 JUNE
MEN'S SINGLES – Quarter-finals: P. McNamee (AUS) d. T. Mayotte (USA) 7–5 7–5; B. Becker (G) d. P. Cash (AUS) 6–4 6–4; J. Kriek (USA) d. R. Simpson (NZ) 6–4 7–6; S. Zivojinovic (YU) d. P. Annacone (USA) 7–6 6–1. *Semi-finals:* Becker d. McNamee 6–4 6–1; Kriek d. Zivojinovic 6–4 6–4. *Final:* Becker d. Kriek 6–2 6–3.
MEN'S DOUBLES – Final: K. Flach (USA) /R. Seguso (USA) d. Cash /J. Fitzgerald (AUS) 3–6 6–3 16–14.

WEST OF ENGLAND CHAMPIONSHIPS ($100,000)

BRISTOL, 10–16 JUNE
MEN'S SINGLES – Quarter-finals: R. Knapp (USA) d. P. Doohan (AUS) 7–6 3–6 6–3; G. Layendecker (USA) d. N. Odizor (NIG) 6–3 6–4; B. Teacher (USA) d. G. Forget (F) 2–6 7–6 6–4; M. Davis (USA) d. M. J. Bates 4–6 7–5 9–7. *Semi-finals:* Layendecker d. Knapp 6–4 6–3; Davis d. Teacher 6–3 7–6. *Final:* Davis d. Layendecker 4–6 6–3 7–5.
MEN'S DOUBLES – Final: E. Edwards (SA) /D. Visser (SA) d. J. G. Alexander (AUS) /R. Simpson (NZ) 6–4 7–6.

HALL OF FAME CHAMPIONSHIPS, NEWPORT, RI ($100,000)

8–14 JULY
MEN'S SINGLES – Quarter-finals: J. Sadri d. S. Davis 6–3 7–5; T. Mayotte d. M. Flur 3–6 6–4 6–2; D. Pate d. P. Annacone 3–6 7–5 6–3; Tom Gullikson d. J. Kriek 7–5 4–6 6–3. *Semi-finals:* Sadri d. Mayotte 6–4 6–3; Gullikson d. Pate 7–6 6–7 7–5. *Final:* Gullikson d. Sadri 6–3 7–6.
MEN'S DOUBLES – Final: P. Doohan (AUS) /S. Giammalva d. Annacone /C. Van Rensburg (SA) 6–1 6–3.

SWISS OPEN ($150,000)

GSTAAD, 8–14 JULY
MEN'S SINGLES – Quarter-finals: J. Nystrom (SW) d. W. Fibak (POL) 7–6 6–0; G. Forget (F) d. H. Gunthardt 6–1 6–4; A. Maurer (G) d. C. Motta (BR) 1–6 6–2 7–6; M. R. Edmondson (AUS) d. R. Viver (EC) 6–4 7–6. *Semi-finals:* Nystrom d. Forget 6–7 6–1 7–6; Maurer d. Edmondson 6–2 3–6 6–3. *Final:* Nystrom d. Maurer 6–4 1–6 7–5 6–3.
MEN'S DOUBLES – Final: Fibak /T. Smid (CZ) d. B. Drewett (AUS) /Edmondson 6–7 6–4 6–4.

SWEDISH OPEN ($80,000)

BASTAD, 15–21 JULY
MEN'S SINGLES – Quarter-finals: M. Wilander d. G. Prpic (YU) 6–1 0–6 6–2; D. Keretic (G) d. H. Sundstrom 6–3 6–3; K. Carlsson d. A. de Minicis (IT) 6–0 6–4; S. Edberg d. S. Simonsson 6–0 6–4.

Semi-finals: Wilander d. Keretic 6–3 4–6 6–4; Edberg d. Carlsson 6–4 6–2. *Final:* Wilander d. Edberg 6–1 6–0.
MEN'S DOUBLES – Final: Edberg /A. Jarryd d. S. Casal (SP) /E. Sanchez (SP) 6–0 7–6.

LIVINGSTON, NJ ($80,000)

22–28 JULY
MEN'S SINGLES – Quarter-finals: J. Kriek d. D. Visser (SA) 6–4 6–0; B. Teacher d. S. Giammalva 6–4 6–3; J. Grabb d. R. Green 6–4 6–4; B. Gilbert d. P. Annacone 6–3 6–2. *Semi-finals:* Teacher d. Kriek 7–6 6–4; Gilbert d. Grabb 6–2 6–2. *Final:* Gilbert d. Teacher 4–6 7–5 6–0.
MEN'S DOUBLES – Final: M. DePalmer /P. Doohan (AUS) d. E. Edwards (SA) /D. Visser (SA) 6–3 6–4.

NETHERLANDS OPEN ($80,000)

HILVERSUM, 22–28 JULY
MEN'S SINGLES – Quarter-finals: K. Carlsson (SW) d. D. Cahill (AUS) 6–2 6–4; M. Oosting d. M. Schapers 6–4 4–6 6–2; R. Osterthun (G) d. T. Smid (CZ) 6–4 6–2; A. Maurer (G) d. H. Van Boeckel 6–1 6–1. *Semi-finals:* Carlsson d. Oosting 6–1 6–4; Osterthun d. Maurer 3–6 7–6 6–4. *Final:* Osterthun d. Carlsson 4–6 4–6 6–4 6–2 6–3.
MEN'S DOUBLES – Final: H. /S. Simonsson (SW) d. C. Limberger (AUS) /M. Woodforde (AUS) 6–3 6–4.

AUSTRIAN OPEN ($150,000)

KITZBUHEL, 5–11 AUGUST
MEN'S SINGLES – Quarter-finals: M. Westphal (G) d. K. Carlsson (SW) 7–6 6–3; M. Vajda (CZ) d. H. Leconte (F) 6–2 6–4; P. Slozil (CZ) d. T. Tulasne (F) 5–7 6–4 6–4; S. Casal (SP) d. E. Sanchez (SP) 7–6 6–1.
Semi-finals: Westphal d. Vajda 7–6 6–3; Slozil d. Casal 6–1 6–3. *Final:* Slozil d. Westphal 7–5 6–2.
MEN'S DOUBLES – Final: Casal /Sanchez d. C. Panatta (IT) /P. Cane (IT) 6–3 3–6 6–2.

SOCIETY BANK CLASSIC ($80,000)

CLEVELAND, 12–18 AUGUST
MEN'S SINGLES – Quarter-finals: B. Gilbert d. M. Doyle 6–1 6–0; B. Schultz d. M. Bauer 6–2 6–3; H. Pfister d. R. Acuna (CH) 5–7 6–2 6–3; B. Drewett (AUS) d. D. Pate 4–6 6–4 7–6. *Semi-finals:* Gilbert d. Schultz 6–4 6–4; Drewett d. Pfister 6–3 7–5. *Final:* Gilbert d. Drewett 6–3 6–2.
MEN'S DOUBLES – Final: L. Palin (FIN) /O. Rahnasto (FIN) d. Pfister /B. Testerman 3–6 7–6 7–6.

BORDEAUX ($80,000)

16–22 SEPTEMBER
MEN'S SINGLES – Quarter-finals: J. L. Clerc (ARG) d. R. Agenor (HA) 6–2 6–4; J. Brown (USA) d. J. Bardou (SP) 6–2 6–2; T. Tulasne d. L. Pimek (CZ) 6–1 6–1; D. Perez (UR) d. F. Maciel (MEX) 6–3 6–3. *Semi-finals:* Brown d. Clerc 6–7 6–3 6–1; Perez d. Tulasne 2–6 6–3 6–2. *Final:* Perez d. Brown 6–4 7–5.
MEN'S DOUBLES – Final: D. Felgate (GB) /S. Shaw (GB) d. Pimek /B. Willenborg (USA) 6–4 5–7 6–4.

GENEVA ($100,000)

16–22 SEPTEMBER
MEN'S SINGLES – Quarter-finals: M. Wilander (SW) d. J. Hlasek 7–5 6–4; H. Leconte (F) d. M. Vajda (CZ) 7–5 6–1; J. Aguilera (SP) d. L. Lavalle (MEX) 7–5 6–1; T. Smid (CZ) d. R. Arguello (ARG) 6–2 6–2. *Semi-finals:* Wilander d. Leconte 3–6 6–3 6–1; Smid d. Aguilera 7–5 6–3. *Final:* Smid d. Wilander 6–4 6–4.
MEN'S DOUBLES – Final: S. Casal (SP) /E. Sanchez (SP) d. C. Kirmayr (BR) /C. Motta (BR) 6–4 4–6 7–5.

When he reached the semi-finals in Delray Beach and the quarter-finals in Hamburg and Rome, the 'silent Swede', Jan Gunnarsson, built the confidence that ultimately helped him to win his first Grand Prix title in Vienna.   (T. Hindley)

MERCEDES CUP ($100,000)

STUTTGART, 9–15 SEPTEMBER
MEN'S SINGLES – Quarter-finals: I. Lendl (CZ) d. R. Agenor (HA) 6–1 6–3; J. L. Clerc (ARG) d. J. Gunnarsson (SW) 6–3 6–3; B. Gilbert (USA) d. A. Maurer 6–0 6–4; T. Smid (CZ) d. U. Riglewski 7–5 7–6. *Semi-finals:* Lendl d. Clerc 6–2 6–2; Gilbert d. Smid 6–4 4–6 7–5. *Final:* Lendl d. Gilbert 6–4 6–0.
MEN'S DOUBLES – Final: Lendl /Smid d. A. Kohlberg (USA) /J. Soares (BR) 3–6 6–4 6–2.

SICILIAN CHAMPIONSHIPS ($80,000)

PALERMO, 9–15 SEPTEMBER
MEN'S SINGLES – Quarter-finals: J. Nystrom (SW) d. R. Arguello (ARG) 7–6 6–4; D. Perez (UR) d. G. Prpic (YU) 6–2 6–3; T. Muster (AU) d. F. Cancellotti 6–3 7–5; T. Tulasne (F) d. C. Pistolesi 6–0 6–4. *Semi-finals:* Nystrom d. Perez 7–6 6–4; Tulasne d. Muster 6–0 6–4. *Final:* Tulasne d. Nystrom 6–3 6–1.
MEN'S DOUBLES – Final: C. Dowdeswell (GB) /Nystrom d. C. Panatta /P. Cane 7–6 4–6 6–4.

GWA MAZDA CLASSIC ($80,000)

BRISBANE, 7–13 OCTOBER
MEN'S SINGLES – Quarter-finals: P. Annacone (USA) d. M. Davis (USA) 6–7 7–6 6–4; S. Youl d. R. Simpson (NZ) 6–3 6–3; K. Evernden (NZ) d. B. Schultz (USA) 6–2 3–6 7–5; G. Layendecker (USA) d. B. Testerman (USA) 6–3 6–4. *Semi-finals:* Annacone d. Youl 6–1 7–6; Evernden d. Layendecker 6–4 6–7 6–1. *Final:* Annacone d. Evernden 6–3 6–3.
MEN'S DOUBLES – Final: B. Drewett /Davis d. Schultz /Testerman 6–2 6–2.

TOULOUSE ($125,000)

7–13 OCTOBER
MEN'S SINGLES – Quarter-finals: Y. Noah d. J. Hlasek (SWZ) 6–3 7–5; G. Forget d. L. Pimek (CZ) 6–2 6–7 9–7; R. Krishnan (IND) d. J. Gunnarsson (SW) 6–4 6–3; T. Smid d. J. Potier 6–5 6–4. *Semi-finals:* Noah d. Forget 6–4 6–2; Smid d. Krishnan 6–7 6–3 6–4. *Final:* Noah d. Smid 6–4 6–4.
MEN'S DOUBLES – Final: R. Acuna (CH) /Hlasek d. Smid /P. Slozil (CZ) 4–6 6–2 9–7.

BASLE ($150,000)

14–20 OCTOBER
MEN'S SINGLES – Quarter-finals: S. Edberg (SW) d. H. Schwaier (G) 6–1 6–4; W. Fibak (POL) d. T. Tulasne (F) 6–4 4–6 6–4; L. Pimek (CZ) d. M. Mecir (CZ) 7–6 1–6 6–2; Y. Noah (F) d. G. Forget (F) 1–6 7–5 7–6. *Semi-finals:* Edberg d. Fibak 6–3 6–2; Noah d. Pimek 5–7 6–2 7–5. *Final:* Edberg d. Noah 6–7 7–6 6–1.
MEN'S DOUBLES – Final: Tim /Tom Gullikson (USA) d. M. Dickson (USA) /T. Wilkison (USA) 4–6 6–4 6–4.

JAPAN OPEN CHAMPIONSHIPS ($125,000)

TOKYO, 14–20 OCTOBER
MEN'S SINGLES – Quarter-finals: J. Arias (USA) d. M. Anger (USA) 6–3 6–3; G. Michibata (C) d. G. Holmes (USA) 6–4 6–4; J. Carlsson (SW) d. J. Canter (USA) 1–6 7–6 6–1; S. Davies (USA) d. S. Giammalva (USA) 6–4 6–2. *Semi-finals:* Arias d. Michibata 5–7 6–3 6–4; Davis d. Carlsson 6–4 6–1. *Final:* Davis d. Arias 6–1 7–6.
MEN'S DOUBLES – Final: Davis /D. Pate (USA) d. Giammalva /Holmes 7–6 6–7 6–3.

TEL AVIV ($80,000)

14–20 OCTOBER
MEN'S SINGLES – Quarter-finals: A. Mansdorf d. F. Segarceanu (RU) 7–5 6–0; B. Gilbert (USA) d. G. Ocleppo (IT) 6–2 6–4; S. Perkis d. E. Jelen (G) 6–1 3–6 6–4; M. J. Bates (GB) d. P. Carlsson (SW) 6–1 6–4. *Semi-finals:* Mansdorf d. Bates 7–5 3–6 6–2; Gilbert d. Perkis 6–2 6–1. *Final:* Gilbert d. Mansdorf 6–3 6–2.
MEN'S DOUBLES – Final: Gilbert /I. Nastase (RU) d. M. Robertson (USA) /Segarceanu 6–3 6–2.

MELBOURNE ($100,000)

21–27 OCTOBER

MEN'S SINGLES – Quarter-finals: P. Annacone (USA) d. W. Masur 3–6 6–4 7–6; C. Van Rensburg (SA) d. M. Woodforde 3–6 7–6 6–1; M. Davis (USA) d. B. Dyke 7–6 6–4; B. Testerman (USA) d. P. McNamara 7–6 4–6 7–5. **Semi-finals:** Annacone d. Van Rensburg 6–7 6–4 6–3; Davis d. Testerman 6–4 6–7 6–4. **Final:** Davis d. Annacone 6–4 6–4.
MEN'S DOUBLES – Final: B. Drewett /M. Mitchell (USA) d. D. Dowlen (USA) /N. Odizor (NIG) 4–6 7–6 6–4.

COLOGNE ($80,000)

21–27 OCTOBER

MEN'S SINGLES – Quarter-finals: R. Krishnan (IND) d. J. M. Lloyd (GB) 3–6 6–3 7–5; M. Dickson (USA) d. H. de la Pena (ARG) 6–3 6–3; P. Lundgren (SW) d. T. Wilkison d. Tom Gullikson (USA) 6–2 6–0. **Semi-finals:** Krishnan d. Dickson 2–6 6–1 7–5; Lundgren d. Wilkison 6–4 1–6 7–6. **Final:** Lundgren d. Krishnan 6–3 6–2.
MEN'S DOUBLES – Final: A. Antonitsch (AU) /M. Schapers (NTH) d. Lundgren /J. Gunnarsson (SW) 6–4 7–5.

HONG KONG ($200,000)

18–24 NOVEMBER

MEN'S SINGLES – Quarter-finals: J. Hlasek (SWZ) d. T. Smid (CZ) 6–2 6–4; A. Gomez (EC) d. M. Anger (USA) 6–1 6–2; B. Schultz (USA) d. L. Lavalle (MEX) 6–3 6–3; A. Krickstein (USA) d. J. Canter (USA) 6–4 6–1. **Semi-finals:** Gomez d. Hlasek 4–6 6–3 7–5; Krickstein d. Schultz 6–3 6–2. **Final:** Gomez d. A. Krickstein 6–3 6–3 3–6 6–4.
MEN'S DOUBLES – Final: B. Drewett /K. Warwick d. Hlasek /Smid 6–3 4–6 6–2.

VIENNA ($100,000)

18–24 NOVEMBER

MEN'S SINGLES – Quarter-finals: L. Pimek (CZ) d. M. Jaite (BR) 7–5 4–6 6–3; A. Maurer (G) d. M. DePalmer (USA) 6–2 4–6 6–3; H. Gunthardt (SWZ) d. R. Agenor (HA) 6–7 6–3 7–5; J. Gunnarsson (SW) d. M. Westphal (G) 6–1 6–2. **Semi-finals:** Pimek d. Maurer 6–3 6–2; Gunnarsson d. Gunthardt 7–6 6–2. **Final:** Gunnarsson d. Pimek 6–7 6–2 6–4 1–6 7–5.
MEN'S DOUBLES – Final: G. Donnelly (USA) /M. DePalmer (USA) d. S. Casal (SP) /E. Sanchez (SP) 6–4 6–3.

SYDNEY ($125,000)

9–15 DECEMBER

MEN'S SINGLES – Quarter-finals: K. Evernden (NZ) d. C. Steyn (SA) 6–7 7–6 7–5; M. Dickson (USA) d. T. Mayotte (USA) 6–3 3–6 7–6; M. Anger (USA) d. B. Schultz (USA) 6–3 6–3; H. Leconte (F) d. W. Masur 6–4 6–3. **Semi-finals:** Evernden d. Dickson 6–4 7–6; Leconte d. Masur 6–4 6–3. **Final:** Leconte d. Evernden 6–7 6–2 6–3.
MEN'S DOUBLES – Final: D. Dowlen (USA) /N. Odizor (NIG) d. Masur /B. Dyke 6–4 7–6.

ADELAIDE ($80,000)

16–22 DECEMBER

MEN'S SINGLES – Quarter-finals: P. Doohan d. A. Mansdorf (IS) 6–3 6–4; W. Masur d. R. Saad (ARG) 0–6 6–4 7–6; E. Edwards (SA) d. L. Shiras (USA) 6–2 6–2; C. Steyn (SA) d. J. Fitzgerald 3–6 7–6 6–2. **Semi-finals:** Doohan d. Masur 6–4 2–0 ret'd; Edwards d. Steyn 7–6 7–6. **Final:** Edwards d. Doohan 6–2 6–4.
MEN'S DOUBLES – Final: M. R. Edmondson/K. Warwick d. N. Aerts (BR)/T. Warneke (USA) 6–4 6–4.

MELBOURNE ($80,000)

22–29 DECEMBER

MEN'S SINGLES – Quarter-finals: J. Canter (USA) d. B. Dyke 6–2 6–3; M. R. Edmondson d. E. Edwards (SA) 6–3 3–6 7–5; M. Kratzman d. W. Scanlon (USA) 6–3 6–4; P. Doohan d. M. Robertson (SA) 7–5 6–1. **Semi-finals:** Canter d. Edmondson 7–6 7–6; Doohan d. Kratzman 6–4 6–3. **Final:** Canter d. Doohan 5–7 6–3 6–4.
MEN'S DOUBLES – Final: D. Cahill /P. Carter d. R. Saad (ARG) /B. Dickinson (USA) 7–6 6–1.

THE NABISCO MASTERS

John Barrett

Ivan Lendl, the gaunt Czech with the life style of an American millionaire, is now unquestionably the best tennis player in the world. By winning the $500,000 Nabisco Masters at New York's Madison Square Garden in January, without dropping a set in four matches, to claim a third Masters title in six consecutive appearances in the final, he dispelled any doubts there might have been about who ruled men's tennis in 1985. Every one of the top men was present, except Jimmy Connors, whose 'flu did not respond in time for him to take part, but none could challenge Lendl's authority.

In the final, which he won 6–2 7–6 6–3 in two hours and 21 minutes of furious hitting against Germany's 18-year-old *wunderkind*, Boris Becker, the world's No. 1 displayed poise and versatility. Here was a man who knew that on the slow Supreme carpet he could contain the awesome power game of Wimbledon's youngest-ever champion, and return that young lion's ferocious serves, bludgeoning drives and diving volleys with interest. Lendl's confidence in moments of crisis was unshakable. His improvement since seeking the guidance of Australia's veteran champion, Tony Roche, early the previous year has been subtle but significant. There is now a greater awareness of when to use the slice backhand to keep the ball low, either as an approach shot or as a means of drawing an opponent wide; there is a greater confidence on the volley – even an eagerness to approach the net at times; there is a greater tactical awareness; and, above all, there is a much greater belief in his own considerable abilities, especially with the serve and the topspin backhand passing shot on key points, which had been particularly evident since September, when he finally won the US Open, after failing in the three previous finals.

For the first time the Masters' field contained 16 players, and for the first time this season-ending climax to the men's year was managed by the Men's International Professional Tennis Council under the direction of Gene Scott, an independent entrepreneur. The first two December Masters in 1970 and 1971, held in Tokyo and Paris under Pepsi-Cola's sponsorship, had been round-robin tournaments. With the change to Commercial Union support in 1972 had come the addition of knock-out semi-finals and final. This formula had continued when Colgate-Palmolive had become the new sponsor in 1977 and had brought the Masters to New York in January 1978. Volvo's first Masters · had come in January 1981 and in the last two years of Volvo's involvement, 1983 and 1984, the discredited round-robin system had given way to a 12-man draw, in which the top four seeds had been given byes – a patently unfair and unsatisfactory format. Now every player would be treated equally.

The 15 players who assembled for the Monday press conference at the Felt Forum (Connors was absent, as he had been the year before) were the points leaders from the 71 tournaments in 23 countries comprising the Nabisco Grand Prix in 1985, with Scott Davis, in 17th position, replacing the injured Miloslav Mecir. When it was finally known the following day that Connors would be unable to take part in his first-round match against Henri Leconte that evening, a hurried search was instigated for a replacement. The next in line on the points table was Kevin Curren but he had already informed the organisers that he would be on vacation. Next was Martin Jaite who was far away in Argentina but who, under the rules, should have been in New York as the official alternate. There will surely be repercussions at the omission. Jimmy Arias, the next choice, was already committed to another event. Accordingly Andres Gomez was

If there had been any doubts about the world leadership, Ivan Lendl silenced them with an utterly commanding performance in New York, where he won the Masters for the third time from six finals. *(R. Adams)*

hurriedly summoned from Washington where he was enjoying an official lunch with the President of Ecuador, Leon Cordero, and the US Secretary of State, George Schultz.

Even before the hurrying Gomez arrived on court there had already been a minor upset. Stefan Edberg, the fifth-seeded Australian Open champion, who looked ill at ease on his first appearance at the Garden, played carelessly against the muscular South African-born Johan Kriek, whom he had twice beaten in 1985, and was bundled out of the tournament 6–2 4–6 6–2, without ever doing his talents full justice. Meanwhile his fellow-Swede, Mats Wilander, the No. 3 seed and one of four singles representatives from the champion country, had disposed of Scott Davis 6–3 6–4 in their first meeting.

Although the Swedes were destined to play no part in the final of the singles, they did make their presence felt in the doubles by providing all four finalists from an original field of eight pairs. Edberg and Jarryd, the second seeds, who had accounted for Slozil and Smid, and then Annacone and Van Rensburg in a glorious 5–7 6–3 7–6 victory, were always a little more positive and decisive than Nystrom and Wilander as they won 6–1 7–6 to take the winners' cheque for $35,000. This win was particularly appropriate for Edberg, who celebrated his 20th birthday on the day of the final. After the presentation ceremony, shyly but successfully, he blew out all the candles on the birthday cake that had been presented to him on court. The losers, who had eliminated Edmondson and Warwick in a thrilling 7–6 4–6 7–6 first-round battle and then the top seeds, Flach and Seguso, in straight sets, earned a reward of $15,000.

Becker won another first-time encounter when, after losing the first set to Paul Annacone's chip-and-charge tactics, he started to drill his passing shots through the Bridgehampton boy's defences. Despite the fact that Annacone was the local man, Becker's dynamic style immediately appealed to the New York public, who cheered the forceful manner of his 3–6 6–3 6–2 victory. As with every arena in which he has played since winning Wimbledon, Beckermania had infected even the sports capital of the world.

Although Gomez had been warned early on Monday morning that he might be required, he arrived in New York with no time to practise. Nor was there time to get nervous, and he was so relaxed in beating Leconte 7–6 6–1, for the first time in three meetings, that he could only smile afterwards about his good fortune. 'I got the phone call at my hotel about four o'clock and caught the five o'clock shuttle', he said. 'It's nice to be back in New York, but don't ask me how I played – I can't remember much about it.' So ended a dramatic opening day.

No-one was prepared for the extraordinary happenings of Wednesday. The day had opened routinely enough with Anders Jarryd (seeded eight) winning a curiously lop-sided domestic battle with Joakim Nystrom (No. 9) 0–6 6–1 6–4. It was Jarryd's fourth win in five meetings against his *Davis Cup* team-mate and their first clash on Supreme. Even the defeat of the No. 7 seed, Yannick Noah, by Tim Mayotte, seeded three places lower, was not really a surprise, for these two big men had never met, and on the day the American was worth his 6–4 6–4 win on the merits of greater serve-and-volley consistency and a greater readiness to exploit the mid-court ball. The third match of the day, a straightforward 6–1 6–0 win by Lendl over fellow-Czech Tomas Smid, to whom he had lost only once (back in 1981) in 10 previous meetings, whetted the appetite for the last of the first-round matches.

The No. 2 seed, John McEnroe, would be opening the defence of his title against fellow-American Brad Gilbert, a 24-year-old Californian who had risen to 18 on the ATP rankings with some impressive performances in 1985 that had included three tournament wins in Livingston, Cleveland and Tel Aviv. However, his season had also included three losses to McEnroe to add to the four previous defeats at the US No. 1's hands since their first meeting at Wimbledon in 1983. This, then, would surely be a gentle pipe-opener for the champion. Imagine the sense of disbelief, outrage almost, among the fans as a thoroughly bad-tempered McEnroe fumbled his way to a 5–7 6–4 6–1 defeat.

To Gilbert's credit, he did find some beautiful passes in the closing stages, as the despairing and clearly unfit McEnroe came charging forward. But the McEnroe of Wednesday, 15 January, 1986, was a pale caricature of the genius who, all agreed, had 12 months earlier on the same court played the best tennis that any man has ever played,

NABISCO GRAND PRIX
...the name of the game.

NABISCO GRAND PRIX

during a golden 11-game spell against Lendl. Gone was the confident aggressive spirit, gone was the timing, gone were the lightning readjustments of body and racket that invent the shots of inspiration you will find in no coaching manual. Here was a man who hated himself for his inability to perform as he knows he can, a man who hated the whole frustrating situation – the howling fans, the court officials, his opponent. The fine of $1,000, imposed by refereee Ken Farrar for John's behaviour that day, was almost irrelevant.

The announcement of John's withdrawal from the circuit for at least 60 days, made on 22 January, came as no surprise. His long-standing association with actress Tatum O'Neal and his impending fatherhood were clearly more important to him than his immediate tennis career. The constant intrusive media pressure surrounding his private life was something which he could no longer face. At the age of 26 he had reached a cross-road in his life. 'My attitude is very bad, very negative . . . I'm not happy with my movement . . . I shouldn't be playing tennis now . . . I'm letting things affect me and I'm embarrassed', he admitted afterwards. 'As a person I'll learn and grow from what is happening', he added. 'I hope others do too. They didn't seem to learn from Borg. Now they see it happening to me.'

Three of the quarter-finals were one-sided affairs. Lendl was always too powerful for Mayotte whose volleying was made to look rather fragile as he went down 6–3 6–3. This was a tenth successive loss to the unyielding Czech for 'Gentleman Tim', who has won only two sets in all those matches. Gomez, smiling more than usual and enjoying the ride on cloud nine, surprised Kriek on this first meeting between them to record a 6–3 6–2 win, earned as much on some outrageous errors from the over-ambitious Kriek as on his own positive virtues of swinging left-handed serves and acutely angled backhand passes. Immediately the match was over, Gomez moved towards the courtside seat occupied by Lucy Hopman, the widow of Harry Hopman who had died suddenly at his home in Florida on 27 December. After embracing Lucy fondly for a moment he was interviewed on court for ESPN television by one of Harry's old pupils, Fred Stolle. 'Mr Hopman was like a father to me, and he and Lucy have helped me so much', said Gomez. Clearly feeling the emotion of the occasion, he added: 'I would like to dedicate this win to both of them.' The gesture, spontaneous and sincere, immediately endeared the likeable giant to everyone who heard it.

Jarryd duly ended Gilbert's dreams of fame and fortune with one of those typical hustling, bustling wins, measured 6–1 6–2, as he bounced around the court as if on springs. This was another of those first encounters of the predictable kind. Becker's 6–4 4–6 6–3 win over Wilander was a gem. Since losing to the Swede in the second round of the French Open last June, Becker had scored three most impressive wins against him – in the Cincinnati final in August, in the fourth match of the *Davis Cup* final that had kept the tie alive in Munich just before Christmas, and in the final of the World Young Masters in Berlin in the first week of January 1986. This was another delightful match, full of contrasts – the all-out attack of the young German against the counter-hitting defence of the Swede. At one stage the German was publicly warned for receiving coaching from Gunther Bosch who was sitting, as usual, with manager Ion Tiriac at the side of the court. If Wilander was depressed by his defeat he had no reason to be. He had actually played well, but the truth is that Becker is better than he is on courts where he can make his pace tell. It will be fascinating to witness their next meeting on clay.

So to the semi-finals, where it became apparent that Lendl and Becker were drawing ahead of the rest of the men's game – just as, in their turns, Borg and Connors had done, and more recently McEnroe and Lendl. The ruthless despatch of Jarryd 6–3 6–4 by Becker indicated that he had moved into that charmed circle at the very top. Here was the *Davis Cup* match that had never materialised because of Jarryd's bout of influenza. Watching the way such a competent competitor was being taken apart for the fourth time in seven months by a lad only two months past his 18th birthday, it was amazing to think that a year earlier Jarryd had led McEnroe 6–2 3–0 and had held a point for 4–0 and another for 4–1 in this very arena. Against the sustained power of Becker's serve (there were seven aces) and the ferocity of his groundstrokes, the Swede was impotent.

For an 11th win in 12 career meetings since 1980, Lendl moved into a higher gear to beat Gomez 6–4 7–5. He had to, for the Ecuadorian was having another good day after announcing, to everyone's amusement, 'I was coming here anyway to watch the semi-finals, and here I am playing in them!' Play he most certainly did, urged on by a small but vociferous group of banner-waving supporters in the gallery. But always his opponent was a trifle more consistent. Lendl's heavy groundstrokes were at their intimidating best, and the booming serve, so often underestimated in assessing the Czech's performance, was becoming ominously grooved. Appropriately the favourite reached his fourth match-point with his 11th ace. It was enough to break Gomez's stout resistance at last, but the tall South American was not at all dismayed. 'I've had some great practice and played the world's No. 1. It's boosted my confidence and I've won a little money ($35,000). It was a good week.' That it most certainly was – for Gomez and for the spectators who had come to appreciate just what an artist the big man is. Happily he seems fully recovered from the shoulder injury that had forced him to retire to Lendl during the 1984 Masters, and had kept him out of the event altogether in 1985. We are surely going to see great things from this talented athlete in 1986.

Although the final was not a great match it was a wonderful example of powerful hitting and tactical awareness by Lendl, who took his time between the points and refused to be rushed by the eager teenager. 'I was in a hurry when I was his age', he said. 'I had to learn from Connors and McEnroe to play slower.' Had Becker been a little less ambitious with some huge shots that just missed the mark, or had he succeeded with a forehand volley when serving for the second set at 5–3 30–30, we might have seen a repeat of their classic duel in the Benson and Hedges final at Wembley the previous November. Another fleeting chance came and went on Lendl's serve at 5–6, 30–40. Lendl saved the set-point with a blistering ace, the sixth and last he would serve in the match. It was a great psychological blow to a young man whose own serve is the foundation of all his victories. Even the nine aces he delivered were not enough, for Lendl played a perfect tie-break, hitting some incredible backhand winners at full stretch from low balls, to astonish the charging Becker. 'He's so fast and when he gets to the ball he still plays a great shot . . . he just couldn't miss with his passing shots in the tie-break. That's probably what I have to learn – to get a little bit faster.'

Throughout the youngster was complaining to Bosch about the tension of the strings in his rackets. But he never stopped trying, even in the third set when he crashed spectacularly through the courtside railing and gashed his right knee, an injury that later required three stitches. That point gave Lendl a 3–0 lead, but after the four-and-a-half-minute injury-break at the change of ends, the favourite seemed to relax his concentration for the only time in the match. Becker's recovery to 3–3 was greeted with tremendous enthusiasm by the 16,227 spectators, but it merely served to jog Lendl's memory about the business in hand. He had come into the tournament with a temperature, and had risen from his bed only to play his matches. The last thing he wanted was a long final.

Three games later it was over. Lendl had won his third title in this historic arena (he had beaten Gerulaitis in 1982 and McEnroe the following year), and was showered with the spoils of victory – a giant cheque for $100,000 from the contributing sponsor Paine Webber, another for $800,000 from Michael Davies, the new chairman of the MIPTC, as the first prize on the Nabisco Grand Prix bonus pool, a magnificent sterling silver trophy designed by Tiffany's of New York, and the keys of a Chrysler car. In a gracious speech Lendl paid tribute to his opponent and to the organisers and sponsors. He seemed relaxed at last, more American now than Czech with his large, comfortable house in Greenwich, Connecticut, guarded by those much publicised six German shepherd dogs.

The crowds, 79,573 for the week, were down on the previous year and somewhat disappointing. The high price of tickets on the last two days – $15 for the upper level, $24 for the high promenade, $30 for the lower promenade and $50 for a box seat – may have been partly responsible, though the lack of American success (Connors absent, McEnroe beaten, only two lesser-known names in the quarter-finals and none in the semi-finals) must also have been a factor. With the next Nabisco Masters coming into the calendar in the first week of December, we shall return at last to the sensible year-end formula

On his 20th birthday, Stefan Edberg (right) and his partner, Anders Jarryd, won the Masters doubles for the first time.   *(R. Adams)*

that had originally been designed for this prestigious event. However, there is talk of reverting to a round-robin system which smacks of pure commercialism. Far better would be a return to an eight-man field playing a knock-out tournament with every match the best of five sets. Unhappily there is no talk of moving the Masters around the world to reflect the different surfaces upon which the Grand Prix tournaments are played – clay, cement, grass and indoor carpet. In all of its 17 years, the Masters has been played only once out of doors, when it went to Kooyong's grass in 1974. Thus it cannot properly claim to reflect the competition for which it purports to be the showcase. Sadly, commercialism is likely to win once again.

NABISCO GRAND PRIX MASTERS ($500,000)

MADISON SQUARE GARDEN, NEW YORK, 13–19 JANUARY, 1986

MEN'S SINGLES – First round: I. Lendl (CZ) d. T. Smid (CZ) 6–1 6–0; T. Mayotte d. Y. Noah (F) 6–4 6–4; A. Gomez (EC) d. H. Leconte (F) 7–6 6–1; J. Kriek d. S. Edberg (SW) 6–2 4–6 6–2; B. Becker (G) d. P. Annacone 3–6 6–3 6–2; M. Wilander (SW) d. S. Davis 6–3 6–4; A. Jarryd (SW) d. J. Nystrom (SW) 0–6 6–1 6–4; B. Gilbert d. J. P. McEnroe 5–7 6–4 6–1. ***Quarter-finals:*** Lendl d. Mayotte 6–3 6–3; Gomez d. Kriek 6–3 6–2; Becker d. Wilander 6–4 4–6 6–3; Jarryd d. Gilbert 6–1 6–2. ***Semi-finals:*** Lendl d. Gomez 6–4 7–5; Becker d. Jarryd 6–3 6–4. ***Final:*** Lendl d. Becker 6–2 7–6 6–3.

MEN'S DOUBLES – Final: Edberg /Jarryd d. Nystrom /Wilander 6–1 7–6.

Left: Joakim Nystrom sensationally beat McEnroe at Dallas. (M. Cole)
Below: After winning the WCT World Doubles in London, Ken Flach (left) and Robert Seguso became the season's best pair, with a top world ranking. (T. Hindley)

THE WCT YEAR

Peter Blackman

Ivan Lendl was untouchable, John McEnroe was again fined and a duo named Ken Flach and Robert Seguso proved that nice guys in tennis can finish first. But the icing on the World Championship Tennis cake was their return to the Grand Prix stage after a four-year absence and the almost immediate decision to increase the schedule. The events in Dallas, New York and London remain, while the addition to the Super Series will be Phoenix this year, which joins Atlanta and Houston, with another location planned for 1987.

The year began with Fuji Film as the new sponsors of the World Doubles and a three-year agreement with Channel 4 to cover that event and the Dallas spectacular. A five-year contract was signed to keep the World Doubles at the Royal Albert Hall until 1990, and in America ABC TV renewed their contract for the Tournament of Champions at Forest Hills, which was sponsored for the first time by Shearson Lehman Brothers.

The WCT Year began in January in London, where the last three days saw almost capacity crowds before whom Flach and Seguso confirmed their emergence as one of the world's most devastating doubles pairings. The 21-year-olds from Southern Illinois University each won £30,000 for their 6–3 3–6 6–3 6–0 win over Heinz Gunthardt of Switzerland and Hungary's Balazs Taroczy, becoming the first all-American team to win the title since McEnroe and Peter Fleming in 1979. All week, in the circular hall with its noble domed roof, spectators were intrigued by the Americans' highly effective method of behind-the-back hand-signals out of view of their opponents. Flach explained: 'We are both day-dreamers and the signals are one way of keeping ourselves intense. We try to keep ourselves pumped up.'

In the final Flach served brilliantly – he held serve throughout the 109-minute contest – while Seguso returned with fearsome accuracy. It was, of course, incidental that as singles performers Flach was ranked 155th in the world, Seguso 209th.

The top half of the draw at the Reunion Arena in Dallas was blown wide open by the totally unexpected defeat of John McEnroe in the quarter-finals of the Buick-backed event. It was a startling upset in which Joakim Nystrom, the lowest-ranked and least fancied of the Swedes, beat him 6–4 7–6 6–3. Nystrom was asked afterwards if the victory had been the biggest thrill of his life. 'In tennis, yes', he answered. 'But it doesn't compare with the birth of my daughter.' McEnroe, the top seed, summed it up this way: 'I just felt very flat, like there was glue on my sneakers.'

Meanwhile, Tim Mayotte, a fifth-year professional from Stanford University, had been moving menacingly through his quarter of the draw, outplaying Andres Gomez in the first round and producing one of his most impressive matches to beat Mats Wilander in the quarters. A fifth set against Nystrom in the semi-finals seemed certain when the Swede led 5–2 in the fourth, but Mayotte launched a blistering counter-attack that took Nystrom by surprise, a combination of punishing service returns and big first serves carrying him through 6–4 4–6 6–2 7–5. Perhaps that effort had drained him of energy by the time he faced Lendl in the final.

The Czech had come to Dallas on the back of a special diet, a written-off Porsche, and a fire-wrecked house, but he put the distractions behind him as he beat Stefan Edberg, who won the first and third sets and lost the tie-break in the second by 10–8. Lendl eased through 3–6 7–6 3–6 6–1 6–2 towards a semi-final meeting with Jimmy Connors. At the start of the second set Connors reached for a smash at the net and doubled up in pain. An old back injury had returned, bringing an abrupt farewell as Connors was forced to retire at 3–6 1–2. In the final Lendl was untouchable as he earned his second WCT title with a series of blistering service games. During the course of his 7–6 6–4 6–1 win, 64.6 per cent of his first serves hit the target, including nine aces and service winners. Mayotte, playing in his first major tournament final, led 3–1 in the first tie-break, but Lendl won six of the next seven points to scramble through. Mayotte took a real battering: in 15 service games including the tie-break, Lendl conceded only 18 points. He served seven love games and in the second set won 17 service points in a row, while in the third he won 12 straight points, including a love break and a love service game back-to-back.

His success completed a marvellous triple in three weeks: Fort Myers on hard courts, Monte Carlo on clay and Dallas on carpet. Other players have won three, even four, tournaments in successive weeks in the Open era, but never on different surfaces. 'There is no way of knowing how good I can get', said an elated Lendl as he accepted the winner's cheque for $150,000.

McEnroe won his fifth event of the year when he collected the WCT Atlanta championship, beating the unseeded Paul Annacone 7–6 (7–2) 7–6 (7–5) 6–2. Annacone, whose route was eased by Kevin Curren's withdrawal from the semi-final owing to a stomach upset, pointed out that he lost the final on the big points. 'That's why McEnroe is where he is', he said. But the man from Tennessee had the consolation of winning the doubles with Christo Van Rensburg.

In Houston McEnroe was fined £2,000 for swearing at Wojtek Fibak, while one of the upsets in the earlier rounds was Vitas Gerulaitis's defeat by Jay Lapidus. But McEnroe was the winner, beating Curren 7–5 6–1 7–6 in a tense final.

McEnroe's game fell apart at Forest Hills, New York, where Lendl produced superlative tennis in the Tournament of Champions final to beat him 6–3 6–3. The American had been dominant in the early stages of this Nabisco Grand Prix Super Series event staged by WCT, in the third round winning 20 of the last 23 points against Martin Jaite; but he was pushed hard in the quarters by Claudio Panatta before winning 3–6 6–2 7–6, and also faced a demanding struggle with Henrik Sundstrom before triumphing 6–2 3–6 6–2.

Lendl powered his way through the lower half, dropping only one set – to Aaron Krickstein in the semi-finals. It was time for the red-hot Lendl to face McEnroe again, and he made mincemeat of him before a capacity 11,230 crowd, stating: 'I'm playing the best tennis of my career.' After falling behind 0–4 at the outset, McEnroe held on to break Lendl's serve in the eighth game, bringing the score to 5–3, only to drop the next game. Lendl, the tournament's 1982 champion, then broke McEnroe's service in the fourth game of the second set to go ahead 3–1 – and McEnroe never recovered. It was a humiliating defeat for the American, who lives only a few miles away at Douglaston. 'He was at his best and I was at my worst', said McEnroe.

VIRGINIA SLIMS SERIES

VIRGINIA SLIMS SERIES REVIEW
VIRGINIA SLIMS SERIES TOURNAMENTS

Pam Shriver won four tournaments in 1985 — more than in any other year — and retained her No. 4 ranking. Two more Grand Slam doubles titles with Navratilova took their tally to 12 since 1981. *(T. Hindley)*

Two players who enjoyed their best seasons to date – Claudia Kohde-Kilsch (left) ended the year ranked five after a rare win against Navratilova and a semi-final finish in Paris, while Zina Garrison, a Wimbledon semi-finalist, was eighth. (T. Hindley, M. Cole)

VIRGINIA SLIMS REVIEW

Barry Newcombe

The 1985–86 Virginia Slims tour reached the end of 1985 with Martina Navratilova and Chris Evert Lloyd intriguingly tied for first place – a fitting conclusion to their personal rivalry which yet again provided a fascinating series of focal points throughout the world. Nobody could shift them from the top places, although Hana Mandlikova made a significant breakthrough by beating Chris and then Martina to snatch the US Open, reminding both of the threat she presents in 1986. Hana's victory at Flushing Meadow was by no means sufficient to give her a handhold on the number one ranking, but she can surely see that crown beckoning her in the end.

Hana's intervention in a world increasingly dominated by Martina's carefully prepared physical assault and Chris's intuitive ground-stroking and massive concentration was one definite alteration in the year. It was the first time since 1981, when the four Grand Slam titles went to four different players, that anyone had prevented Martina or Chris winning, and Hana was the first player since Tracy Austin in 1981 to beat Chris and Martina in successive matches. That achievement alone ended a run of 15 Grand Slam titles which had gone to one or the other, such had been their grip on the women's game.

Martina finished in front because she won two titles – Wimbledon, for the sixth time, and she regained the Australian. She also served for the French title at 5–3 in the final set of a long struggle against Chris, but the Paris clay saw Chris triumph in their 65th meeting and 51st final. The victory in Paris not only put Mrs Lloyd back at No. 1 for the first time for three years, but also maintained her unique record of winning at least one Grand Slam title for 12 years running. 'It's always been a dream of mine to get back to No. 1, but with Martina playing so well in the last two years I didn't think it would be a reality', Chris observed. 'I'm especially proud of the way I hung in there, because in the past I may mentally have given up in the same situation. Having Martina around has given me new goals. My goals for the year were winning a Grand Slam and beating Martina.'

It was Chris's sixth win at Roland Garros – the first was in 1974 – and her last opponent before the final was Argentina's 15-year-old Gabriela Sabatini, whose teenage flair and graceful movement instantly endeared her to the Parisian crowds. She was the youngest player to reach the semi-finals and as Chris pointed out: 'They were on my side 15 years ago. The crowd always wants a new star.' Sabatini downed fourth-seeded Manuela Maleeva to gain the last four, and it was in the quarter-finals that another major upset came when Claudia Kohde-Kilsch inflicted a straight-sets beating on Miss Mandlikova. That top ranking which Mrs Lloyd acquired in Paris was solidly earned, and although she remained top seed for Wimbledon, the US Open, and for Australia, she knew she would have to prove her status on court. It was beyond her in each case.

At Wimbledon, the big two progressed to the final with little difficulty. Chris had some decisively clear-cut margins over her opponents, but Martina had to play a tie-break set in three matches on the way. In the semi-finals, Chris beat the lowest seed, Kathy Rinaldi, and Martina defeated another newcomer to the last four, Zina Garrison, the eighth seed. We also noted the progress of Molly van Nostrand, a qualifier who beat the fourth-seeded Manuela Maleeva on the way to the quarter-finals. Liz Smylie downed Mandlikova in the third round, and had an even stronger voice in doubles play. Teamed with Kathy Jordan, they beat the four-times winners, Martina and Pam Shriver, in the final from a set down and 0–3 behind in the final set. But Martina's triumph in singles gave her a sixth title, a number surpassed only by Dorothea Lambert Chambers, who won seven times and Helen Wills Moody who won eight times.

The Virginia Slims World Championship Series

The Virginia Slims Series unites every major women's tournament — including the Grand Slam events — and culminates in the Virginia Slims Championships at Madison Square Garden. During the year, players compete not only for over 12 million dollars, but also for Virginia Slims points to determine the World Champion of women's tennis.

1986 TOURNAMENTS	DATE
Virginia Slims of Washington	Jan. 6-13
Virginia Slims of New England	Jan. 14-20
Virginia Slims of Kansas	Jan. 20-25
Virginia Slims of Florida	Jan. 27-Feb. 2
Lipton International Players Championships	Feb. 10-23
Virginia Slims of Oklahoma	Feb. 24-Mar. 2
Virginia Slims of California	Feb. 24-Mar. 2
Virginia Slims of Pennsylvania	Mar. 3-9
U.S. Women's Indoors	Mar. 3-9
Virginia Slims of Dallas	Mar. 10-16
Virginia Slims Championships	**Mar. 17-23**
Virginia Slims of Arizona	Mar. 24-30
Chrysler-Plymouth Tournament of Champions	Mar. 31-Apr. 6
Family Circle Magazine Cup	Apr. 7-13
Sunkist WTA Championships	Apr. 14-20
U.S. Clay Courts	Apr. 28-May 4
Virginia Slims of Houston	May 5-11
German Open	May 12-18
French Open	May 26-Jun. 8

1986 TOURNAMENTS	DATE
Pilkington Glass Ladies	Jun. 16-22
Wimbledon	Jun. 23-Jul. 6
Virginia Slims of Newport	Jul. 14-20
Virginia Slims of San Diego	Jul. 28-Aug. 3
Canadian Open	Aug. 4-10
Virginia Slims of Los Angeles	Aug. 11-17
United Jersey Bank Classic	Aug. 18-24
U.S. Open	Aug. 25-Sep. 7
Florida Federal Tennis Open	Sep. 15-21
Virginia Slims of Tulsa	Sep. 22-28
Lynda Carter/ Maybelline Classic	Sep. 22-28
Virginia Slims of New Orleans	Sep. 29-Oct. 5
Porsche Tennis Grand Prix	Oct. 13-19
The Pretty Polly Classic	Oct. 20-26
Virginia Slims of Indianapolis	Oct. 27-Nov. 2
Virginia Slims of New England	Nov. 3-9
Virginia Slims of Chicago	Nov. 10-16
Virginia Slims Championships	**Nov. 17-23**

WORLD CHAMPIONSHIP SERIES
VIRGINIA SLIMS

Shaping the future of women's tennis.

DANGER: Government Health WARNING:
CIGARETTES CAN SERIOUSLY DAMAGE YOUR HEALTH

In the US Open, the 16-year-old West German, Steffi Graf, signalled her arrival in Grand Slam competition with a magnificent run to the semi-finals. She put out Manuela Maleeva in the fourth round and used that as a springboard to defeat Pam Shriver in three momentous tie-break sets in a quarter-final which was the longest women's match at the US Open since the tie-break was introduced in 1970. Yet it was Mandlikova who was to burn brightest of all. 'Finally everything fell into place and I showed I could play', declared Hana after defeating Chris and Martina on successive days, each time in three sets. Her 7–6 1–6 7–6 victory in the final spoke volumes for her concentration and will to win.

The Virginia Slims rankings at the end of 1985 saw Chris and Martina tied for first place. Then came Claudia Kohde-Kilsch, Pam Shriver, and Zina Garrison in the top five, followed by Hana Mandlikova, Manuela Maleeva, Helena Sukova, Steffi Graf and Gabriela Sabatini to complete the top ten. In straight prize-money Martina was out on her own with $1,328,829, a figure that took her career earnings close to $10 million. In addition, her Australian title, earned with a 6–2 4–6 6–2 win over Chris, meant that Martina finished the year at No. 1 on the Hewlett-Packard WTA computer rankings.

Records broken during the year included Sabatini's remarkable performance in tie-breaks – eight won out of nine – and Shriver's total of 21 tie-breaks, more than any other player in the top 50. Garrison became only the eighth player to beat Chris Lloyd on clay (at Amelia Island), and Kohde-Kilsch was only the seventh player in four years to stop Martina when she won their Canadian Open quarter-final.

All four Grand Slam finals went the three-set distance for the first time since the Open era began in 1968, and in doubles Navratilova and Shriver had to be content with the French and Australian titles from their grand Slam challenges. They still won seven tournaments together.

With the glory, wherever it is earned, comes the gold. There were 14 dollar millionairesses listed at the end of 1985, although the status of the leading contenders for the top titles and purses did not alter. Martina Navratilova and the six-million-dollar woman, Chris Lloyd, still led the way.

Fun at Eastbourne, where the players' cabaret includes Bassett, Burgin, Jolissaint, Mesker, Smylie and Jordan. Can you identify them? (T. Hindley)

VIRGINIA SLIMS 1985

DATE	VENUE	SINGLES FINAL	DOUBLES WINNERS
7–13 Jan	Washington, DC	M. Navratilova d. M. Maleeva 6–2 6–2	M. Navratilova /G. Fernandez
14–20 Jan	Denver	P. Louie d. Z. Garrison 6–4 4–6 6–4	M. L. Piatek /R. White
21–27 Jan	Key Biscayne, Fla	Mrs J. M. Lloyd d. M. Navratilova 6–2 6–4	K. Jordan /E. Sayers
28 Jan–3 Feb	Marco Beach, Fla	B. Gadusek d. P. Casale 6–3 6–4	K. Jordan /E. Sayers
4–7 Feb	Delray Beach, Fla	M. Navratilova d. Mrs J. M. Lloyd 6–2 6–4	M. Navratilova /G. Fernandez
18–24 Feb	Oakland, Cal.	H. Mandlikova d. Mrs J. M. Lloyd 6–2 6–4	H. Mandlikova /W. M. Turnbull
25 Feb–3 March	Hershey, Pa.	R. White d. A. Minter 6–7 6–2 6–2	M. L. Piatek /R. White
4–10 March	Princeton, NJ	H. Mandlikova d. C. Lindqvist 6–3 7–5	M. Navratilova /P. H. Shriver
4–10 March	Indianapolis	K. Horvath d. E. Burgin 6–2 6–4	E. Burgin /K. Horvath
11–17 March	Dallas	M. Navratilova d. Mrs J. M. Lloyd 6–3 6–4	B. Potter /S. A. Walsh
18–24 March	New York	M. Navratilova d. H. Sukova 6–3 7–5 6–4	M. Navratilova /P. H. Shriver
	(Virginia Slims Finals)		

The above were part of the 1984–85 Virginia Slims Series.

DATE	VENUE	SINGLES FINAL	DOUBLES WINNERS
25–31 March	Palm Beach Gardens	K. Horvath d. P. Delhees Jauch 3–6 6–3 6–3	J. Russell /A. E. Smith
1–17 April	Seabrook Island, SC	K. Maleeva d. V. Ruzici 6–3 6–3	S. Cherneva /L. Savchenko
1–17 April	Tokyo	—	K. Jordan /E. Smylie
8–14 April	Hilton Head	Mrs J. M. Lloyd d. G. Sabatini 6–4 6–0	R. Fairbank /P. H. Shriver
15–21 April	Amelia Island	Z. Garrison d. Mrs J. M. Lloyd 6–4 6–3	R. Fairbank /H. Mandlikova
22–29 April	Lake Buena Vista	M. Navratilova d. K. Maleeva 6–1 6–0	M. Navratilova /P. H. Shriver
22–29 April	San Diego	A. Croft d. W. M. Turnbull 6–0 7–6	C. Reynolds /W. M. Turnbull
29 April–3 May	Houston	M. Navratilova d. E. Burgin 6–4 6–1	M. Navratilova /E. Burgin
29 April–3 May	Taranto *(Italian Open)*	R. Reggi d. V. Nelson 6–4 6–4	A. M. Cecchini /R. Reggi
6–12 May	Sydney	P. H. Shriver d. D. Balestrat 6–3 6–3	P. H. Shriver /E. Smylie
6–12 May	Barcelona	A. M. Cecchini d. R. Reggi 6–3 6–4	P. Delhees Jauch /P. Medrado
13–19 May	Berlin *(German Open)*	Mrs J. M. Lloyd d. S. Graf 6–4 7–5	C. Kohde-Kilsch /H. Sukova
13–19 May	Melbourne	P. H. Shriver d. K. Jordan 6–4 6–1	P. H. Shriver /E. Smylie
20–26 May	Lugano	B. Gadusek d. M. Maleeva 6–2 6–2	B. Gadusek /H. Sukova
27 May–9 June	Paris *(French Open)*	Mrs J. M. Lloyd d. M. Navratilova 6–3 6–7 7–5	M. Navratilova /P. H. Shriver
10–16 June	Egbaston	P. H. Shriver d. B. Nagelsen 6–1 6–0	T. Holladay /S. A. Walsh Pete
17–22 June	Eastbourne	M. Navratilova d. H. Sukova 6–4 6–3	M. Navratilova /P. H. Shriver
24 June–7 July	Wimbledon	M. Navratilova d. Mrs J. M. Lloyd 4–6 6–3 6–2	K. Jordan /E. Smylie
15–21 July	Bregenz, Austria	V. Ruzici d. M. Jausovec 6–2 6–3	M. Jausovec /V. Ruzici
15–21 July	Newport, RI	Mrs J. M. Lloyd d. P. H. Shriver 6–4 6–1	Mrs J. M. Lloyd /W. M. Turnbull
22–28 July	Indianapolis *(US Clay Courts)*	A. Temesvari d. Z. Garrison 7–6 6–3	K. /M. Maleeva

DATE	VENUE	SINGLES FINAL	DOUBLES WINNERS
29 July–4 Aug	Los Angeles	C. Kohde-Kilsch d. P. H. Shriver 6–3 6–3	C. Kohde-Kilsch /W. M. Turnbull
5–11 Aug	Toronto	Mrs J. M. Lloyd d. C. Kohde-Kilsch 6–2 6–4	M. Navratilova /G. Fernandez
12–18 Aug	Mahwah, NJ	K. Rinaldi d. S. Graf 6–4 3–6 6–4	K. Jordan /E. Smylie
19–25 Aug	Monticello, NY	B. Potter d. H. Kelesi 4–6 6–3 6–2	M. Paz /G. Sabatini
28 Aug–8 Sept	Flushing Meadow *(US Open)*	H. Mandlikova d. M. Navratilova 7–6 1–6 7–6	C. Kohde-Kilsch /H. Sukova
9–15 Sept	Salt Lake City	S. Rehe d. C. Benjamin 6–2 6–4	S. Cherneva /L. Savchenko
16–22 Sept	Chicago	B. Gadusek d. K. Rinaldi 6–1 6–3	K. Jordan /E. Smylie
23–29 Sept	New Orleans	Mrs J. M. Lloyd d. P. H. Shriver 6–4 7–5	Mrs J. M. Lloyd /W. M. Turnbull
30 Sept–6 Oct	Fort Lauderdale	M. Navratilova d. S. Graf 6–0 6–3	G. Fernandez /R. White
7–13 Oct	Indianapolis	B. Gadusek d. P. Casale 6–3 7–6	B. Gadusek /M. L. Piatek
14–20 Oct	Tokyo *(Japan Open)*	G. Sabatini d. L. Gates 6–3 6–4	B. Cordwell /J. Richardson
14–20 Oct	Stuttgart	P. H. Shriver d. C. Lindqvist 6–1 7–5	H. Mandlikova /P. H. Shriver
21–27 Oct	Brighton	Mrs J. M. Lloyd d. M. Maleeva 7–5 6–3	L. McNeil /C. Suire
28 Oct–3 Nov	Zurich	Z. Garrison d. H. Mandlikova 6–1 6–3	H. Mandlikova /A. Temesvari
4–10 Nov	Tampa, Fla	S. Rehe d. G. Sabatini 6–4 6–7 7–5	C. Bassett /G. Sabatini
4–10 Nov	Hilversum	K. Maleeva d. C. Karlsson 6–3 6–2	M. Mesker /C. Tanvier
11–17 Nov	Brisbane	M. Navratilova d. P. H. Shriver 6–4 7–5	M. Navratilova /P. H. Shriver
18–24 Nov	Sydney	M. Navratilova d. H. Mandlikova 3–6 6–1 6–2	H. Mandlikova /W. M. Turnbull
25 Nov–8 Dec	Melbourne *(Australian Open)*	M. Navratilova d. Mrs J. M. Lloyd 6–2 4–6 6–2	M. Navratilova /P. H. Shriver
9–15 Dec	Tokyo	M. Maleeva d. B. Gadusek 7–6 3–6 7–5	C. Kohde-Kilsch /H. Sukova
9–15 Dec	Auckland	A. E. Hobbs d. L. Field 6–3 6–1	A. E. Hobbs /C. Reynolds

SEGMENT 1: 8–28 APRIL

Jim Sarni

FAMILY CIRCLE CUP ($200,000)

Chris Evert Lloyd won her eighth Family Circle Cup, but it was 14-year-old Gabriela Sabatini who stole the show. The Argentine wonder defeated two top ten players: No. 8 Pam Shriver and No. 4 Manuela Maleeva, and then tried to dethrone Evert Lloyd as well – all on the same day. That was a little too much to ask and Evert Lloyd beat Sabatini 6–4 6–0 in the final, winning the last eight games of the match. 'Everyone loves to see someone new on the horizon', Evert Lloyd said. 'She played a good first set against me, hit with a lot of topspin and made very few errors.'

The 30-year-old veteran had to battle both teen-titans of women's tennis at Hilton Head; in the semi-finals she subdued 15-year-old Steffi Graf of West Germany, 6–2 6–1. Graf was the 11th seed at the Family Circle Cup, while Sabatini was still a promising newcomer looking to make her breakthrough. She opened the door with a 5–7 7–5 6–4 suspended quarter-final victory over Pam Shriver, then flung it wide with a 6–1 7–6 (11–9) semi-final victory over Manuela Maleeva.

Rain washed out play for the day on Saturday so, because NBC wanted to complete the tournament on Sunday, three rounds were scheduled on the final day and Sabatini had to take the court a third time. Evert Lloyd, meanwhile, had completed her 6–2 6–0 quarter-final victory over Virginia Ruzici on Friday and had only her semi-final match with Graf on Sunday morning. The crowd inspired Sabatini but the youngster ran out of gas. 'The crowd behind me was one of the extras', Sabatini said. 'They gave me more strength and helped me play better tennis.' Evert Lloyd didn't need any help. She simply played on a full tank the entire week.

There were a few other surprises during the week. Virginia Ruzici upset sixth-seeded Carling Bassett 1–6 6–2 6–3, and Petra Huber eliminated third-seeded Claudia Kohde-Kilsch, the previous year's surprise finalist, 6–1 5–7 6–4.

Although the singles championship was completed on Sunday the doubles final had to be extended to Monday, when Shriver and Rosalyn Fairbank defeated the Soviet Union team of Svetlana Cherveva and Larisa Savchenko 6–4 6–1 for the title.

HILTON HEAD, SC, 8–14 APRIL
WOMEN'S SINGLES – Quarter-finals: Mrs J. M. Lloyd d. V. Ruzici (RU) 6–2 6–0; S. Graf (G) d. P. Huber (AU) 6–1 5–7 7–5; M. Maleeva (BUL) d. B. Potter 5–7 7–5 6–4; G. Sabatini (ARG) d. P. H. Shriver 5–7 7–5 6–4. **Semi-finals:** Lloyd d. Graf 6–2 6–1; Sabatini d. Maleeva 6–1 7–6. **Final:** Lloyd d. Sabatini 6–4 6–0.
WOMEN'S DOUBLES – Final: R. Fairbank (SA) /Shriver d. S. Cherneva (USSR) /L. Savchenko (USSR) 6–4 6–1.

WTA CHAMPIONSHIPS ($250,000)

Chris Evert Lloyd was once invincible on Florida clay. But Martina Navratilova had put a dent in her armour by blasting her 6–2 6–0 at Amelia Island in 1984. She lost the WTA Championships final at Amelia Island again in 1985, but this time it was Zina Garrison who did the damage. Her maiden victory over the clay champion was almost as shocking as Navratilova's crusher, for Garrison humbled Evert Lloyd 6–4 6–3, clinching the match when the top seed double-faulted.

Garrison may have found it hard to believe she was still in the tournament after a terrible scare in her first match against Angeliki Kanellopoulou. The Greek, ranked No. 197, led Garrison 5–3 in the third set before the American managed to pull it out, 4–6 6–2 7–6 (7–5). From there she outlasted West German teenager Steffi Graf 6–7 (7–4) 6–1 6–2 in the quarter-finals, and ousted second-seeded Hana Mandlikova 7–5 6–4 in the semi-finals.

Evert Lloyd, meanwhile, was having her troubles getting to the final. In the quarter-finals, she fought off Argentine teenager Gabriela Sabatini, 6–1 1–6 6–3, and in the semi-finals she rallied to defeat third-seeded Claudia Kohde-Kilsch, 5–7 6–3 6–2. The top seed felt the fatigue of having to play 17 sets in singles and doubles in three days. On Friday night, after her duel with Sabatini, she and Carling Bassett battled with Billie Jean King and Rosie Casals until past midnight.

Evert Lloyd praised Garrison for playing the best match she's ever played against her. 'She moved me around really well', Evert Lloyd said. 'She's a good athlete. She ran down a lot of shots.'

The WTA Championships were filled with thrilling matches. In one of the best, Virginia Ruzici squeezed past Sandra Cecchini, 4–6 6–2 7–6 (9–7). Cecchini led 6–1 in the tie-break, but Ruzici saved five straight match-points. 'It's probably the most dramatic match I've ever played', said Ruzici afterwards.

Evert Lloyd was again a losing finalist when she and Bassett were beaten by Rosalyn Fairbank and Mandlikova in the doubles, 6–1 2–6 6–2.

AMELIA ISLAND, FLORIDA, 15–21 APRIL
WOMEN'S SINGLES – Quarter-finals: Mrs J. M. Lloyd d. G. Sabatini (ARG) 6–1 1–6 6–3; C. Kohde-Kilsch (G) d. K. Horvath 6–1 7–5; Z. Garrison d. S. Graf (G) 6–7 6–1 6–2; H. Mandlikova (CZ) d. V. Ruzici (RU) 6–0 6–2. **Semi-finals:** Lloyd d. Kohde-Kilsch 5–7 6–3 6–2; Garrison d. Mandlikova 7–5 6–4. **Final:** Garrison d. Lloyd 6–4 6–3.
WOMEN'S DOUBLES – Final: R. Fairbank (SA) /Mandlikova d. C. Bassett (C) /Lloyd 6–1 2–6 6–2.

TOURNAMENT OF CHAMPIONS ($200,000)

The event is known as the Tournament of Champions but, for the six years of its history, the tournament has known only one champion. Martina Navratilova has won all six. This time she took only 46 minutes to defeat Katerina Maleeva 6–1 6–0 in the final. Still, the 15-year-old Maleeva put up a better fight than Laura Arraya Gildemeister had done in the 1984 final, when she had lost by the same score in 37 minutes.

Navratilova has won the Tournament of Champions in Orlando on two different surfaces – hard and clay. It doesn't matter if they change the surface, the site, the sponsor or the television network: Navratilova is still the star. 'That shows versatility and longevity', Navratilova said. 'It's fun to win and defend a title again and again.'

Navratilova warmed up for the final with straight-sets victories over Kathleen Horvath, Debby Spence and Claudia Kohde-Kilsch, the third seed. The 15-year-old Bulgarian finalist upset No. 4 seed Pam Shriver in the second round, 7–6 (7–3) 3–6 6–4, and seed No. 6, Bonnie Gadusek, in the semi-finals, 6–1 6–4. In the quarters Gadusek had removed Katerina's elder sister, Manuela, the second seed, so that the 'wrong' Maleeva faced Navratilova, cool in a white, floppy hat, who was loose in a final that she knew she couldn't lose. 'I was playing the points and having a good time', Navratilova said. 'Katerina won $23,000. That's 15 years of wages in Bulgaria.'

The Tournament of Champions marked the return of Regina Marsikova, the Czech who had been unable to leave her native country since the 1981 US Open. Marsikova, a former top ten player, had been involved in a car accident in which there was a fatality, and her passport had been revoked. She lost 7–6 6–1 to Horvath in the first round.

Navratilova and Shriver teamed to win the doubles title 6–3 6–1 over Horvath and Elise Burgin. It was their 92nd consecutive doubles win since losing in the 1983 final to Billie Jean King and Anne Smith.

ORLANDO, FLORIDA, 22–28 APRIL
WOMEN'S SINGLES – Quarter-finals: M. Navratilova d. D. Spence 6–1 6–4; C. Kohde-Kilsch (G) d. C. Lindqvist (SW) 3–6 6–1 6–3; K. Maleeva (BUL) d. A. M. Cecchini (IT) 6–2 6–2; B. Gadusek d. M.

Maleeva (BUL) 6–4 6–2. *Semi-finals:* Navratilova d. Kohde-Kilsch 6–2 6–1; K. Maleeva d. Gadusek 6–1 6–4. *Final:* Navratilova d. K. Maleeva 6–1 6–0.
WOMEN'S DOUBLES – Final: Navratilova /P. H. Shriver d. E. Burgin /K. Horvath 6–3 6–1.

VIRGINIA SLIMS OF HOUSTON ($150,000)

Elise Burgin's first big surprise came when Martina Navratilova asked her to play doubles at the Virginia Slims of Houston. Her second was when she joined Navratilova in the singles final, too.

The Virginia Slims of Houston was billed as the shootout between Navratilova, the big gun in women's tennis, and Zina Garrison, the local kid who had shown her stuff on clay by defeating Chris Evert Lloyd at Amelia Island. But the tournament organisers didn't reckon on Burgin, a left-handed sharpshooter from Baltimore. The unseeded 23-year-old knocked off fourth seed Garrison 7–6 (9–7) 3–6 6–4 in the quarter-finals and then second seed Manuela Maleeva 6–4 7–6 (8–6) in the semi-finals. Meanwhile, Navratilova cruised into the final with a 6–0 6–2 quarter-final victory over Regina Marsikova and a 6–3 6–0 victory over Helena Sukova, the third seed.

In the final, Burgin battled Navratilova to 4-all in the first set, after having two break-points in the fourth game which she failed to convert. Navratilova made her pay by breaking at love for a 5–4 lead, then serving out the set. The rest was easy as the 6–4 6–1 score-line shows. 'Once she got the break, Martina took off and started rolling', Burgin said.

The new doubles team of Navratilova and Burgin proved to be a success as they defeated Manuela Maleeva and Sukova 6–1 3–6 6–3 in the final. 'Elise is so funny', said Navratilova. 'My one concern when I asked her to play doubles was that I would be laughing too hard.' Playing doubles with Navratilova was beneficial to Burgin in more ways than one, for when Navratilova asked her to play, Burgin was suffering from a groin injury and considering pulling out of the tournament. After the invitation, though, her injury got better.

28 APRIL–5 MAY
WOMEN'S SINGLES – Quarter-finals: M. Navratilova d. R. Marsikova (CZ) 6–0 6–2; H. Sukova (CZ) d. M. L. Piatek 6–4 6–1; E. Burgin d. Z. Garrison 7–6 3–6 6–4; M. Maleeva (BUL) d. S. Goles (YU) 6–1 6–4. *Semi-finals:* Navratilova d. Sukova 6–3 6–0; Burgin d. Maleeva 6–4 7–6. *Final:* Navratilova d. Burgin 6–4 6–1.
WOMEN'S DOUBLES – Final: Navratilova /Burgin d. Maleeva /Sukova 6–1 3–6 6–3.

The 19-year-old Hungarian, Andrea Temesvari, won the US Clay Courts for the second time in 1986, although she ended the year two places lower in the rankings at 16.   *(M. Cole)*

SEGMENT 2: 6–19 MAY

John Thirsk, Mike Ward and John Parsons

AUSTRALIAN INDOOR CHAMPIONSHIPS ($200,000)

The inaugural Australian Women's Indoor tennis championships at Sydney's Entertainment Centre will be remembered for three things. Pam Shriver, who is almost as much Australian as she is American through her 12-year association with Aussie coach, Don Candy, returned to the winners' list; Australian Dianne Balestrat proved that former world top tenners can come back to reach a final after a time on the sidelines; and former Wimbledon champion, Evonne Cawley, the famous tennis mother of two, at last made her final curtain call as a serious competitor.

Shriver defeated the 'comeback kid', Balestrat, with what she termed 'the finest big-match serving I can remember' in a 6–3 6–3 final-round victory – her first singles win since her victory at Birmingham, prior to Wimbledon. After 18 months off the tour, the 28-year-old Balestrat had begun her attempt to return to the big time in November 1984. It had been a long road, and she came into the Sydney event ranked 76 and unseeded. After reaching her first final since Boston in 1980, the attractive blonde lefthander finished the Indoor ranked 29, but is still a long way from her glory days of 1979, when she had held a world ranking of four.

The final was over in an hour, the Sydney girl achieving only one break-point in each set, which was not nearly enough to thwart the breath-taking display of serving from Shriver. The difference was that of a competitor who was used to matching strokes with the likes of Evert Lloyd, Navratilova, Mandlikova and Turnbull, and one whose game was back on the drawing board. Shriver picked up the first prizes of $65,685, a neat pay packet after also winning the doubles with Aussie Liz Smylie over the American pairing of Barbara Potter and Sharon Walsh Pete. There was a lovely human touch at the presentation when Shriver emotionally spoke of dedicating the win to Candy's 83-year-old mother, Molly. 'Don's mother had been sick and Don had to come home to Adelaide', Shriver recalled. 'That was a factor in me coming to Australia and playing the tournament. If I can supply a little happiness and a little motivation to work hard, then that's good.'

The tournament centred around Balestrat, particularly after she had dumped the number two seed, Kathy Jordan of the US, in the quarter-finals. World number 12 Jordan, the Wimbledon third-round heroine against Evert Lloyd in 1983 and the same competitor who was runner-up in the 1983 Australian Open, was beaten 3–6 6–0 6–2. Balestrat charged into the final by ripping apart the defences of Gigi Fernandez, 6–1 6–3 in a semi-final. Shriver, who had earlier been down and out mentally and physically through over-exertion, responded to a three-month rest period after a dismal performance on the 1984 Australian grass-court summer circuit. She blitzed all and sundry as a top seed should, duly blasting Alycia Moulton out of contention in the other semi 6–3 4–6 6–2.

The crowds came to watch not only the popular Shriver and the Australian contingent of Balestrat, Thompson, Smylie and Cawley but also the British bombshell, Annabel Croft. The vivacious Croft did a lot of work on court before losing a dramatic 6–4 3–6 6–1 quarter-final to Moulton. Before that match, Croft had played nine sets in 20 hours, able to snatch only three hours' sleep. There must also be mention of another heroine – American Leigh Ann Thompson – a three-set victim of Croft in a match which thrilled the fans late into the night. Attracting attention, too, was the left-handed Sydney teenager, Janine Thompson, who extended Balestrat to 6–2 3–6 6–3 in the second round.

Cawley's appearance was short-lived, coming in a first-round opening-night match. At

33, Cawley no longer has that fleetness of foot, ballerina-like court mobility, flashing backhand, and the natural athletic grace which once thrilled the crowds at the All England Club. Winners can smile, losers can please themselves. Cawley still smiles, even when she loses 6–3 6–2 to Amanda Tobin Dingwall, a player she could have blotted out, back in her halcyon days. – J.T.

SYDNEY, 6–12 MAY
WOMEN'S SINGLES – *Quarter-finals:* D. Balestrat d. K. Jordan (USA) 3–6 6–0 6–2; G. Fernandez (USA) d. B. Potter (USA) 6–3 6–3; A. Moulton (USA) d. A. Croft (GB) 6–4 3–6 6–1; P. H. Shriver (USA) d. R. Fairbank (SA) 7–6 6–2. *Semi-finals:* Balestrat d. Fernandez 6–1 6–3; Shriver d. Moulton 6–3 4–6 6–2. *Final:* Shriver d. Balestrat 6–3 6–3.
WOMEN'S DOUBLES – *Final:* Shriver/E. Smylie d. Potter/S. A. Walsh (USA) 7–5 7–5.

PILKINGTON GLASS CHAMPIONSHIPS ($175,000)

Eastbourne welcomed a new sponsor, Pilkington Glass, for its $175,000 women's tournament, but nothing else changed on the English south coast, where Martina Navratilova, who has a strong liking for the Sussex sea air, found it plain sailing in both singles and doubles. Although the loss of Friday's play to rain meant that the defending champion had to play two matches on the final day, that was no problem for an athlete of her stature. Miss Navratilova needed just over an hour to deal with each opponent, beating Bulgaria's Manuela Maleeva 6–1 6–2 in the semi-finals, and one-time compatriot, Helena Sukova of Czechoslovakia, 6–4 6–3 at the last hurdle.

So with one eye on Wimbledon and the other on her world ranking, Martina took her fourth successive Eastbourne title to ease the pain of Melbourne and Paris. Her only regret after boosting her massive earnings by about £30,000 was that arch-rival Chris Lloyd had given the pre-Wimbledon grass-court event a miss. None the less, the message from Devonshire Park was clear. Martina did not always strike her best form in

Navratilova and Shriver celebrate their 100th consecutive doubles win.   (T. Hindley)

the windy conditions on the final day, but she raised her game on the big points, winning the trials of strength and sounding a warning that she was ready to make Mrs Lloyd pay for defeating her in the 1985 French Open final. The 6ft 1in Miss Sukova, too, had a lot to answer for after destroying the Wimbledon champion's dream of a second singles Grand Slam in Australia the previous November. It had all added up to the loss of the No. 1 world ranking for Martina, and there was little consolation in being made joint top seed with Mrs Lloyd for the 1985 Wimbledon singles championship.

Now Eastbourne provided something of a turning point, and to crown an excellent week's work, Martina combined with Pam Shriver to take the doubles title with a 7–5 6–4 victory over Kathy Jordan and Elizabeth Smylie. On their way to the final, this remarkable partnership chalked up 100 consecutive doubles triumphs. Who would have believed that the two Americans were destined to have the tables turned on them at Wimbledon?

The week began with Carina Karlsson providing another reminder of her 1984 Wimbledon exploits by removing the No. 2 seed, Hana Mandlikova, 7–5 1–6 6–4 in the first round. Miss Mandlikova's concentration in her first grass-court outing of the year was patchy, and the world No. 3 from Czechoslovakia was powerless to counter an awesome array of passing shots as the unseeded Miss Karlsson showed typical contempt for reputations.

British fortunes were mixed in the opening round, where honours went to Annabel Croft, whose spirited comeback earned her a 7–6 (7–5) 7–5 victory over the talented French teenager, Catherine Tanvier. Jo Durie played an awful first set before overcoming the American, Camille Benjamin, 2–6 6–1 6–4, but Britons Sara Gomer, Anne Hobbs and Amanda Brown all went out in straight sets. Day two brought a bitter pill for British tennis when Miss Durie's ailing career took another turn for the worse in a 6–0 6–0 whitewash by the 21-year-old black American, Zina Garrison. And while Miss Durie was still wondering what had hit her, British interest in the singles died when Miss Croft succumbed, 6–1 6–2, to another American, Alycia Moulton.

As for Miss Navratilova, the crowd sensed that the freckled-faced 21-year-old Lori McNeil had come to bury the current Wimbledon queen, not to praise her, but the champion recovered after the shock of losing the first set to win 3–6 6–2 6–0. She went on to book her passage into the quarter-finals with a 6–1 7–5 triumph over Miss Moulton, while Miss Garrison fell in three gruelling sets to Wendy Turnbull of Australia. For the first time in her life, Miss Navratilova paid for a brief outburst next day with a public warning – and later a gentle reprimand from referee Georgina Clark. It happened when the top seed had pensioners scrambling for cover as she despatched a ball angrily into the centre court crowd on her way to a 7–6 6–3 win over West Germany's Bettina Bunge. The heavens opened to drown any hopes of play on semi-finals day, but nothing on a congested Saturday could dampen Miss Navratilova's pursuit of a fourth Eastbourne title and Miss Sukova, who had removed Australia's Wendy Turnbull in the morning, was duly put to the sword. – M.W.

EASTBOURNE, 10–16 JUNE
WOMEN'S SINGLES – Quarter-finals: M. Navratilova (USA) d. B. Bunge (G) 7–6 6–3; M. Maleeva (BUL) d. K. Rinaldi (USA) 6–1 6–0; H. Sukova (CZ) d. B. Potter (USA) 6–0 7–6; W. M. Turnbull (AUS) d. P. Paradis (F) 3–6 6–4 7–5. **Semi-finals:** Navratilova d. Maleeva 6–1 6–2; Sukova d. Turnbull 4–6 7–6 6–4. **Final:** Navratilova d. Sukova 6–4 6–3.
WOMEN'S DOUBLES – Final: Navratilova/P. H. Shriver (USA) d. K. Jordan (USA)/E. Smylie (AUS) 7–5 6–4.

FILA GERMAN OPEN ($150,000)

Looking back, the Fila German Open, which drew large, enthusiastic crowds to the picturesque Rot-Weiss Tennis Club in West Berlin, was a splendidly reliable guide of things to come. Chris Lloyd, for instance, while on the way to regaining a title she had previously held in 1983, was inevitably asked about her hopes and plans for the rest of the year. 'My best hope of beating Martina (Navratilova)', she said when discussing the topic uppermost in most people's minds, 'will be on clay at the French'. It was a prediction which three weeks later was to come true in spectacular fashion.

Three West Germans reached the last eight, which reflected not only the tremendous progress being made by the tennis authorities in that country (before Boris Becker's Wimbledon triumph made it obvious to the whole world), but also the general European advance. It was also marvellous in terms of publicity for the event, with the crowds responding accordingly. The only pity was that all three of the West German quarter-finalists, Steffi Graf, Claudia Kohde-Kilsch and Bettina Bunge, happened to be in the same half, so that inevitably one of them had to disappear at that stage. The victim was Miss Kohde-Kilsch, the defending champion, whom Miss Bunge defeated 7–5 7–6 in an inevitably tense, often nervous match, with the tie-break going to 9–7. In the semi-finals, Miss Graf, who had already built well on a fighting victory over Jo Durie by defeating Etsuko Inoue and Kathy Horvath for the loss of only five games, expertly demonstrated her growing confidence and skill by defeating Miss Bunge 6–1 6–3. The surface benefited the younger girl, whose groundstrokes from the back of the court were superb and more than enough to compensate for the problems which still remain on her serve.

The top eight seeds all reached their allotted places in the quarter-finals but there were close tussles and near upsets along the way. The one set which Miss Graf dropped on her way into the final, for instance, was against Miss Durie, the British player who was still finding it so difficult to regain the form which made her a semi-finalist at both the French Open and US Open in 1983. Miss Durie had won her three previous contests against the talented teenager, and she could hardly have made a more encouraging start. In next to no time Miss Durie found herself leading 5–0 30–15, but just as Miss Graf's stinging forehand began to find its range and rhythm, so her own forehand started to disintegrate. Miss Durie held on to take that opening set 6–3 but was then comprehensively outclassed 6–2 6–3.

Meanwhile, in the top half of the draw, Mrs Lloyd's only serious problem before the stern tussle she was given by Miss Graf in the final, came in her semi-final against Lisa Bonder. The match began with a long and intriguing first set, which the girl from Michigan eventually won 6–3. As has so often happened, however, Mrs Lloyd simply shrugged off that setback like swatting an irritating wasp, and swept imperiously through the next two sets, 3–6 6–0 6–2. In the semi-finals Mrs Lloyd was made to work much harder than one might imagine from a 6–1 6–3 scoreline against the hard-hitting young American, Kathy Rinaldi, whose accuracy and control had been enough to upset Catarina Lindqvist in the previous round.

The final looked as though it might become something of a runaway for Mrs Lloyd when she steamrollered her way to 5–1 in the opening set. Until then Miss Graf, for all her eager endeavour, had simply not been able to get into the match. Suddenly the mood changed. The fourth seed, naturally encouraged on every point by the crowd, recovered to 4–5, retrieving three set-points in the process, before Mrs Lloyd put paid to a full-blooded comeback by serving out the set in the tenth game. Encouraged by those last few games of the first set, however, Miss Graf, spraying her formidable forehand all round the court to good effect, moved into a 3–0 lead in the second, forcing Mrs Lloyd to run and stretch. It was then that Mrs Lloyd's wily experience again became evident as, first defensively and then aggressively, she plundered points from Miss Graf's vulnerable backhand, and the balance rapidly turned back her way as she went on to win 6–4 7–5 for the 136th circuit title of her career.

Miss Graf had to be content with the role of runner-up in both events. Returning after her 88-minute singles final, she partnered Catherine Tanvier in the doubles, but they were beaten 6–4 6–1 by Claudia Kohde-Kilsch and Helena Sukova. – J.P.

BERLIN, 13–19 MAY
WOMEN'S SINGLES – Quarter-finals: Mrs. J. M. Lloyd (USA) d. L. Bonder (USA) 3–6 6–0 6–2; K. Rinaldi (USA) d. C. Lindqvist (SW) 2–6 6–2 6–3; S. Graf d. K. Horvath (USA) 6–1 6–3; B. Bunge d. C. Kohde-Kilsch 7–5 7–6. **Semi-finals:** Lloyd d. Rinaldi 6–1 6–3; Graf d. Bunge 6–1 6–3. **Final:** Lloyd d. Graf 6–4 7–5.
WOMEN'S DOUBLES – Final: Kohde-Kilsch/H. Sukova (CZ) d. Graf/C. Tanvier (F) 6–4 6–1.

SEGMENT 3: 15 JULY–18 AUGUST

Cindy Shmerler and Nora McCabe

VIRGINIA SLIMS OF NEWPORT ($150,000)

After losing in the quarter-finals at Wimbledon to Martina Navratilova, Pam Shriver bemoaned the fact that she hadn't played Chris Evert Lloyd in over two years, implying that she had a realistic chance of beating the world's No. 1. However, when Shriver finally had the opportunity two week later, in the final of the Virginia Slims of Newport, she faced a particularly fired-up Evert Lloyd and won just five games in the match.

The victory not only marked Evert Lloyd's 138th career title and 15th consecutive victory over Shriver, but it was the first time she had played on the grass of the International Tennis Hall of Fame since 1974 when, as a 19-year-old American sweetheart, she won the tournament over fellow-American Betsy Nagelsen. Although she lost no set in the 1985 tournament, she was tested, first by Chinese expatriate Hu Na, whom she beat 6–2 7–5 in the second round, then by semi-finalist Eva Pfaff of West Germany, who held three set-points in the first set before Evert Lloyd prevailed 7–5 6–2. For her part, Shriver was pushed to the limit in her semi-final against Aussie veteran Wendy Turnbull, before pulling out a 6–4 7–6 victory.

In the final, Evert Lloyd put on a brilliant display, proving that even now she can still improve. She passed Shriver 21 times from the backcourt, and in the second set put an amazing 14 of 15 first serves into play. While Shriver broke serve and led 2–0 30–0 in the first set, Evert Lloyd broke right back and never faltered, breaking again in the seventh game and holding her own serve in the eighth, despite being down 0–40.

While Shriver commented after the final that she still thinks she is the heir apparent to the Evert Lloyd–Navratilova throne, she admitted that the Newport experience was humbling. 'People forget how quick she [Evert Lloyd] is on the court', Shriver said. 'Her footwork is as close to perfect as there is.'

After her singles victory, Evert Lloyd teamed with long-time friend Turnbull to defeat Shriver and Elizabeth Smylie 6–4 7–6 to win the doubles title as well. – C.S.

NEWPORT, RI, 15–21 JULY
WOMEN'S SINGLES – Quarter-finals: Mrs J. M. Lloyd d. G. Fernandez 6–1 6–2; E. Pfaff (G) d. B. Cordwell (NZ) 6–4 6–3; W. M. Turnbull (AUS) d. E. Smylie (AUS) 6–7 7–5 6–2; P. Shriver d. L. Antonoplis 6–0 6–2. **Semi-finals:** Lloyd d. Pfaff 7–5 6–2; Shriver d. Turnbull 6–4 7–6. **Final:** Lloyd d. Shriver 6–4 6–1.
WOMEN'S DOUBLES – Final: Lloyd /Turnbull d. Shriver /Smylie 6–4 7–6.

US CLAY COURT CHAMPIONSHIPS ($200,000)

Two years ago, Hungarian heart-throb Andrea Temesvari and American teenager Zina Garrison met in the final of the US Clay Court Championships with Temesvari, the top seed, winning 6–2 6–2. Much has changed since then, but the result was the same when the two faced each other again in the 76th edition of the Clay Courts. This time, though, Temesvari won 7–6 6–3. Once ranked as high as No. 7 in the world, Temesvari has fallen on hard times lately. A series of back injuries over the last year kept her sidelined from the pro tour, and when she did compete she lacked the confidence that was once the trademark of her game. Entering the Clay Courts, Andrea had lost eight of 11 previous matches and found herself ranked 20 on the WTA computer and the fourth seed in the tournament. Garrison, on the other hand, experiencing her best year ever, entered the tournament riding on the crest of a semi-final appearance at Wimbledon and a world ranking of five.

Yet despite the psychological edge Garrison must have had going into the final, she was little match for the suddenly explosive Temesvari, whose high-bouncing topspin forehand continually kept Zina pinned to the backcourt. From 5–6 down and deuce in the first set, Temesvari ran off 17 straight points, winning the tie-break 7–0 and racing to a 2–0 second-set lead before Garrison won another point. But by then it was too late and victory once again belonged to Temesvari.

There were other surprises in the tournament, two of which were provided by American Kate Gompert, a former All-American at Stanford University. First, Gompert upset eighth-seeded Katarina Maleeva of Bulgaria 6–2 6–2 in the round of 16. Then she stunned Katarina's older sister, top-seeded Manuela in the quarter-finals. Temesvari finally sent Gompert packing in the semi-finals, while to gain her berth in the final, Garrison needed just 65 minutes to overpower the Argentine sensation, Gabriela Sabatini.

The Maleeva sisters avenged their singles losses by winning the doubles title with a 3–6 6–3 6–4 victory over Penny Barg and Paula Smith of the United States. – C.S.

INDIANAPOLIS, 21–28 JULY
WOMEN'S SINGLES – Quarter-finals: K. Gompert d. M. Maleeva (BUL) 6–3 1–6 8–6; A. Temesvari (HU) d. R. Reggi (IT) 6–3 7–6; G. Sabatini (ARG) d. D. Spence 6–3 6–3; Z. Garrison d. A. Ivan 6–7 6–1 6–3. **Semi-finals:** Temesvari d. Gompert 6–3 6–4; Garrison d. Sabatini 6–4 6–2. **Final:** Temesvari d. Garrison 7–6 6–3.
WOMEN'S DOUBLES – Final: M. /K. Maleeva (BUL) d. P. Barg /P. Smith 3–6 6–3 6–4.

VIRGINIA SLIMS OF LOS ANGELES ($250,000)

Asfher plane touched down at Los Angeles airport, West German Claudia Kohde-Kilsch turned to her step-father, Jurgen Kilsch, and said, 'Now it is time to do something'. What Claudia meant, explained her step-father later, was that she felt ready to leave her comfortable spot among the world's top ten to begin her assault on the top five. Her timing couldn't have been better, for Kohde-Kilsch entered the Virginia Slims of Los Angeles as the fifth seed, but emerged the tournament's victor, upsetting top-seeded Hana Mandlikova 7–6 7–5 in the quarter-finals and second-seeded Pam Shriver 6–2 6–4 in the final. 'Every shot I hit just felt perfect,' said Claudia, who has also been working hard on her agility and quickness. 'That's the best week of tennis I ever played.'

Kohde-Kilsch's new-found confidence was evident in every match she played. She lost no set throughout the tournament, crushing American Kate Gompert and Laura Gilde-meister of Peru, before squeaking by Mandlikova in an almost bizarre see-saw contest. Down 2–5 in the first set, Claudia used all of her 6ft 0½ in height advantage to serve and volley back to 5–5, then pulled out the tie-break seven points to three. The match quickly looked as though it would extend to three sets when Mandlikova raced to a 5–1 lead in the second set. But Kohde-Kilsch ogain came on strong, winning six straight games for the match and prompting Mandlikova to comment: 'That's never happened to me before. She's like a machine. She's programmed.'

While Kohde-Kilsch was attracting all the attention, Shriver was quietly making her way through her half of the draw, earning straight-sets victories over fellow-Americans Patty Fendick, Peanut Louie, Beth Herr and in the semi-finals fourth-seeded Zina Garrison, whom she edged by 7–6 6–4. But she was no match for the booming Kohde-Kilsch in the final, as Claudia simply over-powered her usually powerful opponent. She broke serve in the first game and again in the seventh, largely on the strength of passing shots that continually caught Shriver off guard. The second set was largely the same, and although Pam saved one match-point and had a point to hold serve at 4–5, a double-fault on the second match-point gave Kohde-Kilsch the title.

Germany had another bright moment in the tournament when Eva Pfaff upset third-seeded Helena Sukova of Czechoslovakia 6–4 6–2 in the round of 16 before being narrowly beaten by eighth-seeded Carling Bassett of Canada 4–6 6–3 6–2 in the quarter-finals. Bassett, in turn, lost to Kohde-Kilsch 6–4 6–4 in the semis.

Experience and youth in the persons of Chris Lloyd (left), still winning tournaments at the age of 30, and the Bulgarian teen-agers, Katerina Maleeva, 16, (below left) and her elder sister, Manuela, 18, who was successful in their four meetings in 1985. (M. Cole, T. Hindley)

To crown her week, Kohde-Kilsch joined partner Sukova to win the doubles title over Mandlikova and Australian Wendy Turnbull 6–4 6–2 in the final. – C.S.

LOS ANGELES, 28 JULY–4 AUGUST
WOMEN'S SINGLES – Quarter-finals: C. Kohde-Kilsch (G) d. H. Mandlikova (CZ) 7–6 7–5; C. Bassett (C) d. E. Pfaff (G) 4–6 6–3 6–2; Z. Garrison d. B. Bunge (G) 1–6 6–3 6–4; P. H. Shriver d. B. Herr 6–1 6–3. **Semi-finals:** Kohde-Kilsch d. Bassett 6–4 6–4; Shriver d. Garrison 7–6 6–4. **Final:** Kohde-Kilsch d. Shriver 6–2 6–4.
WOMEN'S DOUBLES – Final: Kohde-Kilsch /H. Sukova (CZ) d. Mandlikova /W. M. Turnbull (AUS) 6–4 6–2.

CANADIAN OPEN ($250,000)

When the Canadian Open draw was made, nobody dreamed Claudia Kohde-Kilsch would be in the final. Even though the tall West German had mown down Hana Mandlikova and Pam Shriver the week before to win in Los Angeles, no-one in Toronto would have bet a plugged nickel on her surviving her quarter-final contest with Wimbledon champion Martina Navratilova. Rather speculation centred on whether French Open champion Chris Evert Lloyd, top-seeded by virtue of having regained the top ranking, could defend her Player's Challenge title – and in the process beat second-seeded Navratilova, her expected final opponent, for the third time in seven months.

What few took into account was that even great champions like Navratilova find it hard to be super-sharp after a month's lay-off from competitive tennis. Navratilova had seemed invincible for the past three years, and she did little to dispel the myth as she blitzed past Etsuko Inoue and Vicki Nelson with a loss of just four games. For the record, Navratilova played well against Kohde-Kilsch, too. Would that the final – and for that matter most finals – had contained the gripping drama nd technical virtuosity of this quarter-final where, on conclusion, a mere three points separated victor from victim.

Navratilova readily took the first set 6–3 but Kohde-Kilsch, who had worked on taking second serve earlier to add potency to her returns, leaped on Navratilova's second-set errors to take control of the net and claim the second 6–4. In the final set, Navratilova served well enough to win 14 straight points on her own service and came within two points of tying it 4–4. Trailing 3–5, she did not falter, drilling four huge serves across the net. On three of them, Kohde-Kilsch countered with outright winners. Navratilova saved one match-point with a scorching forehand cross-court volley, a shot that normally intimidates lesser lights. On the second, Kohde-Kilsch, who later confessed that she was quaking so badly she'd almost dropped her racket, returned wide to Navratilova's backhand then nipped in and volleyed a winner past Navratilova's outstretched racket.

The fifth-seeded Kohde-Kilsch's stunning upset tended to eclipse other interesting developments. Amid much ballyhoo Gabriela Sabatini made her Canadian debut but disappointed, first in her third-round encounter with US Clay Court champion Andrea Temesvari – a match that disintegrated into an interminable baseline bore – and then, overtired from playing twice in about 12 hours, she was too listless to put up more than token opposition against third-seeded Hana Mandlikova's strong serve-and-volley attack.

Molly Van Nostrand, the delightful American qualifier with the weird half service motion who was the surprise Wimbledon quarter-finalist, bounced sixth-seeded Wendy Turnbull on her way to a quarter-final date with Evert Lloyd, where she was completely outclassed. Canada's own Carling Bassett, seeded eighth, struggled mightily to regain the errant concentration that has plagued her since she learned of her father's cancerous brain tumours. Under the pressure of meeting hometown expectations she simply played up to her ranking before being pasted 6–1 6–1 by fourth-seeded Helena Sukova in the quarters.

Meanwhile, Mandlikova, virtually ignored except to note her new hair cut and trimmer shape, raced to her semi-final joust with Evert Lloyd, where, for a very few perspicacious souls, she hinted at her subsequent startling US Open triumph. In the semis, after a gangbusters' first set, Mandlikova faded as is her wont. Unusually, she rallied, battling back from 0–3 to 3–3 in the final set before wilting in the 35°(C) steambath.

As for the amazing Evert Lloyd, she merely breezed through to the semis as if she'd miraculously turned the clock back ten years to when, as a 20-year-old, she was beating the socks off all comers including Navratilova. Physically in the best shape of her career, she had more than enough stamina to withstand the intense heat and, unlike at Flushing Meadow, enough desire to seize the opportunity created by Navratilova's unexpected loss. In the final, she dispatched Kohde-Kilsch, exhausted after her go-for-broke slugfest with doubles partner Sukova, and claimed a record-setting fourth Canadian Open title.

In the doubles, Navratilova was back in her more accustomed position as winner, joining with Gigi Fernandez to beat Marcella Mesker of the Netherlands and France's Pascale Paradis, 6–4 6–0. – N.McC.

MONTREAL, 5–11 AUGUST
WOMEN'S SINGLES – Quarter-finals: Mrs J. M. Lloyd (USA) d. M. Van Nostrand (USA) 6–2 6–1; H. Mandlikova (CZ) d. G. Sabatini (ARG) 6–3 6–0; H. Sukova (CZ) d. C. Bassett 6–1 6–1; C. Kohde-Kilsch (G) d. M. Navratilova (USA) 3–6 6–4 6–3. **Semi-finals:** Lloyd d. Mandlikova 4–6 6–2 6–4; Kohde-Kilsch d. Sukova 6–4 6–4. **Final:** Lloyd d. Kohde-Kilsch 6–2 6–4.
WOMEN'S DOUBLES – Final: G. Fernandez (USA) /Navratilova d. M. Mesker (NTH) /P. Paradis (F) 6–4 6–0.

UNITED JERSEY BANKS CLASSIC ($150,000)

Kathy Rinaldi has always had a soft spot for Mahwah, the oft-maligned site of the United Jersey Banks Classic. It was there, amid the mountainous splendour of Ramapo College, that Rinaldi turned pro in 1981, aged 14, leaving her tennis youth behind to enter the fire of the women's pro tour. It was fitting, therefore, that Rinaldi should have returned to Mahwah in 1985 to walk away with her first major title in the United States. She did it with a 6–4 3–6 6–4 win over another teenage sensation, Steffi Graf of West Germany.

The tournament was plagued from even before day one, when second seed Zina Garrison was forced to withdraw owing to injury. In fact, none of the top four seeds reached their appointed spots in the semi-finals, as top-seeded Pam Shriver was upset by another teenage professional, Gabriela Sabatini of Argentina, 6–4 7–5; third-seeded Manuela Maleeva of Bulgaria was forced to retire suffering from heat exhaustion during her third-round match against Iva Budarova of Czechoslovakia; and fourth seed Helena Sukova of Czechoslovakia was knocked out by eighth-seeded Catarina Lindqvist of Sweden, 6–1 6–2, in the quarter-finals.

In the resulting semi-final round, the competitors had a combined age of just 71 years. In one semi, the long-awaited showdown between the game's future stars, Sabatini and Graf, age may have been a factor in the injuries that befell both competitors. First, the WTA trainer had to be called to treat a bleeding blister on Sabatini's right toe. Then, at the start of the third set, Graf also started limping, bothered by a pulled muscle in her left leg. Still, the young West German eked out a 4–6 6–0 6–3 win and earned herself a spot in the final against Rinaldi, a 5–7 6–2 6–1 semi-final victor over Lindqvist.

The final was another see-saw battle. Rinaldi won the first set 6–4, but Graf stormed ahead in the second, taking a fast 5–0 lead before Kathy broke back to 3–5 only to lose the set 6–3. After breaking for 2–0 in the third, Rinaldi served for the match at 5–3, but the tenacious Graf broke her serve. When she finally broke again to win the match, a jubilant Rinaldi flashed a broad smile at coach Andy Brandi, with whom she had been working for the last year, as she had been when she first turned pro.

In a clash between top doubles teams, Kathy Jordan and Elizabeth Smylie won the doubles title with a 7–6 6–3 victory over Sukova and Claudia Kohde-Kilsch. – C.S.

MAHWAH, NJ, 12–18 AUGUST
WOMEN'S SINGLES – Quarter-finals: G. Sabatini (ARG) d. P. H. Shriver 6–4 7–5; S. Graf (G) d. K. Jordan 6–4 6–4; C. Lindqvist (SW) d. H. Sukova (CZ) 6–1 6–2; K. Rinaldi d. I. Budarova (CZ) 6–2 6–4. **Semi-finals:** Graf d. Sabatini 4–6 6–0 6–3; Rinaldi d. Lindqvist 5–7 6–2 6–1. **Final:** Rinaldi d. Graf 6–4 3–6 6–4.
WOMEN'S DOUBLES – Final: Jordan /E. Smylie (AUS) d. Sukova /C. Kohde-Kilsch (G) 7–6 6–3.

SEGMENT 4: 16 SEPTEMBER–6 OCTOBER

Jim Martz

VIRGINIA SLIMS OF CHICAGO ($150,000)

Following her US Open championship, Hana Mandlikova crashed to earth much quicker than expected. The return of a back ailment that had flared in April at the Tournament of Champions in Orlando forced her to withdraw from the singles on the second day, after she had won her first doubles match with Wendy Turnbull on the first day. 'I couldn't give 100 per cent, and that wouldn't be fair to the Chicago fans', she said. Cynics could have replied, 'What fans?' Only 16,251 showed up during the entire tournament at the University of Illinois-Chicago Pavilion, tourney problems being compounded when defending champion Pam Shriver, tired from her three-set match with Kim Shaefer in the second round, lost 6–2 6–2 in the quarter-finals to Kathy Jordan.

Meanwhile, Kathy Rinaldi was winning every match in straight sets *en route* to the final, while Bonnie Gadusek was surviving marathons. Rinaldi whipped Gigi Fernandez 6–0 6–4, Mary Lou Piatek 6–1 6–1, Susan Mascarin 6–4 6–3, and Jordan 6–0 7–5. Gadusek squeezed past Janine Thompson 3–6 6–3 6–4, Grace Kim 6–2 6–7 (6–8) 6–4, Elise Burgin 6–4 7–6 (7–4), and Turnbull 7–6 (9–7) 6–2. Yet Gadusek dominated the final 6–1 6–3, winning eight straight games at one stretch while earning her third championship of the year and $27,000. 'Those matches made me match tough', Gadusek said, adding that credit for her success should go to her new coach, Gene Malin of Los Angeles.

Jordan teamed with Elizabeth Smylie to win the doubles title, 6–2 6–2, over JoAnne Russell and Burgin.

16–22 SEPTEMBER
WOMEN'S SINGLES – Quarter-finals: B. Gadusek d. E. Burgin 6–4 7–6; W. M. Turnbull (AUS) d. B. Potter 6–1 6–7 6–3; K. Rinaldi d. S. Mascarin 6–4 6–3; K. Jordan d. P. H. Shriver 6–2 6–2. **Semi-finals:** Gadusek d. Turnbull 7–6 6–2; Rinaldi d. Jordan 6–0 7–5. **Final:** Gadusek d. Rinaldi 6–1 6–3.
WOMEN'S DOUBLES – Final: Jordan /E. Smylie (AUS) d. E. Burgin /J. Russell 6–2 6–2.

VIRGINIA SLIMS OF NEW ORLEANS ($150,000)

For Pam Shriver, this looked like the week she would finally break through and defeat Chris Evert Lloyd after 15 consecutive losses. Recovering quickly from her early exit the previous week at Chicago, she lost only 11 games in eight sets while reaching the final. But Lloyd, eager to protect her No. 1 ranking on the WTA computer, won four matches in straight sets (losing 18 games) before surviving a hard-fought final against Shriver, 6–4 7–5. The tournament was played at the University of New Orleans' Lakefront Arena, and Lloyd was making her first trip to the city in 15 years.

In the final Lloyd proved steadier from the baseline, and fired several passing shots as Shriver approached the net. The turning point came when Lloyd was a break-point down at 3–4 in the second set. She slammed a forehand winner down the line to reach deuce, lofted a perfect lob over a charging Shriver, then won the game with a forehand volley. 'That's what Chris is all about, coming up with the big points', said Shriver.

Zina Garrison, seeded third, bowed in the second round in straight sets to Anne White, and fourth-seeded Kathy Rinaldi, victim of flu and the hard-serving Lisa Bonder, also lost in the second round. Bonder led 7–6 (7–3) 4–3 when Rinaldi asked for the trainer and said she couldn't continue.

Lloyd also won the doubles title, teaming with Wendy Turnbull to capture the final over Mary Lou Piatek and White, 6–1 6–2.

23–29 SEPTEMBER
WOMEN'S SINGLES – Quarter-finals: Mrs J. M. Lloyd d. Mrs K. Shaefer 6–2 6–1; L. Bonder d. C. Reynolds 4–6 6–4 6–1; A. White d. P. Louie 6–4 6–0; P. H. Shriver d. W. M. Turnbull (AUS) 6–2 6–0. **Semi-finals:** Lloyd d. Bonder 6–3 6–1; Shriver d. White 6–3 6–2. **Final:** Lloyd d. Shriver 6–4 7–5. **WOMEN'S DOUBLES – Final:** Lloyd /Turnbull d. M. L. Piatek /A. White 6–1 6–2.

LYNDA CARTER/MAYBELLINE CLASSIC ($150,000)

Martina Navratilova rushed through the final against Steffi Graf as if she were in a hurry to catch a plane. She was indeed pressed in her 4 p.m. match to meet a 7 p.m. flight home to the Dallas area, in order to watch on television the second half of her beloved Dallas Cowboys against the New York Giants. Navratilova disposed of Graf 6–3 6–1 in 58 minutes on the clay court at the Bonaventure Racquet Club, to win this tournament for the second straight year. Graf had trouble handling Navratilova's strong serves, just as she had a month earlier at the US Open, where she was beaten 6–3 6–2. Martina often read Graf's passing shots perfectly and answered with volley winners. 'In the first set, I tried to play my game, but my forehand wasn't going too good and I missed some easy shots', said Graf. 'I was probably tired from yesterday', she added, referring to her 6–3 7–6 (7–1) defeat of Bonnie Gadusek.

On a warm and muggy afternoon, Navratilova jumped to a 3–0 lead. Graf evened the set at 3–3, then Navratilova won nine of ten games as she mixed baseline rallies with serve-and-volley tennis. 'Overall, I'm happy with this week', said Navratilova, who dropped only one set in her first tournament since she had lost the US Open final to Hana Mandlikova.

Gigi Fernandez, one of four Fernandezes in the tournament, teamed with Robin White to win the doubles final over Ros Fairbank and Beverly Mould, 6–2 7–5.

FORT LAUDERDALE, 30 SEPTEMBER–6 OCTOBER
WOMEN'S SINGLES – Quarter-finals: M. Navratilova d. T. Phelps 6–1 5–7 6–3; P. Louie d. M. Torres 7–5 6–7 7–5; S. Graf (G) d. S. Rehe 7–5 4–6 6–2; B. Gadusek d. Mrs D. Balestrat (AUS) 6–3 6–4. **Semi-finals:** Navratilova d. Louie 6–2 6–1; Graf d. Gadusek 6–3 7–6. **Final;** Navratilova d. Graf 6–3 6–1. **WOMEN'S DOUBLES – Final:** G. Fernandez /R. White d. R. Fairbank (SA) /B. Mould (SA) 6–2 7–5.

The game's youngest professional in 1981, aged 14, Kathy Rinaldi has matured to become a fine match-player, as she proved with her first Series win in Mahwah, before ending the year ranked 11. *(T. Hindley)*

SEGMENT 5: 14 OCTOBER–3 NOVEMBER

Jens-Peter Hecht, Jamie Baker and Bryan Cutress

PORSCHE GRAND PRIX ($175,000)

Ever since the Filderstadt tournament has been on the tennis calendar, German tennis fans have been waiting for a home win; the opportunity for that dream to be fulfilled never seemed brighter than in 1985. Claudia Kohde-Kilsch was seeded two, Steffi Graf was the third favourite, and there was no singles entry from Martina Navratilova, Chris Evert Lloyd or Hana Mandlikova. However, Pam Shriver chose this moment to slip into the costume of her doubles partner, Martina, and to play as the world champion had done some years before in Filderstadt. Shriver, in fact, gave little Steffi a double lesson – first on court in a comprehensive semi-final beating which was sweet revenge for her unexpected loss in the US Open, and then in print with a chapter in her new book in which she predicted a bright future for the young German provided that she changed her attitude.

At the start of the week, before the crowds had become too preoccupied with the prospects of a first German win, they adopted a new heroine in America's Sue Mascarin, because of the 21-year-old Floridian's connection with the latest German hero, Boris Becker. She had spent some days the previous week in Monte Carlo practising with Boris, and regardless of what she told interviewers, the writers seemed determined to read between the lines so that her 6–4 7–5 first-round win over Sylvia Hanika inevitably became the result of her practice with Boris.

With the departure of Sue in the second round, at the hands of Barbara Gerken 6–3 7–6, it was time to concentrate on Claudia and Steffi. The former was in a hurry to finish her first match quickly, because she had tickets for the Germany v Portugal soccer match that evening, and she demolished the Czech, Regina Marsikova, 6–2 6–1 in less than an hour. Steffi was equally successful, but had to stay in bed at the hotel afterwards for she had arrived in Filderstadt with a feverish cold.

Thus far the German dream lived on, but the awakening came in the semi-finals. There the previous year's winner, Caterina Lindqvist of Sweden, survived a match-point against Claudia before completing a 2–6 7–6 6–4 win, and Miss Shriver ended Steffi's chance of reaching the final for the second year in a row with a 6–4 6–3 decision. After her match Steffi, visibly upset, told the press that she would never again play in Filderstadt – perhaps never in Germany – because, she said, the spectators did not appear to want to help her. This seemed a curious assessment of the situation and a dangerous attitude to adopt. Perhaps the crowd was less enthusiastic than the Frankfurt fans had been a few days earlier as the German *Davis Cup* team achieved a thrilling victory over Czechoslovakia, but if the German girls expected a reception like that for an individual tournament effort, they were being unrealistic.

The only seeds not to reach their appointed places in the quarter-finals were Andrea Temesvari (five) of Hungary, who lost 6–3 6–4 to Iva Budarova of Czechoslovakia in the second round, and Virginia Ruzici (seven) from Rumania, who fell at the first hurdle 6–3 6–2 to Terry Phelps. Shriver lost no set in defeating Amanda Brown, Sabrina Goles, Budarova and Graf on the way to the final, and there she continued with her devastating serve-and-volley tactics. In a calmly played match, Pam stole the limelight with a 6–1 7–5 win over the title-holder, Lindqvist – a victory that was worth a Porsche car or $32,000 and 200 precious Virginia Slims points. Pam chose the car.

The tournament became a Shriver benefit when Pam, partnering Hana Mandlikova, beat the Scandinavian pair, Carina Karlsson of Sweden and Tine Scheuer-Larsen of Denmark, 6–2 6–1 in the doubles final that was worth $13,000 to the winning pair – enough, thought Pam, for her to buy a little petrol for the car! – J-P.H.

STUTTGART, 14–20 OCTOBER
WOMEN'S SINGLES – Quarter-finals: P. H. Shriver (USA) d. I. Budarova (CZ) 6–2 6–2; S. Graf d. L. Bonder (USA) 7–6 6–2; C. Lindqvist (SW) d. R. Reggi (IT) 4–6 6–3 6–0; C. Kohde-Kilsch d. B. Gerken (USA) 6–4 6–3. **Semi-finals:** Shriver d. Graf 6–4 6–3; Lindqvist d. Kohde-Kilsch 2–6 7–6 6–4. **Final:** Shriver d. Lindqvist 6–1 7–5.
WOMEN'S DOUBLES – Final: H. Mandlikova (CZ) /Shriver d. C. Karlsson (SW) /T. Scheuer-Larsen (D) 6–2 6–1.

PRETTY POLLY CLASSIC ($175,000)

Regal Brighton, after a summer of quite dismal weather, basked in glorious autumnal sunshine for this, the richest indoor women's tournament in Europe. Yet the warmth outside did not deter the vast crowds who gathered at the Brighton Centre. Surely the most notable features of this ever-popular event were the performances of Jo Durie and Annabel Croft, giving Britain two semi-finalists in an international tournament for the first time in six years. Neither was in the world's top 40 at the time, and Jo was emerging from one of the roughest periods of her career. The fact that both failed to make the final was perhaps an anti-climax, for Jo herself had reached the last stage in 1983, and Sue Barker had won the tournament in 1981.

However, the final between the top seed and twice previous champion, Chris Evert Lloyd, and the Bulgarian teenager, Manuela Maleeva, was no let-down. Mrs Lloyd, at 30 playing her consistent, error-free game as well as ever, was made to fight every inch of the way for her 7–5 6–3 win, which put her back ahead of arch-rival Martina Navratilova in the race for the No. 1 world ranking.

It was a British girl, Sally Reeves, who provided the biggest surprise of the tournament. The tiny 22-year-old from Kent, ranked only 185, saw off Corinne Vanier, Marcella Skuherska and Laura Garrone, who had just won the US Open junior title, to reach the main draw of 32. There she met her match as Maleeva took her apart in a 6–2 6–1 win. Britain, though, had a new heroine in Annabel Croft, also from Kent, who put out the younger of the Maleeva sisters, Katerina, 6–2 7–6, to set up a second-round clash with the No. 3 seed, Helena Sukova. This was to prove arguably the best match of the week with Croft coming back from a set down to score an extraordinary victory, 2–6 7–5 6–4, in just under two hours. In 30 games there were 19 service breaks and Croft, who failed to win her own service in the opening set, needed no less than five match-points eventually to win through.

Elsewhere the tournament had lost both the previous year's finalists in the opening round – Sylvia Hanika to Camille Benjamin, who had had to qualify, and JoAnne Russell to Virginia Ruzici, another former Brighton champion. Benjamin's progress was checked in the next round by Christiane Jolissaint in a match interrupted by a faulty fire alarm. The bells rang for more than a minute, and although play was halted it did not affect the Swiss girl's concentration as she won 6–3 6–4 to set up a quarter-final clash with Durie. Britain's No. 1 had a rough ride getting through her first-round match against American Michelle Torres, but she produced a quite devastating performance to provide the upset of the tournament and her best result for more than a year, as she beat second seed Steffi Graf, 6–3 6–3. The party was to continue, too, as in the quarters Durie knocked out Jolissaint and Croft beat Terry Phelps, both with ease.

Mrs Lloyd, meanwhile, had been making steady progress, beating Petra Huber and Pam Casale in straight sets *en route* to the last eight. Then came a most severe test as the favourite was taken to a final-set tie-break – the only one of the week – by Catarina Lindqvist. It was a battle royal with both players contributing to a marvellous match with a spectacular array of passing shots. Lloyd came through notably shaken after seven of the 11 points in the tie-break went against serve. Sadly Annabel Croft was unable to put up such a fight, and the semi-finals did not live up to expectations. Durie went tumbling

By winning in San Diego and beating Sukova in Brighton to reach the semi-finals, Annabel Croft won the No. 1 British ranking, and moved from 82 to 24 in the world ratings.
(A. Evans)

to Maleeva, and once more it was left to the ever-popular Mrs Lloyd to take centre stage. The Bulgarian had upset her once before – in Italy in 1984 – but this time there was to be no fairy tale ending and Mrs Lloyd took her winner's cheque for £23,000.

There was an upset in the doubles when the experienced American left-hander, Barbara Potter, playing with the tall Czech doubles expert, Helena Sukova, ranked nine and four in the world respectively in doubles, lost to America's Lori McNeil, ranked 52, and Catherine Suire, ranked 97, in three sets 4–6 7–6 6–4. – J.B.

BRIGHTON, 21–27 OCTOBER
WOMEN'S SINGLES – Quarter-finals: Mrs J. M. Lloyd (USA) d. C. Lindqvist (SW) 6–2 2–6 7–6; A.

Croft d. T. Phelps (USA) 6–1 6–3; M. Maleeva (BUL) d. B. Potter (USA) 6–2 6–3; J. M. Durie d. C. Jolissaint (SWZ) 6–2 6–3. *Semi-finals:* Lloyd d. Croft 6–3 6–2; Maleeva d. Durie 6–3 7–6. *Final:* Lloyd d. Maleeva 7–5 6–3.
WOMEN'S DOUBLES *– Final:* L. McNeil (USA) /C. Suire (F) d. Potter /H. Sukova (CZ) 4–6 7–6 6–4.

EUROPEAN INDOOR CHAMPIONSHIPS ($150,000)

It was meant to be a successful and fairly easy week for Hana Mandlikova, who had come to Zurich as the US Open champion and was expected to leave with a $27,000 cheque and the European Indoors title. There were certainly some other high-class players in the draw, such as Claudia Kohde-Kilsch, Helena Sukova and Zina Garrison, but none was expected to stop the Czech, whose confidence and reputation had received such a massive boost by the events at Flushing Meadow only a few weeks earlier.

The first hint that something unexpected might be on the way came when the elegant Czech started struggling with her service early in the final against Miss Garrison. Until then she had cruised comfortably through her matches without dropping a set in a run which even Miss Sukova could not halt. Myriam Schropp, Susan Mascarin and Catherine Tanvier had been dismissed at a total cost of only 12 games, and although pushed to a tie-break by Miss Sukova, the top seed won it by seven points to four to complete her 6–2 7–6 semi-final victory. But it was a totally different story in the final. The girl who had so recently beaten Chris Lloyd and Martina Navratilova was in trouble from the start, as Miss Garrison, refusing to be overwhelmed by the reputation of her opponent, went boldly for her shots from the first rally to the last. She had won the title a year earlier and clearly had no intention of relinquishing her hold on it.

The week had started easily enough for Miss Garrison as she demolished Mima Jausovec 6–1 6–1 and Regina Marsikova 6–3 6–2, but she was in serious trouble against Sandra Cecchini in the quarter-finals when she lost a set and trailed 2–4 in the decider. She survived, 3–6 6–1 6–4, and the keenness of the contest put the sharp edge back on her game just in time for the real challenges ahead. Miss Kohde-Kilsch, the second seed, was swept aside 6–3 6–2 in the semi-finals by the pace and skill of the Houston girl, who went on to raise her game even higher in the final.

With Miss Mandlikova below her best, the defending champion hurried into a 3–0 lead, but everyone sat back, confident that the star of the show would quickly take control. They waited in vain, for it took Miss Garrison just 29 minutes to win the first set with a performance that led her opponent to say later: 'This day Zina could have beaten Martina Navratilova or Chris Lloyd.' The second set was little better for the favourite, who managed to salvage only three games from it before having to admit defeat.

Two other upsets in the championship came from Miss Tanvier and Christiane Jolissaint. Miss Tanvier handed a 6–4 6–3 hammering to eighth-seeded Raffaella Reggi, while Miss Jolissaint delighted her home crowd by ousting the big-serving American left-hander, Barbara Potter, before going out in a thrilling three-sets quarter-final to Miss Sukova by 6–3 1–6 6–3.

Miss Mandlikova took some consolation for her singles defeat by winning the doubles title and with it a share of the $10,800. She teamed up with Andrea Temesvari, who had missed the singles because of a fever, to score a thrilling 6–4 3–6 7–5 triumph over the US Open champions, Miss Sukova and Miss Kohde-Kilsch in the final. – B.C.

ZURICH, 28 OCTOBER–3 NOVEMBER
WOMEN'S SINGLES *– Quarter-finals:* H. Mandlikova (CZ) d. C. Tanvier (F) 6–3 6–3; H. Sukova (CZ) d. C. Jolissaint 6–3 1–6 6–3; Z. Garrison (USA) d. S. Cecchini (IT) 3–6 6–1 6–4; C. Kohde-Kilsch (G) d. M. Maleeva (BUL) 6–4 6–2. *Semi-finals:* Mandlikova d. Sukova 6–2 7–6; Garrison d. Kohde-Kilsch 6–3 6–2. *Final:* Garrison d. Mandlikova 6–1 6–3.
WOMEN'S DOUBLES *– Final:* Mandlikova/A. Temesvari (HU) d. Kohde-Kilsch/Sukova 6–4 3–6 7–5.

SEGMENT 6: 4 NOVEMBER–15 DECEMBER

Edward Johnson, Brian Burke and Alan Clarkson

FLORIDA FEDERAL OPEN ($150,000)

The $150,000 Florida Federal Open had a new setting for 1985 – the Bardmoor Country Club, home of Harry Hopman's International tennis. It was particularly appropriate that the man who has contributed so much to the development of so many of the world's leading players should have witnessed, in the last month of his life, an outstanding final between the world's two leading tennis teens, Stephanie Rehe, seeded eight, and Gabriela Sabatini the third favourite. Stephanie, who turned 16 during the tournament, beat the 15-year-old Argentine star 6–4 6–7 7–5, in a battle of mental and physical stamina that lasted almost three hours. Considering the hot, humid conditions and the punishing schedule that Rehe had to endure – her 4–6 6–4 6–4 semi-final win over Carling Bassett had also lasted almost three hours and had finished late on Saturday night – it was a tremendous performance by a girl who had turned pro only after the US Open. The fact that this was the second Virginia Slims title in a month to fall to the Californian schoolgirl suggests that we we are witnessing the emergence of another future champion.

The same could be said of Gabriela. In ten short months as a professional the dark-haired, energetic shot-maker from Buenos Aires, watched at every turn by her coach, Patricio Apey, has astounded onlookers by the maturity of her game and by her dogged determination. Clearly she is also a future champion. Small wonder then that a record crowd of over 5,000 were in attendance to witness the final between these outstanding representatives of the modern game. They knew that Gabriela, after losing a set in her opening match against Melissa Gurney, had cruised past Vicki Nelson, Pam Casale and Anne White without ever being troubled on the fast asphalt court. They also knew that Stephanie had scored straight-sets wins over Gigi Fernandez, local resident Mary Lou Piatek, who has a court in her Bardmoor back garden, and Michelle Torres, before her semi-final against fourth-seeded Bassett.

Despite both girls having been ranked among the world's top five juniors in 1984, this was the first time they had met. Both felt the strain in the deciding set of their marathon final, which was broadcast to a state-wide audience on GGP Sports. The hard courts took their toll on Sabatini's feet, which developed blisters as a result of her running wide to punish Rehe's volleys with piercing passes and needed the attention of the WTA trainer. It was Rehe's legs which suffered and, as she said afterwards: 'I wanted to come to the net and, despite being passed a lot I had to keep on coming in. I knew I had to keep the pressure on her.' The pressure finally paid off as Sabatini became a little tentative.

The first prize of $27,000 was the biggest of Rehe's short career, though the money was the last thing she had been thinking of during the tense closing stages. For Sabatini there was a bonus to her singles prize of $13,500, as well as a measure of consolation, when she and Bassett shared the doubles prize of $10,800, after beating Lisa Bonder and Laura Gildemeister 6–0 6–0 in the final. – E.J.

TAMPA, 4–10 NOVEMBER
WOMEN'S SINGLES – Quarter-finals: G. Sabatini (ARG) d. P. Casale 6–0 6–1; A. White d. L. Bonder 6–2 6–4; C. Bassett (C) d. G. Kim 6–2 7–5; S. Rehe d. M. Torres 6–1 6–2. **Semi-finals:** Sabatini d. White 6–1 6–2; Rehe d. Bassett 4–6 6–4 6–4. **Final:** Rehe d. Sabatini 6–4 6–7 7–5.
WOMEN'S DOUBLES – Final: Bassett /Sabatini d. Bonder /L. Gildemeister (PER) 6–0 6–0.

NATIONAL PANASONIC WOMEN'S CLASSIC ($150,000)

Like the thunderstorms which threatened but bypassed muddy Milton for most of this hot and humid week, so too did any serious challenge to Martina Navratilova, who, for the 12th straight time, bulldozed aside her doubles partner, Pam Shriver, with a 6–4 7–5 victory in the final. The only storm broke at the champion's post-final press conference when, unprompted, she expressed her disappointment that officials had not moved the sponsor's signs from the backdrops at either end of the centre court, thus contravening the rules and impairing her vision. Her outburst may well have signed the death warrant for the tournament, which was under fire earlier in the week from the sponsor and leading players, including Navratilova, Shriver and Wendy Turnbull, about the proposed later date of December 29 to January 4 for 1986.

During the week Martina, playing singles here for the first time, showed why she is the world's best grass-court player. There wasn't a cloud in sight on finals day and the result looked all too predictable, apart from a brief stagger late in the second set when Navratilova, serving for the match at 5–4, dropped her serve for the first time in the match (and only the third time during the week). Shriver saved three match-points in this game, although Martina actually gave them away through unforced errors. Indeed, Shriver hit only one winner in the game. It was a temporary delay as Shriver, who had lost only one service game, served poorly to allow Navratilova to break again for a 6–5 lead. There was no second chance for Shriver as Navratilova served out strongly for the match.

The top four seeds — Navratilova, Shriver, Claudia Kohde-Kilsch and Helena Sukova — took their appointed places in the semi-finals, where Navratilova avenged her Canadian Open quarter-final loss to Kohde-Kilsch with a brutish 6–1 6–4 victory, after the tall West German had come from behind in the quarters to overhaul Brisbane's hometown hero Wendy Turnbull (No. 5 seed) 6–7 (4–7) 6–3 6–1. The only time Martina was remotely troubled was when Australia's Anne Minter had the temerity to break the champion for a 3–0 lead in the second set of their third-round match, before succumbing 6–2 7–5. Minter's young compatriot, Louise Field, was not so lucky, making a quick second-round exit, 6–0 6–1. England's Sara Gomer, who surprised Annabel Croft 6–2 7–5, was no match for Martina in the quarters, going down 6–3 6–1.

Shriver and Sukova, both of whom had strolled through to their semi-final battle without dropping a set, probably provided the match of the tournament. They fired booming serves at each other from their respective great heights, but Sukova, the defending champion, appeared to lack penetration in her returns and Shriver, despite a second-set 'walkabout', triumphed 7–6 (7–3) 1–6 6–2.

Shriver found consolation for her singles defeat when she joined her conqueror to defend their doubles crown, beating Sukova and Kohde-Kilsch in an exciting contest, where again Navratilova served for the match in the second set, before winning 6–4 6–7 (6–8) 6–1. – B.B.

BRISBANE, 11–17 NOVEMBER
WOMEN'S SINGLES – Quarter-finals: M. Navratilova (USA) d. S. Gomer (GB) 6–3 6–1; C. Kohde-Kilsch (G) d. W. M. Turnbull 6–7 6–3 6–1; H. Sukova (CZ) d. E. Burgin (USA) 6–3 6–1; P. H. Shriver (USA) d. L. Savchenko (USSR) 6–2 6–4. **Semi-finals:** Navratilova d. Kohde-Kilsch 6–1 6–4; Shriver d. Sukova 7–6 1–6 6–2. **Final:** Navratilova d. Shriver 6–4 7–5.
WOMEN'S DOUBLES – Final: Navratilova /Shriver d. Kohde-Kilsch /Sukova 6–4 6–7 6–1.

FAMILY CIRCLE NSW OPEN ($150,000)

Martina Navratilova's drive to regain the top ranking in women's tennis gained greater momentum with her 3–6 6–1 6–2 win over Hana Mandlikova in the final of the Family Circle NSW Open at White City. It was her second singles title within a week and fittingly came in the centenary year of the NSW Tennis Association. The magnificent champion triumphed again through her ability to batter the opposition into submission through the sheer quality of her shots and her remarkable athleticism. Few women have had such a profound influence on the sport as Martina, who is the first to acknowledge there is a definite lift in the overall standard of women's tennis, agreeing with the other top competitors that her form is slipping not at all. 'There was a time when I could play badly and still win, but now I have to play well in every match', Martina said, when discussing the overall quality of women's tennis.

An organisers' dream became a reality on the last two days of the tournament when Martina met Helena Sukova in a semi-final and then in the final faced up to Hana Mandlikova, the player who had beaten her for the US title. The stage was set for this enthralling climax when Helena breezed through her three matches against Candy Reynolds, Lea Antonoplis and Dianne Balestrat with the loss of just 17 games in the six sets. With her all-court game working smoothly the big question was whether Helena could repeat her magnificent display of the 1984 Australian Open to beat the World Champion. Helena began by taking advantage of a rather nervous Martina to smack away some fine passing shots and force some unaccustomed errors to take the first set 6–4. But that loss was the spur that goaded Martina to lift her game; hitting the ball with more authority, smacking away a succession of volleys, and returning with more accuracy, Martina forced the breaks to outplay Helena completely in the last two sets for a 4–6 6–3 6–2 victory.

Hana, whose brilliance is a by-word in women's tennis, dropped only 13 games in reaching the semi-final against Claudia Kohde-Kilsch, and what promised to be a stirring contest became a little lop-sided. Few players could have matched shots with Hana in her mood of the first set, in which she broke Claudia's service three times to storm to a 6–0 lead. Playing better tennis in the second set, Claudia was able to snatch five games, but Hana played too well on the big points.

So the repeat of the US Open final was on, and the spectators were enthralled at the drama and the skill displayed by both players. Hana began magnificently, cracking Martina's service and then comfortably staving off the fight-back to win the first set 6–3. But this was not to be a repeat of the US Open; Martina made sure of that. With brilliant tennis she literally blasted Hana out of the match, winning the last two sets 6–1 6–2, dropping just eight points on her service in the last set, losing only 27 points in the 15 games of the final two sets. Hana knew what was coming when Martina hit three winners to break her service in the first game of the third set, and it was simply a matter of time until the final point signalled another triumph for this remarkable player.

However, Hana did have a little to cheer about when she and Wendy Turnbull won an exciting three-set doubles final against Reynolds and Ros Fairbank 3–6 7–6 6–4. – A.C.

SYDNEY, 18–24 NOVEMBER

WOMEN'S SINGLES – Quarter-finals: M. Navratilova (USA) d. W. M. Turnbull 6–4 6–2: H. Sukova (CZ) d. Mrs D. Balestrat 6–1 6–4; C. Kohde-Kilsch (G) d. C. Jolissaint (SWZ) 6–3 3–6 6–3; H. Mandlikova (CZ) d. S. Parkhomenko (USSR) 6–4 6–2. **Semi-finals:** Navratilova d. Sukova 4–6 6–3 6–2; Mandlikova d. Kohde-Kilsch 6–0 7–5. **Final:** Navratilova d. Mandlikova 3–6 6–1 6–2.
WOMEN'S DOUBLES – Final: Mandlikova /Turnbull d. R. Fairbank (SA) /C. Reynolds (USA) 3–6 7–6 6–4.

PAN PACIFIC ($250,000)

TOKYO, 9–15 DECEMBER

WOMEN'S SINGLES – Quarter-finals: C. Kohde-Kilsch (G) d. G. Kim (USA) 6–1 6–1; B. Gadusek (USA) d. C. Bassett (C) 6–3 6–2; M. Maleeva (BUL) d. A. Croft (GB) 6–2 6–2; H. Sukova (CZ) d. S. Rehe (USA) 6–4 6–4. **Semi-finals:** Gadusek d. Kohde-Kilsch 6–4 6–3; Maleeva d. Sukova 6–0 6–2. **Final:** Maleeva d. Gadusek 7–6 3–6 7–5.
WOMEN'S DOUBLES – Final: Kohde-Kilsch /Sukova d. M. Mesker (NTH) /E. Smylie (AUS) 6–0 6–4.

With over $2 million in prize money after almost a decade at the top, the consistent Australian, Wendy Turnbull (33), was a doubles semi-finalist at Wimbledon and the US Open and won four doubles titles in 1985.   *(T. Hindley)*

OTHER VIRGINIA SLIMS TOURNAMENTS

WTA OF PGA ($50,000)

PALM BEACH GARDENS, FLORIDA, 25–31 MARCH

WOMEN'S SINGLES – Quarter-finals: K. Horvath d. G. Sabatini (ARG) 6–2 6–0; R. Reggi (IT) d. T. Scheuer-Larsen (D) 7–6 6–1; T. Phelps d. S. Foltz 7–6 6–2; P. Delhees Jauch (SWZ) d. B. Herr 6–3 6–4. **Semi-finals:** Horvath d. Reggi 6–2 6–3; Delhees Jauch d. Phelps 6–4 6–2. **Final:** Horvath d. Delhees Jauch 3–6 6–3 6–3.
WOMEN'S DOUBLES – Final: J. Russell /A. E. Smith d. Sabatini /L. Gildemeister 1–6 6–1 7–6.

SEABROOK ISLAND, FLORIDA ($75,000)

1–7 APRIL

WOMEN'S SINGLES – Quarter-finals: V. Ruzici (RU) d. N. Dias (BR) 6–1 6–4; T. Scheuer-Larsen (D) d. D. Spence 6–1 6–4; S. Goles (YU) d. S. Foltz 6–2 6–4; K. Maleeva (BUL) d. S. Mascarin 6–1 7–5. **Semi-finals:** Ruzici d. Scheuer-Larsen 6–1 7–5; Maleeva d. Goles 2–6 6–4 6–1. **Final:** K. Maleeva d. Ruzici 6–3 6–3.
WOMEN'S DOUBLES – Final: S. Cherneva (USSR) /L. Savchenko (USSR) d. E. Burgin /L. McNeil 6–1 6–3.

BRIDGESTONE DOUBLES ($175,000)

TOKYO, 1–7 APRIL

WOMEN'S DOUBLES – Semi-finals: K. Jordan (USA) /E. Smylie (AUS) d. A. Kiyomura (USA) /C. Reynolds (USA) 6–4 7–6; B. Nagelsen (USA) /A. White (USA) d. W. M. Turnbull (AUS) /S. A. Walsh (USA) 6–4 4–6 6–3. **Final:** Jordan /Smylie d. Nagelsen /Walsh 4–6 7–5 6–2.

VIRGINIA SLIMS OF SAN DIEGO ($75,000)

22–28 APRIL

WOMEN'S SINGLES – Quarter-finals: W. M. Turnbull (AUS) d. B. Nagelsen 6–4 6–3; M. L. Piatek d. Hu Na 6–1 6–3; M. Gurney d. B. Herr 6–3 6–3; A. Croft (GB) d. R. Fairbank (SA) 6–0 6–3. **Semi-finals:** Turnbull d. Piatek 6–1 6–2; Croft d. Gurney 5–7 6–2 6–3. **Final:** Croft d. Turnbull 6–0 7–6.
WOMEN'S DOUBLES – Final: C. Reynolds /Turnbull d. Fairbank /S. Leo (AUS) 7–5 6–0.

ITALIAN OPEN CHAMPIONSHIPS ($50,000)

TARANTO, 28 APRIL–5 MAY

WOMEN'S SINGLES – Quarter-finals: S. V. Nelson (USA) d. M. Schropp (G) 6–2 6–0; C. Nozzoli d. I. Budarova (CZ) 6–7 6–2 6–0; R. Reggi d. K. Skronska (CZ) 3–6 6–3 6–4; L. Garrone d. I. Cuerto (G) 6–3 4–6 6–2. **Semi-finals:** Nelson d. Garrone 6–4 6–0; Reggi d. Nozzoli 6–0 6–1. **Final:** Reggi d. Nelson 6–4 6–4.
WOMEN'S DOUBLES – Final: A. M. Cecchini /Reggi d. P. Murgo /B. Romano 1–6 6–4 6–3.

SPANISH CHAMPIONSHIPS ($50,000)

BARCELONA, 6–12 MAY

WOMEN'S SINGLES – Quarter-finals: A. M. Cecchini (IT) d. V. Ruzici (RU) 6–4 2–6 7–5; A. Holikova (CZ) d. G. Purdy (USA) 6–7 6–0 6–2; R. Reggi (IT) d. K. Skronska (CZ) 6–3 3–6 6–3; R. Marsikova (CZ) d. L. Plchova (CZ) 6–4 6–1. **Semi-finals:** Cecchini d. Holikova 6–1 6–2; Reggi d. Marsikova 6–4 6–3. **Final:** Cecchini d. Reggi 6–3 6–4.

WOMEN'S DOUBLES – Final: P. Delhees (SWZ) /P. Medrado (BR) d. P. Barg (USA) / A. Villagran (ARG) 6–1 6–0.

VICTORIAN INDOOR CHAMPIONSHIPS ($75,000)

MELBOURNE, 13–19 MAY
WOMEN'S SINGLES – Quarter-finals: P. H. Shriver (USA) d. A. Henricksson (USA) 6–3 6–7 6–4; B. Potter (USA) d. R. Fairbank (SA) 6–2 6–3; A. Croft (GB) d. A. Brown (GB) 6–3 6–4; K. Jordan (USA) d. S. A. Walsh (USA) 6–2 6–4. *Semi-finals:* Shriver d. Croft 7–6 6–2; Jordan d. Potter 7–5 6–3. *Final:* Shriver d. Jordan 6–4 6–1.
WOMEN'S DOUBLES – Final: Shriver /E. Smylie d. Jordan /A. E. Hobbs (GB) 6–2 6–7 6–1.

SWISS OPEN CHAMPIONSHIPS ($100,000)

LUGANO, 20–26 MAY
WOMEN'S SINGLES – Quarter-finals: M. Maleeva (BUL) d. G. Sabatini (ARG) 6–0 6–7 6–2; S. Hanika (G) d. K. Rinaldi (USA) 6–4 6–1; B. Gadusek (USA) d. K. Maleeva (BUL) 6–0 7–6; H. Sukova (CZ) d. K. Horvath (USA) 6–1 6–3. *Semi-finals:* M. Maleeva d. Hanika 6–1 7–6; Gadusek d. Sukova 6–4 1–6 6–4. *Final:* Gadusek d. M. Maleeva 6–2 6–2.
WOMEN'S DOUBLES – Final: Gadusek /Sukova d. B. Bunge (G) /E. Pfaff (G) 6–2 6–4.

EDGBASTON CUP ($125,000)

BIRMINGHAM, 10–16 JUNE
WOMEN'S SINGLES – Quarter-finals: P. H. Shriver (USA) d. A. E. Hobbs 6–4 6–0; E. Burgin (USA) d. R. White (USA) 6–7 6–4 6–4; B. Nagelsen (USA) d. A. Henricksson (USA) 6–3 6–3; S. Mascarin (USA) d. A. Moulton (USA) 7–6 6–4. *Semi-finals:* Shriver d. Burgin 6–4 6–2; Nagelsen d. Mascarin 3–6 7–5 6–1. *Final:* Shriver d. Nagelsen 6–1 6–0.
WOMEN'S DOUBLES – Final: T. Holladay (USA) /S. A. Walsh Pete (USA) d. Burgin /Moulton 6–4 5–7 6–3.

BREGENZ, AUSTRIA ($50,000)

15–21 JULY
WOMEN'S SINGLES – Semi-finals: V. Ruzici (RU) d. P. Keppeler (G) 6–2 6–4; M. Jausovec (YU) d. A. Kanellopoulou (GR) 6–4 3–6 7–6. *Final:* Ruzici d. Jausovec 6–2 6–3.
WOMEN'S DOUBLES – Final: Jausovec /Ruzici d. A. Holikova (CZ) /K. Skronska (CZ) 6–2 6–3.

VIRGINIA SLIMS OF CENTRAL NEW YORK ($75,000)

MONTICELLO, NY, 19–25 AUGUST
WOMEN'S SINGLES – Quarter-finals: H. Sukova (CZ) d. D. Spence 6–4 6–2; H. Kelesi (C) d. V. Ruzici (RU) 1–6 6–2 6–4; S. Hanika (G) d. J. M. Durie (GB) 2–6 7–5 7–6; B. Potter d. A. M. Cecchini (IT) 6–4 6–3. *Semi-finals:* Kelesi d. Sukova 7–6 7–6; Potter d. Hanika 7–6 2–1 ret'd. *Final:* Potter d. Kelesi 4–6 6–3 6–2.
WOMEN'S DOUBLES – Final: M. Paz (ARG) /G. Sabatini (ARG) d. A. Holikova (CZ) /M. Skronska (CZ) 4–6 6–4 6–3.

VIRGINIA SLIMS OF UTAH ($75,000)

9–15 SEPTEMBER
WOMEN'S SINGLES – Quarter-finals: L. Gildemeister (PER) d. R. Fairbank (SA) 3–6 6–2 6–1; C. Benjamin d. P. Fendick 7–5 6–4; S. Rehe d. J. Thompson 6–4 6–4; C. Kuhlman d. E. Rapponi-Longo (ARG) 3–6 7–6 6–4. *Semi-finals:* Benjamin d. Gildemeister 6–4 6–3; Rehe d. Kuhlman 6–3 6–2. *Final:* Rehe d. Benjamin 6–2 6–4.
WOMEN'S DOUBLES – Final: S. Cherneva (USSR) /L. Savchenko (USSR) d. Fairbank /B. Mould (SA) 7–5 6–2.

The left-handed American, Barbara Potter, won her first tournament in three years — the Virginia Slims of New York — although her ranking slipped five places to No. 17. *(T. Hindley)*

VIRGINIA SLIMS OF INDIANAPOLIS ($75,000)

7–13 OCTOBER

WOMEN'S SINGLES – Quarter-finals: B. Gadusek d. M. L. Piatek 6–1 6–4; I. Budarova (CZ) d. H. Kelesi (C) 3–6 6–3 6–2; P. Casale d. C. Reynolds 6–1 6–3; K. Rinaldi d. M. Gurney 6–4 6–3. **Semi-finals:** Gadusek d. Budarova 6–2 6–2; Casale d. Rinaldi 4–6 6–4 6–4. **Final:** Gadusek d. Casale 6–0 6–3.
WOMEN'S DOUBLES – Final: Gadusek /Piatek d. P. Barg /S. Collins 6–1 6–0.

JAPAN OPEN ($50,000)

TOKYO, 14–20 OCTOBER

WOMEN'S SINGLES – Quarter-finals: G. Sabatini (ARG) d. A. Holikova (CZ) 6–0 6–1; L. Drescher (SWZ) d. A. Kanellopoulou (GR) 6–3 6–1; L. Gildemeister (PER) d. A. Holton (USA) 6–3 4–6 6–0; L. Gates (USA) d. M. Schropp (G) 6–4 6–4. **Semi-finals:** Sabatini d. Drescher 1–6 6–3 6–3; Gates d. Gildemeister 6–3 2–6 6–3. **Final:** Sabatini d. Gates 6–3 6–4.
WOMEN'S DOUBLES – Final: B. Cordwell (NZ) /J. Richardson (NZ) d. Gildemeister /B. Herr (USA) 6–4 6–4.

HEWLETT-PACKARD TROPHY ($75,000)

HILVERSUM, 4–10 NOVEMBER

WOMEN'S SINGLES – Quarter-finals: Z. Garrison (USA) d. N. Herreman (F) 6–0 6–2; K. Maleeva (BUL) d. V. Ruzici (RU) 7–5 7–5; T. Scheuer-Larsen (D) d. P. Huber (AU) 6–3 6–1; C. Karlsson (SW) d. C. Tanvier (F) 6–3 6–4. **Semi-finals:** K. Maleeva d. Garrison 6–3 6–2; Carlsson d. Scheuer-Larsen 3–6 3–0 ret'd. **Final:** K. Maleeva d. Karlsson 6–3 6–2.
WOMEN'S DOUBLES – Final: M. Mesker (NTH) /Tanvier d. S. Cecchini (IT) /S. Goles (YU) 6–2 6–2.

AUCKLAND, NEW ZEALAND ($50,000)

9–15 DECEMBER

WOMEN'S SINGLES – Quarter-finals: B. Norton (USA) d. S. Faulkner 6–7 6–4 6–4; L. Field (USA) d. L. Antonoplis (USA) 7–5 6–0; A. E. Hobbs (GB) d. J. Richardson 6–0 6–4; A. M. Fernandez (USA) d. C. Reynolds (USA) 6–7 7–5 7–6. **Semi-finals:** Field d. Norton 6–1 6–1; Hobbs d. Fernandez 7–5 7–6.
Final: Hobbs d. Field 6–3 6–1.
WOMEN'S DOUBLES – Final: Hobbs /Reynolds d. Antonoplis /A. Villagran (ARG) 6–1 6–3.

BURN-OUT

Reginald Brace

Burn-out became a burning topic in 1985 and will continue to smoulder not only in 1986 but as long as gifted young players show a talent to play tennis which is beyond their tender years. The issue is simple in one respect – complex in another. On the one hand it seems unfair to stifle the flair of a fledgling who is clearly ready to vacate the junior nest. If skill is ready to soar, why clip its wings?

In most areas of sport one could agree. Why indeed? Unfortunately in tennis there is grim evidence to indicate that too much adult competition too soon can not only shorten the career of a player but leave a trail of injury and disillusion bordering on despair in its wake. It takes only a little jogging of the memory to prove the perils of precocity on a tennis court. Tracy Austin was a millionaire by the age of 17, a legend in her brief tennis lifetime, before being stricken by back and shoulder injuries related to a childhood spent in pursuit of stardom. Billy Martin, winner of a host of titles from 14 years upwards, was forced into retirement through injuries by the time he was 26. Sweden's Kent Carlsson was sidelined for six months by a knee operation when he was 17 – the legacy of prolonged competition in junior and senior events. Andrea Jaeger was in the world's top ten at 15, and Wimbledon runner-up in 1982, aged 17. Then she dropped out of tennis and worried some of her friends by sending them a Christmas card of herself dressed in Army combat uniform and holding a machine gun.

Some burn-out stories were as chilling as anything out of the Hammer House of Horror. Monika Seles, the Yugoslav prodigy who won the world 12-and-under title in 1984, became a stress victim and underwent a stomach ulcer operation. Lori Kosten, regarded as the best American prospect of her age-group, had a nervous breakdown and quit tennis at the age of 13. Erika Horvath, mother of Kathy, is convinced that the reason her daughter is injury prone is because she and her husband failed to discourage Kathy from playing four or five hours a day when she was a frail eight- and nine-year-old. 'I'd be a liar to say we haven't enjoyed her victories and followed her everywhere, but once a youngster competes she is trapped', said Mrs Horvath at an ITF seminar on burn-out. 'Her life shouldn't be so one-sided.'

Jean-Paul Loth, the French national coach, was once an advocate of intensive play from the earliest possible age. Now he is in favour of a ban preventing under-16s playing in professional tournaments. 'Children must be allowed to grow up as children in a normal fashion', he said. 'Too many of them are growing up in a way that by 17 or 18 they know nothing about anything. You can't talk to them and they can't talk to you. Mentally they are dead, and we have killed them.' Strong words from Jean-Paul but we all know the zombies he is talking about: the over-exposed, over-played and often over-paid young robots of the game.

Parents are frequently at the root of situations which can end in burn-out. The American coach and authority on junior tennis, Ian Russell, says: 'Being a professional tennis player is very prestigious now, and parents of kids with talent think they can guide them along and benefit them in the end. I feel a lot of children are pushed forward at a very young age at the expense of everything else, and it's not good. They should experience a lot of other things.'

Chris Evert Lloyd, who has decorated the game since she was a teenager and remains one of its finest advertisements, believes that children should diversify in sport when they are aged between six and ten, and get serious about tennis only between ten and 12. The time to start playing tournaments is at the age of 12, according to Chris, who

In one of the best matches of the year, Steffi Graf, the outstanding German teenager, beat Pam Shriver to reach the semi-finals at the US Open, and at 16 seemed well able to cope with the pressures. *(T. Hindley)*

The current teen sensation, Gabriela Sabatini (left), now faces the same pressures that drove Andrea Jaeger (right) out of tennis. *(M. Cole)*

urges that players should receive a good education. Homework had a higher priority than tennis in the Evert household, she recalls. 'You really need that education for the rest of your life. If you don't have that camaraderie with kids of your own age, it will affect relationships with people throughout your lifetime. For social and emotional reasons it is important to be with kids your own age, and getting your education is essential.'

One entry in the ITF's burn-out dossier tells of a child who climbed up a tree after losing rather than face the wrath of an irate parent. Mrs Lloyd has this advice to parents: 'When a child is young, vulnerable, very impressionable and conscious of peer pressure, it surely leaves a mark on them. How parents react to this pressure and how much pressure they put on their children can affect the kids for the rest of their lives. I advise parents to be supportive and encouraging and try to understand what their children are going through on the court.'

Dr Jim Lohr, sports psychologist, delivered some sage advice to budding tournament players at an ITF seminar at Disney World, Lake Buena Vista last September. 'Tennis is a game and sometimes we lose sight of that', he said. 'What I am trying to help young developing players to do is to develop a love of the game. Not a love of winning but a love of competition. If you only feel successful when you win, the price you pay because you cannot win the game is too tough. You cannot win and win and win. You must come to a place within yourself where you feel good about yourself because you fought well, because you enjoyed the battle and you enjoyed the competition.'

Losing a tennis match is not, in other words, the end of a young player's world or a reason for embarking on punishing training and practice schedules which can lead to physical and mental problems. But before we move on to the ITF's attempts to extinguish burn-out through special commissions, seminars and rule changes, let us examine the other side of the issue: the young players who are able to set adult targets, hit them and apparently remain normal and healthy. Gabriela Sabatini of Argentina and Steffi Graf of West Germany are glowing examples. Theirs could be the next great rivalry in women's tennis after the Lloyd-Navratilova saga, and there seems to be no immediate obstacle to that happening, despite their early impact on the world game. Boris Becker played and looked like a man when he became Wimbledon's youngest men's champion last summer.

And although the comparison is a little mischievous in that the pressures of 19th century tennis are scarcely comparable with those of the present, Lottie Dod, the first teenage phenomenon of the game, was 15 years 10 months when she won Wimbledon in 1887. She won the title four more times by the age of 21, and then left tennis for golf, field hockey, archery, skating and bob-sledding. No burn-out here – merely a wish to explore other pursuits.

Clearly there must always be room for the extraordinary in tennis: the tyro who is blessed with the rare ability which only champions possess. But just as clearly the ITF was right in providing a platform for many caring people close to the game who saw the burn-out factor as a serious symptom of modern tennis.

A report by a special commission rejected a call from some quarters for a ban on anyone under the age of 16 competing in any professional tournament, but recommended a gradual, carefully monitored entry into the professional game on a limited basis, first at 14 and then on a slightly increased scale at 15. As a result no player under 14 can compete in a professional tournament. For players in the 14–16 age group there are variations in the eligibility rules adopted by the MIPTC and the WIPTC relating to the maximum number of tournaments in which they can compete. But at least action has been taken. A year of earnest effort in tackling burn-out inspired moves born of awareness and concern which should lead to a dramatic improvement.

Junior finalists together at Wimbledon in 1978, pictured here with the Duke and Duchess of Kent, both Hana Mandlikova (left) and Tracy Austin went on to greater triumphs, but Austin's injuries forced her out of the game. *(M. Cole)*

OTHER OFFICIAL PRO TOURNAMENTS

CHALLENGER SERIES
SATELLITE CIRCUITS
WOMEN'S NON-SERIES TOURNAMENTS

The 20-year-old Martin Jaite of Argentina climbed from 54 to 20 in the rankings with one tournament win from three finals and a quarter-final finish in Paris, where he beat Mecir and Gunthardt, but lost to Lendl. *(T. Hindley)*

MEN'S CHALLENGER SERIES

Non Nabisco Grand Prix tournaments carrying ATP points
FINALS

GUARAJA BEACH, SAO PAULO ($50,000)

14–19 JANUARY
SINGLES: J. Avendano (SP) d. R. Saad (ARG) 6–3 6–3.
DOUBLES: M. Tideman (SW) /R. Bathman (SW) d. C. Gattiker (ARG) /G. Tiberti (ARG) 7–6 4–6 6–3.

AGADIR, MOROCCO ($25,000)

21–27 JANUARY
SINGLES: G. Urpi (SP) d. D. Demiguel (SP) 2–6 6–4 6–0.
DOUBLES: P. Cane (SP) /C. Mezzadri (IT) d. J. DeMinicis (SP) /O. Rahnasto (FIN) 6–4 6–4.

OGUN, NIGERIA ($25,000)

11–17 FEBRUARY
SINGLES: G. Oleppo (IT) d. M. Wooldridge (USA) score not available.
DOUBLES: C. Dunk (USA) /B. Strode (USA) d. E. Adams (USA) /Wooldridge score not available.

LAGOS ($75,000)

18–24 FEBRUARY
SINGLES: N. Odizor d. T. Muster (USA) 6–3 6–3.
DOUBLES: E. Adams (USA) /M. Wooldridge (USA) d. P. Elter (G) /P. Feigl (AU) 6–4 6–4.

VINA DEL MAR, CHILE ($25,000)

18–24 FEBRUARY
SINGLES: Hans Gildemeister d. P. Rebolledo 6–3 6–4.
DOUBLES: Hans Gildemeister /B. Prajoux d. R. Acuna /E. Fernandez 7–6 6–3.

CAIRO ($75,000)

25 FEBRUARY–3 MARCH
SINGLES: F. Luna (SP) d. T. Allan (AUS) 6–3 6–4.
DOUBLES: A. Amritraj (IND) /L. Bourne (USA) d. Allan /A. Tous (SP) 6–4 2–6 7–5.

KADUNA, NIGERIA ($25,000)

25 FEBRUARY–3 MARCH
SINGLES: H. P. Kandler (AU) d. A. Gonzalez 2–6 6–4 6–0.
DOUBLES: R. Akel /J. Arons d. Ismail /Vazeos 6–3 6–3.

VIENNA ($25,000)

4–10 MARCH
SINGLES: J. B. Svensson (SW) d. A. DeMinicis 6–0 6–1.
DOUBLES: P. Carlsson (SW) /Svensson d. J. Cihak /DeMinicis 6–3 6–2.

MONTREAL ($25,000)

18–24 MARCH
SINGLES: A. Kohlberg (USA) d. R. Nixon 6–2 2–6 7–6.
DOUBLES: A. Andrews (USA) /T. Warneke (USA) d. K. Evernden /M. Robertson 6–3 7–6.

TUNIS ($75,000)

25–31 MARCH
SINGLES: H. Schwaier (G) d. W. Popp (G) 6–4 6–2.
DOUBLES: Hans Gildemeister (CH) /V. Pecci (PARA) d. D. Mustard (NZ) /J. R. Smith (GB) 2–6 6–4 6–3.

MARRAKESH, MOROCCO ($50,000)

1–7 APRIL
SINGLES: R. Agenor d. R. Osterthun 2–6 6–3 6–4.
DOUBLES: S. Casal (SP) /E. Sanchez (SP) d. A. Fischer /G. Prpic 4–6 6–3 6–1.

SAN LUIS POTOSI, MEXICO ($25,000)

1–7 APRIL
SINGLES: L. Lavalle d. A. Andrews (USA) 4–6 6–3 6–4.
DOUBLES: J. Mattke (USA) /S. Menon (IND) d. R. Akel /J. Arons 7–6 6–3.

CURITIBA, BRAZIL ($25,000)

8–14 APRIL
SINGLES: J. Goes d. G. Guerrero 6–4 6–4.
DOUBLES: D. Campos /L. Mattar d. A. Fillol (CH) /A. Utzinger 7–6 6–3.

RIO DE JANEIRO ($50,000)

15–21 APRIL
SINGLES: G. Barbosa d. M. Henemann 7–5 6–3.
DOUBLES: Barbosa /I. Kley d. M. /A. Hocevar 6–1 6–3.

JERUSALEM ($25,000)

15–21 APRIL
SINGLES: S. Glickstein d. B. Drewett (AUS) 6–4 6–3.
DOUBLES: A. Mansdorf /B. Manson (USA) d. T. Meinecke /R. Osterthun 6–7 6–4 7–6.

BERKELEY, CALIFORNIA ($25,000)

29 APRIL–5 MAY
SINGLES: E. Edwards (SA) d. T. Witsken 6–3 6–4.
DOUBLES: G. Layendecker /G. Michibata (C) d. M. Doyle /J. Mattke 6–4 6–7 7–5.

PAIRIOLI, ITALY ($25,000)

29 APRIL–5 MAY
SINGLES: G. Rivas (ARG) d. S. Colombo 7–6 1–6 7–6.
DOUBLES: C. Mezzadri /P. Parrini d. P. Cane /Colombo 6–4 3–6 6–4.

NAGOYA, JAPAN ($32,672)

29 APRIL–5 MAY
SINGLES: T. Fukui d. L. Palin (FIN) 6–2 6–3.
DOUBLES: S. Menon (IND) /E. Van't Hof (USA) d. H. Shirato /E. Takeuchi 6–3 6–2.

SPRING, TEXAS ($25,000)

13–19 MAY
SINGLES: G. Donnelly d. L. Bourne 5–7 6–4 7–6.
DOUBLES: J. Baxter /G. Michibata (C) d. R. Knapp /M. Wooldridge 6–4 6–3.

TAMPERE, FINLAND ($50,000)

3–9 JUNE
SINGLES: J. B. Svensson (SW) d. M. Cerro (IT) 7–5 7–5.
DOUBLES: D. Campos (BR) /A. DeMincis (BR) d. C. Kirmayr (BR) /A. Mattar (BR) 6–4 1–6 6–3.

DORTMUND ($25,000)

10–16 JUNE
SINGLES: F. Maciel d. E. Masso 7–6 6–2.
DOUBLES: A. Emerson /M. Woodforde d. M. Buckley /A. Barlow 7–6 6–2.

BERGEN, NORWAY ($25,000)

17–22 JUNE
SINGLES: J. B. Svensson (SW) d. P. Svensson (SW) 6–2 7–6.
DOUBLES: J. B. /P. Svensson d. S. Eriksson /M. Lundgren (SW) 7–6 4–6 6–3.

SCHENECTADY, NY ($25,000)

1–7 JULY
SINGLES: M. Maasencamp d. H. Solomon 6–0 3–6 6–3.
DOUBLES: A. Andrews /T. Warneke d. Perren /Schellenger 6–4 7–6.

CAMPOS DE JORDAO, BRAZIL ($50,000)

15–21 JULY
SINGLES: D. Campos d. N. Aerts 6–7 6–3 6–2.
DOUBLES: Campos /C. Kirmayr d. L. Mattar /B. Prajoux (CH) 6–4 3–6 6–4.

ISTANBUL ($25,000)

22–28 JULY
SINGLES: F. Segarceanu (RU) d. A. Dirzu (RU) 6–4 6–3.
DOUBLES: Alfred /Nihssen d. G. Luza /Masso 6–2 6–3.

NEU ULM, GERMANY ($25,000)

29 JULY–4 AUGUST
SINGLES: M. Srejber d. K. Carlsson (SW) 0–6 6–4 6–2.
DOUBLES: J. R. Smith (GB) /D. Mustard (NZ) d. T. Meinecke /R. Osterhun 6–3 4–6 6–4.

WINNETKA, ILLINOIS ($25,000)

5–11 AUGUST
SINGLES: B. Moir d. H. Solomon 2–6 7–5 6–2.
DOUBLES: R. Brown /L. Jensen d. K. Evernden /S. Levine 6–4 6–7 7–6.

OSTEND, BELGIUM ($25,000)

12–18 AUGUST
SINGLES: B. Oresar d. J. A. Rodriguez 6–4 7–6.
DOUBLES: A. Brichant /J. van Langendonck d. M. Cierro /I. Kley 6–2 6–2.

MESSINA, ITALY ($50,000)

2–9 SEPTEMBER
SINGLES: K. Carlsson (SW) d. R. Agenor 6–2 7–6.
DOUBLES: J. Colas /D. de Miguel d. B. Derlin /D. Felgate (AUS) 6–1 7–6.

THESSALONIKI, GREECE ($25,000)

9–15 SEPTEMBER
SINGLES: P. Lundgren (SW) d. S. Zivojinovic (YU) 3–6 6–3 7–6.
DOUBLES: A. Medem /A. Vaudevan d. B. Levine /B. Nealon 6–3 5–7 6–3.

WEST PALM BEACH ($25,000)

23–29 SEPTEMBER
SINGLES: M. Wostenholme (C) d. J. Yzaga 6–2 1–6 6–4.
DOUBLES: D. Tarr /E. Van't Hof d. L. Lavalle /Yzaga 6–2 6–0.

BELO HORIZONTE, BRAZIL ($25,000)

21–27 OCTOBER
SINGLES: T. Muster (AU) d. C. DiLaura 6–1 6–4.
DOUBLES: M. Cierro /J. Goes d. G. Barbosa /I. Kley 6–3 6–4.

PORTO ALEGRE, BRAZIL ($25,000)

28 OCTOBER–3 NOVEMBER
SINGLES: M. Pernfors d. K. Novacek 6–3 6–3.
DOUBLES: Nijssen /Vekemans d. C. Mezzadri /Werner 6–4 2–6 7–6.

BERGEN, NORWAY ($25,000)

28 OCTOBER–3 NOVEMBER
SINGLES: P. Lundgren d. J. Gunnarsson (SW) 5–7 7–6 7–6.
DOUBLES: G. Kalovelonis (GR) /Letts d. J. /P. Carlsson 7–5 6–3.

CURITIBA, BRAZIL ($25,000)

4–10 NOVEMBER
SINGLES: J. Goes d. M. Srejber 6–4 6–4.
DOUBLES: N. Aerts /A. Hocevar d. Nijssen /Vekemans 7–6 6–4.

HELSINKI ($25,000)

11–17 NOVEMBER
SINGLES: A. Chesnokov (USSR) d. E. Jelen 4–6 6–0 6–3.
DOUBLES: R. Bathman (SW) /S. Eriksson d. M. Christensen /P. Kuhgen 6–4 3–6 6–4.

SAO PAULO ($25,000)

11–17 NOVEMBER
SINGLES: F. Maciel d. C. Motta 6–3 6–3.
DOUBLES: C. Kirmayr /Motta d. Keller /Menezes 6–4 3–6 7–6.

BAHIA ($75,000)

25 NOVEMBER–1 DECEMBER
SINGLES: J. Yzaga d. C. Kirmayr 6–2 6–0.
DOUBLES: J. Cihak /T. Nijssen d. E. Sanchez /V. Pecci 6–4 6–3.

RIO DE JANEIRO ($25,000)

2–6 DECEMBER
SINGLES: V. Pecci d. C. Kist 6–2 6–7 6–3.
DOUBLES: C. DiLaura /E. Sanchez d. G. Guerro /G. Tiberti 4–6 6–4 6–2.

MEN'S SATELLITE CIRCUIT 1985

National circuits of four tournaments plus concluding Masters' event. The following were the results of the Masters' singles finals.

DATE	VENUE	SINGLES FINAL
Australia		
26 Feb–2 March	Eppin	S. Youl d. C. Miller 6–4 4–6 6–4
17–20 Nov	Keysborough	P. Doohan d. S. Guy 7–6 7–6
Belgium		
2–6 Oct	Waregem	P. Carlsson d. A. Lane 7–6 6–4
Brazil		
18–24 Feb	Sao Paulo	I. Kley d. R. Viver (EC) 6–4 6–1
Bulgaria		
30 June–3 July	Droujda	L. Bucur d. L. Wallgrehn (SW) 7–6 6–3
Canada		
16–21 July	Chicoutimi	C. Campbell d. H. McDadi 6–2 6–3
Great Britain		
18–24 Feb	Heston	S. Eriksson (SW) d. L. Oundgren (SW) 7–6 4–6 7–5
14–18 May	Lee-on-Solent	M. J. Bates d. C. Allgaardh (SW) 6–2 6–3
India		
5–8 Feb	Poona	G. Lemon (USA) d. B. Cherry (USA) 4–6 6–2 7–5
Italy		
18–22 March	Padora	F. Moscino d. M. Cierro 7–5 6–4
26 Aug–1 Sept	Verona	T. Champion (USA) d. E. Winogradsky (USA) 6–0 7–6
Mexico		
6–12 May	Puerto Vallaria	L. Lavalle d. J. Canter (USA) 4–6 6–1 6–4
Netherlands		
17–21 July	Amersvoort	M. Schapers d. C. Castellan (ARG) 6–4 6–4
Spain		
25–31 March	Gran Canira	I. Werner d. O. Rahnasto (FIN) 6–4 3–6 6–2
1–7 July	Tarragona	D. DeMiguel d. G. Tournant 2–6 6–1 6–0
12–18 Aug	Xativa	C. DiLaura d. B. Uribe 6–4 6–2
16–22 Sept	Valladolid	O. Urnbinati d. W. Bertini 1–6 6–4 6–4
USA		
1–5 May	Mount Pleasant, SC	A. El Mehelmy (EG) d. M. Robertson 6–3 6–4
4–9 June	Hilton Head	M. Wostenholme (C) d. R. Ycaza (EC) 6–2 6–2
26–30 June	Evansville	R. Deppe d. B. Page 6–4 6–2
9–14 July	Sioux City	R. Matuszewski d. J. Gurfein 4–6 7–6 6–3
12–17 Aug	Lebanon, NJ	G. Wilder d. K. Moir (SA) 4–6 6–3 6–4

Britain's Jeremy Bates (right) and Simon Youl of Australia (below) both boosted their rankings with wins on the Satellite circuit in 1985.   (T. Hindley)

| 15–20 Oct | Midland, Texas | T. Witsken d. V. Wilder 5–7 6–4 6–4 |
| 9–15 Dec | Honolulu | G. Michibata d. P. Torre 6–7 6–3 7–5 |

West Germany

18–24 Feb	Munich	W. Popp d. J. B. Svensson (SW) 6–4 6–3
22–27 May	Stanberg	T. Meinecke d. A. A. Volkov (USSR) 4–6 7–6 7–5
17–21 July	Usingen	F. Maciel (SP) d. A. Stepanek 6–3 6–2

WOMEN'S NON-SERIES TOURNAMENTS

FINALS

ARGENTINA

BUENOS AIRES ($10,000)

25–31 MARCH
SINGLES: M. Paz d. M. Perez Roldan 6–3 6–2.
DOUBLES: Perez Roldan /P. Tarabini d. A. Tiezzi /G. Mosca 7–6 6–4.

AUSTRALIA

HOBART ($10,000)

25 FEBRUARY–3 MARCH
SINGLES: B. Cordwell (NZ) d. R. Bryant 4–6 6–3 7–6.
DOUBLES: J. Thompson /L. Field d. M. Turk /C. Carney 6–1 4–6 6–4.

MELBOURNE ($10,000)

4–11 MARCH
SINGLES: V. Marler d. L. O'Neill 6–1 6–2.
DOUBLES: J. Thompson /L. Field d. K. Deed /W. Frazer 6–7 6–0 6–1.

ADELAIDE ($10,000)

11–17 MARCH
SINGLES: L. Field d. B. Cordwell (NZ) 6–3 6–1.
DOUBLES: Cordwell /J. Richardson (NZ) d. J. Thompson /Field 6–2 2–6 6–2.

CANBERRA ($10,000)

29 APRIL–5 MAY
SINGLES: B. Cordwell (NZ) d. R. Bryant 6–2 4–6 6–4.
DOUBLES: B. Perry (NZ) /C. Copeland (USA) d. K. Wenzel (AU) /J. Thompson 6–3 6–4.

NEW SOUTH WALES ($10,000)

28 OCTOBER–3 NOVEMBER
SINGLES: H. Dahlstrom (SW) d. K. Deed 6–4 6–1.
DOUBLES: A. Dingwall /A. Gulley d. C. O'Neill /D. Whytcross 6–4 1–6 6–1.

NEW SOUTH WALES ($25,000)

4–10 NOVEMBER
SINGLES: H. Dahlstrom (SW) d. M. Lundquist (SW) 6–4 3–6 7–6.
DOUBLES: M. Turk /L. Field d. C. O'Neill /D. Whytcross 6–0 7–5.

AUSTRIA

KITZBUHEL ($10,000)

SINGLES: N. Shutte (NTH) d. S. Hack (G) 6–4 6–1.
DOUBLES: H. Fukarkova (CZ) /O. Votavova (CZ) d. N. Bajcikova (CZ) /P. Tesarova (CZ) 7–5 6–3.

BRAZIL

SAO PAOLO ($10,000)

25 FEBRUARY–3 MARCH
SINGLES: H. Dahlstrom (SW) d. M. Paz (ARG) 6–7 6–4 6–4.
DOUBLES: L. Plchova (CZ) /M. Weber d. K. Karlsson (SW) /S. Petterson 6–2 6–2.

CURITIBA ($10,000)

4–10 MARCH
SINGLES: M. Paz (ARG) d. R. Blount (USA) 6–1 6–2.
DOUBLES: P. Hy (HK) /K. Moos (NTH) d. L. Plchova (CZ) /M. Weber 6–3 6–4.

PORTO ALEGRE ($10,000)

11–17 MARCH
SINGLES: L. Plchova (CZ) d. L. Corsata 6–2 6–1.
DOUBLES: M. Perez Roldan (ARG) /P. Tarabini (ARG) d. R. Einy (GB) /L. Gracie (GB) 7–6 3–6 6–4.

BULGARIA

SOFIA ($25,000)

23–29 SEPTEMBER
SINGLES: S. Hack (G) d. H. Fukarkova (CZ).
DOUBLES: M. /K. Maleeva d. I. Brzakova (CZ) /H. Fukarkova (CZ).

FRANCE

LYON ($10,000)

10–16 JUNE
SINGLES: C. Calmek d. F. Bonsignon (IT) 6–7 6–4 6–4.
DOUBLES: M. Perez Roldan (ARG) /P. Tarabini (ARG) d. C. /C. MacGregor (USA) 6–3 6–4.

GREAT BRITAIN

CUMBERLAND ($10,000)

15–21 APRIL
SINGLES: E. Reinach (SA) d. C. Cohen (SWZ) 7–5 7–5.
DOUBLES: E. /M. Reinach (SA) d. L. Gracie /M. Reinhardt (G) 6–2 6–4.

QUEEN'S ($10,000)

22–28 APRIL
SINGLES: K. Okamoto (J) d. D. Moise (RU) 6–4 6–2.
DOUBLES: E. /M. Reinach (SA) d. X. Li (CHI) /N. Zhong (CHI) 2–6 6–2 9–7.

SUTTON ($10,000)

29 APRIL–5 MAY
SINGLES: K. Okamoto (J) d. E. Reinach (SA) 6–4 6–7 6–2.
DOUBLES: X. Li (CHI) /N. Zhong (CHI) d. L. Gracie /M. Reinhardt (G) 6–3 6–3.

BOURNEMOUTH

6–12 MAY
SINGLES: B. Romano (IT) d. D. Van Rensburg (SA) 6–1 6–4.
DOUBLES: X. Li (CHI) /N. Zhong (CHI) d. E. /M. Reinach (SA) 6–8 7–5 6–4.

LEE-ON-SOLENT

13–19 MAY
SINGLES: E. Reinach (SA) d. N. Zhong (CHI) 6–3 6–1.
DOUBLES: E. /M. Reinach (SA) d. B. Borneo /J. Tacon 6–3 6–3.

PETERBOROUGH ($10,000)

4–8 NOVEMBER
SINGLES: C. Dahlman (SW) d. N. Bajcikova (CZ) 7–5 6–2.
DOUBLES: J. Novotna (CZ) /R. Rajchtova (CZ) d. C. Porwik (G) /W. Probst (G) 5–7 6–3 6–4.

QUEEN'S ($10,000)

10–15 NOVEMBER
SINGLES: C. Dahlman (SW) d. N. Jagerman (NTH) 2–6 6–4 6–1.
DOUBLES: C. Singer (G) /P. Tesarova (CZ) d. C. Porwick (G) /W. Probst (G) 5–7 6–4 6–3.

18–22 NOVEMBER
SINGLES: C. Bakkum (NTH) d. J. Novotna (CZ) 5–7 6–3 6–2.
DOUBLES: B. Borneo /J. Tacon d. Novotna /R. Rajchtova (CZ) 6–2 6–3.

TELFORD ($10,000)

25–29 NOVEMBER
SINGLES: C. Porwik (G) d. N. Jagerman (NTH) 6–3 6–4.
DOUBLES: C. Maso (USA) /S. Pendo (USA) d. B. Borneo /Jagerman 4–6 6–2 6–4.

ITALY

CASERTA ($10,000)

15–21 APRIL
SINGLES: L. Garrone d. L. Golarsa 5–7 6–2 6–4.
DOUBLES: D. Murgo /B. Romano d. S. Simmonds /G. Dinu (G) 4–6 7–5 6–4.

MONVISO ($10,000)

22–28 APRIL
SINGLES: L. Golarsa d. P. Tarabini (ARG) 6–4 6–3.
DOUBLES: P. Murgo /B. Romano d. M. Perez Roldan (ARG) /Tarabini 7–6 7–5.

$20,000 Circuit

ADRIA ($5,000)

SINGLES: N. Jagerman (NTH) d. P. Murgo 7–6 6–0.
DOUBLES: R. Rajchtova (CZ) /P. Tesarova (CZ) d. S. Kusuma (IND) /R. Sziszai (HU) 6–4 6–2.

LANCIANI ($5,000)

10–16 JUNE
SINGLES: P. Murgo d. X. Li (CHI) 6–2 4–6 7–5.
DOUBLES: C. Bakkum (NTH) /N. Jagerman (NTH) d. Li /N. Zhong (CHI) 6–4 6–3.

GALATINA ($5,000)

17–23 JUNE
SINGLES: S. la Fratta d. N. Bajcikova (CZ) 7–5 6–0.
DOUBLES: X. Li (CHI) /N. Zhong (CHI) d. Bajcikova /P. Sedleakova (CZ) 3–6 6–2 7–5.

FRANCA-VILLA AL MARE

24–30 JUNE
SINGLES: S. La Fratta d. N. Jagerman (NTH) 6–2 7–5.
DOUBLES: R. Rajchtova (CZ) /A. Nohakova (CZ) d. X. Li (CHI) /N. Zhong (CHI) 6–2 6–4.

Masters

ROME ($5,000)

1–7 JULY
SINGLES: X. Li (CHI) d. P. Murgo 6–1 6–2.
DOUBLES: N. Jagerman (NTH) /C. Bakkum (NTH) d. Li /N. Zhong (CHI) 7–5 4–6 6–1.

SUBIACO ($10,000)

15–21 JULY
SINGLES: B. Romano d. M. Perez Roldan (ARG) 7–6 6–1.
DOUBLES: P. Murgo /Romano d. Perez Roldan /P. Tarabini (ARG) 6–2 6–1.

SEZZE ($10,000)

22–28 JULY
SINGLES: B. Romano (IT) d. M. Perez Roldan (ARG) 6–2 6–4.
DOUBLES: Romano /P. Murgo (IT) d. Perez Roldan /P. Tarabini (ARG) 3–6 6–3 6–2.

JAPAN

TAKANODAI ($25,000)

30 SEPTEMBER–6 OCTOBER
SINGLES: P. Medrado (BR) d. M. Diaz (BR) 6–7 6–1 7–5.
DOUBLES: Medrado /M. Diaz (BR) d. B. Cordwell (NZ) /J. Richardson (NZ) 4–6 6–4 6–4.

SAGA ($10,000)

21–27 OCTOBER ($10,000)

SINGLES: X. Li (CHI) d. Y. Koizumi 6–2 6–3.
DOUBLES: N. Schutte (NTH) /M. Van Der Torre (NTH) d. Li /N. Zhong (CHI) 6–2 6–4.

FUKUOKA ($10,000)

28 OCTOBER–3 NOVEMBER
SINGLES: J. Cummings (USA) d. M. Van Der Torre (NTH) 6–2 6–4.
DOUBLES: N. Schutte (NTH) /Van Der Torre d. E. Ilda /N. Sato 6–3 7–5.

HASAKI ($10,000)

4–10 NOVEMBER
SINGLES: N. Schutte (NTH) d. M. Van Der Torre (NTH) 7–6 6–1.
DOUBLES: N. Zhong (CHI) /E. Ilda d. Van Der Torre /Schutte 7–5 6–3.

MEXICO

$20,000 Circuit

GUADALAJARA ($5,000)

12–18 AUGUST
SINGLES: T. Houk d. S. Rojas 6–3 7–6.
DOUBLES: M. Llamas /L. Becerra d. B. Borbolla /M. Morales 6–1 6–3.

After the Federation Cup of 1982 in California, Hu Na defected to the US, and in 1985 rose from 278 to 96 in the world. (A. Evans)

GUANANJUANTO ($5,000)

19–25 AUGUST
SINGLES: T. Houk d. Yamada 2–6 7–6 6–0.
DOUBLES: M. Llamas /L. Becerra d. J. Newman (USA) /T. Houk 6–2 6–4.

CUERNAVACA ($5,000)

26 AUGUST–1 SEPTEMBER
SINGLES: M. Llamas d. L. Becerra 6–1 4–6 7–5.
DOUBLES: M. Carmen /S. Rojas d. T. Houk /J. Newman (USA) 6–7 6–3 6–0.

Masters

MEXICO CITY ($5,000)

2–8 SEPTEMBER
SINGLES: S. Rojas d. M. Llamas 6–1 6–3.
DOUBLES: Llamas /L. Becerra d. Rojas /M. Casta 6–3 6–2.

SWEDEN

LANSKRONA ($25,000)

8–14 JULY
SINGLES: K. Karlsson d. C. Lindqvist 7–6 6–2.
DOUBLES: J. Hetherington (C) /J. Kaplan (USA) d. L. Field (AUS) /J. Thompson (AUS) 7–5 6–2.

BASTAD ($25,000)

15–21 JULY
SINGLES: M. Lindstrom d. O. Votavova (CZ) 4–6 6–3 7–5.
DOUBLES: E. Ekblom /M. Lindstrom d. L. Corsata (BR) /M. Reinach (SA) 6–3 4–6 6–3.

USA

CHICAGO ($10,000)

31 DECEMBER–6 JANUARY
SINGLES: I. Demongeot (F) d. K. Dreyer 1–6 6–2 6–4.
DOUBLES: L. Lewis /W. Pattenden (C) d. Demongeot /N. Tauziat (F) 4–6 7–6 7–5.

KEY BISCAYNE, FLORIDA

7–13 JANUARY
SINGLES: A. Holikova (CZ) d. K. Kinney 7–5 6–3.
DOUBLES: L. Lewis /W. Pattenden (C) d. E. Ekblom (SW) /M. Van Der Torre (NTH) 5–7 6–4 6–1.

DELRAY BEACH, FLORIDA ($10,000)

14–20 JANUARY
SINGLES: S. Solomon d. S. Almgren (SW) 6–0 6–2.
DOUBLES: E. Ekblom (SW) /M. Van Der Torre (NTH) d. D. Farrell /J. Kaplan 6–3 7–5.

SAN ANTONIO, TEXAS ($10,000)

21–27 JANUARY
SINGLES: S. Gomer (GB) d. E. Eliseenko (USSR) 6–3 6–2.
DOUBLES: I. Demongeot (F) /N. Tauziat (F) d. E. Ekblom (SW) /M. Van Der Torre (NTH) 6–2 6–4.

LANTANA, FLORIDA ($10,000)

3–9 JUNE
SINGLES: H. Cioffe d. L. Gregory (SA) def.
DOUBLES: H. Steden (MEX) /Fernandez d. B. Bowes /B. Callan 6–3 7–5.

BIRMINGHAM, ALABAMA ($10,000)

10–16 JUNE
SINGLES: S. Sloane d. S. Faulkner (AUS) 6–4 6–2.
DOUBLES: S. Hahn /L. Eldredge d. J. Goolding /M. Lindstrom (SW) 6–2 6–4.

FAYETTEVILLE, NC ($10,000)

17–23 JUNE
SINGLES: M. Werdel d. C. Kuhlman 6–3 7–5.
DOUBLES: L. Gates /S. Hahn d. W. Wood /Kuhlman 6–4 6–3.

CHARLESTON, SC ($10,000)

24–30 JUNE
SINGLES: C. Kuhlman d. T. Takago (J) 6–2 6–1.
DOUBLES: Kuhlman /W. Wood d. L. Lewis /W. Pattenden (C) 6–2 6–1.

KEY BISCAYNE, FLORIDA ($25,000)

8–14 JULY
SINGLES: M. Werdel d. H. Cioffi 6–2 6–4.
DOUBLES: L. Corsato (BR) /M. Reinach (SA) d. J. Masters (AUS) /M. Parun (NZ) 6–3 4–6 6–3.

DEARBORN, MICHIGAN ($10,000)

15–21 JULY
SINGLES: J. Young (C) d. K. Dewis (C) 6–0 2–6 6–1.
DOUBLES: C. /C. MacGregor d. A. Grousbeck /A. Nishiya (J) 6–3 2–6 6–2.

COLOMBUS, OHIO ($10,000)

22–28 JULY
SINGLES: A. Nishiya (J) d. M. Werdel 6–0 7–6.
DOUBLES: K. Deed (AUS) /S. Savides d. E. Winston /T. Zambrzycki (BR) 6–2 6–2.

CHATHAM, NJ ($10,000)

29 JULY–4 AUGUST
SINGLES: C. Kuhlman d. A. Nishiya (J) 6–2 6–0.
DOUBLES: Kuhlman /L. Lewis d. E. Barrable (SA) /H. Steden (MEX) 6–1 6–2.

FREEHOLD, NJ ($10,000)

5–11 AUGUST
SINGLES: C. Kuhlman d. D. Hansel 3–6 6–2 6–0.
DOUBLES: L. Allen /R. Reis d. S. Hahn /J. Prah 6–4 6–2.

ROANOKE, VIRGINIA ($25,000)

12–18 AUGUST
SINGLES: A. Smith d. C. Kuhlman 6–2 6–0.
DOUBLES: L. Allen /R. Reis d. L. Eldredge /L. Gates 6–4 6–4.

ATLANTIC BEACH ($25,000)

9–15 SEPTEMBER
SINGLES: L. Golarsa (IT) d. E. Krapl (SWZ) 7–6 6–2.
DOUBLES: J. Goolding /D. Farrell d. L. Field /A. Nishiya (J) 2–6 7–5 6–4.

BOSTON ($10,000)

16–22 SEPTEMBER
SINGLES: B. Norton d. L. Field (AUS) 6–0 6–4.
DOUBLES: Field /L. O'Neill (AUS) d. C. Carney (AUS) /M. Turk (AUS) 6–4 6–1.

BETHESDA, MARYLAND ($25,000)

23–29 SEPTEMBER
SINGLES: J. Forman d. H. Dahlstrom (SW) 6–3 7–5.
DOUBLES: Dailey /M. Reinach (SA) d. D. Hansel /C. Watson.

HAWAII ($10,000)

30 SEPTEMBER–6 OCTOBER
SINGLES: K. Latham d. S. Faulkner (AUS) 7–6 1–6 6–3.
DOUBLES: E. Evans /S. Pendo d. B. Somerville /A. Winston 6–4 6–7 6–2.

7–13 OCTOBER
SINGLES: K. Latham d. Cyn. MacGregor 3–6 6–2 7–6.
DOUBLES: E. Evans /S. Pendo d. MacGregor /W. Ouwendijk 7–6 6–1.

WEST GERMANY

NEUMUNSTER ($10,000)

29 JULY–4 AUGUST
SINGLES: B. Romano (IT) d. H. Ter Riet (NTH) 6–3 0–6 7–5.
DOUBLES: Y. Brzakova (CZ) /M. Pinterova (CZ) d. H. Fukarkova (CZ) /O. Votavova (CZ) 6–0 7–5.

RHEDA WIEDENBRUCKE ($10,000)

12–18 AUGUST
SINGLES: S. Meier d. S. Hack 7–5 6–4.
DOUBLES: C. Porwick /Meier d. L. Gracie (GB) /B. Borneo (GB) 4–6 7–6 6–1.

INTERNATIONAL TEAM COMPETITIONS

WIGHTMAN CUP
WORLD TEAM CUP
BASF EUROPEAN CUP
MAUREEN CONNOLLY BRINKER TROPHY

Though failing to win a Grand Prix title for the first time since 1972, Jimmy Connors contributed to another US success in the World Team Cup in Düsseldorf.　　*(M. Cole)*

Above left to right: *The victorious Wightman Cup team – Anne White, Evert Lloyd, Shriver, Nagelsen, Rinaldi – who beat Britain for the 47th time.* ***Below left to right:*** *Hobbs, Croft, Durie, Gomer, Wade and Mappin (manager).*   *(R. Adams)*

WIGHTMAN CUP

John Parsons

The United States won the Nabisco Wightman Cup in 1985 for the seventh successive year, with one of the most comprehensive victories in the 62-year history of this annual women's competition against Britain. Indeed, it was not until the last of three dead rubbers on the final day that the visitors gathered their solitary set.

Yet in a sense that third day's play, which began with the home team already 4–0 ahead and assured of retaining what is surely one of the most elegant trophies in world tennis, emphasised the special appeal of the Wightman Cup. No matter what the match score may be, it generally manages to evoke a great spirit of competitive and patriotic pride, combined with grace, splendour and ceremony. It was a perfect example of the Wightman Cup being more than just a tennis match but rather a piece of tennis history which an increasing number of influential voices on both sides of the Atlantic want to see preserved. On that last day the competition went from being keen to intense, even though the scores were of no great consequence. The 6,482 crowd, bringing the total for the three days to 14,699 (an increase of 30 per cent on the previous Williamsburg fixture two years earlier) sat back and immensely enjoyed the whole occasion.

Pam Shriver, ranked third in the world at the time, had sped the Americans towards their triumph by crushing the young and nervous British number one, Annabel Croft, 6–0 6–0. Only twice before had a Wightman Cup singles produced such a whitewash score – when Louise Brough beat Jean Walker-Smith in a dead rubber in 1950 and Andrea Jaeger eclipsed Anne Hobbs in 1981. Having produced what the American captain, Mrs Lloyd, said 'probably the most perfect tennis she had ever played', Miss Shriver wondered if she would be able to lift her game again for a match which really did not matter, against Jo Durie. Not only did she win 6–4 6–4, but she was made to do so in a thrilling finish when Miss Durie, despite increasing pain from an injured racket arm, pulled back from 1–4 to 4–5 in the second set. The eighth game, as Miss Durie made it 3–5, lasted 17 minutes, involving 13 deuces as the British player saved four match-points.

In the final doubles, which lasted almost two hours and contained much beautiful tennis, the British team of Hobbs and Durie were given a great ovation when they finally took a set. They lost in the end 6–3 6–7 6–2 to Mrs Lloyd and Miss Shriver but it was a marvellous match with some particularly fine touches from Mrs Lloyd and Miss Hobbs. The tie-break set went to 8–6 and was won on the second opportunity. On the first, at 6–5, Mrs Lloyd spotted Miss Hobbs crossing over a shade early and promptly drove a tremendous two-handed backhand winner past her down the line. It was one of the few times Miss Hobbs was outwitted. Miss Durie clinched the second set-point with a smash.

One of the recurring dilemmas of the Wightman Cup is that the event, especially when it is being staged in the United States, needs the support of the top American players to build up and sustain the degree of enthusiasm in Williamsburg where Dick and Cynthia Anzolut, the professional promoters, and Millie West, the honorary chairman in charge of a veritable army of eager volunteers, do such a magnificent job. When the Americans are at strength, as in 1985, the matches will always be one-sided until Britain also has a crop of players genuinely pressing to be at the very top. The 7–0 result was not entirely unexpected for, apart from having the first- and third-ranked players in the world, both playing two single matches and later a doubles together, even the third American singles competitor, Kathy Rinaldi, in eleventh position was some 17 places ahead of Britain's highest-ranked player, Miss Croft.

Probably the best Britain could have hoped for was a 5–2 defeat. Miss Hobbs was clearly fitter than at any other time in a year which had largely been sacrificed to overcoming a debilitating attack of shingles, and it was felt she might upset Miss Rinaldi. There was optimism too, about the first doubles. In the event, even those modest dreams evaporated and Britain's team manager, Sue Mappin, was left to observe at the end of the first day, with the Americans 2–0 ahead, 'Anything we won would have been a bonus – and in the end we didn't get anything'. With just a tiny slice of luck for Britain it could have been 1–1. On the other hand, the remark remained apt throughout the three days.

On that first day, the British contingent clutched at straws. After the superbly staged opening ceremony, colourful and dignified, Miss Durie won the first six points, four of them with outright winners, in the first rubber against Mrs Lloyd. It was a heady moment, Mrs Lloyd nodding in that appreciative and yet menacing manner she has in acknowledging fine shots. Yet it was too much to hope that it would last. Miss Durie rushed headlong into costly errors in the third game and thereafter, although she played reasonably well and fought for all she was worth, Mrs Lloyd was now superbly in command.

Miss Hobbs, for her part, was nearly able to take advantage of the undoubted nervousness felt by Miss Rinaldi. Despite losing 7–5 7–5, the British player broke back to 5–5 in both sets, but she used so much mental, as well as physical energy simply staying in the match, saving six match-points in that second set, that she did not have enough left to capitalise on the fresh opportunities she created for herself.

The second day was one Britain – and especially Miss Croft – would rather forget. Perhaps it might have been different had Miss Croft taken the break-point she held in the first game. But I doubt it. Three times in that opening game Miss Shriver played crunching forehand volleys which immediately illustrated her confidence and resolve, and in next to no time she was on the rampage. She allowed Miss Croft only ten points in the first set and a meagre 14 in the second. Indeed, not just then, but also against Miss Durie and then in the final doubles with Mrs Lloyd, there was tangible evidence of an altogether sharper Miss Shriver. She was reaching shots with so much time to spare that, particularly on the volley, her response was infinitely more effective than it has been in the past.

After that singles débâcle for Miss Croft, it was hardly surprising that the teenager was still not in the happiest frame of mind or form when she and team captain Virginia Wade, playing her 21st Wightman Cup, were entrusted with the task of trying to keep the contest alive into day three. They stayed with Betsy Nagelsen and Anne White for a while, but drifted to a 6–4 6–1 defeat against opponents whose record together was worthy of a higher reputation.

So once again it was all painfully predictable for Britain, yet the enthusiasm for the event of Miss Shriver and Mrs Lloyd in particular remained undiminished. Both stressed how much they enjoyed the chance to represent their country in an event with such history and tradition, which brought a welcome change from the normal tournament atmosphere in which they play solely for themselves.

Few have represented the United States with greater dignity or success than Mrs Lloyd who, when not in action herself was always to be seen leading her team with much animated gusto from the players' box, while coach Tom Gorman provided what advice was necessary at court-side. She now has a 26–0 singles record over 13 Wightman Cup years to go with her 28–0 record in the *Federation Cup*.

WIGHTMAN CUP

WILLIAMSBURG
USA d. Great Britain 7–0 (Mrs J. M. Lloyd d. J. M. Durie 6–2 6–3; K. Rinaldi d. A. E. Hobbs 7–5 7–5; P. H. Shriver d. A. Croft 6–0 6–0; B. Nagelsen/A. White d. Croft/S. V. Wade 6–4 6–1; Shriver d. Durie 6–4 6–4; Lloyd d. Croft 6–3 6–0; Lloyd/Shriver d. Durie/Hobbs 6–3 6–7 6–2).

AMBRE SOLAIRE WORLD TEAM CUP

Ian Barnes

When they come to chip an epitaph on Jimmy Connors's tombstone it may well be to the effect that he made more great escapes than Harry Houdini, for as a master of the dramatic, he has had no equal at getting out of a tight spot in a dazzling career which has so far lasted more than a dozen years.

Few spots have been tighter than the one he was in at the Rochusclub in Düsseldorf in May when Czechoslovakia were one game — just four points — from dethroning the United States as reigning champions of the Ambre Solaire World Team Cup. Ivan Lendl had soundly beaten John McEnroe 6–7 7–6 6–3 in an enthralling opening match to the final, and Miloslav Mecir led Connors 5–2 in the final set of the second singles. But as Connors has always said: 'No tennis match is over until you are shaking hands.' And this one was far from over. In his determination to dominate, canny Connors called on all his resources literally to power Mecir into submission.

Mecir, the sensation of the early part of the year when he won his first big titles in Rotterdam and Hamburg, was so frustrated that he did not win another game, double-faulting six times in three service games and being reduced to underhand serving at one point, as Connors stormed to a 6–3 2–6 7–5 triumph which kept the match alive. The value of his fight-back was proved when Ken Flach and Robert Seguso beat Lendl and Tomas Smid 6–4 7–6 in the gathering gloom of evening to clinch the Cup and the $200,000 first prize.

It was a superbly exciting climax to another record-making week in Düsseldorf. Media coverage exceeded all the organisers' expectations and the crowds, despite uncertain weather, reached an all-time high at more than 65,000. None will have been disappointed by the quality of the play. Most found a special place in their affections for France's hero, Henri Leconte, the man of the week with victories over Ramesh Krishnan of India, Ivan Lendl, and then the Swedish No. 1, Mats Wilander. His daring play, his frequently outrageous shot-making and the delightfully Gallic manner he brought to the proceedings each time he stepped on court made him the toast of the refreshment stands every time rain interrupted play. He was the only unbeaten player in the tournament, if one discounts Henrik Sundstrom's one victory in the Swedish cause after a severe bout of bronchitis had kept him out of the earlier matches.

Unfortunately for Leconte, his effort was not quite enough. France beat the Czechs, thanks to Thierry Tulasne's fine win over Mecir, but lost to Sweden; the Czechs beat Sweden and everybody in the Red Group beat India, leaving Czechoslovakia, France and Sweden with identical 2–1 records. The Czech team, however, had a 7–2 match record and advanced to the final over Sweden and France who were equal at 5–4.

The United States came through the rival Blue Group unbeaten but far from unchallenged. John McEnroe dropped the opening set of his match against Spain's Juan Aguilera and Connors was frustrated 2–6 7–6 6–1 by the patient José Higueras in a match that rain extended into a second day, leaving Flach and Seguso to secure victory in the doubles.

The Australians, hampered by Pat Cash's back injury which permitted him to play doubles only, were beaten 2–1 and West Germany 3–0 to ensure the holders a place in the final, although the Germans, with home support, were far from a push-over. Hans Schwaier gave McEnroe his toughest work-out of the week before the final and was beaten only by 7–5 7–6. Wolfgang Popp made a brave fight of things against Connors before going down 6–1 6–4, and Flach and Seguso had more than enough to do in putting away Andreas Maurer and Popp by the same score.

Unfortunately for the local fans, a brave show by their men was their only consolation as they lost 2–1 to both Australia and Spain, finishing at the bottom of their round-robin group with just $20,000 to share. How different it might have been had their squad included Boris Becker, who was to win Wimbledon six weeks later. His presence would have served an even earlier warning that the power base in world tennis is moving away from the United States.

McEnroe and Connors cannot go on for ever (or even much longer), and without them the Americans will struggle to hold back the advancing Europeans. Sweden who, like Australia, collected $50,000 as runners-up in the round-robin series, have the strength in depth that used to be America's great asset. Australia have plenty of young players to back Cash when McNamee and Fitzgerald can no longer do their stuff, and the French are enjoying a revival now that Noah and Leconte are adding some consistency to their obvious flair. In a few years we may look back on Düsseldorf 1985 as Connors's – and his country's – last stand.

WORLD TEAM CUP ($500,000)

DÜSSELDORF, 20–26 MAY
ROUND ROBIN BLUE GROUP
Australia d. West Germany 2–1 (P. Cash lost to H. Schwaier 2–6 3–6; P. McNamee d. M. Westphal 6–3 6–3; Cash/J. Fitzgerald d. A. Maurer/W. Popp 6–2 6–1); **USA d. Spain 2–1** (J. P. McEnroe d. J. Aguilera 6–7 6–4 6–4; J. S. Connors lost to J. Higueras 6–2 6–7 1–6; K. Flach/R. Seguso d. Aguilera/Higueras 6–2 6–0); **USA d. Australia 2–1** (McEnroe d. Fitzgerald 6–1 6–0; Connors d. McNamee 6–4 6–2; Flach/Seguso lost to Cash/Fitzgerald 6–4 3–6 4–6); **Spain d. West Germany 2–1** (Aguilera d. Schwaier 7–6 7–6; Higueras d. Westphal 5–7 7–5 6–4; Aguilera/Higueras lost to Maurer/Popp 4–6 2–6); **Australia d. Spain 2–1** (J. Frawley lost to Aguilera 2–6 2–6; McNamee d. Higueras 6–0 4–6 6–3; Cash/Fitzgerald d. Aguilera/Higueras 6–3 6–3); **USA d. West Germany 3–0** (McEnroe d. Schwaier 7–5 7–6; Connors d. Popp 6–1 6–4; Flach/Seguso d. Maurer/Popp 6–1 6–4). **1st:** USA 3 wins; **2nd:** Australia 2 wins; **3rd:** Spain 1 win; **4th:** West Germany no wins.
ROUND ROBIN RED GROUP
France d. India 2–1 (T. Tulasne d. V. Amritraj 6–0 6–1; H. Leconte d. R. Krishnan 6–1 7–6; Leconte/P. Portes lost to V./An. Amritraj 6–7 6–7); **Czechoslovakia d. Sweden 3–0** (I. Lendl d. M. Wilander 6–4 6–3; M. Mecir d. A. Jarryd 2–6 6–3 7–5; Lendl/T. Smid d. Jarryd/Wilander 3–6 6–3 6–4); **Sweden d. India 3–0** (Wilander d. Krishnan 6–4 6–2; Jarryd d. V. Amritraj 6–0 6–2; Jarryd/Wilander d. V./An. Amritraj 6–4 7–6); **France d. Czechoslovakia 2–1** (Tulasne d. Mecir 2–6 6–0 6–4; Leconte d. Lendl 3–6 6–4 6–4; Leconte/Portes lost to Lendl/Smid 4–6 6–4 3–6); **Sweden d. France 2–1** (Wilander lost to Leconte 2–6 4–6; H. Sundstrom d. Tulasne 6–0 3–6 7–6; Wilander/Jarryd d. Leconte/Portes 6–4 6–4); **Czechoslovakia d. India 3–0** (Lendl d. Krishnan 6–2 6–4; Mecir d. V. Amritraj 6–3 6–1; Lendl/Smid d. V./An. Amritraj 6–2 6–3). **1st:** Czechoslovakia 2 wins, 7 rubbers; **2nd:** Sweden 2 wins, 5 rubbers, 12–9 sets; **3rd:** France 2 wins, 5 rubbers, 12–12 sets; **4th:** India no wins.
FINAL: USA d. Czechoslovakia 2–1 (McEnroe lost to Lendl 7–6 6–7 3–6; Connors d. Mecir 6–3 3–6 7–5; Flach/Seguso d. Lendl/Smid 6–4 7–6).

OTHER INTERNATIONAL TEAM EVENTS

BASF EUROPEAN CUP

Formerly King's Cup

Men's European team championship

Group I
ESSEN, WEST GERMANY, 14–20 JANUARY
RED SECTION: Sweden d. Ireland 3–0; Great Britain d. Ireland 2–1 (S. Bale d. S. Sorensen 2–6 7–6 6–2; S. Shaw lost to M. Doyle 3–6 3–6; Bale /Shaw d. Doyle /Sorensen 2–6 6–3 6–2); **Sweden d. Great Britain 3–0** (S. Simonsson d. Bale 6–3 6–4; J. Gunnarsson d. Shaw 6–4 7–6; H. /S. Simonsson d. Bale /M. J. Bates 6–3 6–4).
BLUE SECTION: Switzerland d. Czechoslovakia 2–1; West Germany d. Czechoslovakia 2–1; Switzerland d. West Germany 2–1.
GROUP FINAL: Sweden d. Switzerland 3–0 (T. Hogstedt d. R. Stadler 6–3 6–2; Gunnarsson d. J. Hlasek 7–5 4–6 6–2; H. /S. Simonsson d. Hlasek /Stadler 6–3 3–6 6–3).
RELEGATION MATCH: Czechoslovakia d. Ireland 3–0.
Group II
LOGANO, ITALY, 14–20 JANUARY
GROUP FINAL: Italy d. Netherlands 3–0.
Group III
BUDAPEST, 14–20 JANUARY
GROUP FINAL: Belgium d. Spain 2–1.
Group IV
Yugoslavia d. Poland 2–0.

MAUREEN CONNOLLY BRINKER TROPHY

Women's under-21 team competition between USA and Great Britain

QUEEN'S CLUB, LONDON, 12–14 DECEMBER
USA d. Great Britain 6–5 (A. Hulbert d. S. Reeve 5–7 7–5 6–4, lost to J. Louis 2–6 2–6; R. Reis d. Louis 4–6 7–5 6–0, lost to Reeve 3–6 6–4 3–6; J. Holdren lost to S. Gomer 0–6 1–6, lost to A. Brown 6–3 4–6 3–6; W. Wood d. J. Wood 7–6 6–3; T. Phelps d. A. Brown 6–2 6–2, d. Gomer 6–4 5–7 6–3; Hulbert /Reis d. Louis /J. Wood 4–6 7–5 6–2; Phelps /W. Wood lost to Brown /Gomer 4–6 6–7).

TWO GREAT WIMBLEDON CHAMPIONS

On the occasion of the hundredth Wimbledon Championships in 1986, there follows an appreciation of the achievements of two of the greatest and most loved Wimbledon champions. Ted Tinling pays tribute to the delightful Kitty McKane Godfree, winner of 153 titles in 17 years of competitive tennis and still playing regularly in her 90th year, while Paul Haedens remembers the remarkable 'Bounding Basque', Jean Borotra, one of the French 'Musketeers', who was still competing at the age of 87.

KATHLEEN McKANE GODFREE

May 7, 1986, is the 90th anniversary of the birth of Kathleen McKane Godfree (Kitty or Biddy to her friends), who is one of the greatest tennis champions.

More than six decades ago, in 1924, Kitty won the Wimbledon singles, coming from 4–6 1–4 15–40 down to beat Helen Wills in the final. She also won the mixed doubles with British international, J. B. Gilbert. Two years later, only months after marrying the Wimbledon doubles title-holder, Leslie Godfree, she won the Wimbledon singles a second time, recovering characteristically from a 1–3 30–40 deficit in the third set of the final against the Spanish star, Lili de Alvarez. For good measure she won the mixed doubles again, but this time with her recent bridegroom. No other husband and wife team has ever won the mixed doubles event at Wimbledon.

In her 90th year, Kitty was leading the life of a person half her age, driving herself or bicycling on daily shopping forays and enjoying a happy hour of doubles at Wimbledon at least once every two weeks. 'You see, I have been blessed with marvellously good health', she explained in the relaxed comfort of her south London home.

A compelling Sidney White oil portrait dominates one wall of Kitty's sitting-room. She is portrayed in the compulsory tennis whites of the 1920s, none the less colour-splashed with the ubiquitous 'Lenglen bandeau' of that era. 'Suzanne had such magnetism that we were all copycats then', Kitty reflected, allowing herself an untypical moment of nostalgia. Outside, in the best English tradition, April had framed her home in clouds of white cherry blossom and Kitty's spring garden was a tapestry of crocus and daffodils, surrounded by golden hedges of forsythia. This quiet enclave has been Kitty's home since 1939, interrupted only by the Second World War years, when she was evacuated to Devon, away from London's nightly bombings, with her sons, David and Martin, then aged ten and two.

Since the death of her husband in 1972, Kitty shared her home with Martin, while David's residence is close by. 'And I have two wonderful daughters-in-law to take care of me when necessary', she said happily. However, both daughters-in-law found her an unwilling patient during a bout of pneumonia and pleurisy, when she would worry only about missing an episode of her favourite TV soap operas, *Dynasty* and *Dallas*, and how soon she could resume her tennis and her shopping jaunts.

Kitty was born in London in 1896, one year after her sister, Margaret. Both her parents were keen on outdoor sports, but Kitty's earliest preference was for indoor skating. She became expert so quickly that she earned the British Skating Association's bronze medal at the age of ten. Her parents were also such keen cyclists that in 1906, when called to

At Wimbledon's 1977 Centenary Ball, Kitty McKane Godfree and Jean Borotra, the oldest surviving singles champions, opened the dancing. *(Popperfoto)*

Spanning the eras of Worple Road and Church Road, Kitty McKane was the only player to beat Helen Wills at Wimbledon, and, with her husband Leslie Godfree, the only married pair to win the mixed.

a business meeting in Berlin, her father, John, decided that the whole family should make the 600-mile journey on bicycles. 'Our route was through Holland. It was tulip time and I can still see all those acres of lovely flowers. Our governess, of course, came with us. Our luggage was sent ahead, but we each carried two clothing changes in waterproof packs, as father had planned for us to ride 30 miles every day. One must remember there were no automobiles on the roads in those days. In fact, I don't believe Mr Rolls and Mr Royce had yet met one another', Kitty smiled.

It was while driving cars for the British War Office during the 1914–18 War that Kitty began thinking seriously about tennis. 'Margaret and I had been to a Scottish school where unusual emphasis was put on the outdoor games programme, so afterwards, back in London, we joined a tennis club and I spent every spare moment teaching myself what I hoped would become sound groundstrokes, the basis of good tennis.' Kitty's groundstrokes proved good enough for her to be accepted at the 1919 re-opening of Wimbledon. There she survived three rounds of singles before losing to another player making her Wimbledon debut – her future nemesis, Suzanne Lenglen.

In this first of their many meetings, Kitty was able to take only one game from Lenglen, but her first season's efforts were rewarded when she was invited to join the British team going to Paris for what was then known as the World Covered-Court Championships. She won the women's doubles, taking the first of 107 major doubles and mixed doubles titles she would amass in the next decade.

In the 1920s, London was notoriously short of indoor tennis courts, making the winter months a problem for players unable to make the customary visit to the French Riviera. Kitty solved this problem by adopting badminton as a back-up game in the pursuit of which she would not be dependent on the weather. Again, at this second game she became adept so quickly that she was the national badminton champion in 1919–20, 1920–21, 1921–22 and 1923–24. In addition, Kitty and her sister, Margaret, became national badminton doubles champions in 1923–24, while still improving their tennis enough to reach the 1922 Wimbledon doubles final – the only sisters ever to do so in this century.

Kitty was a member of the British team participating in the 1920 Olympic Games in

Belgium, where she achieved a bronze medal in the singles, a silver in the mixed doubles with Max Woosnam, and a gold for the women's doubles, in which she and her partner, Mrs McNair, had the distinction of winning the semi-final round against Lenglen, partnered by Mlle d'Ayen. Kitty's record in the 1920s makes pages of tennis history. Her name is everywhere, with 1923 the first of her four most outstanding years.

She began this golden era with a triple triumph, winning all three events of the World Covered-Court Championships in Barcelona. Then came the magic sunshine of the French Riviera. 'I loved playing in those historic clubs, particularly Monte Carlo, or Cannes, on the courts laid down by the British Renshaw brothers in 1881, the first in France', she recalled. In May 1923, Kitty reached all three finals of the World Hard-Court Championships in Paris, losing the singles to Lenglen, but again winning the doubles with Mrs Beamish against the famous French star, partnered by Germaine Golding. Two months later, in July, Kitty was Wimbledon runner-up to Suzanne, then in August came the great adventure of travelling to the United States with the first British women's team ever to cross the Atlantic. Wightman Cup fans will know that the Cup was inaugurated in 1923 to coincide with the opening of the Forest Hills stadium. So Kitty enjoyed the double honour of having played not only the first match on the court of the Forest Hills stadium, but also the inaugural match of the Wightman Cup series.

'We left England on 22nd July (on the *Franconia*) and landed in New York's steamy heat on 1st August. Mrs Wightman had made the four-day train journey from her California home in time to meet us. At the draw, Helen Wills' name and mine came first out of the hat, so our match was planned to follow the opening ceremony of the new stadium. However, the President of the US [President Harding] died that week, so the opening was postponed from 10th August to the following day, to allow for his funeral. I remember that I played Helen Wills, who was not quite 18, and that I had two points for the second set, but could not clinch it. Mrs Wightman herself played against us in the doubles. We were badly beaten in that 1923 match, but I am very proud to have been a part of the event which really inaugurated today's international acceptance of women's tennis.' After playing exhibition matches in Canada, the team sailed grandly home on the *Empress of France*.

Kitty felt that since around-the-world tennis has become an accepted fact of most players' lives, it is impossible to recapture the significance of the pioneer sea journey made by the first Wightman Cup team. At that time, only a handful of individual women players had dared the trans-ocean challenge: Mabel Cahill, who went from Ireland to win the US singles in 1891; Marion Jones, who journeyed from California to Wimbledon in 1900; May Sutton, who followed in 1905, 1906 and 1907; and later Elizabeth Ryan, who took up residence in England in 1912.

One recalls also the Norwegian expatriate, Molla Mallory, being quite unable to reproduce in Europe that form which had earned her seven US Championships. Then there was Suzanne Lenglen's disastrous visit to America in 1921. Reading the history books, it seems now that the *Daily Telegraph*'s tennis correspondent, A. Wallis Myers, writing in 1924, put it best: 'Mrs Wightman's inspiration has at last bridged the Atlantic.'

In that first trans-Atlantic team venture, Kitty was determined that Britain would not be denied some success. Partnered by another British team-member, Phyllis Covell, she went on to win the US National doubles title, the first overseas pairing ever to do so.

Asked about the 1924 Olympic Games in Paris, where she was again the top British player, Kitty said: 'The construction of Colombes stadium was still going on as we played, so I remember a lot of noise. Also we could never begin the two o'clock matches as scheduled because of the dressing-room lady's lunch-break. She would lock the door firmly at 12 noon, and not return before two. Little things like that made the whole affair seem very disorganised, in great contrast to today's Championships.' However, these 'little things' did not prevent Kitty from winning bronze and silver medals before adding her name yet again to the following years' rolls of honour.

Destiny has always played a part in the lives of tennis champions, and in this way Kitty was unlucky that her peak years coincided with Lenglen's own zenith. In 1925, Suzanne won Wimbledon with the total loss of five games. She had again thwarted Kitty's hopes in the Paris final, before subjecting Kitty to her only 0 and 0 loss, in the Wimbledon semi-final. None the less, Kitty still made 1925 a memorable year by reaching the US National singles final, leading her British Wightman Cup team to victory at Forest Hills (the only time in 50 years the British have won in America) and then, with Australian Jack Hawkes, beating the legendary partnership of Tilden and Mallory to win the US National mixed doubles at Longwood.

Yet in retrospect, 1926 seems to have provided the ultimate climax to Kitty's seven years of hard work and achievements. The first major happening was her marriage to Leslie Godfree. This took place in January during an innovative three-month tour of South Africa by four British men and four British women. 'We didn't tell any of the others for two weeks', Kitty said, even now making it sound rather a naughty conspiracy. In June, there were the celebrations of Wimbledon's 50th anniversary, and destiny was kinder to Kitty, as Lenglen withdrew from Wimbledon, leaving Kitty the opportunities she most wanted and took — her second singles and mixed doubles titles, plus her third runner-up doubles prize.

As Alan Little says, in his detailed study of Kitty's record, '1927 was not a good year', so it was just as well that marriage had already given Kitty wider horizons. Nevertheless, between two bouts of surgery — for the removal of her tonsils in July and of her appendix in October — she returned to the US in 1927, but was forced to default, unfit, from the national singles, although she managed a repeat of her earlier feat in winning the national doubles title. Later Kitty and Margaret were still winning British tournaments together in 1930, with Kitty on the 1934 Wightman Cup team and still a Wimbledon competitor at the age of 38. In 17 years of competitive play, she won the staggering number of 46 singles titles and 107 doubles titles.

Surveying the wide panorama of Kitty's title-studded career, I asked what was the secret of her success? 'If there was a secret', she replied, 'it was that I was comfortable almost everywhere on the court. My generation had all been to ballroom-dancing classes. These taught me balanced footwork, and I also found skipping very helpful. The early years of hard work gave me confident groundstokes, while badminton taught me to volley and helped enormously on overheads. Then one learned to be patient and when to defend. Equally, when I thought I had managed a really good-length groundshot, I enjoyed moving in.' More recently, Kitty enjoyed experimenting with larger rackets: 'They seem to make the game much easier.'

One of the many joys of a conversation with Kitty is that she has forthright opinions on almost every subject, old or new. Of her visit to the Hollywood set of *Dallas* in 1984, she said: 'I just wished that wicked J.R. would come running down the stairs.' And she seemed to possess instant freeze-frame recall. At the 1984 Olympic Games, representing the Wimbledon Championships, she observed the clash between Mary Decker and Zola Budd, and was able to describe this in detail. Moments later, she could describe, in equal detail, Mrs Lambert Chambers's unlucky match-points against Suzanne Lenglen 67 years earlier. Either way, Kitty fills to perfection the role of tennis's *grande dame*, without any of the usual connotations of the word *grande*. She has always been one very special lady. — Ted Tinling

Ted Tinling and the ITF are grateful to the librarian of the Wimbledon Tennis Museum, Alan Little, for his assistance in the research of this tribute.

JEAN BOROTRA — THE LIVING LEGEND

Between the two world wars, Jean Borotra, at the peak of his tennis career during the era of the French 'Musketeers', was looked upon as a tennis phenomenon. He still was when, at the age of 87, he represented the International Club of France for the hundredth time in their twice-yearly match against the IC of Great Britain in November 1985 in London. What's more, after losing his singles on the first day of this historic meeting against his old friend, Gus Holden (playing the special game of 'singles-doubles' he has

A legend in his own time, the irrepressible Jean Borotra has, since 1929, played in every one of the 100 matches between the International Clubs of Britain and France.

devised to prolong his singles career), he came out on the second day to win a mixed doubles match.

Yvon Petra, a compatriot who won the inaugural post-war Championship at Wimbledon in 1945 (from which Jean was absent), used to say of Jean Borotra: 'He is not an ordinary human being, he is an atmospheric disturbance – a whirlwind.' British *Davis Cup* doubles expert Pat Hughes, in the same vein but more down to earth, said of Jean, 'One of the greatest players in the game and without doubt the finest volleyer'.

Even if these opinions were expressed in the pre-McEnroe era, one wonders if they would not be valid even today. Although the 'Bounding Basque', as he was popularly known, lacked the fast serve of a McEnroe that enables that great champion to follow the ball in to the net with ease, somehow the Frenchman's superhuman gifts of speed and reflex enabled him to achieve the same results behind his gentler delivery. Unable to serve overarm in later years because of a shoulder injury, he developed an underhand serve of great ingenuity. His old friend, Rene Lacoste, wryly observed: 'This changes nothing, you have never had a serve!' In 1928 when Jean won the Australian Championships in singles and in doubles with Jacques 'Toto' Brugnon as his partner, a Sydney journalist wrote of him: 'He waltzes, fox-trots on the court and pounces on the ball like a cat on a mouse.' These gifts he attributes to his Basque origins, for in that region men are either very tough and strongly built, or else slight of build, fleet of foot and with great dexterity. These latter have a wonderful eye, for they are brought up on a daily dose of 'Pelote Basque', which requires great footwork and lightning reactions.

When the First World War broke out in 1914 Jean was just 16. He tried to volunteer for the Bayonne Regiment but was rejected as being too young, so he continued his studies and later attended the Lycée Saint Louis in Paris as a boarder. In 1918, now aged 18, he volunteered for the 121st Horse Artillery Regiment at La Rochelle, and on the day he joined he gave up smoking – for good. A year of action between September 1917 and November 1918 in Alsace, on the Marne, and Champagne earned him two mentions in despatches and the Croix de Guerre. When the war ended he was sent to Germany with the army of occupation. There he was able to play tennis again – a game he had learned in England when, aged almost 14, he had been sent by his widowed mother, Marguerite (his father, Henry, had died unexpectedly when Jean was eight), to an English family, the Wildys, who lived in Kenley. Besides perfecting his English he was also introduced to the delights of lawn tennis in the back garden. He still speaks with warmth of Mrs Wildy, his 'holiday mother', whose kindness instilled a deep love of England and the English that has never dimmed.

In 1919, conscious of the inadequacy of his technique which derived more from pelota than any conventional tennis methods, Jean asked the professional at the Wiesbaden club what he should do. He was advised to grip the racket with the thumb down the back of the handle for his backhand and to use a short sharp swing. This was the only coaching he ever had. The rest of his game was entirely natural, which is why his unorthodox shots were so difficult for his opponents to read. The backhand returns of serve and the backhand volleys came off his racket at awkward angles like pistol shots and demolished many opponents.

When, in November 1919, he was demobbed, his main concern was to secure entry to the École Polytechnic. Thus, for a year, he had no time to play tennis, but when he was admitted in 1920, he started to play once more. Improvement was rapid. Two years later he was playing for France in the *Davis Cup* and a further two years after that he was winning his first Wimbledon.

A summary of his remarkable career reads as follows: five times a Wimbledon singles finalist, winning the title twice (1924, 1926) and the doubles winner three times; the winner of the French singles twice (1924, 1925) and the doubles five times with three different 'Musketeer' partners; the Australian singles and doubles once (1928); and a member of that extraordinary French *Davis Cup* team that ruled the world between 1927 and 1932. Besides these successes there were countless other titles in singles and more still in doubles and mixed doubles, for he excelled in that department of the game. He was an ideal partner, even though he rarely allowed his team-mate to hit more than one shot in four, as he always wanted to dominate his side of the net. He also won innumerable covered-court titles in France, America and England. He won his last important title at the age of 51 – the British Covered Court Championships which he was winning for the tenth time in 1949. Jean also won the mixed title that year with Mrs Bea Walter – now Mrs Seal – the lady who has kindly translated this article.

His life? Equally remarkable. Born on 13 August, 1898, at Domaine de Pouy, near Biarritz in the Basque country, he went to the local school which, in those rural areas, entailed a walk of five kilometres each day. Aged 11 he attended the Lycée in Bayonne which meant a daily cycle ride of 12 miles. Like all Basque boys he played pelota and rugby. After his two years at the École Polytechnic, a military academy and one of France's leading Universities, where he received a degree in engineering, he went on to the Sorbonne, where he received a degree in law, which has proved invaluable in his business career. From then on he travelled the world as a tennis champion and as a successful businessman in the oil industry selling petrol pumps, first for Hardoll and later for Satam when they absorbed the original company. His philosophy was 'work and play' in the true amateur manner. He fitted his business appointments in between his matches and would often phone his clients from the dressing room. He seldom arrived at the tournament ground until a few minutes before his match was due, but he was always on time, never keeping an opponent waiting. At Jubilee Wimbledon in 1926, he actually changed in the taxi on the way from the airport and dashed on to the Centre Court just in time to be presented to King George V and Queen Mary with the other former champions. Jean married Mabel de Forest, the daughter of a British MP, and they had one son, Yves. After the war the marriage was dissolved but Jean and Mabel remained the best of friends.

'Jean's post bag was as large as that of a member of Parliament', wrote Jacques Brugnon. He eventually became the Minister of General Education and Sport, but it was for the Pétain government in Vichy during the German occupation in World War II in which he earned the Croix de Guerre (1939–45) as a soldier in 1940. Because of his Vichy role, Wimbledon refused his entry at the first post-war Championship in 1946. Yet Jean had experienced a harrowing war. Suspected by the Germans of wanting to join the Allied forces in North Africa, he was arrested in Paris at the Gare d'Austerlitz on 22 November, 1942, by the Gestapo and was interrogated. In his bag he carried damning evidence – a French army uniform. There followed two and a half years of imprisonment, at first in solitary confinement at Sachsenhausen, from where he was moved to the ancient fortress of Itter in May, 1943, thanks to the intervention of Rene Lacoste. Believing his fellow 'Musketeer' had either been captured or was dead, Lacoste had asked the King of Sweden to intercede on Jean's behalf with the German authorities. King Gustav, a keen tennis player himself, knew all the 'Musketeers' well and had often partnered them in matches. His message to Hermann Göring had its effect and life became a little more bearable. Three times Jean tried to escape, but he was still in the castle, a prisoner, together with two former Prime Ministers of France, two past Commanders in Chief of the French army, and the sister of General de Gaulle. On 3 May, the SS commander and his men left the fortress: the prisoners were apparently free. However, a small but dedicated SS unit had moved overnight into the valley below the castle. Knowing who the prisoners were, they were determined to execute them. On 4 May, Jean volunteered to go out, disguised as a peasant, to guide the nearby American troops to the castle, avoiding the enemy units. This he did and, clad in a GI uniform, he took part in one of the last skirmishes of the war as the American tanks and infantry ended enemy resistance.

Jean eventually returned to his old way of life and, in 1948, to the Wimbledon public who adored him. Between Jean and the Wimbledon fans there was a sort of love affair. The other French players found it very trying to keep hearing the endless question: 'What time is Borotra on court?' He plucked the public's heart strings like a virtuoso. If he changed his beret, the great crowds on the Centre Court trembled with excitement. He joked with the line-judges, who ruthlessly foot-faulted him on so many occasions. Then, at the end of a long, exhausting rally he would sometimes chase the ball into the stand, leaping over the low wall to land in the lap of an attractive lady spectator who would be ecstatic – especially when he rewarded her enthusiasm by kissing her hand. Above all his matches were either full of drama or full of sympathy and sorrow. Yet he could change his whole attitude like a streak of lightning, which often helped him to win a fifth set.

At the beginning of his career many critics said of Borotra, 'He is fantastic, but he will never last. He will burn himself out the way he plays'. If any of those critics are still alive today – which is extremely doubtful – they would be very surprised to read the following letter which Jean, in his 88th year, sent to his friends early in 1986. He explains that his heart-beats had become so slow – 43 beats per minute – that he decided to have a pacemaker implanted last December. 'Therefore', he says, 'my heart-beat has now gone up to 70 and could, if it becomes necessary, be slowed down or accelerated by remote control. My memory seems to be showing signs of improvement, and I am led to believe that my eyesight and my hearing may also improve. I have even been told that my reflexes on the court might get better, which I refuse to expect.' What a spirit, what a man, what a legend! – Paul Haedens

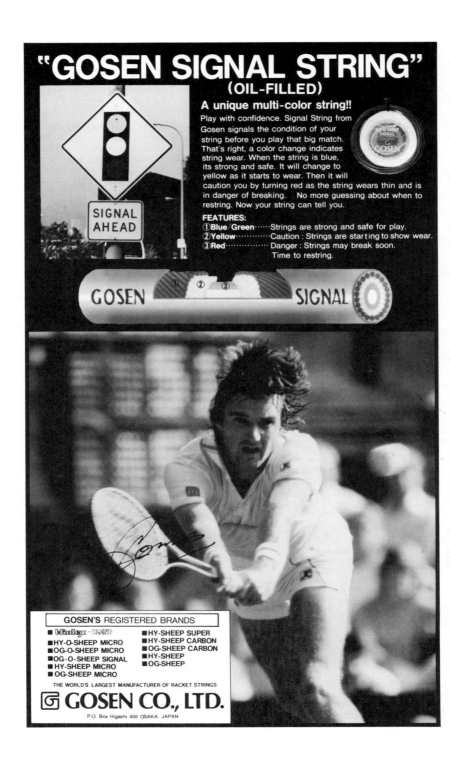

RANKINGS

WORLD RANKINGS
UNDER-21 WORLD RANKINGS
THE ATP YEAR
THE WTA YEAR

Tim Mayotte's major success, the Delray Beach Lipton's tournament, contributed the vital points that lifted him to No. 12 in the world by the year's end — his best finish to date.   *(M. Cole)*

WORLD RANKINGS

Lance Tingay

WORLD RANKINGS 1985

MEN
1 Ivan Lendl (CZ) (2)
2 Mats Wilander (SW) (3)
3 John McEnroe (USA) (1)
4 Boris Becker (G) (—)
5 Stefan Edberg (SW) (—)
6 Jimmy Connors (USA) (4)
7 Anders Jarryd (SW) (—)
8 Kevin Curren (USA) (8)
9 Yannick Noah (F) (—)
10 Joakim Nystrom (SW) (—)
1984 ranking in brackets.

WOMEN
1 Martina Navratilova (USA) (1)
2 Hana Mandlikova (CZ) (3)
3 Chris Evert Lloyd (USA) (2)
4 Pam Shriver (USA) (6)
5 Zina Garrison (USA) (—)
6 Helena Sukova (CZ) (10)
7 Kathy Rinaldi (USA) (—)
8 Claudia Kohde-Kilsch (G) (8)
9 Manuela Maleeva (BUL) (4)
10 Steffi Graf (G) (—)

It was not an easy year for ranking with the great male players producing a hotch-potch of conflicting results. The decline of John McEnroe was striking and, having been at the top, he won none of the four major titles, his best being a semi-final place in France. The four champions of France, Wimbledon, the US and Australia were all different – Mats Wilander, the totally unexpected Boris Becker, Ivan Lendl and Stefan Edberg respectively. Two Swedes were among them but no American.

Lendl won the WCT finals at Dallas as well as the US Open, and so there was little doubt about his status as the number one for the year. He won more tournaments than any rival and never had a really bad loss. He looked and was a commanding, though never invincible, performer and he heads the ranking for the first time at his sixth listing. Who hit the ball harder, or with better control, than this tall Czech? Wilander was not a consistent performer. He suffered at least eight defeats one would not expect from a man of his calibre, but as well as his brilliance in Paris, where he beat Lendl in the final to take the title for the second time, he was in the last four at Flushing Meadow and the losing finalist in Australia. Only at Wimbledon did he fail lamentably. The decline of McEnroe at the Grand Slam events almost justified grading him below the two phenomenal newcomers, Becker and Edberg. None the less only Lendl won more tournaments than McEnroe and one could hardly place him lower.

Becker and Edberg were hard to separate, for the latter had more vital scalps – Lendl and Wilander – in winning Australia than did Becker, who avoided the greatest players at Wimbledon. But at the tail end of the year Becker had a triumph against Edberg and Wilander in the most demanding of all situations; the final round of the *Davis Cup*. Becker had to be ranked the higher.

Jimmy Connors had his worst year for ages. Not since 1973 had he been lower than four but now he is ranked for the 13th time – at six. It was a bad year only in terms of his own old standards, for he was consistent, reaching the semi-finals in France, Wimbledon, the US Open, and at Dallas. The fact that this game warrior was 33 in September 1985 explains much. As always, one might fill the end places in a ranking list of ten with other names without committing violence against sense. The recovery of form by the Frenchman, Yannick Noah, was good to see.

Martina Navratilova takes the top place among women for the fourth year in succession, and the sixth in all, in ranking over 11 years. She was strikingly less ahead of the others than she was, winning but two of the Grand Slam titles – Wimbledon and Australia. Chris

Lloyd beat her to take the French title and Hana Mandlikova overcame her to take the American. These two are clearly in contention for the second place, which falls to the Czech, even though she showed rather more vulnerability. But Mrs Lloyd twice lost to Miss Mandlikova and notably so in the US Championships. Thus in being ranked for the 15th time since 1971, the incomparable Mrs Lloyd drops to third position for the first time since 1979. She was 31 in December 1985, and perhaps the classic values of her game have edged down just a notch. Miss Mandlikova rises to her highest standing ever. She was never more consistent than during 1985 and her genius was more fully exploited than in other years. Pam Shriver, number four, reaches her highest level at her sixth appearance in the ratings, and were doubles skill to count, then Miss Navratilova would have taken her right to the top.

The diminution in standard below the first four is more marked than one would like. Certainly more than six could claim the lower places with some justification. Zina Garrison was always to the fore, and early in the year Helena Sukova seemed to be threatening to climb right to the top. With her background of being a Czech, the nationality of so many super players, and having a mother who was Wimbledon finalist (Vera Sukova in 1962), she would have surprised no-one.

Kathy Rinaldi, once a precocious prodigy, brought herself back to old standards, doing notably well at Wimbledon. Claudia Kohde-Kilsch was again a threat to any player and remains the best German woman despite the rich talent that is growing there. Manuela Maleeva of Bulgaria was not as impressive as in 1984, but the weight of Bulgaria as a tennis force grew none the less as her younger sister, Katerina, became a force, albeit short of top ten rating. Steffi Graf of Germany is the most spectacular newcomer, building on the esteem created by her Olympic Games success in 1984. At Flushing Meadow she was a semi-finalist among the giants.

One may have the impression that American strength has fallen away, dominating less than in some years. Even so three of the top ten men are American by allegiance as are five of the women. But Sweden, with four men, stresses what a boost was given to their game by Bjorn Borg.

LANCE TINGAY'S WORLD RANKINGS 1968–1984

MEN

1968		**1969**		**1970**		**1971**	
1	Laver	1	Laver	1	Newcombe	1	Newcombe
2	Ashe	2	Roche	2	Rosewall	2	Smith
3	Rosewall	3	Newcombe	3	Laver	3	Laver
4	Okker	4	Okker	4	Roche	4	Rosewall
5	Roche	5	Rosewall	5	Okker	5	Kodes
6	Newcombe	6	Ashe	6	Nastase	6	Ashe
7	Graebner	7	Drysdale	7	Richey	7	Okker
8	Ralston	8	Gonzales	8	Ashe	8	Drysdale
9	Drysdale	9	Gimeno	9	Gimeno Pilic	9	Riessen
10	Gonzales	10	Stolle	10	Ralston Taylor	10	Nastase

1972		**1973**		**1974**		**1975**	
1	Smith	1	Newcombe	1	Connors	1	Ashe
2	Nastase	2	Smith	2	Rosewall	2	Orantes
3	Rosewall	3	Nastase	3	Newcombe	3	Connors
4	Laver	4	Kodes	4	Borg	4	Borg
5	Ashe	5	Ashe	5	Nastase	5	Vilas
6	Newcombe	6	Rosewall	6	Smith	6	Nastase
7	Richey	7	Laver	7	Laver	7	Ramirez
8	Orantes	8	Gorman	8	Orantes	8	Newcombe
9	Gimeno	9	Connors	9	Metreveli	9	Laver
10	Kodes	10	Okker	10	Vilas	10	Tanner

1976		**1977**		**1978**		**1979**	
1	Connors	1	Borg	1	Borg	1	Borg
2	Borg	2	Vilas	2	Connors	2	McEnroe
3	Panatta	3	Connors	3	Gerulaitis	3	Connors
4	Nastase	4	Gerulaitis	4	Vilas	4	Gerulaitis
5	Vilas	5	Gottfried	5	Dibbs	5	Tanner
6	Dibbs	6	Stockton	6	Ramirez	6	Vilas
7	Solomon	7	Dibbs	7	Gottfried	7	Pecci
8	Orantes	8	Ramirez	8	Barazzutti	8	Higueras
9	Ramirez	9	Solomon	9	A. Mayer	9	Dibbs
10	Tanner	10	Tanner	10	McEnroe	10	Solomon

1980		**1981**		**1982**		**1983**	
1	Borg	1	McEnroe	1	Connors	1	McEnroe
2	McEnroe	2	Borg	2	Lendl	2	Connors
3	Connors	3	Connors	3	McEnroe	3	Lendl
4	Vilas	4	Lendl	4	Wilander	4	Wilander
5	Gerulaitis	5	Clerc	5	Vilas	5	Noah
6	Lendl	6	Pecci	6	Gerulaitis	6	Arias
7	Solomon	7	G. Mayer	7	Higueras	7	Higueras
8	G. Mayer	8	Vilas	8	Gomez	8	Vilas
9	Teltscher	9	Gerulaitis	9	Noah	9	Clerc
10	Gottfried	10	Teacher	10	Teltscher	10	Gerulaitis

1984	
1	McEnroe
2	Lendl
3	Wilander
4	Connors
5	Gomez
6	Cash
7	Sundstrom
8	Curren
9	Aguilera
10	Krickstein

WOMEN

1968		**1969**		**1970**		**1971**	
1	King	1	Court	1	Court	1	Goolagong
2	Wade	2	Jones	2	King	2	Court
3	Richey	3	King	3	Casals	3	King
4	Bueno	4	Richey	4	Niessen	4	Casals
5	Court	5	Heldman	5	Wade	5	Melville
6	Jones	6	Casals	6	Jones	6	Dalton
7	Tegart	7	Melville	7	Melville	7	Durr
8	Du Plooy	8	Bartkowitz	8	Krantzcke	8	Wade
9	Bowrey	9	Wade	9	Heldman	9	Masthoff
10	Casals	10	Bowrey	10	Durr	10	Evert

1972		**1973**		**1974**		**1975**	
1	King	1	Court	1	Evert	1	Evert
2	Goolagong	2	King	2	King	2	King
3	Evert	3	Evert	3	Goolagong	3	Cawley
4	Court	4	Goolagong	4	Morozova	4	Navratilova
5	Melville	5	Melville	5	Melville	5	Wade
6	Wade	6	Wade	6	Casals	6	Court
7	Casals	7	Casals	7	Wade	7	Morozova
8	Gunter	8	Masthoff	8	Masthoff	8	Sawamatsu
9	Durr	9	Morozova	9	Heldman	9	Heldman
10	Tuero	10	Stove	10	Gunter	10	Reid

America's leading black player, Zina Garrison, was ranked for the first time at No. 5. (A. Evans)

1976		**1977**		**1978**		**1979**	
1	Evert	1	Evert	1	Navratilova	1	Navratilova
2	Cawley	2	Wade	2	Evert	2	Austin
3	Wade	3	King	3	Cawley	3	Evert Lloyd
4	Casals	4	Navratilova	4	Wade	4	King
5	Navratilova	5	Barker	5	King	5	Cawley
6	Fromholtz	6	Reid	6	Turnbull	6	Wade
7	Reid	7	Turnbull	7	Ruzici	7	Fromholtz
8	Barker	8	Casals	8	Jausovec	8	Turnbull
9	Jausovec	9	Stove	9	Marsikova	9	Ruzici
10	Morozova	10	Jausovec	10	Shriver	10	Hanika

1980		**1981**		**1982**		**1983**	
1	Evert Lloyd	1	Austin	1	Navratilova	1	Navratilova
2	Cawley	2	Evert Lloyd	2	Evert Lloyd	2	Evert Lloyd
3	Austin	3	Mandlikova	3	Jaeger	3	Jaeger
4	Navratilova	4	Navratilova	4	Mandlikova	4	Mandlikova
5	Mandlikova	5	Jaeger	5	Potter	5	Hanika
6	King	6	Ruzici	6	Austin	6	Shriver
7	Ruzici	7	Turnbull	7	Shriver	7	Jausovec
8	Jaeger	8	Shriver	8	Bunge	8	Temesvari
9	Turnbull	9	Hanika	9	King	9	King
10	K. Jordan	10	Jausovec	10	Hanika	10	Durie

1984	
1	Navratilova
2	Evert Lloyd
3	Mandlikova
4	Maleeva
5	K. Jordan
6	Shriver
7	Turnbull
8	Kohde-Kilsch
9	Bassett
10	Sukova

21 AND UNDER WORLD RANKINGS

C. M. Jones

Evolution moves slowly, and tennis has always followed the pattern; but 1985 saw an amazing break from the norm in the junior game. It began against bitter opposition when the 21-and-under Young Masters championship was arranged to clash with the World Championship of Tennis only 110 miles away in London. Disputing officials said the event would be a failure, and should not have been scheduled to oppose an established event. However, it was quickly apparent that that Young Masters was a wonderful competition, and praise for the quality of play rang around the world. Additionally, the youngsters created interest and admiration for their knightly sportsmanship, in such fine contrast with much boorish behaviour from their seniors.

More was to come, in the shape of Boris Becker, who, having become the first Young Master, then became the youngest-ever male Wimbledon champion, beating Wilfred Baddeley's record of 19 years 5 months and 23 days in 1891. Becker was just 17 years 7 months and 15 days, younger even than Leonardo Lavalle, the Mexican who won the junior singles final at Wimbledon the same afternoon.

Later in the year Ivan Lendl, no longer a junior, won the US Open, and thus for the first time since Donald Budge brought off the Grand Slam in 1938, those four major events went to men more than six feet tall. Now, almost 50 years later, these four different men – under-21s Becker, Wilander and Edberg – plus Lendl, suggested that greater heights are no longer a handicap and may even be an advantage.

A check with the juniors ranked in the 1976 issue of this year-book shows that the shorter men and those who stood over six feet tall were having equal success. Now, ten years later, players over six feet in height occupy five of the top six positions, suggesting evolution in favour of height. Also more countries are represented – 14 in 1986, compared with 11 in 1976.

Mats Wilander won the Australian and French Opens and told all and sundry that he didn't really wish to be the world number one; maybe number two, but that is very different. Boris Becker has no such limitations in his outlook. He loves tennis, winning, the crowds, competition and the joy of watching a world-class soccer match, given the chance. So which of those two awe-inspiring juniors is the better on the world tennis courts? Becker won Wimbledon; is that better than Wilander's second French title? The computer ratings go for Wilander, but no computer can assess Wilander's frank and, to many, wise philosophy. However, this ranking strives to judge them as tennis competitors and I would go for Becker, who tops these annual rankings ahead of Wilander.

That was the major problem of this year's rankings. There were many lesser ones, and one must commiserate with Pat Cash for the physical troubles he suffered during much of the year. Probably he will climb back . . . But one can never be absolutely sure. Players and their methods change. How long ago is it since any of us saw a top-20 player serve a fault, feel too nervous for a second overarm attempt, and produce an underarm second that wins the point? The 6ft 3in tall Mecir did just that. Perhaps we have many surprises to come in the next two or three years.

The rankings for 1985 have been based on a whole year's results, as distinct from the ATP and WTA computers, which adjust places after every new issue of their newspapers. Only players born in 1964 or later qualify.

Carling Bassett of Canada was a semi-finalist at Delray Beach, but failed to win a tournament in 1985. *(M. Cole)*

MALE
1 Boris Becker (G)
2 Mats Wilander (SW)
3 Stefan Edberg (SW)
4 Miloslav Mecir (CZ)
5 Martin Jaite (ARG)
6 Henrik Sundstrom (SW)
7 Jimmy Arias (USA)
8 Aaron Krickstein (USA)
9 Peter Lundgren (SW)
10 Hans Schwaier (G)

FEMALE
1 Helena Sukova (CZ)
2 Manuela Maleeva (BUL)
3 Steffi Graf (G)
4 Gabriela Sabatini (ARG)
5 Kathy Rinaldi (USA)
6 Carling Bassett (C)
7 Andrea Temesvari (HU)
8 Terry Phelps (USA)
9 Raffaella Reggi (IT)
10 Annabel Croft (GB)

THE ATP YEAR

Alexander McNab

The small word that best describes the big developments at the Association of Tennis Professionals (ATP) in 1985 is *new*. For during the year the men players' guild – in chronological order – granted a new two-year term to its executive director, launched a new two-week tournament in conjunction with the Women's Tennis Association, installed a new computer system, elected a new president and vice president, saw its executive director elected the new chairman of the Men's International Professional Tennis Council, moved into new offices, formulated a new drug-testing programme and watched a new name consolidate his position at the top of the weekly computer rankings.

It all began in January, when the ATP board of directors extended the contract of executive director Mike Davies for two years. Davies, the Welshman who was once Great Britain's No. 1 player, was named executive director in 1983. A month later came the inaugural Lipton International Players Championships in Delray Beach, Florida. The brainchild of former ATP executive director Butch Buchholz, the event was played over a two-week period, with 128-player singles draws for the men and women. Both players' associations own a 10 per cent share of the gross ticket and TV revenues.

The men's draw lacked two of the game's biggest drawing cards – John McEnroe, at the time the ATP's vice president, and Jimmy Connors. There were rain delays and a few other hitches, including an umpire who walked out on a match between Ivan Lendl and Larry Stefanki. Upsets were common, the surprise finalists being young Americans Scott Davis and Tim Mayotte, who came from behind to win in five sets of solid but unscintillating serve-and-volley tennis. In 1986, the Lipton tournament will move to Boca West, the spot it originally planned to call home, and in 1987 the peripatetic event will move again, to another site in nearby Fort Lauderdale.

The ATP gains more recognition for its weekly computer rankings than anything else. The association coordinates entries into all of the world's professional men's tournaments, then collects and tabulates all the results according to an arithmetic formula. This mammoth task used to take hours and hours but now, thanks to an advanced computer system designed and installed by Hewlett-Packard beginning in July, it takes just hours. The totally integrated programmes track entries, collate results and spew out rankings, points tables and statistics in far less time than previously. Moreover, the system can provide members of the tennis press corps with all kinds of fast data about players' records.

A month after the ATP began working with the new computer, two new officers were elected. Matt Doyle, a 27-year-old Yale graduate from Menlo Park, California, and the 1983 winner at Cologne, succeeded South African Ray Moore as president. Word among the players was that they wanted a president who was in the locker room and an active tour player while Moore, aged 39, was around the tournaments, but competed mainly on the over 35s tour. Moore, ATP president since 1983, retained his seat as one of three players' representatives on the Pro Council. His colleagues there were Davies and Harold Solomon, who was chosen to replace Stan Smith. Mats Wilander was elected ATP vice president, succeeding McEnroe, while the two other officers' slots stayed in familiar hands – Jim McManus as secretary and Mike Estep as treasurer.

A few weeks later Davies was elected chairman of the Pro Council, succeeding ITF president Philippe Chatrier, who had held the post since 1979. 'I think it's good for the players when they see an ATP person as chairman', Davies said. 'Philippe has been there for the last six years. Any player who came up during the last six years has seen the

Council under the same chairman.' The biggest challenge facing Davies in his new position, of course, is guiding the Pro Council through the litigious maze of suits and countersuits between it, its administrator Marshall Happer, and former chairman Chatrier, and adversaries Volvo, ProServ and International Management Group. As one wry tennis observer commented on the insanity of the sport's politics, mocking comedian Rodney Dangerfield, 'I went to a lawsuit and a tennis match broke out'.

After the US Open, the ATP moved its offices into a new brown tower just north of the Dallas–Fort Worth expressway in Arlington. The nerve centre of the men's pro game – the computer – is housed in one of the interior offices. Bright green letters and numbers on the black screens of the many brown-grey monitors define the ebb and flow of the world-wide caravan that is the men's pro tour. A room away, the ATP weekly newspaper, *International Tennis Weekly*, is produced. There may be no pro tournaments in Arlington, but the ATP operation there could be considered a mission control centre for the circuit.

The biggest news the ATP made in 1985 was the announcement of the drug-testing programme. In fact, the announcement was made by the Pro council in November, but only after the ATP had recommended it. The ATP claimed to be the first players' association in a major sport to sponsor the passage of a drug-testing programme enforced by the sport's governing body. The testing will be conducted at two of the two-week events in 1986 – the Lipton tournament, the French Open, Wimbledon and the US Open, while the 1987 Australian Open in January of that year will also be part of the rota of possible test sites.

All players in the two tournaments selected must submit to tests or face possible suspension. If a player's test is positive and he refuses treatment, he will also face possible suspension. The tests will be conducted by an independent expert named by the Pro Council and approved by the ATP, and will also be given to the Pro Council and ATP staffs. 'In the long run, (the testing) is good for tennis', said McEnroe.

When the year ended and the final computer rankings were released, the No. 1 spot was firmly in the hands of a new claimant to that pinnacle, Lendl. It was the first time that the Czech star had ended a season at the top of the computer printout. McEnroe, of course, was a dominant No. 1 as the season began, and by a quirk of computer-formula fortune, Lendl briefly ascended to the No. 1 spot for a week in August, following successive final-round *losses* to McEnroe in Stratton and Toronto. He regained the top spot in more legitimate fashion a few weeks later by defeating McEnroe in the US Open final, then consolidated his supremacy with big tournament victories in Sydney, Tokyo and London during the autumn.

ATP 'JAKS' AWARDS 1985

Player of the Year – Ivan Lendl
Doubles Team of the Year – Ken Flach and Robert Seguso
Newcomer of the Year – Jaime Yzaga
Most Improved Player of the Year – Boris Becker
Adidas Sportsmanship Award – Mats Wilander
Hewlett-Packard Computer Award – John McEnroe
Nabisco Grand Prix Points Trophy – Ivan Lendl
CF Humanitarian Award – Mrs Kay McEnroe
ATP Lifetime Achievement Award – Ted Tinling
ATP Media Service Award – Richard Evans

Most Improved Player of the Year was Jaime Yzaga of Peru, the only player to take a set off Lendl at the US Open. *(T. Hindley)*

ATP BOARD 1985–6

Ten ATP board members each serve two-year terms. At the elections held annually in London on the eve of Wimbledon, five places were voted upon resulting in the election of Colin Dowdeswell, Paul McNamee and Ray Moore (all of whom were existing members offering themselves for re-election), plus Harold Solomon and Brian Gottfried. Solomon had been President of ATP from 1980–83 and Moore has been holder of that post since then. Ferdi Taygan had offered himself for re-election but was unsuccessful, and José Higueras retired after his two-year spell. The five Board members whose terms will end in 1986 are Matt Doyle, Mike Estep, Carlos Kirmayr, John McEnroe and Mats Wilander. Of the top 150 members on the ATP Hewlett-Packard singles rankings and the top 100 members on the doubles rankings entitled to vote, 147 did so.

Officers were elected at a meeting in Cincinnati on 18 August. They are: President – Matt Doyle; Vice President – Mats Wilander; Secretary – Jim McManus (a post he has filled since 1977); Treasurer – Mike Estep (for the fourth successive year). Elected to represent ATP on the Men's International Professional Tennis Council were Moore, Solomon, and Michael Davies, the Executive Director who, in September, was elected President on the MIPTC for the first time.

ATP EXECUTIVE DIRECTORS: Jack Kramer, September 1972 – April 1975; Bob Briner, April 1975 – March 1980; 'Butch' Buchholz, March 1980 – Jan. 1982; Michael Davies, Jan. 1983–

HEWLETT-PACKARD ATP RANKINGS AND PRIZE MONEY 1985

In 1985 Hewlett-Packard became the official computer for ATP and WTA rankings. The following tables show year-end rankings in singles and doubles, together with the prize money won by each player ranked in the top 250 in singles and his ranking for the last ten years.

The Hewlett-Packard ATP singles and doubles rankings are based on points awarded for performances at all tournaments with at least $25,000 in prize money, where entry is based upon an approved system of merit, where the conditions laid down for the conduct of tournaments are observed and where there are at least 32 singles players and /or 16 doubles pairs in the draw(s). The level of prize money, the size of the draw and the strength of the field determine the rating a tournament receives, and there are bonus points to be won, on a graded scale, for beating a player ranked in the top 150. A player's ranking, updated weekly, is based upon his average number of points (total points divided by the number of tournaments played) over a moving 12-month period. Until he has played 12 tournaments his total is, nevertheless, divided by 12. Since 1984, when a player has completed 14 tournaments in a 52-week period the divisor becomes 13. After 15 tournaments it becomes 14 and so on until, after completing 27 tournaments (by which time the divisor has become 23), it increases by one more point for every tournament played.

PRIZE MONEY (includes Nabisco Masters in January 1986 and all Nabisco bonuses)
Only once before (in 1983) have three men all earned over $1 million in prize money in a season. The same three — Ivan Lendl ($1,963,074), John McEnroe ($1,455,611) and Mats Wilander ($1,069,697) — repeated that feat in 1985. This was the fourth year in a row that Lendl has passed the magic million mark, aided this time by the $800,000 top prize from the Nabisco Grand Prix bonus pool, but his career earnings of $8,306,592 since 1979 are still $650,096 short of McEnroe's $8,956,688 amassed since he turned professional in June 1978 after winning the NCAA Championships. The record for one season's earnings is still the $2,028,850, set by Lendl in 1982 when, from the lavish WCT circuit alone, he scooped $1,349,000.

The combined earnings of the top ten in 1985 were $8,106,698, a record which exceeds by $370,845 the previous best of $7,735,853 created in 1982. Two other records were set in 1985. Fifteen men earned over $300,000, one more than in 1982, and lower down 108 passed the $50,000 mark, two more than in 1982. The $100,000 barrier was broken by 53 players in 1985, the same number as in 1982.

Note: The prize money figures include earnings from tournaments, circuit bonuses and play-offs plus team events, where the entry is based purely on merit. They include WCT earnings but not rewards from *Davis Cup* ties, invitation tournaments, exhibitions and special events; nor do they include income from contracts or endorsements.

SINGLES	T'MENTS PLAYED	AVGE POINTS	1975	1976	1977	1978	1979	1980	1981	1982	1983	1984	PRIZE MONEY
1 I. Lendl (CZ)	15	165.66	—	—	—	74	20	6	2	3	2	3	$1,963,074
2 J. P. McEnroe (USA)	15	137.53	—	264	21	4	3	2	1	1	1	1	1,455,611
3 M. Wilander (SW)	18	105.12	—	—	—	—	—	283	69	7	4	4	1,069,697
4 J. S. Connors (USA)	14	88.36	1	1	1	1	2	3	3	2	3	2	562,336
5 S. Edberg (SW)	20	79.33	—	—	—	—	—	—	—	523	53	20	719,152
6 B. Becker (G)	20	70.47	—	—	—	—	—	—	—	—	564	65	617,757
7 Y. Noah (F)	19	64.12	—	—	305	49	25	23	12	9	5	10	394,881
8 A. Jarryd (SW)	19	61.12	—	—	—	—	—	182	100	60	19	6	534,822
9 M. Mecir (CZ)	16	51.40	—	—	—	—	—	—	—	215	101	60	245,774
10 K. Curren (USA)	15	48.64	—	—	—	—	—	272	81	20	6	15	235,057
11 J. Nystrom (SW)	21	44.89	—	—	—	—	—	440	73	167	27	11	389,772
12 T. Mayotte (USA)	18	43.94	—	—	387	436	422	171	30	29	16	44	360,842
13 P. Annacone (USA)	20	41.56	—	—	—	—	—	—	—	389	256	94	393,739
14 J. Kriek (USA)	21	41.16	—	—	278	27	35	18	13	12	15	13	303,247
15 A. Gomez (EC)	14	37.77	—	—	—	—	64	43	37	15	14	5	243,767

		T'MENTS PLAYED	AVGE POINTS	1975	1976	1977	1978	1979	1980	1981	1982	1983	1984	PRIZE MONEY
16	H. Leconte (F)	23	36.85	—	—	—	—	—	440	173	28	30	27	259,778
17	S. Davis (USA)	21	36.63	—	—	—	—	465	483	457	193	24	48	257,611
18	B. Gilbert (USA)	24	36.24	—	—	—	—	—	—	282	54	62	23	280,117
19	T. Smid (CZ)	27	34.96	—	154	67	36	28	24	31	23	17	16	394,460
20	M. Jaite (ARG)	19	34.12	—	—	—	—	—	—	—	862	156	54	164,491
21	J. Arias (USA)	21	29.95	—	—	—	—	—	272	81	20	6	14	172,976
22	H. Sundstrom (SW)	18	28.35	—	—	—	—	—	549	315	82	23	7	179,090
23	T. Tulasne (F)	25	26.41	—	—	—	—	—	113	52	98	83	52	171,454
24	E. Teltscher (USA)	11	26.25	—	239	106	42	27	10	8	14	13	9	109,872
25	J. Gunnarsson (SW)	22	26.05	—	—	—	—	392	274	104	143	100	47	152,043
26	D. Pate (USA)	24	25.95	—	—	—	—	—	—	662	203	130	31	177,521
27	P. Lundgren (SW)	11	25.75	—	—	—	—	—	—	—	—	—	276	50,097
28	G. Holmes (USA)	19	25.65	—	—	—	—	—	—	—	308	147	57	103,499
29	J. L. Clerc (ARG)	14	25.23	—	—	—	15	16	8	5	6	8	33	75,764
30	A. Krickstein (USA)	19	24.76	—	—	—	—	—	—	—	—	94	12	159,772
31	M. Anger (USA)	13	24.69	—	—	—	—	—	—	361	289	165	177	93,393
32	A. Maurer (G)	15	24.21	—	—	—	—	151	200	47	143	106	130	112,371
33	J. Hlasek (SWZ)	23	23.20	—	—	—	—	—	—	—	227	179	88	160,724
34	L. Pimek (CZ)	20	22.83	—	—	—	—	—	372	488	219	57	25	117,978
35	S. Zivojinovic (YU)	21	22.63	—	—	—	—	—	—	826	230	281	115	127,660
36	H. Gunthardt (SWZ)	19	22.53	—	203	221	55	52	27	38	85	26	32	254,707
37	M. Leach (USA)	18	22.12	—	—	—	—	—	372	396	143	92	96	104,883
38	S. Casal (SP)	13	21.38	—	—	—	—	—	—	174	159	73	177	103,718
39	G. Vilas (ARG)	14	20.38	2	6	2	3	6	5	6	4	11	28	57,834
40	R. Krishnan (IND)	21	19.79	373	360	414	136	179	53	66	100	84	24	114,596
41	S. Giammalva (USA)	20	19.11	—	—	—	—	—	189	58	79	68	46	112,301
42	J. Lloyd (GB)	21	18.95	93	61	33	66	146	356	225	197	77	37	120,205
43	B. Schultz (USA)	21	18.58	—	—	—	—	—	—	—	—	324	188	85,288
44	T. Wilkison (USA)	29	18.46	—	360	114	54	73	85	67	55	103	39	174,438
45	J. Yzaga (PER)	12	18.41	—	—	—	—	—	—	—	—	—	—	36,377
46	J. Sadri (USA)	26	18.17	—	360	414	84	30	16	48	32	120	30	120,049
47	H. Schwaier (G)	20	17.94	—	—	—	—	—	—	662	434	108	89	96,264
48	K. Carlsson (SW)	15	19.71	—	—	—	—	—	—	—	794	139		55,416
49	P. McNamee (AUS)	12	17.33	—	174	104	120	69	31	89	33	36	68	80,177
50	R. Agenor (HAITI)	16	17.00	—	—	—	—	—	—	—	—	793	416	46,538
51	M. Westphal (G)	16	16.33	—	—	—	—	—	—	662	205	126	73	50,723
52	M. Vajda (CZ)	17	16.25	—	—	—	—	—	—	—	—	201	195	46,160
53	Tom Gullikson (USA)	17	16.18	119	119	60	47	114	64	56	61	60	74	91,003
54	L. Stefanki (USA)	16	16.13	—	—	—	—	—	325	137	223	105	116	103,507
55	D. Perez (UR)	24	16.00	—	—	—	—	—	—	92	121	50	50	106,711
56	R. Seguso (USA)	9	15.50	—	—	—	—	—	—	—	—	146	208	394,908
57	R. Acuna (CH)	12	14.91	—	—	—	232	314	151	264	101	114	151	51,800
58	F. Cancellotti (IT)	16	14.73	—	—	—	—	—	—	415	267	72	26	56,498
59	L. Duncan (USA)	22	14.60	—	—	—	—	—	—	—	—	—	165	89,825
60	K. Flach (USA)	13	14.38	—	—	—	—	—	—	438	314	295	154	367,920
61	G. Forget (F)	21	14.32	—	—	—	—	—	—	—	70	188	36	85,677
62	W. Fibak (POL)	17	14.31	58	14	13	21	15	15	18	22	42	45	85,503
63	M. Davis (USA)	21	14.26	—	—	—	—	—	269	117	141	85	63	123,605
64	E. Sanchez (SP)	19	14.24	—	—	—	—	—	—	—	548	208	112	84,372
65	J. Brown (USA)	20	14.22	—	—	—	—	—	—	408	97	44	100	63,304
66	B. Teacher (USA)	16	14.06	109	81	54	31	61	12	16	18	29	51	56,300
67	P. Cash (AUS)	7	13.92	—	—	—	—	—	—	332	44	38	8	127,244
68	H. Pfister (USA)	10	13.58	252	101	148	29	40	75	25	34	34	87	47,300
69	R. Arguello (ARG)	21	13.57	—	—	—	—	—	365	148	743	49	126	36,854
70	H. de la Pena (ARG)	21	13.52	—	—	—	—	—	—	—	295	90		84,162
71	F. Maciel (MEX)	12	13.42	—	—	—	—	—	—	—	831	269	192	25,903
72	S. Perkis (IS)	19	13.41	—	—	—	—	—	510	509	616	295	75	79,215
73	J. Canter (USA)	18	13.41	—	—	—	—	—	—	—	279	201	239	60,096
74	M. Dickson (USA)	25	13.31	—	—	—	—	—	—	174	40	68	35	90,377

		T'MENTS PLAYED	AVGE POINTS	1975	1976	1977	1978	1979	1980	1981	1982	1983	1984	PRIZE MONEY
75	M. Ingaramo (ARG)	15	13.21	—	—	—	—	—	—	—	285	346	143	32,483
76	G. Michibata (C)	10	13.16	—	—	—	—	—	549	826	172	79	163	26,031
77	C. Steyn (SA)	15	13.14	—	—	—	—	—	—	767	616	177	221	40,775
78	V. Van Patten (USA)	14	12.92	—	—	—	374	44	40	28	48	110	103	50,497
79	J. Aguilera (SP)	16	12.80	—	—	—	—	—	—	225	227	64	19	62,426
80	V. Amritraj (IND)	16	12.80	26	31	46	58	34	20	21	382	144	42	65,412
81	V. Gerulaitis (USA)	15	12.50	15	18	4	5	4	9	9	5	20	17	78,050
82	B. Oresar (YU)	10	12.50	—	—	—	—	—	—	—	—	793	464	23,000
83	M. DePalmer (USA)	19	12.35	—	—	—	—	—	—	618	51	93	103	101,483
84	A. Mansdorf (IS)	17	12.13	—	—	—	—	—	—	—	—	259	268	45,153
85	D. Keretic (G)	17	12.13	—	—	—	—	—	237	138	69	210	142	39,389
86	L. Lavalle (MEX)	10	11.92	—	—	—	—	—	—	—	—	—	741	20,057
87	P. Arraya (PER)	19	11.82	—	—	—	—	—	309	90	36	41	56	37,216
88	B. Testerman (USA)	18	11.82	—	—	—	—	—	383	210	135	194	22	83,041
89	K. Evernden (NZ)	16	11.73	—	—	—	—	—	—	662	—	527	255	67,822
90	S. Youl (AUS)	11	11.67	—	—	—	—	—	—	—	450	153	201	31,856
91	J. Fitzgerald (AUS)	21	11.65	—	—	—	—	301	136	60	78	35	29	142,875
92	C. Panatta (IT)	17	11.56	—	—	—	—	—	482	153	76	71	123	84,805
93	M. Wostenholme (C)	13	11.54	—	—	—	—	—	549	—	329	723	186	24,902
94	P. Fleming (USA)	13	11.46	120	116	47	26	13	38	106	389	32	49	94,782
95	P. Slozil (CZ)	27	11.08	218	310	226	190	82	65	65	49	82	40	190,356
96	J. Goes (BR)	15	11.00	—	—	—	—	—	241	145	117	104	177	21,642
97	F. Segarceanu (RU)	11	10.83	—	—	—	—	—	—	215	125	81	209	25,138
98	T. Muster (AU)	18	10.82	—	—	—	—	—	—	—	—	—	309	34,339
99	J. Bates (GB)	17	10.81	—	—	—	—	—	372	341	329	256	185	34,114
100	M. Schapers (NTH)	20	10.78	—	—	—	—	—	594	300	223	107	78	50,284
101	W. Masur (AUS)	22	10.65	—	—	—	—	—	423	287	125	66	106	87,143
102	P. Doohan (AUS)	22	10.55	—	—	—	—	—	549	415	363	281	84	82,630
103	E. Bengoechea (ARG)	17	10.44	—	—	—	—	—	83	162	279	271	111	38,780
104	T. Moor (USA)	22	10.30	—	71	53	73	38	51	55	122	109	34	69,179
105	M. Flur (USA)	19	10.18	—	—	—	—	—	—	—	—	201	162	50,832
106	N. Odizor (NIG)	15	10.00	—	—	—	—	—	457	204	80	65	110	60,677
107	H. Solomon (USA)	11	9.83	17	8	14	9	8	7	22	66	285	222	21,156
108	V. Pecci (PARA)	22	9.70	55	34	39	46	11	35	17	68	55	38	71,122
109	F. Luna (SP)	16	9.67	—	—	250	340	90	70	79	62	52	70	44,132
110	R. Osterthun (G)	15	9.50	—	—	—	—	—	—	—	669	563	192	42,901
111	R. Green (USA)	24	9.43	—	—	—	—	—	—	—	450	369	40	65,354
112	C. Hooper (USA)	18	9.35	—	—	—	—	—	390	235	30	59	97	52,883
113	M. Edmondson (AUS)	10	9.33	212	35	99	79	72	102	20	24	39	145	120,591
114	B. Dyke (AUS)	10	9.33	—	—	—	—	—	—	306	179	141	292	44,362
115	R. Simpson (NZ)	11	9.33	183	143	120	100	131	76	120	50	97	123	33,526
116	G. Layendecker (USA)	14	9.31	—	—	—	—	—	—	—	—	391	176	46,823
117	S. Eriksson (SW)	13	9.31	—	—	—	—	—	—	—	—	—	306	22,094
118	C. Lewis (NZ)	12	9.17	—	127	151	40	63	66	32	57	25	101	45,896
119	J. Lopez-Maeso (SP)	17	9.06	—	—	—	—	—	118	78	154	219	195	35,851
120	L. Shiras (USA)	22	8.90	—	—	—	—	—	—	—	—	181	61	54,020
121	D. Cahill (USA)	15	8.86	—	—	—	—	—	—	—	831	—	247	32,218
122	J. B. Svensson (SW)	14	8.85	—	—	—	—	—	—	—	831	445	227	38,347
123	C. Kirmayr (BR)	9	8.83	103	119	120	78	60	62	40	53	128	606	17,061
124	G. Urpi (SP)	13	8.69	—	—	—	496	181	115	181	248	135	181	27,108
125	B. Moir (SA)	8	8.67	—	—	—	—	—	752	660	340	292		15,289
126	J. Potier (F)	9	8.67	—	—	—	—	—	—	116	—	301	—	12,380
127	M. Woodforde (AUS)	9	8.67	—	—	—	—	—	—	—	—	661	385	13,897
128	W. Popp (G)	19	8.59	—	—	—	—	—	—	322	310	353	282	46,483
129	M. Purcell (USA)	10	8.59	—	—	—	555	245	28	26	27	28	66	29,060

		T'MENTS PLAYED	AVGE POINTS	1975	1976	1977	1978	1979	1980	1981	1982	1983	1984	PRIZE MONEY
130	E. Edwards (SA)	16	8.47	—	427	250	268	228	106	170	171	129	92	62,475
131	G. Ocleppo (IT)	14	8.46	308	211	212	108	31	94	77	151	46	107	31,752
132	R. Saad (ARG)	15	833	—	—	—	—	—	—	438	617	783	344	31,479
133	T. Benhabiles (F)	28	8.29	—	—	—	—	—	—	—	616	275	71	57,994
134	C. Mezzadri (IT)	15	8.29	—	—	—	—	—	—	—	831	259	150	25,491
135	C. Motta (BR)	15	8.29	—	—	—	—	—	255	232	86	80	109	42,394
136	A. Chesnokov (USSR)	6	8.25	—	—	—	—	—	—	—	—	—	287	15,469
137	G. Prpic (YU)	12	8.08	—	—	—	—	—	—	—	668	563	218	18,698
138	F. Gonzalez (PARA)	18	8.06	308	272	212	61	81	74	98	114	112	83	55,604
139	J. Soares (BR)	12	8.00	—	—	—	—	—	194	101	96	184	147	29,459
140	N. Aerts (BR)	16	7.94	—	—	—	—	—	—	826	399	235	398	21,186
141	P. Rebolledo (CH)	12	7.92	—	—	—	555	301	125	43	129	133	99	12,156
142	J. Avendano (SP)	18	7.89	—	—	—	—	—	269	207	93	127	174	29,853
143	D. Visser (SA)	22	7.75	—	—	—	—	—	—	370	138	135	72	60,921
144	B. Drewett (AUS)	22	7.75	—	193	187	133	89	115	133	116	70	80	67,763
145	H. Gildemeister (CH)	17	7.69	308	193	43	39	14	33	29	35	134	59	57,573
146	C. Kist (BR)	16	7.67	—	—	—	—	—	—	—	—	455	199	13,670
147	C. Di Laura (PER)	8	7.58	—	—	—	—	—	—	571	451	239	344	7,729
148	D. De Miguel (SP)	10	7.50	—	—	—	—	—	—	—	—	—	210	18,125
149	J. Lapidus (USA)	25	7.32	—	—	—	272	184	283	126	39	503	64	56,948
150	J. Fleurian (F)	14	7.31	—	—	—	—	—	—	—	—	—	—	7,334
151	E. Masso (ARG)	13	7.31	—	—	—	—	—	—	—	—	—	292	10,977
152	Tim Gullikson (USA)	11	7.25	172	113	28	18	26	40	50	150	40	108	45,494
153	J. Arrese (SP)	14	7.23	—	—	—	—	—	—	—	831	503	213	24,307
154	H. Van Boeckel (NTH)	17	7.13	—	—	—	—	—	—	—	349	231	143	38,735
155	A. Stepanek (G)	10	7.08	—	—	—	—	—	—	—	—	—	673	1,552
156	M. Oosting (NTH)	14	7.08	—	—	—	—	—	—	—	668	431	344	17,766
157	B. Taroczy (HU)	17	6.94	69	32	32	20	45	19	15	26	51	43	163,167
158	K. Novacek (CZ)	12	6.83	—	—	—	—	—	—	—	—	445	156	16,941
159	T. Nelson (USA)	17	6.81	—	—	—	—	—	—	826	423	206	98	34,810
160	M. Hennemann (BR)	16	6.81	—	—	—	—	—	—	—	—	722	317	11,519
161	S. Simonsson (SW)	19	6.76	—	—	232	340	237	142	144	105	61	121	38,218
162	D. Campos (BR)	17	6.75	—	—	—	—	—	—	662	435	—	276	26,279
163	H. P. Kandler (AU)	12	6.58	—	—	—	—	—	—	207	307	173	370	13,944
164	M. Pernfors (SW)	8	6.58	—	—	—	—	—	—	—	—	—	434	17,155
165	M. Ostoja (YU)	18	6.53	—	—	—	—	—	203	172	156	96	127	36,481
166	J. Carlsson (SW)	8	6.50	—	—	—	—	—	—	—	—	186	245	12,028
167	S. Glickstein (IS)	17	6.44	—	—	—	—	153	57	33	38	43	82	64,557
168	J. Higueras (SP)	12	6.42	46	42	30	14	9	32	36	11	7	21	31,098
169	M. Srejber (CZ)	9	6.42	—	—	—	—	—	—	—	—	793	334	11,459
170	M. Robertson (SA)	11	6.42	—	—	—	—	—	—	826	424	563	434	26,230
171	G. Barbosa (BR)	23	6.40	—	—	—	—	—	356	315	110	186	84	47,936
172	R. Viver (EC)	20	6.33	—	—	—	—	—	325	300	279	214	166	26,626
173	P. Elter (G)	16	6.33	—	310	158	114	119	110	73	81	155	114	26,171
174	V. Wilder (USA)	4	6.25	—	—	—	—	—	—	—	—	—	—	—
175	R. Knapp (USA)	10	6.25	—	—	—	—	—	431	—	—	—	228	12,285
176	J. Frawley (AUS)	24	6.24	—	—	—	—	—	—	—	294	162	67	53,937
177	S. Bonneau (C)	11	6.17	—	—	—	—	—	—	344	743	377	273	10,207
178	M. Mitchell (USA)	22	6.15	—	—	196	220	105	239	180	110	122	53	66,815
179	G. Rivas (ARG)	14	6.08	—	—	—	—	—	—	—	831	603	156	19,820
180	W. Scanlon (USA)	13	6.00	—	52	37	95	43	26	35	71	12	55	23,913
181	J. Navratil (CZ)	20	5.94	—	—	—	—	—	302	191	169	191	93	44,486
182	B. Pils (AU)	11	5.92	—	—	—	—	—	—	246	199	212	266	11,602
183	A. Kohlberg (USA)	11	5.92	—	—	—	—	—	—	225	211	343	218	31,564
184	M. Bauer (USA)	22	5.85	—	—	—	—	—	667	195	89	56	58	51,677
185	G. Muller (SA)	9	5.83	—	—	—	--	—	—	—	—	—	385	10,576

Seeded 8 at Wimbledon, where he beat McEnroe (seed 1) and Connors (seed 3), Kevin Curren lost a golden chance to win a first Grand Slam title when Becker's powerful serve destroyed his confidence.   *(T. Hindley)*

	T'MENTS PLAYED	AVGE POINTS	1975	1976	1977	1978	1979	1980	1981	1982	1983	1984	PRIZE MONEY
186 K. Moir (SA)	10	5.83	—	—	—	—	—	—	752	668	340	292	4,841
187 B. Willenborg (USA)	14	5.77	—	—	—	—	—	283	344	—	235	79	37,562
188 P. Carlsson (SW)	13	5.77	—	—	—	—	—	—	—	273	177	236	13,041
189 T. Champion (F)	8	5.75	—	—	—	—	—	—	—	—	—	434	6,858
190 L. Bourne (USA)	16	5.73	—	—	—	555	336	292	156	73	122	95	39,167
191 T. Meinecke (G)	13	5.69	—	—	—	—	—	—	—	—	602	292	15,606
192 E. Jelen (G)	7	5.58	—	—	—	—	—	—	—	450	250	166	8,301
193 A. El Mehelmy (EG)	9	5.58	—	—	—	—	—	—	826	743	793	451	8,979
194 M. Wooldridge (USA)	14	5.54	—	—	—	—	—	—	662	839	527	184	20,043
195 S. Shaw (GB)	19	5.53	—	—	—	—	—	—	—	669	445	119	37,226
196 T. Allan (AUS)	16	5.47	—	—	—	—	—	—	153	358	153	69	31,519
197 P. Cane (IT)	10	5.42	—	—	—	—	—	—	—	—	353	552	19,856
198 J. Windahl (SW)	6	5.25	—	—	—	—	—	—	467	186	271	302	3,466
199 G. Guerrero (ARG)	9	5.25	—	—	—	—	—	—	253	338	390	317	8,536
200 M. Hocevar (BR)	10	5.25	—	—	—	404	254	50	142	37	142	133	15,750
201 J. Gurfein (USA)	10	5.17	—	—	—	—	—	219	159	118	135	207	11,000
202 A. De Minicis (IT)	21	5.16	—	—	—	—	—	—	752	504	466	236	26,174
203 E. Martins (BR)	13	5.08	—	—	—	—	—	—	408	408	353	210	6,833
204 A. Ganzabal (ARG)	18	5.00	—	—	—	—	—	215	191	92	166	62	29,643
205 M. Kratzman (AUS)	5	5.00	—	—	—	—	—	—	—	616	340	245	13,348
206 T. Hogstedt (SW)	11	5.00	—	—	—	—	371	549	240	88	63	86	20,507
207 C. Pistolesi (IT)	7	4.92	—	—	—	—	—	—	—	—	—	—	8,914
208 R. Reininger (AU)	11	4.92	—	—	—	—	—	325	195	182	259	351	6,814
209 C. Miller (AUS)	14	4.85	—	—	—	—	—	232	251	102	281	191	21,705
210 T. Cain (USA)	13	4.85	—	—	—	—	—	219	382	106	118	182	17,265
211 U. Riglewski (G)	10	4.83	—	—	—	—	—	—	—	—	390	398	7,605
212 B. Derlin (NZ)	13	4.77	—	—	—	—	—	510	171	193	222	135	16,372
213 D. Tarr (SA)	9	4.75	—	—	—	—	—	383	200	133	115	160	12,653
214 S. Bale (GB)	12	4.07	—	—	—	—	—	—	—	—	282		16,893
215 T. Warneke	5	4.67	—	—	—	—	—	—	—	—	—	327	9,321
216 P. Portes (F)	7	4.67	—	—	365	106	101	61	88	254	289	140	19,249
217 D. Cassidy (USA)	19	4.59	—	—	—	—	—	—	509	398	409	76	42,670
218 T. Witsken (USA)	5	4.58	—	—	—	—	—	—	—	—	—	673	7,213
219 I. Kley (BR)	22	4.50	—	—	—	—	—	549	233	431	173	128	35,961
220 B. Dickinson (USA)	8	4.50	—	—	—	—	—	—	—	504	794	434	9,343
221 M. Buckley (USA)	11	4.50	—	—	—	—	—	—	408	369	322	416	6,404
222 M. Cierro (IT)	14	4.46	—	—	—	—	—	—	—	—	603	210	18,550
223 C. Limberger (AUS)	15	4.43	—	—	—	—	—	—	—	—	—	137	23,321
224 J. Rodriguez (SP)	9	4.42	—	—	—	—	—	—	450	240	661	202	14,026
225 J. Bardou (SP)	11	4.42	—	—	—	—	—	—	—	—	—	202	12,319
226 H. McDadi (C)	12	4.25	—	—	—	—	—	—	—	—	661	309	4,359
227 A. Tous (SP)	12	4.25	—	—	—	—	—	—	396	91	195	103	25,034
228 S. Birner (CZ)	12	4.25	—	—	236	157	87	153	63	160	159	182	19,766
229 T. Mmoh (NIG)	9	4.25	—	—	—	—	—	—	—	—	409	375	14,117
230 L. Mattar (BR)	9	4.25	—	—	—	—	—	—	—	—	—	741	5,511
231 M. Doyle (USA)	9	4.25	—	—	—	—	—	249	82	107	99	138	16,395
232 A. Dirzu (RU)	3	4.17	—	—	—	—	—	403	450	415	794	464	2,586
233 C. Castellan (ARG)	7	4.17	—	—	—	—	—	180	179	159	135	171	3,773
234 C. Campbell (SA)	9	4.17	—	—	—	—	—	—	826	669	331	292	2,643
235 T. Nijssen (NTH)	9	4.17	—	—	—	—	—	—	—	—	603	268	8,354
236 A. Antonitsch (AU)	10	4.17	—	—	—	—	—	—	826	831	—	741	11,637
237 F. Roese (BR)	12	4.08	—	—	—	—	—	—	571	258	274	233	9,224
238 R. Nixon (USA)	11	4.08	—	—	—	—	—	—	—	—	391	216	10,128
239 S. Denton (USA)	11	3.92	—	—	—	226	249	403	24	13	58	149	56,929
240 R. Rivera (ARG)	5	3.83	—	—	—	—	—	309	295	267	382	464	343
241 R. Bathman (SW)	10	3.83	—	—	—	—	—	—	662	450	327	370	9,505
242 O. Rahnasto (FIN)	11	3.83	—	—	—	—	—	—	—	314	382	250	6,843

		T'MENTS PLAYED	AVGE POINTS	1974	1975	1976	1977	1978	1979	1980	1981	1982	1983	PRIZE MONEY
243	M. Freeman (USA)	12	3.75	—	—	—	—	—	335	415	343	119	117	23,750
244	L. Jensen (USA)	5	3.75	—	—	—	—	—	—	—	—	—	—	8,339
245	C. Pridham (USA)	6	3.75	—	—	—	—	—	—	—	—	723	464	1,619
246	D. Mustard (NZ)	8	3.75	—	—	—	—	323	344	215	247	170	168	20,755
247	P. McNamara (AUS)	8	3.75	205	193	181	65	48	29	10	10	22	741	29,155
248	L. Bottazzi (IT)	11	3.67	—	—	—	—	—	—	467	349	247	156	12,906
249	J. Berger (USA)	2	3.58	—	—	—	—	—	—	—	—	—	—	13,424
250	J. Grabb (USA)	5	3.58	—	—	—	—	—	—	—	—	—	313	13,200
251	A. Andrews (USA)	7	3.58	—	—	—	—	—	440	215	103	205	195	10,456
252	C. Van Rensburg (SA)	11	3.58	—	—	—	—	—	—	—	548	289	120	231,132

Players who have won more than $1 Million in prize money

1	John McEnroe	$8,956,688	25	Heinz Gunthardt	$1,417,544
2	Ivan Lendl	8,306,592	26	Sherwood Stewart	1,402,915
3	Jimmy Connors	6,815,348	27	José Higueras	1,401,187
4	Guillermo Vilas	5,036,347	28	Manuel Orantes	1,398,303
5	Bjorn Borg	3,607,116	29	Mark Edmondson	1,384,917
6	Mats Wilander	3,281,765	30	Gene Mayer	1,380,531
7	Brian Gottfried	2,781,871	31	Brian Teacher	1,374,969
8	Vitas Gerulaitis	2,764,909	32	Eliot Teltscher	1,374,372
9	Tomas Smid	2,647,404	33	Kevin Curren	1,339,761
10	Wojtek Fibak	2,623,128	34	Balazs Taroczy	1,308,258
11	Raul Ramirez	2,213,581	35	Tom Okker	1,257,200
12	Ilie Nastase	2,068,399	36	Bill Scanlon	1,226,094
13	Eddie Dibbs	2,016,426	37	Vijay Amritraj	1,218,901
14	José-Luis Clerc	1,969,398	38	John Alexander	1,214,079
15	Harold Solomon	1,782,158	39	Anders Jarryd	1,212,999
16	Stan Smith	1,777,618	40	Bob Lutz	1,162,463
17	Johan Kriek	1,748,496	41	Tim Gullikson	1,102,888
18	Peter Fleming	1,730,344	42	Dick Stockton	1,061,773
19	Roscoe Tanner	1,696,108	43	Alexander Mayer	1,056,641
20	Ken Rosewall	1,600,300	44	Paul McNamee	1,054,526
21	Arthur Ashe	1,584,909	45	Peter McNamara	1,022,641
22	Rod Laver	1,564,213	46	Steve Denton	1,020,808
23	Yannick Noah	1,520,637	47	Jimmy Arias	1,015,782
24	Andres Gomez	1,449,584			

DOUBLES

		T'MENTS PLAYED	AVGE POINTS			T'MENTS PLAYED	AVGE POINTS
1	R. Seguso (USA)	22	65.76	15	K. Warwick (AUS)	29	38.43
2	K. Flach (USA)	21	65.38	16	S. Davis (USA)	20	36.61
3	A. Jarryd (SW)	18	65.12	17	A. Gomez (EC)	14	35.92
4	M. Wilander (SW)	16	53.07	18	P. Cash (AUS)	5	34.58
5	P. Annacone (USA)	21	51.26	19	P. Fleming (USA)	11	34.33
6	S. Edberg (SW)	13	47.46	20	P. Slozil (CZ)	27	33.08
7	H. Gunthardt (SWZ)	19	46.35	21	D. Pate (USA)	17	31.94
8	C. Van Rensberg (SA)	26	44.20	22	H. Leconte (F)	13	31.77
9	J. Nystrom (SW)	19	43.70	23	G. Forget (F)	13	29.08
10	B. Taroczy (HU)	18	41.59	24	P. McNamee (AUS)	13	28.85
11	T. Smid (CZ)	26	39.43	25	S. Casal (SP)	21	27.79
12	J. Fitzgerald (AUS)	21	39.30	26	H. Simonsson (SW)	15	27.71
13	Y. Noah (F)	14	38.92	27	E. Sanchez (SP)	25	26.50
14	M. Edmondson (AUS)	21	38.47	28	K. Curren (USA)	11	24.92

		T'MENTS PLAYED	AVGE POINTS			T'MENTS PLAYED	AVGE POINTS
29	M. DePalmer (USA)	26	23.91	65	M. Mitchell (USA)	22	14.60
30	H. Gildemeister (CH)	16	23.87	66	E. Teltscher (USA)	9	14.42
31	P. McNamara (AUS)	12	23.25	67	J. Lloyd (GB)	15	14.20
32	J. Kriek (USA)	15	23.00	68	D. Dowlen (USA)	17	14.13
33	S. Stewart (USA)	12	22.92	69	C. Dowdeswell (GB)	16	14.06
34	J. McEnroe (USA)	4	22.92	70	Tim Gullikson (USA)	18	13.94
35	B. Becker (G)	16	22.27	71	R. Acuna (CH)	17	13.88
36	S. Glickstein (IS)	16	21.87	72	M. Robertson (SA)	19	13.29
37	W. Fibak (POL)	18	21.59	73	B. Testerman (USA)	18	13.18
38	S. Zivojinovic (YU)	17	21.19	74	M. Tideman (SW)	13	13.15
39	S. Giammalva (USA)	19	20.94	75	I. Kley (BR)	25	12.95
40	G. Donnelly	26	20.28	76	T. Nijssen (NTH)	12	12.83
41	R. Van't Hof (USA)	15	19.43	77	C. Dunk (USA)	14	12.61
42	I. Lendl (CZ)	13	19.23	78	E. Edwards (USA)	15	12.43
43	W. Masur (AUS)	19	19.18	79	M. Dickson (USA)	21	12.32
44	P. Cane (IT)	13	19.15	80	C. Motta (BR)	17	12.25
45	A. Mayer (USA)	5	17.83	81	A. Mansdorf (IS)	10	12.17
46	S. Meister (USA)	21	17.62	82	T. Warneke (USA)	10	11.92
47	J. Hlasek (SWZ)	20	17.44	83	G. Barbosa (BR)	24	11.81
48	V. Gerulaitis (USA)	12	17.42	84	C. Hooper (USA)	12	11.58
49	S. Denton (USA)	17	17.31	85	V. Amritraj (IND)	11	11.50
50	N. Odizor (NIG)	14	17.30	86	C. Kirmayr (BR)	9	11.42
51	M. Mortensen (DEN)	20	17.22	87	H. Pfister (USA)	14	11.00
52	T. Wilkison (USA)	29	16.77	88	B. Manson (USA)	10	10.92
53	P. Doohan (AUS)	21	16.68	89	D. Visser (USA)	19	10.83
54	L. Pimek (CZ)	18	16.65	90	L. Warder (AUS)	23	10.75
55	B. Gilbert (USA)	18	16.18	91	E. Fernandez (PR)	15	10.71
56	C. Panatta (IT)	15	16.07	92	J. Soares (BR)	17	10.56
57	V. Pecci (PARA)	19	15.94	93	B. Levine (USA)	13	10.46
58	Tom Gullikson (USA)	16	15.73	94	J. Bates (GB)	13	10.38
59	B. Willenborg (USA)	17	15.63	95	S. Colombo (IT)	12	10.17
60	S. Perkis (IS)	12	15.33	96	D. Felgate (GB)	12	10.17
61	B. Drewett (AUS)	21	15.26	97	P. Svensson (SW)	15	10.07
62	A. Kohlberg (USA)	14	14.85	98	Z. Kuharszky (SWZ)	17	9.94
63	B. Dyke (AUS)	22	14.80	99	D. Graham (AUS)	33	9.94
64	J. Gunnarsson (SW)	20	14.78	100	R. Bathman (SW)	13	9.85

THE WTA YEAR

Jim Bainbridge

Even those who opposed him have to concede that the Women's Tennis Association would not have earned its pre-eminent position in women's sports without Jerry Diamond, and that the WTA will be a much different entity without his presence. After 11 years as the organisation's executive director, the 57-year-old Diamond stepped down on 31 December, to be replaced by former Dade County Manager, Merrett Stierheim. Diamond's hard-nosed business practices and blunt talk eearned him his share of antagonists, but that never bothered him much. The job came first. From early 1974 when he took over as the WTA's second executive director, prize-money on the women's professional tour has risen from less than $1 million to more than $14 million worldwide. He negotiated equal prize money at the US Open and 128-player draws both there and at Wimbledon. He brought in the multi-million dollar sponsorship contracts from Avon, Colgate and Virginia Slims, and he generated additional income by selling endorsements for everything from the WTA's official shoe to an official snackfood.

Apart from making tennis the most lucrative sport in the world for women, all this money allowed the WTA truly to professionalise the circuit. Starting from a point when there was only Diamond, administrative director Grenn Nemhauser, and a secretary in the San Francisco headquarters, the WTA grew to include tour directors, trainers, public relations reps — a full-time staff of 28. By 1983 it was operating a second office in Florida and a European bureau in Marbella, Spain. WTA members now have medical coverage and disability insurance, and in 1985 the WTA Board of Directors created a Health /Medical Committee to help educate members on ways to prevent injury and improve medical care on tour. The WTA has become both a multi-million dollar corporation and a benevolent labour union.

The major business step in Diamond's final year was the adjustment that will make the Virginia Slims Championship Series coincide with the calendar year. There will be two World Championship events in 1986, the first, in March, concluding the 1985 Series, and the second, in November, providing the finale of an abbreviated 1986 Series. The Series will then run from January to November, with the World Championships at Madison Square Garden in New York City. The switch was made with the agreement of the WTA, Virginia Slims and the Women's International Professional Tennis Council (WIPTC) in order to eliminate confusion among the public or media, and also to create a six-week holiday break for the players. During this transition year there will be no Australian Open for women. Having moved from its traditional position at the end of December into January, it will be the first Grand Slam event of the 1987 season. Overall there will be 54 Virginia Slims Series events this year as opposed to 57 in 1985, but the prize money will remain constant at $11,850,000.

In terms of historical significance, the amended Series calendar shared top billing in 1985 with the controversial new rules adopted by the WIPTC concerning the eligibility of players aged 18 or under. An eight-point plan was adopted, incorporating some aspects of proposals offered by the WTA and the International Tennis Federation, intended to form a practical solution to the problems of physical and mental burn-out experienced by teenage players participating in women's tennis. The eligibility restriction is simply the most dramatic example of the growing trend within the WTA to stand as protector and educator for its members.

With the departure of Diamond and the decision to close the San Francisco office, the WTA lost several other long-time employees who were unwilling to make the move 3,000 miles east to Palm Beach, Florida. This group was headed by Nemhauser, the only

WTA employee who had worked for the players' association longer than Diamond, public relations man Joe Page and Michael Kay, managing editor of the WTA newsletter, *Inside Women's Tennis*. Over her 12-year career Nemhauser had become one of the most effective executives in tennis, dealing with every facet of the WTA operation. In initial discussions about how to replace her, it was decided to hire two full-time people and a part-timer to handle the work she had done alone.

By Stierheim's own analysis the WTA operation he inherited is 'in better financial shape than it has been in years', and will benefit further from the consolidation of offices that was completed in January. The agenda that awaits him will likewise serve to consolidate the WTA's gains. The immediate goals are to change the perception that the WTA is strictly an American association, to develop an effective working relationship with the men's Association of Tennis Professionals (ATP), and to create a stronger secondary circuit for the emerging player. The intention is to create more opportunities and allow the developing player the chance to play in the big-money events as soon as her computer ranking was strong enough. Stierheim is committed to meeting with the players frequently to gain a clear picture of how the membership feels about these issues and others that affect the future of the women's game.

'There has been some discussion of reducing the size of the draw in some Slims events to make things easier to manage', says Stierheim. 'Building a strong developmental circuit is one of our primary goals . . . to keep the women's game strong.'

WTA BOARD 1985–6

At the WTA meeting held in New York on the eve of the US Open, Chris Evert Lloyd was re-elected President for a third consecutive year and for the fourth time in all (she had first held the office in 1975–6). The three other office-holders were also re-elected – Kim Shaefer as Vice-President, Marcella Mesker as Secretary and Lele Forood as Treasurer. Two new members, Alycia Mouton and Christiane Jolissaint, were elected to serve on the WTA Board, joining existing members Martina Navratilova, Barbara Jordan, Candy Reynolds, Pam Shriver, JoAnne Russell and Nancy Yeargin. The three delegates elected to represent the WTA on the Women's International Professional Tennis Council were Candy Reynolds, Executive Director Jerry Diamond, and Director of Operations Peachy Kellmeyer, with Director of Player Services Trish Falkener and Lele Forood as Alternates.

The Executive Committee includes the four officers plus Martina Navratilova and Candy Reynolds and there are seven working committees which are, together with their Chairpersons: Disciplinary (Jolissaint); Finance /Marketing (Forood); Goals (John Carroll); Health and Medical (Dr Gary Wadler); International (Mesker); Ranking (Mesker); Tournament (Moulton).

On 30 September, 1985 it was announced that Mr Merrett R. Stierheim, the former Manager for Metropolitan Dade County, Florida, would be replacing Mr Jerry Diamond as the Excutive Director of the WTA from 3 January, 1986.

WTA ANNUAL AWARDS

At the Gala Dinner in aid of the March of Dimes held annually at the Waldorf Astoria Hotel, New York, at the start of the US Open, the following awards were presented based on members' votes:

Most Impressive Newcomer – Gabriela Sabatini
Most Improved Player – Helena Sukova
Writer of the Year – Peter Bodo and Bob Greene
Broadcaster of the Year – Mary Carillo
Player Service Award – Chris Evert Lloyd
David Gray Special Service Award – Ann Haydon Jones
Karen Krantzcke Sportsmanship Award – Peanut Louie
Doubles Team of the Year – Martina Navratilova and Pam Shriver
Player of the Year – Martina Navratilova
A sum of almost $95,000 was presented to the March of Dimes.

HEWLETT-PACKARD WTA RANKINGS AND PRIZE MONEY 1985

The following lists show the WTA singles and doubles rankings, compiled by Hewlett-Packard, as they were on 31 December, 1985. In the past, the rankings have been published at the end of the Virginia Slims season which ends in March. Similarly, the prize money shown is the amount earned to the end of 1985 and, therefore, does not include the bonus payments from the Virginia Slims tour which are not distributed until March. In 1986 the tour is being re-structured so that a reduced circuit will end with the Virginia Slims Championships in November, and from 1987 onwards the full tour will fit into the calendar year.

PRIZE MONEY

The earnings of the leading women players in 1985 remained impressively high – despite the fact that the Virginia Slims bonuses are not included – which indicates the growth of the women's game. For the fourth year in a row Martina Navratilova won more than $1 million in prize money. Although her $1,328,829 is $844,727 lower than the world record of $2,173,556 she set in 1984, that impressive total had included $1 million from the ITF for winning the 'modern' Grand Slam, as well as prize money from the last quarter of the Virginia Slims tour and the season-end bonuses. In real terms, therefore, her performance in 1985 was better than it had been the year before. The combined earnings of the top ten in 1985 were $5,056,713, which is only $76,259 below the 1984 full-season figure. Eight women exceeded $200,000 in earnings, one more than in 1984, but the 22 who broke the $100,000 barrier were one fewer than the previous year. Lower down, too, there were fewer who reached the $50,000 plateau – 52 in 1985 and 54 in 1984. Undoubtedly, however, all these figures would have been exceeded if the true comparison had been made with the extra tournaments and bonus payments included.

Note: The prize money figures include earnings at all recognised tournaments which adopt the WTA guidelines and where entry is based upon merit. They also include earnings from bonus pools, circuit prizes and recognised team events but do not include income from special events, invitation tournaments, exhibitions or product endorsements.

SINGLES

		T'MENTS	POINTS	PRIZE MONEY
1	Martina Navratilova (USA)	17	191.32	$1,328,829
2	Chris Evert Lloyd (USA)	18	175.02	972,782
3	Hana Mandlikova (CZ)	17	103.19	579,847
4	Pam Shriver (USA)	18	89.76	419,686
5	Claudia Kohde-Kilsch (G)	20	87.52	398,120
6	Steffi Graf (G)	13	77.73	168,212
7	Manuela Maleeva (BUL)	19	70.83	271,271
8	Zina Garrison (USA)	20	69.60	274,470
9	Helena Sukova (CZ)	21	65.61	422,387
10	Bonnie Gadusek (USA)	16	61.05	170,700
11	Kathy Rinaldi (USA)	17	57.06	191,750
12	Gabriela Sabatini (ARG)	19	51.56	138,313
13	Catarina Lindqvist (SW)	19	48.44	168,022
14	Wendy Turnbull (AUS)	18	41.60	170,120
15	Carling Bassett (C)	18	39.72	197,591
16	Andrea Temesvari (HU)	13	34.40	101,346
17	Barbara Potter (USA)	17	33.91	128,060
18	Stephanie Rehe (USA)	14	33.28	68,539
19	Kathy Jordan (USA)	15	33.15	184,384

		T'MENTS	POINTS	PRIZE MONEY
20	Anne White (USA)	12	24.55	85,053
21	Sylvia Hanika (G)	15	22.81	51,695
22	Peanut Louie (USA)	19	22.16	73,883
23	Bettina Bunge (G)	17	21.91	90,312
24	Annabel Croft (GB)	21	20.13	69,933
25	Kate Gompert (USA)	14	19.95	32,000
26	Jo Durie (GB)	19	19.57	68,395
27	Elise Burgin (USA)	24	19.49	102,943
28	Katerina Maleeva (BUL)	23	18.88	101,645
29	Terry Phelps (USA)	22	18.70	74,788
30	Dianne Balestrat (AUS)	19	18.06	48,288
31	Eva Pfaff (G)	11	18.04	38,122
32	Robin White (USA)	19	17.84	82,985
33	Christiane Jolissaint (SWZ)	18	17.83	57,992
34	Pam Casale (USA)	20	17.77	67,027
35	Alycia Moulton (USA)	18	17.27	87,175
36	Lisa Bonder (USA)	22	16.94	75,324
37	Debbie Spence (USA)	19	16.92	48,639
38	Rosalyn Fairbank (SA)	23	16.72	106,646
39	Catherine Tanvier (F)	16	16.40	62,174
40	Anne Hobbs (GB)	13	16.03	56,705
41	Virginia Ruzici (RU)	20	15.86	66,154
42	Raffaella Reggi (IT)	22	15.86	56,099
43	Elizabeth Smylie (AUS)	19	15.60	171,469
44	Molly Van Nostrand (USA)	16	14.99	45,397
45	Betsy Nagelsen (USA)	13	14.65	84,049
46	Pascale Paradis (F)	21	14.42	62,677
47	Susan Mascarin (USA)	23	14.37	48,820
48	Helen Kelesi (C)	21	14.11	29,164
49	Sandra Cecchini (IT)	21	13.57	63,365
50	Kathleen Horvath (USA)	19	13.33	84,584
51	Carina Karlsson (SW)	23	12.85	46,329
52	Tine Scheuer-Larsen (D)	18	11.93	41,635
53	Ann Henricksson (USA)	22	11.86	51,890
54	Sabrina Goles (YU)	20	11.82	49,881
55	Larisa Savchenko (USSR)	17	11.77	44,750
56	Michelle Torres (USA)	15	11.66	31,035
57	Iva Budarova (CZ)	24	11.51	44,335
58	Lilian Drescher (SWZ)	17	11.49	32,609
59	Kim Shaefer (USA)	20	11.48	40,573
60	Grace Kim (USA)	27	10.79	38,335
61	Mary Lou Piatek (USA)	18	10.62	53,301
62	Camille Benjamin (USA)	29	10.45	75,248
63	Laura Arraya Gildemeister (PER)	23	10.00	48,997
64	Gigi Fernandez (USA)	18	9.77	92,707
65	Anna Ivan (USA)	8	9.70	11,664
66	Linda Gates (USA)	15	9.52	28,672
67	Candy Reynolds (USA)	13	9.34	49,937
68	Caroline Kuhlman (USA)	11	9.13	20,335
69	Marcella Mesker (NTH)	20	9.12	75,114
70	Belinda Cordwell (NZ)	17	8.92	28,900
71	Mima Jausovec (YU)	13	8.79	30,056
72	Anne Minter (AUS)	25	8.72	54,053
73	Petra Huber (AU)	15	8.56	23,449
74	Svetlana Cherneva (USSR)	10	8.55	22,822
75	Andrea Holikova (CZ)	19	8.54	32,642
76	Angeliki Kanellopoulou (GR)	15	8.44	19,655
77	Sara Gomer (GB)	17	8.44	38,114
78	Barbara Gerken (USA)	24	8.43	34,749

		T'MENTS	POINTS	PRIZE MONEY
79	Vicki Nelson (USA)	23	8.35	36,885
80	Regina Marsikova (CZ)	18	7.97	27,718
81	Melissa Gurney (USA)	12	7.90	21,724
82	Adriana Villagran (ARG)	21	7.85	39,088
83	Patty Fendick (USA)	9	7.73	19,040
84	Lea Antonoplis (USA)	22	7.69	48,032
85	Beth Herr (USA)	23	7.48	47,066
86	Janine Thompson (AUS)	20	7.42	25,714
87	Petra Delhees Jauch (SWZ)	10	7.25	17,325
88	Rene Uys (SA)	17	7.01	29,545
89	Virginia Wade (GB)	9	6.95	31,521
90	Amanda Tobin Dingwall (AUS)	12	6.82	16,225
91	Kristin Kinney (USA)	25	6.69	21,178
92	Petra Keppeler (G)	12	6.65	16,406
93	Lori McNeil (USA)	26	6.61	53,125
94	Leigh Anne Thompson (USA)	17	6.52	18,610
95	Wendy White (USA)	17	6.47	38,887
96	Hu Na (USA)	14	6.41	18,146
97	Myriam Schropp (G)	19	6.31	36,593
98	Etsuko Inoue (J)	25	6.23	31,519
99	Mary Jo Fernandez (USA)	7	6.07	16,381
100	Katerina Skronska (CZ)	19	5.84	30,799
101	Cecilia Fernandez (USA)	13	5.78	11,525
102	Jenny Klitch (USA)	19	5.75	25,605
103	Lisa Spain Short (USA)	22	5.41	25,693
104	Catherine Suire (F)	19	5.29	34,930
105	Isabelle Cueto (G)	17	5.21	16,918
106	Louise Field (AUS)	15	5.20	18,762
107	Amy Holton (USA)	21	5.19	24,366
108	Laura Garrone (IT)	13	5.08	16,818
109	Terry Holladay (USA)	17	5.00	46,578
110	Amanda Brown (GB)	18	4.97	22,998
111	Beverly Bowes (USA)	11	4.93	10,868
112	Natalie Tauziat (F)	15	4.81	15,875
113	JoAnne Russell (USA)	20	4.64	47,729
114	Andrea Betzner (G)	14	4.61	13,339
115	Mercedes Paz (ARG)	21	4.39	37,179
116	Niege Dias (BR)	18	4.33	22,532
117	Masako Yanagi (J)	19	4.30	19,725
118	Yvonne Vermaak (SA)	21	4.23	43,918
119	Beth Norton (USA)	13	4.22	9,900
120	Shawn Foltz (USA)	16	4.22	21,227
121	Sophie Amiach (F)	22	4.17	29,688
122	Marianne Werdel (USA)	12	4.15	13,068
123	Jennifer Mundel (SA)	21	4.02	26,713
124	Tina Mochizuki (USA)	27	3.99	23,208
125	Emilse Rapponi Longo (ARG)	16	3.89	20,737
126	Nathalie Herreman (F)	16	3.76	11,525
127	Elizabeth Minter (AUS)	24	3.76	32,483
128	Kim Sands (USA)	16	3.66	22,185
129	Pat Medrado (BR)	21	3.64	29,744
130	Sharon Walsh Pete (USA)	18	3.58	87,025
131	Marie Calleja (F)	20	3.53	13,462
132	Jenny Byrne (AUS)	19	3.51	18,564
133	Jane Young (USA)	14	3.48	11,318
134	Ginny Purdy (USA)	19	3.46	13,437
135	Isabella Demongeot (F)	19	3.41	22,477
136	Marcela Skuherska (CZ)	24	3.32	31,435
137	Eva Krapl (SWZ)	19	3.20	9,662

Although she won no titles in 1986, Anne White won world-wide publicity with her startling white body-suit at Wimbledon. *(T. Hindley)*

		T'MENTS	POINTS	PRIZE MONEY
138	Maria Lindstrom (SW)	16	3.20	15,777
139	Heather Ludloff (USA)	19	3.17	19,730
140	Gabriela Dinu (G)	14	3.16	9,462
141	Anna Maria Fernandez (USA)	20	3.16	18,657
142	Beverly Mould (SA)	14	3.15	27,415
143	Cecille Calmette (F)	9	3.10	7,475
144	Barbara Jordan (USA)	8	3.02	9,990
145	Julie Richardson (NZ)	17	3.02	14,000
146	Helena Dahlstrom (SW)	16	2.90	14,287
147	Nicole Provis (AUS)	10	2.86	7,975
148	Karoline Karlsson (SW)	18	2.66	12,200
149	Penny Barg (USA)	21	2.65	26,914
150	Csilla Bartos (HU)	17	2.55	9,450
151	Elena Eliseenko (USSR)	13	2.51	8,975
152	Lea Plchova (CZ)	18	2.38	13,160
153	Jane Holdren (USA)	10	2.32	3,025
154	Sally Reeves (GB)	14	2.31	6,872
155	Caterina Nozzoli (IT)	11	2.26	5,800
156	Jane Forman (USA)	23	2.22	14,162
157	Paula Smith (USA)	14	2.22	51,263
158	Rebecca Bryant (AUS)	19	2.21	12,562
159	Monica Lundqvist (SW)	13	2.20	6,812
160	Kathleen Cummings (USA)	27	2.18	16,860
161	Emiko Okagawa (J)	18	2.16	15,945
162	Caryn Copeland (USA)	19	2.16	9,725
163	Michaela Washington (USA)	14	2.12	10,475
164	Silke Meier (G)	8	2.06	5,700
165	Rene Blount (USA)	18	2.05	12,780
166	Laura Golarsa (IT)	12	2.02	8,775
167	Claudia Monteiro (BR)	17	2.00	15,991
168	Karin Stampfli (SWZ)	12	1.97	4,325
169	Sandy Collins (USA)	19	1.97	32,782
170	Eileen Tell (USA)	17	1.93	7,375
171	Micki Schillig (USA)	21	1.85	9,650
172	Akiko Kijimuta (J)	8	1.82	3,425
173	Catrin Jexell (SW)	11	1.81	10,900
174	Pilar Vasquez (PER)	24	1.80	16,300
175	Linda Howell (USA)	9	1.80	10,222
176	Gretchen Rush (USA)	7	1.76	12,473
177	Marianne Groat (C)	19	1.75	9,200
178	Corinne Vanier (F)	24	1.75	17,315
179	Halle Cioffe (USA)	11	1.73	6,425
180	Laura Bernstein (USA)	23	1.64	11,412
181	Stephanie Faulkner (AUS)	14	1.62	5,500
182	Cheryl Jones (USA)	19	1.61	6,712
183	Rosie Casals (USA)	6	1.60	12,064
184	Dee Ann Hansel (USA)	17	1.59	8,500
185	Eleni Rossides (UNK)	7	1.58	5,164
186	Hana Fukarkova (CZ)	12	1.53	6,212
187	Sabine Hack (G)	8	1.49	8,075
188	Olga Votavova (CZ)	16	1.48	9,575
189	Maeve Quinlan (USA)	14	1.48	11,208
190	Federica Bonsignori (IT)	19	1.46	9,150
191	Ann Hulbert (USA)	12	1.45	6,600
192	Vicki Marler (USA)	14	1.44	8,175
193	Susan Leo (AUS)	16	1.43	17,918
194	Rina Einy (GB)	10	1.43	7,878
195	Kristen Dreyer (USA)	17	1.42	5,850
196	Barbara Pollet (A)	7	1.41	3,700

		T'MENTS	POINTS	PRIZE MONEY
197	Emanuel Derly (F)	8	1.33	3,925
198	Kim Steinmetz (USA)	30	1.28	21,783
199	Ronnie Reis (USA)	6	1.25	7,908
200	Elizabeth Ekblom (SW)	15	1.24	8,650

DOUBLES

		T'MENTS PLAYED	AVGE POINTS			T'MENTS PLAYED	AVGE POINTS
1	Pam Shriver (USA)	14	368.95	26	Candy Reynolds (USA)	18	72.84
2	Martina Navratilova (USA)	14	362.65	27	Manuela Maleeva (BUL)	16	72.03
3	Helena Sukova (CZ)	21	254.09	28	Beverly Mould (SA)	16	70.68
4	Claudia Kohde-Kilsch (G)	20	247.16	29	Alycia Moulton (USA)	20	69.39
5	Kathy Jordan (USA)	14	218.29	30	Mary Lou Piatek (USA)	19	67.87
6	Hana Mandlikova (CZ)	18	217.25	31	Terry Phelps (USA)	19	67.36
7	Elizabeth Smylie (AUS)	20	202.09	32	Carling Bassett (C)	16	66.06
8	Wendy Turnbull (AUS)	19	192.98	33	Lori McNeil (USA)	25	65.08
9	Barbara Potter (USA)	12	175.11	34	JoAnne Russell (USA)	17	64.26
10	Gigi Fernandez (USA)	17	150.85	35	Bonnie Gadusek (USA)	13	63.11
11	Chris Evert Lloyd (USA)	13	141.23	36	Terry Holladay (USA)	16	61.43
12	Sharon Walsh Pete (USA)	20	132.26	37	Catherine Tanvier (F)	15	60.83
13	Andrea Temesvari (HU)	14	111.67	38	Jill Hetherington (C)	11	59.70
14	Svetlana Cherneva (USSR)	12	102.79	39	Catherine Suire (F)	18	59.02
15	Rosalyn Fairbank (SA)	22	101.13	40	Pascale Paradis (F)	20	58.97
16	Elise Burgin (USA)	25	97.48	41	Catarina Lindqvist (SW)	11	58.36
17	Eva Pfaff (G)	11	93.50	42	Katerina Maleeva (BUL)	18	57.38
18	Robin White (USA)	19	93.13	43	Laura Gildemeister (PER)	15	55.43
19	Larisa Savchenko (USSR)	15	91.30	44	Zina Garrison (USA)	20	54.95
20	Anne Hobbs (GB)	11	89.68	45	Paula Smith (USA)	24	54.47
21	Marcella Mesker (NTH)	24	88.58	46	Tine Scheuer-Larsen (D)	15	53.03
22	Anne White (USA)	16	84.67	47	Kathleen Horvath (USA)	15	52.84
23	Bettina Bunge (G)	14	79.90	48	Beth Herr (USA)	20	52.70
24	Betsy Nagelsen (USA)	14	77.01	49	Sandra Ceccini (IT)	10	52.35
25	Jo Durie (GB)	19	73.21	50	Steffi Graf (G)	14	52.14

Players who have won more than $1 million in prize money

1	Martina Navratilova	$9,886,474	8 Virginia Wade	1,534,918
2	Chris Evert Lloyd	6,362,163	9 Evonne Goolagong Cawley	1,399,431
3	Hana Mandlikova	2,226,036	10 Andrea Jaeger	1,375,254
4	Wendy Turnbull	2,197,622	11 Rosie Casals	1,319,858
5	Pam Shriver	2,106,584	12 Virginia Ruzici	1,161,626
6	Billie Jean King	1,965,412	13 Kathy Jordan	1,111,820
7	Tracy Austin	1,908,715	14 Betty Stove	1,047,125

MISCELLANEOUS TOURNAMENTS AND SPECIAL EVENTS

MEN

AT & T CHALLENGE OF CHAMPIONS ($1,000,000)

LAS VEGAS, 1–6 JANUARY
MEN'S SINGLES – Final: J. P. McEnroe d. G. Vilas (ARG) 7–5 6–0.
Third Place: Y. Noah (F) d. J. S. Connors 7–6 7–6.

TOKYO

8–12 MAY
MEN'S SINGLES – Semi-finals: B. Borg (SW) d. E. Teltscher (USA) 6–4 6–1; A. Jarryd (SW) d. S. Edberg 6–1 6–2. ***Final:*** Borg d. Jarryd 6–4 6–3.

EUROPEAN CHAMPIONS' CHAMPIONSHIP ($850,000)

ANTWERP, 28 OCTOBER–3 NOVEMBER
MEN'S SINGLES – Quarter-finals: I. Lendl (CZ) d. H. Leconte (F) 4–2 ret'd; A. Jarryd (SW) d. M. Wilander (SW) 1–6 6–2 6–4; B. Becker (G) d. T. Wilkison (USA) 6–2 6–1; J. P. McEnroe (USA) d. M. Dickson (USA) 6–4 6–2. ***Semi-finals:*** Lendl d. Jarryd 6–3 6–2; McEnroe d. Becker 6–4 6–4. ***Final:*** Lendl d. McEnroe 1–6 7–6 6–2 6–2.

WOMEN

FORD CUP ($200,000)

PALM BEACH GARDENS, 5–7 APRIL
WOMEN'S SINGLES – Semi-finals: Mrs J. M. Lloyd d. C. Bassett (C) 6–2 6–1; H. Mandlikova (CZ) d. P. H. Shriver 7–6 7–6. ***Final:*** Lloyd d. Mandlikova 6–3 6–3.

ST LOUIS FESTIVAL

AUGUST
WOMEN'S SINGLES – Final: Mrs J. M. Lloyd d. H. Mandlikova (CZ) 7–6 6–4.

OSAKA

15–17 NOVEMBER
WOMEN'S SINGLES – Final: Mrs J. M. Lloyd (USA) d. M. Maleeva (BUL) 7–5 6–0.

MEN v WOMEN CHALLENGE MATCH

ATLANTIC CITY, 24 AUGUST
M. Navratilova /P. H. Shriver d. V. Gerulaitis /R. L. Riggs 6–2 6–3 6–4.

JUNIORS

ORANGE BOWL INTERNATIONAL CHAMPIONSHIPS

MIAMI BEACH, FLORIDA, 16–23 DECEMBER

BOYS' 18 SINGLES – Quarter-finals: C. Garner d. C. Bergstrom (SW) 6–0 6–4; B. Oresar (YU) d. J. Silva (POR) 6–3 6–4; G. Perez Roldan (ARG) d. C. Allgaardh (SW) 6–2 6–2; C. Pistolesi (IT) d. A. Parker 6–3 6–2. **Semi-finals:** Pistolesi d. Perez Roldan 6–2 6–1; Oresar d. Garner 7–5 6–1. **Final:** Pistolesi d. Oresar 6–0 6–2.

BOYS' 18 DOUBLES – Final: S. Ohta (J) /Garner d. S. Matsouka (J) /M. Kanroji (J) 7–5 6–3.

GIRLS' 18 SINGLES – Quarter-finals: L. Garrone (IT) d. S. Stafford 6–1 3–6 7–6; M. J. Fernandez d. M. Perez Roldan (ARG) 6–4 6–1; P. Tarabini (ARG) d. C. Nozzoli (IT) 6–3 7–6; E. Galphin d. K. Reiter 6–2 6–2. **Semi-finals:** Fernandez d. Garrone 6–1 6–3; Tarabini d. Galphin 6–3 6–2. **Final:** Fernandez d. Tarabini 7–6 6–1.

GIRLS' 18 DOUBLES – Final: Tarabini /Perez Roldan d. R. Zrubakova (CZ) /A. Holikova (CZ) 6–4 6–1.

BOYS' 16 SINGLES – Final: A. Boetsch (F) d. P. Wennberg (SW) 6–3 6–3.

GIRLS' 16 SINGLES – Final: S. Niox Chateau (F) d. A. Dechaume (F) 6–3 6–1.

BELGIAN AMERICAN YOUNG MASTERS 1985 ($150,000)

ICC BERLIN, 1–5 JANUARY, 1986

21 and under

Defending champion Boris Becker of West Germany successfully retained the title he had won 12 months earlier in the inaugural Young Masters. That first tournament had been a knock-out event for 24 players with a best-of-five-sets final. The second tournament was a round-robin event for 16 players in four groups of four players each, prior to knock-out semi-finals for the four group winners and a five-set final. Entry was restricted to players born in 1964 or later. The 12 top-ranked players on the ATP computer rankings of 19 December were accepted direct, and there were four wild cards.

RED GROUP: 1st M. Wilander (SW) d. B. Oresar (YU) 6–1 6–1; d. H. Schwaier (G) 6–0 6–1; d. K. Carlsson (SW) 6–2 6–1. **2nd** Oresar d. Schwaier 5–7 6–4 6–0; d. Carlsson 6–4 3–6 6–3. **3rd** Schwaier d. Carlsson 3–6 4–1 ret'd. **4th** Carlsson.

BLUE GROUP: 1st J. Hlasek (SWZ) d. G. Forget (F) 7–6 6–2; d. H. Sundstrom (SW) 6–2 3–6 6–4; d. T. Muster (AU) 6–4 6–4. **2nd** Forget d. Sundstrom 6–7 6–3 6–4: d. Muster 6–3 6–4. **3rd** Sundstrom d. Muster 6–3 6–7 7–6; **4th** Muster.

GREEN GROUP: 1st B. Becker (G) d. P. Lundgren (SW) 6–4 7–5; d. M. Vajda (CZ) 6–3 6–2; d. J. Brown (USA) 6–7 6–2 6–4. **2nd** Lundgren d. Vajda 6–2 7–5; d. Brown 6–4 6–2; **3rd** Vajda d. Brown 2–6 6–4 6–1. **4th** Brown.

GOLD GROUP: 1st E. Sanchez (SP) d. R. Agenor (HAITI) 6–3 6–4; d. C. Pistolesi (IT) 6–4 6–3; **2nd** J. Carlsson (SW) d. Sanchez 6–3 6–1; d. Pistolesi 3–6 6–3 6–2; **3rd** Agenor d. Carlsson 7–6 6–7 6–1; d. Pistolesi 6–3 6–2. **4th** Pistolesi. (Average of sets won to sets played: Sanchez 66·6%; Carlsson 62·5%; Agenor 57·1%.)

Semi-finals: Wilander d. Hlasek 6–3 7–6; Becker d. Sanchez 6–4 6–4. **Final:** Becker d. Wilander 6–1 7–6 6–0.

Prize Money: Winner $30,000; runner-up $20,000; semi-finalists $14,000; 2nd in group $8,000; 3rd in group $6,000; 4th in group $4,000.

REFERENCE SECTION

BIOGRAPHIES
ALL-TIME GREATS
CHAMPIONSHIP ROLLS

Gabriella Sabatini of Argentina became the youngest ever French Open semi-finalist during a season of tremendous achievement, which lifted her from No. 74 to No. 12 in the world. *(T. Hindley)*

BIOGRAPHIES
Steve Flink

Abbreviations used in this section:

f	final	US CC	US Clay Court Championships
sf	semi-final	D Cup	Davis Cup
qf	quarter-final	Fed Cup	Federation Cup
r /u	runner-up	W Cup	Wightman Cup
def	defaulted	FC Cup	Family Circle Cup
retd	retired	Champ	Championship
fs	final set	Int	International
rr	round-robin	Inv	Invitation
b-p	break-point	Jun	Junior
s-p	set-point	Nat	National
m-p	match-point	Pro	Professional
t-b	tie-break	CS	Colgate Series
1r	first round	TS	Toyota Series
2s	second set	HC	Hard Court
RH	right-handed	VS	Virginia Slims
LH	left-handed	WCT	World Championship Tennis
2HB	2-handed backhand	WTT	World Team Tennis
2HF	2-handed forehand	GP	Grand Prix
BHC	British Hard Court Championships	LIPC	Lipton International Players Championships

Men and women who appear in the top 100 on the ATP and WTA computer rankings are included below, as well as leading doubles players, a few prominent players who compete less than usual nowadays, plus some newcomers. We gratefully acknowledge the assistance of the Nabisco Grand Prix, ATP and WTA in supplying additional biographical information.

1984 ranking is shown in brackets after 1985 ranking.

RICARDO ACUNA (Chile)
Born Santiago, 13 January, 1958, and lives there with wife Kim; RH; 5ft 9in; 150lb; final 1985 ATP ranking 57 (151); 1985 prize money $51,808.
Member of Chilean D Cup team, who reached qf Wimbledon with a hard-fought win over Cash. **1985 HIGHLIGHTS – SINGLES: Wimbledon** qf, unseeded (d. Benhabiles 6–3 4–6 6–1 6–2, Cash [seed 6] 7–6 6–3 3–6 6–7 6–4, Pate 7–5 6–4 6–2, Seguso 6–4 7–6 6–2, lost Connors [seed 3] 6–1 7–6 6–2), **US Open** 1r (lost Fleming 6–4 6–2 7–6); **qf** Cleveland (d. Meister, DeVries, lost Pfister). **1985 HIGHLIGHTS – DOUBLES:** (with Hlasek) **won** Toulouse (d. Slozil /Smid 9–7 fs).

RONALD AGENOR (Haiti)
Born Morocco, 13 November, 1964; lives Bordeaux, France; RH; 5ft 11in; 168lb; final 1985 ATP ranking 50 (416); 1985 prize money $46,538.
Improving rapidly in 1985 he moved up nearly 400 places on the computer. **1985 HIGHLIGHTS – SINGLES: French Open** 1r (lost McEnroe 6–0 6–2 7–5), **US Open** 1r (lost Green 7–6 7–6 6–4); **qf** Marbella (d. Vilas, J. Brown, lost Bengoechea), **qf** Madrid (d.

Nystrom, lost Novacek), *qf* Bologna (d. Luna, lost Tulasne), *qf* Stuttgart (d. Higueras, lost Lendl), *qf* Bordeaux (d. Urpi, lost Clerc).

JUAN AGUILERA (Spain)
Born Barcelona, 22 March, 1962, and lives there; RH; 6ft; 150lb; final 1985 ATP ranking 79 (19); 1985 prize money $62,426.
A distinguished CC player, who leaped 163 places in the rankings across 1983 and in 1984 became probably the most surprising winner of a SS event when he stopped Sundstrom in f of German Open at Hamburg. He moved into the top 20, was seeded at French and US Opens, and coasted through the rest of the year, but his comfortable run came to an end when he was beaten in 3r German Open in 1985. He lost considerable ground and it was not until he reached sf Geneva in the autumn that he began a recovery. *1985 HIGHLIGHTS – SINGLES: French Open* 3r (d. Pecci 6–2 6–3 7–5, C. Lewis 4–6 6–4 6–3 7–5, lost Jarryd [seed 6] 6–4 6–2 6–2); *sf* Geneva (d. Taroczy, Lavalle, lost Smid); *qf* Boston (d. R. Brown, Cancellotti, Mecir 6–4 fs, lost Oresar). *CAREER HIGHLIGHTS – SINGLES: German Open – won 1984* (d. Sundstrom 6–4 2–6 2–6 6–4 6–4).

CHRISTER ALLGAARDH (Sweden)
Born Boras, 20 February, 1967; lives Vasteras; RH; 2HB; 6ft 2in; 171lb; final 1985 ATP ranking 294.
His father, Jan, is a judge and one of his two sisters (Suzanne, 16) plays tennis. Coached by Peter Rosen and Ulf Ericsson he has been Swedish Jun champ in every age group from 12s to 18s. In 1981 won Rolex 14s and in 1985 was third in European 18s as well as playing satellite circuits in Britain and Spain.

VIJAY AMRITRAJ (India)
Born Madras, 14 December, 1953; lives there and Marina Del Rey, Cal.; married Jan 1983, wife's name Shyamala, son Prakash born 1984; RH; 6ft 3in; 160lb; final 1985 ATP ranking 80 (42); 1985 prize money $65,412.
The middle of three brothers (Anand is older, Ashok younger). In 1982, he was the only other world-class player besides Borg to refuse to compete in ten GP tournaments outside GS events, playing only one (Wimbledon) and being forced to qualify before illness late in the summer kept him out for several months. Otherwise, he concentrated solely on WCT tournaments and failed again to do justice to his talent, never even reaching a f and finishing ranked 41 on the Nixdorf computer. Took part of Indian agent in James Bond film *Octopussy* with Roger Moore and in 1983 his mind continued to be preoccupied with the film business, his talent flourishing briefly during the summer. However, in 1984 he won his first GP tournament in four years when he d. T. Mayotte in f Newport. He then pulled off a stunning upset of McEnroe in 1r Cincinnati, and although he could have been more consistent and perhaps won with more frequency, he looked like his old self. In 1985 his singles play was sporadic, but he kept himself in the upper levels of the game with an inspired Wimbledon where he reached last 16 with a fine win over Noah. *1985 HIGHLIGHTS – SINGLES: Wimbledon* last 16, unseeded (d. Canter 6–3 6–4 6–4, Drewett 7–6 6–7 7–6 7–5, Noah [seed 11] 4–6 7–6 6–3 7–6), *US Open* 1r (lost Wilander [seed 3] 6–2 6–4 6–4). *1985 HIGHLIGHTS – DOUBLES:* (with J. Lloyd unless stated) *sf* Queens Club (lost Cash/Fitzgerald 9–7 fs), [Becker] *sf* Rotterdam (lost Gerulaitis/McNamee), *sf* LA (lost Annacone/Van Rensburg 7–6 6–3). *CAREER HIGH-LIGHTS –DOUBLES:* (with Anand Amritraj)*Wimbledon –sf 1976* (lost Gottfried/Ramirez 6–3 7–6 8–6).

MATT ANGER (USA)
Born Walnut Creek, Cal., 20 June, 1963; lives Pleasanton, Cal.; RH; 6ft 2in; 165lb; final 1985 ATP ranking 31 (177); 1985 prize money $93,393.
A former All-American at USC and 1981 Wimbledon jun champ, he made great strides in 1985, winning Johannesburg in the autumn. *1985 HIGHLIGHTS – SINGLES: Wimbledon* 2r (d. Kuharszky 5–7 6–2 6–2 3–6 6–1, lost Becker 6–0 6–1 6–3), *Australian Open* 3r (bye, d. Glickstein 6–2 6–1 5–7 6–2, lost Edberg 5–7 7–6 6–4 7–5); *won* Johannesburg (d. Sadri, Arias 7–5 4–6 7–5, Gilbert 6–4 3–6 6–3 6–2).

PAUL ANNACONE (USA)
Born New York, 20 March, 1963 and lives there; single; RH; 6ft 1in; 175lb; final 1985 ATP ranking 13 (94) singles, 5 (74) doubles; 1985 prize money $383,739.
An All-American at the University of Tennessee in 1982–83, he was one of the favourites to win NCAA singles title in May 1984, but was upset in qf. However, in his first appearance at Wimbledon as a qualifier he surged into qf, winning 7 matches and upsetting Kriek in last 16. Thereafter, much was expected from this gifted touch player, but he was less successful in singles over the second half of the year, although he was impressive in doubles with different partners. In 1985, he made a remarkable surge into top 20 with a sizzling autumn run which included two GP victories in LA and Brisbane. Meanwhile, his singles success somewhat overshadowed some stellar play in doubles. His outstanding record with Van Rensburg pushed him into top 5 on doubles computer and took them to Masters where they lost 1r to Gunthardt /Taroczy. He also lost 1r singles to Becker. **1985 HIGHLIGHTS – SINGLES: French Open** 1r (lost Segarceanu 7–5 6–7 7–6 6–2), **Wimbledon** 2r (d. Goldie 5–7 7–5 6–1 1–6 9–7, lost Nystrom [seed 7] 7–5 7–5 6–3), **US Open** 3r (d. Tom Gullikson 6–4 6–4 3–6 6–1, Fleming 2–6 7–5 7–5 6–1, lost Wilander [seed 3] 6–3 6–7 7–6 6–1), **Australian Open**, seed 12, 3r (d. Green 6–7 7–6 6–4 7–5, lost Wilkison 7–5 6–3 6–3); **won** LA (d. Goldie, Van Patten, S. Davis 6–4 6–2, McEnroe def., Edberg 7–6 6–7 7–6), **won** Brisbane (d. M. Davis 6–4 fs, Youl 6–1 7–6, Everndenn 6–3 6–3); **r/u** Atlanta (d. Sadri, Gilbert 7–6 fs, lost McEnroe 7–6 7–6 6–2), **r/u** Melbourne (d. Cain, Masur, Van Rensburg, lost M. Davis 6–4 6–4); **sf** San Francisco (d. Anger 7–6 fs, Mayotte, lost Edberg 6–1 fs), **sf** Sydney (d. Evernden, Hooper, lost Lendl); **qf** Chicago (d. Kriek, lost McEnroe 6–4 fs), **qf** Queens Club (d. Wilkison, Curren 8–6 fs, lost Zivojinovic), **qf** Newport (lost Pate), **qf** Livingston (lost Gilbert), **qf** Stratton Mountain (d. Pate, lost McEnroe). **1985 HIGHLIGHTS – DOUBLES:** (with Van Rensburg) **French Open** qf, seed 7 (d. Dickson /Wilkison 7–6 6–7 7–5, lost Edberg /Jarryd 6–3 6–2), **Wimbledon** qf, seed 9 (d. Levine /Van't Hof 7–6 6–1 7–6, lost Gunthardt /Taroczy 6–4 2–6 6–4 6–7 24–22), **won Australian Open** (d. Edmondson /Warwick 3–6 7–6 6–4 6–4); **won** LIPC (d. Stewart /Warwick 7–5 7–5 6–4), **won** Atlanta (d. Denton /Smid 6–4 6–3), **won** San Francisco (d. Gilbert /A. Mayer 3–6 6–3 6–4); **r/u** Las Vegas (lost Cash /Fitzgerald 7–6 6–7 7–6), **r/u** Newport (lost Doohan / S. Giammalva), **r/u** LA (d. V. Amritraj /J. Lloyd, lost S. Davis /Van't Hof). **CAREER HIGHLIGHTS – SINGLES: Wimbledon – qf 1984** (d. Kriek, lost Connors 6–2 6–4 6–2). **CAREER HIGHLIGHTS – DOUBLES:** (with Van Rensburg) **Australian Open – won 1985**.

LEA ANTONOPLIS (USA)
Born West Covina, Cal., 20 January, 1959 and lives there; RH; 5ft 5in; 145lb; final 1985 WTA ranking 84 (71); 1985 prize money $48,032.
A member of WTA Board of Directors for the last three years, she is the head of the disciplinary committee. **1985 HIGHLIGHTS – SINGLES: Wimbledon** 1r (lost Wade 6–4 7–5), **US Open** 1r (lost Gates 6–4 6–2), **Australian Open** 1r (lost M. Maleeva [seed 7] 6–1 6–1); **qf** VS Indianapolis (d. Piatek, Washington, lost Gadusek), **qf** VS Newport (d. Moulton 6–4 fs, Copeland, lost Shriver), **qf** New Zealand (d. M. Parun, lost Field).

ROBERTO ARGUELLO (Argentina)
Born Rosario, 12 May, 1963, and lives there with wife Cecelia; ambidextrous; 2HB and 2HF; 5ft 8in; 140lb; final 1985 ATP ranking 69 (126); 1985 prize money $37,854.
The winner of 1981 Orange Bowl title, he is a CC specialist and is rarely seen off that circuit. With three qf appearances in 1985, he returned to the top 100. **1985 HIGHLIGHTS – SINGLES: French Open** 2r (d. M. Davis, lost Smid 6–4 3–6 6–1 6–4), **US Open** 1r (lost Arias 6–1 6–3 6–1); **qf** Buenos Aires (d. Martins, Tiberti, lost Perez), **qf** Nice (d. de la Pena, J. Frawley, lost Perez), **qf** Bari (d. Cihak, Arraya, lost Lopez-Maeso).

JIMMY ARIAS (USA)
Born Grand Island, NY, 16 August, 1964, and lives there; single; RH; 5ft 9in; 145lb; final 1985 ATP ranking 21 (14); 1985 prize money $172,976.
Under the guidance of US teaching pro Nick Bollettieri, he climbed into the top 100 in 1981 after a year which included a terrific victory over Teltscher in USTA Penn circuit

event in Shreveport. Beaten in 1r of six of his eight tournaments in 1982 on GP circuit and 2r of two others, this tenacious, spirited, teenager made a marvellous surge in the summer, reaching f Washington and US CC and won his first GP event (Japan Asian Open) in autumn. He had reached No. 20 at end of 1982 and looked a possible candidate for the top 10 in 1983, when he surged into the top 6 after a year which included four tournament wins (Italian Open, USCC, Florence and Palermo). Following a demanding and debilitating schedule during the spring and summer he came down with mononucleosis in late September. That kept him out of the game until mid-December, when he began playing exhibitions to prepare for the season-ending Masters in January, where he lost 1r to Kriek. He never completely found his former inspiration and efficiency, and although he reached qf French Open, he did not appear in any f. Perhaps he felt the pressure of protecting the No. 5 world ranking he attained early in the season, but whatever the reasons he dropped eight places. Struggling with his confidence early in 1985, he won only four matches in his first five tournaments before being r/u at Las Vegas. He then won no match in his next four events, but demonstrated his resilience and determination as he reached sf Canadian Open, f Japan Open, and sf South African Open and he appeared to be back on track by the end of the year. *1985 HIGHLIGHTS –* *SINGLES: French Open* 1r (lost Saad 6–1 6–4 7–5), *Wimbledon* 1r (lost Lapidus 6–4 6–4 3–6 6–7 7–5), *US Open* 3r (d. Arguello 6–1 6–3 6–1, Mansdorf 6–4 6–7 6–7 6–2 0–1 ret'd, lost Smid [seed 16] 4–6 1–6 6–3 6–3 7–6); *r/u* Las Vegas (d. Cash 7–6 fs, R. Simpson 6–2 fs, Teltscher 7–6 fs, Flach 7–5 fs, lost Kriek 4–6 6–3 6–4 6–2), *r/u* Japan Open (d. Michibata 6–4 fs, lost S. Davis 6–1 7–6); *sf* South African Open (d. Curren, lost Anger), *sf* Canadian Open (d. Curren, Teltscher, lost Lendl); *qf* LA (d. M. Leach, lost Kriek 7–6 fs). *CAREER HIGHLIGHTS – SINGLES: Italian Open – won 1983* (d. Higueras 6–2 6–7 6–1 6–4); *USCC – won 1983* (d. Gomez 6–4 2–6 6–4), *r/u 1982* (lost Higueras 7–5 5–7 6–3); *US Open – sf 1983* (d. Nystrom 6–0 fs, Noah 7–5 fs, lost Lendl 6–2 7–6 6–1). *CAREER HIGHLIGHTS – MIXED DOUBLES:* (with A. Jaeger) *French Open – won 1981* (d. Gonzalez /Teeguarden 4–6 6–3 11–9, McNair /Stove [seed 2] 7–6 6–4).

PABLO ARRAYA (Peru)
Born Buenos Aires, Argentina, 21 October, 1961; lives Lima; single; RH; 5ft 10in; 160lb; final 1985 ATP ranking 87 (56); 1985 prize money $37,216.
Brother of Laura Gildemeister. In Dec. 1979 he was r/u to Viver at Orange Bowl and in 1981 he was r/u to Lendl at Madrid on GP circuit. He beat Arias in Monte Carlo but his best win of 1982 was a stunning 7–6 7–6 dismissal of Wilander at US CC. In 1983 he won Bordeaux on GP circuit and was again a consistent threat on clay. He was less successful in 1984 but managed again to demonstrate his superior CC skills with two wins over German Open champ Aguilera plus one over Sundstrom. In 1985 he played a limited schedule and dropped further down the rankings. *1985 HIGHLIGHTS – SINGLES: French Open* 1r (lost Warneke 3–6 6–1 6–4 7–6); *qf* Marbella (d. Arguello, Cancellotti, lost Duncan), *qf* Washington (d. Ycaza, Gomez, Dickson, lost Jaite).

TRACY AUSTIN (USA)
Born Redondo Beach, Cal., 12 December, 1962 and lives Rolling Hills Estates; RH; 2HB; 5ft 4in; 110lb.
Made history at Wimbledon in 1977 when she became the youngest ever to compete there. Turned pro aged 15 in autumn 1978 at Stuttgart tournament, which she won, having already established herself as one of top 10 players in the world. In 1979 won her first two major champs – Italian and US Opens – becoming the youngest ever to capture the US Open. Ranked 2 in the world behind Navratilova at end 1979, she remained in that position in 1980, surpassed only by Evert Lloyd. Austin won Avon Champs in New York and 9 other tournaments from 13 final-round appearances in 1980, but fell to Goolagong Cawley in Wimbledon sf and lost the most important match of her year to Evert Lloyd in US Open sf. She ended the season with victory in CS Finals in Jan. 1981 (Evert Lloyd had defaulted after one match with flu). In 1981 she had another strong season after overcoming a back injury which kept her out of the game from mid-January until late May. She came back to win US Open for the second time, and TS Champ in Dec, but was beaten in both Wimbledon and Australian Open qf by Shriver. Convincing wins over Evert Lloyd and Navratilova in sf and f of TS Champ earned her No. 1 world ranking in many

eyes, though some experts ranked her second behind Evert Lloyd. When her recurring back injury kept her out of the sport from Jan. to May in 1982, she did not come back to play the outstanding tennis that she had in 1981 and won only one tournament (San Diego). Her best win of the year came over Jaeger at TS Champ, whereupon she lost 6–0 6–0 to an impeccable Evert Lloyd. In 1983 she was again forced out of action by her old back and shoulder injuries. She played the lightest schedule of her pro career, competing in only eight tournaments, her last event being Eastbourne, where she reached sf. Facing Turnbull, she trailed 1–6 0–1 when she felt a pain 'like a knife going through my back', and retired. In the autumn, she went through extensive training with her coach, Tony Roche, in Australia and returned in February 1984 to compete in only 2 tournaments before she was forced to sit out the remainder of the year. Clearly lacking her old sharpness and mental toughness, she was beaten by Potter at Chicago and Casale at US Indoor, but thereafter was confined to TV commentary. She spoke of coming back to the circuit in 1985, but played no tournaments, her future remaining as uncertain as before. **CAREER HIGHLIGHTS – SINGLES: won 1979** (d. Navratilova 7–5 7–5, Evert Lloyd 6–4 6–3), **won 1981** (d. Potter 6–1 6–3, Navratilova 1–6 7–6 7–6), **sf 1980** seed 1 (d. A. Smith, Casals, Hanika, Ruzici [seed 10], Shriver [seed 13], lost Evert Lloyd [seed 3] 4–6 6–1 6–1); **CS Finals – won 1980** seed 3 (d. Ruzici 6–0 6–3, Mandlikova 6–3 6–4 in rr, Turnbull 6–2 6–1 in sf, Jaeger 6–2 6–2 in f), **TS Champ – won 1981** (d. Evert Lloyd 6–1 6–2, Navratilova 2–6 6–4 6–2); **Italian Open – won 1979** (d. Evert Lloyd 6–4 2–6 7–6, Hanika 6–4 1–6 6–3); **Avon Champs – r/u 1979** (lost Navratilova 6–3 3–6 6–2); **Wimbledon – sf 1979** seed 4 (d. Ruzici [seed 10] 6–2 6–4, King [seed 7] 6–4 6–7 6–2, lost Navratilova [seed 1] 7–5 6–1), **sf 1980** seed 2 (d. Moulton, Gregory, Potter, Holladay, Stevens [seed 11] 6–3 6–3, lost Cawley 6–0 0–6 6–4); **French Open – qf 1983** (lost Durie 6–1 4–6 6–0). **CAREER HIGHLIGHTS – MIXED DOUBLES:** (with J. Austin) **Wimbledon – won 1980** (d. Edmondson /Fromholtz [seed 6] 4–6 7–6 6–3), **r/u 1981** (lost McMillan /Stove 4–6 7–6 6–3).

DIANNE FROMHOLTZ BALESTRAT (Australia)
Born Albury, NSW, 10 August, 1956; lives Elanora Heights, NSW; LH; 5ft 4in; 120lb; final 1985 WTA ranking 30 (99); 1985 prize money $48,288.
As a 17-year-old in 1973 she showed great promise, winning 10 minor tournaments. Ever since, this strong, athletic lefthander has been a major force in women's tennis, remaining in the top 10 from 1976–79. In 1980, she was slowed down by an ankle injury but reached French Open sf and US Indoor f. The injury kept her out of the game all winter, but she returned in April 1981 and downed Mandlikova to reach sf Berlin in May. She was involved in a couple of car accidents in 1982, but there were encouraging signs that her considerable talent had not completely diminished as she beat Turnbull, King and Gadusek during the year. In 1983, her incentive seemed gone and most of her good results were on the doubles court, following her marriage to Claude Balestrat in Dec. 1982. She played irregularly again in 1984, but competed more frequently and successfully in 1985, when she entered 19 tournaments, reaching f Sydney indoors and qf Sydney outdoors late in the year to rise 69 places in the rankings. **1985 HIGHLIGHTS – SINGLES: French Open** 1r (lost Spence 6–3 2–6 6–3), **Wimbledon** 2r (d. Dias 6–0 6–2, lost Mandlikova [seed 3] 4–6 6–2 7–5), **Australian Open** 3r (d. Bunge 6–4 6–2, A. Brown 6–0 7–5, lost Evert Lloyd [seed 1] 6–4 6–1); **r/u** Sydney Indoor (d. K. Jordan 6–2 fs, G. Fernandez, lost Shriver 6–3 6–3); **qf** Fort Lauderdale (d. Fairbank, lost Gadusek), **qf** Sydney Outdoor (lost Sukova 6–1 6–4). **CAREER HIGHLIGHTS – SINGLES: Australian Open – r/u Jan. 1977** (d. Krantzcke, lost Reid 7–5 6–2); **South African Open – r/u 1974** (d. DuPlooy 8–6 fs, Court 6–4 6–4, lost Reid 6–3 7–5); **US CC – r/u 1975** (d. Riedel, Ebbinghaus, lost Evert 6–3 6–4); **US Indoor – r/u 1979** (d. Navratilova 6–1 fs, lost Goolagong Cawley 6–3 6–4); **French Open – sf 1979** (d. Ruzici 6–0 6–4, lost Evert Lloyd 6–1 6–3), **sf 1980** seed 5 (d. King 6–1 6–4, lost Ruzici 7–6 6–1); **US Open – sf 1976** (d. Russell, Newberry, Liess, lost Goolagong Cawley 7–6 6–0); **Italian Open – sf 1975** (lost Navratilova 7–6 6–3); **Avon Champs – sf 1979** (d. Stevens, Evert Lloyd 6–2 6–3, lost Austin 7–5 6–2); **US Indoor – r/u 1980** (d. King 7–6 6–3, lost Austin 6–1 2–6 6–2). **CAREER HIGHLIGHTS – DOUBLES: Australian Open –** [Gourlay Cawley] **won Jan. 1977** (d. Reid /Nagelsen 5–7 6–1 7–5); **South African Open –** [Court] **r/u 1974**.

CARLING BASSETT (Canada)
Born Toronto, 9 October, 1967; lives there and Gulf Island Resort, Fla.; RH; 2HB; 5ft 5in; 103lb; final 1985 WTA ranking 15 (11); 1985 prize money $197,591.
After winning Orange Bowl 18 and under in Dec. 1982, she consulted with coach Nick Bollittieri and elected to turn professional. The Orange Bowl triumph, where she beat Maleeva in f, capped a terrific year, during which she played 12 women's tournaments. With sound groundstrokes, a first-rate drop shot off the forehand, and a strong will to win, she is clearly her country's best prospect ever, and in 1982 made her Fed Cup début at No. 2. In 1983, coached by Peter McNamara, she was undoubtedly the 'rookie of the year' in the women's game. Her most notable accomplishments included r/u WTA Champs – where she beat Pfaff, Bunge, Rinaldi and led Evert Lloyd 4–2 fs before losing – and reaching last 16 Wimbledon. Otherwise, she earned her top 20 ranking largely by picking up wins almost every week and reaching qf of big tournaments. Her 1984 record was highly impressive. She reached qf French Open and sf US Open and was ranked in the top 10 by most experts. She made her mark in her second season with her tenacity, sound groundstrokes and feisty determination. She remained in the forefront of the game in 1985, beginning the year with an excellent showing at the inaugural Players Champs in Delray Beach where she eliminated Sabatini and Mandlikova on her way to sf loss to Navratilova. She did not reach that standard again in a major tournament but spent most of the year among the top 15. *1985 HIGHLIGHTS – SINGLES: French Open* last 16 (d. Betzner 7–6 7–6, Mundel 6–3 6–3, Dinu 7–5 6–4, lost Phelps 4–6 6–0 6–2), *Wimbledon* 2r (d. Paz 6–0 3–6 6–3, lost Uys 0–6 7–6 6–3), *US Open* last 16 (d. Budarova 6–0 6–7–5, Paz 6–2 6–1, Gates 6–4 6–4, lost Sukova 4–7 7–6 7–5); *sf* Delray Beach (d. Rehe 6–2 6–3, Sabatini 6–0 6–4, Mandlikova 7–5 6–4, lost Navratilova 6–3 6–3), *sf* Palm Beach (lost Evert Lloyd), *sf* VS LA (d. Pfaff 6–2 fs, lost Kohde-Kilsch), *sf* Tampa (lost Rehe 6–4 fs). *1985 HIGHLIGHTS – DOUBLES:* (with Evert Lloyd) *US Open* qf, seed 8 (d. Horvath /Ruzici 6–4 6–2, lost Garrison /Rinaldi 6–2 6–3); *r/u* Amelia Island (d. Garrison /McNeil 7–6 fs, lost Fairbank /Mandlikova 6–2 fs); *sf* Hilton Head (lost Fairbank /Shriver). *CAREER HIGHLIGHTS – SINGLES: US Open – sf 1984* (lost Evert Lloyd 4–6 6–1 6–0; *French Open – qf 1984* (d. Mandlikova 6–4 6–3, lost Evert Lloyd 6–2 6–2); *Australian Open – qf 1983* (lost Shriver 6–0 6–1).

JEREMY BATES (Great Britain)
Born Solihull, 19 June, 1962, and lives there; RH; 5ft 11in; 160lb; final 1985 ATP ranking 99 (185); 1985 prize money $34,114.
A volatile player, who cracked the top 100 for the first time in 1985. *1985 HIGHLIGHTS – SINGLES: Wimbledon* 1r (lost Flur 6–4 6–4), *Australian Open* 1r (lost Flur 6–7 6–7 7–5 6–4 7–5); *sf* Tel Aviv (lost Mansdorf); *qf* Bristol (d. McCain, Flach, Moor, lost M. Davis).

BORIS BECKER (West Germany)
Born Leiman, 22 November, 1967 and lives there; single; RH; 6ft 1½in; 173lb; final 1985 ATP ranking 6 (65); 1985 prize money $617,757.
The German Nat Jun champ from 1982–84, he is an outstanding prospect with enormous talent; r/u at Orange Bowl 16s 1983, r/u US Open Jun 1984, he proved he was ready for the men's game when he reached qf Australian Open unseeded in Dec. 1984 after 3 months off court following a serious ankle injury at Wimbledon. Confident that successful run, he became the first Young Masters champ in Jan. 1985 and in July he became the youngest men's champion at Wimbledon, the first German, and the first unseeded player to capture the world's most prestigious event. It was probably the most astonishing GS victory achieved by any male in the open era of the game since 1968. He also won Queens Club and ATP Champs, and notched up victories over Edberg and Wilander in D Cup f in Munich. Almost single-handed he led Germany into f for first time since 1970 and only once all year (by Sergio Casal of Spain) was he beaten in D Cup singles. He won the Young Masters again in Jan. 1986 and was r/u to Lendl in Masters, rising from 65th to 6th in the world, although in light of Wimbledon most experts placed him in the top 5. *1985 HIGHLIGHTS – SINGLES: French Open* 2r (d. Gerulaitis 6–3 6–7 6–1 6–1, lost Wilander [seed 4] 6–3 6–2 6–1), *won Wimbledon* unseeded (d. Pfister 4–6 6–3 6–2 6–4, Anger 6–0 6–1 6–3, Nystrom 3–6 7–6 6–1 4–6 9–7, Mayotte 6–3 4–6 6–7 7–6 6–2, Leconte 7–6 3–6 6–3 6–4, Jarryd [seed 5] 2–6 7–6 6–3 6–3, Curren [seed 8] 6–3 6–7

Jimmy Arias, who slipped from a world ranking of 6 in 1983 to 14 a year later and 21 in 1985 – a sign of increasing pressure for the 21-year-old. *(A. Evans)*

7–6 6–4), **US Open** last 16, seed 8 (d. Doohan 6–4 6–1 6–2, van Boeckel 6–3 6–0 6–2, Evernden 7–6 6–3 7–6, lost Nystrom [seed 10] 6–3 6–4 4–6 6–4), **Australian Open** 2r, seed 4 (lost Schapers 3–6 6–4 7–6 4–6 6–3); **D Cup f** (d. Edberg 6–3 3–6 7–5 8–6, Wilander 6–3 2–6 6–3 6–3); **won** Queens (d. Pate 6–3 fs, Cash 6–4 6–4, McNamee, Kriek 6–2 6–3), **won** ATP Cincinnati (d. Sadri 6–4 fs, Pfister 6–4 fs, Nystrom 6–4 7–5, Wilander 6–4 6–2); **r/u** Masters (d. Annacone, Wilander, Jarryd, lost Lendl 6–2 7–6 6–3), **r/u** Wembley (d. Jarryd 7–6 7–6, lost Lendl 6–4 5s); **sf** Italian Open (d. Aguilera, Gunnarsson, lost Noah), **sf** US CC (d. Mecir, lost Lendl 6–2 fs), **sf** Tokyo Seiko (d. Jarryd 7–6 6–4, lost Lendl 7–6 2s). **CAREER HIGHLIGHTS – SINGLES – Wimbledon – won 1985**.

CAMILLE BENJAMIN (USA)
Born Cleveland, 22 June, 1966; lives Bakersfield, Cal.; LH; 2HB; 5ft 9in; 125lb; final 1985 WTA ranking 62 (33); 1985 prize money $75,248.
Ranked No. 1 in the US Girls' 16 in 1981, she played 19 women's tournaments in 1982, which was a remarkable year for her. In 1983 she advanced through the sheer force of her personality and an undeniable flair for the game, with only Leslie Allen and Garrison her superiors among black American players. Thanks largely to a cracking western forehand and extensive reach, she was a dangerous floater in any draw and dismissed Temesvari *en route* to sf Mahwah. In 1984 she was the only unseeded player among the women to advance to a GS sf, to set up a meeting in Paris with five-time and defending champion Evert Lloyd. She failed to win a game but her tournament and her year were successful. She was less so in 1985, but reached f Utah and beat Jordan at VS Florida. **1985 HIGHLIGHTS – SINGLES: French Open** 2r (d. Jexell 4–6 6–3 6–0, lost Hanika 6–0 6–1), **Wimbledon** 2r (d. Eliseenko 6–4 6–0, lost Sabatini [seed 15] 6–3 6–4), **US Open** 3r (d. Demongeot 6–4 6–3, Garrone 6–1 6–2, lost Sukova [seed 7] 6–0 7–5), **Australian Open** 1r (lost Mandlikova [seed 3] 6–2 6–2); **r/u** VS Utah (d. Gildemeister, lost Rehe 6–2 6–4); **sf** VS Pennsylvania (d. W. White 7–5 fs, lost A. Minter); **qf** Marco Island (d. Cecchini, Wade, lost Gadusek 7–6 fs). **CAREER HIGHLIGHTS – SINGLES: French Open – sf 1984** (d. Bonder 6–3 fs, lost Evert Lloyd 6–0 6–0).

CHRISTIAN BERGSTROM (Sweden)
Born Gothenburg, 19 July, 1967, and lives there; RH; 5ft 11in; 143lb; final 1985 ATP ranking 410.
Started playing aged 6, and turned pro in 1984, playing Spanish satellite. On winning Swedish teams in Copa Del Sol 1981, Coupe Jean Becker (now Jean Borotra Cup) 1983 and r/u team in 1985 Valerio Cup. In 1985 he was European 18s champ, was ranked first equal among Swedish 18s with Stenlund, and reached sf US Open jun, ending year No. 2 on ITF jun rankings.

LISA BONDER (USA)
Born Columbus, 16 October, 1965; lives Saline, Mich.; RH; 2HB; 5ft 9in; 128lb; final 1985 WTA ranking 36 (16); 1985 prize money $75,324.
Co-ranked No. 1 with Joni Urban in US 14 and under in 1980, she won Nat 18 singles title in 1981. In 1982, aged 16, she reached sf Italian Open, her final ranking reflecting her reliable baseline play and a solid commitment to the sport. In 1983 this deceptively good player became the toast of Tokyo when she collected two singles titles in that town in the space of one month. First she produced one of the biggest upsets of the year to beat Evert Lloyd indoors in 2r Queen's GP and upended Jaeger in f, then she won the Borden Classic outdoors on cement. Coached by Nick Bollittieri in 1984 her level of play was of such a consistently high standard over the first eight months that she was seeded ninth at US Open. She reached last 16 there, qf French Open, and sf Italian Open, achieving admirable results with her cool, almost effortless style of play. Despite a relapse in the autumn, it was unquestionably her best year. She developed a talent for bad draws in 1985 losing 1r matches to distinguished players including K. Jordan, Turnbull, Temesvari, and Navratilova. Some self-confidence was restored by sf appearance in New Orleans and qf Stuttgart where she upended Durie and Phelps. **1985 HIGHLIGHTS – SINGLES: French Open** 2r (d. Vanier 7–6 2–6 6–0, lost Evert Lloyd [seed 2] 7–5 6–3), **Wimbledon** 1r (lost Navratilova [seed 1] 6–0 6–2), **US Open** 2r (d. Ivan 6–2 4–6 6–3, lost Navratilova

[seed 2] 6–1 6–1); *sf* New Orleans (d. Rinaldi 7–6 4–3 ret'd, Reynolds 6–1 fs, lost Evert Lloyd [seed 1] 6–3 6–1); *qf* Stuttgart (d. Durie 6–1 fs, Phelps 6–4 fs), *qf* Tampa (d. Gadusek 6–1 fs, lost A. White). *CAREER HIGHLIGHTS – SINGLES: French Open – qf 1984* (lost Benjamin 7–6 5–7 6–3); *Italian Open – sf 1982* (d. Rinaldi, lost Evert Lloyd 6–2 6–4); *sf 1984* (lost Evert Lloyd 6–1 6–1).

JIMMY BROWN (USA)
Born Hialeah, Fla., 28 April, 1965; lives Bardmoor Club, Fla.; RH; 2HB; 5ft 11in; 150lb; final 1985 ATP ranking 65 (100); 1985 prize money $63,304.
US Nat 16 champ in 1980, he won Nat 18 CC and Nat 18 Champ in summer 1981, before turning pro in autumn. Gained important experience as member of US D Cup team in Cincinnati as US stopped Argentina to win back the Cup. With impressive CC results, he leaped 311 places on the computer in 1982, and by 1983 he had established himself as one of the most distinguished CC players in the world. On that surface, he defeated Dibbs, Arraya, and Higueras. He played 23 GP events in 1984, but his results were not up to the level of the previous year. However, picking his spots carefully in 1985, he climbed back to a more comfortable place among the top 100. *1985 HIGHLIGHTS – SINGLES: French Open* 1r (lost DePalmer 5–7 6–3 6–7 7–6 6–3); *r/u* Bordeaux (d. Bardou, Clerc 6–1 fs, lost Perez); *sf* Buenos Aires (d. Viver, lost Perez); *qf* Cincinnati (d. Kriek, Benhabiles, Scanlon, lost Wilkison) *qf* Florence (d. Vilas, lost Bengoechea).

IVA BUDAROVA (Czechoslovakia)
Born Duchcov, 31 July, 1960; lives Prague; LH; 5ft 7in; 145lb; final 1985 WTA ranking 57 (56); 1985 prize money $44,335.
A product of the Czech training programme, she represented her country in all the age-group team competitions finally making Fed Cup team in 1980. In 1981 she broke into the top 100 and another successful venture on the Futures circuit in 1982 took her into the top 60. An attractive player, she made further progress in 1983, including a stunning Wimbledon upset of Shriver in 2r. In 1984 she dropped back to No. 56, where she had been in 1982. She did, however, win the Italian Open doubles with Skuherska and was r/u to Maleeva at Swiss Open. Slow to get into the swing of things in 1985, she did better towards the end of the year, beating M. Maleeva, Temesvari and Huber. *1985 HIGHLIGHTS – SINGLES: French Open* 1r (lost Henricksson 3–6 6–3 6–3), *Wimbledon* 1r (lost Mandlikova [seed 3] 6–0 6–1), *US Open* 1r (lost Bassett [seed 15] 6–0 6–7 7–5); *sf* VS Indianapolis (d. Kelesi 6–3 fs, lost Gadusek); *qf* Mahwah (d. M. Maleeva, lost Rinaldi), *qf* Stuttgart (d. Huber 6–3 7–6, Temesvari 6–3 6–4, lost Shriver 6–2 6–2). *CAREER HIGHLIGHTS – DOUBLES:* (with Skuherska) *Italian Open – won 1984* (d. Horvath /Ruzici 7–6 1–6 6–4).

BETTINA BUNGE (West Germany)
Born Adliswick, Switzerland, 13 June, 1963; lives Monte Carlo, Monaco; single; RH; 5ft 7in; 120lb; final 1985 WTA ranking 23 (21); 1985 prize money $90,312.
A German citizen (her father is German), she is a former champ of Peru where she won the Peruvian Nationals aged 13. Although she is eligible to play for Germany in Fed Cup, and produced some of her best tennis of 1980 to beat Barker and Fromholtz at Berlin in that team competition, she remained eligible for US ranking because she lived in America. She is an enormously gifted player, and in 1981 she made impressive progress, reaching the world top 10. While she remained a puzzlingly erratic player in 1982, she consolidated her place among the ten best players in the world, reaching her first Wimbledon sf. Yet she lacked the consistency she will need if she is to move into the top five. After moving up to No. 6 early in 1983, she realised she was becoming hard of hearing, so after leading Germany into Fed Cup f in summer, she withdrew from the circuit, had an operation to correct the problem, and prepared to return in 1984, when she indeed showed flashes of her past glory. However, she was unreliable, and, having spent two years as a member of the top 10, she slipped considerably in 1984. In 1985, at the age of 22, she appeared resigned to the less exclusive territory of the top 25 and it seemed possible that her best tennis was behind her. *1985 HIGHLIGHTS – SINGLES: French Open* 3r (d. Vasquez 6–1 6–1, McNeil 6–1 6–1, lost Graf 6–1 7–6), *Wimbledon* 3r (d. McNeil 6–3 6–3, Cecchini 6–3

6–2, lost Navratilova [seed 1] 7–6 6–3), **US Open** 1r (lost Kim 6–4 6–4), **Australian Open** 1r, seed 12 (lost Balestrat 6–4 6–2); **sf** German Open (d. Kohde-Kilsch 7–5 7–6, lost Graf 6–1 6–3); **qf** VS Dallas (d. Temesvari, lost Sukova 6–3 fs), **qf** Eastbourne (d. Balestrat 6–2 fs, lost Navratilova 7–6 6–3), **qf** VS LA (d. Rinaldi 6–3 6–3, lost Garrison 6–4 fs). **1985 HIGHLIGHTS – DOUBLES:** (with Pfaff) **French Open** qf (lost Nagelsen /A. White 6–1 6–2); **r/u** Swiss Open (d. Burgin /Horvath 6–4 fs, lost Gadusek /Sukova 6–2 6–4); **sf** German Open (lost Graf /Tanvier), **sf** VS LA (lost Mandlikova /Turnbull). **CAREER HIGHLIGHTS – SINGLES: Wimbledon – sf 1982** seed 11 (d. Leslie Allen 6–3 7–5, A. Smith 6–2 3–6 6–0, lost Navratilova [seed 1] 6–2 6–2). **CAREER HIGHLIGHTS – DOUBLES:** (with Kohde) **French Open – sf 1981** (lost Fairbank /Harford 6–2 fs); **Wimbledon – sf 1982** (lost Navratilova /Shriver 6–3 6–4); **US Open – sf 1982** (d. K. Jordan /A. Smith 6–7 7–5 6–3, lost Casals /Turnbull 6–4 6–1).

ELISE BURGIN (USA)
Born Baltimore, 5 March, 1962 and lives there; LH; 2HB; 5ft 4½in; 115lb; final 1985 WTA ranking 27 (51) singles, 16 doubles; 1985 prize money $102,943.
Always among the top of her age group throughout her jun years in US, she beat Horvath *en route* to f 1980 US Open jun event. In 1982 she distinguished herself at Wimbledon, reaching qf doubles with Stanford University friend Alycia Moulton, and upset Bunge in reaching last 16 singles at US Open. Her best performance of 1983 was to reach sf Canadian Open where she upended another old Stanford star, Kathy Jordan, before falling to Evert Lloyd. She remained on essentially the same level in 1984 but in 1985, with a feisty spirit and healthy conviction, she drove her way into the top 30, making her debut in Fed Cup where she helped US reach f. Otherwise her best showing was appearance in f VS Houston with wins over Rehe, Garrison and M. Maleeva. **1985 HIGHLIGHTS – SINGLES: French Open** 2r (d. Klitch 7–5 4–0 ret'd, lost Mandlikova [seed 3] 2–6 6–4 7–5), **Wimbledon** 3r (d. Medrado 7–6 6–2, Villagran 6–0 6–3, lost Durie 7–5 7–5), **US Open** 3r (d. Vermaak 6–0 6–1, Huber 6–4 6–4, lost M. Maleeva [seed 8] 6–4 7–5), **Australian Open** 1r (lost Jolissaint 6–7 6–4 6–2); **r/u** VS Houston (d. Rehe 6–4 fs, Garrison 6–4 fs, M. Maleeva 6–4 7–6, lost Navratilova 6–4 6–1), **r/u** VS Indianapolis (d. Gadusek, lost Horvath 6–2 6–4); **sf** Birmingham (d. Benjamin 6–4 fs, R. White 6–4 fs, lost Shriver). **1985 HIGHLIGHTS – DOUBLES:** [Navratilova] **won** Houston (d. M. Maleeva /Sukova 6–1 3–6 6–3); [Horvath] **r/u** Tourn of Champs (lost Navratilova /Shriver 6–3 6–1), [Russell] **r/u** VS Chicago (lost K. Jordan /Smylie 6–2 6–2).

FRANCESCO CANCELLOTTI (Italy)
Born Perugia, 27 February, 1963, and lives there; RH; 6ft; 165lb; final 1985 ATP ranking 58 (26); 1985 prize money $56,498.
In the year that he turned 20, he proved that his prowess during his jun years was no accident, with a highly successful year on the GP circuit, including a r /u finish at Florence where he was beaten by Arias. By virtue of his first two GP singles titles at Florence and Palermo and some solid performances elsewhere, including a qf finish at his country's Open in Rome, he moved up 46 places on the computer in 1984 and was ranked above all other Italians. He reached last 16 French Open in 1985, but could not maintain his high status of the previous year. **1985 HIGHLIGHTS – SINGLES: French Open** last 16, unseeded (d. Schwaier 6–3 6–2 6–7 3–6 6–0, Saad 6–4 6–4 6–3, Motta 6–3 6–3 3–6 7–6, lost Connors [seed 3] 3–6 6–0 6–4 6–2); **qf** Monte Carlo (d. Fibak, Nystrom 6–2 7–5, lost Lendl 6–2 6–1), **qf** Palermo (lost Muster).

JONATHAN CANTER (USA)
Born Los Angeles, Cal., 4 June, 1965; lives Beverley Hills, Cal.; RH; 6ft 1in; 170lb; final 1985 ATP ranking 73 (239); 1985 prize money $60,096.
At age 14 in 1980 he was the youngest player ever to receive ATP ranking, and was ranked No. 1 in US 18s in 1982. In 1985 he slipped quietly into top 75, ending the year by taking his first GP title in Melbourne. **1985 HIGHLIGHTS – SINGLES: Wimbledon** 1r (lost V. Amritraj 6–3 6–4 6–4), **US Open** 2r (d. Seguso 4–6 6–4 6–3 6–4, lost Odizor 7–6 2–6 6–2 7–6), **Australian Open** 1r (lost Leach 7–5 7–6 5–7 3–6 6–4); **won** Melbourne (d. Visser, Champion, Dyke, Edmondson, Doohan 5–7 6–3 6–4).

KENT CARLSSON (Sweden)
Born Eskilstuma, 3 January, 1968, and lives there; RH; 5ft 11in; 143lb; final 1985 ATP ranking 48 (139); 1985 prize money $49,416.
Father, Lars Jöran, is a postman and coaches a little. A steady, precocious baseliner who looks much like Borg and Wilander did at his age, he won the Orange Bowl in 1983 when he was still only 15. One of 4 players on new SIAB squad under captain Peter Ronsjo – the others are Johan Carlsson (no relation), Jonas Svensson and Helena Dahlström. Had he played more senior tennis in 1984, when an injury curtailed his year, he surely would have taken his place among the top 100 players. However, he added the French Open junior title to his collection, and looked increasingly likely to become an outstanding CC player, with a string of three productive tournaments in the middle of 1985. He lifted himself into the top 50 in 1985 with a run of success featuring sf Bastad, r /u Hilversum and qf Kitzbuhel. *1985 HIGHLIGHTS – SINGLES: French Open* 2r (d. Westphal 6–2 6–1 6–3, lost Gomez [seed 5] 6–2 6–4 6–1); *rlu* Hilversum (d. Benhabiles 6–4 fs, Limberger 6–1 fs, Cahill, Oosting, lost Osterthun 4–6 4–6 6–4 6–2 6–3); *sf* Bastad (d. Casal 6–4 6–2, DeMinicis, lost Edberg 6–4 6–2); *qf* Kitzbuhel (d. Glickstein, Becka, Perez, lost Westphal 7–6 6–3).

SERGIO CASAL (Spain)
Born Barcelona, 8 September, 1962, and lives there; RH; 6ft 2in; 155lb; final 1985 ATP ranking 38 (177) singles, 25 doubles; 1985 prize money $103,718.
When he stopped S. Giammalva and Wilander *en route* to qf 1980 Orange Bowl, it was apparent that he was destined to become a player of note. He went through some growing pains in 1981 and 1982 but was learning in the process. A member of the Galea Cup team as a jun, he became a D Cup squad member in 1982. In 1983, he produced the best tennis of his life. He slipped out of the top 100 in 1984, but returned in 1985, forming a successful doubles partnership with countryman Sanchez. *1985 HIGHLIGHTS – SINGLES: sf* Kitzbuhel (d. Rosenquist, DeMinicis, Cahill, Sanchez, lost Slozil); *qf* Barcelona (lost Wilander 6–1 6–2). *1985 HIGHLIGHTS – DOUBLES:* (with Sanchez) *won* Kitzbuhel (d. Cane /Panatta), *won* Barcelona (d. Gunnarsson /Mortensen 6–3 6–3); *rlu* Munich (lost Edmondson /Warwick), *rlu* Bastad (lost Edberg /Jarryd).

PAM CASALE (USA)
Born Camden, NJ, 20 December, 1963; lives Bradenton, Fla. and Fairfield, NJ; RH; 2HB; 5ft 8in; 127lb; final 1985 WTA ranking 34 (15); 1985 prize money $67,027.
Things started happening quickly for this remarkably hard worker during the 1980 season, when she dominated US Girls' 16s, taking Orange Bowl and Easter Bowl 16s in the process. Summer 1980 she played some satellite tournaments on USTA Penn circuit and in 1981, after capturing Avon Futures Bakersfield, she turned pro. She climbed as high as No. 16 during the year, reaching f Mahwah and Japan Open. A great scrambler and retriever, she has an unorthodox backhand similar to Françoise Durr's. Life grew more complicated for this determined and dedicated baseliner in 1982, when she never quite rose to the level she reached in 1981, and she was uneven in 1983 but remained a player whom none could afford to take lightly. Consistent throughout 1984, she restored herself, reaching sf of 4 tournaments and spending most of the year among the top 25. Two of her best performances took place in her home state of New Jersey, where she upended Austin at US Indoor and Maleeva at Mahwah. She lost some ground in 1985, unable to keep pace with the fast start she made as she reached f of Marco Island in her third event of the year. After a mid-season slumps she returned to top form late in the year when she upset Rinaldi in Indianapolis to reach f, and then concluded year with qf finish in Tampa. *1985 HIGHLIGHTS – SINGLES: French Open* 2r (d. Cummings 6–3 1–6 6–0, lost Tauziat 6–7 7–6 6–2), *Wimbledon* 1r (lost Holikova 5–7 6–1 6–3), *US Open* 2r (d. Rossides 6–3 6–2, lost Garrison [seed 6] 6–2 6–4); *rlu* Marco Island (d. K. Jordan 7–5 6–4, lost Gadusek 6–3 6–4), *rlu* VS Indianapolis (d. Rinaldi 6–4 fs, lost Gadusek 6–0 6–3); *qf* Tampa (d. Phelps 6–4 7–6, lost Sabatini).

PAT CASH (Australia)

Born Melbourne, 27 May, 1965; lives Ringwood; RH; 5ft 11in; 170lb; final 1985 ATP ranking 67 (8) singles, 18 (18) doubles; 1985 prize money $127,244.
One of the world's outstanding jun in 1982 when he won Wimbledon and US Open jun titles. But he found time to test himself among the pros, becoming the youngest ever to win a GP title when he won Melbourne. (Krickstein now holds the record.) Considered by many experts to be the best Australian prospect since Newcombe, he gained significant experience in 1983 when he helped lead Australia to first D Cup success since 1977 as they beat Sweden in Dec. He achieved most of his best results on grass, reaching last 16 Wimbledon and beating Gerulaitis at Queens. He also reached last 16 Australian Open, beating Teacher in a bizarre 5s match before losing to Lendl. Peaking for the occasions which mattered most in 1984, he reached sf Wimbledon and US Open, d. Wilander in both, and was rewarded with a world top 10 ranking. However, he did not win a tournament, lost in qf Australian Open to Kriek, and despite a 'dead rubber' win over Connors in D Cup, he was not the same player outside the gates of Wimbledon and Flushing Meadow. Held back by injuries in 1985, he was sidelined after Wimbledon, where he reached f doubles with Fitzgerald, and missed US and Australian Opens. His ranking slipped drastically as a result. *1985 HIGHLIGHTS – SINGLES: Wimbledon* 2r, seed 6 (d. Nelson 2–6 6–2 7–5 6–7 6–3, lost Acuna 7–6 6–3 3–6 6–7 6–4); *sf* Brussels (d. Nystrom 6–4 6–2, lost Wilander 6–3 7–6); *qf* Rotterdam (lost Nystrom), *qf* Queens Club (d. V. Amritraj, Edmondson, lost Becker 6–4 6–4). *1985 HIGHLIGHTS – DOUBLES:* (with Fitzgerald) *r/u Wimbledon* seed 5 (d. McEnroe /Fleming [seed 1] 7–6 2–6 6–1 6–4, lost Gunthardt /Taroczy 6–4 6–3 4–6 6–3); *won* Las Vegas (lost Annacone /Van Rensburg 7–6 6–7 7–6); *r/u* Queens (d. McNamara /McNamee, lost Flach /Seguso). *CAREER HIGH-LIGHTS – SINGLES: Wimbledon – sf 1984* unseeded (d. Wilander, Motta, Curren, Gomez, lost McEnroe 6–3 7–6 6–4); *US Open – sf 1984* (d. Wilander, lost Lendl [seed 2] 3–6 6–3 6–4 6–7 7–6 after having 1 mp); *Australian Open – qf 1984* (lost Kriek 7–5 6–1 7–6). *CAREER HIGHLIGHTS – DOUBLES:* with Fitzgerald unless stated [McNamee] *Wimbledon – r/u 1984* (lost McEnroe /Fleming 6–2 5–7 6–2 3–6 6–3), *r/u 1985; Australian Open – sf 1984* (lost Nystrom /Wilander 6–4 6–4 2–6 6–3).

ANNA MARIA CECCHINI (Italy)

Born Latina, 28 February, 1965, and lives there; RH; 5ft 5in; 135lb; final 1985 WTA ranking 49 (49); 1985 prize money $63,365.
R /u to Debbie Spence at 1983 Orange Bowl 18s, she was the world No. 2 Jun that year and ranked third among Italy's women. In 1984 she was successful in her first full year on tour and looked capable of becoming the best player in her country since Pericoli, a promise that she kept in 1985, despite a dismal start when she lost eight consecutive 1r matches. Her confidence returned when she stopped Vermaak and Temesvari to reach 3r Amelia Island, and she reached qf French Open unseeded before winning Barcelona. *1985 HIGHLIGHTS – SINGLES: French Open* qf, unseeded (d. Holton 6–0 6–1, Karlsson 6–0 6–1, Jolissaint 7–5 5–7 6–4, Scheuer-Larsen 6–3 6–2, lost Navratilova [seed 1] 6–2 6–2); *won* Barcelona (d. Villagran 7–6 2s, Skuherska, Ruzici 7–5 fs, Holikova, Reggi 6–3 6–4); *qf* VS NY (d. Scheuer-Larsen, lost Potter), *qf* Zurich (d. Holikova, Tauziat, lost Garrison 6–4 fs). *CAREER HIGHLIGHTS – SINGLES: French Open – qf 1985.*

SVETLANA CHERNEVA (Russia)

Born Moscow, 8 October, 1962, and lives there; RH; 5ft 4in; 124lb; final 1985 WTA ranking 74 (122) singles, 14 doubles; 1985 prize money $22,822.
A quarter-finalist in Wimbledon doubles from 1983–85 with countrywoman Savchenko, she was r /u to Mandlikova in 1978 at the European 16-and-under Champs. In 1981 she upset Mandlikova in Fed Cup at Tokyo and in 1985 she worked her way into the top 100 in singles. *1985 HIGHLIGHTS – SINGLES: Wimbledon* 2r qualifying (lost Bryant 1–6 6–2 6–4); *qf* Sydney (d. Marsikova 6–4 fs, Durie, Garrison 6–1 fs, lost Mandlikova). *1985 HIGHLIGHTS – DOUBLES:* (with Savchenko) *Wimbledon* qf, seed 6 (d. Demongeot /Tauziat 4–6 7–6 6–2, lost Mandlikova /Turnbull [seed 4] 6–4 6–3); *r/u* VS Florida (lost K. Jordan /Smylie 6–4 7–6).

JOSÉ-LUIS CLERC (Argentina)
Born Buenos Aires, 16 August, 1958 and lives there with wife Annalie and son Pablo; RH;
6ft 1in; 175lb; final 1985 ATP ranking 29 (33); 1985 prize money $75,764.
In 1981 he dominated the American summer circuit, capturing four consecutive Volvo GP
events and, with a D Cup victory, he built a 28-match winning streak before being
eliminated in last 16 US Open. Clerc captured his first major int title (Italian) in May and
reached sf French Open. He also helped Argentina reach their first D Cup f. By then he
was recognised as one of the 5 best players in the world and had surpassed countryman
Vilas as No. 1 in Argentina. Not so in 1982. An inspired Vilas surpassed him and Clerc
never built the same foundation of confidence. In 1983, he continued in the doldrums
across the first half of the season. With the exception of a narrow 5s win over McEnroe
in D Cup at Buenos Aires and an impressive victory over Wilander at Guaruja Beach, he
never seemed to have his heart in the game until he came alive in the summer and
almost duplicated his 1981 feat of sweeping 4 US clay-court events in succession. After
a change of racket he won Boston and Washington and stopped Gomez to win North
Conway, but his gruelling schedule caught up with him and at US CC he was forced to
retire after losing 1s to countryman Arguello in 3r. In late September he withdrew from
the circuit for the rest of the year, owing to injuries. He was the mystery man of 1984,
seldom playing with any zest or sense of adventure as his ranking slipped substantially.
Only once, when he beat Gomez before losing to Krickstein in US Pro f, did he strike
form. He reached sf Italian Open but there he was trounced by Gomez. In 1985, he
appeared to be a much older man than 27, and while he remained in the same basic
territory on the computer he was no longer the player he had been. *1985 HIGHLIGHTS
– SINGLES: French Open* 3r (d. Lapidus 6–4 6–3 6–1, Ganzabal 6–3 6–3 6–3, lost Noah
[seed 9] 6–1 6–7 6–4 4–6 8–6), *US Open* 1r (lost Edberg [seed 11] 6–4 6–3 6–4); *sf*
Hamburg (d. Gunnarsson, lost Sundstrom), *sf* Munich (d. Mecir 7–5 6–3, lost Nystrom),
sf Stuttgart (d. Gunnarsson, lost Lendl), *sf* Bordeaux (d. Agenor, lost J. Brown). *CAREER
HIGHLIGHTS – SINGLES: USCC – won 1980* (d. Purcell 7–5 6–3), *won 1981* (d. Lendl
4–6 6–4 6–2); *S. American Open – won 1980* (d. Gehring 6–7 2–6 7–5 6–0 6–3), *won
1982; Italian Open – won 1981* (d. A. Panatta, Lendl, Pecci 6–2 6–4 6–0); *US Pro – won
1981* (d. Orantes, Teltscher, Gildemeister 0–6 6–2 6–2), *won 1983* (d. Arias 6–3 6–1);
Nations Cup – on winning ARG team 1980; *Canadian Open – r/u 1978* (d. Gottfried 6–4
fs, lost Dibbs 5–7 6–4 6–1); *French Open – sf 1981* seed 5 (d. Connors [seed 2], lost
Lendl 3–6 6–4 4–6 7–6 6–2), *sf 1982* (lost Wilander 7–5 6–2 1–6 7–5).

JIMMY CONNORS (USA)
*Born East St Louis, Ill., 2 September, 1952; lives Sanibel Island, Fla. and Santa Barbara,
Cal., with wife Patti, son Brett (born 1979) and daughter Aubree (born Dec. 1984); LH;
2HB; 5ft 10in; 155lb; final 1985 ATP ranking 4 (2); 1985 prize money $562,336; career prize
money $6,815,348.*
After rising to No. 1 in the world in 1974, aged 22, when he won Australian Open,
Wimbledon and US Open, as well as 99 of 103 matches, he remained in the top 3 until
1985. Connors was again a unanimous world No. 1 in 1976 when he won his second of
five US Open singles titles. In 1981 he had his least productive year since 1973. He
remained in the world top 5 and finished the year at No. 3, but in terms of what he
accomplished he was the fifth best player behind McEnroe, Borg, Lendl and Clerc. For
the third successive year he reached sf at both Wimbledon and US Open, Borg beating
him on both occasions; a golden opportunity slipped past Connors at Wimbledon when
he led the Swede two sets to love in a classic battle. In a puzzling decision, he declined
to participate in D Cup sf or f and went skiing instead of competing against Argentina in
Cincinnati, thus depriving himself of the chance to add his name to the list of all-time
greats who have helped their nation win the D Cup. In 1982 he made the comeback very
few seasoned observers thought possible, and after an 8-year gap he won his second
Wimbledon singles title by downing defending champion McEnroe. Not since Tilden
(1921 and 1930) had a men's champion re-gained his title after so many years. Seven
weeks later he won his fourth US Open, beating Lendl in 4s and clinching the No. 1 world
ranking. Contrary to what the computers indicated, he was, for the third time,
undoubtedly, the best player in the world. He won 7 of 18 tournaments and reached four
f, five sf, and qf of the remaining two. At 30, following a 6–2 6–2 6–2 loss to Higueras in

French Open qf which brought his streak of defeats in GS events to 10 since the 1978 US Open, he returned to the very top of his sport against some long odds. One last disappointment remained when Lendl thrashed him in sf Masters 6–3 6–1 in 62 minutes. While he did not manage to reach those heights in 1983, he capped another great season by seizing his second consecutive US Open and fifth overall, stopping the favourite Lendl. Connors, trailing 3–5 in 3s, saved a s-p at 4–5 when Lendl served a double-fault, before completing a run of 10 consecutive games to win 6–3 6–7 7–5 6–0. It was his 100th official career singles title, the temperature rose to 100 degrees in the late afternoon at Flushing Meadow, and he had to overcome an intestinal disorder which forced him to leave the court in the middle of 2s. Connors won three additional titles (US Indoor, Las Vegas and Queens Club) but had some setbacks which forced him to relinquish his world champion status to McEnroe. He lost to Roger-Vasselin in qf French Open, fell to Curren in last 16 Wimbledon (the first time in 12 years that he had failed to reach qf there) and lost to Lendl in sf Masters. He finished the year ranked 3 on the computer and was graded either 2 or 3 in the world by most experts. Although unable to add any GS titles in 1984, he was so remarkably consistent that he finished No. 2 on the computer, ranked anywhere from 2 to 4 by the experts. He reached his sixth Wimbledon f where he was crushed by McEnroe, who also removed him from the sf French and US Opens. At Flushing Meadow he pushed his countryman hard and lost narrowly in 5s. At end of year, he lost crucial opening match in D Cup f v Sweden against Wilander when his behaviour embarrassed US contingent, then lost to Lendl in Masters sf for third straight year after leading 5–2 fs and was fined $500 for obscene gesture. After that psychologically damaging defeat by Lendl, he had a dismal start to 1985 which included sf exit to Mecir at US Pro Indoor and a 6–0 6–3 failure against Holmes in qf La Quinta on his favourite surface. He did not win a tournament all year for the first time since 1972. In 15 tournaments he reached only two f (Chicago and Fort Myers) and was eliminated in sf of ten others including Wimbledon, US and French Opens. He remained clearly one of the five best players in the world but looked weary and no longer capable of winning a major event. Nevertheless, his sf US Open was his 11th in succession, and sf Wimbledon his 10th in 12 years. Missed Masters Jan. 1986 owing to flu. *1985 HIGHLIGHTS – SINGLES: French Open* sf, seed 3 (d. Popp 6–4 6–1 7–5, Willenborg 6–1 6–3 6–0, Benhabiles 6–3 4–6 7–5 7–5, Cancellotti 3–6 6–0 6–4 6–2, Edberg 6–4 6–3 7–6, lost Lendl 6–2 6–3 6–1), *Wimbledon* sf, seed 3 (d. S. Simonsson 6–1 6–3 6–4, Evernden 6–3 6–2 6–1, Krishnan 7–5 5–7 7–5 6–2, S. Giammalva 6–3 6–4 6–2, Acuna 6–1 7–6 6–2, lost Curren 6–2 6–2 6–1), *US Open* sf, seed 3 (d. Muller 6–4 6–3 4–6 6–2, Pfister 6–3 6–4 6–2, Tulasne 7–5 6–2 6–4, Edberg 6–4 3–6 6–3 6–4, Gunthardt 6–2 6–2 6–4, lost Lendl 6–2 6–3 7–5); *rlu* Chicago (d. Gilbert 7–5 fs, Gomez, lost McEnroe def.), *rlu* Fort Myers (d. Gomez 6–4 fs, lost Lendl 6–3 6–2); *sf* US Pro Indoor (lost Mecir 6–3 fs), *sf* Memphis (d. Curren, lost Edberg 6–1 6–4), *sf* WCT Dallas (lost Lendl 6–3 2–1 ret'd), *sf* Washington (lost Noah), *sf* Stratton Mountain (lost Lendl 6–4 fs), *sf* Canadian Open (lost McEnroe 6–2 6–3), *sf* Seiko Open Tokyo (lost Wilander def.). *CAREER HIGHLIGHTS – SINGLES: Wimbledon – won 1974* (d. Rosewall 6–1 6–1 6–4), *won 1982* (d. Alexander 7–6 4s, Gitlin 7–5 4s, G. Mayer 6–1 6–2 7–6, Edmondson 6–4 6–3 6–1, McEnroe 3–6 6–3 6–7 7–6 6–4), *rlu 1975* (lost Ashe 6–1 6–1 5–7 6–4), *rlu 1977* (lost Borg 3–6 6–2 6–1 5–7 6–4), *rlu 1978* (lost Borg 6–2 6–2 6–3), *rlu 1984* (d. Lendl 6–7 6–3 7–5 6–1, lost McEnroe 6–1 6–1 6–2), *sf 1979* (lost Borg 6–2 6–3 6–2), *sf 1980* seed 3 (lost McEnroe 6–3 3–6 6–3 6–4), *sf 1981* (d. V. Amritraj 2–6 5–7 6–4 6–3 6–2, lost Borg 0–6 4–6 6–3 6–0 6–4), *sf 1985; US Open – won 1974* (d. Rosewall 6–1 6–0 6–1), *won 1976* (d. Borg 6–4 3–6 7–6 6–4), *won 1978* (d. McEnroe 6–2 6–2 7–5, Borg 6–4 6–2 6–2), *won 1982* (d. Arias 6–4 4–6 6–4 6–1, Nastase 6–3 6–3 6–4, Vilas 6–1 3–6 6–2 6–3, Lendl 6–3 6–2 4–6 6–4), *won 1983* (d. Lendl 6–3 6–7 7–5 6–0), *rlu 1975* (lost Orantes 6–4 6–3 6–3), *rlu 1977* (lost Vilas 2–6 6–3 7–6 6–0), *sf 1979* (lost McEnroe 6–3 6–3 7–5), *sf 1980* seed 3 (lost McEnroe 6–4 5–7 0–6 6–3 7–6), *sf 1981* (lost Borg 6–2 7–5 6–4), *sf 1984* (lost McEnroe 6–4 4–6 7–5 4–6 6–3), *sf 1985; Australian Open – won 1974* (d. Dent 7–6 6–4 4–6 6–3), *rlu 1975* (lost Newcombe 7–5 3–6 6–4 7–6); *Masters – won 1978* (d. Borg 6–4 1–6 6–4), *sf 1979* seed 3 (lost Gerulaitis 7–5 6–2), *sf 1980* seed 4 (lost Borg 6–4 6–7 6–3), *sf 1982* (lost Lendl 6–3 6–1), *sf 1983* (lost Lendl 6–3 6–4), *sf 1984* (lost Lendl 7–6 5–7 7–5); *WCT Finals – won 1977* (d. Stockton 6–7 6–1 6–4 6–3), *won 1980* seed 2 (d. Scanlon, Lendl, McEnroe 2–6 7–6 6–1 6–2); *US CC – won 1974* (d. Borg 5–7 6–3 6–4), *won 1976* (d. Fibak 6–2 6–4), *won 1978* (d. Higueras 7–5 6–1), *won 1979* (d. Vilas 6–1 2–6 6–4), *rlu 1972* (lost Hewitt 6–1 7–6), *rlu*

1977 (lost Orantes 6–1 6–3); *US Pro Indoor – won 1976* (d. Borg 7–6 6–4 6–0), *won 1978* (d. Tanner 6–4 6–2 6–3), *won 1979* (d. Ashe 6–3 6–4 6–1), *won 1980* (d. McEnroe 6–3 2–6 6–3 3–6 6–4); *US Indoor – won 1973* (d. Meiler), *won 1974* (d. McMillan), *won 1975* (d. Gerulaitis 6–1 fs), *won 1978* (d. Tim Gullikson 7–6 6–3), *won 1979* (d. Ashe 6–4 5–7 6–3), *won 1983* (d. G. Mayer 7–5 6–0), *won 1984* (d. Leconte 6–3 4–6 7–5); *South African Open – won 1973* (d. Ashe), *won 1974* (d. Ashe); *French Open – sf 1979* seed 2 (lost Pecci 7–6 6–4 5–7 6–3), *sf 1980* (lost Gerulaitis 6–1 3–6 6–7 6–2 6–4), *qf 1981* (lost Clerc 4–6 6–2 4–6 7–5 6–0), *sf 1985. CAREER HIGHLIGHTS – DOUBLES:* (with Nastase) *Wimbledon – won 1973* (d. Cooper/Fraser 3–6 6–3 6–4 8–9 6–1); *US Open – won 1975* (d. Okker/Riessen); *French Open – r/u 1973* (lost Newcombe/Okker 6–4 fs). *MIXED DOUBLES:* (with Evert) *US Open – r/u 1974* (lost Masters/Teeguarden 6–1 7–6).

BELINDA CORDWELL (New Zealand)

Born Wellington, 21 September, 1965, and lives there; LH; 5ft 9in; 147lb; final 1985 WTA ranking 70 (211); 1985 prize money $22,585.
A rapidly improving player, she emerged in 1985 from the satellites to break into the top 100. *1985 HIGHLIGHTS – SINGLES: Wimbledon* (lost 3r qualifying Van Nostrand 6–1 6–0), *US Open* 3r (d. Lindstrom 6–3 6–4, Werdel 6–2 7–6, lost Garrison [seed 6] 6–4 6–4), *Australian Open* 1r (lost Garrison 6–4 4–6 6–4); *won* Tasmania (d. Turk 7–6 fs, Bryant 7–6 fs); *qf* VS Newport (d. Mochizuki, K. Jordan 6–4 6–3, lost Pfaff).

ANNABEL CROFT (Great Britain)

Born London, 12 July, 1966; lives Farnborough, Kent; RH; 5ft 7in; 120lb; final 1985 WTA ranking 24 (82); 1985 prize money $69,933.
As if by design, she showed her finest colours at Wimbledon in 1984, reaching last 32 and giving Evert Lloyd a thorough test. She then demonstrated her depth as a competitor by winning the Wimbledon Jun title and in the autumn made her W Cup singles début, beating the more experienced American Moulton in 3s. Assisted ably by coach Owen Davidson, she made significant strides in 1985 by winning her first upper-level event in San Diego and reaching sf Brighton, where she surprised Sukova before losing to Evert Lloyd. Moving up 58 places, she had an impressive year, which was marred only by a 6–0 6–0 W Cup beating from Shriver followed by a 6–3 6–0 dismissal by Evert Lloyd. Ended year ranked 1 in GB. *1985 HIGHLIGHTS – SINGLES: French Open* 1r (lost Jausovec 6–2 6–0), *Wimbledon* 1r (lost Hu Na 6–3 7–5), *US Open* 2r (d. Skuherska 6–1 7–5, lost Mandlikova [seed 3] 6–3 6–3), *Australian Open* 1r (lost Kohde-Kilsch [seed 5] 7–5 6–3); *won* VS San Diego (d. Thompson 6–4 fs, Gurney 6–3 fs, Turnbull 6–0 7–6); *sf* Melbourne (d. A. Brown, lost Shriver 7–6 6–2), *sf* Brighton (d. K. Maleeva, Sukova 6–4 fs, Phelps 6–1 6–3, lost Evert Lloyd 6–3 6–2).

KEVIN CURREN (USA)

Born Durban, 2 March, 1958; lives there and Austin, Tex.; RH; 2HF and 2HB; 6ft 1in; 170lb; final 1985 ATP ranking 10 (15) singles, 28 (14) doubles; 1985 prize money $235,057.
The US NCAA champ of 1979 when he played for University of Texas, he was also South African Jun champ 1976. A tenacious competitor and a good athlete, he played his first full year on GP circuit in 1980. His doubles partnership with Texan Steve Denton was one of the best and most successful of the year. Coming together for the first time at Richmond in February, they won 3 of 31 doubles tournaments they played (after meeting at Univ. of Texas, where they never played together). They reached Masters as equal second doubles pair (with McEnroe/Fleming) on Volvo GP. In 1981 he had another great year in doubles with Denton, winning 3 tournaments from 5 finals and reaching Masters again. Coached by Warren Jacques, he was so good in doubles in 1982 that his formidable singles results, taking him up 40 places to 17, were somewhat overshadowed. He captured both Wimbledon and US Open mixed doubles titles with Anne Smith, plus the US Open men's doubles with Denton. In 1983 his gift for playing singles was realised, as he beat Connors for the first time in Brussels and, in one of the outstanding displays of the year, served 33 aces to eliminate defending champion Connors in last 16 Wimbledon, fighting off 3 s-p late in 4s. For the first time in memory, certainly for the first time in a major event, Connors never broke serve in the entire match. Curren reached sf

*Andres Gomez of Ecuador overcame injury to retain his Hong Kong title and later reached
the Masters semi-finals as a replacement for the injured Connors.*   *(T. Hindley)*

Wimbledon where he lost 8–6 fs to an inspired Chris Lewis. An injury forced him out of the US Open and he played a light schedule thereafter. He struggled in 1984 to reach the heights of his 1983 campaign and finally at the end of the year, in Melbourne, he reached his first GS f, removing Lendl in last 16, coming from two sets to love down to beat Testerman in sf, and extending Wilander to 4s before losing f. This helped him move back to the top 15 after spending most of the year ranked below 20. Serving with astonishing skill and power and accuracy, he beat defending champion McEnroe and former titlist Connors back-to-back to reach f Wimbledon in 1985, but after losing 4s f to Becker he was never the same player for the rest of the season. He became a US citizen early in the year. *1985 HIGHLIGHTS – SINGLES: r/u Wimbledon* seed 8 (d. Stefanki 7–6 6–3 6–4, DePalmer 7–5 5–7 6–4 6–4, Mustard 6–3 6–3 7–5, Edberg 7–6 6–3 7–6, McEnroe 6–2 6–2 6–4, Connors 6–2 6–2 6–1, lost Becker 6–3 6–7 7–6 6–4), *US Open* 1r, seed 5 (lost Forget 7–6 6–1 6–2); *won* Toronto Indoor (d. Drewett, Annacone, Schultz, Teltscher, Jarryd 7–6 6–3); *r/u* WCT Houston (d. Annacone, Mayotte, Perkis, lost McEnroe); *sf* WCT Atlanta (d. S. Davis, lost Annacone def.). *1985 HIGHLIGHTS – DOUBLES:* (with Kriek unless stated) *Wimbledon* qf (d. Edberg /Jarryd, lost Cash /Fitzgerald), *US Open* qf (d. Edmondson /Warwick, lost DePalmer /Donnelly 6–1 7–6 4–6 7–6); [Denton] *r/u* Memphis (lost Slozil /Smid), [Fibak] *r/u* Brussels (lost Edberg /Jarryd). *CAREER HIGHLIGHTS –SINGLES: Wimbledon – r/u 1985, sf 1983* (d. Connors 6–3 6–7 6–3 7–6, Mayotte, lost C. Lewis 6–7 6–4 7–6; *Australian Open – r/u 1984* (d. Lendl, S. Davis, Testerman, lost Wilander 6–7 6–4 7–6 6–2). *CAREER HIGHLIGHTS –DOUBLES:* (with Denton) *US Open – won 1982* (d. Amaya /Pfister 6–2 6–7 5–7 6–2 6–4); *US CC – won 1980* (d. Fibak /Lendl 3–6 7–6 6–4), *won 1981; US Pro Indoor – won 1983* (d. McEnroe /Fleming 6–4 7–6); *Wimbledon – sf 1982* (lost McEnroe /Fleming 6–2 6–4 2–6 6–3), *sf 1983* (lost Tim /Tom Gullikson 7–6 6–7 7–6 6–3); *Australian Open – sf 1981* (lost Edmondson /Warwick). *MIXED DOUBLES:* (with A. Smith) *Wimbledon – won 1982* (d. Lloyd /Turnbull 2–6 6–3 7–5); *US Open – won 1981* (d. Denton /Russell 6–4 7–6), *won 1982* (d. Taygan /Potter 6–3 7–6).

MARTY DAVIS (USA)
Born San José, Cal., 15 November, 1958 and lives there; RH; 6ft; 180lb; final 1985 ATP ranking 63 (63); 1985 prize money $123,605.
Won first GP singles title (Honolulu) in 1984 and in 1985 picked up two more GP titles (Bristol and Melbourne Indoor) but too many 1r losses restricted his ranking. *1985 HIGHLIGHTS – SINGLES: French Open* 1r (lost Arguello), *Wimbledon* 1r (lost Gunnarsson 6–3 6–2 3–6 6–3), *US Open* 1r (lost Goldie 6–4 6–3 3–6 7–6); *won* Bristol (d. Masur 7–5 fs, Bates 9–7 fs, Teacher, Layendecker 7–5 fs), *won* Melbourne (d. Bauer 6–3 fs, Kratzman, Dyke, Testerman 6–4 fs, Annacone 6–4 6–4); *qf* Brisbane (d. Hooper, lost Annacone). *1985 HIGHLIGHTS – DOUBLES:* (with Drewett) *won* Brisbane (d. Schultz /Testerman).

SCOTT DAVIS (USA)
Born Santa Monica, Cal., 27 August, 1962, and lives Bardmoor CC, Fla. with his wife Suzy; RH; 6ft 2in; 170lb; final 1985 ATP ranking 17 (48) singles, 16 (49) doubles; 1985 prize money $257,611.
He is the holder of 24 Nat. Jun titles – a new record, surpassing by 4 Dick Stockton's previous record. After graduating from Stanford in late May, he turned pro and had a splendid year in 1983, exploiting his talent beautifully and catapulting into the top 25. He scored a tremendous upset win over Connors in sf Seiko Open, won Maui over Van Patten, was r /u to Fitzgerald at Newport and to Odizor at Taipei. Married to Suzy Jaeger (older sister of Andrea) in the spring of 1984, he was not as successful as he had been the previous year. He nearly upset Lendl in last 16 Wimbledon but lost 7–5 fs, and not until the end of the year when he reached qf Australian Open did he do true justice to his considerable talent. In 1985 he built significantly on his success and was ranked in the top 20 most of the year. He reached sf US Pro Indoor and f Lipton International Players Championships, then won Japan Open in the autumn. Qualified for Masters when Mecir dropped out owing to injury, but lost 1r to Wilander. *1985 HIGHLIGHTS – SINGLES: Wimbledon* 2r (d. Mecir 6–2 6–2 6–3, lost Jarryd [seed 5] 5–7 7–6 7–5 6–4), *US Open* 2r (d. Cierro 6–4 6–0 6–4, lost Teacher 6–3 7–6 6–3), *Australian Open* 1r, seed 9 (lost Zivojinovic 7–5 3–6 6–1 6–3); *won* Japan Open (d. S. Giammalva 6–4 6–2, Carlsson 6–4

6–1, Arias 6–1 7–6); *r/u* Delray Beach (d. Gilbert, Annacone, Flur, Edberg, Smid 6–3 4s, lost Mayotte 6–4 5s); *sf* US Pro Indoor (d. R. Brown 7–5 fs, Schapers, Smid, Teltscher, lost McEnroe), *sf* Chicago (d. Green, Moor, lost McEnroe); *qf* Fort Myers (lost S. Giammalva), *qf* Atlanta (d. Fibak, Pate, lost Curren), *qf* Newport (d. Gonzalez, lost Sadri), *qf* Stratton Mountain (d. Scanlon, Fleming, lost Seguso), *qf* LA (d. Schultz, lost Annacone). *1985 HIGHLIGHTS – DOUBLES:* (with Pate unless stated) *won* Stratton Mountain (d. Flach /Seguso 7–6 fs), [Van't Hof] *won* LA (d. Annacone /Van Rensburg), *won* Japan Open (d. S. Giammalva /Holmes); *r/u* Tokyo Seiko (d. Fitzgerald /Smid, lost Flach /Seguso).

HORACIO de la PENA (Argentina)
Born Buenos Aires, 16 August, 1966, and lives there; LH; 5ft 11in; 138lb; final 1985 ATP ranking 70 (90); 1985 prize money $84,162.
Thanks to proficiency on clay, he moved up 20 places in 1985. *1985 HIGHLIGHTS – SINGLES: French Open* 2r (d. Forget 7–6 5–7 6–1 6–3, lost Motta 6–4 6–2 6–4), *US Open* 3r (d. Palin 3–6 6–3 6–2 4–6 6–4, Panatta 6–7 7–5 7–6 6–3, lost Lendl [seed 2] 6–1 6–1 6–3); *won* Marbella (d. Jaite, Shaw, Duncan); *sf* Buenos Aires (d. Duncan, Ingaramo, lost Jaite); *qf* Cologne (d. Lapidus, Agenor, lost Dickson).

MIKE DePALMER (USA)
Born Tampa, 17 October, 1961; lives Knoxville; LH; 6ft 1in; 175lb; final 1985 ATP ranking 83 (103); 1985 prize money $101,483.
The son of University of Tennessee coach of the same name, he was coached for a time by Nick Bollettieri and then by his father. Always a solid, intelligent player with a sound and complete game, he was overshadowed in jun by S. Davis and Testerman. In 1982 he matured and handled the pressure of GP extremely well, reaching last 32 at US Open, sf Vienna and f Ancona. Playing 24 tournaments in 1983, he looked a better player than his ranking would indicate. After slipping in the rankings in 1984, he returned to last 100 in 1985, when he upset Connors 1r Queens. *1985 HIGHLIGHTS – SINGLES: French Open* 2r (d. J. Brown 5–7 6–3 6–7 7–6 6–3, lost Nystrom 3–6 1–6 7–6 6–3 6–4), *Wimbledon* 2r (d. Viver 6–3 6–3 3–6 6–3, lost Curren [seed 8] 7–5 5–7 6–4 6–4), *US Open* 1r (lost Vajda 2–6 2–6 6–3 7–6 7–6), *Australian Open* 3r (d. Fitzgerald 7–5 6–4 4–6 5–7 14–12, Keretic 6–2 6–2 6–2, lost Zivojinovic 6–7 6–3 6–2 6–4); *sf* Florence (d. Cancellotti, Willenborg, Duncan, lost Arias); *qf* Johannesburg (lost Kriek 4–6 6–3 6–1). *1985 HIGHLIGHTS – DOUBLES:* [Donnelly] *US Open* sf (d. Curren/Kriek [seed 16], lost Flach/Seguso [seed 1] 6–1 6–7 7–5 6–7 7–6); [Doohan] *won* Livingston (d. Edwards/Visser).

MARK DICKSON (USA)
Born Tampa, 8 December, 1959, and lives there with wife Karen; RH; 6ft 3in; 172lb; final 1985 ATP ranking 74 (35); 1985 prize money $98,337.
Unheralded and unknown until late 1982, he worked his way up to the main tours through success on the satellite tour where he won one tournament, reached one f and one sf. Early in 1983 the former Clemson Univ. All-American was in magnificent form, defeating Lendl indoors at Munich and Vilas on clay at Houston. He had his ups and downs but picked a good time to produce some of his best tennis, reaching qf US Open where he bowed in 5s t-b to Scanlon. Capturing his first GP title near the end of 1984 in Toulouse, he moved back into the top 40, winning WCT Houston. He competed with his usual zest in 1985, but a mid-season leg injury slowed him down and he never found his finest form. *1985 HIGHLIGHTS – SINGLES: French Open* 1r (lost Cahill), *US Open* 1r (lost Nelson 7–6 4–6 7–6 7–6), *Australian Open* 2r (d. Bauer 7–6 6–2 7–6, lost Mayotte [seed 8] 6–4 6–4 6–4); *sf* NSW Open Sydney (d. Fitzgerald 7–5 fs, Mansdorf, Mayotte 7–6 fs, lost Evernden 6–4 7–6), *sf* Cologne (d. Benhabiles, de la Pena, lost Krishnan); *qf* WCT Houston (d. S. Giammalva, Arias, lost Perkis), *qf* Florence (d. Elter, lost Casal). *1985 HIGHLIGHTS – DOUBLES:* [Wilkison] *r/u* Basle (d. Slozil /Smid, lost Tim /Tom Gullikson).

LILIAN DRESCHER (Switzerland)
Born Caracas, 23 May, 1965; lives Staag; RH; 5ft 4in; 114lb; final 1985 WTA ranking 58 (80); 1985 prize money $32,609.
A member of the Swiss top 10 since 1980, she moved up to third in her country in 1983 and made further progress in 1984. In 1985 she upset Sukova and Ruzici to reach last 16

Delray Beach where she took a set off Potter. *1985 HIGHLIGHTS – SINGLES: French Open* 1r (lost Sabatini [seed 14] 6–2 6–2), *Wimbledon* 2r (d. Skuherska 6–1 6–2, lost Demongeot 6–4 6–3); *sf* Japan Open (d. Kanellopoulou 6–3 6–1, lost Sabatini 6–3 fs).

LAWSON DUNCAN (USA)
Born Asheville, NC, 26 October, 1964, and lives there; RH; 6ft 1in; 165lb; final 1985 ATP ranking 59 (165); 1985 prize money $89,825.
R /u to Pernfors in 1984 NCAA Champs playing for Clemson. With f appearances in Bari, Marbella and Madrid, he burst into top 60 in 1985. *1985 HIGHLIGHTS – SINGLES: French Open* 2r (d. Fleurian 6–2 6–4 6–4, lost Potier 6–7 6–1 6–1 6–0), *US Open* 1r (lost Evernden 6–4 6–2 6–2); *r/u* Bari (d. Portes, Ganzabal, Jaite, Schwaier, lost Panatta), *r/u* Marbella (d. Potier, Gehring, Arraya, Bengoechea, lost de la Pena), *r/u* Madrid (d. A. Fillol, Tous, Ingaramo, Mansdorf, lost Maurer); *qf* Tourn of Champs (d. Glickstein, Kriek, Rivas, lost Lendl), *qf* Florence (d. Schapers, Ganzabal, lost DePalmer).

JO DURIE (Great Britain)
Born Bristol, 27 July, 1960; lives London; RH; 5ft 11½in; 140lb; final 1985 WTA ranking 26 (24) singles, 25 doubles; 1985 prize money $68,305.
The best of the British jun in 1978, she has improved since then and in 1982 was ranked No. 1 ahead of Wade and Barker. She had led Britain with 6–0 singles record as they won 1980 BP Cup. In 1981, following a successful back operation, she reached last 16 Wimbledon, US Open and Australian Open. Although it was not reflected in her ranking, she was a much better player in 1982 but still missed some good opportunities because she did not have the ability to close out matches. At Wimbledon four m-ps eluded her against an inspired Wade and the week before she waged a superb struggle against Navratilova at Eastbourne. In London in November, playing one of the top two singles spots in W Cup, she led Potter by 1s and 5–1 in 2s t-b but was beaten. However, 1983 was her year. She proceeded to win three tournaments – Mahwah, the British Closed and Sydney – and made her entry among the world's top 10 for the first time near the end of the year. With her distinguished record in the major championships (she reached sf French and US Opens and qf Australian Open) she was regarded by many experts as the fifth best player in the world for the year. Perhaps burdened by larger expectations, and by the death of her father, she was not the same player in 1984. She reached her first Wimbledon qf but was beaten 1r US Open, 2r French and Australian Opens. Her year-end ranking of 24 clearly reflected her decline in form but her good run at Wimbledon and her W Cup performances (she beat Potter and pushed Evert Lloyd into 1s tb) suggested that she could bounce back in 1985, which she did to a degree. She upset Kohde-Kilsch in 2r Wimbledon to reach last 16 and at Brighton she joined countrywoman Croft in sf where she was beaten by M. Maleeva. However, her ranking slipped 2 places during the year. *1985 HIGHLIGHTS – SINGLES: French Open* 1r (lost Derly 7–5 0–6 6–4), *Wimbledon* last 16, unseeded (d. Shaefer 6–3 6–2, Kohde-Kilsch 4–6 6–1 6–2, Burgin 7–5 7–5, lost Potter 7–6 6–7 6–1), *US Open* 1r (lost Hobbs 7–5 6–1), *Australian Open* last 16 (d. A. Minter 6–4 6–4, Gomer 6–3 6–3, lost Kohde-Kilsch [seed 5] 3–6 6–1 6–2); *sf* Brighton (d. Graf 6–2 6–3, Jolissaint, lost M. Maleeva 6–3 7–6); *qf* VS Central NY (d. Drescher 6–4 fs, lost Hanika 7–6 fs [after saving 7 m-ps]). *1985 HIGHLIGHTS – DOUBLES:* (with Evert Lloyd unless stated) *Wimbledon* qf, seed 10 (d. Bunge /Pfaff 5–7 6–4 6–4, lost Navratilova/Shriver [seed 1] 6–4 6–2), [Hobbs]*Australian Open* sf (d. Evert Lloyd/Lindqvist, lost Navratilova /Shriver 7–6 6–2); *sf* German Open (lost Graf /Tanvier). *CAREER HIGHLIGHTS – SINGLES: US Open – sf 1983* (d. Madruga Osses 6–2, lost Evert Lloyd 6–4 6–4); *French Open – sf 1983* (d. Moulton, Shriver, Rinaldi, Austin 6–0 fs, lost Jausovec 6–2 fs); *Australian Open – qf 1983* (lost Navratilova 4–6 6–3 6–4). *CAREER HIGHLIGHTS – DOUBLES:* (with Hobbs unless stated) *Wimbledon – sf 1983* (lost Navratilova /Shriver 6–3 7–5), [Evert Lloyd] *qf 1985* ; *French Open – sf 1983* (lost Fairbank /Reynolds 6–3 6–2); *Australian Open – sf 1985.*

STEFAN EDBERG (Sweden)
Born Vastervik, 19 January, 1966; lives London; RH; 6ft 2in; 158lb; final 1985 ATP ranking 5 (20) singles, 6 (13) doubles; 1985 prize money $719,152.
A remarkably complete player for his age, he achieved the Jun Grand Slam in 1983 – the first player to do so (Butch Buchholz won the 4 titles in 1958 before they were open) – proving his prowess on three different surfaces. Meanwhile, he successfully played 11 men's GP events, finishing the year at 53 in the world. Moving into the world of men's tennis in 1984 on a full-time basis, he enjoyed a sparkling season, dismissing Wilander in a dazzling display to win Milan indoors and then helping lead Sweden to their first D Cup victory since 1975 by clinching the fr triumph over US. Joined by Jarryd, he demonstrated unusual poise as they stopped McEnroe /Fleming in Gothenburg, repeating their win of US Open sf. He did what was expected of him and perhaps more, moving into the top 20 and winning the Olympic demonstration event. Taking 4 GP titles in 1985, he finished the year in style, ending Lendl's 31-match winning streak with a dramatic 9–7 fs triumph in sf Australian Open, then playing flawlessly to take Wilander apart in f. The Australian was the first of what will probably be many GS titles for this fluid player, who went on to lose to Becker in opening match of D Cup f in Munich, but with the pressure on and the score level at 2–2, he came from a set down to stop Westphal 3–6 7–5 6–3 6–4 to clinch the Cup for the Swedes. Edberg's late-season glory lifted him into the top 5 for the first time. At Masters he lost 1r singles to Kriek, but won doubles with Jarryd. *1985 HIGHLIGHTS – SINGLES: French Open* qf, seed 14 (d. C. Panatta 7–6 6–3 6–3, Hlasek 6–2 6–3 6–4, Frawley 7–6 6–3 6–0, Jarryd [seed 6] 6–3 6–7 6–4 6–2), lost Connors [seed 3] 6–4 6–3 7–6), *Wimbledon* last 16, seed 14 (d. Doohan 6–2 6–3 6–4, Wilkison 6–1 7–5 3–6 6–7 9–7, Hooper 6–3 6–4 6–4, lost Curren [seed 8] 7–6 6–3 7–6), *US Open* last 16, seed 11 (d. Clerc 6–3 6–4 6–3, Flach 7–5 6–3 6–4, Gilbert 4–6 6–4 6–1 6–4, lost Connors [seed 4] 6–4 3–6 6–3 6–4), *won Australian Open* seed 5 (d. Schultz 6–3 6–4 7–6, Anger 5–7 7–6 6–4 7–5, Masur 6–7 2–6 7–6 6–4 6–2 [saving 2 mps], Schapers 6–0 7–5 6–4, Lendl [seed 1] 6–7 7–5 6–1 4–6 9–7, Wilander [seed 3] 6–4 6–3 6–3); *won* Memphis (d. Connors 6–1 6–4, Noah 6–1 6–0), *won* San Francisco (d. Gilbert, Annacone 6–1 fs, Kriek 6–2 6–3), *won* Basle (d. Taroczy, Schwaier, Fibak, Noah 6–7 6–4 7–6 6–1); *rlu* Bastad (d. K. Carlsson, lost Wilander 6–1 6–0), *rlu* LA (d. Kriek, lost Annacone 7–6 fs); *sf* Brussels (d. S. Giammalva, lost Jarryd); *sf* Stockholm (d. Casal, lost McEnroe 6–3 7–6). *1985 HIGHLIGHTS – DOUBLES:* (with Jarryd) *French Open* sf, seed 4 (d. Annacone /Van Rensburg 6–3 6–2, lost Glickstein /H. Simonsson 6–3 6–4 6–1); *won* Masters (d. Nystrom /Wilander 6–1 7–6), *won* Bastad (d. Casal /Sanchez), *won* Cincinnati (d. Nystrom /Wilander 4–6 6–2 6–3). *CAREER HIGHLIGHTS – SINGLES: Australian Open – won 1985; French Open – qf 1985. CAREER HIGHLIGHTS – DOUBLES:* (with Jarryd) *US Open – rlu 1984* (d. McEnroe /Fleming 3–6 7–6 7–5 7–6, lost Fitzgerald /Smid 7–6 6–3 6–3); *French Open – sf 1985.*

KELLY EVERNDEN (New Zealand)
Born Gisborne, 21 September, 1961; lives Sydney; RH; 5ft 10in; 155lb; final 1985 ATP ranking 89 (—); 1985 prize money $67,822.
1985 HIGHLIGHTS – SINGLES: Wimbledon 2r (d. Navratil 6–4 6–4 6–4, lost Connors [seed 3] 6–3 6–2 6–1), *US Open* 3r (d. Duncan 6–4 6–2 6–2, Bourne 6–4 6–3 6–4, lost Becker [seed 8] 7–6 6–3 7–6); *rlu* Brisbane (d. Schultz, Layendecker, lost Annacone); *qf* Auckland (d. Shiras, lost Mecir).

ROSALYN FAIRBANK (South Africa)
Born Durban, 2 November, 1960 and lives there; RH; 5ft 8in; 140lb; final 1985 WTA ranking 38 (32) singles, 15 doubles; 1985 prize money $106,646.
An impressive backcourt player with a good flat forehand, she was runner-up to A. Jaeger at 1978 Orange Bowl Jun. At end of 1979 she played extremely well in Australia, taking 22 of 23 matches on satellite circuit, reaching New South Wales Open f. She played well intermittently in 1980 and was still very much a part of the world's top 50 in 1981, when she had an excellent year in doubles with Harford. They were one of the top 5 partnerships in 1981, winning French, Swiss and German Opens and reaching Wimbledon sf. She was perhaps the most improved player in the women's top 50 in 1982, and in 1983, after going through a bad patch, she found her best form at the end of the season, winning Richmond

and reaching qf of five others. Meanwhile, with Candy Reynolds, she won French Open and formed one of the outstanding partnerships in the sport. She hardly did justice to her ability in singles in 1984 when, despite a good win over Shriver in LA, she lost to Turnbull in sf after holding 3 m-ps. Her proudest moments of 1985 came at French Open where she outlasted Garrison 13–11 in fs. She survived mps in that contest again in her 3r triumph over Isabel Cueto, before losing 7–5 fs to Sabatini. But she could not find the same inspiration and intensity to carry her through the rest of the year. *1985 HIGHLIGHTS – SINGLES: French Open* last 16, unseeded (d. Hobbs 7–5 6–2, Garrison [seed 6] 7–6 2–6 13–11, Cueto 4–6 7–6 6–3, lost Sabatini [seed 14] 6–0 1–6 7–5), *Wimbledon* 2r (d. Schropp 7–5 6–4, lost Rinaldi [seed 16] 7–5 6–4), *US Open* 1r (lost Hanika 7–5 6–3), *Australian Open* 1r (lost Evert Lloyd [seed 1] 6–1 6–2); *qf* Sydney Indoor (d. Amiach, lost Shriver 7–6 6–2), *qf* Melbourne (d. Carney, lost Potter), *qf* VS San Diego (d. Rehe 6–2 fs, Howell, lost Croft). *1985 HIGHLIGHTS – DOUBLES:* [Shriver] *won* Hilton Head (d. Cherneva /Savchenko 6–4 6–1), [Mandlikova] *won* Amelia Island (d. Evert Lloyd /Bassett 6–2 fs); [Mould] *r/u* Fort Lauderdale (lost G. Fernandez /R. White 6–2 7–5). *CAREER HIGHLIGHTS – DOUBLES:* (with Harford unless stated) *French Open – won 1981* (d. K. Jordan /A. Smith, Reynolds /P. Smith 6–1 6–3), [Reynolds] *won 1983* (d. Durie /Hobbs, K. Jordan /A. Smith 5–7 7–5 6–2); *US Open –* [Reynolds] *r/u 1983* (d. Burgin /Russell 7–5 fs, King /Walsh 7–5 fs, lost Navratilova /Shriver 6–7 6–1 6–3), *sf 1981* (lost K. Jordan /A. Smith); *Wimbledon – sf 1981* (lost K. Jordan /A. Smith).

PATTY FENDICK (USA)
Born Sacramento, Cal., 31 March, 1965, and lives there; RH; 5ft 5in; 113lb; final 1985 WTA ranking 83 (120); 1985 prize money $19,040.
Boasting a big forehand, she was a member of the 1984 USTA Jun Fed Cup team, after being a member of US Jun W Cup squad in 1982 and 1983. In 1985 she moved comfortably into top 100. *1985 HIGHLIGHTS – SINGLES: Wimbledon* 3r (d. M. Brown 6–4 6–1, Cummings 6–1 6–3, lost Potter 7–6 6–1), *US Open* 1r (lost Graf [seed 11] 4–6 6–1 7–5).

GIGI FERNANDEZ (Puerto Rico)
Born Puerto Rico, 22 February, 1964; lives Largo, Fla.; RH; 5ft 7in; 146lb; final 1985 WTA ranking 64 (27) singles, 10 doubles; 1985 prize money $92,077.
In 1983, after being beaten in 3s t-b in f AIAW Champs by the more experienced Beth Herr, she used that important tournament to launch herself into the forefront of women's tennis, competing in 13 events and showing that she could play good doubles as well, reaching the f US CC with Herr. Buoyed by some praise she received from Navratilova after coming within two points of beating Shriver at Wimbledon in 1984, she took advantage of her 'Lucky Loser' status to reach f Newport. But while she was clearly a better player, her record still lacked consistency as was the case in 1985. Out for two months early in the year with an injury, she was in and out of form and fell in 1r of eight of her last nine tournaments. *1985 HIGHLIGHTS – SINGLES: US Open* 1r (lost Gadusek [seed 14] 6–2 7–5), *Australian Open* 2r (d. Karlsson 6–1 6–4, lost Kohde-Kilsch [seed 5] 6–1 6–2); *sf* Sydney Indoor (d. Potter 6–3 6–3, lost Balestrat); *qf* US Indoor (d. Bassett, lost Navratilova 6–3 fs), *qf* VS Newport (d. Villagran 7–6 7–6, lost Evert Lloyd). *1985 HIGHLIGHTS – DOUBLES:* (with Navratilova unless stated) *won* VS Washington (d. Kohde-Kilsch /Sukova 6–3 fs), *won* LIPC (d. Potter /Walsh Pete 7–5 fs, Jordan /Mandlikova 7–6 6–2), *won* Canadian Open (d. Mandlikova /Turnbull, Mesker /Paradis 6–4 6–0); [R. White] *sf* Sydney Indoor (lost Shriver /Smylie), [R. White] *sf* Mahwah (lost Jordan /Smylie), [R. White] *sf* Pan Pacific Tokyo (lost Mesker /Smylie).

MARY JOE FERNANDEZ (USA)
Born Dominican Republic, 19 August, 1971; lives Miami Beach; RH; 2HB; final 1985 WTA ranking 99; amateur.
One of the truly great prospects for women's tennis, she is a baseliner of the highest order with uncanny court sense, excellent anticipation, a formidable flat forehand, forceful two-handed backhand, and overflowing determination. In 1984, she was the top-ranked US 16-and-under player and became the youngest ever to pass the preliminary round of an upper-level women's event when she beat Teeguarden at Fort Lauderdale in Sept.

1984. She has been coached by Don Petrine Jr, Guillermo Aubone and also works with Fred Stolle. Aubone was replaced late in the year but she continued to work periodically with Stolle, and Heinz Gildemeister took on an active coaching role as well. In 1985 she reached last 16 LIPC upsetting Gadusek, became the youngest to win a match at US Open, and closed the year by capturing Orange Bowl 18s to become the first girl to complete a Grand Slam of that prestigious jun event. Yet her results in the other major jun events were not up to par and she did not fare particularly well on women's tour after Delray Beach. *1985 HIGHLIGHTS – SINGLES: French Open* 1r (lost Mandlikova [seed 3] 6–1 7–5), *US Open* 2r (d. Gomer 6–1 6–4, lost Henricksson 6–1 6–4); *won* Orange Bowl (d. Tarabini 7–6 6–1).

WOJTEK FIBAK (Poland)
Born Poznan, 30 August, 1952; lives Greenwich, Conn. with wife Eva and two children; RH; 6ft; 160lb; final 1985 ATP ranking 62 (45); 1985 prize money $85,503; career prize money $2,627,155.
In 1980 he had his best year since 1976 (when he qualified for Masters and lost fs f to Orantes in Houston), reaching qf Wimbledon, French and US Opens, winning 2 GP tournaments (Dayton, New Orleans) and capturing the richest prize-money tournament of the year at Dubai in Nov. Although not quite as good in 1981, he still performed with unusual consistency and remained firmly entrenched in the world's top 20. He seemed content for much of 1982 to concentrate his energies on helping Lendl to challenge McEnroe and Connors for the world's No. 1 ranking, but after a change of racket in the autumn he finished the year with a series of remarkable performances, including three WCT victories over Vilas. Assisting Lendl still in 1983, as well as looking out for himself, was understandably too much for Fibak as he turned 31. The same could be said about him in 1984, but to his credit he demonstrated an enduring capacity for match play and adroitness when he stopped 16-year-old Krickstein 10–8 fs in 2r French Open. He remained a first-rate competitor in 1985. *1985 HIGHLIGHTS – SINGLES: French Open* 1r (lost Lopez-Maeso 6–0 6–2 6–1), *Wimbledon* 1r (lost M. Leach 7–6 6–4 6–1), *US Open* 1r (lost Leconte 6–4 6–3 6–4); *sf* Toronto Indoor (d. Mayotte 7–5 7–6, Gonzalez 6–4 fs, G. Mayer 6–4 fs, lost Jarryd), *sf* Basle (d. Nystrom, Tulasne, lost Edberg); *qf* Gstaad (d. Leconte, Popp, lost Nystrom 7–6 6–0). *1985 HIGHLIGHTS – DOUBLES:* [Smid] *won* Gstaad (d. Nystrom /Tideman, Drewett /Edmondson); [A. Mayer] *r/u* US Pro Indoor (d. Slozil /Smid, lost Nystrom /Wilander), [Curren] *r/u* Brussels (d. Nystrom /Wilander, lost Edberg /Jarryd). *CAREER HIGHLIGHTS – SINGLES: Masters – r/u 1976* (d. Vilas 8–6 fs, lost Orantes 5–7 6–2 0–6 7–6 6–1 after leading 4–1 4s). *CAREER HIGHLIGHTS – DOUBLES: Australian Open* – [Warwick] *won 1978* (d. Kronk /Letcher 7–6 7–5); *Masters* – [Okker] *r/u 1979* (lost McEnroe /Fleming 6–4 6–2 6–4).

JOHN FITZGERALD (Australia)
Born Cummins, SA, 12 December, 1960; lives Adelaide; single; RH; 6ft 1in; 170lb; final 1985 ATP ranking 91 (29) singles, 12 (17) doubles; 1985 prize money $142,875.
Winner of a $25,000 tournament in Tokyo in 1980, he leapt from a ranking of 301 at end of 1979 to 136 by close of 1979. Overshadowed by the accomplishments of countryman McNamara, he had an impressive 1981, including a big GP victory in Kitzbuhel where he beat Vilas in f. He added Maui to his tournament winner's list in 1982, with Newport (RI) and Stowe in 1983, ending the year as a member of Australia's successful D Cup team with a win against Nystrom on the first day. He continued to play singles for Australia in 1984, but they were beaten 4–1 in Portland by a formidable US contingent led by McEnroe and Connors. Fitzgerald ended the year well by winning last GP event of the year in Sydney. He was not as successful on the 1985 circuit apart from reaching f Wimbledon doubles with Cash. *1985 HIGHLIGHTS – SINGLES: French Open* 1r (lost Viver 5–7 6–4 6–2 6–1), *Wimbledon* 2r (d. T. Giammalva 6–4 7–5 6–1, lost Kriek [seed 9] 3–6 7–6 7–5 6–1), *US Open* 1r (lost van Boeckel 6–2 6–1 3–6 4–6 6–4), *Australian Open 1r (lost DePalmer 7–5 6–4 4–6 5–7 14–12); sf* Auckland (d. Meiler, Drewett, lost Masur), *sf* Sydney (d. M. Davis 6–3 fs, Youl 6–3 fs, lost Leconte). *1985 HIGHLIGHTS – DOUBLES:* (with Cash unless stated) *r/u Wimbledon* seed 5 (d. McEnroe /Fleming [seed 1] 7–6 2–6 6–1 6–4, lost Gunthardt /Taroczy 6–4 6–3 4–6 6–3); *won* Las Vegas (d. Kriek /Lloyd, Annacone /Van Rensburg 7–6 6–7 7–6); *r/u* Queens (d. McNamara /McNamee, lost

Flach /Seguso); [Fleming] *sf* LA (lost S. Davis /Van't Hof). *CAREER HIGHLIGHTS –
DOUBLES:* (with Cash) *Wimbledon – r/u 1985*; *Australian Open – sf 1984* (lost
Nystrom /Wilander 6–4 6–4 2–6 6–3).

KEN FLACH (USA)

*Born St Louis, 24 May, 1963 and lives there; RH; 6ft 1in; 160lb; final 1985 ATP ranking 60
(154) singles, 2 (11) doubles; 1985 prize money $367,920.*
One of the game's outstanding doubles players, he exploded in 1984, winning seven
tournaments in conjunction with long-time partner Seguso. A former All-American at
Southern Illinois Univ. where he was twice NCAA Division II singles champion, he
improved in a big way in 1984. In 1985 the Flach /Seguso duo were victorious in 7 events,
including the US Open. Both partners also made significant strides in singles. *1985
HIGHLIGHTS – SINGLES: Wimbledon* 2r (d. Slozil 6–3 6–7 6–1 7–6, lost Mayotte [seed
16] 6–4 6–4 6–4), *US Open* 2r (d. Lavalle 7–5 6–2 2–6 6–1, lost Edberg [seed 11] 7–5 6–3
6–4); *sf* Las Vegas (d. Moor, V. Amritraj, Lloyd, lost Arias). *1985 HIGHLIGHTS –
DOUBLES:* (with Seguso) *French Open* qf, seed 2 (d. Mustard /J. Smith 6–3 6–3, lost
Glickstein /H. Simonsson 6–2 6–2), *Wimbledon* 1r, seed 3 (lost Felgate /Brown 7–6 6–3
2–6 7–6), *won US Open* seed 1 (d. Leconte /Noah 7–6 6–7 7–6 6–0); *won* Fort Myers (d.
S. Giammalva /Pate 6–2 fs), *won* WCT Forest Hills (d. Gerulaitis /McEnroe 6–4 fs,
Barbosa /Kley 7–5 6–2), *won* Queens Club (d. Cash /Fitzgerald 16–14 fs), *won* US CC (d.
Slozil /Warwick 6–4 6–4), *won* Canadian Open (d. Edberg /Jarryd 5–7 7–6 6–3), *won* Tokyo
Seiko (d. S. Davis /Pate 7–6 fs). *CAREER HIGHLIGHTS – DOUBLES:* (with Seguso) *US
Open – won 1985*; *Italian Open – won 1984* (d. Alexander /M. Leach 3–6 6–3 6–4).

PETER FLEMING (USA)

*Born Summit, NJ, 21 January, 1955; lives London and Seabrook Island, SC; RH; 6ft 5in;
185lb; final 1985 ATP ranking 94 (49) singles, 19 (3) doubles; 1985 prize money $94,782.*
In 1983, this flamboyant shotmaker had the best of both worlds. He collected his third
Wimbledon and US Open doubles titles and sixth successive Masters title along with
McEnroe, but of far more interest was his remarkable rise in singles of more than 350
places. He managed to keep himself in the top 50 in singles in 1984 with success in
Canadian Open, where he beat Jarryd for a place in qf, and Wembley where he reached
sf. In doubles, he won his fourth Wimbledon with McEnroe but they lost their US Open
title in sf at the hands of Edberg and Jarryd, who also inflicted their first D Cup defeat
after 14 victories. In Jan. 1985 they won their seventh successive Masters title and full of
confidence he reached qf Toronto indoors and sf Houston, but thereafter struggled in
singles. With McEnroe cutting back substantially on doubles activity, he found different
partners and won Toronto indoor with Jarryd. At Wimbledon he and McEnroe lost their
chance for a fifth title when they were beaten in sf by Cash and Fitzgerald, and he fell in
qf US Open playing with Denton. *1985 HIGHLIGHTS – SINGLES: Wimbledon* 1r (lost
Gerulaitis 6–2 5–7 6–4 3–6 6–3), *US Open* 2r (d. Acuna 6–4 6–2 7–6, lost Annacone 2–6
7–5 7–6 6–1); *sf* Houston (d. Holmes, Gunnarsson, Shiras, lost McEnroe); *qf* Toronto (d.
Shiras, Hogstedt, lost Jarryd 7–6 6–0). *1985 HIGHLIGHTS – DOUBLES:* (with McEnroe
unless stated) *Wimbledon* sf, seed 1 (d. Tim /Tom Gullikson 6–3 6–4 7–6, lost
Cash /Fitzgerald [seed 5] 7–6 2–6 6–1 6–4), [Denton] *US Open* qf, seed 15 (lost
Nystrom /Wilander [seed 5] 6–3 6–4 6–4); *won* Houston (d. Flach /Seguso 6–4 7–6,
Pfister /Testerman 6–3 6–2), [Jarryd] *won* Toronto (d. Layendecker /Michibata). *CAREER
HIGHLIGHTS – SINGLES: ATP Champs – won 1979* (d. Tanner 6–4 6–2). *CAREER
HIGHLIGHTS – DOUBLES:* (with McEnroe unless stated) *Wimbledon – won 1979* (d.
Gottfried /Ramirez 4–6 6–4 6–2), *won 1981* (d. Lutz /Smith 6–4 6–4 6–4), *won 1983* (d.
Tim /Tom Gullikson 6–4 6–3 6–4), *won 1984* (d. Cash /McNamee 6–2 5–7 6–2 3–6 6–3), *r/u
1978* (lost Hewitt /McMillan 6–1 6–4 6–2), *r/u 1982* (lost McNamara /McNamee 6–3 6–2),
sf 1985; *US Open – won 1979* (d. Smith /Lutz 6–2 6–4), *won 1981* (d. Newcombe /Stolle
6–2 6–2 6–7 5–7 7–6, McNamara /Gunthardt def.), *won 1983* (d. Buehning /Winitsky 6–3
6–4 6–2); *Masters – won 1978* (d. Lutz /Smith 6–4 6–2 6–4), *won 1979* (d. Fibak /Okker
6–4 6–2 6–4), *won 1980* (d. McNamara /McNamee 6–4 6–3), *won 1981* (d. Curren /Denton
6–3 6–3), *won 1982* (d. Stewart /Taygan 7–5 6–3), *won 1983* (d. Slozil /Smid 6–2 6–2), *won
1984* (d. Edmondson /Stewart 6–3 6–1); *Italian Open –* [Smid] *won 1979* (d. Clerc /Nastase
4–6 6–1 7–5).

GUY FORGET (France)
Born Casablanca, 4 January, 1965; lives Paris; LH; single; 6ft 1in; 160lb; final 1985 ATP ranking 61 (36) singles, 23 (213) doubles; 1985 prize money $95,667.
The world's second-best junior in 1982 when he won the Orange Bowl at Miami Beach, he had a difficult time in his first full year on the pro tour in 1983. He had already worked his way up to No. 70 by the end of 1982, making the most of his selected appearances on the men's tour, but a string of 1r losses pushed him back to 188 by end of 1983. His confidence restored in 1984, he turned his game and his psyche around, but his 1985 record was less impressive as he failed to win a match in his first 6 GP appearances during the season, although he improved thereafter. *1985 HIGHLIGHTS – SINGLES: French Open* 1r (lost de la Pena 7–6 5–7 6–1 6–3), *Wimbledon* 1r (lost Bourne 3–6 6–3 6–3 6–4), *US Open* 2r (d. Curren 7–6 6–1 6–2, lost Leconte 6–4 6–4 6–4), *Australian Open* 1r (lost Shiras 6–4 1–6 6–3 6–2); *sf* Gstaad (d. Smid 6–3 fs, Glickstein 7–5 fs, Gunthardt 6–1 6–4, lost Nystrom 7–5 fs), *sf* Toulouse (d. Schapers 7–5 fs, Perez 7–6 6–1, Pimek 9–7 fs, lost Noah); *qf* Bristol (d. Meister, Tim Gullikson, lost Teacher), *qf* Basle (d. Gunnarsson, Birner, lost Noah). *1985 HIGHLIGHTS – DOUBLES:* [Gomez] *won* Stockholm (d. DePalmer /Donnelly); [Courteau] *r/u* Nice (lost Panatta /Slozil).

BONNIE GADUSEK (USA)
Born Pittsburgh, Pa., 11 September 1963; lives Bardmoor Club, Fla.; RH; 2HB; 5ft 7in; 130lb; final 1985 WTA ranking 10 (13); 1985 prize money $170,700.
A former gymnast who suffered a broken neck at 13, she took up tennis shortly after being told by doctors she could no longer continue in that field. Coached from the start by Harry Hopman at his Bardmoor CC tennis camp, in 1981 she won the Easter Bowl 18-and-under title and US Nat 18 HC, then turned pro at the end of the summer. She played consistently in 1982 and gave her best showing at US Open, where she cruised into the qf and took a set off Evert Lloyd. Making a conscientious effort in 1983 to expand her stroke vocabulary, she sacrificed some of her old consistency for a new blend of attack and defence. Watching her in the autumn, it was hard to believe she was the same player as she followed her serve in to the net with surprising frequency. She reached f Italian Open and Deerfield Beach and never underestimated her ability. She won her first tournament of note in 1984 in Marco Island and looked certain to take her place among the top 10. But her season was torn apart by a bout of hypoglycemia which forced her out for several months in the middle of the year and when she returned she had temporarily lost her edge and her confidence. In 1985, however, she won four tournaments, disappointing only in the major championships as she won 46 of her 58 matches and entered the top ten. She was ousted in last 16 French Open by M. Maleeva, by Smith 2r Wimbledon, and by R. White in 3r US Open. *1985 HIGHLIGHTS – SINGLES: French Open* last 16 (d. Dias 6–3 6–2, A. Jaeger 6–1 6–1, Calmett 6–2 6–0, lost M. Maleeva 7–5 6–3), *Wimbledon* 2r (d. Ludloff 6–1 6–1, lost A. Smith 2–6 6–4 6–2), *US Open* 3r (d. G. Fernandez 6–2 7–5, Jausovec 6–0 4–6 6–2, lost R. White 1–6 6–1 6–2); *won* Marco Island (d. Benjamin 7–6 fs, Goles, Casale 6–3 6–4), *won* Lugano (d. Phelps 6–1 6–1, K. Maleeva 6–0 7–6, Sukova 6–4 fs, M. Maleeva 6–2 6–2), *won* VS Chicago (d. Kim 6–4 fs, Burgin, Turnbull 7–6 6–2, Rinaldi 6–1 6–3), *won* VS Indianapolis (d. Casale 6–0 6–3); *r/u* Tokyo (d. Kohde-Kilsch, lost M. Maleeva 7–5 fs); *sf* Orlando (d. M. Maleeva, lost K. Maleeva 6–1 6–4). *CAREER HIGHLIGHTS – SINGLES: US Open – qf 1982* (d. Fromholtz, W. White, Burgin, lost Evert Lloyd [seed 2] 4–6 6–1 6–0); *Italian Open – r/u 1983* (lost Temesvari 6–1 6–0).

ZINA GARRISON (USA)
Born Houston, 16 November, 1963, and lives there; RH; 5ft 4½in; 128lb; final 1985 WTA ranking 8 (9); 1985 prize money $274,470.
Coached by John Wilkerson on public parks in Houston. The second-ranked player in US Girls' 18 division in 1981 behind Andrea Leand, she won Jun Wimbledon title and was r /u to Gadusek at the Easter Bowl and the Nat 18 Hard Courts and was top of ITF Jun rankings. In 1982 she reached qf of her first tournament as a pro – the French Open – and last 16 Wimbledon and US Open. With her natural all-court game, she quickly established herself among the top 20 in the world. In 1983 a long bout of illness hampered her progress. Her mother died just before the US Open but she played with impressive

Jakob Hlasek, the Czech-born Swiss, advanced to 33 in the year-end rankings.
(T. Hindley)

consistency for the rest of the year, which ended on a high note when she reached sf Australian Open. In 1984 she had a year of mixed fortunes, spending most of the year in the top 10, even reaching the top 5. She won her first tournament (Zurich) in the autumn but her GS record held her back as she failed to advance beyond the last 16 and was particularly shaken by 2r loss when her nerves failed her against 1977 champion Wade on Centre Court at Wimbledon, where she was seeded fifth. In 1985, she had her most successful season, giving an excellent account of herself in all GS except French Open, where she lost a marathon contest to Fairbank 13–11 fs. Otherwise, she reached her first Wimbledon sf where she pushed Navratilova in two hard sets. She was beaten again by Navratilova in qf US Open and then fell in 3s to Mandlikova in qf Australian Open. Meanwhile, she captured two tournaments, stopping Evert Lloyd for the first time in f Amelia Island after ousting Mandlikova in sf, then defending her title in Zurich with another win over Mandlikova, *1985 HIGHLIGHTS – SINGLES: French Open* 2r, seed 6 (d. Golder 6–3 6–0, lost Fairbank 7–6 2–6 13–11), *Wimbledon* sf, seed 8 (d. Reinach 6–2 6–1, Phelps 6–3 6–1, Mesker 6–3 6–1, Tanvier 6–1 6–3, Van Nostrand 2–6 6–3 6–0, lost Navratilova [seed 1] 6–4 7–6), *US Open* qf, seed 6 (d. Gerken 7–5 6–3, Casale 6–2 6–4, Cordwell 6–4 6–4, Gompert 6–3 6–2, lost Navratilova [seed 2] 6–2 6–3), *Australian Open* qf, seed 6 (d. Cordwell 6–4 4–6 6–4, Skronska 6–1 6–1, Henricksson 4–6 6–1 6–3, lost Mandlikova [seed 3] 2–6 6–3 6–3); *won* Amelia Island (d. Graf 6–7 6–1 6–2, Mandlikova 7–5 6–4, Evert Lloyd 6–4 6–3), *won* Zurich (d. Cecchini 6–4 fs, Kohde-Kilsch 6–3 6–2, Mandlikova 6–1 6–3); *r/u* VS Denver (d. Nelson 6–3 fs, Washington, Spain Short, Savchenko, lost Louie 6–4 fs), *r/u* US CC (d. Sabatini 6–4 6–2, lost Temesvari 7–6 6–3); *sf* VS California (d. Potter 6–1 fs, lost Evert Lloyd), *sf* Hilversum (d. Herreman, lost K. Maleeva). *1985 HIGHLIGHTS – DOUBLES:* (with McNeil unless stated) [Rinaldi] *US Open* sf, unseeded (d. Bassett /Evert Lloyd 6–2 6–3, lost Kohde-Kilsch /Sukova 5–7 6–4 6–3); *sf* Denver (lost Allen /Walsh Pete 6–3 fs), *sf* Amelia Island (d. Bunge /Kohde-Kilsch 6–4 6–4, lost Bassett /Evert Lloyd 7–6 fs). *CAREER HIGHLIGHTS – SINGLES: USCC – r/u 1983* (lost Temesvari 6–2 6–2), *r/u 1985; Wimbledon – sf 1985; Australian Open – sf 1983* (d. Pfaff, Turnbull 6–2 7–6, lost K. Jordan), *qf 1985; French Open – qf 1982* unseeded (d. Bunge, Herr, Jausovec 7–5 6–1; lost Navratilova 6–3 6–2); *US Open – qf 1985. CAREER HIGHLIGHTS – DOUBLES:* (with Rinaldi) *US Open – sf 1985.*

LINDA GATES (USA)
Born San Francisco, 1 October, 1963; lives Palo Alto; RH; 5ft 9in; 150lb; finl 1985 WTA ranking 66 (260); 1985 prize money $28,672.
The No. 1 player for Stanford University in 1985, she is coached by former circuit player Bill Maze. *1985 HIGHLIGHTS – SINGLES: US Open* 3r (d. Antonoplis 6–4 6–2, Spain Short 6–0 2–6 6–3, lost Bassett 6–4 6–4), *Australian Open* 1r (lost Bryant 2–6 6–4 6–2); *won* New York Satellite (d. C. Fernandez, Goodling 6–1 6–1); *r/u* Japan Open (d. Lindstrom 6–4 fs, Herr, Schropp, Gildemeister 6–3 fs, lost Sabatini 6–3 6–4).

BARBARA GERKEN (USA)
Born Santa Monica, Cal., 3 July, 1964; lives Thousand Oaks, Cal.; RH; 5ft 5in; 125lb; final 1985 WTA ranking 78 (104); 1985 prize money $34,749.
Reached qf US Open in 1981, beating Wendy Turnbull and Jo Durie. Thereafter she was in and out of top form, but played her best tennis for a long time in 1985, rising 26 places in the rankings. A former All-American at UCLA, she is a tenacious back-court performer. *1985 HIGHLIGHTS – SINGLES: Wimbledon* 2r (d. Vanier 6–3 6–2, lost Wade 6–3 6–7 7–5), *US Open* 1r (lost Garrison [seed 6] 7–5 6–3), *Australian Open* 1r (lost A. Brown 6–2 1–6 6–0); *qf* Stuttgart (d. Mascarin, lost Kohde-Kilsch 6–4 6–3).

VITAS GERULAITIS (USA)
Born Brooklyn, NY, 26 July, 1954; lives Kings Point, NY; single; RH; 6ft; 155lb; final 1985 ATP ranking 81 (17); 1985 prize money $78,050; career prize money $2,825,900.
From 1977–79 he carved out a position for himself as one of the top four players in the world and looked capable of making a move for the top when he reached f of 1979 US Open and 1979 Masters (Jan. 1980), followed by a surprising appearance in f of 1980 French Open. By the end of the year he had slipped to 9 and seemed in danger of

dropping further. Early in 1981 he seemed unwilling to work as hard as he used to and his results suffered, but he made a big move back at US Open where he reached sf, removing third-seeded Lendl in last 16. He was suspended for 3 weeks following US Open when fines imposed there took him beyond $5,000 limit. Then, at Masters, where he held m-p in f against Lendl, before losing in fs, he was fined another $1,750. He looked rejuvenated in 1982 and, after winning the Canadian Open over Lendl in August, climbed back to No. 5. But 1983 was a difficult year, despite two tournament triumphs. He was preoccupied at the start by a drug investigation from which he was ultimately cleared. Despite working industriously with his two coaches, Fred Stolle and Harry Hopman, he never really got going, losing in 1r French Open, 2r Wimbledon, and 3r US Open where he fell to the 16-year-old Krickstein after leading two sets to love. He revived briefly in the autumn but fell in 1r of last two events. Thanks to a productive summer and successful autumn, he finished 1984 as a member of the world's top 20 for the 10th consecutive year, 6 of them in the top 10 – a considerable feat and a tribute to his athleticism and durability. He proved at 30 that he is still a remarkable player. In 1985 he looked a good deal older, slipping out of the top 20 to as low as No. 80 by the end of the year as he planned semi-retirement. *1985 HIGHLIGHTS – SINGLES: French Open* 1r (lost Becker 6–3 6–7 6–1 6–1), *Wimbledon* 3r (d. Fleming 6–2 5–7 6–4 3–6 6–3), Sadri 5–7 6–4 3–6 7–6 6–4, lost Gunthardt 6–3 6–7 6–1 3–6 7–5), *US Open* 3r (d. Benhabiles 7–6 3–6 7–5 7–5, Nelson 6–2 3–6 6–2 7–6, lost Noah [seed 7] 6–3 6–4 6–3); *qf* LIPC (d. Alexander, Gildemeister, Mitchell, Benhabiles, lost Gunnarsson 2–6 6–3 6–4 6–2), *qf* Milan (d. Visser, Masur, lost Smid). *1985 HIGHLIGHTS – DOUBLES:* (with McEnroe unless stated) [McNamee] *rlu* Rotterdam (d. V. Amritraj /Becker, lost Slozil /Smid); *sf* Milan (d. Edmondson /Warwick, lost H. Gunthardt /Jarryd), *sf* WCT Forest Hills (lost Flach /Seguso), [C. Lewis] *sf* Florence (lost Graham /Warder). *CAREER HIGHLIGHTS – SINGLES: Australian Open – won 1977* (d. Alexander, J. Lloyd 6–3 7–6 5–7 3–6 6–2); *Italian Open – won 1977* (d. Gottfried 7–5 4s, Zugarelli 6–2 7–6 3–6 7–6), *won 1979* (d. Dibbs, Vilas 6–7 7–6 6–7 6–4 6–2); *WCT Finals – won 1978* (d. Dibbs 6–3 6–2 6–1); *French Open – rlu 1980* seed 5 (d. Connors 6–1 3–6 6–7 6–4 6–4, lost Borg 6–4 6–1 6–2), *qf 1982* (lost Wilander 6–3 6–3 4–6 6–4); *US Open – rlu 1979* (d. Tanner 3–6 2–6 7–6 6–3 6–3, lost McEnroe 7–5 6–4 6–3), *sf 1978* (lost Borg 6–3 6–2 7–6), *sf 1981; Masters – rlu 1979* [Jan. 1980] (d. McEnroe 6–7 7–6 7–6, Connors 7–5 6–2, lost Borg 6–2 6–2), *rlu 1981* [Jan. 1982] (d. Clerc, Vilas, Teltscher, lost Lendl 6–7 2–6 7–6 6–2 6–4); *Wimbledon – sf 1977* (lost Borg 6–4 6–3 6–3 3–6 8–6), *sf 1978* (lost Connors 9–7 6–2 6–1). *CAREER HIGHLIGHTS – DOUBLES:* (with A. Mayer) *Wimbledon – won 1975* (d. C. Dowdeswell /A. Stone 7–5 8–6 6–4).

SAMMY GIAMMALVA (USA)

Born Houston, 24 March, 1963 and lives there; RH; 2HB; 5ft 10in; 160lb; final 1985 ATP ranking 41 (46); 1985 prize money $112,301.

He is brother of Tony and son of Sammy Giammalva, who was three times a member of the US top 10 in the 1950s and a US D Cup player. Ranked No. 1 US 16-and-Under player in 1979, he made a remarkable transition to the 18s in 1980, and was ranked 2 behind Scott Davis, after a marvellous season which included a big triumph at US Nat 18 Champ. Reached the last 32 at his first US Open in 1980, sf Tel Aviv and qf Basle in the autumn. Following the first all-amateur f in the history of GP, in which he beat old friend and jun rival Scott Davis at Napa, in March, 1981, he turned pro and immediately reached f WCT Houston. Before he knew it he was in the top 30 and although he slipped back, he was still considered an outstanding prospect because of his excellent attitude and hardworking nature. After a string of close losses early in 1982 season, his computer ranking dipped so low that he decided wisely to enter some USTA satellite tournaments in summer and autumn. Confidence restored, he came back strongly at the end of the year, working hard under the guidance of his new coach Bob Brett and reaching qf Australian Open. He left the Brett camp in summer 1984 and finished the year in f Sydney when upset Wilander *en route* to sf first Young Masters in Jan. 1985. Later in the year he drove his way convincingly into last 16 Wimbledon with impressive wins over Cox, Testerman and Smid, and he ended the year with his highest-ever ranking of 41. *1985 HIGHLIGHTS – SINGLES: Wimbledon* last 16 (d. B. Cox 6–0 6–4 5–7 6–4, Smid [seed 15] 6–3 6–1 6–2, Testerman 4–6 6–3 7–5 7–6), lost Connors [seed 3] 6–3 6–4 6–3); *sf* Fort Myers (d.

Krickstein, S. Davis 6–2 6–3, lost Lendl); *qf* Brussels (d. Curren, Hooper, lost Edberg), *qf* Tokyo (d. Rudeen, lost S. Davis), *qf* Livingston (d. DePalmer, Harmon, lost Teacher). *1985 HIGHLIGHTS – DOUBLES:* [Doohan] **won** Newport (d. Annacone/Van Rensburg 6–1 6–3); [Pate] *r/u* Fort Myers (lost Flach/Seguso), [Holmes] *r/u* Japan Open (d. Anger/Arias, lost S. Davis/Pate 6–3 fs); [DePalmer] *sf* Toronto (lost Fleming/Jarryd), [Meister] *sf* WCT Tournament Champions (d. Jaite/Pecci, lost Barbosa/Kley). *CAREER HIGHLIGHTS – SINGLES: Australian Open – qf 1982* (d. Johnstone 3–6 6–1 7–5 2–6 6–4, Kleege, Alexander, lost Denton 4–6 6–3 6–3 2–6 6–3).

BRAD GILBERT (USA)
Born Oakland, 9 August, 1961; lives Piedmont, Cal; single; RH, 6ft 1in; 160lb; final 1985 ATP ranking 18 (23); 1985 prize money $280,117.
Brother of Dana Gilbert. He began an impressive 1982 by reaching US Men's Intercollegiate (NCAA) f, losing to M. Leach. A careful analysis of his game by a computer company uncovered some previously unknown weaknesses and he played superbly at the end of the year, beating Teltscher and Gerulaitis. He declined slightly in early 1983, although he more than held his own later in the year. In 1984 he advanced rapidly and consistently into the top 25, playing 25 tournaments and winning 2 GP events (Columbus and Taipei). His surge continued in 1985 when he again captured 2 titles and moved into top 15 for the first time in his career, and finishing the year among the top 20. Qualified for Masters where he d. McEnroe 1r. *1985 HIGHLIGHTS – SINGLES: French Open* 1r (lost Gildemeister 7–5 7–6 6–4), *Wimbledon* 1r (lost Noah [seed 11] 6–4 3–6 7–6 6–7 6–3), *US Open* 3r (d. Van Rensburg 6–2 6–2 6–2, Jensen 6–3 6–2 6–3, lost Edberg [seed 11] 4–6 6–4 6–1 6–4), *Australian Open* 3r, seed 10 (d. Perkis 6–3 6–3 7–6, lost Steyn 2–6 6–4 6–4 7–5); **won** Livingston (d. Annacone 6–3 6–2, Grabb 6–3 6–2, Teacher 4–6 7–5 6–0), **won** Cleveland (d. Doyle, Schultz, Drewett 6–3 6–2); *r/u* Stuttgart (d. Smid, lost Lendl); *qf* Masters (d. McEnroe 5–7 6–4 6–1, lost Jarryd 6–1 6–2), *qf* Memphis (d. Lapidus, lost Edberg), *qf* Houston (d. Zivojinovic, lost McEnroe), *qf* Fort Myers (d. Noah, lost Lendl), *qf* Chicago (lost Connors 7–5 fs), *qf* Atlanta (lost Annacone), *qf* WCT Forest Hills (lost Krickstein 6–3 7–6), *qf* Stratton Mountain (d. Arias, lost Lendl), *qf* LA (d. J. Lloyd, lost McEnroe 6–3 fs). *1985 HIGHLIGHTS – DOUBLES:* (with Van Patten) *sf* Las Vegas (d. Flach/Seguso, Becker/Pate, lost Annacone/Van Rensburg).

LAURA ARRAYA GILDEMEISTER (Peru)
Born Cordoba, Argentina, 12 January, 1964; lives Miami; married Heinz Gildemeister Dec. 1984; RH; 5ft 8in; 126lb; final 1985 WTA ranking 63 (34); 1985 prize money $48,997.
With a background almost as complicated as Bunge's, she was born in Argentina, spent some time in Peru, of which she is a citizen, and lives in Miami. Sister of Pablo. In 1982 she beat Bonder, Nagelsen, Temesvari and Horvath to make her debut in the top 100. Basically a clay-court player and a big hitter, she expanded her game in an effort to become a better all-surface player and moved up 16 places on the computer in 1983, making quiet yet significant progress in 1984. She was r/u to Navratilova at the Tournament of Champions, upended Durie at French Open, and moved up 19 places looking increasingly like a player of sizeable potential, but during her first year of marriage in 1985 she slipped some 30 places on the computer. *1985 HIGHLIGHTS – SINGLES: French Open* 2r (d. Leand 6–3 6–2, lost Kanellopoulou 6–3 6–4), *US* Open 1r (lost A. Jaeger 7–5 2–6 6–1); *r/u* Sao Paulo (d. Bernstein 6–3 fs, Groat, Einy, Medrado, lost Paz 6–4 fs); *sf* VS Utah (d. Mould, Nelson 6–4 fs, Fairbank 6–1 fs, lost Benjamin 6–4 6–3), *sf* Japan Open (d. J. Thompson 7–6 fs, A. Holton 6–0 fs, lost Gates 6–3 fs).

JULIO GOES (Brazil)
Born Baura, 25 October, 1955; lives Sao Paulo; RH; 5ft 11in; 115lb; final 1985 ATP ranking 96 (177); 1985 prize money $21,642.
Playing predominantly Satellite tournaments in 1985, he played D Cup for Brazil but appeared in no GS event.

SABRINA GOLES (Yugoslavia)
Born Zagreb, 3 June, 1965, and lives there; 5ft 7in; 140lb; RH; final 1985 WTA ranking 54
(55); 1985 prize money $49,881.
The top-ranked player in the country, she won Italian Open Jun Champ in 1983, and in
1984 she won a silver medal at Olympic Games, where she upset Kathleen Horvath. She
is a student at Univ. in Zagreb and credited Harry Hopman for most of her fast progress
in 1984. She produced good wins in 1985 over Bonder, K. Maleeva and Louie but lacked
the consistency to progress further. *1985 HIGHLIGHTS – SINGLES: French Open* 1r
(lost Barg 3–6 6–2 6–4), *Wimbledon* 1r (lost Savchenko 6–1 4–6 6–3), *US Open* 2r (d. Uys
7–6 1–6 7–6, lost Moulton 7–5 6–4); *sf* Marco Island (d. Drescher 7–5 fs. Louie, lost
Gadusek 6–4 6–3), *sf* Seabrook (d. Jausovec, Foltz, lost K. Maleeva 6–2 fs); *qf* VS Houston
(d. Rush, lost M. Maleeva).

SARA GOMER (Great Britain)
Born Torquay, 3 May, 1964, and lives there; LH; 6ft 2in; 160lb; final 1985 WTA ranking 77
(128); 1985 prize money $38,114.
A big lefthander, and a former member of British Annie Soisbault and Maureen Connolly
Brinker Cup teams, she lifted her game a notch in 1985 to move up 41 places, and was
picked for British W Cup team. *1985 HIGHLIGHTS – SINGLES: French Open* 1r (lost
Wade 7–6 6–4), *Wimbledon* 2r (d. Mould 6–7 7–6 6–3, lost Potter 6–4 7–5), *US Open* 1r
(lost M.J. Fernandez 6–1 6–4), *Australian Open* 2r (d. Spain Short 6–2 7–6, lost Durie 6–3
6–3); *won* USTA San Antonio (d. Holikova 6–2 fs, McDaniel 6–2 fs, Eliseenko 6–3 6–2);
qf Brisbane (d. Paradis, Croft 6–2 7–5, lost Navratilova 6–3 6–1).

ANDRES GOMEZ (Equador)
Born Guayaquil, 15 March, 1960 and lives there and Bardmoor Club, Fla.; LH; 6ft 3in;
190lb; final 1985 ATP ranking 15 (5) singles, 17 (32) doubles; 1985 prize money $243,767.
The best player in his country, he won his first significant title in 1982 – the Italian Open
– demolishing Teltscher in an awesome display of clay-court aggression, his hard work
and consistency earning him his first place in the Masters. In 1981 he had lost to Connors
in US Open after serving for the match at 5–4 fs. He was a solid performer again in 1983,
playing particularly well on US CC circuit where he was r/u at North Conway and US CC.
In Dallas, he captured his first GP title on cement by wearing down Teacher on a
scorching afternoon. At his second Masters he beat Teltscher, but a torn shoulder muscle
forced him to retire v Lendl. In 1984 even a recurrence of that shoulder problem, which
forced him out of the Masters again in Jan. 1985, could not spoil his most successful year
as a pro. He won his second Italian Open and 4 other GP singles titles including US CC
at Indianapolis, moving into the top 5. He reached qf Wimbledon, French and US Opens,
and his only flaw was an inability to beat those ranked above him, although he did not
meet McEnroe. Out of action for two months in summer 1985, he did not achieve the
same consistently high level he had the previous year, although a late-season triumph in
Hong Kong promised better results for 1986, which he began in style with sf showing at
Masters, where he won a place after Connors withdrew suffering from flu, S. Davis
having already filled the injured Mecir's place. *1985 HIGHLIGHTS – SINGLES: French*
Open 3r, seed 5 (d. Slozil 6–1 3–6 6–3 6–3, K. Carlsson, lost Leconte 6–3 6–4 6–4); *won*
Hong Kong (d. Keretic 6–1 fs, Anger 6–1 6–2, Hlasek 7–5 fs, Krickstein 6–3 6–3 3–6 6–4);
r/u US CC (d. Noah 6–0 6–1, lost Lendl); *sf* Masters (d. Leconte, Kriek, lost Lendl 6–4 7–5),
sf Hamburg (lost Sundstrom); *qf* Sydney (lost Leconte), *qf* Tokyo Seiko (lost Wilander 7–6
fs). *1985 HIGHLIGHTS – DOUBLES:* [Forget] *won* Stockholm (d. DePalmer/Donnelly),
[Gildemeister] *won* Hamburg (d. Gunthardt/Taroczy). *CAREER HIGHLIGHTS – SINGLES:*
Italian Open – won 1982 (d. Noah 6–0 fs, Higueras 6–3 fs, Wilander 5–7 6–4 6–3,
Teltscher 6–2 6–3 6–2), *won 1984* (d. Krickstein 2–6 6–1 6–2 6–2); *French Open – qf*
1984 (lost Lendl [seed 2] 6–3 6–7 6–4 6–3); *Wimbledon – qf 1984* (lost Cash 6–4 6–4 6–7
7–6); *US Open – qf 1984* (lost Lendl [seed 2] 6–4 6–4 6–1). *CAREER HIGHLIGHTS –*
DOUBLES: (with Gildemeister) *Italian Open – won 1981* (d. Manson/Smid 7–5 6–2).

KATE GOMPERT (USA)

Born Ames, Ohio, 11 January, 1963; lives Redwood City, Cal.; LH; 5ft 10in; 136lb; final 1985 WTA ranking 25 (98); 1985 prize money $32,000.
The surprise winner of US Nat 18 Champ in 1980, she returned to defend her title and reached f the following year. A member of US Jun W Cup team in 1981 and became an All-American at Stanford in 1982–83. In 1985, she slipped into the world's top 25 largely as a result of last 16 appearance at US Open and sf US CC, where she eliminated the Maleeva sisters. *1985 HIGHLIGHTS – SINGLES: Wimbledon* 1r (lost Mesker 6–3 4–6 6–4), *US Open* last 16 (d. Medrado 6–3 6–4, Young 6–3 6–1, Holikova 6–4 7–6, lost Garrison [seed 6] 6–3 6–2); *sf* US CC (d. Phelps 6–2 6–4, K. Maleeva 6–2 6–2, M. Maleeva 6–3 1–6 8–6, lost Temesvari).

STEFFI GRAF (West Germany)

Born Bruehl, 14 June, 1969 and lives there; 5ft 5in; 110lb; RH; final 1985 WTA ranking 6 (22); 1985 prize money $168,212.
The youngest player ever to receive a WTA ranking, in 1982 she won European Ladies Circuit Masters, European 14 and Under Champ, German Junior Under 18 Champ and European 12 and Under Champ. This remarkable prodigy gained the essential experience she needed by playing 15 women's events in 1983, turning pro in Sept. and moving into the top 100 in the process. Precocious and gifted, she moved swiftly up the rankings in 1984, when she won the demonstration event in the 1984 Olympic Games in LA and lost narrowly to Durie 9–7 fs at Wimbledon in last 16, then startled journalists by saying she felt she could win Wimbledon within three years. In 1985, she did not win a tournament but reached f of 3 events, and sf of 4 others, including US Open, where she beat Shriver 7–6 6–7 7–6 in qf in the first women's match to extend to the maximum 39 games since the tb was introduced in 1970. By the end of the year she was No. 6 in the world. *1985 HIGHLIGHTS – SINGLES: French Open* last 16, seed 11 (d. Okagawa 7–5 3–6 6–4, Kim 6–0 6–4, Bunge 6–1 7–6, lost Evert Lloyd [seed 2] 6–2 6–3), *Wimbledon* last 16, seed 11 (d. Spain Short 6–7 6–4 6–2, Temesvari 6–3 7–6, Rehe 6–3 6–2, lost Shriver [seed 5] 3–6 6–2 6–4), *US Open* sf, seed 11 (d. Fendick 4–6 6–1 7–5, A. Minter 6–3 7–6, A. White 6–4 6–2, M. Maleeva 6–4 6–2, Shriver [seed 4] 7–6 6–7 7–6, lost Navratilova [seed 2] 6–2 6–3); *r/u* German Open (d. Horvath, Bunge, lost Evert Lloyd 6–4 7–5), *r/u* Mahwah (d. K. Jordan, Sabatini 4–6 6–0 6–3, lost Rinaldi 6–4 3–6 6–4), *r/u* Fort Lauderdale (d. Rehe 6–2 fs, Gadusek, lost Navratilova 6–3 6–1); *sf* LIPC (d. Rinaldi, Temesvari, lost Evert Lloyd 6–4 6–2), *sf* Hilton Head (d. Huber 7–5 fs, lost Evert Lloyd), *sf* Stuttgart (d. Bonder, lost Shriver 6–4 6–3). *CAREER HIGHLIGHTS – SINGLES: US Open – sf 1985.*

TOM GULLIKSON (USA)

Born La Crosse, Wis., 8 September, 1951; lives Palm Coast, Fla. with wife Julie; LH; 5ft 11in; 170lb; final 1985 ATP ranking 53 (74) singles, 58 (35) doubles; 1985 prize money $91,003.
At the start of his pro career he was not as solid or consistent as twin brother Tim, but nevertheless pulled some tremendous upsets, defeating Borg in 1978 and Connors in 1979. A former school teacher, he did not join the circuit until his mid-20s, preferring other sports as a teenager. Playing with assurance in 1982, he had his best year in singles, reaching qf US Open. He was somewhat less effective in 1983 but reached f Bristol and sf Newport. In a terrific year in doubles, with brother Tim, they reached f Wimbledon. Despite another win over Connors indoors in Madrid, his 1984 record was not as good as he would have liked. At long last, in 1985, the year in which he turned 34, he collected his first GP title, on grass at Newport, where he ousted Kriek among others. *1985 HIGHLIGHTS – SINGLES: Wimbledon* 3r (d. Mecir [seed 12] 4–6 6–3 6–4 6–7 6–3, Lapidus 6–7 6–7 6–4 6–2 6–3, lost Seguso 4–6 6–3 7–5 6–2), *US Open* 1r (lost Annacone 6–4 6–4 3–6 6–1); *won* Newport (d. Knapp 6–2 fs, Fitzgerald 6–4 7–6, Kriek [seed 1] 6–3 fs, Pate 7–5 fs, Sadri 6–3 7–6); *qf* Cologne (d. Gunnarsson, Duncan, lost Wilkison). *1985 HIGHLIGHTS – DOUBLES:* (with Tim Gullikson) *Wimbledon* qf (lost McEnroe/Fleming 6–3 6–4 7–6); *sf* Bristol (lost Edwards/Visser). *CAREER HIGHLIGHTS – SINGLES: US Open – qf 1982* (d. Alexander, Hooper, J. Fillol, lost Vilas [seed 4] 6–2 6–1 6–3). *CAREER HIGHLIGHTS – DOUBLES:* (with Tim Gullikson) *Wimbledon – r/u 1983* (d. Mayer/Taygan, S. Giammalva/Sundstrom, Curren/Denton 7–6 6–7 7–6 6–3, lost McEnroe/Fleming 6–4 6–3

6–4), *qf 1985; US Open – sf 1982* (lost Curren/Denton 3–6 6–3 6–2 6–4), *qf 1983* (lost Buehning/Winitsky 2–6 6–7 7–5 7–6 6–3); *Australian Open – sf 1983* (d. Nystrom/Wilander, lost Stewart/Denton 6–4 4–6 6–3).

JAN GUNNARSSON (Sweden)
Born Olofstroem, 30 May, 1962 and lives there; RH; 6ft; 165lb; final 1985 ATP ranking 25 (47); 1985 prize money $152,043.
A finalist at US Open Jun in 1979 and semi-finalist at Pepsi GS Jun in 1980, he finished 3rd in Swedish satellite circuit the same year. In 1983 he made quiet progress and moved into top 100 as his doubles success gave him confidence also in singles. He enjoyed another impressive season in 1984, moving into the top 50 with a record based on consistency rather than flash, and thanks largely to some strong results over the first half of 1985, he kept his ranking in the top 30 most of the year. His most successful performances included sf LIPC and qf German and Italian Opens. He finished the year on a high note with a first GP win in Vienna. *1985 HIGHLIGHTS – SINGLES: French Open* 2r (d. Kuchna 7–6 7–6 7–5, lost Lendl [seed 2] 7–6 6–3 6–2), *Wimbledon* 2r (d. M. Davis 6–3 6–2 3–6 6–3, lost Visser 6–7 6–4 6–4 7–6); *won* Vienna (d. Gunthardt 7–6 6–2, Pimek 6–7 6–2 6–4 1–6 7–5); *sf* LIPC (d. Seguso, Canter, Dyke, Gerulaitis 6–2 4s, lost Mayotte 7–6 6–2 4–6 6–1), *sf* Hamburg (d. Jaite, Birner, Aguilera, lost Clerc); *qf* Rome (d. Gomez 6–3 fs, Ganzabal, Arias 6–3 fs, lost Becker 6–4 6–4), *qf* Toulouse (d. Limberger, Navratil, lost Krishnan). *1985 HIGHLIGHTS – DOUBLES:* (with Lundgren) *r/u* Cologne (lost Antonitsch/Schapers).

HEINZ GUNTHARDT (Switzerland)
Born Zurich, 8 February, 1959 and lives there; single; RH; 5ft 10in; 155lb; final 1985 ATP ranking 36 (32) singles, 7 (9) doubles; 1985 prize money $254,707.
A remarkable all-court player and exceptional doubles player, he won the Wimbledon, French and Italian Jun titles in 1976, but his career probably began in earnest two years later when he won Springfield after getting into the draw as a Lucky Loser. In 1981 he continued to display flashes of great talent but lacked consistency. With Taroczy he won French Open doubles and five other GP titles before losing sf Masters to Curren/Denton. In 1982 unpredictability was again his trademark, as it was in 1983. However, his doubles partnership with Taroczy flourished as they opened the year by taking the Barratt WCT Doubles title in London and going on to win 4 more titles together. Altogether he won 7 doubles championships. Less successful in singles in 1984, he nevertheless moved into the top 10 in doubles. During the year he upset Jarryd at Toulouse and Nystrom on his way to sf US CC, but he continued to be inconsistent. Despite a slight decline in his singles ranking, 1985 was clearly the best year of his tennis life. He played a major role in three of the four GS events, taking the men's doubles at Wimbledon with Taroczy and the mixed at French and US Opens with Navratilova, as well as reaching qf Wimbledon and US Open in singles and last 16 in Paris. *1985 HIGHLIGHTS – SINGLES: French Open* last 16, unseeded (d. Keretic 6–0 6–3 6–4, Viver 1–6 6–1 6–1 6–1, Chesnokov 7–6 4–6 6–4 4–6 8–6, lost Jaite 6–1 6–2 6–3), *Wimbledon* qf, unseeded (d. Teacher 6–4 7–5 4–6 6–2, Zivojinovic 6–4 4–6 4–6 6–3 6–4, Gerulaitis 6–3 6–7 6–1 3–6 7–5, V. Amritraj 6–4 6–4 6–1, lost Jarryd [seed 5] 6–4 6–3 6–2), *US Open* qf, unseeded (d. Krishnan 5–7 6–3 4–6 7–6 6–4, Purcell 6–2 6–2 6–1 6–2, Jaite 6–7 3–6 7–6 6–4 6–1, Leconte 7–6 6–2 3–6 6–4 6–3, lost Connors [seed 4] 6–2 6–2 6–4); *sf* Vienna (d. Agenor 7–5 fs, lost Gunnarsson); *qf* Brussels (d. Gunnarsson. V. Amritraj, lost Wilander), *qf* Gstaad (d. Allan, Forget). *1985 HIGHLIGHTS – DOUBLES:* (with Taroczy unless stated) *won Wimbledon* seed 8 (d. Annacone/Van Rensburg 6–4 2–6 6–4 6–7 24–22, McNamara/McNamee 6–7 6–1 6–2 6–4, Cash/Fitzgerald 6–4 6–3 4–6 6–3); *won* La Quinta (d. Flach/Seguso 3–6 7–6 6–3), [Jarryd] *won* Milan (d. Dyke/Masur 6–2 6–1), *won* WCT Doubles (d. Flach/Seguso, Annacone/Van Rensburg 6–4 1–6 7–6 6–7 6–4); *r/u* Hamburg (d. Nystrom/Wilander, lost Gildemeister/Gomez). *1985 HIGHLIGHTS – MIXED DOUBLES:* (with Navratilova) *won French Open* (d. P. Gonzalez/Smith 6–2 6–4), *won US Open* seed 1 (d. Shiras/Horvath, Fitzgerald/Smylie 6–3 6–4); *won* LIPC (d. Fibak/Bassett). *CAREER HIGHLIGHTS – SINGLES: Wimbledon – qf 1985; US Open – qf 1985. CAREER HIGHLIGHTS – DOUBLES:* (with Taroczy) *French Open – won 1981* (d. Teltscher/Moor 6–2 7–6 6–3), *sf 1982* (lost Gildemeister/Prajoux 4–6 6–2 3–6 6–4 8–6); *Wimbledon – won 1985; Italian*

Open – won 1982 (d. Fibak/Fitzgerald 6–4 4–6 6–3); *German Open – won 1983* (d. Edmondson/Gottfried 7–6 4–6 6–4), *r/u 1984* (lost Edberg/Jarryd 6–3 6–1). *CAREER HIGHLIGHTS – MIXED DOUBLES* (with Navratilova): *French Open – won 1985; US Open – won 1985.*

MELISSA GURNEY (USA)
Born Palos Verdes Peninsula, Cal., 24 June, 1969 and lives there; RH; 5ft 4in; 105lb; final 1985 WTA ranking 81 (84); 1985 prize money $21,724.
Coached by Robert Lansdorp (former coach of Tracy Austin), she was ranked second in the US Girls' 16s in 1983 and third in the 14s the previous year. In 1984, she ventured into women's competition on a limited scale and proved that her potential is enormous, reaching 3r US Open and extending her idol, Evert Lloyd, to 4–6 6–4 6–0 at LA. She played 12 tournaments in 1985, maintaining a high standard and winning 14 of 26 matches, losing mainly to players of a high order such as Sukova, Mandlikova, Rinaldi and Sabatini. *1985 HIGHLIGHTS – SINGLES: Wimbledon* 2r (d. Leo 7–5 6–4, lost Tanvier 6–3 6–4), *US Open* 1r (lost Lindqvist [seed 13] 6–1 6–0); *sf* VS San Diego (d. Holladay, A. Jaeger 6–1 6–0, Herr 6–3 6–3, lost Croft 6–3 fs).

SYLVIA HANIKA (Germany)
Born Munich, 30 November, 1959; lives Ottendichl; LH; 5ft 7¾in; 128lb; final 1985 WTA ranking 21 (17); 1985 prize money $51,695.
An athletic, clever player, she gave notice of things to come when she beat Fromholtz and Goolagong Cawley on way to f of 1979 Italian Open, extending Austin to 6–3 fs. She found a place for herself in the top 20 in 1979 and stayed there in 1980, quietly pulling off impressive wins over Goolagong Cawley and Mandlikova. During the first half of 1981 she played magnificently, capturing an Avon tournament (Seattle) indoors, then moving into her first Grand Slam f at French Open. Thereafter she was less impressive, but her extremely solid record for the year clearly entitled her to a place among the top 6 in the world. Consistent again on the indoor circuit in 1982, she reached a peak at Avon Champs, defeating Turnbull in sf, and producing a stunning display to upset Navratilova for the title. Thereafter she appeared in no other f and suffered a series of surprising defeats, owing, perhaps, to injuries in summer and autumn. With her whirlwind topspin groundstrokes she reached f of 5 tournaments in 1983 and lifted her year-end ranking to 5. It might well have been higher were it not for her strange inability to win tournaments which seemed in her grasp. WTA touring pro at PGA National, Palm Beach, Fla. She did not play well during the first half of 1984 but in the autumn she pulled herself together, found her range, and reached qf US Open. Then she won her first tournament in two years by stopping Russell in f at Brighton. She played reasonably well in 1985 but never struck the top of her game. *1985 HIGHLIGHTS – SINGLES: French Open* last 16, unseeded (d. A. Smith 7–5 6–1, Benjamin 6–0 6–1, Mascarin 6–2 0–6 6–3, lost Kohde-Kilsch [seed 7] 5–7 6–0 6–3), *Wimbledon* 2r (d. Suire 6–4 6–2, lost Paradis 7–6 6–7 6–3); *US Open* 3r (d. Fairbank 7–5 6–2, Leslie Allen 6–0 6–0, lost Mandlikova [seed 3] 6–3 6–4); *sf* Swiss Open (d. Rinaldi 6–4 6–1, lost M. Maleeva 6–1 7–6), *sf* VS Central NY (d. Durie 7–6 fs, lost Potter 7–6 2–1 ret'd); *qf* US Indoor (d. Temesvari, Casale, lost Mandlikova). *CAREER HIGHLIGHTS – SINGLES: French Open – r/u 1981* seed 6 (bye, d. Jevans 6–2 4–6 6–3, Rossi 6–3 6–2, Marsikova 6–1 6–3, Navratilova [seed 2] 6–2 6–4, Jaeger [seed 3] 4–6 6–1 6–4, lost Mandlikova [seed 4] 6–2 6–4); *Avon Champ – won 1982* (d. Turnbull 7–6 fs, Navratilova 1–6 6–3 6–4); *Italian Open – r/u 1979* (d. Tomanova 6–2 6–2, Fromholtz 6–3 1–6 6–2, Goolagong Cawley 7–5 3–6 7–5, lost Austin 6–4 1–6 6–3).

ANN HENRICKSSON (USA)
Born St Paul, Minnesota, 31 October, 1959; lives Mahtomedi, Minnesota; RH; 5ft 5in; 145lb; final 1985 WTA ranking 53 (40); 1985 prize money $51,890.
It was clear from the moment she became an All-American at UCLA as a freshman in 1979 that she was an exceptional player, but injuries and a lack of confidence held her back until 1984. Late in the year she reached f Sydney with a win over Turnbull and cracked the top 50. She proved in 1985 that she clearly belonged in the top 55 with her fast-court prowess. *1985 HIGHLIGHTS – SINGLES: French Open* 2r (d. Budarova 3–6

6–3 6–3, lost Villagran 3–6 6–1 6–4), **Wimbledon** 2r (d. Wood 6–1 7–5, lost W. White 6–4 2–6 6–4), **US Open** 3r (d. Horvath 6–0 6–4, M.J. Fernandez 6–1 6–4, lost Kohde-Kilsch [seed 5] 6–3 6–4), **Australian Open** 3r (d. Byrne 4–6 7–6 6–4, Bonder 3–6 6–3 9–7, lost Garrison [seed 6] 4–6 6–1 6–3); **qf** Melbourne (d. Spain Short, lost Shriver 6–4 fs), **qf** Birmingham (d. Rehe 7–6 7–6, Louie 7–6 6–2, lost Sukova 6–4 6–1).

BETH HERR (USA)
Born Middletown, Ohio, 28 May, 1964; lives Dayton, Ohio; RH; 2HB; 5ft 6in; 125lb; final 1985 WTA ranking 85 (39); 1985 prize money $47,066.
Ranked 6 in US Girls' 18 when she was an Orange Bowl semi-finalist, this baseline stylist had an enormously successful 1982 season in both jun and pro events, winning US Girls' 18 Hard Courts and US Open Jun. Having gained some experience in the women's game in 1981, she reached 3r US Open and sf Tampa in 1982. By then she had enrolled at USC, where she planned to play for their distinguished coach, Dave Borelli, and after winning the 1983 AIAW title in late May, she turned pro and had a reasonably good year. She held her ground in 1984, her best win being a 1r upset of Mandlikova in Zurich in the autumn, but in 1985 she slipped almost 50 places on the computer with only 3 qf appearances and a 17–23 match record for the year. *1985 HIGHLIGHTS – SINGLES: French Open* 2r (d. Mesker 6–1 6–0, lost Scheuer-Larsen 6–3 6–1), *Wimbledon* 2r (d. Antonoplis 6–3 6–4), *US Open* 2r (d. Walsh Pete 6–3 6–2, lost Turnbull [seed 12] 7–5 6–2); *qf* Palm Beach (d. Nelson, A. Smith, lost Jauch), *qf* VS San Diego (d. Spain Short 6–1 fs, Antonoplis, lost Gurney 6–3 6–3), *qf* VS LA (d. Gerken, McNeil, Ivan 6–2 fs, lost Shriver 6–1 6–3).

JAKOB HLASEK (Switzerland)
Born Prague, Czechoslovakia, 12 November, 1964; lives Zurich; 6ft 3in; 165lb; final 1985 ATP ranking 33 (88); 1985 prize money $160,724.
Joining both Olympic and D Cup squads in 1984, he climbed 91 places in the rankings. In 1985 he played a prolific schedule, including 22 tournaments and D Cup for Switzerland, to emerge as one of the least heralded and most improved players of the year. *1985 HIGHLIGHTS – SINGLES: French Open* 2r (d. Elter 6–3 6–2 6–2, lost Edberg [seed 14] 6–3 6–2 6–4), *Wimbledon* 1r (lost Moor 6–3 3–6 6–7 7–6 7–5), *US Open* 1r (lost Yzaga 5–7 7–5 3–6 6–4 6–3), *Australian Open* 3r (d. Limberger 6–4 6–2 6–4, Denton 6–4 5–7 7–5 6–4, lost Lloyd 6–3 6–4 6–3); *r/u* Rotterdam (d. Maurer 7–6 7–6, Krishnan 7–5 7–5); *sf* Milan (d. Wilkison, lost McEnroe), *sf* Hong Kong (d. Smid, lost Gomez 7–5 fs); *qf* Washington (d. Higueras, Arrese, Forget 7–6 fs, lost Connors), *qf* Geneva (d. Slozil, lost Wilander), *qf* Toulouse (d. Tideman, Nastase, lost Noah), *qf* Stockholm (d. Gunthardt, Tulasne, lost Jarryd). *1985 HIGHLIGHTS – DOUBLES:* (with Acuna) *won* Toulouse (d. Slozil/Smid 9–7 fs).

ANNE HOBBS (Great Britain)
Born Nottingham, 21 August, 1959; lives London; RH; 5ft 6in; 120lb; final 1985 WTA ranking 40 (59) singles, 20 doubles; 1985 prize money $56,705.
She was ranked 1 among British jun in 1977 and has made steady climbs ever since. After being ranked 79 at end 1979, she made important progress in 1980, with a win over countrywoman Barker in Manchester f and a good win over Kathy Jordan in W Cup. In 1981 she achieved a thrilling victory over Wade at Wimbledon and reached last 16. But in 1982 she suffered a mystery virus infection after Wimbledon that kept her out of action until Fed Cup. By Nov. she was strong again and, with Durie, she won GB's only point in W Cup match in London. In 1983 she achieved little in singles, but there was no question about her stellar doubles play. First, she won Canadian Open with Jaeger, then partnered Turnbull to reach F Australian Open. Her doubles record in GS tournaments was superb as she reached sf French Open and Wimbledon (with Durie), and qf US Open with Jaeger. Her singles record was disappointing in 1984, but she compensated with another sparkling season in doubles. Her regular partner was Turnbull, with whom she reached her second GS f at US Open, and with five partners, she reached sf or better in 10 tournaments. Her best singles showing was at Wimbledon, where she removed 16th-seeded Bassett before bowing in 3s against 7th seed Maleeva. In 1985 she was again outstanding in doubles, reaching sf Australian Open with Durie. Her first event of the

The muscular South African-born Johan Kriek, who lives in Florida, had a rare win against McEnroe in San Francisco. *(T. Hindley)*

season was Sydney indoors in May, and having picked up confidence and points by winning New Zealand in December over a weak field, she appeared to have the incentive to work hard in 1986 to raise the level of her game. *1985 HIGHLIGHTS – SINGLES: French Open* 1r (lost Fairbank 7–5 6–2), *Wimbledon* 2r (d. Kim 6–4 6–2, lost Shriver [seed 5] 6–3 6–2), *US Open* 3r (d. Durie 7–5 6–1, Casals 2–6 6–3 7–6 [saving 1 mp], lost Shriver 6–2 6–3), *Australian Open* 3r (d. Hu Na 6–2 6–3, Potter 6–4 7–5, lost Navratilova [seed 2] 6–3 6–1). *1985 HIGHLIGHTS – DOUBLES:* (with Durie) *Australian Open* sf (d. Evert Lloyd/Lindqvist 6–4 6–1, lost Navratilova/Shriver 7–6 6–2). *CAREER HIGHLIGHTS – DOUBLES:* (with Durie unless stated) *Australian Open* – (Turnbull) *r/u 1983* (d. Durie/Kiyomura, lost Navratilova/Shriver 6–4 6–7 6–2), *sf 1985; French Open – sf 1983* (d. Kohde-Kilsch/Pfaff, lost Fairbank/Reynolds 6–3 6–2); *Wimbledon – sf 1983* (lost Navratilova/Shriver 7–6 6–4); *US Open* [Turnbull] *r/u 1984* (d. Potter/Walsh 5–7 7–5 6–4, lost Navratilova/Shriver 6–2 6–4); [Jaeger] *qf 1983* (lost Navratilova/Shriver 6–3 6–3).

GREG HOLMES (USA)
Born Covina, Cal., 29 August, 1963; lives Danville, Cal.; RH; 2HF; 2HB; 5ft 7in; 160lb; final 1985 ATP ranking 28 (57); 1985 prize money $103,499.
An All-American at Univ. of Utah, he won the NCAA singles title in May 1983, winning the singles gold medal later that year and representing US in Pan American Games. After reaching last 16 US Open that year (upsetting Vilas in 3r) he turned pro and established himself with his solid, forceful two-handed strokes off both sides, advancing rapidly in 1984 as he moved into the world's top 60. Under the quiet leadership of coach Brian Gottfried, he took more positive steps in 1985, playing his most distinguished tennis on cement to rout Connors in California, take Krickstein apart in Delray Beach, and upset Kriek *en route* to last 16 at US Open. *1985 HIGHLIGHTS – SINGLES: French Open* 2r (d. Perez 6–3 7–5 4–6 6–4, lost J. Frawley 1–6 6–3 3–6 6–3 6–2), *Wimbledon* 3r (d. Sundstrom 6–3 4–6 6–7 6–4 6–2, Schultz 6–4 6–7 6–2 6–3, lost Visser 6–3 4–6 6–7 6–0 10–8), *US Open* last 16, unseeded (d. Motta 6–3 2–6 6–4 6–7 7–6, Kriek [seed 12] 2–6 6–3 6–4 6–1, Ostoja 4–6 6–1 6–2 6–2, lost Wilander [seed 4] 7–6 6–1 7–5), *Australian Open* 2r, seed 16 (lost Woodforde 1–6 6–1 6–4 6–2); *sf* La Quinta (d. Smid, Connors 6–0 6–3, lost Stefanki); *qf* Memphis (d. Kriek, lost Teltscher), *qf* Japan Open (d. Dunk, lost Michibata). *1985 HIGHLIGHTS – DOUBLES:* (with S. Giammalva) *r/u* Japan Open (d. Anger/Arias 7–6 fs, lost S. Davis/Pate 6–3 fs).

ANDREA HOLIKOVA (Czechoslovakia)
Born Jihlova, 15 January, 1968 and lives there; LH; 5ft 6in; 121lb; final 1985 WTA ranking 75 (184); 1985 prize money $33,842.
A former European 12s and 14s titlist, she was ranked 7 among jun in her country at beginning of 1985. She then won Wimbledon Jun and upset Rinaldi (seed 9) in 1r US Open. *1985 HIGHLIGHTS – SINGLES: French Open* 2r (d. Mould 6–2 6–1, lost Calleja 6–2 4–6 6–3), *Wimbledon* 2r (d. Casale 5–7 6–1 6–3, lost Mesker 6–2 6–7 6–3), *US Open* 3r (d. Rinaldi [seed 9] 7–6 7–6, Drescher 6–3 2–6 6–4, lost Gompert 6–4 7–6), *Australian Open* 1r (lost Shriver 6–2 6–3); *won* USTA Key Biscayne (d. Kinney 7–5 6–3); *sf* Barcelona (d. Vasquez 6–3 fs, Jauch 6–2 fs, Purdy 6–2 fs, lost Cecchini).

KATHLEEN HORVATH (USA)
Born Chicago, 25 August, 1965; lives Bardmoor CC, Largo, Fla.; RH; 2HB; 5ft 6½in; 115lb; final 1985 WTA ranking 50 (29); 1985 prize money $84,584.
She was the youngest participant in the history of US Open when, aged 13, she entered the qualifying rounds and played the main draw just after her 14th birthday in 1979. In the same year she captured the Orange Bowl, US Nat 16 and Nat 21 Champs. In 1980 she combined more jun play with some pro tournaments but wisely waited until early 1981 before turning pro, then won the Avon Futures event in Montreal. She had some good jun performances in 1980, sweeping the Pepsi Int at Boca, US Nat 18 CC and the French Jun Champs. Relieved of the pressure of combining jun and women's tennis, she made considerable progress in 1981, winning 3 tournaments, holding two m-ps before losing to Evert Lloyd at Italian Open, and upsetting Jausovec at US Open. In 1982 she never really got going in singles, but with Vermaak won Italian doubles and reached sf French Open.

She took a few months off after 1r loss to Casale at Wimbledon, then suffered a string of 1r losses at the end of year. She was considerably more successful in 1983; she had the distinction of being the only player to beat Navratilova all year, having stopped the world's No. 1 in last 16 French Open. She then lost qf to Jausovec. At Berlin, she was r/u to Evert Lloyd after a string of victories over Gadusek, Leand, Bunge and Jaeger, and in the autumn she won a stirring battle with Bassett to become the first 'Ginny' champion in Honolulu. Perhaps the calming influence of her coach, Harry Hopman, was one of the key reasons for her better play. She broke into the top 10 in spring 1984 and had a highly successful first half of the season including r/u German Open and qf French Open for second straight year. Then her confidence evaporated and, as she was beaten in 1r or 2r in her last five tournaments, her ranking dropped 14 places and continued to do so in 1985, despite her winning two modest events early in the season in Indianapolis and Palm Beach. *1985 HIGHLIGHTS – SINGLES: French Open* 3r (d. Ruzici 6–4 2–6 6–3, Keppeler 7–6 6–1, lost Scheuer-Larsen 6–1 4–6 6–1), *US Open* 1r (lost Henricksson 6–0 6–4); *won* VS Indianapolis (d. Nagelsen, Burgin 6–2 6–4), *won* Palm Beach (d. Sabatini 6–2 6–0, Reggi, Jauch 3–6 6–3 6–3); *qf* German Open (d. Karlsson, lost Graf), *qf* Swiss Open (d. Spence 6–4 fs, Kanellopoulou 6–1 6–2, lost Sukova 6–1 6–3). *1985 HIGHLIGHTS – DOUBLES:* (with Ruzici unless stated) [Burgin] *r/u* Tourn of Champs (lost Navratilova/Shriver 6–3 6–1); *sf* German Open (lost Kohde-Kilsch/Sukova 6–1 fs), *sf* Marco Island (d. Bonder/Temesvari 6–2 fs, lost Potter/Walsh Pete 6–1 fs). *CAREER HIGHLIGHTS – SINGLES: French Open – qf 1983* (d. Navratilova 6–4 0–6 6–3, lost Jausovec 6–1 6–1), *qf 1984* (d. Rinaldi, A. White, lost Navratilova 6–4 6–2). *CAREER HIGHLIGHTS – DOUBLES:* (with Vermaak unless stated) *Italian Open – won 1982* (d. King/Kloss 2–6 6–4 7–6), *r/u 1984* (lost Budarova/Skronska); *French Open – sf 1982* (d. Reynolds/P. Smith 6–2 6–4, lost Navratilova/A. Smith 2–6 6–2 6–2), [Ruzici] *sf 1984* (lost Navratilova/Shriver 6–0 7–6).

PETRA HUBER (Austria)
Born Vienna, 15 November, 1966; lives Brunn Am Gebirge; RH; 5ft 7in; 138lb; final 1985 WTA ranking 73 (48); 1985 prize money $23,449.
Appearing taller than her official height, she produces forceful, elegant, penetrating groundstrokes off both sides. She combined jun and women's tournaments quite successfully in 1983, losing in sf Orange Bowl 18s to Debbie Spence, who also eliminated her in the sf French Jun and looked a likely candidate for the world top 10. In 1984 she upset Temesvari to reach last 16 US Open, gave Bassett a scare before losing their 3r encounter at French Open, and did a good job in her first complete year on the women's tour. She still appeared to be to finding her way around the tour in 1985, looking for the right ingredients to help her win the close matches, but she did beat Kohde-Kilsch, Paradis and Mesker. *1985 HIGHLIGHTS – SINGLES: US Open* 2r (d. Spence 7–6 6–1, lost Burgin 6–4 6–4); *qf* Hilton Head (d. Cecchini, Jausovec 6–4 fs, Kohde-Kilsch 6–4 fs, lost Graf 7–5 fs), *qf* Bregenz (lost Jausovec), *qf* Hilversum (d. Mesker, lost Scheuer-Larsen).

HU NA (China)
Born China, 15 April, 1963; lives Los Angeles, Cal.; RH; 5ft 8in; 128lb; final 1985 WTA ranking 96 (278); 1985 prize money $17,568.
The top-ranked player in China in 1981 and 1982, she was formerly ranked first in jun in her country. In July 1982, following Fed Cup matches in California, she defected to the US. Making slow but significant strides with the help of renowned American teaching pros Nick Bollettieri and Vic Braden, she found herself in the top 100 by the middle of 1985, and was clearly a much improved player strategically. *1985 HIGHLIGHTS – SINGLES: Wimbledon* 3r (d. Croft 6–3 7–5, Plchova 7–5 6–4, lost Uys 6–2 4–6 6–0), *US Open* 2r (d. Pfaff 6–4 6–4, lost Shriver [seed 4] 6–2 7–6); *qf* VS San Diego (d. Quinlan, Tell, lost Piatek).

MARCELO INGARAMO (Argentina)
Born Cortoba, 13 October, 1962 and lives there; LH; 5ft 9in; 152lb; final 1985 ATP ranking 75 (—); 1985 prize money $34,483.
Emerging in 1985 as a legitimate challenger to the best in his country (Vilas and Clerc), he broke into the top 75. *1985 HIGHLIGHTS – SINGLES: French Open* 1r (lost Bengoechea 7–5 2–6 6–4 6–7 6–4); *sf* Washington (d. Mecir, Vilas, lost Jaite); *qf* Buenos Aires (d. H. Simonsson, lost de la Pena), *qf* Madrid (d. Tarr, lost Duncan).

ETSUKO INOUE (Japan)
Born Tokyo, 18 October, 1964 and lives there; RH; 5ft 3in; 114lb; final 1985 WTA ranking 98 (68); 1985 prize money $31,519.
After a distinguished jun career, she graduated to the women's game in 1983, her substantial schedule of 25 tournaments giving her some lessons in match-play. After struggling through much of 1984, she put together a superb series of matches to win the Borden Classic in Tokyo which lifted her morale and her ranking, but she was less successful in 1985 despite wins over Mesker, Schropp and Scheuer-Larsen. *1985 HIGHLIGHTS – SINGLES: French Open* 1r (lost Jolissaint 7–6 6–2), *Wimbledon* 2r (d. Ekblom 6–2 6–1, lost Rehe 6–1 6–3), *US Open* 1r (lost Cecchini 2–6 6–1 6–2), *Australian Open* 2r (d. E. Minter 6–4 7–6, lost Lindqvist [seed 10] 6–4 7–5).

ANNA IVAN (USA)
Born La Jolla, Cal., 17 January, 1966; lives Palo Alto, Cal.; RH; 5ft 5in; 115lb; final 1985 WTA ranking 65 (162); 1985 prize money $11,164.
Ranked seventh in US Girls' 18 in 1983, she won the Nat 18 HC that season. In 1985 she rose swiftly in the women's game, recording impressive wins over Turnbull and Horvath. *1985 HIGHLIGHTS – SINGLES: Wimbledon* (lost 2r qualifying Howell 6–3 6–3), *US Open* 1r (lost Bonder 6–2 4–6 6–3); *qf* US CC (d. Rimes, Arraya Gildemeister 7–5 fs, Horvath 6–4 6–0, lost Garrison 6–7 6–1 6–3).

GORAN IVANISHOVIC (Yugoslavia)
Born Split, 13 September, 1971, and lives there; LH; 5ft 8½in; 112lb.
Began tennis with his father at age 7 and in 1985 won Sport Goofy doubles (with Fuchs), having won his nat singles titles in both 14s and 16s. A finalist (to Kulti) in Rolex 14s having won 12s in 1983.

ANDREA JAEGER (USA)
Born Chicago, 4 June, 1965; lives Bardmoor Club, Fla.; single; RH; 2HB; 5ft 2½in; 100lb.
A brilliant prodigy, she won Orange Bowl 18 title, aged 13, in Dec 1978, and went on to collect important Pepsi Jun 18 title at Boca Raton and US 18 CC in 1979. She turned pro in winter 1980 and far exceeded the expectations even of her Swiss father, Roland, by taking Avon Futures at Las Vegas, then holding her own on Avon Champ circuit. By end of year she had stopped Austin, Navratilova and Mandlikova and was among the top 7 women in the world. In Sept 1981 she was ranked 2 and was firmly established in the world's top 5. In 1982, she had a consistent year and reached her first GS f at French Open, defeating Evert Lloyd in sf before losing to Navratilova. She also reached second US Open sf, and established herself as third-best player in the world. She held her ground in 1983, and was very consistent in GS tournaments, reaching sf French Open, f Wimbledon, and qf US Open, but injury kept her out of the Australian Open. She won one tournament – Marco Island in Florida on clay – and was r/u in five. After playing the first half of 1984, and clearly needing to get away from a game she no longer enjoyed, she left the circuit and attended a junior college in Florida. By the end of the year, her future plans remained uncertain. Playing only five tournaments in 1985, she finished with a 5–5 match record, never advanced beyond the third round of any tournament, and looked miserable most of the time on the court. *1985 HIGHLIGHTS – SINGLES: French Open* 2r (d. Foltz 6–4 7–5, lost Gadusek 6–1 6–1), *US Open* 2r (d. Gildemeister 7–5 2–6 6–1, lost K. Jordan 3–6 6–2 6–2). *CAREER HIGHLIGHTS – SINGLES: French Open – r/u 1982* seed 4 (d. Ruzici 6–1 6–0, Evert Lloyd 6–3 6–1, lost Navratilova 7–6 6–1), *sf 1981* seed 3 (d. Jausovec 4–6 6–2 6–2, lost Hanika 4–6 6–1 6–4), *sf 1983* (d. Arraya 6–0 fs, Hobbs, Rush, lost Evert

Lloyd 6–3 6–1); *US Open – sf 1980* seed 8 (d. DuVall, Nagelsen, Tomanova, Madruga 6–1 6–3, lost Mandlikova [seed 9] 6–1 3–6 7–6), *sf 1982* (lost Evert Lloyd 6–1 6–2); *Australian Open – sf 1982, qf 1981; Wimbledon – r/u 1983* (d. Bassett 6–4 6–3, Potter 6–4 6–1, King 6–1 6–1, lost Navratilova 6–0 6–3), *qf 1980* seed 14 (d. Wade [seed 7] 6–2 7–6, lost Evert Lloyd [seed 3] 6–1 6–1). *CAREER HIGHLIGHTS – MIXED DOUBLES:* (with Arias) *French Open – won 1981, sf 1982.*

MARTIN JAITE (Argentina)
Born Buenos Aires, 9 October, 1964; lives Barcelona, Spain; RH; 5ft 11in; 150lb; final 1985 ATP ranking 20 (54); 1985 prize money $164,491.
With excellent CC results, he burst into top 100 in 1984 and upset Gerulaitis at French Open, gave Connors an interesting test in his D Cup debut for Argentina against US, and reached qf US CC and Barcelona. Following a triumph in his first tournament of 1985 at Buenos Aires, he was a different player, producing good results all year long on the CC circuit and reaching qf French Open. *1985 HIGHLIGHTS – SINGLES: French Open* qf, unseeded (d. Cane 7–5 7–5 6–2, Allan 6–4 6–4 6–3, Mecir [seed 11] 2–6 7–6 6–3 6–4, Gunthardt 6–1 6–2 6–3, lost Lendl [seed 2] 6–4 6–2 6–4), *US Open* 3r (d. Sundstrom [seed 14] 6–4 2–6 6–2 6–3, Perez 6–3 7–6 6–3, lost Gunthardt 6–7 3–6 7–6 6–4 6–1); *won* Buenos Aires (d. Maciel, de la Pena, Perez 6–4 6–3); *r/u* US Pro (d. Solomon, McNamee 6–0 fs, Oresar, lost Wilander 6–2 6–4), *r/u* Washington (d. Yzaga, Pimek, Arraya, Ingaramo, lost Noah 6–4 6–3); *sf* Barcelona (d. Agenor, K. Carlsson, lost Wilander); *qf* US CC (d. Vilas, lost Lendl). *1985 HIGHLIGHTS – DOUBLES:* (with Miniussi) *won* Buenos Aires (d. Bengoechea/Perez). *CAREER HIGHLIGHTS – SINGLES: French Open – qf 1985.*

ANDERS JARRYD (Sweden)
Born Lidkoping, 13 July, 1961 and lives there; single; RH; 2HB; 5ft 11in; 155lb; final 1985 ATP ranking 8 (6) singles, 3 (5) doubles; 1985 prize money $534,822.
Playing second singles in D Cup in 1982, he beat Gottfried in St Louis, giving Wilander the chance to battle McEnroe down to the wire in a 5s classic. He had a wonderful year in doubles with H. Simonsson, but a strange year in singles being dangerous when on form. In 1983 he played with more assurance and produced big wins in different conditions. In sf Canadian Open, on cement, he stunned McEnroe before losing to Lendl in f, and at Wembley, he handed countryman Wilander a rare 1r loss indoors. In doubles, he enjoyed some extraordinary successes with H. Simonsson again, capturing French Open. He improved enormously in 1984, moving swiftly into the world's top 10 and winning two GP tournaments, including Australian Indoor where he dismissed Lendl in straight sets in f. He twice came close to beating McEnroe, being within 2 points of victory at 5–3 in 2s tb in sf Stockholm Open, and led by 1s, 3–0 b-p in qf Masters. His doubles skill was on display with countryman Edberg, with whom he beat McEnroe/Fleming at the US Open sf and in D Cup f where they clinched the first Swedish victory since 1975. In 1985, he slipped from 6 to 8 on the computer, but he made more of a mark in the big tournaments. At Wimbledon, seeded 5th, he nearly lost 1r to Panatta but recovered from 2s to love down to win in 5s, moving comfortably into sf where he lost a hard-fought 4s match to Becker. At US Open he was forced to retire with heat exhaustion late in 3s qf against Wilander. He beat Wilander for his one GP tournament win in Brussels and joined him to win Italian Open doubles. With regular partner Edberg, he was less successful than in 1984 and injury kept him out of D Cup f where he would have joined Edberg again for the doubles. Instead Wilander and Nystrom stepped in and won. However, Jarryd and Edberg won Masters over their compatriots. *1985 HIGHLIGHTS – SINGLES: French Open* last 16, seed 6 (d. McCain 6–4 6–3 7–5, Higueras 6–4 6–1, Aguilera 6–4 6–2 6–2, lost Edberg 6–3 6–7 6–4 6–2), *Wimbledon* sf, seed 5 (d. C. Panatta 4–6 3–6 6–4 6–4 6–3, S. Davis 5–7 7–6 7–5 6–4, Van Patten 6–3 6–3 6–1, Visser 6–1 6–4 6–1, Gunthardt 6–4 6–3 6–2, lost Becker 2–6 7–6 6–3 6–3), *US Open* qf, seed 6 (d. Pernfors 6–3 7–6 6–4, Bauer 6–4 6–3 6–3, Wilkison 6–0 6–1 6–4, Mayotte 7–6 7–6 6–4, lost Wilander [seed 3] 2–6 6–2 5–0 ret'd); *won* Brussels (d. Edberg 6–3 fs, Wilander 6–4 3–6 7–5); *r/u* Toronto Indoor (d. Fibak, lost Curren 7–6 6–3), *r/u* Milan (d. Smid, lost McEnroe 6–4 6–1), *r/u* Stockholm (d. Nystrom 6–3 7–6, lost McEnroe 6–1 6–2); *sf* Masters (d. Nystrom, Gilbert, lost Becker 6–3 6–4), *sf* Wembley (lost Becker 7–6 7–6); *qf* Canadian Open (lost Lendl); *qf* Cincinnati (d. Flur, lost Nystrom), *qf* Barcelona (lost Tulasne), *qf* Seiko (d. Zivojinovic, lost Becker 7–6

6–4). *1985 HIGHLIGHTS – DOUBLES:* (with Edberg unless stated) *French Open* sf, seed 4 (d. Annacone/Van Rensburg 6–3 6–2, lost Glickstein/H. Simonsson 6–3 6–4 6–1); *won* Masters (d. Nystrom/Wilander 6–1 7–6), *won* Bastad (d. Casal/Sanchez), *won* Cincinnati (d. Nystrom/Wilander 4–6 6–2 6–3), [Fleming] *won* Toronto Indoor (d. Layen-decker/Michibata), [Fibak] *won* Brussels (d. Curren/Fibak), [Gunthardt] *won* Milan (d. Gerulaitis/McEnroe, Dyke/Masur), [Wilander] *won* Italian Open (d. Flach/Seguso 4–6 6–3 6–2). *CAREER HIGHLIGHTS – SINGLES: Wimbledon – sf 1985; US Open – qf 1985. CAREER HIGHLIGHTS – DOUBLES:* (with H. Simonsson unless stated) *French Open – won 1983* seed 8 (d. Edmondson/Stewart 7–6 6–4 6–2), [Edberg] *– sf 1985*; *US Open* – [Edberg] *r/u 1984* (d. McEnroe/Fleming 3–6 7–6 7–5 7–6, lost Fitzgerald/Smid 7–6 6–3 6–3); *D Cup* – [Edberg] *f 1984*; *Wimbledon – sf 1983* (lost McEnroe/Fleming 6–2 6–2 6–4).

PETRA DELHEES JAUCH (Switzerland)
Born Zofingen, 28 March, 1959 and lives there; LH; 5ft 9in; 154lb; final 1985 WTA ranking 87 (83); 1985 prize money $13,425.
One of the top 2 players in Switzerland since 1978, she has been a Swiss Fed Cup member since 1976. In one of the least noticed but biggest upsets of the 1984 US Open, she toppled sixth-seeded M. Maleeva in the opening round and reached last 16 before losing to Bassett. The rest of her year was not up to that standard. Unlike most other players ranked near her in 1985, she never lost in 1r during the first half of the season, but having played Barcelona in June she disappeared from the circuit. *1985 HIGHLIGHTS – SINGLES: French Open* 2r (d. Herreman 6–3 6–2, lost Holikova 6–3 2–6 6–2); *r/u* Palm Beach (d. Benjamin, Budarova, Herr, Phelps, lost Horvath 3–6 6–3 6–3.

MIMA JAUSOVEC (Yugoslavia)
Born Maribor, 20 July, 1956 and lives there; single; RH; 5ft 3in; 110lb; final 1985 WTA ranking 71 (87); 1985 prize money $30,056.
A US Open semi-finalist in 1976 and French Open champ in 1977, she gained considerable weight in 1979 and was the victim of various injuries, but returned to form in 1980, reaching US Open qf. In 1981, she had her best year since 1976, perhaps her best ever, defeating Mandlikova twice and beating Jaeger at Wimbledon. While she was not able to keep up the pace and standard of her early-season record, 1982 was still a good year with a triumph on the indoor circuit in LA, and she was always either in or just outside the world's top 10. Despite reaching her third French Open f, she appeared in need of a long rest in 1983, which was a disappointing year. However, in Paris she achieved a win over Hanika and sf triumph over Durie in a contest which she looked likely to lose. Sadly, she slumped to an all-time low by the end of 1984, with little change in 1985, apart from an appearance in f Bregenz, where she lost to Ruzici. *1985 HIGHLIGHTS – SINGLES: French Open* 2r (d. Croft 6–2 6–0, lost Reggi 6–2 7–6), *Wimbledon* 1r (lost Vermaak 6–3 6–4), *US Open* 2r (d. Balestrat 7–5 6–1, lost Gadusek [seed 14] 6–0 4–6 6–2); *r/u* Bregenz (d. Garrone 6–3 fs, Stampfli, Huber 6–3 7–6, Kanellopoulou 7–6 fs, lost Ruzici 6–2 6–3). *CAREER HIGHLIGHTS – SINGLES: French Open – won 1977* (d. Marsikova 6–1 3–6 6–3, Mihai 6–2 6–7 6–1), *r/u 1978* (d. Marsikova, lost Ruzici 6–2 6–2), *r/u 1983* (d. Goles, Hanika, Tanvier, Horvath 6–1 6–1, Durie 6–2 fs, lost Evert Lloyd 6–1 6–2), *qf 1981* (lost Jaeger [seed 3] 4–6 6–2 6–0); *Italian Open – won 1977* (d. Marsikova, Hunt 6–1 6–3), *sf 1975* (d. Masthoff, lost Evert Lloyd 6–2 6–0); *US Open – sf 1976* (d. Wade 6–3 6–3, Gerulaitis, Marcie Louie, Ruzici 6–2 6–1, lost Evert Lloyd 6–3 6–1), *qf 1980* (d. Mesker, Norton, Latham, K. Jordan [seed 11] 7–5 6–3, lost Evert Lloyd 7–6 6–2); *Wimbledon – qf 1981* seed 10 (d. Louie, Jolissaint, Blount, A. Jaeger [seed 5] 6–4 7–6, lost Evert Lloyd [seed 1] 6–2 6–2). *CAREER HIGHLIGHTS – DOUBLES:* (with Ruzici unless stated) *French Open – won 1978* (d. Bowrey/Lovera 5–7 6–4 8–6); *Italian Open – won 1978* (d. Mihai/Nagelsen 6–2 2–6 7–5); *Wimbledon – r/u 1978* (lost Reid/Turnbull 4–6 9–8 6–3); *US Open* – [K. Jordan] *sf 1983* (lost Navratilova/Shriver 6–3 6–2).

CHRISTIANE JOLISSAINT (Switzerland)
Born Vevey, 9 December, 1961; lives Bienne; 5ft 7½in; 145lb; final 1985 WTA ranking 33 (58); 1985 prize money $57,992.
In 1983 she played particularly well in springtime and, adding a fine win over Bunge at Wimbledon, she pulled herself back into top 30 after slumping in 1982. After a disappointing 1984, she restored herself in 1985, moving back to the top 35 with qf appearances in Sydney, Brighton and Zurich. *1985 HIGHLIGHTS – SINGLES; French Open* 3r (d. Inoue 7–6 6–2, Sukova 2–6 6–3 6–0, lost Cecchini 7–5 5–7 6–4), *Wimbledon* 1r (lost Rehe 6–4 6–3), *US Open* 1r (lost Piatek 6–2 6–4), *Australian Open* 2r (d. Burgin 6–7 6–4 6–2, lost Dingwall 6–4 7–6); *qf* Sydney NSW (d. J. Thompson 7–6 7–6, lost Kohde-Kilsch 6–3 fs), *qf* Brighton (d. Benjamin, lost Durie), *qf* Zurich (d. Potter 6–2 fs, lost Sukova 6–3 fs). *CAREER HIGHLIGHTS – DOUBLES:* (with Mesker) *US Open – sf 1984* (d. Kohde-Kilsch/Mandlikova, lost Turnbull/Hobbs 6–4 6–1).

KATHY JORDAN (USA)
Born Bryn Mawr, Pa., 3 December, 1959; lives King of Prussia, Pa.; single; RH; 5ft 8in; 130lb; final 1985 WTA ranking 19 (10) singles, 5 doubles; 1985 prize money $184,384.
A former (1977) US Nat 18 r/u and 1979 AIAW champ, she came within 2 points of upsetting eventual champ Austin in last 16 of 1979 US Open. In 1981 she and Anne Smith had a superb year in doubles as they captured US and Australian Open titles and reached f Wimbledon; they have now won all four Grand Slam doubles titles. Seeking to revamp her unorthodox backhand, which had caused injuries, she took most of autumn 1982 off to work with teaching pro Robert Landsdorp. In 1983 she had her most successful year in singles, reaching f 5 tournaments (including Australian Open) and defeated Evert Lloyd in Wimbledon's biggest upset. At year's end was ranked by most experts in world's top 10. But her doubles partnership with A. Smith ended when Smith announced her departure from the circuit after the French Open. Jordan then played with Jausovec for a while and at year's end teamed with Potter. In fact, Smith returned to circuit part time in 1984 and planned a complete return in 1985 so they were reunited on a part-time basis in doubles and reached their fourth Wimbledon f. In singles, Jordan was forced out of action at each end of the year by shoulder injuries, but in her brief, 11-tournament season she played some outstanding tennis. At Eastbourne she beat Evert Lloyd for the second straight time on grass and at Wimbledon she toppled Shriver to reach sf for the first time. Injuries plagued her again in 1985, forcing her out of Australian Open. Earlier, she beat Evert Lloyd again, in 1r VS Champ – only the fourth time the world No. 2 had lost 1r. Jordan also beat Shriver again, but her highest moments were in doubles. She won Wimbledon for the second time with a new partner, Liz Smylie, beating Navratilova/Shriver in f to end their remarkable 109-match winning streak. It was Jordan's fifth Wimbledon doubles f in six years. *1985 HIGHLIGHTS – SINGLES: Wimbledon* 2r, seed 10 (d. Tacon 6–0 6–2, lost Savchenko 7–5 3–6 6–3), *US Open* last 16 (d. Mesker 2–6 6–1 6–2, Jaeger 3–6 6–2 6–2, Phelps 7–5 6–1, lost Mandlikova [seed 3] 7–5 3–6 6–1); *r/u* Melbourne (d. Potter, lost Shriver 6–4 6–1); *sf* Marco Island (d. Bonder 6–3 fs, lost Casale), *sf* VS Chicago (d. R. White 6–2 fs, Shriver 6–2 6–3, lost Rinaldi 6–0 7–5); *qf* VS Champ (d. Evert Lloyd 6–2 fs). *1985 HIGHLIGHTS – DOUBLES:* (with Smylie unless stated) *won Wimbledon* seed 3 (d. Kohde-Kilsch/Sukova 5–7 6–1 6–4, Navratilova/Shriver 5–7 6–3 6–4); *won* VS Florida (d. Cherneva/Savchenko 6–4 7–6), *won* Marco Island (d. Benjamin/Gadusek 6–3 6–3), *won* Bridgestone (d. Nagelsen/White 4–6 7–5 6–2), *won* Mahwah (d. Kohde-Kilsch/Sukova 7–6 6–3), *won* VS Chicago (d. Burgin/Russell 6–2 6–2); [Mandlikova] *r/u* LIPC (lost Navratilova/G. Fernandez), *r/u* Eastbourne (d. Mandlikova/Turnbull 6–1 fs, lost Navratilova/Shriver 7–5 6–4). *CAREER HIGHLIGHTS – SINGLES: Wimbledon – qf 1983* (d. Evert Lloyd 6–1 7–6, lost King), *sf 1984* (d. Shriver 2–6 6–3 6–4, lost Navratilova 6–3 6–4). *CAREER HIGHLIGHTS – DOUBLES:* (with A. Smith unless stated) *French Open – won 1980* (d. Madruga/Villagran 6–1 6–0); *Wimbledon – won 1980* (d. Casals/Turnbull 3–6 7–6 6–1), *r/u 1981* (d. Fairbank/Harford, lost Navratilova/Shriver 6–3 7–6), *r/u 1982* (lost Navratilova/Shriver 6–4 6–1), *r/u 1984* (d. Potter/Walsh, lost Navratilova/Shriver 6–3 6–1), [Smylie] *r/u 1985*, [Jausovec] *qf 1983* (lost Navratilova/Shriver 3–6 6–3 6–3); *US Open – won 1981* (d. Casals/Turnbull 6–3 6–3), [Jausovec] *sf 1983* (lost Navratilova/Shriver 6–3 6–2); *Australian Open – won 1981* (d. Navratilova/Shriver 6–2 7–5).

CARINA KARLSSON (Sweden)
Born Stockholm, 11 September, 1966, and lives there; RH; 5ft 8in; 125lb; final 1985 WTA ranking 51 (57); 1985 prize money $46,329.
Turned pro April 1984 and immediately won a $10,000 event in Mon Viso, then reached qf Wimbledon. Became a member of the Swedish Fed Cup team in 1984 and acquitted herself well in 1985, reaching f Hilversum late in the year. *1985 HIGHLIGHTS – SINGLES: French Open* 2r (d. Holladay 4–6 6–3 6–1, lost Cecchini 6–0 6–1), *Wimbledon* 1r (lost Plchova 2–6 6–4 6–3), *US Open* 1r (lost Reggi 4–6 6–3 6–3), *Australian Open* 1r (lost G. Fernandez 6–1 6–4); *r/u* Hilversum (d. Garrone, Tanvier, Scheuer-Larsen, lost K. Maleeva 6–3 6–2).

HELEN KELESI (Canada)
Born Victoria, 15 November, 1969, and lives there; RH; 2HB; 5ft 5in; 130lb; final 1985 WTA ranking 48 (—); 1985 prize money $29,164.
Her parents left Czechoslovakia a year before her birth, her mother then being ranked in Canada in 1974, 1975 and 1976. A feisty, gritty backcourt player with a better forehand than two-handed backhand, she came into prominence in summer 1985 when she reached f VS Central NY with a win over Sukova. *1985 HIGHLIGHTS – SINGLES: French Open* 1r (lost Skronska 6–4 2–6 6–1), *Wimbledon* 1r (lost Louie 6–2 6–4), *US Open* 1r (lost A. White 6–3 2–6 6–4); *r/u* VS Central NY (d. Gomer 6–4 fs, K. Maleeva 6–4 fs, Ruzici 1–6 6–2 6–4, Sukova 7–6 7–6, lost Potter 4–6 6–3 6–2); *sf* Delray Beach Satellite (d. Votavova, lost Solomon); *qf* VS Indianapolis (d. Uys 7–5 7–6, Amiach 6–3 fs, lost Horvath).

DAMIR KERETIC (West Germany)
Born Zagreb, Yugoslavia, 6 March, 1960; lives Stuttgart; RH; 5ft 9in; 160lb; final 1985 ATP ranking 85 (142); 1985 prize money $39,389.
Two sf appearances in 1985 helped this German jun champ of 1977 and 1978 to return to the top 100, where he had been ranked in 1982. *1985 HIGHLIGHTS – SINGLES: French Open* 1r (lost H. Gunthardt 6–0 6–3 6–4), *Wimbledon* 1r (lost Visser 7–6 6–4 4–6 7–6 6–3), *Australian Open* 2r (d. Shaw 6–4 2–1 ret'd, lost DePalmer 6–2 6–2 6–2); *sf* Bologna (d. Bottazzi, Kley, Prpic, lost Tulasne), *sf* Bastad (d. Drewett, Kley, Sundstrom, lost Wilander).

GRACE KIM (USA)
Born Ridgwood, NJ, 14 April, 1968; lives Franklin Lakes, NJ; RH; 5ft 4in; 120lb; final 1985 WTA ranking 60 (63); 1985 prize money $38,335.
The top-ranked player in the US Girls' 16 division for 1983, she displayed courage and resilience in 1984 when she emerged from a series of early-season losses in the qual rounds to finish the year at No. 63 in the world. A tireless worker and outstanding retriever, she makes certain that her opponents earn every point. She struggled in and out of the qualifying rounds in 1985 but salvaged her year with qf showings at Tampa and Tokyo. *1985 HIGHLIGHTS – SINGLES: French Open* 2r (d. Eliseenko 6–1 6–2, lost Graf [seed 11] 6–0 6–4), *Wimbledon* 1r (lost Hobbs 6–4 6–2), *US Open* 3r (d. Bunge 6–4 6–4, Piatek 7–6 7–6, lost Evert Lloyd 6–0 6–2); *qf* Tampa (d. Gompert 6–2 fs, Spence, lost Bassett), *qf* Pan Pacific Tokyo (d. Van Nostrand, Henricksson 7–6 fs, lost Kohde-Kilsch).

CLAUDIA KOHDE-KILSCH (West Germany)
Born Saarbrucken, 11 December, 1963, and lives there; RH; 6ft 0½in; 140lb; final 1985 WTA ranking 5 (8) singles, 4 doubles; 1985 prize money $398,120.
In 1979, when she was ranked in the top ten in the world among juniors, she won the German International Jun and reached sf French Jun. Slipping five places on the computer in 1983, she did not fulfil her potential in singles, although she enjoyed a successful year in partnership with Eva Pfaff. When her stepfather officially adopted her in 1983, she was obliged to take his name – Kilsch. She exploited her singles potential fully in 1984, winning German Open and staying inside the top 10 for most of the year. In sf Eastbourne, she led Navratilova 4–2 with a point for 5–2 in fs, but was beaten cleanly by a winning backhand service return and her chance was gone. In doubles, she played wonderfully with both Mandlikova and Sukova. Her best year in singles came in 1985 when, although she won only one tournament (LA), she was one of only 3 players to beat Navratilova (qf Canadian

Open) and achieved sf finishes in French and Australian Opens. Meanwhile, her partnership with Sukova flourished. After losing 7–6 fs to Navratilova/Shriver in f VS Champ, they toppled the formidable duo in f US Open for their first GS crown. *1985 HIGHLIGHTS – SINGLES: French Open* sf, seed 7 (d. Solomon 6–2 6–2, Medrado 6–4 6–4, K. Maleeva 6–4 6–3, Hanika 5–7 6–0 6–3, Mandlikova [seed 3] 6–4 6–4, lost Navratilova [seed 1] 6–4 6–4), *Wimbledon* 2r, seed 6 (d. Nagelsen 7–5 6–1, lost Durie 4–6 6–1 6–2), *US Open* qf, seed 5 (d. Dias 7–6 6–1, Villagran 6–1 6–1, Henricksson 6–3 6–4, Turnbull [seed 12] 5–7 7–5 6–2 [saving 2 mps], lost Evert Lloyd [seed 1] 6–3 6–3), *Australian Open* sf, seed 5 (d. A. Croft 7–5 6–3, G. Fernandez 6–1 6–2, Durie 4–6 6–1 6–2, Lindqvist 6–4 6–0, lost Evert Lloyd [seed 1] 6–1 7–6); *won* VS LA (d. Mandlikova 7–6 7–5, Shriver 6–2 6–4); *r/u* Canadian Open (d. Navratilova 3–6 6–4 6–3, Sukova 6–4 6–3, lost Evert Lloyd 6–2 6–4); *sf* Amelia Island (d. Huber, Horvath, lost Evert Lloyd 6–4 6–2), *sf* Orlando (d. Lindqvist 6–2 fs, lost Navratilova), *sf* Stuttgart (d. Benjamin, Gerken, lost Lindqvist 2–6 7–6 6–4), *sf* Zurich (d. K. Maleeva, lost Garrison), *sf* Brisbane (d. Turnbull 6–1 fs, lost Navratilova), *sf* Sydney (d. Jolissaint 6–3 fs, lost Mandlikova), *sf* Pan Pacific Open Tokyo (d. Kim 7–6 fs, lost Gadusek). *1985 HIGHLIGHTS – DOUBLES:* (with Sukova) *r/u French Open* seed 2 (d. Burgin/Temesvari 6–4 7–5, lost Navratilova/Shriver 4–6 6–2 6–2), *Wimbledon* sf, seed 2 (d. Potter/Walsh Pete 7–6 4–6 6–3, lost K. Jordan/Smylie 5–7 6–1 6–4), *won US Open* seed 2 (d. Garrison/Rinaldi 5–7 6–4 6–3, Navratilova/Shriver 6–7 6–2 6–3), *r/u Australian Open* seed 2 (d. Potter/Walsh Pete 3–6 6–4 6–1, lost Navratilova/Shriver 6–3 6–4); *won* German Open (d. Graf/Tanvier 6–4 6–1), *won* VS LA (d. Mandlikova/Turnbull 6–4 6–2), *won* Pan Pacific Open Tokyo (d. Mesker/Smylie 6–0 6–4); *r/u* VS Washington (lost Navratilova/G. Fernandez 6–3 fs), *r/u* VS Champ (lost Navratilova/Shriver 6–7 6–4 7–6), *r/u* Mahwah (lost K. Jordan/Smylie 7–6 6–3), *r/u* Zurich (d. K./M. Maleeva 6–0 6–1, lost Mandlikova/Temesvari), *r/u* Brisbane (lost Navratilova/Shriver 6–1 fs). *CAREER HIGH-LIGHTS – SINGLES: French Open – sf 1985; Australian Open – sf 1985; US Open – qf 1985. CAREER HIGHLIGHTS – DOUBLES:* (with Sukova unless stated) *US Open – won 1985,* [Bunge] *sf 1982* (d. K. Jordan/A. Smith 6–3 fs, lost Casals/Turnbull 6–4 6–1); *French Open* [Mandlikova] *r/u 1984* (lost Navratilova/Shriver 5–7 6–3 6–2), *r/u 1985; Australian Open –*[Pfaff] *r/u 1982* (d. Casals/Turnbull 6–3 5–7 6–2, Potter/Walsh 7–6 fs, lost Navratilova/Shriver 6–4 6–2), *r/u 1984* (lost Navratilova/Shriver 6–3 6–4), *r/u 1985; Wimbledon –* [Bunge] *sf 1982* (d. Barker/Kiyomura 6–3 3–6 6–4, Piatek/W. White, Blackwood/Leo, lost Navratilova/Shriver 6–3 6–4), *sf 1985.*

KRISTIN KINNEY (USA)

Born Norwalk, Conn., 27 August, 1959; lives New Canaan, Conn.; RH; 5ft 4in; 115lb; final 1985 WTA ranking 91 (181); 1985 prize money $18,650.
A graduate of Princeton University in 1981 where she majored in English, she is one of the best female players ever to emerge from her state. *1985 HIGHLIGHTS – SINGLES: French Open* (lost 3r qualifying Dinu 6–3 6–1), *Wimbledon* 1r (lost W. White 6–3 2–6 6–4), *US Open* (lost 1r qualifying Jane Young 6–3 6–7 6–3); *r/u* USTA Key Biscayne (d. Garrone, Van Der Torre, lost Holikova 7–5 6–3).

AARON KRICKSTEIN (USA)

Born Ann Arbor, Mich., 2 August, 1967, lives Grosse Pointe, Mich.; RH; 2HB; 5ft 10in; 150lb; final 1985 ATP ranking 30 (12); 1985 prize money $159,772.
Always one of the dominant performers in American jun tennis, he was ranked at or near the top of every division from 12s to 18s. He won US Nat 16 in 1982, and Nat 18 in 1983. After a close examination of his goals and priorities, and a meeting with his doctor father and coach Nick Bollettieri, he elected to turn pro in the autumn. The main reason behind his decision was a spectacular US Open where, having been beaten in 1r of all 5 GP tournaments he had played earlier in 1983, he defeated Edberg in 5s t-b in opening round and upended 1979 r/u Gerulaitis in another five-setter before Noah stopped his surprising run of success. Then, in October, he won Tel Aviv for his first GP tournament triumph and at 16 years 2 months and 13 days became the youngest-ever winner of a GP tournament. In 1984 he demonstrated extraordinary courage and resilience after losing 1r or 2r first 8 tournaments. His year turned around when he reached f Italian Open in May and then became the youngest ever to win US Pro Champ in Boston. He added 2 more GP titles by the time he had turned 17, including Wilander and Sundstrom among his more notable

The former Australian Open Junior champion and a Junior quarter-finalist at Wimbledon and the US Open, Australia's Anne Minter has represented her country in the Federation Cup. *(T. Hindley)*

victims. US D Cup captain Arthur Ashe gave him a chance to practise with the team for sf and f rounds, and it seemed likely that he would be a playing member of the squad in the near future, which he was, leading the US past Japan in opening round of 1985 competition. But he suffered a frustrating defeat in Hamburg as Germany upset US in qf, losing in 5s to Schwaier in the pivotal match with a wrist injury as Germany won 3–2. It was an unhappy year for him until he reached f at Hong Kong at the end. *1985 HIGHLIGHTS – SINGLES: French Open* last 16, seed 10 (d. Luna 6–1 4–6 6–4 6–3, Vilas 6–4 3–6 6–1 6–3, McNamee 7–5 5–7 1–6 6–2 6–1, lost Lendl [seed 2] 6–2 6–2 6–0), *Wimbledon* 1r, seed 10 (lost Schultz 6–4 3–6 7–6 6–4); *r/u* Hong Kong (d. Bauer 6–2 fs, Wilkison, Canter, Schultz 6–3 6–2, lost Gomez 6–3 6–3 3–6 6–4); *sf* WCT Forest Hills (d. M. Davis 6–0 fs, Gilbert 6–3 7–6, lost Lendl 6–2 fs); *qf* WCT Dallas (d. Teltscher 7–5 fs, lost Connors). *CAREER HIGHLIGHTS – SINGLES: US Pro – won 1984* (d. Clerc 7–6 3–6 6–4); *Italian Open – r/u 1984* (d. Teltscher, Nystrom, lost Gomez 2–6 6–1 6–2 6–2).

JOHAN KRIEK (USA)
Born Pongola, South Africa, 5 April, 1958; lives Naples, Fla., with wife Tish; RH; 5ft 8in; 155lb; final 1985 ATP ranking 14 (13); 1985 prize money $303,274.
In 1978, aged 20, he gained the confidence to become a world-class player, with good results on satellite American Express circuit and reaching US Open qf. Remained in top 40 through 1979 (when he again reached US Open qf) and then broke into the top 20 in 1980, reaching US Open sf and producing a big win over McEnroe in San Francisco qf. At the start of 1981 he looked very impressive as r/u to McEnroe in WCT Finals. Sidelined for a month by injury, but came back to win Newport in July and ended year by capturing his first GS title in Australian Open. In 1982 the former South African, who became a US citizen that year, blew hot and cold, but won his second straight Australian Open title at the end of the year to qualify for his first Masters where he beat Denton but lost to Connors. In 1983, he beat Connors for the first time in sf Los Angeles and was always a threat to anyone, but he lost his Australian crown to Wilander and again lacked the essential consistency to earn a top 10 world ranking. During 1984 he was ranked as high as No. 7, but by the end of the year he had slipped 6 places, despite qualifying for Masters for the second straight year, and was beaten again by Wilander at Australian Open. He won Bristol and Livingston but was again below par at Wimbledon and US Open and had 3 m-ps in Masters qf before losing to Wilander again. He had a typical year in 1985, full of highs and lows. At his best he beat McEnroe *en route* to f San Francisco, won Las Vegas with wins over Mayotte, Smid and Arias, finished r/u to Becker at Queens, and beat Edberg in 1r Masters. *1985 HIGHLIGHTS – SINGLES: Wimbledon* 3r, seed 9 (d. Pecci 6–4 6–0 4–6 7–5, Fitzgerald 3–6 7–6 7–5 6–1, lost Maurer 6–1 6–4 3–6 6–3), *US Open* 2r, seed 12 (d. McNamee 6–4 6–2 6–4, lost Holmes 2–6 6–3 6–4 6–1), *Australian Open* qf, seed 6 (d. Mustard 6–4 4–6 6–3 6–4, Doohan 7–5 6–4 6–0, Lapidus 6–3 6–4 6–3, lost Wilander [seed 3] 6–3 7–5 6–2); *won* Las Vegas (d. Mayotte 6–3 fs, Smid, Arias 4–6 6–3 6–4 6–2); *r/u* Queens Club (d. Cain 6–1 fs, Ostoja, Krishnan, R. Simpson, Zivojinovic 6–4 6–4, lost Becker 6–2 6–3), *r/u* San Francisco (d. McEnroe 6–1 fs, Green, lost Edberg); *sf* Livingston (lost Teacher), *sf* LA (d. Arias 7–6 fs, lost Edberg); *qf* Masters (d. Edberg 6–2 4–6 6–2, lost Gomez 6–3 6–2). *1985 HIGHLIGHTS – DOUBLES:* (with Curren unless stated) *Wimbledon* qf (d. Edberg/Jarryd, lost Cash/Fitzgerald 6–1 7–5 6–4), *US Open* qf (d. Edmondson/Warwick, lost DePalmer/Donnelly 6–1 7–6 4–6 7–6); [Noah] *won* Chicago (d. Flach/Seguso 3–6 4–6 7–5 6–1 6–4). *CAREER HIGHLIGHTS – SINGLES: Australian Open – won 1981* (d. T. Mayotte, Edmondson, Denton 6–2 7–6 6–7 6–4), *won 1982* (d. McNamee 7–6 7–6 4–6 3–6 7–5 [saving 1 m-p], Denton 6–3 6–3 6–2), *sf 1984* (lost Wilander 6–1 6–0 6–2), *qf 1985; US Indoor – won 1982* (d. Gerulaitis 6–3 fs, Mottram 6–4 fs, McEnroe 6–3 3–6 6–4); *S. African Open – won 1983* (d. Dowdeswell 6–4 4–6 1–6 7–5 6–3); *WCT Final – r/u 1981* (d. Fibak, Tanner 6–4 fs, lost McEnroe 6–1 6–2 6–4); *US Open – sf 1980* (d. Birner, Fleming [seed 9], A. Giammalva, Mottram, Fibak [seed 14], lost Borg [seed 1] 4–6 4–6 6–1 6–1 6–1), *qf 1978* (d. Teacher, lost Gerulaitis 6–2 6–1 6–2), *qf 1979* (d. Pecci, Noah 6–4 5s, lost Gerulaitis 5–7 6–3 6–4 6–3); *Wimbledon – qf 1982* (d. Elter 6–4 5s, Rennert, Saviano, lost McEnroe 4–6 6–2 7–5 6–3); *Masters – qf 1983* (d. Arias, lost McEnroe), *qf 1984* (lost Wilander 6–4 6–3 7–6), *qf 1985.*

RAMESH KRISHNAN (India)
Born Madras, 5 June, 1961 and lives there and Bardmoor Club, Fla.; RH; 5ft 7in; 160lb; final 1985 ATP ranking 40 (24); 1985 prize money $114,596.
Son of former Indian D Cup player Ramanathan who reached Wimbledon sf in 1960 (lost Fraser 6–3 6–2 6–2) and 1961 (lost Laver 6–2 8–6 6–2), Ramesh was the world's best jun in 1979, sweeping the French and Wimbledon Jun crowns. Already during that year he had defeated Fleming at French Open and Dent at US Open – both considerable achievements for an 18-year-old with little experience in men's competition. After a long slump in 1981 brought on by the mistake of playing while injured, this graceful, artistic player delighted US Open crowds as he reached qf and was 2 points away from a two-sets-to-love lead over McEnroe. He won Stuttgart in 1982 but both then and in 1983 he did not realise his potential, often playing dazzling and deceptive tennis but usually losing. He fared better in 1984 and was particularly impressive in the autumn when he upset Wilander to reach sf of Seiko Open in Tokyo. After getting married a few weeks before Wimbledon in 1985, he again saved his best for the end of the season, making up for an otherwise lacklustre year. *1985 HIGHLIGHTS – SINGLES: Wimbledon* 3r (d. Derlin 6–2 7–5 4–6 7–6, Bourne 6–4 7–5 6–2, lost Connors [seed 3] 7–5 5–7 7–5 6–2), *US Open* 1r (lost Gunthardt 5–7 6–3 4–6 7–6 6–4); *r/u* Cologne (d. Ostoja, Svensson, Lloyd 7–5 fs, Dickson, lost Lundgren); *sf* Toulouse (d. Ostoja, Gunnarsson, lost Smid); *qf* LA (d. Stefanki, lost Smid), *qf* Toronto Indoor (d. M. Leach, lost Teltscher). *CAREER HIGHLIGHTS – SINGLES: US Open – qf 1981* (d. S. Smith 6–4 6–3 6–3, M. Davis 6–2 7–5 6–7 6–4, G. Mayer [seed 7] 4–6 1–6 7–6 7–5 ret'd, lost McEnroe [seed 1] 6–7 7–6 6–4 6–2).

CAROLINE KUHLMAN (USA)
Born Covington, 25 August, 1966; lives Lake Side Park, Kentucky; RH; 5ft 8in; 133lb; final 1985 WTA ranking 68 (–); 1985 prize money $19,235.
A former US Jun Fed Cup member, who achieved a good ranking in 1985 based almost entirely on her record in satellite tournaments, as well as 3r showing at US Open, upsetting Temesvari 2r after qualifying. *1985 HIGHLIGHTS – SINGLES: US Open* 3r (d. McNeil 6–1 6–3, Temesvari 2–6 6–2 6–2, lost Moulton 6–4 1–6 7–6); *won* USTA Charleston (d. Takagi 6–2 6–1); *sf* VS Utah (d. Piatek 6–1 fs, Betzner, Rapponi Longo 6–4 fs, lost Rehe).

NIKLAS KULTI (Sweden)
Born Kungsangen, 22 April, 1971; lives Helsingborg; RH; 6ft; 165lb.
Started tennis aged 6 with his father, Lars, an engineer and former footballer. Won Kalle Anka Cup in 1981, and Swedish and European 14s titles in 1985, winning the last three rounds 6–0 6–0 and finishing the year by taking Orange Bowl and Rolex 14s. Member of Salk club and coached by Pavel Strauss.

LEONARDO LAVALLE (Mexico)
Born Mexico City, 14 July, 1967, and lives there; single; LH; 6ft 2in; 170lb; final 1985 ATP ranking 86 (—); 1985 prize money $20,057.
The winner of 1985 Wimbledon Jun Champ, he broke into the men's top 100. *1985 HIGHLIGHTS – SINGLES: US Open* 1r (lost Flach 7–5 6–2 2–6 6–1), *Australian Open* 2r (lost Lendl 6–4 0–6 6–4 6–2); *qf* Geneva (d. Gunthardt, lost Aguilera).

MIKE LEACH (USA)
Born Minneapolis, 9 March, 1960; lives Weston, Mass.; LH; 5ft 11in; 165lb; final 1985 ATP ranking 37 (96); 1985 prize money $104,883.
The NCAA champion of 1982, this former All-American from Univ. of Michigan tested the waters on the pro tour that year and held his own. Then, in 1983, he moved into the top 100, despite a slow start which included 1r and 2r defeats in 10 of his first 11 tournaments, although he reached last 16 Wimbledon with wins over McNamee and Edmondson. After spending 1983 and 1984 located in the 90s on the computer, he produced his most consistent results in 1985 to move into the top 40. *1985 HIGHLIGHTS – SINGLES: French Open* 1r (lost Youl 5–7 6–4 6–4 6–4), *Wimbledon* 2r (d. Fibak 7–6 6–4 6–1, lost Lendl [seed 2] 6–3 1–6 6–2 6–7 6–4), *US Open* 1r (lost Schultz 7–6 6–4 6–2), *Australian Open* 2r (d. Canter 7–5 7–6 5–7 3–6 6–4, lost Wilkison 6–4 6–0 6–2); *sf* Atlanta (d. Edberg,

Denton, Cash, lost McEnroe); *qf* LIPC (d. Arias 7–6 6–3, Wilander 7–5 6–2, lost Mayotte 6–2 6–3 6–2).

HENRI LECONTE (France)
Born Lillers, 4 July, 1963; lives Paris; married; LH; 6ft 1in; 160lb; final 1985 ATP ranking 16 (27); 1985 prize money $259,778.
This enormously talented lefthander came into his own in 1982, playing D Cup doubles with Noah and No. 2 singles for the f v US at Grenoble. He won Stockholm Open over Wilander and enjoyed consistent success all year. It seemed only a matter of time before he would arrive in the world's top 10, but despite two big wins over Lendl in 1983 (at WCT Forest Hills and Australian Indoor) he did not fully deliver what his talent promised. But he will be remembered as the last man to beat Borg in a tournament – 2r Monte Carlo. Ironically, when Borg made another rare appearance at Stuttgart in summer 1984, Leconte beat him again, also scoring notable wins over Smid and G. Mayer to win the event. His enormous skill was on display when he beat Lendl in D Cup and when he nearly ousted Connors in US Indoor f at Memphis. However, he continued to give his coach and advisor, Ion Tiriac, fits of anxiety with his unpredictability. He hardly played in the last quarter of 1984 and seemed to have lost interest in tennis as he approached marriage. However, he made his mark in every GS event in 1985: in Paris he took apart Gomez and Noah to reach the qf; at Wimbledon he upset Lendl (seed 2) before losing to Becker in qf; at US Open, he fell in 5s last 16 to Gunthardt and at Australian Open in the same round he was 2 points from victory, 2 sets to 1 and 5–1 in tb, before losing to McEnroe. He then captured his second GP title of the season in Sydney to qualify for his first Masters, where he lost 1r to Gomez. *1985 HIGHLIGHTS – SINGLES: French Open* qf, unseeded (d. Wilkison 7–5 6–2 6–1, Portes 6–2 6–1 6–3, Gomez [seed 5] 6–3 6–4 6–4, Noah [seed 9] 6–3 6–4 6–7 4–6 6–1, lost Wilander [seed 4] 6–4 7–6 6–7 7–5), *Wimbledon*, qf, unseeded (d. Dunk 6–3 7–6 7–6, Masur 4–6 6–4 7–6 6–3, Lloyd 5–7 6–3 6–4 6–1, Lendl [seed 2] 3–6 6–4 6–3 6–1, lost Becker 7–6 3–6 6–3 6–4), *US Open* last 16 (d. Fibak 6–4 6–3 6–4, Forget 6–4 6–4 6–4, Schwaier 6–2 6–2 6–1, lost Gunthardt 7–6 6–2 3–6 4–6 6–3), *Australian Open* last 16, seed 13 (d. Mansdorf 6–4 6–2 7–5, Sadri 7–6 6–3 7–6, lost McEnroe [seed 2] 5–7 7–6 3–6 7–6 6–1); *won* NSW Open (d. Canter 6–1 fs, Masur, Anger, Evernden 6–7 6–2 6–3); *won* Nice (d. Luna 7–6 6–4, Schwaier 7–5 6–4, Pecci 6–4 6–4); *r/u* Aus. Indoor (d. Gomez, Fitzgerald, lost Lendl 6–4 6–4 7–6); *sf* Geneva (d. Vajda, lost Wilander 6–1 fs), *sf* Barcelona (d. E. Sanchez, lost Tulasne). *1985 HIGHLIGHTS – DOUBLES:* (with Noah) *r/u US Open* seed 12 (d. Nystrom/Wilander, lost Flach/Seguso 7–6 6–7 7–6 6–0). *CAREER HIGHLIGHTS – SINGLES: French Open* – *qf 1985*; *Wimbledon* – *qf 1985*. *CAREER HIGHLIGHTS – DOUBLES:* (with Noah) *French Open* – *won 1984* (d. Gunthardt/Taroczy, Slozil/Smid 6–4 2–6 3–6 6–3 6–2); *US Open* – *r/u 1985*.

IVAN LENDL (Czechoslovakia) **Official World Champion**
Born Ostrava, 7 March, 1960 and lives there and Greenwich, Conn.; single; RH; 6ft 2in; 160lb; final 1985 ATP ranking 1 (3); 1985 prize money $1,963,074; career prize money $8,306,592.
World's outstanding U-18 player in 1978 when he won Orange Bowl (Dec. 1977), Italian, French and Wimbledon Jun titles. Made impressive strides in 1979, including sf appearances at Toronto, Brussels and Buenos Aires. Ranked 20 at end 1979, then, in the middle of 1980, he exploded into first gear, seeming no longer capable of fear and ready to step on court believing he could beat anybody. He was the only player to beat Borg twice (but lost to him in Masters f), and with his lethal hitting from the baseline his scintillating record convinced many that he was the No. 4 player in the world. Led Czechoslovakia to first-ever D Cup success, beating Panatta and Barazzutti and winning doubles with Smid. In 1981 he was brilliant at the end of the year to head GP points table with its $300,000 bonus, capturing 5 consecutive GP tournaments without a rest week to finish world No. 2. He capped an extraordinary year by beating McEnroe and Gerulaitis to win Masters, and extended his unbeaten tournament run to 44 matches before Noah beat him in f La Quinta on 21 Feb. His record for 1982 was equally remarkable. He set an Open Tennis record by winning 106 matches, suffering only 9 defeats and capturing 15 of 23 tournaments. He won WCT Champ and Masters, extending his winning streak over McEnroe to 7 straight matches and was victorious in 2 of 3 clashes with Connors. Yet it

was not enough to earn him the No. 1 ranking because he skipped Wimbledon, lost to Connors in f US Open and lost in last 16 French Open to Wilander. No one performed with more consistency in the big events in 1983, although he won only 7 of 23 tournaments with a match record of 75–16. He reached qf French Open, sf Wimbledon, and was r/u at US Open, Australian Open, and Masters, his inability to win the majors being the only question left unanswered. The US and Australian Open f losses were his third and fourth in GS events. For the second straight year he lost to Connors at Flushing Meadow, after serving a double-fault at 5–4 s-p in 3s at one set all. At Australian Open he lost to Wilander, Noah stopped him at French and McEnroe beat him at Wimbledon and in f Masters – a reversal of their 1982 meeting. But he remained a man of immense talent and only McEnroe had his number, winning four of their six encounters (including Jan. 1984 Masters). He won his first GS title in 1984, coming from two sets to love down to beat McEnroe in the French Open f in Paris. McEnroe had never lost from such a commanding position in a GS event. Otherwise, McEnroe was his nemesis, defeating him in US Pro Indoor, Brussels, WCT Forest Hills, World Team Cup, US Open and f of Masters in Jan. 1985. Lendl lost to Connors in sf Wimbledon, reached his third consecutive US Open f and his fifth consecutive Masters f, but lost to Curren in last 16 Australian Open – the first time since 1981 that he had lost before qf of a GS event. Starting in Sept., he went on the Robert Haas diet and by January, 1985, had lost 15lb and was feeling fitter than ever. Guided ably by Australian Tony Roche and training as hard as anyone in the game, he had a wonderful 1985 season in which he was unanimously ranked No. 1 in the world. The key to his long-awaited rise to the top was his success at Flushing Meadow. Appearing in his fourth consecutive US Open f, he trailed McEnroe 2–5 s-p, but from that point on he was always on the edge of perfection and won the most important match of his year 7–6 6–3 6–4. Earlier in the year, he had won four straight tournaments before Wilander tripped him in French Open f. His 6th loss in 7 GS f left his critics wondering again about his response to pressure, but with his glowing triumph at US Open he set the record straight, winning 4 more consecutive tournaments through the autumn and remaining unbeaten until falling in sf Australian Open to Edberg. He won 11 tournaments across the season ending with Masters, which he took for 3rd time. *1985 HIGHLIGHTS – SINGLES: r/u* **French Open** seed 2 (d. Edwards 6–2 6–3 6–1 Gunnarsson 7–6 6–3 6–2, Potier 6–1 6–2 6–2, Krickstein 6–2 6–2 6–0, Jaite 6–4 6–2 6–4, Connors [seed 3] 6–2 6–3 6–1, lost Wilander [seed 4] 3–6 6–4 6–2 6–2), **Wimbledon** last 16, seed 2 [d. Purcell 6–4 7–6 7–6, M. Leach 6–3 1–6 6–2 6–7 6–4, Glickstein 7–6 4–6 6–3 6–2, lost Leconte 3–6 6–4 6–3 6–1), **won US Open** seed 2 (d. Lapidus 6–2 6–1 6–3, Scanlon 6–2 6–0 6–3, de la Pena 6–1 6–1 6–3, Yzaga 4–6 6–3 6–4 6–0, Noah [seed 7] 6–2 6–2 6–4, Connors [seed 4] 6–2 6–3 7–5, McEnroe [seed 1] 7–6 6–3 6–4), **Australian Open** sf, seed 1 (d. Lavalle 6–4 0–6 6–4 6–2, Testerman 6–3 1–6 6–3 6–2, Steyn 6–3 6–2 6–7 6–2, Lloyd 7–6 6–2 6–1, lost Edberg [seed 5] 6–7 7–5 6–1 4–6 9–7); **won** Masters (d. Smid, Mayotte, Gomez, Becker 6–2 7–6 6–3), **won** Fort Myers (d. Lloyd, Holmes, Gilbert, S. Giammalva, Connors 6–3 6–2), **won** Monte Carlo (d. Sundstrom 7–6 fs, Wilander 6–1 6–4 4–6 6–4), **won** WCT Finals Dallas (d. Edberg 6–2 fs, Connors, Mayotte 7–6 6–4 6–1), **won** WCT Forest Hills (d. Krickstein 6–1 fs, McEnroe 6–3 6–3), **won** US CC (d. Jaite, Becker 5–7 6–2 6–2, Gomez 6–1 6–3), **won** Stuttgart (d. Clerc 6–2 6–2, Gilbert 6–4 6–0), **won** Sydney Indoor (d. Annacone, Leconte 6–4 6–4 7–6), **won** Tokyo Seiko (d. Mayotte, Becker 6–3 7–6, Wilander 6–0 6–4), **won** Wembley (d. Kriek, Pate, Becker 6–7 6–3 4–6 6–4 6–4). *1985 HIGHLIGHTS – DOUBLES:* (with Smid) **won** Stuttgart (d. Kohlberg/Soares). *CAREER HIGHLIGHTS – SINGLES: French Open – won* **1984** (d. Wilander, McEnroe 3–6 2–6 6–4 7–5 7–5), *r/u 1981* (d. McNamee 6–2 4–6 7–6 7–6, McEnroe 6–4 6–4 7–5, Clerc 3–6 6–4 4–6 7–6 6–2, lost Borg 6–1 4–6 6–2 3–6 6–1), *r/u* **1985**; *US Open – won 1985, r/u 1982* (d. McEnroe 6–4 6–4 7–6, lost Connors 6–3 6–2 0–6 6–4), *r/u 1984* (d. Cash 3–6 6–3 6–4 6–7 7–6 [saving 1 mp], lost McEnroe 6–3 6–4 6–4); *Masters – won* **1981** (d. Gerulaitis, Vilas in rr, McEnroe 6–4 6–2, Gerulaitis 6–7 2–6 7–6), **won 1982** (d. Noah 6–4 7–5, Connors 6–3 6–1, McEnroe 6–4 6–4 6–2), *r/u 1980* (d. Mayer 6–3 6–4, lost Borg 6–4 6–2 6–2), *r/u 1983* (d. Connors 6–3 6–4, lost McEnroe 6–3 6–4 6–4), *r/u 1984* (d. Connors, lost McEnroe 7–5 6–0 6–4); *Australian Open – r/u 1983* (d. Mayotte 6–1 7–6 6–3, lost Wilander 6–1 6–4 6–4), *sf 1985; Wimbledon – sf 1983* (d. Tanner, lost McEnroe 7–6 6–4 6–4), *sf 1984* (lost Connors 6–7 6–3 7–5 6–1); *D Cup – 1980 winning team* CZ

d. IT 4–1 in Prague (d. Barazzutti 4–6 6–1 6–1 6–2, [with Smid] d. Bertolucci/Panatta 3–6 6–3 3–6 6–3 6–4, d. Ocleppo 6–3 6–3).

CATARINA LINDQVIST (Sweden)

Born Kristinehamn, 13 June, 1963; lives Hollviksnas; RH; 5ft 5in; 125lb; final 1985 WTA ranking 13 (18); 1985 prize money $168,022.
She was ranked 4 in Sweden in 1981–82, 3 in 1983, and gained important experience as a member of Swedish Fed Cup team 1981–83. While most of her countrymen were stealing the attention, she established herself magnificently in 1984 rising from 114 to 18 on the computer, and the standard was maintained in 1985, when her ranking (13) was the highest ever achieved by a Swedish woman. She closed the season with a dazzling win over Shriver in last 16 Australian Open, having begun the year with a victory at the Ginny Champs in Honolulu, her later victims including Mandlikova, Kohde-Kilsch, Turnbull (twice), Garrison and Sukova. *1985 HIGHLIGHTS – SINGLES: French Open* 2r, seed 9 (d. Savchenko 6–2 6–3, lost Spence 7–5 6–2), *Wimbledon* 1r, seed 12 (lost Potter 6–0 7–5), *US Open* last 16, seed 13 (d. Gurney 6–1 6–0, Holton 6–1 6–2, L. Thompson 7–5 6–0, lost Navratilova [seed 2] 6–4 7–5), *Australian Open* 1f, seed 10 (d. Marsikova 7–5 6–2, Inoue 6–4 7–5, Shriver [seed 4] 3–6 6–3 6–2, lost Kohde-Kilsch [seed 5] 6–4 6–0); *won* Ginny Champs (d. Holladay 6–3 6–1); *r/u* Stuttgart (d. Reggi 6–0 fs, Kohde-Kilsch 6–4 fs, lost Shriver 6–1 7–5); *sf* VS Florida (d. Mandlikova 6–1 fs, lost Navratilova), *sf* VS Dallas (d. Garrison 6–4 7–5, Schropp, lost Evert Lloyd), *sf* Mahwah (d. Sukova 6–1 6–2, lost Rinaldi 6–1 fs); *qf* VS Champs (d. Turnbull, lost Sukova 6–4 6–4), *qf* Orlando (lost Kohde-Kilsch 6–2 fs), *qf* Brighton (lost Evert Lloyd 7–6 fs). *1985 HIGHLIGHTS – DOUBLES:* [Evert Lloyd] *Australian Open* qf (d. Mandlikova/Turnbull 6–3 7–6, lost Durie/Hobbs 6–4 6–1), [Russell] *US Open* qf (d. Bunge/Pfaff 6–7 6–4 6–0, lost Mandlikova/Turnbull 6–1 3–6 6–0). *CAREER HIGHLIGHTS – SINGLES: Australian Open – qf 1985.*

CHRIS EVERT LLOYD (USA)

Born Fort Lauderdale, Fla., 21 December, 1954; lives Amelia Island, Fla., Palm Springs, Cal., and Kingston, Surrey with husband John; RH; 2HB; 5ft 5½in; 120lb; final 1985 WTA ranking 2 (2) singles, 11 doubles; 1985 prize money $972,782; career prize money $6,362,164.
Coached by her father, Jimmy, and Dennis Ralston. After five years (1974–78) ranked 1 in the world, she dropped to 3 in 1979 following her marriage to John Lloyd on 17 April. After a three-month break from the circuit in winter 1980, she returned to win her third Italian Open. By the end of 1980 she had won 58 of 61 matches, her fourth French Open and fifth US Open titles and had moved back to No. 1. She had another great year in 1981, winning her third Wimbledon singles title, and her first since 1976, without the loss of a set, the first woman to do so since Billie Jean King in 1967. She also won her fourth Italian Open title, won WTA Champ and finished the year with a 72–6 record for the best winning percentage of all the women. She won 9 of 15 tournaments, reached the f of three others, sf of three more and never lost to any player outside the world top 5. This record earned her a seventh No. 1 world ranking from most experts and the accolade of World Champion from ITF. Staging a remarkable second half of 1982, she won her sixth US Open, her first Australian Open and had beaten Navratilova in the TS Champ she would have made a strong case to be ranked No. 1 in the world again. However, after a slow start to the season in which she was beaten in French Open sf by Jaeger and Wimbledon f by Navratilova, she won at Flushing Meadow convincingly over Jaeger and Mandlikova and then beat Navratilova for the Australian crown for her 13th and 14th GS titles, moving herself into 3rd place on the all-time list of singles winners of Grand Slam titles. While she had to settle for a No. 2 US and world ranking behind Navratilova, she remained head and shoulders better than anyone else. Representing USA she stretched her amazing Fed Cup record to 28–0 in singles and 15–1 in doubles as US won for 11th time, and in W Cup she remained unbeaten with 22 singles as US took their 44th victory. In 1983 she captured her fifth French Open, but lost her chance of the Grand Slam when K. Jordan beat her in 3r Wimbledon on a day when she was battling a stomach virus. (This was the first time in 35 GS tournaments that she had lost before sf.) In September she reached her 8th US Open f but was beaten by Navratilova, who beat her six times in 1983 dropping only one set in those contests. Her record in 1984 was very similar to the

previous year but ended on a high note when she won Australian Open for second time for her 16th GS triumph in the 40 she has entered since 1971. She was beaten by Navratilova six times without a victory, but lost on only two other occasions (to Maleeva in f Italian Open and K. Jordan in sf Eastbourne) and she was the only player in either the men's or women's game to appear in all four GS f, something even she had never done before. She took 1s from Navratilova in f US Open and reached 15–40 when Martina served for 2s at 5–4. Two W Cup singles wins extended her record in that competition to 24–0. She began 1985 with a rare win v Navratilova in f US Florida – her first since f Australian Open 1982 and after 13 consecutive defeats. Following that initial triumph over Navratilova in Florida, she produced one of her most memorable performances to claim her sixth French Open crown in one of the great matches in the history of women's tennis. Leading by a set, 4–2, 15–40, she could not close the contest, serving for the match at 6–5 in 2s to no avail. Finally, after Martina had erased leads of 2–0, 3–1 and 5–3 in fs, Evert Lloyd rallied from 0–40 at 5–5 to win in a magnificent final. This extended her sequence to 13 straight years of having won at least one GS title. Thereafter, she lost to Navratilova for the fifth time in a Wimbledon f – her seventh personal defeat in 10 Wimbledon f. At US Open she lost sf to Mandlikova, failing for only second time in last decade to reach f. When she lost to Navratilova in 3s f Australian, she lost her chance to become No. 1 in the world for the eighth time, but all in all it had been a very good year, her ten tournament triumphs being the most she had won since 1982. After finishing 0–6 against Navratilova in both 1983 and 1984, she was 2–4 in 1985. **1985 HIGHLIGHTS – SINGLES: won French Open** seed 2 (d. J. Thompson 6–2 6–1, Bonder 7–5 6–3, Kanellopoulou 6–3 7–5, Graf 6–2 6–3, Phelps 6–4 6–0, Sabatini 6–4 6–1, Navratilova 6–3 6–7 7–5), **r/u Wimbledon** seed 1 (d. Piatek 6–1 6–0, Mascarin 6–3 6–0, Byrne 6–2 6–1, A. Smith 6–0 6–4, Potter 6–2 6–1, Rinaldi 6–2 6–0, lost Navratilova 4–6 6–3 6–2), **US Open** sf, seed 1 (d. Thompson 6–1 6–3, Reggi 6–0 6–3, Kim 6–0 6–2, R. White 6–2 6–4, Kohde-Kilsch 6–3 6–3, lost Mandlikova [seed 3] 4–6 6–2 6–3), **r/u Australian Open** seed 1 (d. Fairbank 6–1 6–2, Nagelsen 4–6 6–4 6–0, Balestrat 6–4 6–1, M. Maleeva 6–3 6–3, Kohde-Kilsch 6–1 7–6, lost Navratilova 6–2 4–6 6–2); **won** VS Florida (d. Navratilova 6–2 6–4), **won** Palm Beach (d. Mandlikova 6–3 6–3), **won** Hilton Head (d. Graf 6–2 6–1, Sabatini 6–4 6–0), **won** German Open (d. Bonder 6–2 fs, Rinaldi 6–1 6–3, Graf 6–4 7–5), **won** VS Newport (d. Pfaff 7–5 6–2, Shriver 6–4 6–1), **won** Canadian Open (d. Mandlikova 6–4 fs, Kohde-Kilsch 6–2 6–4), **won** VS New Orleans (d. Bonder 6–3 6–1, Shriver 6–4 7–5), **won** Brighton (d. Lindqvist 6–2 2–6 7–6, Croft, M. Maleeva 7–5 6–3), **won** Lion Cup, Tokyo (d. Maleeva 7–5 6–0); **r/u** LIPC (d. Potter 6–1 fs, Graf 6–4 6–2, lost Navratilova 6–2 6–4), **r/u** VS California (d. Kohde-Kilsch 6–3 6–2, Garrison 6–3 6–2, lost Mandlikova 6–2 6–4), **r/u** VS Dallas (d. Lindqvist, lost Navratilova 6–3 6–4), **r/u** Amelia Island (d. Sabatini 6–3 fs, Kohde-Kilsch 6–2 fs, lost Garrison 6–4 6–3). **1985 HIGHLIGHTS – DOUBLES:** (with Turnbull unless stated) [Paradis] **French Open** qf, seed 11 (d. Horvath/Ruzici 4–6 6–1 6–3, lost Navratilova/Shriver 6–3 6–3), [Durie] **Wimbledon** qf, seed 10 (d. Bunge/Pfaff 5–7 6–4 6–4, lost Navratilova/Shriver 6–4 6–2), [Bassett] **US Open** qf, seed 8 (d. Horvath/Ruzici 6–4 6–2, lost Garrison/Rinaldi 6–2 6–3), [Lindqvist] **Australian Open** qf (d. Mandlikova/Turnbull 6–3 7–6, lost Durie/Hobbs 6–4 6–1); **won** VS Newport (d. Shriver/Smylie 6–4 7–6), **won** VS New Orleans (d. Piatek/A. White 6–1 6–2). **CAREER HIGHLIGHTS – SINGLES: French Open – won 1974** (d. Morozova 6–1 6–2), **won 1975** (d. Navratilova 2–6 6–2 6–0), **won 1979** (d. Turnbull 6–2 6–0), **won 1980** seed 1 (d. Mandlikova 6–3 3–6 6–3, Ruzici 6–0 6–3), **won 1983** (d. Sukova, Mandlikova 4–6 6–3 6–2, Jaeger 6–3 6–1, Jausovec 6–1 6–2), **won 1985, r/u 1973** (lost Court 6–7 7–6 6–4), **r/u 1984,** (lost Navratilova 6–3 6–1), **sf 1981** (lost Mandlikova [seed 5] 7–5 6–4), **sf 1982** (lost Jaeger 6–3 6–1); **Wimbledon – won 1974** (d. Hunt 8–6 5–7 11–9, Masthoff 6–4 6–2, Reid 6–2 6–3, Morozova 6–0 6–4), **won 1976** (d. Navratilova 6–3 4–6 6–4, Goolagong Cawley 6–3 4–6 8–6), **won 1981** (d. Jausovec 6–2 6–2, Shriver 6–3 6–1, Mandlikova 6–2 6–2), **r/u 1973** (d. Court 6–1 1–6 6–1, lost King 6–0 7–5), **r/u 1978** (d. Wade 8–6 6–2, lost Navratilova 2–6 6–4 7–5), **r/u 1979** (d. Goolagong Cawley 6–3 6–2, lost Navratilova 6–4 6–4), **r/u 1980** seed 3 (d. Jaeger 6–1 6–1, Navratilova [seed 1] 4–6 6–4 6–2, lost Goolagong Cawley [seed 4] 6–1 7–6), **r/u 1982** seed 2 (d. King 7–6 2–6 6–3, lost Navratilova 6–2 3–6 6–2), **r/u 1984** (d. Mandlikova 6–1 6–2, lost Navratilova 7–6 6–2), **r/u 1985, sf 1972** (lost Goolagong 4–6 6–3 6–4), **sf 1975** (lost King 2–6 6–2 6–3), **sf 1977** (lost Wade 6–2 4–6 6–1); **US Open – won 1975** (d. Navratilova 6–4 6–4, Goolagong Cawley 5–7 6–4 6–2), **won 1976** (d. Goolagong Cawley 6–3 6–0), **won**

1977 (d. King 6–2 6–0, Stove 6–3 7–5, Turnbull 7–6 6–2), *won 1978* (d. Turnbull 6–3 6–0, Shriver 7–5 6–4), *won 1980* seed 3 (d. Austin [seed 1] 4–6 6–1 6–1, Mandlikova 5–7 6–1 6–1), *won 1982* seed 2 (d. Gadusek 4–6 6–1 6–0, Jaeger 6–1 6–2, Mandlikova 6–3 6–1), *r/u 1979* (d. King 6–1 6–1, lost Austin 6–4 6–3), *r/u 1983* (d. Mandlikova 6–4 6–3, Durie 6–4 6–4, lost Navratilova 6–4 6–3), *r/u 1984* (lost Navratilova 4–6 6–4 6–4), *sf 1971* (d. Eisel 4–6 7–6 6–1 [saved 6 m-ps at 5–6 2s], Durr 2–6 6–2 6–3, Hunt 4–6 6–2 6–3, lost King 6–3 6–2), *sf 1972* (d. Morozova 3–6 6–3 7–6, lost Reid 6–4 6–2), *sf 1973* (lost Court 7–5 2–6 6–2), *sf 1974* (lost Goolagong 6–1 6–7 6–3), *sf 1981* (d. Mandlikova, lost Navratilova 7–6 4–6 6–4), *sf 1985; Australian Open – won 1982* seed 2 (d. King 6–2 6–2, Jaeger 6–1 6–0, Navratilova 6–3 2–6 6–2), *won 1984* (d. Sukova 6–7 6–1 6–3), *r/u 1974* (lost Goolagong 7–6 4–6 6–0), *r/u 1981* (lost Navratilova 6–7 6–4 7–5), *r/u 1985; Italian Open – won 1974* (d. Navratilova 6–3 6–3), *won 1975* (d. Navratilova 6–1 6–0), *won 1980* (d. Ruzici 5–7 6–2 6–3), *won 1981* (d. Ruzici 6–1 6–2), *won 1982* (d. Mandlikova 6–0 6–3), *r/u 1973* (lost Goolagong 7–6 6–0); *CS Champ – won 1977* (d. King 6–2 6–2), *won 1978* (d. Navratilova 6–3 6–3), *VS Champ – won 1972* (d. Reid 7–5 6–4), *won 1973* (d. Richey 6–3 6–3), *won 1975* (d. Navratilova 6–4 6–2), *won 1977* (d. Barker 2–6 6–1 6–1), *r/u 1974* (lost Goolagong 6–3 6–4), *r/u 1976* (lost Goolagong Cawley 6–4 5–7 6–3), *r/u 1984* (lost Navratilova 6–3 7–5 6–1); *US CC – won 1972* (d. Goolagong 7–6 6–1), *won 1973* (d. V. Burton 6–4 6–3), *won 1974* (d. Chanfreau 6–0 6–0), *won 1975* (d. Fromholtz 6–3 6–4), *won 1979* (d. Goolagong Cawley 6–4 6–3); *US Indoor – won 1978* (d. Wade 6–7 6–2 6–4); *South African Open – won 1973* (d. Goolagong 6–3 6–3). *CAREER HIGHLIGHTS – DOUBLES:* (with Navratilova unless stated) *Wimbledon – won 1976* (d. King/Stove 6–1 3–6 7–5); *French Open –* [Morozova] *won 1974* (d. Chanfreau/Ebbinghaus 6–4 2–6 6–1), *won 1975* (d. Anthony/Morozova); *Italian Open –* [Morozova] *won 1974* (w.o. Masthoff/Orth), *won 1975* (d. Barker/Coles), [Ruzici] *r/u 1981* (lost Reynolds/P. Smith 7–5 6–1); *Australian Open –* [Turnbull] *sf 1984* (lost Navratilova/Shriver 6–4 6–3). *MIXED DOUBLES:* (with Connors) *US Open – r/u 1974* (lost Teeguarden/Masters).

JOHN LLOYD (Great Britain)
Born Leigh-on-Sea, 27 August, 1954; lives Amelia Island, Fla., Palm Springs, Cal., and Kingston, Surrey with wife Chris; RH; 5ft 10in; 165lb; 1985 ATP ranking 42 (37); 1985 prize money $120,205.
After rising as high as No. 24 in 1978 after reaching f 1977 Australian Open, the distraction of his marriage to Chris Evert on 17 April, 1979 and a loss of confidence contributed to a long slump in 1979. In 1980 he took most of the second half of the year off to help his wife regain the No. 1 world ranking. Then in 1981 he came up with some good wins, including a five-setter with Dent in 1r Wimbledon, and although injuries kept him out late in the year, he seemed ready to play with his old confidence and enthusiasm as 1982 began. Still troubled by arm injuries in 1982, he never gained the momentum he needed, although he played well in doubles, reaching qf Wimbledon with Stockton. In mixed doubles, he won French Open with Turnbull and they reached f Wimbledon. In 1983, he came out of his long slump and for the first time since 1978 he ended the year in the top 100 having won the Wimbledon mixed doubles title with Turnbull in a long, hard-fought duel against King and Denton. Two months later, gaining a wild-card entry US Open, he reached the last 16, eliminating 10th seed Higueras. At the end of the year, he stopped Denton *en route* to last 16 Australian Open, beat Gerulaitis the next week at Sydney, and had clearly regained confidence. He signed on with Australian coach Bob Brett, training under his tutelage along with Solomon and the Giammalva brothers. His hard work and dedication were further rewarded in 1984, when he reached the highest computer ranking of his career – 23 – and once again his US Open success was the key; he reached qf with upset wins against Kriek and Sundstrom and became the first British man to get that far. Mark Cox had reached same round of US Nationals in 1966. Lloyd also won his second straight Wimbledon mixed title with Turnbull. Although his ranking dropped slightly in 1985, he continued to play some exceptional tennis. He drew 13th seed Mayotte in 2r US Open and lost in 4s, falling substantially on the computer and spending most of the autumn ranked in the 60s and 70s. Then he stopped Smid, Hlasek and Nystrom on his way to qf Australian Open where he lost to Lendl, and climbed back into the top 50 for the second straight year. *1985 HIGHLIGHTS – SINGLES: French Open* 2r (d. Oleppo 6–3 6–3 6–1, lost Benhabiles 6–3 6–2 7–6), *Wimbledon* 3r (d. Popp 6–2 6–4 7–6, Teltscher [seed 13]

6–3 6–4 4–6 3–6 7–5, lost Leconte 5–7 6–3 6–4 6–4), **US Open** 2r (d. Pecci 7–5 7–5 7–5, lost Mayotte [seed 13] 4–6 6–1 7–6 7–5), **Australian Open** qf, unseeded (d. Smid [seed 11] 7–5 6–7 7–6 6–3, Hlasek 6–3 6–4 6–3, Nystrom [seed 7] 6–2 1–6 6–4 6–7 6–4, lost Lendl [seed 1] 7–6 6–2 6–1), **qf** La Quinta (d. Testerman, lost Pimek 6–4 fs), **qf** Las Vegas (d. M. Leach, S. Davis, lost Flach 6–4 fs), **qf** Cologne (lost S. Giammalva 7–5 fs). **1985 HIGHLIGHTS – DOUBLES:** (with V. Amritraj unless stated) **sf** Queens Club (lost Cash/Fitzgerald 9–7 fs), **sf** LA (lost Annacone/Van Rensburg 7–6 6–3), [Kriek] **sf** Las Vegas (lost Cash/Fitzgerald). **CAREER HIGHLIGHTS – SINGLES: Australian Open – r/u 1977** (d. Ball 4–6 6–3 4–6 6–4, Andrew 0–6 6–3 7–6 6–2, Letcher 6–2 6–4 6–2, Newcombe 3–6 6–3 7–5 7–5, Giltinan, lost Gerulaitis 3–6 7–6 5–7 6–3 6–2), **qf 1985; US Open – qf 1984** (d. Kriek [seed 7] 2–6 7–6 6–2 6–3, Sundstrom [seed 9] 4–6 6–4 6–4 6–2, lost Connors 7–5 6–2 6–0). **CAREER HIGHLIGHTS – MIXED DOUBLES:** (with Turnbull) **French Open – won 1982** (d. Motta/Monteiro 6–2 7–6), **sf 1983** (lost Teltscher/B. Jordan 4–6 6–2 6–3); **Wimbledon – won 1983** (d. Shriver/Stolle 6–7 6–3 6–4, King/Denton 6–7 7–6 7–5), **won 1984** (d. Jordan/Denton 6–3 6–3), **r/u 1982** (lost Curren/A. Smith 2–6 6–3 7–5); **US Open – sf 1983** (lost Taygan/Potter 7–6 6–3).

MAREEN 'PEANUT' LOUIE (USA)
Born San Francisco, 15 August, 1960 and lives there; RH; 2HB; 5ft 5in; 115lb; final 1985 WTA ranking 22 (53); 1985 prize money $73,883.
In 1977, this baseline specialist was a finalist in both Wimbledon Jun event and US 18 CC. She is one of five children and her older sister Marcie was ranked 5 in US in 1977 when she won Canadian Open. At end 1980, Peanut was a surprise finalist at Tucson, where she was soundly beaten by Austin. Early in 1981, this tenacious competitor pulled another big surprise by eliminating A. Jaeger at Chicago and followed that with another win over Turnbull at Deerfield Beach in the autumn. In 1985, she revealed a more competitive side of herself and played by far the best tennis of her career, winning her first tournament of the year – Denver – with wins over Sabatini and Garrison. Rinaldi was her victim in qf Florida, and Lindqvist could not contain her when they met at Marco Island. After a mid-season slump, she rebounded with qf appearance at New Orleans and sf showing in Fort Lauderdale. **1985 HIGHLIGHTS – SINGLES: Wimbledon** 2r (d. Kelesi 6–2 6–4, lost Van Nostrand 6–2 6–3), **US Open** 1r (lost Foltz 7–6 6–3); **won** VS Denver (d. Teeguarden 7–6 fs, Drescher, Walsh Pete, Sabatini 6–1 fs, Garrison 6–4 4–6 6–4); **sf** VS Florida (d. Benjamin 6–3 fs, Rinaldi 6–3 6–4, lost Evert Lloyd), **sf** VS Pennsylvania (d. Skuherska, lost R. White 7–5 fs), **sf** Fort Lauderdale (d. M.J. Fernandez 6–4 fs, Torres 7–5 fs, lost Navratilova); **qf** VS New Orleans (d. McNeil, lost A. White), **qf** Marco Island (d. Lindqvist 6–2 fs, lost Goles).

PETER LUNDGREN (Sweden)
Born Sundsvall, 29 January, 1965; lives Stockholm; RH; 5ft 11in; 155lb; final 1985 ATP ranking 27 (276); 1985 prize money $50,097.
The most improved player among the Swedes in 1985, he won his first GP title in Cologne. **1985 HIGHLIGHTS – SINGLES: US Open** 2r (d. Perkis 6–4 7–6 6–2, lost Tulasne 7–6 1–6 7–5 6–3); **won** Cologne (d. Fibak, Prpic, Bates, Wilkison, Krishnan 6–3 6–2); **qf** Stockholm (d. Smid, S. Davis, lost McEnroe). **1985 HIGHLIGHTS – DOUBLES:** (with Gunnarsson) **r/u** Cologne (lost Antonitsch/Schapers).

JOHN McENROE (USA)
Born Wiesbaden, West Germany, 16 February 1959; lives New York; LH; 5ft 11in; 165lb; final 1985 ATP ranking 2 (1) singles, 34 (2) doubles; 1985 prize money $1,455,611; career prize money $8,956,688.
This highly gifted and fiercely competitive lefthander stunned tennis world in 1977 when, as a qualifier, he reached sf of his first Wimbledon. Turned pro in June 1978 after winning NCAA title at first attempt and made a dramatic rise that autumn into the world top 5 taking GP Masters in Jan. 1979, defeating Ashe after being 2 m-ps down. He established himself as the second-best player in the world in 1979 when he won WCT Final Dallas and US Open, and followed in 1980 by playing a superb match in Wimbledon f before losing epic five-set struggle to Borg, saving seven m-ps in the process. Then McEnroe

America's Terry Phelps had some significant highlights in 1986 — she was a quarter-finalist in Paris, beat Rehe and Potter at the US Open, and took a set off Navratilova in Fort Lauderdale. *(T. Hindley)*

stopped Borg in another five-setter in US Open f, depriving the Swede of a shot at the Grand Slam. After a disappointing Masters in which he lost to G. Mayer, Borg and Clerc, he finished the year where he started. After two years ranked 2 behind Borg, he rose to the top in 1981, becoming the first player since Connors in 1974 to win Wimbledon and US Open in the same year. That he beat Borg in both fs was a tribute to his ability to handle the pressure of the big occasion and made many observers wonder why he could not eliminate his many unnecessary outbursts and excessively long arguments with officials. These led to fines of $10,000 being recommended at Wimbledon, later halved by Pro Council and finally quashed following decision of 3-man appeal tribunal on 26 Jan., 1982. For the first time Wimbledon did not make their men's champion an honorary member of All England Club. In addition to 1981 Wimbledon and US Open he helped bring back D Cup to US. During 1981 Lendl became his nemesis; McEnroe lost to him in qf French Open, again in D Cup qf at Flushing Meadow and humiliatingly 6–4 6–2 in sf Masters. Nevertheless, McEnroe was voted World Champion by ITF, following Athlete of the Year accolade by US sportswriters. In GP tournament at Brussels in March 1982, he injured his ankle and by the end of September he had gone 8 months without winning a GP title since the US Pro Indoor in Jan. He lost his Wimbledon title to Connors after coming within 3 points of victory in 4s t-b, but was made a member of AELTC. Went down at US Open for the first time since 1978, losing to Lendl in sf. But then he came alive, won four consecutive GP events, four more D Cup singles matches, and he took a 24-match winning streak into the Masters where he was decisively beaten in straight sets in f by Lendl for the seventh time in succession. He had last beaten Lendl in qf 1980 US Open – his 3rd win in a row since they first met in 1977 French Open junior sf. Scored 4th win from 11 meetings v Lendl in US Pro Indoor f Feb 1983. However, he won his fifth consecutive Masters doubles with Fleming over Stewart and Taygan. In 1983, he won seven tournaments, captured his second Wimbledon singles title in three years, and solidified his claim as the world No. 1 when he closed the season with his most sparkling tennis at the Masters where he stopped Wilander and Lendl to win his second crown. The win over Lendl was his fourth in six meetings across the year but he had much more to prove when he met Wilander. The Swede had beaten him three times on three different surfaces in 1983, removing the New Yorker from qf French Open on clay, f Cincinnati on cement, and sf Australian Open on grass. Another loss on such an occasion could have cost him the No. 1 ranking according to many observers, but he came through when it counted and beat the man who has replaced Borg at the top of the Swedish tennis mountain. Otherwise, McEnroe was superb indoors all year, taking US Pro Indoor and WCT f at Dallas over Lendl as well as Sydney and Wembley (for the fifth time in six years) and finally the Masters. Outdoors he captured WCT Forest Hills Tournament of Champions on clay and Wimbledon. Meanwhile, he and Fleming won Wimbledon, US Open and their sixth consecutive Masters. In 1984 he was almost flawless, winning 82 of 85 matches, 13 of 15 tournaments, including his third Wimbledon and fourth US Open singles titles, his fourth WCT Championship and his third Masters. The only blemishes on his sparkling record were on clay (where he lost French Open f to Lendl after leading two sets to love) and the opening match of the D Cup f against Sweden to Henrik Sundstrom. Otherwise, he lost only to Vijay Amritraj in 1r Cincinnati where he had never intended to play. Meanwhile, despite losses to Edberg/Jarryd in sf US Open and D Cup f, he and Fleming remained the premier pair in the game as they won Wimbledon for the fourth time in six years as well as their seventh consecutive Masters in Jan. 1985. Clearly it was his greatest year and in the 17 years of Open Tennis only Rod Laver in 1969 (GS winner) and Jimmy Connors in 1974 (victorious in three of the four GS events and 99 of 103 matches) have enjoyed success on that level. Sadly he was suspended for 21 days after outburst in sf Stockholm and missed chance of third leg of GS in Australia through wrist injury. Although 1985 was a memorable season off court, it was a disappointing one on court. Late in the year he announced that his close companion, Tatum O'Neal, was expecting their child in May 1986 and that they planned to marry. Perhaps the distraction of this much-publicised relationship hampered him, for although he won 8 of the 16 tournaments he played following the Masters in Jan 85, for the first time since 1982 he won none of the majors. At the French Open he was ousted by Wilander in straight-sets sf, Curren took him apart in Wimbledon qf, and in the most important match he played all year he was stopped by Lendl 7–6 6–3 6–4 in US Open f. For all practical purposes, his year was over, and perhaps the realisation that he could no longer retain the No. 1 world ranking contributed to his making a fool of himself in Australia. His complaints about the court conditions were justified, but he also became involved in a scuffle with a photographer and behaved abrasively during his matches. Finally, after a great escape to beat Leconte in 5s, he lost Australian Open qf to Zivojinovic 6–0 in 5s, only going through the motions in last set. Not since his loss to Connors in the 1983 Wembley final had anyone seen him stop competing like that and it left observers wondering what to expect from him in 1986, which he began in equally listless fashion, losing 1r Masters to Gilbert, after which he announced his intention to take a three-month break. *1985 HIGHLIGHTS – SINGLES: French Open* sf, seed 1 (d. Agenor 6–0 6–2 7–5, Segarceanu 6–2 6–4 6–4, Hocevar 6–2 6–1 6–2, Sundstrom 6–3 7–5 6–2, Nystrom 6–7 6–2 6–2 3–6 7–5, lost Wilander [seed 4] 6–1 7–5 7–5), *Wimbledon* qf, seed 1 (d. McNamara 6–4 6–3 6–4, Odizor 7–6 6–1 7–6, Steyn 6–3 7–5 6–4, Maurer 6–0 6–4 6–2, lost Curren [seed 8], *r/u US Open* seed 1 (d. Glickstein 6–1 6–7 2–6 6–3 7–6, Wostenholme 6–0 7–6 6–1, Schultz 6–3 6–4 6–4, Smid 6–3 7–5 6–2, Nystrom 6–1 6–0 7–5, Wilander [seed 3] 3–6 6–4 4–6 6–3 6–3, lost Lendl [seed 2] 7–6 6–3 6–4), *Australian Open* qf, seed 2 (d. Visser 6–4 6–3 3–6 6–3, Odizor 4–6 6–2 6–4 6–2, Leconte 5–7 7–6 3–6 7–6 6–1, lost Zivojinovic 2–6 6–3 1–6 6–4 6–0); won US Pro Indoor (d. Noah, S. Davis, Mecir 6–3 7–6 6–1), *won* Milan (d. Becker 6–4 6–3, Mansdorf, Leconte, Hlasek, Jarryd 6–4 6–1), *won* Chicago (d. Annacone 6–1 fs, S. Davis, Connors def.), *won* Atlanta (d. Mayotte, Leach, Annacone 7–6 7–6 6–2), *won* Houston (d. Fibak 7–5 fs, Tom Gullikson, Gilbert, Connors, Curren 7–5 6–1 7–6), *won* Stratton Mountain (d. Sadri, Annacone, Seguso, Lendl 7–6 6–2), *won* Stockholm Open (d. Edberg 6–3 7–6, Jarryd 6–1 6–2), *won* Canadian Open (d. Krishnan, Connors, Lendl 7–5 6–3); *r/u* WCT Forest Hills (d. C. Panatta 7–6 fs, Sundstrom 6–2 fs, lost Lendl 6–3 6–3). *1985 HIGHLIGHTS – DOUBLES:* (with Fleming) *Wimbledon* sf, seed 1 (d. Tim/Tom Gullikson 6–3 6–4 7–6, lost Cash/Fitzgerald 7–6 2–6 6–1 6–4); *won* US Pro Indoor (d. Flach/Seguso, Pfister/Testerman). *CAREER HIGHLIGHTS – SINGLES: Wimbledon – won 1981* seed 2 (d. Ramirez, Smith, Kriek, Frawley 7–6 6–4 7–5, Borg 4–6 7–6 7–6 6–4), *won 1983* (d. Lendl 7–6 6–4 6–4, C. Lewis 6–2 6–2 6–2), *won 1984* (d. Connors 6–1 6–1 6–2), *r/u 1980* seed 2 (d. Connors 6–3 3–6 6–3 6–4, lost Borg 1–6 7–5 6–3 6–7 8–6), *r/u 1982* (lost Connors 3–6 6–3 6–7 7–6 6–4), *sf 1977* unseeded after qualifying (lost Connors 6–3 6–3 4–6 6–4); *US Open – won 1979* (d. Connors 6–3 6–3 7–5, Gerulaitis 7–5 6–4 6–3), *won 1980* seed 2 (d. Lendl 4–6 6–3 6–2 7–5, Connors 6–4 5–7 0–6 6–3 7–6, Borg 7–6 6–1 6–7 5–7 6–4), *won 1981* (d. Gerulaitis 5–7 6–3 6–2 4–6 6–3, Borg 4–6 6–2 6–4 6–3), *won 1984* (d. Connors 6–4 4–6 7–5 6–4, Lendl 6–3 6–4 6–1), *r/u 1985, sf 1982* lost Lendl 6–4 6–4 7–6); *WCT Final – won 1979* (d. Connors 6–1 6–4 6–4, Borg 7–5 4–6 6–2 7–6), *won 1981* (d. Kriek 6–1 6–2 6–4), *won 1983* (d. Lendl 6–2 4–6 6–3 6–7 7–6), *won 1984* (d. Connors 6–1 6–2 6–3); *Masters – won 1979* (d. Ashe 6–7 6–3 7–5), *won 1983* (d. Wilander 6–2 7–5, Lendl 6–3 6–4 6–4), *won 1984* (d. Wilander 6–1 6–1, Lendl 7–5 6–0 6–4), *r/u 1982* (d. Vilas, lost Lendl 6–4 6–4 6–2), *sf 1981* (lost Lendl 6–4 6–2); *French Open – r/u 1984* (lost Lendl 3–6 2–6 6–4 7–5 7–5), *sf 1985. CAREER HIGHLIGHTS – DOUBLES:* (with Fleming) *Wimbledon – won 1979* (d. Gottfried/Ramirez 6–2 4s), *won 1981* (d. Smith/Lutz 6–4 6–4 6–4), *won 1983* (d. Tim/Tom Gullikson 6–4 6–3 6–4), *won 1984* (d. Cash/McNamee 6–2 5–7 6–2 3–6 6–3), *sf 1985, r/u 1978* (lost Hewitt/McMillan 6–1 6–4 6–2), *r/u 1982* (lost McNamara/McNamee 6–3 6–1), *sf 1980* (lost McNamara/McNamee 6–3 6–3 6–3), *sf 1985; US Open – won 1979* (d. Smith/Lutz), *won 1981* (d. Newcombe/Stolle 6–2 6–2 6–7 5–7 7–6, McNamara/Gunthardt def.), *won 1983* (d. Buehning/Winitsky 6–3 6–4 6–2), *sf 1984* (lost Edberg/Jarryd 3–6 7–6 7–5 7–6); *Masters – won 1978* (d. Lutz/Smith 6–4 6–2 6–4), *won 1979* (d. Fibak/Okker 6–4 6–2 6–4), *won 1980* (d. McNamara/McNamee 6–4 6–4), *won 1981* (d. Curren/Denton 6–3 6–3), *won 1982* (d. Stewart/Taygan 7–5 6–3), *won 1983* (d. Slozil/Smid 6–2 6–2), *won 1984* (d. Edmondson/Stewart 6–3 6–1).

PETER McNAMARA (Australia)

Born Melbourne, 5 July, 1955; lives Sydney and London; RH; 6ft 1in; 160lb; final 1984 ATP ranking 247 (741) singles, 31 (324) doubles; 1985 prize money $29,155.

A gifted shot-maker, who won his first GP singles title in 1979 in Berlin, then another in 1980 at Brussels. One of the most highly regarded doubles players in the world, following a triumph at Wimbledon in 1980 with countryman Paul McNamee with whom he paired after Wimbledon 1978. In winning the title, they up-ended the two teams who battled it out for the US Open crown in 1979 and 1980 – McEnroe/Fleming and Smith/Lutz. They ended the season by reaching Masters as fourth pair and became first Australians to reach f. In 1981 he became a vastly improved singles player, beating Solomon and Connors to win German Open and Lendl at Nations Cup in Düsseldorf. He went on to reach qf Wimbledon and established himself as one of the world's 10 best players for 1981. He was a part of the top ten for much of 1982, won a second Wimbledon doubles title with McNamee and played No. 1 singles for Australia for the second straight year in D Cup. In 1983, after playing with his usual flair and style to beat Lendl for the Brussels title on 13 March, he injured his knee three days later playing Granat in Rotterdam. After consulting doctors this universally popular player decided to quit the game at the age of 28, but after coaching Carling Bassett in second half of 1983 he underwent surgery with the hope of returning in 1984. His wish was fulfilled when he returned to the game at the 1984 Australian Open after an absence of 21 months. He was beaten by Tim Gullikson in 1r but the following week he reached sf Sydney NSW doubles with Shiras. Hiding the scars left from his surgery, he wore long white trousers which suited his elegant game. Still struggling to find his old form in singles, he resumed his partnership with McNamee to reach sf Wimbledon in 1985. *1985 HIGHLIGHTS – SINGLES: French Open* 1r (lost Higueras 7–5 6–1 6–3), *Wimbledon* 1r (lost McEnroe [seed 1] 6–4 6–3 6–4); *qf* Melbourne (d. Carter, Miller, lost Testerman). *1985 HIGHLIGHTS – DOUBLES:* (with McNamee) *Wimbledon* sf, unseeded (d. Edwards/Strode 6–1 6–4 6–2, lost Gunthardt/Taroczy 6–7 6–1 6–2 6–4); *r/u* US Pro (lost Pimek/Zivojinovic). *CAREER HIGHLIGHTS – SINGLES: German Open – won 1981* (d. Connors 7–6 6–1 4–6 6–4), *r/u 1982* (d. Gomez 7–5 6–1 6–2, lost Higueras 4–6 6–7 7–6 6–3 7–6); *French Open – qf 1982* (d. Solomon 2–6 3–6 7–6 6–1 6–3, Smid 2–6 6–1 7–6 6–3, Gomez 6–1 5–7 6–3 3–6 11–9, lost Clerc 6–2 6–2 6–1), *Wimbledon – qf 1981* (lost Borg). *CAREER HIGHLIGHTS – DOUBLES:* (with McNamee unless stated) *Wimbledon – won 1980* seed 7 (d. Fleming/McEnroe [seed 1] 6–3 6–2 6–3, Lutz/Smith [seed 4] 7–6 6–3 6–7 6–4), *won 1982* (d. Stewart/Taygan 4–6 6–4 6–7 7–6 6–4, McEnroe/Fleming 6–3 6–2), *sf 1981* (lost Lutz/Smith 6–4 2–6 4–6 7–6 6–4), *sf 1985; US Open* – [Gunthardt] *r/u 1981* (lost Fleming/McEnroe def.); *Australian Open – r/u 1980* (lost Edmondson/Warwick 7–5 6–4); *Masters – r/u 1980* (d. Lutz/Smith, lost Fleming/McEnroe 6–3 6–3), *sf 1982* (lost Fleming/McEnroe 6–1 6–3).

PAUL McNAMEE (Australia)
Born Melbourne, 12 November, 1954; lives Sydney and London; RH; 2HB; 5ft 10in; 160lb; final 1985 ATP ranking 49 (68) singles, 24 (19) doubles; 1985 prize money $80,177.
After taking time off between April and August 1979 to switch from one-handed to two-handed backhand under expert guidance of Harry Hopman, he beat Smith in f of a GP tournament in spring 1980. He had some spectacular moments in singles throughout the year, defeating McEnroe in French Open and stopping Gerulaitis twice at end of season. On top of his dramatic rise in singles in 1980, he and McNamara, who paired up after Wimbledon in 1978, were the unexpected winners of Wimbledon doubles title. They ended season by reaching Masters as fourth pair and reaching f – the first Australians to do so. He was injured in 1981 and out of action twice, but in 1982 the great Australian duo regained their Wimbledon title with another victory over McEnroe/Fleming. McNamee also got down to business in singles and highlighted a significant climb in the computer rankings by reaching the last 16 Wimbledon, sf Australian Open and winning WCT Baltimore, over Vilas. Joined by countryman Edmondson, he picked up another GS doubles title when he won the 1983 Australian Open. Undoubtedly the highlight of the year was being a member of the victorious Australian D Cup squad, winning doubles in f v Sweden with Edmondson. Again, in 1984, he was a prime contributor to Australian D Cup effort as they reached sf and lost to US, although it was not otherwise a memorable year. In 1985 he moved up 19 places, achieving peak form in mid-season when he reached sf Queens Club on grass and qf US Pro on clay. But the most pleasant part of his year was the renewal of his partnership with McNamara, with whom he reached sf Wimbledon. *1985 HIGHLIGHTS– SINGLES: French Open* 3r (d. Limberger 6–3 6–4 6–4, Lopez-Maeso 6–0 6–0 6–4, lost Krickstein [seed 10] 7–5 5–7 1–6 6–2 6–1), *Wimbledon* 3r (d. Meister 6–2 6–4 7–6, Saad 6–3 7–6 7–6, lost Mayotte [seed 16] 3–6 4–6 7–6 6–2 6–0), *US* Open 1r (lost Kriek [seed 12] 6–4 6–2 6–4); *sf* Queens Club (d. Mayotte 7–5 7–6, lost

Becker 6–1 6–4), *qf* US Pro (d. Hlasek 6–2 fs, Tulasne 6–4 fs, lost Jaite 6–0 fs). *1985 HIGHLIGHTS – DOUBLES:* (with McNamara unless stated) *Wimbledon* sf, unseeded (d. Slozil/Smid [seed 2], Edwards/Strode 6–1 6–4 6–2, lost Gunthardt/Taroczy [seed 8] 6–7 6–1 6–2 6–4); *r/u* US Pro (d. M. Fancutt/Wilkison, lost Pimek/Zivojinovic 7–6 fs), [Gerulaitis] *r/u* Rotterdam (d. Fibak/Gunthardt, lost Slozil/Smid). *CAREER HIGHLIGHTS – SINGLES: Australian Open – sf 1982* (lost Kriek 7–5 fs). *CAREER HIGHLIGHTS – DOUBLES:* (with McNamara unless stated) *Wimbledon – won 1980* seed 7 (d. Fleming/McEnroe [seed 1] 6–3 6–2 6–3, Lutz/Smith [seed 4] 7–6 6–3 6–7 6–4), *won 1982* (d. Stewart/Taygan 6–4 fs, McEnroe/Fleming 6–3 6–1), [Cash] *r/u 1984* (lost McEnroe/Fleming 6–2 5–7 6–2 3–6 6–3), *sf 1981* (lost Lutz/Smith 6–4 2–6 4–6 7–6 6–4), *sf 1985; Australian Open* – [Edmondson] *won 1983* (d. Stewart/Denton 6–3 7–6), *r/u 1980* (lost Edmondson/Warwick 7–5 6–4), *Masters – r/u 1980* (d. Lutz/Smith 0–6 6–3 6–4, lost Fleming/McEnroe 6–4 6–3).

LORI McNEIL (USA)
Born San Diego, 18 December, 1963; lives Houston; 5ft 6in; 140lb; RH; final 1985 WTA ranking 93 (97); 1985 prize money $53,125.
A member of the 1983 US Jun Fed Cup team, she was ranked 8 that year on US Intercollegiate list and finished 4th on USTA satellite circuit. In 1984, she took a set off Mandlikova in last 16 US Open and in 1985 she achieved some good wins, but not enough to lift her out of the 90s on the computer. *1985 HIGHLIGHTS – SINGLES: French Open* 2r (d. Purdy 6–1 6–0, lost Bunge 6–1 6–1), *Wimbledon* 1r (lost Bunge 6–3 6–3), *US Open* 1r (lost Kuhlman 6–1 6–3), *Australian Open* 1r (lost R. White 6–4 5–7 6–1). *1985 HIGHLIGHTS – DOUBLES:* (with Garrison) *sf* Denver (lost Allen/Walsh Pete 6–3 fs), *sf* Amelia Island (d. Bunge/Kohde-Kilsch 6–4 6–4, lost Bassett/Evert Lloyd 7–6 fs).

FRANCISCO MACIEL (Mexico)
Born Queretaro, 7 January, 1964, and lives there; RH; 6ft 2in; 165lb; final 1985 ATP ranking 71 (192); 1985 prize money $25,903.
A markedly improved player in 1985, he twice reached qf on GP circuit. *1985 HIGHLIGHTS – SINGLES: qf* Buenos Aires (d. Goes, lost Jaite), *qf* Bordeaux (d. Duncan, lost Perez).

KATERINA MALEEVA (Bulgaria)
Born Sofia, 7 May, 1969 and lives there; RH; 2HB; 5ft 5in; 103lb; final 1985 WTA ranking 28 (93); 1985 prize money $101,645.
The younger sister of Manuela, she was an outstanding jun, winning 1984 US Open and being r/u to Sabatini at the French Open and the Orange Bowl. She progressed rapidly, moving into the women's top 100 and reaching qf Zurich. Similar to her sister though less consistent, she possesses a dangerous flat forehand although her two-handed backhand is less solid. Like her sister she is coached by her mother, Yulia Berberian, 9-time former Bulgarian champ. In 1985, her first full year on the women's tour, she produced some sparkling results, winning Seabrook Island and Hilversum, reaching f Orlando, and beating some of the big names like Shriver, Sukova and Garrison. Ironically, her major stumbling block was her sister Manuela whom, in a record for siblings, she met four times, with Manuela winning all in straight sets. *1985 HIGHLIGHTS – SINGLES: French Open* 3r (d. Tell 6–3 7–5, Spain Short 6–1 6–1, lost Kohde-Kilsch [seed 7] 6–4 6–3), *Wimbledon* 1r (lost Temesvari 3–6 7–6 6–4), *US Open* 1r (lost Temesvari 6–2 4–6 6–2), *Australian Open* last 16 (d. Walsh Pete 7–5 6–4, Yanagi 7–5 6–4, lost M. Maleeva [seed 7] 6–2 6–1); *won* Seabrook Island (d. Mascarin 6–1 7–5, Goles 6–1 fs, Ruzici 6–3 6–3), *won* Hilversum (d. Ruzici 7–5 7–5, Garrison 6–3 6–2, Karlsson 6–3 6–2); *r/u* Orlando (d. Shriver 6–4 fs, Cecchini, Gadusek 6–1 6–4, lost Navratilova [seed 1] 6–1 6–0). *1985 HIGHLIGHTS – DOUBLES:* (with M. Maleeva) *won* US CC (d. Barg/P. Smith 6–4 fs), *won* Sofia (d. Brzakova/Fukarkova 6–1 6–2); *sf* Zurich (lost Kohde-Kilsch/Sukova).

MANUELA MALEEVA (Bulgaria)
Born Sofia, 14 February, 1967; RH; 2HB; 5ft 6in; 114lb; final 1984 WTA ranking 7 (6); 1985 prize money $271,271.
A gifted and richly talented player who has an all-court game, excellent touch and an instinct for the volley. Her 1982 season ended unfortunately when, trailing 3–6 3–4 against

Bassett in Orange Bowl f, she was ordered off the court in tears by her mother following a dispute over a line call on game-point at 3–3. Earlier in 1982, she played Fed Cup women's and jun tennis, and wins over Allen and Jausovec at Brisbane signalled her potential. She added Bunge and Mandlikova to her list of notable victims in 1983 and made a rapid rise in the rankings. In 1984 she took command and was (according to many experts) the most improved player of the year. In one of the most significant upsets of the year, she became only the seventh player in Evert Lloyd's 12-year pro career to beat her on clay as she stopped the five-times champion 6–3 6–3 to win Italian Open. Cool and stylish, grown up and ready to deal with her rising status, she also won Swiss Open, US CC and a $300,000 event in Tokyo at the end of the year to make herself one of the keynote performers on the 1984–85 VS circuit. She finished 1984 ranked 6 on the computer, but was given a place in top 5 by most experts. In 1985, she did not fare quite as well but she did manage to win her last tournament of the year, successfully defending her crown in Tokyo. She reached qf French and Australian Opens but had surprising set-backs at Wimbledon and the US Open. Molly Van Nostrand stopped her in last 16 Wimbledon and Steffi Graf routed her in the same round at US Open. However, for the second straight year she finished with a top 10 ranking on the computer. **1985 HIGHLIGHTS – SINGLES: French Open** qf, seed 4 (d. Collins 6–3 6–3, Jauch 6–1 6–2, Calleja 6–0 6–1, Gadusek 7–5 6–3, lost Sabatini 6–3 1–6 6–1), **Wimbledon** last 16, seed 4 (d. Washington 6–0 6–1, Holladay 7–5 3–6 6–3, R. White 6–3 6–3, lost Van Nostrand 7–5 6–2), **US Open** last 16, seed 8 (d. Mascarin 6–1 6–1, Cueto 6–0 7–6, Burgin 6–4 7–5, lost Graf [seed 11] 6–2 6–2), **Australian Open** qf, seed 7 (d. Antonoplis 6–1 6–1, Schropp 6–2 6–3, K. Maleeva 6–2 6–1, lost Evert Lloyd [seed 1] 6–3 6–3); **won** Tokyo Pacific (d. Sukova 6–0 6–2, Gadusek 7–6 3–6 7–5); **r/u** VS Washington (d. K. Jordan, Rinaldi, lost Navratilova 6–3 6–2), **r/u** Swiss Open (d. Sabatini 6–2 fs, Hanika, lost Gadusek 6–2 6–2), **r/u** Lion Cup Tokyo (d. Bassett, lost Evert Lloyd 7–5 6–0), **r/u** Brighton (d. Potter, Durie, lost Evert Lloyd 7–5 6–3); **sf** Hilton Head (d. Potter, lost Sabatini 6–1 7–6), **sf** VS Houston (lost Burgin), **sf** Eastbourne (d. Rinaldi, lost Navratilova). **1985 HIGHLIGHTS – DOUBLES:** (with K. Maleeva) **won** US CC (d. Barg/P. Smith 3–6 6–3 6–4), **won** Sofia (d. Brzakova/Fukarkova 6–1 6–2); **sf** Zurich (lost Kohde-Kilsch/Sukova). **CAREER HIGH-LIGHTS – SINGLES: Italian Open – won 1984** (d. Bassett 6–2 6–2, Evert Lloyd 6–3 6–3); **US CC – won 1984** (d. Bonder 6–4 6–3); **French Open – qf 1985; Wimbledon – qf 1984** (lost Navratilova [seed 1] 6–3 6–2); **Australian Open – qf 1985.**

HANA MANDLIKOVA (Czechoslovakia)
Born Prague, 19 February, 1962; lives there and Boca West, Fla.; single; RH; 5ft 8in; 130lb; final 1985 WTA ranking 3 (3) singles, 6 doubles; 1985 prize money $579,847; career prize money $2,226,036.
After outstanding jun results in 1977 and 1978 (she won Orange Bowl 16s in Dec. 1977 and was r/u to Austin at Wimbledon Jun in 1978, winning French and Italian Jun the same year), she used her considerable natural talent to move up to 17 by end 1979, then, aided by new coach Betty Stove, she enjoyed a spectacular year in 1980, climbing into the top 5. She reached sf French and Italian Opens, f US Open, captured her first major title – Australian Open – at end of year and finished No. 1 in CS bonus pool. She began 1981 with a lack-lustre Avon circuit but found her best form in time to capture the French Open, downing Evert Lloyd sf (ending the American's 64-match winning streak on clay) and Hanika in f. She reached f Wimbledon, beating Navratilova before losing to Evert Lloyd, who also beat her in qf US and Australian Opens. By end of year she seemed back in the doldrums but, although she did not win any tournaments in 1982, she could rise to the occasion. She reached f US Open, sf French Open and TS Champs, and was r/u to Evert Lloyd at Italian Open. True to her curious nature, she had a disappointing year in 1983, again failing to win a tournament. Nevertheless she led Czechoslovakia to victory in Fed Cup and did not lose a match. In 1984, she won five tournaments, all between January and April in a brilliant and productive spell. In January, she won VS Oakland to end Navratilova's 54-match winning streak and twice more she came close to beating her old rival. At Amelia Island, she led 4–2 fs before losing and at French Open she won 1s and had a b-p for 2–0 fs. It was one of her best years as she reached sf French Open and Wimbledon, qf US Open, and kept down her bad losses. After her long series of near misses, she displayed her immeasurable talent in a marvellous 1985 season, with two

wins over Navratilova, two over Evert Lloyd, and a US Open title. In garnering the Open, she not only eliminated the six-time champion Evert Lloyd and two-time winner Navratilova back-to-back, but she became the first woman other than Chris or Martina to win the Open since Tracy Austin in 1981. Navratilova and Evert Lloyd had won the last 15 Grand Slam events between them. Only at Wimbledon, where she fell inexplicably to Smylie in 3r, did she play poorly in a major championship. She was beaten in qf French Open by Kohde-Kilsch and sf Australian Open by Navratilova. At 23, her mind seemed at last to have caught up with her body. *1985 HIGHLIGHTS – SINGLES: French Open* qf, seed 3 (d. M.J. Fernandez 6–1 7–5, Burgin 2–6 6–4 7–5, Garrone 6–3 6–0, Spence 7–6 6–2, lost Kohde-Kilsch [seed 7] 6–4 6–4), *Wimbledon* 3r, seed 3 (d. Budarova 6–0 6–1, Balestrat 4–6 6–2 7–5, lost Smylie 6–1 7–6), *won US Open* seed 3 (d. A. Brown 6–2 6–1, Croft 6–3 6–3, Hanika 6–3 6–4, K. Jordan 7–5 3–6 6–1, Sukova 7–6 7–5, Evert Lloyd [seed 1] 4–6 6–2 6–3, Navratilova [seed 2] 7–6 1–6 7–6), *Australian Open* sf, seed 3 (d. Benjamin 6–2 6–2, Wade 6–2 7–6, Turnbull 6–3 6–4, Garrison 2–6 6–3 6–3, lost Navratilova [seed 2] 6–7 6–1 6–4); *won* VS California (d. Turnbull, Sukova 6–4 6–0, Evert Lloyd 6–2 6–4), *won* US Indoor (d. Navratilova 7–6 6–0, Lindqvist 6–3 7–5); *rlu* Palm Beach (lost Evert Lloyd 6–3 6–3), *rlu* Zurich (d. Sukova, lost Garrison 6–1 6–3); *sf* VS Champs (d. Garrison, lost Navratilova 7–6 7–5), *sf* WTA Champ (d. Ruzici, lost Garrison 7–5 6–4). *1985 HIGHLIGHTS –DOUBLES:* (with Turnbull unless stated) *Wimbledon* sf, seed 4 (d. Cherneva/Savchenko 6–4 6–3, lost Navratilova/Shriver 6–4 6–2), *US Open* sf, seed 4 (d. Lindqvist/Russell 6–1 3–6 6–0, lost Navratilova/Shriver 6–3 6–4); *won* VS California (d. Fairbank/Reynolds 4–6 7–5 6–1), *won* Sydney NSW Open (d. Kohde-Kilsch/Sukova 6–4 fs, Fairbank/Reynolds 6–4 fs), [Temesvari] *won* Zurich (d. Kohde-Kilsch/Sukova 6–4 3–6 7–5), [Fairbank] *won* Amelia Island (d. Evert Lloyd/Bassett 6–2 fs); [K. Jordan] *rlu* LIPC (lost Navratilova/G. Fernandez], *rlu* VS LA (lost Kohde-Kilsch/Sukova 6–4 6–2). *CAREER HIGHLIGHTS – SINGLES: French Open – won 1981* (d. Romanov, Casals, Vasquez, Rinaldi, Evert Lloyd [seed 1], Hanika 6–2 6–4), *sf 1980* seed 7 (d. Redondo, Fairbank, Delhees, Madruga, lost Evert Lloyd [seed 1] 6–7 6–2 6–2), *sf 1982* (d. Austin 7–6 6–7 6–2, lost Navratilova 6–0 6–2), *sf 1984* (lost Navratilova 3–6 6–2 6–2); *US Open – won 1985; rlu 1980* seed 9 (d. Collins, Guissani, P. Smith, Navratilova [seed 2] 7–6 6–4, Hallquist, Jaeger [seed 8] 6–1 3–6 7–6, lost Evert Lloyd 5–7 6–1 6–1), *rlu 1982* (d. Austin 4–6 6–4 6–4, Shriver 6–4 2–6 6–2, lost Evert Lloyd 6–3 6–1), *qf 1981* seed 5 (lost Evert Lloyd 6–1 6–3), *qf 1983* (lost Evert Lloyd 6–4 6–3); *qf 1984* (lost Bassett 6–4 6–3); *Australian Open – won 1980* seed 3 (d. Little, Hallquist, Ruzici [seed 6] 6–1 3–6 6–4, Jausovec 6–4 6–1, Turnbull [seed 4] 6–0 7–5), *qf 1981* (d. Sukova 6–4 7–6, lost Evert Lloyd 6–4 7–6); *Wimbledon – rlu 1981* seed 2 (d. Turnbull, Navratilova, lost Evert Lloyd [seed 1] 6–2, 6–2), *sf 1984* (lost Evert Lloyd 6–1 6–2). *CAREER HIGHLIGHTS –DOUBLES:* (with Turnbull unless stated) *French Open* – [Kohde-Kilsch] *rlu 1984* (lost Navratilova/Shriver 5–7 6–3 6–2); *Wimbledon – sf 1985; US Open – sf 1985.*

AMOS MANSDORF (Israel)
Born Tel Aviv, 20 October, 1965, and lives there; RH; 5ft 8in; 140lb; final 1985 ATP ranking 84 (268); 1985 prize money $45,153.
Former Asian jun champ who was a member of 1984 Israeli Olympic team. *1985 HIGHLIGHTS – SINGLES: US Open* 2r (d. Sadri 7–6 4–6 7–6 6–1, lost Arias 6–4 6–7 6–7 0–1 ret'd), *Australian Open* 2r (d. McNamara 6–7 6–7 6–2 6–4 6–4, lost Leconte [seed 13] 6–4 6–2 7–5); *sf* Madrid (d. Derlin, Gehring, Limberger, lost Duncan). *1985 HIGHLIGHTS – DOUBLES:* (with Perkis) *rlu* South African Open (d. Delatte/DePalmer, lost Dowdeswell/Van Rensburg).

REGINA MARSIKOVA (Czechoslovakia)
Born Prague, 11 December, 1958, and lives there; RH; 5ft 9in; 145lb; final 1985 WTA ranking 80 (—); 1985 prize money $27,718.
After winning German Open 1981 and finishing the year ranked No. 13 in the world, she was involved in a tragic car accident, after which she was not permitted to leave her country until 1985. She was given some well-deserved wildcards and played well over the year, but did not quite reach her old level. *1985 HIGHLIGHTS – SINGLES: French Open* (lost 3r qualifying J. Thompson 6–2 7–5), *US Open* 2r (d. Rapponi-Longo 6–3 6–2,

lost L. Thompson 6–4 2–5 ret'd), *Australian Open* 1r (lost Lindqvist 7–5 6–2); *sf* Barcelona (d. Plchova, lost Reggi); *qf* VS Houston (d, Louie, Klitch, lost Navratilova).

SUSAN MASCARIN (USA)
Born Detroit, 28 June, 1964; lives Boca Raton, Fla.; RH; 2HB; 5ft 8in; 120lb; final 1985 WTA ranking 47 (69); 1985 prize money $48,820.
As the world's No. 1 jun in 1980, she won the Italian, US Open, Easter Bowl and Orange Bowl 18 titles, combining jun competition with impressive results on the women's tour. In 1981 she held her ground, almost always remaining in the top 40, and helped by Australian Owen Davidson's sound advice in 1982, she played some remarkable matches, dismissing King in 1r US Open and handling Leand at US Indoor, but she lacked the consistency and momentum to improve her standing. In 1983, she had her least successful season as her confidence seemed to disintegrate, but she bounced back in 1984, jumping 24 places on the computer and reaching last 16 US Open, where she had to default with an ankle injury. In 1985, she won 24 matches, lost 23, and had a good win over Bassett in Chicago, attracting further attention late in the season when she was seen in the company of Boris Becker. *1985 HIGHLIGHTS – SINGLES: French Open* 3r (d. A. Brown 6–3 7–5, Paradis 6–0 6–2, lost Hanika 6–2 0–6 6–3), *Wimbledon* 2r (d. Scheuer-Larsen 7–6 3–6 6–3, lost Evert Lloyd [seed 1] 6–3 6–0), *US Open* 1r (lost M. Maleeva [seed 8] 6–1 6–1); *sf* Birmingham (d. Kelesi, Croft, A. Minter, Moulton, lost Nagelsen 6–4 fs); *qf* Seabrook (d. Burgin, lost K. Maleeva), *qf* VS Chicago (d. A. Minter, Bassett 7–6 6–4, lost Rinaldi 6–4 6–3).

ANDREAS MAURER (West Germany)
Born Gelsenk-Buer, 8 March, 1958, and lives there; RH; 5ft 7in; 150lb; final 1985 ATP ranking 32 (130); 1985 prize money $112,371.
A member of the top 50 in 1981, he slipped out of the top 100 for the next three years, but returned in style in 1985, reaching last 16 Wimbledon, where he defeated Kriek, and winning Madrid. Played doubles (Becker) in German D Cup team that lost 2–3 to Sweden in Munich f. *1985 HIGHLIGHTS – SINGLES: Wimbledon* last 16, unseeded (d. J. Frawley 7–5 6–3 7–5, Schwaier 6–3 7–5 7–5, Kriek [seed 9] 6–1 6–4 3–6 6–3, lost McEnroe 6–0 6–4 6–2); *won* Madrid (d. H. Gunthardt, Avendano, de Miguel, Novacek, Duncan); *r/u* Gstaad (d. Gerulaitis, Vajda, Motta, Edmondson, lost Nystrom); *sf* Hilversum (d. Van Boeckel, lost Osterthun).

TIM MAYOTTE (USA)
Born Springfield, Mass., 3 August, 1960 and lives there; RH; 6ft 3in; 180lb; final 1985 ATP ranking 12 (44); 1985 prize money $360,842.
A popular young man who won NCAA Champs in 1981 playing for Stanford and was voted ATP Newcomer of the Year. He then joined the pro tour and reached qf Wimbledon. In 1978 he was No. 1 US 18-and-under player and a member of US Sunshine Cup squad. He has had a remarkable run at Wimbledon, reaching qf 1981, sf 1982, and being beaten by Curren in a friendly, spirited qf encounter in 1983, after which Mayotte displayed his rare qualities of sportsmanship by applauding his conqueror. He ended year on high note in sf Australian Open and remained one of the most formidable fast-court players in the world in 1984, but his record and ranking suffered when he lost in 2r Australian Open. In 1985 he worked his way back into the top 20 almost immediately when he won the inaugural LIPC. Down two-sets-to-love in f against S. Davis, he rebounded to win his first GP tournament in style and, although he did not win another the rest of the year, his record was solid. Qualified for Masters where he d. Noah before losing Lendl qf. *1985 HIGHLIGHTS – SINGLES: Wimbledon* last 16, seed 16 (d. Allan 7–5 6–4 6–2, Flach 6–4 6–4 6–4, McNamee 3–6 4–6 7–6 6–2 6–0, lost Becker 6–3 4–6 6–7 7–6 6–2); *US Open* last 16, seed 13 (d. Moor 6–4 6–2 6–4, Lloyd 4–6 6–1 7–6 7–5, Odizor 7–5 6–4 6–3, lost Jarryd [seed 6] 7–6 7–6 6–4), *Australian Open* last 16, seed 8 (d. Dickson 6–4 6–4 6–4, Saad 7–6 6–7 6–4 6–4, lost Zivojinovic 2–6 6–4 6–4 6–4); *won* LIPC (d. Becker 6–2 6–3, M. Davis, Holmes, Leach, Gunnarsson, S. Davis 4–6 4–6 6–3 6–2 6–4); *r/u* WCT Dallas (d. Gomez, Wilander, Nystrom, lost Lendl); *sf* Newport (d. Flur, lost Sadri); *qf* Houston (lost Curren),

qf Chicago (d. Sadri, lost Gomez), *qf* Las Vegas (lost Kriek 4–6 7–6 6–3), *qf* Stratton Mountain (lost Connors), *qf* San Francisco (lost Annacone), *qf* Tokyo Seiko (lost Lendl 6–4 7–5). *CAREER HIGHLIGHTS – SINGLES: LIPC – won 1985*; *Wimbledon – sf 1982* (d. Mayer 3–6 6–7 6–4 6–2 6–4, Mottram 6–2 7–5 6–3, Teacher 6–7 7–6 7–5 3–6 6–1, lost McEnroe [seed 1] 6–1 6–3 6–2), *qf 1981* (d. Mitton, Fancutt, Sadri, A. Mayer 6–3 6–4 7–6, lost Frawley 4–6 7–6 6–3 6–3), *qf 1983* (d. Dickson, Teacher, McCurdy, lost Curren 4–6 7–6 6–2 7–6); *Australian Open – sf 1983* (d. Nystrom, Teltscher, lost Lendl 6–1 7–6 6–3), *qf 1981* (d. Van't Hof, DuPre, lost Kriek 7–6 6–3 7–5).

MILOSLAV MECIR (Czechoslovakia)
Born Bojnice, 19 May, 1964; lives Prievidza; single; RH; 2HB; 6ft 3in; 180lb; final 1985 ATP ranking 9 (60); 1985 prize money $245,774.
Victorious at the 1983 Czech Closed Champ, he made his mark on the 1984 GP tour, reaching f Palermo and Cologne and sf Metz. A deceptive player with a lethal forehand down the line and two-handed backhand crosscourt, he played No. 2 behind Lendl on World Team Cup squad in Düsseldorf in 1985 following a dazzling winter and spring in which he emerged as a vastly improved player who became a delight to watch. In his first outing of the year, he stunned Connors to reach f of US Pro Indoor in Philadelphia, going on to win Rotterdam indoors over Jarryd, Becker, Nystrom and Hlasek, and Hamburg on clay over Nystrom, Wilander and Sundstrom. Following these remarkable successes, he was r/u to Noah at Italian Open where he upended Wilander for a second time in 3 weeks. He looked weary after that and he was never the same player for the rest of the year, but still finished at No. 9 in the world for the year, leaping 51 places and qualifying for Masters, which he missed owing to knee injury, sustained while playing football. *1985 HIGHLIGHTS – SINGLES: French Open* 3r, seed 11 (d. Navratil 6–4 6–2 6–4, Visser 6–2 6–4 6–3, lost Jaite 2–6 7–6 6–3 6–4), *Wimbledon* 1r, seed 12 (lost Tom Gullikson 4–6 6–3 6–4 6–7 6–3), *US Open* 2r, seed 9 (d. Kohlberg 5–7 4–6 7–6 6–3 6–1, lost Pate 6–4 6–0 6–3); *won* Rotterdam (d. McNamee 6–1 fs, Jarryd 6–2 7–6, Becker 6–4 6–2, Nystrom 6–3 6–3, Hlasek 6–1 6–2), *won* German Open (d. Pimek, Nystrom 6–2 6–2, Wilander 6–1 6–2, Sundstrom 6–4 6–1 6–4); *r/u* US Pro Indoor (d. Connors 6–3 fs, lost McEnroe 6–3 7–6 6–1), *r/u* Italian Open (d. Wilander, lost Noah 6–3 3–6 6–2 7–6); *qf* US CC (lost Becker), *qf* Basle (d. Stadler, lost Pimek).

MARCELLA MESKER (Netherlands)
Born The Hague, 23 May, 1959 and lives there; RH; 5ft 10½in; 135lb; final 1985 WTA ranking 69 (37); 1985 prize money $75,114.
In 1982 she played her match of the year to beat Turnbull in Sydney and her greater consistency and growing confidence halved her WTA ranking. She performed at essentially the same level in 1983 but slipped eight places on the computer. Much improved in 1984, she moved into the top 40, upsetting some formidable players on the way – she beat Sukova and Durie *en route* to sf US Indoor and stopped Shriver in Sydney. She had an off year in 1985 and was not once a quarterfinalist, although most observers expected her to regain the top 50 before long. *1985 HIGHLIGHTS – SINGLES: French Open* 1r (lost Herr 6–1 6–0), *Wimbledon* 3r (d. Gompert 6–3 4–6 6–4, Holikova 6–2 6–7 6–3, lost Garrison [seed 7] 6–3 6–1), *US Open* 1r (lost K. Jordan 2–6 6–1 6–2), *Australian Open* 1r (lost Schropp 6–3 6–4). *1985 HIGHLIGHTS – DOUBLES:* (with Paradis) *Australian Open* qf (d. Burgin/Smylie 2–6 6–4 6–3, lost Navratilova/Shriver 6–4 6–2); *r/u* VS Dallas (d. Fairbank/Reynolds 6–3 6–3, lost Potter/Walsh Pete 7–6 fs), *r/u* Canadian Open (lost Fernandez/Navratilova 6–4 6–0). *CAREER HIGHLIGHTS – DOUBLES:* [Jolissaint] *US Open – sf 1984* (d. Kohde-Kilsch/Mandlikova 6–7 6–3 6–4, lost Hobbs/Turnbull 6–4 6–1); *Australian Open –* [Paradis] *qf 1985.*

GLENN MICHIBATA (Canada)
Born Toronto, 13 June, 1962 and lives there; RH; 5ft 6in; 140lb; final 1983 ATP ranking 76 (163); 1985 prize money $26,031.
He is of Japanese descent (but does not speak Japanese), and was formerly coached by the brilliant Allen Fox at Pepperdine University in California, emerging in 1983 as a player of considerable talent and capability. Although his ranking slipped in 1984, he regained his

Pascale Paradis, the tall French No. 1, was coached in 1985 by Virginia Wade, and reached the last 16 at Wimbledon. *(T. Hindley)*

position in the top 80 in 1985. *1985 HIGHLIGHTS – DOUBLES:* (with Layendecker) *r*/*u* Toronto (lost Fleming/Jarryd).

ANNE MINTER (Australia)
Born Melbourne, 4 March, 1963, and lives there; RH; 5ft 4½in; 120lb; 1985 WTA ranking 72 (43); 1985 prize money $54,033.
She plays the flute to state orchestra standard. Won Australian Open Jun in 1980 and 1981, and reached qf both Wimbledon Jun and US Open Jun in 1981. Playing with particular assurance during the summer of 1984, she led Australia into Fed Cup f, then upset Durie at US Open. Meanwhile, her younger sister, Elizabeth, joined her in the top 100. Her record of 21 wins, 25 losses is an accurate reflection of her performance in 1985, when she encountered some difficult draws and lost some close matches, playing less confidently than in 1984. *1985 HIGHLIGHTS – SINGLES: French Open* 2r (d. Schropp 6–2 6–2, lost Calmett 6–1 6–4), *Wimbledon* 2r (d. Vasquez 6–0 6–2, lost Navratilova [seed 1] 6–4 6–1), *US Open* 2r (d. E. Minter 6–3 6–4, lost Graf [seed 11] 6–3 7–6), *Australian Open* 1r (lost Durie 6–4 6–4); *r*/*u* VS Pennsylvania (d. Rehe 7–6 fs, Benjamin, lost R. White 6–2 fs); *qf* Marco Island (d. Graf 6–3 6–1, lost Casale).

ALYCIA MOULTON (USA)
Born Sacramento, Cal., 18 February, 1961; lives Carmichael, Cal.; RH; 5ft 10½in; 145lb; final 1985 WTA ranking 35 (19); 1985 prize money $87,175.
Winner of 1979 jun event at US Open and r/u at Wimbledon Jun the same year, she went to Stanford University and reached f USTA Women's (AIAW) Intercollegiates two years running before capturing the title in her senior year in 1982. In the more demanding world of women's tennis, she exceeded expectations, defeating both Potter and Mandlikova in Australia at the close of the season. In 1983 she was a more improved player than her ranking indicated. Playing particularly well on grass, she was r/u to King at Edgbaston, won Newport, and reached last 16 Eastbourne and Australian Open. Her forceful brand of play, featuring an excellent first serve, lifted her into the top 20 in 1984. She was especially effective on cement where she was r/u to Evert Lloyd at Canadian Open and an upset winner over Bassett in LA. A last-minute replacement for the injured Kathy Jordan, she played her first W Cup match and found the Royal Albert Hall an intimidating arena as she lost 6–1 5–7 6–4 to Annabel Croft – also playing her first match. She had a mixed season in 1985 with some decent results, but she was not as effective a competitor as she had been the previous year. *1985 HIGHLIGHTS – SINGLES: Wimbledon* 3r (d. Herr 6–3 6–4, Reeves 6–2 6–4, lost Rinaldi 7–6 6–4), *US Open* last 16 (d. Mould 6–2 7–5, Goles 7–5 6–4, Kuhlman 6–4 1–6 7–6, lost Shriver [seed 4] 6–2 6–4), *Australian Open* 1r (lost Yanagi 7–5 6–2); *sf* Sydney Indoor (d. Croft 6–1 fs, lost Shriver); *qf* Birmingham (d. Kinney, lost Mascarin 7–6 6–4).

THOMAS MUSTER (Austria)
Born Leibnitz, 21 October, 1967, and lives there; LH; 5ft 11in; 148lb; final 1985 ATP ranking 98 (309); 1985 prize money $34,339.
Gaining more than 200 places on the computer in 1985, he found himself among the top 100 by the end of the year. *1985 HIGHLIGHTS – SINGLES: French Open* 1r (lost Taroczy 7–5 6–3 7–5); *sf* Palermo (d. Ingaramo, Maciel, Cancellotti, lost Tulasne).

BETSY NAGELSEN (USA)
Born St Petersburg, Fla., 23 October, 1956; lives Venice, Fla.; RH; 5ft 9½in; 135lb; final 1985 WTA ranking 45 (77) singles, 24 doubles; 1985 prize money $84,049.
Married Mark McCormack March 1986. Bursting upon the international scene in summer 1974, she stunned Morozova and Wade to reach f of grass-court tournament in Newport, RI. A gifted serve-and-volley player, she seemed to have a glowing future but was beset by back problems in 1975 and it took a long while for her confidence to return. Her record in 1981 was distinguished, including a victory at Surbiton where she beat Navratilova in sf and Hallquist in f, but in 1982 a wrist operation restricted her season, although she continued to work for Australian TV on Channel 9. She was not fully fit in 1983 and 1984, again being denied the chance to play the kind of tennis of which she is clearly capable,

although she played some exceptional doubles, reaching sf US Open with A. White in 1984. Although she was again beset by injuries in 1985, she had a better year, highlighted by her arrival in f Birmingham. **1985 HIGHLIGHTS – SINGLES: French Open** 1r (lost Kanellopoulou 7–5 3–6 6–4), **Wimbledon** 1r (lost Kohde-Kilsch [seed 6] 7–5 6–1), **US Open** 1r (lost Casals 1–0 ret'd), **Australian Open** 2r (d. Reynolds 4–6 6–3 8–6, lost Evert Lloyd [seed 1] 4–6 6–4 6–0); **r/u** Birmingham (d. Yanagi 6–4 fs, Casale, Shaefer 7–5 6–3, Henricksson, Mascarin 6–4 fs, lost Shriver 6–1 6–0); **sf** VS Indianapolis (d. Russell, lost Horvath); **qf** VS San Diego (d. Henricksson 6–3 fs, lost Turnbull). **1985 HIGHLIGHTS – DOUBLES:** (with A. White) **French Open** sf, seed 6 (d. Mandlikova/A. Smith 6–2 6–4, Bunge/Pfaff 6–1 6–2, lost Navratilova/Shriver 6–3 6–4); **r/u** Bridgestone (d. Turnbull/Walsh Pete, lost Jordan/Smylie 4–6 7–5 6–2). **CAREER HIGHLIGHTS – SINGLES: Austalian Open – r/u 1978** (d. Iomanova 6–4 6–4, Matison 7–5 6–4, lost C. O'Neill 6–3 7–6). **CAREER HIGHLIGHTS – DOUBLES: Australian Open** – [Tomanova] **won 1978** (d. Sato/Whytcross 7–5 6–2), [Reid] **r/u 1977** [Jan.] (lost Fromholtz/H. Cawley 5–7 6–1 7–5); **Italian Open** – [Mihai] **r/u 1978** (lost Jausovec/Ruzici 6–2 2–6 7–5); **French Open** – [Navratilova] **sf 1981** (d. Evert Lloyd/Ruzici [seed 6], lost Reynolds/P. Smith [seed 2] 6–4 7–5), [A. White] **sf 1985**; **US Open** [Shriver] **sf 1978** (d. Stove/Evert [seed 3] 6–3 6–2, lost Reid/Turnbull [seed 2] 6–4 1–6 7–5), [A. White] **sf 1984** (d. Evert Lloyd/King 7–6 4–6 6–3, lost Navratilova/Shriver 6–4 7–5).

AMIT NAOR (Israel)
Born Rehovot, 25 July, 1967; lives Ramat Hasharon; RH; 5ft 11in; 185lb; final 1985 ATP ranking 450.
In 1985, his last jun year, he won ITF ranking tournaments in Jerusalem, Tel Aviv and Ulm. He was a finalist in Indianapolis and reached 16s US Open jun and the Orange Bowl. He beat Vijay Amritraj in GP tournament in Tel Aviv in October and turned pro Jan. 1986.

MARTINA NAVRATILOVA (USA) **Official World Champion**
Born Prague, 18 October, 1956; lives Dallas, Texas; single; LH; 5ft 7½in; 145lb; final 1985 WTA ranking 1 (1) singles, 2 doubles; 1985 prize money $1,328,829; career prize money $9,886,474.
After leading Czechoslovakia to victory in Fed Cup 1975, she defected to USA that autumn and became an American citizen in 1981. Always one of the top 5 players in the world since 1975 (when she was r/u to Chris Evert at Italian, French and VS Champs), she won Wimbledon in 1978, 1979, 1982, 1983, 1984 and 1985. In 1979 she captured Avon and CS Champs to earn the No. 1 world ranking. In 1980, however, she did not win a major title. In 1981, for the fifth year in a row, she was one of the world's top 3 players, capturing Avon Champ in New York and Australian Open, but she did not make her mark in the 3 most important tournaments, losing in French Open qf to Hanika, Wimbledon sf to Mandlikova and in an agonisingly close US Open f to Austin. That year she joined forces with Shriver to win Wimbledon, Avon and TS Champs and reach f Australian Open. In 1982 she won 15 of 18 tournaments and 90 of 93 matches, including her third Wimbledon and first French Open titles, but suffered her last two losses on big occasions, dropping US Open qf to Shriver and Australian Open f to Evert Lloyd. She closed the season by winning TS Champ with a 3s win over Evert Lloyd to confirm her status as No. 1 in the world for the second time in her career. She also joined her arch-rival to lead the US to victory in Fed Cup and won the French doubles with A. Smith, plus Wimbledon and Australian doubles titles with Shriver. Nearly invincible in singles and doubles in 1983, she set new records. Her career earnings reached $6,384,089, a record for men and women; her 86 wins against just one singles defeat – by Horvath in Paris – (she won 16 of the 17 tournaments she entered) for a winning percentage of ·988 was a record for the 'Open' era dating back to 1968. No man nor woman in that period has produced such an overwhelming record in a single season and her combined 1982–83 results are as follows: 176 wins, 4 defeats (·977) and 31 tournament victories of the 35 she played. As for her 1983 doubles record, she won 11 of 12 tournaments (52 of 53 matches) with Shriver and altogether with different partners her complete doubles record was 63–1 (13 of 14 tournaments). Her 1984 record was no less impressive. Winning 78 of 80 matches, between her loss to Mandlikova in her first tournament of the year in Oakland and her defeat by Sukova in her last at Melbourne, she won a modern record 74 consecutive matches to eclipse Evert Lloyd's 55. She won a bonus of $1m from the ITF for achieving

a modern GS of four consecutive victories, culminating in her triumph at the French Open in Paris where she played possibly the best match of her career to beat Evert Lloyd in f. She extended her streak of six straight GS events to tie Margaret Court (1969–70) and Maureen Connolly (1952–53) for the women's record, but failed in a bid for a traditional GS when Sukova beat her in sf Australian Open, despite Navratilova saving five m-ps as Sukova served at 6–5 fs. In doubles, she extended her unbeaten run to 83 consecutive matches as she and Shriver won a traditional, calendar-year GS – the first female pair to do so – and extended their unbeaten streak to a record seven GS events. Together they won 11 tournaments and 53 straight matches in 1984. In earning her fourth consecutive No. 1 world ranking in 1985, she had to work harder and struggle longer than before, for not until she beat Evert Lloyd for the Australian crown was the issue settled in her favour. She had another great year, winning her fourth straight Wimbledon singles title (the first woman since Helen Wills Moody in 1927–30 to do so) and her third Australian Open crown to raise her total of GS singles titles to 13. Her singles record of 84–5 and victories in 12 of 17 tournaments extended her totals for the 1982–85 period to: 338 wins, 11 losses and 56 tournament victories of the 67 tournaments she played. In doubles, her record streak of 109 matches, dating back to April of 1983, and the Shriver/Navratilova streak of four consecutive Wimbledons, were broken by Smylie/Jordan in f Wimbledon. Had they won, they would have become the first female pair since Lenglen/Ryan (1919–23) to win five straight Wimbledons. *1985 HIGHLIGHTS – SINGLES: r/u French Open* seed 1 (d. Teeguarden 6–1 6–0, Wade 6–3 6–0, Tanvier 6–0 6–0, Reggi 6–4 6–1, Cecchini 6–2 6–2, Kohde-Kilsch 6–4 6–4, lost Evert Lloyd [seed 2] 6–3 6–7 7–5), *won Wimbledon* seed 1 (d. Bonder 6–0 6–2, A. Minter 6–4 6–1, Bunge 7–6 6–3, Uys 6–2 6–2, Shriver 7–6 6–3, Garrison 6–4 7–6, Evert Lloyd 4–6 6–3 6–2), *r/u US Open* seed 2 (d. Paradis 6–2 6–1, Bonder 6–1 6–1, Cecchini 6–0 6–1, Lindqvist 6–4 7–5, Garrison 6–2 6–3, Graf 6–2 6–3, lost Mandlikova [seed 3] 7–6 1–6 7–6), *won Australian Open* seed 2 (d. Hansel 6–2 6–1, Provis 6–2 6–1, Hobbs 6–3 6–1, Sukova 6–2 6–2, Mandlikova 6–7 6–1 6–4, Evert Lloyd 6–2 4–6 6–2); *won* VS Washington (d. Sukova 6–0 6–4, Garrison 6–1 6–2, M. Maleeva 6–3 6–2), *won* LIPC (d. Lindqvist 6–4 fs, Bunge, Bassett, Evert Lloyd 6–2 6–4), *won* VS Dallas (d. Kohde-Kilsch 6–4 6–3, Sukova 6–2 7–5, Evert Lloyd 6–3 6–4), *won* VS Champ (d. Mandlikova 7–5 7–6, Sukova 6–3 7–5 6–4), *won* Orlando (d. Kohde-Kilsch, K. Maleeva 6–1 6–0), *won* VS Houston (d. Sukova 6–3 6–0, Burgin 6–4 6–1), *won* Eastbourne (d. Bunge 7–6 6–3, M. Maleeva, Sukova 6–4 6–3), *won* Fort Lauderdale (d. Phelps 6–3 fs, Louie, Graf 6–3 6–1), *won* Brisbane (d. Shriver 6–4 7–5), *won* Sydney (d. Sukova 6–2 fs, Mandlikova 3–6 6–1 6–2); *r/u* VS Florida (lost Evert Lloyd 6–2 6–4); *sf* US Indoor (lost Mandlikova 7–6 6–0); *qf* Canadian Open (lost Kohde-Kilsch 3–6 6–4 6–3). *1985 HIGH-LIGHTS – DOUBLES:* (with Shriver unless stated) *won French Open* seed 1 (d. Kohde-Kilsch/Sukova 4–6 6–2 6–2), *r/u Wimbledon* seed 1 (d. Mandlikova/Turnbull 6–4 6–2, lost K. Jordan/Smylie 5–7 6–3 6–4), *r/u US Open* seed 1 (d. Mandlikova/Turnbull 6–3 6–4, lost Kohde-Kilsch/Sukova 6–7 6–2 6–3), *won Australian Open* seed 1 (d. Kohde-Kilsch/Sukova 6–3 6–4), *won* US Indoor (d. Mesker/Smylie 7–5 6–2), *won* VS Champs (d. Kohde-Kilsch/Sukova 6–7 6–4 7–6), *won* Orlando (d. Burgin/Horvath 6–3 6–1), *won* Eastbourne (d. K. Jordan/Smylie 7–5 6–4), *won* Brisbane (d. Kohde-Kilsch/Sukova 6–4 6–7 6–1), [Burgin] *won* Houston (d. M. Maleeva/Sukova 6–1 3–6 6–3), [G. Fernandez] *won* VS Washington (d. Kohde-Kilsch/Sukova 6–3 fs), [G. Fernandez] *won* LIPC (d. Jordan/Mandlikova 7–6 6–2), [G. Fernandez] *won* Canadian Open (d. Mesker/Paradis 6–4 6–0). *CAREER HIGHLIGHTS – SINGLES: French Open – won 1982* (d. Mandlikova 6–0 6–2, Jaeger 7–6 6–1), *won 1984* (d. Mandlikova 3–6 6–2 6–2, Evert Lloyd 6–3 6–1), *r/u 1975* (lost Evert 2–6 6–2 6–0), *r/u 1985*; *Wimbledon – won 1978* (d. Goolagong Cawley 2–6 6–4 6–4, Evert 2–6 6–4 7–5), *won 1979* (d. Austin 7–5 6–1, Evert Lloyd 6–4 6–4), *won 1982* (d. Russell 6–3 6–4, Bunge 6–2 6–2, Evert Lloyd 6–1 3–6 6–2), *won 1983* (d. Vermaak 6–1 6–1, Jaeger 6–0 6–3), *won 1984* (d. Evert Lloyd 7–6 6–2), *won 1985*; *US Open – won 1983* (d. Hanika 6–0 6–3, Shriver 6–2 6–1, Evert Lloyd 6–1 6–3), *won 1984* (d. Evert Lloyd 4–6 6–4 6–4), *r/u 1981* (d. K. Jordan, A. Smith, Evert Lloyd [seed 1], lost Austin [seed 3] 1–6 7–6 7–6), *r/u 1985*; *Australian Open – won 1981* seed 3 (d. Tobin, K. Jordan, Goolagong Cawley, Shriver, Evert Lloyd [seed 1] 6–7 6–4 7–5), *won 1983* (d. Durie 4–6 6–3 6–4, Shriver 6–4 6–3, K. Jordan 6–2 7–6), *won 1985, r/u 1982* (d. Shriver 6–3 6–4, lost Evert Lloyd 6–3 2–6 6–3); *VS Champs – won 1978* (d. Goolagong Cawley 7–6 6–4), *won 1984* (d. Evert Lloyd 6–3 7–5 6–1), *won 1985, r/u 1975* (lost Evert Lloyd 6–4

6–2); *Avon Champs – won 1979* (d. Austin 6–3 3–6 6–2), *won 1981* (d. Jaeger 6–3 7–6), *r/u 1982* (lost Hanika 1–6 6–3 6–4); *TS Finals – won 1982* (d. Evert Lloyd 4–6 6–1 6–2), *r/u 1981* (lost Austin 2–6 6–4 6–2); *Italian Open – r/u 1974* (lost Evert 6–3 6–3), *r/u 1975* (lost Evert 6–1 6–0); *CS Finals – r/u 1978* (lost Evert 6–3 6–3). *CAREER HIGHLIGHTS – DOUBLES:* (with Shriver unless stated) *French Open* – [Evert] *won 1975* (d. Anthony/Morozova, [A. Smith] *won 1982* (d. Casals/Turnbull 6–3 6–4), *won 1984* (d. Kohde-Kilsch/Mandlikova 5–7 6–3 6–2), *won 1985*; *Wimbledon* – [Evert] *won 1976* (d. King/Stove 6–1 3–6 7–5), [King] *won 1979* (d. Stove/Turnbull 5–7 6–3 6–2), *won 1981* (d. K. Jordan/A. Smith 6–3 7–6), *won 1982* (d. K. Jordan/A. Smith 6–4 6–1), *won 1983* (d. Casals/Turnbull 6–2 6–2), *won 1984* (d. K. Jordan/A. Smith 6–3 6–4), *r/u 1985*; *US Open* – [Stove] *won 1977*(d. Richards/Stuart), [King] *won 1978* (d. Stove/Turnbull 7–6 6–4), [King] *won 1980* (d. Shriver/Stove 6–7 7–5), *won 1983* (d. Reynolds/Fairbank 6–7 6–1 6–3), *won 1984* (d. Turnbull/Hobbs 6–2 6–4), [King] *r/u 1979* (lost Stove/Turnbull), *r/u 1985*; *Australian Open* – [Nagelsen] *won 1980* (d. Kiyomura/Reynolds), *won 1982* (d. Kohde/Pfaff 6–4 6–2), *won 1983* (d. Hobbs/Turnbull 6–4 6–7 6–2), *won 1984* (d. Kohde-Kilsch/Sukova 6–3 6–4), [Tomanova] *r/u 1974*, *r/u 1981* (lost K. Jordan/A. Smith 6–2 7–5); *Italian Open* – [Evert] *won 1975* (d. Barker/Coles), [Tomanova] *r/u 1973* (lost Wade/Morozova 7–5 fs); *CS Finals* – [King] *won 1978* (d. Reid/Turnbull, [King] *won 1979* (d. Casals/Evert Lloyd); *TS Champs – won 1981* (d. Casals/Turnbull 6–3 6–4), *won 1982* (d. Reynolds/P. Smith); *US Indoor* – [King] *won 1979* (d. Stove/Turnbull), *won 1984* (d. Durie/Kiyomura Hayashi 6–4 6–3); *Avon Champs – won 1980* (d. Casals/Turnbull 6–3 fs), [King] *won 1981* (d. Potter/Walsh 6–0 7–6), *won 1982* (d. K. Jordan/A. Smith).

VICKI NELSON (USA)
Born Wooster, Ohio, 25 September, 1962, and lives there; RH; 5ft 6in; 120lb; final 1985 WTA ranking 79 (92); 1985 prize money $36,885.
Her grit on court was evident as usual in 1985 and although she produced no sparkling wins, she did lift her ranking a few notches. *1985 HIGHLIGHTS – SINGLES: French Open* 2r (d. Demongeot 6–2 6–2, lost Dinu 4–6 7–6 6–2), *Wimbledon* 1r (lost A. Smith 6–0 6–2), *US Open* 1r (lost Paz 0–6 6–1 6–0; *r/u* Taranto (d. Schropp, Garrone 6–4 6–0, lost Reggi 6–4 6–4).

YANNICK NOAH (France)
Born Sedan, 18 May, 1960; lives Paris and New York with wife Cecilia; RH; 6ft 4in; 180lb; final 1985 ATP ranking 7 (10) singles, 13 (20) doubles; 1985 prize money $394,881.
African father played soccer for Sedan; French mother. Was discovered by Ashe on a goodwill coaching visit to the Cameroons when Noah was only 10. Ashe called Philippe Chatrier, then President of the French Tennis Federation, and suggested he should get Noah to France. The boy duly attended the FFLT school in Nice and made rapid progress, so that now he has become the best black player since Ashe. In 1977 he was Orange Bowl finalist; in 1978 he won two small GP tournaments, swept three more in 1979 and in 1980 reached his first important f (Italian Open, which he lost to Vilas). In 1981 he consolidated his position in the world's top 20 and narrowly missed qualifying for Masters. Moving into the world's top 10 in 1982, he led France into D Cup f where he narrowly missed a win over McEnroe, having stopped Lendl in the decisive match v Czechoslovakia. He won four tournaments across the year, including another big win over Lendl in f Palm Springs ending a 44-match winning streak by the Czech. It was a highly successful year for the Frenchman, who reached his first Masters. In 1983, after successes in Madrid and Hamburg, he became the first Frenchman since Marcel Bernard (1946) to win the French Open and he did so with style and panache. In qf he upset Lendl and in f he stopped defending champion Wilander in as concentrated an effort as he has ever given. That great triumph guaranteed him his rightful place among the top 5 in the world, but he was not prepared for the anguish that exclusive territory would cause him. After Paris he was suspended for 3 weeks and fined for missing a match in the World Team Cup. By the end of the year, he was talking about leaving France to live in New York, the pressures and responsibilities of superstardom becoming too much to endure, as his lacklustre 1r loss to Smid in Masters clearly showed. Married to Cecilia Rodhe in February 1984, the Frenchman adjusted to his new status but was unable to reach the heights of 1983. He played 10 tournaments in the first half of the year but did not return until November. His

early record was impressive as he reached one f, three sf and three qf but his French Open title was taken away by Wilander and he had to settle for the doubles title alongside countryman Leconte. In 1985 he won Italian Open and Washington, remaining at his best on clay. It was a good year for the Frenchman on all surfaces, though, and he reached 2 f indoors, second US Open qf in 3 years, and looked more like the man who had played with such inspiration in 1983, although he fell 1r Masters to Mayotte. *1985 HIGHLIGHTS – SINGLES: French Open* last 16, seed 9 (d. Pimek 6–7 6–1 7–5 6–4, Schapers 6–1 6–1 6–4, Clerc 6–1 6–7 6–4 4–6 8–6, lost Leconte 6–3 6–4 6–7 4–6 6–3), *Wimbledon* 3r, seed 11 (d. Gilbert 6–4 3–6 7–6 6–7 6–3, Edwards 4–6 6–4 7–6 6–2, lost V. Amritraj 4–6 7–6 6–3 7–6), *US Open* qf, seed 7 (d. Bates 6–3 7–6 6–3, Grabb 7–6 6–3 6–2, Gerulaitis 6–3 6–4 6–3, Berger 6–7 6–2 6–3 6–1, lost Lendl [seed 2] 6–2 6–2 6–4); *won Italian Open* (d. Jarryd 6–1 7–5, Clerc 6–1 7–5, Becker 6–3 6–3, Mecir 6–3 3–6 6–2 7–6), *won* Washington (d. Pernfors, Ross, Krickstein 6–2 6–4, Connors 6–2 fs, Jaite 6–4 6–3); *r/u* Memphis (d. Perkis, Teltscher, lost Edberg), *r/u* Basle (d. Forget 7–6 fs, Pimek 7–5 fs, lost Edberg 6–7 6–4 7–6 6–1); *sf* US CC (d. Tulasne, Perez, Schwaier, lost Gomez); *qf* US Pro Indoor (d. Motta, lost McEnroe), *qf* LIPC (d. Tom Gullikson, S. Giammalva, lost Smid), *qf* Stockholm (d. Arias, Sanchez, lost Nystrom). *1985 HIGHLIGHTS – DOUBLES:* [Leconte] *r/u US Open* seed 12 (d. Nystrom/Wilander 6–3 7–6 6–4, lost Flach/Seguso 7–6 6–7 7–6 6–0); [Kriek] *won* Chicago (d. Flach/Seguso 3–6 4–6 7–5 6–1 6–4). *CAREER HIGHLIGHTS – SINGLES: French Open – won 1983* (d. Jarryd 6–1 6–0 6–2, Pecci, DuPre, Alexander, Lendl 7–6 6–2 5–7 6–0, Roger-Vasselin, Wilander 6–2 7–5 7–6), *qf 1981* seed 11 (d. Vilas [seed 6], lost Pecci 3–6 6–4 6–4 6–4), *qf 1982* (d. Fibak 4–6 6–7 6–4 6–4 6–3, lost Vilas 7–6 6–3 6–4), *qf 1984* (lost Wilander 7–6 3–6 2–6 3–6); *Italian Open – won 1985, r/u 1980* (d. Dibbs, Barazzutti, Smid 6–1 6–1, lost Vilas 6–0 6–4 6–4); *US Pro Indoor – sf 1981* (d. Gerulaitis 6–3 fs, lost Fibak 6–2 4s); *US Open – qf 1983* (lost Arias 7–5 fs), *qf 1985*. *CAREER HIGHLIGHTS – DOUBLES:* (with Leconte) *French Open – won 1984* (d. Slozil/Smid 6–4 2–6 3–6 6–3 6–2); *US Open – r/u 1985*.

JOAKIM NYSTROM (Sweden)

Born Skellefta, 10 February, 1963 and lives there; RH; 2HB; 6ft 2in; 155lb; final 1985 ATP ranking 11 (11) singles, 9 (62) doubles; 1985 prize money $309,772.

The Orange Bowl 18-and-under champ of 1980, he fell on hard times in 1982 after a reasonably good 1981. Then, in 1983 he finished the year in the top 30, his one tournament triumph being on grass at Sydney in December, which earned him the chance to play No. 2 singles for Sweden against Australia in D Cup f in Melbourne, where he was beaten by Cash and Fitzgerald as the Swedes fell 3–2. Clearly stronger and more confident in 1984, he won 4 GP tournaments – Gstaad and North Conway on clay and Basle and Cologne indoors – and just missed a top 10 ranking. He qualified for first Masters where he beat Gerulaitis before losing qf to Lendl. At the end of 1985, he found himself with the same ranking as he had in 1984, but this time he had contributed to Sweden's second straight D Cup triumph when he joined Wilander for a critical win over the Germans in D Cup f. Earlier in the year, he beat Gonzalez and Pecci in D Cup qf win over Paraguay. Otherwise he was a formidable competitor, and two of his three duels with Becker were among the year's most memorable matches – at Wimbledon he served for the match at 5–4 and 6–5 in the last set, and at US Open he gained revenge with a 4s triumph. Meanwhile, he picked up GP singles titles in Munich and Gstaad, and qualified for Masters where he lost Jarryd 1r singles but was r/u doubles with Wilander. *1985 HIGHLIGHTS – SINGLES: French Open* qf, seed 7 (d. Beutel 6–2 4–6 6–1 6–0, DePalmer 3–6 1–6 7–6 6–3 6–4, Youl 6–2 6–0 6–2, Gildemeister 7–6 6–1 6–1, lost McEnroe 6–7 6–2 6–2 3–6 7–5), *Wimbledon* 3r, seed 7 (d. Goodall 6–3 6–3 3–6 6–0, Annacone 7–5 7–5 6–3, lost Becker 3–6 7–6 6–1 4–6 9–7), *US Open* qf, seed 10 (d. Hooper 6–4 7–5 6–1, Green 6–3 3–6 6–3 6–0, Goldie 6–0 6–1 1–1 ret'd, Becker [seed 8] 6–3 6–4 4–6 6–4, lost McEnroe [seed 1] 6–1 6–0 7–5), *Australian Open* last 16, seed 7 (d. S. Giammalva 6–3 6–2 5–7 6–4, J. Frawley 4–6 7–5 6–3 6–4, lost Lloyd 6–2 1–6 6–4 6–7 6–4); *won* Munich (d. Benhabiles, Motta, Clerc, Schwaier 6–1 6–0), *won* Gstaad (d. Casal 6–3 fs, S. Simonsson, Fibak, Forget 7–5 fs, Maurer 6–4 1–6 7–5 6–3); *r/u* Palermo (d. Perez, lost Tulasne); *sf* Rotterdam (d. Gunnarsson, Cash, lost Mecir), *sf* WCT Dallas (d. Sundstrom, McEnroe 6–4 7–6 6–4, lost Mayotte), *sf* Cincinnati (d. Purcell 7–6 fs, Hooper, Moor 7–6 fs, Jarryd 6–2 6–1, lost Becker 6–4 7–5), *sf* Stockholm (d. Noah 6–2 7–5, lost Jarryd 6–3 7–6). *1985 HIGHLIGHTS –*

DOUBLES: (with Wilander unless stated) **French Open** sf, seed 6 (d. Giammalva/Willenborg 7–6 6–3, lost Edmondson/Warwick 6–4 6–1 7–5), **US Open** sf, seed 5 (d. Denton/Fleming 6–3 6–4 6–4, lost Leconte/Noah 6–3 7–6 6–4); **won** US Pro Indoor (d. Gunthardt/Taroczy, Fibak/A. Mayer), [Dowdeswell] **won** Palermo (d. Casal/Sanchez); **r/u** Masters (lost Edberg/Jarryd 6–1 7–6), **r/u** Cincinnati (d. Leconte/Noah 6–3 fs, lost Edberg/Jarryd); **sf** Rotterdam (lost Slozil/Smid), **sf** Monte Carlo (d. Gunthardt/Taroczy, lost Glickstein/Perkis), **sf** Hamburg (d. Motta/Willenborg, lost Gunthardt/Taroczy). **CAREER HIGHLIGHTS – DOUBLES:** (with Wilander) **Australian Open – r/u 1984** (d. Cash/Fitzgerald 6–4 6–4 2–6 6–3, lost Edmondson/Stewart 6–2 7–5); **French Open – sf 1985**; **US Open – sf 1985**.

SHIGERU OHTA (Japan)
Born Chigasaki City, 8 January, 1967, and lives there; RH; 5ft 10in; 154lb; final 1985 ATP ranking 792.
His father, Mitsuo, works for Toyota and was former Soft Tennis champ of Japan. Jun champ of Japan since 1984, he joined Nick Bollettieri that year and was a finalist in the Asian Jun Champs (lost Barientos). In 1985 was r/u to Stenlund in the Rolex 18s.

BRUNO ORESAR (Yugoslavia)
Born Zagreb, 21 April, 1967 and lives there; RH; 5ft 10in; 145lb; final 1985 ATP ranking 82 (793); 1985 prize money $23,000.
Started to play, aged 10, at local Mladost club after turning to tennis from soccer for which he was too slight of build. Within a few weeks he won local jun tournament, then 12s Orange Bowl on his first overseas trip in 1979; two years later he won the 14s and, in 1983, the 16s. He has won singles, doubles and mixed in his national Yugoslav Champs in every age group – 12s, 14s, 16s, 18s, 21s and Open. In November 1984 he won Madrid on the Spanish satellite circuit. Seeking to complete a sweep of Orange Bowl crowns in Miami Beach, he lost f of 18s to Pistolesi in 1985. Meanwhile, he asserted himself on GP circuit, moving swiftly into the top 100. **1985 HIGHLIGHTS – SINGLES: US Open** 1r (lost Pate 6–2 6–3 2–6 6–0); **sf** US Pro (d. Ganzabal 6–2 fs, Arias 7–6 7–6, Arguello, Aguilera, lost Jaite). **1985 HIGHLIGHTS – DOUBLES:** (with Prpic) **qf** Palermo (lost Lavalle/Maciel).

CLAUDIO PANATTA (Italy)
Born Rome, 2 February, 1960 and lives there; married, wife Daniela, son Christiano born Dec. 1980; RH; 5ft 10in; 170lb; final 1985 ATP ranking 92 (123); 1985 prize money $84,805.
The younger brother of 1976 French and Italian Open champ Adriano, he was 1978 Italian jun singles and doubles champ and in 1980 he won Italian Nat doubles title with Adriano. In 1982 he appeared in his first GP singles f, losing in Cairo to Drewett, and after a dismal start in 1983 he picked up substantially. Fate was less kind in 1984, when his results were erratic and he lacked inspiration, never quite recovering from a dismal start which included 1r or 2r losses in his first six tournaments. In 1985, he lost a golden opportunity in WCT Tourn of Champs when he fell in 3s t-b to McEnroe. He won Bari and was r/u at Bologna, but 6 1r losses late in the year resulted in a lower ranking than he might have achieved. **1985 HIGHLIGHTS – SINGLES: French Open** 1r (lost Edberg [seed 14] 7–6 6–3 6–3, **Wimbledon** 1r (lost Jarryd [seed 5] 4–6 3–6 6–4 6–4 6–3), **US Open** 2r (d. Tim Gullikson 7–6 6–3 2–6 6–4, lost de la Pena 6–7 7–5 7–6 6–3); **won** Bari (d. Viver, Cancellotti, Pistolesi 7–6 6–0, Lopez-Maeso 6–4 fs, Duncan 6–2 1–6 7–6); **r/u** Bologna (d. Viver, Narducci, Tous, lost Tulasne 6–2 6–0); **qf** WCT Forest Hills (d. Gildemeister, de la Pena, Pate, lost McEnroe 7–6 fs). **1985 HIGHLIGHTS – DOUBLES:** [Slozil] **won** Nice (d. Courteau/Forget), [Ganzabal] **won** Bari (d. Freeman/Warder); [Cane] **r/u** Kitzbuhel (d. Becker/Slozil, lost Hjertquist/P. Svensson). **CAREER HIGHLIGHTS – SINGLES: Italian Open – qf 1984** (d. Arias, lost Gomez).

PASCALE PARADIS (France)
Born Troyes, 24 April, 1966; lives Paris; RH; 5ft 9in; 128lb; final 1985 WTA ranking 46 (28); 1985 prize money $62,677.
One of the brightest stars to emerge on the 1983 tour, she set the pace in the jun, capturing French and Wimbledon Jun and reaching sf US Open Jun, where she also reached last 16 in main draw, with a win over Temesvari. Progressing as rapidly as expected, she moved into the top 30 in 1984, but seemed to be suffering growing pains

in 1985, when only briefly on grass in England did she show her finest form. At Eastbourne, she downed Sabatini on her way to qf and at Wimbledon she removed Turnbull before losing to Sukova in last 16. *1985 HIGHLIGHTS – SINGLES: French Open* 2r (d. Temesvari 7–6 3–6 6–3, lost Mascarin 6–0 6–2), *Wimbledon* last 16, unseeded (d. Okagawa 6–2 6–1, Hanika 7–6 6–7 6–3, Turnbull [seed 14] 2–6 7–5 6–1, lost Sukova [seed 7] 6–4 7–6), *US Open* 1r (lost Navratilova 6–2 6–1), *Australian Open* 1r (lost Dingwall 6–2 5–7 6–2); *sf* Ginny Champs (d. Nagelsen, Sands, lost Holladay 6–3 fs)· *af* Eastbourne (d. Ludloff 6–3 fs, Sabatini 6–3 fs, Karlsson, lost Turnbull 7–5 ts). *1985 HIGHLIGHTS – DOUBLES:* (with Mesker unless stated) [Evert Lloyd] *French Open* qf (d. Horvath/Ruzici 4–6 6–1 6–3, lost Navratilova/Shriver 6–3 6–3), *Australian Open* qf (d. Burgin/Smylie 2–6 6–4 6–3), lost Navratilova/Shriver 6–4 6–2); *r/u* VS Dallas (lost Potter/Walsh Pete 7–6 fs), *r/u* Canadian Open (lost G. Fernandez/Navratilova 6–4 6–0).

DAVID PATE (USA)
Born Los Angeles, 16 April, 1962; lives Las Vegas; RH; 6ft; 170lb; final 1985 ATP ranking 26 (31) singles, 21 (86) doubles; 1985 prize money $177,521.
Twice an All-American at Texas Christian University, he won NCAA doubles title in 1981 with Richter. Meanwhile, he made his presence known quickly on the pro tour and by the end of 1982 was ranked 203 in the world. He moved up 100 notches in 1983 and in 1984 won his first GP event (Tokyo) and without fuss or fanfare drove his way to No. 31. Scheduling himself exclusively on fast courts and playing no CC event all year, he arrived in the top 26 in 1985, claiming Nystrom and Mecir as two of his major scalps as well as taking a set off Lendl at Wembley. *1985 HIGHLIGHTS – SINGLES: Wimbledon* 3r (d. Fulwood 6–3 6–4 6–4, Denton 7–6 6–4 6–4, lost Acuna 7–5 6–4 6–2), *US Open* 3r (d. Oresar 6–2 6–3 2–6 6–0, Mecir [seed 9] 6–4 6–0 6–3, lost Yzaga 6–3 6–3 7–6, *Australian Open* 2r, seed 15 (lost Cahill 3–6 7–6 6–3 6–0); *r/u* La Quinta (d. Nystrom 6–4 fs, Pfister 6–4 fs, Krickstein 6–1 fs, Pimek, lost Stefanki 6–1 6–4 3–6 6–3); *sf* Newport (d. V. Amritraj, Shiras, Annacone 6–3 fs, lost Tom Gullikson 7–5 fs), *sf* Wembley (d. Nystrom 6–2 3–6 7–5, lost Lendl 6–4 6–7 6–3); *qf* Cleveland (lost Drewett). *1985 HIGHLIGHTS –DOUBLES:* (with S. Davis unless stated) *won* Stratton Mountain (d. Annacone/Van Rensburg 7–6 fs, Flach/Seguso 7–6 fs), *won* Japan Open (d. S. Giammalva/Holmes); *r/u* Tokyo Seiko (d. Fitzgerald/Smid, lost Flach/Seguso 7–6 fs), [S. Giammalva] *r/u* Fort Myers (lost Flach/Seguso 6–2 fs).

DIEGO PEREZ (Spain)
Born Montevideo, Uruguay, 9 February, 1962; lives Barcelona; RH; 5ft 10in; 166lb; final 1985 ATP ranking 55 (50); 1985 prize money $106,711.
A member of D Cup Squad in Uruguay, he was ranked 92 at end 1981, slipped to 121 the following year, and then used his superior CC skills to lift himself into top 50 in 1983. His best showing was when he reached sf US Pro with wins over Vilas and Gomez. In 1984 he maintained his position and reached sf Italian Open, while strong performances at each end of 1985 kept him in the top 60. He won Bordeaux in the autumn and upset Becker in 1r Kitzbuhel. *1985 HIGHLIGHTS – SINGLES: French Open* 1r (lost Holmes 6–3 7–5 4–6 6–4), *US Open* 2r (d. Meister 6–3 6–3 6–4, lost Jaite 6–3 7–6 6–3); *won* Bordeaux (d. Tulasne 6–2 fs, J. Brown 6–4 7–6); *r/u* Buenos Aires (d. Arguello, J. Brown, lost Jaite); *sf* Palermo (d. Lavalle, Tous, Prpic, lost Nystrom 7–6 6–4). *1985 HIGHLIGHTS –DOUBLES:* (with Bengoechea) *r/u* Buenos Aires (lost Jaite/Miniussi).

SHACHAR PERKIS (Israel)
Born Haifa, 14 October, 1962 and lives there; single; RH; 6ft 4in; 155lb; final 1985 ATP ranking 72 (75); 1985 prize money $79,215.
By the end of 1984, this ambitious competitor had emerged from nowhere to 75, with a higher ranking than his more experienced countryman, Shlomo Glickstein, with whom he joined forces in the Israeli D Cup squad. He held his ground in 1985 and had a good win over Becker at Memphis. *1985 HIGHLIGHTS – SINGLES: US Open* 1r (lost Lundgren 6–4 7–6 6–2); *sf* Tel Aviv (d. Solomon, Lapidus, Jelen, lost Gilbert), *sf* Houston (d. Krishnan, Moor, Dickson, lost Curren); *qf* Memphis (d. Scanlon, Pate 6–1 fs, Becker 6–4 fs, lost Noah 6–3 fs). *1985 HIGHLIGHTS – DOUBLES:* (with Mansdorf) *r/u* South African Open (d. Delatte/DePalmer, lost Dowdeswell/Van Rensburg).

SHARON WALSH PETE (USA)
Born San Francisco, 24 February, 24 February, 1952; lives Incline Village, Na.; RH; 5ft 8in; 140lb; final 1985 WTA ranking 130 (38) singles, 12 doubles; 1985 prize money $87,025.
A classic Californian serve-and-volley player, she was a finalist at Australian Open in 1979. She was leading US jun in 1970, but seemed to lose confidence when she began entering women's tournaments, yet she has maintained a good standard of play through the years. After a highly successful partnership with Barbara Potter, with whom she reached f 1982 US Open and sf Wimbledon 1983, she started a new alliance with King, reaching sf US and Australian Opens. Meanwhile, Walsh played exceedingly well on the Casals over-30 tour and the hard work lifted her standard on the main tour. In doubles in 1983 she won 6 tournaments with 4 different partners. No wonder many believe she has one of the best forehand volleys in the game. Turning 32 in 1984 she continued to perform exceptionally well in singles and doubles reaching qf Australian Open. She played mostly with Potter in doubles, and with 4 different partners she won 3 tournaments and reached 6 other f. A major force again in doubles in 1985, she reached qf Wimbledon and US Open with Potter. **1985 HIGHLIGHTS – SINGLES: Wimbledon** 1r (lost Van Nostrand 7–5 6–3), **US Open** 1r (lost Herr 6–3 6–2), **Australian Open** 1r (lost K. Maleeva 7–5 6–4); **qf** VS Denver (d. Skuherska, Nagelsen 7–5 fs, lost Louie), **qf** Melbourne (d. Vermaak, Gerken 7–6 fs, lost K. Jordan). **1985 HIGHLIGHTS – DOUBLES:** (with Potter) **Wimbledon** qf, seed 5 (lost Kohde-Kilsch/Sukova 7–6 4–6 6–3), **US Open** qf, seed 5 (d. Mesker/Paradis 3–6 6–1 7–6, lost Kohde-Kilsch/Sukova 6–7 6–4 6–2), **Australian Open** sf (d. Garrison/Wade 6–3 3–6 6–3, lost Kohde-Kilsch/Sukova 3–6 6–4 6–1); **won** VS Dallas (d. Mesker/Paradis); **r/u** Sydney Indoor (d. Jordan/Moulton, lost Shriver/Smylie 7–5 7–5); **sf** LIPC (d. Moulton/P. Smith, lost G. Fernandez/Navratilova 7–5 fs). **CAREER HIGHLIGHTS – SINGLES: Australian Open – r/u 1979** seed 4 (d. Mesker 6–7 6–2 6–4, Gurdal, Sawyer, lost B. Jordan [seed 5] 6–3 6–3). **CAREER HIGHLIGHTS – DOUBLES: US CC –** [P. Hogan] **won 1973** (d. Bonicelli/I. Fernandez 6–4 6–4); **US Open –** [Potter] r/u 1982 (d. Navratilova/Shriver 7–5 2–6 6–4, lost Casals/Turnbull 6–3 6–4); **Italian Open –** [Bruning] **r/u 1977** (lost Cuypers/Kruger 3–6 7–5 6–2); **French Open –** [Piatek] **sf 1982** (lost Casals/Turnbull 6–3 fs); **Wimbledon –** [Potter] **sf 1983** (lost Casals/Turnbull 6–1 6–7 6–4), **sf 1984** (lost K. Jordan/A. Smith 3–6 6–3 6–2); **US Open –** [King] **sf 1983** (lost Fairbank/Reynolds 7–6 2–6 7–5); **Australian Open –** [Potter] **sf 1982** (lost Kohde-Kilsch/Pfaff 5–7 7–5 7–6), [King] **sf 1983** (lost Hobbs/Turnbull 6–4 6–1), **sf 1984** (lost Kohde-Kilsch/Sukova 6–3 6–4), **sf 1985**.

EVA PFAFF (West Germany)
Born Konigstein, 10 February, 1961, and lives there; RH; 5ft 9in; 144lb; final 1985 WTA ranking 31 (31) singles, 17 doubles; 1985 prize money $38,122.
One of the strongest women on the tour, she improved immensely in 1983, being one of the few even to threaten Navratilova, holding 2 m-ps before losing last 16 Canadian Open. But in 1984 she lost ground as an early-season injury kept her out of action. She competed in only 14 events and was unable to produce her best tennis, lacking the consistency to move into the upper echelons. In doubles, though, she was successful with Bunge. After being sidelined again from Feb–March 1985, she endured five consecutive 1r losses, but found her form in Newport when she reached sf. She then fell victim again to injuries after the US Open. **1985 HIGHLIGHTS – SINGLES: French Open** 1r (lost Sukova [seed 5] 6–1 6–2), **Wimbledon** 2r (d. Foltz 6–3 6–3, lost R. White 6–3 6–2), **US Open** 1r (lost Hu Na 6–4 6–4); **sf** Newport (d. Mesker, Gates, Cordwell, lost Evert Lloyd 7–5 6–2); **qf** VS LA (d. Sukova 6–4 6–2, lost Bassett 6–2 fs). **1985 HIGHLIGHTS – DOUBLES:** (with Bunge) **French Open** qf (lost Nagelsen/White 6–1 6–2); **r/u** Swiss Open (d. Burgin/Horvath, lost Gadusek/Sukova); **sf** VS LA (lost Mandlikova/Turnbull), **sf** German Open (d. McNeil/Vanier, lost Graf/Tanvier). **CAREER HIGHLIGHTS – SINGLES: Australian Open – qf 1982** (d. Mandlikova, Durie, lost Jaeger 7–5 6–2).

HANK PFISTER (USA)
Born Bakersfield, Cal., 9 October, 1953; lives Los Gatos, Cal. with wife Kim; RH; 6ft 4in; 185lb; final 1985 ATP ranking 68 (87); 1985 prize money $47,300.
An aggressive player, with one of the best forehands in the game, he has twice won French Open doubles – with Gene Mayer in 1978 and Amaya in 1980. He had an excellent

David Pate was a surprise semi-finalist at Wembley, where he beat Nystrom and took a set off Lendl. *(T. Hindley)*

record when playing for San José State College, and in 1977 he gave notice of his real potential when he beat Smith, Tanner and Nastase to reach sf Nottingham. He had another spectacular week in 1978 at Las Vegas when he downed Ashe, Connors and Tanner on his way to sf, and Vilas was his victim at Sydney in 1979. At Wimbledon in 1980 he upset 14th seed Amaya and reached last 16; at US Open he scored a tremendous upset victory over fifth-seeded Gerulaitis only to lose to Mottram in last 32. He lifted himself back into the top 25 in 1981 with a strong finish, highlighted by reaching sf Australian Open where he was r/u in doubles with Sadri. For the second year in a row, in 1982, he reached sf Australian Open, but m-p slipped away against Denton. However, he did win the grass-court title at Newport, and with Amaya was r/u US Open doubles. Although out of action for much of the latter part of 1983 he did not slip in rankings, but was less fortunate in 1984 and considered quitting the game when injuries plagued him. However, he was r/u at Columbus and still remained in the top 100. He struggled again in 1985, but reaching sf Cleveland and qf Cincinnati helped him improve his standing in the top 100. **1985 HIGHLIGHTS – SINGLES: Wimbledon** 1r (lost Becker 4–6 6–3 6–2 6–4), **US Open** 2r (d. McCain 6–3 6–4 6–4, lost Connors [seed 3] 6–3 6–4 6–2); **sf** Cleveland (d. Pimek, Acuna, lost Drewett); **qf** Cincinnati (d. Sundstrom 6–0 6–1, lost Becker 6–4 fs). **1985 HIGHLIGHTS – DOUBLES:** (with Testerman) **r/u** Houston (lost McEnroe/Fleming), **r/u** Cleveland (d. Gilbert/J. Levine, lost Palin/Rahnasto).

TERRY PHELPS (USA)
Born Brooklyn, 18 December, 1966; lives Larchmont, NY; RH; 2HB; 5ft 8in; 132lb; final 1985 WTA ranking 29 (26); 1985 prize money $74,788.
Ranked third US 16s in 1982, she began testing herself on the women's circuit that year, but her real surge came in 1983 when she moved up 53 places, playing with confidence and determination throughout. Through a long and eventful 1984 she moved quietly forward, playing in 27 events and driving her way into the top 30 by the time she reached her 18th birthday. Although it is not reflected in her ranking, she was perhaps one of the most improved players in 1985. She reached qf French Open upsetting Bassett, beat Rehe and Potter at US Open, and took a set off Navratilova in Fort Lauderdale. Yet in 22 tournaments, she reached qf in only four. **1985 HIGHLIGHTS – SINGLES: French Open** qf, unseeded (d. Uys 6–4 6–4, Derly 6–3 6–2, Tauziat 6–3 4–6 6–2, Bassett [seed 8] 4–6 6–0 6–2, lost Evert Lloyd [seed 2] 6–4 6–0), **Wimbledon** 2r (d. Skronska 6–3 6–3, lost Garrison [seed 8] 6–3 6–1), **US Open** 3r (d. Rehe 6–1 6–4, Potter 5–7 7–5 6–3, lost Jordan 7–5 6–1); **sf** Palm Beach (d. K. Maleeva, Mascarin, Foltz, lost Delhees Jauch); **qf** Fort Lauderdale (d. Kelesi, lost Navratilova 6–3 fs). **CAREER HIGHLIGHTS – SINGLES: French Open – qf 1985**.

MARY LOU PIATEK (USA)
Born Whiting, Ind., 6 August, 1961; lives Munster, Ind.; single; RH; 2HB; 5ft 6in; 125lb; final 1985 WTA ranking 61 (60); 1985 prize money $53,301.
Ranked 1 in US 18s in 1979, she won Wimbledon and Italian Jun titles that year and was finalist at US and French Jun. She went to Trinity Univ. in autumn 1979 and had a good season, turning pro in summer 1980. This impressive back-court shot-maker was among the world top 20 in 1981, the top 40 in 1982, but by the end of 1983 her ranking had slipped to 64, the problem seeming to be a lack of mental toughness in close matches. She played some better matches in 1984, restoring some of her old confidence with success in secondary tournaments, but she lacked consistency as she did in 1985. **1985 HIGHLIGHTS – SINGLES: Wimbledon** 1r (lost Evert Lloyd [seed 1] 6–1 6–0), **US Open** 2r (d. Jolissaint 6–2 6–4, lost Kim 7–6 7–6); **sf** VS San Diego (d. R. White 6–4 fs, Hu Na, lost Turnbull); **qf** VS Denver (d. Inoue 6–4 fs, Gomer, lost Sabatini), **qf** VS Houston (d. Okagawa, lost Sukova), **qf** VS Indianapolis (d. A. Holton, lost Gadusek). **CAREER HIGHLIGHTS – DOUBLES: French Open** – [Walsh] **sf 1982** (d. Madruga Osses/Tanvier 7–6 6–4, lost Casals/Turnbull 6–0 2–6 6–3); **Wimbledon** – [Leand] **qf 1983** (lost Casals/Turnbull 6–3 5–7 6–2).

LIBOR PIMEK (Czechoslovakia)
Born Most, 3 August, 1963; lives Ostrava; RH; 6ft 5in; 172lb; final 1985 ATP ranking 34 (25); 1985 prize money $117,978.
This tall and wiry player was perhaps the most surprising member of the top 60 in 1983, although his schedule was arranged shrewdly to allow him to exploit his CC skills, as it was in 1984, which he concluded as a member of the top 25. He slipped a little in 1985 but continued to enjoy some first-rate results. *1985 HIGHLIGHTS – SINGLES: French Open* 1r (lost Noah [seed 9] 6–7 6–1 7–5 6–4), *US Open* 1r (lost Purcell 6–3 6–4 6–2); *r/u* Vienna (d. Jaite 6–3 fs, Maurer, lost Gunnarsson 7–5 fs); *sf* La Quinta (d. Pecci, Lutz, Higueras, Lloyd 6–4 fs, lost Pate), sf Basle (d. Prpic, Wilkison 6–1 fs, Mecir 6–2 fs, lost Noah 7–5 fs); *qf* Monte Carlo (d. Jaite, lost Wilander), *qf* US Pro (d. Wilkison, lost Vilas), *qf* Bordeaux (d. Courteau, lost Tulasne), *qf* Toulouse (d. Tulasne, lost Forget). *1985 HIGHLIGHTS – DOUBLES:* (with Zivojinovic unless stated) *won* US Pro (d. McNamara/McNamee 7–6 fs); [Willenborg] *r/u* Bordeaux (lost Felgate/Shaw); *sf* US CC (d. Miller/Warder, lost Slozil/Warwick).

CLAUDIO PISTOLESI (Italy)
Born Rome, 25 August, 1967, and lives there; RH; 5ft 9in; 168lb; final 1985 ATP ranking 207 (—); 1985 prize money $8,914.
Although he was r/u Italian Jun and European Jun, he won no major jun championships in 1985 until he captured Orange Bowl 18s in Dec, which gave him the top ITF Jun ranking. *1985 HIGHLIGHTS – SINGLES: won* Orange Bowl (d. Oresar 6–2 6–0); *qf* Bari (d. Navratil, Freeman, lost C. Panatta), *qf* Palermo (d. Bates, Casal, lost Tulasne).

BARBARA POTTER (USA)
Born Waterbury, Conn., 22 October, 1961; lives Woodbury, Conn.; LH; 5ft 9in; 135lb; final 1985 WTA ranking 17 (12) singles, 9 doubles; 1985 prize money $128,060.
A strong lefthander with one of the best serves in the women's game, she is one of the most dangerous players on a fast surface, and twice extended Austin (Wimbledon and Tucson) in 1980. A pro since Jan. 1979, she upset 12th seed Barker at US Open that year. As a junior, she won US Nat 16 doubles and Nat 18 Indoor doubles. Her move up the computer from 10 to 8 in 1982 can be attributed to dedication and improvement and, although her record trailed off late in the season, she had matured as a competitor and had passed her first W Cup test. Playing No. 2 singles, she routed Barker, then recovered from a set down and 1–5 in 2s t-b to beat Durie and clinch the team victory for the US. Despite another qf appearance at Wimbledon 1983 it was simply not her year, but she fared better in 1984, beating Shriver, Garrison, Rinaldi, Temesvari and Sukova. In 1985, she played a less protected schedule and her ranking suffered, but she probably emerged a better player. Effective as usual on fast courts, she beat Lindqvist 1r Wimbledon, where she lost to Evert Lloyd in qf, as she had done in 1982. After removing Sabatini in 1r US Open, she was halted in 3s by Phelps in 2r. Yet she won her first tournament in three years when she took VS Central NY. *1985 HIGHLIGHTS – SINGLES: French Open* 1r, seed 12 (lost Scheuer-Larsen 6–3 6–1), *Wimbledon* qf, unseeded (d. Lindqvist [seed 12] 6–0 7–5, Gomer 6–4 7–5, Fendick 7–6 6–1, Durie 7–6 6–7 6–1, lost Evert Lloyd [seed 1] 6–2 6–1), *US Open* 2r (d. Sabatini [seed 10] 6–4 6–2, lost Phelps 5–7 7–5 6–3); *won* VS Central NY (d. Croft 6–4 7–6, Cecchini, Hanika, Kelesi 4–6 6–3 6–2); *sf* Melbourne (d. Antonoplis 6–3 fs, Fairbank, lost K. Jordan); *qf* LIPC (d. Budarova, Jauch, McNeil, Drescher, lost Evert Lloyd 6–1 fs), *qf* VS California (d. Bunge, R. White, lost Garrison 6–1 fs), *qf* Hilton Head (lost M. Maleeva), *qf* Sydney Indoor (d. Gomer, lost G. Fernandez), *qf* Eastbourne (d. Lindqvist 6–3 fs, lost Sukova), *qf* VS Chicago (d. Fendick, Russell 7–6 7–6, lost Turnbull 6–3 fs), *qf* Brighton (d. Karlsson, lost M. Maleeva). *1985 HIGHLIGHTS – DOUBLES:* (with Walsh Pete unless stated) *Wimbledon* qf, seed 5 (d. Mould/P. Smith 6–3 fs, lost Kohde-Kilsch/Sukova 7–6 4–6 6–3), *US Open* qf, seed 5 (d. Mesker/Paradis 3–6 6–1 7–6, lost Kohde-Kilsch/Sukova 6–7 6–4 6–2), *Australian Open* – sf (lost Kohde-Kilsch/Sukova 3–6 6–4 6–1); *won* VS Dallas (d. Mesker/Paradis 7–6 fs); *r/u* Sydney Indoor (d. K.

Jordan/Moulton, lost Shriver/Smylie), [Sukova] *r/u* Brighton (lost McNeil/Suire 6–4 fs); *sf* LIPC (d. Moulton/P. Smith, lost Fernandez/Navratilova 7–5 fs). *CAREER HIGHLIGHTS – SINGLES: US Open – sf 1981* (d. Leand, Gerken, lost Austin 6–1 6–3); *Wimbledon – qf 1982* (d. Shriver 6–2 6–4, lost Evert Lloyd 6–2 6–1), *qf 1983* (d. Benjamin 6–1 fs, Bonder 7–5 6–4, lost Jaeger 6–4 6–1), *qf 1985*; *Australian Open – qf 1984* (d. Temesvari, lost Navratilova 6–3 6–2). *CAREER HIGHLIGHTS – DOUBLES:* (with Walsh) *US Open – r/u 1982* (d. Navratilova/Shriver 7–5 2–6 6–4, lost Casals/Turnbull 6–3 6–4), *qf 1985*; *Wimbledon – sf 1983* (lost Casals/Turnbull 6–1 6–7 6–4), *sf 1984* (lost K. Jordan/A. Smith 3–6 6–3 6–2), *qf 1985*; *Australian Open – sf 1982* (lost Kohde-Kilsch/Pfaff 5–7 7–5 7–6), *sf 1984* (lost Kohde-Kilsch/Sukova), *sf 1985*. *MIXED DOUBLES:* (with Taygan) *US Open – r/u 1982* (lost Curren/A. Smith), *r/u 1983* (lost Fitzgerald/Sayers 3–6 6–3 6–4).

RAFFAELLA REGGI (Italy)
Born Faenza, 27 November, 1965; lives Ravenna; RH; 2HB; 5ft 5½in; 112lb; final 1985 WTA ranking 42 (62); 1985 prize money $56,099.
Ever since she won Orange Bowl 16s in 1981, it has been clear that she has a flair for the game. She was No. 1 in Italian 16s that year, by the end of 1982 had become the third-best player in the Italian women's division, and in 1983 she established herself as the best player in her country. In 1984, she was impressive early in the season when she reached sf Lugano, qf Italian Open and Florida, although she fell away later. She achieved her best record in 1985, upsetting Rinaldi on her way to last 16 French Open, winning a satellite event in Taranto over Vicki Nelson, reaching qf US CC, and f of another satellite event in Barcelona. *1985 HIGHLIGHTS – SINGLES: French Open* last 16, unseeded (d. Amiach 6–0 4–6 6–0, Jausovec 6–2 7–6, Rinaldi [seed 13] 6–2 6–0, lost Navratilova [seed 1] 6–4 6–1), *US Open* 2r (d. Karlsson 4–6 6–3 6–3, lost Evert Lloyd [seed 1] 6–0 6–3); *won* Taranto (d. Golder, Skronska, Nozzoli, Nelson 6–4 6–4); *r/u* Barcelona (d. Skronska 6–3 fs, Marsikova, lost Cecchini 6–3 6–4); *qf* US CC (d. Uys 6–2 fs, Nelson 6–3 fs, Kelesi 6–4 6–3, lost Temesvari 6–3 7–6), *qf* Stuttgart (d. Russell, Scheuer-Larsen 6–4 fs, lost Lindqvist 6–0 fs).

STEPHANIE REHE (USA)
Born Highland, Cal., November 5, 1969, and lives there; RH; 5ft 11in; 120lb; final 1985 WTA ranking 18 (—); 1985 prize money $68,539.
One of the best American jun players in recent years, she was ranked No. 1 in every age group in her country, winning national champs in 12s, 14s, 16s and 18s. In autumn 1985 she came into her own on the women's tour, capturing VS of Utah over a modest field and closing her season by upsetting Bassett and Sabatini to win Tampa. Those excellent performances lifted her into top 20 only months after she had turned pro. *1985 HIGHLIGHTS – SINGLES: Wimbledon* 3r (d. Jolissaint 6–4 6–3, Inoue 6–1 6–3, lost Graf [seed 11] 6–3 6–2), *US Open* 1r (lost Phelps 6–1 6–4); *won* VS Utah (d. J. Thompson 6–4 6–4, Kuhlman 6–3 6–2, Benjamin 6–2 6–4), *won* Tampa (d. Torres, Bassett 4–6 6–4 6–4, Sabatini 6–4 6–7 7–5); *qf* VS Pennsylvania (d. Tanvier, Shaefer, lost A. Minter 7–6 fs), *qf* Fort Lauderdale (d. Bonder, Sodupe, lost Graf 6–2 fs).

CANDY REYNOLDS (USA)
Born Wichita, Kan., 24 March, 1955; lives Knoxville, Tenn.; RH; 5ft 8in; 150lb; final 1985 WTA ranking 67 (109) singles, 26 (doubles); 1985 prize money $49,937.
A graduate of Univ. of Tennessee, she is one of the world's best doubles players and in 1981 played better singles, reaching sf US Indoor at Minnesota, where she beat Shriver and extended Austin to 3s. In one of 1982's biggest upsets in a major tournament, she beat Mandlikova *en route* to last 16 at Wimbledon and also reached last 16 Australian Open, but did little else in singles. In 1983, she made her Fed Cup début in singles and won 2 contests for the US, losing twice and playing with extraordinary courage and intensity. Although her ranking dropped 34 places, she still had a year to remember and captured the French Open doubles with Fairbank. In 1984 she did not have a particularly good year in singles but she was impressive in doubles again. In 1985 she moved up 42 places, despite a slow start with five straight 1r losses, salvaging her year with qf appearances in VS New Orleans and Indianapolis. *1985 HIGHLIGHTS – SINGLES: US*

Open (lost 1r qualifying Whytcross 3–6 7–6 6–4), *Australian Open* 1r (lost Nagelsen 4–6 6–3 8–6); *qf* VS New Orleans (d. Vermaak 6–2 fs, Gompert, lost Bonder 6–1 fs), *qf* VS Indianapolis (d. Thompson, C. Fernandez, lost Casale), *qf* New Zealand (d. Bartos, lost A. M. Fernandez 7–6 fs). *CAREER HIGHLIGHTS – DOUBLES:* (with P. Smith unless stated) *French Open* – [Fairbank] *won 1983* (d. Durie/Hobbs, K. Jordan/A. Smith 5–7 7–5 6–2), *r/u 1981* (d. Navratilova/Nagelsen, lost Fairbank/Harford 6–1 6–3); *Italian Open – won 1981* (d. Lloyd/Ruzici 7–5 6–1); *US Open* – [Fairbank] *r/u 1983* (d. King/Walsh, lost Navratilova/Shriver 6–4 7–5); *TS Champ – r/u 1982* (lost Navratilova/Shriver 6–4 7–5).

KATHY RINALDI (USA)
Born Jensen Beach, Fla., 24 March, 1967; lives Martin Downs, Fla.; single; RH; 2HB; 5ft 5½in; 110lb; final 1985 WTA ranking 11 (23); 1985 prize money $191,750.
In 1979 she became the first American girl ever to capture a 'Grand Slam' in the 12-and-under division: Nat 12 Indoor, Hard Court, Clay Court and 12 Nat Champ. The following year she won Nat 14 CC and was ranked 3 in the division for the year. In 1981 she became the youngest ever to reach qf of women's French Open and then, after becoming the youngest ever to win a match at Wimbledon (14 years 3 months), she turned pro in July, the youngest to do so. Thanks largely to a consistent record, particularly on clay and cement, she moved into the world top 20 in the first half of 1982 and was consistent again in 1983. In 1984, she slipped back out of the top 20, but showed some spark at the end of the season, taking a set off Navratilova in last 16 Australian Open. She followed up in 1985 with the greatest year of her career, finishing in most experts' top 10, despite her computer placing of 11. She won her first upper-level pro event in Mahwah, with hard-fought 3s triumphs over Lindqvist and Graf. At Wimbledon she proved she could play on grass by surging into sf with upset win over Sukova and during the year she also had wins over Mandlikova, Kohde-Kilsch, Graf, Garrison, and Lindqvist. Reunited with coach Andy Brandi, she seemed much more content with life on the pro circuit. *1985 HIGHLIGHTS – SINGLES: French Open* 3r, seed 13 (d. Mochizuki 6–4 6–0, Skronska 6–4 6–0, lost Reggi 6–2 6–0), *Wimbledon* sf, seed 16 (d. Betzner 6–3 7–5, Fairbank 7–5 6–4, Moulton 7–6 6–4, Smylie 6–2 6–1, Sukova [seed 7] 6–1 1–6 6–1), *US Open* 1r, seed 9 (lost Holikova 7–6 7–6); *won* Mahwah (d. Cordwell, Casale, Budarova, Lindqvist 6–1 fs, Graf 6–4 3–6 6–4); *r/u* VS Chicago (d. K. Jordan, lost Gadusek 6–1 6–3); *sf* VS Washington (d. Kohde-Kilsch 6–1 fs, Casale, Mandlikova 6–4 6–2, lost M. Maleeva 7–6 6–1), *sf* VS Champ (d. Bassett, K. Jordan, lost Sukova), *sf* German Open (d. Lindqvist 6–3 fs, lost Evert Lloyd), *sf* VS Indianapolis (d. Gurney, lost Casale 6–4 fs). *1985 HIGHLIGHTS – DOUBLES:* (with Garrison) *US Open* sf, unseeded (d. Bassett/Evert Lloyd 6–2 6–3, lost Kohde-Kilsch/Sukova 5–7 6–4 6–3). *CAREER HIGHLIGHTS – SINGLES: German Open – r/u 1982* (d. Jausovec 4–6 6–3 7–5, Hanika 6–3 7–5, lost Bunge 6–2 6–2), *sf 1984* (lost Kohde-Kilsch 6–4 6–0); *Wimbledon – sf 1985; French Open – qf 1981* (d. Fromholtz [seed 8], A. Smith [seed 11], lost Mandlikova [seed 4] 6–1 6–3). *CAREER HIGHLIGHTS – DOUBLES:* (with Garrison) *US Open – sf 1985*.

VIRGINIA RUZICI (Rumania)
Born Cimpai-Turzii, 31 January, 1955; lives Bucharest; single; RH; 5ft 8in; 128lb; final 1985 WTA ranking 41 (44); 1985 prize money $66,154; career prize money $1,161,627.
This colourful player and gifted athlete had her best year in 1978 when she won French Open. In 1980 she was French Open finalist and qualified for her second CS Champ. She was only slightly less consistent in 1981, but again was clearly a member of the world's top 10 and joined top eight in TS Champ. In 1982 she was magnificent in the summer, capturing US CC and Monte Carlo titles, although she again had to settle for a ranking just outside the top 10, one place higher than in 1981. She won Detroit in autumn 1983, but it was not one of her vintage years, and in 1984, despite a win over K. Jordan at French Open, to reach last 16 unseeded, her ranking continued to slip, the same being the case in 1985. *1985 HIGHLIGHTS – SINGLES: French Open* 1r (lost Horvath 6–4 2–6 6–3), *Wimbledon* 2r (d. Holton 4–6 6–4 7–5, lost Sukova [seed 7] 6–1 6–4), *US Open* 1r (lost Turnbull [seed 12] 6–4 6–1); *won* Bregenz (d. Marsikova 6–4 fs, Keppeler, Jausovec 6–2 6–3); *r/u* Seabrook (d. Dias 7–5 fs, Scheuer-Larsen, lost K. Maleeva 6–3 6–3); *qf* Hilton Head (d. Bassett 6–3 fs, lost Evert Lloyd), *qf* Amelia Island (d. Cecchini 7–6 fs, lost Mandlikova), *qf* Barcelona (lost Cecchini 7–5 fs). *1985 HIGHLIGHTS – DOUBLES:* (with

Horvath) *sf* German Open (lost Kohde-Kilsch/Sukova 6–1 fs), *sf* Marco Island (d. Bonder/Temesvari, lost Potter/Walsh Pete 6–1 fs). *CAREER HIGHLIGHTS – SINGLES: French Open – won 1978* (d. Bonicelli 8–6 fs, Simon, Jausovec 6–2 6–2), *rlu 1980* seed 8 (lost Evert Lloyd [seed 1] 6–0 6–3); *US CC – won 1982* (d. Madruga Osses, Gadusek, Sukova 6–2 6–0), *rlu 1981* (d. Mascarin, Marsikova, lost Jaeger 6–1 6–0); *Italian Open – rlu 1978* (lost Marsikova 7–5 7–5), *rlu 1980* (lost Evert Lloyd [seed 1] 5–7 6–2 6–2), *rlu 1981* (lost Evert Lloyd 6–1 6–2); *Canadian Open – rlu 1978* (lost Marsikova 7–5 6–7 6–2), *rlu 1980* (lost Evert Lloyd 6–3 6–1). *CAREER HIGHLIGHTS – DOUBLES:* (with Jausovec unless stated) *French Open – won 1978* (d. L. Bowrey/G. Lovera 5–7 6–4 8–6), [Horvath] *sf 1984* (lost Navratilova/Shriver 6–1 7–6); *Italian Open – won 1978* (d. Mihai/Nagelsen 6–2 2–6 7–5), [Wade] *won 1983* (d. Madruga Osses/Tanvier 6–3 2–6 6–1), [Evert Lloyd] *rlu 1981* (lost Reynolds/P. Smith 7–5 6–1, [Horvath] *rlu 1984* (lost Budarova/Skuherska 6–4 fs); *US CC* – [Russell] *won 1981* (d. Barker/P. Smith 6–2 6–2), [Horvath] *won 1983* (d. G. Fernandez/Herr 4–6 7–6 6–2), *rlu 1982* (lost Madruga Osses/Tanvier 7–5 7–6); *Wimbledon – rlu 1978* (lost Reid/Turnbull 4–6 9–8 6–3).

GABRIELA SABATINI (Argentina)
Born Buenos Aires, 16 April, 1970; lives Key Biscayne, Fla.; 5ft 7in; 129lb; final 1985 WTA ranking 12 (74); 1985 prize money $138,313.
The winner in 1984 of French and Italian Jun titles as well as Orange Bowl 18s, where she lost just 9 games in 6 matches, she was the top-ranked player in the world in that category and topped ITF Jun rankings. She began to assert herself in women's tournaments when she reached 3r US CC and US Open and was ranked 74 by the end of the year. A brilliant all-court player with long, fluid, sweeping groundstrokes, she is the best woman player her country has produced. As her coach, Patricio Apey, had predicted, she reached the top 10 during 1985 and finished the year ranked No. 12. She became the youngest semi-finalist in the history of French Open (15 yrs 2 months) when she beat M. Maleeva in 3s qf. In April she had a spectacular run in FC Cup where she upset Garrison, Shriver and M. Maleeva *en route* to f where she lost to Evert Lloyd, the last three matches being played on the same day. In the autumn she won her first tournament over a weak field at Japan Open, and all that remained to be answered about this eager and precocious player was how well could she adapt her game to the faster surfaces, for her 1985 successes were achieved almost entirely on clay. *1985 HIGHLIGHTS – SINGLES: French Open* sf, seed 14 (d. Drescher 6–2 6–2, Barg 6–0 6–2, A. White 6–1 7–6, Fairbank 6–0 1–6 7–5, M. Maleeva [seed 4] 6–3 1–6 6–1, lost Evert Lloyd [seed 2] 6–4 6–1), *Wimbledon* 3r, seed 15 (d. A. Brown 3–6 6–3 6–3, Benjamin 6–3 6–4, lost Tanvier 6–7 6–4 6–1), *US Open* 1r, seed 10 (lost Potter 6–4 6–2); *won* Japan Open (d. Holikova 6–0 6–1, Drescher 6–3 fs, Gates 6–3 6–4); *rlu* Hilton Head (d. Horvath, Garrison 6–4 6–0, Shriver 5–7 7–5 6–4, M. Maleeva 6–1 7–6, lost Evert Lloyd 6–4 6–0), *rlu* Tampa (d. Gurney 6–2 fs, Nelson, Casale, A. White, lost Rehe 6–4 6–7 7–5); *sf* VS Denver (d. McNeil 6–3 fs, Piatek, lost Louie 6–1 fs); *sf* US CC (d. Spence, lost Garrison), *sf* Mahwah (d. Shriver 7–5 6–4, lost Graf 6–3 fs). *CAREER HIGHLIGHTS – SINGLES: French Open – sf 1985*.

JOHN SADRI (USA)
Born Charlotte, 19 September, 1956 and lives there; single; RH; 6ft 2in; 180lb; final 1985 ATP ranking 46 (30); 1985 prize money $128,049.
After a poor 1983 he returned to the top 50 in 1984, thanks to a qf appearance at Wimbledon. In 1985 he held his ground, but seemed unable to produce the serving power that had taken him to the final of the 1979 Australian Open. *1985 HIGHLIGHTS – SINGLES: Wimbledon* 2r (d. Motta 6–3 6–2 6–3, lost Gerulaitis 5–7 6–4 3–6 7–6 6–4), *US Open* 1r (lost Mansdorf 7–6 4–6 7–6 6–1), *Australian Open* 3r (d. Drewett 6–7 7–6 7–6 6–3, lost Leconte 7–6 6–3 7–6); *rlu* Newport (d. Lapidus, R. Simpson, S. Davis 6–3 7–5, Mayotte 6–4 6–3, lost Tom Gullikson); *qf* Rotterdam (d. Fibak, Wilander 6–3 fs, lost Smid), *qf* Milan (d. Green, Slozil, lost Jarryd), *qf* Johannesburg (d. Mansdorf, Visser, lost Anger). *CAREER HIGHLIGHTS – SINGLES: Australian Open – rlu 1979* (d. Warwick 9–7 fs, R. Frawley, Dibley, lost Vilas 7–6 6–3 6–2); *Wimbledon – qf 1984* (d. Gerulaitis 6–3 7–5 6–7 4–6 6–3, lost McEnroe [seed 1] 6–3 6–3 6–1).

EMILIO SANCHEZ (Spain)
Born Madrid, 29 May, 1965; lives Barcelona; RH; 5ft 7½in; 170lb; final 1985 ATP ranking 64 (112) singles, 27 doubles; 1985 prize money $84,372.
Runner-up at Orange Bowl in 1983, he made his mark in 1985 mainly in doubles with countryman Casal. **1985 HIGHLIGHTS – SINGLES: French Open** 3r (d. Prpic 6–3 5–7 2–6 6–1 6–0, Van Boeckel 6–1 6–2 6–4, lost Wilander [seed 4] 3–6 6–4 6–3 6–3); **qf** Munich (d. Elter, Aguilera, lost Perez), **qf** Kitzbuhel (d. Nystrom, Bottazzi, Meinecke, lost Casal), **qf** Barcelona (lost Leconte 6–4 6–4). **1985 HIGHLIGHTS – DOUBLES:** (with Casal) **won** Kitzbuhel (d. Cane/Panatta), **won** Barcelona (d. Gunnarsson/Mortensen 6–3 6–3); **r/u** Munich (lost Edmondson/Warwick), **r/u** Bastad (lost Edberg/Jarryd), **r/u** Palermo (lost Dowdeswell/Nystrom).

LARISA SAVCHENKO (USSR)
Born Lvov, Ukraine, 21 July, 1966, and lives there; RH; 5ft 2in; 139lb; final 1985 WTA ranking 55 (138) singles, 19 doubles; 1985 prize money $44,750.
An outstanding doubles player, in 1985 she reached third straight Wimbledon doubles qf with countrywoman Cherneva. But her progress in singles was even more remarkable as she upset K. Jordan at Wimbledon and Moulton in Australia, ending her season with a win over Croft in Sydney. **1985 HIGHLIGHTS – SINGLES: French Open** 1r (lost Lindqvist [seed 9] 6–2 6–3), **Wimbledon** 3r (d. Goles 6–1 4–6 6–3, K. Jordan [seed 10] 7–5 3–6 6–3, lost Van Nostrand 7–6 3–6 7–5); **sf** VS Denver (d. R. White 6–2 fs, lost Garrison); **qf** Brisbane (d. Moulton 6–4 fs, lost Shriver). **1985 HIGHLIGHTS – DOUBLES:** (with Cherneva) **Wimbledon** qf, seed 6 (d. Demongeot/Tauziat 4–6 7–6 6–2, lost Mandlikova/Turnbull 6–4 6–3); **r/u** VS Florida (lost K. Jordan/Smylie 6–4 7–6).

MICHIEL SCHAPERS (Netherlands)
Born Rotterdam, 11 October, 1959 and lives there; single; RH; 6ft 7in; 176lb; final 1985 ATP ranking 100 (78); 1985 prize money $50,284.
The winner of Dutch Nat Indoor in 1982 and Dutch Nat Outdoor the following year, he moved up 29 places in the world rankings in 1984. In 1985, he saved his best for last, upending Becker in 2r Australian Open where he reached first GS qf. Otherwise he missed French Open, Wimbledon and US Open, and in 15 tournaments had advanced beyond 2r only once. **1985 HIGHLIGHTS – SINGLES: Australian Open** qf, unseeded (d. Popp 6–1 6–7 6–3 1–6 6–3, Becker [seed 4] 3–6 6–4 7–6 4–6 6–3, Van Boeckel 6–2 6–4 7–6, Tim Gullikson 7–6 ret'd, lost Edberg [seed 5] 6–0 7–5 6–4); **qf** Hilversum (d. Sundstrom, lost Oosting).

TINE SCHEUER-LARSEN (Denmark)
Born Olysykke, 13 March, 1966 and lives there; RH; 5ft 6in; 138lb; final 1985 WTA ranking 53 (73); 1985 prize money $41,635.
Winner of Danish Nat Jun Champs four times between 1978 and 1982, she spent most of her time on the satellite circuit in 1983, but in 1984 moved up to a higher level. In 1985, she competed admirably, making her mark despite two 1r losses at start of year and four in the middle of the season. She reached last 16 French Open, sf Seabrook and Hilversum, and moved up 20 places on the computer. **1985 HIGHLIGHTS – SINGLES: French Open** last 16, unseeded (d. Potter [seed 12] 6–3 6–1, Herr 6–3 6–1, Horvath 6–1 4–6 6–1, lost Cecchini 6–3 6–2), **Wimbledon** 1r (lost Mascarin 7–6 3–6 6–3), **US Open** 1r (lost Shriver [seed 4] 6–3 6–3); **sf** Seabrook (d. Spence, lost Ruzici), **sf** Hilversum (d. Cecchini, Huber, lost Karlsson); **qf** Palm Beach (d. Russell, lost Reggi).

MYRIAM SCHROPP (West Germany)
Born Mannheim, 4 April, 1966; lives Hockheim; RH; 5ft 6in; 132lb; final 1985 WTA ranking 97 (54); 1985 prize money $36,593.
A pro since she was 15, she continued to combine jun and women's competition in 1984. One of her best wins was an upset of Sabatini at US Open Jun, but she also upset Tanvier in 1r Australian Open. Already ranked No. 8 in Germany for 1983, she progressed 100 notches on the WTA computer, and in 1985 she beat M. Maleeva at Dallas and Budarova in Marco Island, gaining valuable experience on tour, although her ranking

slipped. *1985 HIGHLIGHTS – SINGLES: French Open* 1r (lost A. Minter 6–2 6–2), *Wimbledon* 1r (lost Fairbank 7–5 6–4), *US Open* 1r (lost Werdel 6–2 6–4), *Australian Open* 2r (d. Mesker 6–3 6–4, lost M. Maleeva [seed 7] 6–2 6–3).

BUD SCHULTZ (USA)
Born Meriden, Conn., 21 August, 1959; lives Boston; RH; 6ft 4in; 190lb; final 1985 ATP ranking 43 (188); 1985 prize money $85,288.
One of the least recognised but most improved members of the top 50 in the world in 1985, he claimed Jarryd and Holmes as two of his major victims and played with increasing assurance. *1985 HIGHLIGHTS – SINGLES: Wimbledon* 2r (d. Krickstein 6–4 3–6 7–6 6–4, lost Holmes 6–4 6–7 6–2 6–3), *US Open* 3r (d. M. Leach 7–6 6–4 6–2, Matuszewski 6–3 6–4 7–6, lost McEnroe [seed 1] 6–0 7–6 6–1); *sf* Cleveland (d. Holmes, Bauer, lost Gilbert); *qf* Toronto Indoor (d. Sadri, lost Curren), *qf* Brisbane (d. Cassidy, lost Evernden). *1985 HIGHLIGHTS – DOUBLES:* (with Testerman) *r1u* Brisbane (d. Bourne/Dyke, lost M. Davis/Drewett).

HANS SCHWAIER (West Germany)
Born Mindelheim, 24 March, 1964; lives Badwörishofen; single; 5ft 10in; 158lb; final 1985 ATP ranking 47 (89); 1985 prize money $96,264.
In 1984, he enjoyed a fruitful autumn, including a particularly good win over Smid in Barcelona, and in 1985 he enjoyed a sparkling early season before coasting through the year to finish in top 50 for first time. A diligent CC player, he scored a crucial win over Krickstein to give Germany a 2–0 lead over US in D Cup qf. Time and again he looked out of position as Krickstein drove him from corner to corner, but, as so often, his excellent defensive play prevailed. *1985 HIGHLIGHTS – SINGLES: French Open* 1r (lost Cancellotti 6–3 6–2 6–7 3–6 6–0), *Wimbledon* 2r (d. Van't Hof 6–3 6–2 6–4, lost Maurer 6–3 7–5 7–5), *US Open* 3r (d. Taroczy 6–7 6–4 7–6 7–6, Mmoh 5–7 6–7 7–5 7–6 6–3, lost Leconte 6–2 6–2 6–1); *r1u* Munich (d. Eberhard, Perez, lost Nystrom); *sf* Nice (d. J. Brown, Zivojinovic, lost Leconte), *sf* Bari (d. Sanchez, de la Pena, lost Duncan); *qf* Basle (d. Dickson, Gunthardt, lost Edberg).

FLORIN SEGARCEANU (Rumania)
Born Bucharest, 29 March, 1961, and lives there; RH; 5ft 11in; 145lb; final 1985 ATP ranking 97 (209); 1985 prize money $25,138.
He is a stylish shotmaker, who has been a member of the Rumanian D Cup team since 1979 and made a steady rise in the international game. Ranked 215 in the world at the end of 1981, he moved up to 125 the following year and cracked the top 100 in 1983, when he gave eventual champion McEnroe cause for concern at Wimbledon when he took the first set of their 2r contest. He faded to 209 in 1984, but returned to the top 100 in 1985. *1985 HIGHLIGHTS – SINGLES: French Open* 2r (d. Annacone 7–5 6–7 7–6 6–2, lost McEnroe 6–2 6–4 6–4).

ROBERT SEGUSO (USA)
Born Minneapolis, 1 May, 1963; lives Sunrise, Fla.; RH; 6ft 3in; 182lb; final 1985 ATP ranking 56 (208) singles, 1 (16) doubles; 1985 prize money $394,908.
An All-American with Flach at Southern Illinois Univ. in 1983, with whom he won several doubles titles in his first full year on the pro tour in 1984, including the WCT London title at end of season which earned them a Masters place. In 1985, he won US Open with Flach and made remarkable strides in singles. The Flach-Seguso duo were again victorious in seven events on the GP tour. *1985 HIGHLIGHTS – SINGLES: Wimbledon* last 16, unseeded (d. Harmon 6–4 6–3 6–0, Bauer 6–3 6–4 6–4, Tom Gullikson 4–6 6–3 7–5 6–2, lost Acuna 6–4 7–6 6–2), *US Open* 1r (lost Canter 4–6 6–4 6–3 6–4); *sf* Stratton Mountain (d. Kriek 7–6 7–6, Masur 7–5 fs, Dowdeswell 6–4 fs, S. Davis 6–2 7–6, lost McEnroe). *1985 HIGHLIGHTS – DOUBLES:* (with Flach) *French Open* qf, seed 2 (d. Mustard/J. Smith 6–3 6–3, lost Glickstein/H. Simonsson 6–2 6–2), *Wimbledon* 1r, seed 3 (lost Felgate/Brown 7–6 6–3 2–6 7–6), *won US Open* seed 1 (d. Leconte/Noah 7–6 6–7 7–5 6–0); *won* Fort Myers (d. S. Giammalva/Pate 6–2 fs), *won* WCT Forest Hills (d. Gerulaitis/McEnroe 6–4 fs, Barbosa/Kley 7–5 6–2), *won* Queens Club (d. Cash/Fitzgerald

16–14 fs), **won** US CC (d. Slozil/Warwick 6–4 6–4), **won** Canadian Open (d. Edberg/Jarryd 5–7 7–6 6–3), **won** Tokyo Seiko (d. S. Davis/Pate 7–6 fs). *CAREER HIGHLIGHTS – DOUBLES:* (with Flach) *US Open – won 1985*; *Italian Open – won 1984* (d. Alexander/M. Leach 3–6 6–3 6–4).

KIM JONES SHAEFER (USA)
Born Columbus, Ga., 28 September, 1957; lives Alexandria, Va.; married to Len Shaefer, a computer expert; RH; 5ft 8in; 135lb; final 1985 WTA ranking 60 (66); 1985 prize money $40,573.
With almost no warning, she came through a strong field to win the 1983 US Indoor, beating Ruzici, Garrison, Shriver and Hanika, the latter being easily dismissed in front of a US TV audience. Although she did not play with that kind of audacity for the rest of the year, she proved that she can clearly be an outstanding tennis player. Her record in 1984 and 1985 was reasonably good but she could not match her golden week of 1983. Nevertheless, she increased her activities by serving on the board of the WTA where she took on a significant role on the computer-ranking committee, and 1985 finished on a happy note when she learned she was expecting her first child in 1986. *1985 HIGHLIGHTS – SINGLES: Wimbledon* 1r (lost Durie 6–2 6–2), *US Open* 1r (lost Torres 7–6 6–7 6–2); *qf* VS New Orleans (d. Piatek, lost Evert Lloyd). *CAREER HIGHLIGHTS – SINGLES: US Indoor – won 1983* (d. Ruzici 2–6 6–3 6–2, Garrison 6–3 6–0, Shriver 6–3 3–6 6–0, Hanika 6–4 6–3).

STEPHEN SHAW (Great Britain)
Born Enfield, Middlesex, 1 January, 1963 and lives there; single; RH; 6ft 3in; 178lb; final 1985 ATP ranking 195 (119); 1985 prize money $37,226.
In 1984 he won $25,000 satellite event in Thessaloniki, was r/u at Sutton, and became a member of the British D Cup and King's Cup teams. Moving close to the neighbourhood of the top 100 by the end of 1984, he slipped back in 1985 and finished just on the sunny side of the top 200. *1985 HIGHLIGHTS – SINGLES: French Open* 1r (lost Zivojinovic 4–6 6–2 2–6 6–3 8–6), *Wimbledon* 1r (lost C. Lewis 6–4 6–2 6–3); *sf* Marbella (d. Ostoja, Perez, Ganzabal, lost de la Pena). *1985 HIGHLIGHTS – DOUBLES:* (with Felgate) *won* Bordeaux (d. Pimek/Willenborg).

PAM SHRIVER (USA)
Born Baltimore, 4 July, 1962; lives Lutherville, Md; single; RH; 5ft 11in; 130lb; final 1985 WTA ranking 4 (4) singles, 1 doubles; 1985 prize money $419,686; career prize money $2,106,584.
In summer 1978, aged 16, she stunned tennis world by reaching f US Open, beating Navratilova in two tense sf t-bs before losing f to Evert. The following year she suffered a nagging shoulder injury. Hurt her shoulder again in Adelaide in Dec. 1980, and was forced to pull out of tournament. Qualified for CS Finals but finished in last place. In 1981 she consolidated a place for herself in the world's top 7 and played with tremendous consistency throughout the year. She ended a long personal jinx by beating old jun rival Austin twice – in qf Wimbledon and Australian Open. With Navratilova formed top doubles pair in 1981, winning 9 titles from 11 finals (including Wimbledon) plus TS Champs. Troubled by illness in winter 1981–82, she did not compete with the same intensity and skill but she was one of only 3 players to beat Navratilova, coming from a set down and 2 points from defeat in qf 1982 US Open to stop her doubles partner. Meanwhile, she continued to prosper in doubles with Navratilova, winning a second Wimbledon crown and a first Australian. In 1983 she added a third consecutive Wimbledon and second straight Australian Open crown with Navratilova, and together they won their first US Open. In fact, the Navratilova/Shriver duo was beaten only once all year (by King/A. Smith in f Orlando) as they won 11 of 12 tournaments and 52 of 53 matches. In singles Shriver was very solid through the year, reaching sf US and Australian Opens for the second year in a row. In addition, she won Atlanta and Brisbane, and moved up to fourth in the world. She won Chicago and Birmingham at the beginning of the year but lost to Jordan in qf Wimbledon and fell unexpectedly to Turnbull in qf US Open. In between, she nearly beat Navratilova for the fourth time in her career, reaching b-p at 5–5

Australia's Elizabeth Sayers Smylie beat Mandlikova at Wimbledon where, with Kathy Jordan, she won the doubles, and later at the US Open she won the mixed with countryman John Fitzgerald. *(A. Evans)*

fs in f Mahwah. In doubles she and Navratilova extended their winning streak to 83 straight matches and seven consecutive GS tournaments from Wimbledon 1983, and with their triumph at the Australian Open they became the first women's doubles team to achieve a traditional calendar year Grand Slam. However, she grew tired of tennis, and wisely took a three-month break from the game after the Australian Open, returning in March 1985 to win more tournaments than she had in any other year. Her record was of a high order and only in the majors did she do less than expected. At Wimbledon, she reached qf where she fell to Navratilova, at US Open Graf stopped her in a brilliant qf struggle and Lindqvist surprised her in last 16 Australian Open. She picked up two more GS doubles titles with Navratilova to lift their total to 12, but they lost their bid for a fifth consecutive Wimbledon when they were halted in f by Smylie and Jordan, ending their record winning streak at an astounding 109 matches. In pursuit of a third straight US Open, they fell in the f to Kohde-Kilsch and Sukova, but they took their fourth Australian and second French crowns in a row. *1985 HIGHLIGHTS – SINGLES: Wimbledon* qf, seed 5 (d. A. White 6–3 6–7 6–3, Hobbs 6–3 6–2, Wade 6–2 5–7 6–2, Graf [seed 11] 3–6 6–2 6–4), lost Navratilova [seed 1] 7–6 6–3), *US Open* qf, seed 4 (d. Scheuer-Larsen 6–3 6–3, Hu Na 6–2 7–6, Hobbs 6–2 6–3, Moulton 6–2 6–4, lost Graf [seed 11] 7–6 6–7 7–6), *Australian Open* last 16, seed 4 (d. Holikova 6–3 6–3, Bryant 6–4 6–1, lost Lindqvist [seed 10] 3–6 6–3 6–2); *won* Sydney Indoor (d. Moulton, Balestrat 6–3 6–3), *won* Melbourne (d. Croft 7–6 6–2, K. Jordan 6–4 6–1), *won* Birmingham (d. Burgin, Nagelsen 6–1 6–0), *won* Stuttgart (d. Graf 6–4 6–3, Lindqvist 6–1 7–5); *r/u* VS Newport (d. Turnbull, lost Evert Lloyd 6–4 6–1), *r/u* VS LA (d. Garrison 7–6 6–4, lost Kohde-Kilsch 6–2 6–4), *r/u* VS New Orleans (d. Turnbull 6–2 6–0, A. White 6–3 6–2, lost Evert Lloyd 6–4 7–5), *r/u* Brisbane (d. Sukova 6–2 fs, lost Navratilova 6–4 7–5). *1985 HIGHLIGHTS – DOUBLES:* (with Navratilova unless stated) *won French Open* seed 1 (d. Nagelsen/A. White 6–3 6–4, Kohde-Kilsch/Sukova 4–6 6–2 6–2), *r/u Wimbledon* seed 1 (d. Mandlikova/Turnbull 6–4 6–2, lost K. Jordan/Smylie 5–7 6–3 6–4), *r/u US Open* seed 1 (d. Mandlikova/Turnbull 6–3 6–4, lost Kohde-Kilsch/Sukova 6–7 6–2 6–3), *won Australian Open* seed 1 (d. Durie/Hobbs 7–6 6–2, Kohde-Kilsch/Sukova 6–3 6–4); *won* US Indoor (d. Mesker/Smylie 7–5 6–2), *won* VS Champs (d. Kohde-Kilsch/Sukova 6–7 6–4 7–6), *won* Orlando (d. Burgin/Horvath), *won* Eastbourne (d. K. Jordan/Smylie 7–5 6–4), [Fairbank] *won* Hilton Head (d. Cherneva/Savchenko 6–4 6–1), *won* Brisbane (d. Kohde-Kilsch/Sukova 6–4 6–7 6–1); [Smylie] *r/u* Newport (lost Evert Lloyd/Turnbull). *CAREER HIGHLIGHTS – SINGLES: US Open – r/u 1978* (d. Reid, Hunt, Navratilova 7–6 7–6, lost Evert 7–5 6–4), *sf 1982* (d. Navratilova 1–6 7–6 6–2, lost Mandlikova 6–4 2–6 6–2), *sf 1983* (d. Jaeger 7–6 6–3, lost Navratilova 6–2 6–1); *Wimbledon – sf 1981* seed 7 (d. Ekblom, Little, Coles, Durie, Austin [seed 3] 7–5 6–4, lost Evert Lloyd [seed 1] 6–3 6–1); *Australian Open – sf 1981* seed 6 (d. Desfor, Durie, Austin [seed 2] 7–5 7–6, lost Navratilova [seed 3] 6–3 7–5), *sf 1982* (lost Navratilova 6–3 6–4, *sf 1983* (d. Bassett 6–0 6–1, lost Navratilova 6–4 6–3). *CAREER HIGHLIGHTS – DOUBLES:* (with Navratilova unless stated) *French Open – won 1984* (d. Kohde-Kilsch/Mandlikova 5–7 6–3 6–2), *won 1985*; *Wimbledon – won 1981* (d. K. Jordan/A. Smith 6–3 7–6), *won 1982* (d. K. Jordan/A. Smith 6–4 6–1), *won 1983* (d. Casals/Turnbull 6–2 6–2), *won 1984* (d. K. Jordan/A. Smith 6–3 6–4), *r/u 1985*; *US Open – won 1983* (d. Fairbank/Reynolds 6–7 6–1 6–3), *won 1984* (d. Turnbull/Hobbs 6–2 6–4), [Stove] *r/u 1980* (lost King/Navratilova 7–6 7–5), *r/u 1985*; *sf 1982* (lost Potter/Walsh 7–5 2–6 6–4); *Australian Open – won 1982* (d. Kohde/Pfaff 6–4 6–2), *won 1983* (d. Hobbs/Turnbull 6–4 6–7 6–2), *won 1984* (d. Kohde-Kilsch/Sukova 6–3 6–4), *won 1985, r/u 1981* (lost K. Jordan/A. Smith 6–2 7–5), *TS Champs – won 1982* (d. P. Smith/Reynolds 6–4 7–5).

KATERINA SKRONSKA (Czechoslovakia)
Born Prague, 22 January, 1958, and lives there; RH; 5ft 6in; 134lb; final 1985 WTA ranking 100 (79); 1985 prize money $30,799.
A student of economics in University in Prague, she has been a member of Czech Fed Cup since 1980 and turned pro in 1981. She dropped 21 places in 1985, but held on to the last slot in the top 100. *1985 HIGHLIGHTS – SINGLES: French Open* 2r (d. Kelesi 6–4 2–6 6–1), lost Rinaldi [seed 13] 6–4 6–0), *Wimbledon* 1r (lost Phelps 6–3 6–3), *US Open* 2r (d. Amiach 6–4 6–7 6–2, lost Torres 3–6 6–2 6–0); *qf* Taranto (d. Villagran, lost Reggi 6–4 fs).

PAVEL SLOZIL (Czechoslovakia)
Born Opava, 29 December, 1955; lives Prague with wife Jana and daughter Jane; 5ft 8in; 155lb; final 1985 ATP ranking 95 (40) singles, 20 (8) doubles; 1985 prize money $190,356.
Although overshadowed by Lendl, he is a fine ambassador for Czech tennis. In 1980 he played No. 2 singles behind Lendl on Czech D Cup team v Rumania and Argentina, helping to lead his country to its first-ever triumph in the competition. Selecting a schedule which kept him on clay most of 1982, he moved up into the world top 50. He was remarkably successful in doubles, winning 7 tournaments with 3 different partners (Smid, Stewart and Leconte). In 1983 he pulled off one of the year's largest upsets when he removed Lendl from 1r WCT Delray Beach, but otherwise he was less successful in singles than in 1982. However, his doubles skills were even more remarkable. He won 9 tournaments with 4 different partners (Smid, H. Gunthardt, C. Lewis and Fibak), and with Smid reached f Masters. In 1984, he picked up six more GP doubles titles with four different partners (Smid, Taygan, Wilkinson and Willenborg) but it was with his countryman Smid with whom he had his most regular success. In the meantime, he finished the year at his highest singles ranking of 40, which he was unable to maintain in 1985, when he concentrated on doubles, reaching Masters once more with Smid. ***1985 HIGHLIGHTS – SINGLES: French Open*** 1r (lost Gomez 6–1 3–6 6–3 6–3), ***Wimbledon*** 1r (lost Flach 6–3 6–7 6–1 7–6), *US Open* 2r (d. Gonzalez 6–3 6–4 6–4, lost Wilkison 6–1 6–3 6–1). ***1985 HIGHLIGHTS – DOUBLES:*** (with Smid unless stated) *won* Memphis (d. Curren/Denton), *won* Rotterdam (d. Nystrom/Wilander, Gerulaitis/McNamee), *won* Monte Carlo (d. Glickstein/Perkis), [C. Panatta] *won* Nice (d. Courteau/Forget); *r/u* Toulouse (lost Acuna/Hlasek), [Warwick] *r/u* Indianapolis (lost Flach/Seguso). *CAREER HIGHLIGHTS – DOUBLES:* (with Smid unless stated) *US Pro* – [Ramirez] *won 1981* (d. Gildemeister/Gomez 6–4 7–6); *German Open* – *won 1982* (d. Jarryd/Simonsson 6–4 6–3); *French Open* – *r/u 1984* (lost Leconte/Noah 6–4 2–6 3–6 6–3 6–2); *sf 1983* (lost Jarryd/Simonsson 6–2 6–4 6–4); *Masters* – *sf 1982* (d. Curren/Denton 7–6 7–6, lost McEnroe/Fleming 6–3 6–4).

TOMAS SMID (Czechoslovakia)
Born Plzen, 20 May, 1956; lives Prague; son Tomas (born 1979); RH; 6ft 3in; 175lb; final 1985 ATP ranking 19 (26) singles, 11 (1) doubles; 1985 prize money $394,460.
The third-best player in his country after Lendl (with whom he joined forces in 1980 to help Czechoslovakia win D Cup) and Mecir. Planning a schedule which brought out the best in him, Smid had a superb 1982 when he captured two WCT tournaments, was r/u at a third and on GP tour was twice a finalist. Qualified for Masters doubles with countryman Slozil. Moving into the world's top 20 in 1983, he was enormously consistent across the year, the only flaws in his record being losses in 2r French Open, 1r Wimbledon, and 2r US Open. He did reach qf Australian Open at the end of the year and at Masters he beat Noah and took a set off Connors, while in doubles with Slozil he lost in f to Fleming and McEnroe. In 1984 he reached Masters for the second year in a row and achieved more than his ranking reflects. Perhaps he might have made a bid for the top 10 had he played less, but he is an incurable 'workaholic' and he nosed out McEnroe from the No. 1 doubles position. Ubiquitous again in 1985, he won Geneva with a rare victory over Wilander and kept himself in the top 20 with a solid record, qualifying for Masters, where he lost 1r Lendl. Meanwhile, his doubles partnership with Slozil prospered and he won Stuttgart with Lendl. ***1985 HIGHLIGHTS – SINGLES: French Open*** last 16, seed 13 (d. Tous 7–6 6–3 6–3, Arguello 6–4 3–6 6–1 6–4, Cahill 6–2 6–1 6–1, lost Wilander [seed 4] 6–3 6–4 6–4), ***Wimbledon*** 2r (d. R. Simpson 6–4 6–7 7–5 7–6, lost Giammalva 6–3 6–1 6–2), *US Open* last 16, seed 16 (d. Flur 6–3 7–5 6–2, Vilas 6–2 6–2 6–1, Arias 4–6 1–6 6–3 6–3 7–6, lost McEnroe [seed 1] 6–3 7–5 6–2), *Australian Open* 2r, seed 11 (lost Lloyd 7–5 6–7 7–6 6–3); *won* Geneva (d. Aguilera, Wilander 6–4 6–4); *r/u* Toulouse (d. Benhabiles, Eriksson, Potier, Krishnan, lost Noah 6–4 6–4); *sf* LIPC (d. Van Patten 7–5 fs, Jarryd 6–1 6–4, Noah 6–3 6–3 7–5, lost S. Davis), *sf* Rotterdam (d. Gunthardt, Bale, Sadri, lost Hlasek), *sf* Milan (d. C. Panatta, Gerulaitis, lost Jarryd), *sf* Las Vegas (d. Becker 7–6 fs, lost Kriek), *sf* Stuttgart (lost Gilbert). ***1985 HIGHLIGHTS – DOUBLES:*** (with Slozil unless stated) *won* Memphis (d. Curren/Denton), *won* Rotterdam (d. Nystrom/Wilander, Gerulaitis/McNamee), *won* Monte Carlo (d. Glickstein/Perkis), [Fibak] *won* Gstaad (d. Drewett/Edmondson), [Lendl] *won* Stuttgart (d. Kohlberg/Soares); [Denton] *r/u* Atlanta

(lost Annacone/Van Rensburg), *r/u* Toulouse (lost Acuna/Hlasek). *CAREER HIGHLIGHTS – SINGLES: Wimbledon – qf 1984* (lost Lendl 6–1 7–6 6–3), *Australian Open – qf 1983* (d. Fitzgerald, lost Lendl [seed 1] 7–6 2–6 6–1 6–2). *CAREER HIGHLIGHTS – DOUBLES: US Open* – [Fitzgerald] *won 1984* (d. Edberg/Jarryd 7–6 6–3 6–3); *Italian Open* [Fleming] *won 1979* (d. Clerc/Nastase 7–5 fs), [Manson] *r/u 1981* (lost Gildemeister/Gomez 7–5 6–2); *German Open* – [Slozil] *won 1982* (d. Jarryd/H. Simonsson 6–4 6–3); *French Open* – [Slozil] *r/u 1984* (lost Leconte/Noah 6–4 2–6 3–6 6–3 6–2); *Masters* – [Slozil] *r/u 1983* (lost McEnroe/Fleming 6–2 6–2).

ELIZABETH SAYERS SMYLIE (Australia)
Born Perth, 1 April, 1963; lives Hilton Head, SC; RH; 5ft 7in; 128lb; final 1985 WTA ranking 43 (31) singles, 7 doubles; 1985 prize money $171,469.
She was considered one of the 10 best jun in 1981, and has wins to her credit over Temesvari, Jausovec and Barker. A first-rate doubles player, she captured US Open mixed doubles crown with fellow-Australian Fitzgerald in 1983 and while her prowess in doubles was increasingly evident in 1984, she also made notable progress in singles and was married during the year to Peter Smylie, a tennis pro at Palmetto Dunes in Hilton Head. In 1985, she entered a new realm as a singles player, dismissing Mandlikova at Wimbledon, but her doubles play was outstanding. Forming a new partnership with K. Jordan, she won Wimbledon and they became the first pair to beat the Navratilova/Shriver duo in more than two years and 109 matches. The emergence of Smylie and Jordan along with the advance of Sukova and Kohde-Kilsch added new life to women's doubles at the top. *1985 HIGHLIGHTS – SINGLES: Wimbledon* last 16, unseeded (d. Leand 6–1 6–2, Russell 6–4 6–2, Mandlikova [seed 3] 6–1 7–6, lost Rinaldi 6–2 6–1), *US Open* 1r (lost A. Holton 5–7 6–4 6–1), *Australian Open* 2r (d. Suire 6–2 4–6 6–3, lost Turnbull [seed 9] 6–0 6–0); *qf* VS Newport (d. Richardson 6–4 fs, lost Turnbull 6–2 fs). *1985 HIGHLIGHTS – DOUBLES:* (with K. Jordan unless stated) *won Wimbledon* seed 3 (d. Kohde-Kilsch/Sukova 5–7 6–1 6–4, Navratilova/Shriver 5–7 6–3 6–4); *won* VS Florida (d. Cherneva/Savchenko 6–4 7–6), *won* Marco Island (d. Benjamin/Gadusek), *won* Bridgestone (d. Nagelsen/A. White 6–2 fs), *won* Mahwah (d. Kohde-Kilsch/Sukova 7–6 6–3), *won* VS Chicago (d. Burgin/Russell 6–2 6–2); *r/u* Eastbourne (lost Navratilova/Shriver 7–5 6–4), [Shriver] *r/u* Newport (lost Evert Lloyd/Turnbull). *1985 HIGHLIGHTS – MIXED DOUBLES:* (with Fitzgerald) *r/u US Open* (lost Navratilova/Gunthardt 6–3 6–4). *CAREER HIGHLIGHTS – DOUBLES:* [K. Jordan] *Wimbledon – won 1985*; [B. Jordan] *French Open – sf 1984* (lost Kohde-Kilsch/Mandlikova 6–7 6–3 6–4). *MIXED DOUBLES:* (with Fitzgerald unless stated) *US Open – won 1983* (d. Taygan/Potter 3–6 6–3 6–4), *r/u 1984* (lost M. Maleeva/Tom Gullikson 2–6 7–5 6–4), *r/u 1985; Wimbledon* – [Stewart] *sf 1984* (lost J. Lloyd/Turnbull 6–1 5–7 6–2).

DEBBIE SPENCE (USA)
Born San José, Cal., 9 August, 1967 and lives Cerritos, Cal.; RH; 2HB; 5ft 3in; 115lb; final 1985 WTA ranking 37 (47); 1985 prize money $84,639.
The top-ranked American 18-and-under player in 1983, she was r/u at the French Open Jun, and closed the year by winning Orange Bowl with 3s victories over Huber and Cecchini. Meanwhile, she fared well in women's events, reaching qf Tampa, and in 1984, playing her first full season on the pro tour, she distinguished herself with her deceptive backcourt skill and courage. Her CC skills were fully apparent in 1985 when she reached last 16 French Open and qf Orlando and US CC. *1985 HIGHLIGHTS – SINGLES: French Open* last 16, unseeded (d. Balestrat 6–3 2–6 6–3, Lindqvist [seed 9] 7–5 6–2, Villagran 6–0 6–1, lost Mandlikova [seed 3] 7–6 6–2), *US Open* 1r (lost Huber 7–6 6–1); *sf* Ginny Champs (d. Piatek 6–3 fs, Leand, lost Lindqvist 6–3 fs); *qf* Seabrook (d. Savchenco, Reggi, lost Scheuer-Larsen 6–1 6–4), *qf* Orlando (d. Hanika, lost Navratilova 6–1 6–4), *qf* US CC (d. Torres, lost Sabatini), *qf* VS Central NY (d. Shaefer, lost Sukova).

MILAN SREJBER (Czechoslovakia)
Born Prague, 30 December, 1963, and lives there; RH; 6ft 8in; 210lb; final 1985 ATP ranking 169; 1985 prize money $11,459.
Has neither coach nor manager. Ranked 10 in Czechoslovakia. Did not play competitive tennis as a jun, starting at age 19 on Satellite circuits on clay in Europe and S America.
1985 HIGHLIGHTS – SINGLES: won Finnish Challenger; **r/u** Brazil Challenger.

LARRY STEFANKI (USA)
Born Elmhurst, Ill., 23 July, 1957; lives Menlo Park, Cal.; RH; 5ft 10in; 150lb; final 1985 ATP ranking 54 (116); 1985 prize money $103,507.
A former All-American at Berkeley, Cal., he won La Quinta – his home club – on a wild-card in 1985, and made his way into the top 100. **1985 HIGHLIGHTS – SINGLES: Wimbledon** 1r (lost Curren 7–6 6–3 6–4); **won** La Quinta (d. Aguilera, S. Davis, Benhabiles, Holmes, Pate).

ULF STENLUND (Sweden)
Born Falun, 21 January, 1967; lives Hedemora; RH; 5ft 10in; 150lb; final 1985 ATP ranking 273.
He reached sf Kalle Anka Cup and in 1984 left school and won Swedish jun title over C. Bergstrom. He then won Finnish satellite circuit and in last jun tournament won Rolex 18s over Shigeru Ohta.

CHRISTO STEYN (South Africa)
Born Springs, 1 May, 1961; lives Klerksdorp; RH; 6ft 1in; 175lb; final 1985 ATP ranking 77 (221); 1985 prize money $40,775.
1985 HIGHLIGHTS – SINGLES: Wimbledon 3r (d. Barbosa 6–4 6–4 6–2, C. Lewis 3–6 7–6 6–4 6–4, lost McEnroe 6–3 7–5 6–4), **Australian Open** last 16, unseeded (d. Derlin 6–4 6–3 6–3, Warder 6–4 3–6 6–3 6–2, Gilbert [seed 10] 2–6 6–4 6–4 7–5, lost Lendl [seed 1] 6–3 6–2 6–7 6–2).

HELENA SUKOVA (Czechoslovakia)
Born Prague, 23 February, 1965 and lives there; RH; 6ft 1½in; 139lb; final 1985 WTA ranking 9 (7) singles, 3 doubles; 1985 prize money $422,387.
Daughter of late 1962 Wimbledon finalist Vera Sukova, she made a splash in Australia in 1981, upsetting Anne Smith and Barbara Potter to reach last 16 Australian Open before losing to countrywoman Hana Mandlikova. Like Mandlikova, she is tall and enormously talented with a wonderful flair for the game. Earlier in the year she was r/u to Gadusek at French Open Jun. In 1982 she acquainted herself with the women's game and was rewarded by a rise of 49 places in the computer rankings, her major victims including Potter, Rinaldi, Jausovec, Leand and Fairbank. In 1983 she was victorious in 80 per cent of her singles matches and joined Mandlikova to lead Czechoslovakia to their second Fed Cup championship. Her consistent record took her into the world top 20. She played an ambitious schedule of 24 tournaments in 1984, but saved her best for the end of the year when she beat Navratilova in sf Australian Open to reach her first major f, then extended Evert Lloyd to 3s before succumbing to the American's consistency and experience. In beating Navratilova, she not only came from behind but also refused to panic when her adversary saved five m-ps as Sukova served for the match at 6–5. She thoroughly deserved her 1–6 6–3 7–5 triumph and, moving into the top 10, was r/u to Navratilova in VS Champs March 1985. Her record continued to be impressive in 1985, but she did not win a singles tournament, 7 of her 21 defeats being at the hands of Navratilova. However, in a formidable doubles partnership with Kohde-Kilsch, she won US Open and reached f French and Australian Opens. **1985 HIGHLIGHTS – SINGLES: French Open** 2r, seed 5 (d. Pfaff 6–1 6–2, lost Jolissaint 2–6 6–3 6–0), **Wimbledon** qf, seed 7 (d. Jexell 6–3 6–3, Ruzici 6–1 6–4, W. White 6–1 6–4, Paradis 6–4 7–6, lost Rinaldi (seed 16) 6–1 1–6 6–1), **US Open** qf, seed 7 (d. Mundel 6–1 6–0, Bowes 6–3 6–1, Benjamin 6–0 7–5, Bassett 4–6 7–6 7–5, lost Mandlikova 7–6 7–5), **Australian Open** qf, seed 8 (d. J. Thompson 6–4 6–4, R. White 6–4 6–3, Dingwall 6–3 6–1, lost Navratilova 6–2 6–2); **r/u** VS Champs (d. Kohde-Kilsch 7–6 7–6, Lindqvist 6–4 6–4, Rinaldi 6–4 6–2, lost Navratilova 6–3 7–5 6–4), **r/u**

Eastbourne (d. Potter, Turnbull 6–4 fs, lost Navratilova 6–4 6–3); *sf* VS California (d. Spence 6–1 fs, Temesvari, lost Mandlikova), *sf* VS Dallas (d. Bunge 6–3 fs, lost Navratilova), *sf* VS Houston (d. Piatek, lost Navratilova), *sf* Swiss Open (d. Mascarin 6–0 fs, Burgin, Horvath, lost Gadusek 6–4 fs), *sf* Canadian Open (d. Bassett 6–1 6–1, lost Kohde-Kilsch 6–4 6–4), *sf* VS Central NY (d. Spence, lost Kelesi 7–6 7–6), *sf* Zurich (d. Jolissaint 6–3 fs, lost Mandlikova 6–2 7–6), *sf* Brisbane (d. Burgin, lost Shriver 6–2 fs), *sf* Pan Pacific, Tokyo (d. Rehe, lost Maleeva 6–0 6–2). *1985 HIGHLIGHTS – DOUBLES* (with Kohde-Kilsch unless stated): *r/u French Open* seed 2 (d. Burgin/Temesvari 6–4 7–5, lost Navratilova/Shriver 4–6 6–2 6–2), *Wimbledon* sf, seed 2 (d. Potter/Walsh Pete 7–6 4–6 6–3, lost Jordan/Smylie 5–7 6–1 6–4), *won US Open* seed 2 (d. Garrison/Rinaldi 5–7 6–4 6–3, Navratilova/Shriver 6–7 6–2 6–3) *r/u Australian Open* seed 2 (lost Navratilova/Shriver 6–3 6–4); *won* German Open (d. Graf/Tanvier 6–4 6–1), *won* VS LA (d. Mandlikova/Turnbull 6–4 6–2), *won* Pan Pacific Tokyo (d. Mesker/Smylie 6–0 6–4); *r/u* VS Washington (lost Fernandez/Navratilova 6–3 fs), *r/u* VS Champ (lost Navratilova/Shriver 6–7 6–4 7–6), *r/u* Mahwah (lost Jordan/Smylie 7–6 6–3), *r/u* Zurich (lost Mandlikova/Temesvari 7–5 fs), *r/u* Brisbane (lost Navratilova/Shriver 6–1 fs), [Potter] *r/u* Brighton (lost McNeil/Suire 6–4 fs). *CAREER HIGHLIGHTS – SINGLES: Australian Open – r/u 1984* (d. Kohde-Kilsch, Shriver, Navratilova 1–6 6–3 7–5, lost Evert Lloyd 6–7 6–1 6–3); *VS Champ – r/u 1985; US Open – qf 1984* (d. K. Jordan, lost Navratilova). *CAREER HIGHLIGHTS – DOUBLES:* (with Kohde-Kilsch) *US Open – won 1985; French Open – r/u 1985; Australian Open – r/u 1984* (lost Navratilova/Shriver), *r/u 1985; Wimbledon – sf 1985*.

HENRIK SUNDSTROM (Sweden)
Born Lunde, 29 February, 1964; lives Bjarred; single; RH; 2HB; 6ft 2in; 160lb; final 1985 ATP ranking 22 (7); 1985 prize money $179,098.
Moving out of the jun ranks in 1982 he did well in his 15 appearances, especially during the first half of the year. He was r/u to Wilander at Swedish Open, and beat Smid and Gunthardt at Hilversum to reach sf. He followed in 1983 with regularly fine performances fully deserving his top-25 status, but no-one was quite prepared for his rapid ascent into the top 10 in 1984, when he won three GP tournaments, beat Wilander twice, and had D Cup wins over Lendl and McEnroe on opening days when his country was not counting on him. He recovered from two sets to love, 0–3, 0–40 to beat Lendl and saved 4 s-p against McEnroe in f at Gothenburg on his way to a 13–11 6–4 6–3 success. His only flaw was in the major championships, Connors beating him in qf French Open, Edmondson ousting him in 5s Wimbledon, and Lloyd upsetting him in last 16 US Open. Qualified for Masters but fell to Jarryd 1r. Owing to persistent injuries, he declined in 1985, slipping out of the top 20. *1985 HIGHLIGHTS – SINGLES: French Open* last 16, seed 12 (d. Urpi 6–3 6–3 6–1, Flur 6–1 2–6 6–4 6–2, Taroczy 6–3 6–4 6–4, lost McEnroe (seed 1) 6–3 7–5 6–2), *Wimbledon* 1r, (lost Holmes 6–3 4–6 7–6 4–6 2), *US Open* 1r, seed 14 (lost Jaite 6–4 2–6 6–2 6–3), *Australian Open* 2r, seed 14 (lost Dyke 6–2 6–2 6–3); *r/u* Hamburg (d. Maurer, Gomez, Clerc, lost Mecir 6–4 6–1 6–4); *sf* WCT Forest Hills (d. Dickson, Moor, lost McEnroe 6–2 fs); *qf* Italian Open (d. Pistolesi, Cancellotti, lost Wilander). *1985 HIGHLIGHTS – DOUBLES:* (with Navratil) *r/u* Nancy (lost Freeman/Harmon).

CATHERINE TANVIER (France)
Born Toulouse, 28 May, 1965; lives Cap d'Agde; RH; 2HB; 5ft 8½in; 114lb; final 1985 WTA ranking 39 (30); 1985 prize money $62,174.
Emerging from the French qualifying circuits in 1981, she made her mark on the Avon Futures circuit. A former winner of French 14 (1979) and 16 (1980) Nationals, she had cracked world's top 100 by end 1981. Her decline in the rankings in 1983 was misleading, for she grew as a player and showed promise for 1984. Her outstanding performances were reaching last 16 French Open, f Stuttgart (where she beat Ruzici for the third time during the year) and a narrow defeat against Evert Lloyd in qf Brighton, where she led 5–4 in fs. WTA touring pro at Marbella Don Carlos Tennis Centre in Spain. Although she still did not seem to be doing full justice to her remarkable talent, she moved up three places during 1984, but in 1985, although she upset Shriver at US Indoor as well as removing Sabatini to reach last 16 Wimbledon, she slipped nine places in the rankings. *1985 HIGHLIGHTS – SINGLES: French Open* 3r (d. Skuherska 6–2 6–3, Sands 6–4 6–4, lost Navratilova [seed 1] 6–0 6–0), *Wimbledon* last 16, unseeded (d. Groat 6–3 6–2, Gurney

6–3 6–4, Sabatini [seed 15] 6–7 6–4 6–1, lost Garrison [seed 8] 6–1 6–3), **US Open** 1r (lost R. White 0–6 7–6 6–4); *sf* US Indoor (d. R. White, Paradis, Shriver 7–6 6–3, lost Lindqvist); *qf* Zurich (d. Reggi, lost Mandlikova). **CAREER HIGHLIGHTS –DOUBLES:** (with Madruga Osses) *Italian Open – r/u 1983* (lost Wade/Ruzici 6–1 fs); **French Open – sf 1983** (d. Allen/Evert Lloyd, Casals/Turnbull 6–1 6–1, lost K. Jordan/A. Smith 6–4 6–4).

BALAZS TAROCZY (Hungary)
Born Budapest, 9 May, 1954 and lives there with wife Bori; RH; 6ft; 170lb; final 1985 ATP ranking 157 (43) singles, 10 (12) doubles; 1985 prize money $163,167.
Ranked 1 in his country since 1973. In 1981 he enjoyed a superb year, performing particularly well on his favourite clay-court surfaces in spring. In doubles (with Gunthardt) won 6 GP titles, including a first French Open, plus the WCT Barratt World Doubles (Jan. 1982). By comparison 1982 paled for him but he won Hilversum for the fifth straight year, triumphed at Nice in a marathon duel with Noah, and took the Italian Open doubles title with Gunthardt. Playing only 11 tournaments in 1983 owing to injury, he slipped down on the computer. In 1984, he moved up eight places and continued to excel in doubles with Gunthardt. In US CC he reached f in singles, and was disqualified in doubles f with Gunthardt. Against Flach/Seguso they were penalised a game point when down a set and 6–5, which meant they lost the match. In 1985 he won Wimbledon with Gunthardt but declined in singles. **1985 HIGHLIGHTS – SINGLES: French Open** 3r (d. Muster 7–5 6–3 7–5, Vajda 4–6 6–3 6–7 6–4 6–4, lost Sundstrom [seed 12] 6–3 6–4 6–7 6–3), **Wimbledon** 1r (lost Hooper 7–5 7–6 6–3), **US Open** 1r (lost Schwaier 6–7 6–4 7–6 7–5). **1985 HIGHLIGHTS – DOUBLES:** (with Gunthardt unless stated) **won Wimbledon** seed 8 (d. Annacone/Van Rensburg 6–4 2–6 6–4 6–7 24–22, McNamara/McNamee 6–7 6–1 6–2 6–4, Cash/Fitzgerald 6–4 6–3 4–6 6–3); **won** La Quinta (d. Flach/Seguso 3–6 7–6 6–3), **won** WCT Doubles (d. Flach/Seguso, Annacone/Van Rensburg 6–4 1–6 7–6 6–7 6–4); [Graham] *r/u* Washington (lost Gildemeister/Pecci), *r/u* Hamburg (d. Nystrom/Wilander, lost Gildemeister/Gomez). **CAREER HIGHLIGHTS – SINGLES: Dutch Open – won 1978** d. Barazzutti 6–3 6–2 6–0, Okker 2–6 6–1 6–2 6–4), **won 1979** (d. Kodes 4–6 6–3 7–5 6–7 6–3, Smid 6–2 6–2 6–1), **won 1980** (d. Ismail 6–3 6–2), **won 1981** (d. Gunthardt 6–4 4s), **won 1982** (d. Teacher 6–3 6–1, Mottram 7–6 6–7 6–3 7–6); **French Open – qf 1976** lost Ramirez 7–5 fs), **qf 1981** lost Borg [seed 1] 6–3 6–3 6–2). **CAREER HIGHLIGHTS – DOUBLES:** (with Gunthardt) **French Open – won 1981** (d. Teltscher/Moor 6–2 7–6 6–3), **sf 1982** (d. Edmondson/Manson 6–3 6–4, lost Gildemeister/Prajoux 4–6 6–2 3–6 6–4 8–6); **Wimbledon – won 1985; Italian Open – won 1982** (d. Fibak/Fitzgerald 6–4 4–6 6–3); **German Open – won 1983** (d. Edmondson/Gottfried 7–6 4–6 6–4), *r/u 1984* (lost Flach/Seguso 7–6 6–5 disqualified).

BRIAN TEACHER (USA)
Born San Diego, 23 December, 1954; lives Los Angeles; RH; 6ft 3in; 175lb; final 1985 ATP ranking 66 (51); 1985 prize money $56,300.
Towards the end of 1980 he played the most consistent, impressive tennis of his career, crowning a superb two-month spell with a first major title in Australia. Forced by illness and injuries to miss the end of the 1981 season in Australia, and unable to defend his Australian Open crown, he nevertheless had another fine year which included a win over Connors in San Francisco. In 1982 he finished strongly, winning a WCT event in Dortmund, reaching qf Australian Open and San Francisco, and f Maui. In 1983 he won Columbus and Munich WCT crowns but was less successful in 1984, when he was r/u at Bristol and Gstaad but won no tournament. As he moved closer to his 31st birthday in 1985, he had similar results. **1985 HIGHLIGHTS – SINGLES: Wimbledon** 1r (lost Gunthardt 6–4 7–5 6–7 6–2), **US Open** 3r (d. Ganzabal 6–1 6–4 7–5, S. Davis [seed 15] 6–3 7–6 6–3, lost Berger 4–6 7–6 6–4 7–6), **Australian Open** 2r (d. Evernden 7–6 6–2 4–6 3–6 15–13, lost Testerman 6–1 6–7 7–6 7–6); *r/u* Livingston (d. Honey 6–3 fs, Cain 6–2 fs, S. Giammalva, Kriek 7–6 6–4, lost Gilbert 4–6 7–5 6–0); *sf* Bristol (d. Nelson 6–3 fs, Flur 6–4 fs, Forget 6–4 fs, lost M. Davis 6–3 7–6). **CAREER HIGHLIGHTS – SINGLES: Australian Open – won 1980** (d. Warwick 7–5 7–6 6–3), **qf 1982** (d. M. Leach 7–5 fs, Bauer 6–3 fs, Dent, lost Pfister 7–6 fs); **Wimbledon – qf 1982** seed 11 (d. Glickstein 6–2 5s, R. Frawley, S. Simonsson 6–3 4s, Wilander [seed 7] 6–4 6–4 6–3, lost T. Mayotte 6–7 7–6 7–5 3–6 6–1).

ELIOT TELTSCHER (USA)
Born Palos Verdes Estates, Cal., 15 March, 1959, and lives there; single; RH; 5ft 10in; 140lb; final 1985 ATP ranking 24 (9); prize money $109,872.
After breaking into the world's top 10 in 1980, he proved he belonged there in 1981. Despite reaching f Italian Open in 1982, the tenacious Californian with the small physique and large heart did not perform with the same high level of consistency as he had the previous two years, reaching only one more f, in Melbourne. Not particularly confident across the first half of the season, he finished 1983 by playing better tennis. For the third time in four years, he reached qf US Open on his best surface (cement) but again had the misfortune to meet Connors. In 1984 he elected to skip Wimbledon and French Open but ended the year in high gear, capturing South African Open over Gerulaitis, and his consistent efforts were rewarded with another Masters berth, where he beat Smid but lost to Connors. He played only D Cup and 12 tournaments, winning none, in 1985, to end the year with his lowest ranking since 1979. From 1980–84 he had always been in the top 15, three times finishing in the top 10. *1985 HIGHLIGHTS – SINGLES: French Open* 2r, seed 8 (d. Campos 6–2 6–3 6–3, lost Chesnokov 5–7 7–5 6–3 6–4), *Wimbledon* 2r, seed 13 (d. Ocleppo 5–7 7–6 7–6 6–0, lost Lloyd 6–3 6–4 3–6 4–6 7–5); *sf* Memphis (d. Holmes, lost Noah 7–5 fs), *sf* Toronto Indoor (d. Krishnan, lost Curren); *qf* US Pro Indoor (d. Mayotte, lost S. Davis), *qf* Fort Myers (lost Gomez), *qf* Las Vegas (d. Annacone, lost Arias 7–6 fs), *qf* Canadian Open (d. S. Giammalva, lost Arias), *qf* San Francisco (d. V. Amritraj, lost Green). *CAREER HIGHLIGHTS – SINGLES: South African Open – won 1984,* (d. Gerulaitis 6–3 6–1 7–6); *Italian Open – r/u 1982* seed 4 (d. Nystrom, Maurer, Mottram 6–4 6–3, Dibbs 6–2 6–2, Arraya 6–3 fs, lost Gomez 6–2 6–3 6–2); *US Open – qf 1980* (d. Davis, Pecci, Ocleppo, Gottfried, lost Connors 6–1 3–6 6–3 6–0), *qf 1981* seed 8 (d. Amaya, Austin, V. Amritraj, Gottfried [seed 16], lost Connors [seed 4] 6–3 6–1 6–2), *qf 1983* (d. S. Giammalva, Jarryd, Holmes, lost Connors 7–6 6–2 6–2). *CAREER HIGHLIGHTS – DOUBLES:* (with Moor) *French Open – r/u 1981* (d. Feigl/Martin, lost Gunthardt/Taroczy 6–2 7–6 6–3). *MIXED DOUBLES:* (with B. Jordan) *French Open – won 1983* (d. Allen/Strode 6–2 6–3).

ANDREA TEMESVARI (Hungary)
Born Budapest, 26 April, 1966 and lives there; 5ft 6½in; 115lb; final 1985 WTA ranking 16 (14); 1985 prize money $101,346.
Coached by father Otto, a former Olympic basketball player, she was WTA 'Most Impressive Newcomer' in 1982. That year she gave notice of things to come when she reached f Swiss Open, but her rapidly improving skills took nearly everyone by storm in 1983 as she emerged as one of the 5 best CC players, and she provided women's tennis with a new star as she appeared in tournaments around the world looking glamorous and several years older than she is. She won Italian Open, US CC and Hittfeld, dominating with her heavily topspun groundstrokes and superior ball control. She is best woman player to emerge from Hungary since Kormoczi. WTA touring pro at Marbella Don Carlos Tennis Centre, Spain. As is frequently the case, once she reached the top 10, she found it hard to stay there. In 1984 she was not the same disciplined competitor as in the year before, but although she reached no f, she produced flashes of her best tennis, and by the end of the year had worked her way back to No. 14. Her results were uneven in 1985, but she won her first tournament in two years, winning US CC for second time with another win over Garrison in f. *1985 HIGHLIGHTS – SINGLES: French Open* seed 15, 1r (lost Paradis 7–6 3–6 6–3), *Wimbledon* 2r (d. K. Maleeva 3–6 7–6 6–4, lost Graf [seed 11] 6–3 7–6), *US Open* 2r, seed 16 (d. K. Maleeva 6–2 4–6 6–2, lost Kuhlman 2–6 6–2 6–2); *won* US CC (d. Reggi 6–3 7–6, Gompert, Garrison 7–6 6–3); *qf* LIPC (d. Turnbull 6–4 6–3, lost Graf 6–2 6–1), *qf* VS California (d. Fairbank, Tanvier, lost Sukova 7–6 6–2). *1985 HIGHLIGHTS – DOUBLES:* (with Mandlikova) *won* Zurich (d. Kohde-Kilsch/Sukova 6–4 3–6 7–5). *CAREER HIGHLIGHTS – SINGLES: Italian Open – won 1983* (d. Maleeva, Sukova, Rinaldi 6–0 6–0, Gadusek 6–1 6–0), *US CC – won 1983* (d. Jausovec, Horvath, Ruzici 6–2 6–2, Garrison 6–2 6–2), *won 1985*.

BEN TESTERMAN (USA)
Born Knoxville, Tenn., 2 February, 1962 and lives there; LH; 6ft 3in; 180lb; final 1985 ATP ranking 88 (22); 1985 prize money $83,041.
A former All-American at University of Tennessee and one of the outstanding American jun of the late 1970s, he was ranked No. 1 in every age group (12s, 14s, 16s), only S. Davis and S. Giammalva surpassing him in 18s. He was r/u to Davis for 1979 US Nat 18 Champ and to Giammalva the following year. Slow to get started in the pro game. A devout Christian, he found the right formula in 1984 and made dramatic progress, leaping 172 places on the computer to 22, and reaching sf Australian Open where he led Curren two sets to love. He also reached sf US Indoor at Memphis early in the year by beating Curren before losing a good battle with Connors. He struggled at the beginning of 1985, losing ground on the computer, but his improved play during the indoor circuit in Australia gave promise for 1986. *1985 HIGHLIGHTS – SINGLES: Wimbledon* 3r (d. Miller 3–6 6–3 6–4 6–2, Shiras 6–4 6–7 4–6 6–1 7–5, lost S. Giammalva 4–6 6–3 7–5 7–6), *US Open* 1r (lost Scanlon 7–6 7–6 0–6 5–7 6–3), *Australian Open* 3r (d. Cain 7–6 6–3 7–6, Teacher 6–1 6–7 7–6 7–6, lost Lendl [seed 1] 6–3 1–6 6–3 6–2); *sf* Melbourne (d. Cassidy, Bourne, McNamara, lost M. Davis 6–4 fs); *qf* Brisbane (d. McPherson, Freeman, lost Layendecker), *qf* Sydney Indoor (d. Alexander, Nelson, lost Lendl). *1985 HIGHLIGHTS – DOUBLES:* (with Pfister unless stated) *r/u* Houston (d. Gitlin/Manson, lost McEnroe/Fleming), [Schultz] *r/u* Brisbane, (d. Bourne/Dyke, lost M. Davis/Drewett), *r/u* Cleveland (d. Gilbert/J. Levine, lost Palin/Rahnasto). *CAREER HIGHLIGHTS – SINGLES: Australian Open – sf 1984* (lost Curren 2–6 4–6 6–3 6–4 6–4).

JANINE THOMPSON (Australia)
Born Sydney, 12 September, 1967, and lives there; LH; 5ft 4in; 125lb; final 1985 WTA ranking 86 (251); 1985 prize money $25,714.
One of the bright young prospects from her country, she made significant progress in 1985 and looked a likely candidate for the top 50. *1985 HIGHLIGHTS – SINGLES: French Open* 1r (lost Evert Lloyd [seed 2] 6–1 6–1), *Wimbledon* 1r (lost Holladay 6–1 6–3), *US Open* 1r (lost Evert Lloyd [seed 1] 6–1 6–3), *Australian Open* 1r (lost Sukova 6–4 6–4); *qf* VS Utah (d. Casals, Balestrat, lost Rehe 6–4 6–4).

LEIGH THOMPSON (USA)
Born Hampton, Va., 8 January, 1964; lives Kingsmill-on-the-James, Va.; RH; 5ft 7½in; 118lb; final 1985 WTA ranking 94 (215); 1985 prize money $18,610.
One of the most surprising winners of a major league tournament over the last two decades, she won Mahwah in 1982 with wins over Jaeger and Bunge among others. She had a disappointing year in 1984 but rebounded in 1985 to claim a place for herself again in the top 100. *1985 HIGHLIGHTS – SINGLES: US Open* 3r (d. Collins 6–1 3–6 6–1, Marsikova 6–4 2–5 ret'd, lost Lindqvist [seed 13] 7–5 6–0).

MICHELLE TORRES (USA)
Born Chicago, Ill., 27 June, 1967; lives Northfield, Ill.; RH; 5ft 4in; 107lb; RH; 2HB; final 1985 WTA ranking 56 (20); 1985 prize money $31,035.
Ranked 5 in US Girls' 14 for 1981, she concentrated her energies in 1982 on women's tournaments, where she reached qf US CC and had wins over K. Jordan and Norton. She finished 1981 ranked 31 places higher, having carefully chosen her schedule to exhibit her solid baseline style in the places where she could make the most of it. Curiously, she played better tennis in women's tournaments than she did in the juniors, but the mixture seemed to agree with her. During the first half of 1984, she again combined jun with women's tennis before turning pro in the autumn. In her first event as a pro, she was r/u to Navratilova in Fort Lauderdale where she beat Bonder and Rinaldi. Then, a few weeks later, she upset Bassett to win Tampa and on the basis of these two outstanding tournaments she surged into the top 20 at the end of the year. She was unable to maintain that level in 1985, when she advanced no further than qf anywhere, but she still remained a player no-one could take for granted. *1985 HIGHLIGHTS – SINGLES: French Open* 1r (lost Medrado 6–2 6–2), US Open 3r (d. Shaefer 7–6 6–7 6–2, Skronska 3–6 6–2

One of the year's most successful pairs, America's Paul Annacone (left) and his South African partner, Christo Van Rensburg, who ended the year with their first Grand Slam win in Melbourne. (T. Hindley)

6–0, lost Turnbull [seed 12] 7–6 6–1), **qf** Fort Lauderdale (d. Mascarin, Nelson, lost Louie 7–5 fs), **qf** Tampa (d. A. Holton, Villagran, lost Rehe).

THIERRY TULASNE (France)
Born Aix-les-Bains, 12 July, 1963; lives Paris; RH; 2HB; 5ft 10in; 160lb; final 1985 ATP ranking 23 (52); 1985 prize money $171,454.
The world's best jun in 1980, he won the Italian and Wimbledon Jun titles, and shocked more than a few people when he beat Gerulaitis (twice former Italian Open champ) in 2r 1980 Italian Open. His enormous potential was evident in early 1981, when he swept to sf US Pro Indoor and took Tanner to 5s. Later in the year, at Cincinnati, he beat Tanner and won Swedish Open at Bastad. With the swift advance of countrymen Noah, Leconte, and Forget, Tulasne was left in the shadows in 1982 and slipped down 46 places on the computer, doing little better in 1983 and 1984. Suddenly, in the second half of 1985, it all came together for him, and at 22 he became the player it had seemed for years he would become, surging into the top 25. He won 3 GP events, beat Wilander twice and scored other notable victories over Nystrom and Jarryd after having lost in either 1r or 2r of his first 10 tournaments that year. **1985 HIGHLIGHTS – SINGLES: French Open** 1r (lost Wilander [seed 4] 6–1 6–4 6–2), **US Open** 3r (d. Navratil 6–7 6–3 6–7 6–3 6–0, Lundgren 7–6 1–6 7–5 6–3, lost Connors [seed 4] 7–5 6–2 6–4); **won** Bologna (d. Agenor 6–4 fs, Keretic, C. Panatta 6–2 6–0), **won** Palermo (d. Pistolesi 6–1 6–0, Muster, Nystrom 6–3 6–1), **won** Barcelona (d. Taroczy 6–2 fs, Keretic, Jarryd 7–6 6–0, Leconte, Wilander 0–6 6–2 3–6 6–4 6–0); **sf** Bordeaux (d. Pimek, lost Perez); **qf** Basle (d. Krishnan, lost Fibak). **CAREER HIGHLIGHTS – SINGLES: US Pro Indoor – sf 1981** (d. S. Giammalva 6–2 fs, Sadri 7–6 6–3, lost Tanner 7–6 3–6 3–6 6–4 6–4).

WENDY TURNBULL (Australia)
Born Brisbane, 25 November, 1952; lives Sandgate; single; RH; 5ft 3in; 120lb; final 1985 WTA ranking 14 (5) singles, 8 doubles; 1985 prize money $170,120; career prize money $2,197,622.
A late bloomer, she produced a dazzling string of upsets over Casals, Wade and Navratilova to reach 1977 US Open f and remained in the world's top 10 until 1985. In 1981 she had her most erratic year as a singles player since 1977, failing to qualify for either the Avon or TS Champs and suffering more bad losses than usual. A strong finish highlighted her 1982 season, as she picked up two tournament victories at Brisbane and Richmond, although, troubled by tennis elbow, she had not been up to par in the middle of the season. She played marvellous doubles with Casals, picking up a second US Open title, as well as winning her second French mixed title and reaching first Wimbledon f. In 1983 she was her usual self, winning Boston singles, taking mixed title with John Lloyd at Wimbledon, where she also reached f women's doubles with Casals, and was finalist at Australian Open with Hobbs. She had a terrific year in 1984, winning her second consecutive Wimbledon mixed title with Lloyd, reaching sf US and Australian Open singles, and finishing the year ranked 5. In 1985, when she turned 33, she spent most of the year around No. 12 and 14, losing her only f to Croft in San Diego. However, she played her usual brand of superb doubles with regular partner Mandlikova and occasional partner Evert Lloyd. **1985 HIGHLIGHTS – SINGLES: Wimbledon** 3r, seed 14 (d. Rush 7–5 6–3, E. Minter 7–5 7–5, lost Paradis 2–6 7–5 6–1), **US Open** last 16, seed 12 (d. Ruzici 6–4 6–1, Herr 7–5 6–2, Torres 7–6 6–1, lost Kohde-Kilsch [seed 5] 5–7 7–5 6–2 after having 2 mps]), **Australian Open** last 16, seed 9 (d. Leo 6–0 6–0, Smylie 6–0 6–0, lost Mandlikova 6–3 6–4); **rlu** VS San Diego (d. Ludloff 6–2 fs, Kinney, Nagelsen, Piatek, lost Croft 6–0 7–6); **sf** Eastbourne (d. Garrison 7–6 6–4, Paradis 7–5 fs, lost Sukova 4–6 7–6 6–4), **sf** VS Newport (d. Smylie 6–2 fs, lost Shriver 6–4 7–6), **sf** VS Chicago (d. Potter 6–3 fs, lost Gadusek 7–6 6–2). **1985 HIGHLIGHTS – DOUBLES:** (with Mandlikova unless stated) **Wimbledon** sf, seed 4 (d. Cherneva/Savchenko 6–4 6–3, lost Navratilova/Shriver 6–4 6–2), **US Open** sf, seed 4 (d. Lindqvist/Russell 6–1 3–6 6–0, lost Navratilova/Shriver 6–3 6–4); **won** VS California (d. Fairbank/Reynolds 4–6 7–5 6–1), **won** Sydney NSW (d. Fairbank/Reynolds 3–6 7–6 6–4), [Evert Lloyd] **won** VS Newport (d. Shriver/Smylie 6–4 7–6), [Evert Lloyd] **won** VS New Orleans (d. Piatek/A. White 6–1 6–2); **rlu** VS LA (lost Kohde-Kilsch/Sukova 6–4 6–2). **CAREER HIGHLIGHTS – SINGLES: French Open – rlu 1979** (d. Mandlikova 6–3 6–3, Marsikova 6–4 6–3, lost Evert Lloyd 6–2 6–0), **qf 1980** seed

3 (lost Ruzici [seed 8] 6–2 6–0); *US Open – r/u 1977* (d. Casals 4–6 6–0 6–0, Wade 6–2 6–1, Navratilova 2–6 7–5 6–4, lost Evert 7–6 6–2), *sf 1978* (lost Evert 6–3 6–0), *sf 1984* (d. Shriver 2–6 6–3 6–3, lost Navratilova 6–4 6–1); *Australian Open – sf 1981* seed 7 (d. Jaeger 6–3 7–6, lost Evert Lloyd 6–4 7–6), *sf 1984* (d. Graf, lost Evert Lloyd 6–3 6–3); *Wimbledon – qf 1980* seed 6 (lost Goolagong Cawley 6–3 6–3), *qf 1981* seed 6 (lost Mandlikova [seed 2] 6–0 6–0). *CAREER HIGHLIGHTS – DOUBLES:* (with Stove unless stated) *French Open – won 1979* (d. Wade/Durr 3–6 7–5 6–4), [Casals] *r/u 1982* (lost Navratilova/A. Smith 6–3 6–4); *Wimbledon –* [Reid] *won 1978* (d. Jausovec/Ruzici 4–6 9–8 6–3), *r/u 1979* (lost King/Navratilova 5–7 6–3 6–2), [Casals] *r/u 1980* (lost K. Jordan/A. Smith 3–6 7–6 6–1), [Casals] *r/u 1983* (d. Potter/Walsh 6–1 6–7 6–4, lost Navratilova/Shriver 6–2 6–2), [Mandlikova] *sf 1985; US Open – won 1979* (d. King/Navratilova 7–5 6–2), [Casals] *won 1982* (d. Potter/Walsh 6–3 6–4), [Casals] *r/u 1981* (d. Navratilova/Shriver 6–4 fs, lost A. Smith/K. Jordan 6–3 6–3), [Hobbs] *r/u 1984* (lost Navratilova/Shriver 6–2 6–4), [Mandlikova] *sf 1985; Italian Open – won 1979* (d. Goolagong Cawley/Reid 6–3 6–4); *CS Final –* [Casals] *won 1980* (d. Stove/Shriver 6–4 6–4, Reynolds/P. Smith 6–3 4–6 7–6); *TS Champ –* [Casals] *r/u 1981* (lost Navratilova/Shriver 6–3 6–4); *Australian Open –* [Hobbs] *r/u 1983* d. Durie/Kiyomura, King/Walsh 6–4 6–1, lost Navratilova/Shriver 6–4 6–7 6–2). *MIXED DOUBLES:* (with J. Lloyd unless stated) *French Open –* [Hewitt] *won 1979* (d. Tiriac/Ruzici 6–3 2–6 6–1), *won 1982* (d. Motta/Monteiro 6–2 7–6); *Wimbledon – won 1983,* (d. Denton/King 6–7 7–6 7–5), *won 1984* (d. Denton/Jordan 6–3 6–3), *r/u 1982* (lost Curren/A. Smith 2–6 6–3 7–5); *US Open –* [Riessen] *won 1980* (d. McMillan/Stove 7–6 6–2).

RENE UYS (South Africa)
Born Bloemfontein, 26 July, 1964 and lives there; RH; final 1985 WTA ranking 88 (70); 1985 prize money $29,545.
A finalist in Wimbledon Jun 1981, she returned to school in 1982 to get her high-school diploma. In 1983 she won the South African GC and in 1984 reached sf South African Open. Her 1985 season was a mixed one, but she produced her best when it mattered most, driving her way into last 16 Wimbledon with hard-fought 3s wins over Bassett and Hu Na. *1985 HIGHLIGHTS – SINGLES: French Open* 1r (lost Phelps 6–4 6–4), *Wimbledon* last 16, unseeded (d. Louis 7–6 4–6 6–2, Bassett [seed 13] 0–6 7–6 6–3, Hu Na 6–2 4–6 6–0, lost Navratilova [seed 1] 6–2 6–2), *US Open* 1r (lost Goles 7–6 1–6 7–6).

MARIAN VAJDA (Czechoslovakia)
Born Povazska, 24 March, 1965; lives Bratislava; RH; 5ft 8in; 150lb; final 1985 ATP ranking 52 (–); 1985 prize money $46,160.
Coming from nowhere in 1985, he narrowly missed cracking the top 50 at the end of the year. *1985 HIGHLIGHTS – SINGLES: French Open* 2r (d. Van Patten 6–4 3–6 4–6 6–3 6–3, lost Taroczy 4–6 6–3 6–7 6–4 6–4), *Wimbledon* 1r (lost Bauer 5–7 7–6 7–5 6–2), *US Open* 2r (d. DePalmer 2–6 2–6 6–3 7–6 7–5, lost Goldie 1–6 6–3 6–2 6–2); *sf* Kitzbuhel (d. Duncan, Perkis, Leconte, lost Westphal); *qf* Geneva (d. Jaite, K. Carlsson, lost Leconte).

MOLLY VAN NOSTRAND (USA)
Born Bright Waters, NY, 12 March, 1965, and lives there; RH; 2HF; 2HB; 5ft 9in; 130lb; final 1985 WTA ranking 44 (112); 1985 prize money $45,397.
The No. 2 player in US Girls' 16s in 1981, she was r/u at Nat. 16 Indoors and HC that year. An aggressive baseliner, she drives the ball fiercely with her two-handed strokes off both sides. At Wimbledon 1985 she upset M. Maleeva to reach qf and nearly toppled Garrison before falling in 3s. *1985 HIGHLIGHTS – SINGLES: Wimbledon* qf, unseeded (d. Walsh Pete 7–5 6–3, Louie 6–2 6–3, Savchenko 7–6 3–6 7–5, M. Maleeva [seed 4] 7–5 6–2, lost Garrison [seed 8] 2–6 6–3 6–0), *US Open* 2r (d. W. White 7–6 6–1, lost Cecchini 6–4 6–4), *Australian Open* 1r (lost Wade 6–3 5–7 6–2); *qf* Canadian Open (d. Durie, Turnbull 7–5 fs, Kinney, lost Evert Lloyd 6–2 6–1).

VINCE VAN PATTEN (USA)
Born Brooklyn, NY, 17 October, 1957; lives Snowmass, Col.; RH; 2HB; 5ft 11in; 155lb; final 1985 ATP ranking 78 (103); 1985 prize money $50,497.
A former actor and son of actor Dick Van Patten, star of the popular TV series 'Eight is Enough'. An exciting, unorthodox player, he has an impressive 2HB and can volley brilliantly. He played his first GP tournament, aged 21, in Maui, and was voted 'Newcomer of the Year' in 1979. Made a significant leap in 1981 as he picked just the right moment to explode with the full glory of his talent. Coming into the Seiko Open in November, unseeded and with his computer ranking as low as 83, he beat Clerc, Gerulaitis, McEnroe and Edmondson, winning the tournament and shooting up to No. 26 the following week. In 1982 he did not produce such a dream tournament and his ranking slipped 20 places, although he did reach f 2 GP events during the year. He languished outside the top 100 in 1983 and 1984, but in 1985 he returned. *1985 HIGHLIGHTS – SINGLES: French Open* 1r (lost Vajda 6–4 3–6 4–6 6–3 6–3), *Wimbledon* 3r (d. Elter 6–3 6–7 7–5 6–4, Mitchell 7–5 6–3 6–2, lost Jarryd [seed 5] 6–3 6–3 6–1), *US Open* 1r (lost Wilkison 6–3 6–3 4–6 7–6); *qf* Tokyo (lost Connors 7–5 6–2). *1985 HIGHLIGHTS – DOUBLES:* (with Gilbert) *sf* Las Vegas (d. Flach/Seguso, Becker/Pate, lost Annacone/Van Rensburg).

CHRISTO VAN RENSBURG (South Africa)
Born Uitenhage, 23 October, 1962, and lives there; RH; 6ft 1in; 165lb; final 1985 ATP ranking 252 singles, 8 doubles; 1985 prize money $231,132.
Although in 1985 this 1983 South African jun champ failed to win 1r singles in GP tournaments, he and Annacone, who first came together to win NSW Open Dec. 1984, formed one of the best doubles partnerships of the season. In 1985, with 4 GP titles to their credit, including Australian Open, they finished the season seeded third at Masters, one week after reaching f WCT World Doubles in London. *1985 HIGHLIGHTS DOUBLES:* (with Annacone unless stated) *French Open* qf, seed 7 (d. Dickson/Wilkison, lost Edberg/Jarryd 6–3 6–2), *Wimbledon* qf, seed 9 (lost Gunthardt/Taroczy 6–4 2–6 6–4 6–7 22–24), *won Australian Open* (d. Edmondson/Warwick 3–6 7–6 6–4 6–4); *won* LIPC (d. Stewart/Warwick 7–5 7–5 6–4), *won* Atlanta (d. Denton/Smid 6–4 6–3), *won* San Francisco (d. Gilbert/A. Mayer 3–6 6–3 6–4), [Dowdeswell] *won* Johannesburg (d. Mansdorf/ Perkis 3–6 7–6 6–4); *r/u* Las Vegas (lost Cash/Fitzgerald 7–6 6–7 7–6), *r/u* Newport (lost Doohan/S. Giammalva), *r/u* LA (d. V. Amritraj/J. Lloyd, lost S. Davis/Van't Hof). *CAREER HIGHLIGHTS – DOUBLES:* (with Annacone) *Australian Open – won 1985.*

GUILLERMO VILAS (Argentina)
Born Buenos Aires, 17 August 1952; lives Mar Del Plata; single; LH; 5ft 11in; 165lb; final 1985 ATP ranking 39 (28); 1985 prize money $57,834; career prize money $5,072,427.
Since 1974, when he burst into prominence to become one of the world top 5 after surprisingly capturing GP Masters on grass in Melbourne, he remained one of the top 10 until 1983. After a glorious year in 1977, when he won French and US Opens and unfolded a GP record streak of 50 straight wins (earning him the top world ranking from some experts), he appeared to have lost some of his drive and initiative. Nevertheless, he did win back-to-back Australian Open titles in 1978 and 1979, and in 1980 was one of only four men to defeat Borg. Vilas did not play particularly well in the major tournaments in 1981, but his overall record, which consisted mainly of clay-court tournaments, was remarkable once again. He won 4 GP events and reached the f of 5 others, as well as leading Argentina into their first D Cup f. Then, in an outstanding 1982, he won his first 5 GP tournaments, and 31 straight matches on that tour, going on to reach his 4th French Open f, the US Open sf and the Masters, adding two more titles to his collection. He beat Connors in 2 of 3 battles and Lendl in both their confrontations. Only one crucial defeat (the French Open f against Wilander) kept him from an even more productive and spectacular season in which he finished second to Connors in GP points race. However, 1983 was an agonizing year in which he was given notice by the Pro Council, shortly before Wimbledon, that he faced a one-year suspension and a fine of $20,000 for allegedly accepting a $60,000 guarantee to play in Rotterdam. A hearing took place in Rotterdam and New York in December before a three-man committee of Forrest Hainline, Bill Talbert and Vic Seixas, the decision being announced in Jan. 1984 that the fine should stand, although the suspension was not enforced. Understandably, it was not a pleasant year

for Vilas on court either. He did win two WCT tournaments (Richmond and Delray Beach) and another on the GP circuit (Kitzbuhel), but he fell to Higueras in qf French Open, Odizor in 1r Wimbledon, and Holmes in 3r US Open. In 1984, looking like a defeated man, he wandered unhappily through the season without advancing beyond sf of any tournament, and his ranking dropped to 28, his lowest since the middle of 1974. He continued to have problems early in 1985 but some good CC results mid-season were enough to keep him in the top 40. *1985 HIGHLIGHTS – SINGLES: French Open* 2r (d. Masur 6–3 6–2 6–2, lost Krickstein [seed 10] 6–4 3–6 6–1 6–3), *US Open* 2r (d. Masur 7–6 6–7 6–4 3–6 6–1, lost Smid [seed 16] 6–2 6–2 6–1); *sf* US Pro (d. Krickstein 7–6 6–1, Arraya 6–4 6–2, Pimek 6–4 6–2, lost Wilander); *qf* Hamburg (d. Cancellotti, lost Wilander), *qf* Washington (d. Tulasne, Cancellotti, Clerc, lost Ingaramo). *CAREER HIGHLIGHTS – SINGLES: French Open – won 1977* (d. S. Smith, Fibak 6–4 6–0 6–4, Ramirez 6–2 6–0 6–3, Gottfried 6–0 6–3 6–0), *rlu 1975* (lost Borg 6–2 6–3 6–4), *rlu 1978* (lost Borg 6–1 6–1 6–3), *rlu 1982* (d. Noah 7–6 6–3 6–4, Higueras 6–1 6–3 7–6, lost Wilander 1–6 7–6 6–0 6–4); *US Open – won 1977* (d. Moore 6–1 6–1 6–0, Solomon 6–2 7–6 6–2, Connors 2–6 6–3 7–6 6–0), *sf 1982* (d. Denton 3–6 4–6 7–6 6–3 6–3, Tom Gullikson, lost Connors 6–1 3–6 6–2 6–3); *Australian Open – won 1978* (d. Roche, Pfister, Marks 6–4 6–4 3–6 6–3), *won 1979* (d. Amaya, Sadri 7–6 6–3 6–2), *rlu 1977* (lost Tanner 6–3 6–3 6–3); *Masters – won 1974* (d. Newcombe, Borg, Parun, Ramirez, Nastase 7–6 6–2 3–6 3–6 6–4), *sf 1977* (d. Connors 6–4 3–6 7–5 in rr, lost Borg 6–3 6–3), *sf 1982* (d. Gomez, lost McEnroe 6–3 6–3); *South African Open – won 1977* (d. Smith, Mottram 7–6 6–3 6–4), *rlu 1982* (lost Gerulaitis 7–6 6–2 4–6 7–6); *Italian Open – won 1980* seed 1 (d. Ramirez, Teltscher, Noah 6–0 6–4 6–4), *rlu 1976* (lost Panatta 2–6 7–6 6–2 7–6), *rlu 1979* (lost Gerulaitis 6–7 7–6 6–7 6–4 6–2); *Nations Cup – won 1980* (d. Barazzutti, Gehring, Lendl in rr, Borg 6–3 1–6 6–1 in sf, Barazzutti 6–3 6–2 in f as Argentina won); *US Pro – won 1982* (d. Noah 6–3 6–2, Purcell 6–4 6–0).

ADRIANA VILLAGRAN (Argentina)
Born Buenos Aires, 7 August, 1956, and lives there; RH; 5ft 6in; 130lb; final 1985 WTA ranking 82 (85); 1985 prize money $39,088.
1985 HIGHLIGHTS – SINGLES: French Open 3r (d. Einy 6–2 6–0, Henricksson 3–6 6–1 6–4, lost Spence 6–0 6–1), *Wimbledon* 2r (d. Klitch 6–7 6–4 6–3, lost Burgin 6–0 6–3), *US Open* 2r (d. Kanellopoulou 7–6 3–6 6–4, lost Kohde-Kilsch [seed 5] 6–1 6–1); *qf* Sao Paulo (d. Betzner, lost Sabatini).

VIRGINIA WADE (Great Britain)
Born Bournemouth, 10 July, 1945; lives New York City; single; RH; final 1985 WTA ranking 89 (61); 1985 prize money $31,521; career prize money $1,534,918.
In 1981 this former US (1968), Italian (1971), Australian (1972) and centenary Wimbledon (1977) champion began to phase out of the game, cutting down her schedule, enjoying her work as a television commentator for both CBS in US and BBC in Britain and not taking her losses as hard as she used to. Nevertheless, she teamed with Barker to help lead Britain into Fed Cup f for the first time since 1972. There was little change in 1982, although she produced a burst of inspiration at Deerfield Beach in October, looking like the Wade of old as she beat Hanika. Her next best performance was at Wimbledon, where in 1r she fought on Centre Court as if she owned it, saving 4 m-ps to beat Durie before bowing quietly on an outside court against Marjorie Blackwood. Became first woman elected to committee of All England Club. In 1983 she reached qf Wimbledon for the first time since 1978 with a sudden burst of inspired play. She came from a set and 1–5 down to beat Leand and saved 1 m-p to stop Pfaff before Vermaak woke her from her dream. In the autumn, she played extremely well again to reach the f British Closed, where she pushed Durie long and hard before losing in 3s. Picking and choosing her appearances carefully, she played only 11 tournaments in 1984, but at Wimbledon she produced a remarkable upset only two weeks before turning 39, beating fifth-seeded Garrison on Centre Court in 2r before losing 3r narrowly to Karlsson 11–9 fs. In 1985, she played her 24th and conceivably last Wimbledon singles in a row and departed in typically grand style with 3s 3r loss to Shriver. In Melbourne, competing in her final GS singles event, she eliminated Wimbledon qf Van Nostrand in 1r before losing respectably to Mandlikova. This was remarkable stuff from a woman who had turned 40 in July. Her

The high spot of 1985 for Elise Burgin came at Houston, where she lost in the final to Navratilova, with whom she won the doubles. *(D. Horton)*

priorities now have taken her outside the court to the commentary box and the committee room, but her record over a quarter of a century in international tennis will have earned her a high status in Britain and in the game at large. *1985 HIGHLIGHTS – SINGLES: French Open* 2r (d. Gomer 7–6 6–4, lost Navratilova [seed 1] 6–3 6–0), *Wimbledon* 3r (d. Antonoplis 6–4 7–5, Gerken 6–3 6–7 7–5, lost Shriver [seed 5] 6–2 5–7 6–2), *Australian Open* 2r (d. Van Nostrand 6–3 5–7 6–2, lost Mandlikova [seed 3] 6–2 7–6). *CAREER HIGHLIGHTS: – SINGLES: Wimbledon – won 1977* (d. Casals 7–5 6–2, Evert 6–2 4–6 6–1, Stove 4–6 6–3 6–1), *sf 1974* (lost Morozova 1–6 7–5 6–4), *sf 1976* (d. Reid, lost Goolagong Cawley 6–1 6–2), *sf 1978* (lost Evert 8–6 6–2); *US Open – won 1968* (d. Casals, Tegart, A. Jones 7–5 6–1, King 6–4 6–2), *sf 1969* (d. Heldman, lost Court 7–5 6–0), *sf 1970* (d. Durr, lost Casals 6–2 6–7 6–2), *sf 1975* (lost Goolagong Cawley 7–5 6–1); *Australian Open – won 1972* (d. Harris, Goolagong 6–4 6–4); *Italian Open – won 1971* (d. Neumanova 7–5 fs, Hoesl 6–4 6–3, Masthoff 6–4 6–4); *South African Open – r/u 1968* (lost Court), *r/u 1972* (lost Goolagong 4–6 6–3 6–0). *CAREER HIGHLIGHTS – DOUBLES: (with Court unless stated) French Open – won 1973* (d. Durr/Stove 6–2 6–3); *US Open – won 1973* (d. King/Casals 3–6 6–3 7–5), *won 1975* (d. King/Casals 7–5 2–6 7–6), *r/u 1972* (lost Durr/Stove 6–3 1–6 6–3), [Morozova] *r/u 1976* (lost Boshoff/Kloss 6–1 6–4); *Australian Open – won 1973* (d. Reid/Harris 6–4 6–4); *Italian Open –* [Morozova] *won 1973* (d. Tomanova/Navratilova 3–6 6–2 7–5), *won 1968* (d. DuPlooy/Walkden 6–2 7–4), [Ruzici] *won 1983* (d. Madruga Osses/Tanvier 6–3 6–2 6–1); *Wimbledon –* (Durr) *r/u 1970* (lost King/Casals 6–2 6–3); *South African Open –* [Evert] *r/u 1973* (lost Boshoff/Kloss 7–6 2–6 6–1). *MIXED DOUBLES: (with Mulligan) South African Open – won 1972* (d. McMillan/Pretorious 6–0 4–6 6–4).

MICHAEL WESTPHAL (Germany)
Born Hamburg, 19 February, 1965 and lives there; RH; 6ft 3in; 172lb, final 1985 ATP ranking 51 (73); 1985 prize money $50,723.
He has been in the German D Cup Squad since 1983, and in 1985 he nearly pulled off a huge upset in f v Sweden at Munich when he took first set from Edberg with score 2–2 in matches. However, Edberg deprived Westphal of the memory of a lifetime with a 4s triumph. A r/u showing in Kitzbuhel helped to improve his ranking. *1985 HIGHLIGHTS – SINGLES: French Open* 1r (lost K. Carlsson 6–2 6–1 6–3); *r/u* Kitzbuhel (d. K. Carlsson, Muster, lost Slozil); *qf* Monte Carlo (d. Luna, Wilkison, Arias, lost Sundstrom).

ANNE WHITE (USA)
Born Charleston, West Va., 28 September, 1961; lives St Petersburg, Fla; RH; 5ft 11in; 140lb; final 1985 WTA ranking 20 (45) singles, 22 (14) doubles; 1985 prize money $85,053.
Having already made her mark internationally, and with one year remaining at USC, she turned pro in summer 1981. She was a finalist at US 18 Hard Courts in 1979, and is a protégée of Nick Bollettieri. Without any spectacular results, she managed to achieve her highest year-end ranking in 1983 by virtue of applying herself assiduously. She remained essentially on the same level in singles in 1984, but was more formidable than ever in doubles, capturing 3 events with Allen and reaching sf US Open with Nagelsen. On all levels, 1985 was a memorable year, in which she achieved her highest year-end singles ranking, reached sf French Open in doubles with Nagelsen, and created a stir at Wimbledon when she appeared for her 1r match with Shriver in a white body-suit. *1985 HIGHLIGHTS – SINGLES: French Open* 3r (d. Schmid 6–2 4–6 9–7, Suire 6–0 7–6, lost Sabatini [seed 14] 6–1 7–6), *Wimbledon* 1r (lost Shriver [seed 5] 6–3 6–7 6–3), *US Open* 3r (d. Kelesi 6–3 2–6 6–4, Foltz 6–4 6–1, lost Graf [seed 11] 6–4 6–2); *sf* VS New Orleans (d. Garrison 6–2 6–2, Louie, lost Shriver), *sf* Tampa (d. Bonder, lost Sabatini). *1985 HIGHLIGHTS – DOUBLES:* (with Nagelsen) *French Open* sf, seed 6 (d. Bunge/Pfaff 6–1 6–2, lost Navratilova/Shriver 6–3 6–4); *r/u* Bridgestone (d. Turnbull/Walsh Pete, lost Jordan/Smylie 4–6 7–5 6–2). *CAREER HIGHLIGHTS – DOUBLES:* (with Nagelsen) *French Open – sf 1985; US Open – sf 1984* (d. Evert Lloyd/King 7–6 4–6 6–3, lost Navratilova/Shriver 6–4 7–5).

ROBIN WHITE (USA)
Born San Diego, Cal., December 12, 1963; lives San José, Cal.; RH; 5ft 4in; 120lb; final 1985 WTA ranking 32 (105) singles, 18 doubles; 1985 prize money $82,895.
One of the most improved players on the tour in 1985, she reached last 16 US Open, beating Gadusek. A student at Pepperdine University for one year, she left to pursue a pro tennis career in 1983. She won five nat jun doubles titles in the various age group categories. In 1984 she reached f Wimbledon Plate and in 1985 began her rise into the top 35 by taking VS of Hershey. *1985 HIGHLIGHTS – SINGLES: Wimbledon* 3r (d. Collins 6–2 6–2, Pfaff 6–3 6–2, lost M. Maleeva [seed 4] 6–3 6–3), *US Open* last 16, unseeded (d. Tanvier 0–6 7–6 6–4, Keppeler 6–2 6–2, Gadusek [seed 14] 1–6 6–1 6–2, lost Evert Lloyd [seed 1] 6–2 6–4), *Australian Open* 2r (d. McNeil 6–4 5–7 6–1, lost Sukova [seed 8] 6–4 6–3); *won* VS Hershey (d. Klitch 6–4 fs, Smylie 7–6 6–3, Louie 6–7 6–4 7–5, A. Minter 6–7 6–2 6–2); *qf* VS Denver (d. Cecchini 6–2 fs, K. Cummings, lost Savchenko 6–2 fs), *qf* Birmingham (d. Savchenko 6–4 fs, Gerken, Drescher, lost Burgin 6–4 fs). *1985 HIGH-LIGHTS – DOUBLES:* (with G. Fernandez unless stated) [Piatek] *won* VS Denver (d. Walsh Pete/Leslie Allen 1–6 6–4 7–5), [Piatek] *won* VS Hershey (d. Louie/Minter); *sf* Sydney Indoor (lost Shriver/Smylie), sf Mahwah (lost Jordan/Smylie), *sf* Pan Pacific Tokyo (lost Mesker/Smylie).

WENDY WHITE (USA)
Born Atlanta, 29 September, 1960 and lives there; single; RH; 5ft 6in; 125lb; final 1985 WTA ranking 95 (67); 1985 prize money $38,877.
A crowd-pleaser at 1978 US Open when she and K. Jordan reached doubles qf, she had an excellent 1980 season playing for Rollins college in Florida, sweeping AIAW Champ title in June. She turned pro the next week and immediately beat Ruzici at Eastbourne before losing to Austin in last 16. During 1981 and 1982 she established herself as a reliable performer who could not be taken lightly by the top players. She expanded her game in 1983 and looked more capable in the forecourt, but her ranking virtually stood still. Her results were below par in both singles and doubles in 1984 and 1985. *1985 HIGHLIGHTS – SINGLES: French Open* 1r (lost Tauziat 6–0 6–7 6–2), *Wimbledon* 3r (d. Kinney 6–3 2–6 6–4, Henricksson 6–4 2–6 6–4, lost Sukova [seed 7] 6–1 6–4), *US Open* 1r (lost Van Nostrand 7–6 6–1); *qf* VS Pennsylvania (d. Vermaak, Washington 6–1 fs, lost Benjamin 7–5 fs).

MATS WILANDER (Sweden)
Born Vaxjo, 22 August, 1964; lives Monte Carlo, Monaco; RH; 2HB; 5ft 10in; 155lb; final 1985 ATP ranking 3 (4) singles, 4 (26) doubles; 1985 prize money $1,069,697; career prize money $3,141,665.
European Jun Champ in 1981, he followed victory over Jimmy Brown (USA) in French Open Jun f that year by reaching 3r Wimbledon and, in November, his first GP final (Bangkok) to end year comfortably established among the top 100 men. But no-one could have been prepared for what he would become in 1982. In the most astonishing achievement of the Open Tennis era, he won French Open with victories over Lendl, Gerulaitis, Clerc and Vilas. That was his first GP tournament win and he became the youngest, at 17 years 9 months and 6 days, ever to win that GS event and the first unseeded player since 1947. The placid Swede continued to improve exceptionally fast in 1983, winning more tournaments than anyone else in men's tennis (9), and making a major breakthrough when he won Australian Open with back-to-back triumphs over McEnroe and Lendl. Had he won the Masters, some authorities could have awarded him the No. 1 world ranking, but he was prevented by a sf loss to McEnroe (his first in four 1983 meetings with the American). Nevertheless, he was the only top player to win tournaments on clay (6), grass (1), indoor (1) and cement (1). The only significant flaw in his 1983 record was a 3r loss to Tanner at Wimbledon. While he was ranked 4 on the computer at the end of the year, most experts placed him either second or third, based on his capturing of Australian Open, beating McEnroe three out of four times, winning the most tournaments and displaying the most consistency. In addition, he led Sweden to D Cup f and did not lose a D Cup match all year. In 1984, he took longer to find his peak form but finished the year on a high note with a second consecutive Australian Open title and another D Cup success as Sweden stopped US in f with Wilander routing Connors

in the critical opening match. He remained at No. 4 despite winning only three events and being beaten twice by countryman Sundstrom, once by Edberg, and by Cash in 2r Wimbledon and qf US Open. However, he beat Connors three times without a loss and won a GS title for the third straight year. Again in 1985 he led Sweden to victory in D Cup, putting the finishing touches to another productive season. He achieved a private goal when he collected his fourth GS and second French Open title, stopping McEnroe and Lendl back-to-back in Paris, having won no tournament all year until then. He was a victim of Zivojinovic in 1r at Wimbledon, but bounced back to reach sf US Open (where he lost narrowly to McEnroe in 5 sets), and f Australian, where he lost for only the second time to countryman Edberg. Had he managed to beat Edberg he would have earned the No. 1 world ranking from some experts. *1985 HIGHLIGHTS – SINGLES: won French Open* seed 4 (d. Tulasne 6–1 6–4 6–2, Becker 6–3 6–2 6–1, Sanchez 3–6 6–4 6–3 6–3, Smid 6–3 6–4 6–4, Leconte 6–4 7–6 6–7 7–5, McEnroe [seed 1] 6–1 7–5 7–5, Lendl [seed 2] 3–6 6–4 6–2 6–2), *Wimbledon* 1r, seed 4 (lost Zivojinovic 6–2 5–7 7–5 6–0), *US Open* sf, seed 3 (d. V. Amritraj 6–2 6–4 6–4, Foxworth 6–3 7–5 6–3, Annacone 6–3 6–7 7–6 6–1, Holmes 7–6 6–1 7–5, Jarryd 2–6 6–2 5–0 ret'd, lost McEnroe [seed 1] 3–6 6–4 4–6 6–3 6–3), *r/u Australian Open* seed 3 (d. Muller 3–6 6–3 7–6 6–4, Shiras 6–2 6–3 6–2, Wilkison 7–6 6–3 6–3, Kriek 6–3 7–5 6–2, Zivojinovic 7–5 6–1 6–3, lost Edberg 6–4 6–3 6–3); *won* US Pro (d. Sundstrom, Vilas, Jaite 6–2 6–4), *won* Bastad (d. Keretic, Edberg 6–1 6–0); *r/u* Brussels (d. Cash, lost Jarryd 7–5 fs), *r/u* Monte Carlo (d. Krickstein, lost Lendl 6–1 6–4 4–6 6–4), *r/u* Cincinnati (d. Edberg, Wilkison, lost Becker 6–4 6–2), *r/u* Geneva (lost Smid 6–4 6–4), *r/u* Barcelona (lost Tulasne 0–6 6–2 3–6 6–4 6–0), *r/u* Tokyo Seiko (d. Gomez 7–6 fs, Connors def., lost Lendl 6–0 6–4); *sf* Italian Open (lost Mecir 6–2 6–4), *sf* German Open (lost Mecir 6–2 6–4); *qf* Masters (lost Becker 6–4 4–6 6–3). *1985 HIGHLIGHTS – DOUBLES:* (with Nystrom unless stated) *French Open* sf, seed 6 (d. Giammalva/Willenborg 7–6 6–3, lost Edmondson/Warwick 6–4 6–1 7–5), *US Open* sf, seed 5 (d. Denton/Fleming 6–3 6–4 6–4, lost Leconte/Noah [seed 12] 6–3 7–6 6–4); [Jarryd] *won* Italian Open (d. Flach/Seguso 4–6 6–3 6–2), *won* US Pro Indoor (d. Gunthardt/Taroczy, Fibak/A. Mayer); *r/u* Cincinnati (lost Edberg/Jarryd), *r/u* Masters (lost Edberg/Jarryd 6–1 7–6); *sf* Rotterdam (lost Slozil/Smid), *sf* Monte Carlo (d. Gunthardt/Taroczy, lost Glickstein/Perkis, *sf* Hamburg (d. Motta/Willenborg, lost Gunthardt/Taroczy). *CAREER HIGHLIGHTS – SINGLES: French Open – won 1982* unseeded (d. Lendl 4–6 7–5 3–6 6–4 6–2, Gerulaitis 6–3 6–3 4–6 6–4, Clerc 7–5 6–2 1–6 7–5, Vilas 1–6 7–6 [saving one s-p] 6–0 6–4), *won 1985, r/u 1983* (d. Sundstrom, McEnroe 1–6 6–2 6–4 6–0, Higueras, lost Noah 6–2 7–5 7–6), *sf 1984* (lost Lendl 6–3 6–3 7–5); *Australian Open – won 1983* (d. McEnroe 4–6 6–3 6–4 6–3, Lendl 6–1 6–4), *won 1984* (d. Curren 6–7 6–4 7–6 6–2), *r/u 1985; US Open – qf 1984* (lost Cash 7–6 6–4 2–6 6–3), *sf 1985; Masters – sf 1983* (lost McEnroe 6–2 6–4), *sf 1984* (lost McEnroe 6–1 6–1). *CAREER HIGHLIGHTS – DOUBLES: (with Nystrom) Australian Open – r/u 1984* (lost Cash/Fitzgerald 6–4 6–4 2–6 6–3); *French Open – sf 1985; US Open – sf 1985*.

TIM WILKISON (USA)
Born Shelby, NC, 21 November, 1959; lives Asheville, NC; LH; 5ft 11in; 160lb; final 1985 ATP Ranking 44 (39); 1985 prize money $174,438.
A finalist in US Nat 21 Champs in summer 1977, and a former US Nat 16 Champ, he is a stocky, determined serve-and-volleyer and was a finalist in Maui in 1980. In 1981 he won NSW Open and he opened 1982 with another tournament win at Auckland, Following an off year in 1983, he had his greatest season in 1984, winning Vienna and reaching f North Conway and Basle. He appeared in 26 tournaments in 1985, winning Nancy, reaching sf ATP Champs and Cologne, and last 16 Australian Open, as well as giving Edberg a scare in 2r Wimbledon. *1985 HIGHLIGHTS – SINGLES: Wimbledon* 2r (d. Ostoja 6–4 6–0 2–6 7–6, lost Edberg [seed 14] 6–1 7–5 3–6 6–7 9–7), *US Open* 3r (d. Van Patten 6–3 6–3 4–6 7–6, Slozil 6–1 6–3 6–1, lost Jarryd [seed 6] 6–0 6–1 6–4), *Australian Open* last 16, unseeded (d. Zverev 6–2 6–3 6–0, Leach 6–4 6–0 6–2, Annacone [seed 12] 7–5 6–3 6–3, lost Wilander [seed 3] 7–6 6–3 6–3); *won* Nancy (d. Portes, Zivojinovic 4–6 7–6 9–7); *sf* Cologne (d. Hooper, Tom Gullikson, lost Lundgren), *sf* Cincinnati (d. Anger, Jaite, Noah, J. Brown, lost Wilander); *qf* Milan (d. Mecir, McNamee, lost Hlasek). *1985 HIGHLIGHTS – DOUBLES:* [Dickson] *r/u* Basle (d. Slozil/Smid, lost Tim/Tom Gullikson).

MARTIN WOSTENHOLME (Canada)
Born Toronto, 11 October, 1962; lives Oakville, Ontario; RH; 6ft; 165lb; final 1985 ATP ranking 93 (186); 1985 prize money $24,902.
The No 1. player for Yale University from 1980 to 1984, he was also the Canadian No. 1 in 1984. In 1985, a qf finish in Johannesburg fuelled his rise into the top 100. *1985 HIGHLIGHTS – SINGLES: US Open* 2r (d. Gildemeister 6–4 6–3 3–6 3–6 6–3, lost McEnroe 6–0 7–6 6–1); *qf* Johannesburg (d. Stefanki, Shaw, lost Gilbert).

SIMON YOUL (Australia)
Born Simons Plans, Tasmania, 1 July, 1965, and lives there; RH; 6ft 1in; 170lb; final 1985 ATP ranking 90 (201); 1985 prize money $31,856.
Victorious at French, Wimbledon and US Open Jun Champs in doubles in 1983, he was a member of the 1984 Australian Olympic team and 1985 made his mark on the GP circuit. *1985 HIGHLIGHTS – SINGLES: French Open* 3r (d. Leach 5–7 6–4 6–4 6–4, Bengoechea 2–6 7–5 7–6 1–6 7–5, lost Nystrom 6–2 6–0 6–2); *sf* Brisbane (d. R. Simpson, lost Annacone), *sf* Sydney (d. Schultz, lost Fitzgerald).

JAIME YZAGA (Peru)
Born Lima, 23 October, 1967, and lives there; RH; 5ft 7in; 134lb; final 1985 ATP ranking 45 (–); 1985 prize money $36,377.
Two months after reaching sf Wimbledon jun, he reached last 16 US Open where he was the only player to take a set off Lendl. *1985 HIGHLIGHTS – SINGLES: US Open* last 16, unseeded (d. Hlasek 5–7 7–5 3–6 6–4 6–3, Cassidy 6–7 6–3 6–7 6–1 7–5, Pate 6–3 6–3 7–6, lost Lendl [seed 2] 4–6 6–3 6–4 6–0).

SLOBODAN ZIVOJINOVIC (Yugoslavia)
Born Belgrade, 23 July, 1963; lives Hamburg, West Germany; RH; 6ft 6in; 200lb; final 1985 ATP ranking 35 (115); 1985 prize money $127,660.
Yugoslav nat champ in 12, 13, 14, 16, 18 and 21 categories, he shot into top 35 in 1985, when he beat Wilander at Wimbledon, and ended the year in style with sf place in Australian Open, defeating McEnroe in qf. *1985 HIGHLIGHTS – SINGLES: French Open* 2r (d. Shaw 4–6 6–2 2–6 6–3 8–6, lost Gildemeister 5–7 7–6 6–3 7–5), *Wimbledon* 2r (d. Wilander [seed 4] 6–2 5–7 7–5 6–0, lost H. Gunthardt 6–4 4–6 4–6 6–3 6–4), *US Open* 1r (lost Foxworth 6–7 6–4 4–6 6–3 6–3), *Australian Open* sf, unseeded (bye, d. S. Davis [seed 9] 7–6 3–6 6–1 6–3, DePalmer 6–7 6–3 6–2 6–2, Mayotte [seed 8] 2–6 6–4 6–4 6–4, McEnroe [seed 2] 2–6 6–3 1–6 6–4 6–0, lost Wilander [seed 3] 7–5 6–1 6–3); *rlu* Nancy (d. Soares, Kandler, Pils, Hooper, lost Wilkison); *sf* Queens (d. Leconte, Acuna, Annacone, lost Kriek); *qf* Nice (d. Portes, Maurer, lost Schwaier). *1985 HIGHLIGHTS – DOUBLES:* (with Pimek) *won* US Pro (d. McNamara/McNamee 7–6 fs); *sf* USCC (lost Slozil/Warwick).

A former junior champion and the winner of the junior title at Wimbledon and in Italy, Mary Lou Piatek has never quite become the player she promised to be and is now ranked 61 in the world. *(T. Hindley)*

ALL-TIME GREATS

David Gray and John Barrett

WILMER LAWSON ALLISON (USA)
Born 8 /1 /04. Died 30 /4 /77. One of the greatest and most spectacular of American doubles specialists, he also gained some notable singles successes. Possessing a fierce smash, a serve 'with the kick of a Texas mustang', considerable power on the volley, and a fine backhand drive, he found an ideal doubles partner in John Van Ryn. They won at Wimbledon in **1929–30** and were runners-up in **1935.** They took the US title in **1931** and **1935** and reached the final in **1930|32|34|36.** His singles form was less consistent, but on his day he could play brilliantly. He defeated Perry to win the US title in **1935,** and in **1930,** after beating Cochet, he was runner-up to Tilden at Wimbledon. Between **1929–35** he played in 45 D Cup rubbers, winning 18 out of 29 singles and 14 of his 16 doubles.

JOSEPH ASBOTH (Hungary)
Born 18 /9 /17. A stylish righthander whose victory in the **1947** French singles, when he beat Petra, Tom Brown and Sturgess, was Hungary's most important tennis success before their victory in the Saab King's Cup in 1976; 7 times nat champ; 6 times winner of the Hungarian int title; he played 1st at Wimbledon in **1939** and impressed those who saw him against Austin in 1 r. Lost to Bromwich in the **1948** sfs. From **1938–57** he played 41 D Cup rubbers in 16 ties.

ARTHUR ROBERT ASHE (USA)
Born 10 /7 /43. A cool, thoughtful, dogged competitor, he was the first black American to win the Wimbledon men's singles title and, in **1968,** playing as an amateur, he became the first US Open champion. Always happier on fast courts, he tried hard to succeed on clay but endured regular disappointments in Paris and never progressed further than the semi-finals **(1971)** in Rome. He was a semi-finalist at Wimbledon **1968–69** before surprising Connors in the **1975** final. He defeated Okker to win the US title in **1968** but in **1972** lost to Nastase after leading by two sets to one and 4–2 in the final. He won Australian singles **1970** and the WCT title **1975.** Refused a visa to South Africa in 1970, he broke through apartheid laws to play in Johannesburg **1973,** losing to Connors in the final and winning the doubles with Okker. After missing most of the 1977 season, he regained his place among the leaders of the circuit in **1978** and reached match-point against McEnroe in the Masters final. Between **1963** and **1978,** he appeared in 18 Davis Cup ties, winning 27 out of 32 singles and one of two doubles. US Davis Cup captain **1980–85,** following his retirement from active play owing to a heart condition that had necessitated triple by-pass surgery.

CILLY AUSSEM (Germany)
Born 4 /1 /09. Died 22 /3 /63. Later the Contessa della Corta Brae. The only German to win the women's singles at Wimbledon. Her strokes were not strong but she was a model of steadiness and persistence. 'Quite small and more of a girl in appearance with round brown eyes and a cherub face', wrote Helen Wills. 'Her agility on court and the distance that she covers in spite of her shortness are really astonishing.' **1931** – when the Californian did not compete – was her best year. She beat Betty Nuthall in the French f and then defeated Hilde Krahwinkel in Wimbledon's only all-German final. That was a disappointing match, because both women were handicapped by blistered feet. Her

victory compensated for an unlucky failure in *1930.* Then she slipped and sprained an ankle at 4–4 in the fs of her sf against Elizabeth Ryan and had to be carried from the court.

HENRY WILFRED AUSTIN (Great Britain)
Born 20 /8 /06. Bunny Austin's Wimbledon record was remarkable (and unlucky), but his most important contribution to British tennis was in the D Cup. The possessor of elegant groundstrokes, which compensated for a lack of power in his serving and smashing, he played many of the crucial singles, alongside Perry, in Britain's successful campaigns in the 1930s. A former Cambridge Univ captain, he played in 24 ties between *1929–37,* winning 36 of his 48 rubbers, all singles. He won 8 rubbers out of 12 and 5 out of 8 'live' rubbers in his 6 Challenge Rounds. At Wimbledon he failed only once to reach the qf or go further between *1929–39.* R /u to Vines *1932* and Budge *1938,* in sf *1929* and *1936|37,* and r /u to Henkel in *1937* French singles.

WILFRED BADDELEY (Great Britain)
Born 11 /1 /1872. Died 30 /1 /1929. Youngest winner–at 19 years, 5 months and 23 days–of Wimbledon singles in *1891* until Becker in 1985. Also won singles in *1892|95,* and doubles (with twin brother Herbert) *1891|94|95|96.*

MARCEL BERNARD (France)
Born 18 /6 /14. Shrewd and stylish, a canny lefthander with considerable touch, he is one of only two French players to have won in Paris since the days of the 'Musketeers' (the other is Noah, 1983); demonstrated his promise early, reaching the French singles sf and, with Boussus, the doubles in *1932,* still in sufficient form to be chosen for the French D Cup team in *1956.* In *1946* he won 5 set matches against Petra in the sf and Drobny in the final to take the French title; in sf on 3 other occasions; won the doubles with Borotra *(1936)* and with Petra *(1946)* and the mixed with Lollette Payot *(1935)* and Billie Yorke *(1936).* Between *1935–56* he played 42 D Cup rubbers in 25 ties and he has also served as president of the French Tennis Federation.

PAULINE MAY BETZ (USA)
Born 6 /8 /19. Now Mrs Addie. An agile, athletic competitor, who might have gained many more titles if the war had not interrupted international competition. She was ranked eighth in the US in *1939* and was the most successful player in wartime competitions there, winning the national title from *1942–44.* She won Wimbledon at a cost of only 20 games in *1946,* defeating Louise Brough 6–2 6–4 in the final. She and Miss Hart were runners-up to Miss Brough and Miss Osborne in the doubles and, if she was disappointed in Paris, where Miss Osborne beat her 1–6 8–6 7–5 in the final, after saving two match-points with drop-shots at 5–6 in the second set, she asserted her supremacy again at Forest Hills by defeating Doris Hart 11–9 6–3 in the final. Soon afterwards she turned professional.

BLANCHE BINGLEY (Great Britain)
Born 3 /11 /1863. Died 6 /8 /1946. Became Mrs Hillyard. One of the determined pioneers of women's tennis. She competed in the first women's tournament at Wimbledon in *1884* and lost to Maud Watson, the eventual champion, in sfs. The following year Miss Watson defeated her in f, but she avenged those failures by beating the champion in the challenge round in *1886.* That was the first of her six victories. Further successes followed in *1889,* *1894, 1897, 1899* and *1900.* Only Lottie Dod, who retired in 1893, troubled her until Mrs Sterry ended her supremacy in 1901. Like many early players, her game was founded on a powerful forehand and strict command of length. A reluctant volleyer who invariably ran round her backhand, she was so quick and so fit that she was difficult to outmanoeuvre. She wore white gloves to give her a better grip and her follow-through on the forehand was said to have been so complete 'that her left shoulder was often a mass of bruises from the impact of the racket'. She married Commander G. W. Hillyard, secretary of the All England Club from 1907–24; altogether she competed in the championships 24 times.

PENELOPE DORA HARVEY BOOTHBY (Great Britain)
Born 2 /8 /1881. Died 22 /2 /1970. Became Mrs Green. One of the group of players from the county of Middlesex who dominated the early years of women's tennis at Wimbledon. She won one of the most exciting of the pre-1914 f, defeating Miss A. M. Morton 6–4 4–6 8–6 ('Few closer or more interesting struggles have ever been witnessed on the famous old court', wrote G. W. Hillyard) in **1909**, and lost the most dismal in the history of the championships to Mrs Lambert Chambers, who beat her 6–0 6–0, in the **1911** challenge round. Mrs Lambert Chambers had beaten her by the same score at the Beckenham tournament two weeks earlier and had allowed her only four games in the challenge round in **1910**. Somewhat fortunately she and Mrs McNair became Wimbledon's first women's doubles champions in 1913. They were down 2–6 2–4 to Mrs Lambert Chambers and Mrs Sterry in the final when Mrs Sterry fell and retired with a torn tendon. She and Mrs McNair were also semi-finalists in **1922.**

BJORN BORG (Sweden)
Born 6 /6 /56. One of the coolest match players the game has ever known, he matured early, winning his first important title, the **1974** Italian Open, shortly before his 18th birthday and the first of his six French Championships just after it. With fierce topspin on both his forehand and his double-handed backhand, a powerful serve and speedy court coverage plus an indomitable will to win, he was virtually invincible on European clay between **1974** and **1981** adding the French Open in **1975, 1978, 1979, 1980** and **1981** and a second Italian title in **1978** as well as the US Pro Championship on US clay in **1974, 1975** and **1976**. Never an instinctive volleyer, he confounded those observers who thought his game was unsuited to grass by setting a modern record at Wimbledon where he won five successive titles between **1976** and **1980**. Only William Renshaw, in the days of the Challenge Round, won more (1881–86). He learned to win indoors, taking the WCT title in **1976** and the Masters twice **(1979** and **1980)** and leading Sweden to their first D Cup success, a 3–2 victory over Czechoslovakia in Stockholm in **1975**. But he never solved the problems of the high, fast bounce and positive foothold of US hard courts. Four times he was beaten in the US Open final, twice by Connors **(1978, 1979)** and twice by McEnroe **(1980, 1981)**, the last three being on asphalt at Flushing Meadow. By the autumn of **1981** this great champion felt burnt out and virtually retired from the mainstream, restricting his play to exhibitions and special events. Although he attempted two comebacks, in **1982** and **1984**, he could no longer make the total commitment that had once made him supreme and turned to other interests. His legacy to Swedish tennis is immeasurable for he sparked the flame that has burned so brightly ever since through Wilander, Sundstrom, Jarryd, Nystrom and now Edberg. His style of errorless, counter-attacking topspin inspired a whole generation of players around the world. – J.B.

JEAN BOROTRA (France)
Born 13 /8 /1898. A brilliantly agile volleyer and a shrewd player. One of the 'Four Musketeers' who won the D Cup for France from **1927–32**. Enthusiastic and popular, he continued to play competitive lawn tennis long past his 70th year, regularly appearing for France in International Club matches against Britain. Won Wimbledon singles **1924** and **1926** and doubles (with R. Lacoste) **1925** and (with J. Brugnon) **1932/33**. French singles **1924/31,** and doubles **1925/28/29/34/36**. Won Australian singles and doubles **1928**. Had long and spectacular covered court record, winning French singles title 12 times, British 11, and US 4. Played 54 D Cup rubbers **1922–47,** winning 36 in 32 ties.

MAUREEN CONNOLLY BRINKER (USA)
Born 17 /9 /34. Died 21 /6 /69. The most determined and concentrated of post-war women's champions she hit her groundstrokes with remorseless accuracy. Won US singles in **1951** at the age of 16 and thereafter lost only 4 matches – 2 to Doris Hart, one to Shirley Fry, and another to Beverley Fleitz – before she broke her leg in a riding accident in 1954 and retired. She was never beaten in singles at Wimbledon, winning **1952/53/54**. US singles **1951/52/53**. French singles **1953/54** and (with Mrs H. C. Hopman) doubles **1954**.

Three great American post-war Wimbledon champions. **Right:** Maureen Connolly, undefeated from 1952–1954. **Below:** Pauline Betz (left), the first post-war winner in 1946, with her victim, Louise Brough, who won in 1948, 1949, 1950 and 1955.   (A. Cole)

Australian singles and doubles (with Julie Sampson) *1953.* Italian singles *1954.* She won all 9 of her W Cup rubbers and in *1953* she was the first woman to bring off the Grand Slam of the 4 major singles titles.

JOHN EDWARD BROMWICH (Australia)
Born 14 /11 /18. A gracefully unorthodox player whose career might have been even more successful if it had not been interrupted by World War II. Ambidextrous but using both hands on the forehand, he used a very light, softly strung racket to control the ball with great subtlety. He won the Australian singles in *1939* and regained the title from Quist in *1946.* Those were his only major singles victories, although he was agonisingly close to success in f of *1948* Wimbledon when he lost to Falkenburg after leading 5–2 in the fs and holding three match-points. But it was in doubles, mostly with Quist or Sedgman, that he earned most honours. He won at Wimbledon in *1948* (with Sedgman) *I50* (with Quist), took the US title three times, and he and Quist ruled in Australia from *1938–40* and *1946–50.* Won the Wimbledon mixed with Louise Brough, *1947I48,* and played in 53 D Cup rubbers between *1937–50.*

SIR NORMAN EVERARD BROOKES (Australia)
Born 14 /11 /1877. Died 10 /1 /1968. The first overseas winner of men's singles at Wimbledon. Left-handed and a notable volleyer, he lost in Challenge Round on first to H. L. Doherty in Challenge Round on first visit to Wimbledon 1905. Won singles and doubles (with A. F. Wilding) *1907* and *1914.* With Wilding won the D Cup for Australasia in *1907.* Between *1905–20* he played 39 rubbers and was 6 times a member of a side which won the Challenge Round. Returned to Wimbledon in *1924* at 46 and reached the 4r.

ALTHEA LOUISE BROUGH (USA)
Born 11 /3 /23. Now Mrs Clapp. An aggressive server and volleyer, she played a major part in establishing American domination of women's tennis immediately after World War II. Won Wimbledon singles *1948I49I50* and again in *1955* after the retirement of Maureen Connolly, who beat her in *1952* and *1954* f, US in *1947,* and Australian, *1950.* She and Margaret Osborne du Pont formed a redoubtable doubles partnership, winning 5 times at Wimbledon and 3 times in Paris, and holding the US title from *1942–50* and *1955I56I57.* She was mixed doubles champ at Wimbledon *1946I47I48I50* and took all 3 titles in *1948* and *1950.* She played 22 W Cup rubbers between *1946–57* and was never beaten.

JACQUES BRUGNON (France)
Born 11 /6 /1895. Died 20 /3 /1978. The doubles specialist of the 'Four Musketeers', he gained most of his early success with Cochet and then formed a partnership with Borotra, which was still capable of reaching the *1939* French f, when he was 44 and Borotra 40, and coming three times within a point of the title. He and Borotra returned to Wimbledon and reached the 3r in *1948.* Won Wimbledon doubles *1926I28* (Cochet) *I32I33* (Borotra). Between *1927–34* won French doubles 3 times with Cochet and twice with Borotra. Also Australian doubles (with Borotra) in *1928.* Reached singles sf at Wimbledon, *1926.* Played 31 D Cup doubles and 6 singles *1921–34.*

JOHN DONALD BUDGE (USA)
Born 13 /6 /15. The first player to bring off the Grand Slam of the 4 historic singles titles in one year – *1938.* A relentless competitor with a majestic backhand he won all 3 titles at Wimbledon in *1937* and *1938.* Won doubles (with G. Mako) and mixed (with Alice Marble). US singles *1937I38* and doubles (with Mako) *1936I38.* French and Australian singles *1938* and between *1935–38* won 25 out of 29 D Cup rubbers in 11 ties. Turned professional in *1938.*

MARIA ESTHER ANDION BUENO (Brazil)
Born 11 /10 /39. The most gracefully artistic of post-war women's champions. For nearly a decade her rivalry with Margaret Court provided the principal excitement of the women's game, but at the end she was plagued by injury. Won Wimbledon singles *1959I60I64,*

and doubles (with Althea Gibson) *1958,* (with Darlene Hard) *1960I63,* (with Billie Jean King) *I65,* and (with Nancy Gunter) *I66.* US singles *1959I63I64I66* and doubles (with Darlene Hard) *1960I62,* (with Nancy Gunter) *I66,* and (with Margaret Court) *I68.* French doubles (with Darlene Hard) *1960.* Australian doubles (with Christine Janes) *1960.* Italian singles, *1958I61I65.*

MAY SUTTON BUNDY (USA)
Born in Plymouth, England, 25 /9 /1886. Died 4 /10 /1975. In *1905* the first overseas player to win a Wimbledon title. The seventh and youngest child of a British naval officer, Captain A. de G. Sutton, she learnt tennis on asphalt courts after her family moved to California in 1893. She was forceful and vigorous with a disconcerting top-spin forehand. F. R. Burrow commented: 'She took a deep breath before every stroke and then hit the ball with all her force to the accompaniment of a very audible expiration.' After winning the US singles and doubles in *1904* she went, aged 18, to Wimbledon *1905* and defeated the holder, Miss Douglass, in the Challenge Round. Miss Douglass regained the title the following year, but then lost a third battle with the Californian in *1907.* After winning the US Clay Court singles *1912,* Miss Sutton married Thomas Bundy, 3 times a US doubles champ. She played doubles in the *1925* W Cup and in *1929* returned to Wimbledon at 42 to defeat Eileen Bennett, seeded 4, and reach the qf. She was still playing 44 years later. Her daughter Dorothy represented the US 3 times in the W Cup and won the Australian singles 1938 and a nephew, John Doeg, was US champ in 1930.

DOROTHEA LAMBERT CHAMBERS (Great Britain)
Born 3 /9 /1878. Died 7 /1 /1960. Née Douglass. The most successful British woman player before 1914, she won Wimbledon singles 7 times and lost dramatically to Suzanne Lenglen in *1919* Challenge Round after holding 2 match-points. Played in *1926* W Cup – 23 years after first success at Wimbledon. The daughter of an Ealing vicar, she became a coach in *1928.* Won Wimbledon singles *1903I04I06I10I11I13I14.*

HENRI COCHET (France)
Born 14 /12 /01. The great instinctive genius of lawn tennis, swift and imaginative, a master of the volley and half-volley, whose play could rise to dizzy heights and sometimes slip to unexpected disaster. Won Wimbledon singles *1927I29* and doubles (with J. Brugnon) *1926I28.* US singles *1928.* French singles *1922I26I28I30I32* and doubles (with Brugnon) *1927I30I32.* With the other 'Musketeers', he played successfully in 6 Challenge Rounds. Between *1922* and *1933,* when he turned professional, he won 44 D Cup rubbers out of 58 in 26 ties. After the war reinstated as an amateur.

ASHLEY JOHN COOPER (Australia)
Born 15 /9 /36. A strong and determined competitor who maintained Australia's command of the international game after Hoad and Rosewall turned professional. After being overwhelmed by Hoad in the *1957* f at Wimbledon, he returned to beat Fraser in a stern test of endurance in *1958.* He was US champion *1958* and won Australia *1957–58.* His doubles victories included Australia *1958,* France *1957–58* and US *1958.* He played singles when Australia successfully defended the D Cup in *1957* and *1958,* winning one rubber in each match. He beat Seixas and lost to Mackay *1957* and beat Mackay and lost to Olmedo *1958.*

CHARLOTTE COOPER (Great Britain)
Born 22 /9 /1870. Died 10 /10 /1970. Became Mrs Sterry. One of the first successful women volleyers, she won at Wimbledon *1895I96I98I1901I08.* Overshadowed at first by Mrs Hillyard – her first three victories were gained in years when the older player did not compete – she defeated her at last in *1901,* the year of her marriage, after losing to Mrs Hillyard in four previous matches at the championships. In *1902* she lost in the famous re-played challenge round to Muriel Robb (they stopped at 4–6 13–11 on the first evening, then began again and Miss Robb won 7–5 6–1) and then regained the title in *1908* after

beating Mrs Lambert Chambers in the quarter-finals. She reached the all-comers' final in **1912** and took Mrs McNair to 9–7 in the third set of a qf in **1913.** Her attacking spirit delighted her contemporaries. 'Her smiling good temper and sportsmanship made her as popular a player as ever went on to the Centre Court', wrote Burrow. 'She had a constitution like the proverbial ostrich. She never knew what it was to be tired and was never sick or sorry', said Hillyard.

BARON GOTTFRIED VON CRAMM (Germany)
Born 7 /7 /09. Died in car accident in Egypt 9 /11 /76. An elegant stylist and Germany's most successful player. Won French singles **1934|36** and doubles (with H. Henkel) **1937,** and German singles **1932|33|34|35|48|49** and doubles **1948|49|53|55.** Like F. S. Stolle, he was losing singles finalist at Wimbledon for 3 successive years – 1935–37. Won Wimbledon mixed (with Hilda Krahwinkel) **1933** and US doubles (with Henkel) **1937.** Won 82 D Cup rubbers out of 102 in 37 ties between **1932–53.**

JOHN HERBERT CRAWFORD (Australia)
Born 22 /3 /08. Classic stylist, he beat H. E. Vines in **1933** in one of the greatest of all Wimbledon f. Won Wimbledon doubles (with A. K. Quist) **1935.** French singles **1933** and doubles (with Quist) **1935,** Australian singles **1931|33** and doubles (with H. C. Hopman) **1929|30,** (with E. F. Moon) **1932,** and (with V. B. McGrath) **1935.** Won 36 out of 58 D Cup rubbers between **1928–37.**

DWIGHT FILLEY DAVIS (USA)
Born 5 /7 /1879. Died 28 /11 /1945. The donor of the D Cup, the trophy at stake in the international team championship. A Harvard undergraduate, he played against the British Isles in the first two matches of that competition, winning a single and partnering Holcombe Ward successfully in the doubles in **1900** and, with Ward again, losing to the Dohertys in the doubles in **1902.** A lefthander, he won the US doubles with Ward from **1899–1901,** retiring undefeated, and also the all-comers' final at Wimbledon in **1901,** only to fall to the Dohertys. He was President of the US LTA in **1923,** US Secretary of War 1925–29 and later Governor-General of the Philippines.

MAX DECUGIS (France)
Born 24 /9 /1882. Died 6 /9 /1978. The first great French player. He spent his schooldays in England and won his first tournaments there. Short, quick, and wiry, he was an aggressive competitor, whom Lawrie Doherty described as 'the most promising young player in the world'. He dominated French tennis from **1903,** when he won in Paris for the first time, to the outbreak of World War I, winning the singles title 8 times in 12 years and the doubles from **1902–14** and again in **1920** when the Champs were resumed. He was still playing well enough to reach the singles final in **1923** when he was 41. By that time the age of the 'Musketeers' was dawning. Although he competed regularly at Wimbledon, he never progressed beyond the singles sf **(1911|12)** but, with Gobert, he gained France's first title by winning the doubles in **1911.**

CHARLOTTE DOD (Great Britain)
Born 24 /9 /1871. Died 27 /6 /1960. The first lawn tennis prodigy. Won the first of 5 Wimbledon titles in **1887** at the age of 15 years and 10 months. When she retired, she became an international golfer and hockey player. Nicknamed 'the Little Wonder', she won Wimbledon singles **1887|88|91|92|93.**

HUGH LAURENCE DOHERTY (Great Britain)
Born London 8 /10 /1875. Died 21 /8 /1919. Learnt game with elder brother, Reginald Frank ('Reggie'), at Westminster School. Played for Cambridge Univ against Oxford in 1896–98 and developed into one of the most spectacular, aggressive, stylish, and successful of British players. 'Lawrie' Doherty was celebrated for smashing and volleying, and for speed about the court. With his brother, formed one of the greatest doubles partnerships

in the history of the game. Won all-comers' singles at Wimbledon, *1898,* and singles champ *1902–06.* Doubles champ (with R. F. Doherty) *1897—1901, 1903–05.* First overseas player to win US singles, *1903,* and doubles, *1902I03.* In 5 D Cup challenge rounds, *1902–06,* he was never beaten, winning 7 singles rubbers and 5 doubles.

REGINALD FRANK DOHERTY (Great Britain)
Born London 14 /10 /1872. Died 29 /12 /1910. The senior partner of the great Doherty combination and the most notable stylist of early lawn tennis. Contemporary observers called his backhand, produced with back swing, full follow-through and remarkable touch, 'a model of perfection'. Was Wimbledon singles champ *1897–1900* and doubles champ *1897–1901* and *1903–05.* Reached the doubles challenge round at Wimbledon for first time with H. A. Nisbet in 1896. Thereafter he and his brother, H. L. Doherty, were beaten only by S. H. Smith and F. L. Riseley at Wimbledon. They lost to this pair in 1902, then beat them in the next three challenge rounds before falling to them again in 1906. The Dohertys won the US doubles in *1902I03.* Won South African singles and doubles, *1909.*

JAROSLAV DROBNY (Great Britain)
Born 12 /10 /21. Exiled himself from Czechoslovakia in 1949, became an Egyptian subject in 1950 and a naturalised Briton in 1960. One of the great post-war clay court competitors with tremendous left-hand serve and smash, and delicate touch, he played in some of Wimbledon's most dramatic and emotional matches and eventually won the singles in *1954* at the age of 33. In *1946* he beat Kramer, the favourite; he lost to Schroeder in the *1949* f; in *1950* he let a two-set lead slip against Sedgman; Mottram surprised him in *1951;* he fell to Sedgman again in the *1952* f; and in *1953* he never recovered from beating Patty 8–6 16–18 3–6 8–6 12–10 in Wimbledon's second longest singles. The following year, when his chance seemed to be slipping away, he beat Rosewall, then 19, in f. He won in Paris in *1951I52* (after another series of dramatic failures), Italy *1950I51I53* and Germany *1950.* In *1946I47I48I49* he played in 43 D Cup rubbers, and won 37.

FRANCOISE DURR (France)
Born 25 /12 /42. Now Mrs Browning. The outstanding French woman player of the 1960s and 1970s. Shrewd and unorthodox, particularly in her serve and on the backhand, she excelled in doubles. She gained her major singles successes in *1967* when she won the French and German titles and reached the US semi-finals, but in doubles won a host of titles with a variety of partners, including five successive French victories – with Gail Sheriff (later Mrs Chanfreau and now Mrs Lovera) *1967* and *1970I71,* and with Ann Jones, *1968I69.* Won US doubles *1972* with Betty Stove, and Italian and South African titles *1969* with Jones. She failed, however, in six Wimbledon doubles finals between *1965* and *1975.* Won Wimbledon mixed doubles with Tony Roche *1976* and the French with Jean-Claude Barclay in *1968, 1971* and *1973.*

ROY STANLEY EMERSON (Australia)
Born 3 /11 /36. A remarkable athlete, 'lean, keen, and trained to the last ounce', who led Australia's international challenge for five years after Laver turned professional in 1962. A Queenslander, he won Wimbledon singles *1964I65* but injury in 1966 spoilt his chance of equalling Perry's record of three successive titles. Won the doubles with Fraser *1959I61,* US singles *1961I64* and doubles *1959I60* (with Fraser) and *1965I66* (with Stolle), Australian singles *1961* and *1963I64I65I66I67* and doubles *1960I66.* On clay courts won the French singles *1963I67,* Italian *1959I61I66* and German *1967* and his most interesting doubles achievement was to take the French title from *1960* to *1965* with five different partners, Fraser *1960I62,* Laver *1961,* Santana *1963,* Fletcher *1964,* and Stolle *1965.* He won 36 of his 40 D Cup rubbers and played in 9 successive challenge rounds between *1959* and *1967.*

ROBERT FALKENBURG (USA)

Born 29 /1 /26. Won the US Junior Championship in *1943–44* and came to Europe in *1947* with the reputation of possessing the fastest service in the US. He won at Queen's Club, but lost to Pails in qf at Wimbledon and then won the doubles with Kramer, defeating Mottram and Sidwell in f. The following year he won one of Wimbledon's most dramatic f, defeating Bromwich 7–5 0–6 6–2 3–6 7–5 after saving three match-points as 3–5 in 5s. He was born in New York, learnt most of his tennis in Los Angeles and moved to Brazil, for whom he played in D Cup on a residential qualification.

NEALE ANDREW FRASER (Australia)

Born 3 /10 /33. A consistently aggressive lefthander, with a plain, direct serve and volley game, he was trained by Hopman, winning 18 of 21 D Cup rubbers between *1958* and *1963*, and later captained the Australian team which recaptured the trophy at Cleveland in *1973* and at Melbourne in *1978 and 1983*. Fraser started his Wimbledon career in the qualifying competition and ended by winning the singles in *1960* after a remarkable escape in the qf. Buchholz, who had held 5 match-points against him, retired with cramp. doubles with Emerson *1959|61* and mixed with du Pont in *1962* – the year in which he and his brother, John, a Melbourne doctor, both reached the singles sf. Neither got through to the f. He won the US singles *1959|60* and doubles *1957|59|60,* the French doubles *1958|60|62,* and Australian doubles *1957|58|62.*

SHIRLEY JUNE FRY (USA)

Born 30 /6 /27. Now Mrs Irvin. A persistent competitor, whose most notable performances were in doubles. She was first ranked in the top ten in the US in 1944, but she did not gain her two major singles successes until *1956* when she won both Wimbledon and Forest Hills. Until then she had always been thwarted by fellow-Americans. She won the Wimbledon doubles from *1951–53* with Doris Hart, losing only four games in capturing the title in *1953* and beat Helen Fletcher and Jean Quertier 6–0 6–0 in sf and Julie Sampson and Maureen Connolly by the same score in f. They won the US title *1951–54.* Her other successes included the Wimbledon mixed, with Seixas, *1956,* the Australian singles and doubles, with Althea Gibson, *1957,* and the French singles, *1951,* and doubles, with Hart, *1950–53.* She played in six W Cup contests, winning 10 matches and losing twice.

ALTHEA GIBSON (USA)

Born 25 /8 /27. Now Mrs Darbin. The first black player to dominate international lawn tennis, relying on fierce serving and considerable strength and reach. Won Wimbledon singles *1957|58* and doubles (with Angela Buxton) *1957* and (with Maria Bueno) *|58.* US singles *1957|58.* French singles and doubles (with Angela Buxton) *1956.* Australian doubles (with Shirley Fry) *1957.* Italian singles *1956.* W Cup *1957|58,* turned professional *1958.*

ANDRE HENRI GOBERT (France)

Born 30 /9 /1890. Died 6 /12 /1951. Wallis Myers described him as 'perhaps the greatest indoor player of all time'. With Decugis, he gained France's first Wimbledon title by defeating the holders, Ritchie and Wilding, in *1911*. Although they were beaten by Dixon and Roper Barrett the following year, the brilliant Gobert's compensation was a place in the all-comers' singles f in which he lost to the experienced A. W. Gore. He won the French covered court title from *1911–13* and again in *1920* and the British covered court event in *1911–12* and again from *1920–22*. He first played in D Cup in *1911* and his career ended when the 'Musketeers' arrived in *1922.* He also won two Olympic gold medals in *1912.*

RICHARD (PANCHO) GONZALES (USA)

Born 9 /5 /28. A dramatic and spectacular competitor, who was undoubtedly the best player in the world for most of the 1950s. He turned pro in 1949 after winning the US singles in *1948|49,* taking the US Clay Court title *1948|49,* the US indoor title *1949,* and winning the doubles in Paris and at Wimbledon – in his only amateur appearances there – in *1949* with Parker. Thereafter he played his brilliant, angry tennis away from the main arenas of the game until, at last, open competition was allowed. By then he was 40, but he played one last great match for the Wimbledon crowd. In *1969* he beat Pasarell 22–24 1–6 16–14 6–3 11–9 in 5hr 12min – the longest singles seen at Wimbledon.

EVONNE FAY GOOLAGONG (Australia)
Born 31 /7 /51. Now Mrs Roger Cawley (married in 1975). One of the most naturally gifted of champions, she was the first of her Aborigine race to excel at the game. Suddenly, in *1971* at the age of 19, 3 years before her coach Vic Edwards had forecast she would, she swept through both the French Championships and Wimbledon on a cloud of inspiration to win her first major titles. Although she reached the Wimbledon final again the following year and twice more, in *1975* and *1976*, it was not until *1980* that she won again – four years after the birth of her daughter, Kelly. This was the first win by a mother since Dorothea Lambert-Chambers's success in 1914. The nine-year gap between her championships was also the greatest since Bill Tilden's wins in 1921 and 1930. She was always more at home on faster surfaces where her beautifully instinctive volleying paid handsome dividends and she won her native Australian Open on that surface four times – *1974, 1975, 1976, 1978*. She was always a competent player on clay but tended to be rather erratic as her famous 'walkabouts' led to extravagant errors. Nevertheless, besides the French Open in *1971* she also won the Italian title in *1973*. The other highlights of her singles career were the victories in the South African Championships *(1972)* and the Virginia Slims Champs *(1974, 1976)*. She was a good doubles player and won once at Wimbledon *(1974)*, four times in Melbourne *(1971, 1974, 1975, 1976)* and twice in Johannesburg *(1971, 1972)*. In seven years of Fed Cup duty for Australia from *1971* to *1982* she won 33 of the 38 rubbers she contested in 24 ties. – J.B.

ARTHUR WENTWORTH GORE (Great Britain)
Born 2 /1 /1868. Died 1 /12 /1928. Wimbledon's oldest champ and probably the most persistent and industrious competitor in the history of the Champs. He played there for the first time in 1888 and although the Dohertys, Brookes, and Wilding were among his contemporaries, won the singles 3 times *1901* and *1908|09* and, at the age of 44 years and 6 months, won the right to challenge Wilding for the title in *1912.* That was his seventh appearance in the challenge round in 13 years. He was almost entirely a forehand player, hitting the ball flat with the racket in a dead line with his outstretched arm. His lightness of foot enabled him to protect his backhand which was no more than a safe push. He competed at every Wimbledon between *1888–1927* and captained the first British D Cup team at Boston in 1900, reaching sf US Champs on that trip.

KAREN HANTZE (USA)
Born 11 /12 /42. Now Mrs Susman. One of the new generation of aggressive Californians who arrived on the international scene at the start of the 1960s, she won the doubles at Wimbledon with the 17-year-old Billie Jean Moffitt in *1961* and then defeated Vera Sukova in the *1962* singles final. Marriage and motherhood restricted her tennis, but she won US doubles (again with Moffitt) *1964.* She played W Cup *1960–62* and *1965,* winning six of her nine matches, and Fed Cup *1965.*

DARLENE R. HARD (USA)
Born 6 /1 /36. An energetic volleyer, a shrewd tactician, and one of the best doubles players of her generation, she won the US singles in *1960* and *1961* and the French singles *1960,* but she failed in both her Wimbledon finals, losing to Althea Gibson in *1957* and Maria Bueno *1960.* She won the Wimbledon doubles, with Gibson *1957*, Jeanne Arth *1959*, and twice with Bueno *(1960, 1963)* and the mixed in *1957* (with Rose), *1959–60* (with Laver). She won the US doubles six times and the French doubles three times. Perhaps her most surprising American success came in *1969,* some years after she had retired

from regular competition, when she and Francoise Durr defeated Margaret Court and Virginia Wade 0–6 6–3 6–4 in f.

DORIS HART (USA)
Born 20 /6 /25. In spite of childhood illness which impeded her movement, she became one of the subtlest and most graceful of post-war competitors. Won Wimbledon singles *1951,* doubles (with Pat Todd) *1947* and (with Shirley Fry) *1951|52|53.* US singles *1954|55* and doubles (with Shirley Fry) *1951|52|53|54.* French singles *1950|52* and doubles (with Pat Todd) *1948* and (with Shirley Fry) *1950|51|53.* Australian singles *1949* and doubles (with Louise Brough) *1950.* Italian singles *1951|53* and South African singles *1952.* Also won many mixed titles, notably with E. V. Seixas at Wimbledon *1953|54|55.* Turned professional *1955.*

ADRIANNE SHIRLEY HAYDON (Great Britain)
Born 17 /10 /38. Now Mrs Jones. A shrewd, persistent lefthander, who reached sf at Wimbledon 7 times in 10 years, she captured the title at last in *1969* after beating Margaret Court in sf and Billie Jean King, to whom she had been r /u in *1967,* in f. She achieved international fame as a table tennis player, but decided to concentrate on lawn tennis after being r /u in three events in the 1957 World Table Tennis Champs. She won the French title in *1961|66,* Rome in *1966* and was twice r /u at Forest Hills *1961|67.* She took the French doubles (with Francoise Durr) in *1968|69* and won the Wimbledon mixed with Stolle in *1969.* Her W Cup record – 15 successful rubbers out of 32 in 12 matches – is another remarkable illustration of her tenacity and consistency.

ROBERT ANTHONY JOHN HEWITT (South Africa)
Born 12 /1 /40 in Sydney, Australia. He moved to South Africa in the early 1960s and started to represent that country when his residential qualification matured in 1967. A big brooding volcano of a man, he had deceptively fine touch and became one of the greatest right-court returners of the serve of modern times. He enjoyed two careers – first with fellow-Australian Fred Stolle and then with South Africa's Frew McMillan. With Stolle he won Wimbledon twice *(1962|64)* the Australian Championship twice *(1963|64)* and the Italian twice *(1963|64)* and with McMillan he added three more Wimbledon crowns *(1967|74|78),* two German *(1967|70),* one French *(1972),* one US *(1977),* one Masters *(1977)* and one WCT *(1974)* title as well as the Italian in *1967* and four at home in South Africa *(1967|70|72|74).* He registered four major mixed doubles successes with three different partners, winning in Australia with Jan Lehane in *1961,* in Paris with Billie Jean King in *1970* and twice at Wimbledon with his pupil, Greer Stevens, in *1977* and *1979*. He represented South Africa in D Cup *1967–74* and was a member of the successful team of *1974* that won by default from India. – J.B.

LEWIS ALAN HOAD (Australia)
Born 23 /11 /34. Capable of generating fierce power with great ease, he was one of the 'boy wonders' Harry Hopman produced to beat the US in the *1953* D Cup match. The other was Rosewall, 21 days his senior, who was to thwart his attempt on the Grand Slam in *1956* by beating him at Forest Hills, in the last of the 4 great f. That year Hoad had won the Australian and French titles, and had beaten Rosewall at Wimbledon. In *1957* he defeated Ashley Cooper in one of the most devastating Wimbledon f ever and then turned professional, but constant back trouble spoilt his pro career and also ended his attempt to return to the circuit when the game was opened to the pros. He won the Wimbledon doubles in *1953|55|56,* the US doubles in *1956,* the French doubles in *1953,* and the Australian doubles in *1953|56|57.* He won 17 rubbers out of 21 in D Cup play between *1953–56.*

HAZEL HOTCHKISS (USA)

Born 20 /12 /1886. Died 5 /12 /1974. Became Mrs G. Wightman. One of the most remarkable and enthusiastic competitors that the game has known. She was the donor of the W Cup and a considerable influence in American tennis for more than 60 years. She gained the first of her four US singles titles *(1909/10/11/19)* in 1909 and won the US indoor doubles for the 10th *(1919/21/24/27/28/29/30/31/33/43)* and last time in 1943. A remarkable volleyer with great speed about the court, she and Helen Wills were never beaten in doubles. They won the Wimbledon doubles in *1924* and the US doubles — a title which she had won on 4 other occasions — in *1924–28.* She captained the first US W Cup team in 1923 and between *1923–31* won 3 doubles rubbers in 5 matches.

HELEN HULL JACOBS (USA)

Born 6 /8 /08. A tenacious competitor, notable for duels with fellow-Californian, Helen Wills Moody, 5 times a Wimbledon finalist between *1929–39* but won only in *1936.* US singles *1932/33/34/35* and doubles (with Sarah Palfrey Fabyan) *1930/34/35.* Italian singles *1934.*

WILLIAM JOHNSTON (USA)

Born 2 /11 /1894. Died 1 /6 /1946. 'Little Bill', a Californian, small in physique but a brilliant volleyer and the possessor of a formidable top-spin forehand, was 'Big Bill' Tilden's principal rival at home in the first half of the 1920s. He defeated McLoughlin to win the US singles in *1915,* the first year at Forest Hills, lost to Williams in the *1916* final and then regained the title by beating Tilden in straight sets in *1919.* Tilden gained his revenge the following year and, although Johnston reached the final five times between *1920* and *1925,* Tilden always frustrated him. He beat Hunter in the *1923* Wimbledon final, losing only one set in the tournament. He won the US doubles with Griffin *1915/16* and *1920* and played in eight D Cup challenge rounds, winning 18 of his 21 D Cup rubbers.

BILLIE JEAN MOFFITT KING (USA)

Born 22 /11 /43. Perhaps the most important single figure in the history of tennis, as player, stateswoman, innovator and entrepreneur (usually with lawyer husband Larry King, whom she married in 1965), she has worked tirelessly to gain recognition and respect for the women's game. One of the founders of the women's pro tour in *1970*, twice President of the Women's Tennis Association, and the prime mover behind Team Tennis, she has been involved in most aspects of the game. As a player her natural exuberance and bubbling personality suited her attacking serve-and-volley game and made her a fearsome opponent. She will best be remembered for her 'Battle of the Sexes' against Bobby Riggs at the Houston Astrodome on 20 September, *1973* where the world's largest-ever crowd of 30,492 and some 50 million more around the world on TV, saw her win 6–4 6–3 6–3. In *1979* she achieved her 20th Wimbledon title to pass the record she had jointly shared with fellow-Californian Elizabeth Ryan who, ironically, had died on the eve of that unique achievement. Her unparalleled record comprises 6 singles — *1966, 1967, 1968, 1972, 1973* and *1975*; 10 women's doubles — *1961, 1962, 1965, 1967, 1968, 1970, 1971, 1972, 1973* and *1979*; 4 mixed doubles — *1967, 1971, 1973* and *1974*. She first played at Wimbledon in *1961* and won the doubles with Karen Hantze. At her last appearance in *1983* she was competing for the 22nd year (she had not entered in *1981*) and reached the mixed doubles final with Steve Denton when she played her 265th and last match at Wimbledon. It was also her 29th final and, as they lost to John Lloyd and Wendy Turnbull 7–5 in the final set, she was losing at that stage for only the 9th time. She was almost as successful in her own US Championships where she won 12 titles, 4 each in singles — *1967, 1971, 1972, 1974*, doubles — *1964, 1967, 1968, 1970* and mixed — *1967, 1971, 1973, 1976* and, in addition she became the only woman to win US National titles on all four surfaces — grass, clay, hard and indoor — a feat she repeated in doubles with Rosie Casals with whom she had most of her major doubles successes. She won the French Open singles and doubles in *1972* and the mixed in *1967* and *1970* and was successful in singles and mixed at the Australian Open in *1968*, the first year of open tennis. Her 39 Grand Slam titles put her second only to Margaret Court who won 66. She was also the singles and doubles champion of Italy *(1970)* and of Germany *(1971)* and won the South African title 3 times *(1966, 1967, 1969)*. With 21 winning rubbers from 26 played in 9 W Cup matches between *1961* and *1978*, plus 52 wins from 58 rubbers in 6 years of Fed Cup play from *1963* to *1979* she contributed hugely to American dominance in those team competitions. – J.B.

JAN KODES (Czechoslovakia)
Born 1 /3 /46. A dogged, industrious player with great strength and determination. He won his first major victories on clay, winning the French singles *1970/71* and reaching the Italian final *1970/71/72*, but he won the Wimbledon singles in the boycott year of *1973* and was runner-up in the US Champs *1971/73*. Having served his apprenticeship in European junior team competitions (he was on a winning Galea Cup team), he first represented Czechoslovakia in D Cup in *1966*, took them to the final in *1975* and was a member of their winning team in *1980*.

HILDE KRAHWINKEL (West Germany)
Born 26 /3 /08. Now Mrs Sperling. A tall German, later Danish by marriage, whose dogged ability to retrieve from the back of the court turned her matches into long tests of endurance. She won the German indoor title in *1929* and then, emerging rapidly as an international player, lost to Cilly Aussem in the only all-German women's f at Wimbledon *1931*. She reached the final again in *1936*, losing 6–2 4–6 7–5 to Helen Jacobs, and altogether she was in qf (or better) 8 times. She won the French singles *1935–37*, defeating Mrs Mathieu in each of the three f, the Italian title *1935* and she was German singles champ *1933/35/37/39*. There was no competition in 1936. Her last important victory was in the Scandinavian indoor final in *1950*.

JACK ALBERT KRAMER (USA)
Born 1 /8 /21. A methodical and powerful exponent of the serve and volley game. Played for the US in the last pre-war D Cup challenge round against Australia. Won Wimbledon singles title in *1947* after losing dramatically to the then unknown Jaroslav Drobny in 1946. Won doubles *1946/47*. Won US singles *1946/47* and doubles *1940/41/43/47*. Turned pro *1947* and then controlled pro tennis for 15 years. Still appears occasionally as a television commentator and was executive director of ATP Sept. 1972–April 1975.

RENE LACOSTE (France)
Born 2 /7 /04. In spite of ill health, he became the best groundstroke player and most astute tactician of pre-war lawn tennis. Won Wimbledon singles *1925/28* and doubles (with J. Borotra) *1925*. Won US singles *1926/27*, French singles *1925/27/29* and French doubles (with Borotra) *1924/25/29*. Played in 51 D Cup rubbers between *1923–28* and won the crucial rubbers of the *1927* challenge round which brought France the trophy for the first time, when he beat Tilden and Johnston in the singles.

ARTHUR D. LARSEN (USA)
Born 6 /4 /25. A graceful, elegant lefthander with exquisite touch and some notable eccentricities, he was famous for his dressing-room superstitions, his physical twitches and his rituals on court. He was known as Tappy because he would have a lucky number for the day and would always tap the baseline, the umpire's chair – even his own toe – with his racket the required number of times before continuing. He won US singles *1950*, US Clay Courts *1952* and US Indoor *1953*. A motor-cycle accident in which he suffered severe head injuries ended his career in 1957.

RODNEY GEORGE LAVER (Australia)
Born 9 /8 /38. The first player to achieve the Grand Slam twice and the master of the old professional circuit, with Rosewall as his great rival, in its last days. A lefthander, red-haired like Budge, with a spectacularly aggressive style, he brought off the slam of the

Right: The first Grand Slam winner, Don Budge (1938). (A. Cole) ***Below:*** Pictured in Paris, the winning British Davis Cup team of 1933 – Bunny Austin, Pat Hughes, Dan Maskell (coach), Harry Lee, Fred Perry and Anthony Sabelli (Secretary, LTA).

four major singles titles, as an amateur, in *1962* and then, as a professional, in *1969.* Disciplined, unassuming, quick and light in movement, he could produce sudden bombardments of shots, heavy with spin, which totally disconcerted his opponents. Born at Rockhampton, Queensland, 'Rocket' was a perfect nickname for the first tennis millionaire. If he had not turned professional in 1963, he would have won many more of the traditional titles. As it was, he won the singles at Wimbledon *1961l62* and *1968l69,* the doubles with Emerson *1971* and the mixed, with Darlene Hard, *1959l60.* He took the US singles and French singles *1962* and *1969,* also winning the French doubles with Emerson and the mixed with Hard in *1961.* His Australian singles victories came in *1960, 1962* and *1969,* with doubles *1959l61* (Mark) and *1969* (Emerson). He was Italian singles champion *1962* and *1971,* German champion *1961l62* and a member of the undefeated Australian D Cup team from *1959–62.* He returned to D Cup in *1973,* collecting three more rubbers in Australia's 5–0 victory over the US in the final at Cleveland.

SUZANNE LENGLEN (France)
Born 24 /5 /1899. Died 4 /7 /1938. The most exciting, and successful of women players. She survived 2 match-points to win at Wimbledon in *1919* against Mrs Lambert Chambers and thereafter lost only in a controversial match to Molla Mallory (US) in 1921 US Champs until her retirement in 1926. Quarrelled with the Wimbledon referee in 1926 and turned pro. Won Wimbledon singles and doubles (with Elizabeth Ryan) *1919l20l21l22l23l25.* French singles and doubles (with various partners) *1920l21l22l23l25l26.*

KATHLEEN McKANE (Great Britain)
Born 7/5/1896. Now Mrs Godfree. A fine match-player with a quick, aggressive game, she achieved the notable distinction of winning the Wimbledon singles twice – even though she was a contemporary of Suzanne Lenglen and Helen Wills. In Lenglen's absence, she beat the Californian (a feat which no other player achieved in the next 14 years at Wimbledon) in the *1924* final after trailing by a set and 1–4, and in *1926* she regained the title after being within a point of 1–4 in the third set against Lili d'Alvarez. She won the Wimbledon mixed (with Gilbert) in *1924* and in *1926* (with her husband, Leslie Godfree). She was r /u to Miss Wills at Forest Hills in 1925 after beating Elizabeth Ryan and Molla Mallory, and she won the US doubles in *1923* (with Mrs Covell) *l27* (with Miss Harvey). She won 7 rubbers out of 17 in 7 W Cup matches between *1923–34.*

CHARLES ROBERT McKINLEY (USA)
Born 5 /1 /41. An energetic and athletic match-player, who won the Wimbledon singles title in *1963* without meeting another seeded player in the course of the tournament. He was runner-up to Laver in *1961,* a disappointing competitor in *1962* but in *1963* bounced back to take the title. In the US Championships he never progressed further than the semi-finals, failing three times at that stage, but, with Ralston, he won the doubles in *1961* and *1963–64.* He played in 16 D Cup matches between *1960* and *1965* and won 29 of his 38 rubbers.

MAURICE EVANS McLOUGHLIN (USA)
Born 7 /1 /1890. Died 10 /12 /1957. 'The Californian Comet' was the first notable exponent of the cannonball service. Fiercely effective with volley and smash, he was US champ in *1912–13* and his appearance at Wimbledon was, as a contemporary remarked, a sign of the way the modern game was developing. His spectacular style had considerable appeal. When he met Wilding for the title in *1913,* 'there was such an indecent crush round the barriers of the Centre Court that, to avoid serious injury, several ladies had to be lifted over by policemen into the security of the arena'. Wilding beat him 8–6 6–3 10–8, but McLoughlin had the consolation of winning 2 rubbers in the American capture of the D Cup from Britain at Wimbledon. In the *1914* challenge round at Forest Hills he beat both Brookes and Wilding, but Australasia took the trophy. He did not play after the war. His aggressive style was said to have burnt him out.

FREW DONALD McMILLAN (South Africa)

Born 20 /5 /42 in Springs, a small Transvaal town. A gifted and unusual doubles player who invariably wore a peaked white cloth cap and held the racket with two hands on both sides to produce just the right blend of disguise, finesse and power. His partnership with ex-patriate Australian Bob Hewitt was particularly fruitful and they became one of the three greatest pairs of the post-Second World War years. Together they won their native South African title four times *(1967|70|72|74)* and succeeded at Wimbledon three times *(1967|72|78)*. They won once each the French *(1972)*, the US *(1977)*, the Masters *(1977* played in Jan '78), the WCT *(1974)* and the Italian *(1967)* titles and won the German twice *(1967|70)*. But it was in mixed doubles that he won his first and last major championships. In *1966* he partnered Annette Van Zyl to the French title and in *1981* he captured the Wimbledon mixed for the second time with Betty Stove, with whom he had been successful in 1978 — the same year they won a second US Open together *(1977|78)*. He played D Cup from *1965* to *1976* and was a member of the only team ever to win the famous trophy by default — from India in 1974. — J.B.

ALICE MARBLE (USA)

Born 28 /9 /13. A brilliant server and volleyer whose career was interrupted by ill health and the war. Won Wimbledon singles *1939* and doubles (with Sarah Palfrey Fabyan) *1938|39*. US singles *1936|38|39|40* and doubles (with Sarah Palfrey Fabyan) *1937|38|39|40*. Turned pro *1941*.

SIMONE MATHIEU (France)

Born 31 /1 /08. Died 7 /1 /80. A formidable clay court player, she succeeded Lenglen as the leader of the women's game in France. She was junior champ — as a married woman — at 18, and 3 years later reached the French f, losing 6–3 6–4 to Wills. She was r /u again in *1933|36|37* before she won at last in *1938,* defeating Landry, and then retained her title *1939* against Jedrzejowska. She won the French doubles 6 times and the Wimbledon doubles twice with Ryan *1933|34* and once with Yorke *1937.* Her soundness from the baseline carried her 4 times to the singles sf.

HELEN WILLS MOODY (USA)

Born 6 /10 /05. Later Mrs A. Roark. Lenglen's successor as ruler of Wimbledon. A relentless baseliner, she won the singles 8 times in 9 attempts, losing only to Kitty McKane in 1924. Between *1927–32* she won all the major singles champs, except Australia, without losing a set. Won Wimbledon singles *1927|28|29|30|32|33|35|38* and doubles (with Hazel Wightman) *1924* and (with Elizabeth Ryan) *|27|30*. US singles *1923|24|25|27|28|29|31,* and doubles (with Mrs J. B. Jessup) *1922,* (with Hazel Wightman) *|24|28,* and (with Mary K. Browne) *|25*. French singles *1928|29|30|32* and doubles (with Elizabeth Ryan) *1930|31|32*.

ANGELA MORTIMER (Great Britain)

Born 21 /4 /32. Now Mrs Barrett. Britain's first post-war Wimbledon singles champ. Coached by Arthur Roberts at Torquay, she used an armoury of firmly controlled ground-strokes most effectively and considerable determination enabled her to overcome a certain frailty of physique. Her first notable success was the capture of the French title in *1955* — the first British victory in Paris since Peggy Scriven won in 1934 — and in the same year she won the Wimbledon doubles (with Anne Shilcock). She won the Australian title in *1958,* after travelling there to recover from illness, and 6 months later was r /u to Althea Gibson at Wimbledon. She won the title in *1961* by beating Christine Truman in the first all-British f of the modern Wimbledon. She won 5 rubbers out of 16 in 6 W Cup matches and became W Cup captain *1964–70*.

ILIE NASTASE (Rumania)

Born 19 /8 /46. One of the most gifted shot-makers and fluid movers in the game's history, he never quite fulfilled his enormous potential. His two Grand Slam titles were won on different surfaces – on grass in New York in *1972* and on clay in Paris the following year. He could also play beautifully indoors as his four Masters titles in *1971, 1972, 1973, 1975* testify. Sadly for his many admirers, a childlike and sometimes mischievous streak was his undoing on many occasions, particularly towards the end of his playing days when he fell foul of authority for his behaviour. Throughout his career the showman in him struggled constantly with the athlete so that there was often a lack of steel about his match play. This failing, and an inability to put the ball away with his somewhat lightweight volleys, cost him two chances to win the Wimbledon title – in *1972* when Smith beat him and in *1976* when Borg won the first of his five titles. His lightning reflexes made him an excellent doubles player and he won major titles in Paris *(1970)* and Rome *(1970* and *1972)*, at Wimbledon *(1973)* and in New York *(1975)*. He also won two mixed titles at Wimbledon with Rosie Casals *(1970, 1972)*. His biggest disappointment was his failure to lead Rumania to victory in the *1972* D Cup final against the Americans on clay in Bucharest where his loss to Smith in the opening rubber proved decisive. – J.B.

JOHN DAVID NEWCOMBE (Australia)

Born 23 /5 /44. The supreme exponent of the simple, rugged style in modern tennis. Splendidly confident and with great strength of personality, Newcombe relied upon a heavy service, forceful volleying and solid, powerful groundstrokes. His best singles successes were on grass – Wimbledon *1967, 1970/71,* US Championships *1967, 1973,* and Australia *1973, 1975* – but he also won, by doggedness and determination, the German *(1968)* and Italian *(1969)* titles. He and Roche formed the most successful of modern doubles partnerships, winning Wimbledon in *1965, 1968–70,* and *1974.* When Roche was injured in *1966,* Fletcher replaced him at short notice and he and Newcombe won the title. He won the US doubles with Roche *1967,* with Taylor *1971,* and with Davidson *1973,* France twice with Roche *(1967, 1969)* and once with Okker *(1973)* and Australia four times with Roche *(1965, 1967, 1971* and *1976)* and once with Anderson *(1973).* In *1981*, aged 37, he and Stolle (42) took McEnroe /Fleming to 5s tie-break in US Open sf. He first played in the Davis Cup in *1963* and finally against Italy in Rome, *1976,* but perhaps his best performance was in *1973* when he and Laver inflicted a 5–0 defeat upon the United States at Cleveland.

BETTY NUTHALL (Great Britain)

Born 23 /6 /11. Now Mrs Shoemaker. An aggressive and attractive competitor, with a remarkable record as a junior, she never progressed beyond qf at Wimbledon but gained her most impressive victories abroad. At 16, after beating Molla Mallory, No. 6 seed, at Wimbledon in *1927,* she astonished the tennis world by reaching f at F Hills, where Helen Wills beat her 6–1 6–4. In *1930* she became the first British player to win that title with a 6–4 6–1 victory over Mrs Harper. She won the US doubles *1930/31/33* and mixed *1929/31* and the French doubles *1931* and mixed *1931/32.* Her only British success in a nat singles event was the capture of the HC title in *1927.* She won the HC doubles *1926/28/31/32* and the mixed in *1927.* She played in 8 W Cup matches between *1927* and *1939,* winning 6 rubbers and losing 7.

ALEJANDRO OLMEDO (USA)

Born 24 /3 /36. The son of a groundsman in Peru, this superb natural athlete rose like a comet in *1958* to win D Cup for America in Brisbane almost single-handed. Selected by the captain, Perry T. Jones, Olmedo had rewarded him with two singles wins and a share with Ham Richardson in the doubles win that had sealed the victory. Success in the Australian Championships confirmed the quality of his play as he beat Neale Fraser in four sets. Six months later 'The Chief', as he was popularly known, won the *1959*

Wimbledon from Rod Laver for the loss of only two sets, with one of the most competent displays of power tennis seen since the war. After taking part in the unsuccessful defence of D Cup where he lost to Fraser but beat Laver again, he reached the final of the US Championships but failed once more against Fraser. Immediately he turned professional. – J.B.

MANUEL ORANTES (Spain)

Born 6 /2 /49. A consummate artist on European clay whose exquisite touch and gentle, generous manners made him an international favourite. A left-hander who, after leading Spain to two Galea Cup victories in **1968** and **1969**, won his first two important titles in **1972** – the German and Italian Opens. His best year was **1975** for, besides winning a second German title, the Canadian Open and the first of his two US Clay Court crowns (he won the second in **1977**, he was triumphant on the clay at Forest Hills. After recovering miraculously to defeat Vilas in a night-time semi-final, having trailed one set to two and 0–5 in the fourth, he was back on court 15 hours later to thrash Jimmy Connors 6–4 6–3 6–3 in a near-perfect display of the clay-court art. In **1976** he won the Spanish Open and at the year's end won Masters in Houston against Fibak with another brave recovery, coming back from one set to two and 1–4. He played in the losing Spanish team in the D Cup challenge round of **1967** in Brisbane but led his country to victory in the World Team Cup in Düsseldorf 11 years later. – J.B.

MARGARET OSBORNE (USA)

Born 4 /4 /18. Now Mrs du Pont. One of the finest of American doubles players and a formidably successful competitor in singles. With her splendidly consistent serving and her strength and skill at the net, she did much to set the pattern for the period of American supremacy in women's tennis, which began in 1946. Won Wimbledon singles in **1947,**Forest Hills **1948|49|50** and Paris in **1946|49**. She and Louise Brough won the Wimbledon doubles in **1946|48|49|50|54**. They ruled the US doubles from **1942–50** and **1955–57,** and held the French title **1946|47|49**. She won the Wimbledon mixed with Neale Fraser in **1962** – 15 years after her first singles victory.

SARAH PALFREY (USA)

Born 18 /9 /12. Now Mrs Danzig, formerly Mrs Fabyan, and Mrs Cooke. A fine volleyor with a sweeping backhand and a notable doubles player, she partnered Alice Marble to victory at Wimbledon in **1938|39** and won the US doubles title with a variety of partners – Betty Nuthall, Helen Jacobs (3 times), Alice Marble (4 times) and Margaret Osborne – 9 times between **1930–41**. She won the US singles in **1941|45** and was r/u to Helen Jacobs in **1934|35**. She was the US mixed champion on 4 occasions. She played in 10 W Cup matches and won 14 rubbers out of 21.

ADRIANO PANATTA (Italy)

Born 9 /7 /50. Without doubt, 1976 was the *annus mirabilis* of Panatta's career. Until then he had always been dashing and stylish, but had never made full use of his talent. In **1976**, however, he lived dangerously and survived brilliantly. In Rome he became the first home player to win in Italy for 15 years after frustrating Warwick no fewer than 11 times at m-p in the first round. In Paris, against Hutka, he again faced a first-round m-p and again went on to take the championship. Four months later, when Italy won D Cup for the first time, Panatta played a major role in their victory. Paris, Rome and D Cup – this was Panatta's year! He was also the leading player in the Italian teams which reached the **1977**, **1979** and **1980** D Cup finals. He reached the French sf in **1973** and **1975** and was runner-up in Rome **1978** and Hamburg **1972**.

GERALD L. PATTERSON (Australia)

Born 17 /12 /1895. Died 13 /6 /1967. Formidably aggressive with a cannonball service modelled on McLoughlin's, he was the dominating player when international competition was resumed in 1919. After being r /u to O'Hara Wood in the *1914* Australian singles, he became Wimbledon's first post-war champ by defeating Brookes in *1919*. He lost his Wimbledon title to Tilden in *1920* but regained it against Lycett in *1922*. R /u doubles in *1922* (O'Hara Wood) and *1928* (Hawkes) and won the mixed with Suzanne Lenglen in *1920*. He won the Australian singles in his fourth final in *1927*. Between *1919–28* he played 46 D Cup rubbers for Australia and Australasia and won 4 out of 12 challenge round rubbers. He was a nephew of Dame Nellie Melba and was the first man to win the Wimbledon singles by playing through when the challenge round was abolished there in 1922.

J. EDWARD PATTY (USA)

Born 11 /2 /24. An American who lived in Paris and developed his game there, 'Budge' Patty, with his elegant, effective forehand volley, was one of the great post-war stylists. *1950* – when he won both the Wimbledon and French singles – was the peak of his career, but his rivalry with Drobny captured the public's imagination. The most notable of their long and dramatic matches was in the third round at Wimbledon in 1953. After 4½ hours Patty lost 8–6 16–18 3–6 8–6 12–10 after holding 6 match-points. He had beaten the Czech at Wimbledon in *1947* and 3 years later by 6–1 6–2 3–6 5–7 7–5 in his French f. The last of their meetings was in *1954*. Drobny, on his way to the title, won a 4-set sf. Patty won his last title there in *1957* when he and Mulloy, then aged 43, beat Hoad and Fraser to take the men's doubles. He won the Italian singles *1954,* and the German singles *1953/54* and doubles *1953/54/55*.

FRANK A. PARKER (USA)

Born 31 /1 /16. Shrewd, persistent, and accurate in spite of a certain lightness of shot, he shared with Trabert the distinction, rare for an American, of winning the French title twice. At his best on slow courts, he was ranked in the first 10 in the US for 17 consecutive years between *1933*, the year of the first of his 5 US Clay Court victories, and *1949* when he turned pro. His victories in Paris were in *1948/49*, and in *1949* he won the doubles in Paris and Wimbledon with Gonzales. He won the US singles in *1944* and *1945* as an Army sergeant and the doubles with Kramer in *1943*. He played in the D Cup challenge round against Britain in *1937* when the US regained the trophy after 10 years and in the *1939* and *1948* challenge rounds. He was beaten only twice in 14 D Cup rubbers.

FREDERICK JOHN PERRY (Great Britain)

Born 18 /5 /09. A US citizen. The most successful modern British player, an aggressive competitor with boundless self-confidence and a remarkable running forehand. Won Wimbledon singles *1934/35/36* – the first player since A. F. Wilding (1910–13) to take the title 3 years in succession – and mixed (with Dorothy Round) *1935/36*. US singles *1933/34/36*. French singles *1935* and doubles (with G. P. Hughes) *1933*. Australian singles *1934* and doubles (with Hughes) *1934*. Won 45 out of 52 D Cup rubbers, 34 out of 38 singles, between *1931–36*. Turned pro in *1936*.

YVON FRANCOIS MARIE PETRA (France)

Born 8 /3 /16 in Indo-China. Died 11 /9 /84. Wimbledon's first post-war men's singles champion. Reached mixed f at Wimbledon *1937* with Simone Mathieu and won French doubles *1938* with Destremau, defeating Budge and Mako in f. Between 1942, when he was released from a prisoner-of-war camp, and 1945, he consolidated his reputation as France's most aggressive competitor in wartime domestic competitions. At Wimbledon, *1946,* his strength, flair and, notably, the consistency of his heavy serving gained this formidably built player an unexpected title. Drobny beat Kramer, the favourite, in 4r. Petra disposed of Pails, the other expected finalist, in qf and then won 5s matches against Tom

Brown and Geoff Brown. That was the peak of his career. Marcel Bernard beat him in the French sf – played in July that year – and his consolation was a doubles victory, partnered by Bernard, over Morea and Segura in f. Patty beat him easily on the second day at Forest Hills and in *1947* he lost to Tom Brown in qf at Wimbledon.

NICOLA PIETRANGELI (Italy)
Born 11 /9 /33. A master of the European clay court style, he was born in Tunis (of a French father and Russian mother) and between *1954* and *1972* played in 163 D Cup rubbers for Italy, more than anyone in history. Won most rubbers (120), played most singles (109) and won most (78), played most doubles (54), and won most (42), and played in most ties (66). Appeared in the *1960/61* challenge rounds against Australia, but won only one 'dead' singles. Won French singles *1959/60* and doubles (with Sirola), Italian singles *1957/61,* and German singles *1960.* Reached sf at Wimbledon, *1960,* and doubles final (with Sirola) *1956.*

DR JOSHUA PIM (Ireland)
Born 20 /6 /1869. Died 13 /4 /1942. A robust, adventurous competitor, regarded by contemporary critics as one of the great geniuses of early tennis. 'When Pim was at his best he was virtually unplayable', wrote Wallis Myers. 'It is scarcely exaggerating to say that he could hit a coin placed anywhere on the court.' He reached sf at Wimbledon *1890,* losing to Hamilton, who became Wimbledon's first Irish champ, then lost in *1891* to Wilfred Baddeley in the all-comers' f and again in *1892* challenge round. He gained his revenge, however, by beating Baddeley in the 2 following Wimbledon f. Pim won the Irish title for the 3rd and last time in *1895* but then played little first-class tennis until he was controversially picked for the D Cup match against USA at New York in 1902. He was preferred to Lawrie Doherty, lost both his singles badly and the British Isles were beaten 3–2. 'Although still very good, Pim had no more than a shadow of his former skill, but alas! a great deal more than the shadow of his former weight', wrote Commander Hillyard.

ADRIAN KARL QUIST (Australia)
Born 4 /8 /13. A shrewd, graceful doubles player, whose victories at Wimbledon were separated by a gap of 15 years. Won with J. H. Crawford in *1935* and, when almost a veteran, with J. E. Bromwich *1950.* Held Australian title from *1936–50,* winning twice with D. P. Turnbull and 8 times with Bromwich. Won US doubles (with Bromwich) *1939,* French doubles (with J. H. Crawford) *1935,* and Australian singles *1936/40/48.* Won 42 out of 55 D Cup rubbers in 28 ties between *1933–48.*

WILLIAM CHARLES RENSHAW (Great Britain)
Born 3 /1 /1861. Died 12 /8 /1904. The first great champ. Learnt on asphalt at school at Cheltenham with twin brother, Ernest, a more graceful but less determined competitor. They were the first spectacular players and their skill – particularly in volleying and smashing – brought crowds to Wimbledon and contributed considerably to the development of lawn tennis as a spectator sport. 'Willie' Renshaw was singles champ at Wimbledon from *1881–86* and in *1889.* He held the doubles, with Ernest, in *1884/85/86/88/89.* Ernest won the singles title in *1888* and was beaten by William in the challenge rounds of 1882 and 1883.

NANCY ANN RICHEY (USA)
Born 23 /8 /42. Later Mrs Gunter. A Texan, famous for her shorts and peaked cap, she was, like her brother, George Clifford Richey, a tenacious baseliner, impressive on clay. Her determination occasionally brought unexpected success on grass. She reached the *1969* US final, losing 6–2 6–2 to Margaret Court. She won Australia *1967,* beating Lesley Turner, another clay-court specialist, in the final. At Wimbledon she reached qf seven times in nine years *1964–72* but was semi-finalist only in *1968.* She won Wimbledon doubles with Maria Bueno *1966.* On clay she won French singles *1968,* beating Ann

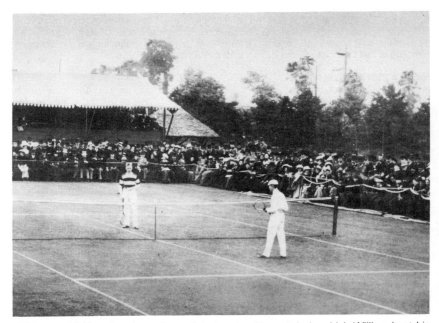

William and Ernest Renshaw pictured during the title match, in which William beat his brother, at the Worple Road ground in Wimbledon in 1883.

Jones to avenge a defeat in the *1966* final, but the best evidence of her quality was her record in US Clay Courts. She won Indianapolis from *1963–68* and even as late as *1975* led Chris Evert 7–5 5–0 in the semi-finals there, twice reaching match-point before retiring with cramp at 2–4 in the final set. She played Wightman Cup from *1962–68* and Federation Cup *1964–69.*

ROBERT LARIMORE RIGGS (USA)
Born 25 /2 /18. A shrewd, confident match-player, with remarkable versatility of shot, he won all 3 titles on his first appearance at Wimbledon in *1939.* He also won Forest Hills in *1939,* but lost to McNeill in the French f. He turned pro in 1941 and later became a notable competitor in veterans' events, but his greatest fame came at the age of 55. Profiting from the Women's Lib controversy, he challenged and beat Margaret Court 6–2 6–1 in a singles match in Ramona, Cal, and then lost to Billie Jean King 6–4 6–3 6–3, before a record television audience of almost 50 million and 30,492 paying spectators at the Houston Astrodome in September 1973.

ANTHONY DALTON ROCHE (Australia)
Born 17 /6 /45. Strong, rugged and a fine volleyer, he was the lefthander in one of Wimbledon's most successful doubles partnerships. He won the doubles with John Newcombe in *1965,* from *1968–70* (the first hat-trick of titles since the Dohertys 1903–5) and in *1974.* Other doubles victories included US *1967,* French *1967–69.* Australia *1965/67/71/76/77* and Italy *1965/71.* He did not achieve as much as expected in singles, partly because of injury. The extraordinary operation on his left elbow, performed without knife or anaesthetic in the Philippines by a faith healer, received worldwide publicity. He never reached an Australian final in spite of numerous attempts, but was runner-up to Laver at Wimbledon in *1968* and lost two US Open finals: *1969* when Laver beat him to

complete the Grand Slam and **1970** to Rosewall. His most successful year was **1966** when he won French and Italian titles. Played Davis Cup **1964–78** but did not play singles in a final until he beat Panatta in the opening match **1977**.

KENNETH ROBERT ROSEWALL (Australia)
Born 2 /11 /34. For a quarter of a century Rosewall's grace and easy, economical style delighted the connoisseurs and the only regret about his long and distinguished career is that, in spite of four finals over a period of 20 years, he never won the Wimbledon singles title. He began as a Hopman prodigy and it was not until the end of **1979** that he retired from Grand Prix tennis. In **1953,** aged 18, he won the Australian and French singles and, with Hoad, the French and Wimbledon doubles. In **1954** he lost to Drobny in the Wimbledon final. Hoad beat him in the **1956** Wimbledon final, but Rosewall avenged that defeat in the US final, frustrating Hoad in the last leg of his attempt on the Grand Slam. Turning professional in **1957,** he took over the leadership of the professional circuit from Gonzales until Laver's arrival in **1963.** Rosewall's skills endured. In **1968** he won the first open tournament at Bournemouth and then recaptured some of his former titles. He regained the French singles and doubles (with Stolle) in **1968.** In **1970** – after 14 years and aged 35 – he won the US title again and reached his fourth final at Forest Hills in **1974.** The gap between his Australian successes was even wider. After his victories in **1953** and **1955,** he won again in **1971** and **1972.** But Wimbledon always eluded him. Newcombe beat him in **1970,** his third final, and Connors overwhelmed him in the **1974** final.

DOROTHY EDITH ROUND (Great Britain)
Born 13 /7 /09. Died 12 /11 /82. Became Mrs Little. Determined and efficient, possessing a fine forehand drive and shrewd drop-shot, she was one of the two British women's singles champs at Wimbledon between the wars. She gained her first notable victory there against Lili d'Alvarez in **1931,** was r /u to Helen Wills Moody in **1933,** then beat Helen Jacobs to win the title in **1934** and regained it against Jadwiga Jedrzejowska in **1937.** She won the Australian singles in **1935** and the Wimbledon mixed in **1934** (with Miki) and **1935|36** (with Perry). She won 4 of her 13 W Cup rubbers between **1931–36.**

ELIZABETH RYAN (USA)
Born 5 /2 /1892. Died 6 /7 /1979. Suzanne Lenglen's doubles partner and the winner of 19 Wimbledon titles – 12 doubles and 7 mixed. A determined competitor with a cunningly chopped forehand and a great appetite for match-play, she was regarded by contemporaries as 'the best player never to win a great singles championship'. With a variety of partners, she won the Wimbledon doubles **1914|19|20|21|22|23|25|26|27|30|33|34** and the mixed **1919|21|23|27|28|30|32.** US doubles in **1926,** the French doubles **1930|32|33|34.**

JOHN WILLIAM VAN RYN (USA)
Born 30 /6 /06. Formed one of the most famous of all doubles partnerships with Wilmer Allison. Pat Hughes described their combination as 'a perfect blending of styles . . . Van Ryn dipped the ball over from the right court and his partner stepped in at the psychological moment for the final volley'. George Lott thought that their deep personal friendship and knowledge of each other's movements and reactions played an important part in their success. With Allison, Van Ryn succeeded at Wimbledon in **1929–30** and took the US title in **1931** and **1935.** He won Paris and Wimbledon with Lott in **1931.** In the **1929** D Cup challenge round he and Allison beat Cochet and Borotra and in the **1932** match they defeated Cochet and Brugnon. He was a member of the US team from **1929–36** and won 29 of his 32 rubbers in 24 matches. He lost only two of his 24 D Cup doubles.

MANUEL SANTANA (Spain)
Born 10 /5 /38. Learnt the game as a ballboy and, after a period in which he was the most admired clay court player in Europe, won US singles **1965**, and Wimbledon singles **1966**. Possessed a remarkable forehand and great delicacy of touch. Won French singles **1961** and **1964,** defeating Pietrangeli in both finals, and doubles (with Emerson) **1963,** and South African singles **1967**. The most successful Spanish player in history, he won 91 D Cup rubbers out of 119 between **1958** and **1973.**

RICHARD SAVITT (USA)
Born 4 /3 /27. His talent was discovered in the classic fashion by a complete stranger who saw him playing in a public park, and after a modest junior career he became a powerful exponent of the serve and volley game. Concentrating on tennis after a basketball injury in 1949, he rose rapidly on the US ranking-list, moving up from 16th to 6th after reaching sf at Forest Hills, **1950,** with victories over Seixas and Bromwich. His remarkable year was **1951**. He won both the Australian and Wimbledon titles, defeating McGregor in both finals. This was his first trip to Europe and he never achieved the same kind of success again, although he played some memorable matches, notably sf against Rosewall at Forest Hills, **1956,** and a vain defence of his US indoor title in a three-hour f in **1959**. He was a member of the US D Cup team in 1951, but was not chosen to play in the challenge round against Australia.

FREDERICK RUDOLPH SCHROEDER (USA)
Born 20 /7 /21. A powerful Californian whose aggressive serve-and-volley game brought him much success on fast surfaces. The US National Junior Champion in **1939**, he won the NCAA Championships from Stanford in **1942** and the same year won the US Championships, defeating Frank Parker in the final. In **1949** he reached the final again but lost in five sets to Pancho Gonzales. Earlier that same year, on his only visit to Wimbledon he had won the singles in heroic fashion after surviving four five-set matches. In the first round he had beaten his doubles partner, Gardnar Mulloy, 7–5 in the fifth (later they reached the doubles final and lost to Gonzales and Parker). In the quarter-finals he had been match-point down to Frank Sedgman and, despite being foot-faulted on his first serve, had followed in his second serve to hit a winning volley and finally won 9–7 in the final set. Only Boris Becker in 1985 played more games (292) than Schroeder did that year (291). In doubles he won the US Championships with Jack Kramer in **1940, 1941** and **1947** and the mixed with Louise Brough in **1942**. A distinguished member of the US D Cup team between **1946** and **1951**, he played in six challenge rounds, winning eight of his 11 singles and one of his four doubles. – J.B.

FRANK ALLAN SEDGMAN (Australia)
Born 29 /10 /27. A superb volleyer who seemed to glide about the court, he was Australia's first post-war Wimbledon singles champ and, with Ken McGregor, he achieved the grand slam of the 4 major doubles titles in **1953**. Won Wimbledon singles **1952** and doubles (with J. E. Bromwich) **1948** and (with McGregor) l**51**l**52**. US singles **1951**l**52** and doubles (with Bromwich) **1950** and (with McGregor) l**51.** French doubles (with McGregor) **1951**l**52**. Australian singles **1949**l**50** and (with McGregor) doubles **1951**l**52**. Italian singles and doubles (with McGregor) **1952**. Won 25 D Cup rubbers out of 28 between **1949–52.** Turned pro in **1953.**

FRANCISCO 'PANCHO' SEGURA (Ecuador)
Born 20 /6 /21. An unorthodox showman who made his reputation in his pro years – he achieved little as an amateur. Won the US Clay Court title in **1944** and the US Indoor in **1946,** but made little mark at Wimbledon, losing to Tom Brown and to Drobny in his two singles appearances. He turned pro in 1947 and immediately became one of the great entertainers of the pro game. With his double-fisted forehand, his deadly lobs, his scuttling speed about the court, and his beaming smile, he was a most popular competitor

for 20 years. If he did not win as many titles as he deserved, he was always capable of testing players of the quality of Kramer, Rosewall, and Gonzales.

ELIAS VICTOR SEIXAS (USA)
Born 30 /8 /23. A doggedly successful American competitor. Won Wimbledon singles *1953* and mixed *1953|54|55|56,* 3 times with Doris Hart and once with Shirley Fry. US singles *1954* and doubles (with M. G. Rose) *1952* and (with M. A. Trabert) *|54.* French doubles (with Trabert) *1954|55.* Played in 7 successive D Cup challenge rounds and won 38 out of 55 rubbers in 19 ties between *1951–57.*

MARGARET SMITH (Australia)
Born 16 /7 /42. Now Mrs Court. In 1970 she became the second woman to achieve the Grand Slam of the major singles championships, having brought off a unique mixed doubles slam with Fletcher in *1963.* A powerful athlete, superbly fit, with a heavy service, great stamina and a formidable reach on the volley, she won a record number of 62 GS titles – and would have won more if she had not been afflicted by occasional and often inexplicable losses of confidence. Her major singles successes were Wimbledon *1963, 1965, 1970,* US Championships *1962, 1965, 1969, 1970, 1973,* French Championships *1962, 1964, 1969, 1970, 1973,* and Australia *1960–66, 1969–71* and *1973.* She was also three times the holder of the Italian, German and South African titles. In addition, she won the doubles at Wimbledon twice and the mixed five times, the US doubles five times and the mixed on eight occasions, the French four times in doubles and mixed, and she held eight Australian doubles and two mixed titles. She toured successfully, with the help of her husband, Barry, with two children, but retired in 1977 when she found that she was expecting a third baby.

STANLEY ROGER SMITH (USA)
Born 14 /12 /46. The very epitome of the All-American boy with his tall straight-backed figure, his fair hair and his clean-cut good looks, he became a national hero in *1972,* as well as the world's No. 1 player, when he won a magnificent Wimbledon final against Nastase and then beat the Rumanian again in the opening rubber of the D Cup final on unfriendly clay in Bucharest to launch the United States towards an improbable victory against the odds. Earlier, in *1969,* he had won the US Nationals and the following year had beaten Laver and Rosewall to capture the first-ever Masters which, that year, was a round-robin competition. When he won the US Open in *1971* on the grass of Forest Hills he was perfecting the serve-and-volley technique that made him such an awkward opponent. Although his groundstrokes were never his strength, he used them intelligently to secure the few breaks of serve that were necessary as he blanketed the net to secure his own service games. His doubles partnership with Lutz was one of the best American pairings there has ever been. They are the only pair to have won US National titles on all four surfaces – grass, clay, hard and indoor. Four times they won the US Open – *1968, 1974, 1978, 1980* and in *1977* they were successful both in South Africa and the US Pro at Boston. In D Cup they are the only American pair to have won three Challenge Round rubbers and two in the Final Round. Overall his D Cup record is 34 wins and 7 losses in 23 ties. – J.B.

FREDERICK SYDNEY STOLLE (Australia)
Born 8 /10 /38. Former Sydney bank clerk, regarded primarily as doubles specialist, who by diligence and determination became one of the most successful singles players of the 1960s. Powerful serving and volleying, added to dogged consistency in return of service on the backhand, compensated for his lack of mobility and flexibility. Shared with Von Cramm the unlucky distinction of losing in 3 successive Wimbledon singles f, falling to McKinley *(1963)* and Emerson *(1964|65).* Was also r /u to Lundquist in *1964* Italian f, but won French singles *1965* and US and German titles *1966.* Established himself first as a doubles player with Hewitt. They won Australia *1963|64,* Wimbledon *1962|64* and Italy *1963|64.* With Emerson, who had dominated him in singles, won French and US doubles

1965 and Australia, Italy and US *1966.* In *1981,* aged 42, he and Newcombe (37) took McEnroe /Fleming to 5s tie-break in US Open sf. Became contract professional *1967* and reached Wimbledon doubles f with Rosewall *1968.* Between *1964–66* he won 13 out of his 16 D Cup rubbers. Coached NY Sets to victory in World Team Tennis competition *1976.*

ERIC WILLIAM STURGESS (South Africa)
Born 10 /6 /20. South Africa's most successful singles competitor and their nat champ on no fewer than 11 occasions, beginning a sequence of victories in *1939/40* and continuing in *1946, 1948–54,* and *1957.* Outside Johannesburg his major achievement was the capture of the German singles *1952;* r /u in Paris *1947* and *1951* and lost to Gonzales in *1948* US f. Twice he was in Wimbledon sf, but in spite of speed, steadiness, and elegance, he lacked the weight of shot to win in the highest class and his second service was vulnerable. He won the French doubles with Fannin *1947* and a number of mixed titles, notably Wimbledon *1949* (with Sheila Summers) and *1950* (with Louise Brough), and F Hills *1949* (with Brough).

WILLIAM F. TALBERT (USA)
Born 4 /11 /18. An expert in the practice, technique and strategy of doubles. The best right-court player of his generation, his most important victories were gained with Mulloy, with whom he won the US doubles *1942/45/46/48*, and a total of 84 out of 90 tournaments in ten years. With a variety of partners, he won US Clay Court doubles *1942/44/45/46* and the US Indoor Doubles *1949/50/51/52/54*. Abroad, with the young Trabert, also from Cincinnati, he won French and Italian doubles *1950*. He was runner-up to Parker in US singles *1944/45* and US Indoor champion *1948/51*. He won nine of his ten D Cup rubbers *1946–53*, from *1953–57* he captained the US D Cup team and later became Tournament Director of the US Open. All this was achieved despite the disability of diabetes.

WILLIAM TATUM TILDEN (USA)
Born 10 /2 /1893. Died 5 /6 /1953. For many critics the greatest player and student of match-strategy in the history of the game. Tall, with a long reach and a long stride, great strength and versatility of shot, and a powerful sense of drama, Tilden did not win a major title until he was 27. Then won Wimbledon singles *1920/21/30,* and doubles (with F. T. Hunter) *1927,* and US singles *1920/21/22/23/24/25/29*, and doubles *1918/21/22/23/27*. Was first Italian champ in *1930* and played D Cup from *1920–30* winning 34 rubbers out of 41 and 21 out of 28 in challenge rounds. Between *1920–26* won 13 successive challenge round singles. Turned pro in *1931.*

MARION ANTHONY TRABERT (USA)
Born 16 /8 /30. Won Wimbledon singles *1955* and US singles *1953/55* without losing a set. Won French singles *1954/55,* and doubles victories included US in *1954* (with E. V. Seixas), French *1950* (with W. F. Talbert) and *1954/55* (with Seixas) and Italian *1950* (with Talbert). Won 27 out of 35 D Cup rubbers between *1951–55.* Turned pro in *1955.*

CHRISTINE CLARA TRUMAN (Great Britain)
Born 16 /1 /41. Now Mrs Janes. Britain's most popular post-war player. She possessed a powerful forehand, a disconcerting ability to hit her way out of crises, a remarkable capacity for unorthodox volleying, and temperament and court manners that made her a model for every schoolgirl in the country. She was always regarded as a potential Wimbledon champ and reached sf at the age of 16 at her first Wimbledon, where she lost to Althea Gibson, the eventual winner. Afterwards came a series of spectacular failures until she reached the *1961* f, only to fall to Angela Mortimer. Her best performances were a victory over Miss Gibson in the *1958* W Cup match, which helped to give Britain the trophy for the first time since the war, and the capture of the French and Italian singles titles in *1959.* She and her sister, Nell, formed an aggressively effective – and

sometimes erratic – doubles partnership. She won 10 rubbers out of 25 in 11 W Cup matches.

LESLEY ROSEMARY TURNER (Australia)

Born 16 /8 /1942. Now Mrs Bowrey. Clever, strong and persistent, she gained her principal successes on European clay courts. In *1961* on her first European tour she lost to Maria Bueno in the Italian final and was runner-up again *1962* and *1964* before winning the title *1967|68*. She won the French singles *1963,* defeating Ann Jones, and *1965,* beating Margaret Court, and was runner-up *1962* and *1967*. She reached the Australian final *1964* and *1967*. In doubles, with Margaret Court, she won Wimbledon *1964,* Paris *1964|65* and Australia *1965*. Also took the Australian doubles title, with Judy Tegart, *1964* and *1967* and the US doubles, with Darlene Hard, *1961.* Won Wimbledon mixed doubles with Fred Stolle *1961* and *1964.*

H. ELLSWORTH VINES (USA)

Born 28 /9 /11. The possessor of a fine forehand and one of the fastest services of all time. Defeated Bunny Austin in *1932* 6–4 6–2 6–0 in one of the shortest Wimbledon f and lost title next year in a classic f against Jack Crawford. Won US singles *1931|32* and Australian doubles *1933*. Played D Cup *1932|33,* winning 13 rubbers out of 16. Turned pro *1934.*

SARAH VIRGINIA WADE (Great Britain)

Born 10 /7 /45. A spectacular and dramatic competitor, at her 16th attempt she finally achieved her ambition of winning the women's singles at Wimbledon in the Centenary year of *1977*. Until then her career had been an extravagant mixture of bitter disappoint-ments, many of the worst endured at Wimbledon, and dazzling successes. Her first major success was gained at US Open *1968* when she defeated Billie Jean King 6–4 6–2 in the final. She won the Australian title, beating Evonne Goolagong, in *1972* and gained her only major clay-court success in *1971*, when she defeated Helga Masthoff in the Italian final. Her best doubles victories – France *1973*, US *1973|75*, Australia *1975* and Italy *1968* – were won with Margaret Court, but she also succeeded in Rome *1971* with Mrs Masthoff and *1973* with Olga Morozova. She also holds the record for the most appearances of any player of any nation in both Fed Cup (100 rubbers in 57 ties) and the W Cup (56 rubbers in 20 ties).

ANTHONY FREDERICK WILDING (New Zealand

Born 31 /10 /1883. Killed in action in Belgium 9 /5 /1915. Coached by his father, a notable cricketer, he won the champ of Canterbury, New Zealand, at the age of 17 and went to Cambridge Univ for which he played *1904–05.* He became one of the great heroes of Edwardian tennis, winning the singles champ at Wimbledon *1910|11|12|13*. Won doubles (with N. E. Brookes) in *1907* and (with M. J. G. Ritchie) *|08|10.* He won 21 of the 30 D Cup rubbers which he played for Australasia between *1905–14.*

SIDNEY BURR BEARDSLEE WOOD (USA)

Born 1 /11 /11. A nephew of the late Julian Myrick, a former President of the US LTA and the prime mover in 1913 in the development of Forest Hills as the national centre of tennis in the US, he made his first appearance at Wimbledon, aged 15, in *1927,* playing Lacoste on the Centre Court. In *1931,* aged 19 years and 243 days, he became Wimbledon's second youngest champion. He won by default. Frank Shields fell in 4s of his sf against Borotra and damaged an ankle. Shields won, but was not fit enough to play in f. A shrewd strategist and a graceful stroke-maker, Wood was r/u to Allison at Forest Hills in *1935* but lost 6–2 6–2 6–3 in one of the tournament's most disappointing finals.

CHAMPIONSHIP ROLLS

FRENCH CHAMPIONSHIPS

Up to 1924 entry was restricted to members of French clubs. In 1925 entry was open to all amateurs. The Championships became 'open' in 1968.

MEN'S SINGLES

1891	H. Briggs	1903–04	M. Decugis	1920	A. H. Gobert
1892	J. Schopfer	1905–06	M. Germot	1921	J. Samazeuilh
1893	L. Riboulet	1907–09	M. Decugis	1922	H. Cochet
1894–96	A. Vacherot	1910	M. Germot	1923	P. Blanchy
1897–1900	P. Ayme	1911	A. H. Gobert	1924	J. Borotra
1901	A. Vacherot	1912–14	M. Decugis		
1902	M. Vacherot	1915–19	*Not held*		

	CHAMPION	RUNNER-UP	SCORE				
1925	R. Lacoste	J. Borotra	7–5	6–1	6–4		
1926	H. Cochet	R. Lacoste	6–2	6–4	6–3		
1927	R. Lacoste	W. T. Tilden	6–4	4–6	5–7	6–3	11–9
1928	H. Cochet	R. Lacoste	5–7	6–3	6–1	6–3	
1929	R. Lacoste	J. Borotra	6–3	2–6	6–0	2–6	8–6
1930	H. Cochet	W. T. Tilden	3–6	8–6	6–3	6–1	
1931	J. Borotra	C. Boussus	2–6	6–4	7–6	6–4	
1932	H. Cochet	G. de Stefani	6–0	6–4	4–6	6–3	
1933	J. H. Crawford	H. Cochet	8–6	6–1	6–3		
1934	G. von Cramm	J. H. Crawford	6–4	7–9	3–6	7–5	6–3
1935	F. J. Perry	G. von Cramm	6–3	3–6	6–1	6–3	
1936	G. von Cramm	F. J. Perry	6–0	2–6	6–2	2–6	6–0
1937	H. Henkel	H. W. Austin	6–1	6–4	6–3		
1938	J. D. Budge	R. Menzel	6–3	6–2	6–4		
1939	W. D. McNeill	R. L. Riggs	7–5	6–0	6–3		
1940–45	*Not held*						
1946	M. Bernard	J. Drobny	3–6	2–6	6–1	6–4	6–3
1947	J. Asboth	E. W. Sturgess	8–6	7–5	6–4		
1948	F. A. Parker	J. Drobny	6–4	7–5	5–7	8–6	
1949	F. A. Parker	J. E. Patty	6–3	1–6	6–1	6–4	
1950	J. E. Patty	J. Drobny	6–1	6–2	3–6	5–7	7–5
1951	J. Drobny	E. W. Sturgess	6–3	6–3	6–3		
1952	J. Drobny	F. A. Sedgman	6–2	6–0	3–6	6–3	
1953	K. R. Rosewall	E. V. Seixas	6–3	6–4	1–6	6–2	
1954	M. A. Trabert	A. Larsen	6–4	7–5	6–1		
1955	M. A. Trabert	S. Davidson	2–6	6–1	6–4	6–2	
1956	L. A. Hoad	S. Davidson	6–4	8–6	6–3		
1957	S. Davidson	H. Flam	6–3	6–4	6–4		
1958	M. G. Rose	L. Ayala	6–3	6–4	6–4		
1959	N. Pietrangeli	I. C. Vermaak	3–6	6–3	6–4	6–1	
1960	N. Pietrangeli	L. Ayala	3–6	6–3	6–4	4–6	6–3
1961	M. Santana	N. Pietrangeli	4–6	6–1	3–6	6–0	6–2
1962	R. G. Laver	R. S. Emerson	3–6	2–6	6–3	9–7	6–2
1963	R. S. Emerson	P. Darmon	3–6	6–1	6–4	6–4	
1964	M. Santana	N. Pietrangeli	6–3	6–1	4–6	7–5	
1965	F. S. Stolle	A. D. Roche	3–6	6–0	6–2	6–3	
1966	A. D. Roche	I. Gulyas	6–1	6–4	7–5		
1967	R. S. Emerson	A. D. Roche	6–1	6–4	2–6	6–2	
1968	K. R. Rosewall	R. G. Laver	6–3	6–1	2–6	6–2	
1969	R. G. Laver	K. R. Rosewall	6–4	6–3	6–4		
1970	J. Kodes	Z. Franulovic	6–2	6–4	6–0		
1971	J. Kodes	I. Nastase	8–6	6–2	2–6	7–5	
1972	A. Gimeno	P. Proisy	4–6	6–3	6–1	6–1	

	FIRST PRIZE (in French francs)
1968	15,000
1969	35,000
1970	56,000
1971	48,000
1972	48,000

1973	I. Nastase	N. Pilic	6–3	6–3	6–0			70,000
1974	B. Borg	M. Orantes	2–6	6–7	6–0	6–1	6–1	120,000
1975	B. Borg	G. Vilas	6–2	6–3	6–4			120,000
1976	A. Panatta	H. Solomon	6–1	6–4	4–6	7–6		130,000
1977	G. Vilas	B. E. Gottfried	6–0	6–3	6–0			190,000
1978	B. Borg	G. Vilas	6–3	6–1	6–3			210,000
1979	B. Borg	V. Pecci	6–3	6–1	6–7	6–4		208,200
1980	B. Borg	V. Gerulaitis	6–4	6–1	6–2			221,000
1981	B. Borg	I. Lendl	6–1	4–6	6–2	3–6	6–1	250,000
1982	M. Wilander	G. Vilas	1–6	7–6	6–0	6–4		400,000
1983	Y. Noah	M. Wilander	6–2	7–5	7–6			500,000
1984	I. Lendl	J. P. McEnroe	3–6	2–6	6–4	7–5	7–5	1,058,600
1985	M. Wilander	I. Lendl	3–6	6–4	6–2	6–2		1,338,200

WOMEN'S SINGLES

1897–99	Mlle F. Masson	1906	Mme F. Fenwick	1915–19	*Not held*
1900	Mlle Y. Prevost	1907	Mme de Kermel	1920–23	Mlle S. Lenglen
1901	Mme P. Girod	1908	Mme F. Fenwick	1924	Mlle D. Vlasto
1902–03	Mlle F. Masson	1909–12	Mlle J. Matthey		
1904–05	Mlle K. Gillou	1913–14	Mlle M. Broquedis		

(Up to 1924 entry was restricted to members of French clubs. In 1925 entry was open to all amateurs.)

	CHAMPION	RUNNER-UP	SCORE			
1925	Mlle S. Lenglen	Miss K. McKane	6–1	6–2		
1926	Mlle S. Lenglen	Miss M. K. Browne	6–1	6–0		
1927	Mlle K. Bouman	Mrs G. Peacock	6–2	6–4		
1928	Miss H. N. Wills	Miss E. Bennett	6–1	6–2		
1929	Miss H. N. Wills	Mme R. Mathieu	6–3	6–4		
1930	Mrs F. S. Moody	Miss H. H. Jacobs	6–2	6–1		
1931	Frl C. Aussem	Miss B. Nuthall	8–6	6–1		
1932	Mrs F. S. Moody	Mme R. Mathieu	7–5	6–1		
1933	Miss M. C. Scriven	Mme R. Mathieu	6–2	4–6	6–4	
1934	Miss M. C. Scriven	Miss H. H. Jacobs	7–5	4–6	6–1	
1935	Mrs H. Sperling	Mme R. Mathieu	6–2	6–1		
1936	Mrs H. Sperling	Mme R. Mathieu	6–3	6–4		
1937	Mrs H. Sperling	Mme R. Mathieu	6–2	6–4		
1938	Mme R. Mathieu	Mme N. Landry	6–0	6–3		
1939	Mme R. Mathieu	Miss J. Jedrzejowska	6–3	8–6		
1940–45	*Not held*					
1946	Miss M. E. Osborne	Miss P. M. Betz	1–6	8–6	7–5	
1947	Mrs P. C. Todd	Miss D. J. Hart	6–3	3–6	6–4	
1948	Mme N. Landry	Miss S. J. Fry	6–2	0–6	6–0	
1949	Mrs W. du Pont	Mme N. Adamson	7–5	6–2		
1950	Miss D. J. Hart	Mrs P. C. Todd	6–4	4–6	6–2	
1951	Miss S. J. Fry	Miss D. J. Hart	6–3	3–6	6–3	
1952	Miss D. J. Hart	Miss S. J. Fry	6–4	6–4		
1953	Miss M. Connolly	Miss D. J. Hart	6–2	6–4		
1954	Miss M. Connolly	Mme G. Bucaille	6–4	6–1		
1955	Miss A. Mortimer	Mrs D. P. Knode	2–6	7–5	10–8	
1956	Miss A. Gibson	Miss A. Mortimer	6–0	12–10		
1957	Miss S. J. Bloomer	Mrs D. P. Knode	6–1	6–3		
1958	Mrs Z. Kormoczy	Miss S. J. Bloomer	6–4	1–6	6–2	
1959	Miss C. C. Truman	Mrs Z. Kormoczy	6–4	7–5		
1960	Miss D. R. Hard	Miss Y. Ramirez	6–3	6–4		
1961	Miss A. S. Haydon	Miss Y. Ramirez	6–2	6–1		
1962	Miss M. Smith	Miss L. R. Turner	6–3	3–6	7–5	
1963	Miss L. R. Turner	Mrs P. F. Jones	2–6	6–3	7–5	
1964	Miss M. Smith	Miss M. E. Bueno	5–7	6–1	6–2	
1965	Miss L. R. Turner	Miss M. Smith	6–3	6–4		FIRST
1966	Mrs P. F. Jones	Miss L. Richey	6–3	6–1		PRIZE
1967	Mlle F. Durr	Miss L. R. Turner	4–6	6–3	6–4	*(in French francs)*
1968	Miss N. Richey	Mrs P. F. Jones	5–7	6–4	6–1	5,000
1969	Mrs B. M. Court	Mrs P. F. Jones	6–1	4–6	6–3	10,000
1970	Mrs B. M. Court	Miss H. Niessen	6–2	6–4		17,800
1971	Miss E. Goolagong	Miss H. Gourlay	6–3	7–5		13,500
1972	Mrs L. W. King	Miss E. Goolagong	6–3	6–3		13,500
1973	Mrs B. M. Court	Miss C. M. Evert	6–7	7–6	6–4	25,000
1974	Miss C. M. Evert	Mrs O. Morozova	6–1	6–2		40,000
1975	Miss C. M. Evert	Miss M. Navratilova	2–6	6–2	6–1	40,000
1976	Miss S. Barker	Miss R. Tomanova	6–2	0–6	6–2	30,000

1977	Miss M. Jausovec	Miss F. Mihai	6–2	6–7	6–1			35,000
1978	Miss V. Ruzici	Miss M. Jausovec	6–2	6–2				100,000
1979	Mrs C. Evert Lloyd	Miss W. M. Turnbull	6–2	6–0				126,900
1980	Mrs C. Evert Lloyd	Miss V. Ruzici	6–0	6–3				178,500
1981	Miss H. Mandlikova	Miss S. Hanika	6–2	6–4				200,000
1982	Miss M. Navratilova	Miss A. Jaeger	7–6	6–1				300,000
1983	Mrs C. Evert Lloyd	Miss M. Jausovec	6–1	6–2				375,000
1984	Miss M. Navratilova	Mrs C. Evert Lloyd	6–3	6–1				791,600
1985	Mrs C. Evert Lloyd	Miss M. Navratilova	6–3	6–7	7–5			1,262,700

MEN'S DOUBLES

	CHAMPIONS	RUNNERS-UP	SCORE				
1925	J. Borotra/R. Lacoste	J. Brugnon/H. Cochet	7–5	4–6	6–3	2–6	6–3
1926	H. O. Kinsey/V. Richards	J. Brugnon/H. Cochet	6–4	6–1	4–6	6–4	
1927	J. Brugnon/H. Cochet	J. Borotra/R. Lacoste	2–6	6–2	6–0	1–6	6–4
1928	J. Borotra/J. Brugnon	R. de Buzelet/H. Cochet	6–4	3–6	6–2	3–6	6–4
1929	J. Borotra/R. Lacoste	J. Brugnon/H. Cochet	6–3	3–6	6–3	3–6	8–6
1930	J. Brugnon/H. Cochet	H. C. Hopman/J. Willard	6–3	9–7	6–3		
1931	G. M. Lott/J. Van Ryn	N. G. Farquharson/V. G. Kirby	6–4	6–3	6–4		
1932	J. Brugnon/H. Cochet	M. Bernard/C. Boussus	6–4	3–6	7–5	6–3	
1933	G. P. Hughes/F. J. Perry	V. B. McGrath/A. K. Quist	6–2	6–4	2–6	7–5	
1934	J. Borotra/J. Brugnon	J. H. Crawford/V. B. McGrath	11–9	6–3	2–6	4–6	9–7
1935	J. H. Crawford/A. K. Quist	V. B. McGrath/D. P. Turnbull	6–1	6–4	6–2		
1936	M. Bernard/J. Borotra	G. P. Hughes/C. R. D. Tuckey	6–2	3–6	9–7	6–1	
1937	G. Von Cramm/H. Henkel	N. G. Farquharson/V. G. Kirby	6–4	7–5	3–6	6–1	
1938	B. Destremau/Y. Petra	J. D. Budge/G. Mako	3–6	6–3	9–7	6–1	
1939	C. Harris/W. D. McNeil	J. Borotra/J. Brugnon	4–6	6–4	6–0	2–6	10–8
1940–1945	*Not held*						
1946	M. Bernard/Y. Petra	E. Morea/F. Segura	7–5	6–3	0–6	1–6	10–8
1947	E. Fannin/E. W. Sturgess	T. P. Brown/O. W. Sidwell	6–4	4–6	6–4	6–3	
1948	L. Bergelin/J. Drobny	H. C. Hopman/F. A. Sedgman	8–6	6–1	12–10		
1949	R. A. Gonzales/F. Parker	E. Fannin/E. W. Sturgess	6–3	8–6	5–7	6–3	
1950	W. F. Talbert/M. A. Trabert	J. Drobny/E. W. Sturgess	6–2	1–6	10–8	6–2	
1951	K. McGregor/F. A. Sedgman	G. Mulloy/R. Savitt	6–2	2–6	9–7	7–5	
1952	K. McGregor/F. A. Sedgman	G. Mulloy/R. Savitt	6–3	6–4	6–4		
1953	L. A. Hoad/K. R. Rosewall	M. G. Rose/C. Wilderspin	6–2	6–1	6–1		
1954	E. V. Seixas/M. A. Trabert	L. A. Hoad/K. R. Rosewall	6–4	6–2	6–1		
1955	E. V. Seixas/M. A. Trabert	N. Pietrangeli/O. Sirola	6–1	4–6	6–2	6–4	
1956	D. W. Candy/R. M. Perry	A. J. Cooper/L. A. Hoad	7–5	6–3	6–3		
1957	M. J. Anderson/A. J. Cooper	D. W. Candy/M. G. Rose	6–3	6–0	6–3		
1958	A. J. Cooper/N. A. Fraser	R. N. Howe/A. Segal	3–6	8–6	6–3	7–5	
1959	N. Pietrangeli/O. Sirola	R. S. Emerson/N. A. Fraser	6–3	6–2	14–12		
1960	R. S. Emerson/N. A. Fraser	J. L. Arilla/A. Gimeno	6–2	8–10	7–5	6–4	
1961	R. S. Emerson/R. G. Laver	R. N. Howe/R. Mark	3–6	6–1	6–1	6–4	
1962	R. S. Emerson/N. A. Fraser	W. P. Bungert/C. Kuhnke	6–3	6–4	7–5		
1963	R. S. Emerson/M. Santana	G. L. Forbes/A. Segal	6–2	6–4	6–4		
1964	R. S. Emerson/K. N. Fletcher	J. D. Newcombe/A. D. Roche	7–5	6–3	3–6	7–5	
1965	R. S. Emerson/F. S. Stolle	K. N. Fletcher/R. A. J. Hewitt	6–8	6–3	8–6	6–2	
1966	C. E. Graebner/R. D. Ralston	I. Nastase/I. Tiriac	6–3	6–3	6–0		
1967	J. D. Newcombe/A. D. Roche	R. S. Emerson/K. N. Fletcher	6–3	9–7	12–10		
1968	K. R. Rosewall/F. S. Stolle	R. S. Emerson/R. G. Laver	6–3	6–4	6–3		
1969	J. D. Newcombe/A. D. Roche	R. S. Emerson/R. G. Laver	4–6	6–1	3–6	6–4	6–4
1970	I. Nastase/I. Tiriac	A. R. Ashe/C. Pasarell	6–2	6–4	6–3		
1971	A. R. Ashe/M. C. Riessen	T. W. Gorman/S. R. Smith	6–8	4–6	6–3	6–4	11–9
1972	R. A. J. Hewitt/F. D. McMillan	P. Cornejo/J. Fillol	6–3	8–6	3–6	6–1	
1973	J. D. Newcombe/T. S. Okker	J. S. Connors/I. Nastase	6–1	3–6	6–3	5–7	6–4
1974	R. D. Crealy/O. Parun	R. C. Lutz/S. R. Smith	6–3	6–2	3–6	5–7	6–1
1975	B. E. Gottfried/R. Ramirez	J. G. Alexander/P. Dent	6–2	2–6	6–2	6–4	
1976	F. McNair/S. E. Stewart	B. E. Gottfried/R. Ramirez	7–6	6–3	6–1		
1977	B. E. Gottfried/R. Ramirez	W. Fibak/J. Kodes	7–6	4–6	6–3	6–4	
1978	G. Mayer/H. Pfister	J. Higueras/M. Orantes	6–3	6–2	6–2		
1979	A. A./G. Mayer	R. Case/P. Dent	6–4	6–4	6–4		
1980	V. Amaya/H. Pfister	B. E. Gottfried/R. Ramirez	1–6	6–4	6–4	6–3	
1981	H. Gunthardt/B. Taroczy	T. Moor/E. Teltscher	6–2	7–6	6–3		
1982	S. E. Stewart/F. Taygan	H. Gildemeister/B. Prajoux	7–5	6–3	1–1 ret'd		
1983	A. Jarryd/H. Simonsson	M. R. Edmondson/S. E. Stewart	7–6	6–4	6–2		
1984	H. Leconte/Y. Noah	P. Slozil/T. Smid	6–4	2–6	3–6	6–3	6–2
1985	M. R. Edmondson/K. Warwick	S. Glickstein/H. Simonsson	6–3	6–4	6–7	6–3	

WOMEN'S DOUBLES

	CHAMPIONS	RUNNERS-UP	SCORE		
1925	S. Lenglen/D. Vlasto	E. Colyer/K. McKane	6–1	9–11	6–2
1926	S. Lenglen/D. Vlasto	E. Colyer/L. A. Godfree	6–1	6–1	
1927	E. L. Heine/G. Peacock	P. Saunders/P. H. Watson	6–2	6–1	
1928	E. Bennett/P. H. Watson	S. Deve/A. Lafaurie	6–0	6–2	
1929	L. de Alvarez/K. Bouman	E. L. Heine/A. Neave	7–5	6–3	
1930	F. S. Moody/E. Ryan	S. Barbier/S. Mathieu	6–3	6–1	
1931	B. Nuthall/E. F. Whittingstall	C. Aussem/E. Ryan	9–7	6–2	
1932	F. S. Moody/E. Ryan	B. Nuthall/E. F. Whittingstall	6–1	6–3	
1933	S. Mathieu/E. Ryan	S. Henrotin/C. Rosambert	6–1	6–3	
1934	S. Mathieu/E. Ryan	H. H. Jacobs/S. Palfrey	3–6	6–4	6–2
1935	M. C. Scriven/K. Stammers	N. Adamoff/H. Sperling	6–4	6–0	
1936	S. Mathieu/A. M. Yorke	S. Noel/J. Jedrzejowska	2–6	6–4	6–4
1937	S. Mathieu/A. M. Yorke	D. Andrus/S. Henrotin	3–6	6–2	6–2
1938	S. Mathieu/A. M. Yorke	A. Halff/N. Landry	6–3	6–3	
1939	J. Jedrzejowska/S. Mathieu	A. Florian/H. Kovac	7–5	7–5	
1940–1945	*Not held*				
1946	L. Brough/M. Osborne	P. Betz/D. Hart	6–4	0–6	6–1
1947	L. Brough/M. Osborne	D. Hart/P. C. Todd	7–5	6–2	
1948	D. Hart/P. C. Todd	S. Fry/M. A. Prentiss	6–4	6–2	
1949	L. Brough/W. du Pont	J. Gannon/B. Hilton	7–5	6–1	
1950	S. Fry/D. Hart	L. Brough/W. du Pont	1–6	7–5	6–2
1951	S. Fry/D. Hart	B. Bartlett/B. Scofield	10–8	6–3	
1952	S. Fry/D. Hart	H. Redick-Smith/J. Wipplinger	7–5	6–1	
1953	S. Fry/D. Hart	M. Connolly/J. Sampson	6–4	6–3	
1954	M. Connolly/N. Hopman	M. Galtier/S. Schmitt	7–5	4–6	6–0
1955	B. Fleitz/D. R. Hard	S. J. Bloomer/P. Ward	7–5	6–8	13–11
1956	A. Buxton/A. Gibson	D. R. Hard/D. Knode	6–8	8–6	6–1
1957	S. J. Bloomer/D. R. Hard	Y. Ramirez/R. M. Reyes	7–5	4–6	7–5
1958	Y. Ramirez/R. M. Reyes	M. K. Hawton/T. D. Long	6–4	7–5	
1959	S. Reynolds/R. Schuurman	Y. Ramirez/R. M. Reyes	2–6	6–0	6–1
1960	M. E. Bueno/D. R. Hard	R. Hales/A. Haydon	6–2	7–5	
1961	S. Reynolds/R. Schuurman	M. E. Bueno/D. R. Hard	w.o.		
1962	S. Price/R. Schuurman	J. Bricka/M. Smith	6–4	6–4	
1963	P. F. Jones/R. Schuurman	R. A. Ebbern/M. Smith	7–5	6–4	
1964	M. Smith/L. R. Turner	N. Baylon/H. Schultze	6–3	6–1	
1965	M. Smith/L. R. Turner	F. Durr/J. Lieffrig	6–3	6–1	
1966	M. Smith/J. A. M. Tegart	J. Blackman/F. Toyne	4–6	6–1	6–1
1967	F. Durr/G. Sheriff	A. M. Van Zyl/P. Walkden	6–2	6–2	
1968	F. Durr/P. F. Jones	R. Casals/L. W. King	7–5	4–6	6–4
1969	F. Durr/P. F. Jones	M. Court/N. Richey	6–0	4–6	7–5
1970	F. Durr/G. Chanfreau	R. Casals/L. W. King	6–1	3–6	6–3
1971	F. Durr/G. Chanfreau	H. Gourlay/K. Harris	6–4	6–1	
1972	L. W. King/B. Stove	W. Shaw/F. E. Truman	6–1	6–2	
1973	M. Court/S. V. Wade	F. Durr/B. Stove	6–2	6–3	
1974	C. Evert/O. Morozova	G. Chanfreau/K. Ebbinghaus	6–4	2–6	6–1
1975	C. Evert/M. Navratilova	J. Anthony/O. Morozova	6–3	6–2	
1976	F. Bonicelli/G. Lovera	K. Harter/H. Masthoff	6–4	1–6	6–3
1977	R. Marsikova/P. Teeguarden	R. Fox/H. Gourlay	5–7	6–4	6–2
1978	M. Jausovec/V. Ruzici	N. Bowey/G. Lovera	5–7	6–4	8–6
1979	B. Stove/W. M. Turnbull	F. Durr/S. V. Wade	6–4	7–6	
1980	K. Jordan/A. E. Smith	I. Madruga/I. Villagran	6–1	6–0	
1981	R. Fairbank/T. Harford	C. Reynolds/P. Smith	6–1	6–3	
1982	M. Navratilova/A. E. Smith	R. Casals/W. M. Turnbull	6–3	6–4	
1983	R. Fairbank/C. Reynolds	K. Jordan/A. E. Smith	5–7	7–5	6–2
1984	M. Navratilova/P. H. Shriver	C. Kohde-Kilsch/H. Mandlikova	5–7	6–3	6–2
1985	M. Navratilova/P. H. Shriver	C. Kohde-Kilsch/H. Sukova	4–6	6–2	6–2

MIXED DOUBLES

	CHAMPIONS	RUNNERS-UP	SCORE		
1925	J. Brugnon/Miss S. Lenglen	H. Cochet/Miss D. Vlasto	6–2	6–2	
1926	J. Brugnon/Miss S. Lenglen	J. Borotra/Mrs Le Besnerais	6–4	6–3	
1927	J. Borotra/Miss M. Broquedis	W. T. Tilden/Miss L. de Alvarez	6–4	2–6	6–2
1928	H. Cochet/Miss E. Bennett	F. T. Hunter/Miss H. Wills	3–6	6–3	6–3
1929	H. Cochet/Miss E. Bennett	F. T. Hunter/Miss H. Wills	6–3	6–2	
1930	W. T. Tilden/Miss C. Aussem	H. Cochet/Mrs F. Whittingstall	6–4	6–4	

1931	P. D. B. Spence/Miss B. Nuthall	H. W. Austin/Mrs D. C. Shepherd-Barron	6–3	5–7	6–3
1932	F. J. Perry/Miss B. Nuthall	S. B. Wood/Mrs F. S. Moody	6–4	6–2	
1933	J. H. Crawford/Miss M. C. Scriven	F. J. Perry/Miss B. Nuthall	6–2	6–3	
1934	J. Borotra/Miss C. Rosambert	A. K. Quist/Miss E. Ryan	6–2	6–4	
1935	M. Bernard/Miss L. Payot	A. M. Legeay/Mrs S. Henrotin	4–6	6–2	6–4
1936	M. Bernard/Miss A. M. Yorke	A. M. Legeay/Mrs S. Henrotin	7–5	6–8	6–3
1937	Y. Petra/Mrs S. Mathieu	R. Journu/Miss M. Horne	7–5	7–5	
1938	D. Mitic/Mrs S. Mathieu	C. Boussus/Miss N. Wynne	2–6	6–3	6–4
1939	E. T. Cooke/Mrs S. Fabyan	F. Kukuljevic/Mrs S. Mathieu	4–6	6–1	7–5
1940–1945	*Not held*				
1946	J. E. Patty/Miss P. M. Betz	T. P. Brown/Miss D. Bundy	7–5	9–7	
1947	E. W. Sturgess/Mrs S. P. Summers	C. Caralulis/Miss J. Jedrzejowska	6–0	6–0	
1948	J. Drobny/Mrs P. C. Todd	F. A. Sedgman/Miss D. Hart	6–3	3–6	6–3
1949	E. W. Sturgess/Mrs S. P. Summers	G. D. Oakley/Miss J. Quertier	6–1	6–1	
1950	E. Morea/Miss B. Scofield	W. F. Talbert/Mrs P. C. Todd	w.o.		
1951	F. A. Sedgman/Miss D. Hart	M. G. Rose/Mrs T. D. Long	7–5	6–2	
1952	F. A. Sedgman/Miss D. Hart	E. W. Sturgess/Miss S. Fry	6–8	6–3	6–3
1953	E. V. Seixas/Miss D. Hart	M. G. Rose/Miss M. Connolly	4–6	6–4	6–0
1954	L. A. Hoad/Miss M. Connolly	R. N. Hartwig/Mrs J. Patorni	6–4	6–3	
1955	G. L. Forbes/Miss D. R. Hard	L. Ayala/Miss J. Staley	5–7	6–1	6–2
1956	L. Ayala/Mrs T. D. Long	R. N. Howe/Miss D. R. Hard	4–6	6–4	6–1
1957	J. Javorsky/Miss V. Puzejova	L. Ayala/Miss E. Buding	6–3	6–4	
1958	N. Pietrangeli/Miss S. J. Bloomer	R. N. Howe/Miss L. Coghlan	9–7	6–8	6–2
1959	W. A. Knight/Miss R. Ramirez	R. G. Laver/Miss R. Schuurman	6–4	6–4	
1960	R. N. Howe/Miss M. Bueno	R. S. Emerson/Miss A. Haydon	1–6	6–1	6–2
1961	R. G. Laver/Miss D. R. Hard	J. Javorsky/Miss V. Puzejova	6–0	2–6	6–3
1962	R. N. Howe/Miss R. Schuurman	F. S. Stolle/Miss L. R. Turner	3–6	6–4	6–4
1963	K. N. Fletcher/Miss M. Smith	F. S. Stolle/Miss L. R. Turner	6–1	6–2	
1964	K. N. Fletcher/Miss M. Smith	F. S. Stolle/Miss L. R. Turner	6–3	6–4	
1965	K. N. Fletcher/Miss M. Smith	J. D. Newcombe/Miss M. Bueno	6–4	6–4	
1966	F. D. McMillan/Miss A. M. Van Zyl	C. Graebner/Mrs P. F. Jones	1–6	6–3	6–2
1967	O. K. Davidson/Mrs L. W. King	I. Tiriac/Mrs P. F. Jones	6–3	6–1	
1968	J. C. Barclay/Miss F. Durr	O. K. Davidson/Mrs L. W. King	6–1	6–4	
1969	M. C. Riessen/Mrs. B. M. Court	J. C. Barclay/Miss F. Durr	7–5	6–4	
1970	R. A. J. Hewitt/Mrs L. W. King	J. C. Barclay/Miss F. Durr	3–6	6–3	6–2
1971	J. C. Barclay/Miss F. Durr	T. Lejus/Miss W. Shaw	6–2	6–4	
1972	K. Warwick/Miss E. Goolagong	J. C. Barclay/Miss F. Durr	6–2	6–4	
1973	J. C. Barclay/Miss F. Durr	P. Dominguez/Miss B. Stove	6–1	6–4	
1974	I. Molina/Miss M. Navratilova	M. Lara/Mrs R. M. Darmon	6–3	6–3	
1975	T. Koch/Miss·F. Bonicelli	J. Fillol/Miss P. Teeguarden	6–4	7–6	
1976	K. Warwick/Miss I. Kloss	C. Dowdeswell/Miss L. Boshoff	5–7	7–6	6–2
1977	J. P. McEnroe/Miss M. Carillo	I. Molina/Miss F. Mihai	7–6	6–3	
1978	P. Slozil/Miss R. Tomanova	P. Dominguez/Miss V. Ruzici	7–6 ret'd		
1979	R. A. J. Hewitt/Miss W. M. Turnbull	I. Tiriac/Miss V. Ruzici	6–3	2–6	6–3
1980	W. Martin/Miss A. E. Smith	S. Birner/Miss R. Tomanova	2–6	6–4	8–6
1981	J. Arias/Miss A. Jaeger	F. D. McNair/Miss B. Stove	7–6	6–4	
1982	J. M. Lloyd/Miss W. M. Turnbull	C. Motta/Miss C. Monteiro	6–2	7–6	
1983	E. Teltscher/Miss B. Jordan	C. Strode/Miss L. Allen	6–2	6–3	
1984	R. L. Stockton/Miss A. E. Smith	L. Warder/Miss A. Minter	6–2	6–4	
1985	H. P. Gunthardt/Miss M. Navratilova	F. Gonzalez/Miss P. Smith	2–6	6–3	6–2

WIMBLEDON CHAMPIONSHIPS

For the years 1913, 1914, and 1919–23 inclusive, these records include the 'World's Championship on Grass' granted to the LTA by the ILTF. This title was then abolished. Prior to 1922 the holder did not compete in the Championship but met the winner of the singles in the Challenge Round. The Challenge Round was abolished in 1922 and the holder subsequently played through. Modified 'seeding' was introduced in 1924. Full 'seeding', as we know it today, was first practised in 1927. The Championships became 'open' in 1968.

There was a tie-break at 8–all in the years 1971–1978. Thereafter the tie-break was played at 6–all.
Holders did not defend the title.

MEN'S SINGLES

	CHAMPION	RUNNER-UP	SCORE		
1877	S. W. Gore	W. C. Marshall	6–1	6–2	6–4
1878	P. F. Hadow	S. W. Gore	7–5	6–1	9–7
1879*	J. T. Hartley	V. St L. Goold	6–2	6–4	6–2

1880	J. T. Hartley	H. F. Lawford	6–3 6–2 2–6 6–3		
1881	W. Renshaw	J. T. Hartley	6–0 6–1 6–1		
1882	W. Renshaw	E. Renshaw	6–1 2–6 4–6 6–2 6–2		
1883	W. Renshaw	E. Renshaw	2–6 6–3 6–3 4–6 6–3		
1884	W. Renshaw	H. F. Lawford	6–0 6–4 9–7		
1885	W. Renshaw	H. F. Lawford	7–5 6–2 4–6 7–5		
1886	W. Renshaw	H. F. Lawford	6–0 5–7 6–3 6–4		
1887*	H. F. Lawford	E. Renshaw	1–6 6–3 3–6 6–4 6–4		
1888	E. Renshaw	H. F. Lawford	6–3 7–5 6–0		
1889	W. Renshaw	E. Renshaw	6–4 6–1 3–6 6–0		
1890	W. J. Hamilton	W. Renshaw	6–8 6–2 3–6 6–1 6–1		
1891*	W. Baddeley	J. Pim	6–4 1–6 7–5 6–0		
1892	W. Baddeley	J. Pim	4–6 6–3 6–3 6–2		
1893	J. Pim	W. Baddeley	3–6 6–1 6–3 6–2		
1894	J. Pim	W. Baddeley	10–8 6–2 8–6		
1895*	W. Baddeley	W. V. Eaves	4–6 2–6 8–6 6–2 6–3		
1896	H. S. Mahony	W. Baddeley	6–2 6–8 5–7 8–6 6–3		
1897	R. F. Doherty	H. S. Mahony	6–4 6–4 6–3		
1898	R. F. Doherty	H. L. Doherty	6–3 6–3 2–6 5–7 6–1		
1899	R. F. Doherty	A. W. Gore	1–6 4–6 6–2 6–3 6–3		
1900	R. F. Doherty	S. H. Smith	6–8 6–3 6–1 6–2		
1901	A. W. Gore	R. F. Doherty	4–6 7–5 6–4 6–4		
1902	H. L. Doherty	A. W. Gore	6–4 6–3 3–6 6–0		
1903	H. L. Doherty	F. L. Riseley	7–5 6–3 6–0		
1904	H. L. Doherty	F. L. Riseley	6–1 7–5 8–6		
1905	H. L. Doherty	N. E. Brookes	8–6 6–2 6–4		
1906	H. L. Doherty	F. L. Riseley	6–4 4–6 6–2 6–3		
1907*	N. E. Brookes	A. W. Gore	6–4 6–2 6–2		
1908*	A. W. Gore	H. Roper Barrett	6–3 6–2 4–6 3–6 6–4		
1909	A. W. Gore	M. J. G. Ritchie	6–8 1–6 6–2 6–2 6–2		
1910	A. F. Wilding	A. W. Gore	6–4 7–5 4–6 6–2		
1911	A. F. Wilding	H. Roper Barrett	6–4 4–6 2–6 6–2 ret'd		
1912	A. F. Wilding	A. W. Gore	6–4 6–4 4–6 6–4		
1913	A. F. Wilding	M. E. McLoughlin	8–6 6–3 10–8		
1914	N. E. Brookes	A. F. Wilding	6–4 6–4 7–5		
1915–18 *Not held*					
1919	G. L. Patterson	N. E. Brookes	6–3 7–5 6–2		
1920	W. T. Tilden	G. L. Patterson	2–6 6–2 6–3 6–4		
1921	W. T. Tilden	B. I. C. Norton	4–6 2–6 6–1 6–0 7–5		
(Challenge Round abolished)					
1922*	G. L. Patterson	R. Lycett	6–3 6–4 6–2		
1923*	W. M. Johnston	F. T. Hunter	6–0 6–3 6–1		
1924	J. Borotra	R. Lacoste	6–1 3–6 6–1 3–6 6–4		
1925	R. Lacoste	J. Borotra	6–3 6–3 4–6 8–6		
1926	J. Borotra	Howard Kinsey	8–6 6–1 6–3		
1927	H. Cochet	J. Borotra	4–6 4–6 6–3 6–4 7–5		
1928	R. Lacoste	H. Cochet	6–1 4–6 6–4 6–2		
1929	H. Cochet	J. Borotra	6–4 6–3 6–4		
1930	W. T. Tilden	W. L. Allison	6–3 9–7 6–4		
1931*	S. B. Wood	F. X. Shields	w.o.		
1932	H. E. Vines	H. W. Austin	6–4 6–2 6–0		
1933	J. H. Crawford	H. E. Vines	4–6 11–9 6–2 2–6 6–4		
1934	F. J. Perry	J. H. Crawford	6–3 6–0 7–5		
1935	F. J. Perry	G. von Cramm	6–2 6–4 6–4		
1936	F. J. Perry	G. von Cramm	6–1 6–1 6–0		
1937*	J. D. Budge	G. von Cramm	6–3 6–4 6–2		
1938	J. D. Budge	H. W. Austin	6–1 6–0 6–3		
1939*	R. L. Riggs	E. T. Cooke	2–6 8–6 3–6 6–3 6–2		
1940–45 *Not held*					
1946*	Y. Petra	G. E. Brown	6–2 6–4 7–9 5–7 6–4		
1947	J. A. Kramer	T. Brown	6–1 6–3 6–2		
1948*	R. Falkenburg	J. E. Bromwich	7–5 0–6 6–2 3–6 7–5		
1949	F. R. Schroeder	J. Drobny	3–6 6–0 6–3 4–6 6–4		
1950*	J. E. Patty	F. A. Sedgman	6–1 8–10 6–2 6–3		
1951	R. Savitt	K. McGregor	6–4 6–4 6–4		
1952	F. A. Sedgman	J. Drobny	4–6 6–2 6–3 6–2		
1953*	E. V. Seixas	K. Nielsen	9–7 6–3 6–4		
1954	J. Drobny	K. R. Rosewall	13–11 4–6 6–2 9–7		
1955	M. A. Trabert	K. Nielsen	6–3 7–5 6–1		
1956*	L. A. Hoad	K. R. Rosewall	6–2 4–6 7–5 6–4		
1957	L. A. Hoad	A. J. Cooper	6–2 6–1 6–2		
1958*	A. J. Cooper	N. A. Fraser	3–6 6–3 6–4 13–11		

1959*	A. Olmedo	R. G. Laver	6–4	6–3	6–4	
1960*	N. A. Fraser	R. G. Laver	6–4	3–6	9–7	7–5
1961	R. G. Laver	C. R. McKinley	6–3	6–1	6–4	
1962	R. G. Laver	M. F. Mulligan	6–2	6–2	6–1	
1963*	C. R. McKinley	F. S. Stolle	9–7	6–1	6–4	
1964	R. S. Emerson	F. S. Stolle	6–1	12–10	4–6	6–3
1965	R. S. Emerson	F. S. Stolle	6–2	6–4	6–4	

							FIRST
1966	M. Santana	R. D. Ralston	6–4	11–9	6–4		PRIZE
1967	J. D. Newcombe	W. P. Bungert	6–3	6–1	6–1		(£)
1968	R. G. Laver	A. D. Roche	6–3	6–4	6–2		2,000
1969	R. G. Laver	J. D. Newcombe	6–4	5–7	6–4	6–4	3,000
1970	J. D. Newcombe	K. R. Rosewall	5–7	6–3	6–2	3–6 6–1	3,000
1971	J. D. Newcombe	S. R. Smith	6–3	5–7	2–6	6–4 6–4	3,750
1972*	S. R. Smith	I. Nastase	4–6	6–3	6–3	4–6 7–5	5,000
1973*	J. Kodes	A. Metreveli	6–1	9–8	6–3		5,000
1974	J. S. Connors	K. R. Rosewall	6–1	6–1	6–4		10,000
1975	A. R. Ashe	J. S. Connors	6–1	6–1	5–7	6–4	10,000
1976	B. Borg	I. Nastase	6–4	6–2	9–7		12,500
1977	B. Borg	J. S. Connors	3–6	6–2	6–1	5–7 6–4	15,000
1978	B. Borg	J. S. Connors	6–2	6–2	6–3		19,000
1979	B. Borg	R. Tanner	6–7	6–1	3–6	6–3 6–4	20,000
1980	B. Borg	J. P. McEnroe	1–6	7–5	6–3	6–7 8–6	20,000
1981	J. P. McEnroe	B. Borg	4–6	7–6	7–6	6–4	21,600
1982	J. S. Connors	J. P. McEnroe	3–6	6–3	6–7	7–6 6–4	41,667
1983	J. P. McEnroe	C. J. Lewis	6–2	6–2	6–2		66,600
1984	J. P. McEnroe	J. S. Connors	6–1	6–1	6–2		100,000
1985	B. Becker	K. Curren	6–3	6–7	7–6	6–4	130,000

WOMEN'S SINGLES

	CHAMPION	RUNNER-UP	SCORE		
1884	Miss M. Watson	Miss L. Watson	6–8	6–3	6–3
1885	Miss M. Watson	Miss B. Bingley	6–1	7–5	
1886	Miss B. Bingley	Miss M. Watson	6–3	6–3	
1887	Miss C. Dod	Miss B. Bingley	6–2	6–0	
1888	Miss C. Dod	Mrs G. W. Hillyard	6–3	6–3	
1889*	Mrs G. W. Hillyard	Miss H. Rice	4–6	8–6	6–4
1890*	Miss H. Rice	Miss M. Jacks	6–4	6–1	
1891*	Miss C. Dod	Mrs G. W. Hillyard	6–2	6–1	
1892	Miss C. Dod	Mrs G. W. Hillyard	6–1	6–1	
1893	Miss C. Dod	Mrs G. W. Hillyard	6–8	6–1	6–4
1894*	Mrs G. W. Hillyard	Miss L. Austin	6–1	6–1	
1895*	Miss C. Cooper	Miss H. Jackson	7–5	8–6	
1896	Miss C. Cooper	Mrs W. H. Pickering	6–2	6–3	
1897	Mrs G. W. Hillyard	Miss C. Cooper	5–7	7–5	6–2
1898*	Miss C. Cooper	Miss L. Martin	6–4	6–4	
1899	Mrs G. W. Hillyard	Miss C. Cooper	6–2	6–3	
1900	Mrs G. W. Hillyard	Miss C. Cooper	4–6	6–4	6–4
1901	Mrs A. Sterry	Mrs G. W. Hillyard	6–2	6–2	
1902	Miss M. E. Robb	Mrs A. Sterry	7–5	6–1	
1903*	Miss D. K. Douglass	Miss E. W. Thomson	4–6	6–4	6–2
1904	Miss D. K. Douglass	Mrs A. Sterry	6–0	6–3	
1905	Miss M. Sutton	Miss D. K. Douglass	6–3	6–4	
1906	Miss D. K. Douglass	Miss M. Sutton	6–3	9–7	
1907	Miss M. Sutton	Mrs Lambert Chambers	6–1	6–4	
1908*	Mrs A. Sterry	Miss A. M. Morton	6–4	6–4	
1909*	Miss D. P. Boothby	Miss A. M. Morton	6–4	4–6	8–6
1910	Mrs Lambert Chambers	Miss D. P. Boothby	6–2	6–2	
1911	Mrs Lambert Chambers	Miss D. P. Boothby	6–0	6–0	
1912*	Mrs D. R. Larcombe	Mrs A. Sterry	6–3	6–1	
1913*	Mrs Lambert Chambers	Mrs R. J. McNair	6–0	6–4	
1914	Mrs Lambert Chambers	Mrs D. R. Larcombe	7–5	6–4	
1915–18	*Not held*				
1919	Mlle S. Lenglen	Mrs Lambert Chambers	10–8	4–6	9–7
1920	Mlle S. Lenglen	Mrs Lambert Chambers	6–3	6–0	
1921	Mlle S. Lenglen	Miss E. Ryan	6–2	6–0	
(Challenge Round abolished)					
1922	Mlle S. Lenglen	Mrs F. Mallory	6–2	6–0	
1923	Mlle S. Lenglen	Miss K. McKane	6–2	6–2	
1924	Miss K. McKane	Miss H. N. Wills	4–6	6–4	6–4

1925	Mlle S. Lenglen	Miss J. Fry	6–2	6–0		
1926	Mrs L. A. Godfree	Sta E. de Alvarez	6–2	4–6	6–3	
1927	Miss H. N. Wills	Sta E. de Alvarez	6–2	6–4		
1928	Miss H. N. Wills	Sta E. de Alvarez	6–2	6–3		
1929	Miss H. N. Wills	Miss H. H. Jacobs	6–1	6–2		
1930	Mrs F. S. Moody	Miss E. Ryan	6–2	6–2		
1931*	Frl C. Aussem	Frl H. Krahwinkel	6–2	7–5		
1932*	Mrs F. S. Moody	Miss H. H. Jacobs	6–3	6–1		
1933	Mrs F. S. Moody	Miss D. E. Round	6–4	6–8	6–3	
1934*	Miss D. E. Round	Miss H. H. Jacobs	6–2	5–7	6–3	
1935	Mrs F. S. Moody	Miss H. H. Jacobs	6–3	3–6	7–5	
1936*	Miss H. H. Jacobs	Mrs S. Sperling	6–2	4–6	7–5	
1937	Miss D. E. Round	Miss J. Jedrzejowska	6–2	2–6	7–5	
1938*	Mrs F. S. Moody	Miss H. H. Jacobs	6–4	6–0		
1939*	Miss A. Marble	Miss K. E. Stammers	6–2	6–0		
1940–45	*Not held*					
1946*	Miss P. M. Betz	Miss A. L. Brough	6–2	6–4		
1947*	Miss M. E. Osborne	Miss D. J. Hart	6–2	6–4		
1948	Miss A. L. Brough	Miss D. J. Hart	6–3	8–6		
1949	Miss A. L. Brough	Mrs W. du Pont	10–8	1–6	10–8	
1950	Miss A. L. Brough	Mrs W. du Pont	6–1	3–6	6–1	
1951	Miss D. J. Hart	Miss S. J. Fry	6–1	6–0		
1952	Miss M. Connolly	Miss A. L. Brough	6–4	6–3		
1953	Miss M. Connolly	Miss D. J. Hart	8–6	7–5		
1954	Miss M. Connolly	Miss A. L. Brough	6–2	7–5		
1955*	Miss A. L. Brough	Mrs J. G. Fleitz	7–5	8–6		
1956	Miss S. J. Fry	Miss A. Buxton	6–3	6–1		
1957*	Miss A. Gibson	Miss D. R. Hard	6–3	6–2		
1958	Miss A. Gibson	Miss A. Mortimer	8–6	6–2		
1959*	Miss M. E. Bueno	Miss D. R. Hard	6–4	6–3		
1960	Miss M. E. Bueno	Miss S. Reynolds	8–6	6–0		
1961*	Miss A. Mortimer	Miss C. C. Truman	4–6	6–4	7–5	
1962	Mrs J. R. Susman	Mrs V. Sukova	6–4	6–4		
1963*	Miss M. Smith	Miss B. J. Moffitt	6–3	6–4		
1964	Miss M. Smith	Miss M. Smith	6–4	7–9	6–3	
1965	Miss M. Smith	Miss M. E. Bueno	6–4	7–5		FIRST
1966	Mrs L. W. King	Miss M. E. Bueno	6–3	3–6	6–1	PRIZE
1967	Mrs L. W. King	Mrs P. F. Jones	6–3	6–4		(£)
1968	Mrs L. W. King	Miss J. A. M. Tegart	9–7	7–5		750
1969	Mrs P. F. Jones	Mrs L. W. King	3–6	6–3	6–2	1,500
1970*	Mrs B. M. Court	Mrs L. W. King	14–12	11–9		1,500
1971	Miss E. Goolagong	Mrs B. M. Court	6–4	6–1		1,800
1972	Mrs L. W. King	Miss E. Goolagong	6–3	6–3		2,400
1973	Mrs L. W. King	Miss C. M. Evert	6–0	7–5		3,000
1974	Miss C. M. Evert	Mrs O. Morozova	6–0	6–4		7,000
1975	Mrs L. W. King	Mrs R. A. Cawley	6–0	6–1		7,000
1976*	Miss C. M. Evert	Mrs R. A. Cawley	6–3	4–6	8–6	10,000
1977	Miss S. V. Wade	Miss B. F. Stove	4–6	6–3	6–1	13,500
1978	Miss M. Navratilova	Miss C. M. Evert	2–6	6–4	7–5	17,100
1979	Miss M. Navratilova	Mrs C. Evert Lloyd	6–4	6–4		18,000
1980	Mrs R. A. Cawley	Mrs C. Evert Lloyd	6–1	7–6		18,000
1981	Mrs C. Evert Lloyd	Miss H. Mandlikova	6–2	6–2		19,440
1982	Miss M. Navratilova	Mrs C. Evert Lloyd	6–1	3–6	6–2	37,500
1983	Miss M. Navratilova	Miss A. Jaeger	6–0	6–3		60,000
1984	Miss M. Navratilova	**Mrs** C. Evert Lloyd	7–6	6–2		90,000
1985	Miss M. Navratilova	**Mrs** C. Evert Lloyd	4–6	6–3	6–2	117,000

MEN'S DOUBLES

	CHAMPIONS	RUNNERS-UP	SCORE				
1884	E./W. Renshaw	E. W. Lewis/E. L. Williams	6–3	6–1	1–6	6–4	
1885	E./W. Renshaw	C. E. Farrer/A. J. Stanley	6–3	6–3	10–8		
(Challenge Round instituted)							
1886	E./W. Renshaw	C. E. Farrer/A. J. Stanley	6–3	6–3	4–6	7–5	
1887*	P. Bowes-Lyon	E. Barret-Smith/J. H. Crispe	7–5	6–3	6–2		
	H. W. W. Wilberforce						
1888	E./W. Renshaw	P. Bowes-Lyon	2–6	1–6	6–3	6–4	6–3
		H. W. W. Wilberforce					
1889	E./W. Renshaw	G. W. Hillyard/E. W. Lewis	6–4	6–4	3–6	0–6	6–1

Year	Winners	Runners-up	Score				
1890*	J. Pim/F. O. Stoker	G. W. Hillyard/E. W. Lewis	6–0	7–5	6–4		
1891	H./W. Baddeley	J. Pim/F. O. Stoker	6–1	6–3	1–6	6–2	
1892	H. S. Barlow/E. W. Lewis	H./W. Baddeley	4–6	6–2	8–6	6–4	
1893	J. Pim/F. O. Stoker	H. W. Barlow/E. W. Lewis	4–6	6–3	6–1	2–6	6–0
1894*	H./W. Baddeley	H. S. Barlow/C. H. Martin	5–7	7–5	4–6	6–3	8–6
1895	H./W. Baddeley	W. V. Eaves/E. W. Lewis	8–6	5–7	6–4	6–3	
1896	H./W. Baddeley	R. F. Doherty/H. A. Nisbet	1–6	3–6	6–4	6–2	6–1
1897	H. L./R. F. Doherty	H./W. Baddeley	6–4	4–6	8–6	6–4	
1898	H. L./R. F. Doherty	C. Hobart/H. A. Nisbet	6–4	6–4	6–2		
1899	H. L./R. F. Doherty	C. Hobart/H. A. Nisbet	7–5	6–0	6–2		
1900	H. L./R. F. Doherty	H. A. Nisbet/H. Roper Barrett	9–7	7–5	4–6	3–6	6–3
1901	H. L./R. F. Doherty	D. F. Davis/H. Ward	4–6	6–2	6–3	9–7	
1902	F. L. Riseley/S. H. Smith	H. L./R. F. Doherty	4–6	8–6	6–3	4–6	11–9
1903	H. L./R. F. Doherty	F. L. Riseley/S. H. Smith	6–4	6–4	6–4		
1904	H. L./R. F. Doherty	F. L. Riseley/S. H. Smith	6–3	6–4	6–3		
1905	H. L./R. F. Doherty	F. L. Riseley/S. H. Smith	6–2	6–4	6–8	6–3	
1906	F. L. Riseley/S. H. Smith	H. L./R. F. Doherty	6–8	6–4	5–7	6–3	6–3
1907*	N. E. Brookes/A. F. Wilding	K. Behr/B. C. Wright	6–4	6–4	6–2		
1908*	M. J. G. Ritchie/A. F. Wilding	A. W. Gore/H. Roper Barrett	6–1	6–2	1–6	1–6	9–7
1909*	A. W. Gore/H. Roper Barrett	S. N. Doust/H. A. Parker	6–2	6–1	6–4		
1910	M. J. G. Ritchie/A. F. Wilding	A. W. Gore/H. Roper Barrett	6–1	6–1	6–2		
1911	M. Decugis/A. H. Gobert	M. J. G. Ritchie/A. F. Wilding	9–7	5–7	6–3	2–6	6–2
1912	C. P. Dixon/H. Roper Barrett	M. Decugis/A. H. Gobert	3–6	6–3	6–4	7–5	
1913	C. P. Dixon/H. Roper Barrett	H. Kleinschroth/F. W. Rahe	6–2	6–4	4–6	6–2	
1914	N. E. Brookes/A. F. Wilding	C. P. Dixon/H. Roper Barrett	6–1	6–1	5–7	8–6	
1915–1918	*Not held*						
1919*	P. O'Hara Wood/R. V. Thomas	R. W. Heath/R. Lycett	6–4	6–2	4–6	6–2	
1920*	C. S. Garland/R. N. Williams	A. R. F. Kingscote/J. C. Parke	4–6	6–4	7–5	6–2	
1921*	R. Lycett/M. Woosnam	A. H./F. G. Lowe	6–3	6–0	7–5		
(Challenge Round abolished)							
1922	J. O. Anderson/R. Lycett	P. O'Hara Wood/G. L. Patterson	3–6	7–9	6–4	6–3	11–9
1923	L. A. Godfree/R. Lycett	E. Flaquer/Count de Gomar	6–3	6–4	3–6	6–3	
1924	F. T. Hunter/V. Richards	W. M. Washburn/R. N. Williams	6–3	3–6	8–10	8–6	6–3
1925	J. Borotra/R. Lacoste	R. Casey/J. Hennessey	6–4	11–9	4–6	1–6	6–3
1926	J. Brugnon/H. Cochet	H. Kinsey/V. Richards	7–5	4–6	6–3	6–2	
1927	F. T. Hunter/W. T. Tilden	J. Brugnon/H. Cochet	1–6	4–6	8–6	6–3	6–4
1928	J. Brugnon/H. Cochet	J. B. Hawkes/G. L. Patterson	13–11	6–4	6–4		
1929	W. L. Allison/J. Van Ryn	I. G. Collins/J. C. Gregory	6–4	5–7	6–3	10–12	6–4
1930	W. L. Allison/J. Van Ryn	J. H. Doeg/G. M. Lott	6–3	6–3	6–2		
1931	G. M. Lott/J. Van Ryn	J. Brugnon/H. Cochet	6–2	10–8	9–11	3–6	6–3
1932	J. Borotra/J. Brugnon	G. P. Hughes/F. J. Perry	6–0	4–6	3–6	7–5	7–5
1933	J. Borotra/J. Brugnon	R. Nunoi/J. Satoh	4–6	6–3	6–3	7–5	
1934	G. M. Lott/L. R. Stoefen	J. Borotra/J. Brugnon	6–2	6–3	6–4		
1935	J. H. Crawford/A. K Quist	W. L. Allison/J. Van Ryn	6–3	5–7	6–2	5–7	7–5
1936	G. P. Hughes/C. R. D. Tuckey	C. E. Hare/F. H. D. Wilde	6–4	3–6	7–9	6–1	5–4
1937	J. D. Budge/G. Mako	G. P. Hughes/C. R. D. Tuckey	6–0	6–4	6–8	6–1	
1938	J. D. Budge/G. Mako	H. Henkel/G. von Metaxa	6–4	3–6	6–3	8–6	
1939	E. T. Cooke/R. L. Riggs	C. E. Hare/F. H. D. Wilde	6–3	6–4	6–3	9–7	
1940–1945	*Not held*						
1946	T. Brown/J. A. Kramer	G. E. Brown/D. Pails	6–4	6–4	6–2		
1947	R. Falkenburg/J. A. Kramer	A. J. Mottram/O. W. Sidwell	8–6	6–3	6–3		
1948	J. E. Bromwich/F. A. Sedgman	T. Brown/G. Mulloy	5–7	7–5	7–5	9–7	
1949	R. A. Gonzales/F. A. Parker	G. Mulloy/F. R. Schroeder	6–4	6–4	6–2		
1950	J. E. Bromwich/A. K. Quist	G. E. Brown/O. W. Sidwell	7–5	3–6	6–3	3–6	6–2
1951	K. McGregor/F. A. Sedgman	J. Drobny/E. W. Sturgess	3–6	6–2	6–3	3–6	6–3
1952	K. McGregor/F. A. Sedgman	E. V. Seixas/E. W. Sturgess	6–3	7–5	6–4		
1953	L. A. Hoad/K. R. Rosewall	R. N. Hartwig/M. G. Rose	6–4	7–5	4–6	7–5	
1954	R. N. Hartwig/M. G. Rose	E. V. Seixas/M. A. Trabert	6–4	6–4	3–6	6–4	
1955	R. N. Hartwig/L. A. Hoad	N. A. Fraser/K. R. Rosewall	7–5	6–4	6–3		
1956	L. A. Hoad/K. R. Rosewall	N. Pietrangeli/O. Sirola	7–5	6–2	6–1		
1957	G. Mulloy/B. Patty	N. A. Fraser/L. A. Hoad	8–10	6–4	6–4	6–4	
1958	S. Davidson/U. Schmidt	A. J. Cooper/N. A. Fraser	6–4	6–4	8–6		
1959	R. Emerson/N. A. Fraser	R. Laver/R. Mark	8–6	6–3	1–6	9–7	
1960	R. H. Osuna/R. D. Ralston	M. G. Davies/R. K. Wilson	7–5	6–3	10–8		
1961	R. Emerson/N. A. Fraser	R. A. J. Hewitt/F. S. Stolle	6–4	6–8	6–4	6–8	8–6
1962	R. A. J. Hewitt/F. S. Stolle	B. Jovanovic/N. Pilic	6–2	5–7	6–2	6–4	
1963	R. H. Osuna/A. Palafox	J. C. Barclay/P. Darmon	4–6	6–2	6–2	6–2	
1964	R. A. J. Hewitt/F. S. Stolle	R. Emerson/K. N. Fletcher	7–5	11–9	6–4		FIRST
1965	J. D. Newcombe/A. D. Roche	K. N. Fletcher/R. A. J. Hewitt	7–5	6–3	6–4		PRIZE
1966	K. N. Fletcher/J. D. Newcombe	W. W. Bowrey/O. K. Davidson	6–3	6–4	3–6	6–3	*(£ per*
1967	R. A. J. Hewitt/F. D. McMillan	R. Emerson/K. N. Fletcher	6–2	6–3	6–4		*team)*
1968	J. D. Newcombe/A. D. Roche	K. R. Rosewall/F. S. Stolle	3–6	8–6	5–7	14–12	6–3	800

1969	J. D. Newcombe/A. D. Roche	T. S. Okker/M. C. Riessen	7–5 11–9 6–3			1,000
1970	J. D. Newcombe/A. D. Roche	K. R. Rosewall/F. S. Stolle	10–8 6–3 6–1			1,000
1971	R. Emerson/R. Laver	A. R. Ashe/R. D. Ralston	4–6 9–7 6–8 6–4 6–4			750
1972	R. A. J. Hewitt/F. D. McMillan	S. R. Smith/E. Van Dillen	6–2 6–2 9–7			1,000
1973	J. S. Connors/I. Nastase	J. R. Cooper/N. A. Fraser	3–6 6–3 6–4 8–9 6–1			1,000
1974	J. D. Newcombe/A. D. Roche	R. C. Lutz/S. R. Smith	8–6 6–4 6–4			2,000
1975	V. Gerulaitis/A. Mayer	C. Dowdeswell/A. J. Stone	7–5 8–6 6–4			2,000
1976	B. E. Gottfried/R. Ramirez	R. L. Case/G. Masters	3–6 6–3 8–6 2–6 7–6			3,000
1977	R. L. Case/G. Masters	J. G. Alexander/P. C. Dent	6–3 6–4 3–6 8–9 6–4			6,000
1978	R. A. J. Hewitt/F. D. McMillan	P. Fleming/J. P. McEnroe	6–1 6–4 6–2			7,500
1979	P. Fleming/J. P. McEnroe	B. E. Gottfried/R. Ramirez	4–6 6–4 6–2 6–2			8,000
1980	P. McNamara/P. McNamee	R. C. Lutz/S. R. Smith	7–6 6–3 6–7 6–4			8,400
1981	P. Fleming/J. P. McEnroe	R. C. Lutz/S. R. Smith	6–4 6–4 6–4			9,070
1982	P. McNamara/P. McNamee	P. Fleming/J. P. McEnroe	6–3 6–2			16,666
1983	P. Fleming/J. P. McEnroe	T. E./T. R. Gullikson	6–4 6–3 6–4			26,628
1984	P. Fleming/J. P. McEnroe	P. Cash/P. McNamee	6–2 5–7 6–2 3–6 6–3			40,000
1985	H. P. Gunthardt/B. Taroczy	P. Cash/J. Fitzgerald	6–4 6–3 4–6 6–3			47,500

WOMEN'S DOUBLES

	CHAMPIONS	RUNNERS-UP	SCORE		
1913	R. J. McNair/D. P. Boothby	A. Sterry/D. Lambert Chambers	4–6 2–4 ret'd		
1914	A. M. Morton/E. Ryan	G. Hannam/D. R. Larcombe	6–1 6–3		
1915–1918	*Not held*				
1919	S. Lenglen/E. Ryan	D. Lambert Chambers/D. R. Larcombe	4–6 7–5 6–3		
1920	S. Lenglen/E. Ryan	D. Lambert Chambers/D. R. Larcombe	6–4 6–0		
1921	S. Lenglen/E. Ryan	A. E. Beamish/G. Peacock	6–1 6–2		
1922	S. Lenglen/E. Ryan	K. McKane/A. D. Stocks	6–0 6–4		
1923	S. Lenglen/E. Ryan	J. Austin/E. L. Colyer	6–3 6–1		
1924	H. Wightman/H. N. Wills	B. C. Covell/K. McKane	6–4 6–4		
1925	S. Lenglen/E. Ryan	A. V. Bridge/C. G. McIlquham	6–2 6–2		
1926	M. K. Browne/E. Ryan	L. A. Godfree/E. L. Colyer	6–1 6–1		
1927	H. N. Wills/E. Ryan	E. L. Heine/G. Peacock	6–3 6–2		
1928	P. Saunders/M. Watson	E. Bennett/E. H. Harvey	6–2 6–3		
1929	L. R. C. Michell/M. Watson	B. C. Covell/D. C. Shepherd-Barron	6–4 8–6		
1930	F. S. Moody/E. Ryan	E. Cross/S. Palfrey	6–2 9–7		
1931	D. C. Shepherd-Barron/P. E. Mudford	D. Metaxa/J. Sigart	3–6 6–3 6–4		
1932	D. Metaxa/J. Sigart	H. H. Jacobs/E. Ryan	6–4 6–3		
1933	S. Mathieu/E. Ryan	F. James/A. M. Yorke	6–2 9–11 6–4		
1934	S. Mathieu/E. Ryan	D. B. Andrus/S. Henrotin	6–3 6–3		
1935	F. James/K. E. Stammers	S. Mathieu/H. Sperling	6–1 6–4		
1936	F. James/K. E. Stammers	S. Fabyan/H. H. Jacobs	6–2 6–1		
1937	S. Mathieu/A. M. Yorke	P. King/E. Pittman	6–3 6–3		
1938	S. Fabyan/A. Marble	S. Mathieu/A. M. Yorke	6–2 6–3		
1939	S. Fabyan/A. Marble	H. H. Jacobs/A. M. Yorke	6–1 6–0		
1940–1945	*Not held*				
1946	A. L. Brough/M. E. Osborne	P. M. Betz/D. J. Hart	6–3 2–6 6–3		
1947	D. J. Hart/P. C. Todd	A. L. Brough/M. E. Osborne	3–6 6–4 7–5		
1948	A. L. Brough/W. du Pont	D. J. Hart/P. C. Todd	6–3 3–6 6–3		
1949	A. L. Brough/W. du Pont	G. Moran/P. C. Todd	8–6 7–5		
1950	A. L. Brough/W. du Pont	S. J. Fry/D. J. Hart	6–4 5–7 6–1		
1951	S. J. Fry/D. J. Hart	A. L. Brough/W. du Pont	6–3 13–11		
1952	S. J. Fry/D. J. Hart	A. L. Brough/M. Connolly	8–6 6–3		
1953	S. J. Fry/D. J. Hart	M. Connolly/J. Sampson	6–0 6–0		
1954	A. L. Brough/W. du Pont	S. J. Fry/D. J. Hart	4–6 9–7 6–3		
1955	A. Mortimer/J. A. Shilcock	S. J. Bloomer/P. E. Ward	7–5 6–1		
1956	A. Buxton/A. Gibson	F. Muller/D. G. Seeney	6–1 8–6		
1957	A. Gibson/D. R. Hard	K. Hawton/T. D. Long	6–1 6–2		
1958	M. E. Bueno/A. Gibson	W. du Pont/M. Varner	6–3 7–5		
1959	J. Arth/D. R. Hard	J. G. Fleitz/C. C. Truman	2–6 6–2 6–3		
1960	M. E. Bueno/D. R. Hard	S. Reynolds/R. Schuurman	6–4 6–0		
1961	K. Hantz/J. R. Moffitt	J. Lehane/M. Smith	6–3 6–4		
1962	B. J. Moffitt/J. R. Susman	L. E. G. Price/R. Schuurman	5–7 6–3 7–5		
1963	M. E. Bueno/D. R. Hard	R. A. Ebbern/M. Smith	8–6 9–7		
1964	M. Smith/L. R. Turner	B. J. Moffitt/J. R. Susman	7–5 6–2		FIRST
1965	M. E. Bueno/B. J. Moffitt	F. Durr/J. Lieffrig	6–2 7–5		PRIZE
1966	M. E. Bueno/N. Richey	M. Smith/J. A. M. Tegart	6–3 4–6 6–4		(£ per
1967	R. Casals/L. W. King	M. E. Bueno/N. Richey	9–11 6–4 6–2		team)
1968	R. Casals/L. W. King	F. Durr/P. F. Jones	3–6 6–4 7–5		500
1969	B. M. Court/J. A. M. Tegart	P. S. A. Hogan/M. Michel	9–7 6–2		600

1970	R. Casals/L. W. King	F. Durr/S. V. Wade	6–2	6–3		600
1971	R. Casals/L. W. King	B. M. Court/E. Goolagong	6–3	6–2		450
1972	L. W. King/B. Stove	D. E. Dalton/F. Durr	6–2	4–6	6–3	600
1973	R. Casals/L. W. King	F. Durr/B. Stove	6–1	4–6	7–5	600
1974	E. Goolagong/M. Michel	H. F. Gourlay/K. M. Krantzcke	2–6	6–4	6–3	1,200
1975	A. Kiyomura/K. Sawamatsu	F. Durr/B. Stove	7–5	1–6	7–5	1,200
1976	C. Evert/M. Navratilova	L. W. King/B. Stove	6–1	3–6	7–5	2,400
1977	H. Gourlay-Cawley/J. C. Russell	M. Navratilova/B. Stove	6–3	6–3		5,200
1978	G. E. Reid/W. Turnbull	M. Jausovec/V. Ruzici	4–6	9–8	6–3	6,500
1979	L. W. King/M. Navratilova	B. Stove/W. M. Turnbull	5–7	6–3	6–2	6,930
1980	K. Jordan/A. E. Smith	R. Casals/W. M. Turnbull	4–6	7–5	6–1	7,276
1981	M. Navratilova/P. H. Shriver	K. Jordan/A. E. Smith	6–3	7–6		7,854
1982	M. Navratilova/P. H. Shriver	K. Jordan/A. E. Smith	6–4	6–1		14,450
1983	M. Navratilova/P. H. Shriver	R. Casals/W. M. Turnbull	6–2	6–2		23,100
1984	M. Navratilova/P. H. Shriver	K. Jordan/A. E. Smith	6–3	6–4		34,700
1985	K. Jordan/E. Smylie	M. Navratilova/P. H. Shriver	5–7	6–3	6–4	41,100

MIXED DOUBLES

	CHAMPIONS	RUNNERS-UP	SCORE		
1913	Hope Crisp/Mrs C. O. Tuckey	J. C. Parke/Mrs D. R. Larcombe	3–6	5–3 ret'd	
1914	J. C. Parke/Mrs D. R. Larcombe	A. F. Wilding/Mlle M. Broquedis	4–6	6–4	6–2
1915–1918	*Not held*				
1919	R. Lycett/Miss E. Ryan	A. D. Prebble/Mrs D. Lambert Chambers	6–0	6–0	
1920	G. L. Patterson/Mlle S. Lenglen	R. Lycett/Miss E. Ryan	7–5	6–3	
1921	R. Lycett/Miss E. Ryan	M. Woosnam/Miss P. L. Howkins	6–3	6–1	
1922	P. O'Hara Wood/Mlle S. Lenglen	R. Lycett/Miss E. Ryan	6–4	6–3	
1923	R. Lycett/Miss E. Ryan	L. S. Deane/Mrs D. C. Shepherd-Barron	6–4	7–5	
1924	J. B. Gilbert/Miss K. McKane	L. A. Godfree/Mrs D. C. Shepherd-Barron	6–3	3–6	6–3
1925	J. Borotra/Mlle S. Lenglen	H. L. de Morpurgo/Miss E. Ryan	6–3	6–3	
1926	L. A./Mrs Godfree	H. Kinsey/Miss M. K. Browne	6–3	6–4	
1927	F. T. Hunter/Miss E. Ryan	L. A./Mrs Godfree	8–6	6–0	
1928	P. D. B. Spence/Miss E. Ryan	J. H. Crawford/Miss D. Akhurst	7–5	6–4	
1929	F. T. Hunter/Miss H. N. Wills	I. G. Collins/Miss J. Fry	6–1	6–4	
1930	J. H. Crawford/Miss E. Ryan	D. Prenn/Frl H. Krahwinkel	6–1	6–3	
1931	G. M. Lott/Mrs L. A. Harper	I. G. Collins/Miss J. C. Ridley	6–3	1–6	6–1
1932	E. Maier/Miss E. Ryan	H. C. Hopman/Mlle J. Sigart	7–5	6–2	
1933	G. von Cramm/Frl H. Krahwinkel	N. G. Farquharson/Miss M. Heeley	7–5	8–6	
1934	R. Miki/Miss D. E. Round	H. W. Austin/Mrs D. C. Shepherd-Barron	3–6	6–4	6–0
1935	F. J. Perry/Miss D. E. Round	H. C./Mrs Hopman	7–5	4–6	6–2
1936	F. J. Perry/Miss D. E. Round	J. D. Budge/Mrs S. Fabyan	7–9	7–5	6–4
1937	J. D. Budge/Miss A. Marble	Y. Petra/Mme S. Mathieu	6–4	6–1	
1938	J. D. Budge/Miss A. Marble	H. Henkel/Mrs S. Fabyan	6–1	6–4	
1939	R. L. Riggs/Miss A. Marble	F. H. D. Wilde/Miss N. B. Brown	9–7	6–1	
1940–1945	*Not held*				
1946	T. Brown/Miss A. L. Brough	G. E. Brown/Miss D. Bundy	6–4	6–4	
1947	J. E. Bromwich/Miss A. L. Brough	C. F. Long/Mrs N. M. Bolton	1–6	6–4	6–2
1948	J. E. Bromwich/Miss A. L. Brough	F. A. Sedgman/Miss D. J. Hart	6–2	3–6	6–3
1949	E. E. Sturgess/Mrs S. P. Summer	J. E. Bromwich/Miss A. L. Brough	9–7	9–11	7–5
1950	E. W. Sturgess/Miss A. L. Brough	G. E. Brown/Mrs P. C. Todd	11–9	1–6	6–4
1951	F. A. Sedgman/Miss D. J. Hart	M. G. Rose/Mrs N. M. Bolton	7–5	6–2	
1952	F. A. Sedgman/Miss D. J. Hart	E. Morea/Mrs T. D. Long	4–6	6–3	6–4
1953	E. V. Seixas/Miss D. J. Hart	E. Morea/Miss S. J. Fry	9–7	7–5	
1954	E. V. Seixas/Miss D. J. Hart	K. R. Rosewall/Mrs W. du Pont	5–7	6–4	6–3
1955	E. V. Seixas/Miss D. J. Hart	E. Morea/Miss A. L. Brough	8–6	2–6	6–3
1956	E. V. Seixas/Miss S. J. Fry	G. Mulloy/Miss A. Gibson	2–6	6–2	7–5
1957	M. G. Rose/Miss D. R. Hard	N. A. Fraser/Miss A. Gibson	6–4	7–5	
1958	R. N. Howe/Miss L. Coghlan	K. Nielsen/Miss A. Gibson	6–3	13–11	
1959	R. Laver/Miss D. R. Hard	N. A. Fraser/Miss M. E. Bueno	6–4	6–3	
1960	R. Laver/Miss D. R. Hard	R. N. Howes/Miss M. E. Bueno	13–11	3–6	8–6
1961	F. S. Stolle/Miss L. R. Turner	R. N. Howe/Miss E. Buding	11–9	6–2	
1962	N. A. Fraser/Mrs W. du Pont	R. D. Ralston/Miss A. S. Haydon	2–6	6–3	13–11
1963	K. N. Fletcher/Miss M. Smith	R. A. J. Hewitt/Miss D. R. Hard	11–9	6–4	
1964	F. S. Stolle/Miss L. R. Turner	K. N. Fletcher/Miss M. Smith	6–4	6–4	FIRST
1965	K. N. Fletcher/Miss M. Smith	A. D. Roche/Miss J. A. M. Tegart	12–10	6–3	PRIZE
1966	K. N. Fletcher/Miss M. Smith	R. D. Ralston/Mrs L. W. King	4–6	6–3	6–3	(£ per
1967	O. K. Davidson/Mrs L. W. King	K. N. Fletcher/Miss M. E. Bueno	7–5	6–0	team)
1968	K. N. Fletcher/Mrs B. M. Court	A. Metreveli/Miss O. Morozova	6–1	14–12	450
1969	F. S. Stolle/Mrs P. F. Jones	A. D. Roche/Miss J. A. M. Tegart	6–3	6–2	500
1970	I. Nastase/Miss R. Casals	A. Metreveli/Miss O. Morozova	6–3	4–6	9–7	500

1971	O. K. Davidson/Mrs L. W. King	M. C. Rieseen/Mrs B. M. Court	3–6	6–2	15–13	375
1972	I. Nastase/Miss R. Casals	K. Warwick/Miss E. Goolagong	6–4	6–4		500
1973	O. K. Davidson/Mrs L. W. King	R. Ramirez/Miss J. Newberry	6–3	6–2		500
1974	O. K. Davidson/Mrs L. W. King	M. J. Farrell/Miss L. J. Charles	6–3	9–7		1,000
1975	M. C. Riessen/Mrs B. M. Court	A. J. Stone/Miss B. Stove	6–4	7–5		1,000
1976	A. D. Roche/Miss F. Durr	R. L. Stockton/Miss R. Casals	6–3	2–6	7–5	2,000
1977	R. A. J. Hewitt/Miss G. R. Stevens	F. D. McMillan/Miss B. Stove	3–6	7–5	6–4	3,000
1978	F. D. McMillan/Miss B. Stove	R. O. Ruffels/Mrs L. W. King	6–2	6–2		4,000
1979	R. A. J. Hewitt/Miss G. R. Stevens	F. D. McMillan/Miss B. Stove	7–5	7–6		4,200
1980	J. R. Austin/Miss T. Austin	M. R. Edmondson/Miss D. L. Fromholtz	4–6	7–6	6–3	4,420
1981	F. D. McMillan/Miss B. Stove	J. R. Austin/Miss T. Austin	4–6	7–6	6–3	4,770
1982	K. Curren/Miss A. E. Smith	J. M. Lloyd/Miss W. M. Turnbull	2–6	6–3	7–5	6,750
1983	J. M. Lloyd/Miss W. M. Turnbull	S. Denton/Mrs L. W. King	6–7	7–6	7–5	12,000
1984	J. M. Lloyd/Miss W. M. Turnbull	S. Denton/Miss K. Jordan	6–3	6–3		18,000
1985	P. McNamee/Miss M. Navratilova	J. Fitzgerald/Mrs E. Smylie	7–5	4–6	6–2	23,400

US NATIONAL CHAMPIONSHIPS 1881–1969

Holders did not defend the title

MEN'S SINGLES

	CHAMPION	RUNNER-UP	SCORE				
1881	R. D. Sears	W. E. Glyn	6–0	6–3	6–2		
1882	R. D. Sears	C. M. Clark	6–1	6–4	6–0		
1883	R. D. Sears	J. Dwight	6–2	6–0	9–7		
1884	R. D. Sears	H. A. Taylor	6–0	1–6	6–0	6–2	
1885	R. D. Sears	G. M. Brinley	6–3	4–6	6–0	6–3	
1886	R. D. Sears	R. L. Beeckman	4–6	6–1	6–3	6–4	
1887	R. D. Sears	H. W. Slocum	6–1	6–3	6–2		
1888	*H. W. Slocum	H. A. Taylor	6–4	6–1	6–0		
1889	H. W. Slocum	Q. A. Shaw	6–3	6–1	4–6	6–2	
1890	O. S. Campbell	H. W. Slocum	6–2	4–6	6–3	6–1	
1891	O. S. Campbell	C. Hobart	2–6	7–5	7–9	6–1	6–2
1892	O. S. Campbell	F. H. Hovey	7–5	3–6	6–3	7–5	
1893	*R. D. Wrenn	F. H. Hovey	6–4	3–6	6–4	6–4	
1894	R. D. Wrenn	M. F. Goodbody	6–8	6–1	6–4	6–4	
1895	F. H. Hovey	R. D. Wrenn	6–3	6–2	6–4		
1896	R. D. Wrenn	F. H. Hovey	7–5	3–6	6–0	1–6	6–1
1897	R. D. Wrenn	W. V. Eaves	4–6	8–6	6–3	2–6	6–2
1898	*M. D. Whitman	D. F. Davis	3–6	6–2	6–2	6–1	
1899	M. D. Whitman	J. P. Paret	6–1	6–2	3–6	7–5	
1900	M. D. Whitman	W. A. Larned	6–4	1–6	6–2	6–2	
1901	*W. A. Larned	B. C. Wright	6–2	6–8	6–4	6–4	
1902	W. A. Larned	R. F. Doherty	4–6	6–2	6–4	8–6	
1903	H. L. Doherty	W. A. Larned	6–0	6–3	10–8		
1904	*H. Ward	W. J. Clothier	10–8	6–4	9–7		
1905	B. C. Wright	H. Ward	6–2	6–1	11–9		
1906	W. J. Clothier	B. C. Wright	6–3	6–0	6–4		
1907	*W. A. Larned	R. LeRoy	6–2	6–2	6–4		
1908	W. A. Larned	B. C. Wright	6–1	6–2	8–6		
1909	W. A. Larned	W. J. Clothier	6–1	6–2	5–7	1–6	6–1
1910	W. A. Larned	T. C. Bundy	6–1	5–7	6–0	6–8	6–1
1911	W. A. Larned	M. E. McLoughlin	6–4	6–4	6–2		
(Challenge Round abolished)							
1912	M. E. McLoughlin	W. F. Johnson	3–6	2–6	6–2	6–4	6–2
1913	M. E. McLoughlin	R. N. Williams	6–4	5–7	6–3	6–1	
1914	R. N. Williams	M. E. McLoughlin	6–3	8–6	10–8		
1915	W. M. Johnston	M. E. McLoughlin	1–6	6–0	7–5	10–8	
1916	R. N. Williams	W. M. Johnston	4–6	6–4	0–6	6–2	6–4
1917	*Not held*						
1918	R. L. Murray	W. T. Tilden	6–3	6–1	7–5		
1919	W. M. Johnston	W. T. Tilden	6–4	6–4	6–3		
1920	W. T. Tilden	W. M. Johnston	6–1	1–6	7–5	5–7	6–3
1921	W. T. Tilden	W. F. Johnson	6–1	6–3	6–1		
1922	W. T. Tilden	W. M. Johnston	4–6	3–6	6–2	6–3	6–4
1923	W. T. Tilden	W. M. Johnston	6–4	6–1	6–4		

1924	W. T. Tilden	W. M. Johnston	6–1	9–7	6–2	
1925	W. T. Tilden	W. M. Johnston	4–6	11–9	6–3	4–6	6–3
1926	P. Lacoste	J. Borotra	6–4	6–0	6–4	
1927	R. Lacoste	W. T. Tilden	11–9	6–3	11–9	
1928	H. Cochet	F. T. Hunter	4–6	6–4	3–6	7–5	6–3
1929	W. T. Tilden	F. T. Hunter	3–6	6–3	4–6	6–2	6–4
1930	J. H. Doeg	F. X. Shields	10–8	1–6	6–4	16–14
1931	H. E. Vines	G. M. Lott	7–9	6–3	9–7	7–5
1932	H. E. Vines	H. Cochet	6–4	6–4	6–4	
1933	F. J. Perry	J. H. Crawford	6–3	11–13	4–6	6–0	6–1
1934	F. J. Perry	W. L. Allison	6–4	6–3	1–6	8–6
1935	W. L. Allison	S. B. Wood	6–2	6–2	6–3	
1936	F. J. Perry	J. D. Budge	2–6	6–2	8–6	1–6	10–8
1937	J. D. Budge	C. Von Cramm	6–1	7–9	6–1	3–6	6–1
1938	J. D. Budge	G. Mako	6–3	6–8	6–2	6–1
1939	R. L. Riggs	S. W. van Horn	6–4	6–2	6–4	
1940	W. D. McNeill	R. L. Riggs	4–6	6–8	6–3	6–3	7–5
1941	R. L. Riggs	F. Kovacs	5–7	6–1	6–3	6–3
1942	F. R. Schroeder	F. A. Parker	8–6	7–5	3–6	4–6	6–2
1943	J. R. Hunt	J. A. Kramer	6–3	3–6	10–8	6–0
1944	F. A. Parker	W. F. Talbert	6–4	3–6	6–3	6–3
1945	F. A. Parker	W. F. Talbert	14–12	6–1	6–2	
1946	J. A. Kramer	T. P. Brown	9–7	6–3	6–0	
1947	J. A. Kramer	F. A. Parker	4–6	2–6	6–1	6–0	6–3
1948	R. A. Gonzales	E. W. Sturgess	6–2	6–3	14–12	
1949	R. A. Gonzales	F. R. Schroeder	16–18	2–6	6–1	6–2	6–4
1950	A. Larsen	H. Flam	6–3	4–6	5–7	6–4	6–3
1951	F. A. Sedgman	E. V. Seixas	6–4	6–1	6–1	
1952	F. A. Sedgman	G. Mulloy	6–1	6–2	6–3	
1953	M. A. Trabert	E. V. Seixas	6–3	6–2	6–3	
1954	E. V. Seixas	R. N. Hartwig	3–6	6–2	6–4	6–4
1955	M. A. Trabert	K. R. Rosewall	9–7	6–3	6–3	
1956	K. R. Rosewall	L. A. Hoad	4–6	6–2	6–3	6–3
1957	M. J. Anderson	A. J. Cooper	10–8	7–5	6–4	
1958	A. J. Cooper	M. J. Anderson	6–2	3–6	4–6	10–8	8–6
1959	N. A. Fraser	A. Olmedo	6–3	5–7	6–2	6–4
1960	N. A. Fraser	R. G. Laver	6–4	6–4	9–7	
1961	R. S. Emerson	R. G. Laver	7–5	6–3	6–2	
1962	R. G. Laver	R. S. Emerson	6–2	6–4	5–7	6–4
1963	R. H. Osuna	F. Froehling	7–5	6–4	6–2	
1964	R. S. Emerson	F. S. Stolle	6–4	6–2	6–4	
1965	M. Santana	E. C. Drysdale	6–2	7–9	7–5	6–1
1966	F. S. Stolle	J. D. Newcombe	4–6	12–10	6–3	6–4
1967	J. D. Newcombe	C. Graebner	6–4	6–4	8–6	
1968	A. R. Ashe	R. C. Lutz	4–6	6–3	8–10	6–0	6–4
1969	S. R. Smith	R. C. Lutz	9–7	6–3	6–1	

WOMEN'S SINGLES

	CHAMPION	RUNNER-UP	SCORE				
1887	Miss E. Hansell	Miss L. Knight	6–1	6–0		
1888	Miss B. L. Townsend	Miss E. Hansell	6–3	6–5		
1889	Miss B. L. Townsend	Miss L. D. Voorhes	7–5	6–2		
1890	Miss E. C. Roosevelt	Miss B. L. Townsend	6–2	6–2		
1891	Miss M. E. Cahill	Miss E. C. Roosevelt	6–4	6–1	4–6	6–3
1892	Miss M. E. Cahill	Miss E. H. Moore	5–7	6–3	6–4	4–6	6–2
1893	*Miss A. Terry	Miss A. Schultze	6–1	6–3		
1894	Miss H. Hellwig	Miss A. Terry	7–5	3–6	6–0	3–6	6–3
1895	Miss J. Atkinson	Miss H. Hellwig	6–4	6–2	6–1	
1896	Miss E. H. Moore	Miss J. Atkinson	6–4	4–6	6–2	6–2
1897	Miss J. Atkinson	Miss E. H. Moore	6–3	6–3	4–6	3–6	6–3
1898	Miss J. Atkinson	Miss M. Jones	6–3	5–7	6–4	2–6	7–5
1899	*Miss M. Jones	Miss M. Banks	6–1	6–1	7–5	
1900	*Miss M. McAteer	Miss E. Parker	6–2	6–2	6–0	
1901	Miss E. H. Moore	Miss M. McAteer	6–4	3–6	7–5	2–6	6–2
1902	Miss M. Jones	Miss E. H. Moore	6–1	1–0 ret'd		
1903	Miss E. H. Moore	Miss M. Jones	7–5	8–6		

1904	Miss M. G. Sutton	Miss E. H. Moore	6–1 6–2	
1905	*Miss E. H. Moore	Miss H. Homans	6–4 5–7 6–1	
1906	*Miss H. Homans	Mrs M. Barger-Wallach	6–4 6–3	
1907	*Miss E. Sears	Miss C. Neely	6–3 6–2	
1908	Mrs M. Barger-Wallach	Miss E. Sears	6–3 1–6 6–3	
1909	Miss H. Hotchkiss	Mrs M. Barger-Wallach	6–0 6–1	
1910	Miss H. Hotchkiss	Miss L. Hammond	6–4 6–2	
1911	Miss H. Hotchkiss	Miss F. Sutton	8–10 6–1 9–7	
1912	*Miss M. K. Browne	Miss Eleanora Sears	6–4 6–2	
1913	Miss M. K. Browne	Miss D. Green	6–2 7–5	
1914	Miss M. K. Browne	Miss M. Wagner	6–2 1–6 6–1	
1915	*Miss M. Bjurstedt	Mrs G. W. Wightman	4–6 6–2 6–0	
1916	Miss M. Bjurstedt	Mrs L. H. Raymond	6–0 6–1	
1917	*Not held*			
1918	Miss M. Bjurstedt	Miss E. E. Goss	6–4 6–3	
(Challenge Round abolished)				
1919	Mrs G. W. Wightman	Miss M. Zinderstein	6–1 6–2	
1920	Mrs F. Mallory	Miss M. Zinderstein	6–3 6–1	
1921	Mrs F. Mallory	Miss M. K. Browne	4–6 6–4 6–2	
1922	Mrs F. Mallory	Miss H. N. Wills	6–3 6–1	
1923	Miss H. N. Wills	Mrs F. Mallory	6–2 6–1	
1924	Miss H. N. Wills	Mrs F. Mallory	6–1 6–3	
1925	Miss H. N. Wills	Miss K. McKane	3–6 6–0 6–2	
1926	Mrs F. Mallory	Miss E. Ryan	4–6 6–4 9–7	
1927	Miss H. N. Wills	Miss B. Nuthall	6–1 6–4	
1928	Miss H. N. Wills	Miss H. H. Jacobs	6–2 6–1	
1929	Miss H. N. Wills	Mrs P. H. Watson	6–4 6–2	
1930	Miss B. Nuthall	Mrs L. A. Harper	6–1 6–4	
1931	Mrs F. S. Moody	Mrs F. Whittingstall	6–4 6–1	
1932	Miss H. H. Jacobs	Miss C. A. Babcock	6–2 6–2	
1933	Miss H. H. Jacobs	Mrs F. S. Moody	8–6 3–6 3–0 ret'd	
1934	Miss H. H. Jacobs	Miss S. Palfrey	6–1 6–4	
1935	Miss H. H. Jacobs	Mrs S. P. Fabyan	6–2 6–4	
1936	Miss A. Marble	Miss H. H. Jacobs	4–6 6–3 6–2	
1937	Miss A. Lizane	Miss J. Jedrzejowksa	6–4 6–2	
1938	Miss A. Marble	Miss N. Wynne	6–0 6–3	
1939	Miss A. Marble	Miss H. H. Jacobs	6–0 8–10 6–4	
1940	Miss A. Marble	Miss H. H. Jacobs	6–2 6–3	
1941	Mrs S. P. Cooke	Miss P. M. Betz	7–5 6–2	
1942	Miss P. M. Betz	Miss A. L. Brough	4–6 6–1 6–4	
1943	Miss P. M. Betz	Miss A. L. Brough	6–3 5–7 6–3	
1944	Miss P. M. Betz	Miss M. E. Osborne	6–3 8–6	
1945	Mrs S. P. Cooke	Miss P. M. Betz	3–6 8–6 6–4	
1946	Miss P. M. Betz	Miss P. C. Todd	11–9 6–3	
1947	Miss A. L. Brough	Miss M. E. Osborne	8–6 4–6 6–1	
1948	Mrs W. D. du Pont	Miss A. L. Brough	4–6 6–4 15–13	
1949	Mrs W. D. du Pont	Miss D. J. Hart	6–4 6–1	
1950	Mrs W. D. du Pont	Miss D. J. Hart	6–4 6–3	
1951	Miss M. Connolly	Miss S. J. Fry	6–3 1–6 6–4	
1952	Miss M. Connolly	Miss D. J. Hart	6–3 7–5	
1953	Miss M. Connolly	Miss D. J. Hart	6–2 6–4	
1954	Miss D. J. Hart	Miss A. L. Brough	6–8 6–1 8–6	
1955	Miss D. J. Hart	Miss P. E. Ward	6–4 6–2	
1956	Miss S. J. Fry	Miss A. Gibson	6–3 6–4	
1957	Miss A. Gibson	Miss A. L. Brough	6–3 6–2	
1958	Miss A. Gibson	Miss D. R. Hard	3–6 6–1 6–2	
1959	Miss M. E. Bueno	Miss C. C. Truman	6–1 6–4	
1960	Miss D. R. Hard	Miss M. E. Bueno	6–4 10–12 6–4	
1961	Miss D. R. Hard	Miss A. S. Haydon	6–3 6–4	
1962	Miss M. Smith	Miss D. R. Hard	9–7 6–4	
1963	Miss M. E. Bueno	Miss M. Smith	7–5 6–4	
1964	Miss M. E. Bueno	Mrs C. Graebner	6–1 6–0	
1965	Miss M. Smith	Miss B. J. Moffitt	8–6 7–5	
1966	Miss M. E. Bueno	Miss N. Richey	6–3 6–1	
1967	Mrs L. W. King	Mrs P. F. Jones	11–9 6–4	
1968	Mrs B. M. Court	Miss M. E. Bueno	6–2 6–2	
1969	Mrs B. M. Court	Miss S. V. Wade	4–6 6–3 6–0	

MEN'S DOUBLES

Holders did not defend the title.

CHAMPIONS	RUNNERS-UP	SCORE				
1881 C. M. Clark/F. W. Taylor	A. Van Rennselaer/A. E. Newbold	6–5	6–4	6–5		
1882 J. Dwight/R. D. Sears	W. Nightingale/G. M. Shields	6–2	6–4	6–4		
1883 J. Dwight/R. D. Sears	A. Van Rennselaer/A. E. Newbold	6–0	6–2	6–2		
1884 J. Dwight/R. D. Sears	A. Van Rennselaer/W. V. R. Berry	6–4	6–1	8–10	6–4	
1885 J. S. Clark/R. D. Sears	W. P. Knapp/H. W. Slocum	6–3	6–0	6–2		
1886 J. Dwight/R. D. Sears	G. M. Brinley/H. A. Taylor	7–5	5–7	7–5	6–4	
1887 J. Dwight/R. D. Sears	H. W. Slocum/H. A. Taylor	6–4	3–6	2–6	6–3	6–3
1888 O. S. Campbell/V. G. Hall	C. Hobart/E. P. MacMullen	6–4	6–2	6–4		
1889 H. W. Slocum/H. A. Taylor	O. S. Campbell/V. G. Hall	6–1	6–3	6–2		
1890 V. G. Hall/C. Hobart	C. W. Carver/J. A. Ryerson	6–3	4–6	6–2	2–6	6–3
(Challenge Round instituted)						
1891 O. S. Campbell/R. P. Huntington	V. G. Hall/C. Hobart	6–3	6–4	8–6		
1892 O. S. Campbell/R. P. Huntingdon	V. G. Hall/E. L. Hall	6–4	6–2	4–6	6–3	
1893 C. Hobart/F. H. Hovey	O. S. Campbell/R. P. Huntington	6–3	6–4	4–6	6–2	
1894 C. Hobart/F. H. Hovey	C. B. Neel/S. R. Neel	6–3	8–6	6–1		
1895 M. G. Chase/R. D. Wrenn	C. Hobart/F. H. Hovey	7–5	6–1	8–6		
1896* C. B./S. R. Neel	M. G. Chase/R. D. Wrenn	6–3	1–6	6–1	3–6	6–1
1897 L. E. Ware/P. Sheldon	H. S. Mahony/H. A. Nisbet	11–13	6–2	9–7	1–6	6–1
1898 L. E. Ware/P. Sheldon	D. F. Davis/H. Ward	1–6	7–5	6–4	4–6	7–5
1899 D. F. Davis/H. Ward	L. E. Ware/P. Sheldon	6–4	6–4	6–3		
1900 D. F. Davis/H. Ward	F. B. Alexander/R. D. Little	6–4	9–7	12–10		
1901 D. F. Davis/H. Ward	L. E. Ware/B. C. Wright	6–3	9–7	6–1		
1902 H. L./R. F. Doherty	D. F. Davis/H. Ward	11–9	12–10	6–4		
1903 H. L./R. F. Doherty	L. Collins/L. H. Waldner	7–5	6–3	6–3		
1904* H. Ward/B. C. Wright	K. Collins/R. D. Little	1–6	6–2	3–6	6–4	6–1
1905 H. Ward/B. C. Wright	F. B. Alexander/H. H. Hackett	6–3	6–1	6–2		
1906 H. Ward/B. C. Wright	F. B. Alexander/H. H. Hackett	6–3	3–6	6–3	6–3	
1907* F. B. Alexander/B. C. Wright	W. J. Clothier/W. A. Larned	6–3	6–1	6–4		
1908 F. B. Alexander/H. H. Hackett	R. D. Little/B. C. Wright	6–1	7–5	6–2		
1909 F. B. Alexander/H. H. Hackett	G. J. James/M. E. McLoughlin	6–4	6–1	6–0		
1910 F. B. Alexander/H. H. Hackett	T. C. Bundy/T. W. Hendrick	6–1	8–6	6–3		
1911 R. D. Little/G. F. Touchard	F. B. Alexander/H. H. Hackett	7–5	13–15	6–2	6–4	
1912 T. C. Bundy/M. E. McLoughlin	R. D. Little/G. F. Touchard	3–6	6–2	6–1	7–5	
1913 T. C. Bundy/M. E. McLoughlin	C. J. Griffin/J. R. Strachan	6–4	7–5	6–1		
1914 T. C. Bundy/M. E. McLoughlin	G. M. Church/D. Mathey	6–4	6–2	6–4		
1915 C. J. Griffin/W. M. Johnston	T. C. Bundy/M. E. McLoughlin	6–2	3–6	4–6	6–3	6–3
1916 C. J. Griffin/W. M. Johnston	W. Dawson/M. E. McLoughlin	6–4	6–3	5–7	6–3	
1917 Not held						
(Challenge Round abolished)						
1918 V. Richards/W. T. Tilden	F. B. Alexander/B. C. Wright	6–3	6–4	3–6	2–6	6–2
(Challenge Round restored)						
1919 N. E. Brookes/G. L. Patterson	V. Richards/W. T. Tilden	8–6	6–3	4–6	6–2	
(Challenge Round abolished)						
1920 C. J. Griffin/W. M. Johnston	W. E. Davis/R. Roberts	6–2	6–2	6–3		
1921 V. Richards/W. T. Tilden	W. M. Washburn/R. N. Williams	13–11	12–10	6–1		
1922 V. Richards/W. T. Tilden	P. O'Hara Wood/G. L. Patterson	4–6	6–1	6–3	6–4	
1923 B. I. C. Norton/W. T. Tilden	W. M. Washburn/R. N. Williams	3–6	6–2	6–3	5–7	6–2
1924 H./R. Kinsey	P. O'Hara Wood/G. L. Patterson	7–5	5–7	7–9	6–3	6–4
1925 V. Richards/R. N. Williams	J. B. Hawkes/G. L. Patterson	6–2	8–10	6–4	11–9	
1926 V. Richards/R. N. Williams	A. H. Chapin/W. T. Tilden	6–4	6–8	11–9	6–3	
1927 F. T. Hunter/W. T. Tilden	W. M. Johnston/R. N. Williams	10–8	6–3	6–3		
1928 J. F. Hennessey/G. M. Lott	J. B. Hawkes/G. L. Patterson	6–2	6–1	6–2		
1929 J. H. Doeg/G. M. Lott	B. Bell/L. N. White	10–8	16–14	6–1		
1930 J. H. Doeg/G. M. Lott	W. L. Allison/J. Van Ryn	8–6	6–3	4–6	13–15	6–4
1931 W. L. Allison/J. Van Ryn	B. Bell/G. S. Mangin	6–4	8–6	6–3		
1932 K. Gledhill/H. E. Vines	W. L. Allison/J. Van Ryn	6–4	6–3	6–2		
1933 G. M. Lott/L. R. Stoefen	F. A. Parker/F. X. Shields	11–13	9–7	9–7	6–3	
1934 G. M. Lott/L. R. Stoefen	W. L. Allison/J. Van Ryn	6–4	9–7	3–6	6–4	
1935 W. L. Allison/J. Van Ryn	J. D. Budge/G. Mako	6–4	6–2	3–6	2–6	6–1
1936 J. D. Budge/G. Mako	W. L. Allison/J. Van Ryn	6–4	6–2	6–4		
1937 G. Von Cramm/H. Henkel	J. D. Budge/G. Mako	6–4	7–5	6–4		
1938 J. D. Budge/G. Mako	J. E. Bromwich/A. K. Quist	6–3	6–2	6–1		
1939 J. E. Bromwich/A. K. Quist	J. H. Crawford/H. C. Hopman	8–6	6–1	6–4		
1940 J. A. Kramer/F. R. Schroeder	G. Mulloy/H. J. Prussoff	6–4	8–6	9–7		
1941 J. A. Kramer/F. R. Schroeder	G. Mulloy/W. Sabin	9–7	6–4	6–2		

1942	G. Mulloy/W. F. Talbert	F. R. Schroeder/S. B. Wood	9–7	7–5	6–1
1943	J. A. Kramer/F. A. Parker	D. Freeman/W. F. Talbert	6–2	6–4	6–4
1944	R. Falkenburg/W. D. McNeill	F. Segura/W. F. Talbert	7–5	6–4	3–6	6–1
1945	G. Mulloy/W. F. Talbert	R. Falkenburg/J. Tuero	12–10	8–10	12–10	6–2
1946	G. Mulloy/W. F. Talbert	G. Guernsey/W. D. McNeill	3–6	6–4	2–6	6–3	20–18
1947	J. A. Kramer/F. R. Schroeder	W. F. Talbert/O. W. Sidwell	6–4	7–5	6–3
1948	G. Mulloy/W. F. Talbert	F. A. Parker/F. R. Schroeder	1–6	9–7	6–3	3–6	9–7
1949	J. Bromwich/O. W. Sidwell	F. A. Sedgman/G. Worthington	6–4	6–0	6–1
1950	J. Bromwich/F. A. Sedgman	G. Mulloy/W. F. Talbert	7–5	8–6	3–6	6–1
1951	K. McGregor/F. A. Sedgman	D. Candy/M. G. Rose	10–8	6–4	4–6	7–5
1952	M. G. Rose/E. V. Seixas	K. McGregor/F. A. Sedgman	3–6	10–8	10–8	6–8	8–6
1953	R. N. Hartwig/M. G. Rose	G. Mulloy/W. F. Talbert	6–4	4–6	6–2	6–4
1954	E. V. Seixas/M. A. Trabert	L. A. Hoad/K. R. Rosewall	3–6	6–4	8–6	6–3
1955	K. Kamo/A. Miyagi	G. Moss/W. Quillian	6–3	6–3	3–6	1–6	6–4
1956	L. A. Hoad/K. R. Rosewall	H. Richardson/E. V. Seixas	6–2	6–2	3–6	6–4
1957	A. J. Cooper/N. A. Fraser	G. Mulloy/J. E. Patty	4–6	6–3	9–7	6–3
1958	A. Olmedo/H. Richardson	S. Giammalva/B. McKay	3–6	6–3	6–4	6–4
1959	R. S. Emerson/N. A. Fraser	E. Buchholz /A. Olmedo	3–6	6–3	5–7	6–4	7–5
1960	R. S. Emerson/N. A. Fraser	R. G. Laver/R. Mark	9–7	6–2	6–4
1961	C. McKinley/R. D. Ralston	A. Palafox/R. H. Osuna	6–3	6–4	2–6	13–11
1962	A. Palafox/R. H. Osuna	C. McKinley/R. D. Ralston	6–4	10–12	1–6	9–7	6–3
1963	C. McKinley/R. D. Ralston	A. Palafox/R. H. Osuna	9–7	4–6	5–7	6–3	11–9
1964	C. McKinley/R. D. Ralston	G. Stilwell/M. Sangster	6–3	6–2	6–4
1965	R. S. Emerson/F. S. Stolle	F. Froehling/C. Pasarell	6–4	10–12	7–5	6–3
1966	R. S. Emerson/F. S. Stolle	C. Graebner/R. D. Ralston	6–4	6–4	6–4
1967	J. D. Newcombe/A. D. Roche	O. K. Davidson/W. W. Bowrey	6–8	9–7	6–3	6–3
1968	R. C. Lutz/S. R. Smith	R. A. J. Hewitt/R. J. Moore	6–4	6–4	9–7
1969	R. D. Crealy/A. Stone	W. W. Bowrey/C. Pasarell	9–11	6–3	7–5

WOMEN'S DOUBLES

	CHAMPIONS	RUNNERS-UP	SCORE
1889	Not available		
1890	E. C. Roosevelt/G. W. Roosevelt	B. L. Townsend/M. Ballard	6–1 6–2
1891	M. E. Cahill/W. F. Morgan	E. C. Roosevelt/G. W. Roosevelt	2–6 8–6 6–4
1892	M. E. Cahill/A. M. McKinley	A. H. Harris/A. R. Williams	6–1 6–3
1893	H. Butler/A. M. Terry	A. L. Schultz/Stone	6–4 6–3
1894	J. P. Atkinson/H. R. Helwig	A. R. Williams/A. C. Wistar	6–4 7–5
1895	J. P. Atkinson/H. R. Helwig	E. H. Moore/A. R. Williams	6–2 6–2 12–10
1896	J. P. Atkinson/E. H. Moore	A. R. Williams/A. C. Wistar	6–4 7–5
1897	J. P. Atkinson/K. Atkinson	F. Edwards/E. J. Rastall	6–2 6–1 6–1
1898	J. P. Atkinson/K. Atkinson	C. B. Neely/M. Weimar	6–1 2–6 4–6 6–1 6–2
1899	J. W. Craven/M. McAteer	M. Banks/E. J. Rastall	6–1 6–1 7–5
1900	H. Champlin/E. Parker	M. McAteer/M. Weimar	9–7 6–2 6–2
1901	J. P. Atkinson/M. McAteer	M. Jones/E. H. Moore	w.o.
1902	J. P. Atkinson/M. Jones	M. Banks/N. Closterman	6–2 7–5
1903	E. H. Moore/C. B. Neely	M. Jones/M. Hall	6–4 6–1 6–1
1904	M. Hall/M. G. Sutton	E. H. Moore/C. B. Neely	3–6 6–3 6–3*
1905	H. Homans/C. B. Neely	V. Maule/M. F. Oberteuffer	6–0 6–1
1906	Mrs L. S. Coe/Mrs D. S. Platt	C. Boldt/H. Homans	6–4 6–4
1907	C. B. Neely/M. Weimer	E. Wildey/N. Wildey	6–1 2–6 6–4
1908	M. Curtis/E. Sears	C. B. Neely/M. Steever	6–3 5–7 9–7
1909	H. V. Hotchkiss/E. E. Rotch	D. Green/L. Moyes	6–1 6–1
1910	H. V. Hotchkiss/E. E. Rotch	A. Browning/E. Wildey	6–4 6–4
1911	H. V. Hotchkiss/E. Sears	D. Green/F. Sutton	6–4 4–6 6–2
1912	M. K. Browne/D. Green	Mrs M. Barger-Wallach/Mrs F. Schmitz	6–2 5–7 6–0
1913	M. K. Browne/Mrs R. H. Williams	D. Green/E. Wildey	12–10 2–6 6–3
1914	M. K. Browne/Mrs R. H. Williams	Mrs E. Raymond/E. Wildey	8–6 6–2
1915	E. Sears/Mrs G. W. Wightman	Mrs G. L. Chapman/Mrs M. McLean	10–8 6–2
1916	M. Bjurstedt/E. Sears	Mrs E. Raymond/E. Wildey	4–6 6–2 10–8
1917	*Not held*		
	(Challenge Round abolished)		
1918	E. E. Goss /M. Zinderstein	M. Bjurstedt /Mrs J. Rogge	7–5 8–6
	(Challenge Round restored)		
1919	E. E. Goss /M. Zinderstein	E. Sears /Mrs G. W. Wightman	9–7 9–7
	(Challenge Round abolished)		
1920	E. E. Goss/M. Zinderstein	H. Baker/E. Tennant	13–11 4–6 6–3
1921	M. K. Browne/Mrs L. Williams	H. Gilleaudeau/Mrs L. G. Morris	6–3 6–2
1922	J. B. Jessup/H. N. Wills	Mrs F. I. Mallory/E. Sigourney	6–4 7–9 6–3
1923	Mrs B. C. Covell/K. McKane	E. E. Goss/Mrs G. W. Wightman	2–6 6–2 6–1

There is some doubt about the accuracy of this result.

1924	Mrs G. W. Wightman/H. N. Wills	E. E. Goss/Mrs J. B. Jessup	6–4 6–3	
1925	M. K. Browne/H. N. Wills	Mrs T. C. Bundy/E. Ryan	6–4 6–3	
1926	E. E. Goss/E. Ryan	M. K. Browne/Mrs A. H. Chapin	3–6 6–4 12–10	
1927	Mrs L. A. Godfree/E. H. Harvey	J. Fry/B. Nuthall	6–1 4–6 6–4	
1928	Mrs G. W. Wightman/H. N. Wills	E. Cross/Mrs L. A. Harper	6–2 6–2	
1929	Mrs L. R. C. Michell/Mrs P. H. Watson	Mrs B. C. Covell/Mrs D. C. Shepherd-Barron	2–6 6–3 6–4	
1930	B. Nuthall/S. Palfrey	E. Cross/Mrs L. A. Harper	3–6 6–3 7–5	
1931	B. Nuthall/Mrs E. F. Whittingstall	H. H. Jacobs/D. E. Round	6–2 6–4	
1932	H. H. Jacobs/S. Palfrey	A. Marble/Mrs M. Painter	8–6 6–1	
1933	F. James/B. Nuthall	Mrs F. S. Moody/E. Ryan	w.o.	
1934	H. H. Jacobs/S. Palfrey	Mrs D. B. Andrus/C. A. Babcock	4–6 6–3 6–4	
1935	H. H. Jacobs/Mrs M. Fabyan	Mrs D. B. Andrus/C. A. Babcock	6–4 6–2	
1936	C. A. Babcock/Mrs J. Van Ryn	H. H. Jacobs/Mrs M. Fabyan	9–7 2–6 6–4	
1937	Mrs M. Fabyan/A. Marble	C. A. Babcock/Mrs J. Van Ryn	7–5 6–4	
1938	Mrs M. Fabyan/A. Marble	J. Jedrzejowska/Mrs R. Mathieu	6–8 6–4 6–3	
1939	Mrs M. Fabyan/A. Marble	Mrs S. H. Hammersley/K. E. Stammers	7–5 8–6	
1940	Mrs M. Fabyan/A. Marble	D. M. Bundy/Mrs J. Van Ryn	6–4 6–3	
1941	Mrs E. T. Cooke/M. E. Osborne	D. M. Bundy/D. J. Hart	3–6 6–1 6–4	
1942	A. L. Brough/M. E. Osborne	P. M. Betz/D. J. Hart	9–7 6–2 6–1	
1943	A. L. Brough/M. E. Osborne	P. M. Betz/D. J. Hart	6–4 6–3	
1944	A. L. Brough/M. E. Osborne	P. M. Betz/D. J. Hart	4–6 6–4 6–3	
1945	A. L. Brough/M. E. Osborne	P. M. Betz/D. J. Hart	6–4 6–4	
1946	A. L. Brough/M. E. Osborne	Mrs P. C. Todd/Mrs M. A. Prentiss	6–1 6–3	
1947	A. L. Brough/M. E. Osborne	Mrs P. C. Todd/D. J. Hart	5–7 6–4 7–5	
1948	A. L. Brough/Mrs W. D. du Pont	Mrs P. C. Todd/D. J. Hart	6–4 8–10 6–1	
1949	A. L. Brough/Mrs W. D. du Pont	S. J. Fry/D. J. Hart	6–4 10–8	
1950	A. L. Brough/Mrs W. D. du Pont	S. J. Fry/D. J. Hart	6–2 6–3	
1951	S. J. Fry/D. J. Hart	N. Chaffee/Mrs P. C. Todd	6–4 6–2	
1952	S. J. Fry/D. J. Hart	A. L. Brough/M. Connolly	10–8 6–4	
1953	S. J. Fry/D. J. Hart	A. L. Brough/Mrs W. D. du Pont	6–2 7–9 9–7	
1954	S. J. Fry/D. J. Hart	A. L. Brough/Mrs W. D. du Pont	6–4 6–4	
1955	A. L. Brough/Mrs W. D. du Pont	S. J. Fry/D. J. Hart	6–3 1–6 6–3	
1956	A. L. Brough/Mrs W. D. du Pont	Mrs B. R. Pratt/S. J. Fry	6–3 6–0	
1957	A. L. Brough/Mrs W. D. du Pont	A. Gibson/D. R. Hard	6–2 7–5	
1958	J. M. Arth/D. R. Hard	A. Gibson/M. E. Bueno	2–6 6–3 6–4	
1959	J. M. Arth/D. R. Hard	S. Moore/M. E. Bueno	6–2 6–3	
1960	M. E. Bueno/D. R. Hard	D. M. Catt/A. A. Haydon	6–1 6–1	
1961	D. R. Hard/L. Turner	E. Buding/Y. Ramirez	6–4 5–7 6–0	
1962	R. Ebbern/M. Smith	Mrs J. B. Susman/B. J. Moffitt	4–6 6–3 6–2	
1963	M. E. Bueno/D. R. Hard	M. E. Bueno/D. R. Hard	4–6 10–8 6–3	
1964	Mrs J. B. Susman/B. J. Moffitt	M. Smith/L. Turner	3–6 6–2 6–4	
1965	N. Richey/Mrs C. Graebner	Mrs J. B. Susman/B. J. Moffitt	6–4 6–4	
1966	M. E. Bueno/N. Richey	R. Casals/Mrs L. W. King	6–3 6–4	
1967	R. Casals/Mrs L. W. King	M. A. Eisel/Mrs D. Fales	4–6 6–3 6–4	
1968	M. E. Bueno/M. Smith	S. V. Wade/Mrs G. M. Williams	6–3 7–5	
1969	Mrs B. M. Court/S. V. Wade	Mrs P. W. Curtis/V. Ziegenfuss	6–1 6–3	

MIXED DOUBLES

Not recognised as an official championship

	CHAMPIONS	RUNNERS-UP	SCORE	
1887*	J. S. Clark/Miss V. Stokes	Not known		
1888*	J. S. Clark/Miss M. Wright	P. Johnson/Miss A. Robinson	1–6 6–5 6–4 6–3	
1889*	J. S. Clark/Miss M. Wright	Not known		
1890*	R. Beach/Miss M. E. Cahill	Not known		
1891*	M. R. Wright/Miss M. E. Cahill	C. T. Lee/Miss G. W. Roosevelt	6–4 6–0 7–5	
1892	C. Hobart/Miss M. E. Cahill	R. Beach/Miss E. H. Moore	6–1 6–3	
1893	C. Hobart/Miss E. C. Roosevelt	R. N. Wilson/Miss Bankson	6–1 4–6 10–8 6–1	
1894	E. P. Fischer/Miss J. P. Atkinson	A. Remak/Mrs McFaddon	6–2 6–2 6–1	
1895	E. P. Fischer/Miss J. P. Atkinson	M. Fielding/Miss A. R. Williams	4–6 6–1 6–2	
1896	E. P. Fischer/Miss J. P. Atkinson	M. Fielding/Miss A. R. Williams	6–2 6–3 6–3	
1897	D. L. Magruder/Miss L. Henson	R. A. Griffin/Miss M. Banks	6–4 6–3 7–5	
1898	E. P. Fischer/Miss C. B. Neely	J. A. Hill/Miss H. Chapman	Not known	
1899	A. L. Hoskins/Miss E. J. Rastall	J. P. Gardner/Miss J. W. Craven	6–4 6–0 ret'd	
1900	A. Codman/Miss M. J. Hunnewell	G. Atkinson/Miss T. Shaw	11–9 6–3 6–1	
1901	R. D. Little/Miss M. Jones	C. Stevens/Miss M. McAteer	6–4 6–4 7–5	
1902	W. C. Grant/Miss E. H. Moore	A. L. Hoskins/Miss E. J. Rastall	6–2 6–1	

Year	Winners	Runners-up	Score		
1903	H. F. Allen/Miss H. Chapman	W. H. Rowland/Miss C. B. Neely	6–4	7–5	
1904	W. C. Grant/Miss E. H. Moore	F. B. Dallas/Miss M. Sutton	6–2	6–1	
1905	C. Hobart/Mrs Hobart	E. B. Dewhurst/Miss E. H. Moore	6–2	6–4	
1906	E. B. Dewhurst/Miss S. Coffin	J. B. Johnson/Miss M. Johnson	6–3	7–5	
1907	W. F. Johnson/Miss M. Sayres	H. M. Tilden/Miss N. Wildey	6–1	7–5	
1908	N. W. Niles/Miss E. E. Rotch	R. D. Little/Miss L. Hammond	6–4	4–6	6–4
1909	W. F. Johnson/Miss H. V. Hotchkiss	R. D. Little/Miss L. Hammond	6–2	6–0	
1910	J. R. Carpenter/Miss H. V. Hotchkiss	H. M. Tilden/Miss E. Wildey	6–2	6–2	
1911	W. F. Johnson/Miss H. V. Hotchkiss	H. M. Tilden/Miss E. Wildey	6–4	6–4	
1912	R. N. Williams/Miss M. K. Browne	W. J. Clothier/Miss E. Sears	6–4	2–6	11–9
1913	W. T. Tilden/Miss M. K. Browne	C. S. Rogers/Miss D. Green	7–5	7–5	
1914	W. T. Tilden/Miss M. K. Browne	J. R. Rowland/Miss M. Myers	6–1	6–4	
1915	H. C. Johnson/Mrs G. W. Wightman	I. C. Wright/Miss M. Bjurstedt	6–0	6–1	
1916	W. E. Davis/Miss E. Sears	W. T. Tilden/Miss F. A. Ballin	6–4	7–5	
1917	*Not held*				
(Challenge Round abolished)					
1918	I. C. Wright /Mrs G. W. Wightman	F. B. Alexander /Miss M. Bjurstedt	6–2	6–4	
(Challenge Round restored)					
1919	V. Richards /Miss M. Zinderstein	W. T. Tilden /Miss F. A. Ballin	2–6	11–9	6–1
(Challenge Round abolished)					
1920	W. F. Johnson/Mrs G. W. Wightman	C. Biddle/Mrs F. I. Mallory	6–4	6–3	
1921	W. M. Johnston/Miss M. K. Browne	W. T. Tilden/Miss F. I. Mallory	3–6	6–4	6–3
1922	W. T. Tilden/Mrs F. I. Mallory	H. Kinsey/Miss H. N. Wills	6–4	6–3	
1923	W. T. Tilden/Mrs F. I. Mallory	J. B. Hawkes/Miss K. McKane	6–3	2–6	10–8
1924	V. Richards/Miss H. N. Wills	W. T. Tilden/Miss F. I. Mallory	6–8	7–5	6–0
1925	J. B. Hawkes/Miss K. McKane	V. Richards/Miss E. H. Harvey	6–2	6–4	
1926	J. Borotra/Miss E. Ryan	R. Lacoste/Mrs G. W. Wightman	6–4	7–5	
1927	H. Cochet/Miss E. Bennett	R. Lacoste/Mrs G. W. Wightman	2–6	6–0	6–2
1928	G. M. Lott/Miss B. Nuthall	H. W. Austin/Mrs B. C. Covell	6–3	6–3	
1930	W. L. Allison/Miss E. Cross	F. X. Shields/Miss M. Morrill	6–4	6–4	
1931	G. M. Lott/Miss B. Nuthall	W.L. Allison/Mrs L. A. Harper	6–3	6–3	
1932	F. J. Perry/Miss S. Palfrey	H. E. Vines/Miss H. H. Jacobs	6–3	7–5	
1933	H. E. Vines/Miss E. Ryan	G. M. Lott/Miss S. Palfrey	11–9	6–1	
1934	G. M. Lott/Miss H. H. Jacobs	L. R. Stoefen/Miss E. Ryan	4–6	13–11	6–2
1935	E. Maier/Mrs M. Fabyan	R. Menzel/Miss K. E. Stammers	6–3	3–6	6–4
1936	G. Mako/Miss A. Marble	J. D. Budge/Mrs M. Fabyan	6–3	6–2	
1937	J. D. Budge/Mrs M. Fabyan	Y. Petra/Mme S. Henrotin	6–2	8–10	6–0
1938	J. D. Budge/Miss A. Marble	J. E. Bromwich/Miss T. Coyne	6–1	6–2	
1939	H. C. Hopman/Miss A. Marble	E. T. Cooke/Mrs M. Fabyan	9–7	6–1	
1940	R. L. Riggs/Miss A. Marble	J. A. Kramer/Miss D. M. Bundy	9–7	6–1	
1941	J. A. Kramer/Mrs E. T. Cooke	R. L. Riggs/Miss P. M. Betz	4–6	6–4	6–4
1942	F. R. Schroeder/Miss A. L. Brough	A. D. Russell/Miss P. C. Todd	3–6	6–1	6–4
1943	W. F. Talbert/Miss M. E. Osborne	F. Segura/Miss P. M. Betz	10–8	6–4	
1944	W. F. Talbert/Miss M. E. Osborne	W. D. McNeill/Miss D. M. Bundy	6–2	6–3	
1945	W. F. Talbert/Miss M. E. Osborne	R. Falkenburg/Miss D. J. Hart	6–4	6–4	
1946	W. F. Talbert/Miss M. E. Osborne	R. Kimbrell/Miss A. L. Brough	6–3	6–4	
1947	J. Bromwich/Miss A. G. Moran	F. Segura/Miss A. G. Moran	6–3	6–1	
1948	T. P. Brown/Miss A. L. Brough	W. F. Talbert/Mrs W. D. du Pont	6–4	6–4	
1949	E. W. Sturgess/Miss A. L. Brough	W. F. Talbert/Mrs W. D. du Pont	4–6	6–3	7–5
1950	K. McGregor/Mrs W. D. du Pont	F. A. Sedgman/Miss D. J. Hart	6–4	3–6	6–3
1951	F. A. Sedgman/Miss D. J. Hart	M. G. Rose/Miss S. J. Fry	6–3	6–2	
1952	F. A. Sedgman/Miss D. J. Hart	L. A. Hoad/Mrs T. C. Long	6–3	7–5	
1953	E. V. Seixas/Miss D. J. Hart	R. N. Hartwig/Miss J. A. Sampson	6–2	4–6	6–4
1954	E. V. Seixas/Miss D. J. Hart	K. R. Rosewall/Mrs W. D. du Pont	4–6	6–1	6–1
1955	E. V. Seixas/Miss D. J. Hart	L. A. Hoad/Miss S. J. Fry	9–7	6–1	
1956	K. R. Rosewall/Mrs W. D. du Pont	L. A. Hoad/Miss D. R. Hard	9–7	6–1	
1957	K. Nielsen/Miss A. Gibson	R. N. Howe/Miss D. R. Hard	6–3	9–7	
1958	N. A. Fraser/Mrs W. D. du Pont	A. Olmedo/Miss M. E. Bueno	6–3	3–6	9–7
1959	N. A. Fraser/Mrs W. D. du Pont	R. Mark/Miss J. Hopps	7–5	13–15	6–2
1960	N. A. Fraser/Mrs W. D. du Pont	A. Palafox/Miss M. E. Bueno	6–3	6–2	
1961	R. Mark/Miss M. Smith	R. D. Ralston/Miss D. R. Hard	w.o.		
1962	F. S. Stolle/Miss M. Smith	F. Froehling/Miss L. Turner	7–5	6–2	
1963	K. Fletcher/Miss M. Smith	E. Rubinoff/Miss J. Tegart	3–6	8–6	6–2
1964	J. D. Newcombe/Miss M. Smith	E. Rubinoff/Miss J. Tegart	10–8	4–6	6–3
1965	F. S. Stolle/Miss M. Smith	F. Froehling/Miss J. Tegart	5–2	6–2	
1966	O. K. Davidson/Mrs D. Fales	E. Rubinoff/Miss C. A. Aucamp	6–1	6–3	
1967	O. K. Davidson/Mrs L. W. King	S. R. Smith/Miss R. Casals	6–3	6–2	
1968	P. W. Curtis/Miss M. A. Eisel	R. N. Perry/Miss T. A. Fretz	6–4	7–5	
1969	P. Sullivan/Miss P. S. A. Hogan	T. Addison/Miss K. Pigeon	6–4	2–6	12–10

US OPEN CHAMPIONSHIPS

Played at West Side Club, Forest Hills, New York, on grass courts 1968–74, on Har-Tru courts 1975–77.
Played at National Tennis Centre, Flushing Meadow, New York, on cement courts, 1978 on.

MEN'S SINGLES

	CHAMPION	RUNNER-UP	SCORE					WINNER'S PRIZE ($)
1968	A. R. Ashe	T. S. Okker	14–12	5–7	6–3	3–6	6–3	15,000
1969	R. G. Laver	A. D. Roche	7–9	6–3	6–1	6–2		16,000
1970	K. R. Rosewall	A. D. Roche	2–6	6–4	7–6	6–3		20,000
1971	S. R. Smith	J. Kodes	3–6	6–3	6–2	7–6		15,000
1972	I. Nastase	A. R. Ashe	3–6	6–3	6–7	6–4	6–3	25,000
1973	J. D. Newcombe	J. Kodes	6–4	1–6	4–6	6–2	6–3	25,000
1974	J. S. Connors	K. R. Rosewall	6–1	6–0	6–1			22,500
1975	M. Orantes	J. S. Connors	6–4	6–3	6–3			25,000
1976	J. S. Connors	B. Borg	6–4	3–6	7–6	6–4		30,000
1977	G. Vilas	J. S. Connors	2–6	6–3	7–6	6–0		33,000
1978	J. S. Connors	B. Borg	6–4	6–2	6–2			38,000
1979	J. P. McEnroe	V. Gerulaitis	7–5	6–3	6–3			39,000
1980	J. P. McEnroe	B. Borg	7–6	6–1	6–7	5–7	6–4	46,000
1981	J. P. McEnroe	B. Borg	4–6	6–2	6–4	6–3		60,000
1982	J. S. Connors	I. Lendl	6–3	6–2	4–6	6–4		90,000
1983	J. S. Connors	I. Lendl	6–3	6–7	7–5	6–0		120,000
1984	J. P. McEnroe	I. Lendl	6–3	6–4	6–1			160,000
1985	I. Lendl	J. P. McEnroe	7–6	6–3	6–4			187,500

WOMEN'S SINGLES

	CHAMPION	RUNNER-UP	SCORE			WINNER'S PRIZE ($)
1968	Miss S. V. Wade	Mrs L. W. King	6–4	6–2		6,000
1969	Mrs B. M. Court	Miss N. Richey	6–2	6–2		6,000
1970	Mrs B. M. Court	Miss R. Casals	6–2	2–6	6–1	7,500
1971	Mrs L. W. King	Miss R. Casals	6–4	7–6		5,000
1972	Mrs L. W. King	Miss K. Melville	6–3	7–5		10,000
1973	Mrs B. M. Court	Miss E. Goolagong	7–6	5–7	6–2	25,000
1974	Mrs L. W. King	Miss E. Goolagong	3–6	6–3	7–5	22,500
1975	Miss C. M. Evert	Mrs R. A. Cawley	5–7	6–4	6–2	25,000
1976	Miss C. M. Evert	Mrs R. A. Cawley	6–3	6–0		30,000
1977	Miss C. M. Evert	Miss W. Turnbull	7–6	6–2		33,000
1978	Miss C. M. Evert	Miss P. Shriver	7–5	6–4		38,000
1979	Miss T. A. Austin	Miss C. M. Evert	6–4	6–3		39,000
1980	Mrs J. M. Lloyd	Miss H. Mandlikova	5–7	6–1	6–1	46,000
1981	Miss T. A. Austin	Miss M. Navratilova	1–6	7–6	7–6	60,000
1982	Mrs J. M. Lloyd	Miss H. Mandlikova	6–3	6–1		90,000
1983	Miss M. Navratilova	Mrs J. M. Lloyd	6–1	6–3		120,000
1984	Miss M. Navratilova	Mrs J. M. Lloyd	4–6	6–4	6–4	160,000
1985	Miss H. Mandlikova	Miss M. Navratilova	7–6	1–6	7–6	187,500

MEN'S DOUBLES

	CHAMPIONS	RUNNERS-UP	SCORE					
1968	R. C. Lutz/S. R. Smith	A. R. Ashe/A. Gimeno	11–9	6–1	7–5			
1969	K. R. Rosewall/F. S. Stolle	C. Pasarell/R. D. Ralston	2–6	7–5	13–11	6–3		
1970	P. Barthes/N. Pilic	R. S. Emerson/R. G. Laver	6–3	7–6	4–6	7–6		
1971	J. D. Newcombe/R. Taylor	S. R. Smith/E. van Dillen	6–7	6–3	7–6	4–6	5–3 (tie-break)	
1972	E. C. Drysdale/R. Taylor	O. K. Davidson/J. D. Newcombe	6–4	7–6	6–3			
1973	O. K. Davidson/J. D. Newcombe	R. G. Laver/K. R. Rosewall	7–5	2–6	7–5	7–5		
1974	R. C. Lutz/S. R. Smith	P. Cornejo/J. Fillol	6–3	6–3				
1975	J. S. Connors/I. Nastase	T. S. Okker/M. C. Riessen	6–4	7–6				
1976	T. S. Okker/M. C. Riessen	P. Kronk/C. Letcher	6–4	6–4				
1977	R. A. J. Hewitt/F. D. McMillan	B. E. Gottfried/R. Ramirez	6–4	6–0				
1978	R. C. Lutz/S. R. Smith	M. C. Riessen/S. E. Stewart	1–6	7–5	6–3			
1979	P. Fleming/J. P. McEnroe	R. C. Lutz/S. R. Smith	6–2	6–4				
1980	R. C. Lutz/S. R. Smith	P. Fleming/J. P. McEnroe	7–6	3–6	6–1	3–6	6–3	
1981	P. Fleming/J. P. McEnroe	H. Gunthardt/P. McNamara	w.o.					
1982	K. Curren/S. Denton	V. Amaya/H. Pfister	6–2	6–7	5–7	6–2	6–4	
1983	P. Fleming/J. P. McEnroe	F. Buehning/V. Winitsky	6–3	6–4	6–2			
1984	J. Fitzgerald/T. Smid	S. Edberg/A. Jarryd	7–6	6–3	6–3			
1985	K. Flach/R. Seguso	H. Leconte/Y. Noah	7–6	6–7	7–6	6–0		

WOMEN'S DOUBLES

	CHAMPIONS	RUNNERS-UP	SCORE		
1968	M. E. Bueno/Mrs B. M. Court	R. Casals/Mrs L. W. King	4–6	9–7	8–6
1969	F. Durr/D. R. Hard	Mrs B. M. Court/S. V. Wade	0–6	6–4	6–4
1970	Mrs B. M. Court/Mrs D. Dalton	R. Casals/S. V. Wade	6–3	6–4	
1971	R. Casals/Mrs D. Dalton	Mrs J. B. Chanfreau/F. Durr	6–3	6–3	
1972	F. Durr/B. Stove	Mrs B. M. Court/S. V. Wade	6–3	1–6	6–3
1973	Mrs B. M. Court/S. V. Wade	R. Casals/Mrs L. W. King	3–6	6–3	7–5
1974	R. Casals/Mrs L. W. King	F. Durr/B. Stove	7–6	6–7	6–4
1975	Mrs B. M. Court/S. V. Wade	R. Casals/Mrs L. W. King	7–5	2–6	7–5
1976	L. Boshoff/I. Kloss	O. Morozova/S. V. Wade	6–1	6–4	
1977	M. Navratilova/B. Stove	R. Richards/B. Stuart	6–1	7–6	
1978	Mrs L. W. King/M. Navratilova	Mrs G. E. Reid/W. M. Turnbull	7–6	6–4	
1979	B. Stove/W. M. Turnbull	Mrs L. W. King/M. Navratilova	7–5	6–3	
1980	Mrs L. W. King/M. Navratilova	P. H. Shriver/B. Stove	7–6	7–5	
1981	K. Jordan/A. E. Smith	R. Casals/W. M. Turnbull	6–3	6–3	
1982	R. Casals/W. M. Turnbull	B. Potter/S. A. Walsh	6–4	6–4	
1983	M. Navratilova/P. H. Shriver	R. Fairbank/C. Reynolds	6–7	6–1	6–3
1984	M. Navratilova/P. H. Shriver	A. E. Hobbs/W. M. Turnbull	6–2	6–4	
1985	C. Kohde-Kilsch /H. Sukova	M. Navratilova /P. H. Shriver	6–7	6–2	6–3

MIXED DOUBLES

	CHAMPIONS	RUNNERS-UP	SCORE		
1968	*Not held*				
1969	M. C. Riessen/Mrs B. M. Court	R. D. Ralston/Miss F. Durr	7–5	6–3	
1970	M. C. Riessen/Mrs B. M. Court	F. D. McMillan/Mrs D. Dalton	6–4	6–4	
1971	O. K. Davidson/Mrs L. W. King	R. R. Maud/Miss B. Stove	6–3	7–5	
1972	M. C. Riessen/Mrs B. M. Court	I. Nastase/Miss R. Casals	6–3	7–5	
1973	O. K. Davidson/Mrs L. W. King	M. C. Riessen/Miss B. M. Court	6–3	3–6	7–6
1974	G. Masters/Miss P. Teeguarden	J. S. Connors/Miss C. M. Evert	6–1	7–6	
1975	R. L. Stockton/Miss R. Casals	F. S. Stolle/Mrs L. W. King	6–3	7–6	
1976	P. Dent/Mrs L. W. King	F. D. McMillan/Miss B. Stove	3–6	6–2	7–5
1977	F. D. McMillan/Miss B. Stove	V. Gerulaitis/Mrs L. W. King	6–2	3–6	6–3
1978	F. D. McMillan/Miss B. Stove	R. O. Ruffels/Mrs L. W. King	6–3	7–6	
1979	R. A. J. Hewitt/Miss G. Stevens	F. D. McMillan/Miss B. Stove	6–3	7–5	
1980	M. C. Riessen/Miss W. M. Turnbull	F. D. McMillan/Miss B. Stove	7–5	6–2	
1981	K. Curren/Miss A. E. Smith	S. Denton/Miss J. Russell	6–4	7–6	
1982	K. Curren/Miss A. E. Smith	F. Taygan/Miss B. Potter	6–7	7–6	7–6
1983	J. Fitzgerald/Miss E. Sayers	F. Taygan/Miss B. Potter	3–6	6–3	6–4
1984	Tom Gullikson/Miss M. Maleeva	J. Fitzgerald/Miss E. Sayers	2–6	7–5	6–4
1985	H. Gunthardt/Miss M. Navratilova	J. Fitzgerald/Mrs E. Smylie	6–3	6–4	

AUSTRALIAN CHAMPIONSHIPS

MEN'S SINGLES

	CHAMPION	RUNNER-UP	SCORE				
1905	R. W. Heath	A. H. Curtis	4–6	6–3	6–4	6–4	
1906	A. F. Wilding	F. N. Fisher	6–0	6–0	6–4		
1907	H. M. Rice	H. A. Parker	6–3	6–4	6–4		
1908	F. B. Alexander	A. W. Dunlop	3–6	3–6	6–0	6–2	6–3
1909	A. F. Wilding	E. F. Parker	6–1	7–5	6–2		
1910	R. W. Heath	H. M. Rice	6–4	6–3	6–2		
1911	N. E. Brookes	H. M. Rice	6–1	6–2	6–3		
1912	J. C. Parke	A. E. Beamish	3–6	6–2	1–6	6–1	7–5
1913	E. F. Parker	H. A. Parker	2–6	6–1	6–3	6–2	
1914	A. O'Hara Wood	G. L. Patterson	6–4	6–3	5–7	6–1	
1915	F. G. Lowe	H. M. Rice	4–6	6–1	6–1	6–4	
1916–18	*Not held*						
1919	A. R. F. Kingscote	E. O. Pockley	6–4	6–0	6–3		
1920	P. O'Hara Wood	R. V. Thomas	6–3	4–6	6–8	6–1	6–3
1921	R. H. Gemmell	A. Hedeman	7–5	6–1	6–4		
1922	J. O. Anderson	G. L. Patterson	6–0	3–6	3–6	6–3	6–2

Year	Champion	Runner-up	Score				
1923	P. O'Hara Wood	C. B. St John	6–1	6–1	6–3		
1924	J. O. Anderson	R. E. Schlesinger	6–3	6–4	3–6	5–7	6–3
1925	J. O. Anderson	G. L. Patterson	11–9	2–6	6–2	6–3	
1926	J. B. Hawkes	J. Willard	6–1	6–3	6–1		
1927	G. L. Patterson	J. B. Hawkes	3–6	6–4	3–6	18–16	6–3
1928	J. Borotra	R. O. Cummings	6–4	6–1	4–6	5–7	6–3
1929	J. C. Gregory	R. E. Schlesinger	6–2	6–2	5–7	7–5	
1930	E. F. Moon	H. C. Hopman	6–3	6–1	6–3		
1931	J. H. Crawford	H. C. Hopman	6–4	6–2	2–6	6–1	
1932	J. H. Crawford	H. C. Hopman	4–6	6–3	3–6	6–3	6–1
1933	J. H. Crawford	K. Gledhill	2–6	7–5	6–3	6–2	
1934	F. J. Perry	J. H. Crawford	6–3	7–5	6–1		
1935	J. H. Crawford	F. J. Perry	2–6	6–4	6–4	6–4	
1936	A. K. Quist	J. H. Crawford	6–2	6–3	4–6	3–6	9–7
1937	V. B. McGrath	J. E. Bromwich	6–3	1–6	6–0	2–6	6–1
1938	J. D. Budge	J. E. Bromwich	6–4	6–2	6–1		
1939	J. E. Bromwich	A. K. Quist	6–4	6–1	6–3		
1940	A. K. Quist	J. H. Crawford	6–3	6–1	6–2		
1941–45 *Not held*							
1946	J. E. Bromwich	D. Pails	5–7	6–3	7–5	3–6	6–2
1947	D. Pails	J. E. Bromwich	4–6	6–4	3–6	7–5	8–6
1948	A. K. Quist	J. E. Bromwich	6–4	3–6	6–3	2–6	6–3
1949	F. A. Sedgman	J. E. Bromwich	6–3	6–2	6–2		
1950	F. A. Sedgman	K. McGregor	6–3	6–4	4–6	6–1	
1951	R. Savitt	K. McGregor	6–3	2–6	6–3	6–1	
1952	K. McGregor	F. A. Sedgman	7–5	12–10	2–6	6–2	
1953	K. R. Rosewall	M. G. Rose	6–0	6–3	6–4		
1954	M. G. Rose	R. N. Hartwig	6–2	0–6	6–4	6–2	
1955	K. R. Rosewall	L. A. Hoad	9–7	6–4	6–4		
1956	L. A. Hoad	K. R. Rosewall	6–4	3–6	6–4	7–5	
1957	A. J. Cooper	N. A. Fraser	6–3	9–11	6–4	6–2	
1958	A. J. Cooper	M. J. Anderson	7–5	6–3	6–4		
1959	A. Olmedo	N. A. Fraser	6–1	6–2	3–6	6–3	
1960	R. G. Laver	N. A. Fraser	5–7	3–6	6–3	8–6	8–6
1961	R. S. Emerson	R. G. Laver	1–6	6–3	7–6	6–4	
1962	R. G. Laver	R. S. Emerson	8–6	0–6	6–4	6–4	
1963	R. S. Emerson	K. N. Fletcher	6–3	6–3	6–1		
1964	R. S. Emerson	F. S. Stolle	6–3	6–4	6–2		
1965	R. S. Emerson	F. S. Stolle	7–9	2–6	6–4	7–5	6–1
1966	R. S. Emerson	A. R. Ashe	6–4	6–8	6–2	6–3	
1967	R. S. Emerson	A. R. Ashe	6–4	6–1	6–4		
1968	W. W. Bowrey	J. M. Gisbert	7–5	2–6	9–7	6–4	

Year	Champion	Runner-up	Score					FIRST PRIZE (US $)
1969	R. G. Laver	A. Gimeno	6–3	6–4	7–5			5,000
1970	A. R. Ashe	R. D. Crealy	6–4	9–7	6–2			3,800
1971	K. R. Rosewall	A. R. Ashe	6–1	7–5	6–3			10,000
1972	K. R. Rosewall	M. J. Anderson	7–6	6–3	7–5			2,240
1973	J. D. Newcombe	O. Parun	6–3	6–7	7–5	6–1		8,750
1974	J. S. Connors	P. Dent	7–6	6–4	4–6	6–3		9,750
1975	J. D. Newcombe	J. S. Connors	7–5	3–6	6–4	7–5		12,489
1976	M. Edmondson	J. D. Newcombe	6–7	6–3	7–6	6–1		32,000
1977	(Jan) R. Tanner	G. Vilas	6–3	6–3	6–3			32,000
1977	(Dec) V. Gerulaitis	J. M. Lloyd	6–3	7–6	5–7	3–6	6–2	28,000
1978	G. Vilas	J. Marks	6–4	6–4	3–6	6–3		41,000
1979	G. Vilas	J. Sadri	7–6	6–3	6–2			50,000
1980	B. Teacher	K. Warwick	7–5	7–6	6–3			65,000
1981	J. Kriek	S. Denton	6–2	7–6	6–7	6–4		65,000
1982	J. Kriek	S. Denton	6–3	6–3	6–2			70,000
1983	M. Wilander	I. Lendl	6–1	6–4	6–4			77,500
1984	M. Wilander	K. Curren	6–7	6–4	7–6	6–2		100,000
1985	S. Edberg	M. Wilander	6–4	6–3	6–3			100,000

WOMEN'S SINGLES

	CHAMPION	RUNNER-UP	SCORE		
1922	Mrs M. Molesworth	Miss E. F. Boyd	6–3	10–8	
1923	Mrs M. Molesworth	Miss E. F. Boyd	6–1	7–5	
1924	Miss S. Lance	Miss E. F. Boyd	6–3	3–6	6–4
1925	Miss D. Akhurst	Miss E. F. Boyd	1–6	8–6	6–4
1926	Miss D. Akhurst	Miss E. F. Boyd	6–1	6–3	
1927	Miss E. F. Boyd	Mrs S. Harper	5–7	6–1	6–2

1928	Miss D. Akhurst	Miss E. F. Boyd	7–5 6–2	
1929	Miss D. Akhurst	Miss L. M. Bickerton	6–1 5–7 6–2	
1930	Miss D. Akhurst	Mrs S. Harper	10–8 2–6 7–5	
1931	Mrs C. Buttsworth	Mrs J. H. Crawford	1–6 6–3 6–4	
1932	Mrs C. Buttsworth	Miss K. Le Messurier	9–7 6–4	
1933	Miss J. Hartigan	Mrs C. Buttsworth	6–4 6–3	
1934	Miss J. Hartigan	Mrs M. Molesworth	6–1 6–4	
1935	Miss D. E. Round	Miss N. M. Lyle	1–6 6–1 6–3	
1936	Miss J. Hartigan	Miss N. Wynne	6–4 6–4	
1937	Miss N. Wynne	Mrs V. Westacott	6–3 5–7 6–4	
1938	Miss D. M. Bundy	Miss D. Stevenson	6–3 6–2	
1939	Mrs V. Westacott	Mrs H. C. Hopman	6–1 6–2	
1940	Mrs N. Bolton	Miss T. Coyne	5–7 6–4 6–0	
1941–45	*Not held*			
1946	Mrs N. Bolton	Miss J. Fitch	6–4 6–4	
1947	Mrs N. Bolton	Mrs H. C. Hopman	6–3 6–2	
1948	Mrs N. Bolton	Miss M. Toomey	6–3 6–1	
1949	Miss D. J. Hart	Mrs N. Bolton	6–3 6–4	
1950	Miss A. L. Brough	Miss D. J. Hart	6–4 3–6 6–4	
1951	Mrs N. Bolton	Mrs T. D. Long	6–1 7–5	
1952	Mrs T. D. Long	Miss H. Angwin	6–2 6–3	
1953	Miss M. Connolly	Miss J. Sampson	6–3 6–2	
1954	Mrs T. D. Long	Miss J. Staley	6–3 6–4	
1955	Miss B. Penrose	Mrs T. D. Long	6–4 6–3	
1956	Miss M. Carter	Mrs T. D. Long	3–6 6–2 9–7	
1957	Miss S. J. Fry	Miss A. Gibson	6–3 6–4	
1958	Miss A. Mortimer	Miss L. Coghlan	6–3 6–4	
1959	Mrs S. J. Reitano	Miss R. Schuurman	6–2 6–3	
1960	Miss M. Smith	Miss J. Lehane	7–5 6–2	
1961	Miss M. Smith	Miss J. Lehane	6–1 6–4	
1962	Miss M. Smith	Miss J. Lehane	6–0 6–2	
1963	Miss M. Smith	Miss J. Lehane	6–2 6–2	
1964	Miss M. Smith	Miss L. R. Turner	6–3 6–2	
1965	Miss M. Smith	Miss M. E. Bueno	5–7 6–4 5–2 ret'd	
1966	Miss M. Smith	Miss N. Richey	w.o.	FIRST
1967	Miss N. Richey	Miss L. R. Turner	6–1 6–4	PRIZE
1968	Mrs L. W. King	Mrs B. M. Court	6–1 6–2	(US $)
1969	Mrs B. M. Court	Mrs L. W. King	6–4 6–1	2,000
1970	Mrs B. M. Court	Miss K. Melville	6–1 6–3	700
1971	Mrs B. M. Court	Miss E. Goolagong	2–6 7–5 7–6	1,800
1972	Miss S. V. Wade	Miss E. Goolagong	6–4 6–4	1,200
1973	Mrs B. M. Court	Miss E. Goolagong	6–4 7–5	5,700
1974	Miss E. Goolagong	Miss C. M. Evert	7–6 4–6 6–0	9,000
1975	Miss E. Goolagong	Miss M. Navratilova	6–3 6–2	8,115
1976	Mrs E. Cawley	Miss R. Tomanova	6–2 6–2	12,000
1977	(Jan) Mrs G. Reid	Miss D. Fromholtz	7–5 6–2	12,000
1977	(Dec) Mrs E. Cawley	Mrs H. Cawley	6–3 6–0	9,000
1978	Miss C. O'Neil	Miss B. Nagelsen	6–3 7–6	6,000
1979	Miss B. Jordan	Miss S. Walsh	6–3 6–3	10,000
1980	Miss H. Mandlikova	Miss W. M. Turnbull	6–0 7–5	32,000
1981	Miss M. Navratilova	Mrs C. Evert Lloyd	6–7 6–4 7–5	34,000
1982	Mrs C. Evert Lloyd	Miss M. Navratilova	6–3 2–6 6–3	40,000
1983	Miss M. Navratilova	Miss K. Jordan	6–2 7–6	75,000
1984	Mrs J. M. Lloyd	Miss H. Sukova	6–7 6–1 6–3	100,000
1985	Miss M.Navratilova	Mrs J. M. Lloyd	6–2 4–6 6–2	100,000

MEN'S DOUBLES

	CHAMPIONS	RUNNERS-UP	SCORE			
1905	R. Lycett/T. Tachell	E. T. Barnard/B. Spence	11–9	8–6	1–6	4–6 6–1
1906	R. W. Heath/A. F. Wilding	C. C. Cox/H. A. Parker	6–2	6–4	6–2	
1907	W. A. Gregg/H. A. Parker	H. M. Rice/G. W. Wright	6–2	3–6	6–3	6–2
1908	F. B. Alexander/A. W. Dunlop	G. G. Sharpe/A. F. Wilding	6–3	6–2	6–1	
1909	J. P. Keane/E. F. Parker	C. Crooks/A. F. Wilding	1–6	6–1	6–1	9–7
1910	A. Campbell/H. M. Rice	R. W. Heath/J. L. O'Dea	6–3	6–3	6–2	
1911	H. W. Heath/R. Lycett	J. J. Addison/N. E. Brookes	6–2	7–5	6–0	
1912	C. P. Dixon/J. C. Parke	A. E. Beamish/F. G. Lowe	6–0	6–4	6–2	
1913	A. H. Hedemann/E. F. Parker	H. Parker/R. Taylor	8–6	4–6	6–4	6–4
1914	A. Campbell/G. L. Patterson	R. W. Heath/A. O'Hara Wood	7–5	3–6	6–3	6–3

Year	Winners	Runners-up	Score				
1915	H. M. Rice/C. V. Todd	F. G. Lowe/C. St John	8–6	6–4	7–9	6–3	
1916–1918	Not held						
1919	P. O'Hara Wood/R. V. Thomas	J. O. Anderson/A. H. Lowe	7–5	6–1	7–9	3–6	6–3
1920	P. O'Hara Wood/R. V. Thomas	H. Rice/R. Taylor	6–1	6–0	7–5		
1921	S. H. Eaton/R. H. Gemmell	E. Stokes /N. Breasly	7–5	6–3	6–3		
1922	J. B. Hawkes/G. L. Patterson	J. O. Anderson/N. Peach	8–10	6–0	6–0	7–5	
1923	P. O'Hara Wood/C. B. St John	H. Rice/J. Bullough	6–4	6–3	3–6	6–0	
1924	J. O. Anderson/N. E. Brookes	P. O'Hara Wood/G. L. Patterson	6–2	6–4	6–3		
1925	P. O'Hara Wood/G. L. Patterson	J. O. Anderson/F. Kalms	6–4	8–6	7–5		
1926	J. B. Hawkes/G. L. Patterson	J. O. Anderson/P. O'Hara Wood	6–1	6–4	6–2		
1927	J. B. Hawkes/G. L. Patterson	I. McInnes/P. O'Hara Wood	8–6	6–2	6–1		
1928	J. Borotra/J. Brugnon	E. F. Moon/J. Willard	6–2	4–6	6–4	6–4	
1929	J. H. Crawford/H. C. Hopman	R. O. Cummings/E. F. Moon	6–1	6–8	4–6	6–1	6–3
1930	J. H. Crawford/H. C. Hopman	J. Fitchett/J. B. Hawkes	8–6	6–1	2–6	6–3	
1931	C. Donohoe/R. Dunlop	J. H. Crawford/H. O. Hopman	8–6	6–2	5–7	7–9	6–4
1932	J. H. Crawford/E. F. Moon	H. C. Hopman/G. L. Patterson	12–10	6–3	4–6	6–4	
1933	K. Gledhill/H. E. Vines	J. H. Crawford/E. F. Moon	6–4	10–8	6–2		
1934	G. P. Hughes/F. J. Perry	A. K. Quist/D. P. Turnbull	6–8	6–3	6–4	3–6	6–3
1935	J. H. Crawford/V. B. McGrath	G. P. Hughes/F. J. Perry	6–4	8–6	6–3		
1935	J. H. Crawford/V. B. McGrath	G. P. Hughes/F. J. Perry	6–4	8–6	6–2		
1936	A. K. Quist/D. P. Turnbull	J. H. Crawford/V. B. McGrath	6–8	6–2	6–1	3–6	6–2
1937	A. K. Quist/D. P. Turnbull	J. E. Bromwich/J. E. Harper	6–2	9–7	1–6	6–8	6–4
1938	J. E. Bromwich/A. K. Quist	H. Henkel/G. Von Cramm	7–5	6–4	6–0		
1939	J. E. Bromwich/A. K. Quist	C. F. Long/D. P. Turnbull	6–4	7–5	6–2		
1940	J. E. Bromwich/A. K. Quist	J. H. Crawford/V. B. McGrath	6–3	7–5	6–1		
1941–1945	Not held						
1946	J. E. Bromwich/A. K. Quist	M. Newcombe/L. A. Schwartz	6–4	6–2	6–3		
1947	J. E. Bromwich/A. K. Quist	F. A. Sedgman/G. Worthington	6–1	6–3	6–1		
1948	J. E. Bromwich/A. K. Quist	C. Long/F. A. Sedgman	1–6	6–8	9–7	6–3	8–6
1949	J. E. Bromwich/A. K. Quist	G. Brown/O. W. Sidwell	6–8	7–5	6–2	6–3	
1950	J. E. Bromwich/A. K. Quist	J. Drobny/E. W. Sturgess	6–3	5–7	4–6	6–3	8–6
1951	K. McGregor/F. A. Sedgman	J. E. Bromwich/A. K. Quist	11–9	2–6	6–3	4–6	6–3
1952	K. McGregor/F. A. Sedgman	D. Candy/M. G. Rose	6–4	7–5	6–3		
1953	L. A. Hoad/K. R. Rosewall	D. Candy/M. G. Rose	9–11	6–4	10–8	6–4	
1954	R. N. Hartwig/M. G. Rose	N. A. Fraser/C. Wilderspin	6–3	6–4	6–2		
1955	E. V. Seixas/M. A. Trabert	L. A. Hoad/K. R. Rosewall	6–3	6–2	2–6	3–6	6–1
1956	L. A. Hoad/K. R. Rosewall	D. Candy/M. G. Rose	10–8	13–11	6–4		
1957	N. A. Fraser/L. A. Hoad	M. J. Anderson/A. Cooper	6–3	8–6	6–4		
1958	A. Cooper/N. A. Fraser	R. S. Emerson/R. Mark	6–5	6–8	3–6	6–3	7–5
1959	R. G. Laver/R. Mark	D. Candy/R. N. Howe	9–7	6–4	6–2		
1960	R. G. Laver/R. Mark	R. S. Emerson/N. A. Fraser	1–6	6–2	6–4	6–4	
1961	R. G. Laver/R. Mark	R. S. Emerson/M. F. Mulligan	6–3	7–5	3–6	7–9	6–2
1962	R. S. Emerson/N. A. Fraser	R. A. J. Hewitt/F. S. Stolle	4–6	4–6	6–1	6–4	11–9
1963	R. A. J. Hewitt/F. S. Stolle	K. N. Fletcher/J. D. Newcombe	6–2	3–6	6–3	3–6	6–3
1964	R. A. J. Hewitt/F. S. Stolle	R. S. Emerson/K. N. Fletcher	6–4	7–5	3–6	4–6	14–12
1965	J. D. Newcombe/A. D. Roche	R. S. Emerson/F. S. Stolle	3–6	4–6	13–11	6–3	6–4
1966	R. S. Emerson/F. S. Stolle	J. D. Newcombe/A. D. Roche	7–9	6–3	6–8	14–12	12–10
1967	J. D. Newcombe/A. D. Roche	W. W. Bowrey/O. K. Davidson	3–6	6–3	7–5	6–8	8–6
1968	R. D. Crealy/A. J. Stone	T. Addison/R. Keldie	10–8	6–4	6–3		
1969	R. S. Emerson/R. G. Laver	K. R. Rosewall/F. S. Stolle	6–4	6–4	6–4		
1970	R. C. Lutz/S. R. Smith	J. G. Alexander/P. Dent	6–3	8–6	6–3		
1971	J. D. Newcombe/A. D. Roche	T. S. Okker/M. C. Riessen	6–2	7–6			
1972	O. K. Davidson/K. R. Rosewall	R. Case/G. Masters	3–6	7–6	6–3		
1973	M. J. Anderson/J. D. Newcombe	J. G. Alexander/P. Dent	6–3	6–4	7–6		
1974	R. Case/G. Masters	S. Ball/R. Giltinan	6–7	6–3	6–4		
1975	J. G. Alexander/P. Dent	R. Carmichael/A. J. Stone	6–3	7–6			
1976	J. D. Newcombe/A. D. Roche	R. Case/G. Masters	7–6	6–4			
1977	A. R. Ashe/A. D. Roche	C. Pasarell/E. Van Dillen	6–4	6–4			
1977 (Dec)	R. O. Ruffels/A. J. Stone	J. G. Alexander/P. Dent	7–6	7–6			
1978	W. Fibak/K. Warwick	P. Kronk/C. Letcher	7–6	7–5			
1979	P. McNamara/P. McNamee	P. Kronk/C. Letcher	7–6	6–2			
1980	M. R. Edmondson/K. Warwick	P. McNamara/P. McNamee	7–5	6–4			
1981	M. R. Edmondson/K. Warwick	H. Pfister/J. Sadri	6–3	6–7	6–3		
1982	J. G. Alexander/J. Fitzgerald	A. Andrews/J. Sadri	6–4	7–6			
1983	M. R. Edmondson/P. McNamee	S. Denton/S. E. Stewart	6–3	7–6			
1984	M. R. Edmondson/S. E. Stewart	J. Nystrom/M. Wilander	6–2	6–2	7–5		
1985	P. Annacone /C. Van Rensburg	M. R. Edmondson/K. Warwick	3–6	7–6	6–4	6–4	

WOMEN'S DOUBLES

	CHAMPIONS	RUNNERS-UP	SCORE		
1922	E. F. Boyd/M. Mountain	St George/H. S. Utz	1–6	6–4	7–5
1923	E. F. Boyd/S. Lance	M. Molesworth/H. Turner	6–1	6–4	
1924	D. Akhurst/S. Lance	K. Le Mesurier/P. O'Hara Wood	7–5	6–2	
1925	D. Akhurst/R. Harper	E. F. Boyd/K. Le Mesurier	6–4	6–3	
1926	E. F. Boyd/P. O'Hara Wood	D. Akhurst/M. Cox	6–3	6–8	8–6
1927	L. M. Bickerton/P. O'Hara Wood	E. F. Boyd/R. Harper	6–3	6–3	
1928	D. Akhurst/E. F. Boyd	K. Le Mesurier/D. Weston	6–3	6–1	
1929	D. Akhurst/L. M. Bickerton	R. Harper/P. O'Hara Wood	6–2	3–6	6–2
1930	E. Hood/M. Molesworth	M. Cox/R. Harper	6–3	0–6	7–5
1931	L. M. Bickerton/R. Cozens	A. Lloyd/H. S. Utz	6–0	6–4	
1932	C. Buttsworth/J. H. Crawford	K. Le Mesurier/D. Weston	6–2	6–2	
1933	M. Molesworth/V. Westacott	J. Hartigan/J. Van Ryn	6–3	6–3	
1934	M. Molesworth/V. Westacott	J. Hartigan/U. Valkenborg	6–8	6–4	6–4
1935	E. M. Dearman/N. M. Lyle	L. M. Bickerton/N. Hopman	6–3	6–4	
1936	T. Coyne/N. Wynne	M. Blick/K. Woodward	6–2	6–4	
1937	T. Coyne/N. Wynne	N. Hopman/V. Westacott	6–2	6–2	
1938	T. Coyne/N. Wynne	D. M. Bundy/D. E. Workman	9–7	6–4	
1939	T. Coyne/N. Wynne	M. Hardcastle/V. Westacott	7–5	6–4	
1940	T. Coyne/N. Bolton	J. Hartigan/E. Niemeyer	7–5	6–2	
1941–1945	*Not held*				
1946	M. Bevis/J. Fitch	Not available			
1947	N. Bolton/T. D. Long	M. Bevis/J. Fitch	6–3	6–3	
1948	N. Bolton/T. D. Long	M. Bevis/N. Jones	6–3	6–3	
1949	N. Bolton/T. D. Long	D./M. Toomey	6–0	6–1	
1950	L. Brough/J. J. Hart	N. Bolton/T. D. Long	6–3	2–6	6–3
1951	N. Bolton/T. D. Long	J. Fitch/M. Hawton	6–2	6–1	
1952	N. Baker/T. D. Long	R. Baker/M. Hawton	6–1	6–1	
1953	M. Connolly/J. Sampson	M. Hawton/B. Penrose	6–3	6–2	
1954	M. Hawton/B. Penrose	H. Redick-Smith/J. Wipplinger	6–3	8–6	
1955	M. Hawton/B. Penrose	N. Hopman/A. Thiele	7–5	6–1	
1956	M. Hawton/T. D. Long	M. Carter/B. Penrose	6–3	5–7	9–7
1957	S. J. Fry/A. Gibson	M. Hawton/F. Muller	6–2	6–1	
1958	M. Hawton/T. D. Long	L. Coghlan/A. Mortimer	7–5	6–8	6–2
1959	S. Reynolds/R. Schuurman	L. Coghlan/A. Reitano	7–5	6–4	
1960	M. E. Bueno/C. Truman	L. Robinson/M. Smith	6–2	5–7	6–2
1961	M. Reitano/M. Smith	M. Hawton/J. Lehane	6–3	3–6	7–5
1962	E. Ebbern/M. Smith	D. R. Hard/M. Reintano	6–4	6–4	
1963	R. Ebbern/M. Smith	J. Lehane/L. R. Turner	6–1	6–3	
1964	J. A. M. Tegart/L. R. Turner	R. Ebbern/M. Smith	6–4	6–4	
1965	M. Smith/L. R. Turner	R. Ebbern/B. J. Moffitt	1–6	6–2	6–3
1966	C. Graebner/N. Richey	M. Smith/L. R. Turner	6–4	7–5	
1967	J. A. M. Tegart/L. R. Turner	L. Robinson/E. Terras	6–0	6–2	
1968	K. Krantzcke/K. Melville	J. A. M. Tegart/L. R. Turner	6–4	3–6	6–2
1969	B. M. Court/J. A. M. Tegart	R. Casals/L. W. King	6–4	6–4	
1970	B. M. Court/D. Dalton	K. Krantzcke/K. Melville	6–3	6–4	
1971	B. M. Court/E. F. Goolagong	J. Emmerson/L. Hunt	6–0	6–0	
1972	H. Gourlay/K. Harris	P. Coleman/K. Krantzcke	6–2	6–3	
1973	B. M. Court/S. V. Wade	K. Harris/K. Melville	6–4	6–4	
1974	E. F. Goolagong/M. Michel	K. Harris/K. Melville	7–5	6–3	
1975	E. F. Goolagong/M. Michel	B. M. Court/O. Morozova	7–6	7–6	
1976	E. F. Cawley/H. Gourlay	W. W. Bowrey/R. Tomanova	8–1 (one set)		
1977	D. Fromholtz/H. Gourlay	B. Nagelsen/G. E. Reid	5–7	6–1	7–5
1977	(Dec) E. F. Cawley/H. Cawley div'd with M. Guerrant/G. E. Reid				
1978	B. Nagelsen/R. Tomanova	N. Sato/P. Whytcross	7–5	6–2	
1979	D. D. Chaloner/D. R. Evers	L. Harrison/M. Mesker	6–2	1–6	6–0
1980	B. Nagelsen/M. Navratilova	A. Kiyomura/C. Reynolds	6–4	6–4	
1981	K. Jordan/A. E. Smith	M. Navratilova/P. H. Shriver	6–2	7–5	
1982	M. Navratilova/P. H. Shriver	C. Kohde/E. Pfaff	6–4	6–2	
1983	M. Navratilova/P. H. Shriver	A. E. Hobbs/W. M. Turnbull	6–4	6–7	6–2
1984	M. Navratilova/P. H. Shriver	C. Kohde-Kilsch/H. Sukova	6–3	6–4	
1985	M. Navratilova/P. H. Shriver	C. Kohde-Kilsch/H. Sukova	6–3	6–4	

MIXED DOUBLES

	CHAMPIONS	RUNNERS-UP	SCORE		
1922	J. B. Hawkes/Miss E. F. Boyd	H. S. Utz/Mrs Utz	6–1	6–1	
1923	H. M. Rice/Miss S. Lance	C. St John/Miss M. Molesworth	2–6	6–4	6–4
1924	J. Willard /Miss D. Akhurst	G. M. Hone /Miss E. F. Boyd	6–3	6–4	
1925	J. Willard /Miss D. Akhurst	R. E. Schlesinger /Mrs R. Harper	6–4	6–4	
1926	J. B. Hawkes /Miss E. F. Boyd	J. Willard /Miss D. Akhurst	6–2	6–4	
1927	J. B. Hawkes /Miss E. F. Boyd	J. Willard /Miss Y. Anthony	6–1	6–3	
1928	J. Borotra /Miss D. Akhurst	J. B. Hawkes /Miss E. F. Boyd	w.o		
1929	E. F. Moon /Miss D. Akhurst	J. H. Crawford /Miss M. Cox	6–0	7–5	
1930	H. C. Hopman /Miss N. Hall	J. H. Crawford /Miss M. Cox	11–9	3–6	6–3
1931	J. H. Crawford/Mrs Crawford	A. Willard/Mrs V. Westacott	Not available		
1932	J. H. Crawford/Mrs Crawford	J. Satoh/Mrs P. O'Hara Wood	6–8	8–6	6–3
1933	J. H. Crawford/Mrs Crawford	H. E. Vines/Mrs J. Van Ryn	3–6	7–5	13–11
1934	E. F. Moon/Miss J. Hartigan	R. Dunlop/Mrs V. Westacott	6–3	6–4	
1935	C. Boussus/Miss L. Bickerton	V. G. Kirby/Mrs Bond	1–6	6–3	6–3
1936	H. C. Hopman/Mrs Hopman	A. A. Kay/Miss M. Blick	6–2	6–0	
1937	H. C. Hopman/Mrs Hopman	D. P. Turnbull/Miss D. Stevenson	3–6	6–3	6–2
1938	J. E. Bromwich/Miss J. Wilson	C. Long/Miss N. Wynne	6–3	6–2	
1939	H. C. Hopman/Mrs Hopman	J. E. Bromwich/Miss J. Wilson	6–8	6–2	6–3
1940	C. Long/Mrs N. Bolton	H. C. Hopman/Mrs Hopman	7–5	2–6	6–4
1941–1945	*Not held*				
1946	C. Long/Mrs N. Bolton	J. Bromwich/Miss J. Fitch	6–0	6–4	
1947	C. Long/Mrs N. Bolton	J. E. Bromwich/Miss J. Fitch	6–3	6–3	
1948	C. Long/Mrs N. Bolton	O. W. Sidwell/Mrs T. D. Long	7–5	4–6	8–6
1949	F. A. Sedgman/Miss D. J. Hart	J. E. Bromwich/Miss J. Fitch	6–1	5–7	12–10
1950	F. A. Sedgman/Miss D. J. Hart	E. W. Sturgess/Miss J. Fitch	6–3	2–6	6–3
1951	G. A. Worthington/Mrs T. D. Long	J. May/Miss C. Proctor	4–6	6–3	6–2
1952	G. A. Worthington/Mrs T. D. Long	T. Warhurst/Mrs A. R. Thiele	9–7	7–5	
1953	R. N. Hartwig/Miss J. Sampson	H. Richardson/Miss M. Connolly	6–4	6–3	
1954	R. N. Hartwig/Mrs T. D. Long	J. E. Bromwich/Miss B. Penrose	8–6	9–7	
1955	G. A. Worthington/Mrs T. D. Long	L. A. Hoad/Miss J. Staley	6–2	6–1	
1956	N. A. Fraser/Miss B. Penrose	R. S. Emerson/Mrs M. Hawton	6–2	6–4	
1957	M. J. Anderson/Miss F. Muller	W. A. Knight/Miss J. Langley	7–5	3–6	6–1
1958	R. N. Howe/Mrs M. Hawton	A. Newman/Miss A. Mortimer	9–11	6–1	6–2
1959	R. Mark/Miss S. Reynolds	R. G. Laver/Miss R. Schuurman	4–6	13–11	6–1
1960	T. Fancutt/Miss J. Lehane	R. Mark/Mrs M. Reitano	6–2	7–5	
1961	R. A. J. Hewitt/Miss J. Lehane	J. Pearce/Mrs M. Reitano	9–7	6–2	
1962	F. S. Stolle/Miss L. R. Turner	R. Taylor/Miss D. R. Hard	6–3	9–7	
1963	K. N. Fletcher/Miss M. Smith	F. S. Stolle/Miss L. R. Turner	7–5	5–7	6–4
1964	K. N. Fletcher/Miss M. Smith	M. J. Sangster/Miss J. Lehane	6–1	6–2	
1965	J. D. Newcombe/Miss M. Smith div'd with O. K. Davidson/Miss R. Ebbern				
1966	A. D. Roche/Miss J. A. Tegart	W. W. Bowrey/Miss R. Ebbern	6–1	6–3	
1967	O. K. Davidson/Miss L. R. Turner	A. D. Roche/Miss J. A. M. Tegart	9–7	6–4	
1968	R. D. Crealy/Mrs L. W. King	A. J. Stone/Mrs B. M. Court	6–2	9–7	
1969	M. C. Riessen/Mrs B. M. Court div'd with F. S. Stolle/Mrs P. F. Jones				
1970–84	*Not held*				

US CLAY COURT CHAMPIONSHIPS

* Played as 'Patriotic Tournament' without championship status.

MEN'S SINGLES

	CHAMPION	RUNNER-UP	SCORE				
1910	M. H. Long	W. M. Hall	6–0	6–1	6–1		
1911	W. T. Hayes	P. Siverd	7–5	6–2	6–1		
1912	R. N. Williams	W. T. Hayes	6–3	6–1	8–6		
1913	J. R. Strachan	W. M. Hall	6–0	6–4	4–6	6–4	
1914	C. J. Griffin	E. Fottrell	3–6	6–8	8–6	6–0	6–2
1915	R. N. Williams	G. M. Church	7–5	6–3	2–6	8–6	
1916	W. E. Davis	C. B. Doyle	6–2	7–5	6–3		
1917*	S. Hardy	C. S. Garland	3–6	6–1	1–6	6–3	6–3
1918	W. T. Tilden	C. S. Garland	6–4	6–4	3–6	6–2	
1919	W. M. Johnston	W. T. Tilden	6–0	6–1	4–6	6–2	
1920	R. Roberts	V. Richards	6–3	6–1	6–3		
1921	W. T. Hayes	A. Squair	6–0	6–2	6–4		

1922	W. T. Tilden	Z. Shimizu	6–5	6–3	6–1	
1923	W. T. Tilden	M. Alonso	6–2	6–8	6–1	7–5
1924	W. T. Tilden	H. B. Snodgrass	6–2	6–1	6–1	
1925	W. T. Tilden	G. M. Lott	3–6	6–3	2–6	6–2 8–6
1926	W. T. Tilden	B. I. C. Norton	w.o.			
1927	W. T. Tilden	J. Hennessey	5–4	6–1	6–2	
1928	*Not held*					
1929	E. Pare	J. B. Hall	6–4	6–3	4–6	3–6 6–1
1930	B. M. Grant	W. F. Coen	6–2	4–6	6–2	6–4
1931	H. E. Vines	K. Gledhill	6–3	6–3	6–3	
1932	G. M. Lott	B. M. Grant	3–6	6–2	3–6	6–3 6–3
1933	F. A. Parker	G. Mako	6–3	6–3	6–3	
1934	B. M. Grant	J. D. Budge	6–2	8–6	6–3	
1935	B. M. Grant	F. A. Parker	4–6	6–1	3–6	6–3 6–0
1936	R. L. Riggs	F. A. Parker	6–1	6–8	6–4	
1937	R. L. Riggs	J. R. Hunt	6–3	4–6	6–3	6–4
1938	R. L. Riggs	G. Mulloy	6–4	5–7	4–6	6–1 7–5
1939	F. A. Parker	G. Mulloy	6–3	6–0	5–7	6–3
1940	D. McNeill	R. L. Riggs	6–1	6–4	6–9	6–3
1941	F. A. Parker	R. L. Riggs	6–3	7–5	6–8	4–6 6–3
1942	S. Greenberg	H. W. Everett	5–7	7–5	7–9	7–5 8–6
1943	S. Greenberg	W. F. Talbert	6–1	4–6	6–3	6–3
1944	F. Segura	W. F. Talbert	6–1	2–6	7–5	6–3
1945	W. F. Talbert	F. Segura	6–4	4–6	6–2	2–6 6–2
1946	F. A. Parker	W. F. Talbert	6–4	6–4	6–2	
1947	F. A. Parker	F. R. Schroeder	8–6	6–2	6–4	
1948	R. A. Gonzales	C. Carter	7–5	6–2	6–3	
1949	R. A. Gonzales	F. A. Parker	6–1	3–6	8–6	6–3
1950	H. Flam	F. R. Schroeder	6–1	6–2	6–2	
1951	M. A. Trabert	A. Larsen	6–8	2–6	6–4	6–3 8–6
1952	A. Larsen	R. Savitt	4–6	6–4	6–2	6–4
1953	E. V. Seixas	H. Richardson	6–2	6–4	6–3	
1954	B. Bartzen	M. A. Trabert	6–2	4–6	6–0	6–2
1955	M. A. Trabert	B. Bartzen	10–8	6–1	6–4	
1956	H. Flam	E. Moylan	3–6	6–3	1–6	6–3 6–3
1957	E. V. Seixas	H. Flam	1–6	8–6	6–1	6–3
1958	B. Bartzen	S. Giammalva	3–6	7–5	6–2	6–2
1959	B. Bartzen	W. Reed	6–0	8–6	7–5	
1960	B. MacKay	B. Bartzen	4–6	7–5	6–4	6–0
1961	B. Bartzen	D. Dell	6–1	2–6	6–2	6–0
1962	C. R. McKinley	F. S. Stolle	6–3	8–6	6–4	
1963	C. R. McKinley	R. D. Ralston	6–2	6–2	6–4	
1964	R. D. Ralston	C. R. McKinley	6–2	6–2	6–1	
1965	R. D. Ralston	C. Richey	6–4	4–6	6–4	6–3
1966	C. Richey	F. A. Froehling	13–11	6–1	6–3	
1967	A. R. Ashe	M. C. Riessen	4–6	6–3	6–1	7–5
1968	C. Graebner	S. R. Smith	6–3	7–5	6–0	
1969	Z. Franulovic	A. R. Ashe	8–6	6–3	6–4	
1970	C. Richey	S. R. Smith	6–2	10–8	3–6	6–1
1971	Z. Franulovic	C. Richey	6–3	6–4	0–6	6–3
1972	R. A. J. Hewitt	J. S. Connors	7–6	6–1	6–2	
1973	M. Orantes	R. Ramirez	6–4	6–1	6–4	
1974	J. S. Connors	B. Borg	5–7	6–3	6–4	
1975	M. Orantes	A. R. Ashe	6–2	6–2		
1976	J. S. Connors	W. Fibak	6–2	6–4		
1977	M. Orantes	J. S. Connors	6–1	6–3		
1978	J. S. Connors	J. Higueras	7–5	6–1		
1979	J. S. Connors	G. Vilas	6–1	2–6	6–4	
1980	J. L. Clerc	M. Purcell	7–5	6–3		
1981	J. L. Clerc	I. Lendl	4–6	6–4	6–2	
1982	J. Higueras	J. Arias	7–6	5–7	6–3	
1983	J. Arias	A. Gomez	6–4	2–6	6–4	
1984	A. Gomez	B. Taroczy	6–0	7–6		
1985	I. Lendl	A. Gomez	6–1	6–3		

WOMEN'S SINGLES

	CHAMPION	RUNNER-UP	SCORE	
1912	Miss M. Sutton	Miss M. K. Browne	6–4	6–2
1913	*Not held*			

1914	Miss M. K. Browne	Miss R. H. Williams	6–1	3–6	6–2		
1915	Miss M. Bjurdstedt	Mrs G. W. Wightman	3–6	6–1	6–3		
1916	Miss M. Bjurdstedt	Miss M. Guthrie	6–3	6–3			
1917*	Miss R. Sanders	Mrs W. Ellis	6–1	6–3			
1918	Miss C. B. Neely	Mrs A. Yager	6–4	6–2			
1919	Miss C. Gould	Miss C. B. Neely	6–4	6–2			
1920	Miss M. Zinderstein	Miss C. Gould	6–0	6–1			
1921	Mrs B. E. Cole	Mrs F. Godfrey	6–0	6–3			
1922	Mrs H. Bickle	Miss L. Bancroft	3–6	6–1	7–5		
1923	Miss M. MacDonald	Miss L. Scharman	7–5	1–6	6–4		
1924–39	*Not held*						
1940	Miss A. Marble	Miss G. W. Wheeler	7–5	6–0			
1941	Miss P. M. Betz	Miss M. Arnold	6–3	6–1			
1942	*Not held*						
1943	Miss P. M. Betz	Miss N. Corbett	6–1	6–0			
1944	Miss D. M. Bundy	Miss M. Arnold	7–5	6–4			
1945	Mrs S. P. Cooke	Miss P. M. Betz	6–3	7–5			
1946	Miss B. Krase	Mrs V. W. Kovacs	10–8	6–4			
1947	Mrs M. A. Prentiss	Miss D. Head	6–1	6–1			
1948	Mrs M. Rurac	Miss D. Head	1–6	7–5	6–3		
1949	Mrs M. Rurac	Miss B. Baker	2–6	9–7	6–3		
1950	Miss D. J. Hart	Miss S. J. Fry	6–1	6–3			
1951	Miss D. Head	Mrs P. C. Todd	4–6	6–2	6–2		
1952	Miss A. Kanter	Mrs L. Davidson	6–4	6–3			
1953	Miss M. Connolly	Miss A. Gibson	6–4	6–4			
1954	Miss M. Connolly	Miss D. J. Hart	6–3	6–1			
1955	Mrs D. H. Knode	Miss B. Breit	6–4	6–3			
1956	Miss S. J. Fry	Miss A. Gibson	7–5	6–1			
1957	Miss A. Gibson	Miss D. R. Hard	6–2	6–3			
1958	Mrs D. H. Knode	Miss K. Fageros	6–3	6–8	6–2		
1959	Miss S. Moore	Miss S. Reynolds	6–2	2–6	6–3		
1960	Mrs D. H. Knode	Miss G. Thomas	6–3	6–3			
1961	Miss E. Buding	Miss K. Hantze	6–4	2–6	6–4		
1962	Miss D. Floyd	Miss C. Caldwell	6–3	6–1			
1963	Miss N. Richey	Miss V. Palmer	6–1	6–1			
1964	Miss N. Richey	Miss C. Caldwell	6–2	6–1			
1965	Miss N. Richey	Miss J. M. Heldman	5–7	6–3	9–7		
1966	Miss N. Richey	Miss S. De Fina	6–2	6–2			
1967	Miss N. Richey	Miss R. Casals	6–2	6–3			
1968	Miss N. Richey	Miss L. Tuero	6–3	6–3			
1969	Mrs G. Chanfreau	Miss L. Tuero	6–2	6–2			
1970	Miss L. Tuero	Mrs G. Chanfreau	7–5	6–1			
1971	Mrs L. W. King	Miss L. Tuero	6–4	7–5			
1972	Miss C. M. Evert	Miss E. F. Goolagong	7–6	6–1			
1973	Miss C. M. Evert	Miss V. Burton	6–4	6–3			
1974	Miss C. M. Evert	Mrs G. Lovera	6–0	6–0			
1975	Miss C. M. Evert	Miss D. Fromholtz	6–3	6–4			
1976	Miss K. May	Miss B. Cuypers	6–4	4–6	6–2		
1977	Miss L. DuPont	iss N. Richey	6–4	6–3			
1978	Miss D. Gilbert	Miss V. Gonzalez	6–2	6–3			
1979	Mrs J. M. Lloyd	Mrs E. Cawley	6–4	6–3			
1980	Mrs J. M. Lloyd	Miss A. Jaeger	6–4	6–3			
1981	Miss A. Jaeger	Miss V. Ruzici	6–1	6–0			
1982	Miss V. Ruzici	Miss H. Sukova	6–2	6–0			
1983	Miss A. Temesvari	Miss Z. Garrison	6–2	6–2			
1984	Miss M. Maleeva	Miss L. Bonder	6–4	6–3			
1985	Miss A. Temesvari	Miss Z. Garrison	7–6	6–3			

MEN'S DOUBLES

	CHAMPIONS	RUNNERS-UP	SCORE				
1910	F. G. Anderson/W. T. Hayes	M. H. Long/A. Scribner	2–6	3–6	6–1	6–3	6–3
1911	H. G. Whitehead/J. H. Winston	F. G. Anderson/W. T. Hayes	6–3	2–6	7–5	6–1	
1912	H. H. Hackett/W. M. Hall	H. G. Whitehead/J. H. Winson	4–6	6–1	6–0	6–1	
1913	C. J. Griffin/J. R. Strachan	W. M. Hall/F. Harris	w.o.				
1914	N. Browne/C. Wayne	E. Fottrell/C. J. Griffin	6–3	6–4	6–3		
1915	G. M. Church/D. Mathey	W. M. Washburn/R. N. Williams	6–3	2–6	6–3		
1916	G. M. Church/D. Mathey	W. Davis/H. V. D. Johns	7–5	6–0	6–2		
1917*	C. S. Garland/S. Hardy	H. T. Emerson/W. H. Hopple	6–4	6–2	6–3		

Year	Winners	Runners-up	Score				
1918	C. S. Garland/S. Hardy	R. H. Burdick/W. T. Hayes	6–4	1–6	6–2	7–9	6–2
1919	S. Hardy/W. M. Johnston	A. Gravem/R. Kinsley	6–3	6–1	2–6	6–3	
1920	V. Richards/R. Roberts	R. Burdick/W. T. Hayes	6–2	6–2	7–5		
1921	W. T. Hayes/C. B. Herd	R. Burdick/J. Hennessey	6–1	6–3	6–2		
1922	F. Bastian/R. Burdick	J. Hennessey/W. Wesbrook	6–3	3–6	7–5	5–7	6–4
1923	H./R. Kinsey	J. Hennessey/W. Wesbrook	6–4	13–11	6–3		
1924	H./R. Kinsey	W. T. Tilden/S. Wiener	6–4	7–5	6–2		
1925	H. Snodgrass/W. Wesbrook	W. T. Tilden/S. Wiener	6–1	6–2	6–1		
1926	L. Thalheimer/L. N. White	H. Chapin/B. I. C. Norton	w.o.				
1927	J. Hennessey/R. N. Williams	W. T. Tilden/S. Wiener	6–4	6–3	3–6	9–7	
1928	*Not held*						
1929	J. G. Hall/F. Mercur	B. Gerschakoff/A. Kussman	10–12	3–6	6–2	9–7	6–4
1930	J. G. Hall/F. Mercur	W. Brown/H. Coggeshell	3–6	6–3	7–5	6–2	
1931	K. Gledhill/H. E. Vines	B. Barnes/B. Bell	6–3	7–9	10–8	9–7	
1932	B. M. Grant/G. M. Lott	C./E. Sutter	6–4	6–4	1–6	4–6	6–3
1933	G. Mako/J. Tidball	R. Bryan/J. McDiarmid	6–2	2–6	7–5	4–6	6–0
1934	J. D. Budge/G. Mako	R. Bryan/J. McDiarmid	4–6	6–3	6–4	6–4	
1935	B. Bell/J. G. Hall	R. Bruan/J. McDiarmid	6–4	6–4	5–7	9–11	6–2
1936	R. L. Riggs/W. Sabin	E. McCauliff/J. McDiarmid	4–6	6–2	7–5	6–4	
1937	E. McCauliff/J. McDiarmid	N. Bickett/N. Burgess	3–6	6–3	11–13	7–5	6–1
1938	J. R. Hunt/L. Wetherel	E. Cooke/C. Hare	6–4	8–6	6–2		
1939	G. Mako/F. A. Parker	J. H. Doeg/W. Sabin	6–3	3–6	6–3	6–4	
1940	R. Harmon/R. C. Peacock	W. D. McNeill/F. A. Parker	w.o.				
1941	J. A. Kramer/F. R. Schroeder	J. R. Hunt/C. Oliwine	6–4	7–5	6–1		
1942	W. Reedy/W. F. Talbert	C. Mattman/G. Richards	6–3	6–3	6–3		
1943	E. Cochell/R. Kimbrell	S. Greenberg/W. F. Talbert	1–6	6–3	6–4	6–2	
1944	F. Segura/W. F. Talbert	H. Manire/H. Wrobbel	6–3	6–1	5–7	6–1	
1945	F. Segura/W. F. Talbert	E. Cooke/H. Surface	6–4	7–5	6–2		
1946	G. Mulloy/W. F. Talbert	J. Cushingham/R. Falkenburg	12–10	6–2	6–4		
1947	F. R. Schroeder/J. Tuero	S. Greenberg/E. V. Seixas	6–3	3–6	2–6	8–6	6–4
1948	T. Chambers/S. Match	T. P. Brown/R. A. Gonzales	1–6	7–5	6–3		
1949	S. Match/E. V. Seixas	R. A. Gonzales/H. Stewart	6–1	1–6	5–7	8–6	9–7
1950	H. Flam/A. Larsen	F. R. Schroeder/M. A. Trabert	3–6	1–6	6–2	6–2	6–4
1951	H. Richardson/M. A. Trabert	H. Burrows/S. Clark	3–6	8–6	6–2	6–2	
1952	G. Golden/A. Larsen	N. Brown/H. Stewart	6–2	6–4	8–6		
1953	B. Bartzen/G. Holden	A. Larsen/G. Worthington	8–6	2–6	8–6	6–4	
1954	E. V. Seixas/M. A. Trabert	B. Bartzen/A. Larsen	6–3	11–9	6–2		
1955	H. Richardson/M. A. Trabert	B. Bartzen/E. Moylan	6–1	6–2			
1956	F. Contreras/A. Olmedo	H. Flam/A. Larsen	6–3	5–7	6–4		
1957	A. J. Cooper/N. A. Fraser	H. Flam/E. V. Seixas	4–6	7–5	6–4	6–3	
1958	S. Giammalva/B. MacKay	B. Bartzen/G. Golden	6–2	6–4	5–7	3–6	6–0
1959	B. Bartzen/G. Golden	W. Bond/R. D. Ralston	12–10	6–2	6–4		
1960	R. A. J. Hewitt/M. F. Mulligan	R. Earnhart/M. C. Riessen	6–3	6–2	11–13	6–4	
1961	C. R. McKinley/R. D. Ralston	R. Earnhart/M. C. Riessen	6–3	6–4	6–2		
1962	R. Earnhart/M. C. Riessen	C. Crawford/F. S. Stolle	6–4	6–2	6–3		
1963	C. Graebner/M. C. Riessen	C. R. McKinley/R. D. Ralston	6–4	0–6	6–4	5–7	6–3
1964	C. R. McKinley/R. D. Ralston	C. Graebner/M. C. Riessen	6–1	6–4	6–2		
1965	C. Graebner/M. C. Riessen	R. D. Ralston/H. Richardson	3–6	6–3	6–1 ret'd		
1966	C. Graebner/R. D. Ralston	F. A. Froehling/C. Pasarell	6–1	8–10	6–4	6–8	6–4
1967	C. Graebner/M. C. Riessen	J. Brown/B. Tobin	6–2	6–4	6–4		
1968	R. C. Lutz/S. R. Smith	M. Mosur/M. C. Riessen	3–6	6–2	6–4	6–2	
1969	W. W. Bowrey/C. Graebner	R. D. Crealy/A. J. Stone	6–4	4–6	6–4		
1970	A. R. Ashe/C. Graebner	I. Nastase/I. Tiriac	2–6	6–4	6–4		
1971	Z. Franulovic/J. Kodes	C. Graebner/E. Van Dillen	7–6	5–7	6–3		
1972	R. A. J. Hewitt/F. D. McMillan	O. Cornejo/J. Fillol	6–2	6–3			
1973	R. Carmichael/F. D. McMillan	M. Orantes/I. Tiriac	6–3	7–4			
1974	J. S. Connors/I. Nastase	J. Fassbender/H. J. Pohmann	6–7	6–3	6–4		
1975	J. Gisbert/M. Orantes	W. Fibak/H. J. Pohmann	7–5	6–0			
1976	B. E. Gottfried/R. Ramirez	F. McNair/S. E. Stewart	6–2	6–2			
1977	P. Cornejo/J. Fillol	R. D. Crealy/C. Letcher	6–7	6–4	6–3		
1978	G. Mayer/H. Pfister	J. Borowiak/C. J. Lewis	6–3	6–0			
1979	J. P. McEnroe/G. Mayer	J. Kodes/T. Smid	6–4	7–6			
1980	K. Curren/S. Denton	W. Fibak/I. Lendl	3–6	7–6	6–4		
1981	K. Curren/S. Denton	R. Ramirez/V. Winitsky	6–3	5–7	7–5		
1982	S. E. Stewart/F. Taygan	R. Venter/B. Willenborg	6–4	7–5			
1983	M. R. Edmondson/S. E. Stewart	C. Kirmayr/C. Motta	6–3	6–2			
1984	K. Flach/R. Seguso	H. Gunthardt/B. Taroczy	7–6	7–5			
1985	K. Flach/R. Seguso	P. Slozil/K. Warwick	6–4	6–4			

WOMEN'S DOUBLES

	CHAMPIONS	RUNNERS-UP	SCORE		
1914	M. K. Brown/Mrs R. Williams	M. Dodd/M. Lyons	6–1	6–2	
1915–16	*Not held*				
1917*	Mrs C. Gregg/R. Sanders	Mrs W. Ellis/A. Levy	6–4	6–2	
1918	B. Esch/Mrs R. Field	C. B. Neely/Mrs A. Yager	6–4	4–6	6–4
1919	C. B. Neely/K. Vorhees	C. Gould/Mrs H. Peters	6–4	6–2	
1920	F. Ballin/E. Tennant	B. Esch/C. Gould	6–3	6–2	
1921	Mrs B. E. Cole/Mrs F. Godfrey	L. Bancroft/Mrs E. V. Lynch	6–3	8–6	
1922	L. Bancroft/Mrs F. Godfrey	Mrs H. Bickle/H. Hooker	3–6	7–5	6–1
1923	Mrs R. Leqchman/E. Sigourney	M. MacDonald/L. Scharman	6–1	6–0	
1924–39	*Not held*				
1940	M. Arnold/A. Marble	H. I. Bernard/G. W. Wheeler	7–5	6–1	
1941	B. Bradley/Mrs J. S. Gallagher	D. J. Hart/N. Sheer	4–6	8–6	6–4
1942	*Not held*				
1943	P. M. Betz/N. Corbett	M. Hernando/M. Siriwaitis	6–3	6–3	
1944	P. M. Betz/D. J. Hart	M. Warnold/C. Wolf	8–6	6–3	
1945	P. M. Betz/D. J. Hart	M. Arnold/Mrs S. P. Cooke	3–6	6–4	9–7
1946	S. J. Fry/Mrs M. A. Prentiss	Mrs V. W. Kovacs/B. Scofield	6–4	6–1	
1947	G. Moran/Mrs M. A. Prentiss	S. J. Fry/B. Krase	6–4	6–4	
1948–49	*Not held*				
1950	S. J. Fry/D. J. Hart	B. Baker/Mrs M. Rurac	2–6	6–4	6–4
1951	Mrs M. Rurac/Mrs P. C. Todd	D. Head/A. Kanter	3–6	6–2	6–2
1952	Mrs L. Davidson/D. Popple	A. Kanter/J. Merciadis	7–5	6–4	
1953	A. Kanter/Mrs T. D. Long	M. Connolly/J. Sampson	6–3	6–0	
1954	M. Connolly/D. J. Hart	A. Gibson/E. Norton	6–3	6–2	
1955	J. Hopps/Mrs D. H. Knode	B. Breit/P. Shaffer	6–2	3–6	6–3
1956	S. J. Fry/Mrs D. H. Knode	M. Hernandez/Y. Ramirez	6–2	6–1	
1957	A. Gibson/D. R. Hard	J. Arth/K. Fageros	6–3	6–0	
1958	K. Fageros/Mrs D. H. Knode	M. Hernandez/M. Montgomery	2–6	6–5 ret'd	
1959	S. Reynolds/R. Schuurman	J. Arth/J. Hopps	4–6	6–0	6–3
1960	D. R. Hard/B. J. Moffitt	J. Bricka/C. Hanks	6–3	6–4	
1961	J. Bricka/C. Hanks	D. Floyd/B. Gunderson	6–3	6–2	
1962	S. Behlmar/D. R. Hard	C. Hanks/M. Montgomery	6–2	6–3	
1963	M. E. Bueno/D. R. Hard	C. Caldwell/B. J. Moffitt	6–2	6–2	
1964	Mrs C. Graebner/N. Richey	J. Danilovich/S. Shrader	6–1	6–4	
1965	Mrs C. Graebner/N. Richey	R. Casals/J. M. Heldman	7–5	6–4	
1966	K. Krantzcke/K. Melville	E. Emanuel/M. Godwin	1–6	6–4	6–4
1967	K. Krantzcke/K. Melville	R. Casals/Mrs L. W. King	6–4	6–1	
1968	N. Richey/V. Ziegenfuss	J. Bartkowicz/S. De Fina	6–2	6–0	
1969	Mrs W. W. Bowrey/Mrs G. Chanfreau	E. Burrer/L. Tuero	6–0	10–8	
1970	P. Austin/M. Cooper	M. Gengler/A. Lebedeff	2–6	6–3	7–5
1971	Mrs D. E. Dalton/Mrs L. W. King	J. M. Heldman/L. Tuero	6–1	6–2	
1972	E. F. Goolagong/L. Hunt	Mrs B. M. Court/P. Teeguarden	6–2	6–1	
1973	P. S. A. Hogan/S. A. Walsh	F. Bonicelli/I. Fernandez	6–4	6–4	
1974	Mrs G. Chanfreau/J. M. Heldman	C. M./J. C. Evert	6–3	6–1	
1975	F. Bonicelli/I. Fernandez	Mrs G. Chanfreau/J. M. Heldman	3–6	7–5	6–3
1976	L. Boshoff/I. Kloss	L. DuPont/W. M. Turnbull	6–2	6–3	
1977	L. Boshoff/I. Kloss	M. Carillo/W. Overton	5–7	7–5	6–3
1978	H. Anliot/Mrs H. Sparre-Viragh	B. Hallquist/S. McInerney	6–3	6–1	
1979	K. Jordan/A. E. Smith	P. Johnson/P. Smith	6–1	6–0	
1980	A. E. Smith/P. Smith	V. Ruzici/R. Tomanova	6–4	3–6	6–4
1981	J. Russell/V. Ruzici	S. Barker/P. Smith	6–2	6–2	
1982	I. Madruga Osses/C. Tanvier	J. Russell/V. Ruzici	7–5	7–6	
1983	K. Horvath/V. Ruzici	G. Fernandez/B. Herr	4–6	7–6	6–2
1984	B. Mould/P. Smith	E. Burgin/J. Russell	6–2	7–5	
1985	K. /M. Maleeva	P. Barg /P. Smith	2–6	6–3	6–4

MIXED DOUBLES

This event was staged intermittently

	CHAMPIONS	RUNNERS-UP	SCORE		
1912	F. Harris/Miss M. Sutton	R. N. Williams/Miss M. K. Browne	6–3	2–6	6–2
1915	H. Johnson/Mrs G. W. Wightman	P. D. Siverd/Miss C. Cassel	6–2	6–0	
1916	G. Church/Miss M. Bjurdstedt	C. Doyle/Mrs H. Bickle	6–1	6–2	
1917*	H. Cordes/Miss R. Sanders	C. S. Garland/Miss L. Hofer	6–1	6–2	
1923	A. J. Castle/Miss M. MacDonald	A. Misner/Miss E. Sigourney	6–1	7–5	
1945	E. Cooke/Mrs J. P. Cooke	W. F. Talbert/Miss P. M. Betz	7–5	4–6	6–3

ITALIAN CHAMPIONSHIPS

Staged in Milan 1930 to 1934. Moved to the Foro Italico in Rome in 1935. Not held 1936 to 1949 because of the Abyssinia War and World War II. In 1961 the tournament was staged in Turin. Men's and women's events were held at different dates in 1979. In 1980 the women's events moved to Perugia.

MEN'S SINGLES

	CHAMPION	RUNNER-UP	SCORE			
1930	W. T. Tilden	H. L. de Morpurgo	6–1	6–1	6–2	
1931	G. P. Hughes	H. Cochet	6–4	6–3	6–2	
1932	A. Merlin	G. P. Hughes	6–1	5–7	6–0	8–6
1933	E. Sertorio	A. Martin Legeay	6–3	6–1	6–3	
1934	G. Palmieri	G. de Stefani	6–3	6–0	7–5	
1935	W. Hines	G. Palmieri	6–3	10–8	9–7	
1936–49	*Not held*					
1950	J. Drobny	W. F. Talbert	6–4	6–3	7–9	6–2
1951	J. Drobny	G. Cucelli	6–3	10–8	6–1	
1952	F. A. Sedgman	J. Drobny	7–5	6–3	1–6	6–4
1953	J. Drobny	L. A. Hoad	6–2	6–1	6–2	
1954	J. E. Patty	E. Morea	11–9	6–4	6–4	
1955	F. Gardini	G. Merlo	6–1	1–6	3–6	5–6 ret'd
1956	L. A. Hoad	S. Davidson	7–5	6–2	6–0	
1957	N. Pietrangeli	G. Merlo	8–6	6–2	6–4	
1958	M. G. Rose	N. Pietrangeli	5–7	8–6	6–4	1–6	6–2
1959	L. Ayala	N. A. Fraser	6–3	1–6	6–3	6–3
1960	B. MacKay	L. Ayala	7–5	7–5	0–6	0–6	6–1
1961	N. Pietrangeli	R. G. Laver	6–8	6–1	6–1	6–2
1962	R. G. Laver	R. S. Emerson	6–1	1–6	3–6	6–3	6–1
1963	M. F. Mulligan	B. Jovanovic	6–2	4–6	6–3	8–6
1964	J. E. Lundquist	F. S. Stolle	1–6	7–5	6–3	6–1
1965	M. F. Mulligan	M. Santana	1–6	6–4	6–3	6–1
1966	A. D. Roche	N. Pietrangeli	11–9	6–1	6–2	
1967	M. F. Mulligan	A. D. Roche	6–3	0–6	6–4	6–1
1968	T. S. Okker	R. A. J. Hewitt	10–8	6–8	6–1	1–6	6–0
1969	J. D. Newcombe	A. D. Roche	6–3	4–6	6–2	5–7	6–3
1970	I. Nastase	J. Kodes	6–3	1–6	6–3	8–6
1971	R. G. Laver	J. Kodes	7–5	6–3	6–3	
1972	M. Orantes	J. Kodes	4–6	6–1	7–5	6–2
1973	I. Nastase	M. Orantes	6–1	6–1	6–1	
1974	B. Borg	I. Nastase	6–3	6–4	6–2	
1975	R. Ramirez	M. Orantes	7–6	7–5	7–5	
1976	A. Panatta	G. Vilas	2–6	7–6	6–2	7–6
1977	V. Gerulaitis	A. Zugarelli	6–2	7–6	3–6	7–6
1978	B. Borg	A. Panatta	1–6	6–3	6–1	4–6	6–3
1979	V. Gerulaitis	E. Dibbs	6–7	7–6	6–7	6–4	6–2
1980	G. Vilas	Y. Noah	6–0	6–4	6–4	
1981	J. L. Clerc	V. Pecci	6–3	6–4	6–0	
1982	A. Gomez	E. Teltscher	6–2	6–3	6–2	
1983	J. Arias	J. Higueras	6–2	6–7	6–1	6–4
1984	A. Gomez	A. Krickstein	2–6	6–1	6–2	6–2
1985	Y. Noah	M. Mecir	6–3	3–6	6–2	7–6

WOMEN'S SINGLES

	CHAMPION	RUNNER-UP	SCORE		
1930	Miss E. de Alvarez	Miss L. Valerio	3–6	8–6	6–0
1931	Mrs L. Valerio	Mrs D. Andrus	2–6	6–2	6–2
1932	Miss I. Adamoff	Miss L. Valerio	6–4	7–5	
1933	Miss E. Ryan	Miss I. Adamoff	6–1	6–1	
1934	Miss H. Jacobs	Miss L. Valerio	6–3	6–0	
1935	Miss H. Sperling	Miss L. Valerio	6–4	6–1	
1936–49	*Not held*				
1950	Mrs A. Bossi	Miss P. J. Curry	6–4	6–4	
1951	Miss D. J. Hart	Miss S. J. Fry	6–3	8–6	
1952	Miss S. Partridge	Miss M. P. Harrison	6–3	7–5	
1953	Miss D. J. Hart	Miss M. Connolly	4–6	9–7	6–3

1954	Miss M. Connolly	Miss P. E. Ward	6–3	6–0		
1955	Miss P. E. Ward	Miss E. Vollmer	6–4	6–3		
1956	Miss A. Gibson	Mrs S. Kormoczy	6–3	7–5		
1957	Miss S. J. Bloomer	Mrs D. P. Knode	1–6	9–7	6–2	
1958	Miss M. E. Bueno	Miss L. Coghlan	3–6	6–3	6–3	
1959	Miss C. C. Truman	Miss S. Reynolds	6–0	6–1		
1960	Mrs S. Kormoczy	Miss A. S. Haydon	6–4	4–6	6–1	
1961	Miss M. E. Bueno	Miss L. R. Turner	6–4	6–4		
1962	Miss M. Smith	Miss M. E. Bueno	8–6	5–7	6–4	
1963	Miss M. Smith	Miss L. R. Turner	6–3	6–4		
1964	Miss M. Smith	Miss L. R. Turner	6–1	6–1		
1965	Miss M. E. Bueno	Miss N. Richey	6–1	1–6	6–3	
1966	Mrs P. F. Jones	Miss A. Van Zyl	8–6	6–1		
1967	Miss L. R. Turner	Miss M. E. Bueno	6–3	6–3		
1968	Mrs W. W. Bowrey	Mrs B. M. Court	2–6	6–2	6–3	
1969	Miss J. M. Heldman	Miss K. Melville	7–5	6–4		
1970	Mrs L. W. King	Miss J. M. Heldman	6–1	6–3		
1971	Miss S. V. Wade	Mrs H. Masthoff	6–4	6–4		
1972	Miss L. Tuero	Mrs O. Morozova	6–4	6–3		
1973	Miss E. F. Goolagong	Miss C. M. Evert	7–6	6–0		
1974	Miss C. M. Evert	Miss M. Navratilova	6–3	6–3		
1975	Miss C. M. Evert	Miss M. Navratilova	6–1	6–0		
1976	Miss M. Jausovec	Miss L. Hunt	6–1	6–3		
1977	Miss J. Newberry	Miss R. Tomanova	6–3	7–6		
1978	Miss R. Marsikova	Miss V. Ruzici	7–5	7–5		
1979	Miss T. A. Austin	Miss S. Hanika	6–4	1–6	6–3	
1980	Mrs J. M. Lloyd	Miss V. Ruzici	5–7	6–2	6–2	
1981	Mrs J. M. Lloyd	Miss V. Ruzici	6–1	6–2		
1982	Mrs J. M. Lloyd	Miss H. Mandlikova	6–0	6–3		
1983	Miss A. Temesvari	Miss B. Gadusek	6–1	6–0		
1984	Miss M. Maleeva	Mrs J. M. Lloyd	6–3	6–3		
1985	Miss R. Reggi	Miss V. Nelson	6–4	6–4		

MEN'S DOUBLES

CHAMPIONS	RUNNERS-UP	SCORE				
1930 W. F. Coen/W. T. Tilden	H. L. de Morpurgo/P. Gaslini	6–0	6–3	6–3		
1931 A. del Bono/G. P. Hughes	H. Cochet/A. Merlin	3–6	8–6	4–6	6–4	6–3
1932 G. P. Hughes/G. de Stafani	J. Bonte/A. Merlin	6–2	6–2	6–4		
1933 J. Lesuer/A. M. Legeay	G. Palmieri/E. Sertorio	6–2	6–4	6–2		
1934 G. Palmieri/G. L. Rogers	G. P. Hughes/G. de Stefani	3–6	6–4	9–7	0–6	6–2
1935 J. H. Crawford/V. B. McGrath	J. Borotra/J. Brugnon	4–6	4–6	6–4	6–2	6–2
1936–49 Not held						
1950 W. F. Talbert/M. A. Trabert	J. E. Patty/O. W. Sidwell	6–3	6–1	4–6 ret'd		
1951 J. Drobny/R. Savitt	G. Cucelli/M. Del Bello	6–2	7–9	6–1	6–3	
1952 J. Drobny/F. A. Sedgman	G. Cucelli/M. Del Bello	3–6	7–5	3–6	6–3	6–2
1953 L. A. Hoad/K. R. Rosewall	J. Drobny/J. E. Patty	6–2	6–4	6–2		
1954 J. Drobny/E. Morea	M. A. Trabert/E. V. Seixas	6–4	0–6	3–6	6–3	6–4
1955 A. Larsen/E. Morea	N. Pietrangeli/O. Sirola	6–1	6–4	4–6	7–5	
1956 J. Drobny/L. A. Hoad	N. Pietrangeli/O. Sirola	11–9	6–2	6–3		
1957 N. A. Fraser/L. A. Hoad	N. Pietrangeli/O. Sirola	6–1	6–8	6–0	6–2	
1958 A. Jancso/K. Nielsen	L. Ayala/D. Candy	8–10	6–3	6–2	1–6	9–7
1959 R. S. Emerson/N. A. Fraser	N. Pietrangeli/O. Sirola	8–6	6–4	6–4		
1960 N. Pietrangeli/O. Sirola	R. S. Emerson/N. A. Fraser	3–6	7–5	2–6	11–11 ret'd	
1961 R. S. Emerson/N. A. Fraser	N. Pietrangeli/O. Sirola	6–2	6–4	11–9		
1962 N. A. Fraser/R. G. Laver	K. N. Fletcher/J. D. Newcombe	11–9	6–2	6–4		
1963 R. A. J. Hewitt/F. S. Stolle	N. Pietrangeli/O. Sirola	6–3	6–3	6–1		
1964 R. A. J. Hewitt/F. S. Stolle	A. D. Roche/J. D. Newcombe	7–5	6–3	3–6	7–5	
1965 A. D. Roche/J. D. Newcombe	C. Barnes/T. Koch	1–6	6–4	2–6	12–10 ret'd	
1966 R. S. Emerson/F. S. Stolle	N. Pietrangeli/E. C. Drysdale	6–4	12–10	6–3		
1967 R. A. J. Hewitt/F. D. McMillan	W. W. Bowrey/O. K. Davidson	6–3	2–6	6–3	9–7	
1968 T. S. Okker/M. C. Riessen	A. Stone/N. Kalogeropoulos	6–3	6–4	6–2		
1969 A. D. Roche/J. D. Newcombe	T. S. Okker/M. C. Riessen	6–4	1–6 ret'd			
1970 I. Nastase/I. Tiriac	W. W. Bowrey/O. K. Davidson	0–6	10–8	6–3	6–8	6–1
1971 A. D. Roche/J. D. Newcombe	A. Gimeno/R. Taylor	6–4	6–4			
1972 I. Nastase/I. Tiriac	L. A. Hoad/F. D. McMillan	3–6	3–6	6–4	6–3	5–3 ret'd
1973 J. D. Newcombe/T. S. Okker	R. Case/G. Masters	6–3	6–2	6–4		
1974 B. E. Gottfried/R. Ramirez	J. Gisbert/I. Nastase	6–3	6–2	6–3		
1975 B. E. Gottfried/R. Ramirez	J. S. Connors/I. Nastase	6–4	7–6	2–6	6–1	

1976	B. E. Gottfried/R. Ramirez	G. Masters/J. D. Newcombe	7–6	5–7	6–3	3–6	6–3
1977	B. E. Gottfried/R. Ramirez	F. McNair/S. E. Stewart	7–6	6–7	7–5		
1978	V. Pecci/B. Prajoux	J. Kodes/T. Smid	6–7	7–6	6–1		
1979	P. Fleming/T. Smid	J. L. Clerc/I. Nastase	4–6	6–1	7–5		
1980	M. R. Edmondson/K. Warwick	B. Taroczy/E. Teltscher	7–6	7–6			
1981	H. Gildemeister/A. Gomez	B. Manson/T. Smid	7–5	6–2			
1982	H. Gunthardt/B. Taroczy	W. Fibak/J. Fitzgerald	6–4	4–6	6–3		
1983	F. Gonzalez/V. Pecci	J. Gunnarsson/M. Leach	6–2	6–7	6–4		
1984	K. Flach/R. Seguso	J. G. Alexander/M. Leach	3–6	6–3	6–4		
1985	A. Jarryd/M. Wilander	K. Flach/R. Seguso	4–6	6–3	6–2		

WOMEN'S DOUBLES

	CHAMPIONS	RUNNERS-UP	SCORE		
1930	E. de Alvarez/L. Valerio	C. Anet/M. Neufeld	7–5	5–7	7–5
1931	A. Luzzatti/J. Prouse	Mrs D. Andrus Burke/L. Valerio	6–3	1–6	6–3
1932	C. Rosambert/L. Payot	Mrs D. Andrus Burke/L. Valerio	7–5	6–3	
1933	I. Adamoff/Mrs D. Andrus Burke	E. Ryan/L. Valerio	6–3	1–6	6–4
1934	H. H. Jacobs/E. Ryan	I. Adamoff/Mrs D. Andrus Burke	7–5	9–7	
1935	E. M. Dearman/N. Lyle	C. Aussem/E. Ryan	6–2	6–4	
1936–49	*Not held*				
1950	J. Quertier/J. Walker-Smith	B. E. Hilton/K. L. A. Tuckey	1–6	6–3	6–2
1951	S. J. Fry/D. J. Hart	L. Brough/T. D. Long	6–1	7–5	
1952	N. Hopman/Mrs T. D. Long	N. Migliori/V. Tonoli	6–2	6–8	6–1
1953	M. Connolly/J. Sampson	S. J. Fry/D. J. Hart	6–8	6–4	6–4
1954	P. E. Ward/E. M. Watson	N. Adamson/G. Bucaille	3–6	6–3	6–4
1955	C. Mercellis/P. E. Ward	M. Muller/B. Penrose	6–4	10–8	
1956	M. Hawton/Mrs T. D. Long	A. Buxton/D. R. Hard	6–4	6–8	9–7
1957	M. Hawton/Mrs T. D. Long	Y. Ramirez/R. M. Reyes	6–1	6–1	
1958	S. J. Bloomer/C. Truman	M. Hawton/Mrs T. D. Long	6–3	6–2	
1959	Y. Ramirez/R. M. Reyes	M. E. Bueno/J. Hopps	4–6	6–4	6–4
1960	M. Hellyer/Y. Ramirez	S. J. Brasher/A. Haydon	6–4	6–4	
1961	J. Lehane/L. R. Turner	M. Reitano/M. Smith	2–6	6–1	6–1
1962	M. E. Bueno/D. R. Hard	S. Lazzarino/L. Pericoli	6–4	6–4	
1963	R. Ebbern/M. Smith	S. Lazzarino/L. Pericoli	6–2	6–3	
1964	L. R. Turner/M. Smith	S. Lazzarino/L. Pericoli	6–1	6–2	
1965	M. Schacht/A. Van Zyl	S. Lazzarino/L. Pericoli	2–6	6–2	12–10
1966	N. Baylon/A. Van Zyl	Mrs P. F. Jones/E. Starkie	6–3	1–6	6–2
1967	R. Casals/L. R. Turner	S. Lazzarino/L. Pericoli	7–5	7–5	
1968	Mrs B. M. Court/S. V. Wade	A. Van Zyl/P. Walkden	6–2	7–5	
1969	F. Durr/Mrs P. F. Jones	R. Casals/Mrs L. W. King	6–3	3–6	6–2
1970	R. Casals/L. W. King	F. Durr/S. V. Wade	6–2	3–6	9–7
1971	Mrs H. Masthoff/S. V. Wade	Mrs L. Bowrey/H. Gourlay	5–7	6–2	6–2
1972	L. Hunt/Mrs O. Morozova	Mrs G. Chanfreau/R. Vido	6–3	6–4	
1973	Mrs O. Morozova/S. V. Wade	M. Navratilova/R. Tomanova	3–6	6–2	7–5
1974	C. M. Evert/Mrs O. Morozova	H. Masthoff/H. Orth	w.o.		
1975	C. M. Evert/M. Navratilova	S. Barker/G. Coles	6–1	6–2	
1976	L. Boshoff/I. Kloss	M. Simionescu/V. Ruzici	6–1	6–2	
1977	B. Cuypers/M. Kruger	B. Bruning/S. A. Walsh	3–6	7–5	6–2
1978	M. Jausovec/V. Ruzici	F. Mihai/B. Nagelsen	6–2	2–6	7–5
1979	B. Stove/W. M. Turnbull	Mrs E. Crawley/G. E. Reid	6–3	6–4	
1980	H. Mandlikova/R. Tomanova	I. Madruga/I. Villagran	6–4	6–4	
1981	C. Reynolds/P. Smith	Mrs J. M. Lloyd/V. Ruzici	7–5	6–1	
1982	K. Horvath/Y. Vermaak	Mrs L. W. King/I. Kloss	2–6	6–4	7–6
1983	V. Ruzici/S. V. Wade	I. Madruga Osses/C. Tanvier	6–3	2–6	6–1
1984	I. Budarova/M. Skuherska	K. Horvath/V. Ruzici	7–6	1–6	6–4
1985	A. M. Cecchini/R. Reggi	P. Murgo/B. Romano	1–6	6–4	6–3

MIXED DOUBLES

	CHAMPIONS	RUNNERS-UP	SCORE		
1930	H. L. de Morpurgo/Miss E. de Alvarez	G. P. Hughes/Miss L. Valerio	4–6	6–4	6–2
1931	G. P. Hughes/Miss L. Valerio	A. del Bono/Mrs D. Andrus Burke	6–0	6–1	
1932	J. Bonte/Miss L. Payot	A. del Bono/Mrs D. Andrus Burke	6–1	6–2	
1933	A. M. Legeay/Mrs D. Andrus Burke	E. Gabrowitz/Miss Y. Orlandini	6–4	6–3	
1934	H. M. Culley/Miss E. Ryan	F. Puncec/Miss R. Couquerque	6–1	6–3	
1935	H. C. Hopman/Miss J. Jedrzejowska	G. P. Hughes/Miss E. M. Dearman	6–3	1–6	6–3
1936–49	*Not held*				

1950	A. K. Quist/Miss G. Moran div'd with G. Cucelli/Miss A. Bossi	6–3 1–1 unf.
1951	F. Ampon/Miss S. J. Fry	L. Bergelin/Miss D. J. Hart	8–6 3–6 6–4
1952	K. Nielsen/Miss A. McGuire	E. Migone/Mrs M. J. de Riba	4–6 6–3 6–3
1953	E. V. Seixas/Miss D. J. Hart	M. G. Rose/Miss M. Connolly	6–4 6–4
1954	E. V. Seixas/Miss M. Connolly div'd with M. A. Trabert/Miss B. M. Kimbrell	3–6 11–9 3–3 unf.
1955	E. Morea/Miss P. E. Ward div'd with M. G. Rose/Miss B. Penrose	
1956	L. Ayala/Mrs T. D. Long	G. Fachini/Miss S. J. Bloomer	6–4 6–3
1957	L. Ayala/Mrs T. D. Long	R. N. Howe/Miss S. J. Bloomer	6–1 6–1
1958	G. Fachini/Miss S. J. Bloomer	L. Ayala/Mrs T. D. Long	4–6 6–2 9–7
1959	F. Contreras/Miss R. M. Reyes	W. A. Knight/Miss Y. Ramirez	9–7 6–1
1960	Not held	
1961	R. S. Emerson/Miss M. Smith	R. A. J. Hewitt/Miss J. Lehane	6–1 6–1
1962	F. S. Stolle/Miss L. R. Turner	S. Davidson/Miss M. Schacht	6–4 6–1
1963	Not held	
1964	J. D. Newcombe/Miss M. Smith	T. Koch/Miss M. E. Bueno	3–6 7–5 6–2
1965	J. E. Mandarino/Miss M. Coronado	V. Zarazua/Miss E. Subirats	6–1 6–1
1966	Not held	
1967	W. W. Bowrey/Miss L. R. Turner	F. D. McMillan/Miss F. Durr	6–2 7–5
1968	M. C. Riessen/Mrs B. M. Court	T. S. Okker/Miss S. V. Wade	8–6 6–3
1969–85	Not held	

SOUTH AFRICAN CHAMPIONSHIPS

MEN'S SINGLES

	CHAMPION	RUNNER-UP	SCORE
1891	L. A. Richardson	L. Winslow	Not available
1892	L. A. Richardson	R. Davis	Not available
1893	W. L. Edwards	L. A. Richardson	Not available
1894	L. Giddy	W. T. Edmonds	Not available
1895	L. Giddy	S. Bayly	Not available
1896	L. Giddy	H. R. Eaton	Not available
1897	L. Giddy	Not available	
1898	L. Giddy	Not available	
1899	L. G. Heard	Not available	
1900–02	Not held		
1903	R. W. G. Clarke	Not available	
1904	P. W. Sherwell	Not available	
1905	H. A. Kitson	Not available	
1906	J. Richardson	Not available	
1907	A. Rowan	Not available	
1908	H. A. Kitson	V. R. Gauntlett	6–2 5–7 6–2 7–9 6–2
1909	R. F. Doherty	Not available	
1910	A. F. Wilding	Not available	
1911	H. A. Kitson	Father Kelly	6–4 6–3 6–2
1912	G. H. Dodd	Not available	
1913	H. A. Kitson	Not available	
1914	C. L. Winslow	Not available	
1915–19	Not held		
1920	B. I. C. Norton	Not available	
1921	L. B. Raymond	M. Davies	6–3 6–0 6–1
1922	L. B. Raymond	Not available	
1923	L. B. Raymond	J. Condon	6–3 7–5 4–6 6–2
1924	L. B. Raymond	Not available	
1925	I. J. Richardson	Not available	
1926	J. Condon	C. R. Blackbeard	6–0 6–3 6–2
1927	G. Eaglestone	Not available	
1928	G. Eaglestone	Not available	
1929	C. J. J. Robbins	Not available	
1930	L. B. Raymond	C. J. J. Robbins	6–2 5–7 6–3 6–4
1931	L. B. Raymond	M. Bertrams	6–3 4–6 6–4 6–2
1932	M. Bertram	C. J. J. Robbins	2–6 9–7 9–7 6–1
1933	C. J. J. Robbins	V. G. Kirby	6–1 1–6 4–6 9–7 6–4
1934	N. G. Farquharson	R. Malcolm	4–6 6–2 6–3 14–12
1935	N. G. Farquharson	V. G. Kirby	6–0 6–4 6–1
1936	N. G. Farquharson	M. Bertram	6–4 6–4 1–6 6–3
1937	J. Pallada	V. G. Kirby	6–2 0–6 4–6 6–1 6–0
1938	N. G. Farquharson	V. G. Kirby	4–6 4–6 6–3 7–5 6–0
1939	E. W. Sturgess	E. E. Fannin	6–2 9–7 3–6 6–8 7–5

1940	E. W. Sturgess	R. H. M. Bertram	6–2	2–6	6–0	6–2
1941–45	*Not held*					
1946	E. W. Sturgess	N. G. Farquharson	6–0	6–2	6–3	
1947	E. Fannin	E. W. Sturgess	6–1	6–2	1–6	0–6 6–4
1948	E. W. Sturgess	A. J. Mottram	6–3	6–4	6–8	6–1
1949	E. W. Sturgess	G. E. Brown	4–6	6–4	6–2	7–5
1950	E. W. Sturgess	A. Larsen	6–1	6–1	3–6	6–1
1951	E. W. Sturgess	S. Levy	6–3	6–2	7–5	
1952	E. W. Sturgess	S. Levy	6–2	6–2	6–3	
1953	E. W. Sturgess	W. R. Seymour	6–1	6–3	6–3	
1954	E. W. Sturgess	J. Drobny	5–7	6–4	6–3	8–6
1955	W. R. Seymour	G. L. Forbes	1–6	9–7	6–1	8–6
1956	I. C. Vermaak	T. Johansson	6–2	4–6	3–6	6–3 8–6
1957	E. W. Sturgess	G. Koening	9–7	6–3	6–1	
1958	U. Schmidt	T. Ulrich	1–6	12–10	6–2	6–8 6–2
1959	G. L. Forbes	I. C. Vermaak	6–3	6–4	6–2	
1960	E. Buchholz	J. Frost	6–1	7–5	6–3	
1961	G. L. Forbes	J. C. Mayers	8–6	3–6	4–6	6–4 6–4
1962	R. Mark	G. L. Forbes	6–1	6–1	2–6	8–6
1963	W. P. Bungert	G. L. Forbes	6–4	6–4	8–6	
1964	A. A. Segal	G. L. Forbes	4–6	7–5	6–3	6–3
1965	E. C. Drysdale	J. C. Couder	1–6	6–3	6–4	1–6 6–3
1966	R. S. Emerson	R. A. J. Hewitt	6–3	2–6	3–6	6–4 7–5
1967	M. Santana	J. Leschly	2–6	6–2	4–6	6–3 6–4
1968	T. S. Okker	M. C. Riessen	12–10	6–1	6–4	
1969	R. G. Laver	T. S. Okker	6–3	10–8	6–3	
1970	R. G. Laver	F. D. McMillan	4–6	6–2	6–1	6–2
1971	K. R. Rosewall	F. S. Stolle	6–4	6–0	6–4	
1972	C. Richey	M. Orantes	6–4	7–5	3–6	6–4
1973	J. S. Connors	A. R. Ashe	6–4	7–6	6–3	
1974	J. S. Connors	A. R. Ashe	7–6	6–3	6–1	
1975	H. Solomon	B. E. Gottfried	6–2	6–4	5–7	6–1
1976	H. Solomon	B. E. Gottfried	6–2	6–7	6–3	6–4
1977	G. Vilas	C. J. Mottram	7–6	6–3	6–4	
1978	Tim Gullikson	H. Solomon	2–6	7–6	7–6	6–7 6–4
1979	A. Pattison	V. Pecci	2–6	6–3	6–2	6–3
1980	K. Warwick	F. Buehning	6–2	6–1	6–2	
1981	V. Gerulaitis	J. Borowiak	6–4	7–6	6–1	
1982	V. Gerulaitis	G. Vilas	7–6	6–2	4–6	6–3
1983	J. Kriek	C. Dowdeswell	6–4	4–6	1–6	7–5 6–3
1984	E. Teltscher	V. Gerulaitis	6–3	6–2	7–6	
1985	M. Anger	B. Gilbert	6–4	3–6	6–3	6–2

WOMEN'S SINGLES

	CHAMPION	RUNNER-UP	SCORE
1891	Miss H. Grant	Miss Blackburn	Not available
1892	Miss H. Grant	Mrs McLagon	Not available
1893	Miss H. Grant	Mrs McLagon	Not available
1894	Miss H. Grant	Miss B. Grant	Not available
1895	Miss R. Biddulph	Miss Fry	Not available
1896	Mrs H. Green	Miss L. Biddulph	Not available
1897	Miss N. Hickman	Not available	
1898	Miss N. Hickman	Not available	
1899	Miss N. Hickman	Not available	
1900–02	*Not held*		
1903	Miss F. Kuys	Not available	
1904	Mrs H. A. Kirby	Not available	
1905	Mrs H. A. Kirby	Not available	
1906	Mrs H. A. Kirby	Not available	
1907	Mrs H. A. Kirby	Not available	
1908	Miss M. Kelly	Mrs Gillmore	6–2 6–1
1909	Mrs G. Washington	Not available	
1910	Mrs H. A. Kirby	Not available	
1911	Mrs G. Washington	Miss M. Kelly	6–0 6–1
1912	Mrs H. A. Kirby	Not available	
1913	Miss M. Coles	Not available	
1914	Miss O. Mathias	Not available	
1915–19	*Not held*		
1920	Mrs C. L. Winslow	Not available	

1921	Miss N. Edwards	Mrs W. F. du Plessis	6–1	6–2	
1922	Mrs T. J. McJannett	Not available			
1923	Mrs C. K. Pitt	Mrs Moor	6–4	6–3	
1924	Mrs I. E. Peacock	Not available			
1925	Mrs I. E. Peacock	Not available			
1926	Mrs I. E. Peacock	Miss A. de Smit	6–2	6–1	
1927	Mrs T. J. McJannett	Not available			
1928	Miss E. L. Heine	Not available			
1929	Mrs T. J. McJannett	Not available			
1930	Miss R. D. Tapscott	Mrs V. Everett	7–5	6–2	
1931	Miss E. L. Heine	Miss W. Miller	6–3	6–3	
1932	Mrs E. Heine Miller	Mrs F. H. Lowe	6–0	6–3	
1933	Mrs C. J. J. Robbins	Mrs F. H. Lowe	6–4	3–6	6–1
1934	Mrs C. J. J. Robbins	Mrs F. H. Lowe	6–0	6–3	
1935	Mrs A. Allister	Mrs C. J. J. Robbins	6–4	6–3	
1936	Mrs E. Heine Miller	Mrs V. Everett	6–2	4–6	6–4
1937	Mrs E. Heine Miller	Mrs A. Neave	6–4	4–6	6–0
1938	Mrs C. J. J. Robbins	Miss O. Craze	6–4	6–4	
1939	Miss O. Craze	Miss S. Piercey	4–6	6–3	6–4
1940	Miss O. Craze	Miss S. Piercey	4–6	6–4	6–4
1941–45	*Not held*				
1946	Mrs M. Muller	Mrs O. Plessis	6–4	6–4	
1947	Mrs M. Muller	Mrs S. P. Summers	6–2	6–8	6–2
1948	Mrs S. P. Summers	Mrs M. Menzies	6–1	6–4	
1949	Mrs S. P. Summers	Mrs T. D. Long	6–1	6–1	
1950	Miss S. J. Fry	Miss D. J. Hart	4–6	7–5	6–3
1951	Mrs S. P. Summers	Mrs H. Redick-Smith	8–6	2–6	7–5
1952	Miss D. J. Hart	Mrs J. Whipplinger	6–1	7–5	
1953	Mrs H. Redick-Smith	Mrs J. Whipplinger	6–2	6–2	
1954	Mrs H. Redick-Smith	Miss G. Love	4–6	6–3	6–2
1955	Mrs H. Redick-Smith	Miss L. van der Westhuizen	6–4	6–3	
1956	Miss D. Kilian	Miss G. Love	4–6	7–5	6–4
1957	Mrs W. Brewer	Miss G. Love	8–10	6–2	6–3
1958	Miss B. Carr	Mrs A. A. Segal	3–6	7–5	6–4
1959	Miss S. Reynolds	Mrs B. Vukovich	6–0	8–6	
1960	Mrs B. Vukovich	Miss S. Reynolds	6–1	2–6	12–10
1961	Miss S. Reynolds	Miss L. Hutchings	6–4	7–5	
1962	Mrs A. A. Segal	Miss J. Forbes	6–1	7–5	
1963	Miss A. Van Zyl	Miss M. Hunt	6–4	2–6	6–3
1964	Miss D. R. Hard	Mrs P. F. Jones	6–3	7–5	
1965	Miss C. C. Truman	Miss A. Van Zyl	6–2	6–3	
1966	Mrs L. W. King	Miss M. Smith	6–3	6–2	
1967	Mrs L. W. King	Miss M. E. Bueno	7–5	5–7	6–2
1968	Mrs B. M. Court	Miss S. V. Wade	6–4	6–4	
1969	Mrs L. W. King	Miss N. Richey	6–3	6–4	
1970	Mrs B. M. Court	Mrs L. W. King	6–4	1–6	6–3
1971	Mrs B. M. Court	Miss E. F. Goolagong	6–3	6–1	
1972	Miss E. F. Goolagong	Miss S. V. Wade	4–6	6–3	6–0
1973	Miss C. M. Evert	Miss E. F. Goolagong	6–3	6–3	
1974	Miss K. Melville	Miss D. Fromholtz	6–3	7–5	
1975	Mrs A. du Plooy	Miss B. Cuypers	6–3	3–6	6–4
1976	Miss B. Cuypers	Miss L. DuPont	6–7	6–4	6–1
1977	Miss L. Boshoff	Miss B. Cuypers	6–1	6–4	
1978	Miss B. Cuypers	Miss L. Siegel	6–1	6–0	
1979	Miss B. Cuypers	Miss T. Harford	7–6	6–2	
1980	Miss L. J. Charles	Miss R. R. Uys	7–5	6–4	
1981	Miss K. Horvath	Miss K. Rinaldi	7–6	6–4	
1982–83	*Not held*				
1984	Mrs J. M. Lloyd	Miss A. Jaeger	6–3	6–0	
1985	*Not held*				

MEN'S DOUBLES

	CHAMPIONS	RUNNERS-UP	SCORE
1903	J. Orr/P. W. Sherwell	Not available	
1904	P. H. Hobbs/P. W. Sherwell	Not available	
1905	M. Hathorn/H. A. Kitson	Not available	
1906	D./S. Cockerell	Not available	
1907	A. Rowan/F. L. Scholtz	Not available	

Year	Champions	Runners-up	Score
1908	V. R. Gauntlett/H. A. Kitson	A. Rowan/F. L. Scholtz	6–2 6–2 7–5
1909	R. F. Doherty/G. W. Hillyard	Not available	
1910	V. R. Gauntlett/H. A. Kitson	Not available	
1911	F. E. Cochran/H. A. Kitson	E. Tapscott/J. Walscott	w.o.
1912	F. E. Cochran/C. N. Davis	Not available	
1913	F. E. Cochran/H. A. Kitson	Not available	
1914	F. E. Cochran/H. A. Kitson	Not available	
1915–19	*Not held*		
1920	B. I. C. Norton/L. B. Raymond	Not available	
1921	M. S. Davies/P. D. B. Spence	G. Eaglestone/A. Whiteley	Not available
1922	H. Hatton/W. F. Upton	Not available	
1923	C. R./D. Blackbeard	G. Eaglestone/C. H. Golborne	11–9 4–6 6–3 ret'd
1924	J. Condon/L. B. Raymond	Not available	
1925	M. S. Davies/I. J. Richardson	Not available	
1926	C. R. Blackbeard/C. L. Winslow	J. Condon/R. Le Suer	6–3 6–4 9–7
1927	F. H. Lowe/F. R. Shaw	Not available	
1928	G. Eaglestone/C. V. Kirby	Not available	
1929	R. W. Cornell/R. Klemp	Not available	
1930	J. Condon/V. G. Kirby	R. Malcolm/L. B. Raymond	7–5 6–1 10–8
1931	N. G. Farquharson/V. G. Kirby	F. H. Lowe/F. R. Shaw	4–6 8–6 2–6 6–0 6–1
1932	N. G. Farquharson/R. Malcolm	J. Condon/L. B. Raymond	6–4 1–6 6–1 6–4
1933	N. G. Farquharson/V. G. Kirby	J. Condon/R. Malcolm	5–7 6–2 6–4 12–10
1934	J. Condon/R. Malcolm	N. G. Farquharson/H. Silson	4–6 9–7 8–6
1935	N. Farquharson/R. Musgrove	M. Bertram/C. H. Robbs	6–4 7–5 4–6 6–3
1936	N. G. Farquharson/V. G. Kirby	M. Bertram/C. H. Robbs	6–3 8–6 6–2
1937	N. G. Farquharson/V. G. Kirby	J. Pallada/F. Puncec	1–6 2–6 6–4 7–5 6–4
1938	M. Bertram/E. Fannin	K. Hedley/F. H. Lowe	6–1 6–1 12–10
1939	N. G. Farquharson/V. G. Kirby	Not available	
1940	M. Bertram/E. Fannin	Not available	
1941–45	*Not held*		
1946	G. Ballance/E. W. Sturgess	N. G. Farquharson/V. G. Kirby	2–6 6–1 6–4 6–3
1947	E. Fannin/E. W. Sturgess	N. G. Farquharson/V. G. Kirby	6–3 10–8 10–8
1948	R. Fannin/E. W. Sturgess	N. Cockburn/S. Levy	6–3 6–2 7–5
1949	G. E. Brown/T. Warhurst	N. G. Cockburn/E. W. Sturgess	2–6 6–4 4–6 6–3 6–4
1950	A. Larsen/E. V. Seixas	P. Buckley/L. Norgarb	6–4 6–2 7–5
1951	L. Norgarb/E. W. Sturgess	N. Cockburn/S. Levy	9–7 6–3 3–6 6–4
1952	N. Cockburn/E. W. Sturgess	I. G. Ayre/D. Candy	6–4 8–6 3–6 6–3
1953	N. Cockburn/E. W. Sturgess	O. Williams/B. M. Woodroffe	9–7 8–6 6–4
1954	J. Drobny/J. E. Patty	A. Segal/E. W. Sturgess	6–2 6–3 4–6 3–6 6–3
1955	A. Segal/E. W. Sturgess	T. T. Fancutt/I. C. Vermaak	1–6 6–4 6–1 6–4
1956	S. Davidson/T. Johansson	E. W. Sturgess/B. M. Woodroffe	3–6 9–7 7–5 6–2
1957	N. A. Fraser/E. W. Sturgess	I. C. Vermaak/B. M. Woodroffe	6–4 6–2 2–6 5–7 6–3
1958	E. W. Sturgess/O. Williams	G. L. Forbes/A. Segal	6–4 5–7 8–6 7–5
1959	G. L. Forbes/A. Segal	A. Gaetner/B. M. Woodroffe	6–3 13–11 3–6 6–3
1960	G. L. Forbes/A. Segal	E. Buchholz/J. Frost	6–3 4–6 6–4 6–4
1961	G. L. Forbes/A. Segal	A. Gaetner/J. Mayers	14–12 6–3 12–10
1962	R. Mark/J. Mayers	G. Koenig/E. W. Sturgess	4–6 6–2 6–3 6–2
1963	G. L. Forbes/A. Segal	W. P. Bungert/W. Stuck	6–3 15–17 6–3 9–7
1964	K. Diepram/E. C. Drysdale	G. L. Forbes/A. Segal	6–3 6–4 6–4
1965	K. Diepram/F. D. McMillan	E. C. Drysdale/W. Stuck	10–8 6–4 1–6 6–2
1966	R. S. Emerson/F. S. Stolle	G. L. Forbes/A. Segal	6–3 3–6 6–3 7–5
1967	R. A. J. Hewitt/F. D. McMillan	W. W. Bowrey/O. K. Davidson	6–1 6–4 6–4
1968	T. S. Okker/M. C. Riessen	R. A. J. Hewitt/F. D. McMillan	6–2 6–3 3–6 4–6 6–3
1969	R. A. Gonzales/R. J. Moore	R. A. J. Hewitt/F. D. McMillan	6–3 4–6 6–1 6–3
1970	R. A. J. Hewitt/F. D. McMillan	E. C. Drysdale/R. Taylor	6–3 6–3 6–2
1971	K. R. Rosewall/F. S. Stolle	R. A. J. Hewitt/F. D. McMillan	5–7 6–2 6–1 6–2
1972	R. A. J. Hewitt/F. D. McMillan	G. Goven/R. J. Moore	6–2 6–2 6–4
1973	A. R. Ashe/T. S. Okker	L. A. Hoad/R. Maud	6–2 4–6 6–2 6–4
1974	R. A. J. Hewitt/F. D. McMillan	T. S. Okker/M. C. Riessen	7–6 6–4 6–3
1975	R. A. J. Hewitt/F. D. McMillan	K. Meiler/C. Pasarell	7–5 6–4
1976	B. E. Gottfried/S. E. Stewart	J. Gisbert/S. R. Smith	1–6 6–1 6–2 7–6
1977	R. C. Lutz/S. R. Smith	R. J. Moore/P. Fleming	6–3 7–5 6–7 7–6
1978	R. J. Moore/P. Fleming	R. A. J. Hewitt/F. D. McMillan	6–3 7–6
1979	R. A. J. Hewitt/F. D. McMillan	M. Cahill/C. J. Mottram	1–6 6–1 6–4
1980	R. C. Lutz/S. R. Smith	H. Gunthardt/P. McNamee	6–7 6–3 6–4
1981	T. Moor/J. Yuill	F. Buehning/R. Simpson	6–3 5–7 6–4 6–7 12–10
1982	B. E. Gottfried/F. D. McMillan	S. Glickstein/A. Pattison	6–2 6–2
1983	S. Meister/B. Teacher	A. Gomez/S. E. Stewart	6–7 7–6 6–2
1984	T. Delatte/F. Gonzalez	E. Teltscher/S. Meister	7–6 6–1
1985	C. Dowdeswell/C. Van Rensburg	A. Mansdorf/S. Perkis	3–6 7–6 6–4

WOMEN'S DOUBLES

	CHAMPIONS	RUNNERS-UP	SCORE
1905	Mrs Auret/Mrs H. A. Kirby	Not available	
1906	Mrs Stevenson/Mrs G. Washington	Not available	
1907	Mrs H. A. Kirby/A. Tudhope	Not available	
1908	Mrs J. Reid/A. Tudhope	Mrs Middleton/Mrs G. Washington	2–6 6–2 7–5
1909	M. Kelly/Mrs G. Washington	Not available	
1910	Mrs J. Reid/A. Tudhope	Not available	
1911	O. Mathias/Mrs G. Washington	M. Kelly/A. Pringle	4–6 6–2 6–1
1912	M. Coles/A. Tudhope	Not available	
1913	M. Coles/A. Tudhope	Not available	
1914	Mrs Botting/O. Mathias	Not available	
1915–19	*Not held*		
1920	N. Edwards/Mrs C. K. Pitt	Not available	
1921	E. Kellar/W. Vesfeld	Mrs Ellis/A. Gradwell	7–5 6–3
1922	Mrs H. A. Kirby/Mrs C. L. Winslow	Not available	
1923	Mrs T. J. McJannett/Mrs McArthur	Mrs Beck/Mrs W. F. du Plessis	4–6 6–2 6–2
1924	Mrs Moor/Mrs I. E. Peacock	Not available	
1925	A. Foote/Mrs I. E. Peacock	Not available	
1926	Mrs E. C. Hall/A. de Smit	Mrs F. H. Lowe/Mrs I. E. Peacock	6–2 6–0
1927	W. Miller/A. Williams	Not available	
1928	Mrs T. J. McJannett/A. de Smit	Not available	
1929	Mrs T. J. McJannett/Mrs Tanner	Not available	
1930	D. Cole/R. D. Tapscott	Mrs V. Everett/A. Hopkins	6–4 6–4
1931	D. Cole/Mrs E. L. Heine	Not available	
1932	F. H. Lowe/Mrs E. Heine Miller	Mrs V. Everett/A. de Smit	6–1 6–3
1933	Mrs E. C. Hall/D. Kitson	Not available	
1934	D. Kitson/A. de Smit	Mrs F. H. Lowe/K. Rodd	9–7 5–7 6–4
1935	Mrs A. Allister/D. Kitson	Mrs C. J. J. Robbins/Mrs F. H. Lowe	6–3 6–3
1936	E. M. Dearman/N. M. Lyle	R. M. Hardwick/F. James	6–3 6–4
1937	Mrs E. Heine Miller/M. Morphew	Mrs F. H. Lowe/S. Piercey	9–7 6–3
1938	Mrs E. Heine Miller/M. Morphew	O. Craze/S. Piercey	6–4 6–4
1939	Mrs E. Heine Miller/M. Morphew	Not available	
1940	O. Craze/S. Piercey	Not available	
1941–45	*Not held*		
1946	Mrs M. Muller/Mrs O. Plessis	J. Austin/B. Nichols	6–2 4–6 8–6
1947	Mrs E. Heine Miller/J. Scott	M. Morphew/Mrs O. Plessis	4–6 6–3 6–2
1948	Mrs B. E. Hilton/Mrs M. Menzies	Mrs M. Muller/Mrs S. P. Summers	6–1 6–3
1949	J. Fitch/Mrs T. D. Long	Mrs B. Bartlett/M. Morphew	6–0 6–4
1950	S. J. Fry/D. J. Hart	Mrs S. P. Summers/Mrs E. Watermeyer	6–3 0–6 6–2
1951	Mrs M. Muller/Mrs H. Redick-Smith	Mrs B. Bartlett/Mrs E. Watermeyer	6–4 6–2
1952	S. J. Fry/D. J. Hart	Mrs H. Redick-Smith/Mrs S. P. Summers	7–5 7–5
1953	Mrs H. Redick-Smith/Mrs S. P. Summers	Mrs T. Hale/Mrs R. Stevens	11–13 6–3 6–3
1954	Mrs T. Hale/Mrs R. Stevens	Mrs H. Redick-Smith/Mrs J. Wipplinger	6–2 3–6 9–7
1955	Mrs B. Bartlett/G. Love	D. Kilian/L. van der Westhuizen	6–4 6–2
1956	Mrs B. Bartlett/G. Love	D. Kilian/L. van der Westhuizen	6–3 6–8 8–6
1957	Mrs B. Bartlett/G. Love	Mrs T. Hale/Mrs T. T. Fancutt	6–2 6–4
1958	S. Reynolds/R. Schuurman	S. J. Bloomer/L. Brough	4–6 8–6 6–3
1959	Mrs T. Hale/Mrs D. Shaw	S. Reynolds/R. Schurman	6–3 6–4
1960	S. Reynolds/R. Schuurman	Mrs A. Segal/Mrs B. Vukovich	13–11 7–9 6–1
1961	S. Reynolds/R. Schuurman	J. Lehane/Mrs M. Reitano	6–1 6–1
1962	M. Hunt/A. Van Zyl	J. Forbes/Mrs G. L. Forbes	7–5 6–8 6–4
1963	M. Hunt/A. Van Zyl	A. Betlehem/Mrs B. Vukovich	6–2 9–7
1964	M. E. Bueno/D. R. Hard	M. Hunt/A. Van Zyl	6–4 6–8 6–0
1965	Mrs L. E. G. Price/C. C. Truman	Mrs A. Segal/A. Van Zyl	6–3 6–2
1966	M. Smith/A. Van Zyl	Mrs C. Graebner/Mrs L. W. King	6–4 6–4
1967	R. Casals/Mrs L. W. King	M. E. Bueno/J. A. M. Tegart	4–6 6–1 6–3
1968	Mrs A. Du Ploy/P. M. Walkden	Mrs B. M. Court/S. V. Wade	0–6 6–4 7–5
1969	F. Durr/Mrs P. F. Jones	N. Richey/S. V. Wade	6–2 3–6 6–4
1970	R. Casals/Mrs L. W. King	K. Krantzcke/K. Melville	6–2 6–2
1971	Mrs B. M. Court/E. F. Goolagong	B. Kirk/L. Rossouw	6–3 6–2
1972	E. F. Goolagong/H. Gourlay	W. M. Shaw/Mrs G. Williams	6–1 6–4
1973	L. Boshoff/I. Kloss	C. M. Evert/S. V. Wade	7–6 2–6 6–1

1974	I. Kloss/K. Melville	Mrs B. M. Court/D. Fromholtz	6–2 6–3
1975	D. Boshoff /I. Kloss	L. Du Pont /S. A. Walsh	4–6 6–3 6–3
1976	L. Du Pont /V. Ziegenfuss	Y. Vermaak/Mrs E.Vlotman	6–1 6–4
1977	L. Boshoff /I. Kloss	B. Cuypers/M. Kruger	6–1 6–4
1978	L. Charles /T. Harford	A, McDade /E. Vlatman	6–2 6–3
1979	L. J. Charles/T. Harford	F. Durr/M. Kruger	6–1 6–3
1980	S. Rollinson/J. Mundel	L. Gordon/N. Gregory	6–3 6–2
1981	B. Mould/R. Uys	I. Kloss/Y. Vermaak	6–4 1–6 6–3
1982	*Not held*		
1983	*Not held*		
1984	R. Fairbank /B. Mould	S. Collins /A. Leand	6–1 6–2
1985	*Not held*		

MIXED DOUBLES

	CHAMPIONS	RUNNERS-UP	SCORE
1903	V. M. Lumsden/Miss M. E. Lumsden	Not available	
1904	H. A. Kirby/Mrs H. A. Kirby	Not available	
1905	M. Hathorn/Mrs H. A. Kirby	Not available	
1906	H. A. Kitson/Mrs H. A. Kirby	Not available	
1907	H. A. Kitson/Mrs H. A. Kirby	Not available	
1908	V. R. Gauntlett/Mrs J. Reid	H. A. Kitson/Miss M. Kelly	7–5 6–2
1909	A. Rowan/Miss M. Kelly	Not available	
1910	H. A. Kitson/Mrs H. A. Kirby	Not available	
1911	H. A. Kitson/Miss O. Mathias	S. L. Taylor-Taswell/Miss Wells	6–2 6–4
1912	F. E. Cochran/Miss O. Mathias	Not available	
1913	F. E. Cochran/Mrs G. Washington	Not available	
1914	C. L. Winslow/Miss O. Mathias	Not available	
1915–19	*Not held*		
1920	C. L. Winslow/Mrs C. L. Winslow	Not available	
1921	L. B. Raymond/Miss N. Edwards	R. Le Suer/Miss W. Versfeld	6–1 6–1
1922	G. Eaglestone/Miss Parker	Not available	
1923	I. J. Richardson/Mrs Moor	R. Le Suer/Mrs Beck	6–8 6–1 6–3
1924	L. B. Raymond/Miss A. Foote	Not available	
1925	V. G. Kirby/Mrs I. E. Peacock	Not available	
1926	I. J. Richardson/Mrs V. Everett	J. Haywood/Mrs I. E. Peacock	6–4 6–2
1927	I. J. Richardson/Mrs V. Everett	Not available	
1928	G. Eaglestone/Miss A. de Smit	Not available	
1929	M. J. Connor/Miss Stone	Not available	
1930	N. G. Farquharson/Miss E. L. Heine	L. B. Raymond/Mrs V. Everett	0–6 6–2 6–2
1931	F. H. Lowe/Miss W. Miller	N. G. Farquharson/Miss E. L. Heine	6–4 6–2
1932	V. G. Kirby/Miss A. de Smit	G. Eaglestone/Mrs E. Heine Miller	8–6 7–9 6–3
1933	R. J. Malcolm/Miss D. Cole	F. H. Lowe/Mrs F. H. Lowe	3–6 7–5 6–3
1934	N. G. Farquharson/Miss A. de Smit	J. Condon/Mrs F. H. Lowe	6–1 2–6 6–1
1935	F. H. Lowe/Mrs F. H. Lowe	J. Hendrie/Miss K. Rodd	6–3 6–3
1936	N. G. Farquharson/Miss W. Miller	V. G. Kirby/Mrs A. Allister	6–3 6–3
1937	N. G. Farquharson/Miss W. Miller	V. G. Kirby/Mrs V. Everett	6–3 8–6
1938	N. G. Farquharson/Miss W. Miller	V. G. Kirby/Miss M. Morphew	7–9 8–6 6–3
1939	N. G. Farquharson/Miss W. Miller	Not available	
1940	E. W. Sturgess/Miss S. Piercey	Not available	
1941–45	*Not held*		
1946	E. W. Sturgess/Mrs S. P. Summers	N. G. Farquharson/Mrs E. Heine Miller	2–6 6–4 10–8
1947	E. W. Sturgess/Mrs S. P. Summers	E. Fanin/Mrs M. Muller	6–4 6–3
1948	E. W. Sturgess/Mrs S. P. Summers	N. G. Farquharson/Mrs E. Heine Miller	6–4 6–1
1949	G. E. Brown/Mrs J. Fitch	E. W. Sturgess/Mrs S. P. Summers	6–0 7–5
1950	E. V. Seixas/Miss D. J. Hart	E. W. Sturgess/Mrs S. P. Summers	6–3 4–6 6–3
1951	E. W. Sturgess/Mrs S. P. Summers	N. Cockburn/Miss B. Bartlett	6–4 6–3
1952	D. Candy/Mrs N. Bolton	B. M. Woodroffe/Mrs T. Hale	6–2 6–3
1953	E. W. Sturgess/Mrs S. P. Summers	B. M. Woodroffe/Mrs T. Hale	2–6 6–3 6–4
1954	W. R. Seymour/Mrs H. Redick-Smith	A. Segal/Mrs J. Wipplinger	w.o.
1955	W. R. Seymour/Mrs H. Redick-Smith	B. M. Woodroffe/D. Kilian	6–4 6–4
1956	J. Hurry/Miss G. Love	S. Davidson/Miss P. E. Ward	1–6 7–5 6–3
1957	G. L. Forbes/Miss J. Forbes	O. Williams/Miss S. Reynolds	10–8 6–3
1958	G. L. Forbes/Miss J. Forbes	B. M. Woodroffe/Mrs T. Hale	6–2 3–6 6–3
1959	G. L. Forbes/Miss J. Forbes	B. Farrer/Mrs B. Bartlett	6–4 7–5
1960	R. N. Howe/Mrs B. Vukovich	A. Gaetner/Miss S. Reynolds	6–3 6–3
1961	R. Weedon/Miss M. Hunt	A. Gaetner/Miss R. Schuurman	4–6 6–0 6–1
1962	N. Pietrangeli/Mrs L. E. G. Price	B. M. Woodroffe/Mrs T. Hale	6–3 6–3

1963	G. L. Forbes/Miss J. Forbes	D. Phillips/Miss I. Frohling	6–2	7–5	
1964	R. Mark/Miss D. R. Hard	F. D. McMillan/Miss M. Hunt	3–6	6–4	6–4
1965	F. D. McMillan/Mrs L. E. G. Price	D. Dell/Miss F. Durr	8–6	9–7	
1966	F. S. Stolle/Miss M. Smith	F. D. McMillan/Mrs L. W. King	6–4	5–7	6–4
1967	O. K. Davidson/Mrs L. W. King	K. N. Fletcher/Miss M. E. Bueno	6–1	6–3	
1968	M. C. Riessen/Miss P. M. Walkden	R. A. J. Hewitt/Mrs B. M. Court	6–8	6–4	6–4
1969	T. S. Okker/Mrs A. Du Ploy	R. R. Maud/Miss S. V. Wade	8–6	5–7	6–4
1970	M. C. Riessen/Mrs B. M. Court	F. D. McMillan/Miss P. M. Walkden	7–5	3–6	7–5
1971	F. S. Stolle/Mrs B. M. Court	R. O. Ruffels/Mrs P. M. Walkden	6–3	7–6	
1972	M. F. Mulligan/Miss S. V. Wade	F. D. McMillan/Mrs Q. Pretorius	6–0	4–6	6–4
1973	J. Fassbender/Miss E. F. Goolagong	B. Mitton/Miss I. Kloss	6–3	6–2	
1974	M. Riessen/Mrs B. M. Court	J. Fassbender/Miss I. Kloss	6–0	6–2	
1975	B. Bertram/Miss I. Kloss	S. Cornchon/Miss J. Russell	div'd		
1976	R. A. J. Hewitt/Miss B. Nagelsen	D. Joubert/Mrs A. Du Ploy	6–2	7–6	
1977	C. Dowdeswell/Miss L. Boshoff	S. E. Stewart/Miss I. Kloss	6–4	4–6	7–5
1978	B. Mitton/Miss B. Cuypers	D. Joubert/Mrs A. Du Plooy	6–3	6–2	
1979	S. Carnahan /Miss M. Depalmer	S. Van Der Merwe /Miss Y. Vermaak	div'd		
1980–85	*Not held*				

THE *DAVIS CUP*

The International Men's Team Championship of the World was initiated in 1900 when the British Isles, then comprising Great Britain and Ireland, challenged the United States for the trophy presented by Dwight F. Davis. The competition was enlarged in 1904 when Belgium and France took part. Each tie has comprised two players engaged in reverse singles plus a doubles match with the best of five sets throughout.

From 1900 to 1971 the Champion Nation stood out until challenged by the winner of a knock-out competition between the challenging nations and had the choice of venue. The format was changed in 1972 with all nations taking part in a knock-out event. The format was amended in 1981, when the competition became sponsored by NEC. The Champion Nation was the winner of the World Group of 16 nations. Other nations competed in four zonal groups, two European, an American and an Eastern Zone, with the four winners earning promotion to the World Group. The four bottom nations of the top group, as decided by a relegation round, fell back to the zonal competition.

Between 1900 and 1984 the total number of participating nations was 72, including Hawaii and Estonia which have ceased to exist as distinct tennis nations.

CHALLENGE ROUNDS (In playing order)

1900 USA d. British Isles 3–0, Boston: M. D. Whitman d. A. W. Gore 6–1 6–3 6–2; D. F. Davis d. E. D. Black 4–6 6–2 6–4 6–4; Davis/H. Ward d. Black/H. Roper Barrett 6–4 6–4 6–4; Davis div'd with Gore 9–7 9–9.
1901 *Not held*
1902 USA d. British Isles 3–2, Brooklyn, New York: W. A. Larned lost to R. F. Doherty 6–2 6–3 3–6 4–6 4–6; M. D. Whitman d. J. Pim 6–1 6–1 1–6 6–0; Larned d. Pim 6–3 6–2 6–3; Whitman d. R. F. Doherty 6–1 7–5 6–4; D. F. Davis/H. Ward lost to R. F./H. L. Doherty 6–3 8–10 3–6 4–6.
1903 British Isles d. USA 4–1, Boston: H. L. Doherty d. R. D. Wrenn 6–0 6–3 6–4; R. F. Doherty lost to W. A. Larned ret'd; R. F./H. L. Doherty d. R. D./G. L. Wrenn 7–5 9–7 2–6 6–3; H. L. Doherty d. Larned 6–3 6–8 6–0 2–6 7–5; R. F. Doherty d. R. D. Wrenn 6–4 3–6 6–3 6–8 6–4.
1904 British Isles d. Belgium 5–0, Wimbledon: H. L. Doherty d. P. de Borman 6–4 6–1 6–1; F. L. Riseley d. W. Lemaire 6–1 6–4 6–2; R. F./H. L. Doherty d. de Borman/Lemaire 6–0 6–1 6–3; H. L. Doherty w.o. Lemaire; Riseley d. de Borman 4–6 6–2 8–6 7–5.
1905 British Isles d. USA 5–0, Wimbledon: H. L. Doherty d. H. Ward 7–9 4–6 6–1 6–2 6–0; S. H. Smith d. W. A. Larned 6–4 6–4 5–7 6–4; R. F./H. L. Doherty d. Ward/B. Wright 8–10 6–2 6–2 4–6 8–6; Smith d. W. J. Clothier 4–6 6–1 6–4 6–3; H. L. Doherty d. Larned 6–4 2–6 6–8 6–4 6–2.
1906 British Isles d. USA 5–0, Wimbledon: S. H. Smith d. R. D. Little 6–4 6–4 6–1; H. L. Doherty d. H. Ward 6–2 8–6 6–3; R. F./H. L. Doherty d. Little/Ward 3–6 11–9 9–7 6–1; Smith d. Ward 6–1 6–0 6–4; H. L. Doherty d. Little 3–6 6–3 6–8 6–1 6–3.
1907 Australasia d. British Isles 3–2, Wimbledon: N. E. Brookes d. A. W. Gore 7–5 6–1 7–5; A. F. Wilding d. H. Roper Barrett 1–6 6–4 6–3 7–5; Brookes/Wilding lost to Gore/Roper Barrett 6–3 6–4 5–7 2–6 11–13; Wilding lost to Gore 6–3 3–6 5–7 2–6; Brookes d. Roper Barrett 6–2 6–0 6–3.

1908 Australasia d. USA 3–2, Melbourne: N. E. Brookes d. F. B. Alexander 5–7 9–7 6–2 4–6 6–3; A. F. Wilding lost to B. Wright 6–3 5–7 3–6 1–6; Brookes/Wilding d. Alexander/Wright 6–4 6–2 5–7 1–6 6–4; Brookes lost to Wright 6–0 6–3 5–7 2–6 10–12; Wilding d. Alexander 6–3 6–4 6–1.

1909 Australasia d. USA 5–0, Sydney: N. E. Brookes d. M. E. McLoughlin 6–2 6–2 6–4; A. F. Wilding d. M. H. Long 6–2 7–5 6–1; Brookes/Wilding d. Long/McLoughlin 12–10 9–7 6–3; Brookes d. Long 6–4 7–5 8–6; Wilding d. McLoughlin 3–6 8–6 6–2 6–3.

1910   Not held

1911 Australasia d. USA 5–0, Christchurch, NZ: N. E. Brookes d. B. Wright 6–4 2–6 6–3 6–3; R. W. Heath d. W. A. Larned 2–6 6–1 7–5 6–2; Brookes/A. W. Dunlop d. Wright/M. E. McLoughlin 6–4 5–7 7–5 6–4; Brookes d. McLoughlin 6–4 3–6 4–6 6–3 6–4; Heath w.o. Wright.

1912 British Isles d. Australasia 3–2, Melbourne: J. C. Parke d. N. E. Brookes 8–6 6–3 5–7 6–2; C. P. Dixon d. R. W. Heath 5–7 6–4 6–4 6–4; A. E. Beamish/Parke lost to Brookes/A. W. Dunlop 4–6 1–6 5–7; Dixon lost to Brookes 2–6 4–6 4–6; Parke d. Heath 6–2 6–4 6–4.

1913 USA d. British Isles 3–2, Wimbledon: M. E. McLoughlin lost to J. C. Parke 10–8 5–7 4–6 6–1 5–7; R. N. Williams d. C. P. Dixon 8–6 3–6 6–2 1–6 7–5; H. Hackett/McLoughlin d. Dixon/H. Roper Barrett 5–7 6–1 2–6 7–5 6–4; McLoughlin d. Dixon 8–6 6–3 6–2; Williams lost to Parke 2–6 7–5 7–5 4–6 2–6.

1914 Australasia d. USA 3–2, Forest Hills, NY: A. F. Wilding d. R. N. Williams 7–5 6–2 6–3; N. E. Brookes lost to M. E. McLoughlin 15–17 3–6 3–6; Brookes/Wilding d. T. C. Bundy/McLoughlin 6–3 8–6 9–7; Brookes d. Williams 6–1 6–2 8–10 6–3; Wilding lost to McLoughlin 2–6 3–6 6–2 2–6.

1915–18   Not held

1919 Australasia d. British Isles 4–1, Sydney: G. L. Patterson d. A. H. Lowe 6–4 6–3 2–6 6–3; J. O. Anderson lost to A. R. F. Kingscote 5–7 2–6 4–6; N. E. Brookes/Patterson d. A. E. Beamish/Kingscote 6–0 6–0 6–2; Patterson d. Kingscote 6–4 6–4 8–6; Anderson d. Lowe 6–4 5–7 6–3 4–6 12–10.

1920 USA d. Australasia 5–0, Auckland: W. T. Tilden d. N. E. Brookes 10–8 6–4 1–6 6–4; W. M. Johnston d. G. L. Patterson 6–3 6–1 6–1; Johnston/Tilden d. Brookes/Patterson 4–6 6–4 6–0 6–4; Johnston d. Brookes 5–7 7–5 6–3 6–3; Tilden d. Patterson 5–7 6–2 6–3 6–3.

1921 USA d. Japan 5–0, Forest Hills, NY: W. M. Johnston d. I. Kumagae 6–2 6–4 6–2; W. T. Tilden d. Z. Schimidzu 5–7 4–6 7–5 6–2 6–1; W. Washburn/R. N. Williams d. Kumagae/Shimidzu 6–2 7–5 4–6 7–5; Tilden d. Kumagae 9–7 6–4 6–1; Johnston d. Shimidzu 6–3 5–7 6–2 6–4.

1922 USA d. Australasia 4–1, Forest Hills, NY: W. T. Tilden d. G. L. Patterson 7–5 10–8 6–0; W. M. Johnston d. J. O. Anderson 6–1 6–2 6–3; V. Richards/Tilden lost to P. O'Hara Wood/Patterson 4–6 0–6 3–6; Johnston d. Patterson 6–2 6–2 6–1; Tilden d. Anderson 6–4 5–7 3–6 6–4 6–2.

1923 USA d. Australia 4–1, Forest Hills, NY: W. M. Johnston lost to J. O. Anderson 6–4 2–6 6–2 5–7 2–6; W. T. Tilden d. J. B. Hawkes 6–4 6–2 6–1; Tilden/R. N. Williams d. Anderson/Hawkes 17–15 11–13 2–6 6–3 6–2; Johnston d. Hawkes 6–0 6–2 6–1; Tilden d. Anderson 6–2 6–3 1–6 7–5.

1924 USA d. Australia 5–0, Philadelphia: W. T. Tilden d. G. L. Patterson 6–4 6–2 6–3; V. Richards d. P. O'Hara Wood 6–3 6–2 6–4; W. M. Johnston/Tilden d. O'Hara Wood/Patterson 5–7 6–3 0–6 4–6 6–1; Tilden d. O'Hara Wood 6–2 6–1 6–1; Richards d. Patterson 6–3 7–5 6–4.

1925 USA d. France 5–0, Philadelphia: W. T. Tilden d. J. Borotra 4–6 6–0 2–6 9–7 6–4; W. M. Johnston d. R. Lacoste 6–1 6–1 6–8 6–3; V. Richards/R. N. Williams d. Borotra/Lacoste 4–6 6–4 6–3; Tilden d. Lacoste 3–6 10–12 8–6 7–5 6–2; Johnston d. Borotra 6–1 6–4 6–0.

1926 USA d. France 4–1, Philadelphia: W. M. Johnston d. R. Lacoste 6–0 6–4 0–6 6–0; W. T. Tilden d. J. Borotra 6–2 6–3 6–3; V. Richards/R. N. Williams d. J. Brugnon/H. Cochet 6–4 6–4 6–2; Johnston d. Borotra 8–6 6–4 9–7; Tilden lost to Lacoste 4–4 6–4 6–8 6–8.

1927 France d. USA 3–2, Philadelphia: R. Lacoste d. W. M. Johnston 6–3 6–2 6–2; H. Cochet lost to W. T. Tilden 4–6 6–2 2–6 6–8; J. Borotra/J. Brugnon lost to F. Hunter/Tilden 6–3 3–6 3–6 6–4 0–6; Lacoste d. Tilden 6–4 4–6 6–3; Cochet d. Johnston 6–4 4–6 6–2 6–4.

1928 France d. USA 4–1, Paris: R. Lacoste lost to W. T. Tilden 6–1 4–6 4–6 6–2 3–6; H. Cochet d. J. Hennessey 5–7 9–7 6–3 6–0; J. Borotra/Cochet d. F. Hunter/Tilden 6–4 6–8 7–5 4–6 6–2; Lacoste d. Hennessey 4–6 6–1 7–5 6–3; Cochet d. Tilden 9–7 8–6 6–4.

1929 France d. USA 3–2, Paris: H. Cochet d. W. T. Tilden 6–3 6–1 6–2; J. Borotra d. G. M. Lott 6–1 3–6 6–4 7–5; Borotra/Cochet lost to W. Allison/J. Van Ryn 1–6 6–8 4–6; Cochet d. Lott 6–1 3–6 6–0 6–3; Borotra lost to Tilden 6–4 1–6 4–6 5–7.

1930 France d. USA 4–1, Paris: J. Borotra lost to W. T. Tilden 6–2 5–7 4–6 5–7; H. Cochet d. G. M. Lott 6–4 6–2 6–2; J. Brugnon/Cochet d. W. Allison/J. Van Ryn 6–3 7–5 1–6 6–2; Borotra d. Lott 5–7 6–3 2–6 6–2 8–6; Cochet d. Tilden 4–6 6–3 6–1 7–5.

1931 France d. Great Britain 3–2, Paris: H. Cochet d. H. W. Austin 3–6 11–9 6–2 6–4; J. Borotra lost to F. J. Perry 6–4 8–10 0–6 6–4 4–6; J. Brugnon/Cochet d. G. P Hughes/C. H. Kingsley 6–1 5–7 6–3 8–6; Cochet d. Perry 6–4 1–6 9–7 6–3; Borotra lost to Austin 5–7 3–6 6–3 7–5.

1932 France d. USA 3–2, Paris: H. Cochet d. W. Allison 5–7 7–5 3–6 7–5 6–2; J. Borotra d. H. E. Vines 6–4 6–2 2–6 6–4; J. Brugnon/Cochet lost to Allison/J. Van Ryn 3–6 13–11 5–7 6–4 4–6; Borotra d. Allison 1–6 3–6 6–4 6–2 7–5; Cochet lost to Vines 6–4 6–0 5–7 6–8 2–6.

1933 Great Britain d. France 3–2, Paris: H. W. Austin d. A. Merlin 6–3 6–4 6–0; F. J. Perry d. H. Cochet 8–10 6–4 8–6 3–6 6–1; G. P. Hughes/H. G. N. Lee lost to J. Borotra/J. Brugnon 3–6 6–8 2–6; Austin lost to Cochet 7–5 4–6 6–4 4–6 4–6; Perry d. Merlin 4–6 8–6 6–2 7–5.

1934 Great Britain d. USA 4–1, Wimbledon: F. J. Perry d. S. B. Wood 6–1 4–6 5–7 6–0 6–3; H. W. Austin d. F. X. Shields 6–4 6–4 6–1; G. P. Hughes/H. G. N. Lee lost to G. M. Lott/L. Stoefen 5–7 0–6 6–4 7–9; Perry d. Shields 6–4 4–6 6–2 15–13; Austin d. Wood 6–4 6–0 6–8 6–3.

1935 Great Britain d. USA 5–0, Wimbledon: F. J. Perry d. J. D. Budge 6–0 6–8 6–3 6–4; H. W. Austin d. W. Allison 6–2 2–6 4–6 6–3 7–5; G. P. Hughes/C. R. D. Tuckey d. Allison/J. Van Ryn 6–2 1–6 6–8 6–3 6–3; Perry d. Allison 4–6 6–4 7–5 6–3; Austin d. Budge 6–2 6–4 6–8 7–5.

1936 Great Britain d. Australia 3–2, Wimbledon: H. W. Austin d. J. H. Crawford 4–6 6–3 6–1 6–1; F. J. Perry d. A.

K. Quist 6–1 4–6 7–5 6–2; G. P. Hughes/C. R. D. Tuckey lost to Crawford/Quist 4–6 6–2 5–7 8–10; Austin lost to Quist 4–6 6–3 5–7 2–6; Perry d. Crawford 6–2 6–3 6–3.

1937 USA d. Great Britain 4–1, Wimbledon: F. A. Parker lost to H. W. Austin 3–6 2–6 5–7; J. D. Budge d. C. E. Hare 15–13 6–1 6–2; Budge/G. Mako d. C. R. D. Tuckey/F. H. D. Wilde 6–3 7–5 7–9 12–10; Parker d. Hare 6–2 6–4 6–2; Budge d. Austin 8–6 3–6 6–4 6–3.

1938 USA d. Australia 3–2, Philadelphia: R. L. Riggs d. A. K. Quist 4–6 6–0 8–6 6–1; J. D. Budge d. J. E. Bromwich 6–2 6–3 4–6 7–5; Budge/G. Mako lost to Bromwich/Quist 6–0 3–6 4–6 2–6; Budge d. Quist 8–6 6–1 6–2; Riggs lost to Bromwich 4–6 6–4 0–6 2–6.

1939 Australia d. USA 3–2, Philadelphia: J. E. Bromwich lost to R. L. Riggs 4–6 0–6 5–7; A. K. Quist lost to F. A. Parker 3–6 6–2 4–6 6–1 5–7; Bromwich/Quist d. J. R. Hunt/J. Kramer 5–7 6–2 7–5 6–2; Quist d. Riggs 6–1 6–4 3–6 3–6 6–4; Bromwich d. Parker 6–0 6–3 6–1.

1940–45 Not held

1946 USA d. Australia 5–0, Melbourne: F. R. Schroeder d. J. E. Bromwich 3–6 6–1 6–2 0–6 6–3; J. Kramer d. D. Pails 8–6 6–2 9–7; Kramer/Schroeder d. Bromwich/A. K. Quist 6–2 7–5 6–4; Kramer d. Bromwich 8–6 6–4 6–4; G. Mulloy d. Pails 6–3 6–3 6–4.

1947 USA d. Australia 4–1, Forest Hills, NY: J. Kramer d. D. Pails 6–2 6–1 6–2; F. R. Schroeder d. J. E. Bromwich 6–4 5–7 6–3 6–3; Kramer/Schroeder lost to Bromwich/C. F. Long 4–6 6–2 2–6 4–6; Schroeder d. Pails 6–3 8–6 4–6 9–11 10–8; Kramer d. Bromwich 6–3 6–2 6–2.

1948 USA d. Australia 5–0, Forest Hills, NY: F. A. Parker d. O. W. Sidwell 6–4 6–4 6–4; F. R. Schroeder d. A. K. Quist 6–3 4–6 6–0 6–0; G. Mulloy/W. F. Talbert d. C. F. Long/Sidwell 8–6 9–7 2–6 7–5; Parker d. Quist 6–2 6–2 6–3; Schroeder d. Sidwell 6–2 6–1 6–1.

1949 USA d. Australia 4–1, Forest Hills, NY: F. R. Schroeder d. O. W. Sidwell 6–1 5–7 4–6 6–2 6–3; R. A. Gonzales d. F. A. Sedgman 8–6 6–4 9–7; G. Mulloy/W. F. Talbert lost to J. E. Bromwich/Sidwell 6–3 6–4 8–10 7–9 7–9; Schroeder d. Sedgman 6–4 6–3 6–3; Gonzales d. Sidwell 6–1 6–3 6–3.

1950 Australia d. USA 4–1, Forest Hills, NY: F. A. Sedgman d. T. Brown 6–0 8–6 9–7; K. McGregor d. F. R. Schroeder 13–11 6–3 6–4; J. E. Bromwich/Sedgman d. G. Mulloy/Schroeder 4–6 6–4 6–2 4–6 6–4; Sedgman d. Schroeder 6–2 6–2 6–2; McGregor lost to Brown 11–9 10–8 9–11 1–6 4–6.

1951 Australia d. USA 3–2, Sydney: M. G. Rose lost to E. V. Seixas 3–6 4–6 7–9; F. A. Sedgman d. F. R. Schroeder 6–4 6–3 4–6 6–4; K. McGregor/Sedgman d. Schroeder/M. A. Trabert 6–2 9–7 6–3; Rose lost to Schroeder 4–6 11–13 5–7; Sedgman d. Seixas 6–4 6–2 6–2.

1952 Australia d. USA 4–1, Adelaide: F. A. Sedgman d. E. V. Seixas 6–3 6–4 6–3; K. McGregor d. M. A. Trabert 11–9 6–4 6–1; McGregor/Sedgman d. Seixas/Trabert 6–3 6–4 1–6 6–3; Sedgman d. Trabert 7–5 6–4 10–8; McGregor lost to Seixas 3–6 6–8 8–6 3–6.

1953 Australia d. USA 3–2, Melbourne: L. A. Hoad d. E. V. Seixas 6–4 6–2 6–3; K. R. Rosewall lost to M. A. Trabert 3–6 4–6 4–6; R. Hartwig/Hoad lost to Seixas/Trabert 2–6 4–6 4–6; Hoad d. Trabert 13–11 6–3 2–6 3–6 7–5; Rosewall d. Seixas 6–2 2–6 6–3 6–4.

1954 Australia d. USA 3–2, Sydney: M. A. Trabert d. L. A. Hoad 6–4 2–6 12–10 6–3; E. V. Seixas d. K. R. Rosewall 8–6 6–8 6–4 6–3; Seixas/Trabert d. Hoad/Rosewall 6–2 4–6 6–2 10–8; Trabert lost to Rosewall 7–9 5–7 3–6; Seixas lost to R. Hartwig 6–4 3–6 2–6 3–6.

1955 Australia d. USA 5–0, Forest Hills, NY: K. R. Rosewall d. E. V. Seixas 6–3 10–8 4–6 6–2; L. A. Hoad d. M. A. Trabert 4–6 6–3 6–3 8–6; R. Hartwig/Hoad d. Seixas/Trabert 12–14 6–4 6–3 3–6 7–5; Rosewall d. H. Richardson 6–4 3–6 6–1 6–4; Hoad d. Seixas 7–9 6–1 6–4 6–4.

1956 Australia d. USA 5–0, Adelaide: L. A. Hoad d. H. Flam 6–2 6–3 6–3; K. R. Rosewall d. E. V. Seixas 6–2 7–5 6–3; Hoad/Rosewall d. S. Giammalva/Seixas 1–6 6–1 7–5 6–4; Hoad d. Seixas 6–2 7–5 6–3; Rosewall d. Giammalva 4–6 6–1 8–6 7–5.

1957 Australia d. USA 3–2, Melbourne: A. J. Cooper d. E. V. Seixas 3–6 7–5 6–1 1–6 6–3; M. J. Anderson d. B. MacKay 6–3 7–5 3–6 7–9 6–3; Anderson/M. G. Rose d. MacKay/Seixas 6–4 6–4 8–6; Cooper lost to MacKay 6–1 6–4 4–6 3–6; Anderson lost to Seixas 3–6 6–4 3–6 6–0 11–13.

1958 USA d. Australia 3–2, Brisbane: A. Olmedo d. M. J. Anderson 8–6 2–6 9–7 8–6; B. MacKay lost to A. J. Cooper 6–4 3–6 2–6 4–6; Olmedo/H. Richardson d. Anderson/N. A. Fraser 10–12 3–6 16–14 6–3 7–5; Olmedo d. Cooper 6–3 4–6 6–4 8–6; MacKay lost to Anderson 5–7 11–13 9–11.

1959 USA d. Australia 3–2, Forest Hills, NY: N. A. Fraser d. A. Olmedo 8–6 6–8 6–4 8–6; R. G. Laver lost to B. MacKay 5–7 4–6 1–6; R. S. Emerson/Fraser d. E. Buchholz/Olmedo 7–5 7–5 6–4; Laver lost to Olmedo 7–9 6–4 8–10 10–12; Fraser d. MacKay 8–6 3–6 6–2 6–4.

1960 Australia d. Italy 4–1, Sydney: N. A. Fraser d. O. Sirola 4–6 6–3 6–3 6–3; R. G. Laver d. N. Pietrangeli 8–6 6–4 6–3; R. S. Emerson/Fraser d. Pietrangeli/Sirola 10–8 5–7 6–3 6–4; Laver d. Sirola 9–7 6–2 6–3; Fraser lost to Pietrangeli 9–11 3–6 6–1 2–6.

1961 Australia d. Italy 5–0, Melbourne: R. S. Emerson d. N. Pietrangeli 8–6 6–4 6–0; R. G. Laver d. O. Sirola 6–1 6–4 6–3; Emerson/N. A. Fraser d. Pietrangeli/Sirola 6–2 6–3 6–4; Emerson d. Sirola 6–2 6–3 4–6 6–2; Laver d. Pietrangeli 3–6 3–6 4–6 6–3 8–6.

1962 Australia d. Mexico 5–0, Brisbane: N. A. Fraser d. A. Palafox 7–9 6–3 6–4 11–9; R. G. Laver d. R. H. Osuna 6–2 6–1 7–5; R. S. Emerson/Laver d. Osuna/Palafox 7–5 6–2 6–4; Fraser d. Osuna 3–6 11–9 6–1 3–6 6–4; Laver d. Palafox 6–1 4–6 6–4 8–6.

1963 USA d. Australia 3–2, Adelaide: R. D. Ralston d. J. D. Newcombe 6–4 6–1 3–6 4–6 7–5; C. R. McKinley lost to R. S. Emerson 3–6 6–3 5–7 5–7; McKinley/Ralston d. Emerson/N. A. Fraser 6–3 4–6 11–9 11–9; Ralston lost to Emerson 2–6 3–6 6–3 2–6; McKinley d. Newcombe 10–12 6–2 9–7 6–2.

1964 Australia d. USA 3–2, Cleveland, Ohio: R. S. Stolle lost to C. R. McKinley 1–6 7–9 6–4 2–6; R. S. Emerson d. R. D. Ralston 6–3 6–1 3–6; Emerson/Stolle lost to McKinley/Ralston 4–6 6–4 6–4 3–6 4–6; Stolle d. Ralston 7–5 6–3 3–6 9–11 6–4; Emerson d. McKinley 3–6 6–2 6–4 6–4.

1965 Australia d. Spain 4–1, Sydney: F. S. Stolle d. M. Santana 10–12 3–6 6–1 6–4 7–5; R. S. Emerson d. J. Gisbert

6–3 6–2 6–2; J. D. Newcombe/A. D. Roche d. J. L. Arilla/Santana 6–3 4–6 7–5 6–2; Emerson lost to Santana 6–2 3–6 4–6 13–15; Stolle d. Gisbert 6–2 6–4 8–6.

1966 Australia d. India 4–1, Melbourne: F. S. Stolle d. R. Krishnan 6–3 6–2 6–4; R. S. Emerson d. J. Mukerjea 7–5 6–4 6–2; J. D. Newcombe/A. D. Roche lost to Krishnan/Mukerjea 6–4 5–7 4–6 4–6; Emerson d. Krishnan 6–0 6–2 10–8; Stolle d. Mukerjea 7–5 6–8 6–3 5–7 6–3.

1967 Australia d. Spain 4–1, Brisbane: R. S. Emerson d. M. Santana 6–4 6–1 6–1; J. D. Newcombe d. M. Orantes 6–3 6–3 6–2; Newcombe/A. D. Roche d. Orantes/Santana 6–4 6–4 6–4; Newcombe lost to Santana 5–7 4–6 2–6; Emerson d. Orantes 6–1 6–1 2–6 6–4.

1968 USA d. Australia 4–1, Adelaide: C. Graebner d. W. W. Bowrey 8–10 6–4 8–6 3–6 6–1; A. R. Ashe d. R. O. Ruffels 6–8 7–5 6–3 6–3; R. C. Lutz/S. R. Smith d. J. G. Alexander/Ruffels 6–4 6–4 6–2; Graebner d. Ruffels 3–6 8–6 2–6 6–3 6–11; Ashe lost to Bowrey 6–2 3–6 9–11 6–8.

1969 USA d. Rumania 5–0, Cleveland, Ohio: A. R. Ashe d. I. Nastase 6–2 15–13 7–5; S. R. Smith d. I. Tiriac 6–8 6–3 5–7 6–4 6–4; R. C. Lutz/Smith d. Nastase/Tiriac 8–6 6–1 11–9; Smith d. Nastase 4–6 4–6 6–4 6–1 11–9; Ashe d. Tiriac 6–3 8–6 3–6 4–0 ret'd.

1970 USA d. West Germany 5–0, Cleveland, Ohio: A. R. Ashe d. W. Bungert 6–2 10–8 6–2; C. Richey d. C. Kuhnke 6–3 6–4 6–2; R. C. Lutz/S. R. Smith d. Bungert/Kuhnke 6–3 7–5 6–4; Richey d. Bungert 6–4 6–4 7–5; Ashe d. Kuhnke 6–8 10–12 9–7 13–11 6–4.

1971 USA d. Rumania 3–2, Charlotte, NC: S. R. Smith d. I. Nastase 7–5 6–3 6–1; F. A. Froehling d. I. Tiriac 3–6 1–6 6–1 6–3 8–6; Smith/E. Van Dillen lost to Nastase/Tiriac 5–7 4–6 8–6; Smith d. Tiriac 8–6 6–3 6–0; Froehling lost to Nastase 3–6 1–6 6–1 4–6.

Challenge Round abolished

FINAL ROUND SCORES

1972 USA d. Rumania 3–2, Bucharest: S. R. Smith d. I. Nastase 11–9 6–2 6–3; T. Gorman lost to I. Tiriac 6–4 6–2 4–6 3–6 2–6; Smith/E. Van Dillen d. Nastase/Tiriac 6–2 6–0 6–3; Smith d. Tiriac 4–6 6–2 6–4 2–6 6–0; Gorman lost to Nastase 1–6 2–6 7–5 8–10.

1973 Australia d. USA 5–0, Cleveland, Ohio (indoors): J. D. Newcombe d. S. R. Smith 6–1 3–6 6–3 3–6 6–4; R. G. Laver d. T. Gorman 8–10 8–6 8–6 3–6 1; Laver/Newcombe d. Smith/E. Van Dillen 6–1 6–2 6–4; Newcombe d. Gorman 6–2 6–1 6–3; Laver d. Smith 6–3 6–4 6–2.

1974 South Africa w.o. India

1975 Sweden d. Czechoslovakia 3–2, Stockholm (indoors): O. Bengtson lost to J. Kodes 4–6 6–2 5–7 4–6; B. Borg d. J. Hrebec 6–1 6–3 6–0; Bengtson/Borg d. Kodes/V. Zednik 6–4 6–4 6–4; Borg d. Kodes 6–4 6–2 6–2; Bengtson lost to Hrebec 6–1 3–6 1–6 4–6.

1976 Italy d. Chile 4–1, Santiago: C. Barazzutti d. J. Fillol 7–5 4–6 7–5 6–1; A. Panatta d. P. Cornejo 6–3 6–1 6–3; P. Bertolucci/Panatta d. Cornejo/Fillol 3–6 6–2 9–7 6–3; Panatta d. Fillol 8–6 6–4 3–6 10–8; A. Zugarelli lost to B. Prajoux 4–6 4–6 2–6.

1977 Australia d. Italy 3–1, Sydney: A. D. Roche d. A. Panatta 3–6 4–6 4–6 4; J. G. Alexander d. C. Barazzutti 6–2 8–6 4–6 6–2; Alexander/P. Dent lost to P. Bertolucci/Panatta 4–6 4–6 5–7; Alexander d. Panatta 6–4 4–6 2–6 8–6 11–9; Roche div'd with Barazzutti 12–12.

1978 USA d. Great Britain 4–1, Palm Springs, California: J. P. McEnroe d. J. M. Lloyd 6–1 6–2 6–2; B. E. Gottfried lost to C. J. Mottram 6–4 6–2 8–10 4–6 3–6; R. C. Lutz/S. R. Smith d. M. Cox/D. A. Lloyd 6–2 6–2 6–3; McEnroe d. Mottram 6–2 6–2 6–1; Gottfried d. J. M. Lloyd 6–1 6–2 6–4.

1979 USA d. Italy 5–0, San Francisco (indoors): V. Gerulaitis d. C. Barazzutti 6–3 3–2 ret'd; J. P. McEnroe d. A. Panatta 6–2 6–3 6–4; R. C. Lutz/S. R. Smith d. P. Bertolucci/Panatta 6–4 12–10 6–2; McEnroe d. A. Zugarelli 6–4 6–3 6–1; Gerulaitis d. Panatta 6–1 6–3 6–3.

1980 Czechoslovakia d. Italy 4–1, Prague (indoors): T. Smid d. A. Panatta 3–6 3–6 6–3 6–4 6–4; I. Lendl d. C. Barazzutti 4–6 6–1 6–1 6–2; Lendl/Smid d. P. Bertolucci/Panatta 3–6 6–3 3–6 6–3 6–4; Smid lost to Barazzutti 6–3 3–6 2–6; Lendl d. G. Ocleppo 6–3 6–3.

1981 USA d. Argentina 3–1, Cincinnati (indoors): J. P. McEnroe d. G. Vilas 6–3 6–2 6–2; R. Tanner lost to J. L. Clerc 5–7 3–6 6–8; P. Fleming/McEnroe d. Clerc/Vilas 6–3 4–6 6–4 4–6 11–9; McEnroe d. Clerc 7–5 5–7 6–3 3–6 6–3; Tanner div'd with Vilas 11–10.

1982 USA d. France 4–1, Grenoble (indoors): J. P. McEnroe d. Y. Noah 12–10 1–6 3–6 6–2 6–3; G. Mayer d. H. Leconte 6–2 6–2 7–9 6–4; P. Fleming/McEnroe d. Leconte/Noah 6–3 6–4 9–7; Mayer lost to Noah 1–6 0–6; McEnroe d. Leconte 6–2 6–3.

1983 Australia d. Sweden 3–2, Melbourne: P. Cash lost to M. Wilander 3–6 6–4 7–9 3–6; J. Fitzgerald d. J. Nystrom 6–4 6–2 4–6 6–4; M. R. Edmondson/P. McNamee d. A. Jarryd/H. Simonsson 6–4 6–4 6–2; Cash d. Nystrom 6–4 6–1 6–1; Fitzgerald lost to Wilander 8–6 0–6 1–6.

1984 Sweden d. USA 4–1, Gothenburg: M. Wilander d. J. S. Connors 6–1 6–3 6–3; H. Sundstrom d. J. P. McEnroe 13–11 6–4 6–3; S. Edberg/A. Jarryd d. P. Fleming/McEnroe 7–5 5–7 6–2 7–5; Wilander lost to McEnroe 3–6 7–6 3–6; Sundstrom d. J. Arias 3–6 8–6 6–3.

1985 Sweden d. West Germany 3–2, Munich: (M. Wilander d. M. Westphal 6–3 6–4 10–8; S. Edberg lost to B. Becker 3–6 6–3 5–7 6–8; Wilander /J. Nystrom d. Becker /A. Maurer 6–4 6–2 6–1; Wilander lost to Becker 3–6 6–2 3–6 3–6; Edberg d. Westphal 3–6 7–5 6–4 6–3.

ZONE WINNERS QUALIFYING FOR WORLD GROUP

	EUROPEAN ZONE A	EUROPEAN ZONE B	AMERICAN ZONE	EASTERN ZONE
1981	Spain	USSR	Chile	India
1982	Ireland	Denmark	Paraguay	Indonesia
1983	West Germany	Yugoslavia	Ecuador	India
1984	USSR	Spain	Chile	Japan
1985	Denmark	Great Britain	Mexico	New Zealand

DAVIS CUP *STALWARTS*
(Players participating in 100 or more rubbers)

	TOTAL MATCHES PL'D	WON	SINGLES PL'D	WON	DOUBLES PL'D	WON	TIES	YEARS
N. Pietrangeli (IT)	163	120	109	78	54	42	66	1954–72
I. Nastase (RU)	146	110	96	74	50	36	51	1966–85
J. Brichant (B)	120	71	79	52	41	19	42	1949–65
M. Santana (SP)	119	91	85	69	34	22	46	1958–73
T. Koch (BR)	118	75	77	46	41	29	44	1962–81
J. E. Mandarino (BR)	*109	67	*73	41	36	26	42	1961–76
I. Tiriac (RU)	109	70	68	40	41	30	43	1959–77
A. Panatta (IT)	103	65	65	38	38	27	39	1970–83
G. von Cramm (G)	102	82	69	58	33	24	37	1932–53
W. Bungert (G)	†102	66	†79	52	23	14	43	1958–71
U. Schmidt (SW)	102	66	69	44	33	22	38	1955–64
P. Washer (B)	102	66	64	46	38	20	39	1946–61
T. Ulrich (D)	101	45	65	31	36	14	40	1948–77
A. Metreveli (USSR)	†100	73	†67	51	33	22	36	1963–79

* Including one unfinished rubber. † Including two unfinished rubbers.

FEDERATION CUP

International Women's Team Championship, staged on a knock-out basis at one venue with each tie comprising two singles and one doubles match.

FINAL ROUNDS

1963 USA d. Australia 2–1, Queen's Club, London, 18–21 June: D. R. Hard lost to M. Smith 3–6 0–6; B. J. Moffitt d. L. R. Turner 5–7 6–0 6–3; Hard/Moffitt d. Smith/Turner 3–6 13–11 6–3.

1964 Australia d. USA 2–1, Germantown Cricket Club, Philadelphia, 2–5 September: M. Smith d. B. J. Moffitt 6–2 6–3; L. R. Turner d. N. Richey 7–5 6–1; Smith/Turner lost to Moffitt/Mrs J. R. Susman 6–4 5–7 1–6.

1965 Australia d. USA 2–1, Kooyong Stadium, Melbourne, 12–18 January: L. R. Turner d. Mrs C. Graebner 6–3 2–6 6–3; M. Smith d. B. J. Moffitt 6–4 8–6; Smith/J. M. Tegart lost to Graebner/Moffitt 5–7 6–4 4–6.

1966 USA d. West Germany 3–0, Turin, 11–15 May: J. M. Heldman d. H. Niessen 4–6 7–5 6–1; Mrs L. W. King d. E. Buding 6–3 3–6 6–1; Mrs C. Graebner/Mrs King d. Buding/H. Schultse 6–4 6–2.

1967 Great Britain 2–0, Rot-Weiss Club, Berlin, 7–11 June: R. Casals d. S. V. Wade 9–7 8–6; Mrs L. W. King d. Mrs P. F. Jones 6–3 6–4; Casals/Mrs King div'd with Mrs Jones/Wade 6–8 9–7.

1968 Australia d. Netherlands 3–0, Stade Roland Garros, Paris, 23–26 May: K. A. Melville d. M. Jansen 4–6 7–5 6–3; Mrs B. M. Court d. A. Suurbeck 6–1 6–3; Court/Melville d. Suurbeck/L. Venneboer 6–3 6–8 7–5.

1969 USA d. Australia 2–1, Athens, 19–25 May: N. Richey d. K. A. Melville 6–4 6–3; J. M. Heldman lost to Mrs B. M. Court 1–6 6–8; J. Bartkowicz/Richey d. Court/J. M. Tegart 6–4 6–4.

1970 Australia d. West Germany 3–0, Freiburg, Germany, 19–24 May: K. M. Krantzcke d. Mrs H. Hoesl 6–2 6–3; Mrs D. E. Dalton d. H. Niessen 4–6 6–3 6–3; Dalton/Krantzcke d. Hoesl/Niessen 6–2 7–5.

1971 Australia d. Great Britain 3–0, Perth, Australia, 26–29 December 1970: Mrs B. M. Court d. Mrs P. F. Jones 6–8 6–3 6–2; E. F. Goolagong d. S. V. Wade 6–4 6–1; Court/L. Hunt d. W. M. Shaw/Wade 6–4 6–4.

1972 South Africa d. Great Britain 2–1, Ellis Park, Johannesburg, 19–26 March: Mrs Q. C. Pretorius lost to S. V. Wade 3–6 2–6; B. Kirk d. W. M. Shaw 4–6 7–5 6–0; Kirk/Pretorius d. Wade/Mrs G. M. Williams 6–1 7–5.

1973 Australia d. South Africa 3–0, Bad Homburg, Germany, 30 April–6 May: E. F. Goolagong d. Mrs Q. C. Pretorius 6–0 6–2; P. Coleman d. B. Kirk 10–8 6–0; Goolagong/J. Young d. Kirk/Pretorius 6–1 6–2.

1974 USA d. Australia 2–1, Naples, 13–19 May: E. F. Goolagong d. J. M. Heldman 6–1 7–5; D. L. Fromholtz lost to C. M. Evert 6–2 5–7 3–6; Goolagong/J. Young d. Heldman/A. Walsh 7–5 8–6.

1975 Czechoslovakia d. Australia 3–0, Aix-en-Provence, 6–11 May: M. Navratilova* d. E. F. Goolagong 6–3 6–4; R. Tomanova d. H. Gourlay 6–4 6–2; Navratilova/Tomanova d. D. L. Fromholtz/Gourlay 6–3 6–1.

1976 USA d. Australia 2–1, Spectrum Stadium, Philadelphia, 22–29 August: R. Casals lost to Mrs G. Reid 6–1 3–6 5–7; Mrs L. W. King d. Mrs E. Cawley 7–6 6–4; Casals/King d. Cawley/Reid 7–5 6–3.

1977 USA d. Australia 2–1, Devonshire Park, Eastbourne, 13–18 June: Mrs L. W. King d. D. L. Fromholtz 6–1 2–6 6–2; C. M. Evert d. Mrs G. Reid 7–5 6–3; Casals/Evert lost to Reid/W. M. Turnbull 3–6 3–6.

1978 USA d. Australia 2–1, Kooyong Stadium, Melbourne, 27 November–3 December: T. A. Austin lost to Mrs G. Reid 3–6 3–6; C. M. Evert d. W. M. Turnbull 3–6 6–1 6–1; Evert/Mrs L. W. King d. Reid/Turnbull 4–6 6–1 6–4.

1979 USA d. Australia 3–0, Madrid, 30 April–6 May: T. A. Austin d. Mrs G. Reid 6–3 6–0; Mrs J. M. Lloyd d. D. L. Fromholtz 2–6 6–3 8–6; R. Casals/Mrs L. W. King d. Reid/W. M. Turnbull 3–6 6–3 8–6.

1980 USA d. Australia 3–0, Rot-Weiss Club, Berlin, 19–25 May: Mrs J. M. Lloyd d. D. L. Fromholtz 4–6 6–1 6–1; T. A. Austin d. W. M. Turnbull 6–2 6–3; R. Casals/K. Jordan d. Fromholtz/S. Leo 2–6 6–4 6–4.

1981 Great Britain 3–0, Tokyo, 9–15 November: Mrs J. M. Lloyd d. S. V. Wade 6–3 6–1; Mrs J. M. Lloyd d. S. Barker 6–2 6–1; R. Casals/K. Jordan d. J. M. Durie/Wade 6–4 7–5.

1982 USA d. West Germany 3–0, Santa Clara, California, 19–25 July: Mrs J. M. Lloyd d. C. Kohde 2–6 6–1 6–3; M. Navratilova* d. B. Bunge 6–4 6–4; Lloyd/Navratilova d. Bunge/Kohde 3–6 6–1 6–2.

1983 Czechoslovakia d. West Germany 2–1, Zurich, 18–24 July: H. Sukova d. C. Kohde 6–4 2–6 6–2; H. Mandlikova
d. B. Bunge 6–2 3–0 ret'd; I. Budarova/M. Skuherska lost to E. Pfaff/Kohde 6–3 2–6 1–6.
1984 Czechoslovakia d. Australia 2–1, Sao Paulo, 15–22 July: H. Sukova lost to A. Minter 5–7 5–7; H. Mandlikova
d. E. Sayers 6–1 6–0; Mandlikova/Sukova d. W. Turnbull/Sayers 6–2 6–2.
1985 Czechoslovakia d. USA 2–1, Nagoya, 7–13 October: H. Sukova d. E. Burgin 6–3 6–7 6–4; H. Mandlikova d. K.
Jordan 7–5 6–1; A. Holikova /R. Marsikova lost to Burgin /Jordan 2–6 3–6.
* *M. Navratilova became a US citizen in 1981.*

FEDERATION CUP *STALWARTS*
(Players participating in 30 or more rubbers)

	TOTAL RUBBERS PL'D	WON	SINGLES PL'D	WON	DOUBLES PL'D	WON	TIES	YEARS
S. V. Wade (GB)	*100	66	56	36	*44	30	57	1967–83
Mrs L. W. King (US)	*58	52	29	25	*29	27	36	1963–67,76–79
B. Stove (NTH)	55	41	26	21	29	20	29	1964,66,69–72,76–79,82,83
Mrs H. Masthoff (G)	53	35	31	21	22	14	31	1965–67,69,70,72–77
W. W. Turnbull (AUS)	53	39	23	17	30	22	37	1977–85
Mrs G. E. Reid (AUS)	45	35	23	19	22	16	28	1967–69,76–79
D. M. Fromholtz (AUS)	45	34	33	24	12	10	36	1974–83
S. Barker (GB)	45	32	24	16	21	16	27	1974–82
Mrs J. M. Lloyd (USA)	43	42	28	28	15	14	28	1977–82
H. Mandlikova (CZ)	42	35	29	25	13	10	32	1978–85
Mrs B. M. Court (AUS)	40	35	20	20	20	15	20	1963–65,68,69,71
R. Casals (USA)	*38	34	9	8	*29	26	29	1967,76–81
Mrs E. Cawley (AUS)	38	33	24	21	14	12	24	1971–76,82
F. Durr (F)	*35	22	18	12	17	10	18	1963–67,71,72
Mrs P. F. Jones (GB)	*34	21	17	10	*17	11	18	1963–67,71
J. M. Heldman (USA)	30	21	19	13	11	8	19	1966,69,70,74,75

* *Including one unfinished rubber.*

WIGHTMAN CUP

Women's team contest between USA and Great Britain, each match comprising five singles and two
doubles, with reverse singles played between the two top players.

1923 USA d. Great Britain 7–0, Forest Hills: H. Wills d. K. McKane 6–2 7–5, d. Mrs R. Clayton 6–2 6–3; Mrs F.
Mallory d. Clayton 6–1 8–6, d. McKane 6–2 6–3; E. Goss d. Mrs W. G. Beamish 6–2 0–6 7–5; Mrs G. W.
Wightman/Goss d. McKane/Mrs B. C. Covell 10–8 5–7 6–4; Mallory/Wills d. Beamish/Clayton 6–3 6–2.
1924 Great Britain d. USA 6–1, Wimbledon: Mrs B. C. Covell d. H. Wills 6–2 6–4, d. Mrs F. Mallory 6–2 5–7 6–3; K.
McKane d. Mallory 6–3 6–3, d. Wills 6–2 6–2; Mrs W. G. Beamish d. E. Goss 6–1 8–10 6–3; Covell/Mrs D. C.
Shepherd-Barron d. Mrs M. Z. Jessup/Goss 6–2 6–2; McKane/E. Colyer lost to Mrs G. W. Wightman/Wills 6–2
2–6 4–6.
1925 Great Britain d. USA 4–3, Forest Hills: K. McKane d. Mrs F. Mallory 6–4 5–7 6–0, lost to H. Wills 1–6 6–1 7–9;
J. Fry lost to Wills 0–6 5–7, lost to Mallory 3–6 0–6; Mrs R. Lambert Chambers d. Goss 7–5 3–6 6–1; Lambert
Chambers/E. H. Harvey d. Mallory/Mrs T. C. Bundy 10–8 6–1; McKane/E. Colyer d. Wills/M. K. Browne 0–6 6–3.
1926 USA d. Great Britain 4–3, Wimbledon: E. Ryan d. J. J. Fry 6–1 6–3, lost to Mrs L. A. Godfree 1–6 7–5 4–6; M.
K. Browne lost to Godfree 1–6 5–7, lost to Fry 6–3 0–6 4–6; Mrs M. Z. Jessup d. Mrs D. C. Shepherd-Barron 6–1
5–7 6–4; Jessup/E. Goss d. Mrs R. Lambert Chambers/Shepherd-Barron 6–4 6–2; Browne/Ryan d. Godfree/E.
L. Colyer 3–6 6–2 6–4.
1927 USA d. Great Britain 5–2, Forest Hills: H. Wills d. J. Fry 6–2 6–0, d. Mrs L. A. Godfree 6–1 6–1; Mrs F. Mallory
d. Godfree 6–4 6–2, d. J. Fry 6–2 11–9; H. H. Jacobs lost to B. Nuthall 3–6 6–2 1–6; E. Goss/Mrs A. H. Chapin
lost to G. Sterry/Mrs J. Hill 7–5 5–7 5–7; Wills/Mrs G. W. Wightman d. Godfree/E. H. Harvey 6–4 4–6 6–3.
1928 Great Britain d. USA 4–3, Wimbledon: Mrs P. H. Watson lost to H. Wills 1–6 2–6, d. Mrs F. Mallory 2–6 6–1
6–2; E. Bennett d. Mallory 6–1 6–3, lost to Wills 3–6 2–6; B. Nuthall lost to H. H. Jacobs 3–6 1–6; E. H.
Harvey/P. Saunders d. E. Goss/Jacobs 6–4 6–1; Bennett/Watson d. Wills/P. Anderson 6–2 6–1.
1929 USA d. Great Britain 4–3, Forest Hills: H. Wills d. Mrs P. H. Watson 6–1 6–4, d. B. Nuthall 8–6 8–6; H. H.
Jacobs d. Nuthall 7–5 8–6, lost to Watson 3–6 2–6; E. Goss d. Mrs L. R. C. Michell 6–3 3–6 6–3; Wills/Goss lost
to Watson/Michell 4–6 1–6; Mrs G. W. Wightman/Jacobs lost to Mrs B. C. Covell/Mrs D. C. Shepherd-Barron
2–6 1–6.
1930 Great Britain d. USA 4–3, Wimbledon: J. Fry lost to H. Wills 1–6 1–6, lost to H. H. Jacobs 0–6 3–6; Mrs P. H.
Watson d. Jacobs 2–6 6–2 6–4, lost to Wills 5–7 1–6; P. Mudford d. S. Palfrey 6–0 6–2; Fry/E. H. Harvey d.
Palfrey/E. Cross 2–6 6–2 6–4; Watson/Mrs L. A. Godfree d. Jacobs/Wills 7–5 1–6 6–4.
1931 USA d. Great Britain 5–2, Forest Hills: Mrs F. S. Moody d. P. Mudford 6–1 6–4, d. B. Nuthall 6–4 6–2; H. H.
Jacobs d. Nuthall 8–6 6–4, d. Mudford 6–4 6–2; Mrs L. A. Harper d. D. E. Round 6–3 4–6 9–7; S. Palfrey/Mrs G.
W. Wightman lost to Mudford/Mrs D. C. Shepherd-Barron 4–6 8–10; Moody/Harper lost to Nuthall/Mrs Fearnley
Whittingstall 6–8 7–5 3–6.
1932 USA d. Great Britain 4–3, Wimbledon: H. H. Jacobs d. D. E. Round 6–4 6–3, lost to Mrs Fearnley Whittingstall

4–6 6–2 1–6; Mrs F. S. Moody d. Fearnley Whittingstall 6–2 6–4, d. Round 6–2 6–3; Mrs L. A. Harper lost to Mrs M. R. King 6–3 1–6 1–6; Harper/Jacobs d. Mrs L. R. C. Michell/Round 6–4 6–1; Moody/Palfrey lost to Fearnley Whittingstall/B. Nuthall 3–6 6–1 8–10.

1933 USA d. Great Britain 4–3, Forest Hills: H. H. Jacobs d. D. E. Round 6–4 6–2, d. M. Scriven 5–7 6–2 7–5; S. Palfrey d. Scriven 6–3 6–1, lost to Round 4–6 8–10; C. Babcock lost to B. Nuthall 6–1 1–6 3–6; Jacobs/Palfrey d. Round/M. Heeley 6–4 6–2; A. Marble/Mrs J. Van Ryn lost to Nuthall/F. James 5–7 2–6.

1934 USA d. Great Britain 5–2, Wimbledon: S. Palfrey d. D. E. Round 6–3 3–6 8–6, d. M. Scriven 4–6 6–2 8–6; H. H. Jacobs d. Scriven 6–1 6–1, d. Round 6–4 6–4; C. Babcock lost to B. Nuthall 7–5 3–6 4–6; Babcock/J. Cruickshank lost to N. Lyle/E. M. Dearman 5–7 5–7; Jacobs/Palfrey d. Mrs L. A. Godfree/Nuthall 5–7 6–3 6–2.

1935 USA d. Great Britain 4–3, Forest Hills: H. H. Jacobs lost to K. Stammers 7–5 1–6 7–9, d. D. E. Round 6–3 6–2; Mrs E. B. Arnold lost to Round 0–6 3–6, d. Stammers 6–2 1–6 6–3; S. Palfrey d. Mrs M. R. King 6–0 6–3; Jacobs/Palfrey d. Stammers/F. James 6–3 6–2; Mrs D. B. Andrus/C. Babcock lost to N. Lyle/E. M. Dearman 6–3 4–6 1–6.

1936 USA d. Great Britain 4–3, Wimbledon: H. H. Jacobs lost to K. Stammers 10–12 1–6, lost to D. E. Round 3–6 3–6; S. Palfrey lost to Round 3–6 4–6, d. Stammers 6–3 6–4; C. Babcock d. M. Hardwick 6–4 4–6 6–2; Babcock/Mrs J. Van Ryn d. N. Lyle/E. M. Dearman 6–2 1–6 6–3; Jacobs/Palfrey d. Stammers/F. James 1–6 6–3 7–5.

1937 USA d. Great Britain 6–1, Forest Hills: A. Marble d. M. Hardwick 4–6 6–2 6–4, d. K. Stammers 6–3 6–1; H. H. Jacobs d. Stammers 6–1 4–6 6–4, d. Hardwick 2–6 6–4 6–2; S. Palfrey d. M. Lumb 6–3 6–1; Marble/Palfrey d. E. M. Dearman/J. Ingram 6–3 6–2; Mrs J. Van Ryn/D. M. Bundy lost to Stammers/F. James 3–6 8–10.

1938 USA d. Great Britain 5–2, Wimbledon: A. Marble lost to K. Stammers 6–3 5–7 3–6, d. M. Scriven 6–3 3–6 6–0; Mrs F. S. Moody d. Scriven 6–0 7–5, d. Stammers 6–2 3–6 6–3; S. Fabyan d. M. Lumb 5–7 6–2 6–3; Marble/Fabyan d. Lumb/F. James 6–4 6–2; Moody/D. Bundy lost to E. M. Dearman/J. Ingram 2–6 5–7.

1939 USA d. Great Britain 5–2, Forest Hills: A. Marble d. M. Hardwick 6–3 6–4, d. K. Stammers 3–6 6–3 6–4; H. H. Jacobs lost to Stammers 2–6 6–1 3–6, d. Hardwick 6–2 6–2; S. Fabyan lost to V. Scott 3–6 4–6; M. Arnold/D. M. Bundy d. B. Nuthall/N. Brown 6–3 6–1; Marble/Fabyan d. Stammers/Mrs S. H. Hammersley 7–5 6–2.

1940–45   *Not held.*

1946 USA d. Great Britain 7–0, Wimbledon: P. M. Betz d. Mrs J. Bostock 6–2 6–4, d. Mrs M. Menzies 4–6 6–4; M. Osborne d. Bostock 6–1 6–4, d. Menzies 6–3 6–2; L. Brough d. J. Curry 8–6 6–3; Brough/Osborne d. Bostock/Mrs M. Halford 6–2 6–1; Betz/D. Hart d. Mrs B. Passingham/M. Lincoln 6–1 6–3.

1947 USA d. Great Britain 7–0, Forest Hills: M. Osborne d. Mrs J. Bostock 6–4 2–6 6–2, d. Mrs M. Menzies 7–5 6–2; L. Brough d. Menzies 6–4 6–2, d. Bostock 6–4 6–4; D. Hart d. Mrs B. Hilton 4–6 6–3 7–5; Hart/Mrs P. C. Todd d. J. Gannon/J. Quertier 6–1 6–2; Brough/Osborne d. Bostock/Hilton 6–1 6–4.

1948 USA d. Great Britain 6–1, Wimbledon: Mrs W. du Pont d. Mrs J. Bostock 6–4 8–6, d. Mrs B. Hilton 6–3 6–4; L. Brough d. Hilton 6–1 6–1, d. Bostock 6–2 4–6 7–5; D. Hart d. J. Gannon 6–1 6–4; Brough/du Pont d. Mrs M. Menzies/Hilton 6–2 6–2; Hart/Mrs P. C. Todd lost to Bostock/Mrs N. W. Blair 3–6 4–6.

1949 USA d. Great Britain 7–0, Merion Cricket Club, Philadelphia: D. Hart d. Mrs J. Walker-Smith 6–3 6–1, d. Mrs B. Hilton 6–1 6–3; Mrs W. du Pont d. Hilton 6–1 6–3, d. Walker-Smith 6–4 6–2; B. Baker d. J. Quertier 6–4 7–5; Hart/S. Fry d. Quertier/Mrs N. W. Blair 6–1 6–2; G. Moran/Mrs P. C. Todd d. Hilton/K. Tuckey 6–4 8–6.

1950 USA d. Great Britain 7–0, Wimbledon: Mrs W. du Pont d. Mrs B. Hilton 6–3 6–4, d. Mrs J. Walker-Smith 6–3 6–2; L. Brough d. Hilton 2–6 6–2 7–5, d. Walker-Smith 6–0 6–0; D. Hart d. J. Curry 6–2 6–4; Hart/Mrs P. C. Todd d. Walker-Smith/J. Quertier 6–2 6–3; Brough/du Pont d. Hilton/K. Tuckey 6–2 6–0.

1951 USA d. Great Britain 6–1, Longwood Cricket Club, Boston: D. Hart d. J. Quertier 6–4 6–4, d. Mrs J. Walker-Smith 6–4 2–6 7–5; S. Fry d. Walker-Smith 6–1 6–4; lost to Quertier 3–6 6–8; M. Connolly d. K. Tuckey 6–1 6–3; Mrs P. C. Todd/N. Chaffee d. Mrs J. Mottram/P. Ward 7–5 6–3; Fry/D. Hart d. Quertier/Tuckey 6–3 6–3.

1952 USA d. Great Britain 7–0, Wimbledon: D. Hart d. Mrs J. Rinkel-Quertier 6–3 6–3, d. Mrs J. Walker-Smith 7–5 6–2; M. Connolly d. Walker-Smith 3–6 6–1 7–5, d. Rinkel-Quertier 9–7 6–2; S. Fry d. S. Partridge 8–6 8–6; Fry/Hart d. H. Fletcher/Rinkel-Quertier 8–6 6–4; L. Brough/Connolly d. Mrs J. Mottram/P. Ward 6–0 6–3.

1953 USA d. Great Britain 7–0, Westchester Club, Rye, NY: M. Connolly d. A. Mortimer 6–1 6–1, d. H. Fletcher 6–1 6–1; Hart d. Fletcher 6–4 7–5, d. Mortimer 6–1 6–1; S. Fry d. Rinkel-Quertier 6–2 6–4; L. Brough/Connolly d. Mortimer/A. Shilcock 6–2 6–3; Fry/Hart d. Fletcher/Rinkel-Quertier 6–2 6–1.

1954 USA d. Great Britain 6–0, Wimbledon: M. Connolly d. H. Fletcher 6–1 6–3, d. A. Shilcock 6–2 6–2; Hart d. Shilcock 6–4 6–1, d. Fletcher 6–1 6–8 6–2; L. Brough d. A. Buxton 8–6 6–2; L. Brough/Mrs W. du Pont d. Buxton/P. Hird 2–6 6–4 7–5; S. Fry/Hart v. Fletcher/Shilcock not played.

1955 USA d. Great Britain 6–1, Westchester Club, Rye, NY: D. Hart lost to A. Mortimer 4–6 6–1 5–7, d. S. J. Bloomer 7–5 6–3; L. Brough d. Bloomer 6–2 6–4, d. Mortimer 6–0 6–2; Mrs D. Knode d. A. Buxton 6–3 6–3; Brough/Mrs W. du Pont d. Bloomer/P. Ward 6–3 6–3; S. Fry/Hart d. Buxton/Mortimer 3–6 6–2 7–5.

1956 USA d. Great Britain 5–2, Wimbledon: L. Brough d. A. Mortimer 3–6 6–4 7–5, d. A. Buxton 3–6 6–3 6–4; S. Fry d. Buxton 6–2 6–8 7–5, lost to Mortimer 4–6 3–6; Mrs D. Knode lost to S. J. Bloomer 4–6 4–6; B. Baker/Knode d. Bloomer/P. Ward 6–1 6–4; Brough/Fry d. Buxton/Mortimer 6–2 6–2.

1957 USA d. Great Britain 6–1, Sewickley, Pennsylvania: A. Gibson d. S. J. Bloomer 6–4 4–6 6–2, d. C. Truman 6–4 6–2; Mrs D. Knode d. Truman 6–2 11–9, d. Bloomer 5–7 6–1 6–2; D. R. Hard lost to A. Haydon 3–6 6–3 4–6; Gibson/Hard d. Bloomer/S. M. Armonstrong 6–3 6–4; L. Brough/W. du Pont d. Haydon/A. Shilcock 6–4 6–1.

1958 Great Britain d. USA 4–3, Wimbledon: S. J. Bloomer lost to A. Gibson 3–6 4–6, lost to Mrs D. Knode 4–6 2–6; C. Truman d. Knode 6–4 6–4, d. Gibson 2–6 6–3 6–4; A. Haydon d. M. Arnold 6–3 5–7 6–3; Bloomer/Truman d. K. Fageros/Knode 6–2 6–3; A. Shilcock/P. Ward lost to Gibson/J. Jopps 4–6 6–3 3–6.

1959 USA d. Great Britain 4–3, Sewickley, Pennsylvania: Mrs B. Fleits d. A. Mortimer 6–2 6–1, d. C. Truman 6–4 6–4; D. R. Hard lost to Truman 4–6 6–2 3–6, d. Mortimer 6–3 6–8 6–4; S. Moore lost to A. Haydon 1–6 1–6; J. Arth/Hard d. S. J. Bloomer/Truman 9–7 9–7; J. Hopps/Moore lost to Haydon/Mortimer 2–6 4–6.

1960 Great Britain d. USA 4–3, Wimbledon: A. Haydon d. K. Hantze 2–6 11–9 6–1, lost to D. R. Hard 7–5 2–6 1–6; C. Truman lost to Hard 6–4 3–6 4–6, d. Hantze 7–5 6–3; A. Mortimer d. J. Hopps 6–8 6–4 6–1; Haydon/Mortimer lost to Hard/Hantze 0–6 0–6; S. J. Bloomer/Truman d. Hopps/Mrs D. Knode 6–4 9–7.

1961 USA d. Great Britain 6–1, Saddle & Cycle Club, Chicago: K. Hantze d. C. Truman 7–9 6–1 6–1, d. A. Haydon 6–1 6–4; B. J. Moffitt d. Haydon 6–4 6–4, lost to Truman 3–6 2–6; J. Bricka d. A. Mortimer 10–8 4–6 6–3; Hantze/Moffitt d. Truman/D. M. Catt 7–5 6–2; Mrs W. du Pont/M. Varner w.o. Mortimer/Haydon.

1962 USA d. Great Britain 4–3, Wimbledon: D. R. Hard d. C. Truman 6–2 6–2, d. A. Haydon 6–3 6–8 6–4; Mrs J. R. Susman lost to Haydon 8–10 5–7, d. Truman 6–4 7–5; N. Richey lost to D. M. Catt 1–6 5–7; Mrs W. du Pont/M. Varner d. Catt/E. Starkie 6–2 3–6 6–2; Hard/B. J. Moffitt lost to Haydon/Truman 4–6 3–6.

1963 USA d. Great Britain 6–1, Cleveland Skating Club, Cleveland: D. R. Hard lost to Mrs P. F. Jones 1–6 6–0 6–8, d. C. Truman 6–3 6–0; B. J. Moffitt d. Truman 6–4 19–17, d. Jones 6–4 4–6 6–3; N. Richey d. D. M. Catt 14–12 6–3; Hard/Moffitt d. Truman/Jones 4–6 7–5 6–2; Richey/Mrs D. Fales d. Catt/E. Starkie 6–4 6–8 6–2.

1964 USA d. Great Britain 5–2, Wimbledon: N. Richey d. D. M. Catt 4–6 6–4 7–5, d. Mrs P. F. Jones 7–5 11–9; B. J. Moffitt d. Jones 4–6 6–4 6–3, d. Catt 6–3 4–6 6–3; C. Caldwell d. E. Starkie 6–4 1–6 6–3; Caldwell/Moffitt lost to Catt/Jones 2–6 6–4 0–6; Richey/Mrs D. Fales lost to A. Mortimer/Starkie 6–2 3–6 4–6.

1965 USA d. Great Britain 5–2, Clarke Stadium, Cleveland: B. J. Moffitt lost to Mrs P. F. Jones 2–6 4–6, d. E. Starkie 6–3 6–2; N. Richey d. Starkie 6–1 6–0, lost to Jones 4–6 6–8; Mrs C. Graebner d. S. V. Wade 3–6 10–8 6–4; Graebner/Richey d. F. E. Truman/Starkie 6–1 6–0; Moffitt/Mrs J. R. Susman d. Jones/Wade 6–3 8–6.

1966 USA d. Great Britain 4–3, Wimbledon: N. Richey lost to Mrs P. F. Jones 6–2 4–6 3–6, d. S. V. Wade 2–6 6–2 7–5; Mrs L. W. King d. Wade 6–3 6–3, d. Jones 5–7 6–2 6–3; M. A. Eisel lost to W. Shaw 2–6 3–6; King/J. Albert lost to Jones/Wade 5–7 2–6; Richey/Eisel d. R. Bentley/E. Starkie 6–1 6–2.

1967 USA d. Great Britain 6–1, Clarke Stadium, Cleveland: Mrs L. W. King d. S. V. Wade 6–3 6–2, d. Mrs P. F. Jones 6–1 6–2; N. Richey d. Jones 6–2 6–2, d. Wade 3–6 8–6 6–2; R. Casals lost to C. Truman 6–3 5–7 1–6; Casals/King d. Jones/Wade 10–8 6–4; M. A. Eisel/Mrs C. Graebner d. W. Shaw/Mrs J. Williams 8–6 12–10.

1968 USA d. USA 4–3, Wimbledon: Mrs C. Janes lost to N. Richey 1–6 6–8, lost to M. A. Eisel 4–6 3–6; S. V. Wade d. Eisel 6–0 6–1, d. Richey 6–4 2–6 6–3; W. Shaw lost to J. Bartkowicz 5–7 6–3 4–6; Shaw/Wade d. Eisel/Richey 5–7 6–4 6–3; Janes/F. E. Truman d. S. De Fina/K. Harter 6–3 2–6 6–3.

1969 USA d. Great Britain 5–2, Clarke Stadium, Cleveland: J. M. Heldman d. S. V. Wade 3–6 6–1 8–6, d. W. Shaw 6–3 6–4; N. Richey d. Shaw 8–6 6–2, lost to Wade 3–6 6–2 4–6; J. Bartkowicz d. Mrs C. Janes 8–6 6–0; Mrs P. Curtis/V. Ziengenfuss lost to Janes/F. E. Truman 1–6 6–3 4–6; Heldman/Bartkowicz d. Shaw/Wade 6–4 6–2.

1970 USA d. Great Britain 4–3, Wimbledon: Mrs L. W. King d. S. V. Wade 8–6 6–4, d. Mrs P. F. Jones 6–4 6–2; N. Richey lost to Jones 3–6 3–6, lost to Wade 3–6 2–6; J. M. Heldman d. Mrs G. Williams 6–3 6–2; Mrs P. Curtis/Heldman lost to Jones/Williams 3–6 2–6; King/J. Bartkowicz d. W. Shaw/Wade 7–5 6–8 6–2.

1971 USA d. Great Britain 4–3, Clarke Stadium, Cleveland: C. Evert d. W. Shaw 6–0 6–4, d. S. V. Wade 6–1 6–1; J. M. Heldman lost to Wade 5–7 5–7; V. Ziegenfuss d. Shaw 6–4 4–6 6–3; K. Pigeon lost to Mrs G. Williams 5–7 6–3 4–6; Mrs P. Curtis/Ziegenfuss d. Mrs C. Janes/F. E. Truman 6–1 6–4; Mrs C. Graebner/Evert lost to Wade/Williams 8–10 6–4 1–6.

1972 USA d. Great Britain 5–2, Wimbledon: W. Overton lost to Mrs G. Williams 3–6 6–3 3–6, lost to S. V. Wade 6–8 5–7; C. Evert d. Wade 6–4 6–4, d. Williams 6–2 6–3; P. S. A. Hogan d. C. Molesworth 6–8 6–4 6–2; Evert/Hogan d. W. Shaw/F. E. Truman 7–5 6–4; Overton/V. Ziegenfuss d. Wade/Williams 6–3 6–3.

1973 USA d. Great Britain 5–2, Longwood Cricket Club, Boston: C. Evert d. S. V. Wade 6–4 6–2, d. V. Burton 6–3 6–0; P. S. A. Hogan d. Burton 6–4 6–3, lost to Wade 2–6 2–6; L. Tuero d. G. Coles 7–5 6–2; Evert/M. Redondo lost to Coles/Wade 3–6 4–6; J. Evert/Hogan d. L. Beaven/L. Charles 6–3 4–6 8–6.

1974 Great Britain d. USA 6–1, Deeside Leisure Centre, Queensferry, North Wales (indoors): S. V. Wade d. J. M. Heldman 5–7 9–7 6–4, d. J. Newberry 6–1 6–3; G. Coles d. Newberry 4–6 6–1 6–3, d. Heldman 6–0 6–4; S. Barker d. J. Evert 4–6 6–4 6–1; Barker/Charles d. Newberry/B. Nagelsen 4–6 6–2 6–1; Coles/Wade lost to Heldman/M. Schallau 5–7 4–6.

1975 Great Britain d. USA 5–2, Public Auditorium, Cleveland (indoors): S. V. Wade d. M. Schallau 6–2 6–2; lost to C. Evert 3–6 5–7; G. Coles lost to Evert 4–6 1–6, d. Schallau 6–3 7–6; S. Barker d. J. Newberry 6–4 7–5; Mrs P. F. Jones/Wade d. Newberry/J. Anthony 6–2 6–3; Coles/Barker d. Evert/Schallau 7–5 6–4.

1976 USA d. Great Britain 5–2, Crystal Palace, London (indoors): C. Evert d. S. V. Wade 6–2 3–6 6–2, d. S. Barker 2–6 6–2 6–2; R. Casals lost to Barker 6–1 3–6 2–6, lost to Wade 6–3 7–9 ret'd; T. Holladay d. G. Coles 3–6 6–1 6–4; Casals/Evert d. Barker/Wade 6–5 7 6–1; Mrs M. Guerrant/A. Kiyomura d. S. Mappin/L. Charles 6–2 6–2.

1977 USA d. Great Britain 7–0, Oakland, California (indoors): C. Evert d. S. V. Wade 7–5 7–6, d. S. Barker 6–1 6–2; Mrs L. W. King d. Barker 6–1 6–4, d. Wade 6–4 3–6 8–6; R. Casals d. M. Tyler 6–2 3–6 6–4; King/J. Russell d. S. Mappin/L. Charles 6–0 6–1; Casals/Evert d. Barker/Wade 6–2 6–4.

1978 Great Britain d. USA 4–3, Albert Hall, London (indoors): S. Barker lost to C. Evert 2–6 1–6, d. T. Austin 6–3 3–6 6–0; S. V. Wade d. Austin 3–6 7–5 6–3, lost to Evert 0–6 1–6; M. Tyler d. P. H. Shriver 5–7 6–2 6–3; S. Mappin/A. E. Hobbs lost to Mrs L. W. King/Austin 2–6 6–4 2–6; Barker/Wade d. Evert/Shriver 6–0 5–7 6–4.

1979 USA d. Great Britain 7–0, Palm Beach West, Florida: Mrs J. M. Lloyd d. S. Barker 7–5 6–2, d. S. V. Wade 6–1 6–1; T. Austin d. Wade 6–1 6–4, d. Barker 6–4 6–2; K. Jordan d. A. E. Hobbs 6–4 6–7 6–2; Austin/A. Kiyomura d. J. M. Durie/D. A. Jevans 6–3 6–1; Lloyd/R. Casals d. Barker/Wade 6–0 6–1.

1980 USA d. Great Britain 5–2, Albert Hall, London (indoors): Mrs J. M. Lloyd d. S. Barker 6–1 6–2, d. S. V. Wade 7–5 3–6 7–5; A. Jaeger d. Wade 6–6 3 6–2, lost to Barker 3–6 5–7; K. Jordan lost to A. E. Hobbs 6–4 4–6 1–6; Lloyd/R. Casals d. Hobbs/G. Coles 6–3 6–3; A. E. Smith/Jordan d. Barker/Wade 6–4 7–5.

1981 USA d. Great Britain 7–0, International Amphitheatre, Chicago (indoors): T. Austin d. S. Barker 7–5 6–3, d. S. V. Wade 6–3 6–1; Mrs J. M. Lloyd d. Wade 6–1 6–3, d. Barker 6–3 6–0; A. Jaeger d. A. E. Hobbs 6–0 6–0; Jaeger/P. H. Shriver d. J. M. Durie/Hobbs 6–1 6–3; Lloyd/R. Casals d. G. Coles/Wade 6–3 6–3.

1982 USA d. Great Britain 6–1, Albert Hall, London (indoors): B. Potter d. S. Barker 6–2 6–2, d. J. M. Durie 5–7 7–6 6–2; Mrs J. M. Lloyd d. Durie 6–2 6–2, d. Barker 6–4 6–3; A. E. Smith d. S. V. Wade 6–3 7–6; R. Casals/Smith lost to Durie/A. E. Hobbs 3–6 6–2 3–6; Potter/S. A. Walsh d. Barker/Wade 2–6 6–4 6–4.

1983 USA d. Great Britain 6–1, Williamsburg, Virginia (indoors): M. Navratilova d. S. Barker 6–2 6–0, d. J. M. Durie 6–3 6–3; P. H. Shriver d. Durie 6–3 6–2, d. Barker 6–0 6–1; K. Rinaldi d. S. V. Wade 6–3 6–2; C. Reynolds/P. Smith lost to Barker/Wade 5–7 6–3 1–6; Navratilova/Shriver d. Durie/A. Croft 6–2 6–1.

1984 USA d. Great Britain 5–2, Albert Hall, London (indoors): Mrs J. M. Lloyd d. A. E. Hobbs 6–2 6–2; A. Moulton

lost to A. Croft 1–6 7–5 4–6; B. Potter lost to J. M. Durie 3–6 6–7; Lloyd/Moulton d. A. Brown/S. V. Wade 6–2 6–2; Potter d. Hobbs 6–1 6–3; Lloyd d. Durie 7–6 6–1; Potter/S. A. Walsh d. Durie/Hobbs 7–6 4–6 9–7.
1985 USA d. Great Britain 7–0, Williamsburg, Virginia (indoors): Mrs J. M. Lloyd d. J. M. Durie 6–2 6–3; K. Rinaldi d. A. E. Hobbs 7–5 7–5; P. H. Shriver d. A. Croft 6–0 6–0; B. Nagelsen /A. White d. Croft /S. V. Wade 6–4 6–1; Shriver d. Durie 6–4 6–4; Lloyd d. Croft 6–3 6–0; Lloyd /Shriver d. Durie /Hobbs 6–3 6–7 6–2.

WIGHTMAN CUP STALWARTS
(Players participating in 10 or more ties or playing 20 or more rubbers)

	TOTAL RUBBERS		SINGLES		DOUBLES			
	PL'D	WON	PL'D	WON	PL'D	WON	TIES	YEARS
S. V. Wade (GB)	56	19	35	12	21	7	21	1965–85
Mrs J. M. Lloyd (USA)	38	34	26	26	12	8	13	1971–73,75–82,84–85
Mrs P. F. Jones (GB)	32	16	21	10	11	6	13	1957–67,70,75
Mrs F. S. Moody (USA)	30	21	20	18	10	3	10	1923–25,27,29–32,38
H. H. Jacobs (USA)	30	19	22	14	8	5	12	1927–37,39
Mrs G. T. Janes (GB)	27	12	21	10	11	6	11	1957–63,67–69,71
S. Barker (GB)	27	9	18	5	9	4	10	1974–83
Mrs L. W. King (USA)	26	21	16	14	10	7	10	1961–67,70,77,78
D. Hart (USA)	24	22	15	14	9	8	10	1946–55
A. L. Brough (USA)	22	22	12	12	10	10	10	1946–48,50,52–57
Mrs S. P. Fabyan (USA)	21	14	11	7	10	7	10	1930–39
N. Richey (USA)	21	12	16	9	5	3	9	1962–70

EUROPEAN CUP

Formerly King's Cup

International Men's Team Championship on Indoor Courts. It was staged on a knock-out basis 1936–38, 1952–74, on a league basis 1976–83 with ties home and away. From 1984 the ties in each division were held concurrently at one venue. The Challenge Round system was used in the two opening years, with 1937 the only Challenge Round.

FINALS
1936 France d. Sweden 4–1, Stockholm: J. Borotra d. K. Schroeder 2–6 6–2 6–1 6–3, d. C. Oestberg 6–1 6–3 7–5; B. Destremau d. Schroeder 3–6 7–5 6–2 6–4, d. Oestberg 6–2 6–2 6–4; C. Boussus/J. Brugnon lost to Oestberg/Schroeder 2–6 6–3 4–6 6–3 4–6.
1937 France d. Sweden 5–0, Paris: B. Destremau d. K. Schroeder 8–6 1–6 2–6 11–9 8–6, d. N. Rohlsson 1–6 1–6 6–3 6–1 6–0; Y. Petra d. Rohlsson 6–1 6–4 6–2, d. Schroeder 6–3 3–6 6–3 6–4; H. Bolelli/J. Lesueur d. Schroeder/H. Wallen 10–8 6–4 6–4.
1938 Germany d. Denmark 5–0, Hamburg: R. Menzel d. H. Plougmann 6–3 6–2 8–6; H. Henkel d. I. Gerdes 6–4 6–0 6–3, d. Plougmann 6–2 6–1 6–3; R. Redl d. Gerdes 6–3 6–3 6–2; Henkel/Menzel d. Gerdes/Plougmann 6–0 6–4 6–2.
1939–51 *Not held*
1952 Denmark won: Details not available
1953 Denmark won: Details not available
1954 Denmark d. Sweden 3–2
1955 Denmark d. Italy 3–2
1956 Sweden d. France 4–1
1957 Sweden won: Details not available
1958 Sweden d. Denmark 3–2
1959 Denmark won: Details not available
1960 Denmark d. West Germany 2–1
1961 Sweden d. Denmark 2–1
1962 Denmark d. Italy 3–0
1963 Yugoslavia d. Denmark 3–0
1964 Great Britain d. Sweden 3–0, Stockholm: M. J. Sangster d. J. E. Lundquist 13–15 10–8 12–10; R. Taylor d. B. Holmstrom 6–3 9–7; Sangster/R. K. Wilson d. Holmstrom/L. Olander 4–6 12–10 6–4.

1965 Great Britain d. Denmark 2–1, Torquay: R. K. Wilson lost to J. Leschly 1–6 4–6; M. Cox d. C. Hedelund 6–4 6–3; A. R. Mills/Wilson d. Leschly/Hedelund 3–6 6–2 6–4 12–10.
1966 Great Britain d. Italy 3–0, Milan: R. Taylor d. N. Pietrangeli 6–4 6–4; M. J. Sangster d. G. Maioli 7–9 6–4 11–9; Sangster/R. K. Wilson d. D. di Maso/Maioli 6–4 6–1.
1967 Great Britain d. Sweden 2–1, Stockholm: R. Taylor d. O. Bengtson 2–6 6–3 9–7; R. K. Wilson d. M. Carlstein 8–6 6–2; M. Cox/Taylor lost to Bengtson/B. Homstrom 4–6 7–9.
1968 Sweden d. Netherlands 2–1, Bratislava: O. Bengtson lost to T. S. Okker 12–14 4–6; M. Carlstein d. J. Hordijk 6–4 6–3; Bengtson/Carlstein d. N. Fleury/Okker 1–6 4–6 7–5 6–3 6–4.
1969 Czechoslovakia d. Sweden 2–1, Cologne: V. Zednik d. H. Zahr 6–4 7–5; J. Kukal d. O. Bengtson 6–1 5–7 11–9; Kukal/Zednik lost to Bengtson/H. Nerell 4–6 4–6.
1970 France d. Denmark 2–1, Copenhagen: J. B. Chanfreau d. J. Ulrich 6–3 8–6; G. Goven lost to J. Leschly 1–6 3–6; Chanfreau/Goven d. Ulrich/Leschly 2–6 6–4 7–5.
1971 Italy d. Spain 2–1, Ancona: A. Panatta lost to M. Orantes 2–6 3–6; N. Pietrangeli d. J. Gisbert 7–9 8–6 6–4; Panatta/Pietrangeli d. Gisbert/Orantes 4–6 8–6 6–3 6–4.
1972 Spain d. Hungary 3–0, Madrid: A. Gimeno d. S. Baranyi 10–8 6–2; J. Gisbert d. B. Taroczy 6–1 7–9 6–3; J. Herrera/A. Munoz d. R. Machan/Taroczy 6–4 3–6 7–5.
1973 Sweden d. Italy 2–1, Hanover: L. Johansson d. A. Zugarelli 6–4 6–3; B. Borg d. A. Panatta 4–6 6–2 8–6; Borg/Johansson lost to P. Bertolucci/Zugarelli 6–3 5–7 4–6.
1974 Italy d. Sweden 3–0, Ancona: Details not available
1975 Not held
1976 Hungary 11 wins, Great Britain 10 wins (played entirely as round robin, each tie home and away). Hungarian team: P. Szoke, B. Taroczy. British team: M. Cox, J. M. Lloyd, C. J. Mottram, R. Taylor.
1977 Sweden d. West Germany 5–1: 3–0 Stockholm, 2–1 Kiel.
1978 Sweden d. Hungary 3–3 (9–7 sets), Uppsala: T. Svensson d. P. Szoke 6–2 6–4; O. Bengtson lost to B. Taroczy 6–7 6–7; Bengtson/Svensson lost to Szoke/Taroczy 6–7 4–6; **Debrecen:** Svensson d. Szoke 6–2 6–2; Bengtson d. Taroczy 6–4 7–6; Bengtson/Svensson lost to Szoke/Taroczy 3–6 6–3 3–6.
1979 Czechoslovakia d. Hungary 4–2: 2–1 Pecs; 2–1 Chrudim.
1980 Czechoslovakia d. Hungary 5–1, Chrudim: T. Smid d. R. Machan 6–4 6–2; I. Lendl d. B. Taroczy 6–2 6–1; Smid/P. Slozil d. P. Szoke/Machan 6–4 7–5; **Debrecen:** Smid d. J. Benyik 6–2 3–6 6–2; Lendl d. Machan 6–0 6–2; Smid/Slozil lost to Machan/Szoke 6–3 3–6 2–6.
1981 West Germany d. USSR 3–3 (9–7 sets): Details not available
1982 West Germany d. Czechoslovakia 2–1, Dortmund: K. Eberhard lost to J. Navratil 4–6 1–6; U. Pinnder d. P. Slozil 6–4 6–4; C. Zipf/H. D. Beutel d. Navratil/Slozil 6–3 6–4.
1983 West Germany d. Czechoslovakia 2–1, Uppsala: H. J. Schwaier lost to L. Pimek 6–4 2–6 3–6; M. Westphal d. J. Navratil 3–6 6–2 6–3; E. Jelen/W. Popp d. Navratil/Pimek 6–1 1–6 7–6.
1984 Czechoslovakia d. Sweden 2–1, Essen: M. Mecir d. J. Gunnarsson 7–6 6–4; L. Pimek lost to J. Nystrom 3–6 5–7; Pimek/J. Navratil d. Gunnarsson/Nystrom 3–6 6–2 6–4.
1985 Sweden d. Switzerland 3–0, Essen: T. Hogstedt d. R. Stadler 6–3 6–2; J. Gunnarsson d. J. Hlasek 7–5 4–6 6–2; H. /S. Simonsson d. Hlasek /Stadler 6–3 3–6 6–3.

WORLD TEAM CUP

Eight-nation men's team event, qualification by individual ATP rating. Formerly Nations Cup.

FINALS
Played at Kingston, Jamaica
1975 USA d. Great Britain 2–1: R. Tanner d. R. Taylor 6–3 2–6 6–4; A. R. Ashe lost to C. J. Mottram 5–7 7–5 1–6; Ashe/Tanner d. Mottram/Taylor 6–1 1–6 6–4.
1976–77 Not held
Played at Düsseldorf
1978 Spain d. Australia 2–1: J. Higueras d. J. D. Newcombe 6–2 6–3; M. Orantes d. P. Dent 6–3 6–4; Higueras/Orantes lost to Dent/Newcombe 6–7 4–6.
1979 Australia d. Italy 2–1: J. G. Alexander d. C. Barazzutti 6–2 6–0; P. Dent lost to A. Panatta 3–6 3–6; Alexander/Dent d. P. Bertolucci/Panatta 6–3 7–6.
1980 Argentina d. Italy 3–0: G. Vilas d. C. Barazzutti 6–3 6–2; J. L. Clerc d. A. Panatta 7–6 6–3; Clerc/Vilas d. P. Bertolucci/Panatta 6–2 6–3.
1981 Czechoslovakia d. Australia 2–1: I. Lendl lost to P. McNamara 3–6 4–6; T. Smid d. P. McNamee 6–4 7–6; Lendl/Smid d. McNamara/McNamee 6–4 6–3.
1982 USA d. Australia 2–1: G. Mayer d. K. Warwick 7–6 6–2; E. Teltscher d. P. McNamara 6–4 7–6; Mayer/S. E. Stewart lost to M. R. Edmondson/McNamara 1–6 1–6.
1983 Spain d. Australia 2–1: J. Higueras d. M. R. Edmondson 6–2 6–4; M. Orantes d. P. Cash 6–3 6–2; A. Gimenez/Higueras lost to Cash/Edmondson 5–7 6–4 1–6.
1984 USA d. Czechoslovakia 2–1: J. P. McEnroe d. I. Lendl 6–3 6–2; J. Arias lost to T. Smid 6–4 6–7 4–6; P. Fleming/McEnroe d. Lendl/Smid 6–1 6–2.
1985 USA d. Czechoslovakia 2–1: J. P. McEnroe lost to I. Lendl 7–6 6–7 3–6; J. S. Connors d. M. Mecir 6–3 3–6 7–5; K. Flach /R. Seguso d. Lendl /T. Smid 6–3 7–6

MEN'S GRAND PRIX WINNERS

	SINGLES	BONUS	DOUBLES	BONUS	SPONSOR
1970	C. Richey	$25,000	—		Pepsi-Cola
1971	S. R. Smith	$25,000	—		Pepsi-Cola
1972	I. Nastase	$50,000	—		Commercial Union
1973	I. Nastase	$55,000	—		Commercial Union
1974	G. Vilas	$100,000	—		Commercial Union
1975	G. Vilas	$100,000	J. Gisbert	$25,000	Commercial Union
1976	R. Ramirez	$150,000	R. Ramirez	$40,000	Commercial Union
1977	G. Vilas	$300,000	R. A. J. Hewitt	$85,000	Colgate
1978	J. S. Connors	*$300,000	W. Fibak	$90,000	Colgate
1979	J. P. McEnroe	$300,000	S. E. Stewart	$90,000	Colgate
1980	J. P. McEnroe	$300,000	S. R. Smith	$90,000	Volvo
1981	I. Lendl	$300,000	H. Gunthardt	$90,000	Volvo
1982	J. S. Connors	$600,000	S. E. Stewart	$150,000	Volvo
1983	M. Wilander	$600,000	P. Fleming	$150,000	Volvo
1984	J. P. McEnroe	$600,000	T. Smid	$150,000	Volvo
1985	I. Lendl	$800,000	R. Seguso	$165,000	Nabisco

Neither Connors nor second-placed B. Borg had played enough tournaments to qualify for the bonus payment, which was awarded to third-placed E. Dibbs.

MEN'S GRAND PRIX MASTERS WINNERS

SINGLES

	VENUE	WINNER	RUNNER-UP	SCORE	FIRST PRIZE
1970	Tokyo	S. R. Smith	R. G. Laver	Round-Robin	$10,000
1971	Paris	I. Nastase	S. R. Smith	Round-Robin	$15,000
1972	Barcelona	I. Nastase	S. R. Smith	6–3 6–2 3–6 2–6 6–3	$15,000
1973	Boston	I. Nastase	T. S. Okker	6–3 7–5 4–6 6–3	$15,000
1974	Melbourne	G. Vilas	I. Nastase	7–6 6–2 3–6 3–6 6–4	$40,000
1975	Stockholm	I. Nastase	B. Borg	6–2 6–2 6–1	$40,000
1976	Houston	M. Orantes	W. Fibak	5–7 6–2 0–6 7–6 6–1	$40,000
1977*	New York	J. S. Connors	B. Borg	6–4 1–6 6–4	$100,000
1978*	New York	J. P. McEnroe	A. R. Ashe	6–7 6–3 7–5	$100,000
1979*	New York	B. Borg	V. Gerulaitis	6–2 6–2	$100,000
1980*	New York	B. Borg	I. Lendl	6–4 6–2 6–2	$100,000
1981*	New York	I. Lendl	V. Gerulaitis	6–7 2–6 7–6 6–2 6–4	$100,000
1982*	New York	I. Lendl	J. P. McEnroe	6–4 6–4 6–2	$100,000
1983*	New York	J. P. McEnroe	I. Lendl	6–3 6–4 6–4	$100,000
1984*	New York	J. P. McEnroe	I. Lendl	7–5 6–0 6–4	$100,000
1985*	New York	I. Lendl	B. Becker	6–2 7–6 6–3	$100,000

Played in January of the following year.

DOUBLES

	WINNERS	RUNNERS-UP	SCORE
1970	S. R. Smith/A. R. Ashe	R. G. Laver/J. Kodes	Round-Robin
1971–74	Not held		
1975	J. Gisbert/M. Orantes	J. Fassbender/H. J. Pohmann	Round-Robin
1976	F. McNair/S. E. Stewart	B. E. Gottfried/R. Ramirez	6–3 5–7 5–7 6–4 6–4
1977*	R. A. J. Hewitt/F. D. McMillan	R. C. Lutz/S. R. Smith	7–5 7–6 6–3
1978*	P. Fleming/J. P. McEnroe	W. Fibak/T. S. Okker	6–4 6–2 6–4
1979*	P. Fleming/J. P. McEnroe	W. Fibak/T. S. Okker	6–3 7–6 6–1
1980*	P. Fleming/J. P. McEnroe	P. McNamara/P. McNamee	6–4 6–3
1981*	P. Fleming/J. P. McEnroe	K. Curren/S. Denton	6–3 6–3
1982*	P. Fleming/J. P. McEnroe	S. E. Stewart/F. Taygan	6–2 6–2
1983*	P. Fleming/J. P. McEnroe	P. Slozil/T. Smid	6–2 6–2
1984*	P. Fleming/J. P. McEnroe	M. R. Edmondson/S. E. Stewart	6–3 6–1
1985*	A. Jarryd/S. Edberg	J. Nystrom/M. Wilander	6–1 7–6

Played in January of the following year.

WOMEN'S WORLD SERIES

	WINNER	BONUS	DOUBLES WINNERS	SPONSOR
1971	Mrs L. W. King	$10,000	—	Pepsi-Cola
1972	Mrs L. W. King	$20,000	—	Commerical Union
1973	Miss C. M. Evert	$23,000	—	Commercial Union
1974–76	*Not held*			
1977	Miss C. M. Evert	$100,000	Miss M. Navratilova/Miss B. Stove	Colgate
1978	Miss C. M. Evert	$100,000	Mrs G. E. Reid/Miss W. M. Turnbull	Colgate
1979	Mrs J. M. Lloyd	$115,000	Miss B. Stove/Miss W. M. Turnbull	Colgate
1980	Miss H. Mandlikova	$115,000	Miss K. Jordan/Miss A. E. Smith	Colgate
1981	Miss M. Navratilova	$125,000	Miss R. Casals/Miss W. M. Turnbull	Toyota
1982	Miss M. Navratilova	$130,000	Miss R. Casals/Miss W. M. Turnbull	Toyota
1983	Miss M. Navratilova	$150,000	Miss M. Navratilova/Miss P. H. Shriver	Virginia Slims
1984	Miss M. Navratilova	$150,000	Miss M. Navratilova/Miss P. H. Shriver	Virginia Slims

WOMEN'S INTERNATIONAL SERIES CHAMPIONSHIPS

SINGLES

	VENUE	WINNER	RUNNER-UP	SCORE			FIRST PRIZE
1977	Palm Springs	Miss C. M. Evert	Mrs L. W. King	6–2	6–2		$75,000
1978	Palm Springs	Miss C. M. Evert	Miss M. Navratilova	6–3	6–3		$75,000
1979*	Landover, Maryland	Miss M. Navratilova	Miss T. A. Austin	6–2	6–1		$75,000
1980*	Palm Springs	Miss T. A. Austin	Miss A. Jaeger	6–2	6–2		$75,000
1981	East Rutherford, NJ	Miss T. A. Austin	Miss M. Navratilova	2–6	6–4	6–2	$75,000
1982	East Rutherford, NJ	Miss M. Navratilova	Mrs J. M. Lloyd	4–6	6–1	6–2	$75,000
1983*	Madison Square Garden, NY	Miss M. Navratilova	Mrs J. M. Lloyd	6–3	7–5	6–1**	$125,000
1984*	Madison Square Garden, NY	Miss M. Navratilova	Miss H. Sukova	6–3	7–5	6–4**	$125,000

* Played in the following year.   *** Best of five sets.*

DOUBLES

	WINNERS	RUNNERS-UP	SCORE		
1977	Miss F. Durr/Miss S. V. Wade	Mrs H. Gourlay Cawley/Miss J. Russell	6–1	4–6	6–4
1978	Mrs L. W. King/Miss M. Navratilova	Mrs G. E. Reid/Miss W. M. Turnbull	6–3	6–4	
1979*	Mrs L. W. King/Miss M. Navratilova	Miss R. Casals/Mrs J. M. Lloyd	6–4	6–3	
1980*	Miss R. Casals/Miss W. M. Turnbull	Miss C. Reynolds/Miss P. Smith	6–3	4–6	7–6
1981	Miss M. Navratilova/Miss P. H. Shriver	Miss R. Casals/Miss W. M. Turnbull	6–3	6–4	
1982	Miss M. Navratilova/Miss P. H. Shriver	Miss C. Reynolds/Miss P. Smith	6–4	7–5	
1983*	Miss M. Navratilova/Miss P. H. Shriver	Miss J. M. Durie/Miss A. Kiyomura	6–3	6–1	
1984*	Miss M. Navratilova/Miss P. H. Shriver	Miss C. Kohde-Kilsch/Miss H. Sukova	6–7	6–4	7–6

* Played in the following year.

GRAND SLAMS

The Grand Slam denotes holding the four championship titles of Australia, France, Wimbledon and the United States at the same time (originally in the same season)

MEN'S SINGLES
J. D. Budge: Wimbledon, US 1937, Australia, France, Wimbledon, US 1938
R. G. Laver: Australia, France, Wimbledon, US 1962
R. G. Laver: Australia, France, Wimbledon, US 1969

WOMEN'S SINGLES
Miss M. Connolly: Wimbledon, US 1952, Australia, France, Wimbledon, US 1953
Mrs B. M. Court: US 1969, Australia, France, Wimbledon, US 1970, Australia 1971
Miss M. Navratilova: Wimbledon, US, Australia 1983, France, Wimbledon, US 1984

MEN'S DOUBLES
F. A. Sedgman: (With J. E. Bromwich) US 1950, (with K. McGregor) Australia, France, Wimbledon, US 1951, Australia, France, Wimbledon 1952
K. McGregor: (With F. A. Sedgman) Australia, France, Wimbledon, US 1951, Australia, France, Wimbledon 1952

WOMEN'S DOUBLES
Miss A. L. Brough: (with Mrs W. du Pont) France, Wimbledon, US 1949, (with Miss D. J. Hart) Australia 1950
Miss M. E. Bueno: (With Miss C. C. Truman) Australia 1960, (with Miss D. R. Hard) France, Wimbledon, US 1960
Miss M. Navratilova/Miss P. H. Shriver: Wimbledon, US, Australia 1983, France, Wimbledon, US, Australia 1984, France 1985

MIXED DOUBLES
Miss M. Smith: (With F. S. Stolle) US 1962, (with K. N. Fletcher) Australia, France, Wimbledon, US 1963, Australia, France 1964
K. N. Fletcher: (With Miss M. Smith) Australia, France, Wimbledon, US 1963, Australia, France 1964
O. K. Davidson: (With Mrs D. Fales) US 1966, (with Miss L. R. Turner) Australia 1967, (with Mrs L. W. King) France, Wimbledon, US 1967
Mrs L. W. King: (With O. K. Davidson) France, Wimbledon, US 1967, (with R. D. Crealy) Australia 1968

JUNIOR SINGLES
E. H. Buchholz: Australia, France, Wimbledon, US 1958 (*Note:* the US event was not then conducted as an international event)
S. Edberg: France, Wimbledon, US, Australia 1983

ITF VETERAN CHAMPIONS

	1981 SAO PAULO	1982 POERTSCHACH	1983 BAHIA	1984 CERVIA	1985 MELBOURNE
MEN					
45+ Singles	S. Davidson	I. Gulyas	I. Gulyas	I. Gulyas	I. Barclay
45+ Doubles	S. Davidson/ H. Stewart	J. Morton/ J. Nelson	K. Fuhrmann/ F. Seeman	K. Fuhrmann/ F. Seeman	A. Duesler/J. Nelson
55+ Singles	S. Clark	R. McCarthy	R. McCarthy	G. Merlo	H. Stewart
55+ Doubles	S. Clark/ T. Johansson	A. Hussmuller/ L. Legenstein	A. Hussmuller/ L. Legenstein	J. Morton/ H. Stewart	J. Morton/H. Stewart
60+ Singles	—	T. Johansson			R. Sorlein
60+ Doubles	—	T. Johansson/ A. Ritzenberg			T. Johansson/V. Zabrodsky
65+ Singles	—	F. Klein	R. San Martin	G. Mulloy	J. Gilchrist
65+ Doubles	—	J. Becker/ F. Klein	F. Barboza/ H. H. Pizani	G. Mulloy/ F. Klein	F. Klein/A. Ritzenberg
WOMEN					
40+ Singles	E. de Molina	R. Drisaldi	H. Masthoff	H. Masthoff	H. Orth
40+ Doubles	N. Reed/ M. S. Plante	—	H. Masthoff/ H. Orth	H. Masthoff/ H. Orth	J. Dalton/H. Orth
45+ Doubles	—	C. Hillebrand/ N. Reed	—	—	—
50+ Singles	A. Cury	E. Slytermann	I. de Pla	C. Mazzoleni	I. Michael
50+ Doubles	—	E. Slytermann/ I. Burmester	G. Barboza/ J. Borzone	H. Brabenec/ P. Wearne	A. Fotheringham/A. Pilkinghorne

Margaret Smith Court achieved the traditional Grand Slam in mixed doubles with Fletcher in 1963 – the only pair to do so – and in singles in 1970. *(A. Cole)*

DUBLER CUP

International Men's Team Championship for Over 45s

FINALS

	VENUE*	WINNERS	RUNNERS-UP	SCORE
1958	Monte Carlo	Italy	West Germany	3–1
1959	Zurich	Switzerland	Italy	4–1
1960	Merano, Italy	Italy	Switzerland	5–0
1961	Bologna	Italy	Austria	4–1
1962	Merano, Italy	Italy	France	3–2
1963	Merano, Italy	Italy	Belgium	4–1
1964	Merano, Italy	Italy	West Germany	5–0
1965	Merano, Italy	Italy	Sweden	3–0
1966	Florence	Sweden	Italy	4–1
1967	Avesta, Sweden	France	Sweden	3–2
1968	Paris	USA	France	5–0
1969	St Louis	USA	Sweden	4–1
1970	Cleveland	USA	Sweden	4–1
1971	La Costa, California	USA	Sweden	3–2
1972	Le Touquet	USA	France	4–1
1973	New York	Australia	USA	3–1
1974	New York	USA	Australia	3–2
1975	New York	Australia	USA	5–0
1976	Alassio, Italy	Italy	Canada	3–2
1977	New York	USA	France	4–1
1978	New York	USA	Australia	4–1
1979	Vienna	Austria	USA	3–2
1980	Cervia, Italy	Sweden	Austria	2–1
1981	Buenos Aires	USA	Great Britain	2–1
1982	Athens	USA	Great Britain	2–1
1983	New York	USA	West Germany	2–1
1984	Bastad	West Germany	USA	3–0
1985	Perth	West Germany	Australia	2–1

* From 1958 to 1979 the early rounds were played zonally

AUSTRIA CUP

International Men's Team Competition for Over 55s

	VENUE	WINNERS	RUNNERS-UP	FINAL SCORE
1977	Baden b. Wien	Great Britain	Austria	2–1
1978	Brand (Austria)	USA	Sweden	2–1
1979	Brand (Austria)	USA	Sweden	3–0
1980	Brand (Austria)	USA	Sweden	2–1
1981	Poertschach	USA	Sweden	3–0
1982	Cervia, Italy	Australia	USA	2–1
1983	New York	Australia	USA	2–1
1984	Poertschach	USA	Australia	2–1
1985	Perth	Australia	USA	3–0

YOUNG CUP

International Women's Team Competition for Over 40s

	VENUE	WINNERS	RUNNERS-UP	FINAL SCORE
1977	Malmo	Argentina	Not available	
1978	Ancona	Italy	Not available	
1979	Cannes	West Germany	USA	3–0
1980	Bad Wiessee, Germany	West Germany	Italy	3–0
1981	Bad Wiessee, Germany	France	Italy	2–1
1982	Brand, Austria	France	Italy	3–0
1983	Cervia, Italy	West Germany	France	2–1
1984	Cervia, Italy	USA	France	3–0
1985	Poertschach, Austria	West Germany	France	3–0

MARIA ESTHER BUENO CUP

International Women's Team Competition for Over 50s

	VENUE	WINNERS	RUNNERS-UP	FINAL SCORE
1983	Poertschach	Great Britain	USA	2–1
1984	Le Touquet, France	USA	France	3–0
1985	Bremen	USA	Great Britain	3–0

ITALIA CUP

International Men's Team Competition for Over 35s

	VENUE	WINNERS	RUNNERS-UP	FINAL SCORE
1982	Cervia, Italy	Italy	USA	2–1
1983	Cervia, Italy	West Germany	USA	2–1
1984	Brand, Austria	West Germany	France	2–1
1985	Reggio Calabria, Italy	USA	Italy	2–0

BRITANNIA CUP

International Men's Team Competition for Over 65s

	VENUE	WINNERS	RUNNERS-UP	FINAL SCORE
1979	Queen's Club, London	USA	Great Britain	3–0
1980	Frinton-on-Sea	USA	Sweden	3–0
1981	Hurlingham Club, London	USA	Sweden	3–0
1982	New York	USA	Canada	3–0
1983	Poertschach	USA	Australia	3–0
1984	Poertschach	USA	Australia	3–0
1985	Poertschach	USA	Australia	3–0

THE CRAWFORD CUP

International Men's Team Competition for Over 75s

	VENUE	WINNERS	RUNNERS-UP	FINAL SCORE
1983	Brand, Austria	USA	Sweden	3–0
1984	Helsinki, Finland	USA	Great Britain	3–0
1985	Brand, Austria	USA	Australia	3–0

FRENCH INTERNATIONAL JUNIOR CHAMPIONSHIPS

BOYS' SINGLES

	WINNER	RUNNER-UP	SCORE		
1974	C. Casa (F)	U. Marten (G)	2–6	6–1	6–4
1975	C. Roger-Vasselin (F)	P. Elter (G)	6–1	6–2	
1976	H. Gunthardt (SWZ)	J. L. Clerc (ARG)	4–6	7–6	6–4
1977	J. P. McEnroe (USA)	R. Kelly (AUS)	6–1	6–1	
1978	I. Lendl (CZ)	P. Hjertquist	7–6	6–4	
1979	R. Krishnan (IND)	B. Testerman (USA)	2–6	6–1	6–0
1980	H. Leconte (F)	A. Tous (SP)	7–6	6–3	
1981	M. Wilander (SW)	J. Brown (USA)	7–5	6–1	
1982	T. Benhabiles	L. Courteau (F)	7–6	6–2	
1983	S. Edberg (SW)	F. Fevrier (F)	6–4	7–6	
1984	K. Carlsson (SW)	M. Kratzman (AUS)	6–3	6–3	
1985	J. Yzaga (PER)	T. Muster (AU)	2–6	6–3	6–0

GIRLS' SINGLES

	WINNER	RUNNER-UP	SCORE		
1974	M. Simionescu (RU)	S. Barker (GB)	6–3	6–3	
1975	R. Marsikova (CZ)	L. Mottram (GB)	6–3	5–7	6–2
1976	M. Tyler (GB)	M. Zoni (IT)	6–1	6–3	
1977	A. E. Smith (USA)	H. Strachonova (CZ)	6–3	7–6	
1978	H. Mandlikova (CZ)	M. Rothschild	6–1	6–1	
1979	L. Sandin (SW)	M. L. Piatek (USA)	6–3	6–1	
1980	K. Horvath (USA)	K. Henry (USA)	6–2	6–2	
1981	B. Gadusek (USA)	H. Sukova (CZ)	6–7	6–1	6–4
1982	M. Maleeva (BUL)	P. Barg (USA)	7–5	6–2	
1983	P. Paradis (F)	D. Spence (USA)	7–6	6–3	
1984	G. Sabatini (ARG)	K. Maleeva (BUL)	6–3	5–7	6–3
1985	L. Garrone (IT)	D. Van Rensburg (SA)	6–1	6–3	

BOYS' DOUBLES

	WINNERS	RUNNERS-UP	SCORE		
1983	M. Kratzman (AUS)/S. Youl (AUS)	A. Chesnokov (USSR)/A. Olkhovski (USSR)	6–2	6–3	
1985	P. Korda (CZ) /C. Suk (CZ)	V. Godrichidze (USSR)/V. Volkov (USSR)	4–6	6–0	7–5

GIRLS' DOUBLES

	WINNERS	RUNNERS-UP	SCORE		
1983	C. Anderholm (SW)/H. Olsson (SW)	K./M. Maleeva (BUL)	6–4	6–1	
1985	M. Perez (ARG)/P. Tarabini (ARG)	A. Holikova (CZ)/R. Szrubakova (CZ)	6–3	5–7	6–4

INTERNATIONAL WIMBLEDON JUNIOR CHAMPIONSHIPS

The event originated as an invitation tournament, boys' singles in 1947 and girls' singles in 1948. It became a championship event in 1975.

BOYS' SINGLES

	WINNER	RUNNER-UP	SCORE		
1975	C. J. Lewis (NZ)	R. Ycaza (EC)	6–1	6–4	
1976	H. Gunthardt (SWZ)	P. Elter (G)	6–4	7–5	
1977	V. Winitsky (USA)	E. Teltscher (USA)	6–1	1–6	8–6
1978	I. Lendl (CZ)	J. Turpin (USA)	6–3	6–4	
1979	R. Krishnan (IND)	D. Siegler (USA)	6–3	6–4	
1980	T. Tulasne (F)	H. D. Beutel (G)	6–4	3–6	6–4
1981	M. Anger (USA)	P. Cash (AUS)	7–6	7–5	
1982	P. Cash (AUS)	H. Sundstrom (SW)	6–4	6–7	6–3
1983	S. Edberg (SW)	J. Frawley (AUS)	6–3	7–6	
1984	M. Kratzman (AUS)	S. Kruger (SA)	6–4	4–6	6–3
1985	L. Lavalle (MEX)	E. Velez (MEX)	6–4	6–4	

GIRLS' SINGLES

	WINNER	RUNNER-UP	SCORE		
1975	N. Y. Chmyreva (USSR)	R. Marsikova (CZ)	6–4	6–3	
1976	N. T. Chmyreva (USSR)	M. Kruger (SA)	6–3	2–6	6–1
1977	L. Antonoplis (USA)	Mareen Louie (USA)	6–5	6–1	
1978	T. A. Austin (USA)	H. Mandlikova (CZ)	6–0	3–6	6–4
1979	M. L. Piatek (USA)	A. Moulton (USA)	6–1	6–3	
1980	D. Freeman (AUS)	S. Leo (AUS)	7–6	7–5	
1981	Z. Garrison (USA)	R. Uys (SA)	6–4	3–6	6–0
1982	C. Tanvier (F)	H. Sukova (CZ)	6–2	7–5	
1983	P. Paradis (F)	P. Hy (HK)	6–2	6–1	
1984	A. N. Croft (GB)	E. Reinach (SA)	3–6	6–3	6–2
1985	A. Holikova (CZ)	J. Byrne (AUS)	7–5	6–1	

BOYS' DOUBLES

	WINNERS	RUNNERS-UP	SCORE		
1982	P. Cash (AUS)/F. Frawley (AUS)	R. Leach (USA)/J. Ross (USA)	6–3	6–2	
1983	M. Kratzman (AUS)/S. Youl (AUS)	M. Nastase (RU)/O. Rahnasto (FIN)	6–4	6–4	
1984	R. Brown (USA)/R. Weiss (USA)	M. Kratzman (AUS)/J. Svensson (SW)	1–6	6–4	11–9
1985	A. Moreno (MEX)/J. Yzaga (PER)	P. Korda (CZ)/C. Suk (CZ)	7–6	6–4	

GIRLS' DOUBLES

	WINNERS	RUNNERS-UP	SCORE		
1982	B. Herr (USA)/P. Barg (USA)	B. S. Gerken (USA)/G. Rush (USA)	6–1	6–4	
1983	P. Fendick (USA)/P. Hy (HK)	C. Anderholm (SW)/H. Olsson (SW)	6–1	7–5	
1984	C. Kuhlman (USA)/S. Rehe (USA)	V. Milvidskaya (USSR)/L. Savchenko (USSR)	6–3	5–7	6–4
1985	L. Field (AUS) /J. Thompson (AUS)	E. Reinach (SA) /J. Richardson (NZ)	6–1	6–2	

US INTERNATIONAL JUNIOR CHAMPIONSHIPS

BOYS' SINGLES

	WINNER	RUNNER-UP	SCORE		
1974	W. Martin (USA)	F. Taygan (USA)	6–4	6–2	
1975	H. Schonfield (USA)	C. J. Lewis (NZ)	6–4	6–3	
1976	Y. Ycaza (EC)	J. L. Clerc (ARG)	6–4	5–7	6–0
1977	V. Winitsky (USA)	E. Teltscher (USA)	6–4	6–4	
1978	P. Hjertquist (SW)	S. Simonsson (SW)	7–6	1–6	7–6
1979	S. Davis (USA)	J. Gunnarsson (SW)	6–3	6–1	
1980	M. Falberg (USA)	E. Korita (USA)	6–0	6–2	
1981	T. Hogstedt (SW)	H. Schwaier (G)	7–5	6–3	
1982	P. Cash (AUS)	G. Forget (F)	6–3	6–3	
1983	S. Edberg (SW)	S. Youl (AUS)	6–2	6–4	
1984	M. Kratzman (AUS)	B. Becker (G)	6–3	7–6	
1985	T. Trigueiro (USA)	J. Blake (USA)	6–2	6–3	

GIRLS' SINGLES

	WINNER	RUNNER-UP	SCORE		
1974	I. Kloss (SA)	M. Jausovec (YU)	6–4	6–3	
1975	N. T. Chmyreva (USSR)	G. Stevens (SA)	6–7	6–2	6–2
1976	M. Kruger (SA)	L. Romanov (RU)	6–3	7–5	
1977	C. Casabianca (ARG)	L. Antonoplis (USA)	6–3	2–6	6–2
1978	L. Siegel (USA)	I. Madruga (ARG)	6–4	6–4	
1979	A. Moulton (USA)	M. L. Piatek (USA)	7–6	7–6	
1980	S. Mascarin (USA)	K. Keil (USA)	6–3	6–4	
1981	Z. Garrison (USA)	K. Gompert (USA)	6–0	6–3	
1982	B. Herr (USA)	G. Rush (USA)	6–3	6–1	
1983	E. Minter (AUS)	M. Werdel (USA)	6–3	7–5	
1984	K. Maleeva (BUL)	N. Sadupe (USA)	6–1	6–2	
1985	L. Garrone (IT)	A. Holikova (CZ)	6–2	7–6	

BOYS' DOUBLES

	WINNERS	RUNNERS-UP	SCORE		
1982	J. Canter (USA)/M. Kures (USA)	P. Cash (AUS)/J. Frawley (AUS)	7–6	6–3	
1983	M. Kratzman (AUS)/S. Youl (AUS)	P. McEnroe (USA)/B. Pearce (USA)	6–1	7–6	
1984	L. Lavelle (MEX)/M. Nastase (RU)	J. Icaza (PER)/A. Moreno (MEX)	7–6	1–6	6–1
1985	J. Blake (USA)/D. Yates (USA)	P. Flynn (USA)/D. McPherson (USA)	3–6	6–3	6–4

GIRLS' DOUBLES

	WINNERS	RUNNERS-UP	SCORE		
1982	P. Barg (USA)/B. Herr (USA)	A. Hulbert (AUS)/B. Randall (AUS)	1–6	7–5	7–6
1983	A. Hulbert (AUS)/B. Randall (AUS)	N. Riva (USSR)/L. Savchenko (USSR)	6–4	6–2	
1984	G. Sabatini (ARG)/M. Paz (MEX)	S. MacGregor (USA)/S. London (USA)	6–4	3–6	6–2
1985	R. Zrubakova (CZ) /A. Holikova (CZ)	P. Tarabini (ARG) /M. Perez Roldan (ARG)	6–4	2–6	7–5

ORANGE BOWL

International 18 and Under Championship

BOYS' SINGLES

	WINNER	RUNNER-UP	SCORE				
1974	W. Martin (USA)	T. Smid (CZ)	6–7	4–6	6–2	6–1	7–6
1975	F. Luna (SP)	B. E. Gottfried (USA)	6–4	6–4			
1976	J. P. McEnroe (USA)	E. Teltscher (USA)	7–5	6–1			
1977	I. Lendl (CZ)	Y. Noah (F)	4–6	7–6	6–3		
1978	G. Urpi (SP)	S. van der Merwe (SA)	6–3	6–1			
1979	R. Viver (EC)	P. Arraya (PER)	7–6	6–4			
1980	J. Nystrom (SW)	C. Castellan (ARG)	7–5	7–6			
1981	R. Arguello (ARG)	R. Joaquim (BR)	6–2	6–1			
1982	G. Forget (F)	J. Bardou (SP)	7–5	2–6	6–1		
1983	K. Carlsson (SW)	E. Sanchez (SP)	6–2	6–4			
1984	R. Brown (USA)	J. Berger (USA)	6–3	6–3			
1985	C. Pistolesi (IT)	B. Oresar (YU)	6–2	6–0			

GIRLS' SINGLES

	WINNER	RUNNER-UP	SCORE		
1974	L. Epstein (USA)	C. Penn (USA)	6–1	6–2	
1975	L. Epstein (USA)	S. McInerny (USA)	6–2	6–1	
1976	M. Kruger (SA)	A. E. Smith (USA)	2–6	6–3	6–4
1977	A. E. Smith (USA)	H. Strachonova (CZ)	7–6	7–5	
1978	A. Jaeger (USA)	R. Fairbank (SA)	6–1	6–3	
1979	K. Horvath (USA)	P. Murgo (IT)	7–5	6–0	
1980	S. Mascarin (USA)	R. Sasak (YU)	6–3	3–6	6–4
1981	P. Barg (USA)	H. Fukarkova (CZ)	6–2	6–3	
1982	C. Bassett (C)	M. Maleeva (BUL)	6–4	4–3 ret'd	
1983	D. Spence (USA)	A. Cecchini (IT)	2–6	7–5	6–4
1984	G. Sabatini (ARG)	K. Maleeva (BUL)	6–1	6–3	
1985	M. J. Fernandez (USA)	P. Tarabini (ARG)	7–5	6–1	

GALEA CUP

International Men's Team Competition for Under 21s.

FINAL ROUNDS

Played at Deauville

1950 *Italy d. France 4–1:* U. Bergamo d. R. L. Haillet 6–2 6–3, d. A. Lemyze 8–10 7–5 7–5; F. Gardini d. Lemyze 6–1 6–2; A. Parri lost to F. Nys 3–6 2–6; Gardini/H. Clerici d. Lemyze/Nys 6–1 6–3.

1951 *France d. West Germany 5–0:* A. Lemyze d. B. Pottinger 8–6 10–8; R. L. Haillet d. F. Feldbausch 6–4 6–4; G. Pilet d. C. Biederlack 1–6 6–2 6–2; P. Darmon d. J. Gulcz 6–4 1–6 6–1; Haillet/Lemyze d. Feldbausch/Pottinger 6–1 6–3 6–1.

Played at Vichy

1952 *Italy d. France 4–1:* N. Pietrangeli d. X. Perreau-Saussine 6–8 6–2 6–2, d. G. Pilet 7–5 6–1; A. Maggi lost to Pilet 3–6 6–2 3–6, d. Perreau-Saussine 6–4 7–5; Maggi/Pietrangeli d. J. N. Grinda/Pilet 10–8 6–3 6–3.

1953 *Italy d. France 4–1:* G. Pilet d. N. Pietrangeli 5–7 6–1 6–0, d. S. Jacobini 6–2 6–4; J. N. Grinda d. Jacobini 6–0 6–2, d. Pietrangeli 6–4 6–1; P. Darmon/Pilet lost to M. Pirro/Pietrangeli 3–6 5–7 7–9.

1954 *Italy d. Yugoslavia 3–2:* S. Jacobini d. L. Jagec 6–2 7–5, d. L. Backor 6–4 7–5; M. Pirro lost to Backor 6–3 4–6 4–6, lost to Jagec 0–6 5–7; Jacobsini/Pirro d. Backor/Jagec 10–8 4–6 6–4 6–3.

1955 *Italy d. Spain 5–0:* S. Jacobini d. A. Gimeno 3–6 6–3 6–4; F. Bonetti d. J. Moure 6–1 6–4; G. Morelli d. Moure 6–2 6–4; M. Drisaldi d. Santana 6–4 6–4; Drisaldi/Jacobini d. A. Arilla/Gimeno 6–3 6–4 2–6 6–1.

1956 *Spain d. Italy 4–1:* M. Santana d. F. Bonetti 6–3 5–7 7–5, d. G. Bonairi 4–6 6–5 7–5; A. Gimeno d. Bonetti 6–3 6–2, d. Bonairi 5–7 6–2 6–3: A. Arilla/A. Maggi 6–1 4–6 3–6 3–6.

1957 *Spain d. Italy 4–1:* M. Santana d. G. Morelli 9–7 6–4, d. E. Casini 6–4 6–4; A. Gimeno d. F. Bonetti 6–3 6–4; J. L. Arilla lost to Morelli 3–6 6–8; A. Arilla/Gimeno d. Bonetti/A. Maggi 6–4 6–3 6–3.

1958 *Spain d. West Germany 3–2:* M. Santana d. W. Bungert 6–3 7–5 4–6 6–0, lost to D. Eklebe 1–6 5–7 6–1 3–6; A. Arilla d. Eklebe 6–1 9–7 4–6 7–5; J. Gisbert lost to W. Stuck 0–6 2–6 2–0–6; A. Arilla/Santana d. Eklebe/Stuck 7–6 6–3 6–3.

1959 *West Germany d. USSR 4–1:* W. Stuck d. A. Pontanin 6–3 6–0 6–1, d. T. Lejus 6–4 6–1 6–0; W. Bungert d. Lejus 6–3 6–2; L. Sanders lost to Pontanin 4–6 3–6 6–1 7–5 2–6; Bungert/Stuck d. Lejus/S. Likachev 6–4 5–7 3–6 7–5 6–4.

1960 *France d. USSR 3–2:* A. Bresson d. S. Likachev 6–3 6–2 6–4, d. T. Lejus 2–6 3–6 6–0 6–3; C. Duxin lost to Lejus 5–7 4–6 8–10, lost to Likachev 2–6 3–6 1–6; D. Contet/F. Jauffret d. Lejus/Likachev 6–6 6–2 4–6 6–2.

1961 *France d. Spain 3–2:* C. Duxin lost to J. Gisbert 1–6 3–6 2–6, d. T. Casado 6–2 2–6 1–6–1; F. Jauffret d. Casado 6–3 6–2 6–3, lost to Gisbert 6–1 4–6 3–6 6–4 3–6; D. Contet/Jauffret d. J. L. Arilla/Gisbert 6–2 6–0 6–2.

1962 *France d. USSR 3–2:* J. C. Barclay d. S. Mdzinarichvili 6–4 6–2 6–4, d. A. Metreveli 6–4 6–2 8–6; F. Jauffret lost to Metreveli 6–3 2–6 3–6 4–6, d. Mdzinarichvili 8–6 6–1 0–6 6–2; C. Duxin/Jauffret lost to Mdzinarichvili/Metreveli 6–3 6–4 6–5 5–7.

1963 *Czechoslovakia d. Italy 3–2:* S. Koudelka lost to G. Maioli 3–6 6–4 3–6 5–7; d. G. Di Maso 6–4 6–2 6–2; M. Holecek d. Di Maso 6–4 11–9 6–4, d. Maioli 6–0 6–3 8–6; Holecek/Koudelka lost to Di Maso/Maioli 6–8 4–6 9–7 7–9.

1964 *USSR d. Czechoslovakia 3–2:* A. Metreveli d. J. Kodes 6–3 6–3 4–6 17–15, d. S. Koudelka 6–1 6–4 6–1; A. Ivanov lost to Koudelka 6–4 8–10 6–8 2–6, lost to Kodes 7–5 6–4 8–10 6–8 3–6; Ivanov/Metreveli d. Koudelka/F. Pala 6–4 5–7 9–7 8–6.

1965 *Czechoslovakia d. USSR 3–2:* J. Kodes lost to A. Ivanov 5–7 6–3 6–3 2–6 1–6, d. V. Korotkov 6–2 5–7 7–5 6–1; M. Laudin d. Korotkov 6–2 9–7 6–0, lost to Ivanov 8–10 2–6 2–6; Kodes/J. Stoces d. Ivanov/Korotkov 6–2 6–3 6–1.

1966 *Czechoslovakia d. USSR 4–1:* J. Kodes d. S. Kakoulia 6–3 6–1 6–1; M. Laudin d. V. Korotkov 6–2 3–6 6–1 6–4, lost to Kakoulia 1–6 0–6 7–5 3–6; Kodes/J. Medonos d. A. Egorov/Korotkov 6–4 6–3 6–1.

1967 *France d. Great Britain 3–1:* J. B. Chanfreau d. G. Battrick 6–4 3–6 4–6 7–5, d. D. A. Lloyd 6–2 6–3 6–8 7–5; G. Goven d. D. A. Lloyd 3–6 6–3 6–2 6–2; Goven/Chanfreau d. Battrick/Lloyd 8–10 6–3 6–4 6–2.

1968 *Spain d. France 3–2:* M. Orantes d. G. Goven 6–4 6–2 6–3, d. P. Proisy 6–1 10–8 6–3; A. Munoz lost to Proisy 6–4 9–11 6–8 6–3 1–6, d. Goven 6–2 3–6 6–3 4–6 7–5; Munoz/Orantes lost to Goven/P. Dominguez 1–6 6–0 1–6 1–6.

1969 *Spain d. Czechoslovakia 3–2:* A. Munoz d. P. Hutka 1–6 6–3 6–1 6–3; M. Orantes d. J. Hrebec 6–2 6–4 7–5;

J. Gisbert lost to Hutka 2–6 6–2 3–6 4–6; A. Muntanola lost to J. Pisecki 3–6 1–6 5–7; Munoz/Orantes d. Hrebec/Hutka 5–7 6–3 6–1 6–4.

1970 *Czechoslovakia d. Spain 3–2:* I. Pisecki lost to A. Munoz 7–5 4–6 4–6 2–6, d. A. Riba 6–1 6–2 6–2; J. Hrebec d. Riba 6–3 6–2 6–0, lost to Munoz 3–6 3–6 8–6 1–6; Hrebec/Pisecki d. Munoz/Riba 6–3 6–2 6–0.

1971 *Sweden d. France 5–0:* K. Johansson d. J. Lovera 6–1 0–6 6–1 6–3, d. E. Deblicker 10–12 6–4 6–3 1–6 7–5; T. Svensson d. Deblicker 6–2 6–2 6–2, d. Lovera 5–7 7–5 8–6; K./L. Johansson d. D. Naegelen/J. F. Caujoulle 6–4 6–4 6–2.

1972 *Great Britain d. Spain 4–1:* C. J. Mottram d. J. Herrera 6–1 4–6 6–0 2–6 7–5; S. Warboys d. J. Higueras 6–2 6–2 1–6 6–3, d. Herrera 6–3 6–2 0–6 2–6 7–5; J. M. Lloyd d. Higueras 6–2 10–8; Mottram/Warboys lost to Higueras/J. Moreno 6–3 3–6 4–6 6–1 5–7.

1973 *Spain d. Great Britain 4–1:* J. Higueras d. J. M. Lloyd 4–6 6–2 6–2 0–6 6–4; J. Moreno d. C. J. Mottram 3–6 3–6 6–3 6–1 6–3, d. Lloyd 6–1 6–1 6–3; Higueras/Moreno lost to S. Warboys/M. J. Farrell 7–9 3–6 2–6.

1974 *Czechoslovakia d. Spain 4–1:* P. Slozil d. S. Cabeza 6–4 6–2 6–1; T. Smid d. J. Soler 0–6 6–4 6–0 11–9, d. J. Garcia 6–3 1–6 6–3; J. Granat lost to A. Gimenez 4–6 2–6; Slozil/Smid d. Gimenez/Soler 6–4 6–2 6–4.

1975 *Czechoslovakia d. Spain 3–2:* T. Smid d. A. Gimenez 6–1 4–6 3–6 6–2 6–2, d. M. Mir 3–6 8–6 6–2 7–5; P. Slozil d. Mir 8–6 3–6 6–3 6–2, lost to A. Gimenez 4–6 8–6 1–6 5–7; Slozil/Smid lost to Gimenez/Mir 8–6 6–4 3–6 2–6 1–6.

1976 *West Germany d. Italy 3–2:* W. Zirngibl lost to F. Merlone 2–6 2–6 7–5 4–6, d. G. Ocleppo 6–1 6–1 6–4; P. Elter lost to Ocleppo 2–6 2–6 6–2 4–6, d. Merlone 6–3 3–6 6–4 6–4; U. Marten/K. Eberhard d. V. Vattuone/G. Marchetti 3–6 6–3 6–4 6–4.

1977 *Argentina d. France 3–2:* F. Dalla Fontana lost to C. Roger-Vasselin 4–6 6–1 4–6 4–6, d. C. Casa 6–3 7–6 6–3; J. L. Clerc lost to Casa 4–6 5–7 6–2 4–6, d. Roger-Vasselin 3–6 6–3 6–0 6–4; Clerc/A. Gattiker d. D. Bedel/Noah 2–6 4–6 7–5 6–1 6–4.

1978 *France d. Czechoslovakia 4–1:* Y. Noah d. D. Kulhaj 6–1 6–4 6–4; P. Portes d. I. Lendl 8–6 4–6 6–2 6–2; G. Morreton lost to Lendl 3–6 13–15; Portes d. M. Lacek 6–2 6–1; Morreton/Noah d. Kulhaj/Lendl 9–7 6–1 5–7 3–6 6–4.

1979 *France d. Czechoslovakia 3–2:* Y. Noah d. M. Lacek 6–3 6–1, d. D. Pohl 6–3 6–2 6–2; P. Portes lost to I. Lendl 1–6 3–6 5–7; T. Pham lost to Lacek 3–6 1–6; Noah/Portes d. Lacek/Lendl 14–12 5–7 8–6 7–5.

1980 *France d. Spain 3–2:* T. Tulasne d. A. Tous 6–4 6–3 6–2, d. J. B. Avendano 6–2 6–2 6–1; J. Potier lost to Avendano 6–8 2–6 2–6, lost to Tous 2–6 3–6; H. Leconte/Potier d. Avendano/Tous 6–0 7–5 3–6 6–1.

1981 *West Germany d. Australia 5–0:* C. Zipf d. G. Whitecross 5–7 7–5 9–11 6–2 6–2, d. C. Miller 8–6 3–6 11–9; H. D. Beutel d. Miller 3–6 8–6 6–2 6–1, d. Whitecross 6–4 6–2; Beutel/Zipf d. P. Doohan/Miller 6–4 7–5 6–2.

1982 *Australia d. Spain 3–2:* P. Cash d. A. Tous 4–6 6–2 8–10 6–4 6–1, lost to S. Casal 0–6 1–6; C. Miller d. Casal 6–4 1–6 9–7 6–3, lost to Tous 5–7 1–6; Cash/Miller d. Casal/M. Jaite 6–4 6–1 6–4.

1983 *France d. Spain 5–0:* G. Forget d. J. Bardou 6–2 6–2 5–7 4–6 10–8, d. M. Jaite 7–6 6–3; L. Courteau d. Jaite 6–4 10–8 3–6 6–2, d. Bardou 6–3 4–6 6–4; Courteau/Forget d. Bardou/Jaite 6–2 6–3 6–4.

1984 *Czechoslovakia d. Argentina 4–1:* M. Mecir d. G. Garetto 6–3 2–6 6–8 6–0 6–2; M. Vajda d. E. Masso 6–2 8–6 6–2; Mecir d. Masso 7–5 6–3; Garetto d. Vajda 9–7 6–1; Mecir/K. Novacek d. Masso/Mena 6–4 6–4 6–1.

1985 *Italy d. USA 3–2:* P. Cane d. L. Jensen 6–2 6–1 8–6; C. Pistolesi lost to R. Reneberg 3–6 3–6 3–6; Cane /M. Fioroni lost to Jensen /B. Pearce 1–6 6–3 1–6 2–6; Pistolesi d. Pearce 10–8 4–6 4–6 6–1 6–1; Cane d. Reneberg 6–3 6–0 6–4.

VALERIO CUP

International Team Championship for boys aged 18 and under. Played zonally with the final stages in Lesa, Italy.

FINALS

1970 *Sweden d. France 4–1:* L. Johansson d. F. Caujolle 10–8 6–3; T. Svensson d. E. Naegelen 6–4 6–0; R. Norbeg lost to E. Deblicker 4–6 0–6; M. Stig d. A. Collinot 6–3 6–1; Johansson/Stig d. Deblicker/Naegelen 6–3 6–3.

1971 *Italy d. West Germany 4–0:* M. Consolini d. U. Pinner 6–2 1–0 ret'd; N. Gasparini d. R. Gehring 6–1 3–6 6–0; C. Borea d. A. Hongsag 3–6 4–6 6–3; C. Barazzutti v L. Jelitto 5–1 abandoned; Barazzutti/Gasparini d. Gehring/Jelitto 6–4 6–4.

1972 *Czechoslovakia d. USSR 3–2:* I. Hora lost to V. Borisov 6–4 7–9 5–7; P. Slozil d. A. Machavez 6–2 2–6 6–4; Slozil/J. Granat d. A. Bogomolov/Borisov 6–3 7–5; T. Smid lost to K. Pugaev 3–6 8–6 4–6; Granat d. Bogomolov 6–3 6–4.

1973 *Czechoslovakia d. USSR 4–1:* A. Jankowski lost to V. Borisov 6–4 2–3 ret'd; P. Slozil d. A. Machavez 6–3 5–7 6–4: J. Granat d. K. Pugaev 3–6 6–4 6–3; T. Smid d. V. Katsnelson 6–4 6–4; Jankowski/Slozil d. Borisov/Pugaev 6–8 10–8 6–3.

1974 *Italy d. Italy 3–2:* L. Fargas d. A. Meneschincheri 6–1 6–1; A. Capitan /M. Mir lost to A. Marchetti/A. Vattuone 6–3 4–6 3–6; M. Mir lost to G. Ocleppo 4–2 6–2 6–1; A. Torralbo d. Vattuone 9–11 6–4 6–3; Capitan d. G. Marchetti 8–6 3–6 6–3.

1975 *Italy d. USSR 3–2:* G. Ocleppo d. S. Baranov 7–5 6–5 ret'd; A. Spiga d. S. Molodoikov 6–4 6–8 6–0; A. Merlone d. V. Gruzman 6–2 0–6 6–3; A. Meneschincheri lost to S. Elerdashvili 9–11 4–6; Ocleppo/Merlone lost to Baranov/Gruzman 5–7 4–6.

1976 *West Germany d. France 4–1:* P. Elter d. P. Portes 6–3 6–2; W. Popp lost to Y. Noah 3–6 0–6; J. Henn d. J. Kuentz 6–2 6–2; A. Maurer d. G. Geniau 6–4 6–3; Elter/Popp d. G. Moretton/Noah 6–3 3–6 6–3.

1977 *Italy d. Rumania 5–0:* G. Rinaldini d. E. Pana 6–1 6–1; M. Rivaroli d. L. Mancas 6–2 6–4; N. Canessa d. A. Dirzu 6–3 2–6 6–4; P. Parrini d. F. Segarceanu 6–1 6–0; Canessa/Parrini d. Dirzu/Segarceanu 7–5 6–2.

1978 *Sweden d. Italy 3–2:* M. Wennberg d. F. Moscino 6–2 6–2; P. Hjertquist/S. Simonsson d. M. Alciati/C. Panatta 6–1 6–3; Hjertquist d. M. Ferrari 6–1 6–3; Simonsson lost to Alciati 4–6 1–6; A. Jarryd lost to Panatta 0–6 1–6.

1979 *Sweden d. West Germany 4–1:* S. Simonsson d. H. D. Beutel 6–4 6–0; T. Svensson d. C. Zipf 2–6 6–4 6–4; A. Jarryd d. K. Vogel 6–2 7–5; J. Gunnarsson d. A. Schulz 7–5 6–4; Simonsson/Svensson lost to Beutel/Zipf 3–6 6–2 6–8.
1980 *Spain d. France 4–1:* J. Aguilera d. T. Pham 6–4 1–6 6–3; A. Tous/S. Casal d. J. Potier/J. M. Piacentile 6–2 3–6 6–4; Tous lost to Potier 1–6 6–7; R. Mensua d. P. Kuchna 6–4 6–1; Casal d. Miacentile 6–1 6–1.
1981 *Sweden d. Italy 3–2:* H. Sundstrom d. S. Ercoli 6–4 6–2; J. Nystrom/M. Tideman lost to L. Botazzi/F. Cancellotti 6–1 3–6 4–6; Nystrom d. Botazzi 6–3 6–2; T. Hogstedt lost to Cancellotti 4–6 1–6; Tideman d. S. Colombo 6–2 7–6.
1982 *Italy d. Spain 3–2:* S. Ercoli lost to M. Jaite 2–6 6–7; M. Fiorini d. D. de Miguel 6–2 7–5; P. Cane d. E. Sanchez 6–1 3–6 6–4; M. Zampieri lost to J. Bardou 4–6 4–6; Cane/Fioroni d. Bardou/Jaite 4–6 6–3 8–6.
1983 *Sweden d. Spain 4–1:* J. Svensson d. G. R. Fernando 4–6 6–4 7–5; J./K. Carlsson d. D. de Miguel/J. Bardou 6–2 1–6 6–2; J. Carlsson lost to Bardou 4–6 2–6; K. Carlsson d. E. Sanchez 3–6 6–0 6–1; P. Lundgren d. L. F. Garcia 6–3 6–4.
1984 *Italy d. France 3–1:* F. Ricci d. G. Tournant 6–4 3–6 7–5; N. Devide d. P. Gardarein 6–3 6–4; I. Cappelloni d. O. Cayla 7–5 7–6; Gardarein/Winogradski d. Devide/Pistolesi 5–7 6–4 6–4.
1985 *Italy d. Sweden 3–2:* A. Baldoni lost to D. Engel 2–6 1–6; C. Pistolesi /S. Mezzadri d. C. Allgaardh /T. Nydahll 6–4 6–4; Pistolesi d. Allgaardh 6–3 6–4; U. Colombini d. C. Bergstrom 7–6 6–2; O. Camporese lost to U. Stenlund 0–6 3–6.

JEAN BOROTRA CUP

International Team Championship for boys aged 16 and under; originally the Jean Becker Cup. Finals played in Le Touquet.

1972 *Spain d. France 4–1:* Details not available.
1973 *Italy d. West Germany 3–2:* Details not available.
1974 *West Germany d. Italy 4–1:* Details not available.
1975 *Czechoslovakia d. Italy 3–2:* M. Lacek d. G. Rinaldini 7–5 6–1; I. Lendl d. A. Ciardi 6–1 6–3; J. Kucera d. P. Parreni 6–4 6–4; Lacek/Kucera lost to Parreni/A. Rivaroli 4–6 4–6; Lendl/A. Vantuch lost to Ciardi/Rinaldini 6–1 4–6 3–6.
1976 *Sweden d. Czechoslovakia 3–2:* P. Hjertquist lost to I. Lendl 6–0 3–6 4–6; S. Simonsson d. A. Vikopa 6–3 6–0; H. Johansson d. T. Pitra 6–3 6–2; Simonsson/A. Fritzner lost to Lendl/J. Kerezek 6–4 3–6 1–6; Hjertquist/Johansson d. Pitra/J. Vikopal 6–3 6–2.
1977 *Italy d. Sweden 3–2:* A. Costa d. A. Jarryd 7–5 6–2; A. Giacomini lost to S. Simonsson 1–6 1–6; A. Moscino d. S. Svensson 6–4 6–4; Giacomini/A. Odling lost to Simonsson/Jarryd 3–6 4–6; Costa/Moscino d. Svensson/M. Wennberg 6–2 6–4.
1978 *Sweden d. France 3–2:* S. Svensson d. T. Tulasne 6–4 6–2; H. Simonsson lost to J. Potier 6–3 2–6 7–9 disqualified; J. Gunnarsson d. T. Pham 6–2 5–7 6–2; M. Wilander lost to J. L. Cotard 2–6 7–5 4–6; Svensson/Simonsson d. Cotard/J. M. Piacentile 6–3 6–1.
1979 *Sweden d. France 4–1:* J. Windahll lost to T. Tulasne 2–6 1–6; M. Wilander d. H. Leconte 6–2 1–6 6–3; T. Hogstedt d. P. Kuchna 6–2 6–1; J. Sjogren d. J. M. Piacentile 6–1 6–1; Hogstedt/Wilander d. Leconte/Piacentile 3–6 6–3 6–4.
1980 *Sweden d. Czechoslovakia 3–0:* M. Wilander d. M. Mecir 3–6 6–1 6–1; A. Mansson d. K. Novacek 6–3 6–3; H. Sundstrom/Wilander d. Mecir/B. Stankovic 6–3 3–0 ret'd.
1981 *France d. Sweden 3–2:* T. Benhabiles d. S. Edberg 6–4 6–4; F. Hamonet d. J. B. Svensson 6–0 6–2; T. Chamsion lost to P. Svensson 2–6 2–0–6; O. Cayla lost to A. Henricsson 6–1 4–6 3–6; Hamonet/G. Forget d. Edberg/P. Svensson 6–4 1–6 6–2.
1982 *Sweden d. Spain 4–1:* J. Svensson d. J. Maso 6–2 6–2; S. Edberg d. F. Garcia 6–4 6–4; P. Svensson d. J. M. Oltra 6–2 6–1; J. Carlsson lost to S. Castello 5–7 1–6; Edberg/P. Svensson d. Garcia/Oltra 6–2 6–1.
1983 *Sweden d. USSR 3–2:* D. Engel d. V. Gabritchidze 7–5 6–1; K. Carlsson d. A. Volkov 6–2 6–4; C. Allgaardh d. A. Tchernetsky 7–5 6–3; C. Bergstrom lost to I. Metreveli 6–0 6–7 3–6; Carlsson/Allgaardh d. Volkov/Metreveli 6–3 6–7 6–3.
1984 *Italy d. Sweden 4–1:* P. Chinellato lost to T. Nydhal 4–6 6–4 3–6; O. Camporese d. H. Holm 6–4 6–0; A. Baldoni d. A. Rosen 6–4 6–0; S. Sorensen d. N. Utgren 6–2 6–4; Baldoni /E. Rossi d. T. Nydal /P. Henricsson 7–6 1–6 6–3.
1985 *Sweden d. France 3–2:* P. Henricsson lost to A. Boetsch 3–6 2–6; P. Wennberg d. P. Ventura 6–2 6–2; N. Utgren d. S. Blanquie 6–1 6–2; M. Zeile d. C. Sebastiani 6–1 6–3; Henricsson /Utgren lost to Boetsch /R. Pedros 2–6 6–3 4–6.

COPA DEL SOL

International Team Championship for boys aged 14 and under. Played in zones with finals in Barcelona.

1979 *Italy d. France 3–2:* M. Fioroni d. M. Cartier 6–0 6–2; G. Possani d. G. Forget 6–7 7–5 6–3; A. Paris lost to T. Benhabiles 0–6 5–7; L. Baglioni lost to F. Hamonet 0–6 0–6; Possani/Paris d. Benhabiles/Hamonet 6–1 6–4.
1980 *Sweden d. Italy 4–1:* P. Svensson d. R. Salemme 6–4 7–6; S. Edberg d. F. Ricci 7–5 6–3; R. Lofquist d. F. Filippi 6–3 6–4; J. Svensson lost to P. Poggioli 4–6 2–6; Edberg/P. Svensson d. Filippi/A. Vacca 6–4 6–3.
1981 *Sweden d. Israel 3–2:* T. Johansson lost to A. Naor 2–6 6–7; C. Allgaardh lost to G. Blom 4–6 6–2 4–6; K. Carlsson d. R. Weinberg 6–0 6–0; C. Bergstrom d. M. Osherov 2–6 7–5 7–5; Allgaardh/Carlsson d. Blom/Osherov 6–2 6–1.
1982 *Sweden d. West Germany 4–1:* H. Kolm d. U. Kraft 6–1 6–0; K. Carlsson d. O. Sachau 6–0 6–0; P. Ekstrand lost to I. Kroll 0–6 2–6; T. Nydahl d. C. Guhl 6–0 1–6 6–1; Carlsson/Nydahl d. Guhl/Kraft 6–1 6–4.
1983 *Sweden d. West Germany 3–2:* U. Persson d. H. Stang 6–2 6–2; P. Henricsson d. P. Pfleger 6–4 6–1; U. Eriksson lost to U. Kraft 7–6 3–6 2–6; P. Wennberg lost to L. Orzessek 2–6 3–6; Henricsson/M. Urgren d. Kraft/Orzessek 6–2 6–3.

1984 West Germany d. Spain 4–1: S. Scheider d. F. Alfonso 6–3 4–6 7–5; F. Loddenkemper/A. Thoms d. J. Olivert/S. Bruguera 6–3 6–2; Loddenkemper d. Olivert 7–6 7–6; D. Richter d. A. Martinez 6–1 7–5; A. Thoms lost to Bruguera 3–6 6–2 4–6.
1985 Austria d. Italy 5–0: G. Bohm d. F. Casa 6–4 6–2; T. Buchmayer/O. Fuchs d. S. Pescosolido/F. Pisilli 6–2 6–3; Buchmayer d. Pescosolido 6–3 4–6 6–4; Fuchs d. Pisilli 6–3 7–6; H. Prilled d. M. Ardinghi 6–2 6–1.

ANNIE SOISBAULT CUP

International Team Championship for women aged 20 and under. Played zonally with final stages in Le Touquet.

1965 Netherlands d. France 2–1: M. Jansen lost to J. Venturino 1–6 1–6; B. Stove d. C. Spinoza 6–1 1–6 6–3; Jansen/Stove d. Spinoza/Venturino 10–8 6–4.
1966 France d. Netherlands 2–1: A. A. Seghers lost to A. Bakker 4–6 7–5 2–6; J. Venturino d. M. Jansen 6–4 6–4; Seghers/Venturino d. Bakker/Jansen 7–5 6–8 6–4.
1967 Netherlands d. France 2–1: A. Bakker lost to O. de Roubin 3–6 0–1 ret'd; A. Suurbeck d. N. Cazeaux 8–6 6–2; Bakker/Suurbeck d. Cazeaux/de Roubin 6–0 6–0.
1968 USSR d. Czechoslovakia 3–0: O. Morozova d. M. Holubova 6–2 10–8; R. Islanova d. K. Vaneckova 7–5 6–2; Morozova/A. Eremeeva d. Holubova/Vaneckova 6–3 6–2.
1969 USSR d. Hungary 3–0: O. Morozova d. J. Szorenyi 6–0 6–1; S. Yansone d. A. Graczol 4–6 6–4 6–2; Yansone/E. Izopajitis d. Szorenyi/A. Barogh 8–6 6–1.
1970 USSR d. France 3–0: E. Izopajitis d. N. Fuchs 6–3 6–1; M. Kroshina d. A. M. Cassaigne 4–6 6–1 9–7; Izopajitis/K. Zincevic d. Fuchs/M. C. Brochard 6–4 2–6 6–3.
1971 France d. Czechoslovakia 2–1: N. Fuchs d. M. Kozeluhova 6–2 6–3; F. Guedy lost to R. Tomanova 4–6 1–6; M. C. Brochard/Fuchs d. Kozeluhova/Tomanova 1–6 7–5 6–3.
1972 USSR d. Great Britain 2–1: M. Kroshina d. G. L. Coles 6–3 6–4; E. Biriukova d. V. Burton 6–2 4–6 6–3; Biriukova/E. Granatuzova lost to L. J. Charles/Coles 3–6 2–6.
1973 Great Britain d. USSR 2–1: G. L. Coles d. M. Kroshina 7–5 4–6 6–3; S. Barker d. E. Granaturova 6–4 7–5; Barker/Coles lost to Granaturova/Kroshina 4–6 6–3 3–6.
1974 Czechoslovakia d. Great Britain 2–1: M. Navratilova d. G. L. Coles 6–1 6–2; R. Tomanova lost to S. Barker 3–6 2–6; Navratilova/Tomanova d. Baker/Coles 6–2 6–8 7–5.
1975 Great Britain d. Rumania 2–1: S. Barker d. V. Ruzici 4–6 6–4 6–2; L. J. Mottram lost to M. Simionescu 4–6 9–7 1–6; Barker/Mottram d. Ruzici/Simionescu 6–4 6–0.
1976 Czechoslovakia d. Great Britain 2–1: H. Strachonova lost to M. Tyler 7–5 4–6 4–6; R. Marsikova d. L. J. Mottram 6–2 6–4; Marsikova/K. Skronska d. Mottram/B. L. Thompson 6–3 8–10 6–1.
1977 Czechoslovakia d. Switzerland 3–0: H. Strachonova d. A. M. Ruegg 6–0 6–3; R. Marsikova d. M. Simmen 6–0 4–6 6–0; Marsikova/H. Mandlikova d. Ruegg/Simmen 8–6 6–4.
1978 USSR d. Switzerland 3–0: N. Chmyreva d. A. M. Ruegg 6–4 6–4; Eliseenko d. P. Delhees 7–5 6–4; Chmyreva/Eliseenko d. Ruegg/M. Simmen 6–1 6–0.
1979 Czechoslovakia d. Great Britain 2–1: H. Mandlikova d. A. E. Hobbs 4–6 6–3 6–3; I. Budarova lost to J. M. Durie 6–8 6–4 6–8; Budarova/Mandlikova d. Durie/D. Jevans 1–6 6–2 6–3.
1980 Czechoslovakia d. Australia 2–1: I. Budarova d. S. Leo 6–4 6–4; M. Skuherska lost to D. Evers 0–6 3–6; Budarova/Skuherska d. Evers/M. Sawyer 6–3 6–3.
1981 Netherlands d. USSR 2–0: M. Van Der Torre d. J. Salnikova 6–1 6–4; N. Shutte d. O. Zaitzeva 6–1 6–4.
1982 USSR d. Great Britain 2–1: O. Zaitseva d. S. Walpole 6–2 6–4; N. Reva d. A. Brown 6–1 6–3; J. Kashevarova/Zaitseva lost to Brown/J. Salmon 5–7 6–0 2–6.
1983 France d. Czechoslovakia 2–1: P. Paradis d. H. Fukarkova 7–5 1–6 6–2; N. Herreman d. O. Votavova 6–4 6–0; Paradis/P. Thanh lost to Fukarkova/Votavova 6–4 3–6 4–6.
1984 USA d. Czechoslovakia 3–0: G. Rush d. O. Votavova 6–3 6–1; D. Spence d. A. Holikova 6–2 7–5; Rush/N. Kuhlman d. Votavova/Holikova 6–3 6–2.
1985 Czechoslovakia d. Argentina 3–0: A. Holikova d. P. Tarabini 3–6 7–5 6–4; O. Votavova d. M. Perez Roldan 0–6 6–3 6–2; Holikova /J. Novotna d. Tarabini /Perez Roldan 7–5 7–5.

QUEEN SOFIA CUP

International Team Championship for girls aged 18 and under. Played zonally with the final stages in Spain.

FINALS
1972 Rumania d. West Germany 3–2: F. Mihai d. A. Spiedel 6–4 7–5; V. Ruzici/M. Simionescu d. B. Portcheller/B. Kasler 8–6 6–1; Ruzici d. Portcheller 2–6 6–0 6–1; Simionescu lost to Kasler 4–6 3–6; M. Neuweiller lost to K. Pohmann 4–6 3–6.
1973 Great Britain d. Spain 4–1: B. L. Thompson d. G. Nogues 6–4 6–4; L. J. Mottram d. J. Mateo 6–3 12–10; S. Barker d. J. Alvarez 7–5 6–0; Barker/Mottram d. Mateo/C. Chillida 6–2 6–2; J. Potterton lost to Chillida 3–6 6–0 6.
1974 Czechoslovakia d. France 4–1: L. Plchova d. M. Cozaux 6–4 6–1; Y. Brzakova lost to B. Simon 6–8 6–2 4–6; H. Strachonova d. C. Gimmig 6–3 6–0; R. Marsikova d. F. Thibault 8–4 6–4; Brzakova/A. Kulankova d. Thibault/A. Duguy 9–7 4–6 6–4.
1975 Great Britain d. Czechoslovakia 4–1: M. Tyler d. A. Kulhankova 6–1 3–6 6–3; C. Harrison d. J. Kopekova 6–3 6–3; L. J. Mottram d. H. Strachonova 2–6 11–9 6–3; J. Cottrell lost to K. Skronska 1–6 1–6; A. Cooper/Cottrell d. Skronska/Kulhankova 1–6 6–4 6–4.

1976 **Great Britain d. Switzerland 3–1:** J. M. Durie d. C. Jolissaint 4–6 6–3 6–4; A. Cooper lost to M. Simmen 6–4 0–6 4–6; C. Harrison d. A. Ruegg 6–4 6–7 6–2; M. Tyler d. P. Delhees 6–2 6–2.
1977 **Czechoslovakia d. Sweden 5–0:** H. Mandlikova d. M. Wiedel 6–2 6–2; I. Budarova d. H. Brywe 6–1 6–1; Mandlikova/Budarova d. A. C. Mansson/A. Nilsson 6–1 6–3; M. Skuherska d. Nilsson 6–0 6–4; H. Strachonova d. Mansson 6–3 7–5.
1978 **Czechoslovakia d. Sweden 5–0:** M. Skuherska d. L. Jacobson 6–3 6–2; H. Mandlikova d. H. Brywe 6–1 6–1; I. Budarova/Mandlikova d. Jacobson/L. Sandin 6–3 6–1; I. Petru d. A. Nilsson 6–1 6–2; Budarova d. Sandin 6–3 5–7 7–5.
1979 **Czechoslovakia d. Switzerland 3–1:** I. Bendlova d. P. Frey 6–1 6–1; M. Skuherska/I. Petru lost to C. Jolissaint/I. Villiger 3–6 4–6; Skuherska. Villiger 3–6 6–1 6–1; I. Novakova d. Jolissaint 6–7 6–3 6–3; Petru v C. Pasquale 5–7 abandoned.
1980 **Switzerland d. USSR 3–2:** K. Stampfli d. J. Kashevarova 6–3 6–3; I. Villiger/L. Drescher lost to O. Zaitseva/S. Cherneva 4–6 5–7; Villiger d. Zaitseva 6–2 7–5; C. Pasquale lost to Cherneva 4–6 7–5 7–9; Drescher d. J. Salnikova 7–6 6–4.
1981 **Sweden d. Czechoslovakia 3–2:** B. Bjort d. P. Dutkova 6–2 6–3; M. Lindstrom/C. Lindqvist d. H. Sukova/M. Pazderova 6–3 6–3; C. Jexell lost to Pazderova 6–3 2–6 0–6; Lindqvist d. N. Piskackova 6–2 6–2; Lindstrom lost to Sukova 6–7 3–6.
1982 **Italy d. Czechoslovakia 4–1:** R. Reggi d. I. Petru 6–3 6–4; N. Virgintino lost to H. Fukarkova 7–5 2–6 3–6; A. Cecchini d. P. Dutkova 7–6 7–6; F. Bonsignori d. A. Souckova 6–3 6–0; Reggi/Virgintino d. Petru/Fukarkova 7–5 4–6 6–2.
1983 **Italy d. Czechoslovakia 4–1:** L. Ferrando d. A. Souckova 6–0 6–3; B. Romano/N. Virgintino d. A. Holikova/Souckova 6–3 6–7 6–3; A. M. Cecchini d. O. Votavova 6–7 6–3 6–1; Virgintino d. P. Tesarova 6–3 6–1; S. Dalla Valle lost to Holikova 5–7 3–6.
1984 **Sweden d. Czechoslovakia 3–2:** H. Dahlstrom d. O. Votavova 6–3 6–3; A. Karlsson d. A. Holikova 6–3 6–0; A. Souckova d. M. Lundquist 7–5 7–5; K. Karlsson d. P. Tesarova 6–1 6–2; Votavova/Holikova d. Lundquist/Olsson 6–4 6–2.
1985 **Italy d. Sweden 4–1:** L. Lapi lost to C. Dahlman 0–6 1–6; L. Garrone/L. Golarsa d. A. K. Ollson/M. Lundquist 6–1 6–3; Garrone d. H. Dahlstrom 6–2 6–7 6–2; C. Nozzoli d. Ollson 6–4 6–4; Golarsa d. Lundquist 6–2 6–0.

HELVETIA CUP

International Team Championship for girls aged 16 and under. Played zonally with final stages at Leysin, Switzerland.

FINALS
1977 **Italy d. Switzerland 3–2:** P. Cigognani lost to C. Jolissaint 0–6 3–6; B. Rossi d. I. Villiger 6–3 6–7 8–6; M. Calabria d. K. Stampfli 6–1 6–2; P. Murgo d. C. Pasquale 6–3 6–3; Rossi/Murgo lost to Jolissaint/Villiger 4–6 3–6.
1978 **Bulgaria d. West Germany 3–2:** M. Condova d. C. Kohde 1–6 6–3 7–5; A. Veltcheva d. Haas 6–3 5–7 6–4; I. Chichkova d. Hammig 6–3 6–0; I. Christova d. Wilmsmeyer 3–6 7–6 6–3; Condova/Veltcheva d. Kohde/Haas 3–6 6–2 6–2.
1979 **Sweden d. France 5–0:** C. Lindqvist d. I. Vernhes 6–7 6–3 6–0; B. Bjork d. C. Vanier 4–6 6–3 6–3; A. Flodin d. S. Gardette 6–0 6–1; H. Olsson/K. Marivall d. M. Callejo/Vanier 6–3 6–3; Olsson d. Calleja 6–2 6–1.
1980 **Sweden d. West Germany 3–2:** C. Anderholm d. M. Schropp 6–1 6–2; H. Olsson lost to K. Reuter 5–7 4–6; M. Schultz d. P. Keppeler 6–4 6–4; N. Nielson d. M. Reinhard 6–7 6–3 6–2; Olsson/Schultz lost to Reuter/Reinhard 6–1 4–6 5–7.
1981 **Sweden d. Italy 3–2:** A. Bjork lost to F. Sollenti 2–6 6–7; H. Olsson/C. Anderholm d. R. Reggi/F. Virgintino 0–6 6–2 6–1; Olsson d. A. M. Cecchini 6–4 7–5; Anderholm d. Reggi 6–3 3–6 6–4; I. Sjogreen lost to Virgintino 0–6 0–6.
1982 **USSR d. France 3–2:** I. Fishkina d. I. Demongeot 6–1 6–2; L. Savchenko/V. Milvidskaya lost to P. Paradis/N. Phan-Thanh 4–6 7–5 4–6; N. Bykova lost to Paradis 1–6 2–6; Savchenko d. Phan-Thanh 6–2 6–3; Mildvidskaya d. N. Herreman 6–1 6–4.
1983 **USSR d. Sweden 3–2:** A. Kuzmina d. A. K. Olsson 6–3 1–6 6–3; V. Milvidskaya d. H. Dahlmstrom 3–6 6–2 6–4; I. Fischkina lost to M. Lundquist 4–6 4–6; I. Fateeva lost to E. Helmersson 2–6 3–6; Fishkina/Mildvidskaya d. Dahlstrom/Lundquist 6–4 7–5.
1984 **Czechoslovakia d. West Germany 4–1:** R. Wlona lost to M. Gartner 7–6 3–6 4–6; J. Novotna/R. Rajchrotova d. S. Meier/R. Weiser 6–0 7–6; Novotna d. Meier 7–5 6–2; Rajchrotova d. Weiser 6–3 4–6 6–1; P. Sedkackova d. S. Hack 6–4 4–6 6–2.
1985 **West Germany d. Sweden 4–1:** M. Schurhoff d. M. Ekstrand 6–2 4–6 6–4; M. Gartner /S. Hack lost to M. Strandlund /M. Nilsson 3–6 3–6; Gartner /J. Jonerup 7–6 6–2; Hack d. Strandlund 6–1 6–1; W. Probst d. M. Nilsson 6–1 6–1.

EUROPA CUP

International Team Championship for girls under 14.

FINALS
1981 **West Germany d. France 3–2, Winterslag, Belgium:** I. Cueto d. J. Clerin 6–3 2–6 6–1; R. Wieser lost to E. Folcher 1–6 6–3 1–6; S. Graf d. M. Phan-Thanh 7–5 6–3; S. Luidinant d. E. Grousseau 6–2 6–2; Graf/Wieser lost to Folcher/Grousseau 6–4 2–6 1–6.

1982 Sweden d. West Germany 3–2, Mons, Belgium: C. Dahlman d. S. Meier 7–5 7–5: H. Dahlstrom d. B. Herget 6–0 6–4; E. Helmersson lost to I. Cueto 3–6 7–6 0–6; I. Mattiasson lost to E. Walliser 5–7 2–6; Dahlstrom/Helmersson d. Cueto/Walliser 6–2 6–2.

1983 West Germany d. France 3–2, Lee-on-Solent, Hampshire: N. Vassen d. S. N. Chateau 4–6 6–3 6–2; W. Probst d. M. C. Rolet 7–5 5–7 ret'd; S. Hack lost to C. Bourdais 6–3 2–6 0–6; M. Gartner d. A. Dechaume 6–4 4–6 7–5; Gartner/Vassen lost to Bourdais/Dechaume 3–6 1–6.

1984 France d. Sweden 4–1: S. Dussault lost to A. Narbe 0–6 6–4 3–6; A. Dechaume/E. Derly d. M. Ekstrand/H. Johnsson 6–3 6–3; Dechaume d. Ekstrand 7–5 6–2; Derly d. Salsgard 6–4 3–6 6–1; M. Laval d. Johnsson 6–4 6–4.

1985 USSR d. Italy 3–2: N. Zvereva d. A. Dell'Orso 6–2 4–6 6–4; T. Tchernysova lost to F. Romano 3–6 2–6; E. Brihovec lost to S. Favini w.o.; A. Blumberga d. G. Boschiero 6–3 4–6 6–4; Zvereva/Tchernysova d. Boschiero/Dell'Orso 6–4 6–3.

US INTERCOLLEGIATE CHAMPIONSHIPS

MEN'S SINGLES

	WINNER	RUNNER-UP	SCORE				
1883	Spring: J. S. Clark (Harvard)	Not available					
1883	Autumn: H. A. Taylor (Harvard)	Not available					
1884	W. P. Knapp (Yale)	Not available					
1885	W. P. Knapp (Yale)	Not available					
1886	G. M. Brinley (Trinity, Con.)	Not available					
1887	P. S. Sears (Harvard)	Not available					
1888	P. S. Sears (Harvard)	Not available					
1889	R. P. Huntington (Yale)	Not available					
1890	F. H. Hovey (Harvard)	Not available					
1891	F. H. Hovey (Harvard)	Not available					
1892	W. A. Larned (Cornell)	Not available					
1893	M. G. Chace (Brown)	Not available					
1894	M. G. Chace (Yale)	Not available					
1895	M. G. Chace (Yale)	Not available					
1896	M. D. Whitman (Harvard)	Not available					
1897	S. G. Thompson (Princeton)	Not available					
1898	L. E. Ware (Harvard)	Not available					
1899	D. F. Davis (Harvard)	Not available					
1900	R. D. Little (Princeton)	Not available					
1901	F. B. Alexander (Princeton)	Not available					
1902	W. J. Clothier (Harvard)	Not available					
1903	E. B. Dewhurst (U of Penn)	Not available					
1904	R. LeRoy (Columbia)	Not available					
1905	E. B. Dewhurst (U of Penn)	Not available					
1906	R. LeRoy (Columbia)	Not available					
1907	G. P. Gardner (Harvard)	Not available					
1908	N. W. Niles (Harvard)	Not available					
1909	W. F. Johnson (U of Penn)	Not available					
1910	R. A. Holden (Yale)	Not available					
1911	E. H. Whitney (Harvard)	Not available					
1912	G. M. Church (Princeton)	Not available					
1913	R. N. Williams (Harvard)	Not available					
1914	G. M. Church (Princeton)	Not available					
1915	R. N. Williams (Harvard)	Not available					
1916	G. C. Caner (Harvard)	Not available					
1917–18	*Not held*	Not available					
1919	C. S. Garland (Yale)	K. Reid (Cornell)	4–6	6–1	6–2	2–6	6–3
1920	L. M. Banks (Yale)	D. P. Robinson (Harvard)	6–3	6–4	6–3		
1921	P. Neer (Stanford)	J. B. Fenno (Harvard)	3–6	6–1	6–4	1–6	6–1
1922	R. N. Williams (Yale)	W. Brown (Washington)	6–3	6–1	7–5		
1923	C. H. Fischer (Phil. Osteo.)	G. R. Emerson (Columbia)	6–2	6–3	6–2		
1924	W. Scott (Washington)	Not available					
1925	E. G. Chandler (California)	O. Holman	6–4	6–3	1–6	6–3	
1926	E. G. Chandler (California)	Not available					
1927	W. Allison (Texas)	B. Gorchakoff (Occidental)	6–1	6–1	6–1		
1928	H. Siligson (Lehigh)	Not available					
1929	B. Bell (Texas)	Not available					
1930	C. Sutter (Tulane)	Not available					
1931	K. Gledhill (Stanford)	Not available					
1932	C. Sutter (Tulane)	Not available					
1933	J. Tidball (UCLA)	R. Murphy (Hamilton)	8–6	9–7	8–6		
1934	G. Mako (USC)	Not available					

1935	W. Hess (Rice)	Not available				
1936	E. Sutter (Tulane)	Not available				
1937	E. Sutter (Tulane)	Not available				
1938	F. D. Guernsey (Rice)	Not available				
1939	F. D. Guernsey (Rice)	Not available				
1940	D. McNeill (Kenyon Coll)	Not available				
1941	J. R. Hunt (US Naval Acad)	Not available				
1942	F. R. Schroeder (Stanford)	Not available				
1943	F. Segura (Miami)	Not available				
1944	F. Segura (Miami)	Not available				
1945	F. Segura (Miami)	Not available				
1946	R. Falkenburg (USC)	Not available				
1947	G. Larned (Wm & Mary)	Not available				
1948	H. E. Likas (U of San Francisco)	Not available				
1949	J. Tuero (Tulane)	Not available				
1950	H. Flam (USC)	Not available				
1951	M. A. Trabert (U of Cincinnati)	Not available				
1952	H. Stewart (USC)	Not available				
1953	H. Richardson (Tulane)	Not available				
1954	H. Richardson (Tulane)	R. Perry (UCLA)	6–1	6–2	6–3		
1955	J. Aguero (Tulane)	W. Quillian (Washington)	6–1	4–6	6–1	6–0	
1956	A. Olmedo (USC)	J. Frost (Stanford)	2–6	6–4	6–2	6–1	
1957	B. McKay (U of Michigan)	S. Giammalva (Texas)	6–4	3–6	6–2	3–6	6–3
1958	A. Olmedo (USC)	J. Douglas (Stanford)	6–3	3–6	6–4	6–1	
1959	W. Reed (San José State)	D. Dell (Yale)	7–5	3–6	6–2	4–6	6–3
1960	L. Nagler (UCLA)	W. Reed (San José State)	3–6	8–6	6–4	3–6	6–4
1961	A. Fox (UCLA)	Not available				
1962	R. H. Osuna (USC)	Not available				
1963	R. D. Ralston (USC)	Not available				
1964	R. D. Ralston (USC)	Not available				
1965	A. R. Ashe (UCLA)	Not available				
1966	C. Pasarell (UCLA)	S. R. Smith (USC)	6–4	3–6	2–6	6–3	6–1
1967	R. C. Lutz (USC)	J. Fillol (Miami)	6–0	6–0	6–8	2–6	6–2
1968	S. R. Smith (USC)	R. C. Lutz (USC)	3–6	6–1	6–0	6–2	
1969	J. Loyo-Mayo (USC)	M. Estep (Rice)	6–1	6–2	6–3		
1970	J. Borowiak (UCLA)	R. Tanner (Stanford)	10–8	9–7	7–5		
1971	J. S. Connors (UCLA)	R. Tanner (Stanford)	6–3	4–6	6–4	6–4	
1972	R. L. Stockton (Trinity, Texas)	B. E. Gottfried (Trinity, Texas)	4–6	6–4	6–3	6–2	
1973	A. A. Mayer (Stanford)	R. Ramirez (USC)	6–3	6–1	6–4		
1974	J. Whitlinger (Stanford)	G. Hagey (USC)	1–6	6–3	6–3	6–1	
1975	W. Martin (UCLA)	G. Hardie (S Methodist U)	0–6	1–6	6–3	6–3	6–3
1976	W. Scanlon (Trinity, Texas)	P. Fleming (UCLA)	5–7	7–6	6–3	6–2	
1977	M. Mitchell (Stanford)	A. Graham (UCLA)	6–4	1–6	6–3	6–4	
1978	J. P. McEnroe (Stanford)	J. Sadri (NC State)	7–6	7–6	5–7	7–6	
1979	K. Curren (Texas)	E. Iskersky (Trinity, Texas)	Not available				
1980	R. Van't Hof (USC)	P. Rennert (Stanford)	6–3	7–5			
1981	T. Mayotte (Stanford)	J. Gurfein (Stanford)	6–3	6–3			
1982	M. Leach (Michigan)	B. Gilbert (Pepperdine)	7–5	6–3			
1983	G. Holmes (Utah)	F. Pahlett	6–3	6–2			
1984	M. Pernfors (Georgia)	L. Duncan (Clemson)	6–3	7–6			
1985	M. Pernfors (Georgia)	G. Bezecny (Georgia)	6–3	6–2			

MEN'S DOUBLES

	WINNERS	RUNNERS-UP	SCORE
1883	Spring: J. S. Clark/H. A. Taylor (Harvard)	Not available	
1883	Autumn: R. E. Presbrey/H. A. Taylor (Harvard)	Not available	
1884	W. P. Knapp/W. V. S. Thorne (Yale)	Not available	
1885	W. P. Knapp/A. L. Shipman (Yale)	Not available	
1886	W. P. Knapp/W. L. Thacher (Yale)	Not available	
1887	P. S. Sears/Q. A. Shaw (Harvard)	Not available	
1888	V. G. Hall/O. S. Campbell (Columbia)	Not available	
1889	O. S. Campbell/A. E. Write (Columbia)	Not available	
1890	S. T. Chase/Q. A. Shaw (Harvard)	Not available	
1891	F. H. Hovey/R. D. Wrenn (Harvard)	Not available	
1892	F. B. Winslow/R. D. Wrenn (Harvard)	Not available	
1893	C. R. Budlong/M. G. Chace (Brown)	Not available	
1894	M. G. Chace/A. E. Foote (Yale)	Not available	
1895	M. G. Chace/A. E. Foote (Yale)	Not available	

Year	Winners	Runners-up	Score
1896	W. M. Scudder/L. E. Ware (Harvard)	Not available	
1897	M. D. Whitman/L. E. Ware (Harvard)	Not available	
1898	M. D. Whitman/L. E. Ware (Harvard)	Not available	
1899	D. F. Davis/H. Ward (Harvard)	Not available	
1900	F. B. Alexander/R. D. Little (Princeton)	Not available	
1901	H. A. Plummer/S. L. Russell (Yale)	Not available	
1902	W. J. Clothier/E. W. Leonard (Harvard)	Not available	
1903	E. Clapp/B. Colston (Harvard)	Not available	
1904	K. H. Behr/G. Bodman (Yale)	Not available	
1905	E. B. Dewhurst/H. B. Register (U of Penn)	Not available	
1906	E. B. Wells/A. Spaulding (Yale)	Not available	
1907	A. S. Dabney/N. W. Niles (Harvard)	Not available	
1908	H. M. Tilden/A. Thayer (U of Penn)	Not available	
1909	W. F. Johnson/A. Thayer (U of Penn)	Not available	
1910	B. N. Dell/D. Mathey (Princeton)	Not available	
1911	C. T. Butler/D. Mathey (Princeton)	Not available	
1912	G. M. Church/W. H. Mace (Princeton)	Not available	
1913	J. J. Armstrong/W. M. Washburn (Harvard)	Not available	
1914	R. Harte/W. N. Williams (Harvard)	Not available	
1915	R. Harte/R. N. Williams (Harvard)	Not available	
1916	R. Harte/G. C. Caner (Harvard)	Not available	
1917–18	*Not held*	Not available	
1919	C. S. Garland/K. N. Hawkes (Yale)	J. B. Morse/K. R. L. Simmons (Yale)	6–1 5–7 6–3 7–5
1920	A. Wilder/L. Wiley (Yale)	C. E. Granger/M. Drumwright (Texas)	2–6 6–8 6–1 7–5 6–3
1921	E. W. Feibleman/J. B. Fenno (Harvard)	W. Bates/E. Levy (California)	6–4 7–5 10–12 3–6 6–4
1922	J. Davis/P. Neer (Stanford)	L. E. Williams/G. M. Wheeler (Yale)	8–6 6–4 6–4
1923	L. Thalheimer/L. N. White (Texas)	L. E. Williams/A. W. Jones (Yale)	11–9 6–3 9–11 5–7 6–1
1924	L. Thalheimer/L. N. White (Texas)	Not available	
1925	G. Hillis/G. Stratford (California)	A. W. Jones/C. Watson (Yale)	7–5 7–5 3–6 6–3
1926	E. G. Chandler/T. Stow (California)	Not available	
1927	K. Appel/J. Van Ryn (Princeton)	B. Gorchakoff/N. Craig (Occidental)	6–3 7–5 5–7 6–4
1928	A. Herrington/R. McElvenny (Stanford)	Not available	
1929	G. Gorchakoff/A. Kussman (Occidental)	Not available	
1930	D. Muehleisen/R. Muench (California)	Not available	
1931	B. Barnes/K. Kamrath (Texas)	Not available	
1932	J. Coughlin/K. Gledhill (Stanford)	Not available	
1933	J. Coughlan/S. Lee (Stanford)	K. Kamrath/S. Williams (Texas)	6–2 11–13 6–4 6–2
1934	G. Mako/G. P. Castlen (USC)	Not available	
1935	R. Bennett/P. Newton (California)	Not available	
1936	W. B. Dey/W. Seward (Stanford)	Not available	
1937	R. Bennett/P. Newton (California)	Not available	
1938	J. R. Hunt/L. Wetherell (USC)	Not available	
1939	D. Imhoff/R. Peacock (California)	Not available	
1940	L. A. Dee/J. Wade (Stanford)	Not available	
1941	C. E. Olewine/C. H. Mattmann (USC)	Not available	
1942	L. A. Dee/F. R. Schroeder (Stanford)	Not available	
1943	W. Driver/J. Hickmann (Texas)	Not available	
1944	P. Kelley/J. Hickmann (Texas)	Not available	
1945	T. Burke/F. Segura (Miami)	Not available	
1946	R./T. Falkenburg (USC)	Not available	
1947	R. Curtis/S. Match (Rice)	Not available	
1948	B. Bartzen/F. Kovalaski (Wm & Mary)	Not available	
1949	J. Brink/F. Fisher (Washington)	Not available	
1950	H. Flam/G. Garrett (UCLA)	Not available	
1951	E. Cohel/H. Stewart (USC)	Not available	
1952	H. Ditzler/C. Mayne (UCLA)	Not available	
1953	L. Huebner/R. Perry (UCLA)	Not available	
1954	R. Livingston/R. Perry (UCLA)	J. Grigry/A. Cleveland (USC)	6–4 6–0 3–6 8–6
1955	F. Contreras/J. Reyes (USC)	S. Giammalva/J. Hernandez (Texas)	6–3 4–6 2–6 7–5 15–13
1956	F. Contreras/A. Olmedo (USC)	M. Franks/J. Lesch (UCLA)	2–6 1–6 6–3 11–9 6–4
1957	C. Henry/R. Holmberg (Tulane)	B. MacKay/R. Potter (Michigan)	6–3 7–9 6–4 6–4
1958	E. Atkinson/A. Olmedo (USC)	J. Douglas/D. Nelson (Stanford)	6–3 6–1 6–3
1959	C. Henry/R. Holmberg (Tulane)	M. Brown/W. Heinbecker (Notre Dame)	6–3 6–3 6–2
1960	A. Fox/L. Nagler (UCLA)	B. Delgado/G. Grant (USC)	6–3 6–4 6–2
1961	R. Earnhart/R. H. Osuna (USC)	Not available	
1962	R. Earnhart/R. H. Osuna (USC)	Not available	
1963	R. D. Ralston/R. H. Osuna (USC)	Not available	

1964	R. D. Ralston/W. Bond (USC)	Not available				
1965	A. R. Ashe/I. Crookenden (UCLA)	Not available				
1966	C. Pasarell/I. Crookenden (UCLA)	T. Edlefsen/S. R. Smith (USC)	10–8	6–4		
1967	R. C. Lutz/S. R. Smith (USC)	J. Loyo-Mayo/C. Hobson (USC)	6–2	9–7		
1968	R. C. Lutz/S. R. Smith (USC)	R. Barth/S. Tidball (UCLA)	6–1	7–5		
1969	M. Lara/J. Loyo-Mayo (USC)	S. Avoyer/R. C. Lutz (USC)	7–5	6–4	12–10	
1970	O. Cramer/L. Garcia (Miami)	R. Rippner/R. Tanner (Stanford)	6–2	7–5	6–1	
1971	J. Borowiak/H. Rahim (UCLA)	B. McKinley/R. L. Stockton (Trinity, Texas)	7–6	7–6		
1972	A. A. Mayer/R. Tanner (Stanford)	P. Gerken/B. E. Gottfried (Trinity, Texas)	6–1	3–6	6–3	6–4
1973	A. A. Mayer/J. Delaney (Stanford)	F. McNair/R. McKee (N Carolina)	6–3	3–6	7–5	6–3
1974	J. Whitlinger/J. Delaney (Stanford)	J. Andrews/S. Menon	6–4	6–4	4–6	6–4
1975	B. Manson/B. Walts (USC)	W. Martin/B. Teacher (UCLA)	6–1	6–4	7–6	
1976	P. Fleming/F. Taygan (UCLA)	B. Manson/C. J. Lewis (USC)	6–0	6–2	6–4	
1977	B. Manson/C. J. Lewis (USC)	J. Austin/B. Nichols (UCLA)	6–2	6–3	6–7	6–3
1978	J. Austin/B. Nichols (UCLA)	G. Plock/K. Curren (Texas)	6–4	6–4	6–2	
1979	E. Iskersky/B. McCowan (Trinity, Texas)	Not available				
1980	R. Harmon/M. Purcell (Tennessee)	A. Giammalva/J. Benson (Trinity, Texas)	7–6	7–6		
1981	D. Pate/K. Richter (TCU)	P. Doohan/P. Serret (Arkansas)	6–7	6–3	6–4	
1982	P. Doohan/P. Serret (Arkansas)	A. Miller/O. Malmquist (Georgia)	7–6	5–7	6–2	
1983	A. Miller/O. Malmquist (Georgia)	K. Flach/R. Seguso (S Illinois)	6–3	6–4		
1984	J./K. Jones (Pepperdine)	R. Leach/T. Pawsat (S California)	6–3	7–6		
1985	C. DiLaura /K. Jones (Pepperdine)	C. Beckman/R. Deppe (Texas)	7–5	7–6		

WOMEN'S SINGLES

	WINNER	RUNNER-UP	SCORE		
1958	D. R. Hard (Pomona)	O. McHaney (Rollins)	6–3	6–4	
1959	D. Floyd (Wm & Mary)	C. Looper (San Bernadino)	6–0	6–2	
1960	L. Vail (Oakland City)	S. Butt (British Columbia)	6–0	6–0	
1961	T. A. Fretz (Occidental)	Not available			
1962	R. Allison (Alabama)	Not available			
1963	R. Allison (Alabama)	Not available			
1964	J. Albert (Stanford)	Not available			
1965	M. Henreid (UCLA)	Not available			
1966	C. Martinez (San Francisco State)	J. Danilovitch	4–6	7–5	6–4
1967	O. Rippy (Odessa Jr)	P. Lamm (Miami)	6–1	6–3	
1968	E. Burrer (Trinity, Texas)	M. Michell (Arizona State)	3–6	7–5	7–5
1969	E. Burrer (Trinity, Texas)	P. Richmond (Arizona State)	6–1	6–4	
1970	L. DuPont (N Carolina)	Not available			
1971	P. Richmond (Arizona State)	M. Michell (Arizona State)	6–1	6–2	
1972	J. Metcalf (Redlands)	Not available			
1973	J. Metcalf (Redlands)	T. Watanabe	6–1	6–0	
1974	C. Meyer (Marymount)	L. Morse	6–4	2–6	7–6
1975	S. Tolleson (Trinity, Texas)	L. Forood (Stanford)	5–7	6–0	6–1
1976	B. Hallquist (USC)	M. Hann	6–4	6–4	
1977	B. Hallquist (USC)	D. Desfor (USC)	6–3	1–6	6–2
1978	S. Margolin (USC)	B. Jordan (Stanford)	6–3	6–2	
1979	K. Jordan (Stanford)	W. White (Rollins)	6–4	7–5	
1980	W. White (Rollins)	A. Moulton (Stanford)	5–7	6–3	6–0
1981	A. M. Fernandez (Rollins)	A. Moulton (Stanford)	6–3	6–1	
1982	A. Moulton (Stanford)	M. Schillig (San Diego State)	4–6	6–1	6–4
1983	B. Herr (USC)	G. Fernandez (Clemson)	3–6	6–2	7–6
1984	L. Spain (Georgia)	L. Gates (Stanford)	7–5	3–6	6–2
1985	L. Gates (Stanford)	G. Rush (Trinity)	7–6	6–2	

WOMEN'S DOUBLES

	WINNERS	RUNNERS-UP	SCORE		
1958	S. Metzger (St Mary's & Notre Dame)/E. Puetz (Webster)	J. Hagan/O. McHaney (Rollins)	6–1	4–6	6–3
1959	J. Pniewski/P. Saganski (Michigan State)	B. Brown/D. Floyd (Wm & Mary)	6–0	5–7	6–0
1960	S. Butt (British Columbia)/L. Vail (Oakland City)	C. Lenahan (Florida State)/S. Sterret (Illinois)	6–3	6–1	
1961	T. A. Fretz (Occidental)/M. Sherar (Yakima Valley)	Not available			

1962	C. Hanks/L. Yeomans (Stanford)	Not available		
1963	R. Allison (Alabama)/J. Bricka (Washington, Mo)	Not available		
1964	C. Jaster/C. Loop (Cal State LA)	Not available		
1965	N. Falkenburg/C. Goeltz (Mary Baldwin)	Not available		
1966	Y. Stockwell/L. Weiss (USC)	M. Henreid/M. Shapiro (UCLA)	6–1 6–2	
1967	J. Albert/J. Anthony (Stanford)	P. Rippy/B. Vest (Trinity, Texas)	6–2 6–3	
1968	E. Burrer/B. Vest (Trinity, Texas)	C. Gay/M. Michell (Arizona State)	6–2 6–3	
1969	E. Burrer/B. Vest (Trinity, Texas)	P. Austin/P. Lamm (Miami)	6–1 6–4	
1970	C. Capozzi/P. Farmer (Odessa Jr)	Not available		
1971	M. Michell/P. Richmond (Arizona State)	M. Cooper/M. Schallau (Rollins)	6–2 6–4	
1972	M. Michell/P. Richmond (Arizona State)	Not available		
1973	C. Beene/L. Rupert (Lamar)	M. Hamm/D. Stockton (Trinity, Texas)	1–6 6–3	6–4
1974	A. Lebedeff/K. Reinke (San Diego State)	L. Morse/J. Nachand	7–5 7–6	
1975	J. Russell/D. Stockton (Trinity, Texas)	S. Stap/S. Tolleson (Trinity, Texas)	6–1 6–2	
1976	S. Hagey/D. Morrison (Stanford)	P. Smith/C. Thomas (UCLA)	6–3 6–4	
1977	J. Appelbaum/T. Saglankik (USC)	A. Ellis/K. McDaniel (Louisiana State)	7–6 6–0	
1978	J./S. Acker (Florida)	B. Hallquist/S. McInerney (USC)	6–2 6–7	6–3
1979	K. Jordan/A. Moulton (Stanford)	B. Hallquist/S. McInerney (USC)	6–3 6–2	
1980	T. Lewis/A. White (USC)	A. M. Fernandez/S. McInerney (USC)	6–4 7–6	
1981	C. Copeland/A. Moulton (Stanford)	K. Henry/L. Siegel (USC)	6–3 6–3	
1982	L. Lewis/H. Ludloff (UCLA)	K. O'Brian/H. Manset (UCLA)	6–4 4–6	7–5
1983	L. Allen/G. Rush (Trinity, Texas)	E. Burgin/L. Gates (Stanford)	6–2 6–4	
1984	L. Gates/E. Burgin (Stanford)	E. Minter/L. Lewis (UCLA)	6–3 6–4	
1985	L. Gates/L. A. Eldredge (Stanford)	G. Rush/L. Sassano (Trinity)	6–4 6–3	

INDEX